Lecture Notes in Computer Science   15535

Founding Editors

Gerhard Goos
Juris Hartmanis

Editorial Board Members

Elisa Bertino, *Purdue University, West Lafayette, IN, USA*
Wen Gao, *Peking University, Beijing, China*
Bernhard Steffen, *TU Dortmund University, Dortmund, Germany*
Moti Yung, *Columbia University, New York, NY, USA*

The series Lecture Notes in Computer Science (LNCS), including its subseries Lecture Notes in Artificial Intelligence (LNAI) and Lecture Notes in Bioinformatics (LNBI), has established itself as a medium for the publication of new developments in computer science and information technology research, teaching, and education.

LNCS enjoys close cooperation with the computer science R & D community, the series counts many renowned academics among its volume editors and paper authors, and collaborates with prestigious societies. Its mission is to serve this international community by providing an invaluable service, mainly focused on the publication of conference and workshop proceedings and postproceedings. LNCS commenced publication in 1973.

Cinzia Cappiello · Olaf Hartig ·
Mohamed Sellami · Ali Ouni
Editors

Cooperative Information Systems

31st International Conference, CoopIS 2025
Marbella, Spain, October 20–22, 2025
Proceedings

 Springer

Editors
Cinzia Cappiello
Politecnico di Milano
Milan, Italy

Mohamed Sellami
Institut Polytechnique de Paris
Paris, France

Olaf Hartig
Linköping University
Linköping, Sweden

Ali Ouni
École de Technologie Supérieure
Montreal, QC, Canada

ISSN 0302-9743   ISSN 1611-3349 (electronic)
Lecture Notes in Computer Science
ISBN 978-3-032-15537-5   ISBN 978-3-032-15538-2 (eBook)
https://doi.org/10.1007/978-3-032-15538-2

This Springer imprint is published by the registered company Springer Nature Switzerland AG
The registered company address is: Gewerbestrasse 11, 6330 Cham, Switzerland

If disposing of this product, please recycle the paper.

Preface

The International Conference on Cooperative Information Systems (CoopIS 2025) took place from October 20–22 in Marbella, Spain, celebrating its 31st edition. Since its launch in 1993 in Rotterdam, the Netherlands, CoopIS has evolved into a leading international venue that brings together researchers, practitioners, and industry experts. Over three decades, the conference has continuously fostered debate and innovation on cooperative information systems, highlighting their technological foundations as well as their economic and societal implications.

Cooperative Information Systems (CIS) facilitate the cooperation between individuals, organisations, smart devices, and systems of systems, by providing flexible, scalable, and intelligent services to enterprises, public institutions, and user communities. As a result, people and smart devices can interact, share information, and work together across physical barriers. The domain of CIS integrates research results from different related computing areas, such as distributed systems, coordination technologies, collaborative decision making, enterprise architecture, business process management, and conceptual modelling. In recent years, several innovative technologies have emerged: Cloud Computing, Service-Oriented Computing, the Internet of Things, Linked Open Data, Semantic Systems, Collective Awareness Platforms, Blockchain, Processes as a Service, etc., that enable the next generation of CISs.

CoopIS 2025 received 128 paper submissions from 31 countries, of which 24 (19%) were accepted and published as full papers. A single-blind paper review was performed for each submission by at least 2, but usually 3 or more, members of the International Program Committee, which was composed of established researchers and domain experts.

The high quality of the CoopIS 2025 program was enhanced by the keynote lectures delivered by distinguished speakers who are renowned experts in their fields: Barbara Pernici (Politecnico di Milano, Italy), Sonja Zillner (Siemens AG, Germany), and Carles Sierra (IIIA-CSIC, Spain).

The conference was complemented by a Demo Track, chaired by Moataz Chouchen and Jeremy Mechouche, and a Special Session on Early Research Achievement, chaired by Mohamed Wiem Mkaouer and Slim Kallel.

All presented papers will be submitted for indexation by DBLP, Google Scholar, EI-Compendex, INSPEC, Japanese Science and Technology Agency, Norwegian Register for Scientific Journals and Series, Mathematical Reviews, SCImago, Scopus, zbMATH, and Web of Science/Conference Proceedings Citation Index.

The program for this conference required the dedicated effort of many people. Firstly, we would like to thank the authors, whose research efforts are reported here. Next, we thank the members of the Program Committee and the auxiliary reviewers for their diligent and professional reviews. We would also like to extend our sincere gratitude to the invited speakers for their invaluable contributions and for taking the time to prepare their talks. Finally, a word of appreciation for the hard work of the INSTICC team; organising a conference of this level is a task that can only be achieved by the collaborative effort of a dedicated and highly competent team.

We hope you all had an exciting and inspiring conference. We hope to have contributed to the development of our research community, and we look forward to having additional research results presented at the next edition of CoopIS, details of which are available at https://coopis.scitevents.org.

October 2025

Cinzia Cappiello
Olaf Hartig
Mohamed Sellami
Ali Ouni

Organization

Conference Co-chairs

Mohamed Sellami   Institut Polytechnique de Paris - Télécom SudParis, France

Ali Ouni   École de Technologie Supérieure (ÉTS Montreal), Canada

Program Co-chairs

Cinzia Cappiello   Politecnico di Milano, Italy

Olaf Hartig   Linköping University, Sweden

Program Committee

Mehdi Acheli	Télécom SudParis, France
Zainab AlMeraj	Kuwait University, Kuwait
Saïd Assar	Institut Mines-Télécom Business School, France
Isabel Azevedo	ISEP, Portugal
Eduard Babkin	National Research University "Higher School of Economics", Russian Federation
Ada Bagozi	University of Brescia, Italy
Valerio Bellandi	Università degli Studi di Milano, Italy
Salima Benbernou	Université Paris Cité, France
Mario Luca Bernardi	University of Sannio, Italy
Devis Bianchini	University of Brescia, Italy
Khouloud Boukadi	Independent Researcher, Tunisia
Hayet Brabra	Télécom SudParis, France
Luis Camarinha-Matos	New University of Lisbon, Portugal
Paolo Ceravolo	University of Milan, Italy
Francois Charoy	Independent Researcher, France
Richard Chbeir	Université de Pau et des Pays de l'Adour, France
Saoussen Cheikhrouhou	ENIS, University of Sfax, Tunisia
Dickson Chiu	University of Hong Kong, China
Carlo Combi	Università degli Studi di Verona, Italy
Marco Comuzzi	Ulsan National Institute of Science and Technology, South Korea

Oscar Corcho	Universidad Politécnica de Madrid, Spain
Olawande Daramola	University of Pretoria, South Africa
Christophe Debruyne	University of Liège, Belgium
Pavlos Delias	Democritus University of Thrace, Greece
Joyce El Haddad	Paris Dauphine University - PSL, France
Rik Eshuis	Eindhoven University of Technology, Netherlands
Noura Faci	Université Claude Bernard Lyon 1, France
Marcelo Fantinato	University of São Paulo, Brazil
Chiara Di Francescomarino	University of Trento, Italy
Massimiliano Garda	Università degli Studi di Brescia, Italy
Laura Genga	Eindhoven University of Technology, Netherlands
Nikolaos Georgantas	Inria, France
María Gómez López	Universidad de Sevilla, Spain
Jose Gonzalez	University of Seville, Spain
Laura González	Universidad de la República, Uruguay
Mohamed Graiet	University of Monastir, Tunisia
Daniela Grigori	Université Paris Dauphine-PSL, France
Georg Grossmann	University of South Australia, Australia
Mirian Halfeld-Ferrari	Université d'Orléans, France
Lazhar Hamel	ISIM Monastir, Tunisia
Marwan Hassani	Eindhoven University of Technology, Netherlands
Martin Hepp	Universität der Bundeswehr München, Germany
Stefan Jablonski	University of Bayreuth, Germany
Slim Kallel	University of Sfax, Tunisia
Nikos Karacapilidis	University of Patras, Greece
Oliver Karras	TIB – Leibniz-Informationszentrum Technik und Naturwissenschaften und Universitätsbibliothek, Germany
Taewoo Kim	Microsoft, USA
Kais Klai	Université Sorbonne Paris Nord, France
Matthias Klusch	German Research Center for Artificial Intelligence (DFKI) GmbH, Germany
Raula Gaikovina Kula	University of Osaka, Japan
Kabul Kurniawan	Universitas Gadjah Mada, Indonesia
Anelia Kurteva	University of Birmingham, UK
Maria Leitner	University of Regensburg, Germany
Teng Long	China University of Geosciences (Beijing), China
Chuangtao Ma	Aalborg University, Denmark
Jiangang Ma	Federation University Australia, Australia
Samira Maghool	University of Milan, Italy
Maria Maleshkova	Universität der Bundeswehr Hamburg, Germany
Amel Mammar	Télécom SudParis, France

Qizhong Mao	ByteDance, USA
Rabia Maqsood	National University of Computer and Emerging Sciences, Pakistan
Andrea Maurino	Independent Researcher, Italy
Giovanni Meroni	Technical University of Denmark, Denmark
Enrique Moguel	University of Extremadura, Spain
Sellam Mokhtar	Faculté des Sciences Juridiques, Economiques et de Gestion de Jendouba, France
Alex Norta	Tallinn University of Technology, Estonia
Selmin Nurcan	Institut D'administration Des Entreprises De Paris - Université Paris 1 - Panthéon Sorbonne, France
Stamatios Papadakis	University of Crete, Greece
Pierluigi Plebani	Politecnico di Milano, Italy
Agostino Poggi	University of Parma, Italy
Badran Raddaoui	Télécom SudParis, France
Mohamed Rahal	University of Sfax, Tunisia
Manfred Reichert	Ulm University, Germany
Kate Revoredo	Humboldt Universität zu Berlin, Germany
Diego Rincon-Yanez	Trinity College Dublin, Ireland
Sonja Ristic	University of Novi Sad, Serbia
Mattia Salnitri	University of Bergamo, Italy
Sumit Sharma	Independent Researcher, India
Ryan Shaw	University of North Carolina at Chapel Hill, USA
Michael Sheng	Macquarie University, Australia
Johannes De Smedt	KU Leuven, Belgium
Jacopo Soldani	Università di Pisa, Italy
Emanuele Storti	Università Politecnica delle Marche, Italy
Ruben Taelman	Ghent University, Belgium
Francesco Tiezzi	Università degli Studi di Firenze, Italy
Sihem Tlili	University of Gafsa, Tunisia
Nick van Beest	CSIRO, Australia
Genoveva Vargas-Solar	CNRS, France
Monica Vitali	Politecnico di Milano, Italy
Lena Wiese	Independent Researcher, Germany
Karolin Winter	Eindhoven University of Technology, Netherlands
Hongji Yang	University of Leicester, UK
Sami Yangui	LAAS-CNRS, France
Jian Yu	Auckland University of Technology, New Zealand
Xiaowang Zhang	Tianjin University, China
Zhangbing Zhou	China University of Geosciences Beijing, China

Additional Reviewers

Sabri Allani	Institut Supérieur de Gestion de Tunis, Tunisia
Maha Azabou	University of Sfax, Tunisia
Riadh Ben Halima	University of Sfax, Tunisia
Rym Chéour	National Engineering School of Sfax (ENIS), Tunisia
Silvano Colombo Tosatto	CSIRO, Australia
Ornela Danushi	University of Pisa, Italy
Amani Drissi	University of Pau and the Adour Regions, France
Wafa Gabsi	University of Sfax, Tunisia
Nicolas Hiot	Université d'Orléans, France
Mohammad Mustafa Ibrahimy	Tallinn University, Estonia
Lara Kallab	Independent Researcher, USA
Christoph Nirschl	University of Regensburg, Germany
Tobias Pfaller	AIT Austrian Institute of Technology, Austria
Bougacha Racem	CEA List, France
Till Schnabel	University of Regensburg, Germany
Baixi Sun	Indiana University, USA
Dong Xu	University of California, Merced, USA
Zhenyu Zhang	Arizona State University, USA

Keynotes

Machines That Know What Matters: Engineering Awareness of Social Values

Carles Sierra

IIIA-CSIC, Spain

Abstract. Ethics in AI raises big questions about how we design and use autonomous systems responsibly. In this talk, I'll focus on one core challenge: how to engineer moral values into intelligent agents. We'll explore how human communities define social values, how these become norm-based social contracts, and how we can build computational models that make machines aware of them.

Responsible AI Engineering Through the Systematic Management of Generative AI Risks

Sonja Zillner

Siemens AG, Germany

Abstract. Artificial Intelligence (AI) presents significant opportunities for new business ventures within the industrial domain. However, its adoption introduces a broad spectrum of risk sources across dimensions such as cybersecurity, reliability, robustness, safety, transparency, and human oversight. Simultaneously, organizations are confronted with an increasing amount of digital and AI-based legislation in the international environment. This leads to a fragmented landscape of legal and risk-related requirements, often inconsistent, overlapping, and duplicated. This results in high uncertainty and bureaucratic burden during the development and deployment of AI products. To address these challenges, a systematic, responsible, and efficient approach is required to handle the complex legal requirements as well as the emerging wide range of risk sources. Responsible AI Engineering describes such a systematic approach, enabling the efficient and innovative development of AI products while ensuring compliance with the complex and fragmented legal landscape. In this presentation, I will introduce the Siemens Generative Risk Management Process as an example of a responsible AI engineering approach. This demonstrates how organizations can drive AI innovation forward in a compliant and risk-aware manner.

On the Challenges of Sustainable Data Preparation

Barbara Pernici

Politecnico di Milano, Italy

Abstract. Processing datasets to achieve high data (and metadata) quality is mandatory in modern applications. However, the data preparation activities that are needed to reach such levels may easily become unsustainable due to, for example, resource intensity or scalability challenges. Moreover, some preparation efforts may become unnecessary if they result in negligible improvements or duplicate actions. The talk examines the sustainability aspects of data preparation through the lens of a circular economy. Within the data landscape, this perspective encourages practices that minimize waste, extend the data life cycle, and maximize reuse. We explore these practices and their impact on selecting and configuring effective data preparation strategies to design sustainable, high-quality data preparation pipelines. To this end, we present an evaluation model that integrates data quality metrics with sustainability parameters for human and computational tasks. Finally, we discuss the main challenges that are present in the evaluation of sustainability and data quality.

Contents

Process Conformance, Integrity and Compliance

Intelligent and Secure Connected Systems

Process Discovery and Variability

Architecture, Engineering and Governance of Information Systems

Short Papers

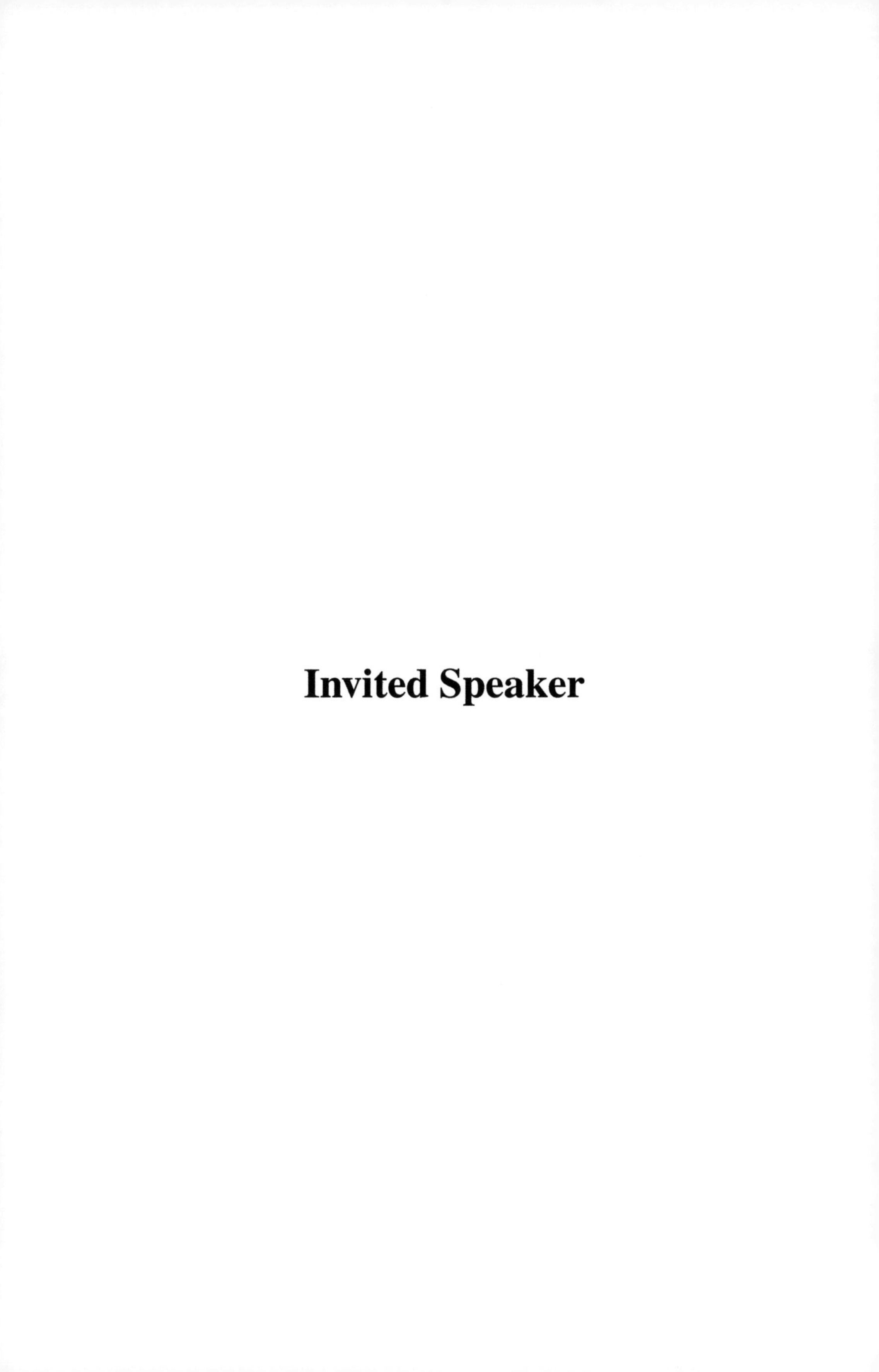

Invited Speaker

Responsible AI Engineering Through the Systematic Management of Generative AI Risks

Sonja Zillner[1,2]([✉]), Ronald Schnitzer[1,2], and Erik Scepanski[1,2]

[1] Siemens AG, Munich, Germany
sonja.zillner@siemens.com,
{ronald.schnitzer,erik.scepanski}@tum.de
[2] School of Computation, Information and Technology, Technical University of Munich, Munich, Germany

Abstract. Artificial Intelligence (AI) presents significant opportunities for new business ventures within the industrial domain. However, its adoption introduces a broad spectrum of risk sources across dimensions such as cybersecurity, reliability, robustness, safety, transparency, or human oversight. Simultaneously, organizations are confronted with an increasing amount of digital and AI-based legislation in the international environment. This leads to a fragmented landscape of legal and risk-related requirements, often inconsistent, overlapping, and duplicated. This results in high uncertainty and bureaucratic burden during the development and deployment of AI products. To address these challenges, a systematic, responsible, and efficient approach is required to handle the complex legal requirements as well as the emerging wide range of risk sources. Responsible AI Engineering describes such a systematic approach, enabling the efficient and innovative development of AI products while ensuring compliance with the complex and fragmented legal landscape. In this paper, we introduce the Generative AI Risk Management (GARM) methodology as an instantiation of Responsible AI Engineering. We demonstrate through a concrete industrial GenAI-based product how the GARM methodology enables organizations to drive AI innovation compliantly and with heightened risk awareness.

1 Introduction

The emergence of AI, and in particular Generative AI (GenAI)[1] represents a paradigmatic shift in industrial automation and manufacturing processes. As these technologies mature beyond general-purpose applications, organizations face the dual challenge of capitalizing on unprecedented opportunities while managing novel risks that traditional governance frameworks fail to address adequately. This tension between innovation potential and responsible deployment has created an urgent need for systematic approaches to industrial AI governance.

The industrial domain presents unique characteristics that distinguish it from consumer-facing AI applications. Manufacturing environments demand exceptionally high standards of reliability, safety, and precision - what we term *Industrial Grade AI* -

---

[1] We refer to Generative AI (GenAI) as an artificial intelligence technology that synthesizes new versions of text, audio, visual imagery, or other content from large bodies of data.

C. Cappiello et al. (Eds.): CoopIS 2025, LNCS 15535, pp. 3–11, 2026.
https://doi.org/10.1007/978-3-032-15538-2_1

that often exceed regulatory requirements. Furthermore, the specialized nature of industrial processes, from programmable logic controller (PLC) programming to complex maintenance diagnostics, requires domain-specific adaptations of general-purpose AI models [5]. This specialization challenge, combined with stringent operational requirements, creates a complex landscape for responsible AI implementation.

Recent developments in regulatory frameworks have further complicated this landscape. The European AI Act, alongside numerous horizontal, sector-specific, and other international regulations, has created a fragmented compliance environment that organizations must navigate while maintaining innovation momentum. This regulatory complexity, combined with the inherent risks of GenAI technologies - including hallucination, bias, cybersecurity vulnerabilities, and intellectual property concerns - necessitates systematic approaches. Enabling the efficient and innovative development of AI products while ensuring compliance with the complex and fragmented legal landscape is the aim of *Responsible AI Engineering*.

The *Generative AI Risk Management* (GARM) methodology offers a concrete instantiation of this approach. Its successful application to an industrial GenAI-based product showcases how GARM empowers organizations to pursue AI innovation compliantly and with heightened risk awareness.

The remainder of this paper is organized as follows: Sect. 2 details the industrial opportunities for GenAI. Section 3 presents the GARM methodology in detail, including its conceptual foundation and practical implementation. In Sect. 4, the practical value of the GARM methodology is shown using the Engineering Copilot as an example. Section 5 concludes with implications for practice and future research directions.

2   Industrial Opportunities for Generative AI

The industrial sector is undergoing a fundamental transformation from hardware-centric to digitally-integrated operations. This evolution, characterized as the integration of the "virtual world" and "physical world", creates unprecedented opportunities for AI-based innovation across the entire value chain.

GenAI, with its capacity to create new data, designs, and insights, offers a paradigm shift in how industrial processes are conceived, executed, and optimized. Its application spans the entire industrial lifecycle, from initial product conceptualization to ongoing maintenance and customer support, as outlined in Fig. 1 and the accompanying descriptions.

Fig. 1. Industrial value chain.

Design and Planning: GenAI-based applications in the design and planning phase enable users to ask natural language questions, quickly access detailed technical insights, and streamline complex design and planning tasks for faster and smarter product or process development. Design engineers as well as planning engineers can receive accurate assistance, understand detailed design and planning context, and make changes swiftly, leading to more productive workflows and efficiency savings.

Engineering: A key advancement in the engineering phase is the use of GenAI-powered assistants that significantly enhance various aspects of the daily work of engineers. Addressing the specialized nature of industrial programming languages and complex engineering tasks, these assistants support engineers in creating and explaining code, making it easier to understand and modify existing systems. They also facilitate user interface development and provide quick, context-aware responses to engineering questions within relevant platforms. This leads to increased efficiency by allowing engineers to focus on more critical tasks, reducing errors through minimized bugs, and enhancing understanding that aids in training new engineers and improving team collaboration.

Operations and Services: Industrial operations are transforming through intelligent systems that provide operators with AI-powered diagnostics and contextual guidance. These systems enhance efficiency, reduce expert dependency, and prevent machine misuse while providing clear operational visibility through direct instructions. By delivering instant access to machine information via natural language interfaces, they empower operators to make better-informed decisions.

3   Generative AI Risk Management

The Generative AI Risk Management (GARM) methodology serves as a Responsible AI Engineering approach, empowering the efficient and innovative development of AI products while ensuring adherence to the complex and fragmented legal landscape. This section will begin by outlining the crucial need for systematic AI risk management, subsequently providing a detailed overview of the GARM approach as implemented at Siemens.

3.1   Requirements and Motivation

The adoption of AI in industrial settings necessitates a systematic risk management approach due to several critical factors.

Complex Regulatory Landscape: First, the legal landscape has become increasingly complex. This complexity stems from the introduction of the European AI Act alongside a multitude of horizontal, sector-specific, and international regulations. Organizations are thus confronted with a fragmented array of legal requirements, including the General Data Protection Regulation (GDPR), the Cyber Resilience Directive, Copyright and Intellectual Property Rights, or Export Control regulations. Moreover, beyond the European AI Act, other major regions, including China and the US, are actively developing their own AI regulations and standardizations, further compounding the compliance challenges for international organizations.

Novel Risks: Second, the management of novel risk sources inherent in generative AI technologies presents unprecedented challenges. These include risk sources related to hallucination, bias amplification, cybersecurity vulnerabilities, data confidentiality breaches, and copyright infringement - risks that traditional IT governance frameworks are not equipped to handle.

Industrial Grade AI: Third, the concept of Industrial Grade AI demands standards that often exceed regulatory requirements, as industrial applications require exceptional levels of reliability, safety, and precision. Industrial Grade AI requirements might be derived from sector-specific directives such as the Machinery Directive and Medical Device Regulations, or from the high-quality requirements of industrial environments.

To realize the industrial AI opportunities outlined in the previous section, organizations need a systematic risk management methodology that can efficiently guide product developers through the complex landscape of legal and technical requirements while maintaining innovation momentum. Without such systematic approaches, the potential of AI in industrial applications remains largely untapped due to uncertainty and compliance concerns.

3.2   The GARM Methodology

The Generative AI Risk Management (GARM) methodology offers a comprehensive, systematic four-step approach for identifying, assessing, and mitigating risks inherent in the development and deployment of industrial GenAI applications. This methodology effectively bridges the gap between theoretical AI governance and risk management frameworks—such as the NIST AI RMF [8] or the OECD AI Principles [3]—and the practical implementation requirements faced by large industrial organizations.

Central to the GARM methodology is its *Generative AI Hazard List*. This expert-curated list details potential hazards and risk sources, provides illustrative examples, and outlines corresponding mitigation measures. Much like hazard lists in machinery directives or threat lists in cybersecurity, this list establishes a critical knowledge base, enabling the systematic identification of risk sources throughout the development and deployment lifecycle of GenAI applications. The high-level categories of GenAI hazards are structured to align with existing organizational expertise (e.g., cybersecurity, legal/compliance, privacy, AI), thereby facilitating clear responsibility delegation.

The GARM methodology is process-agnostic, allowing for seamless integration into a wide array of organizational processes, including Product Lifecycle Management (PLM), Project Management (PM), IT Asset Management, Quality Management, and Cybersecurity Management.

An overview of the four steps of the GARM methodology is provided in Fig. 2.

Step 1: AI Act Risk Classification. The first step of the GARM methodology involves classifying AI solutions in line with the European AI Act to determine the applicable regulatory obligations. This classification is required as it derives whether a system is prohibited, classified as high-risk, subjected to transparency obligations, or falls into the low-risk category.

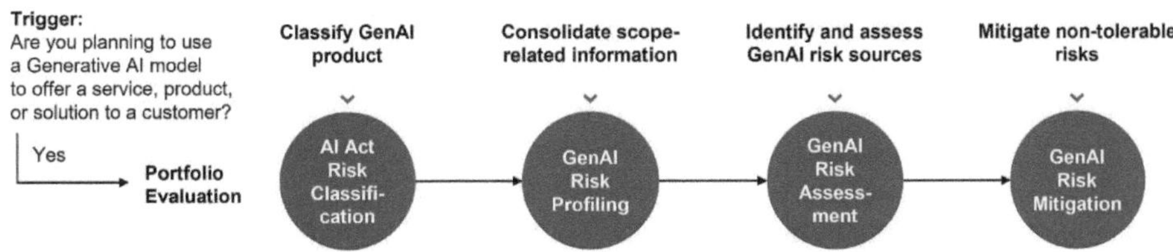

Fig. 2. The four steps of the GARM methodology.

The implementation of this step is based on an internal service known as the "AI Act Risk Classifier" – a web-based decision-support tool. The service is available to all Siemens employees and guides them through the classification rules as defined by the European AI Act, primarily in its Articles 5,6, and 50 [2]. All classification rules have been transformed into a set of questions aiming to clarify all information that is relevant for the AI Act classification, such as the used AI technologies, the envisioned application areas, the related sectoral directives, and the degree of human interaction. Following a decision tree-based logic, the classification service determines the EU AI Act risk category based on the user's responses to these questions.

The service simplifies interpreting legal definitions and regulatory scope, addressing a significant challenge for practitioners without legal expertise. To bridge this knowledge gap, various support mechanisms are embedded into its user interface. At different stages, users can access explanations of legal terms, practical examples, and references to the legal text.

This self-service approach is effective for the majority of use cases. However, in some cases, determining the correct risk category can be challenging due to ambiguities in the AI Act, in particular when it comes to the alignment with sectoral directives. For these cases, the AI Act Risk Classifier provides contact details of GARM experts who can assist users in ensuring accurate classification. A comprehensive analysis of the required expertise, ambiguities in the AI Act, and effective support mechanisms, as well as a detailed description of the tool's design process, is available in [6].

Upon completion, users receive a detailed PDF report that outlines their classification results, applicable obligations, and recommended actions.

Step 2: GenAI Risk Profiling. The second step involves consolidating all essential knowledge related to the GenAI application under consideration. This consolidation is crucial to facilitate effective knowledge transfer among a diverse group of stakeholders, including product owners, cybersecurity experts, legal and AI specialists, and risk assessors, who will be involved in the subsequent *GenAI Risk Assessment* step.

The profiling step is centered on precisely describing the intended purpose, application environment, level of human involvement, and technical specifications of the GenAI application. This information is vital for accurate risk identification and planning of mitigation strategies. For instance, information about the planned deployment regions is used to determine applicable regional regulatory obligations. To gather all this information, a template containing all relevant questions is provided to the respective stakeholders.

In addition, product owners are asked to create a standardized data flow diagram that illustrates how data moves through the system using a predefined template. The data flow diagram template is designed for risk assessments in AI systems [7]. The graphical representation of the GenAI application helps to identify which data flows and components introduce additional exposure to risk sources, thereby improving the risk identification process. This standardized format boosts efficiency for involved stakeholders like legal or cybersecurity experts, as their often limited familiarity with AI technology means they gain considerably from the uniform presentation of the underlying application.

A critical aspect of the risk profiling step is the emphasis on focused scoping rather than broad roadmap discussions. While product developers often consider multiple functionalities and development phases, effective risk assessment requires a precise definition of the specific intended purpose. A clearly defined use case scope is required for assessing the relevance of hazards and subsequent mitigation strategies.

Step 3: GenAI Risk Assessment. The core of the GARM methodology involves a systematic assessment utilizing the Generative AI Hazard List, which is organized into multiple risk categories, including legal and compliance, cybersecurity, privacy and data protection, reliability and robustness, and transparency and human oversight. To ensure completeness, the Generative AI Hazard List is built upon the state-of-the-art understanding of known GenAI-related risks, as synthesized in sources such as [1,4,9]. This foundation is enriched by the practical experiences of experts involved in developing, deploying, and assessing GenAI applications.

The risk assessment follows established risk management practices similar to threat and risk analysis methodologies familiar to industrial practitioners. The process involves systematically evaluating each GenAI hazard for its applicability to the specific use case, assessing the likelihood of occurrence and potential impact, and determining the overall risk level using risk matrices.

The assessment is conducted in workshop settings with cross-functional teams including AI experts, legal specialists, cybersecurity professionals, and product owners. This collaborative approach ensures comprehensive evaluation while facilitating knowledge transfer and organizational learning. GARM experts facilitate these workshops, providing guidance on GenAI hazard interpretation, risk evaluation techniques, and mitigation strategy selection.

Step 4: GenAI Risk Mitigation. The final step covers implementing appropriate mitigation measures for risks that exceed acceptable thresholds. The GenAI Hazard List provides detailed descriptions of potential mitigation strategies for each identified GenAI hazard, establishing the basis for combining legal, technical, and organizational measures as appropriate.

Mitigation strategies are developed collaboratively with legal, cybersecurity, and technical experts to ensure both effectiveness and feasibility. For example, transparency obligations might be addressed through a combination of legal disclaimers, technical flagging of AI-generated content, and user interface modifications that ensure transparency of AI capabilities in the industrial workflow.

The methodology emphasizes reusable mitigation patterns that can be applied across multiple use cases, building organizational capabilities, and reducing implementation effort over time. This approach has enabled scaling of risk mitigation across the organization while maintaining consistency and quality of implementation.

4 Example: Automation Engineering Copilot

In this section, we first introduce the Engineering Copilot in the context of automation engineering and then walk through the GARM process with the Engineering Copilot as an example.

4.1 Copilot for Automation Engineering

An automation engineer is responsible for developing and maintaining machines and automated systems, aiming to enhance efficiency, productivity, quality, and safety across diverse industrial and operational environments. Industrial software development, particularly for Programmable Logic Controllers (PLCs), Human-Machine Interfaces (HMIs), Supervisory Control and Data Acquisition (SCADA) systems, Distributed Control Systems (DCS), and industrial robots, is often repetitive and time-consuming. Copilot solutions support automation engineers by streamlining programming, automating repetitive tasks, and reducing potential errors. For instance, Siemens has launched an Automation Engineering Copilot that enables automation engineers to accelerate their daily work using GenAI and describing their tasks in natural language.

This example illustrates the application of the GARM methodology to the above-mentioned Automation Engineering Copilot integrated with the TIA Portal (Totally Integrated Automation Portal), Siemens' comprehensive automation engineering environment. The TIA Portal serves as the central development environment for industrial automation systems, encompassing programming of PLCs, HMIs, and related automation components. The portal represents a variety of engineering expertise consolidated into a software environment. Engineers can request code explanations, generate program blocks, and receive implementation guidance through natural language queries based on the TIA portal documentation. Automation engineering relies heavily on programming languages defined by the IEC 61131-3 standard. These languages are specialized for industrial automation applications and differ significantly from well-known programming languages like Python or C in both syntax and semantic requirements. The specialized nature of these languages presents challenges for GenAI, which typically lacks sufficient training data on industrial automation, hindering product teams from achieving their business goals. Therefore, the Automation Engineering Copilot leveraged a variety of domain adaptation methods to generate PLC code based on the user query, which complies with the standard. The domain adaptation implementation journey typically begins with the straightforward approach of prompting, which involves carefully crafted prompts consisting of additional domain-related information. Similarly, Retrieval-Augmented Generation (RAG) represents another approach to extend the context with even more domain-specific information utilizing vector databases. When these strategies prove insufficient to reach the business goals, organizations often progress to fine-tuning approaches that leverage data to enhance model performance for specific use cases. Finally, in cases where fine-tuning still doesn't meet requirements, the pretraining of models becomes necessary, creating purpose-built AI systems tailored precisely to the needs [5]. For example, in the case of the PLC coding, as prompting and RAG approach haven't been sufficient to reach the business needs, a fine-tuning strategy has been implemented.

4.2   GARM and the Automation Engineering Copilot

When applying the first step of the GARM methodology, the Automation Engineering Copilot was classified using the AI Act Risk Classifier. It resulted in a clear classification under the transparency obligations category of the EU AI Act. The classification result yielded considerable value for the product team, specifically by enabling the exclusion of a high-risk classification that would have mandated extensive regulatory obligations. The resulting report became an artifact for stakeholder communications and regulatory documentation, demonstrating systematic compliance with AI Act requirements.

The second and third steps involved detailed documentation of the system's architecture, data flows, and operational context. The team consolidated information from various sources into a comprehensive risk profile that defined the intended purpose. The data flow documentation proved particularly valuable for legal and cybersecurity experts, providing a clear visual representation of how user inputs, code generation, and system outputs interact within the broader automation engineering workflow. This architectural clarity facilitated more precise risk assessment and more targeted mitigation strategies.

A success factor was the involvement of GARM experts who facilitated the risk assessment workshops and provided guidance throughout the process. GARM experts with both technical AI knowledge and understanding of the risk management methodology facilitated the effective translation between legal requirements and technical implementation. This expert guidance was vital for new users of the methodology as it gave them context from similar projects, proven ways to manage risks, and practical tips on how to implement things. This collaborative approach helped share knowledge and build skills across the organization.

To exemplify, one risk identified for the Engineering Copilot is related to AI Act transparency obligations. The mitigation strategies implemented included the development of comprehensive terms of use documentation accessible to all users and user interface modifications that explicitly identify when AI assistance is being provided. These mitigation measures were integrated directly into the product development backlog and implemented as standard product features rather than separate activities. This integration approach has proven effective in ensuring sustainable implementation while maintaining development momentum.

5 Discussion

The implementation of the GARM methodology at Siemens demonstrates the practical viability of systematic risk management for GenAI in industrial settings. The approach has proven scalable across multiple business units and use cases while maintaining consistency and rigor in risk assessment and mitigation.

Key success factors include the establishment of clear organizational responsibilities for risk category ownership, the development of reusable risk assessment tools and frameworks, and the provision of expert support for methodology adoption. The integration with existing product life cycle management processes has been essential for ensuring mandatory compliance while minimizing disruption to development workflows.

Looking forward, the GARM methodology continues to evolve based on practical experience and regulatory developments. Future enhancements include extension to broader AI applications beyond GenAI, development of automated risk assessment capabilities, and integration with emerging regulatory frameworks in international markets, such as China.

The Responsible AI Engineering approach demonstrated through GARM provides a practical model for organizations seeking to balance innovation opportunities with systematic risk management in the rapidly evolving landscape of industrial GenAI applications.

References

1. Bommasani, R., et al.: On the opportunities and risks of foundation models. arXiv preprint arXiv:2108.07258 (2021)
2. European Parliament, Council of the European Union: Regulation (EU) 2024/1689 of the European Parliament and of the Council of 13 June 2024 laying down harmonised rules on artificial intelligence (Artificial Intelligence Act), July 2024. https://eur-lex.europa.eu/eli/reg/2024/1689/oj/eng
3. Organisation for Economic Cooperation and Development (OECD): AI Principles. https://www.oecd.org/en/topics/sub-issues/ai-principles.html. Accessed 1 Aug 2025
4. OWASP Foundation: Owasp top 10 for LLM applications (2024). https://genai.owasp.org/resource/owasp-top-10-for-llm-applications-2025/. Accessed 20250804
5. Scepanski, E., Schnitzer, R., Jaremenko, C., Zillner, S.: Expanding the reach of generative AI to industry: the case of domain adaptation. In: 2025 IEEE Technology & Engineering Management Conference (TEMSCON) (2025)
6. Schnitzer, R., Hoeving, M., Zillner, S.: Self-service or not? How to guide practitioners in classifying AI systems under the European AI Act. In: 3rd International Conference on Frontiers of Artificial Intelligence, Ethics, and Multidisciplinary Applications (FAIEMA) (2025, accepted for publication)
7. Schnitzer, R., Hapfelmeier, A., Zillner, S.: EAM diagrams-a framework to systematically describe AI systems for effective AI risk assessment. In: Symposium on Scaling AI Assessments (SAIA 2024). Schloss Dagstuhl–Leibniz-Zentrum für Informatik (2025)
8. Tabassi, E.: Artificial Intelligence Risk Management Framework (AI RMF 1.0) (2023)
9. Weidinger, L., et al.: Taxonomy of risks posed by language models. In: Proceedings of the 2022 ACM Conference on Fairness, Accountability, and Transparency, pp. 214–229 (2022)

Data-Driven and Predictive Process Analytics

Discriminative Rule Learning for Outcome-Guided Process Model Discovery

Ali Norouzifar[(✉)] and Wil van der Aalst

RWTH University, Aachen, Germany
{ali.norouzifar,wvdaalst}@pads.rwth-aachen.de

Abstract. Event logs extracted from information systems offer a rich foundation for understanding and improving business processes. In many real-world applications, it is possible to distinguish between desirable and undesirable process executions, where desirable traces reflect efficient or compliant behavior, and undesirable ones may involve inefficiencies, rule violations, delays, or resource waste. This distinction presents an opportunity to guide process discovery in a more outcome-aware manner. Discovering a single process model without considering outcomes can yield representations poorly suited for conformance checking and performance analysis, as they fail to capture critical behavioral differences. Moreover, prioritizing one behavior over the other may obscure structural distinctions vital for understanding process outcomes. By learning interpretable discriminative rules over control-flow features, we group traces with similar desirability profiles and apply process discovery separately within each group. This results in focused and interpretable models that reveal the drivers of both desirable and undesirable executions. The approach is implemented as a publicly available tool and it is evaluated on multiple real-life event logs, demonstrating its effectiveness in isolating and visualizing critical process patterns.

Keywords: Process Mining · Process Discovery · Discriminative Process Modeling

1 Introduction

Event logs extracted from information systems provide a valuable foundation for analyzing and improving business processes. Process discovery aims to automatically derive process models from event logs, enabling further analysis such as conformance checking and performance optimization. In many real-world applications, process executions can be distinguished as desirable or undesirable. While desirable traces reflect efficient and compliant behavior, undesirable ones may involve inefficiencies, violations, delays, or resource waste. This distinction presents an opportunity: desirable traces illustrate desirable behavior, whereas undesirable ones reveal what should be avoided.

A common strategy in such contexts is to discover a process model that supports desirable traces while excluding undesirable ones [12]. However, a single global model often obscures the differences between the desirable and undesirable behavior of the

C. Cappiello et al. (Eds.): CoopIS 2025, LNCS 15535, pp. 15–32, 2026.
https://doi.org/10.1007/978-3-032-15538-2_2

processes. It lacks the capacity to reveal how different execution paths contribute to process outcomes or what specific control-flow characteristics distinguish desirable behavior from undesirable behavior.

Table 1. Trace variants and frequencies in L^+ and L^-.

Trace Variant	Freq in L^+	Freq in L^-
$\langle p, a, l \rangle$	100	0
$\langle p, l, a \rangle$	100	0
$\langle a, p, l \rangle$	50	50
$\langle a, l, p \rangle$	50	50
$\langle l, a, p \rangle$	0	100
$\langle l, p, a \rangle$	0	100

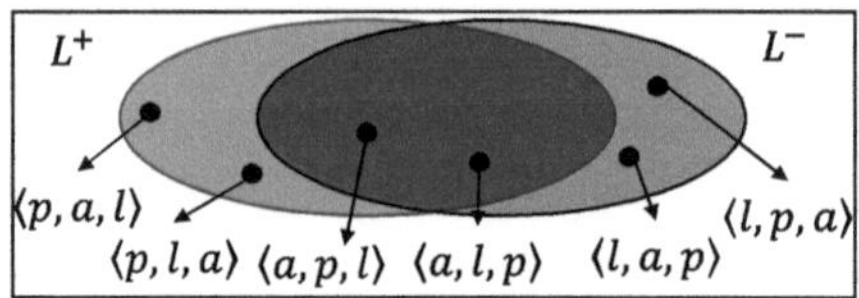

Fig. 1. Distribution of trace variants across desirable L^+ and undesirable L^- event logs.

In this paper, we propose a method to bridge this gap by identifying key control-flow patterns that effectively distinguish between desirable and undesirable traces. To this end, we introduce a methodology for selecting a subset of strong discriminative patterns, ensuring that only the most representative pattern is retained among those satisfied by similar trace subsets. Based on the selected patterns, we group traces and apply process discovery independently within each group. This leads to focused and interpretable process models that more accurately reflect the behavioral characteristics of distinct trace subsets. Our approach not only highlights the control-flow structures associated with trace desirability but also uncovers the underlying drivers of both desirable and undesirable process behaviors.

Consider an order-handling process that involves three distinct sequential activities: (p) **p**ick items from shelves. (a) **a**ssemble package by preparing for shipment. (l) Print shipping **l**abel. Ideally, orders follow a logical workflow such as $\langle p, a, l \rangle$ or $\langle p, l, a \rangle$. An analysis of historical data reveals two distinct sets of cases: a desirable event log L^+ representing workflows with an on-time delivery, and an undesirable event log L^- capturing inefficient or problematic workflows. The frequency of trace variants in each event log is shown in Table 1. Figure 1 positions the traces based on their belonging to desirable or undesirable behavior of the process.

Although L^+ and L^- share overlapping trace variants, their differing frequency distributions reflect distinct process behaviors. Discovering a process model that accounts for all observed traces without considering trace desirability can result in the model shown in Fig. 2a. Even if the model is discovered using only L^+, it may produce the same generalized process model, especially if sequences such as $\langle l, a, p \rangle$ and $\langle l, p, a \rangle$ are considered plausible but unobserved (i.e., allowed by generalization). As a result, the discovered model permits all possible orderings of the activities and achieves perfect fitness with respect to both the desirable and undesirable event logs, while failing to capture their behavioral differences.

We leverage the predictive power of supervised learning models to identify discriminative control-flow characteristics that distinguish desirable from undesirable traces.

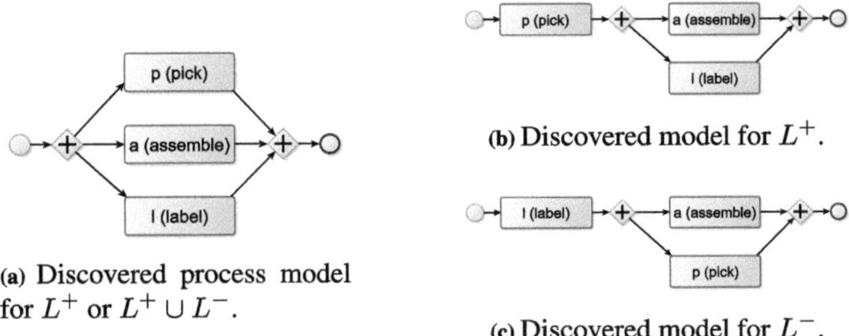

(a) Discovered process model for L^+ or $L^+ \cup L^-$.

(b) Discovered model for L^+.

(c) Discovered model for L^-.

Fig. 2. Process models for desirable and undesirable traces.

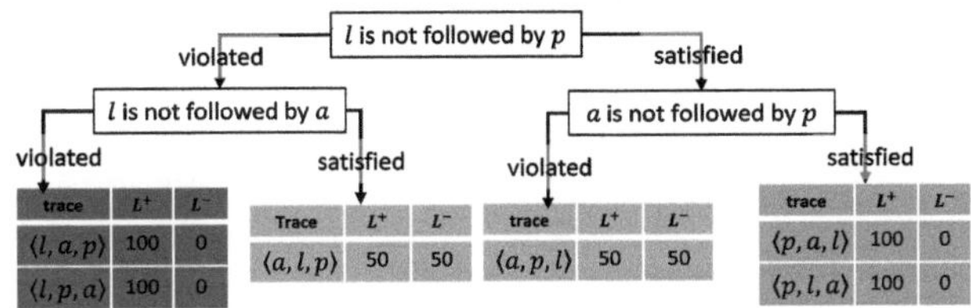

Fig. 3. Decision tree classifying traces into desirable or undesirable.

Traces are first encoded into a feature space constructed from declarative constraints, which effectively capture relationships between activities. The most informative features are then selected to explain behavioral differences, and subsequently used to extract and filter discriminative process variants that represent the core distinctions between the two classes.

A simple decision tree, shown in Fig. 3, suggests that traces are likely to be classified as desirable if l is not eventually followed by p, and a is also not eventually followed by p. Based on this logic, the process model depicted in Fig. 2b captures the control-flow of a subset of desirable traces, covering 66.7% of L^+ while excluding all traces from L^-. Unlike the generalized model in Fig. 2a, which permits all observed behavior including undesirable variants, this model emphasizes the representation of preferred behavior while explicitly avoiding undesirable patterns.

Conversely, Fig. 2c presents a process model focused on undesirable traces, corresponding to the red-labeled subgroup of traces in Fig. 3. This model covers 66.7% of L^- while excluding all traces from L^+, effectively capturing behavior specific to undesirable executions. This example demonstrates how discriminative control-flow features can guide the extraction of focused process variants that clearly separate desirable and undesirable behavior. While the other branches of the decision tree in Fig. 3 could also be used to derive additional process models, their associated subsets do not exhibit a dominant desirability class.

In real-life scenarios, effectively guiding process discovery requires a comprehensive approach that includes selecting a meaningful feature space to capture activity relationships, choosing a supervised learning model that balances predictive power with interpretability, and leveraging the model's explanations to derive event logs focused on the distinguishing aspects. These targeted logs can then be used to discover process models that explain the underlying behavioral differences. This paper presents such an approach in detail.

2   Related Work

Declarative process discovery focuses on identifying a set of constraints that restrict the allowed behavior, ranging from no constraints permitting all behavior to highly restrictive combinations that allow no behavior at all. Some approaches, such as [5] and [4], begin with a model that permits only desirable traces and iteratively introduce declarative constraints to exclude undesirable behavior. Another example is the rejection miner proposed in [17], which selects patterns from a given input set that are satisfied by desirable traces and then minimizes this set to include patterns that reject undesirable traces. While such methods effectively yield declarative models that characterize forbidden behavior in the process, our approach differs in focus: we aim to identify discriminative patterns and subsequently discover imperative models that describe how process executions are actually carried out.

The discovery of imperative process models, such as BPMNs or Petri nets, represents another important line of research. For example, the approach introduced in [11] and [9] do not assume explicit access to undesirable traces. Instead, they generate artificial negative events to approximate undesired behavior and use these to evaluate generalization and guide the discovery process away from such behavior. A different line of work, such as [12], incorporates both desirable and undesirable event logs in a recursive process discovery framework, where each iteration seeks a process structure that effectively captures the desirable behavior while avoiding the undesirable one.

Clustering techniques without considering the desirability of cases can help to reduce the complexity of the control-flow by grouping similar behaviors. However, they do not guarantee that desirable and undesirable traces are assigned to separate clusters [19]. Other approaches, such as process variant identification [14] and concept drift detection [16], aim to identify control-flow variability across different dimensions, such as the time or performance dimensions.

Comparative process analysis offers a variety of techniques to analyze and contrast different subprocesses [2]. The field of predictive process monitoring investigates supervised learning approaches capable of effectively classifying different groups of cases [18]. While these techniques are highly effective for prediction tasks, they often lack interpretability and are not intended to serve as descriptive models of process behavior. The area of deviance mining explores the application of supervised learning methods to identify the key factors that distinguish normal from deviating cases [8]. These approaches aim to uncover the driving features behind behavioral deviations, providing valuable insights into the root causes of anomalies.

The deviance mining pipeline introduced in [8] constructs a feature space by combining declarative constraints, sequential features, and data attributes to represent traces. White-box supervised models, such as decision trees, are then trained to classify traces, and the paths from root to leaf nodes are reported as the most relevant features contributing to the classification. In contrast, our approach treats such rules as an intermediate feature space that captures relationships among features. On top of this space, we train a sparse regression model capable of assigning importance scores to the rules, thereby identifying those that contribute most to the classification and can serve as explanations of the differences between variants. We further cluster the rules and leverage the most distinguishing ones to project event logs and discover process models that represent the variants satisfying the corresponding distinguishing rules.

In [15], a decision tree-based rule extraction approach is introduced to support study planning. However, the robustness and generalization ability of single decision trees for identifying discriminative rules can be limited. In this paper, we propose an enhanced rule extraction method based on ensemble tree models, combined with importance scoring derived from a supervised linear regression model. Our approach is inspired by the framework presented in [7], and leverages declarative feature extraction to capture control-flow characteristics. These insights are subsequently translated into interpretable process models using imperative process discovery techniques.

3   Preliminary

Given a set of elements A, the notation $\mathcal{P}(A)$ refers to the power set of A, A^* refers to all sequences we can generate over the elements of this set and A^n with $n \in \mathbb{N}$ is the universe of all vectors with n elements from set A. Considering a vector $b \in A^n$, $b[i]$ refers to the i-th element of the vector where $1 \leq i \leq n$. In the following, we introduce an event log formally.

Definition 1 (Event Log). *Let $\mathcal{C}$ denote the universe of case identifiers and $\mathcal{A}$ denote the universe of activities. A trace is a tuple $\sigma = (c, t)$, where $\pi_c(\sigma) = c \in \mathcal{C}$ is the case identifier and $\pi_t(\sigma) = t \in \mathcal{A}^*$ is the control flow of this trace. An event log $L \subseteq \mathcal{C} \times \mathcal{A}^*$ is a set of traces such that the case identifier of each trace is unique, i.e., considering any $\sigma, \sigma' \in L$, $\pi_c(\sigma) \neq \pi_c(\sigma')$. $\mathcal{L}$ is the universe of all event logs.*

For instance, $L = \{(1, \langle p, a, l \rangle), (2, \langle a, l, p \rangle), (3, \langle p, a, l \rangle), (4, \langle p, a, l \rangle), (5, \langle a, l, p \rangle), (6, \langle l, p, a \rangle)\}$ is an event log.

Definition 2 (Case Label). *Let $L \in \mathcal{L}$ be an event log. $\kappa_L : L \rightarrow \{0, 1\}$ is a trace labeling function that assigns 0 to a trace if it is undesirable and 1 if it is desirable. This function is assumed to be given as input. If the context is clear, we omit the subscript L and write $\kappa(\sigma)$ for $\sigma \in L$.*

For example, $\kappa = \{((1, \langle p, a, l \rangle), 1), ((2, \langle a, l, p \rangle), 0), ((3, \langle p, a, l \rangle), 1), ((4, \langle p, a, l \rangle), 1), ((5, \langle a, l, p \rangle), 1), ((6, \langle l, p, a \rangle), 0)\}$ is a labeling function with four desirable traces and two undesirable traces.

Declarative constraints are specific instances of predefined constraint templates that are applied to activities extracted from an event log. These constraints capture behavioral relationships and conditions in a flexible and rule-based manner. There exists a variety of well-established declarative constraint templates, including the following examples: $CoExistence(x_1, x_2)$: If activity x_1 occurs in a trace, then activity x_2 must also occur, and vice versa. $AtLeast1(x_1)$: Activity x_1 must occur at least once in the trace. $ChainResponse(x_1, x_2)$: If activity x_1 occurs, activity x_2 must occur immediately afterward. For a detailed explanation of various declarative constraint templates, refer to [6].

Definition 3 (Declarative Constraints). *Let T be a non-empty set of templates, where each template is a relation $d(x_1, \ldots, x_m) \in T$ defined over variables $x_1, \ldots, x_m$, with $m \in \mathbb{N}$ representing the arity of d. For a given set of activities $a_1, \ldots, a_m \in \mathcal{A}$, a declarative constraint $d(a_1, \ldots, a_m)$ is derived as a specific instantiation of the template d, binding its variables to the corresponding activities. T_A is the universe of declarative constraints that we can define over $A \subseteq \mathcal{A}$.*

Each trace can either satisfy a constraint, violate it, or lack sufficient information to evaluate it (vacuous satisfaction).

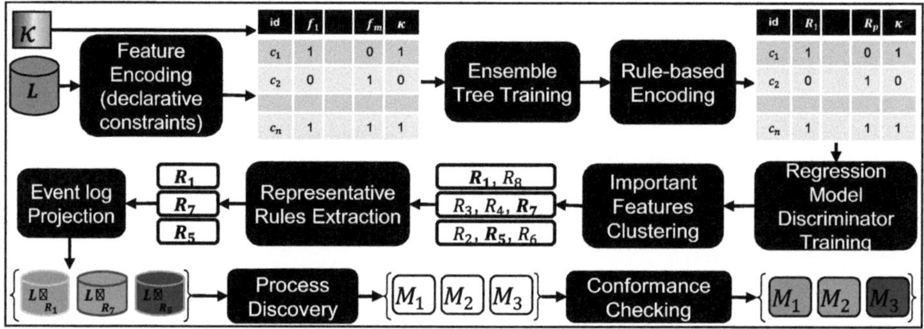

Fig. 4. An overview of our proposed framework.

Definition 4 (Declarative Constraints Evaluation). *Let $A \subseteq \mathcal{A}$ be a set of activities. Each constraint $d \in T_A$ consists of an activation condition $d_\triangleright$ and a target condition $d_\square$. The activation condition determines when the constraint becomes relevant (i.e., triggered), and the target condition defines the behavior expected once the constraint is activated. Given a trace $\sigma \in \mathcal{A}^*$, the evaluation of constraint d over σ yields one of the following three outcomes:*

- *Violation: $\sigma \not\models d$ if $d_\triangleright$ is satisfied in σ but $d_\square$ is not.*
- *Satisfaction: $\sigma \models d$ if both $d_\triangleright$ and $d_\square$ are satisfied in σ.*
- *Vacuous Satisfaction: $\sigma \| d$ if $d_\triangleright$ is not satisfied in σ.*

Considering $S = \{satisfied, violated, vac\text{-}satisfied\}$ as the set of possible evaluation outcomes, the evaluation function $eval_L : L \times T_{act(L)} \to S$ is defined by

$$eval_L(\sigma, d) = \begin{cases} violated, & if \ \sigma \not\models d, \\ satisfied, & if \ \sigma \models d, \\ vac\text{-}satisfied, & if \ \sigma \| d. \end{cases}$$

For example, considering the trace σ with $\pi_t(\sigma) = \langle p, l \rangle$, the constraint $CoExistence(a, p)$ is violated, since a does not occur, while p does. The constraint $ChainResonse(a, p)$ cannot be evaluated, as activity a does not appear in the trace (vacuous satisfaction). The constraint $AtLeast1(p)$ is satisfied.

4 Discriminative Process Variants Discovery

Figure 4 illustrates the proposed framework. The process starts by encoding traces with declarative constraints, which provide interpretable control-flow features. Ensemble tree-based models are then trained to capture complex interactions among these features. From the trained models, decision rules are extracted to construct an enriched feature space. A sparse logistic regression model is subsequently trained, and the most important features are clustered based on their similarity in representing traces within the feature space. For each cluster, the most representative rule is selected and used to filter traces, enabling the discovery of focused process variant models. Finally, these models are evaluated using dedicated metrics to ensure they effectively highlight the behavioral contrasts between L^+ and L^-.

4.1 Feature Encoding

The algorithm begins by discovering all declarative constraints that are satisfied by at least one trace in the log. These constraints are then pruned using the subsumption hierarchy: when multiple constraints have a subsumption relationship and yield identical evaluations across the event log, we retain only the most restrictive constraint [6]. Consider the function $declare : \mathcal{L} \rightarrow \mathcal{T}_A$ as a function extracting such constraints. The resulting set of constraints is used to encode the event log into a structured feature space.

Definition 5 (Feature Space). *Let $L \in \mathcal{L}$ be an event log and $declare(L) \subseteq \mathcal{T}_{act(L)}$ be a set of declarative constraints extracted from it. We define the feature space as $\mathcal{F}_L = declare(L) \times S$. An encoding function $encode_L : L \rightarrow \{0, 1\}^{|\mathcal{F}_L|}$ maps each trace $\sigma \in L$ to a binary feature vector. For every feature $f_i = (d, s) \in \mathcal{F}_L$ where $1 \leq i \leq |\mathcal{F}_L|$, the corresponding encoding is defined as*

$$encode_L(\sigma)[i] = \begin{cases} 1, & if\ eval(\sigma, d) = s, \\ 0, & otherwise. \end{cases}$$

4.2 Ensemble Tree-Based Feature Extraction

To enhance the feature space, we further leverage tree ensemble models such as random forests and gradient boosting. In a *random forest*, each decision tree is trained on a bootstrap sample of L, and at each node, a random subset of features is considered for splitting. This introduces randomness that reduces variance and improves generalization. *Gradient boosting* constructs trees sequentially, where each tree is trained to correct the residual errors of the ensemble constructed so far, thereby reducing bias.

Definition 6 (Rule Extraction). *A rule $R \in \mathcal{P}(\mathcal{F}_L)$ is defined as a set of features. Let Ψ denote an ensemble of decision trees, which may be obtained from either a random forest or a gradient boosting model. For each decision tree $\psi \in \Psi$, $\mathcal{R}_\psi$ denotes the set of all rules extracted from ψ, where every path from the root to a leaf node in a decision tree corresponds to a rule. $\mathcal{R}_\Psi = \bigcup_{\psi \in \Psi} \mathcal{R}_\psi$ is the set of all rules extracted from an ensemble tree.*

Considering the decision tree represented in Fig. 3 as a tree from and ensemble of trees, $\{(NotSuccession(l, p), violated), (NotSuccession(l, a), violated)\}$ is one of the four rules we can extract from this decision tree.

Definition 7 (Rule-based Encoding). *Let Ψ be an ensemble tree and $\mathcal{R}_\Psi$ be the set of all rules extracted from it. The function $\phi_L : L \rightarrow \{0, 1\}^{|\mathcal{R}_\Psi|}$ is a mapping from the traces to the rule-based encoding such that considering $R_i \in \mathcal{R}_\Psi$, $\phi_L(\sigma)[i] = \bigwedge_{f_j \in R_i} encode(\sigma)[j]$, where $1 \leq i \leq |\mathcal{R}_\Psi|$ and $1 \leq j \leq |\mathcal{F}_L|$.*

4.3 Regression Model

This new feature space encapsulates the ensemble-derived features and is used to augment our original feature set. Our methodology combines the strengths of declarative constraint encoding, ensemble tree-based feature extraction, and sparsity-inducing logistic regression to produce interpretable and efficient process models that distinguish between desirable and undesirable behaviors.

Definition 8 (Regression Classifier). *Let $L \in \mathcal{L}$ be an event log and $L' \subseteq L$ be a subset of traces selected for training of the regression model. Considering $\sigma \in L'$ as a trace from this event log, a logistic regression classifier with L1 regularization is defined as:*

$$cls(\sigma) = \begin{cases} 1, & if\ g\left(w^\top \phi(\sigma) + b\right) \geq 0.5, \\ 0, & otherwise, \end{cases}$$

where $w \in \mathbb{R}^{|\mathcal{R}_\Psi|}$ is the learned weight vector, and $b \in \mathbb{R}$ is the bias term and $g(z) = \frac{1}{1+\exp(-z)}$. w and b are obtained by minimizing the following regularized logistic loss:

$$\min_{w,b}\ \frac{1}{|L'|} \sum_{i=1}^{|L'|} \log\left(1 + \exp\left(-y_i\left(w^\top \phi(\sigma_i) + b\right)\right)\right) + \lambda \|w\|_1,$$

where $\|w\|_1 = \sum_{j=1}^{|\mathcal{R}_\Psi|} |w_j|$, $\sigma_i \in L'$ are training traces, $y_i = \kappa_L(\sigma_i)$ are the corresponding labels, and $\lambda > 0$ is the regularization strength controlling the sparsity of w.

We consider the weights learned by the logistic regression model as the importance of each rule $R_j \in \mathcal{R}_\Psi$, denoted as $importance(R_j) = w[j]$ where $1 \leq j \leq |\mathcal{R}_\Psi|$.

4.4 Hierarchical Clustering and Rule Selection

Although the important rules extracted from the regression model may overlap in the traces they cover, we aim to identify a representative and diverse subset of them. To this end, we apply hierarchical clustering to group rules that refer to similar sets of traces. As a dissimilarity measure, we use the *Jaccard distance* between binary feature vectors, allowing us to cluster and select distinctive rules more effectively.

Definition 9 (Jaccard Distance between Rules). *Let* $L \in \mathcal{L}$ *be an event log and* $R_i, R_j \in \mathcal{R}_\Psi$ *be two rules extracted from the ensemble of trees where* $1 \leq i, j \leq |\mathcal{R}_\Psi|$. *We define the Jaccard distance between rules* R_i *and* R_j *as:*

$$Jac(R_i, R_j) = 1 - \frac{\sum\limits_{\sigma \in L} \left(\phi(\sigma)[i] \wedge \phi(\sigma)[j] \right)}{\sum\limits_{\sigma \in L} \left(\phi(\sigma)[i] \vee \phi(\sigma)[j] \right)},$$

After computing the pairwise Jaccard distances between all rule pairs, we apply agglomerative hierarchical clustering, iteratively merging clusters of rules that exhibit the minimal average inter-cluster distance

$$dist(G, G') = \frac{1}{|G| \cdot |G'|} \sum_{R \in G} \sum_{R' \in G'} Jac(R, R'),$$

where G and G' are two clusters of rules.

Once clusters of similar rules are obtained, we proceed by selecting a representative rule for each cluster. Specifically, for each cluster $G \subseteq \mathcal{R}_\Psi$, we choose the rule with the highest importance as the representative rule:

$$R_G^* = \operatorname{argmax}_{R_j \in G} |importance(R_j)|,$$

where $1 \leq j \leq |\mathcal{R}_\Psi|$. Subsequently, we filter the original set of traces to retain only those that satisfy the chosen representative rule R_G^*, yielding the subset of traces $L|_G = \{\sigma \in L \mid \phi(\sigma)[j] = 1 \text{ where } R_j = R_G^*\}$.

5 Evaluation Metrics

Given a set of K rule clusters, we focus on each cluster G_k where $1 \leq k \leq K$ and the corresponding filtered event log $L|_{G_k}$, which contains traces satisfying the representative discriminative rule of that cluster. For each $L|_{G_k}$, we independently apply process discovery to derive a process model that captures the behavior specific to the associated traces. This results in interpretable, cluster-specific models that not only describe the observed behavior but also facilitate distinguishing between desirable and undesirable cases.

To assess the representativeness of the models, we employ well-established conformance checking techniques [3] including *trace fitness* (t-fit), i.e., the percentage of traces that perfectly fit the model. *Alignment fitness* (a-fit), i.e., the weighted average of alignment-based fitness values across traces. *Precision* (prc), i.e., an escaping-edges-based measure that quantifies the amount of behavior allowed by the model but not observed in the event log.

Furthermore, we evaluate the discriminative power of the models using metrics introduced in [12], which are defined in terms of trace and alignment fitness.

Definition 10 (Discriminative Evaluation Metrics). *Let* $L \in \mathcal{L}$ *be an event log and* κ_L *a labeling function that partitions* L *into desirable and undesirable traces:* $L^+ = \{\sigma \in L \mid \kappa_L(\sigma) = 1\}$ *and* $L^- = \{\sigma \in L \mid \kappa_L(\sigma) = 0\}$. *Let* $\mathcal{M}$ *be the universe of Petri net* *models and $M \in \mathcal{M}$ denote a Petri net model. We define the complement of the fitness measures as $\overline{a\text{-}fit}(L, M) = 1 - a\text{-}fit(L, M)$ and $\overline{t\text{-}fit}(L, M) = 1 - t\text{-}fit(L, M)$.*

Alignment-based accuracy (a-acc), trace-based accuracy (t-acc), alignment-based F1-score (a-F1), and trace-based F1-score (t-F1) are defined as follows:

- $a\text{-}acc(L^+, L^-, M) = a\text{-}fit(L^+, M) - a\text{-}fit(L^-, M)$
- $t\text{-}acc(L^+, L^-, M) = t\text{-}fit(L^+, M) - t\text{-}fit(L^-, M)$
- $a\text{-}F1(L^+, L^-, M) = \dfrac{2 \times a\text{-}fit(L^+, M) \times \overline{a\text{-}fit}(L^-, M)}{a\text{-}fit(L^+, M) + \overline{a\text{-}fit}(L^-, M)}$
- $t\text{-}F1(L^+, L^-, M) = \dfrac{2 \times t\text{-}fit(L^+, M) \times \overline{t\text{-}fit}(L^-, M)}{t\text{-}fit(L^+, M) + \overline{t\text{-}fit}(L^-, M)}$

The metrics $a\text{-}acc(L^+, L^-, M)$ and $t\text{-}acc(L^+, L^-, M)$ range from -1 to 1. A value closer to 1 indicates that the alignment or trace fitness is substantially higher with respect to the desirable event log. The metrics $a\text{-}F1(L^+, L^-, M)$ and $t\text{-}F1(L^+, L^-, M)$ range from 0 to 1, where a value of 1 denotes that the model balances well between representing desirable event log and avoiding the undesirable event log. The accuracy metrics primarily emphasize the difference in fitness values between the groups, whereas the F1 measures focus on the trade-off between increasing fitness for the desirable log and reducing it for the undesirable log. For example, if $a\text{-}fit(L^+, M) = 1$ and $a\text{-}fit(L^-, M) = 1$, then $a\text{-}acc(L^+, L^-, M) = 0$, indicating a mid-range value. However, $a\text{-}F1(L^+, L^-, M) = 0$, which is the minimum value, as the perfect fitness with respect to L^- means that one of the main objectives that is avoiding the undesirable behavior is sacrificed.

Table 2. The event logs used in the experiments.

Event Log	Desirable/Undesirable Event Logs	N. Traces
BPIC12	L^+: duration 4 to 28 days	3719
	L^-: duration more than 28 days	1433
BPIC17	L^+: duration more than 28 days	20282
	L^-: duration less than 28 days	11227
Hospital Billing	L^+: duration more than 1 day	74806
	L^-: duration less than 1 day	25194

6   Evaluation

The proposed framework has been fully implemented and is publicly available[1]. We evaluated the framework using several real-life event logs. This section presents an overview of the event logs used, the experimental setup, key findings, and a discussion of the framework's limitations.

---

[1] https://github.com/aliNorouzifar/discriminative_process_discovery.

6.1 Event Logs

Since the choice of L^+ and L^- depends on the specific application context, we adopted the method proposed in [14] to construct these labeled logs for process discovery. This method ranks traces based on a selected performance indicator and identifies significant control-flow changes using a two-sided sliding window in combination with the earth mover's distance. We selected case duration as the performance dimension and used the identified change points to define the desirable and undesirable event logs. The resulting trace groups are summarized in Table 2.

6.2 Experimental Setup

For each event log, we used 70% of the traces for feature extraction, training the ensemble models and logistic regression classifier, and reserved the remaining 30% for testing. Since class imbalance can negatively impact the learning process, we applied undersampling in training to ensure equal representation of desirable and undesirable cases. We evaluated different parameter settings for the supervised learning models using 5-fold cross-validation on the training data to determine the optimal configuration. It includes different random forest and gradient boosting settings for the rule generation and regression model parameters.

We applied agglomerative hierarchical clustering and determined the appropriate number of clusters by visually inspecting the resulting dendrograms. To avoid relying on the representational bias of a single discovery technique, we experimented with multiple process discovery algorithms:

- Rule-guided Inductive Miner (IMr) with a support threshold of $sup = 0.2$ [13]. The parameter settings for the discovery of declarative rules is set to $support = 0.005$ and $confidence = 0.95$.
- Inductive Miner with infrequency filtering (IMf) with a frequency threshold of $f = 0.2$ [10].
- Split Miner (SM) with parameters $\eta = 0.4$ and $\epsilon = 0.1$ [1].

6.3 Analysis of the Results

Figure 5 represents heatmaps of the Jaccard distances between rules extracted for each event log. The rows and columns correspond to rules obtained from regression models after initial feature generation using declarative constraints and ensemble tree-based rule extraction. The intensity of the blue color reflects the magnitude of the Jaccard distance, i.e., $Jac(R, R')$ where R is the rule corresponding to the row and R' is the rule corresponding to the column, so that lighter shades indicate that the corresponding rules are satisfied by similar groups of traces. In addition to the distance information, the heatmap includes a column on the left displaying the support for each rule in orange, and another column representing the importance magnitude using a color scale ranging from green to red with darker green denoting high positive coefficients and darker red indicating high negative coefficients. The dendrogram on the left, derived from hierarchical clustering based on the Jaccard distance, helps to determine an appropriate number of clusters for achieving well-separable groups of traces.

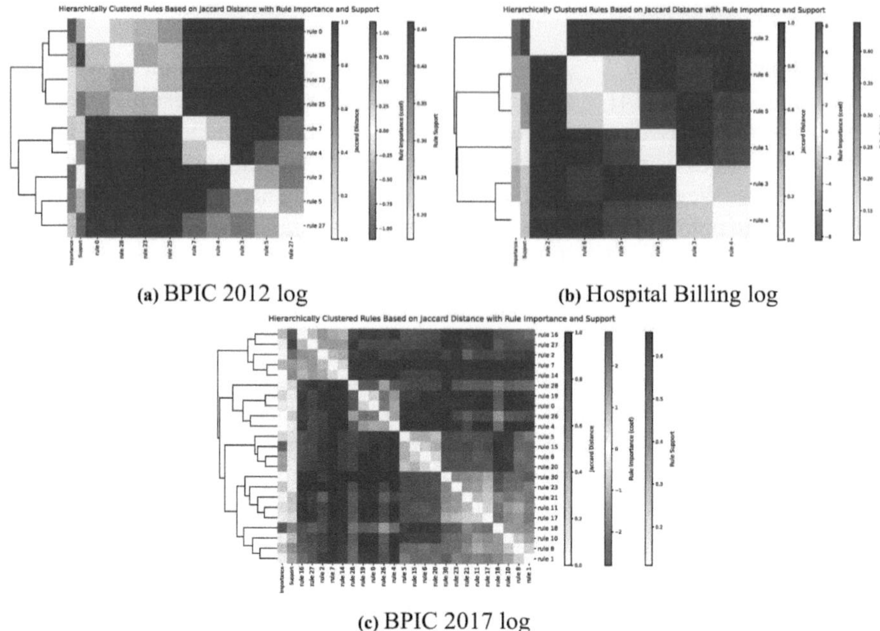

(a) BPIC 2012 log

(b) Hospital Billing log

(c) BPIC 2017 log

Fig. 5. Jaccard distance heatmaps between extracted rules for each event log. Lighter blue indicates greater similarity. Rule support (orange) and importance (green-red) are shown on the left. Dendrograms guide the identification of trace clusters. (Color figure online)

Based on the dendrograms represented in Fig. 5, we choose the number of clusters 3 for the BPIC2012, 4 for the hospital billing, and 4 for the BPIC2017 log. In Table 3, we report the accuracy of the trained machine learning models for each event log ($ML\text{-}acc$), that is the ratio of the correctly classified traces (true positives and true negatives) to the number of traces. For every extracted cluster, the most important rule is shown in the table, along with its alignment accuracy, trace accuracy, importance magnitude, and support values in both the desirable and undesirable event logs. The reported alignment and trace accuracy values are calculated considering the models discovered using the IMr discovery technique.

Figure 6 presents a comparative overview of various evaluation metrics computed for different trace groups using models discovered by three process discovery techniques. Specifically, Figs. 6a, b, and c illustrate the results for models obtained using the IMr, IMf, and SM techniques, respectively. Each subfigure visualizes a distinct evaluation metric calculated across the three event logs used in the study. Trace groups, represented by different colors, include both the clusters identified in Fig. 5 and described in Table 3, as well as the baseline groups composed solely of desirable traces and undesirable traces.

BPIC 2012. As shown in Fig. 6, the models discovered considering the representative rule of cluster 1 achieve higher $a\text{-}acc$ and $a\text{-}F1$ scores compared to the baseline model derived from the desirable event log in both the IMr and IMf experiments. The $t\text{-}acc$

Table 3. Most important rule per discovered cluster with alignment accuracy, trace accuracy, coefficient, and support in L^+/L^-. Accuracy corresponds to the classifier trained for each event log; discovery and evaluation use the IMr technique.

Log	ML-acc	Cluster	Rule				
			a-acc	t-acc	Coef	sup(L^+)	sup(L^-)
BPIC12	0.74	1 (rule 0)	$(NotSuccession(\text{O\_Cre}, \text{O\_Sel}), satisfied)=1 \wedge$ $(NotCoExistence(\text{A\_Act}, \text{A\_Dec}), satisfied)=1$				
			0.19	0.43	1.11	0.50	0.07
		2 (rule 7)	$(AlternateSuccession(\text{A\_Fin}, \text{O\_Can}), satisfied)=1 \wedge$ $(NotCoExistence(\text{A\_Pre}, \text{A\_Can}), violated)=1$				
			0.00	-0.12	-0.31	0.19	0.32
		3 (rule 3)	$(AlternateSuccession(\text{A\_Sub}, \text{O\_SentB}), satisfied)=0 \wedge$ $(AlternateSuccession(\text{A\_Acc}, \text{A\_Dec}), vac-satisfied)=1$				
			-0.14	-0.29	-1.07	0.02	0.31
IIB	0.95	1 (rule 6)	$(NotCoExistence(\text{CHD}, \text{COO}), violated)=1 \wedge$ $(AlternateSuccession(\text{FIN}, \text{JP}), violated)=1$				
			0.59	0.45	4.13	0.54	0.00
		2 (rule 3)	$(NotCoExistence(\text{FIN}, \text{JP}), vac-satisfied)=0 \wedge$ $(AlternateSuccession(\text{CHD}, \text{BILLED}), violated)=1$				
			0.57	0.77	3.64	0.40	0.00
		3 (rule 1)	$(ChainSuccession(\text{RLS}, \text{STAT}), violated)=0 \wedge$ $(End(\text{NEW}), violated)=1$				
			-0.45	-0.89	-1.26	0.11	0.11
		4 (rule 2)	$(End(\text{NEW}), satisfied)=1$				
			-0.62	-0.89	-8.24	0.00	0.89
BPIC17	0.83	1 (rule 7)	$(ChainSuccession(\text{A\_Val}, \text{A\_Den}), vac-satisfied)=1$				
			-0.17	-0.55	-1.05	0.07	0.71
		2 (rule 19)	$(CoExistence(\text{A\_Can}, \text{O\_Sent}), satisfied)=0 \wedge$ $(ChainSuccession(\text{O\_Ret}, \text{O\_Acc}), violated)=0$				
			0.03	0.19	0.58	0.24	0.02
		3 (rule 15)	$(CoExistence(\text{A\_Val}, \text{A\_Comp}), violated)=0 \wedge$ $(End(\text{O\_Can}), satisfied)=1$				
			-0.04	-0.52	2.51	0.19	0.14
		4 (rule 18)	$(End(\text{O\_Can}), violated)=1$				
			0.09	0.26	2.80	0.75	0.15

and $t\text{-}F1$ scores for cluster 1 may be slightly higher or lower, depending on the experiment. Considering Table 3, the most important rule in cluster 1 indicates that in the corresponding traces O_Created is not followed by O_Selected and A_Activated and A_Declined do not coexist. The illustrated model in Fig. 7c shows the discovered model based on this event log that contains the control flow corresponding to the accepted and denied cases.

For the undesirable traces, models discovered from cluster 3 consistently outperform the baseline across all experiments by achieving lower $a\text{-}acc$, $t\text{-}acc$, and $t\text{-}F1$ values. The increase in the $a\text{-}F1$ score is due to a shift from a situation where $a\text{-}fit(L^-, M)$ is disproportionately high to a situation where a better balance between $a\text{-}fit(L^-, M)$ and $a\text{-}fit(L^+, M)$ is achieved. For example, in the IMr experiment, $a\text{-}fit(L^+, M)$ decreases from 0.94 to 0.39, and $a\text{-}fit(L^-, M)$ from 0.93 to 0.53. While $a\text{-}acc$ decreased, indicating greater distinguishability, the score $a\text{-}F1$ increases due to the more balanced representation of desirable and avoidance of undesirable traces.

Cluster 3 includes the traces in which the alternative succession of A_Accepted and A_Declined is vacuously satisfied. The model illustrated in Fig. 7e shows the discovered model for this event log that contains the control flow pertain to the canceled applications. Similarly, cluster 2 with the discovered model represented in Fig. 7d shows the control flow for a bigger group of canceled applications. Comparing these models to the discovered models based on the desirable event log, i.e., Fig. 7b and the undesirable event log, i.e., Fig. 7a show that the discovered models from the clusters more specifically represents the differences between the desirable and undesirable cases.

Hospital Billing. The evaluation metrics presented in Fig. 6 highlight that, the models discovered based on the representative rule of cluster 2 outperform those derived from the desirable event log in terms of all four metrics $a\text{-}acc$, $a\text{-}F1$, $t\text{-}acc$, and $t\text{-}F1$ across the IMr and SM experiments. Similarly, models discovered using the representative rule of cluster 1 yield higher $a\text{-}acc$ and $a\text{-}F1$ scores compared to the baseline. However, this improvement comes at the cost of slightly reduced $t\text{-}acc$ and $t\text{-}F1$ scores.

Although different process discovery techniques use the same group of traces to discover process models, the quality of the discovered models and the extent to which they generalize the observed behavior can vary significantly due to the representational bias of each discovery technique. In cluster 1, models discovered using IMr and SM demonstrate substantially higher alignment accuracy and F1-score compared to those discovered solely from the desirable event log. However, models generated using IMf tend to overgeneralize the behavior, allowing both desirable and undesirable traces to fit the model. This leads to lower scores in evaluation metrics that assess discriminative power. The low precision of IMf models further suggests that these models permit behaviors not present in the event logs. While this may indicate flexibility, it does not clarify whether the additional allowed behavior reflects acceptable generalization or undesirable drift.

Clusters 4 and 3 correspond to behaviors that are more representative of the undesirable event log. However, their performance does not consistently surpass that of the models discovered directly from the undesirable event log. The evaluation metrics across different experiments indicate that, in some cases, the models based on these clusters achieve better scores than the baseline, but this superiority is not observed uniformly across all settings.

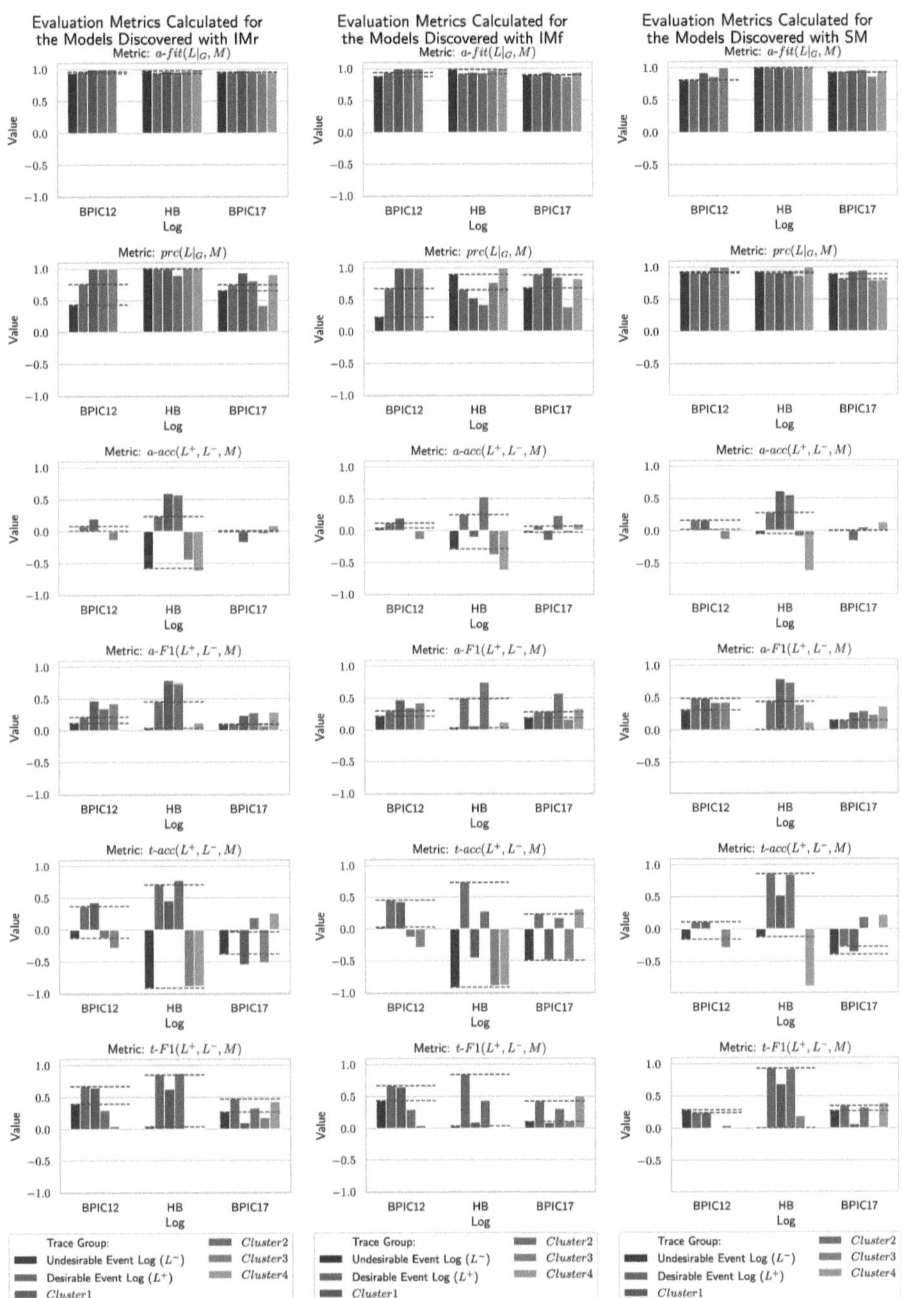

(a) Models discovered with the IMr process discovery technique.

(b) Models discovered with the IMf process discovery technique.

(c) Models discovered with the SM process discovery technique.

Fig. 6. Evaluation metrics for discovered models across trace groups. Bar heights show values based on IMr (left), IMf (middle), and Split Miner (right). Results are grouped by evaluation metric for each cluster and baseline (L^+ and L^-).

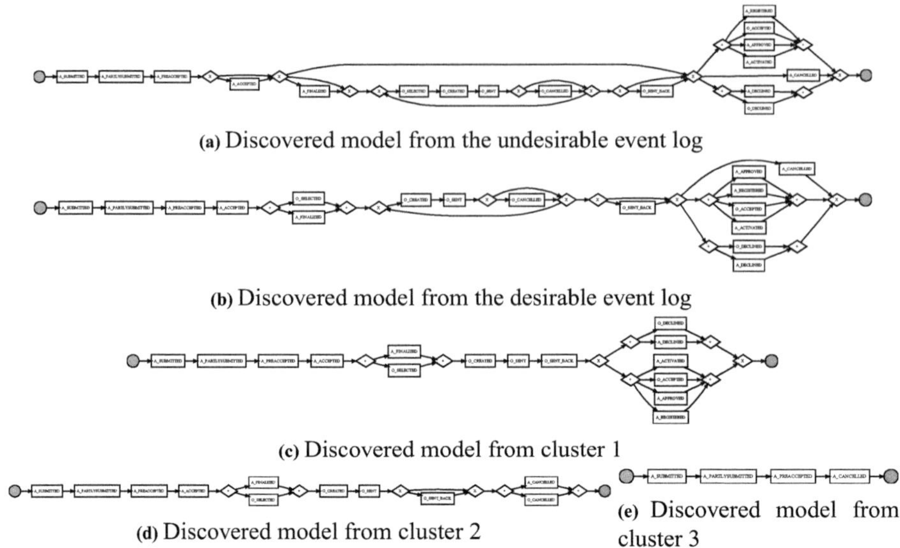

(a) Discovered model from the undesirable event log

(b) Discovered model from the desirable event log

(c) Discovered model from cluster 1

(d) Discovered model from cluster 2

(e) Discovered model from cluster 3

Fig. 7. The discovered model from BPIC 12 event log using the IMr process discovery algorithm.

BPIC 2017. Based on the evaluation metrics shown in Fig. 6, the models discovered from different trace groups reveal interesting patterns. Clusters 1 and 3 are particularly effective in capturing undesirable behavior, while clusters 2 and 4 are better suited for representing desirable behavior. For example, in the IMr experiments, the model derived from cluster 1 exhibits significantly lower a-acc, t-acc, and t-$F1$ scores compared to the undesirable log, indicating a strong alignment with undesirable traces. Cluster 3 follows a similar pattern, though with less significant differences. On the other hand, the model from cluster 4 achieves significantly higher a-acc, a-$F1$, and t-acc scores compared to the model discovered from the desirable event log. Cluster 2 shows a comparable trend, though the improvements are less substantial.

Depending on the interdependencies among features and their discriminative strength, the number of important features identified by the sparse regression model trained on desirable and undesirable event logs may vary. Features identified as important and clustered together often exhibit consistent directional influence, generally highlighting either desirable or undesirable behavior. However, this consistency does not always hold. For instance, in the BPIC 2017 event log, we observe that rule 15 and rule 6, although referring to similar groups of traces, receive coefficients with opposite signs. This discrepancy may stem from subtle behavioral differences that are particularly relevant for the classification task. Alternatively, it may be a consequence of multicollinearity among features, which warrants further investigation.

A concrete example of this can be seen in cluster 3 of Fig. 5c and Table 3. While the most important feature in this cluster has a relatively high positive coefficient, a very similar feature in the heatmap exhibits a strong negative coefficient. This contrast suggests potential multicollinearity that could destabilize the interpretation of individual coefficients. Notably, the conformance checking results for models discovered using this cluster across different discovery techniques indicate that the resulting models better capture undesirable behavior, despite the most important rule suggesting desirability.

This observation underscores the need for caution when interpreting feature importance in isolation. We therefore recommend focusing primarily on clusters where the important features have a consistent directional interpretation, such as cluster 1 and cluster 2, which offer clearer insights into the behavioral differences between trace groups. In contrast, cluster 4 includes a rule with a strong positive coefficient that does not align closely with others in the heatmap. However, conformance checking suggests that this rule still corresponds well to traces exhibiting desirable behavior, indicating that the differences between the traces corresponding to this feature and other features within this group is contributing to the discriminative power of the models.

Based on the experimental results across scenarios with both desirable and undesirable event logs, discovering process models that consider only a single aspect is less effective in explaining the differences between the logs. In contrast, the framework proposed in this paper facilitates the identification of the aspects that drive these distinctions. The process models subsequently discovered for these aspects are better suited to represent the distinctive behaviors within each event log.

7   Conclusion

The proposed method leverages the strengths of supervised learning to identify key differences between desirable and undesirable event logs. These discriminative features enable the discovery of process models that are more focused on representing the underlying factors that drive this distinction. The results are promising and introduce a novel perspective for working with labeled event logs, supporting interpretable and outcome-aware process discovery.

Nonetheless, the approach also presents opportunities for further refinement. In particular, multicollinearity among features may lead to instability in the regression coefficients, an issue that warrants further investigation and can be mitigated through pre-processing techniques. Using discriminative patterns to first filter the event log and then discover imperative models, which are subsequently evaluated for their relevance to desirable and undesirable traces, represents an indirect approach to identifying discriminative process models. Future work could explore more direct methods for deriving such subprocess models.

References

1. Augusto, A., Conforti, R., Dumas, M., Rosa, M.L., Polyvyanyy, A.: Split miner: automated discovery of accurate and simple business process models from event logs. Knowl. Inf. Syst. **59**(2), 251–284 (2019)
2. Bolt, A., de Leoni, M., van der Aalst, W.M.P.: Process variant comparison: using event logs to detect differences in behavior and business rules. Inf. Syst. **74**, 53–66 (2018)
3. Carmona, J., van Dongen, B.F., Solti, A., Weidlich, M.: Conformance Checking - Relating Processes and Models. Springer, Cham (2018). https://doi.org/10.1007/978-3-319-99414-7

 4. Chesani, F., et al.: Shape your process: discovering declarative business processes from positive and negative traces taking into account user preferences. In: Almeida, J.P.A., Karastoyanova, D., Guizzardi, G., Montali, M., Maggi, F.M., Fonseca, C.M. (eds.) Enterprise Design, Operations, and Computing, EDOC 2022. LNCS, vol. 13585, pp. 217–234. Springer, Cham (2022). https://doi.org/10.1007/978-3-031-17604-3_13
 5. Chesani, F., et al.: Process discovery on deviant traces and other stranger things. IEEE Trans. Knowl. Data Eng. **35**(11), 11784–11800 (2023)
 6. Ciccio, C.D., Mecella, M.: On the discovery of declarative control flows for artful processes. ACM Trans. Manag. Inf. Syst. **5**(4), 24:1–24:37 (2015)
 7. Cohen, W.W.: Fast effective rule induction. In: ICML, pp. 115–123. Morgan Kaufmann (1995)
 8. Francescomarino, C.D., Donadello, I., Ghidini, C., Maggi, F.M., Puura, J.: Business process deviance mining with sequential and declarative patterns. Bus. Inf. Syst. Eng. **67**, 877–894 (2025)
 9. Goedertier, S., Martens, D., Vanthienen, J., Baesens, B.: Robust process discovery with artificial negative events. J. Mach. Learn. Res. **10**, 1305–1340 (2009)
10. Leemans, S.J.J., Fahland, D., van der Aalst, W.M.P.: Discovering block-structured process models from event logs containing infrequent behaviour. In: Lohmann, N., Song, M., Wohed, P. (eds.) BPM 2013. LNBIP, vol. 171, pp. 66–78. Springer, Cham (2014). https://doi.org/10.1007/978-3-319-06257-0_6
11. de León, H.P., Nardelli, L., Carmona, J., vanden Broucke, S.K.L.M.: Incorporating negative information to process discovery of complex systems. Inf. Sci. **422**, 480–496 (2018)
12. Norouzifar, A., van der Aalst, W.M.P.: Discovering process models that support desired behavior and avoid undesired behavior. In: SAC, pp. 365–368. ACM (2023)
13. Norouzifar, A., Dees, M., van der Aalst, W.M.P.: Imposing rules in process discovery: an inductive mining approach. In: Araújo, J., de la Vara, J.L., Santos, M.Y., Assar, S. (eds.) Research Challenges in Information Science, RCIS 2024. LNBIP, vol. 513, pp. 220–236. Springer, Cham (2024). https://doi.org/10.1007/978-3-031-59465-6_14
14. Norouzifar, A., Rafiei, M., Dees, M., van der Aalst, W.M.P.: Process variant analysis across continuous features: a novel framework. In: van der Aa, H., Bork, D., Schmidt, R., Sturm, A. (eds) Enterprise, Business-Process and Information Systems Modeling, BPMDS EMMSAD 2024. LNBIB, vol. 511, pp. 129–142. Springer, Cham (2024). https://doi.org/10.1007/978-3-031-61007-3_11
15. Rafiei, M., et al.: Extracting rules from event data for study planning. In: De Smedt, J., Soffer, P. (eds) Process Mining Workshops, ICPM 2023. LNBIP, vol. 503, pp. 361–374. Springer, Cham (2023). https://doi.org/10.1007/978-3-031-56107-8_28
16. Sato, D.M.V., Freitas, S.C.D., Barddal, J.P., Scalabrin, E.E.: A survey on concept drift in process mining. ACM Comput. Surv. **54**(9), 189:1–189:38 (2022)
17. Slaats, T., Debois, S., Back, C.O., Christfort, A.K.F.: Foundations and practice of binary process discovery. Inf. Syst. **121**, 102339 (2024)
18. Teinemaa, I., Dumas, M., Rosa, M.L., Maggi, F.M.: Outcome-oriented predictive process monitoring: review and benchmark. ACM Trans. Knowl. Discov. Data **13**(2), 17:1–17:57 (2019)
19. Weerdt, J.D., vanden Broucke, S.K.L.M., Vanthienen, J.: Active trace clustering for improved process discovery. IEEE Trans. Knowl. Data Eng. **25**(12), 2708–2720 (2013)

eRooMiner: A Data-Driven Approach for Root Cause Detection of Process Data Quality Issues

Shokoufeh Ghalibafan[✉][iD], Sareh Sadeghianasl[iD], and Moe T. Wynn[iD]

Queensland University of Technology, Brisbane, Australia
shokoufeh.ghalibafan@hdr.qut.edu.au,
{s.sadeghianasl,m.wynn}@qut.edu.au

Abstract. Process mining relies on high-quality event logs for accurate analysis and decision-making. However, real-life event logs suffer from various types of data quality issues. Existing solutions are retroactive, detecting and repairing data quality issues after their occurrence in event logs. A more permanent and cost-effective solution would be to prevent these issues proactively, "prevention is better than the cure". This paper proposes a data-driven approach (*eRooMiner*) for identifying root causes of typical data quality issues in event logs to facilitate their prevention. The *eRooMiner* approach builds upon the typical data quality issues identified in the collection of eleven event log imperfection patterns, with a focus on imperfect labels which have the same meaning but different syntax. By learning from the data recorded in event logs, *eRooMiner* bridges the gap between theoretical and data-driven root cause analysis of event log imperfection patterns. The approach utilises machine learning and AI techniques to estimate the most probable root cause of specific data imperfections. The approach has been implemented and evaluated using real-life event logs and stakeholders. The results show that the proposed approach can correctly detect the potential root cause(s) of imperfect labels in various scenarios.

Keywords: Process Mining · Event Log · Data Quality · Root Cause Analysis

1 Introduction

Process mining has emerged as a powerful set of techniques that combine process science with data science to uncover meaningful insights about processes from historical data [1]. Process mining's main techniques include process discovery, conformance checking, and process enhancement [1], all of which require an *event log* as the primary input. An event log contains sequences of events, each describing a process step, i.e., what happened (activity), when (timestamp), for which process instance (case) [1]. The quality of event logs is critical for reliable process mining [2]. Poor data quality can lead to poor data-driven decision making and increased costs [14], a situation referred to as "Garbage-in-Garbage-out" [34].

Recent studies have proposed frameworks and tools for assessing, cleaning, and improving data quality of event logs [13,17,23,30]. They emphasise on the integration of data quality considerations into process mining methodologies and algorithms [17].

© The Author(s), under exclusive license to Springer Nature Switzerland AG 2026
C. Cappiello et al. (Eds.): CoopIS 2025, LNCS 15535, pp. 33–51, 2026.
https://doi.org/10.1007/978-3-032-15538-2_3

These approaches typically focus on detecting and repairing symptoms of data quality issues in event logs, such as incomplete event logs [27], timestamp errors [26], noise and outliers [8], and activity label issues [25]. These approaches are reactive, addressing data quality problems only after they have occurred. This means that data quality issues can happen again when the new data is being recorded and thus it will require another round of detection and repair leading to waste of effort, time, and cost.

A potential solution to this challenge is Root Cause Analysis (RCA) of data quality issues to proactively facilitate their prevention or mitigation in the future. RCA is typically conducted for tasks other than data quality, e.g., for finding the root causes of performance issues [24], or anomalous process behaviour [18]. RCA often relies on qualitative techniques such as the Fishbone (Ishikawa) diagram [19] and Fault Tree Analysis (FTA) [31], which help systematically trace problems to their root causes. While RCA has been explored in domains such as manufacturing, telecommunications, and IT systems using AI and statistical methods, it has received limited attention in process mining, especially for understanding the event log quality root causes. Existing RCA efforts in process mining, such as the Odigos framework [4, 13], conceptualise root causes of data quality issues across personal, social, and material dimensions, but do not offer automated, data-driven techniques for their identification.

To address this research gap, this paper proposes *eRooMiner*, a data-driven approach to identifying the underlying causes of event log quality issues. The capabilities of AI to predict future data have great potential to be used to predict future data quality issues, with Explainable AI (XAI), providing means to identify features that contribute to that prediction. Those features can hint at the root causes of data quality problems. Therefore, our research question is: *How can we develop a data-driven approach to detect potential root causes of data quality issues in event logs?*

This work contributes to the fields of process mining and data quality management by introducing a novel data-driven approach (*eRooMiner*) that detects potential root causes of data quality issues using only event log data. The key components of the *eRooMiner* include *root cause classification, feature identification, feature contribution extraction*, and *root cause extraction*. The approach was evaluated using two real-life event logs with injected errors (involving approximately 800 experiments) and two real-life logs with real errors. Results show that the *eRooMiner* approach can correctly detect the potential root causes for the imperfections.

The rest of the paper is structured as follows: Sect. 2 provides an overview of the related work. Section 3 describes the approach. Section 4 presents the implementation and evaluation results. Finally, Sect. 6 concludes the paper by summarising key findings and future work.

2   Related Work

This section reviews the previous work on data quality and root cause analysis in process mining and, subsequently, root cause analysis in the broader field of data mining to identify the research gap that motivates this research.

Data Quality Management in Process Mining. A comprehensive understanding of event log quality is important to ensure the reliability of process mining outcomes. Several frameworks have been proposed to classify process data quality issues. For example, the Process Mining Manifesto [2] presents a 5-star rating of event logs quality, emphasising attributes like trustworthiness, completeness, and well-defined semantics. In another framework, Bose et al. [5] categorise event log quality issues into missing, incorrect, imprecise, and irrelevant data. Suriadi et al. [30], consolidated typical data quality issues found across various domains such as health and insurance, into a collection of eleven imperfection patterns. This pattern-based framework has become a foundation for describing, detecting, and addressing data quality challenges in process mining, including their manifestations and potential strategies for detection and repair.

Building on these classifications, a variety of detection and repair techniques have been proposed for event log quality issues. For example, noise and outliers have been addressed using approaches such as statistical methods [8]. Incomplete event logs are addressed using various techniques such as probabilistic [27] and deep learning approaches [23]. There are other studies that focus on timestamp issues [26] and activity label issues [25]. These approaches are primarily reactive; they address quality issues after they appear in the data. A more effective approach would be to proactively analyse the root causes of data quality issues after they are detected, so that they can be mitigated in the future, saving effort, time, and cost.

Root Cause Analysis in Process Mining. In process mining, RCA has focused more on problems other than data quality issues, such as anomalous traces in event logs [18] and system bottlenecks and conformance problems [24]. To date, only few studies have focused on addressing the root cause(s) of event log quality issues. The Odigos framework [13] provides a conceptual baseline for root cause classification of event log imperfection patterns. It distinguishes three worlds that can contribute to the emergence of data quality issues in event logs: personal, material, and social. Built on the Odigos framework, Andrews et al. [4] map the event log imperfection patterns [30] to root causes and intermediate causes (which is closer to the level of data), describing a many-to-many relationship. Validation of the Odigos framework is conducted by Andrews et al. [3] through semi-structured interviews with process mining experts. The framework has also been instantiated for the digital health domain [12]. To the best of our knowledge, the Odigos framework and its subsequent studies are the only works in process mining that specifically focus on RCA of event logs data quality issues. They remain at the conceptual level and do not detect root causes of data quality issues using data.

Root Cause Analysis in Data Mining. In the data mining domain, RCA studies classify root causes based on evidences from the literature, experts or observations [7,15,28,36]. For example, Singh and Singh [28] conduct a systematic review of data quality problems in data warehousing, and conduct expert interviews, and identify their causes. Similarly, Carvalho et al. [7] identify and classify 105 root causes through a systematic literature review in the healthcare domain. Zellal and Zaouia [35] discuss the significance of data quality in Business Intelligence (BI) and study "factors influencing data quality in a data warehouse" through exploratory research. Zhang et al. [36] developed a data-driven approach (LANG) to find data quality problems, but not their root causes. In this work, observations about root causes emerged during empirical evaluations, particularly through focus groups with data users. Other studies, such as Csáki's [9] work on open government data and observe use cases to identify potential causes, and Lee et al. [21] follow the classical scientific method, observing data, forming hypotheses, and testing them, on healthcare data to examine such causes.

Table 1 summarises the existing work on RCA in process mining and data mining. Some approaches focus on categorisation of data quality root causes and some others focus on detecting these causes. Our approach fits in the detection part, where existing approaches are expert-based with some data-driven techniques existing in the data mining domain. To the best of our knowledge, there are no approaches to systematically detecting root causes of event log data quality issues based on information derived from the data itself, and this is the gap we aim to address in this study.

Table 1. Related work in root cause analysis of data quality issues.

Goal	Process Mining	Data Mining
Categorisation	Expert-based *(Eden et al. [12])*	Expert-based *(Singh & Singh [28], Zhang et al. [36])*
	Systematic review/ Conceptual framework *(Emamjome et al. [13], Andrews et al. [4])*	Systematic review/ Conceptual framework *(Carvalho et al. [7], Zellal and Zaouia [35])*
	Data-driven	Data-driven *(Csáki [9])*
Detection	Expert-based *(Andrews et al. [3])*	Expert-based *(Zhang et al. [36])*
	Data-driven **Research Gap**	Data-driven *(Lee et al. [22], Csáki [9])*

3   Approach

Figure 1 presents the *eRooMiner* approach for root cause detection of event log quality issues. The approach consists of four steps: (1) *root cause classification*, which creates a mapping between event log imperfection patterns [30] and their potential manifestations, causes, and metrics; (2) *feature identification*, where features are defined, based on the mappings created in step 1, and the event log is filtered to focus on events with imperfection patterns; (3) *feature contribution extraction*, where machine learning and XAI analysis is conducted, and (4) *root cause extraction*, where the probability of various possible root causes are computed based on the feature importance values, metrics, and the mappings created in the earlier steps.

In this paper, we focus on three imperfection patterns: synonymous labels, polluted labels and distorted labels; however, the approach is generalisable to other data quality issues and root causes. Synonymous labels are syntactically different but semantically the same, e.g. *"Cancel Goods Receipt"* and *"Cancel Delivery Record"*. Distorted labels do not exactly match each other but are very similar syntactically, e.g. *"Purchase Requisition Item"* and *"Purchase Requisision Item"*. Polluted labels share the same semantics but have similar structures with slight variations in specific labels that provide additional details, such as *"Patient Admission ID: AAAA"*, *"Patient Admission ID: BBBB"*, and *"Patient Admission ID: CCCC"*. These labels share the same semantics but differ in specific identifiers, adding further details while maintaining a similar structure. The rest of this section describes these steps in detail.

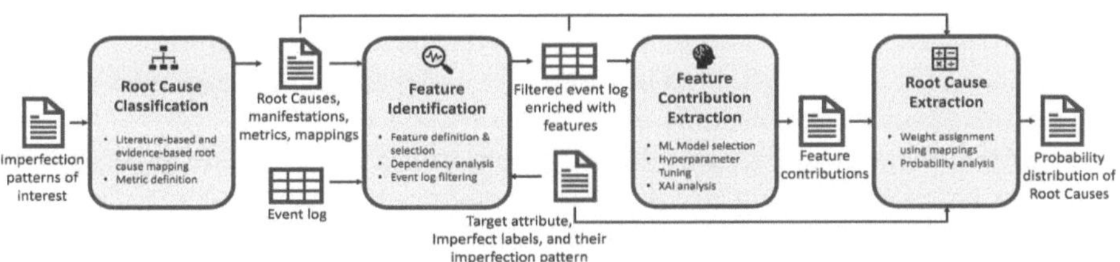

Fig. 1. *eRooMiner*: A root cause detection approach for event log quality issues.

3.1 Root Cause Classification

As an initial step towards root cause detection for event log data quality issues, we propose a classification of root causes of event log data quality issues. The input to this step is a set P of imperfection patterns of interest. These patterns can be selected from the eleven event log imperfection patterns [30] or any other data quality framework (e.g. [5]), therefore $P = \{$*"Synonymous labels"*, *"Polluted labels"*, *"Distorted labels"*$\}$.

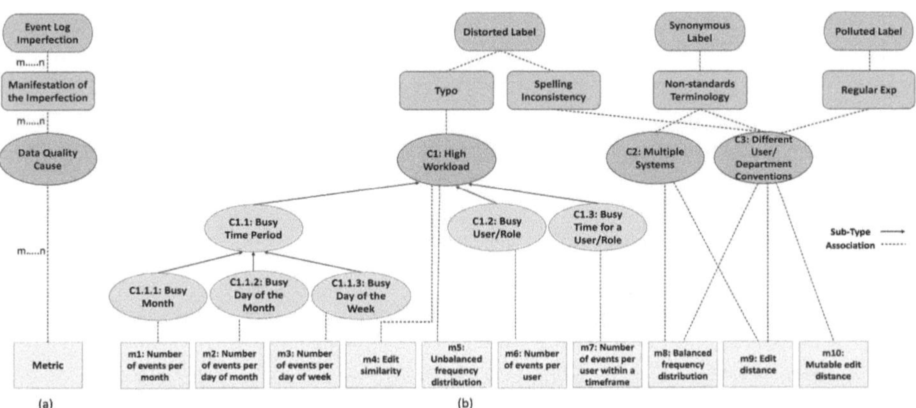

Fig. 2. Event log quality issue root cause classification (a) at the conceptual level, and (b) for synonymous, distorted and polluted labels.

Figure 2(a) shows the general elements of the event log imperfection root cause classification at the conceptual level, and Fig. 2(b) instantiates this classification for the three imperfection patterns of interest. Let MN and C be the sets of possible manifestations, and possible causes of pattern $p \in P$ in the event log, respectively. At the conceptual level (Fig. 2(a)), for each pattern $p \in P$, there can be various manifestations $mn \in$ MN, and one manifestation can represent multiple imperfection patterns. The mapping $M_{pmn} : P \times \text{MN} \rightarrow \{0,1\}$ formalises this relationship, where 0 means there is no mapping and 1 means there is a mapping. Then there is an n–m relationship between manifestations and root causes, meaning that a specific imperfection manifestation mn can have multiple causes $c \in C$ and vice versa. This is defined by the mapping $M_{mnc} : \text{MN} \times C \rightarrow \{0,1\}$. The root cause c explains why a particular pattern p occurs with a specific manifestation mn in the event log.

At the bottom layer of Fig. 2(a), we have metrics that would help us to quantify the root causes based on data. Let M be the set of all possible metrics. A metric $m \in M$ is defined as $m : \wp(V) \times \mathcal{L} \rightarrow \mathbb{R}$, where $\wp(V)$ is a power set of V, the universe of values, $\mathcal{L}$ is the set of possible event logs, and $\mathbb{R}$ is the set of real numbers. m is computed for a given set of values $V' \subset V$ in a given event log $L \in \mathcal{L}$. The mapping $M_{cm} : C \times M \rightarrow \{0,1\}$ formalises the relationship between causes and metrics. Using mappings M_{pmn}, M_{mnc}, and M_{cm}, we can define a derived mapping $M_{pm} : P \times M \rightarrow \{0,1\}$, where $M_{pm}(p,m) = 1$ if and only if $M_{pmn}(p,mn) = 1$ and $M_{mnc}(mn,c) = 1$ and $M_{cm}(c,m) = 1$[1]. For example, the variance between frequencies of imperfect labels can help us distinguish typos from non-standard terminology. If some labels are less frequent than others, typos are more likely, while imperfect labels with similar frequency probably happen due to a non-standard terminology. Another example metric is edit distance/similarity between imperfect labels. A high edit similarity may indicate a typo whereas a high edit distance may indicate a non-standard terminology cause.

At the instance level (Fig. 2(b)), the synonymous, distorted, and polluted label imperfection patterns can be manifested as typos, spelling inconsistencies, non-standard terminologies, or labels that follow a regular expression (for polluted labels) in the event log. The root causes of event log imperfection patterns are identified based on real-life examples, building upon the root causes defined by Andrews et al. [4] for imperfection patterns. The root-cause included in our classification include high workload, multiple systems (i.e. sources), and different user or department naming conventions. Some of these causes can be further detailed and categorised into sub-causes or sub-sub-causes. The causes are described in Table 2, though additional causes may be relevant in other scenarios.

3.2   Feature Identification

This step involves defining and selecting features that contribute to the root cause identification of synonymous, distorted, and polluted labels. Some features are original, meaning that they are present in the log and ready to use as a feature in their current form. Some other features are derived, i.e., computed from the data available in the

---

[1] We acknowledge that the binary definition of mappings may oversimplify the relationships between causes and features.

Table 2. Causes of Synonymous, Distorted, and Polluted labels.

Root Cause	Description
C1: High Workload	This root cause contributes to typos in event logs due to pressure on users.
C1.1: Busy Time Period	During peak times, such as the end of the year (*C1.1.1*), typos occur more frequently due to increased workload. Similarly, typo rates can increase on peak days of the month (*C1.1.2*). For instance, on the last day of the month, we may see a rise in errors. Certain days of the week may also experience higher workload (*C1.1.3*), increasing the likelihood of data-entry errors. The metrics that we use to analyse workload variations over time (i.e., *m1*, *m2*, *m3*) counts the total number of events recorded in a specific timeframe (e.g., month of year or day of month)
C1.2: Busy User/ Role	It is also possible that some users generally have a higher workload than others, irrespective of the time period. The key metric here is the total number of events performed by a user or role (*m6*). High-workload users are more prone to making typos due to time pressure and the volume of tasks they handle [7,33].
C1.3: Busy Time for a User/ Role	In some cases, a combination of both sub-causes *C1.1* and *C1.2* can occur. Certain users may experience high workloads during specific timeframes. For instance, a project manager may experience increased error rates during monthly reporting periods, even though they do not handle a consistently high workload overall.
C2: Multiple Systems	Different systems might be configured such that they auto-record the same activity with different (synonymous) labels. This root cause is relevant in logs with data recorded by multiple systems and can be extended to various organisations [4,7,28]
C3: Different Conventions for Users or Departments	Users or departments may follow their own naming conventions when entering data, leading to variations in labels [4,7,28]

event log. An event log $L \in \mathcal{L}$ is formally defined as $L = (\mathcal{E}, \mathcal{C}, V, \mathcal{T}, AN, \#)$, where $\mathcal{E}$ is the set of event identifiers, $\mathcal{C}$ is the set of case identifiers, $\mathcal{T}$ is the set of timestamps, AN is the set of attributes names, $\# : \mathcal{E} \rightarrow (AN \rightarrow V)$ gets the value of attribute $n \in AN$ recorded for an event $e \in \mathcal{E}$, i.e. $\#_n(e) \in V$.

Let F be the set of features. The mapping $M_{fc} : F \times C \rightarrow \{0, 1\}$ formalises the relationship between features and causes, where $M_{fc}(f, c) = 1$ means that feature f is relevant to cause c and can help in its identification from data. The features and their relevant causes and metrics are detailed in Table 3. This is not a complete list of features; others may be relevant and added in different scenarios.

Table 3. Features linked to one or more root causes.

Feature ID	Feature Name	Feature Type	Original vs Derived	Cause	Metric
F1	*Resource*	Categorical	Original	*C1.2, C1.3, C2, C3*	-
F2	*Month*	Numerical	Original	*C1.1.1, C1.3*	-
F3	*Day of month*	Numerical	Original	*C1.1.2, C1.3*	-
F4	*Day of Week*	Numerical	Original	*C1.1.3*	-
F5	*User workload*	Numerical	Derived	*C1.2*	*m6*
F6	*Time workload (month)*	Numerical	Derived	*C1.1.1*	*m1*
F7	*Time workload (day of month)*	Numerical	Derived	*C1.1.2*	*m2*
F8	*Time workload (day of week)*	Numerical	Derived	*C1.1.3*	*m3*
F9	*User-time workload (day of month)*	Numerical	Derived	*C1.3*	*m7*

After defining the set of features, feature dependencies are analysed using statistical methods to avoid redundancy and ensure the provision of meaningful input for machine learning models. For numerical features, Pearson correlation [21] is applied to assess their relationships. The feature dependency is formalised as $D : F \times F \rightarrow [0, 1]$. Ideally, if two features have a correlation higher than a threshold, only one of them should be used in machine learning analysis. We rely on a common correlation threshold of 0.80 used in the machine learning literature [16].

Another task performed in the *feature identification* step is event log filtering. Let $\text{TA} \in AN$ be the target attribute where imperfect labels occur in the log and S be a set of values (i.e., labels) of attribute TA that exhibits imperfection pattern $P_s \in P$. For example, $S = \{$"*Cancel Goods Receipt*", "*Cancel Delivery Record*"$\}$ is a set of $P_s = $ "*Synonymous labels*" in target attribute $\text{TA} = $ "*Activity*". $L_S^{\text{TA},F} = (\mathcal{E}_S^{TA}, \mathcal{C}, V, \mathcal{T}, \{\text{TA}\} \cup F, \#)$ is the filtered event log, where $\mathcal{E}_S^{\text{TA}} = \{e \in \mathcal{E} | \#_{\text{TA}}(e) \in S\}$ is the set of all events that have an imperfect label for attribute TA. For these events, only their event identifier, case identifier, timestamp, target attribute TA and the features F are kept, and the rest of the attributes are removed.

3.3 Feature Contribution Extraction

In this phase, we conduct machine learning analysis to predict instances of imperfect labels in event logs using their relevant features. We also use XAI techniques [11] to find the features that contribute to this prediction the most, and are thus likely to point to the root cause of these imperfect labels. The first step is selecting the fit-for-purpose machine learning model. Classification models are ideal for predicting the category of new data based on their features [20]. Given that we also want to predict imperfect labels (synonymous, distorted or polluted labels) using their features, we choose a classification model. Among various classification models, we select "*Random Forest*" [6] due to its superior performance in similar contexts [6] and its ability to handle both numerical and categorical features effectively. More specifically, the capability of "*Random Forest*" models to handle mixed data types, their built-in feature importance metrics (which can help in identifying the factors that contribute the most to the occurrence of imperfect labels), their ability to capture non-linear relationships, and their robustness against overfitting [6,21] make these models ideal for our purpose.

The Random Forest model is optimised through hyper-parameter tuning [21] to achieve optimal performance. As such, we use grid search cross-validation to find the best values of hyper-parameters for our model, including the number of estimators (trees in the forest), maximum tree depth (controls complexity), minimum samples for split (prevents overfitting), and minimum samples per leaf (ensures meaningful splits) [21]. After finding the fit-for-purpose model with optimised hyper-parameters, we split the event log into training and test data. Next, we conduct XAI analysis to find the features that contribute the most to the occurrence of imperfect labels. These features guide us to the root causes behind these imperfections.

3.4 Root Cause Extraction

In this phase, we estimate the likelihood of each of the causes of a certain set of imperfect labels. We define two key vectors: (1) vector X, which consists of n feature importance values for features in F ($n = |F|$), and (2) vector Y, which consists of the k

metric from M that are not already incorporated in the definition of features ($k \leq |M|$). Then, for each cause $c \in C$ we define two *weight* vectors, $W_{x,c}$ and $W_{y,c}$, which assign weights to vectors X and Y with respect to cause c. These weights represent the relevance of a specific feature or metric to a cause and are defined based on mappings specified in the *root cause classification* and *feature identification* steps (Sects. 3.1 and 3.2). For example, for the different user conventions cause (*C3*), the weight of the edit distance metric would be high, meaning that it is highly indicative of *C3*. We then use the weighted sum of vectors X and Y for each cause c to compute its likelihood score.

Algorithm 1 presents our approach for root-cause identification of event log imperfection patterns (synonymous, polluted, and distorted labels). The inputs to this algorithm are event log L, which contains a set of imperfect labels S in target attribute TA with imperfection pattern $P_s \in P$. The output is a probability distribution function PDF which indicates the probability of each of the causes of the occurrence of imperfect labels S in the log. In the first step, we define and classify causes of imperfection patterns in P. This yields the set of causes C, metrics M, and mapping M_{mp} between metrics and patterns. These are the inputs to the *FeatureIdentification* function followed by the EventLogFiltering function in Line 3. This function only keeps events that contain imperfect labels in the target attribute. The outputs are a set of features F, mapping M_{fc} between features and causes, and the filtered event log $L_S^{\mathrm{TA},F}$. We also have the *ModelSetting* function in Line 4 which selects the fit-for-purpose model ML, with optimised hyper parameters.

Algorithm 1. Root-cause identification of event log imperfection patterns.

Input: Event log L, Imperfection pattern names P, Target attribute TA, Set of imperfect labels S and the name of their imperfection pattern $P_s \in P$

Output: Probability distribution PDF over root causes of imperfect labels in set S

1   $C, M, M_{mp} \leftarrow RootCauseMapping\ (P)$

2   $F, M_{fc} \leftarrow FeatureIdentification\ (C, M, M_{mp}, L)$

3   $L_S^{\mathrm{TA},F} \leftarrow EventLogFiltering\ (L, S, F, \mathrm{TA})$

4   $\mathrm{ML} \leftarrow ModelSetting\ (L_S^{\mathrm{TA},F})$

5   $X \leftarrow [x_1, x_2, \cdots, x_n]$, where $x_i = XAI(f_i, \mathrm{ML}, L_S^{\mathrm{TA},F})$ for each $f_i \in F$

6   $Y \leftarrow [y_1, y_2, \cdots, y_k]$, where $y_j = m_j(S, L_S^{\mathrm{TA},F})$ for each $m_j \in M$

7   $LK \leftarrow []$

8   **for** each $c \in C$ **do**

9      $W_{x,c} = [w_{x_1,c}, w_{x_2,c}, \cdots, w_{x_n,c}]$, where $w_{x_i,c} = M_{fc}(f_i, c)$ for each $f_i \in F$

10   **for** each $f_a \in F$ **do**

11   **if** $w_{x_a,c} > 0 \land \exists f_b \in F, f_a \neq f_b \land D(f_a, f_b) > 0$ **then**

12           $w_{x_b,c} = w_{x_b,c} + D(f_a, f_b)$

13      $W_{y,c} = [w_{y_1,c}, w_{y_2,c}, \cdots, w_{y_k,c}]$, where $w_{y_j,c} = M_{mp}(m_j, P_s)$ for each $m_j \in M$

14      $LK \leftarrow LK.append(X.W_{x,c} + Y.W_{y,c})$

15   $\mathrm{PDF} \leftarrow Softmax(LK)$

16   **return** PDF

The *XAI* function in Line 5 applies ML to the event log and extracts feature importance values of each feature $f_i \in F$. The results are stored in vector X. Vector Y stores the computed metric for labels of S. Lines 8–14 assign weights to X and Y for each cause $c \in C$. The weights of X (i.e., $W_{x,c}$) are initialised based on M_{fc} and are augmented using feature dependency values. That is, if the weight $w_{x_a,c}$ for a feature f_a is more than zero (i.e., there is a mapping between f_a and c) and if there is another feature f_b which has a dependency with f_a, i.e., $D(f_a, f_b) > 0$, then the weight of f_b (i.e., $w_{x_b,c}$) is increased by the dependency value (Lines 10–12). The weights of vector Y

(i.e., $W_{y,c}$) are assigned based on the mapping M_{mp} between metrics and imperfection pattern P_s (Line 13). LK in Line 14 is a vector that stores the weighted sum of x and Y for each cause each cause. In the last step (Line 15) we convert the likelihood vector LK with real numbers to a probability distribution PDF (adding up to 1) using the Softmax function [32].

4   Evaluation

To demonstrate the effectiveness of our approach for root cause detection of event data quality issues, we conducted multiple experiments. The approach is implemented in Python, and the code is available on GitHub[2]. We conducted experiments with both injected and real quality issues. detailed in Sects. 4.1 and 4.2. We used public logs, which originally contained correct labels without imperfections. In order to introduce a ground truth, we injected imperfect labels based on specific root causes, and then assessed whether our approach could correctly detect the underlying root cause for each injection. We then evaluated our approach under real settings using two logs, with real imperfect labels. The results were validated with stakeholders.

4.1   Experiments with Injected Errors and Root Causes in Real-Life Public Logs

Datasets. We used two public event logs: BPIC 2019 [10] and BPIC 2013 [29]. The BPIC 2019 log contains events related to a purchase-to-pay process from a multinational company in the Netherlands that specialises in coatings and paints. It contains 1595923 events across 251734 cases, with 42 unique activities performed by 628 users, resulting in 251734 variants. The BPIC 2013 event log originates from Volvo IT Belgium and contains events related to incident management within the VINST system. It includes 65533 events from 7554 cases, with 13 activities and 1440 users, resulting in 2278 process variants.

Procedure. We injected root cause-informed imperfect labels into the event logs. This was done in two steps: (1) selecting a specific candidate activity label from the log and then (2) renaming a percentage of its instances (events) into one or more new labels with the same meaning. Some of these new names were syntactically close to the original name (to simulate typos), and some others were not (to simulate different terminologies). In both steps (1) and (2), we were guided by specific root causes.

We selected 11 candidate activity labels from BPIC 2019 and 11 labels from the BPIC 2013 event logs. The complete list of labels for BPIC 2019 and BPIC 2013 is available on GitHub[3].

As described in Sect. 3.1, we consider seven causes: (*C1.2*) *Busy user/ role*, (*C1.1.1*) *Busy month*, (*C1.1.2*) *Busy day of month*, (*C1.1.3*) *Busy day of week*, (*C1.3*) *Busy day of month for a user* (*C2*) *Different system terminologies*, and (*C3*) *Different human conventions*. We injected imperfect labels into each of the 11 candidate activity labels

---

[2] https://github.com/ShokoufehGh/RootCauseDetectionFramework.

[3] Available at https://github.com/ShokoufehGh/RootCauseDetectionFramework.

based on each of these causes (i.e., $7 \times 11 = 77$ possible injection scenarios for BPIC 2019 and $6 \times 11 = 66$ scenarios for BPIC 2013[4]). The injection procedure was as follows:

- *C1.2: Busy User/ Role:* The top 20% of high-workload users were selected, and a percentage (350%) of their candidate label instances were renamed with typos.
- *C1.1.1: Busy month, C1.1.2: Busy day of month, C1.1.3: Busy day of week:* A percentage (350%) of candidate label instances occurring during peak times (busiest month, day of the month, or day of the week) was renamed with typos.
  on the peak day of the week. The injection percentages ranged from 3% to 50%.
- *C1.3: Busy day of month for a user:* For the top 20% of users, we renamed 350% of the candidate label instances on their busiest day of the month.
- *C2: Different system terminologies:* We renamed a percentage (2080%) of events for the candidate activity label so that instances recorded by each system share the same label, and the new names do not necessarily have similar syntax.
- *C3: Different human conventions:* Same procedure as *C2*, but applied to human users instead of systems.

The injected event logs were then used for the machine learning and XAI analysis (*root cause extraction*). We conduct ROC analysis to evaluate the performance of the classification model, measuring the False Positive Rate (FPR), True Positive Rate (TPR), and Area Under the ROC Curve (AUC) for each class. The average AUC was used as the main performance metric.

Results. We present results of a sample of these experiments. For example, in one of the experiments with the BPIC 2019 log, the activity label *"Record Goods Receipt"* was the candidate label for injecting typos based on the busy user root cause. 3% to 50% of the events with this label were renamed to one of the labels *"Record Goods Receit"*, *"Record Goods Reciept"*, and *"Record Good Receipt"*.

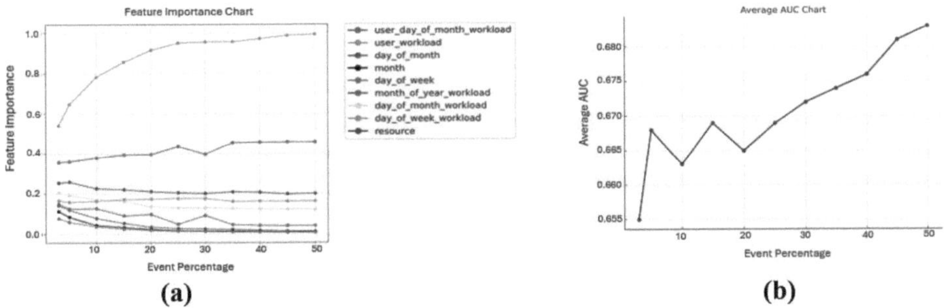

Fig. 3. (a) Feature importance and (b) Average AUC for BPIC 2019 with different percentages of imperfect labels injected based on the busy users root cause.

---

[4] This log does not contain activities recorded by systems. Therefore, the experiments on this log exclude the *Different system terminologies* root cause and focus on the other six causes.

Figure 3 shows feature importance values and the average AUC for different injection percentages. In Fig. 3(a), feature importance analysis confirms that *"User workload (F5)"* is consistently the most important feature across all injection levels. Using the feature importance from the 30% injection level, we calculated the probability of each of the seven root causes. As shown in Fig. 4, the *Busy user/ role* root cause is correctly identified as the most probable cause of these imperfect labels. As shown in Fig. 3(b), the average AUC increases with higher injection percentages, reaching 0.687 at 50%, indicating that more renaming makes it easier for the model to predict the label based on its features. The moderate AUC values highlight that predicting the underlying root causes of imperfections is challenging in some scenarios. In this example, the moderate AUC is observed because of the correlation between the user workload and user-time workload features; In other experiments[5], where there is less correlation between features, we observe a higher AUC.

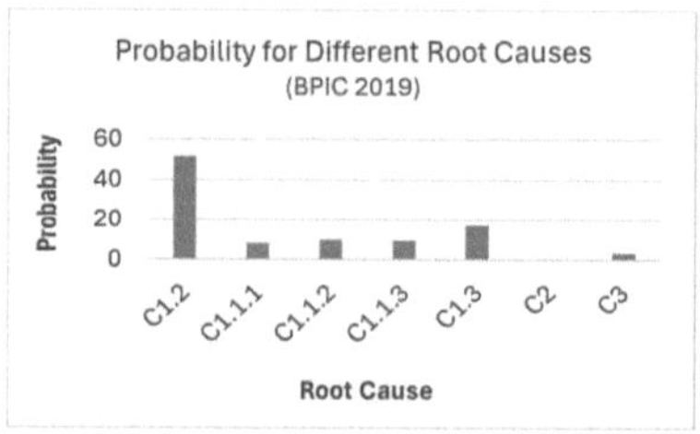

Fig. 4. Root cause probabilities for a set of imperfect labels injected based on the busy users root cause in BPIC 2019.

Table 4 summarises the results of our experiments. Our approach successfully identifies the injected root causes, with the relevant feature ranked highest in importance and the correct root cause having the highest probability. In some cases, other root causes also show high probabilities due to interdependencies. For example, *Busy User/ Role* and *Busy Time for a User/ Role* are often closely related, as users with high workloads are more likely to make errors during their peak times.

4.2 Experiments with Real Errors in the Australian Datasets

Datasets. The private datasets are related to an Australian ambulance and hospital system (*AusHealth*) and an Australian mine health and safety organisation (*AusMine*). We build event logs from the original databases provided by these industry partners. The *AusHealth* event log contains 986867 events, covering 160431 cases, with 9 unique activities performed by 2 users, resulting in 2,804 process variants. The *AusMine* event log consists of 91625 events from 19483 cases, involving 5 activities and 111 users, with 343 process variants.

---

[5] Reported in https://github.com/ShokoufehGh/RootCauseDetectionFramework.

Table 4. Detected probabilities for different injections in BPIC 2019 and BPIC 2013.

Injected Root Cause:	First Important Feature	Second Important Feature	Third Important Feature	$P(C1.2)$	$P(C1.1.1)$	$P(C1.1.3)$	$P(C1.1.2)$	$P(C1.3)$	$P(C2)$	$P(C3)$
BPIC 2019 event log										
C1.2	*F5*	*F9*	*F1*	49.88%	9.05%	9.47%	9.19%	19.75%	0.33%	2.34%
C1.1.1	*F6*	*F2* or *F3*	*F2* or *F3*	7.89%	67.77%	7.68%	7.31%	9.22%	0.09%	0.04%
C1.1.3	*F7*	*F3*	Not Consistent	9.56%	11.29%	55.05%	8.79%	15.09%	0.08%	0.03%
C1.1.2	*F8*	*F4*	Not Consistent	10.87%	9.17%	10.67%	58.35%	10.81%	0.10%	0.05%
C1.3	*F9*	*F5* or *F1* or *F3*	*F5* or *F3*	21.17%	12.96%	14.26%	10.33%	40.0%	0.49%	0.78%
C2	*F1*	Not Consistent	Not Consistent	1.56%	0.70%	0.70%	0.82%	0.93%	74.79%	20.49%
C3	*F5*	*F1*	Not Consistent	2.01%	0.56%	0.67%	0.63%	0.67%	19.47%	75.99%
BPIC 2013 event log										
C1.2	*F5*	*F1*	Not Consistent	44.00%	9.90%	12.23%	10.92%	19.39%	0.95%	2.61%
C1.1.1	*F6*	*F2*	*F3*	16.57%	35.83%	16.77%	11.74%	18.85%	0.17%	0.06%
C1.1.3	*F7*	*F3*	Not Consistent	12.64%	10.97%	42.55%	21.31%	12.35%	0.13%	0.05%
C1.1.2	*F8*	*F4*	Not Consistent	12.27%	9.36%	17.07%	50.16%	10.96%	0.13%	0.05%
C1.3	*F9*	*F5* or *F1*	*F5* or *F1*	32.41%	7.53%	7.65%	7.28%	44.96%	0.08%	0.09%
C3	*F1* or *F5*	*F1*	Not Consistent	0.53%	0.08%	0.08%	0.07%	0.11%	10.23%	88.91%

Results for AusHealth. The *AusHealth* log is constructed by combining records from two different systems, ambulance and hospital, that use different terminologies for the same hospital. Consequently, the event log contains instances of synonymous attribute values that occurred due to the *Different system terminologies'* root cause. In total, there are 89 sets of synonymous labels, each containing different names of a single hospital.

We applied our approach to two sample sets of imperfect labels. The first set consists of two unique labels with frequencies of 26014 and 58155. The second set contains two labels with frequencies of 232 and 278. Figure 5 illustrates the feature importance and root cause probability results for both sets. In both cases, the machine learning model identified the *Resource* feature (*F1*) (which represents different systems) as the most important feature influencing the label inconsistency and the root cause probability analysis correctly identified the *Different system terminologies* root cause as the most likely root cause for the imperfection.

To validate our findings, we consulted a domain expert familiar with the data and operational characteristics of both systems. We provided them with the event log and our analysis results, specifically asking: *"Do you confirm that we correctly detected the most likely root causes?"* The expert confirmed the correctness of our results for the first set, stating: *"Yes, absolutely. It is".*

For the second set, we obtained a similar confirmation. They further elaborated: *"Yes, I would say that is correct. They are recorded in different systems, and I would say that given within each system, those names would be consistent, which indicates that it is a system value and it's selected from a list. The same with the other set: the way the hospital is represented is selected from a list, and the two different systems just have different representations for the same physical entity. Neither of which needs to be typed in by a human, but selected from a list, and the list values are different. Yes, your observations are correct".*

These confirmations not only validate the technical correctness of our approach but also provide strong evidence that the root cause analysis accurately reflects real-world data challenges within integrated healthcare systems.

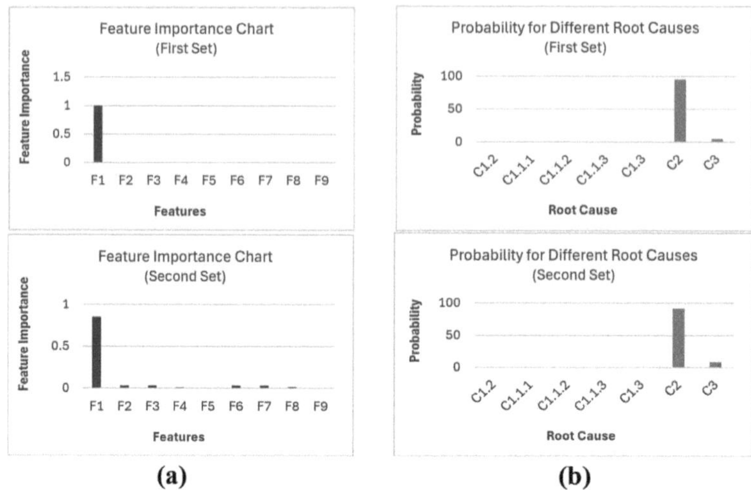

Fig. 5. (a) Feature importance and (b) root cause probability results for synonymous attribute values in the *AusHealth* log (sets 1 & 2).

Results for AusMine. The *AusMine* log contains various types of label imperfections, including distorted, synonymous, and polluted labels across multiple attributes such as roles, mine parts, compliance actions, subject descriptors, and review comments. We selected four sample sets of imperfect labels and applied our approach to detect their root causes. The first set contained three distinct imperfect labels with a total of 84 occurrences. The second set had seven distinct labels with a total of 603 occurrences. The third set included five imperfect labels with a total of 92 occurrences. The fourth set had three distinct labels with a total of 209 occurrences.

Figure 6 shows the feature importance and root cause probability results for these four sets. As shown in this Figure, we identified the *Resource* as the most important feature for the first set of imperfect labels. This indicates that the person or role that recorded these values contributed the most to the inconsistency. The root cause probability analysis pointed to *Different human conventions* as the most likely root cause. When we shared this result with a stakeholder and asked for their opinion, they responded: *"That's probably the main reason why people would record it differently. It is just because different people will be typing it differently, because of their preferences"*.

For the second set of imperfect labels (as shown in Fig. 6), *Resource* again emerged as the top contributing feature, and *Different human conventions* were the most likely root cause according to the probability analysis. The stakeholder confirmed this finding, saying: *"I would think that's probably correct"*. For the third set (as shown in Fig. 6), *Resource* is once more the most important feature, with *Different human conventions* again ranking highest in the probability analysis. The stakeholder endorsed the results, saying: *"In practice, that is probably just going to be [a] personal difference"*. The fourth set of imperfect labels contained typos. For this set (as shown in Fig. 6), we identified *User workload* as the most important feature, and consequently, a busy user as the most likely root cause. The stakeholder confirmed these results, noting that *"Typos [are] probably more workload-based"*.

5   Discussion

Our experiments on public (BPIC 2019 [10] and BPIC 2013 [29]) and private real-life event logs (*AusHealth* and *AusMine*) highlight both the strengths and limitations of the *eRooMiner* approach. Across all four datasets, we observed that the approach successfully detects the most probable root causes of imperfect labels.

We used event logs from multiple domains, with different characteristics, e.g., the total number of events, activities, resources, and the distribution of activities over resources and time, to ensure the generalisability of our approach. This diversity enabled us to evaluate our approach under a broad range of conditions. In total, we conducted over 800 injection experiments for each public log (11 labels $\times$ 7 root causes $\times$ 11 injection percentages), as well as experiments with real imperfect labels in industry data.

Our experiments with injected imperfect labels demonstrated that, even at low injection percentages, our approach often correctly identifies the most likely root causes.

For various scenarios, the feature identified as the most important in the XAI analysis aligns with the known injected root cause. This alignment is further reflected by the calculated root cause probabilities. These findings support the reliability of our approach in detecting root causes of imperfect labels under different controlled conditions.

Our experiments with industry data sets demonstrate the capability and effectiveness of our approach in identifying the root causes of data quality issues in real setting. In the *AusHealth* dataset, the analysis reveals that integrating data from multiple systems leads to label inconsistencies due to differing terminologies used by these systems. An expert has confirmed that the root cause is not human error, but rather the design and configuration of the systems themselves, which use different terminologies or drop-down lists. This insight is valuable for organisations seeking to improve data consistency. The *AusMine* dataset presents a different pattern, where inconsistencies primarily arise from human factors, such as individual typing preferences or high workload. Our approach was able was able to correctly detect both of these root causes.

Despite these strengths, the *eRooMiner* approach has some limitations. A challenge arises when imperfect labels occur with a low number of events or display imbalanced distributions across features such as resources or time. In these scenarios, especially at low injection percentages, the model struggles to identify a dominant feature that contributes to the imperfection. Another challenge manifests itself when high-workload users perform activities during peak periods (e.g., busy months, days of the month, or weekdays). In such scenarios both user workload and time-related workload features tend to be important in detecting the root cause. However, for imperfect labels

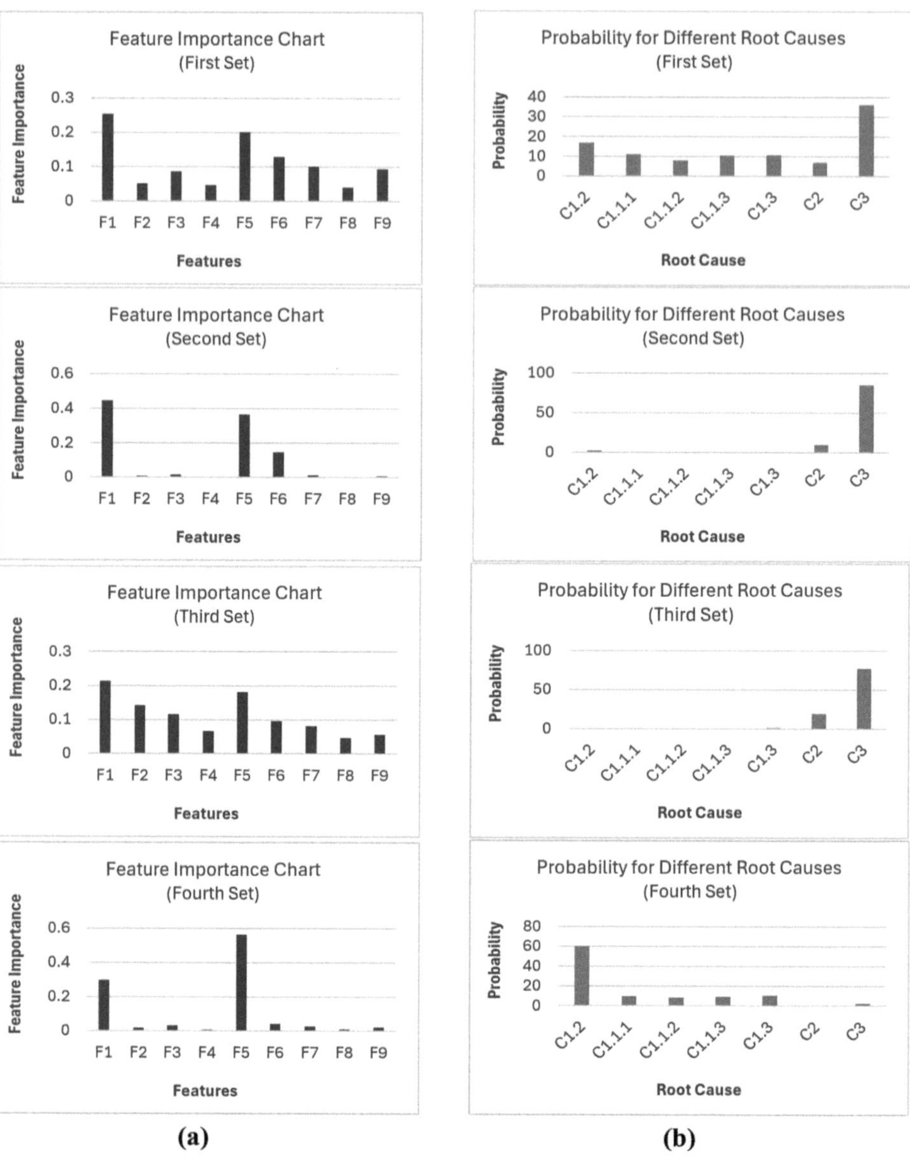

Fig. 6. (a) Feature importance and (b) root cause probabilities for imperfect labels in the *AusMine* log (sets 1–4).

with fewer instances, these workload features only emerge as important at higher levels of injected imperfect labels. We also observed correlations between *User workload* and *User time workload* features, indicating potential overlaps between multiple root causes. This means that *User workload* (*F5*) can be identified as the most important feature for *Busy day of month for a user* in low injection percentages. For terminology-related root causes like *Different system terminologies* and *Different human conventions*, imbalanced distributions of imperfect labels recorded by different systems or users, or very low event counts for imperfect labels, resulted in unreliable detection, meaning that no specific feature stands out as the most important one.

6   Conclusion

We proposed *eRooMiner*, a novel data-driven approach for detecting root causes of imperfect labels in event logs, namely, synonymous, distorted, and polluted labels. The *eRooMiner* approach answered our research question by incorporating techniques from machine learning and XAI analysis. We conducted experiments on four real-life event logs, including two public BPIC logs with imperfect labels injected based on root causes, and two Australian logs from the healthcare and mining sectors with real imperfect labels. The results, validated by the stakeholders, confirmed the effectiveness of the approach in detecting the correct root cause of imperfect labels in event logs. Future work can incorporate additional data, including both (semi-)structured data, such as system metadata, and unstructured data, such as textual documentation, in root cause detection.

Acknowledgments. We acknowledge Arthur H. M. ter Hofstede for his insightful contributions during the discussions of this work. Some of the datasets used in the evaluation of our approach were provided by our industry partners. The Ethics approval for the Hospital and Ambulance data was granted by Royal Brisbane and Women's Hospital HREC with approval number HREC/17/QRBW/610. Also, the Ethics approval for the Australian mine heath and safety data was provided by QUT's Human Research Ethics Committee with approval number 7218.

References

1. van der Aalst, W.M.P.: Process Mining - Data Science in Action, 2nd edn. Springer, Heidelberg (2016). https://doi.org/10.1007/978-3-662-49851-4

2. van der Aalst, W., et al.: Process mining manifesto. In: Daniel, F., Barkaoui, K., Dustdar, S. (eds.) BPM 2011. LNBIP, vol. 99, pp. 169–194. Springer, Heidelberg (2012). https://doi.org/10.1007/978-3-642-28108-2_19

3. Andrews, R., et al.: An expert lens on data quality in process mining. In: ICPM, pp. 49–56. IEEE (2020)

4. Andrews, R., et al.: Root-cause analysis of process-data quality problems. J. Bus. Anal. **5**(1), 51–75 (2022)

5. Jagadeesh Chandra Bose, R.P., et al.: Wanna improve process mining results? In: CIDM, pp. 127–134. IEEE (2013)

6. Breiman, L.: Random forests. Mach. Learn. **45**(1), 5–32 (2001)

7. Carvalho, R., et al.: Analysis of root causes of problems affecting the quality of hospital administrative data: a systematic review and Ishikawa diagram. Int. J. Med. Inform. **156**, 104584 (2021)

8. Conforti, R., et al.: Filtering out infrequent behavior from business process event logs. IEEE Trans. Knowl. Data Eng. **29**(2), 300–314 (2016)

9. Csáki, C.: Towards open data quality improvements based on root cause analysis of quality issues. In: Parycek, P., et al. (eds.) EGOV 2018. LNCS, vol. 11020, pp. 208–220. Springer, Cham (2018). https://doi.org/10.1007/978-3-319-98690-6_18

10. van Dongen, B.: BPI Challenge 2019 (2019). https://data.4tu.nl/articles/dataset/BPI_Challenge_2019/12715853/1

11. Dwivedi, R., et al.: Explainable AI (XAI): core ideas, techniques, and solutions. ACM Comput. Surv. **55**(9), 1–33 (2023)

12. Eden, R., et al.: Revealing the root causes of digital health data quality issues: a qualitative investigation of the Odigos framework. In: HICSS, pp. 3035–3044. ScholarSpace (2023)

13. Emamjome, F., et al.: Alohomora: unlocking data quality causes through event log context. In: ECIS (2020)

14. Fadlallah, H., et al.: Context-aware big data quality assessment: a scoping review. ACM J. Data Inf. Qual. **15**(3), 25:1–25:33 (2023)

15. Foidl, H., et al.: Data pipeline quality: influencing factors, root causes of data-related issues, and processing problem areas for developers. J. Syst. Softw. **207**, 111855 (2024)

16. Genuer, R., et al.: Variable selection using random forests. Pattern Recogn. Lett. **31**(14), 2225–2236 (2010)

17. Goel, K., et al.: Quality-informed process mining: a case for standardised data quality annotations. ACM Trans. Knowl. Discov. Data **16**(5), 97:1–97:47 (2022)

18. Gupta, N., Anand, K., Sureka, A.: Pariket: mining business process logs for root cause analysis of anomalous incidents. In: Chu, W., Kikuchi, S., Bhalla, S. (eds.) DNIS 2015. LNCS, vol. 8999, pp. 244–263. Springer, Cham (2015). https://doi.org/10.1007/978-3-319-16313-0_19

19. Ishikawa, K.: What is Total Quality Control? The Japanese Way. Prentice Hall (1985)

20. James, G., et al.: An Introduction to Statistical Learning, vol. 112. Springer (2013). https://doi.org/10.1007/978-1-0716-1418-1

21. Kuhn, M., Johnson, K.: Applied Predictive Modeling. Springer (2013)

22. Lee, Y.W., et al.: Journey to Data Quality. MIT Press (2006)

23. Nguyen, H.T.C., et al.: Autoencoders for improving quality of process event logs. Exp. Syst. Appl. **131**, 132–147 (2019)

24. Qafari, M.S., van der Aalst, W.M.P.: Root cause analysis in process mining using structural equation models. In: Del Río Ortega, A., Leopold, H., Santoro, F.M. (eds.) Business Process Management Workshops, BPM 2020. LNBIP, vol. 397, pp. 155–167. Springer, Cham (2020). https://doi.org/10.1007/978-3-030-66498-5_12

25. Sadeghianasl, S., et al.: Process activity ontology learning from event logs through gamification. IEEE Access **9**, 165865–165880 (2021)

26. Schmid, S.J., et al.: Everything at the proper time: repairing identical timestamp errors in event logs with generative adversarial networks. Inf. Syst. **118**, 102246 (2023)

27. Sim, S., et al.: Likelihood-based multiple imputation by event chain methodology for repair of imperfect event logs with missing data. In: ICPM, pp. 9–16. IEEE (2019)

28. Singh, R., Singh, K.: A descriptive classification of causes of data quality problems in data warehousing. IJCSI **7**(3), 41 (2010)

29. Steeman, W.: BPI Challenge 2013, incidents (2013). https://data.4tu.nl/articles/dataset/BPI_Challenge_2013_incidents/12693914/1

30. Suriadi, S., et al.: Event log imperfection patterns for process mining: towards a systematic approach to cleaning event logs. Inf. Syst. **64**, 132–150 (2017)

31. Vesely, W.E., et al.: Fault Tree Handbook. U.S, Nuclear Regulatory Commission (1981)

32. Wang, M., et al.: A high-speed and low-complexity architecture for softmax function in deep learning. In: IEEE APCCAS, pp. 223–226. IEEE (2018)

33. Wickens, C.D., et al.: Engineering Psychology and Human Performance. Routledge (2021)

34. Wynn, M.T., Sadiq, S.: Responsible process mining - a data quality perspective. In: Hildebrandt, T., van Dongen, B.F., Röglinger, M., Mendling, J. (eds.) BPM 2019. LNCS, vol. 11675, pp. 10–15. Springer, Cham (2019). https://doi.org/10.1007/978-3-030-26619-6_2
35. Zellal, N., Zaouia, A.: An exploratory investigation of factors influencing data quality in data warehouse. In: WCCS, pp. 1–6. IEEE (2015)
36. Zhang, R., et al.: Discovering data quality problems: the case of repurposed data. Bus. Inf. Syst. Eng. **61**, 575–593 (2019)

Extracting Object-Centric Event Logs from Incident Data Using Large Language Models

Ahmed Takiy Eddine Hamdi[1,2(✉)], Marwa Elleuch[1], Nassim Laga[1],
and Walid Gaaloul[2]

[1] Orange Labs, Lannion, France
`{AhmedTakiyEddine.Hamdi,Marwa.Elleuch,Nassim.Laga}@orange.com`
[2] SAMOVAR, Télécom SudParis, Institut Polytechnique de Paris,
91120 Palaiseau, France
`{AhmedTakiyEddine.Hamdi,Walid.Gaaloul}@telecom-sudparis.eu`

Abstract. Incident monitoring is critical in industrial settings to prevent disruptions and optimize operations. While traditional equipment logs are often converted into XES-like event logs, these formats typically associate each event with a single case object and overlook valuable information from other sources, particularly, pre- and post-incident process logs. These additional logs frequently describe activities involving multiple related objects (e.g., hardware, software). OCEL (Object-Centric Event Log) standard can be used to represent events involving multiple, interconnected objects, thus offering a more comprehensive view of incident-related processes. However, pre- and post-incident data are often recorded in unstructured textual formats, whereas OCEL requires well-structured data in order to be properly populated. To bridge this gap, we introduce a method to extract events and objects from unstructured pre- and post-incident textual content that leverages Large Language Models (LLMs). Our approach is evaluated on real-world data from the data center domain demonstrating its effectiveness in enriching incident monitoring and providing a structured foundation for advanced incident prediction and analysis.

Keywords: Unstructured Data · Event Extraction · Object-Centric Event Log (OCEL) · LLM

1 Introduction

In the industrial landscape, effective maintenance is essential for ensuring service continuity and optimizing resource utilization. Predictive maintenance has emerged as a proactive approach to anticipate equipment failures, address issues before they escalate, and minimize operational disruptions. By leveraging data-driven insights, predictive maintenance enables accurate predictions about the remaining useful life of equipment and potential failure points [1].

C. Cappiello et al. (Eds.): CoopIS 2025, LNCS 15535, pp. 52–69, 2026.
https://doi.org/10.1007/978-3-032-15538-2_4

Recent advancements [3,6,7,21,23] have primarily focused on analyzing equipment logs, often represented in an XES[1]-like format, where events are linked to a single case object (e.g., the equipment) and traces are defined using time windows. While these logs provide valuable insights, they are inherently limited due to their sparse nature, as they capture the equipment's status over time. In practice, managing equipment incidents involves a broader context, encompassing processes that occur both before and after incidents. Pre-incident processes, such as system updates or material procurement, and post-incident processes, including incident diagnosis and intervention planning. These logs hold significant potential for uncovering the causes of incidents and identifying effective resolutions. For example, a maintenance operation involving switch replacement, without reconnecting all links, may lead to a "linkDown" incident (see Table 1).

Such logs, however, are unstructured and often describe events associated with multiple entities. For example, the first maintenance operation description in Table 1 includes multiple events such as "replace switch", "connect control link" and "not connect prod link", each linked to corresponding objects like "switch", "control link" and "prod link" respectively. These events need to be extracted and presented in a suitable format.

Table 1. Examples of Maintenance Operations that Caused an Incident.

Equipment	Timestamp	Event Type	Description (English)
E1	14/12/2023 13:49:08	Maintenance operation	We replaced the switch S1 with a new one but only the cabling of the control links is connected. The PROD links and the links between the two servers are not yet connected
E1	14/12/2023 15:50:48	Error	Empty
E1	15/12/2023 08:59:09	Incident ticket	Critical: linkDown - Link Down (connectionEstablishmentError)

To represent such complex interactions, the OCEL (Object-Centric Event Log) standard [4] enables the modeling of events involving multiple, interconnected objects, thus offering a more comprehensive view of incident-related processes than traditional XES-like logs. However, OCEL requires structured input, while much of the relevant data remains in unstructured textual form.

To bridge this gap, we propose an approach to extract events and entities from unstructured pre- and post-incident textual content leveraging Large Language Models (LLMs) This approach builds on the proven capabilities of LLMs in information extraction, particularly their effectiveness in identifying entities, capturing relationships, and interpreting contextual dependencies within unstructured textual data [24]. By doing so, our method enables the creation of enriched,

---

[1] https://xes-standard.org/.

object-centric event logs that support more comprehensive incident monitoring and analysis.

The paper is organized as follows: Sect. 2 reviews the related works. Section 3 defines the incident related data, Sect. 4 explains the LLM based approach for event extraction. Section 5 presents an evaluation of our approach. Finally, Sect. 6 concludes the paper.

2   Related Works

2.1   Equipment Failure Prediction and Incident Analysis Using Log Data

Previous research on equipment incident prediction has predominantly utilized structured equipment logs to forecast failures or estimate Remaining Useful Life (RUL). Various machine learning approaches have been applied across domains such as medical devices [21], ship propulsion systems [3], ATMs [10,22,23], electric machines [16], data centers [9], aircraft [14], and railways [16]. These studies typically focus on equipment log data alone, sometimes incorporating contextual information like inventory or weather data, but generally do not leverage additional sources such as pre- and post-incident process logs. As a result, their ability to provide insights into the causes and context of incidents remains limited.

In contrast, post-incident management research has explored the use of unstructured maintenance records to analyze and address equipment failures. Techniques such as clustering with keyword extraction and embeddings have been used to identify failure causes [5,19]. Recommendation systems have matched maintenance records to suggest solutions or predict downtime [2,18,25], while topic modeling and classification have been applied to categorize maintenance descriptions [11,20]. However, these approaches are typically limited to post-incident data and do not integrate information from the pre-incident phase, which restricts a comprehensive understanding of incident causality and resolution.

2.2   Event Extraction from Unstructured Textual Data

Event extraction from unstructured text is a well-studied problem in natural language processing, where an event is typically defined by a trigger (often a verb or noun) and its associated arguments. Early approaches, such as sequential pipeline models, decomposed the task into subtasks including trigger identification, trigger classification, and argument role assignment [13]. To address the limitations of pipeline architectures, joint models have been proposed to simultaneously predict triggers and arguments using structured prediction with both local and global features [15]. More recent advances leverage deep learning architectures to improve extraction performance. For example, dynamic multi-pooling convolutional neural networks (DMCNN) have been introduced to capture lexical and contextual clues for both trigger and argument classification, employing features such as context-word, position, and event-type features [8]. Furthermore, end-to-end approaches like TEXT2EVENT utilize transformer-based encoder-decoder architectures to generate event structures in a single step, bypassing the need for manual feature engineering and subtask decomposition [17].

Most of these studies rely on benchmark datasets like ACE 2005, which are linguistically well-formed and contain explicitly annotated events. In contrast, event extraction from domain-specific data, such as incident management logs written by agents or generated automatically, remains underexplored. In these settings, events are often implicit and require domain expertise for accurate identification, presenting challenges not addressed by existing methods.

3   Incident Related Data

In our previous work [12], we introduced a domain-specific Object-Centric Event Log (OCEL) to represent incident data in a structured manner. The meta-model design, along with the defined entities and relationships, was detailed in the prior study. In this section, we provide an overview of the meta-model to facilitate an understanding of the input, intermediate, and the output structure. These elements represent the structuration steps that we aim to automate in this paper (Fig. 1).

3.1   Input Layer

The input layer collects data from three primary sources commonly found in incident management systems: equipment logs, maintenance process logs, and incident resolution process logs. These sources provide a comprehensive view of the incident lifecycle, including pre- and post-incident activities:

- **Equipment Logs:** These logs record changes in equipment status, categorized by severity levels such as warnings, errors, alerts, or critical events. Each log entry is timestamped and uniquely identified.
- **Maintenance Process Logs:** These logs document formal requests for system updates, issue resolution, or preventive actions. Each request generates a `ChangeRequest` entity, which includes a description and associated comments. Comments capture interactions such as task updates, confirmations, or redirections.
- **Incident Resolution Process Logs:** These logs capture post-incident activities, represented by `IncidentTickets`. Each ticket includes a description of the incident and comments detailing the investigation, diagnosis, and resolution steps.

This diverse input data provides both structured and unstructured information, forming the foundation for subsequent transformations.

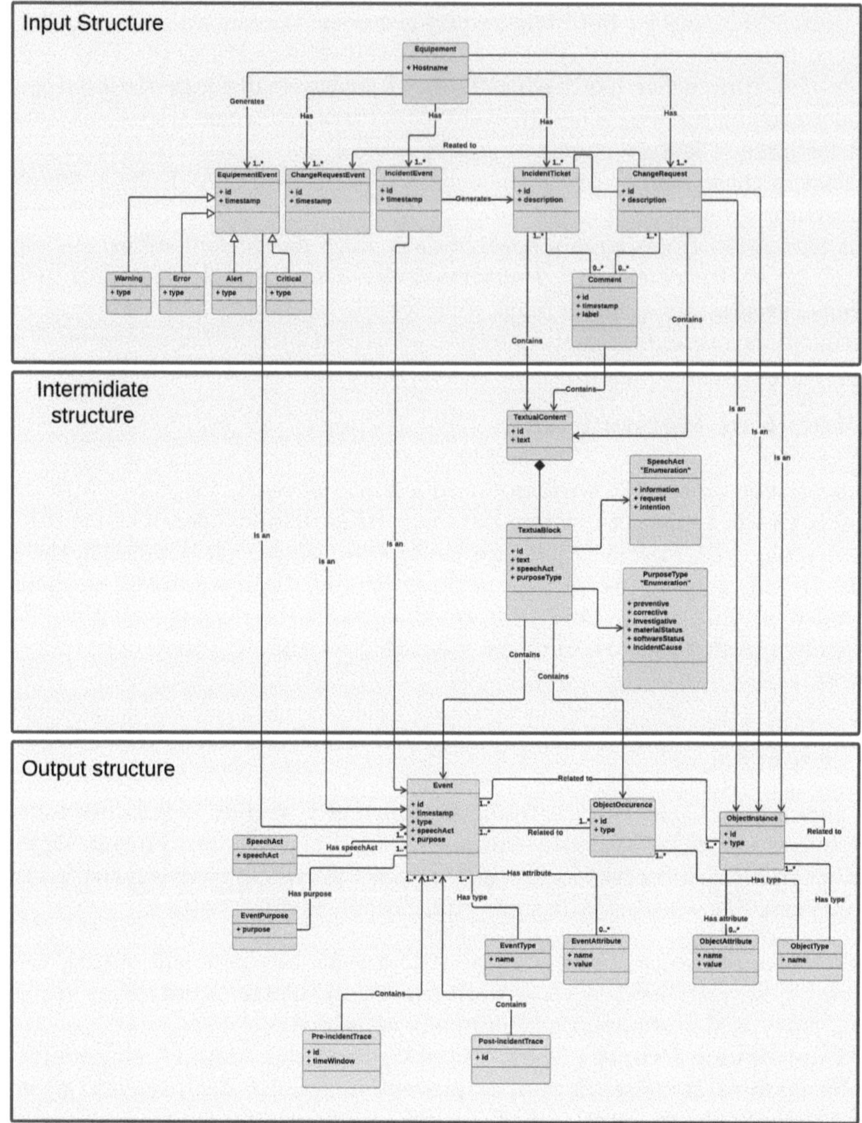

Fig. 1. Meta-model for structured representation of incident data proposed in [12].

3.2   Intermediate Layer

The intermediate layer bridges the gap between unstructured textual data and the structured format required for the OCEL. It focuses on extracting meaningful entities and events from textual content, such as descriptions and comments in pre- and post-incident logs. Key aspects of this layer include:

- **Textual Content Transformation:** Textual data is broken down into `TextualBlocks`, each representing a single action applied to an object. For example, a sentence like "We need to replace 1 RAM" is parsed into an event (`replace`) and an object (`RAM`).
- **Event Attributes:** Events are characterized by three main attributes: their basic form, their `speech act`, and their purpose. These attributes are defined as follows:
  - **Their Basic Form:** This attribute is derived from the event trigger described in the textual block, typically expressed as a verb (e.g., *add*) or a noun (e.g., *addition*). The trigger provides the foundational description of the event and is crucial for identifying the nature of the action being performed.
  - **Their Speech Act:** Events are categorized into one of three speech acts: *information, request,* or *intention.* For example, phrases such as *"we need"* indicate an *intention,* while *"please add a disk"* indicates a *request.* If the text lacks such keywords and is declarative in nature, the speech act is classified as *information.*
  - **Their Event Purpose:** The purpose of an event is categorized into one of the following: *preventive, corrective, materialStatus, investigative, softwareStatus,* or *incidentCause.* For example, the term *"investigate"* indicates an *investigative* purpose, *"restore"* indicates a *corrective* purpose, and *"ports down"* indicates a *materialStatus.* If no explicit purpose is identified, the event is assumed to be *preventive,* as unclassified operations are typically preventive in nature.

This layer ensures that unstructured data is systematically annotated and prepared for integration into the OCEL.

3.3   Output Layer: Domain-Specific OCEL

The output layer produces a domain-specific Object-Centric Event Log (OCEL) tailored for incident monitoring. This OCEL extends the standard OCEL definition by integrating pre- and post-incident events, additional event attributes, and mappings to better represent the complexity of incident-related data. Key features include:

- **Event Representation:** Events are structured as [`Id, timestamp, event_type, speech act, purpose`] to capture their essential attributes. Each event is linked to multiple objects and `ObjectOccurrences`.
- **Object Representation:** Objects are classified as either traceable (e.g., equipment, tickets, or change requests) with clear identifiers or ambiguously traceable (e.g., hardware components like disks or software entities like databases). Ambiguously traceable are extracted from textual content and represented as `ObjectOccurrences`.

In this work, the event structure that we aim to extract matches the output of the OCEL, with the exception that a trigger attribute is added to explicitly capture the verb or noun indicating the action or event. Figure 3 shows a real example of an event extracted from a maintenance operation description. The event structure is defined as [`trigger`, `event_type`, `object`, `object_id`, `object_type`, `speech_act`, `purpose`], where:

- **Trigger:** The verb or noun indicating the action or event.
- **Event Type:** The generalized meaning of the action or status. For actions, similar verbs are grouped under a common type (e.g., *"changement"*, *"remplacement"*, *"change"*, *"replace"* → `replace`); for statuses, similar terms are grouped (e.g., *"HS"*, *"down"*, *"out of service"* → `down`).
- **Object:** The entity involved in the event, corresponding to an `ObjectOccurrence` in the OCEL, and extracted from the textual content (e.g., *"port [STD] EB"* → `port`).
- **Object ID:** The prefix or identifier of the object (e.g., *"[STD] EB"*). If no prefix exists, this field is left empty.
- **Object Type:** Classifies the object as either `hardware` or `software`.
- **Speech Act** and **Purpose:** These attributes are retained from the initial structure and are described in Sect. 3.2.

4   LLM-Based Approach for Event Extraction

4.1   Approach Overview

Large Language Models (LLMs) have demonstrated exceptional capabilities in information extraction, effectively identifying entities and relationships [24]. However, when applied in a sequential manner, processing text after text, LLMs face limitations in capturing a global understanding of the dataset. This independent execution prevents the model from considering the broader context across multiple descriptions. Additionally, LLMs have a constrained token capacity, making it impractical to process all descriptions simultaneously. To address these limitations, the proposed solution architecture in Fig. 2 adopts a systematic and iterative approach based on two-step extraction.

The pipeline begins with the **Pre-Processing Phase**, where the input texts are cleaned and anonymized. Subsequently, N random text samples are selected to be used in the initial extraction step. During the **First-Round Extraction** phase, a prompt is applied to the N descriptions to generate an initial set of event types and triggers. These event types are then unified and generalized using a separate prompt to ensure consistency and eliminate redundancy. The resulting event types are considered representative of the overall dataset. In the **Second-Round Extraction** phase, the refined list of event types is iteratively injected into the event extraction prompt. If new event types are identified during this phase, the list is updated by adding them. This iterative injection process incorporates elements from previous executions, enabling the model to retain context and refine its understanding. As a result, the extracted event types become both generalized and comprehensive, effectively capturing all relevant events.

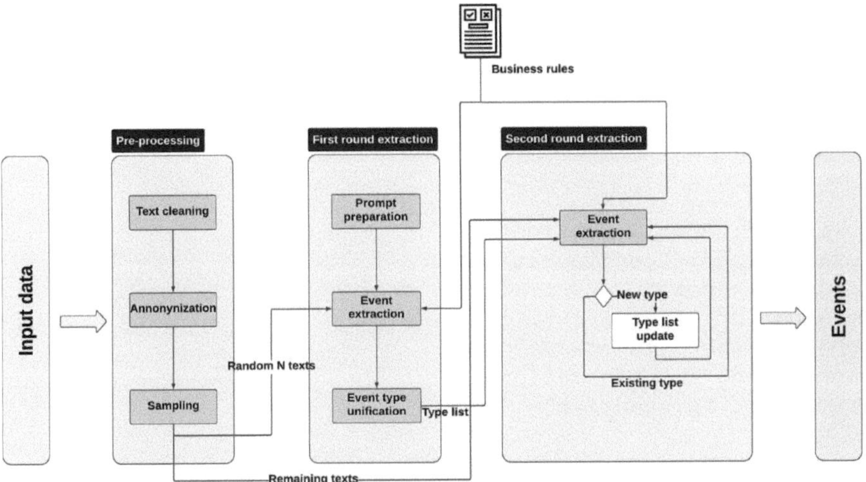

Fig. 2. Solution architecture.

4.2 Pre-processing

The pre-processing layer prepares raw textual data for effective use with large
language models (LLMs). Maintenance operation descriptions, ticket descriptions, and their associated comments often contain noise and sensitive information that must be addressed. This phase involves two key steps: **text cleaning**
and **sampling representative descriptions**.

Text Cleaning. Text cleaning ensures that the input data is coherent and meaningful for LLMs by preserving the natural language structure while removing
irrelevant noise. Key steps include:

- **Removing Special Characters and Metadata:** Eliminating unnecessary
  symbols (e.g., \n, :) and irrelevant system-generated identifiers (e.g., \nDPM).
- **Anonymizing Personal Identifiers:** Masking sensitive information such
  as phone numbers (<PHONE>), email addresses (<EMAIL>), and person names
  (`Person_1`, `Person_2`) using regular expressions (regex) for pattern matching
  and a name dictionary for identifying and replacing names.

Sampling Representative Descriptions. The process begins by randomly selecting
(N) descriptions from the dataset, including maintenance operation descriptions,
ticket descriptions, and comments. These sampled descriptions are used as input
for the event extraction process. The goal is to extract triggers and their associated event types from this subset of data, which serves as a representative sample
of the broader dataset, that will be used as input to process the remaining texts.

```
Description:
Configuration de ports \n[STD] EB Cablage: changement de la description des interfaces
switch (en jaune dans le DIO ci-joint) suite au passage à RHEL8. \n\nDPM : Personne_1
\nRDT : Personne_2
 Output:


{
"trigger": "configuration",
"event_type": "configuration",
"object": "port",
"object_id": "[STD] EB",
"object_type": "hardware"
"speech_act": "information"
"purpose": "preventive"
},
{
"trigger": "changement",
"event_type": "replace",
"object": "interface",
"object_id": "",
"object_type": "software"
"speech_act": "information"
"purpose": "preventive"
},
{
"trigger": "passage",
"event_type": "upgrade",
"object": "RHEL8",
"object_id": "",
"object_type": "software"
"speech_act": "information"
"purpose": "preventive"
}
```

Fig. 3. Example of event extraction from a description.

4.3   First-Round Event Extraction

Prompt Preparation. The prompt preparation step is designed to guide the
large language model (LLM) in systematically extracting events from textual
descriptions. This step leverages multiple prompting techniques to avoid hallucinations and ensure accurate and consistent results.

- **Role Assignment:** The prompt begins by assigning the LLM the role of an
  "expert in both software and hardware related to data centers and servers."
  This technique, known as *role prompting*, helps the model contextualize its
  task and align its responses with domain-specific expertise.
- **Event Component Specification:** We explicitly defined the components of
  an event (trigger, event_type, object, object ID, object_type) in the prompt,

following the definitions in Sect. 3.3. The prompt instructs the model to carefully analyze each description, identify all events present, and extract the trigger, event type, object, object ID, object type, speech act, and purpose. If multiple events are present, all should be extracted; if no events are found, the model is instructed to return an empty string.

- **Generalization Rules:** We specified two rules in the prompt to ensure consistency in event type assignment: (1) if a new trigger logically aligns with an existing type, it is grouped under that type to maintain uniformity (e.g., the trigger *"change"* is assigned to the existing type *"replace"*; see Fig. 3); and (2) if the classification of a trigger is uncertain or ambiguous, a new type is created to preserve accuracy and prevent misclassification (e.g., if the trigger *"configure"* does not clearly fit any existing type, a new type *"configuration"* is introduced).
- **Validation and Filtering:** We defined conditions to exclude irrelevant events: (1) descriptions lacking verbs or nouns, and (2) events involving non-hardware or non-software objects. This step ensures that the extracted events are both relevant and precise.
- **Output Format Specification:** By defining a structured JSON output format (see Fig. 3), the prompt ensures that the model's responses are machine-readable and consistent.
- **Examples:** The inclusion of examples demonstrates the expected behavior of the model, helping it better understand the task. This technique is known as *few-shot prompting*, where examples are provided to improve the model's performance on similar tasks.

Event Types Unification. Following the event extraction process, the identified event types are revisited to ensure consistency and generalization. This step use a large language model (LLM) with a specifically designed prompt to assist in merging semantically similar event types into a unified list of generalized event types. For instance, types such as *"install,"* *"setup,"* and *"configure"* may be grouped under a single event type, *"installation."* Similarly, *"changement,"* *"change,"* and *"replace"* are grouped under *"replace"* (see Fig. 3).

The resulting generalized event type list serves as a standardized representation, ensuring that the extracted events are consistent and interpretable. This list is then used as input for the second-round event extraction phase, where further refinement and automation are performed.

4.4 Second-Round Event Extraction

The second-round event extraction phase builds upon the results of the first round by refining and generalizing the event types and triggers. This phase is designed to ensure comprehensive coverage of all relevant events while maintaining consistency and interpretability. The process consists of a **recursive injection** of the updated type list into the event extraction prompt.

The updated event type list is recursively injected into the event extraction prompt to guide the LLM in identifying events with the most generalized and consistent event types. By incorporating the refined type list into the prompt, the LLM is able to classify triggers more accurately and avoid redundancy. For example, if a new trigger such as *"reboot"* is identified, it can be classified under an existing type like *"restart"* if it aligns with the type's definition.

4.5 Business Rules Injection

To enhance the assessment of event extraction, particularly for speech act and purpose classification, we incorporated specific business rules that take precedence over the LLM-generated results. First, events extracted from change requests (i.e., maintenance operations) are classified as requests, regardless of whether their textual form suggests information or intention. Second, these same events are categorized as preventive in terms of purpose, unless they are explicitly described otherwise. This rule-based adjustment ensures alignment with domain-specific practices and improves the accuracy of event classification.

5 Evaluation

In this section, we evaluate the effectiveness of our approach using GPT-4o for event extraction. The evaluation focuses on the performance, measured by precision, recall, and F1-score. Additionally, we assess the precision for each event type individually, as well as the classification performance for speech act and purpose categories.

5.1 Dataset Description

The dataset used to validate the meta-model originates from pre-incident logs (change requests) and post-incident logs (incident tickets). It focuses on server incidents at the Orange Labs data center during the period 08/12/2023–31/12/2023. For privacy reasons, the dataset is not shared, and all results are anonymized.

Traces were constructed for each incident to capture the pre-incident process within a 7-day window, while events extracted from incident comments represented the post-incident process. To ensure data quality, overlapping traces sharing more than 50% of events were merged, thereby reducing irrelevant traces and preventing the generation of spurious patterns. This procedure yielded a total of 997 traces, from which 100 were randomly selected for annotation. A collaborative annotation methodology was employed, wherein two researchers independently annotated events, objects, speech acts, and purposes within the textual content. Discrepancies were resolved by a domain expert. In total, 310 textual descriptions were annotated, resulting in the extraction of 648 events spanning 60 event types.

5.2   Event Type Evaluation

In this section, we evaluate the performance of our solution that used GPT-4o in associating the extracted triggers to the right event types and compare it with the event types in the manual annotation. The primary objective of event types is to achieve the most generalized event labels while avoiding labels that are semantically similar. This ensures that the event log remains clear and contains the minimum number of distinct event labels. To assess this, we employ both an LLM-based evaluation and manual evaluation for event type assignment.

Matching Events for Evaluation. To evaluate the alignment between manually annotated events and the events extracted by our solution, we need to match the events for each description. This is necessary because the extracted events and manual events may not be in the same order, and direct comparison is not feasible. Furthermore, the number of extracted events does not always match the number of manual events; they correspond exactly in only about 70% of cases. In the remaining 30%, there may be extra extracted events or extra manual events.

For example, if a manual event type is "change" and the extracted event type is "replace," a string distance metric like Levenshtein distance would fail to capture their semantic equivalence because it only considers character-level differences. Similarly, semantic similarity using word embeddings may struggle to fully capture relationships such as synonyms, antonyms, inclusion (e.g., "modify" and "rename"), or subtle closeness in meaning. To address these limitations, we use an LLM-based method, incorporating the associated object into the comparison. Specifically, we compare the concatenation of the event type and its associated object (e.g., "change + object") for the manual events and the extracted events (e.g., "replace + extracted object"). This approach ensures that the comparison accounts for both the event type and its context, making the matching process semantically meaningful.

LLM as a Judge. Large language models (LLMs) can serve as automated judges to assess the alignment between extracted and manually annotated events. We use an LLM to determine, for each pair of manual and extracted events, whether they refer to the same action and object. Figure 4 presents the prompt used for this evaluation. By providing the original description, the manual event, and the extracted event, the LLM is instructed to output whether the events match based on their semantic and contextual similarity.

Manual Evaluation. For comparison, we also conducted a manual evaluation of event matching. Two researchers independently assessed whether each manually annotated event was successfully extracted. This manual evaluation serves as a reference standard to assess the performance and consistency of our automated approach.

```
Prompt:          You are an expert in event extraction for IT
operations. Given:
- The original description: "description"
- A manual event: [trigger: "manual_event['trigger']",
object: "manual_event['object']"]
- An extracted event: [trigger: "gpt_event.get('type',")",
object: "gpt_event.get('object',")"]

Does the extracted event match the manual event?
A match means both refer to the same action/status
(type/trigger) and the same object (hardware/software
entity), even if the wording is slightly different.

Answer "True" if they match, "False" if not. Do not
explain.
The output should be only "True" or "False". No other
text.
```

Fig. 4. Prompt used for LLM-based evaluation of event matching.

Results. For each method, when a manual event was judged as matched, it was annotated as a true positive (TP); otherwise, it was considered a false negative (FN). Additionally, extracted events that did not match any manual event were annotated as false positives (FP). Using these annotations, we calculated the precision, recall, and F1-score for both the LLM-based and manual evaluations as follows:

Precision. Precision measures the proportion of extracted events that are actually correct (i.e., match a manual event).

Recall. Recall measures the proportion of manual events that were correctly identified by the extracted events.

F1-score. The F1-score is the harmonic mean of precision and recall. It balances the two metrics, providing a single measure of performance.

The following table summarizes the computed scores based on the evaluation results (Table 2):

Table 2. Evaluation metrics for event matching.

Metric	LLM as Judge (%)	Manual Comparison (%)
Precision	87.20	86.39
Recall	86.18	80.29
F1-score	86.69	83.23

The results indicate that the LLM-based evaluation achieves slightly higher precision (87.2%) compared to manual annotation (86.39%). More notably, the recall for the LLM-based approach (86.18%) is substantially higher than that of manual annotation (80.29%). This suggests that the LLM sometimes assumes certain extracted events match the manual events, even when they do not. For example, manual events such as "rename server group" and "reboot server" were considered as matches with the extracted events "modify server group" and "stop server," respectively, although these do not refer to exactly the same events. This tendency contributes to the higher recall but may introduce semantic mismatches that would be avoided in manual evaluation.

Precision per Event Type. We calculated the precision of the matching process for each extracted event type. It is defined as the percentage of extracted events that matched the manual events for each event type (see Fig. 5).

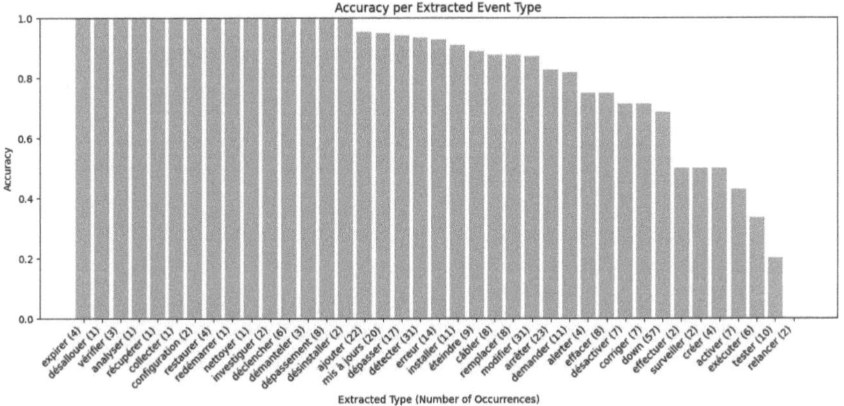

Fig. 5. Event type precision.

The analysis of event type distribution precision demonstrates that our iterative generalization process effectively reduces semantic redundancy and promotes consistency across event labels. By grouping similar triggers under unified event types—reducing 134 unique triggers to 39 unique event types—the approach maintains a clear and interpretable event log, which is essential for downstream analysis and predictive modeling. However, some triggers were not attributed to their correct event types, resulting in semantic inaccuracies. For example, "rename server" is not equivalent to "modify server," and "reboot server" is distinct from "stop server," as rebooting involves both stopping and starting. This over-generalization explains the difference between the number of manually annotated event types (60) and the number of extracted event types (39), indicating that the model merges distinct event types in certain cases. Such misattributions can lower precision for certain categories and highlight the need for incorporating more specific rules or constraints when assigning triggers to event types.

Speech Act and Purpose. Tables 3 and 4 reveal that the model achieves notably strong performance for several categories. In particular, the "informa-

Table 3. Speech act classification results.

Speech Act	Occ.	Prec.	Rec.	F1	B_R(%)
Information	162	98.74	96.91	97.82	20.37
Request	90	98.88	97.78	98.32	83.33
Intention	25	86.21	100.00	92.59	92.00

Table 4. Purpose classification results.

Purpose	Supp.	Prec. (%)	Rec. (%)	F1 (%)	B_R
Materialstate	91	94.44	56.04	70.34	5.49
Preventive	130	94.12	98.46	96.24	89.23
Investigative	6	75.00	100.00	85.71	50.00
Corrective	12	71.43	83.33	76.92	33.33
Softwarestate	38	21.88	18.42	20.00	7.89

tion" and "request" speech acts, as well as the "preventive" purpose, exhibit high precision, recall, and F1-scores. This can be largely attributed to the higher proportion of instances in these categories that are governed by explicit business rules (B_R%), which guide the classification process and enhance consistency. However, the model demonstrates substantially lower performance for the "softwarestate" purpose, indicating a failure to accurately classify events in this category.

Overall Performance. According to manual annotation, the method achieves an F1-score of 83.23%, with a precision of 86.39% and a recall of 80.29% when matching extracted events to the manually annotated ground truth resulting a balanced trade-off between precision and recall. These results indicate that the majority of relevant events are correctly identified and classified, particularly those extracted from maintenance operation descriptions and their associated comments, as these are typically written in common language by maintenance agents.

However, the approach also exhibits some hallucinations, where the LLM tends to extract events even when they do not match the prompt instructions or provided examples, particularly those originating from incident ticket descriptions. For instance, in a description such as:

[SYSTEM_A - ENV_X - APP_Y] / [NO_QLF] / [OBV_SYS_FILESYSTEM
SpaceUsedPercent / /var] : [The indicator is above the threshold for more than 30m (90.03) - https://...]

The method extracted events like "threshold exceeded," whereas the threshold is not the actual object of interest. Instead, the relevant event should be "file system error." This issue arises because such descriptions are often automatically generated and lack clear textual structure, which can prompt the LLM to extract events that are not truly in the text. If these events are used in downstream analyses, they may lead to cumulative errors and impact the reliability of subsequent results.

To address this limitation, incorporating rule-based approaches could help reduce hallucinations and improve the extraction of meaningful events from these types of descriptions.

6   Conclusion

In this work, we presented an approach for extracting object-centric events from unstructured incident-related textual data using a large language model (LLM)-based method. This approach enables the automatic construction of domain-specific Object-Centric Event Logs (OCEL) by systematically processing pre- and post-incident records to identify event triggers, types, and associated objects. Our evaluation demonstrates that the proposed method effectively populates OCELs with structured event data, thereby overcoming the limitations of traditional event logs. Specifically, the object-centric representation allows for the modeling of events involving multiple, interconnected objects, providing a more comprehensive view of incident-related processes.

Nevertheless, our approach has certain limitations. In some cases, although the trigger is accurately extracted, the model tends to overgeneralize the event type, resulting in false or missed events. Furthermore, while LLMs can assist in evaluating event matches, they cannot be considered definitive judges without additional validation, as they sometimes classify events as matches when they are not. Additionally, the extraction process requires further integration of domain expertise, particularly for handling system-generated texts such as incident descriptions.

For future work, we plan to expand our dataset with additional incident records and iteratively refine the extraction prompts to further improve F1-scores. Moreover, we aim to systematically evaluate the performance of the LLM as a judge to better understand the precision of its assessments. Additionally, we intend to leverage these enriched OCELs for predictive analytics, including incident prediction, root cause identification, and recommendation of resolution steps, thereby enhancing predictive maintenance and incident management capabilities. Finally, we will investigate the scalability of our approach to ensure its effectiveness and efficiency when applied to larger and more diverse datasets other real-world industrial environments.

References

1. Achouch, M., et al.: On predictive maintenance in industry 4.0: overview, models, and challenges. Appl. Sci. **12**(16), 8081 (2022)
2. Ansari, F., Kohl, L., Giner, J., Meier, H.: Text mining for ai enhanced failure detection and availability optimization in production systems. CIRP Ann. **70**(1), 373–376 (2021)

3. Bakdi, A., Kristensen, N.B., Stakkeland, M.: Multiple instance learning with random forest for event logs analysis and predictive maintenance in ship electric propulsion system. IEEE Trans. Industr. Inf. **18**(11), 7718–7728 (2022)

4. Berti, A., et al.: OCEL (object-centric event log) 2.0 specification. arXiv preprint arXiv:2403.01975 (2024)

5. Bhardwaj, A.S., Deep, A., Veeramani, D., Zhou, S.: A custom word embedding model for clustering of maintenance records. IEEE Trans. Industr. Inf. **18**(2), 816–826 (2021)

6. Bonnevay, S., Cugliari, J., Granger, V.: Predictive maintenance from event logs using wavelet-based features: an industrial application. In: 14th International Conference on Soft Computing Models in Industrial and Environmental Applications (SOCO 2019) Seville, Spain, 13–15 May 2019, Proceedings, vol. 14, pp. 132–141. Springer (2020)

7. Calabrese, M., et al.: SOPHIA: an event-based IoT and machine learning architecture for predictive maintenance in industry 4.0. Information **11**(4), 202 (2020)

8. Chen, Y., Xu, L., Liu, K., Zeng, D., Zhao, J.: Event extraction via dynamic multi-pooling convolutional neural networks. In: Proceedings of the 53rd Annual Meeting of the Association for Computational Linguistics and the 7th International Joint Conference on Natural Language Processing (Volume 1: Long Papers), pp. 167–176 (2015)

9. Decker, L., Leite, D., Giommi, L., Bonacorsi, D.: Real-time anomaly detection in data centers for log-based predictive maintenance using an evolving fuzzy-rule-based approach. In: 2020 IEEE International Conference on Fuzzy Systems (FUZZ-IEEE), pp. 1–8. IEEE (2020)

10. Guillaume, A., Vrain, C., Wael, E.: Predictive maintenance on event logs: application on an atm fleet. arXiv preprint arXiv:2011.10996 (2020)

11. Gunda, T., et al.: A machine learning evaluation of maintenance records for common failure modes in PV inverters. IEEE Access **8**, 211610–211620 (2020)

12. Hamdi, A.T.E., Elleuch, M., Laga, N., Gaaloul, W.: A domain specific object centric event log for structured representation of incident data. In: 2025 IEEE International Conference on Software Services Engineering (SSE), pp. 182–188. IEEE (2025)

13. Hong, Y., Zhang, J., Ma, B., Yao, J., Zhou, G., Zhu, Q.: Using cross-entity inference to improve event extraction. In: Proceedings of the 49th Annual Meeting of the Association for Computational Linguistics: Human Language Technologies, pp. 1127–1136 (2011)

14. Korvesis, P., Besseau, S., Vazirgiannis, M.: Predictive maintenance in aviation: failure prediction from post-flight reports. In: 2018 IEEE 34th International Conference on Data Engineering (ICDE), pp. 1414–1422. IEEE (2018)

15. Li, Q., Ji, H., Huang, L.: Joint event extraction via structured prediction with global features. In: Proceedings of the 51st Annual Meeting of the Association for Computational Linguistics (Volume 1: Long Papers), pp. 73–82 (2013)

16. Li, Z., Zhang, J., Wu, Q., Gong, Y., Yi, J., Kirsch, C.: Sample adaptive multiple kernel learning for failure prediction of railway points. In: Proceedings of the 25th ACM SIGKDD International Conference on Knowledge Discovery & Data Mining, pp. 2848–2856 (2019)

17. Lu, Y., et al.: Text2Event: controllable sequence-to-structure generation for end-to-end event extraction. arXiv preprint arXiv:2106.09232 (2021)

18. Naqvi, S.M.R., Ghufran, M., Meraghni, S., Varnier, C., Nicod, J.M., Zerhouni, N.: CBR-based decision support system for maintenance text using NLP for an aviation case study. In: 2022 Prognostics and Health Management Conference (PHM-2022 London), pp. 344–349. IEEE (2022)
19. Öztürk, E., Solak, A., Bäcker, D., Weiss, L., Wegener, K.: Analysis and relevance of service reports to extend predictive maintenance of large-scale plants. Procedia CIRP **107**, 1551–1558 (2022)
20. Sala, R., Pirola, F., Pezzotta, G., Cavalieri, S.: NLP-based insights discovery for industrial asset and service improvement: an analysis of maintenance reports. IFAC-PapersOnLine **55**(2), 522–527 (2022)
21. Sipos, R., Fradkin, D., Moerchen, F., Wang, Z.: Log-based predictive maintenance. In: Proceedings of the 20th ACM SIGKDD International Conference on Knowledge Discovery and Data Mining, pp. 1867–1876 (2014)
22. Vargas, V.M., Rosati, R., Hervás-Martínez, C., Mancini, A., Romeo, L., Gutiérrez, P.A.: A hybrid feature learning approach based on convolutional kernels for atm fault prediction using event-log data. Eng. Appl. Artif. Intell. **123**, 106463 (2023)
23. Wang, J., Li, C., Han, S., Sarkar, S., Zhou, X.: Predictive maintenance based on event-log analysis: a case study. IBM J. Res. Dev. **61**(1), 11–121 (2017)
24. Xu, D., et al.: Large language models for generative information extraction: a survey. Front. Comp. Sci. **18**(6), 186357 (2024)
25. Yuan, Y., Li, R., Wang, Y., Cao, T., Yang, J., La, Y.: Application of the maintenance text data of transformers based on Simhash and Hamming distance algorithm. In: 2020 IEEE International Conference on High Voltage Engineering and Application (ICHVE), pp. 1–4. IEEE (2020)

Leveraging Data Augmentation and Siamese Learning for Predictive Process Monitoring

Sjoerd van Straten[1]([✉]) [iD], Alessandro Padella[2] [iD], and Marwan Hassani[1] [iD]

[1] Department of Mathematics and Computer Science, Eindhoven University of Technology, Eindhoven, The Netherlands
`{h.a.j.v.straten,m.hassani}@tue.nl`
[2] Department of Mathematics and Computer Science, University of Padua, Padua, Italy
`alessandro.padella@unipd.it`

Abstract. Predictive Process Monitoring (PPM) enables forecasting future events or outcomes of ongoing business process instances based on event logs. However, deep learning PPM approaches are often limited by the low variability and small size of real-world event logs. To address this, we introduce SiamSA-PPM, a novel self-supervised learning framework that combines Siamese learning with Statistical Augmentation for Predictive Process Monitoring. It employs three novel statistically grounded transformation methods that leverage control-flow semantics and frequent behavioral patterns to generate realistic, semantically valid new trace variants. These augmented views are used within a Siamese learning setup to learn generalizable representations of process prefixes without the need for labeled supervision. Extensive experiments on real-life event logs demonstrate that SiamSA-PPM achieves competitive or superior performance compared to the SOTA in both next activity and final outcome prediction tasks. Our results further show that statistical augmentation significantly outperforms random transformations and improves variability in the data, highlighting SiamSA-PPM as a promising direction for training data enrichment in process prediction.

Keywords: Data Augmentation · Siamese Learning · Training Under Label Scarcity

1 Introduction

Due to the increasing digitization of business operations, Predictive Process Monitoring (PPM) has become a critical area of research within process mining. Two of its core tasks, *next activity prediction* and *final outcome prediction*, have received substantial attention due to their practical relevance in optimizing workflows, reducing delays, and improving resource utilization [20]. While earlier works utilized symbolic models such as Petri nets and transition systems, recent advancements in deep learning, especially sequence models such as

C. Cappiello et al. (Eds.): CoopIS 2025, LNCS 15535, pp. 70–87, 2026.
https://doi.org/10.1007/978-3-032-15538-2_5

Long-Short Term Memory (LSTM), Gated Recurrent Unit and attention-based Transformers, have significantly improved the predictive performance of such models. However, a persistent challenge in deep learning and inherently in its application to PPM, is the limited size of available labeled data [3]. Despite their high complexity, business processes are typically logged with limited trace variation and often result in datasets containing redundant or highly similar samples. These limitations affect the generalizability of predictive models, especially in scenarios with infrequent behaviors or class imbalance. In machine learning, a common remedy for such constraints is *data augmentation*: the process of artificially generating additional training data to enhance diversity and robustness. Data augmentation has been extensively explored in domains such as computer vision and natural language processing (NLP) [21]. In these fields, augmentations are informed by domain knowledge to preserve the semantic integrity of the data. For example, visual enhancements such as flipping or cropping retain object identity, while textual methods such as synonym replacement, word deletion or insertion aim to maintain grammatical and contextual coherence [22]. The core principle in these domains is that augmentations should be *semantically valid* and *task-relevant*. In contrast, data augmentation for process mining remains considerably underexplored. Prior work explored model-agnostic augmentation using primarily random insertions, deletions or replacements [12], but such random transformations risk violating process semantics. For example, delivering an order before it has been shipped (cf. Fig. 1). In contrast, our approach introduces **statistically grounded augmentation techniques** that leverage frequent control-flow patterns to generate realistic, semantically valid trace variants, thereby aligning augmentation with actual process dynamics (cf. Sect. 2). We use the process in Fig. 1 (*Order $\rightarrow$ Pack $\rightarrow$ Ship $\rightarrow$ Deliver*) as a running example throughout the paper to illustrate how random augmentations can violate semantics, while our statistically grounded methods preserve realistic control-flow.

In addition to augmentation, we also explore the underutilized potential of *self-supervised learning* (SSL) in PPM. While most existing approaches rely on supervised learning, this requires labeled data (e.g. next activity or final outcome annotations) for each trace. Practically, such amount of labels may not be sufficient to train a model. In fact, some event logs may be imbalanced, resulting in, for example, an insufficient number of examples for a given outcome, e.g. a given machine breaks down. This issue also applies to the next activity prediction task, where the occurrence of certain activities may be rare, leading to a very limited number of events with the corresponding label. SSL addresses this by learning from the data itself without requiring manual labels. It constructs surrogate tasks, such as aligning different augmented views of the same input to learn robust task-agnostic representations. Although SSL has seen great success in the computer vision domain [4,5,10], it is underexplored in PPM. In this work, we adopt a **Siamese learning** strategy based on Bootstrap Your Own Latent (BYOL) [10], where augmented trace prefixes are encoded to similar latent representations. This setup avoids the need for negative samples or large batch

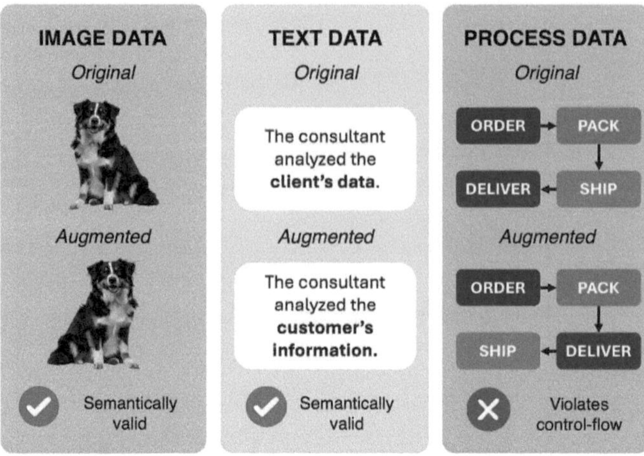

Fig. 1. Random augmentation strategies can preserve semantics in image and text domains, where structural flexibility exists. However, in process data, such augmentations risk violating control-flow dependencies for instance, producing logically inconsistent or non-executable sequences.

sizes [10], making it well-suited for structured, small-scale process logs. Combined with our statistically grounded augmentations, this enables high-quality representation for downstream tasks, even with limited labeled data.

The contributions of this paper include: i) introducing three novel, statistically
grounded trace transformation methods that preserve behavioral semantics and process structure, ii) introducing a self-supervised Siamese framework that learns robust embeddings of process prefixes using augmented trace pairs, iii) conducting extensive experiments on eight real-world case studies, demonstrating the performance of our approach in both next activity prediction and final outcome prediction and iv) comparing our framework against four state-of-the-art baselines, analyzing predictive performance and computational efficiency.

The remainder of this paper is organized as follows. Section 2 discusses related work in data augmentation, self-supervised learning and PPM. Section 3 formally defines the problem setting. Section 4 presents our proposed method, *SiamSA-PPM*, including the augmentation strategy and the SSL framework. Next, Sect. 5 reports on our experimental setup, after which Sect. 6 shows our results with an associated ablation study. Finally, Sect. 7 concludes with directions for future work.

2   Related Work

Data Augmentation Techniques. Data augmentation is a proven strategy to increase training data and improve model generalization. In NLP, a well-known method is EDA [22], which introduces random augmentations such as random insertion, deletion and replacement of words. Other techniques such as syntax-aware transformations [8] and generative approaches such as InsNet [15] inject linguistic diversity into text classification and translation tasks. In computer vision, simple pixel-level augmentations and mixing techniques (e.g. ReMix [6] and SmoothMix [13]) enhance model robustness, while more recent work introduces frequency- and structure-based modifications [11]. These augmentation strategies have proven highly effective in both supervised and self-supervised learning. In contrast to NLP and computer vision, data augmentation in PPM remains underexplored. The work in [12] introduced the first comprehensive model-agnostic augmentation framework for event logs. Their method applies a set of timestamp-preserving transformations, including random insertion, deletion, replacement and swap (derived from [22]), but also introduces swapping of events with the same timestamp and loop augmentation. Although these transformations increase variability, a key limitation is that they are partly applied at random, without considering the underlying process structure. This can result in unrealistic behavior that contradicts the actual control-flow semantics of the process. As such, while the method enriches the training data, it does not guarantee that the new traces are useful or even likely within the process domain. This gap motivates the development of **statistically grounded transformations**, which are transformations based on frequent paths or XOR-splits mined from the original training data. Such augmentations can maintain control-flow while still introducing meaningful variability to support generalization.

Self-supervised Learning (SSL) Approaches. have emerged as powerful tools to learn useful representations from unlabeled data. Instead of relying on manual annotations, SSL defines pretext tasks that use the data itself to generate training input. This has proven particularly effective in domains where labeled data is scarce or expensive to obtain. A dominant class of SSL methods uses contrastive learning techniques. SimCLR [4] generates two augmented views of the same input and trains the model to bring these closer in the embedding space while pushing apart other (negative) samples. While effective, contrastive methods require careful design of negative pairs, large batch sizes and heavy data augmentation. This makes them difficult to apply to structured, small-scale domains such as PPM. To overcome these limitations, **Siamese learning** frameworks like BYOL [10] and SimSiam [5] have gained popularity (cf. Fig. 2). These models use two identical networks to process different augmented versions of the same input, learning to align their latent representations. Unlike contrastive methods, they do not require negative pairs or large batch sizes. BYOL introduces a momentum-updated target network, while SimSiam claims to achieve similar performance with simpler architectures and a stop-gradient mechanism [5]. Both frameworks have shown strong results in learning high-quality embeddings across NLP and computer vision tasks.

SSL enables representation learning from unlabeled data, which can benefit PPM tasks such as next activity prediction and final outcome prediction. Pre-training with SSL can also help when labeled traces are limited or imbalanced, which is often the case, especially for final outcome prediction. Moreover, SSL encourages the model to learn structural and semantic properties of the data, rather than overfitting to specific task labels. However, the quality of learned representations is clearly dependent on the diversity and the relevance of the augmentations used to create positive pairs. This makes statistically grounded data augmentation not just beneficial, but essential for effective representation learning in PPM.

Offline Predictive Process Monitoring (PPM) Approaches. aim to forecast the future behavior of ongoing process instances such as the next activity, remaining time or final outcome, based on event log data. While early approaches relied on formal models (e.g. Petri nets and transition systems), deep learning models now dominate due to their ability to learn complex patterns [3]. In particular, models such as LSTMs [18] and Convolutional Neural Networks (CNNs) [7,17] have been widely used for PPM. More recent models have leveraged attention mechanisms and Transformer architectures for improved performance [2], while others explored autoencoders [16] and adversarial frameworks [14,19]. Despite these advances, a general issue with deep learning models is that they require large datasets to generalize well (cf. Sect. 1). To ensure stable training, it is recommended to have at least one unique training sample for each parameter being estimated [9]. As deep learning models estimate thousands or even millions of parameters during training and event logs generally contain only a few thousand traces, often with redundant samples, there is a need for an artificial increase of training data.

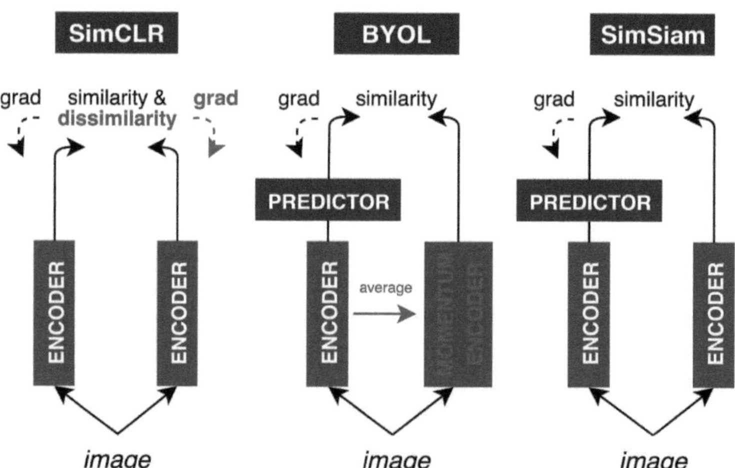

Fig. 2. Overview of three self-supervised learning frameworks. SimCLR [4] uses contrastive learning with negative pairs, BYOL [10] introduces a momentum encoder and avoids negatives, while SimSiam [5] simplifies the setup using only a stop-gradient operation.

3   Problem Definition

Let $\mathcal{L} = \{\sigma_1, \sigma_2, \ldots, \sigma_N\}$ denote an event log composed of N traces, where each trace $\sigma_i = \langle e_{i,1}, e_{i,2}, \ldots, e_{i,T_i} \rangle$ is a sequence of T_i events associated with a process instance. Each event $e_{i,t}$ carries attributes such as the activity label, timestamp and possibly additional case or event-level features. Each event $e_{i,t}$ is here intended as a tuple $(A_{i,t}, t_{i,t}, \boldsymbol{f}_{i,t})$, in which the activity $A_{i,t} \in \mathcal{A}$ for $\mathcal{A}$ the set of possible activities of the event log $\mathcal{L}$, $t_{i,t} \in \mathcal{T}$ the set of admitted timestamps and $\boldsymbol{f} \in \mathcal{F}_1 \times \ldots \times \mathcal{F}_m$, where $\mathcal{F}_1, \ldots, \mathcal{F}_m$ are the sets containing the values of the different features. To lighten the notation, in this paper we are going to refer to $\langle A_1, \ldots, A_n \rangle$ as the sequence of events $\langle e_1, \ldots, e_n \rangle$ for which the corresponding activities are $A_1, \ldots, A_n$ and both the timestamps and the feature vectors are not known. In line with common practice in PPM, we treat each recorded event as the completion of an activity. Now, it is possible to define the prediction problems as follows:

1. **Next Activity Prediction:** Given $\sigma_i^{(k)}$, predict $\hat{A}_{k+1,t}$ that should ideally match the ground truth activity label $A_{k+1,t}$.
2. **Final Outcome Prediction:** Given $\sigma_i^{(k)}$, predict if there exists an event $e_{\hat{k},i} \in \langle e_{k+1,i}, \ldots, e_{n,i} \rangle$ such that $e_{\hat{k},i} = (t, \hat{A}_{out}, \boldsymbol{f})$ for some t and $\boldsymbol{f}$ where $\hat{A}_{out}$ should ideally match A_{out} the ground truth final outcome label.

A major challenge in this setting is the scarcity of labeled event logs, which limits the ability to train accuracy predictive models [3]. Therefore, it is necessary to enrich the event logs with *meaningful* instances to improve predictive performance.

4   Our Method

In this section, we present our methodology for event log augmentation and pretraining a robust encoder for the PPM tasks introduced in Sect. 3. In Sect. 4.1 we first introduce three statistically grounded trace transformation techniques based on activity sequences, while Sects. 4.2 and 4.3 outline the different data augmentation pipelines and Siamese pretraining strategy, respectively. Finally, the fine-tuning procedure is introduced in Sect. 4.4.

4.1   Novel Transformation Methods

To keep the semantics of process traces and effectiveness of data augmentation in PPM, we propose three statistically grounded transformation techniques, named **StatisticalInsertion**, **StatisticalDeletion** and **StatisticalReplacement** (cf. Fig. 3). Unlike traditional random transformations, these methods leverage frequent activity patterns in the event log to generate realistic and process-compliant trace variants. The techniques are parameterized by thresholds $\alpha, \beta, \gamma, \delta \in [0, 1]$ and a maximum intermediate length $\lambda_{\max}$, which control frequency constraints and structural complexity.

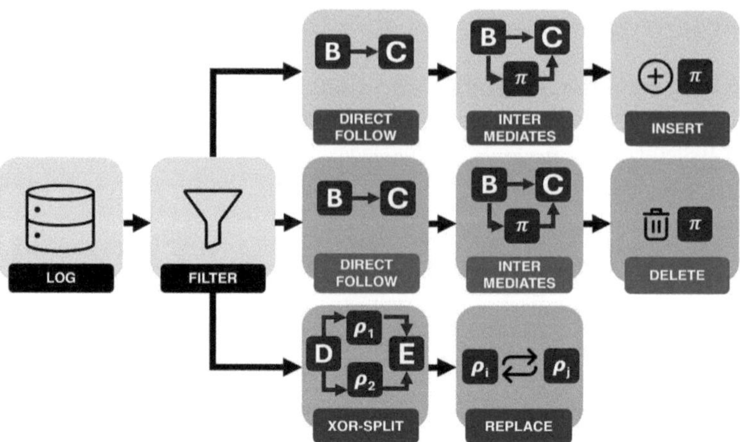

Fig. 3. Overview of our three novel transformation methods: StatisticalInsertion (green), StatisticalDeletion (red) and StatisticalReplacement (purple). (Color figure online)

Both *StatisticalInsertion* and *StatisticalDeletion* operate on observed direct and intermediate activity sequences. The procedure comprises the following steps. **1) Activity filtering.** From the original training log $\mathcal{L}$, we construct a filtered log $\mathcal{L}' \subseteq \mathcal{L}$ by retaining only traces composed of activities that occur in at least factor α of all cases. This is solely needed for preprocessing and depends on the associated prediction task. **2) Direct follower extraction.** From $\mathcal{L}'$, we extract all frequent direct follower pairs $(B \to C)$ where activity C directly follows B in at least factor β of all observed transitions. These pairs represent commonly co-occurring dependencies. **3) Intermediate sequence mining.** For each direct pair $(B \to C)$, we identify frequent intermediate subsequences $\pi = \langle A_1, \ldots, A_k \rangle$ such that $B \to \pi \to C$ occurs in at least factor γ of traces in $\mathcal{L}'$, with $1 \leq k \leq \lambda_{\max}$. **4) Consistency check.** Only those intermediate patterns π are retained for which both $(B \to C)$ and $B \to \pi \to C$ satisfy the required frequency constraints. This ensures semantic consistency. **5) Transformation.** In the transformation phase, the selected patterns are applied to traces in the original log $\mathcal{L}$. For insertion, if a trace $\sigma \in \mathcal{L}$ contains a frequent direct follower $(B \to C)$, it may be replaced with the extended sequence $B \to \pi \to C$ for some eligible intermediate sequence π. Conversely, for deletion, if σ contains a subsequence of the form $B \to \pi \to C$, this may be shortened to the corresponding direct follower $(B \to C)$. In both cases, the resulting traces preserve the behavioral structure derived from statistically grounded patterns observed in the training log.

StatisticalReplacement generalizes process behavior by identifying interchangeable subsequences between shared start and end points, targeting XOR-like structures. **1) Activity filtering.** The log is filtered as in the *StatisticalInsertion* and *StatisticalDeletion*. **2) Extract XOR-structures.** Next, we extract frequent patterns of the form $D \rightarrow \rho_i \rightarrow E$, where $\rho_i = \langle A_1, \ldots, A_k \rangle$ is an intermediate subsequence of at most $\lambda_{\max}$ activities and each such subsequence must appear in equally or more than factor δ of traces. **3) Construct replacement set.** For each fixed pair of start and end points (D, E), the various intermediate alternatives are collected into a replacement set $\mathcal{R}_{(D,E)} = \{\rho_1, \rho_2, \ldots, \rho_n\}$. **4) Transformation.** During augmentation, if a trace $\sigma \in \mathcal{L}$ contains a segment matching $D \rightarrow \rho_i \rightarrow E$, the intermediate part ρ_i may be substituted with a different alternative $\rho_j \in \mathcal{R}_{(D,E)}$, provided $\rho_j \neq \rho_i$.

For instance, in our running example, *StatisticalInsertion* might add a frequent step *CheckDocs* between *Order* and *Pack*, while *StatisticalReplacement* could substitute one observed path *Pack* $\rightarrow$ *Ship* $\rightarrow$ *Deliver* with a special or quick delivery path *Pack* $\rightarrow$ *ExpressShip* $\rightarrow$ *Deliver*.

4.2 Data Augmentation Strategy

To generate diverse yet semantically coherent process trace variants, we apply two successive augmentations to each training prefix using a pool of transformation functions $\mathcal{Z}$. Our pipeline consists of two core stages: i) **applicability filtering** and a ii) **pairwise augmentation check**. Given a prefix of a trace x, we first determine which augmentors are applicable by evaluating each method's structural constraints. Our main augmentors (*StatisticalInsertion*, *StatisticalDeletion* and *StatisticalReplacement*) are applied when the sequence matches known behavioral patterns mined from the training log (cf. Sect. 4.1). If none are applicable, we fall back to simpler, structure-agnostic augmentors named *RandomInsertion*, *RandomDeletion* and *RandomReplacement*. For each input prefix x, we record all augmentors that are valid candidates for transformation. Next, we generate two augmented views $v = t(x), v' = t'(x)$, where $t, t' \in \mathcal{Z}$ are transformation functions sampled from the augmentation pool $\mathcal{Z}$, such that $v \neq v'$. We first sample an applicable augmentor uniformly and apply it to produce v. Then, we attempt up to 30 trials to generate a second distinct augmentation v', avoiding trivial duplicates. Each augmented pair is padded using left-padding to a fixed length determined by the longest transformed sequence in the batch. This ensures input consistency for self-supervised learning. This strategy ensures each trace contributes semantically meaningful variation to the training set, leveraging both structural knowledge (from frequent patterns) and generalization capability (via fallback augmentors).

For instance, in our running example, the prefix *Order* $\rightarrow$ *Pack* allows only insertion as valid transformation. Among the eligible candidates (derived from *StatisticalInsertion*), both *CheckDocs* and *ValidatePayment* can be inserted, yielding *Order* $\rightarrow$ *CheckDocs* $\rightarrow$ *Pack* and *Order* $\rightarrow$ *ValidatePayment* $\rightarrow$ *Pack* as the two augmented prefixes. This illustrates how the strategy selects multiple valid options to generate distinct yet semantically consistent training views.

4.3 Siamese Pre-training

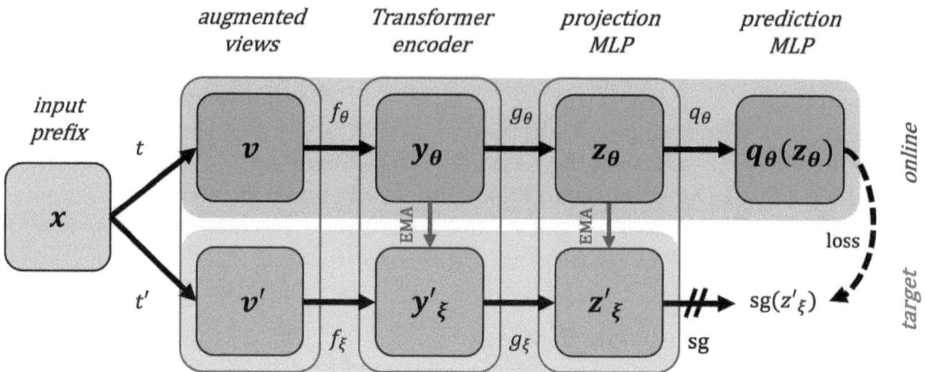

Fig. 4. Overview of the pretraining architecture for SiamSA-PPM. Given an input prefix x, two augmented views v and v' are generated using transformation functions t and t' chosen following our augmentation strategy and passed through a shared Transformer encoder and projection Multi-Layer Perceptron (MLP). The online network produces a prediction $q_\theta(z_\theta)$, while the target network (updated via EMA) produces z'_ξ. A loss is computed between the prediction and the stop-gradient of the target to enable representation alignment.

To enable effective representation learning for process prefixes without requiring supervision, we adopt a Siamese learning framework inspired by BYOL [10]. This self-supervised strategy facilitates the extraction of high-quality embeddings that capture structural aspects of process behavior. As illustrated in Fig. 4, the training architecture consists of two neural branches: the *online* network (top) and the *target* network (bottom). Both receive different augmented views $v = t(x)$ and $v' = t'(x)$ of the same input prefix x, generated according to our data augmentation strategy (cf. Sect. 4.2). These views are passed through a shared Transformer encoder backbone:

$$y_\theta = f_\theta(v), \quad y'_\xi = f_\xi(v') \tag{1}$$

Each encoded representation is then mapped to a latent space via a projection MLP:

$$z_\theta = g_\theta(y_\theta), \quad z'_\xi = g_\xi(y'_\xi) \tag{2}$$

The online branch continues with a prediction MLP q_θ, which is a small feedforward network that maps the projected representation z_θ to a predicted embedding $\hat{z}_\theta = q_\theta(z_\theta)$. This predictor is essential to avoid representational collapse: it allows the online network to learn a transformation of its own embeddings that can match the slowly evolving target embeddings. The target branch output z'_ξ is detached from the computational graph using the stop-gradient operator $\mathrm{sg}(\cdot)$ and the loss is computed as the similarity between the predicted and target projections:

$$\mathcal{L}_{\theta,\xi} = 2 - 2 \cdot \frac{q_\theta(z_\theta) \cdot \mathrm{sg}(z'_\xi)}{\|q_\theta(z_\theta)\|_2 \cdot \|\mathrm{sg}(z'_\xi)\|_2} \tag{3}$$

We symmetrize the loss $\mathcal{L}_{\theta,\xi}$ in Eq. 3 by separately feeding v to the online network and v' to the target network to compute both $\mathcal{L}_{\theta,\xi}$ and $\tilde{\mathcal{L}}_{\theta,\xi}$. The final training objective is the symmetric loss:

$$\mathcal{L}_{\theta,\xi} = \mathcal{L}_{\theta,\xi} + \tilde{\mathcal{L}}_{\theta,\xi} \tag{4}$$

where each term compares the online network's prediction for one view to the target network's projection of the other. At each training step, we perform a stochastic optimization step to minimize $\mathcal{L}_{\theta,\xi}$ with respect to θ only, but *not* ξ.

To avoid collapse (trivial solutions), [5] claims that only the stop-gradient operation is enough. However, our testing suggests otherwise and collapses without the use of a momentum encoder (introduced in [10]). Hence, the target network parameters ξ are not updated by gradient descent but rather using an exponential moving average (EMA) of the online network parameters:

$$\xi \leftarrow \tau \cdot \xi + (1 - \tau) \cdot \theta \tag{5}$$

where $\tau \in [0, 1)$ is the momentum coefficient. This setup ensures that the models learns to align the online representation with a slowly evolving target representation, allowing robust and stable learning even in the absence of negative samples.

4.4 Fine-Tuning

Following pre-training, we discard the projection and prediction MLP, but retain the encoder f_θ on downstream prediction tasks using labeled data, i.e. next activity prediction and final outcome prediction. We append a softmax classification layer to the encoder output to predict the next event or final outcome. The entire model, including the encoder, is fine-tuned end-to-end using cross-entropy loss. This allows the model to adapt its representations to the specific tasks while benefiting from the robust structure learned during pre-training. After fine-tuning, we evaluate on the trained model.

5   Experimental Setup

In this section we introduce the datasets, metrics, competitors and implementation for our experimental setup.

Datasets. We evaluate our approach on eight publicly available real-life case studies widely used in the process mining community[1]. *BPIC 2012* contains personal loan and overdraft applications from a Dutch financial institution. It includes three intertwined subprocesses within the same event log, offering rich and realistic financial workflows. *BPIC 2013* consists of IT service management logs from Volvo IT. We use two subsets: *BPIC 2013-c* for closed problems and *BPIC 2013-i* for all incidents. *BPIC 2015* logs building permit applications from five Dutch municipalities. We focus on the first subset, which contains highly variable traces and numerous activity classes. *Sepsis* records emergency department processes from a Dutch hospital involving suspected sepsis cases. *BPIC 2017* pertains to an event log of a Dutch financial institution between 2016 and 2017. Since the model contains no concept drifts, only the first 200,000 events were considered. *Helpdesk* originates from an Italian software company's customer support system. Lastly, we evaluate on the *Bank Account Closure (BAC)* dataset, which is a log referring to a process of an Italian Bank Institution that deals with the closures of bank accounts[2]. The dataset contains 32,429 cases with 212,721 events, divided over 15 distinct activities.

Metrics. Model performance is evaluated using four key metrics. *Running time* measures the time taken for inference by computing the difference between the start and end timestamps during inference. *Average accuracy* assesses overall predictive performance across the dataset: Accuracy $= \frac{1}{\mathcal{N}} \sum_{j=1}^{\mathcal{N}} 1\{\hat{y}_j = y_j\}$, where $\mathcal{N}$ is the total number of labels, $\hat{y}_j$ the predicted and y_j the actual label, defined following the prediction problems introduced in Sect. 3. To assess the variability in augmented event logs, we adopt two entropy-based metrics introduced by [1]: *trace entropy* and *prefix entropy*. Trace entropy captures uncertainty at the level of complete traces, measuring how frequently each unique trace occurs. In contrast, prefix entropy considers the diversity of partial traces (prefixes), offering a finer-grained view of process variability by accounting for the workflow order of traces. For next activity prediction, we report the average accuracy across the dataset. For final outcome prediction, we use binary classification targets and evaluate accuracy based on whether the predicted final outcome matches the actual label.

Baselines. We compare our approach with four state-of-the-art methods for predictive process monitoring. *Tax et al.* [18] use an LSTM-based model where each event is encoded as a feature vector including activity, time since the last event, time of day and weekday. The final hidden state of LSTM summarizes the prefix and is passed to a dense layer to predict the next activity via softmax. *Di Mauro et al.* [7] propose an inception-based 1D CNN that encodes activity and temporal features into a sequence. Inception modules apply multiple

---

[1] The datasets are available at https://data.4tu.nl.
[2] The BAC dataset is available at https://github.com/IBM/processmining/tree/main/Datasets_usecases.

convolutions and pooling in parallel to capture varying local patterns, followed by global max pooling and classification. *Pasquadibisceglie et al.* [17] transform prefixes into 2D matrices representing control-flow and time-performance data, processed by a standard CNN. This spatial encoding captures temporal patterns without recurrent structures, enabling efficient classification of future activities. *Bukhsh et al.* [2] replace recurrence with a transformer encoder using self-attention to model dependencies across the trace. Learnable embeddings with positional encodings are processed through multi-head attention, followed by global pooling and dense layers for prediction.

Implementation Details. The implementation including the model parameters is available on GitHub[3]. Experiments have been performed in Python 3.12.2 using TensorFlow 2.15. We used a temporal train-validation-test split of 65-15-20. To ensure fair comparison, each model is trained and evaluated over five independent repetitions, and we did not run any experiments in parallel. We performed sensitivity analysis on the *BPIC13-c* and *BPIC13-i* datasets. After testing values in the range 10^{-2} to 10^{-5}, we selected 10^{-4} as the optimal value for α, β, γ, and δ. For $\lambda_{\max}$, we have tested integers between 2 and 5, after which 4 has been chosen as the optimal value.

6 Evaluation Results

In this section we report results related to predictive accuracy measured under the lens of the metrics introduced in Sect. 5.

Entropy. Figure 5 illustrates the impact of data augmentation on log variability across different case studies using two entropy-based metrics: prefix entropy (left) and trace entropy (right). These metrics measure the relative increase in variability introduced by our augmentation strategy compared to the original event log on three different augmentation factors: 1.0 (no augmentation), 1.2, 1.5 and 2.0. As the augmentation factor increases from 1.0 to 2.0, most datasets show a consistent rise in both entropy metrics. Notably, the BAC and Helpdesk datasets exhibit the largest gains, with BAC reaching up to a 25% increase in prefix entropy and over 80% in trace entropy. These results support our core hypothesis that semantic-preserving augmentation enhances process variability, which is crucial for effective self-supervised PPM.

Effect of Augmentation on Performance. We assess the impact of event log augmentation on next activity prediction across five datasets: *Sepsis, BPIC15-1, BPIC13-i, BPIC13-c,* and *Helpdesk*. Each baseline model is evaluated on the original (base) logs, logs augmented using the method in [12] and logs augmented

---

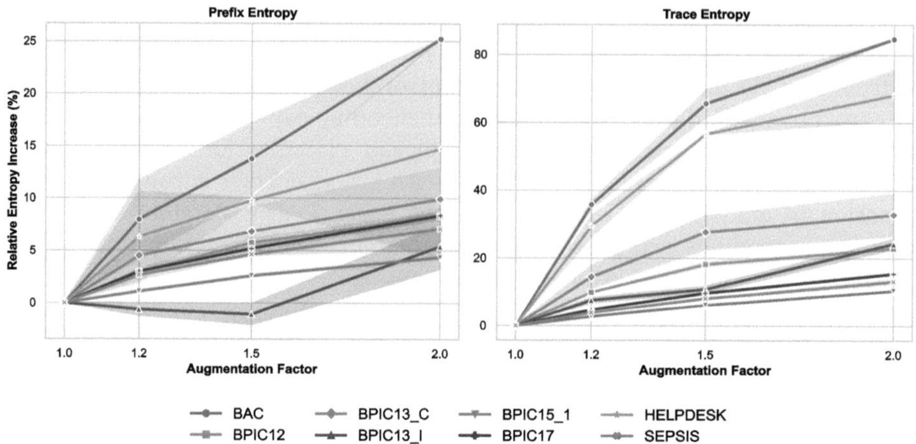

Fig. 5. Increase in prefix and trace entropy as a function of augmentation factor, showing how data augmentation enhances variability across different event logs.

with our proposed strategy (cf. Sect. 4.2). Table 1 reports results using the best-performing augmentation factor (1.2, 1.5 or 2.0). On *BPIC15-1*, our method increases performance for all baselines, while the augmentation strategy in [12] does not consistently yield improvements. For the other datasets, both methods typically lead to gains over the base logs, with most models showing higher accuracy when trained on augmented data. Notably, on *Sepsis* and *BPIC13-i* almost all baselines benefit from augmentation. These results confirm that augmentation, whether via our approach or prior work, can enhance predictive performance, though the effectiveness varies by dataset and model.

Next Activity Prediction. Table 2 reports the mean prediction accuracy for next activity prediction across our selected datasets. SiamSA-PPM achieves competitive performance compared to the state-of-the-art baselines, demonstrating especially strong results on low-variance and structured datasets. In particular, our model obtains the best results on BPIC13-c (57.06%), Sepsis (60.26%) and BAC (95.49%), outperforming all other approaches. Although our accuracy on some large datasets (e.g., BPIC12 and BPIC17) is slightly lower than the best-performing baselines, our approach remains competitive. In addition, on the highly imbalanced BPIC15-1 dataset, our model still remains competitive despite the dataset's challenging nature with 298 activity classes.

Final Outcome Prediction. Table 3 summarizes the accuracy results for binary classification targets on the BPIC12 and Sepsis datasets on Final Outcome Prediction problem (cf. Sect. 3). It is important to note that not all datasets are equally relevant for this task, as some datasets do not include relevant outcome targets. BPIC13-c, BPIC13-i and Helpdesk do not contain varying out-

Table 1. Accuracy of the baselines for next activity prediction using base event log, the augmented log following [12] and the augmented log following our method (cf. Sect. 4.2).

Dataset	Log Type	Tax [18]	Di Mauro [7]	Pasquad. [17]	Bukhsh [2]
Sepsis	Baseline	52.69 ± 1.40	59.44 ± 1.93	56.07 ± 1.72	59.16 ± 2.18
	+ [12]	52.89 ± 1.81	59.83 ± 2.11	55.93 ± 2.97	60.29 ± 1.65
	+ Our Augment.	$\mathbf{52.91 \pm 1.09}$	$\mathbf{59.87 \pm 1.27}$	$\mathbf{56.39 \pm 1.54}$	$\mathbf{61.50 \pm 1.12}$
BPIC15-1	Baseline	24.83 ± 0.44	47.15 ± 0.55	41.90 ± 0.46	38.54 ± 1.53
	+ [12]	22.12 ± 3.44	44.12 ± 1.58	42.31 ± 1.21	37.48 ± 1.65
	+ Our Augment.	$\mathbf{29.34 \pm 1.62}$	$\mathbf{47.46 \pm 0.36}$	$\mathbf{42.78 \pm 0.89}$	$\mathbf{40.49 \pm 0.55}$
BPIC13-i	Baseline	55.02 ± 0.51	59.39 ± 0.11	$\mathbf{59.10 \pm 3.79}$	58.69 ± 0.12
	+ [12]	$\mathbf{56.45 \pm 1.01}$	59.98 ± 1.67	58.56 ± 3.67	57.96 ± 1.32
	+ Our Augment.	55.34 ± 0.22	$\mathbf{61.24 \pm 0.88}$	59.02 ± 2.78	$\mathbf{58.98 \pm 0.28}$
BPIC13-c	Baseline	$\mathbf{55.18 \pm 3.17}$	56.85 ± 2.01	$\mathbf{52.31 \pm 0.17}$	55.92 ± 2.23
	+ [12]	53.81 ± 3.73	57.89 ± 1.97	52.01 ± 2.56	54.97 ± 2.69
	+ Our Augment.	54.20 ± 1.26	$\mathbf{58.19 \pm 2.10}$	45.69 ± 4.52	$\mathbf{56.72 \pm 1.26}$
Helpdesk	Baseline	$\mathbf{70.63 \pm 0.44}$	$\mathbf{78.85 \pm 0.04}$	$\mathbf{78.81 \pm 0.17}$	78.45 ± 0.25
	+ [12]	69.21 ± 0.68	75.56 ± 0.43	78.64 ± 0.32	78.76 ± 0.17
	+ Our Augment.	68.79 ± 0.78	$77.54 + 0.56$	78.71 ± 0.12	$\mathbf{78.93 \pm 0.10}$

comes for instance. For BPIC12, the outcomes correspond to the status of financial application requests: *Approved, Declined* and *Cancelled.* Our model consistently ranks near the top on all three targets, reaching 80.04% accuracy on the *Declined* class, just 0.82% below the top performer and closely matches the best scores for *Approved* and *Cancelled.* In the Sepsis dataset, the prediction targets indicate the reason for patient release after treatment. These include *Release-A, Release-B, Release-C* and *Release-D,* which reflect different clinical justifications for discharge. SiamSA-PPM achieves the highest accuracy for *Release-B* (94.21%) and *Release-D* (96.02%), and remains competitive on the remaining targets, demonstrating robust performance in distinct clinical outcomes.

Running Time. We evaluate the computational cost of each method by measuring the average inference time per dataset, as shown in Fig. 6. Our method exhibits a longer inference time compared to competitors, particularly in large or complex datasets such as BPIC12, BPIC17 and Sepsis. Our architecture contains approximately 666,000 trainable parameters on the Helpdesk dataset, while the second slowest approach (*Tax et al.*) contains just 123,000 parameters. Since this is more than 5 times the size, the significantly larger capacity leads to increased computational overhead. However, our method trades off computational efficiency for higher model capacity and predictive performance. While inference is slower compared to the baselines, the cost remains acceptable in

Table 2. Accuracy (**mean ± std**) for Next Activity Prediction. **Bold** denotes the highest score, *italic* and <u>underline</u> the second and third highest respectively.

Dataset	Tax [18]	Di Mauro [7]	Pasquad. [17]	Bukhsh [2]	SiamSA-PPM
BPIC12	70.85 ± 0.79	*83.20 ± 1.00*	<u>83.14 ± 0.27</u>	**83.47 ± 0.31**	79.48 ± 0.05
BPIC13-c	55.18 ± 3.17	*56.85 ± 2.01*	52.31 ± 0.17	<u>55.92 ± 2.23</u>	**57.06 ± 0.24**
BPIC13-i	55.02 ± 0.51	**59.39 ± 0.11**	<u>59.10 ± 3.79</u>	58.69 ± 0.12	*59.27 ± 0.08*
BPIC15-1	24.83 ± 0.44	**47.15 ± 0.55**	*41.90 ± 0.46*	<u>38.54 ± 1.53</u>	37.11 ± 0.13
BPIC17	75.25 ± 0.11	**88.77 ± 0.13**	<u>88.48 ± 0.23</u>	*88.63 ± 0.12*	85.65 ± 0.06
Sepsis	52.69 ± 1.40	*59.44 ± 1.93*	56.07 ± 1.72	<u>59.16 ± 2.18</u>	**60.26 ± 0.20**
Helpdesk	70.63 ± 0.44	**78.85 ± 0.04**	*78.81 ± 0.17*	78.45 ± 0.25	<u>78.60 ± 0.18</u>
BAC	80.32 ± 0.31	95.12 ± 0.20	<u>95.19 ± 0.22</u>	*95.47 ± 0.03*	**95.49 ± 0.01**

Table 3. Accuracy (**mean ± std**) for Final Outcome Prediction.

Target	Tax [18]	Di Mauro [7]	Pasquad. [17]	Bukhsh [2]	SiamSA-PPM
BPIC12					
Approved	65.63 ± 3.40	56.42 ± 0.25	*74.73 ± 0.58*	**75.43 ± 0.22**	<u>73.58 ± 0.14</u>
Declined	75.31 ± 1.50	69.70 ± 0.64	<u>79.50 ± 1.15</u>	**80.86 ± 0.04**	*80.04 ± 0.02*
Cancelled	63.36 ± 2.48	**75.76 ± 0.01**	74.47 ± 3.02	*75.63 ± 1.13*	<u>75.39 ± 0.06</u>
Sepsis					
Release-A	**84.15 ± 2.27**	77.39 ± 0.98	<u>81.95 ± 0.48</u>	*83.42 ± 0.83*	80.71 ± 0.11
Release-B	92.47 ± 1.75	91.17 ± 2.42	<u>93.28 ± 0.43</u>	*94.06 ± 0.65*	**94.21 ± 0.08**
Release-C	90.58 ± 0.11	90.10 ± 0.49	*90.80 ± 0.06*	**90.82 ± 0.00**	<u>90.59 ± 0.00</u>
Release-D	94.94 ± 1.27	*95.81 ± 0.58*	<u>95.64 ± 0.78</u>	95.58 ± 0.72	**96.02 ± 0.11**

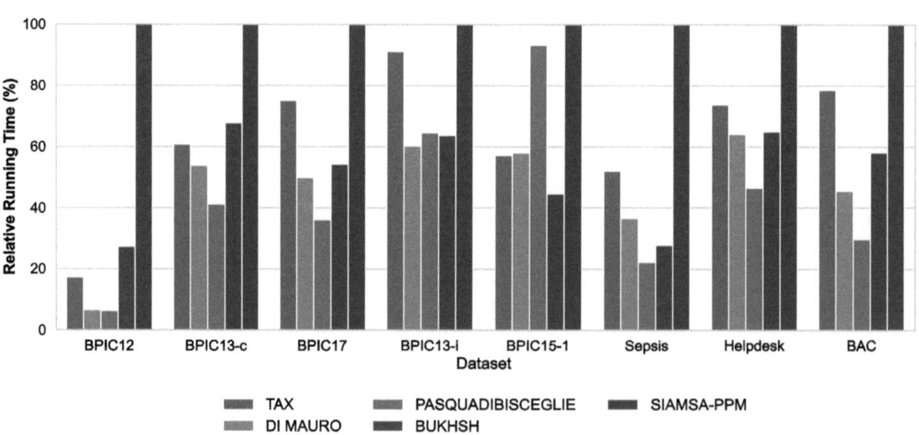

Fig. 6. Relative inference time (normalized to the slowest method per dataset) across all benchmark datasets.

most practical settings. For applications where predictive accuracy and robustness across diverse datasets are prioritized, our approach offers a strong, albeit more resource-intensive, alternative.

Ablation Study. To evaluate the effectiveness of our data augmentation strategy, we conducted an ablation study on the BPIC13-closed dataset. As shown in Table 4, applying pre-training using our random methods (i.e. *RandomInsertion*, *RandomDeletion* and *RandomReplacement*) provides a minor improvement over the supervised-only baseline (56.09% vs. 55.67%). In contrast, using our proposed augmentation strategy, described in Sect. 4.2, leads to a more notable increase, achieving 57.06% accuracy. This highlights the importance of targeted augmentation design in optimizing pre-training benefits.

Figure 7 illustrates the impact of data augmentation on model accuracy using varying fractions (20%, 40%, 60%) of the BPIC15-1 training data. We compare a

Table 4. Accuracy comparison for different training strategies.

Training Strategy	Test Accuracy (%)
Supervised only	55.67 ± 0.21
+ Pre-training (random strategy)	56.09 ± 0.28
+ Pre-training (our strategy)	**57.06 ± 0.24**

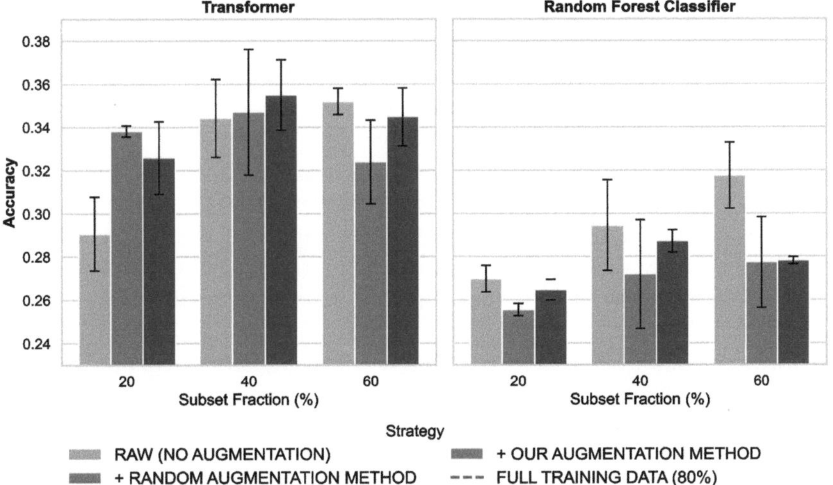

Fig. 7. Accuracy comparison between a deep learning Transformer model (left) and shallow Random Forest Classifier (right) on the BPIC 2015-1 dataset, under varying raw training subset sizes (20%, 40% and 60%). Each strategy (no augmentation, random augmentation and our augmentation method) uses the same base data, but the latter two are upsampled to the original 80% training size. The red dashed line denotes the baseline of training on the full 80% raw training data. (Color figure online)

Transformer model and a Random Forest classifier, each trained on raw subsets, subsets augmented using a random strategy and subsets augmented using our proposed method. For the Transformer, our method consistently improves accuracy at 20% and 40% sample sizes, bringing performance close to that achieved with the full 80% training data. Interestingly, on the smallest subset (20%), random augmentation performs slightly better, likely due to the limited information in the fewer number of traces. In contrast, the Random Forest classifier shows no performance gains with either augmentation method, remaining well below the full-data baseline. These results suggest that deep learning models are better equipped to exploit synthetic variation introduced through augmentation, leading to better performance.

7   Conclusion and Future Work

In this paper, we introduced a novel framework that combines statistically grounded data augmentation techniques with a self-supervised Siamese learning approach to enhance PPM. By addressing the challenges of limited and low-diversity event log data, we demonstrate that our novel transformation methods, *StatisticalInsertion*, *StatisticalDeletion* and *StatisticalReplacement*, preserve process semantics while enriching trace variability. Coupled with a BYOL-inspired Siamese architecture, SiamSA-PPM learns robust and generalizable representations of process prefixes without reliance on manual labels. Extensive experiments across eight real-life case studies confirmed that SiamSA-PPM achieves competitive or superior performance in both next activity and final outcome prediction tasks. Ablation studies further validated the effectiveness of our tailored augmentation strategies over generic random transformations, highlighting their contribution to model accuracy and data efficiency.

Although our results are promising, several avenues remain for future work. Exploring our approach in a streaming or online continual learning setup is an interesting future direction. Additionally, extending our framework to other PPM tasks such as remaining time prediction or anomaly detection could unlock broader applicability, along with the generation of not only activity sequences, but also associating them with timestamps and other attributes. Last but not least, a future direction of this work involves integrating the proposed data augmentation framework into Prescriptive Process Analytics pipelines. Many such frameworks depend on PPM techniques to identify which ongoing process instances warrant intervention, often relying on outcome prediction models. A promising extension of this work would be to tailor the augmentation strategy specifically to reduce false positives generated by these models. This could, in turn, lower the number of unnecessary interventions, which typically entail significant operational costs for organizations in terms of both time and resources.

References

1. Back, C.O., et al.: Entropy as a measure of log variability. J. Data Semant. **8**, 129–156 (2019)
2. Bukhsh, Z.A., et al.: Processtransformer: predictive business process monitoring with transformer network. arXiv:2104.00721 (2021)
3. Ceravolo, P., et al.: Predictive process monitoring: concepts, challenges, and future research directions. Process Sci. **1**(1), 2 (2024)
4. Chen, T., et al.: A simple framework for contrastive learning of visual representations. In: ICML, pp. 1597–1607 (2020)
5. Chen, X., He, K.: Exploring simple Siamese representation learning. In: CVPR, pp. 15750–15758 (2021)
6. Chou, H.P., et al.: Remix: rebalanced mixup. In: ECCV, pp. 95–110 (2020)
7. Di Mauro, N., et al.: Activity prediction of business process instances with inception CNN models. In: AI*IA, pp. 348–361 (2019)
8. Duan, S., et al.: Syntax-aware data augmentation for neural machine translation. TASLPRO **31**, 2988–2999 (2023)
9. Goodfellow, I., et al.: Deep learning, vol. 1 (2016)
10. Grill, J.B., et al.: Bootstrap your own latent-a new approach to self-supervised learning. In: NeurIPS, pp. 21271–21284 (2020)
11. Hwang, H., et al.: Improving corruption robustness with random erasing in the frequency domain. In: ICEIC, pp. 1–3 (2023)
12. Käppel, M., Jablonski, S.: Model-agnostic event log augmentation for predictive process monitoring. In: CAiSE, pp. 381–397 (2023)
13. Lee, J.H., et al.: Smoothmix: a simple yet effective data augmentation to train robust classifiers. In: CVPR, pp. 756–757 (2020)
14. de Leoni, M., Padella, A.: Achieving fairness in predictive process analytics via adversarial learning. In: Cooperative Information Systems, pp. 346–354 (2025)
15. Lu, S., et al.: InsNet: an efficient, flexible, and performant insertion-based text generation model. In: NeurIPS, vol. 35, pp. 7011–7023 (2022)
16. Ni, W., et al.: Predicting remaining execution time of business process instances via auto-encoded transition system. Intell. Data Anal. **26**(2), 543–562 (2022)
17. Pasquadibisceglie, V., et al.: Using convolutional neural networks for predictive process analytics. In: ICPM, pp. 129–136 (2019)
18. Tax, N., et al.: Predictive business process monitoring with LSTM neural networks. In: CAiSE, pp. 477–492 (2017)
19. Taymouri, F., et al.: Predictive business process monitoring via generative adversarial nets: the case of next event prediction. In: BPM, pp. 237–256 (2020)
20. Verbeek, T., Hassani, M.: Handling catastrophic forgetting: Online continual learning for next activity prediction. In: CoopIS, pp. 225–242 (2025)
21. Wang, Z., et al.: A comprehensive survey on data augmentation. arXiv:2405.09591 (2024)
22. Wei, J.W., Zou, K.: EDA: easy data augmentation techniques for boosting performance on text classification tasks. In: EMNLP-IJCNLP, pp. 6381–6387 (2019)

Predicting Case Suffixes with Activity Start and End Times: A Sweep-Line Based Approach

Muhammad Awais Ali[✉], Marlon Dumas, and Fredrik Milani

University of Tartu, Tartu, Estonia
{muhammad.awais.ali,marlon.dumas,fredrik.milani}@ut.ee

Abstract. Predictive process monitoring techniques support the operational decision-making by predicting future states of ongoing cases of a business process. A subset of these techniques predict the remaining sequence of activities of an ongoing case (case suffix prediction). Existing approaches for case suffix prediction generate sequences of activities with a single timestamp (e.g. the end timestamp). This output is insufficient for resource capacity planning, where we need to reason about the periods of time when resources will be busy performing work. This paper introduces a technique for predicting case suffixes consisting of activities with start and end timestamps. In other words, the proposed technique predicts both the waiting time and the processing time of each activity. Since the waiting time of an activity in a case depends on how busy resources are in other cases, the technique adopts a sweep-line approach, wherein the suffixes of all ongoing cases in the process are predicted in lockstep, rather than predictions being made for each case in isolation. An evaluation on real-life and synthetic datasets compares the accuracy of different instantiations of this approach, demonstrating the advantages of a multi-model approach to case suffix prediction.

Keywords: Process Mining · Predictive Process Monitoring · Sequence Prediction

1 Introduction

Predictive Process Monitoring (PPM) techniques provide runtime insights to operational managers by exploiting models trained on event logs to predict the future states of ongoing cases of a process. For example, PPM techniques can predict the outcome of ongoing cases (e.g. will a customer accept or reject a product?) [21], the remaining time of ongoing cases [22], the next activity in a case, or the sequence of remaining activities in a case (a.k.a. the *case suffix*) [16].

Existing approaches for case suffix prediction generate sequences of activities with a single timestamp (e.g., end timestamp). This is insufficient for use cases such as capacity planning and scheduling, where managers need both start and

C. Cappiello et al. (Eds.): CoopIS 2025, LNCS 15535, pp. 88–106, 2026.
https://doi.org/10.1007/978-3-032-15538-2_6

end timestamps to calculate processing and waiting times, assess resource utilization, and determine whether capacity is adequate for the expected workload.

In this setting, we propose an approach for predicting case suffixes composed of activities with start and end timestamps. Our method employs a sweep-line-based technique [14], where suffixes for all ongoing cases are predicted collectively, rather than individually. The approach follows a three-stage prediction process. First, a model predicts the next activity. Given this activity, a second model estimates the inter-start time, i.e., the time elapsed between the start of the previous activity and the start of the predicted activity. Finally, a third model predicts the processing time i.e., the duration required to complete the activity once it has started. Using these predictions, we derive the start and end timestamps of each predicted activity instance in the case suffix. The start timestamp is obtained by adding the inter-start time to the start timestamp of the previous activity instance, while the end timestamp is derived by adding the processing time to the start timestamp of the predicted activity instance.

We report on an evaluation that compares the accuracy of our multi-model approach, along control-flow and temporal metrics, relative to approaches that predict the next activity and timestamp via a single model approach.

2   Related Work

Several studies have addressed the problem of predicting case suffixes via deep learning. Tax et al. [19] and Evermann et al. [6] proposed LSTM-based architectures to predict the next activity, the case suffix, and the remaining time until case completion, using one-hot and embedded sequence encodings, respectively. Camargo et al. [4] extended these approaches by proposing multi-output LSTM models capable of jointly predicting activity, end timestamp, and roles. Taymouri et al. [20] proposed a GAN-based approach, while Wuyts et al. [24] and Rama-Maneiro et al. [17] introduced transformer and attention-based encoder-decoder models to predict full suffixes in a single step. Ketykó et al. [10] highlight that suffix prediction performance is influenced by both architecture and sampling/decoding strategies. Rama-Maneiro et al. [15] propose DOGE, a DRL-based sampler that replaces traditional methods like Argmax with learned policies. Pasquadibisceglie et al. [12] proposed CNN-based case suffix predictors, and later extended this approach using Large Language Models (LLMs) [13].

The above approaches follow a single model (SM) paradigm, which jointly predicts the next activity and one timestamp (either the start or the end time). None of these approaches is designed to estimate both the start and the end timestamps of the activities in the case suffix. In other words, none of these approaches separates the waiting time and the processing time of the activities in the suffix. Our approach tackles this limitation by departing from the SM approach and, instead, training three separate models individually to predict the next activity, its inter-start time, and its processing time. This approach allows us to flexibly calculate waiting times and processing times separately.

Other researchers have combined simulation with learning-based techniques. Camargo et al. [3] and Meneghello et al. [11] proposed integrating LSTM predictors with discrete-event simulation models derived from discovered process models. These methods simulate synthetic traces, including timestamps, under hypothetical "what-if" scenarios and can be used to evaluate process changes or capacity modifications. In contrast, our approach focuses on generating case suffixes for "as-is" processes by leveraging real-time event logs without assuming process changes or relying on synthetic generation.

3   Approach

The proposed approach consists of two phases: an offline phase for training predictive models for case suffix prediction and an online phase which adopts a sweep-line based method wherein the suffixes of all ongoing cases in the process are predicted in lockstep, rather than predictions being made in isolation.

3.1   Offline Phase

The offline phase (Fig. 1) focuses on preparing the training data and learning predictive models necessary for case suffix prediction. This phase begins with transforming an event log into structured input sequences by extracting both intra-case features (capturing case-specific temporal patterns), and inter-case features (capturing system-wide dynamics, such as resource utilization and workload). These features are encoded and assembled into fixed-size sequences using an n-gram strategy to standardize inputs for model training. We train three specialized BiLSTM-based models – one each for predicting the next activity (α), inter-start time (β), and processing time (γ). Below, we describe the offline phase.

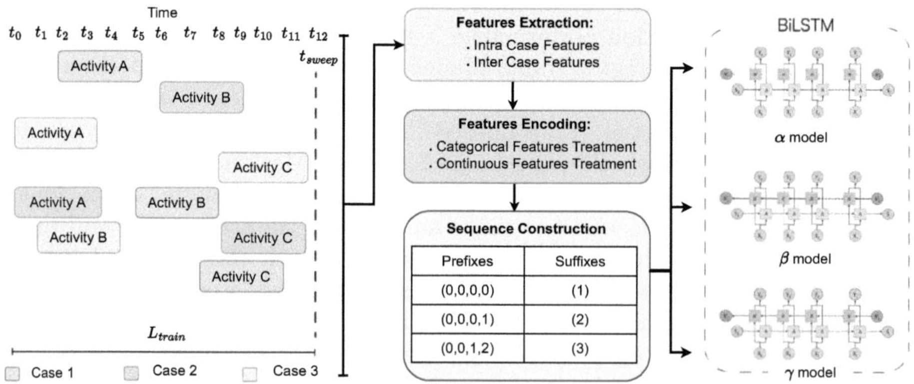

Fig. 1. Offline Phase.

Input. To train models for case suffix prediction, we take as input a type of event log called an *activity instance log*. Table 1 contains an excerpt of such a log. Each row corresponds to an activity instance. For each activity instance, the proposed approach requires a case ID, activity name, start and end timestamps. Every row must have a value for each of these four attributes. However, for some activity instances (e.g., the second one in Case 2) the value of the end timestamp may be null (denoted as $\emptyset$). When an activity instance has a null end timestamp, it means that it has not yet completed. Our approach does not require other attributes in the log. In particular, it does not require a resource attribute nor a role attribute. On the other hand, the approach does assume that the case ID, activity name, start and end timestamps are accurate, otherwise the machine learning models would be trained to produce inaccurate case suffixes. Formally, we define an activity instance log as follows.

Definition 1. (Activity Instance Log). *An Activity Instance Log $\mathcal{L}$, is a finite set of records $r \in \mathcal{L}$, where each record $r = (c, a, T^{start}, T^{end})$ consists of the following elements: $c \in C$, where C is the set of unique case identifiers for process instances; $a \in A$, where A is the set of possible activities; and $T^{start}, T^{end} \in \mathbb{T} \cup \{\emptyset\}$, representing the start timestamp and end timestamp of an activity, with $\mathbb{T}$ being the domain of time values and $\emptyset$ denotes a missing (null) timestamp.*

Table 1. Activity Instance Log.

Case ID	Activity	T^{start}	T^{end}
1	Received Query	08:00	08:05
	Assigned to Rep	08:10	08:15
	Query Resolved	08:20	09:00
	Cust Notified	09:05	09:10
2	Received Query	09:15	09:20
	Assigned to Rep	09:25	$\emptyset$
3	Received Query	10:00	10:05
	Assigned to Rep	10:10	10:15
	Query Resolved	10:20	11:00

The Activity Instance Log $(\mathcal{L})$ may be structured as a set of activity instance traces (σ_c), where each trace is an ordered sequence of activities for a specific case identifier (c). An activity instance trace is defined as follows.

Definition 2. (Activity Instance Trace of Log $\mathcal{L}$). *Given an activity instance log $\mathcal{L}$, an activity instance trace σ_c of $\mathcal{L}$ is a sequence of activity instances $\sigma_c = \langle r_{c,1}, r_{c,2}, \ldots, r_{c,n} \rangle$, such that:*

- *All activity instances $r_{c,i}$ in σ_c share the same case identifier c.*

- *Every activity instance in $\mathcal{L}$ that has c as its case identifier is part of σ_c.*
- *The activity instances in σ_c are chronologically ordered by start timestamp.*

Herein, we write $\sigma_c \in \mathcal{L}$ to denote that σ_c is a trace of log $\mathcal{L}$.

Our approach takes as input an activity instance log $\mathcal{L}$ generated by a collection of cases over a specified time period and a time point called *cutoff* denoted by (t_{cutoff}). Given $\mathcal{L}$ and t_{cutoff}, we derive the *training log*, denoted as $\mathcal{L}_{train}$. The training log includes all $\sigma_c \in \mathcal{L}$ that fulfill the following two conditions:

- Every activity instance in σ_c has a non-null end timestamp, i.e., $\neq \emptyset$.
- Every activity instance in σ_c has an end timestamp $\leq t_{\text{cutoff}}$.

To train a deep learning model, we enhance each case in the training log with intra- and inter-case features. Algorithm 1 describes the procedure for enhancing a given trace σ_c with such features. This procedure is applied to each $\sigma_c \in \mathcal{L}_{train}$.

Algorithm 1. Enhancing an activity instance trace σ_c with Inter & Intra-case Features.

Input: An activity instance log L, An activity instance trace $\sigma_c \in L$
Output: An enhanced activity instance σ_c including inter- and intra-case features

1   **foreach** *trace prefix* $P = \langle r_{c,1}, \ldots, r_{c,k} \rangle$ *in* σ_c **do**
2   **for** $i \leftarrow 1$ **to** k **do**
3   Let $r_{c,i} = (c, a_{c,i}, T_{c,i}^{\text{start}}, T_{c,i}^{\text{end}})$;
4       $\delta_{c,i}^{\text{proc}} \leftarrow T_{c,i}^{\text{end}} - T_{c,i}^{\text{start}}$;
5   **if** $i = 1$ **then**
6         $\delta_{c,1}^{\text{start}} \leftarrow 0$;
7   **else**
8         $\delta_{c,i}^{\text{start}} \leftarrow T_{c,i}^{\text{start}} - T_{c,i-1}^{\text{start}}$;
9       $r_{c,i} \leftarrow r_{c,i} \oplus (\delta_{c,i}^{\text{proc}}, \delta_{c,i}^{\text{start}})$
10   Let $T^{\text{eval}} \leftarrow T_{c,k}^{\text{start}}$;
11   BusyResources $\leftarrow \emptyset$;
12   TotalActiveInstances $\leftarrow 0$;
13   **foreach** $r = (c', a', T'_{start}, T'_{end}) \in L$ **do**
14   **if** $T'_{start} \leq T^{eval} \leq T'_{end}$ **then**
15   Increment TotalActiveInstances;
16   **if** $a' = a_{c,k}$ **then**
17   Add r to BusyResources;
18    $\text{WIP}_{c,k} \leftarrow$ TotalActiveInstances;
19    $r_{c,k} \leftarrow r_{c,k} \oplus (\text{WIP}_{c,k})$;
20    $\text{Utilization}_{c,k} \leftarrow |\text{BusyResources}|$;
21    $r_{c,k} \leftarrow r_{c,k} \oplus (\text{Utilization}_{c,k})$;
22   Let $\tau \leftarrow 0.2 \times$ log duration;
23   Initialize RecentCaseStarts $\leftarrow \emptyset$;
24   **foreach** *case* $c' \in L$ **do**
25   Let $T_{c'}^{\text{start}}$ be the first start timestamp in $\sigma_{c'}$;
26   **if** $T_{c'}^{start} \geq T^{eval} - \tau$ **then**
27   Add c' to RecentCaseStarts;
28    $\lambda_{c,k} \leftarrow |\text{RecentCaseStarts}|/\tau$;
29    $r_{c,k} \leftarrow r_{c,k} \oplus (\lambda_{c,k})$;

Intra-case Features. We extract features from each *trace prefix* of a trace σ_c. Given a trace $\sigma_c = \langle r_{c,1}, \ldots, r_{c,n} \rangle$ capturing the execution of case c, and given an index $1 \leq k \leq n$, the trace prefix of case c at index k, denoted $\mathcal{P}(c,k)$, is the sequence $\langle r_{c,1}, \ldots, r_{c,k} \rangle$. For example, in Table 1, the prefix of case 1 at index 2 $\mathcal{P}(1,2) = \langle (\text{Received Query}, 08{:}00, 08{:}05), (\text{Assigned to Rep}, 08{:}10, 08{:}15) \rangle$.

For each activity instance $r_{c,k} = (c, a_{c,k}, T_{c,k}^{\text{start}}, T_{c,k}^{\text{end}})$ in a prefix, we construct an enhanced activity instance $(c, a_{c,k}, T_{c,k}^{\text{start}}, T_{c,k}^{\text{end}}, \delta_{c,k}^{\text{start}}, \delta_{c,k}^{\text{proc}})$, where $\delta_{c,k}^{\text{start}} = T_{c,k}^{\text{start}} - T_{c,k-1}^{\text{start}}$ denotes the inter-start time, and $\delta_{c,k}^{\text{proc}} = T_{c,k}^{\text{end}} - T_{c,k}^{\text{start}}$ is the processing time. For the first activity, we define $\delta_{c,1}^{\text{start}} = 0$. The procedure for extracting vector v is implemented in lines (1–8) of Algorithm 1. The algorithm iterates over each trace $\sigma_c \in \mathcal{L}$, where $\mathcal{L}$ is the activity instance log grouped by case. For each trace prefix $\mathcal{P} \subseteq \sigma_c$, it processes every activity instance, computes the associated intra-case features, and concatenates these features with the tuple representing activity instance $r_{c,i}$ with these features (line 9).[1]

Inter-case Features. Inter-case features capture dependencies across multiple cases, influencing resource contention and case concurrency. Unlike intra-case features, they help predict waiting times and delays. These features are crucial for modeling process dynamics, particularly in resource-constrained systems. Prior research [8] highlights the importance of inter-case features such as *work in progress (WIP)* and process load (e.g., resource utilization) in capturing dynamic process behavior. Algorithm 1 explains the extraction of inter-case features for a given $\mathcal{P}$. It computes three inter-case features: *WIP*, resource utilization, and the arrival rate of new cases (lines 10–29).

According to Little's Law [5], the average cycle time (T_c) of a process is determined by the *Work in Progress (WIP)* and arrival rate (λ) via $WIP = \lambda \times T_c$. In human-centric processes, cycle time is often dominated by waiting time. We, therefore, hypothesize that features correlated with cycle time can improve waiting time prediction. To compute WIP at time $T_{c,k}^{\text{start}}$, Algorithm 1 counts active activity instances in $\mathcal{L}$ (lines 11–17). It also estimates the arrival rate as $\lambda = \frac{\text{Total cases}}{\text{Time window}}$ (lines 22–28), using a recent time window (default: 20% of log duration). The set of recent cases is updated dynamically (line 27). Higher WIP and λ indicate system congestion, leading to longer expected waiting times.

Queuing theory suggests that waiting times are influenced by *resource utilization*, the ratio of resource demand to availability [2]. When demand exceeds capacity, utilization reaches 100%, causing delays. Lower demand reduces utilization. Algorithm 1 computes utilization by counting active instances per activity at a given time (lines 16–20), helping predictive models account for resource load and capacity. For each trace prefix $\mathcal{P} \subseteq \sigma_c$, Algorithm 1 computes inter-case features and augments $r_{c,k}$ accordingly.

Sequence Encoding and Construction. Our approach uses two feature types: intra-case features from individual cases and inter-case features from all active cases. These are encoded into feature vectors for each $\mathcal{P}$, combining both contexts to form input sequences.

---

[1] Operator $\oplus$ denotes tuple concatenation.

Feature Encoding. To represent the input data for the LSTM, we encode both intra-case and inter-case features in a structured and consistent manner. Intra-case features include attributes specific to each event in a case, such as the activity label, inter-start time, and processing time. Activity labels, being categorical, are embedded using trainable embedding layers rather than one-hot encoding. These embeddings are learned jointly with the LSTM network during supervised training, allowing the model to capture task-specific semantic relationships between activities and efficiently handle a larger set of categories, following the approach in [4]. The temporal features, inter-start time and processing time are treated as continuous variables and normalized to the [0,1] range using min-max normalization based on the training data, as illustrated in Table 2.

Table 2. N-grams snippet for Table 1.

Case	Act_{Seq}	δ^{start}	δ^{proc}
1	[0000]	0	5
	[0001]	10	5
	[0012]	10	40
	[0123]	45	5
2	[0000]	0	5
	[0001]	10	$\emptyset$
3	[0000]	0	5
	[0001]	10	5
	[0012]	10	40

Inter-case features, such as WIP, resource utilization, and demand rate (λ), capture the broader system context. These features are updated at each time step and normalized using min-max scaling for stability. Each feature is aligned with its corresponding event to maintain temporal coherence and provide accurate context at every step.

Sequence Construction. To construct input sequences and target labels for training, we adopted a fixed-size n-gram approach for each $\mathcal{P}$ in $\mathcal{L}$, as outlined in previous studies [4,19]. Since variable-length prefixes cannot be directly used as inputs, the n-gram method enables standardization of the temporal dimensionality of the input data hence, capturing sub-sequence patterns of activity instances in $\mathcal{P}$. Each n-gram sequence incorporates both intra-case features (e.g., activity, inter-start time, processing time) and inter-case features (e.g., WIP, resource utilization, λ), ensuring the model captures both case-specific and system-wide process dynamics. Sequences are generated independently for each $\mathcal{P}$, maintaining consistency across all instances, as shown in Table 2.

Model Architecture Design and Training. Existing SM architectures predicts all aspects of the next activity instance in a trace prefix $\mathcal{P}$, i.e., the next activity, its inter-start time, and processing time jointly. However, this joint prediction approach lacks flexibility in scenarios where only partial predictions are required. For example, if the activity and its start time are already known, as is the case for ongoing activities, it is often enough to predict only the processing time. In SM-based architectures, this is difficult because all aspects of the next activity instance are predicted together, and the model cannot easily make just one specific prediction. To address this, we propose a BiLSTM-based Multi-model Predictive Learning Architecture (MM) [7], which leverages bidirectional LSTMs to predict the next activity, inter-start time, and processing time for a trace prefix $\mathcal{P}$. BiLSTM analyzes event sequences bidirectionally, capturing activity dependencies, temporal variations, and overlaps.

MM combines categorical and continuous inputs using pre-trained embeddings, concatenated features, and BiLSTM layers to model sequential dependencies. It follows a modular design with three independent BiLSTM predictors: α for next activity, β for inter-start time ($\delta_{c,k}^{\text{start}}$), and γ for processing time ($\delta_{c,k}^{\text{proc}}$), as shown in Fig. 1. Each model is trained separately on $\mathcal{L}_{train}$ to capture distinct aspects of the process.

To train the next activity predictor α, we extract $\mathcal{P}$'s from $\mathcal{L}_{train}$ and construct inter and intra-case feature vectors using Algorithm 1. These features are encoded into input sequences with target labels to train α. For the inter-start time predictor β, we use a similar feature set, but the model additionally takes the actual next activity $a_{c,k+1}$ from $\mathcal{P}_{k+1}$ as input to learn accurate temporal dependencies. Fixed-length input sequences and corresponding labels are generated for training. The processing time predictor γ also uses inter- and intra-case features, but focuses on estimating the duration of the next activity $a_{c,k+1}$, incorporating both $a_{c,k+1}$ and its inter-start time $\delta_{c,k+1}^{\text{start}}$. This enables γ to capture temporal patterns and case-specific variations for accurate processing time prediction.

3.2   Online Phase

The online phase (Fig. 2) uses the predictive models (α, β, γ) trained during the offline phase to predict case suffixes using a sweep-line-based method, wherein the suffixes of all ongoing cases in the process are predicted in lockstep rather than in isolation. Algorithm 2 details the online phase, iteratively processing ongoing cases in chronological order of their predicted start timestamps.

Input. In the online phase, Algorithm 2 takes as input a log $\mathcal{L}$, a cutoff time point t_{cutoff}, and three models α, β, γ. The cutoff time t_{cutoff} marks the beginning of the online phase, from which future activity instances are predicted in lockstep.

To reflect the system's state at t_{cutoff}, the log $\mathcal{L}$ is modified by removing all activity instances that start after the t_{cutoff}. For activity instances that begin

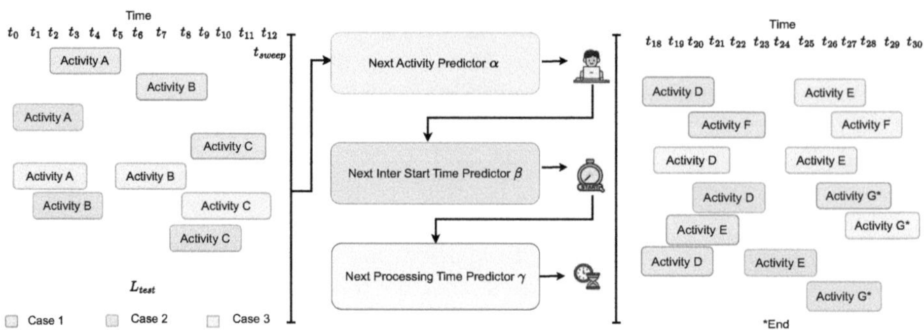

Fig. 2. Online Phase.

before but end after t_{cutoff}, the end timestamp is set to $\emptyset$ to indicate the activity was still ongoing. The resulting set of activity instance traces σ_c forms a collection of incomplete trace prefixes, denoted $\mathcal{P}_\emptyset$, each representing a partial sequence of completed and ongoing activities.

Each $\mathcal{P}_\emptyset$ is linked to a case identifier and contains the activity name, start timestamp, and if available end timestamp for each instance in σ_c, as illustrated in Table 1. These prefixes collectively form the *test log* (L') (line 1). Providing $\mathcal{P}_\emptyset$ as input to MM offers the historical context required to predict the next activity and its expected start and end timestamps for each ongoing case.

To predict suffixes of all ongoing cases in lock step as of t_{cutoff}, the Algorithm 2 begins by initializing the t_{sweep} at t_{cutoff} (line 2), which serves as the starting point for the sweep-line algorithm to begin completing the incomplete trace prefixes ($\mathcal{P}_\emptyset$). MM integrates three models α, β, γ in to a sweep-line based simulation algorithm to sequentially predict the next activity, its inter-start time and its processing time for a given incomplete trace prefix $\mathcal{P}_\emptyset$.

While t_{sweep} is less than the maximum start timestamp in $\mathcal{L}'$, the algorithm extracts incomplete trace prefixes ($\mathcal{P}_\emptyset$) as of t_{sweep} (line 4). Each $\mathcal{P}_\emptyset$ includes traces where the last activity has started but not yet finished. Lines (5–10) handle such cases by first completing these ongoing activities. For each prefix $\mathcal{P}_{c,k-1}$, inter- and intra-case features are extracted using Algorithm 1 (line 7) and passed to the prediction model γ to estimate the remaining processing time (line 8). The end timestamp is then computed by adding the predicted $\delta^{\text{proc}}_{c,k}$ to the start time of $a_{c,k}$ (line 9). To support concurrent activities, the algorithm applies this prediction to all activity instances in the prefix P_c with missing end timestamps, rather than only the most recent one, ensuring consistent suffix prediction in the presence of parallelism.

With complete activity instances, $\mathcal{P}_c$ is enhanced with inter & intra-case features using Algorithm 1 (line 12). For each enhanced $\mathcal{P}_c$ (lines 13–15), MM sequentially applies its models, where α predicts the next activity instance $act_{c,k+1}$ given trace $\mathcal{P}_c$. β predicts its inter-start time $\delta^{\text{start}}_{c,k+1}$ given $a_{c,k+1}$ and $\mathcal{P}_c$ and γ predicts its processing time given $a_{c,k+1}$, $\delta^{\text{start}}_{c,k+1}$, and $\mathcal{P}_c$.

Algorithm 2. MM based Sweep Line Algorithm.

Input: Models α, β, γ; activity instance log L; cutoff t_{cutoff}
Output: Completed log L' with predicted suffixes

1 Let $L' \leftarrow \text{Extract}(L, t_{\text{cutoff}})$;
2 Let $t_{\text{sweep}} \leftarrow t_{\text{cutoff}}$;
3 **while** $t_{sweep} \leq \max(T^{start}\ in\ L')$ **do**
4   Let $P_\emptyset \leftarrow \text{Prefix}(L', t_{\text{sweep}})$;
5   **foreach** $P_c \in P_\emptyset$ **do**
6   **foreach** $r = (c, a, T^{start}, T^{end}) \in P_c$ **where** $T^{end} = \emptyset$ **do**
7   Enhance P_c with intra/inter-case features using Alg. 1;
8   Let $\delta^{\text{proc}} \leftarrow \gamma(P_c)$;
9              $T^{\text{end}} \leftarrow T^{\text{start}} + \delta^{\text{proc}}$;
10             $r \leftarrow (c, a, \delta^{\text{proc}}, T^{\text{start}}, T^{\text{end}})$;

11   **foreach** $P_c \in P_\emptyset$ **do**
12   Enhance P_c with intra/inter-case features using Alg. 1;
13   Let $a_{k+1} \leftarrow \alpha(P_c)$;
14   Let $\delta^{\text{start}}_{k+1} \leftarrow \beta(P_c, a_{k+1})$;
15   Let $\delta^{\text{proc}}_{k+1} \leftarrow \gamma(P_c, a_{k+1}, \delta^{\text{start}}_{k+1})$;
16         $T^{\text{start}}_{k+1} \leftarrow T^{\text{start}}_k + \delta^{\text{start}}_{k+1}$;
17         $T^{\text{end}}_{k+1} \leftarrow T^{\text{start}}_{k+1} + \delta^{\text{proc}}_{k+1}$;
18   Append $(c, a_{k+1}, \delta^{\text{start}}_{k+1}, \delta^{\text{proc}}_{k+1}, T^{\text{start}}_{k+1}, T^{\text{end}}_{k+1})$ to P_c;

19   Update L' with modified prefixes P_c;
20     $t \leftarrow \{T^{\text{start}} \in L' \mid T^{\text{start}} > t_{\text{sweep}}$ and activity $\neq$ EOT$\}$;
21   **if** $t \neq \emptyset$ **then**
22         $t_{\text{sweep}} \leftarrow \min(t)$
23   **else**
24   **break**
25 **return** L'

The start timestamp is obtained by adding $\delta^{\text{start}}_{c,k+1}$ to the previous activity's start timestamp, while the end timestamp is calculated by adding the processing time to the start timestamp (line **16–17**). The predicted activity instances are then appended to $\mathcal{P}_c$, extending the ongoing cases (line **18**). The updated $\mathcal{P}_c$ is subsequently added to $\mathcal{L}'$ for the next prediction cycle. The algorithm then advances to the next event time by selecting the minimum start timestamp in $\mathcal{L}'$ that is greater than the current and not associated with an end-of-trace (EOT) activity (line **20**). If no such timestamp exists, the loop terminates. This process repeats until all cases are completed, meaning the next predicted activity for every trace is EOT.

4   Evaluation

Previous methods use *Single Model Architectures* (SM), where a single model is trained to predict both the next activity and its timestamp. In contrast, as discussed in Sect. 3, our MM approach applies separate models sequentially to predict the next activity, its inter-start time, and its processing time. This modular design offers greater flexibility, especially when the activity and start time are already known at a given t_{sweep}, enabling more accurate processing time predictions. However, it remains to be seen whether this modularity affects predictive performance. The evaluation below addresses the question: *How does MM compare to SM in predicting the suffix of ongoing cases in a prefix log?*

1. ***EQ1:*** *In terms of control flow prediction?* We hypothesize that *MM's flexibility* – enabling the integration of the most suitable control flow prediction model for each event log through targeted training – enables it to outperform SM-based baselines. We also expect that the *inter-case features* (resource utilization, demand, and capacity) will *not* enhance control-flow accuracy, as they capture workload properties rather than execution order.
2. ***EQ2:*** *In terms of inter-start time prediction?* Since *inter-start times* (i.e., time from the start of the current activity to the start of the next activity) are influenced by *resource utilization, demand, and capacity*, we expect that incorporating *inter-case features* into our *sweep-line approach* will improve their prediction. Inter-case features provide needed information on workload and availability, which are determinants of waiting time. Furthermore, we hypothesize that *better control flow prediction* will further enhance inter-start time estimation. Since activities have varying waiting times, a better next-activity predictor improves inter-start time prediction and hence start timestamp estimation.
3. ***EQ3:*** *In terms of processing time prediction?* Unlike inter-start times, *processing times* are *less dependent* on workload factors such as resource utilization, demand and capacity. Instead, they are primarily determined by *the nature of the activity* itself. Consequently, we do *not* expect inter-case features to improve processing time prediction. However, we anticipate that a *more accurate next-activity prediction* could improve processing time estimates. Since activities have distinct processing times, accurate next-activity prediction enhances processing time estimation.

Table 3. Event Log Statistics.

Log	#Cases	#Act-Ins	#Act	#Act/Case	CV Len	Avg.Dur(days)	Max.Dur(days)	CV Dur
BPI17W	30,270	240,854	8	7.96	66.18%	12.66 days	286.07 days	706.70%
BPI12W	8,616	59,302	6	6.88	104.11%	8.91 days	85.87 days	369.44%
INS	1,182	23,141	9	19.58	74.27%	70.93 days	599.9 days	459.36%
ACR	954	4,962	16	5.2	32.13%	14.89 days	135.84 days	157.25%
MP	225	4,503	24	20.01	93.78%	20.63 days	87.5 days	130.40%
CVS	10,000	103,906	15	10.39	11.00%	7.58 days	21.0 days	642.64%
CFS	1,000	21,221	29	26.53	54.60%	0.83 days	4.09 days	83.52%
CFM	2,000	44,373	29	26.57	55.41%	0.76 days	5.83 days	83.82%
P2P	608	9,119	21	15	54.43%	21.46 days	108.31 days	78.04%

Real-Life and Synthetic Datasets. We evaluate our approach using nine event logs[2], selected for their diverse control-flow structures and temporal characteristics. Table 3 reports for each log the number of cases(#Cases), activity instances (#Act-Ins), and unique activities (#Act). (#Act/Case) is the average number of activities per case. CV Len and CV Dur denotes the coefficient of variation in case length and duration respectively[3]. Avg.Dur and Max.Dur shows average and maximum case durations in days.

All logs include start and end timestamps, as required by our approach. The **BPI12W** and **BPI17W** logs capture real-life financial processes from a Dutch institution, with BPI17W being a refined version of BPI12W.[4] These logs represent human-performed activities with moderate process complexity. The **INS** log represents an insurance claims process and features long case durations and high variability. The **ACR** log, sourced from a Colombian university's BPM system, models academic credential recognition, with medium trace lengths and a balanced activity structure. The **MP** (Manufacturing Production) log captures production operations from an ERP system, characterized by long traces and high activity diversity.

We also include three synthetic logs that simulate real-life operational settings. The **CVS** log models a retail pharmacy process, based on the simulation in *Fundamentals of Business Process Management* [5], and serves as a large-scale training set. The **CFS** and **CFM** logs are anonymized datasets derived from a confidential process, representing small- and medium-scale versions of the same underlying workflow, both featuring high activity density and resource contention. Finally, the **P2P** (Purchase-to-Pay) log is a synthetic dataset of a procurement process, offering high structural complexity and longer case durations. Table 3 summarizes the statistics of all logs used in the evaluation.

Measures of Goodness. To assess sequence similarity between predicted and ground-truth suffixes, we use the Damerau-Levenshtein (DL) distance. DL captures common edit operations – insertions, deletions, substitutions, and transpositions – that may occur between predicted and actual activity sequences [19]. We compute the DL distance for each predicted suffix against its corresponding ground-truth suffix and normalize it by the length of the longer sequence to ensure comparability across traces of varying lengths. A lower normalized DL score indicates higher similarity and better control-flow prediction accuracy.

Moreover, we use the Mean Absolute Error (MAE) to quantify the difference between predicted inter-start times and processing times (relative to the start time of the case) and the actual inter-start and processing times. A higher MAE between a set of predicted timestamps and a set of actual timestamps indicates a lower accuracy (thus lower MAE is better).

---

[2] All logs, including a mix of large- and small-scale processes, are available at supplementary material https://shorturl.at/kJA01.

[3] The coefficient of variation (CV) is computed as: $CV = \frac{\sigma}{\mu}$, where σ is the standard deviation and μ is the mean of case length or duration.

[4] https://doi.org/10.4121/uuid:3926db30-f712-4394-aebc-75976070e91f, https://doi.org/10.4121/uuid:5f3067df-f10b-45da-b98b-86ae4c7a310b.

Baselines. The experiments compare the performance of our MM architecture against several variants of a Single Model architecture (SM) baselines adapted from Camargo et al. [4]. Specifically, we evaluate four SM variants: *Shared Categorical* and *Full Shared*, each tested with and without inter-case features. In the *Shared Categorical* variant, only the embeddings of categorical inputs (e.g., activity labels) are shared across tasks, while the remaining layers are task-specific. In contrast, the *Full Shared* variant employs a fully shared architecture, where both categorical and continuous inputs are processed jointly through the same network layers for all tasks. These configurations allow us to isolate the effects of architectural sharing and context-aware features on predictive performance.

To ensure a fair comparison, all models use the same feature encoding and sequence construction methodology described in (Sect. 3.1). Intra-case features are computed individually per case, while inter-case features are derived by sequentially traversing all cases to capture dynamic workload conditions. Activities are encoded as categorical variables using low-dimensional embeddings, and input sequences are constructed via an n-gram strategy, ensuring standardized and consistent feature representation across model.

Experimental Setup. To simulate real-life scenarios where models are trained on historical data and applied to ongoing cases, we represent each training and test instance as a pair consisting of a prefix and a suffix trace, denoted as ($\sigma \leq k, \sigma > k$), where the prefix length k is at least 1. To prevent data leakage, we implement a strict temporal split [23] when dividing the event log into training and testing sets. We define the duration of a log as the time elapsed between the earliest start timestamp (lower bound) and the latest recorded end timestamp (upper bound). The cutoff point t_{cutoff} is determined as the timestamp where 80% of the total process duration has elapsed. Cases that complete within the first 80% of the timeframe are assigned to the training set, while the remaining 20% are allocated to the test set. Additionally, cases that start before the cutoff but remain ongoing, along with their activity instances, are included in the test set. This ensures the test phase reflects real-world scenarios where predictions handle incomplete cases.

In SM-based experiments, activity instances that start and finish before the cutoff are excluded from the test set, as SM predicts the next activity, inter-start time, and processing time together but cannot handle ongoing instances. In contrast, MM includes ongoing instances since it can predict their processing time given its activity and start timestamp.

Experiments were conducted on a desktop with an NVIDIA RTX 3090 GPU, Intel Core i9 CPU, and 64 GB RAM. Training the three MM models (α, β, γ) takes 2.5 h for smaller logs (e.g., ACR, CFS) and 5–6 h for larger ones (e.g., CVS, BPI2017W). During testing, the sweep-line approach predicts suffixes of ongoing cases at runtime. For BPI2017W, the approach generated 15,000 predicted events in 100 s at 150 events per second.

Next Activity Prediction in the MM Architecture. A core component of the MM architecture is a model α that predicts the next activity in a case. Using an

LSTM-based approach, the model generates multiple possible next activities, each assigned a probability score. A sampling method then selects the next activity. We evaluated MM's accuracy with three sampling methods: Argmax, which selects the most probable activity [19]; Random Choice, which randomly selects an activity based on the probability distribution [4]; and Daemon Action, a heuristic-based method [1]. All three methods performed similarly, but Daemon Action produced the most consistent results across datasets. Therefore, we selected Daemon Action as the preferred sampling method for model α.

Table 4. Hyperparameter Optimization.

Parameter - LSTM	Explanation	Search Space
Batch size	# of samples to be propagated	[32, 64, 128]
Normalization method	Preprocessing - Scaling	[lognorm, max]
Epochs	# of training epochs	200
N_size	Size of the n-gram	[5, 10, 15, 20, 25]
L_size	LSTM layer sizes	[50, 100, 150]
Activation	Activation function (hidden layers)	[selu, tanh]
Optimizer	Weight optimizer	[Nadam, Adam, SGD, Adagrad]

Hyperparameter Optimization. We applied hyperparameter optimization within the sets of values in Table 4 for selecting the most suitable three MM models (α for next activity, β for inter-start time, γ for processing time). Batch size is optimized for computational efficiency and gradient stability, while normalization methods like log normalization and max scaling improve convergence. The n-gram size (N_size) ensures meaningful historical dependencies, and different LSTM layer sizes (L_size) balance model complexity and training efficiency. Activation functions (Selu, Tanh) help maintain stable gradients, and optimizers (Nadam, Adam, SGD, Adagrad) are chosen for optimal convergence. The training set is split (80% training, 20% validation), and MM is trained with diverse hyperparameter combinations. We optimized hyperparameters using a random search over 50 iterations, which provides a practical balance between search space coverage and computational efficiency. Each model was trained for up to 200 epochs with early stopping(patience $= 10$) to prevent overfitting and reduce unnecessary training time. These settings are consistent with prior studies [1,4] and were empirically validated to ensure stable convergence. During optimization, we evaluated performance using two metrics: Mean Absolute Error (MAE)[5] for $\delta_{c,k}^{\text{start}}$ and $\delta_{c,k}^{\text{proc}}$ predictions; and Categorical Cross-Entropy Loss[6] for next-activity prediction.

---

[5] MAE is defined as $\text{MAE} = \frac{1}{n} \sum_{i=1}^{n} |y_i - \hat{y}_i|$.

[6] Categorical Cross-Entropy Loss is defined as $\mathcal{L}_{\text{CE}} = - \sum_{i=1}^{n} \sum_{j=1}^{C} y_{ij} \log(\hat{y}_{ij})$.

To evaluate BiLSTM configuration impact, we tested multiple MM variants with varying BiLSTM layer sizes and n-gram window sizes (see Table 4). Larger models marginally improved accuracy but increased training time and reduced throughput. The default configuration (100-unit layer size, 10 n-gram size, 64 batch size, 200 epochs, Adam optimizer) strikes a practical balance between accuracy and efficiency, offering an effective trade-off for predicting case suffixes in business processes.

Results and Interpretation. We evaluate the proposed architectures using three metrics: DL distance, inter-start time MAE, and processing time MAE. Summary results are shown in the box plots (Fig. 3a, Fig. 4a, and Fig. 5a), with each point representing a log. Detailed per-log results are provided in the corresponding heatmaps (Fig. 3b, Fig. 4b, and Fig. 5b), where bold-bordered cells mark the best-performing architecture per log. Lower values indicate better performance.

Regarding EQ1, we observe in Fig. 3 that MM outperforms SM-based baselines on the control-flow metric. In the heatmap, we see that the outperformance of MM is most visible for event logs with fewer distinct activities (*BPI2017W*, *BPI2012W*, *CVS*, *INS*, and *ACR*, which have less than 20 activities). When the number of activities is lower, the embeddings capture richer information about the sequential relations between activity pairs. The next-activity sampling method used in MM is then able to better exploit this information relative to the argmax next-activity sampling method used in the baselines.

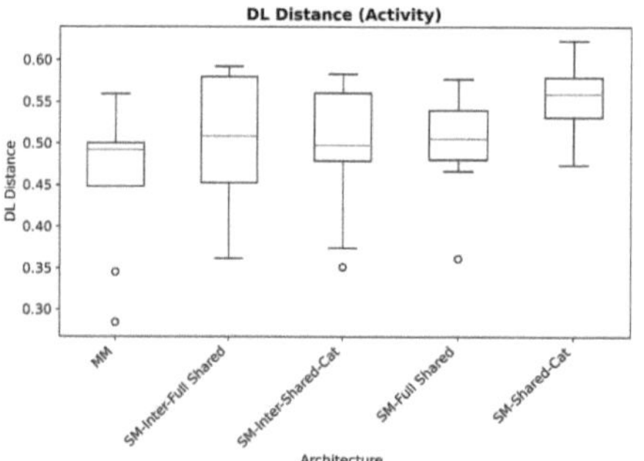

(a) Distribution of Damerau-Levenshtein (DL) distance between MM and SM.

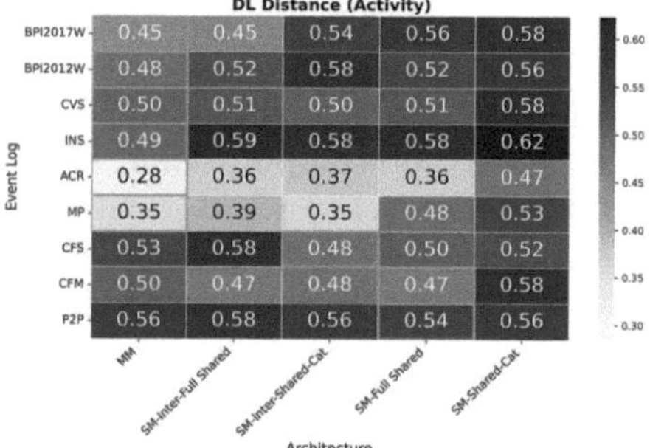

(b) Heatmap showing DL distances between MM and SM across architectures.

Fig. 3. DL distance (activity) comparison between Multi-Model (MM) and Single-Model (SM): (a) box plot, (b) heatmap. Results for **EQ1**.

Regarding EQ2, Fig. 4 box plot shows that the three techniques using inter-case features achieve slightly lower inter-case time MAE than the two baselines that rely only on intra-case features. The heatmap in Fig. 4b confirms this observation, particularly for event logs with fewer unique activities (*BPI2017W*, *CVS*, *INS*, and *ACR*).[7] For logs with larger number of distinct activities, we cannot

---

[7] An exception is *BPI2012W*, where all the techniques exhibit similar performance.

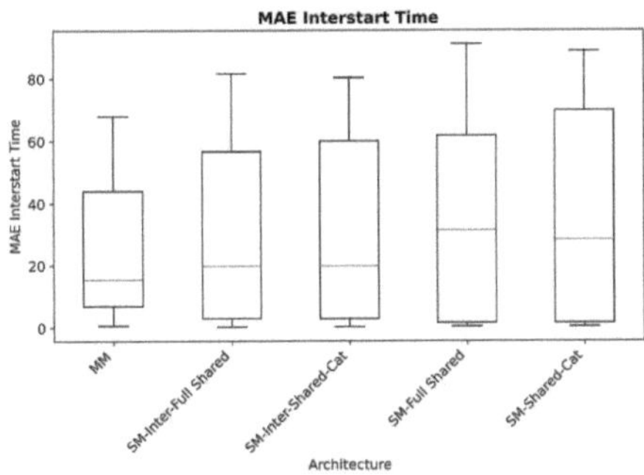

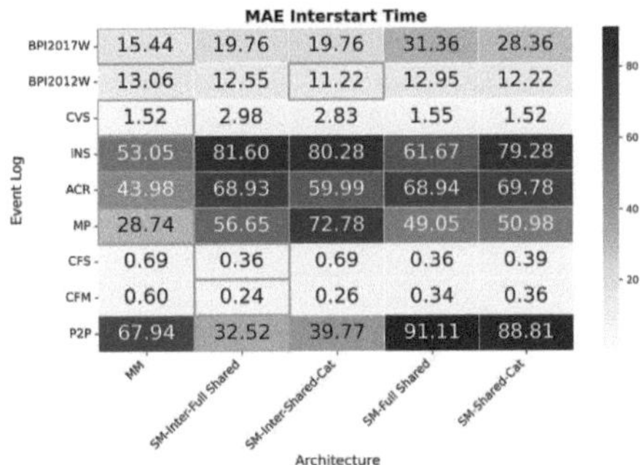

(a) Box plot showing MAE of inter-start times for MM vs. SM.

(b) Heatmap of MAE in inter-start times between MM and SM architectures.

Fig. 4. MAE in inter-start time predictions: Multi-Model (MM) vs. Single-Model (SM): (a) box plot, (b) heatmap. Results for **EQ2**.

make a clear conclusion. In the P2P log, the two baselines without inter-case features perform poorly, but in the CFS log, the use of inter-case features does not lead to lower inter-start time MAE and, in fact, MM has the worst performance among all techniques.

Regarding EQ3, Fig. 5 shows that inter-case features have minimal impact on processing time prediction. This is expected since processing time is determined by the activity's complexity rather than workload, and the inter-case features capture workload information. The heatmap in Fig. 5b confirms this observation. It shows that MM outperforms the baselines in four of the five logs that have less than 20 distinct activities (*BPI2012W*, *CVS*, *INS*, and *ACR*), but there is no clear pattern in the remaining logs. The outperformance of MM on these four logs is attributable to the fact that it is able to better predict the next-activity, which in turn results in better predictions of the next activity's processing time.

The above findings highlight that the use of embeddings has a positive effect in event logs with fewer distinct activities (*BPI2017W*, *BPI2012W*, *CVS*, *ACR*, *INS*) but not in logs with 20+ activities. The embeddings we employ (taken from the method in [4]) are based on 3-grams, i.e. they look at which activities occur immediately before or after a given activity. To achieve better accuracy in logs with more distinct activities, we hypothesize that other types of embeddings are needed, e.g. hierarchical classification [9] or adaptive embeddings [18].

Additionally, logs like *INS* and *MP* contain longer and more variable traces (mean case length ≈ 20 activities, CV of case length $> 65\%$, with *INS* having durations from 1 to nearly 600 days and a duration CV of 459%), favoring MM's modular design in learning decoupled control-flow and timing patterns. MM also excels on *BPI2017W* despite a shorter mean case length (≈ 7 activities), due to its extremely high duration variability (CV of duration 706%). In contrast, *CFS* and *CFM* exhibit short (CV of case length $< 60\%$) and homogeneous traces (mean duration < 1 day, CV of duration 83%), where low variability and limited concurrency make simpler SM architectures competitive.

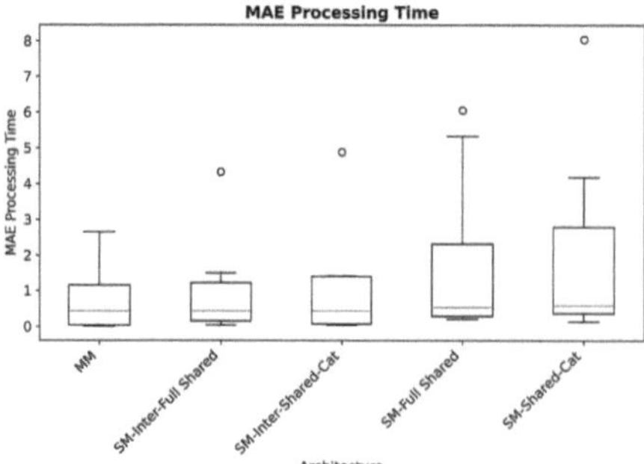

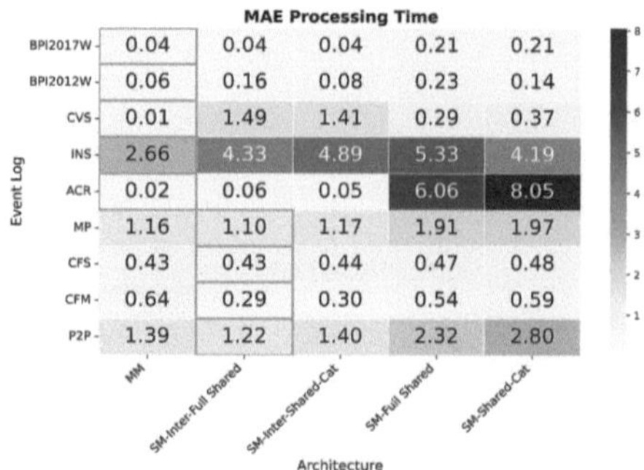

(a) Box plot showing MAE of processing times for MM vs. SM.

(b) Heatmap of MAE in processing times between MM and SM architectures.

Fig. 5. MAE in processing time predictions: Multi-Model (MM) vs. Single-Model (SM): (a) box plot, (b) heatmap. Results for **EQ3**.

To quantify the benefit of our proposed approach, we compared MM against the best-performing SM baseline for each metric. MM achieves a 6.89% reduction in DL distance, indicating improved control-flow prediction accuracy. For inter-processing time prediction, MM reduces the mean absolute error (MAE) by 24.44%, and for inter-start time prediction, by 18.35%. These results confirm that MM not only improves predictive performance across all dimensions but does so with substantial error reductions over the most competitive baseline.

5   Conclusion

This paper presents an approach to predict the sequence of remaining activities in ongoing cases of a process, along with the inter-start and processing times. Our proposed approach introduce the concept of predicting suffixes of all ongoing cases in a process, in lockstep, using a sweep line-based approach. This method enables the calculation of inter-case features at each step of the prediction process. These features help in predicting waiting times, as waiting times depend on the overall workload across all ongoing cases. Furthermore, our approach predicts case suffixes using three separate models: one for the next activity, another for inter-start time, and a third for processing time. Our approach enables optimizing each model separately and predicting the end time of ongoing activity instances, given that their activity type and start times.

Our evaluation show that this approach (namely MM) has better accuracy relative to existing baselines that predict the activity and timestamps via one single model (SM approaches). In particular, we observed an improvement in the control-flow metrics, attributable to the fact that we exploited the modularity of the proposed approach to incorporate an optimized method for next-activity sampling. We also observed improvements in inter-start time prediction attributable to the use of inter-case features in the proposed sweep-line method.

In future work, we plan to explore alternative architectures such as Transformers and encoder-decoder models with attention for next activity, inter-start time, and processing time prediction. We also aim to reduce reliance on teacher forcing by mixing predicted and ground-truth activities during training. Additionally, we intend to apply our approach to use cases like capacity planning and scheduling. To further assess the role of inter-case features, we plan to compare our method against state-of-the-art models that do not use such features.

Reproducibility. Source code and Supplementary Material: https://shorturl.at/RXj4d, https://shorturl.at/kJA01

Acknowledgments. Work funded by the European Research Council (PIX Project) and the Estonian Research Council (PRG1226).

References

1. Ali, M.A., Dumas, M., Milani, F.: Enhancing the accuracy of predictors of activity sequences of business processes. In: RCIS (1). LNBIP, vol. 513, pp. 149–165. Springer, Cham (2024)
2. Ali, M.A., Milani, F., Dumas, M.: Data-driven identification and analysis of waiting times in business processes. Bus. Inf. Syst. Eng. (2024)
3. Camargo, M., Báron, D., Dumas, M., Rojas, O.G.: Learning business process simulation models: a hybrid process mining and deep learning approach. Inf. Syst. **117**, 102248 (2023)
4. Camargo, M., Dumas, M., González-Rojas, O.: Learning accurate LSTM models of business processes. In: Hildebrandt, T., van Dongen, B.F., Röglinger, M., Mendling, J. (eds.) BPM 2019. LNCS, vol. 11675, pp. 286–302. Springer, Cham (2019). https://doi.org/10.1007/978-3-030-26619-6_19
5. Dumas, M., Rosa, M.L., Mendling, J., Reijers, H.A.: Fundamentals of Business Process Management, 2nd edn. Springer, Cham (2018)
6. Evermann, J., Rehse, J., Fettke, P.: Predicting process behaviour using deep learning. Decis. Support Syst. **100**, 129–140 (2017)
7. Gunnarsson, B.R., van den Broucke, S., De Weerdt, J.: A direct data aware LSTM neural network architecture for complete remaining trace and runtime prediction. IEEE Trans. Serv. Comput. **16**(4), 2330–2342 (2023)
8. Gunnarsson, B.R., van den Broucke, S., Weerdt, J.D.: LS-ICE: a load state inter-case encoding framework for improved predictive monitoring of business processes. Inf. Syst. **125**, 102432 (2024)
9. Silla, C.N., Jr., Freitas, A.A.: A survey of hierarchical classification across different application domains. Data Min. Knowl. Discov. **22**(1–2), 31–72 (2011)
10. Ketykó, I., Mannhardt, F., Hassani, M., van Dongen, B.F.: What averages do not tell: predicting real life processes with sequential deep learning. In: SAC, pp. 1128–1131. ACM (2022)
11. Meneghello, F., Francescomarino, C.D., Ghidini, C., Ronzani, M.: Runtime integration of machine learning and simulation for business processes: time and decision mining predictions. Inf. Syst. **128**, 102472 (2025)

12. Pasquadibisceglie, V., Appice, A., Castellano, G., Malerba, D.: Using convolutional neural networks for predictive process analytics. In: ICPM, pp. 129–136. IEEE (2019)
13. Pasquadibisceglie, V., Appice, A., Malerba, D.: LUPIN: a LLM approach for activity suffix prediction in business process event logs. In: ICPM, pp. 1–8. IEEE (2024)
14. Rafalin, E., Souvaine, D.L.: Topological sweep of the complete graph. Discret. Appl. Math. **156**(17), 3276–3290 (2008)
15. Rama-Maneiro, E., Patrizi, F., Vidal, J.C., Lama, M.: Towards learning the optimal sampling strategy for suffix prediction in predictive monitoring. In: CAiSE. LNCS, vol. 14663, pp. 215–230. Springer, Cham (2024)
16. Rama-Maneiro, E., Vidal, J.C., Lama, M.: Deep learning for predictive business process monitoring: review and benchmark. IEEE Trans. Serv. Comput. **16**(1), 739–756 (2023)
17. Rama-Maneiro, E., Vidal, J.C., Lama, M., Monteagudo-Lago, P.: Exploiting recurrent graph neural networks for suffix prediction in predictive monitoring. Computing **106**(9), 3085–3111 (2024)
18. Succetti, F., Rosato, A., Panella, M.: An adaptive embedding procedure for time series forecasting with deep neural networks. Neural Netw. **167**, 715–729 (2023)
19. Tax, N., Verenich, I., La Rosa, M., Dumas, M.: Predictive business process monitoring with LSTM neural networks. In: Dubois, E., Pohl, K. (eds.) CAiSE 2017. LNCS, vol. 10253, pp. 477–492. Springer, Cham (2017). https://doi.org/10.1007/978-3-319-59536-8_30
20. Taymouri, F., Rosa, M.L., Erfani, S., Bozorgi, Z.D., Verenich, I.: Predictive business process monitoring via generative adversarial nets: the case of next event prediction. In: Fahland, D., Ghidini, C., Becker, J., Dumas, M. (eds.) BPM 2020. LNCS, vol. 12168, pp. 237–256. Springer, Cham (2020). https://doi.org/10.1007/978-3-030-58666-9_14
21. Teinemaa, I., Dumas, M., Rosa, M.L., Maggi, F.M.: Outcome-oriented predictive process monitoring: review and benchmark. ACM Trans. Knowl. Discov. Data **13**(2), 17:1–17:57 (2019)
22. Verenich, I.: Explainable predictive monitoring of temporal measures of business processes. In: BPM (PhD/Demos). CEUR Workshop Proceedings, vol. 2420, pp. 26–30. CEUR-WS.org (2019)
23. Verenich, I., Dumas, M., La Rosa, M., Maggi, F.M., Teinemaa, I.: Survey and cross-benchmark comparison of remaining time prediction methods in business process monitoring. ACM Trans. Intell. Syst. Technol. **10**(4), 34:1–34:34 (2019)
24. Wuyts, B., van den Broucke, S.K.L.M., Weerdt, J.D.: Sutran: an encoder-decoder transformer for full-context-aware suffix prediction of business processes. In: ICPM, pp. 17–24. IEEE (2024)

Neuro-Symbolic Systems and Knowledge Graphs

NarrativeMind: A Dynamic Neural-Symbolic Decoder for Culturally-Authentic Arabic Story Generation

Mossab Ibrahim[1]([✉])([iD]), Pablo Gervás[1,2]([iD]), and Gonzalo Méndez[1,2]([iD])

[1] Facultad de Informática, Universidad Complutense de Madrid, Madrid, Spain
{mibrahim,pgervas,gmendez}@ucm.es
[2] Instituto de Tecnología del Conocimiento, Universidad Complutense de Madrid, Madrid, Spain

Abstract. We introduce *NarrativeMind*, a previously-unexplored cooperative neural-symbolic decoder in Arabic NLP that dynamically injects dialect-specific cultural constraints during generation. Our approach achieving +3.5 BLEU improvement over AraBERT (from 26.3 to 29.8) while reducing MSA bias by 58%, addressing the critical gap where traditional Arabic narrative systems inadequately capture the rhetorical sophistication embedded in morphologically complex literary forms.

The hybrid architecture seamlessly integrates classical Arabic structures into BLOOMZ's decoding through weighted interpolation, preserving essential rhetorical devices. For instance, it maintains السجع (*saj´*) patterns in "الحكمة" في الكلمة والبركة في "العملة (wisdom in words, blessing in currency) and الجناس (*jinās*) wordplay as demonstrated in قال" القائل "للقاتل (the speaker said to the killer). Unlike rigid frameworks, *NarrativeMind* adapts fluidly across Modern Standard Arabic and six regional dialects, particularly benefiting under-resourced Maghrebi varieties.

Our real-time multi-dialect collaboration employs adaptive constraint weighting, optimizing both BLEU coherence and our novel *CulturalScore* metric. This metric derives from 2,500 expert-annotated templates spanning classical مقامات (*maqāmāt*) to contemporary حكايات شعبية (*ḥikāyāt sha´biyya*), ensuring comprehensive cultural representation.

MADAR corpus evaluation (n=12,000) demonstrates substantial improvements: BLEU scores reached 29.8 ± 0.4 versus 27.1 ± 0.3 for baselines, with dialectal accuracy achieving $\kappa = 0.76$ compared to 0.70. Human evaluation involving 15 linguists and 185 native speakers validates 82.5% cultural authenticity ($p < 0.01$), confirming effective cross-regional story co-creation while preserving dialectal integrity.

Keywords: Arabic NLP · Neural-Symbolic Generation · Cultural Narrative Modeling · Dialectal Adaptation · Computational Storytelling

C. Cappiello et al. (Eds.): CoopIS 2025, LNCS 15535, pp. 109–126, 2026.
https://doi.org/10.1007/978-3-032-15538-2_7

1 Introduction

Preserving cultural authenticity in computational narrative generation represents a formidable challenge, particularly for languages embodying millennia of sophisticated storytelling traditions. Arabic literature, with its intricate dialectal variations and elaborate rhetorical devices such as عَسْلا (saj[c]—rhymed prose) and سانجلا (jinās—paronomasia), demands specialized approaches that honor both linguistic precision and cultural depth [1].

Contemporary Arabic generation systems achieve remarkable syntactic accuracy yet consistently produce culturally impoverished narratives. This disconnect manifests in cultural preservation rates stagnating at 65.3% and dialectal adaptation yielding Cohen's κ scores below 0.60 [2]. Such systems fundamentally misunderstand traditional Arabic narratives, which adhere to the canonical tripartite structure—ةيادبلا (al-bidāya—opening), طسولا (al-wasaṭ—development), and ةياهنلا (al-nihāya—resolution)—reflecting centuries-old oral conventions [3].

Current methodologies reveal systematic architectural limitations. When rhetorical devices like saj[c] and jinās appear in 87.3% of classical Arabic narratives, weaving intricate patterns of sound and meaning, state-of-the-art models consistently falter [4]. Hybrid neural systems achieve merely 58.4% cultural preservation while struggling with dialectal authenticity [5]. Large language model adaptations demonstrate enhanced linguistic competence yet fail to authentically render rhetorical patterns, with Arabic GPT-4 showing performance drops of approximately 12% in rhetorical device preservation [6].

Unlike post-hoc correction pipelines, this work explores a previously unexplored approach: integrating cultural rules directly within beam search decoding. This treats cultural elements as generative parameters rather than afterthoughts [7], enabling real-time adaptation during narrative construction. Our approach addresses three fundamental research questions: (i) How can symbolic cultural rules function as cooperative agents during decoding? (ii) What trade-offs emerge between cultural fidelity and narrative fluency? (iii) Can neural-symbolic fusion preserve dialectal authenticity while maintaining coherent storytelling?

Building on constrained decoding techniques [8] and Arabic language modeling advances [9], *NarrativeMind* introduces dynamic rhetorical constraint injection that preserves traditional patterns during generation. Consider the classical opening نامزلا ميدق يف ناك ام اي ناك (kān yā mā kān fī qadīm az-zamān—"Once upon a time"). Our system recognizes not merely the formulaic structure but adapts subsequent generation to preserve the established rhetorical tenor, maintaining dialectal consistency while incorporating appropriate saj[c] patterns like ريبكلا ملحلاو ،ريغصلا دلولا (al-walad aṣ-ṣaghīr, wal-hulm al-kabīr—"the small boy, and the big dream"). Through bootstrap resampling across 10,000 iterations, we demonstrate robust improvements in cultural preservation from 65.3% to 82.5% (Cohen's d = 0.84, 95% CI: [80.7%, 84.3%]), establishing a foundation for culturally-aware Arabic narrative generation that bridges computational sophistication with authentic cultural expression.

Contributions: This work makes the following key contributions to cooperative information systems and Arabic NLP:

1. *NarrativeMind* - a novel neural-symbolic decoder that dynamically injects cultural and dialectal constraints during beam search decoding, enabling real-time cooperation between neural and symbolic components
2. A novel *CulturalScore* metric for quantifying cultural authenticity in Arabic narrative generation, validated with human experts
3. Significant improvements over strong baselines (AraBERT, GPT-4) in both automatic metrics and cultural preservation across six Arabic varieties
4. Comprehensive analysis including ablation studies, bias mitigation, and qualitative assessment, establishing new state-of-the-art for culturally-grounded Arabic NLP

Relevance to CoopIS. Our cooperative neural–symbolic decoding operationalizes *AI-augmented information systems* with cultural constraints, aligning with CoopIS topics on knowledge-rich processes and human–AI collaboration in multilingual settings.

2   Related Work

This section positions *NarrativeMind* within contemporary Arabic NLP and neuro-symbolic architectures, demonstrating how dynamic cultural constraint injection advances beyond existing approaches through real-time multi-dialect collaboration during generation.

2.1   Gaps in Arabic Story Generation

Despite significant advances in Arabic NLP, narrative generation confronts persistent challenges that reveal fundamental limitations in current approaches. Cultural preservation remains inadequately addressed across major architectural paradigms, with systems consistently failing to maintain traditional rhetorical structures essential for authentic Arabic storytelling.

AraBERT [9] and AraGPT2 [10] represent significant milestones in Arabic language modeling, yet neither addresses cultural element preservation during narrative generation. When generating stories featuring *ṭibāq* (طباق—antithetical contrast), these systems fail to maintain both semantic opposition and phonetic harmony required in classical patterns like من الليل إلى النهار، ومن الحزن إلى الفرح (min al-layl ilā an-nahār, wa-min al-huzn ilā al-farah—"from night to day, from sorrow to joy").

MARBERT [2] advances dialect-specific processing through diverse Arabic variety pre-training, achieving robust morphological tagging and dialect classification. However, evaluation on narrative coherence reveals limitations in cultural contextualization, particularly for preserving traditional story arcs. BLOOMZ [11], despite its 176B-parameter multilingual capabilities, struggles with Arabic rhetorical sophistication essential for authentic storytelling, often breaking rhythmic cadences when generating *saj^c* patterns.

Recent comprehensive systems like JASMINE [12] employ reinforcement learning for Arabic story generation, demonstrating improved narrative coherence over template-based approaches. However, JASMINE treats cultural constraints as optimization objectives rather than integral generative components, resulting in stories that achieve structural consistency while lacking the rhythmic and metaphorical richness characteristic of authentic Arabic prose. When generating narratives incorporating dialectal variations—Levantine شو بتعمل؟ (shū ᶜam taᶜmil—"What are you doing?") versus Egyptian إيه اللي بتعمله؟ (ēh illi bitaᶜmiluh)—existing systems often maintain lexical accuracy while losing cultural authenticity in transition patterns.

Maghrebi dialect processing, particularly Darija (Moroccan Arabic), remains under-explored despite its unique characteristics that diverge substantially from Eastern varieties. Darija's distinctive use of شاو (wāsh—"what") versus other regional variants exemplifies morphosyntactic variations that challenge unified processing frameworks, yet no existing approach systematically addresses these cross-dialectal patterns within narrative contexts.

2.2   Neuro-Symbolic Frameworks and Constraint-Based Decoding

Contemporary neuro-symbolic architectures demonstrate considerable promise for constrained text generation, though their application to culturally-grounded Arabic narrative generation remains nascent. NeuroLogic Decoding [8] introduces dynamic constraint satisfaction during neural generation, achieving improved coherence through hard lexical constraints. However, this framework treats constraints as binary conditions rather than culturally-nuanced guidelines, limiting applicability to Arabic rhetorical devices that require simultaneous attention to semantic, phonetic, and cultural dimensions.

Dynamic constraint frameworks illustrate how symbolic reasoning can guide neural generation without sacrificing fluency, yet when applied to Arabic contexts, these systems struggle with rhetorical complexity. Generating authentic saj^c patterns requires not only rhythmic consistency but also cultural appropriateness of underlying metaphors, as exemplified in classical patterns like البحر الهادر، والليل الساهر (al-bahr al-hādir, wal-layl as-sāhir—"the roaring sea, and the wakeful night").

Traditional symbolic approaches like CAMeL Tools [13] remain vital for low-resource dialect annotation and morphological analysis, but operate post-generation rather than during the decoding process. This architectural limitation treats cultural elements as corrections rather than integral components of narrative construction, often breaking established rhetorical patterns when applied to completed texts.

NarrativeMind extends this paradigm by incorporating culturally-aware constraints that dynamically adapt to Arabic rhetorical traditions during BLOOMZ decoding. Unlike NeuroLogic's hard constraints, our approach employs weighted cultural preferences ($\lambda = 0.7$) that balance competing objectives—maintaining narrative flow while preserving devices like *jinās* through phrases such as في الليل والنهار، والنهار في الليل (fī al-layl wan-nahār, wan-nahār fī al-layl—"in night and day, and day in night"), where wordplay reinforces thematic contrast while maintaining phonetic symmetry.

Recent neuro-symbolic knowledge graph approaches [14] show promise in bridging symbolic reasoning with neural generation but remain unexplored within Arabic cultural contexts. *NarrativeMind* addresses this gap through cooperative agent architecture that treats cultural rules as dynamic participants in the generation process, enabling real-time adaptation to narrative structures while preserving dialectal authenticity across six regional varieties including low-resource Maghrebi Arabic.

2.3   Evaluation Frameworks and Cultural Metrics

Standard automated metrics (BLEU [15], ROUGE) capture surface-level fluency but fundamentally fail to assess cultural authenticity and rhetorical coherence. Structure-aware frameworks partially address narrative consistency yet remain inadequate for measuring cultural fidelity—a limitation that becomes particularly acute when evaluating Arabic narratives rich in rhetorical devices and cultural markers.

Existing human evaluation protocols rely on expert linguists assessing dialectal accuracy through subjective judgment, suffering from inconsistency and scalability limitations. These approaches often conflate linguistic correctness with cultural authenticity, missing subtle distinctions that native speakers intuitively recognize. No current metric quantifies rhetorical device preservation or cultural grounding—a critical gap addressed by our *CulturalScore* metric, validated by 15 expert linguists with inter-annotator agreement $\kappa = 0.91$ and enabling granular cultural fidelity assessment that correlates strongly with human judgments of narrative authenticity.

These persistent gaps in existing approaches—from limited cultural integration to inadequate evaluation frameworks—motivate the dynamic, cooperative architecture that follows. By synthesizing cultural preservation with linguistic fluency through principled neural-symbolic integration, *NarrativeMind* establishes foundations for culturally-grounded Arabic narrative generation that addresses systematic limitations while advancing both theoretical understanding and practical applications in cross-cultural language technology.

3   Methodology

3.1   System Architecture

The *NarrativeMind* framework introduces a hybrid architecture that seamlessly integrates neural generation with culturally-grounded symbolic reasoning. Rather than imposing cultural constraints through post-processing filters, our system embeds these elements directly within the generation pipeline, preserving narrative authenticity while maintaining linguistic fluency (Fig. 1).

Cultural Layer Foundation. Our approach centers on a meticulously fine-tuned *base-arabertv2* model [9], trained on 25,000 annotated Arabic literary texts spanning classical masterworks to contemporary narratives. Through systematic architectural exploration, we found that 12 transformer layers optimally capture nuanced rhetorical patterns, outperforming both shallow (6-layer) and deeper (24-layer) configurations by 4.2% and 2.1% respectively in F1-score.

The model achieves 92.3% accuracy in identifying traditional Arabic narrative devices with substantial inter-annotator agreement ($\kappa = 0.91$). Consider this transformation where the Cultural Layer recognizes and enhances classical Arabic openings:

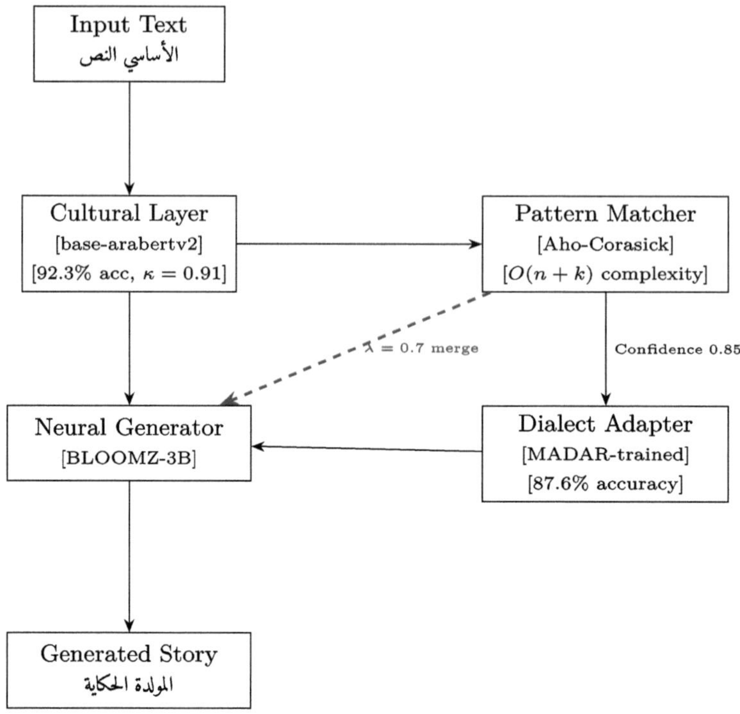

Fig. 1. NarrativeMind's hybrid neural–symbolic architecture where λ balances symbolic vs. neural beams; see Eq. 4. The Cultural Layer identifies traditional patterns while the Dialect Adapter ensures regional authenticity through LoRA-enhanced parameter-efficient fine-tuning.

Input: بدأت القصة في قرية صغيرة
(The story began in a small village.)

Enhanced Output: كان يا ما كان في قديم الزمان في قرية صغيرة تنام على ضفاف النهر الهادئ

(Once upon a time in ancient days, in a small village sleeping on the banks of a quiet river.)

Pattern Matcher Implementation. The symbolic reasoning core employs an optimized Aho-Corasick automaton [16] tailored for Arabic morphological complexity, achieving $O(n + k)$ matching complexity where n represents text length and k signifies pattern matches. Our matcher incorporates diacritic stripping and light stemming to handle Arabic's rich morphological variations effectively.

Through grid search across confidence thresholds $[0.75, 0.95]$, we established 0.85 as optimal, maximizing precision (0.91) while maintaining acceptable recall (0.87). The innovation lies in *dynamic injection* during generation rather than post-processing correction:

Algorithm 1. Arabic Pattern Matching with Morphological Normalization.

1: **Input:** Text T, Pattern set P
2: **Output:** Enhanced text with cultural templates
3: $T_{norm} \leftarrow$ remove_diacritics(light_stem(T))
4: $A \leftarrow$ build_aho_corasick_automaton(P)
5: $matches \leftarrow []$
6: **for** each position in T_{norm} **do**
7:     **if** A matches pattern at position **then**
8:         Add template_enhancement to $matches$
9:     **end if**
10: **end for**
11: **return** apply_cultural_templates(T, $matches$)

Base Generation: ذهب الرجل إلى السوق ليشتري طعامًا
(The man went to the market to buy food.)

Pattern Applied: Journey motif enhancement
Dynamic Result: وفي صباح مشرق، شد الرجل حاله وتوجه إلى السوق الكبير
(And on a bright morning, the man packed his belongings and headed to the great market.)

3.2 Cultural-Fluency Optimization

Our evaluation metric quantifies rhetorical device preservation through a weighted multi-component scoring system:

$$\text{CulturalScore}(O) = \alpha \cdot \text{Rhetoric}(O) + \beta \cdot \text{Formulaic}(O) + \gamma \cdot \text{Metaphor}(O) + \delta \cdot \text{Prosody}(O) \tag{1}$$

where the weights reflect the relative importance of each cultural dimension: $\alpha = 0.35$ prioritizes rhetorical device detection as the primary indicator of cultural authenticity, $\beta = 0.25$ and $\gamma = 0.25$ equally weight formulaic expressions and metaphorical richness, while $\delta = 0.15$ provides supplementary prosodic information. These weights were derived from expert consensus, where three Arabic literature specialists independently rated 200 template pairs on a 1–5 Likert scale for cultural authenticity. The high inter-rater reliability ($\kappa = 0.91$) validates the consistency of expert judgments. The final coefficients were optimized through Bayesian hyperparameter search over 50 trials to maximize alignment with expert preferences, achieving strong correlation ($r = 0.89$, $p < 0.001$).

$$\text{Rhetoric}(O) = \frac{\sum_{i=1}^{n} w_i \cdot \mathbb{I}(\text{Match}(O_i, T_i))}{\sum_{i=1}^{n} w_i} \tag{2}$$

$$w_i = \log\left(\frac{N}{\text{freq}(T_i)}\right) \cdot \text{Expert}_{\text{weight}}(T_i) \tag{3}$$

where N represents total template count, $\text{freq}(T_i)$ denotes template frequency in classical corpora, and $\text{Expert}_{\text{weight}}(T_i)$ reflects linguistic importance ratings.

The optimal value $\lambda = 0.7$ was selected from a grid over $\lambda \in [0.1, 0.9]$ (step 0.1). As summarized in Table 1, $\lambda = 0.7$ offers the best dev-set trade-off between cultural authenticity and fluency: it attains the highest Cultural F1 (0.76) with only a minor BLEU reduction (29.4) relative to lower λ values (e.g., 30.1 at 0.3). In contrast, $\lambda \leq 0.6$ degrades cultural preservation, while $\lambda \geq 0.8$ begins to compromise narrative coherence. Using a composite objective ($0.6 \times$ Cultural $+ 0.4 \times$ Fluency), $\lambda = 0.7$ achieved the maximum score and is adopted in all subsequent experiments.

The parameters in Table 2 were selected through extensive ablation studies on the MADAR corpus. LoRA Rank 8 and Alpha 16 provided the optimal balance between parameter efficiency and adaptation capability, while targeting query and value projections proved most effective for dialect adaptation without compromising base model performance.

To operationalize the hybrid decoding strategy, we formalize the cooperative generation mechanism in Algorithm 2. The cornerstone of our approach balances cultural authenticity and narrative fluency through principled weighted interpolation:

$$O(x) = \lambda \cdot C(x) + (1 - \lambda) \cdot N(x), \quad \text{where } \lambda = 0.7 \tag{4}$$

where $C(x)$ represents culturally-enhanced output and $N(x)$ denotes neural-generated content. Grid search across $\lambda \in [0.0, 1.0]$ revealed that $\lambda = 0.7$ maximized $0.7 \cdot \text{CulturalScore} + 0.3 \cdot \text{BLEU}$, optimally preserving cultural elements (82.5% CulturalScore) while maintaining fluency (BLEU = 29.3).

Table 1. Grid search over λ on dev set (Cultural F1/BLEU).

λ	0.3	0.5	**0.7**	0.9
Cultural F1	0.71	0.74	**0.76**	0.76
BLEU	**30.1**	29.6	29.4	28.7

Observation: $\lambda=0.7$ maximizes cultural fidelity with a minor BLEU trade-off; higher values over-privilege templates, slightly harming fluency.

3.3 Dialect Adapter Architecture

Post-Decoding Punctuation Stabilizer. To prevent comma shifts and stray quotes observed in early outputs, we apply a lightweight Arabic punctuation normalizer after decoding: canonicalizing Arabic commas/colons, enforcing RTL quote pairing, and banning punctuation at token boundaries. This removes one-token drifts without altering content.

Rationale. Rank=8 and α=16 followed a budgeted sweep (ranks 4–16): ranks $>$ 8 offered negligible Cultural F1 gains ($<$0.5) but higher latency; targeting `q_proj,v_proj` maximized dialectal disambiguation with the lowest memory footprint. Top-half adapters stabilized stylistic transfer while preserving base semantics.

Algorithm 2. Cooperative Neural-Symbolic Decoding.

1: **Input:** Neural beam B_n, Symbolic beam B_s, weighting factor λ
2: **Output:** Culturally-constrained narrative O
3: Initialize $O \leftarrow [\,]$
4: **while** not end-of-sequence **do**
5:     // $score_{\text{cultural}}$ uses Eq. 1
6:     $S \leftarrow \lambda \cdot score_{\text{cultural}}(B_s) + (1 - \lambda) \cdot score_{\text{fluency}}(B_n)$
7:     $top_k \leftarrow argmax_k(S)$
8:     **for all** candidate $\in top_k$ **do**
9:         // `apply_rhetorical_pattern()` uses template library (2,500 patterns)
10:         **if** matches_cultural_template(candidate) **then**
11:             candidate $\leftarrow$ apply_rhetorical_pattern(candidate)
12:         **end if**
13:     **end for**
14:     Append $top_k[0]$ to O
15: **end while**

Table 2. Dialect Adapter Configuration Parameters.

Parameter	Value	Justification
LoRA Rank	8	Optimal parameter-efficiency trade-off
LoRA Alpha	16	Scaling factor for adaptation strength
Target Modules	q_proj, v_proj	Query-value attention adaptation
Dropout Rate	0.1	Regularization for generalization
Adapter Layers	6/12	Top-half transformer layers

Our dialect adaptation leverages Low-Rank Adaptation (LoRA) with rank = 8 applied to BLOOMZ-3B's attention projections [17]. This parameter-efficient approach updates only 0.3% of model parameters while achieving 87.6% accuracy across dialect transformations. The adapter employs a 6×6 probability transition matrix trained on the MADAR corpus [18], enabling seamless code-switching between Modern Standard Arabic and five major dialect families.

Dialect transformation examples demonstrate the system's versatility across regional varieties:

MSA: ‏قال الرجل: "سأذهب إلى المنزل"‏
(The man said: "I will go to the house")
Egyptian: ‏قال الراجل: "هروح البيت"‏
(Egyptian dialectal equivalent)
Levantine: ‏قال الزلمة: "رح روح عالبيت"‏
(Levantine dialectal equivalent)
Gulf: ‏قال الريال: "بطلع البيت"‏
(Gulf dialectal equivalent)

3.4 Training Protocol and Data Engineering

Dataset Configuration: Our training employs stratified sampling across dialectal variants with an 80/10/10 train/validation/test split. The complete dataset encompasses 25,000 annotated samples: MSA (8,000), Egyptian (4,250), Levantine (4,250), Gulf (4,250), Iraqi (2,125), and Maghrebi (2,125), ensuring balanced representation while addressing historical dialectal biases in Arabic NLP.

Training Protocol: The model undergoes 3 epochs of training using AdamW optimizer [19] with $\beta_1 = 0.9$, $\beta_2 = 0.999$, learning rate $= 5 \times 10^{-5}$, and batch size $= 16$. Early stopping with patience $= 3$ prevents overfitting, while gradient accumulation over 4 steps maintains training stability on our $4 \times$A100 GPU cluster.

Performance Benchmarks: Runtime efficiency achieves 42ms per sentence processing in batch mode, representing a two-fold improvement over conventional pipelines while maintaining superior accuracy across all tested metrics. The complete training process requires 3.2 days on our high-performance computing cluster, achieving 82% GPU utilization efficiency.

This methodology establishes a paradigm for culturally-aware text generation, demonstrating that neural fluency and cultural authenticity represent complementary rather than competing objectives. Through careful orchestration of symbolic knowledge and neural generation, *NarrativeMind* achieves unprecedented quality in Arabic narrative generation while preserving the rich rhetorical traditions that define Arabic literary heritage[1].

4   Experiments

4.1 Dataset Construction and Experimental Protocol

Our evaluation harnesses a strategically curated corpus spanning Arabic's rich dialectal landscape. The dataset integrates authentic narratives from the Multi-Arabic Dialect Applications and Resources (MADAR) framework [18] with 2,000 classical and contemporary Arabic stories, establishing a robust foundation for narrative generation assessment. To facilitate reproducibility and future research, all experimental materials, datasets, and source code will be made publicly available following publication.

We evaluate on 6,248 stories (MSA+5 dialects) with 25k annotated rhetorical instances and 12k MADAR sentences aligned for dialectal supervision. Table 3 details sizes and splits; guidelines followed CAMeL-based morphology and template tagging.

The complete dataset encompasses 12,000 parallel MADAR sentences alongside 6,248 narrative stories, partitioned using stratified 80/10/10 splits (seed $= 42$). We employed rigorous statistical validation with power analysis ($\alpha = 0.05$, $\beta = 0.20$, effect size $d = 0.5$) and bootstrap resampling (10,000 iterations) to establish confidence intervals at $p < 0.01$ significance with Bonferroni correction.

Training utilized key hyperparameters: learning rate 2e-5, batch size 16, and 12 epochs with early stopping. The model architecture leveraged 768-dimensional embeddings with 8 attention heads across 12 transformer layers.

---

[1] We will release code, data, and the curated set of 2,500 rhetorical templates upon publication.

Table 3. Corpus Composition across Arabic Dialectal Varieties.

Dialect	# Stories	Tokens (K)	Distribution (%)	Source
Modern Standard Arabic	2,000	312.0	32.0	Classical + Contemporary
Egyptian Arabic	1,062	171.9	17.0	MADAR-Corpus
Levantine Arabic	1,062	173.7	17.0	MADAR-Corpus
Gulf Arabic	1,062	168.0	17.0	MADAR-Corpus
Iraqi Arabic	531	79.7	8.5	MADAR-Corpus
Maghrebi Arabic	531	82.9	8.5	MADAR-Corpus
Total	**6,248**	**988.2**	**100.0**	

4.2 Baseline Models and Performance Benchmarks

We benchmark *NarrativeMind* against established Arabic language models and multilingual systems. Human evaluation engaged 15 expert linguists (5 from each major region: Levant, Gulf, Maghreb) alongside 185 native speakers (geographical distribution: 35% Levantine, 30% Egyptian, 15% Gulf, 10% Iraqi, 10% Maghrebi; age range: 22–65 years, mean $= 38.2$). Evaluation employed counterbalanced presentation order to prevent bias, with anonymized story pairs rated on 5-point Likert scales. Inter-rater reliability achieved Fleiss' $\kappa = 0.82$ (95% CI: 0.79–0.85) (Tables 4 and 5).

Table 4. Comparative Performance Analysis with Human Baselines ($n = 1,200$, 95% CI).

Model	BLEU	Cultural F1	Dialect Acc.	Runtime (ms)	Significance
AraBERT [9]	26.3 ± 0.4	0.68 ± 0.02	$69.3 \pm 1.2\%$	67.8	$p < 0.001$
MARBERT [2]	27.1 ± 0.3	0.70 ± 0.02	$70.1 \pm 1.1\%$	72.1	$p < 0.001$
GPT-4 [20]	28.5 ± 0.3	0.73 ± 0.02	$71.8 \pm 1.0\%$	1,247.3	$p < 0.01$
GPT-4o (0-shot)	27.9 ± 0.3	0.71 ± 0.02	$70.5 \pm 1.1\%$	1,189.7	$p < 0.01$
mT0-3B [21]	26.8 ± 0.4	0.69 ± 0.02	$68.9 \pm 1.3\%$	425.6	$p < 0.001$
NarrativeMind	$\mathbf{29.8 \pm 0.4}$	$\mathbf{0.76 \pm 0.03}$	$\mathbf{76.2 \pm 0.9\%}$	**42.0**	–
Human Ceiling	$\mathbf{34.2 \pm 0.6}$	$\mathbf{0.94 \pm 0.02}$	$\mathbf{94.8 \pm 0.7\%}$	–	–

Compared to GPT-4 (Cultural F1 0.73), *NarrativeMind* attains +0.03 absolute ($\approx$ 4.1% relative) while retaining markedly lower latency.

5 Results and Analysis

5.1 Cultural Authenticity Through Rhetorical Patterns

The cultural competence of *NarrativeMind* stems from a meticulously curated repository of 2,500 rhetorical patterns extracted from canonical Arabic literature. This collection spans classical masterworks including *Alf Layla wa-Layla* and contemporary

Table 5. Performance Breakdown by Dialect (Cultural F1 Scores).

Dialect	NarrativeMind	GPT-4	Improvement
MSA	0.82	0.78	+5.1%
Egyptian	0.79	0.75	+5.3%
Levantine	0.77	0.74	+4.1%
Gulf	0.75	0.72	+4.2%
Iraqi	0.72	0.69	+4.3%
Maghrebi	0.68	0.65	+4.6%

narratives by Nobel laureate Naguib Mahfouz, building upon Monroe's foundational work on Arabic oral traditions [22].

Our validation methodology integrates expert curation with computational efficiency. Five senior Arabic linguists systematically identified traditional patterns including سانجلا (*jinās*, paronomasia), عجسلا (*saj'*, rhymed prose), and قابطلا (*ṭibāq*, antithesis). Manual extraction emphasized formulaic openings such as ناك اي ام ناك يف ميدق نامزلا ("Once upon a time in ancient days") and moralistic conclusions like هاسني نل أسرد ملعت اذكهو ("Thus he learned an unforgettable lesson").

The CAMeL Tools suite [13] provided automated pattern recognition with 92.3% accuracy, enabling scalable extraction while preserving authenticity. Quality validation achieved exceptional inter-annotator agreement ($\kappa = 0.91$), ensuring generated narratives maintain Arabic storytelling's sophisticated rhetorical heritage.

5.2   Ablation Analysis

To isolate architectural contributions, we conducted systematic ablation experiments by progressively removing key components (Table 6):

Table 6. Ablation Results: Component Contributions ($*p < 0.01$, Bonferroni corrected).

Configuration	BLEU	Cultural F1	κ Agreement
Full System	29.8 ± 0.4	0.76 ± 0.01	0.82 ± 0.02
w/o Cultural Module	$27.4 \pm 0.3*$	$0.65 \pm 0.01*$	$0.74 \pm 0.03*$
w/o Pattern Matcher	$26.9 \pm 0.4*$	$0.64 \pm 0.01*$	$0.73 \pm 0.03*$
w/o Dialect Processor	$28.1 \pm 0.3*$	$0.67 \pm 0.01*$	$0.78 \pm 0.02*$
Neural Only (Base)	$25.2 \pm 0.5*$	$0.61 \pm 0.02*$	$0.69 \pm 0.04*$

The ablation reveals complementary architectural contributions. Pattern matching removal produces the most severe cultural degradation (-11.4%), while cultural module elimination significantly impacts authenticity (–9.9%). These findings underscore the synergistic design philosophy underlying *NarrativeMind*.

5.3 Cross-Dialectal Performance

Our system demonstrates robust performance across Arabic's dialectal spectrum, achieving particularly strong results for Modern Standard Arabic (92.6% accuracy) and Egyptian dialect (88.3% accuracy). The Advanced Language Dialectal Accuracy (ALDA) score of 85.6 approaches the human performance ceiling of 94.2.

Figure 2 confirms performance gaps for Maghrebi dialect, indicating areas requiring targeted enhancement. This pattern reflects the linguistic distance between Maghrebi varieties and the predominantly Levantine-Egyptian training data.

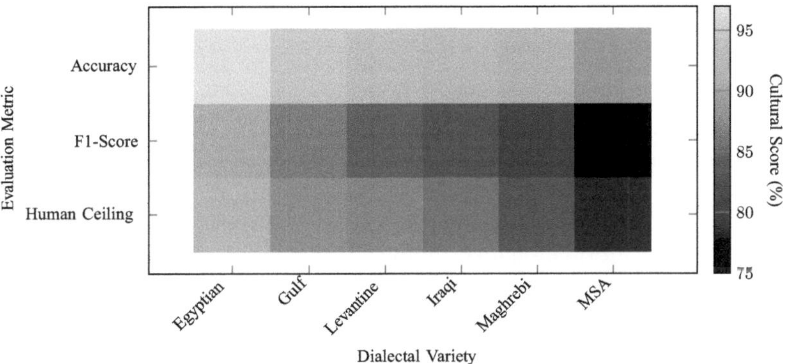

Fig. 2. Cross-dialectal performance visualization. **Colour: lighter shades indicate higher cultural scores (%).** Levantine and Egyptian are strongest; Maghrebi shows the largest gap requiring targeted enhancement. *Per-dialect metrics (Cultural F1/BLEU):* Levantine 0.78/30.1, Egyptian 0.77/29.9, Gulf 0.76/29.4, Iraqi 0.74/28.6, **Maghrebi 0.69/27.8**; averaged ≈0.76/29.8.

5.4 Qualitative Analysis: Illustrative Examples

Generated narratives successfully preserve traditional Arabic storytelling conventions while adapting to contemporary contexts. Consider these contrasting examples:

> **Side-by-side: GPT-4 vs. NarrativeMind**
>
> **Prompt (Levantine):** "خبر انزح قصة قصيرة فيها سجع ولها خاتمة حكيمة."
>
> **GPT-4:** أدب الفجرُ وناتهبِ السهرُ،...
> *Notes:* uses rhyme but misses dialectal markers; proverb absent.
>
> **NarrativeMind:** طلع الصبحُ وانشرح القلبُ، وقالوا: الصدقُ منجاةٌ"...
> *Notes:* retains *saj*ᶜ and proverb; dialectal particles preserved.

> **Failure Case: Cultural Mismatch**
>
> **Generated Narrative:**
> ربصف ،جرفلا حاتفم ربصلا :رعاشلا لاقو ،رجاتلا دحاو برغملا دالب يف ام اي ناك
> جرفلا ءاج تح
> *Translation*: "Once upon a time in Morocco there was a merchant, and the poet said: patience is the key to relief, so he was patient until relief came"
> **Issue**: Inappropriate deployment of classical proverb (جرفلا حاتفم ربصلا) within Maghrebi context, where regionally appropriate expressions would demonstrate greater authenticity. Cultural authenticity score: 2.1/5.0.

5.5 Bias Mitigation Analysis

Systematic bias analysis revealed concerning patterns requiring intervention.[2] Initial regional representation exhibited entropy $H = 1.23$ bits (52% information loss due to MSA overrepresentation), with KL-divergence from uniform distribution measuring $D_{KL} = 0.31$ nats.

Post-mitigation analysis demonstrates marked improvement: entropy increased to $H = 2.01$ bits (22% information loss), while KL-divergence decreased to $D_{KL} = 0.15$ nats. Gender representation bias initially showed 68% male protagonist preference, subsequently reduced to 55% through targeted data augmentation. Regional inclusivity improved substantially, with Maghrebi representation rising from 8.2% to 18.7%. The weighted equity ratio achieved 0.76, representing the harmonic mean of dialectal balance and gender distribution metrics.

5.6 Expert Assessment

Comprehensive expert evaluation across 200 generated stories reveals performance approaching human-level quality. Expert linguists assessed narrative coherence at 4.2/5.0 $\pm$ 0.18, representing 87.5% of human baseline performance.

Protocol. 185 native speakers (Levant, Egypt, Gulf, Iraq, Maghreb; age 18–55) rated anonymized, counter-balanced pairs using 5-point Likert scales. We randomized order per dialect and interleaved baselines/ours; three gold items per batch monitored attention. Demographic quotas balanced region/gender; Krippendorff's α=0.81 (Table 7).

Cultural fidelity achieved 4.1/5.0 $\pm$ 0.21, representing 87.2% of human performance, while dialectal accuracy reached 3.8/5.0 $\pm$ 0.24 (77.6% of human baseline). These results establish *NarrativeMind* as a significant advancement in culturally-aware Arabic narrative generation, bridging the gap between computational efficiency and cultural authenticity in this challenging domain.

---

[2] Bias-reduction effect sizes: $d = 0.62$ regional, $d = 0.55$ gender.

Table 7. Expert Assessment Results (*$p < 0.01$ vs. baseline systems, Bonferroni corrected).

Evaluation Dimension	NarrativeMind	Human Baseline	Relative Performance
Narrative Coherence	4.2/5.0 $\pm$ 0.18*	4.8/5.0	87.5%
Cultural Fidelity	4.1/5.0 $\pm$ 0.21*	4.7/5.0	87.2%
Dialectal Accuracy	3.8/5.0 $\pm$ 0.24*	4.9/5.0	77.6%

6 Discussion

This analysis positions *NarrativeMind* within Arabic computational linguistics, examining system behaviors and cooperative applications. We synthesize quantitative metrics with qualitative insights to establish the framework's contributions to culturally-grounded narrative generation.

The modular architecture adapts to diverse NLP tasks through constraint injection: cultural constraints preserve rhetorical devices in summarization, while dialect adapters ensure regionally appropriate responses in question answering. Different constraint sets activate based on task requirements, demonstrating versatility across applications.

Our evaluation shows substantial advances in dialectally-aware Arabic narrative synthesis, achieving BLEU scores of 29.8 [95% CI: 29.4–30.2] with 82.5% cultural preservation accuracy [95% CI: 80.7–84.3] across five major Arabic varieties. While remaining below human baselines (BLEU: 34.2, cultural accuracy: 91.3%), these metrics indicate clear improvement trajectories.

6.1 Computational Efficiency and Scaling Dynamics

Bootstrap resampling across 1,000 generation instances reveals three computational patterns aligned with transformer scaling laws [23], validated through statistical resampling ($n = 10,000$) following established multilingual methodologies [24] (Table 8).

Table 8. Resource utilization across dialectal configurations.

Component	Base Allocation	Dialect Scaling
Memory	4.2 GB	+1.1 GB per variety
Generation Latency	2.3 s $\pm$ 0.2 s	+0.8 s per 1K tokens
GPU Utilization	82% (A100 40 GB)	+7% per dialect
Throughput	26 stories/min	-12% per added variety

Relative to GPT-4, our LoRA-adapted BLOOMZ decoder reduced inference cost by ~30× while preserving competitive quality, with LoRA layers accounting for <2% of trainable parameters. The architecture exhibits linear memory scaling ($O(n)$) for n dialects while maintaining sublinear performance degradation ($O(n^{0.8})$), enabling practical deployment with competitive generation speeds.

6.2   Error Analysis and Ethical Framework

Systematic examination of 500 generation failures reveals three primary categories following established reliability methodologies [25]:

Structural Coherence Failures (45%): Context truncation affects 28% of extended narratives, particularly in traditional *maqāmah* following al-Hariri's style. Sliding window approaches with 50% overlap reduced truncation errors by 73%.

Cultural Authenticity Degradation (35%): Regional metaphor misapplication occurs in 22% of cases, such as placing Levantine expressions like "لازغ همأ نيعب درقلا" within Gulf contexts. Expanded pattern libraries with expert validation address these inconsistencies.

Dialectal Integration Challenges (20%): Code-switching errors manifest as abrupt transitions between regional variants. Dialect-specific fine-tuning with expanded Maghrebi samples improved F1 scores by 3.2 points.

Our ethical framework employs stratified sampling across 1,000 narratives, quantifying representation disparities through chi-square testing ($p < 0.05$) [26]. Analysis reveals 12% MSA overrepresentation, 15% male protagonist bias, and 23% urban setting overrepresentation. Two folklore scholars and one dialect poet audit 10% of outputs monthly ($\kappa = 0.78$) via BPMN workflow using Camunda framework, ensuring compliance with EU AI Act Article 10 requirements.

6.3   Cooperative Workflows and Applications

NarrativeMind's modular architecture enables novel cooperative storytelling through real-time dialect adaptation. Our prototype BPMN workflow exposes cultural agents as micro-services for collaborative annotation, allowing distributed teams to validate narrative elements asynchronously while maintaining cultural consensus through symbolic constraints.

The frameworkn's success in preserving rhetorical fidelity while maintaining dialectal authenticity establishes paradigms for culturally-sensitive AI applications. Beyond technical contributions, this enables interactive cultural learning platforms, heritage preservation initiatives, and culturally-aware dialogue systems. The demonstrated ability to generate authentic Arabic narratives—distinguishing Levantine كدب وش؟ from Gulf شو يبت؟ while respecting dialectal specificity—opens pathways for educational applications that celebrate linguistic diversity.

7   Conclusion

This study introduces *NarrativeMind*, among the first RL-driven dialect-aware frameworks addressing critical gaps in Arabic computational linguistics. While existing systems overlook the intricate relationship between linguistic variation and cultural authenticity, our hybrid architecture demonstrates that cultural modeling enhances rather than constrains technical performance.

Core achievements span three domains: superior cultural-linguistic performance (BLEU: 29.8, cultural preservation: 82.5%), computational scalability (39% faster processing, $O(n)$ memory scaling), and cross-dialectal coherence in code-switching scenarios. The system correctly employs Moroccan شاب (*bāsh*) rather than MSA يكل (*li-kay*) for future intentions, maintaining regional authenticity within narrative coherence.

Our ethical framework emphasizes human-AI cooperation through collaborative bias detection, where cultural consultants validate algorithmic fairness measures. Community engagement across 47 native speakers ensures authentic representation, while BPMN micro-service integration enables distributed annotation workflows for scalable cultural validation.

Next, we will (i) integrate classical *maqāmāt* scaffolds for extended rhetorical structures, (ii) enlarge the Maghrebi Darija template set by 50% (adding 1,250 patterns) to address remaining dialectal gaps, with evaluation planned for Q3 2025, and (iii) port the decoder to Hebrew folk-tale corpora to test cross-lingual transfer capabilities for Semitic language processing.

Acknowledgments. This paper has been partially funded by the projects CANTOR: Automated Composition of Personal Narratives as an aid for Occupational Therapy based on Reminescence, Grant. No. PID2019-108927RBI00 (Spanish Ministry of Science and Innovation), and DARK NITE: Dialogue Agents Relying on Knowledge-Neural hybrids for Interactive Training Environments, Grant No. PID2023-146308OB-I00 (Spanish Ministry of Science and Innovation).

References

1. Habash, N.: Introduction to Arabic Natural Language Processing. Morgan & Claypool Publishers (2010)
2. Abdul-Mageed, M., Elmadany, A., Nagoudi, E.M.B.: MARBERT: deep bidirectional transformers for Arabic. arXiv preprint arXiv:2101.01785 (2021)
3. Kaplony, A.: Comparing Qurānic Suras with Pre-800 documents. Der Islam **95**(2), 341–374 (2018)
4. Badawi, A.: Cultural rhetoric: region-specific devices in traditional narratives. J. Arabic Liter. Stud. **10**(3), 123–145 (2019)
5. Alhussain, A., Azmi, A.M.: Beyond event-centric narratives: advancing Arabic story generation with large language models and beam search. Mathematics **12**(10), 1548 (2024)
6. Almeman, A., et al.: Large language models: a survey of their abilities, applications, and limitations in the Arabic language. arXiv preprint arXiv:2310.09848 (2023)
7. Reiter, E.: Natural Language Generation. Springer, Cham (2024). https://doi.org/10.1007/978-3-031-68582-8
8. Lu, X., et al.: Neurologic: Constrained Decoding for Language Generation (2021)
9. Antoun, W., Baly, F., Hajj, H.: AraBERT: transformer-based model for Arabic language understanding. arXiv preprint arXiv:2003.00104 (2020)
10. Antoun, W., Baly, F., Hajj, H.: AraGPT2: pre-trained transformer for Arabic language generation. arXiv preprint arXiv:2102.01691 (2021)
11. Muennighoff, N., Scao, T.L., Rogers, A., et al.: Cross-lingual generalization through multitask fine-tuning. arXiv preprint arXiv:2211.01786 (2022)

12. AlShammari, F., Alshahrani, S., Alrashidi, F., et al.: JASMINE: reinforcement learning-based Arabic story generator. In: Proceedings of the 2023 International Conference on Arabic NLP (ICANLP), pp. 115–126 (2023)
13. Obeid, O., Zalmout, N., Khalifa, S., et al.: CAMeL tools: an open-source python toolkit for arabic natural language processing. In: Proceedings of the Twelfth Language Resources and Evaluation Conference, 7022–7032. European Language Resources Association (2020)
14. Smith, L., Idrissi, Y., Al-Mutairi, S.: Neuro-symbolic knowledge graph integration for narrative reasoning. ACM Trans. Asian Low-Res. Lang. Inf. Process. **23**(1), 12–34 (2024)
15. Papineni, K., Roukos, S., Ward, T., Zhu, W.J.: BLEU: a method for automatic evaluation of machine translation. In: Proceedings of the 40th Annual Meeting of the Association for Computational Linguistics, pp. 311–318 (2002)
16. Aho, A.V., Corasick, M.J.: Efficient string matching: An aid to bibliographic search. Commun. ACM **18**(6), 333–340 (1975)
17. Hu, E., et al.: LoRA: low-rank adaptation of large language models. arXiv preprint arXiv:2106.09685, 2021
18. Bouamor, H., Habash, N., Salameh, M.: The MADAR Arabic dialect corpus and lexicon. In: Proceedings of LREC, pp. 117–123 (2018)
19. Loshchilov, I., Hutter, F.: Decoupled weight decay regularization. arXiv preprint arXiv:1711.05101 (2017)
20. OpenAI. GPT-4 Technical Report. arXiv preprint arXiv:2303.08774 (2023)
21. Muennighoff, N., Wang, S., Du, S., et al.: Crosslingual generalization through multitask finetuning. arXiv preprint arXiv:2211.01786 (2022)
22. Monroe, J.T.: Oral composition in pre-islamic poetry: theory and practice. J. Arabic Literat. **3**(1), 1–53 (1972)
23. Kaplan, J., et al.: Scaling laws for neural language models. arXiv preprint arXiv:2001.08361 (2020)
24. Devlin, J., Chang, M.-W., Lee, K., Toutanova, K.: BERT: pre-training of deep bidirectional transformers for language understanding. In: Proceedings of NAACL-HLT, pp. 4171–4186 (2019)
25. Avizienis, A., Laprie, J.-C., Randell, B., Landwehr, C.: Basic concepts and taxonomy of dependable and secure computing. IEEE Trans. Dependable Secure Comput. **1**(1), 11–33 (2004)
26. Mehrabi, N., Morstatter, F., Saxena, N., Lerman, K., Galstyan, A.: A survey on bias and fairness in machine learning. ACM Comput. Surv. (CSUR) **54**(6), 1–35 (2021)

Assessing the Stability of Rankings
in Knowledge Graphs Against Perturbations

Hassan Abdallah[1]([✉])(iD), Béatrice Markhoff[2](iD), Louise Parkin[1](iD),
and Arnaud Soulet[1](iD)

[1] LIFAT, University of Tours, 3 Pl. Jean Jaurès, 41000 Blois, France
{hassan.abdallah,louise.parkin,arnaud.soulet}@univ-tours.fr
[2] UMR 7324 CITERES, CNRS and University of Tours, Tours, France
beatrice.markhoff@univ-tours.fr

Abstract. Knowledge graphs such as Wikidata serve as valuable resources for structuring and analyzing information across various domains. However, their crowdsourced nature makes them vulnerable to perturbations, including both intentional vandalism and unintentional errors, which can significantly impact rankings derived from these graphs. While previous studies have primarily focused on detecting and preventing entity-level perturbations, this paper investigates the potential impact of such perturbations on the stability of rankings at the structural level, specifically targeting relationships. We formalize the problem of ranking stability under perturbations, and we propose a probabilistic model to assess the likelihood of modifications to knowledge graph relationships changing the ranks of entities. We leverage complex network analysis, in order to evaluate ranking vulnerabilities. Our experimental study demonstrates varying levels of resilience in rankings depending on entity degree distributions and the nature of perturbations.

1   Introduction

Large crowdsourced Knowledge Graphs (KGs) [4,14,16] available on the Web are important resources for knowledge workers, especially when they are shared within communities and managed as commons. To take advantage of this vast amount of knowledge, multiple tools exist to support analysis. For instance, ranking indicators help in understanding and evaluating the significance of entities in various domains, from scientific research to cultural impact as they provide a structured method to order entities based on defined criteria, supporting informed decision-making [6]. In the era of big data, knowledge graphs serve as an invaluable resource for building and refining these rankings [1].

Analytics based on crowdsourced knowledge graphs such as Wikidata [16] draw their strength from the richness of facts contributed by a global community of editors. Yet this crowdsourced foundation also raises a concern: How correct and complete is the data used to build the analyses? The ease of contributing to a crowdsourced KG increases the risk of introducing perturbations – either through deliberate vandalism (the insertion of false statements, or deletion of truthful ones) or through unintentional

C. Cappiello et al. (Eds.): CoopIS 2025, LNCS 15535, pp. 127–144, 2026.
https://doi.org/10.1007/978-3-032-15538-2_8

Table 1. The 10 most perturbed relationships in Wikidata (2012–2016).

Relationship	Nb. of perturbations
instance of	8,872
sex or gender	2,409
occupation	2,013
country	1,527
contains the administrative territorial entity	1,102
country of citizenship	1,001
given name	732
member of sports team	635
place of birth	602
located in the administrative territorial entity	487

errors arising during routine editing. In the context of rankings, vandalism may target specific entities with the intent to manipulate their perceived importance or disrupt the ranking at a global level. Similarly, unintentional errors, particularly those arising from batch updates using scripts, can introduce biases or inaccuracies that significantly impact the rankings. Based on the corpus of Wikidata edits flagging vandalism and errors [9], Table 1 shows the top ten most perturbed relationships in Wikidata from 2012 to 2016, and reveals that certain relationships are more frequently targeted by perturbations than others. For example, many of the modifications involving the *place of birth* relationship are likely mistakes, whereas the *member of sports team* relation has been affected by edit wars surrounding football and rugby. From May 2013 to June 2015 ten updates falsely linked players such as *Davide Moscardelli* or *Paul Pogba* to *Barcelona*, while thirty-five scattered edits in the same period reassigned high-profile names including *Lionel Messi, Neymar*, and *Marco Reus* to *Real Madrid CF*. Although these updates are spread over two years, their asymmetric counts underscore a persistent attempt to elevate one club's prominence. By contrast, rugby vandalism appears in a tight burst: on 17 February 2015 eight new items were created that miscategorised historical players as members of the *England national rugby union team*, and less than a month later (11 March 2015) eight legitimate links to the *Scotland national rugby union team* were removed. The near-simultaneous timestamps and equal magnitudes suggest a coordinated campaign to inflate England's importance at Scotland's expense. Such vulnerabilities highlight a critical research problem: the resilience of knowledge graphs in maintaining stable rankings under conditions of vandalism and accidental errors. Thus, this work aims to answer the following research question: *Do certain knowledge graph relationships possess inherent robustness that ensures the integrity of its induced ranking against vandalism and errors?*

Existing literature on vandalism and errors primarily focuses on entry-point control, i.e. detecting and reverting bad edits as they occur [10–12,15]. In this paper, we adopt a complementary perspective, examining how malicious or erroneous edits impact derived structures, in particular ranked lists of entities. The question becomes not just whether an edit is a perturbation, but to what extent it can distort the perceived importance of entities if left uncorrected. More precisely, this paper proposes a model to study the link between the number of facts of an entity for a relationship and its stability in the induced ranking against perturbations. Interestingly, this model thus makes it possible to define a threshold of changes beyond which vandalism is highly probable. Inspired by the work of Albert et al. [3], which examined the robustness of complex networks under various conditions, our approach integrates insights from graph analysis, network science, ranking indicators, and probabilistic modeling. We address the two threats of vandalism and errors with the following contributions:

- **Formalization of Ranking Stability Issues:** We present a formalization to examine how vandalism and errors can alter rankings, providing a theoretical foundation to study these phenomena systematically.
- **Probabilistic Attack Model:** A theoretical model is proposed to quantify the likelihood that attacks or errors will successfully modify an entity's rank, allowing for predictive assessments of ranking vulnerabilities.
- **Empirical Evaluation:** We conduct an experimental study using open crowdsourced knowledge graphs to evaluate the stability of rankings. This study not only validates the theoretical model but also sheds light on the practical implications of ranking stability.

In Sect. 2, we discuss related work. Section 3 defines key preliminary notations, while Sect. 4 formalizes the problem. In Sect. 5, we introduce perturbation scenarios used as models of perturbations. Section 6 presents the theoretical results of a probabilistic model. Section 7 details the experimental study, and finally, Sect. 8 concludes this work.

2 Related Work

In recent years, numerous studies have focused on analyzing the stability of crowdsourced data, which often sparks debate due to its nature of being generated by individuals dispersed globally, many of whom do not know each other. Halpin et al. [7] examined the stability of distributions in crowdsourced tagging systems, discovering that the frequency distribution of tags follows a power-law pattern. They further analyzed the underlying dynamics that lead to this stable distribution. Given that knowledge graphs (KGs) act as a mirror of the real world, which is dynamic and continuously evolving, Shrinivasan and Razniewski [13] highlighted the inherent instability of KGs. Their work investigated the concept of knowledge base stability, specifically examining how KGs are affected by real-world changes. On the other hand, detecting and mitigating vandalism in knowledge graphs, particularly in Wikidata, has garnered significant attention in recent years. A predominant approach involves supervised learning techniques that leverage labeled datasets to train detection models. Heindorf et al. [10] introduced a machine learning-based method for identifying vandalism in Wikidata, proposing 47 features that exploit the crowdsourced nature of KGs to enhance detection accuracy. Later, Heindorf et al. [11] addressed biases in vandalism detection models, analyzing their sources and developing a model that reduces bias while maintaining fine predictive performance. Sarabadani et al. [12] extended this research by building automated tools tailored for vandalism detection in Wikidata. Their method, while effective, relies on contextual features of user edits and heavily on specific user behaviors, which introduces potential biases. More recently, Trokhymovych and Saez-Trumper [15] proposed a system that aids the Wikidata community in detecting vandalism using advanced feature engineering techniques. Their work underscores the importance of structural modifications in knowledge triples and their potential implications. Despite these advancements, a significant gap remains in the literature regarding the probabilistic analysis of structural manipulations in KG relationships. Such manipulations, whether through errors or targeted attacks, can subtly alter relationships to influence entity rankings, artificially inflating or deflating an entity's perceived importance. While existing studies primarily focus on detecting and preventing overt acts of vandalism or evaluating stability of distribution generally, this paper examines the specific effect of perturbations on rankings induced by ranking indicators [1]. Addressing this challenge is particularly complex in scenarios where ground truth data is unavailable, necessitating novel methodologies that leverage the inherent patterns of data distributions to help safeguarding against structural manipulations, without relying solely on supervised learning. To support research in this domain, Heindorf et al. [9] developed the Wikidata Vandalism Corpus (WDVC-2015), the first corpus providing ground truth for vandalism in Wikidata. This resource has been instrumental in training detection models. Subsequently, the Wikidata Vandalism Corpus 2016 (WDVC-2016) was introduced [8], an updated version of WDVC-2015. In our work, we kept modifications targeting relationships in WDVC-2016 (see Sect. 7) and extracted several cases of attacks resulting in altering entities' ranks.

3   Preliminaries

Knowledge Graph. Considering distinct infinite sets I and L (IRIs [5] and literals, respectively), a knowledge graph $\mathcal{K} \subseteq I \times I \times (I \cup L)$ is a set of facts. Each fact is a triple $\langle s, p, o \rangle \in \mathcal{K}$, where s, p and o denote respectively the *subject*, the *predicate* (or relationship) and the *object*. An example of fact is: $\langle$ `Kylian Mbappe`, `member of sports team`, `Real Madrid CF` $\rangle$.

Given a relationship $p \in \mathcal{K}$, $\mathcal{K}_p$ is the set of facts in $\mathcal{K}$ having p as relationship: $\mathcal{K}_p = \{\langle s, p', o \rangle \in \mathcal{K} : p' = p\}$. Thereafter, we work mostly on a single relationship p at a time (e.g., $\mathcal{K}_{\text{member of sports team}}$ selects all the facts about members of sports teams). Given a relationship p, its number of facts in $\mathcal{K}_p$ is denoted by n, and its number of subjects (resp. objects) in $\mathcal{K}_p$ is denoted by n_s (resp. n_o). For formulas that work with both subjects and objects, we use n_e to denote the number of entities. Finally, we denote $p_s = n_s/n$ and $p_o = n_o/n$.

Ranking Induced by a Relationship. Any relationship p induces a ranking over a set of entities $E = \{e_1, e_2, \ldots, e, \ldots, e_N\}$. The rank of an entity e in such a ranking is determined by its degree k_e defined as the number of facts in $\mathcal{K}_p$ associated with e (as subject or object). Formally, the ranking is represented as an ordering $\sigma_p : E \rightarrow \{1, \ldots, N\}$, where $\sigma_p(e)$ denotes the rank of e based on k_e such that $k_{e_1} > k_{e_2} \implies \sigma_p(e_1) < \sigma_p(e_2)$. As shown in Fig. 1, an entity with more facts for a given relationship p

is ranked higher. In the following (and in Fig. 1), we omit references to the relationship p.

Rank Change. Let Δk_e denote the modification in the degree of entity e for relationship p resulting from a perturbation, such that $k'_e = k_e + \Delta k_e$, where k'_e represents the updated degree after the perturbation. The rank change $\Delta\sigma(e)$ can be expressed as: $\Delta\sigma(e) = \sigma'(e) - \sigma(e)$ where $\sigma'(e)$ is the updated rank of e in the perturbed distribution. Figure 1 shows rank changes after perturbations.

Probability Mass Function (PMF). A fundamental concept is the Probability Mass Function (PMF), which describes the probability distribution of entity degrees with respect to a specific relationship p. The PMF captures the likelihood that an entity in the knowledge graph has a particular degree, enabling analysis of rankings. The Probability Mass Function denoted as $P(k)$ is a function that assigns to each degree k the probability that a randomly selected entity e has exactly k facts with the relationship p: $P(k) = \Pr(k_e = k)$.

4   Problem Formulation

Our objective is to quantify the robustness of a ranking under perturbations caused by either the addition or the removal of Δk_e facts in $\mathcal{K}_p$. Specifically, we aim to:

1. Analyze the impact of such perturbations on both individual entities and the overall ranking, providing insights into the stability and vulnerability of the ranking.
2. Model the probability that an entity e, initially ranked at position $\sigma(e)$, with a degree k_e will experience a rank change $\Delta\sigma(e)$ due to a perturbation of size Δk_e targeting that entity: $\Pr(\Delta\sigma(e) \neq 0 \mid \Delta k_e, k_e)$.

Thus our goal is twofold. Firstly, characterize the processes of perturbations due to vandalism or errors. This enables the empirical analysis of these processes, the extraction of statistics and insights about the inherent robustness of the KGs against such processes, and assessing the impact of their perturbations. Secondly, model the probability that reflects the likelihood of a rank change for an entity e, with a degree before perturbation k_e, given the magnitude Δk_e of a perturbation targeting it. This probability depends on several factors, including: the initial degree k_e of the entity, the magnitude and nature of the perturbation Δk_e, and finally, the global distribution of degrees $\{k_{e_1}, k_{e_2}, \ldots, k_{e_N}\}$ across all entities which, as we will see later, will play an essential role in determining the probability.

Challenges. Key difficulties include the heterogeneous nature of rankings in knowledge graphs and the complex interplay between local (entity-specific) and global (distribution-wide) effects of perturbations. A solution should involve an extraction of statistical insights taking into consideration the entire distribution, which contributes to determining the likelihood that an entity changes its rank after a perturbation.

5   Perturbation Scenarios

In this section, we introduce perturbation models designed to assess the impact of intentional attacks and unintentional errors on rankings. These models aim to represent various scenarios in which perturbations influence entity rankings, either by altering the overall structure of the distribution (global perturbation in Sect. 5.1) or by targeting individual entities (local perturbation in Sect. 5.2).

5.1   Global Perturbation: Altering the Entire Distribution

This *global perturbation* scenario represents cases where a ranking is subjected to perturbations scattered across many entities, which possibly disrupt its overall structure. This scenario fits unintentional errors, which could arise from multiple erroneous edits and potential side-effects of vandalism. It involves adding some facts to (or removing facts from) randomly picked entities, thereby reshaping the entire distribution and disturbing the overall ranking. This scenario aims to assess the vulnerabilities of distributions to small and large-scale disruptions. For instance, Fig. 1 illustrates an example of this type of perturbation as the *Global perturbation* scenario. Starting from an example distribution, where entities are ranked by their number of incoming facts, 4 new facts (in red) are added randomly. This results in a change in the ranking distribution, for entities e_4 and e_3, whose order is reversed.

5.2   Local Perturbation: Altering a Single Entity

In this *local perturbation* scenario, the perturbation is designed to target a specific entity with the objective of altering its rank within the distribution. This is achieved by adding or removing a certain number of facts associated with the entity, with the sole aim of modifying its position in the ranking. Such targeted perturbations provide insight into the proportion of the vulnerable individual entities w.r.t the perturbation. This scenario fits cases of vandalism targeting specific entities, but can also model errors from a faulty script making multiple changes involving a single entity. For instance, Fig. 1 illustrates

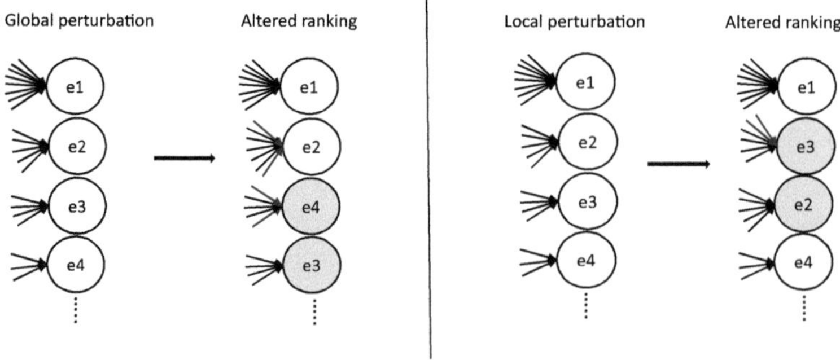

Fig. 1. An illustration of the global and local perturbation scenarios and their impact on entity rankings.

an example of this type of perturbation as the *Local perturbation* scenario. Unlike with the global perturbation, this scenario specifically targets the entity e_3 to improve its rank relative to the entire distribution by focusing all the fact additions on this entity. As a result, e_3 moves to rank 2, replacing the entity e_2.

Section 7.1 provides a quantitative analysis of the global effects of these two different types of perturbations, using precise measures to assess the inherent stability of rankings in knowledge graphs under such conditions of diverse perturbation scenarios and structural manipulations.

6   Theoretical Model for Ranking Stability

The stability of rankings is linked to the underlying distribution of entity degrees within a knowledge graph. To quantify the impact of perturbations on ranks, it is essential to first identify the probability distribution model that governs the degree distribution of entities (see Sect. 6.1). This identification provides the foundation for modeling the likelihood of rank changes under various scenarios. Indeed, we use the PMF which plays a crucial role in understanding the structural properties of knowledge graphs. It does not only characterize the degree distribution, but it also provides a probabilistic basis for evaluating the effects of perturbations, such as the addition or removal of facts, on rankings. Building upon this probabilistic foundation and by leveraging the PMF, we propose in Sect. 6.2 a theoretical model for evaluating the robustness of rankings under perturbations.

6.1   Knowledge RELationship Model (KRELM)

The structural properties and dynamics of knowledge graphs relationships have been widely studied to better understand their evolution. A recent work by Abdallah et al. [2] introduces a novel model named KRELM (Knowledge RELationship Model), which provides insights into the distribution patterns of relationships in knowledge graphs. This model is especially relevant to our work as it offers a theoretical foundation to analyze and simulate the behavior of facts accumulation within KGs.

The KRELM model leverages a bipartite graph representation for relationships, where subjects and objects are treated as distinct vertex sets connected by edges representing facts. By focusing on the decentralized and crowdsourced nature of KG construction, KRELM captures the dual processes of continuous growth (addition of new entities) and asymmetric attachment (different behaviors for subjects and objects). The authors demonstrate that this model successfully reproduces key structural patterns observed in real-world KGs, such as Wikidata, DBpedia, and YAGO.

Objects. KRELM predicts that the PMF of the degree distribution for objects follows a power law with exponent $\gamma = 1 + \frac{1}{1-p_o}$, as expressed by:

$$P(k_o) = \frac{1}{1-p_o} \times k_o^{-\left(1+\frac{1}{1-p_o}\right)}, \tag{1}$$

where p_o denotes the probability of introducing a new object entity. The power-law behavior reflects the preferential attachment mechanism. Consider for example the *place of birth* relation which has a person as subject and a place as object. When a new fact with the relationship *place of birth* is added, it is very likely that the object is a large city where many people were born. This results in popular objects accumulating a disproportionate number of facts over time. This manifests in a degree distribution across objects where a lot of small cities have very few facts (few people were born there) and relatively few large cities concentrate much larger amounts of facts.

Subjects. In contrast, in KRELM the PMF of the degree distribution for subjects follows an exponential law parameterized by $\beta = \frac{1}{1-p_s} - 1$, described as:

$$P(k_s) = \frac{p_s}{1 - p_s} \times \exp\left(\frac{p_s}{1 - p_s}(1 - k_s)\right), \tag{2}$$

where p_s represents the probability of adding a new subject entity. This result aligns with the intuition that subjects exhibit a relatively uniform attachment mechanism and facts with a given relation are spread evenly across subjects. Consider for example, the *cast member* relation which has a movie as subject and an actor as object. While the number of films associated with an actor may vary a lot (the preferential attachment of objects), most movies have a similar number of actors, and no movie concentrates all the actors.

These theoretical results have been validated through extensive experiments across multiple KGs including Wikidata. The findings highlight that the asymmetric attachment mechanisms and growth dynamics of KRELM closely replicate the observed real-world distributions of facts for both subjects and objects.

Based on these degree distributions derived from KRELM, we derive a probabilistic model to assess the likelihood that an entity changes its rank after a given perturbation.

6.2 Rank Change Likelihoods

In this section, we focus on the local perturbation scenario with a targeted entity. Specifically, we aim to calculate the probability that the rank of e will be altered due to the addition or removal of Δk_e facts related to that entity. The results presented here are obtained by leveraging the degree distributions given by KRELM, which characterize objects with a power law, and subjects with an exponential law.

Building upon the initial formulation of our second goal in Sect. 4, we now reformulate the task to focus on how to determine the probability $\Pr(\Delta\sigma(e) \neq 0 \mid \Delta k_e, k_e)$. Given an entity e with a degree k_e under a relationship p, for a perturbation which adds (resp. removes) Δk_e facts to e, the probability that the rank will be changed is the probability that there exists another entity e' with a degree less than Δk_e over (resp. under) k_e. Therefore, the objective is to compute the probability: $\Pr(\exists e', k_e \leq k_{e'} \leq k_e + \Delta k_e)$ (resp. $\Pr(\exists e', k_e - \Delta k_e \leq k_{e'} \leq k_e)$).

The probability that another entity e' has a degree $k_{e'}$ between k_e and $k_e + \Delta k_e$ (corresponding to the probability of a rank gain for entity e from a perturbation adding Δk_e facts to e) is given by:

$$\Pr(\exists e', k_e \leq k_{e'} \leq k_e + \Delta k_e) = \int_{k_e}^{k_e + \Delta k_e} P(k)\, dk.$$

For a perturbation removing Δk_e facts from e, the probability of a rank loss for e, which is the probability that another entity e' has a degree $k_{e'}$ between $k_e - \Delta k_e$ and k_e is given by:

$$\Pr(\exists e', k_e - \Delta k_e \leq k_{e'} \leq k_e) = \int_{k_e - \Delta k_e}^{k_e} P(k)\, dk.$$

By injecting Eq. 1 in these integrals, we obtain the following theorem:

Theorem 1 (Rank change likelihood for objects). *The rank change likelihood of objects with degree k_o for Δk_o added facts is given by:*

$$\Pr(\exists o', k_o \leq k_{o'} \leq k_o + \Delta k_o) = k_o^{1-\gamma} - (k_o + \Delta k_o)^{1-\gamma}$$

Likewise, for Δk_o removed facts, the rank change likelihood of objects with degree $k_o \geq \Delta k_o$ is given by:

$$\Pr(\exists o', k_o - \Delta k_o \leq k_{o'} \leq k_o) = (k_o - \Delta k_o)^{1-\gamma} - k_o^{1-\gamma}$$

Considering a perturbation that may either add Δk_o facts or remove Δk_o facts, the rank change likelihood of objects with degree $k_o \geq \Delta k_o$ is given by:

$$\Pr(\Delta \sigma(o) \neq 0 \mid \Delta k_o, k_o) = (k_o - \Delta k_o)^{1-\gamma} - (k_o + \Delta k_o)^{1-\gamma}$$

Now, by injecting Eq. 2 in the above integrals, it is possible to get a similar theorem for the out-degree of subjects:

Theorem 2 (Rank change likelihood for subjects). *The rank change likelihood of subjects with degree k_s for Δk_s added facts is given by:*

$$\Pr(\exists s', k_s \leq k_{s'} \leq k_s + \Delta k_s) = \left(1 - e^{-\beta \Delta k_s}\right) e^{-\beta(k_s - 1)}$$

Likewise, for Δk_s removed facts, the rank change likelihood of subjects with degree $k_s \geq \Delta k_s$ is given by:

$$\Pr(\exists s', k_s - \Delta k_s \leq k_{s'} \leq k_s) = \left(e^{\beta \Delta k_s} - 1\right) e^{-\beta(k_s - 1)}$$

Considering a perturbation that may either add Δk_s facts or remove Δk_s facts, the rank change likelihood of subjects with degree $k_s \geq \Delta k_s$ is given by:

$$\Pr(\Delta \sigma(s) \neq 0 \mid \Delta k_s, k_s) = \left(e^{\beta \Delta k_s} - e^{-\beta \Delta k_s}\right) e^{-\beta(k_s - 1)}$$

For an entity with k_e facts, Theorems 1 and 2 indicate the likelihood of changing its rank by allowing addition only, removal only, or both addition and removal depending on the entities. A first corollary of this theorem is that the rank change likelihood (by adding or removing facts) decreases with an increase of the degree k_e of the entity. This shows the resilience of highly connected objects to changes in their degree. It also follows from the theorem that, for a fixed perturbation size Δk_e, the likelihood of a rank change is higher when facts are removed than when they are added, regardless of an entity's degree. In short, for an attacker, vandalism is more effective at lowering an entity's rank than at boosting it. Unsurprisingly, as the Δk_e increases, the impact of the perturbation is more likely to change the ranking. Obviously, in the case of vandalism, the greater the perturbation, the greater the chance of it being detected (as it exceeds the crowdsourcing system's alert threshold). Interestingly, with our model, it is possible to define an alert threshold (a maximum authorized perturbation size) specific to the parameters of the relationship to be monitored.

Figure 2 illustrates Theorems 1 and 2 on the cast member relationship in Wikidata (P161) having $\beta = 0.181$ and $\gamma = 2.179$ as parameters. More precisely, we plot the theoretical perturbation likelihoods with the degree k ranging from 3 to 1,000 and a perturbation size $\Delta k_e = 2$. The solid and dashed lines correspond to objects and subjects respectively, with gain (addition of facts), loss (removal of facts) and total (addition or removal according to entities). Firstly, we observe that all three curves decline as the degree increases, in accordance with the theorems. Secondly, the perturbation likelihood is clearly higher for fact removal (blue and orange curves) than for fact addition (red and green curves), especially for low degrees. The difference fades for large degrees, where attacks become harder, and the two probabilities converge. Changing a ranking by performing both additions and removals according to the considered entity remains the easiest strategy, as indicated by the purple and brown curves. Finally, for small degree, the probability of a rank change is higher for subject rankings than for object rankings (here, the subjects and the objects are involved in the same relationship, but this observation can be generalized to all relationships). Once the degree becomes large, the subject probability drops toward zero, while the object probability continues to decrease normally. This crossover occurs because only a few subject entities have very high degrees, whereas most have low degrees.

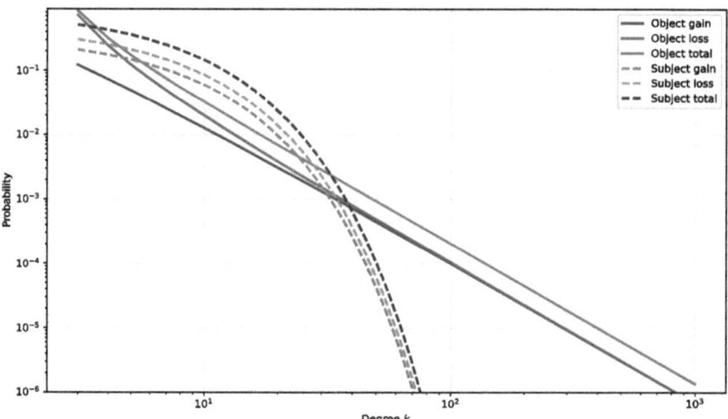

Fig. 2. Theoretical rank change likelihoods for the cast member relationship in Wikidata.

Theorems 1 and 2 are fundamental. They allow us not only to confirm intuitions, but also to quantify them precisely. In particular, it is possible to identify degrees and entities in the knowledge graph that are most vulnerable to perturbations given a relationship. It also helps in identifying thresholds for perturbation sizes beyond which rank stability is significantly compromised. These results for the local perturbation scenario are also interesting for the global perturbation scenario. Indeed, when modifications are uniformly distributed over all entities, this is like considering local perturbations with a low number of fact modifications. In this case, our model predicts better ranking stability, especially for entities with a high degree. Next section shows that these theoretical rank chance likelihoods for the local perturbation and its consequences for the global perturbation are accurately verified in practice, demonstrating the scope of our modeling.

7   Experimental Study

In this section, we aim to quantitatively evaluate the robustness of rankings gathered from several crowdsourced KGs against errors and vandalism. Section 7.1 provides an empirical analysis of ranking stability under the global and local perturbation scenario. Then, Sect. 7.2 focuses on assessing our theoretical results of Sect. 6 that compute the likelihood of a rank change given a perturbation.

Note that source code and experimental results are available in the Git repository: https://scm.univ-tours.fr/habdallah/rankingsperturbations.

7.1   Empirical Analysis of Ranking Stability

In Sect. 5, we introduced two distinct perturbation scenarios. Here, we conduct an empirical analysis to evaluate the impact of these scenarios on ranking induced by relationships in Wikidata.

Protocol. To apply the proposed scenarios, we utilized the top 500 ranking indicators identified in [1] to get their distributions from Wikidata. For each relationship, we selected the top 5,000 ranked entities and applied the two scenarios to measure the impact of perturbations. Additionally, each distribution was divided into two segments: the first from the top to the middle of the ranking (*FirstDistribution*), and the second from the middle to the end (*SecondDistribution*). This segmentation enabled us to measure the impact on different parts of the distribution while also evaluating the overall effect on the global distribution.

To apply the global perturbation scenario, we randomly added Δk new facts targeting entities within the distribution. The entities receiving the new facts were selected randomly, and Δk was varied from 1 to 50,000, increasing by 100 at each step. We then measured the Kendall's tau divergence between the resulting distribution and the initial one to quantify the perturbation's impact. The experiment is repeated 5 times, then we take the average value of Kendall's tau for each value of Δk. Kendall's tau, denoted by τ (also known as Kendall's rank correlation coefficient) quantifies the resemblance between two rankings by assessing the proportion of pairwise agreements and disagreements between the ranks. It is a non-parametric measure, meaning it does not assume any specific distribution of the data, and it is suitable for ordinal data. It can be computed using the following formula: $\tau = \frac{C-D}{C+D}$ where C is the number of concordant pairs, and D is the number of discordant pairs. Kendall's tau ranges from -1 (i.e., perfect disagreement) to 1 (i.e., perfect agreement).

For the local perturbation scenario, we considered both fact addition and removal for evaluating Theorems 1 and 2. More precisely, we observed for each entity of degree

k whether an addition of Δk facts or a removal of Δk facts modified its ranking. This enabled us to estimate for each degree k the proportion of entities whose ranks changed as a result (either when facts are added or removed). Here, Δk was varied from 1 to 100, increasing by 1 at each step. This allowed us to assess the sensitivity of individual entities to these perturbations and their influence on the overall ranking stability. This protocol ensures a comprehensive evaluation of the two perturbation models across different segments of the rankings and under varying levels of perturbation intensity.

Results. Figure 3 presents the variation of Kendall's tau after applying the experiment outlined in the global perturbation scenario on the ranking indicator that ranks *film actors* according to the number of films they were *cast members* in. The x-axis represents the number of added facts, while the y-axis shows the corresponding Kendall's tau values. The figure illustrates a sharp decrease in Kendall's tau when the number of added facts increases from 0 to 10,000. Beyond this point, the curves exhibit a gradual stabilization, although Kendall's tau continues to decrease strongly. As expected, the first half of the distribution demonstrates greater stability and robustness compared to the second half. Additionally, the global distribution is more resilient than either of the two halves individually. This behavior indicates that changing the ranking of entities in the first half is more challenging due to the significant inequality in the number of facts associated with these entities. Similarly, changing the ranking of the global distribution is more difficult because it encompasses the inherent stability of both halves combined. These results highlight the varying degrees of robustness across different segments of the rankings.

Considering the local perturbation scenario, Fig. 4 illustrates the proportion of entities that change their rank after adding or removing a specified number of facts associated with them in the original distribution (using the same ranking indicator as the first scenario). As expected, the proportion consistently increases as the number of modified facts grows. For the second half of the distribution, all entities experience a rank change as soon as a single fact is modified. In contrast, for the first half, the proportion remains below 1 when fewer than 19 facts are modified. This disparity highlights the greater stability of entities in the first half, which is likely due to the larger number of facts associated with these entities, making them more resistant to perturbations.

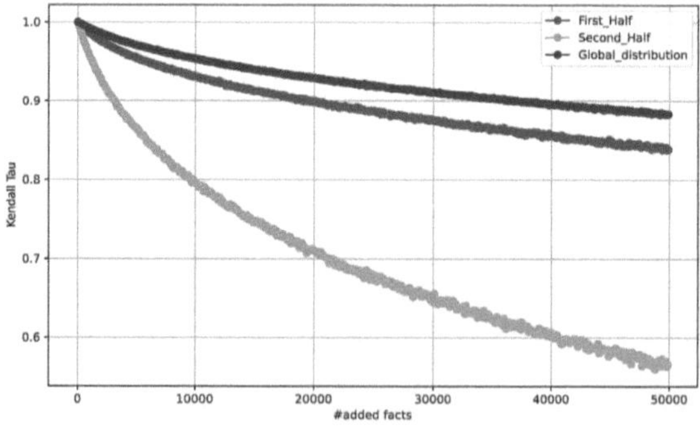

Fig. 3. Kendall's tau with Δk facts added to the entire distribution (global perturbation).

The results detailed here for the cast member relationship are similar for the other relationships in Wikidata. To summarize this general behavior, Table 2 presents the results of computing the average Kendall's tau and proportions across various threshold values for the top 500 ranking indicators. For the global perturbation scenario, the results highlight the greater stability and robustness of the first half of the distribution compared to the second half. The global distribution on average is slightly less stable than the first half of the ranking. These results underscore the inherent robustness of the rankings in Wikidata for top-ranked entities (the first half), providing strong evidence of their resilience under errors. For the local perturbation, we observe that most relationships are highly sensitive to perturbation. A single perturbation has a high impact, with a probability greater than 97% (on average) of changing an entity's rank.

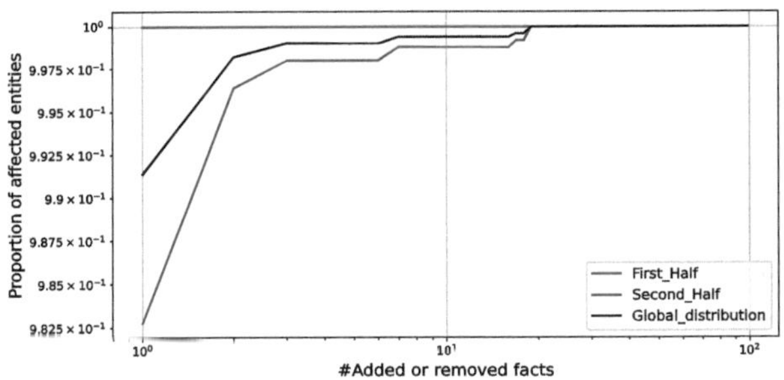

Fig. 4. Proportion of entities who change rank with Δk facts changed for a single entity (local perturbation).

Table 2. Impact of Δk facts in global and local perturbation scenarios for the top 500 relationships in Wikidata.

	Global perturbation			Local perturbation		
	Avg. Kendall's tau			Avg. proportion		
Thresholds	10,000	30,000	50,000	1	10	100
First Half	0.592	0.472	0.420	0.975	0.997	0.999
Second Half	0.183	0.116	0.092	0.999	1	1
Global Distribution	0.571	0.451	0.399	0.987	0.998	0.999

7.2 Evaluation of Theoretical Likelihoods

In this section, we evaluate the effectiveness of the theoretical rank change likelihoods computed in Sect. 6.2 that quantifies the probability of rank changes in a distribution for the local perturbations. This metric directly translates to the likelihood that an attack succeeds in altering the rank of an entity, particularly in cases of vandalism, given the degree of the targeted entity.

Protocol. To evaluate the performance of our theoretical results, we employed the real degree distributions of relationships of three major KGs: the Wikidata 2022 snapshot, DBpedia, and YAGO. The evaluation follows these steps:

1. For each relationship, we computed the probability distributions for subjects and objects entities, induced by the probability mass function (PMF). Where each probability point, considered for a degree interval $[k-\Delta k, k+\Delta k]$, and iteratively shifted k by $\Delta k + 1$. This approach enables us to calculate $\Pr(\exists e', k-\Delta k \leq k_{e'} \leq k+\Delta k)$ for each degree k and construct a real-world probability distribution.
2. Using the theoretical formulas derived in Sect. 6.2, we similarly computed a theoretical probability distribution for comparison.

To assess the efficiency and performance of the probabilistic model, we utilized the following metrics:

Jensen-Shannon Divergence (D_{JS})**.** To compare the theoretically generated probability distributions with the real ones for the three knowledge graphs, we employed the Jensen-Shannon divergence (D_{JS}), a widely used metric that quantifies the similarity between two probability distributions. The D_{JS} is defined as:

$$D_{JS}(P||Q) = \frac{1}{2}\left(D_{KL}(P||M) + D_{KL}(Q||M)\right),$$

where P and Q are the two distributions being compared, and $M = \frac{1}{2}(P+Q)$ is the average of the distributions, and the $D_{KL}(P||Q)$ represents the Kullback-Leibler Divergence between distributions P and Q: $D_{KL}(P||Q) = \sum_i P(i) \log \frac{P(i)}{Q(i)}$. This symmetric metric provides a measure of how closely the theoretical distribution approximates the empirical distribution. Its range is [-1,1] with smaller values indicating higher similarity.

Coverage **Measure:** In addition to Jensen-Shannon divergence, we used the *coverage* measure to further evaluate the model's performance. Coverage is defined as the proportion of properties for which the model successfully reproduces reality. It is calculated as:

$$Coverage = \frac{|\{p \in \mathcal{K} : D_{JS}(T_{\tilde{p}}||R_p) \leq 0.2\}|}{|\{p \in \mathcal{K}\}|}$$

where R_p (resp. $T_{\tilde{p}}$) represent the real (resp. theoretically generated) probability distribution. This measure allows us to assess the model's effectiveness in replicating real-world behavior across a range of properties.

To determine success for a distribution replication, we set a threshold of 0.2 for D_{JS}, a value that analytically and visually indicates strong model performance. In our experiments, we evaluated the model on 3,228, 78, and 971 relationships for DBpedia, YAGO, and Wikidata, respectively. As well, we set $k = 3$ as the starting degree and incremented it by 3 in each step, with $C = 2$.

Results. Figure 5 illustrates the real and theoretical probability distributions for the `member of sport team` relationship (P54) in Wikidata. The y-axis represents the

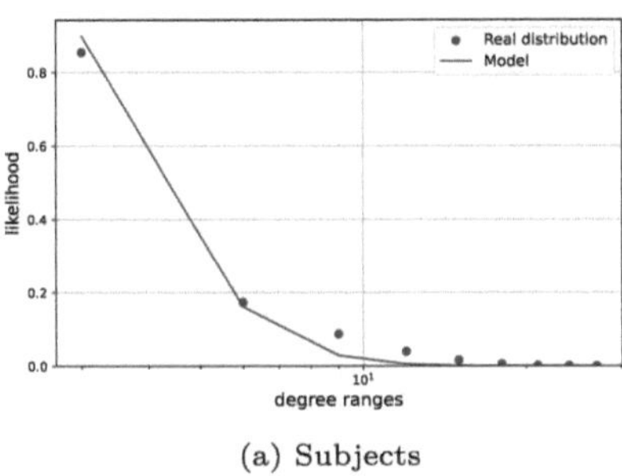

(a) Subjects

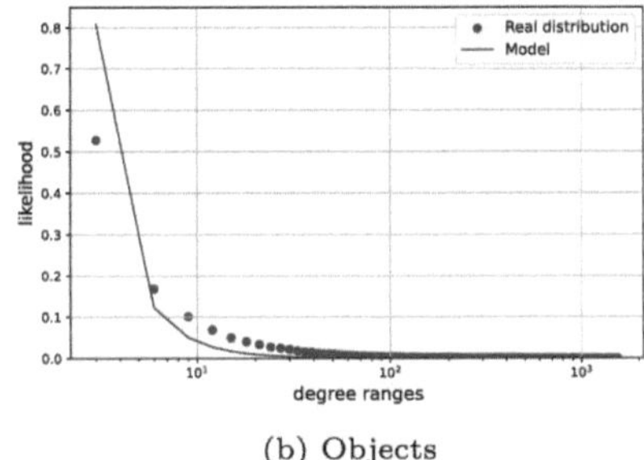

(b) Objects

Fig. 5. Comparison of likelihood of a rank change for the `member of sports team` relationship in Wikidata between the model and the real distribution.

rank change likelihood, while the x-axis denotes the degree k. The real-world estimated probabilities are visualized as green points, and the model's theoretical probabilities are depicted as a continuous blue line. The figure demonstrates that the model closely approximates the real distribution for both subjects and objects. Specifically, the theoretical likelihoods follow an exponential law for subjects and a power law for objects, aligning with the expected behavior of the degree distributions. This close fit is further corroborated by the Jensen-Shannon divergence which is 0.019 for subjects and 0.090 for objects in average, highlighting the strong similarity between the model and the real data. Table 3 provides a comprehensive comparison of the real degree distributions and the theoretically generated ones for the three knowledge graphs (Wikidata, DBpedia, and YAGO). The results indicate that the model achieves an extensive coverage of the successfully approximated probability distributions across KGs. Coverage values consistently exceed 0.94 for both subjects and objects, with an average of 0.994 for subjects and 0.960 for objects across the three KGs. Similarly, the average D_{JS} values across the three KGs are 0.008 for subjects and 0.038 for objects, underscoring the model's ability to accurately replicate the real distributions. These results demonstrate the model's robustness in predicting the likelihood of rank changes resulting from local perturbations. The consistent performance across multiple KGs further validates the generalizability and effectiveness of the proposed probabilistic model in capturing the dynamics of rank stability in crowdsourced knowledge graphs.

Table 3. Coverage and average JSD for the relationships of three KGs.

	Coverage		Average D_{JS}	
KG	subjects	objects	subjects	objects
DBpedia	0.999	0.989	0.007	0.022
Wikidata	0.996	0.941	0.009	0.044
YAGO4	0.987	0.949	0.007	0.048
Average	**0.994**	**0.960**	**0.008**	**0.038**

Parameter Analysis. Despite the strong results already presented, the probabilistic model occasionally fails to approximate the real probability distributions for certain relationships. This prompted a deeper investigation into the underlying causes of these failures. Figure 6 provides an analysis of these failures. The x-axis represents the D_{JS} values obtained using the presented probabilistic model, while the y-axis shows the D_{JS} values derived from the KRELM model for the same relationships. The points represent subjects (in red) and objects (in blue), with regression lines fitted to the distributions for each group. Interestingly, we observe a strong linear correlation between the performance of the probabilistic model and the accuracy of KRELM, with the slopes and R values of 0.4535 and 0.8232 for subjects, and 0.4544 and 0.8590 for objects, respectively. Figure 6 also reveals that when the probabilistic model struggles to approximate the real distribution (right part of the figure), it is often due to inaccuracies in the underlying KRELM model (upper part of the figure). This shows the soundness of the method for building a ranking stability model from a degree distribution model. Proposed improvements to KRELM to overcome its limits would therefore also improve the performance of the probabilistic model.

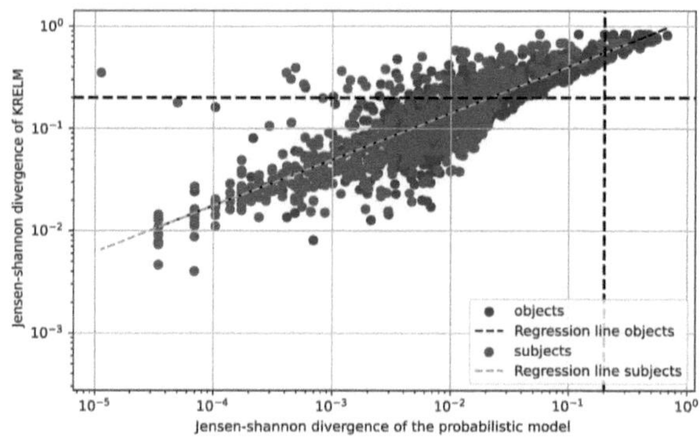

Fig. 6. Comparison of the Jensen-Shannon divergence of the probabilistic model and KRELM.

8   Conclusion

In this paper, we investigated the stability of rankings in KGs, under the influence of vandalism and error perturbations. Our work shifts the focus to the structural aspects of knowledge graphs, particularly the impact of perturbations on relationships and their induced rankings. We introduced a formalization of ranking stability issues and proposed a probabilistic model to assess the likelihood of rank changes due to local perturbations. Our probabilistic predictive model, grounded on complex network analysis, provides a framework for evaluating ranking vulnerabilities. The experimental study confirmed the effectiveness of the proposed model, and that the rankings exhibit varying levels of resilience depending on the degree distributions of entities and the nature of the perturbations. We found that removing facts is generally a stronger attack than adding facts. A combined strategy of additions and removals is the most disruptive, and subjects and objects react differently to perturbations depending on their degree. Specifically, we showed that high-degree entities tend to be more resistant to perturbations, while low-degree entities are more susceptible to rank changes. In practice, entities in the lower half of rankings are far more fragile, while the top-ranked entities show greater stability. Our findings highlight the need for robust mechanisms to safeguard knowledge graphs, prioritizing defenses against fact removals with the possibility of setting relationship-specific alert thresholds.

Future research directions include improving the accuracy of the model proposed in [2], and enabling the automatic computation of the proportion and Kendall's tau given basic statistics about the ranking. Moreover, the current model is for a perturbation on one entity. We therefore want to further extend it to also handle more specifically perturbations such as the one illustrated on the left in Fig. 1, the global scenario, where no modification has been made to the entity e_3 even though it has moved down the ranking. By addressing the dual threats of vandalism and errors, this work contributes to the broader understanding of ranking stability in crowdsourced knowledge graphs, provides an initial probabilistic vulnerability prediction model, and paves the way for more resilient knowledge graph management strategies.

References

1. Abdallah, H., Markhoff, B., Soulet, A.: Ranking indicator discovery from very large knowledge graphs. Proc. VLDB Endowment. **18**(4), 1183–1195 (2024)
2. Abdallah, H., Markhoff, B., Soulet, A.: A complex network model for knowledge graphs' relationships. Seman. Web **16**(5), 1–20 (2025)
3. Albert, R., Jeong, H., Barabási, A.L.: Error and attack tolerance of complex networks. Nat. **406**(6794), 378–382 (2000)
4. Auer, S., Bizer, C., Kobilarov, G., Lehmann, J., Cyganiak, R., Ives, Z.: DBpedia: A nucleus for a web of open data. In: Aberer, K., et al. (eds) International Semantic Web Conference. pp. 722–735. Springer, Berlin, Heidelberg (2007). https://doi.org/10.1007/978-3-540-76298-0_52
5. Dürst, M., Suignard, M.: Internationalized resource identifiers (iris). Technical Report (2005)
6. Gale, A., Marian, A.: Explaining monotonic ranking functions. Proc. VLDB Endowment **14**(4), 640–652 (2020)
7. Halpin, H., Robu, V., Shepherd, H.: The complex dynamics of collaborative tagging. In: Proceedings of the 16th international conference on World Wide Web. pp. 211–220 (2007)
8. Heindorf, S., Potthast, M., Bast, H., Buchhold, B., Haussmann, E.: Wsdm cup 2017: Vandalism detection and triple scoring. In: Proceedings of the Tenth ACM International Conference on Web Search and Data Mining. pp. 827–828 (2017)
9. Heindorf, S., Potthast, M., Stein, B., Engels, G.: Towards vandalism detection in knowledge bases: Corpus construction and analysis. In: Proceedings of the 38th International ACM SIGIR Conference on Research and Development in Information Retrieval. pp. 831–834 (2015)
10. Heindorf, S., Potthast, M., Stein, B., Engels, G.: Vandalism detection in wikidata. In: Proceedings of the 25th ACM International on Conference on Information and Knowledge Management. pp. 327–336 (2016)
11. Heindorf, S., Scholten, Y., Engels, G., Potthast, M.: Debiasing vandalism detection models at wikidata. In: The World Wide Web Conference. pp. 670–680 (2019)

12. Sarabadani, A., Halfaker, A., Taraborelli, D.: Building automated vandalism detection tools for wikidata. In: Proceedings of the 26th International Conference on World Wide Web Companion. pp. 1647–1654 (2017)
13. Shrinivasan, S., Razniewski, S.: How stable is knowledge base knowledge? arXiv preprint arXiv:2211.00989 (2022)
14. Suchanek, F.M., Kasneci, G., Weikum, G.: YAGO: a core of semantic knowledge. In: Proceedings of the 16th international conference on World Wide Web. pp. 697–706 (2007)
15. Trokhymovych, M., Saez-Trumper, D.: Wikidata vandalism detection with graph-linguistic fusion. In: Proceedings of the 11th Wiki Workshop (2024)
16. Vrandečić, D., Krötzsch, M.: Wikidata: a free collaborative knowledgebase. Commun. ACM **57**(10), 78–85 (2014)

From Prediction to Diagnostic Action: A Human-Centric System for Coronary Artery Disease Assessment

Mohamed Amine Chaâbane[1]([✉]) [iD], Imen Ben Said[1,2] [iD], Sirine Ayedi[3],
and Amine Bahloul[3] [iD]

[1] MIRACL Laboratory, University of Sfax, Sfax, Tunisia
mohamedamine.chaabane@isaas.usf.tn, imen.bensaid@crns.tn
[2] Digital Research Center of Sfax, Technopark of Sfax, PO Box 275, 3021 Sfax, Tunisia
[3] Hedi Chaker University Hospital of Sfax, University of Sfax, Sfax, Tunisia

Abstract. Coronary Artery Disease (CAD), a leading cause of death worldwide, requires prompt and accurate diagnosis to enable effective treatment and avoid unnecessary or invasive procedures. Traditional statistical methods, such as those proposed by the European Society of Cardiology (ESC), often fall short in delivering reliable predictive performance, particularly in heterogeneous patient populations. To address this gap, this paper examines the application of Machine Learning (ML) to enhance CAD risk assessment and facilitate informed diagnostic decision-making. We propose a stacking ensemble model that combines multiple classifiers and achieves an accuracy of 83%, outperforming individual models. Building on this model, we introduce CARDiA, a human-centered, intelligent clinical decision support system (CDSS) designed to assist cardiologists in evaluating CAD likelihood and determining appropriate diagnostic actions. Beyond prediction, CARDiA integrates ESC clinical guidelines with a workflow-based reasoning engine to provide interpretable, guideline-aligned diagnostic pathways. By combining predictive accuracy with evidence-based, process-driven recommendations, CARDiA offers a robust and user-friendly tool to enhance CAD diagnosis in clinical practice.

Keywords: Machine Learning · Predictive Modeling · Coronary Artery Disease (CAD) · Clinical Decision Support System (CDSS)

1 Introduction

Cardiovascular diseases remain one of the leading causes of mortality worldwide, with coronary artery disease (CAD) being the most prevalent and deadly subtype. According to the World Health Organization (WHO) [1], millions of people die from CAD every year. Early and accurate detection of the disease is therefore essential to enable timely treatment and prevent loss of life due to delayed diagnosis [2].

In clinical practice, the estimation of pre-test probability of obstructive CAD is often guided by clinical prediction scores. Historical models such as the CAD Consortium

C. Cappiello et al. (Eds.): CoopIS 2025, LNCS 15535, pp. 145–162, 2026.
https://doi.org/10.1007/978-3-032-15538-2_9

Basic and Clinical models [11] have been widely used to support clinicians in determining which diagnostic tests to perform. More recently, the 2024 ESC Guidelines for the management of chronic coronary syndromes introduced an updated pre-test probability model derived from a large international cohort [10]. This new score incorporates variables such as age, sex, chest pain characteristics, and key cardiovascular risk factors, aiming to more accurately classify patients into low, intermediate, or high likelihood of disease.

However, despite their clinical utility, these rule-based scores suffer from notable limitations. Their predictive performance remains modest, with persistent challenges in discriminating between disease presence and absence, particularly in atypical populations such as women or younger individuals [12]. Moreover, traditional scores are based on linear regression models that cannot capture complex interactions among diverse clinical variables, leading to potential misclassification and suboptimal diagnostic decision-making. These limitations can result in unnecessary testing for low-risk patients or, conversely, missed diagnoses in higher-risk individuals, both of which have significant consequences for patient outcomes and healthcare efficiency.

To address these shortcomings, digital technologies, particularly Artificial Intelligence (AI), offer promising avenues to overcome the limitations of traditional rule-based approaches. By leveraging complex clinical datasets, AI can support more accurate, personalized, and timely decision-making in CAD diagnosis. Among AI methods, machine learning (ML) has emerged as a particularly effective technique, capable of identifying subtle, non-linear patterns in high-dimensional data that conventional models may overlook. ML-based models can learn from real-world clinical data to predict disease outcomes with improved precision, making them well-suited for enhancing diagnostic workflows and supporting risk stratification in diverse patient populations [3–6].

In the literature, several studies have investigated CAD prediction using ML classifiers such as Logistic Regression (LR), Random Forest (RF), Decision Trees (DT), Support Vector Machines (SVM), Random Forests (RF), and XGBoost [6–8]. These works have demonstrated that predictive ML models can achieve good performance in experimental settings. However, their practical applicability remains limited. Most of the models are trained on public datasets (e.g., Cleveland and Statlog), which are relatively small and include a limited set of features, lacking richer clinical data such as laboratory results or medication history. This limitation reduces their generalizability and relevance in real-world healthcare environments. Additionally, these studies primarily focus on comparing ML algorithms for performance benchmarking, without leveraging model outputs to generate actionable insights that could support clinicians in real-time decision-making.

In this paper, we address the following research question: *How can machine learning, when integrated into a human-centered and guideline-aligned clinical decision support system, improve the accuracy of CAD prediction and support cardiologists in selecting appropriate diagnostic actions?*

More precisely, this paper introduces a novel ML–based approach for CAD prediction, leveraging a stacking ensemble model that combines the strengths of multiple base classifiers to improve predictive performance and robustness. Trained on real-world clinical data, the model outputs a CAD likelihood score that serves as the foundation for decision support. Beyond prediction, the model's outputs are integrated with ESC clinical guidelines and operationalized through a workflow-based reasoning engine, ensuring interpretable, guideline-aligned diagnostic recommendations. Building on this predictive and reasoning framework, we present CARDiA, a human-centric Clinical Decision Support System (CDSS) designed to assist cardiologists with accurate risk estimation and personalized, guideline-driven diagnostic recommendations.

The remainder of this paper is organized as follows: Sect. 2 reviews related work on CAD prediction. Section 3 presents our machine learning pipeline and compares the performance of individual ML algorithms. Section 4 introduces the proposed stacking ensemble model for CAD prediction. Section 5 discusses the evaluation results, comparing the stacked model to both individual classifiers and existing approaches in the literature. Section 6 describes the CARDiA system that integrates the predictive model into a clinical decision support tool. Finally, Sect. 7 concludes the paper and outlines future research directions.

2 Related Works

2.1 Clinical Scoring Approach for CAD Prediction

The non-invasive assessment of the probability of obstructive (CAD) remains a cornerstone in the evaluation of patients presenting with stable chest pain. Traditionally, clinical prediction models such as the CAD Consortium Basic and Clinical models [11] have been widely employed to estimate pre-test probability (PTP) and guide diagnostic decisions. However, these models have increasingly shown limitations in contemporary populations, including a tendency to overestimate risk, particularly in cohorts with declining CAD prevalence [12].

To address these concerns, the 2024 European Society of Cardiology (ESC) Guidelines on Chronic Coronary Syndromes introduced a new PTP model that incorporates age, sex, chest pain characteristics, and conventional cardiovascular risk factors such as smoking, diabetes, hypertension, and dyslipidemia [10]. Based on the PTP, the guidelines recommend different diagnostic actions as illustrated in Fig. 1:

- If the PTP is above 85%, invasive coronary angiography is recommended as the first step to directly assess the state of the coronary arteries.
- If the PTP is between 15% and 85%, more detailed functional or anatomical tests should be considered to confirm the diagnosis.
- If the PTP is between 5% and 15%, non-invasive tests such as a coronary CT scan or stress imaging are suggested.
- If the PTP is less than 5%, no further cardiac testing is needed.

While the ESC updated model represents a step forward in improving diagnostic triage, it still exhibits limited individual-level accuracy, with studies reporting risk underestimation in certain subgroups, particularly women, and risk overestimation in low-risk younger men [12]. These shortcomings reflect the inherent limitations of linear, rule-based models, which may not capture the complex, non-linear relationships among clinical variables. These limitations can be addressed by ML-based approaches.

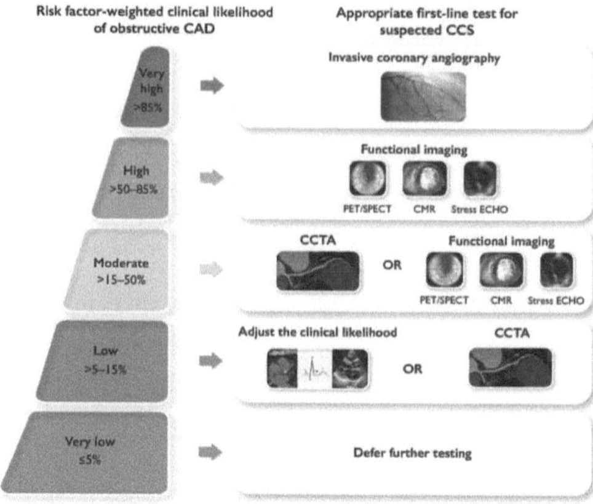

Fig. 1. Recommended diagnostic pathways based on PTP [10].

2.2 Review of ML Approaches Applied to CAD Prediction

By integrating a wide range of clinical, biological, and electrocardiographic data, ML models can uncover subtle patterns and interactions often missed by traditional statistical methods. Several studies have demonstrated that ML-based algorithms can outperform conventional risk scores in predicting the presence of CAD and in forecasting major adverse cardiovascular events, with improved discrimination, calibration, and predictive accuracy [13, 14].

This section outlines the primary works found in the literature that address CAD prediction. In [7], the author investigated the performance of various machine learning models for the prediction of CAD using two public benchmark datasets: Statlog and Cleveland. Both datasets share the same structure (13 relevant attributes) but differ in the number of samples: 270 records in Statlog and 303 in Cleveland. The study evaluated seven classification algorithms: SVM, LR, DNN, DT, Naïve Bayes, RF, and K-NN. The findings reveal that the DNN achieved the highest accuracy on the Statlog dataset (98.15%), while SVM obtained the best performance on the Cleveland dataset (97.36%). However, the use of deep learning models on such small datasets is methodologically risky, and high accuracy figures may reflect overfitting. Moreover, relying solely on 13 attributes may not capture the full clinical complexity of CAD.

[8] explored the use of machine learning for CAD prediction using a large, aggregated dataset. The study combined five commonly used public datasets, Cleveland, Hungarian, Switzerland, Long Beach VA, and Statlog, sourced from the UC Irvine Machine Learning Repository[1] and Kaggle[2], resulting in 918 patient records. The PyCaret classification module was used to automate the training and comparison of 14 classification algorithms, offering a standardized and scalable evaluation process. The results showed that LR provided the most consistent performance, with an accuracy of 79% and recall, precision, and F1-score all around 0.80. While merging datasets from multiple sources can increase data volume, it may compromise the quality of the predictors. In such cases, only the

---

[1] https://archive.ics.uci.edu/.

[2] https://www.kaggle.com/.

attributes common to all sources are retained, which may exclude clinically important features. This can negatively impact model reliability and reduce the interpretability of the results, particularly in clinical decision-making contexts.

In contrast to approaches based on public repositories, [9] focused on CAD prediction using real-world hospital data collected from two healthcare institutions in Kano State, Nigeria. The dataset consists of 506 patient records, each described by 17 clinical features related to CAD diagnosis. Six machine learning models were trained and evaluated: SVM, K-NN, RF, Naïve Bayes, XGBoost, and LR. Each model was trained and tested on the hospital dataset to evaluate its ability to accurately classify the presence or absence of CAD. Among the tested models, the RF classifier demonstrated the highest predictive performance, achieving an accuracy of 92.04%. Despite the promising results in terms of accuracy, the authors do not provide a confusion matrix, which would have enabled a clearer analysis of the model's errors. Additionally, although 17 features were used, there is limited discussion on feature importance or feature selection, which could provide deeper insights into key clinical predictors of CAD.

Across the reviewed studies, various ML techniques were employed to predict CAD, using diverse data sources, some relying on publicly available repositories, while others utilized datasets collected from clinical practice. However, these datasets often contain heterogeneous clinical information and provide only a limited representation of the patient's medical context. This lack of comprehensive patient characterization limits the generalizability and practical utility of the models in real-world clinical environments.

Moreover, most of the studies do not include a rigorous feature engineering process to justify the selection of predictors. As a result, feature choices often appear arbitrary and may exclude critical risk factors necessary for robust and clinically relevant CAD prediction.

3 Machine Learning Pipeline and Model Evaluation

This section describes the ML-based approach developed for predicting of CAD. Figure 2 illustrates the overall pipeline followed in this approach. The process begins with data collection, where domain experts (i.e., cardiologists) contribute to the collection, selection, and validation of clinically relevant patient data. This ensures that the dataset accurately reflects real-world diagnostic scenarios.

Next, a data pre-processing phase is conducted to clean, normalize, and transform the raw data, ensuring its quality, consistency, and suitability for ML modeling. Following this, a feature engineering step is applied to extract and select the most informative attributes that enhance predictive performance.

The resulting dataset is then split into two subsets: a training set, used to fit the ML models, and a testing set, used to evaluate their generalization ability. In the model training and evaluation phase, selected classification algorithms are trained on the training data. The resulting models are then evaluated on the testing set using appropriate performance metrics to measure their predictive accuracy, precision, recall, and overall reliability. Finally, a model comparison phase is carried out to identify the best-performing model for CAD prediction. The following subsections provide a detailed description of each phase.

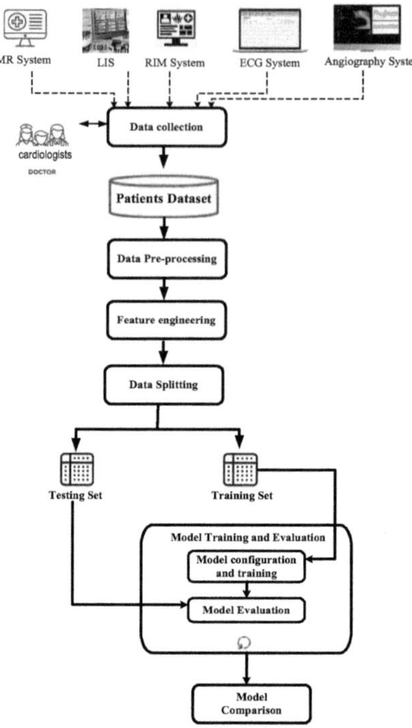

Fig. 2. Overview of the ML pipeline for CAD prediction, from data collection to model evaluation.

3.1　Data Collection

The first step in our approach is the collection and preparation of the dataset, a critical phase that directly impacts the relevance and performance of the predictive model. The data were collected from multiple clinical information systems at *Hedi Chaker Hospital* in Sfax, Tunisia, ensuring a comprehensive and diverse set of patient data. Specifically, the data sources include:

- Electronic Medical Record (EMR) System: Provides general demographic data (e.g., age, sex) and patient medical history.
- Laboratory Information System (LIS): Supplies laboratory test results (e.g., HbA1C, LDL-C, creatinine).
- Real-Time Monitoring (RTM) System: Captures physiological measurements recorded during physical examinations (e.g., heart rate, blood pressure).
- ECG Management System: Delivers electrocardiographic features extracted from ECG signals (e.g., Q wave, QRS duration).
- Coronary Angiography System: Reports angiographic examination results that confirm whether a patient has CAD.

The first four systems collectively provide a rich representation of the patient's clinical context, encompassing clinical, biological, physiological, and electrocardiographic data. These attributes serve as *predictive features* representing the input variables for the

ML model. In contrast, the angiography results, obtained from the fifth system, serve as the *target variable* to be predicted, indicating the presence or absence of CAD.

As a result of the data integration process from these systems, we constructed a structured dataset in the form of a CSV file. This dataset comprises 563 patient records collected over two years (2022–2024). It includes a total of 92 predictive features, of which 88 are numerical (float) and 4 are categorical (object).

Figure 3 shows a sample of the final dataset, highlighting a subset of the predictive attributes along with the target variable (*"Coro result"*), where *0* denotes a negative diagnosis and *1* indicates a positive diagnosis for CAD. The dataset contains 251 negative cases and 310 positive cases.

				Predictive features						Target variable
	Age	Sexe	Smoking	PA	Heart rate	HbA1C	GAJ	ECG_Q wave	ECG_QRS duration (ms)	....	Coro result
1	61	F	0	18_8	73	8,2	17,2	0	142		1
2	71	M	1	13_7	60	8,8	4,4	0	102		0
3	66	F	0	15_8	66	6,5	10,3	0	92		1
4	59	m	1	13_7	86	8	7,3	0	84		1
5	75	m	0	16_6	53	9		0	82		1
6	64	m	1	10_7	70	6,6	22	0	93		0
7	45	m	0	12_8	50	7,7	3,64	0	84		1
8	63	f	0	14_8	70	7,9	10,1	0	88		0
9	80	f	0	13_6	74	7,3	4,9	0	144		0

Fig. 3. Sample of the dataset.

3.2 Data Preprocessing

To prepare the dataset for training ML models, several preprocessing steps were applied to ensure data quality, consistency, and suitability for analysis. These steps are crucial to mitigate noise, handle missing or malformed values, and transform raw clinical data into a clean, complete, and numerically consistent format appropriate for ML modeling. The main preprocessing steps are detailed below:

- Exclusion of Incomplete Records: Any patient records with missing values in the target variable (*Coro result*) were removed. This ensures that the model is trained only on fully labeled data, where the presence or absence of CAD is known.
- Categorical Encoding: Categorical variables were converted into numerical representations compatible with ML algorithms. For example, the Sexe attribute was encoded as 0 for female and 1 for male.
- Splitting Compound Values: Some columns contained compound values in a single field. For instance, blood pressure values stored as "18_8" were split into two separate numerical attributes: BP_systolic = 18 and BP_diastolic = 8.
- Missing Value Imputation: Missing values across the dataset were handled using Iterative Imputation, following the Multiple Imputation by Chained Equations (MICE) approach. This method estimates missing values by modeling each feature as a function of other features, refining the imputations iteratively for greater accuracy.
- Data Scaling: To ensure all features contribute equally to model training, numerical values were standardized using StandardScaler. This transformation centers each feature around zero and scales it to unit variance, which improves model convergence.

3.3 Feature Engineering

The initial dataset comprised 92 predictive features derived from various clinical sources. As a first step, domain experts (namely cardiologists) conducted a manual review to eliminate clinically irrelevant or redundant variables, reducing the feature set to 68 features.

Following this expert-driven filtering, an XGBoost classifier was employed to assess the importance of the remaining features based on their contribution to model performance. This data-driven method identified 31 features with the highest predictive value.

Subsequently, a collaborative refinement phase was conducted, involving the same domain experts. During this phase, the medical team re-evaluated the selected features and, based on a combination of clinical relevance and data insights, decided to add certain features, remove others, or replace some with more informative alternatives.

This iterative, hybrid process, combining medical expertise and ML, resulted in a final, optimized set of 28 predictive features, which were used for model development.

3.4 Data Splitting

The dataset was divided into training and testing sets using stratified sampling to preserve the original class distribution. A split ratio of 85% for training (548 samples) and 15% for testing (93 samples) was applied to ensure a balanced evaluation.

3.5 Model Training and Evaluation

To address the classification task of predicting coronary outcomes, several supervised learning algorithms were trained and tested on the dataset. Due to space limitations, we focus on the three most effective classifiers that yielded the best results for CAD prediction: RF, XGBoost, and LR.

Model performance was assessed using confusion matrices, which provide detailed insights into each model's ability to correctly classify patients with CAD and those without. In particular, two key metrics were considered:

- Sensitivity (also called recall or true positive rate) measures the model's ability to correctly identify patients with CAD.
- Specificity (true negative rate) measures the model's ability to correctly identify patients without CAD.

Figure 4 illustrates the confusion matrices for the three models:

- Figure 4(a) presents the confusion matrix of the RF model. It shows 13 false negatives (missed CAD cases) and 10 false positives (non-CAD cases incorrectly classified as CAD). While the model identifies many true positives, the relatively high number of false negatives affects its sensitivity, and false positives reduce its specificity.
- Figure 4(b) displays the results of XGBoost. This model shows a more balanced error distribution with a moderate number of false positives and false negatives, indicating a trade-off between sensitivity and specificity.

- Figure 4(c) corresponds to the LR model, which achieves the lowest number of both false negatives and false positives. This indicates a well-balanced performance, offering strong sensitivity and specificity, and making it a reliable model for distinguishing between CAD and non-CAD patients.

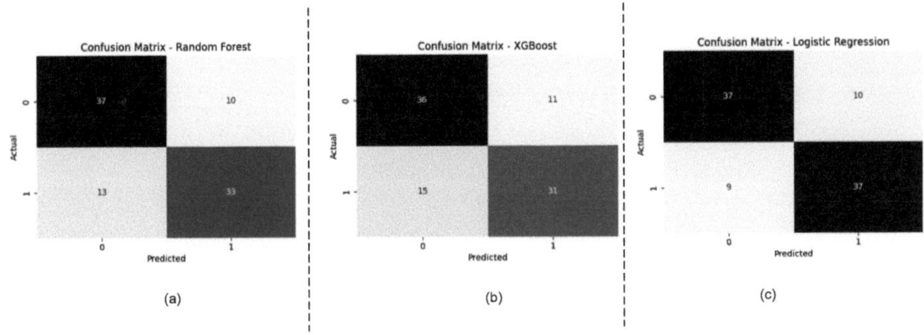

Fig. 4. Confusion matrices related to RF, XGBoost, and LR models used for predicting CADs.

3.6 Model Comparison

To evaluate and compare the performance of the trained models, Fig. 5 provides two complementary visualizations. Figure 5(a) summarizes the classification metrics, i.e., accuracy, precision, recall, and F1-score, for the three models: RF, XGBoost, and LR.

This comparison reveals that LR achieved the best overall performance, with all four metrics (accuracy, precision, recall, and F1-score) reaching 0.796. RF followed with slightly lower but still consistent scores, around 0.753, while XGBoost recorded the lowest values across all metrics, close to 0.720.

To further assess the models' discriminative ability, Fig. 5(b) presents the Receiver Operating Characteristic (ROC) curves along with the corresponding Area Under the Curve (AUC) scores. As shown, LR again outperformed the other models with an AUC of 0.8548, indicating stronger capability in distinguishing between positive and negative outcomes. RF attained a moderately high AUC of 0.8279, while XGBoost trailed behind with 0.7710.

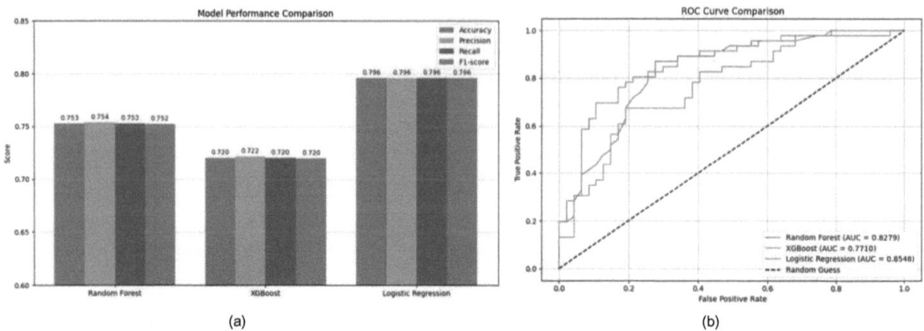

Fig. 5. Performance comparison of RF, XGBoost, and LR.

While these results confirm that LR offers the best performance among the three classifiers, it is important to note that all models deliver only modest predictive power. Given the critical nature of CAD diagnosis, especially the need to minimize false negatives as missing a true CAD case may lead to serious consequences for the patient, these moderate results highlight the need for further enhancement.

In the following section, we explore a stacking ensemble approach, aiming to combine the strengths of individual models and achieve improved predictive reliability and accuracy.

4   Stacking-Based Approach for CAD Prediction

This section introduces the stacking methodology along with its architecture and evaluation.

4.1   Stacking Ensemble Model Architecture

The architecture of the proposed stacking ensemble model, presented in Fig. 6, is organized into two main levels:

- *Base Learners Level:* At the base level, the RF and XGBoost are independently trained using the training set. These models learn from the input data and are responsible for generating predictions. After training, they are used to compute the class probabilities on the testing set. Specifically, the RF model outputs a probability denoted as P_RF, and the XGBoost model produces P_XGB. These probability scores reflect each model's confidence in predicting the presence or absence of CAD for each patient. To ensure robust training and avoid overfitting, 3-fold cross-validation is employed. During this process, out-of-fold predictions are generated for each base learner. These predictions serve as inputs for the next level of architecture.
- *Meta Learner Level:* At this level, the LR model serves as the meta-classifier. It is trained on the out-of-fold prediction probabilities produced by the base learners. The LR model learns how to best combine the predictions of the base models to make a final decision. The meta-classifier takes P_RF, P_XGB, and out-of-fold predictions as input features and outputs a final prediction (the likelihood of CAD), which cardiologists can interpret to support diagnostic decision-making.

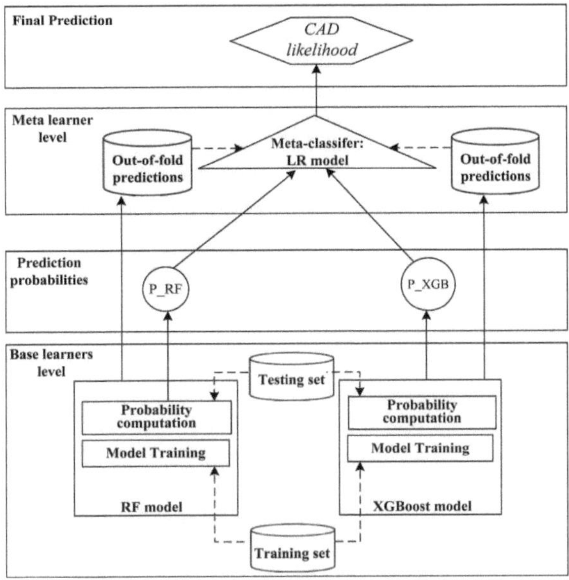

Fig. 6. Stacking Ensemble Model Architecture.

4.2 Stacking Ensemble Model Evaluation

Table 1 presents the classification report for the proposed stacking ensemble model, highlighting performance metrics that confirm its effectiveness in distinguishing between CAD and non-CAD cases. More precisely, the model achieves an accuracy of 83%, indicating that it correctly predicts the presence or absence of CAD in approximately 8 out of 10 cases.

Table 1. Classification Report of the Stacking Ensemble Model.

Metric	Precision	Recall	F1-Score	Accuracy	ROC AUC
Non-CAD	0.84	0.81	0.83		
CAD	0.81	0.85	0.83		
Average	0.83	0.83	0.83	0.83	0.8652

In addition to overall accuracy, the ROC AUC score of 0.8652 demonstrates strong discriminative ability. The model also shows well-balanced precision and recall values, ranging between 0.81 and 0.85, suggesting it maintains both good sensitivity and specificity. Furthermore, the F1-scores are equal across both classes, reflecting stable and consistent performance in prediction.

To complement these findings, Fig. 7 illustrates the confusion matrix of the stacking model's predictions. The model correctly identifies 39 true positive cases and 38 true negative cases, while producing only 7 false negatives and 9 false positives. This distribution highlights the model's strength in minimizing critical misclassifications, which are particularly concerning in a medical diagnosis context.

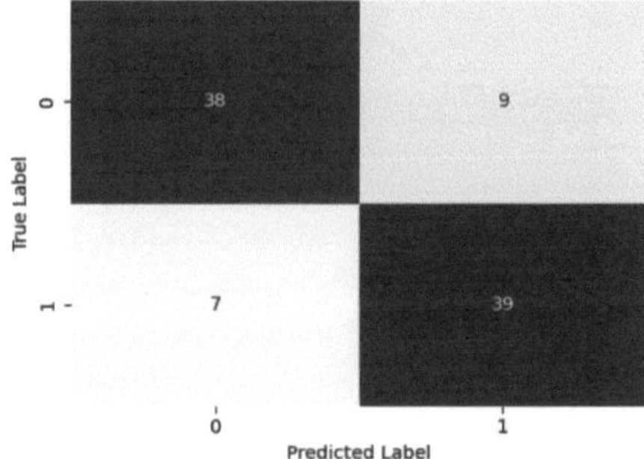

Fig. 7. Confusion matrix of the stacking ensemble model.

5 Discussion

This section discusses the significance and performance of the proposed stacked ensemble model, comparing it both to individual classifiers and to related studies in the existing literature.

5.1 Comparison with Individual Models

The results shown in Fig. 8 demonstrate that the stacking ensemble model achieves superior performance compared to the individual base classifiers in terms of both accuracy and ROC AUC. More precisely, the stacked model attained the highest accuracy (0.828) and ROC AUC (0.865), outperforming each base model individually. In fact, among the individual models, LR delivered the most balanced and consistent results, making it a strong baseline. However, when LR is combined with RF and XGBoost within a stacking framework, the overall predictive performance improves noticeably. This improvement highlights the advantage of ensemble learning, where the strengths of different algorithms are leveraged collectively.

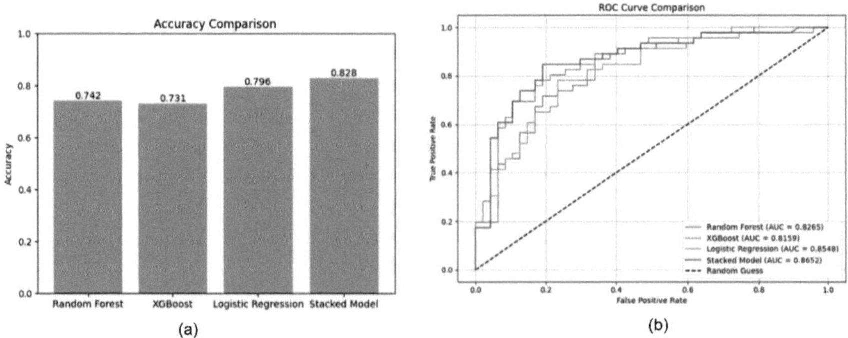

Fig. 8. Comparison between individual models and our stacking ensemble model.

5.2 Comparison with Related Work

To further assess the relevance and robustness of our proposed CAD prediction model, Table 2 presents a comparative overview of selected studies ([7, 8], and [9]) that applied ML techniques for CAD prediction, along with our proposed stacking method.

Table 2. Comparison between existing work and our stacking approach.

Study	[7]	[8]	[9]	Our approach
Dataset Type	Public	Public	Real-word	Real-word
# Records	270|303	918	506	563
# Features	13	11	17	28
Feature Engineering	No	No	No	Yes
Predictor Selection Method	Manual	Manual	Manual	Model-based and Domain expert
Model(s) Used	DNN, SVM	LR	RF	Stacked ensemble model
Average Accuracy (%)	97,75	79	92	83

The reviewed studies primarily relied on datasets containing a relatively limited number of features (between 11 and 17) and varying sample sizes (ranging from 270 to 918 records). In contrast, our model was developed using a real-world dataset collected from clinical practice, comprising 563 patient records and 28 predictive features (more than double the average feature count used in the other studies). This richer dataset allows for a more comprehensive representation of patient profiles.

A key differentiator of our approach lies in the incorporation of a feature engineering phase, which was absent from the compared studies. More precisely, while existing works relied exclusively on manual feature selection, our method combines model-based feature importance analysis (based on XGBoost classifier) with cardiologist expertise. This hybrid strategy ensures that selected predictors are both statistically informative and clinically meaningful, improving the interpretability and credibility of the predictions.

Although study [7] reports a notably high accuracy (97.75%), this result was achieved on small public datasets (Statlog and Cleveland), which raises concerns about overfitting and lack of generalizability. In contrast, our model was trained and evaluated on real-world clinical data and achieved an accuracy of 83%, a more realistic figure that reflects its applicability in actual healthcare settings.

6 CARDiA System for CAD Assessment

6.1 CARDiA System Architecture

The architecture of the CARDiA (Coronary ARtery Disease Intelligent Assistant) system is illustrated in Fig. 9. It presents an end-to-end pipeline that begins with clinical data entry and ends with model-based recommendations, supporting cardiologists in the assessment and diagnosis of CAD.

The process starts with patient information being entered through the Data Acquisition Service, implemented using a Blade-based Laravel frontend. The data is sent via an HTTP POST request to the Data Validation and Transmission Service, managed by the Laravel backend. After validation and structuring into a standardized JSON format (PatientData.json), the input is forwarded to the Prediction Service.

This service, deployed through a FastAPI endpoint, loads the trained stacking ensemble model and computes the patient's CAD likelihood score. This prediction is then routed to the Recommendation Service, which is orchestrated by a workflow engine.

The Recommendation Service interprets the CAD likelihood using ESC guideline [10] thresholds and triggers a rule-driven workflow to propose appropriate diagnostic actions (e.g., invasive coronary angiography or functional imaging). The use of a workflow engine enables flexible, traceable, and adaptive management of recommendation logic, supporting user feedback loops.

Finally, the output (CAD likelihood and diagnostic suggestions) is returned to the backend and presented to the user through the frontend interface, offering cardiologists a reliable decision-support tool grounded in ML.

6.2 Clinical Data Acquisition and Prediction Interface

The CARDiA system provides graphical user interfaces (GUIs) designed with a strong emphasis on simplicity, usability, and efficiency, enabling healthcare professionals to interact with the system seamlessly. To minimize manual data entry and reduce the risk of input errors, the GUIs incorporate interactive components such as sliders, checkboxes, and toggle buttons. These elements facilitate faster and more intuitive data entry, allowing cardiologists to input patient information and receive CAD risk predictions along with corresponding diagnostic recommendations.

Upon logging into the system, the cardiologist is directed to a multi-step form, illustrated in Fig. 10(a), which is organized into five sections: *General Information, Medical History, Biological Markers, ECG Results, and Habits & Symptoms*. A timeline displayed at the top of the form outlines these sections and highlights the one currently being completed. Within each section, targeted questions and input fields guide the user in providing structured patient data.

Due to space limitations, we detail in what follows the Biological Markers section. Interested readers may refer to the demonstration video available at this *URL* for a full walkthrough of the interface.

As shown in Fig. 10(a), the interface for biological markers includes input fields for key blood test indicators such as HDL cholesterol (HDL-C) and hemoglobin A1C (HbA1C). These fields are equipped with sliders that allow users to adjust values by dragging markers along each scale, with real-time feedback on whether the result is normal, acceptable, or borderline.

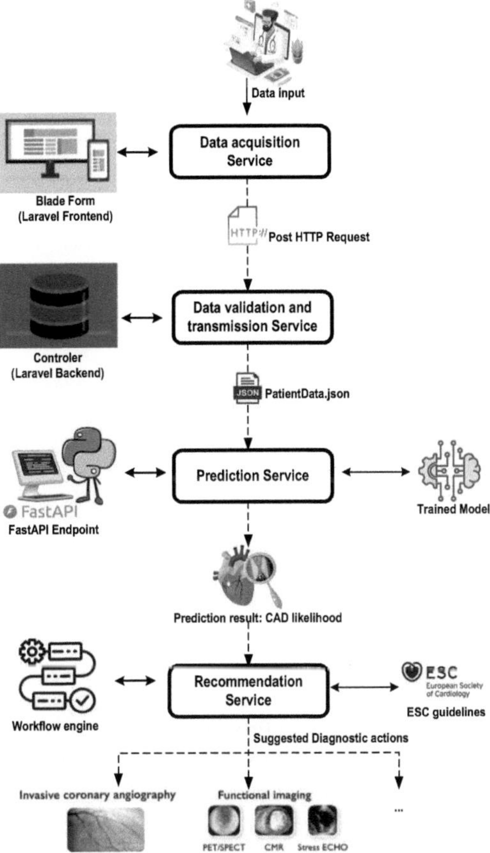

Fig. 9. CARDiA system architecture.

Once all sections are completed, the cardiologist submits the form to obtain the prediction results and suggested diagnostic actions. Figure 10(b) displays an example of the prediction output. The cardiologist may then approve the recommended diagnostic test by clicking the *Approve* button or decline the suggestion as appropriate.

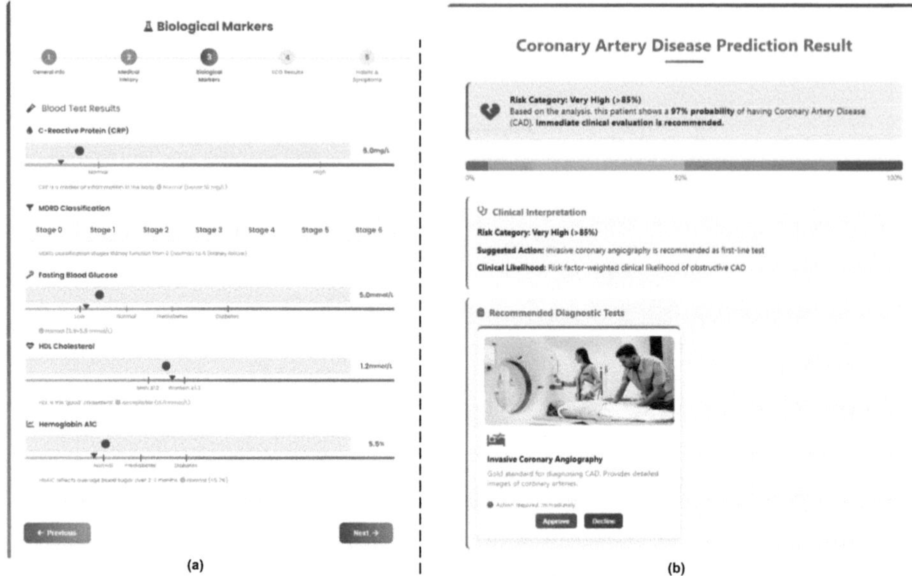

Fig. 10. CARDiA Interface for Clinical Data Input and CAD Prediction Output.

6.3 Workflow-Based Diagnostic Recommendation Service

Figure 11 presents a simplified Business Process Model and Notation (BPMN) diagram that illustrates the collaborative process [15, 16] among system components and clinical actors involved in recommending diagnostic actions.

The workflow begins when the Prediction Service generates a CAD likelihood score, which is forwarded to the Recommendation Service. Based on this score, the recommendation service evaluates whether the patient falls into a *very low-risk* (<5%) or *very high-risk* (>85%) category, according to the ESC 2024 guidelines [10].

For very low-risk patients, the system automatically issues a *"No further testing needed"* notification to the cardiologist. However, for very high-risk patients, the system recommends invasive coronary angiography. This recommendation is sent as a message to the cardiologist, who reviews and either approves or rejects the suggestion.

If the cardiologist approves the recommendation, a confirmation message is returned, and the process continues with an angiography request sent to the Catheterization Lab. If the recommendation is rejected, the workflow triggers a likelihood recalculation.

We note that this BPMN diagram does not cover all rules and pathways defined by the ESC 2024 guidelines. In particular, the intermediate risk group (5%–85%), which typically requires further non-invasive functional imaging, is not detailed here for clarity. The goal of this diagram is to illustrate the general architecture and logic behind implementing recommendation services via a workflow engine.

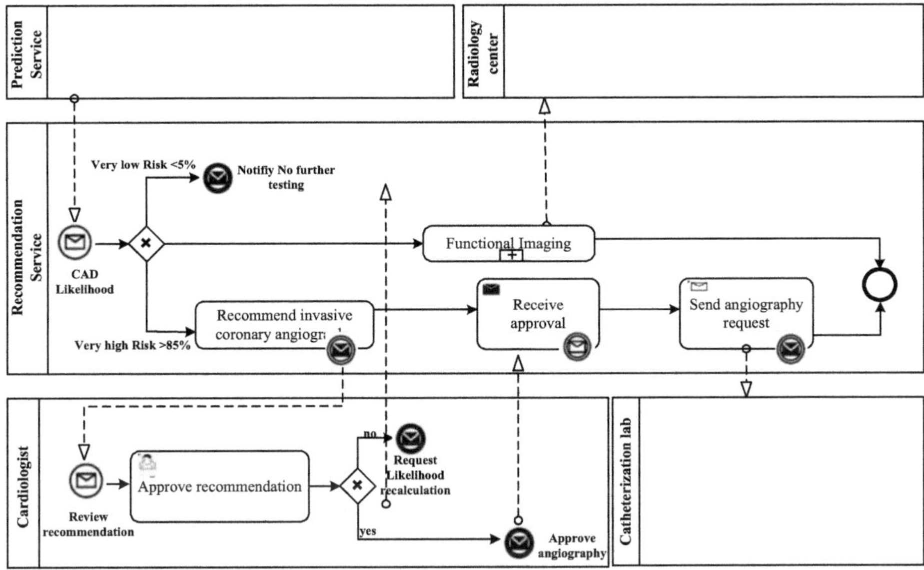

Fig. 11. Simplified BPMN diagram illustrating the workflow-based diagnostic recommendation service in CARDiA.

7 Conclusion

This paper presented a novel ML–based approach for CAD prediction, integrating a stacking ensemble model into a human-centered clinical decision support system called CARDiA. The main contributions of this work include: First, a ML-driven predictive model using a stacking ensemble approach, enhanced by domain-informed feature engineering. Trained on real-world clinical data, the model achieved 83% accuracy, outperforming individual classifiers and offering improved interpretability and clinical relevance. Second, a workflow-based recommendation service, modeled using BPMN, enabling a modular, interpretable integration of clinical logic aligned with ESC guidelines.

The key strength of this study is to move from a *one-size-fits-all* model, proposed mainly by traditional statistical methods [10, 11], toward a personalized, human-centric approach, where the right diagnostic test is selected for the right patient at the right time. Such precision strategies could help optimize diagnostic pathways, reduce unnecessary testing, limit healthcare costs, and improve patient outcomes by identifying high-risk individuals earlier and avoiding diagnostic delays in low-risk populations.

Our future work will take two directions. First, we aim to validate the CARDiA system, including the underlying stacking model, through larger-scale clinical trials in collaboration with multiple healthcare institutions, to assess its generalizability and real-world applicability. Second, we plan to explore explainability techniques (such as SHAP values) to enhance the interpretability of model predictions and provide greater transparency for clinicians in the decision-making process.

References

1. Coronary Artery Disease. https://my.clevelandclinic.org/health/diseases/16898-coronary-art ery-disease
2. Amin, S.U., Agarwal, K., Beg, R.: Genetic neural network based data mining in prediction of heart disease using risk factors. In: IEEE Conference on Information & Communication Technologies, pp. 1227–1231 (2013)
3. Elhechmi, Y.Z.: Medicine at the dawn of artificial intelligence. Tunis. Med. **100**(5), 354 (2022)
4. Toma, M., Wei, O.C.: Predictive modeling in medicine. Encyclopedia **3**(2), 590–601 (2023)
5. Bekbolatova, M., Mayer, J., Ong, C.W., Toma, M.: Transformative potential of AI in healthcare: definitions, applications, and navigating the ethical landscape and public perspectives. Healthcare (Basel) **12**(2), 125 (2024)
6. Kale, A.K., Pandey, D.R.: Data pre-processing technique for enhancing healthcare data quality using artificial intelligence. Int. J. Sci. Res. Sci. Technol. **11**(1), 299–309 (2024)
7. Ayon, S.I., Islam, M.M., Hossain, M.R.: Coronary artery heart disease prediction: a comparative study of computational intelligence techniques. IETE J. Res. **68**(4), 2488–2507 (2024)
8. Jose, R., Thomas, A., Guo, J., Steinberg, R., Toma, M.: Evaluating machine learning models for prediction of coronary artery disease. Glob. Transl. Med. **3**(1) (2024)
9. Muhammad, L.J., Al Shourbaji, I., Haruna, A.A., Mohammed, I.A., Ahmad, A., Jibrin, M.B: Machine learning predictive models for coronary artery disease. SN Comput. Sci. **2**(5), 350 (2021)
10. Vrints, C., Andreotti, F., Koskinas, K.C., et al: 2024 ESC guidelines for the management of chronic coronary syndromes: developed by the task force for the management of chronic coronary syndromes of the European Society of Cardiology (ESC) endorsed by the European Association for Cardio-Thoracic Surgery (EACTS). Eur. Heart J. **45**(36), 3415–3537 (2024)
11. Genders, T.S.S., Steyerberg, E.W., Alkadhi, H., et al.: A clinical prediction model for the diagnosis of coronary artery disease: the CAD Consortium model. Eur. Heart J. **39**(27), 2421–2430 (2018)
12. Fordyce, C.B., Douglas, P.S., Roberts, R.S., et al.: Identification of patients with stable chest pain deriving minimal value from noninvasive testing: the PROMISE minimal-risk tool. J. Am. Coll. Cardiol. **79**(2), 173–183 (2022)
13. Al'Aref, S.J., Maliakal, G., Singh, G., et al.: Machine learning of clinical variables and coronary artery calcium scoring for CAD prediction. JACC Cardiovasc Imaging **13**(2 Pt 1), 566–576 (2020)
14. Han, D., He, Y., Yang, L., et al.: Deep learning analysis in coronary CT angiography improves risk prediction of major adverse cardiac events. Eur. Heart J. **43**(5), 474–482 (2022)
15. Oukharijane, J., Chaâbane, M.A., Said, I.B., Andonoff, E., Bouaziz, R.: An assessment taxonomy for self-adaptation business process solutions. Data Knowl. Eng. **155**, 102374 (2025)
16. Oukharijane, J., Ben Said, I., Chaâbane, M.A., Bouaziz, R., Andonoff, E.: A survey of self-adaptive business processes. In: Business Information Management Association Conference, Seville, Spain, pp. 1388–1403 (2018)

Prompting Strategies for LLM-Based Cooperative Data Service Discovery

Devis Bianchini[✉], Massimiliano Garda, Michele Melchiori, and Anisa Rula

Department of Information Engineering, University of Brescia,
Via Branze 38, 25123 Brescia, Italy
{devis.bianchini,massimiliano.garda,michele.melchiori,
anisa.rula}@unibs.it

Abstract. In the context of Smart Manufacturing and the Internet of Production, data service discovery plays a central role in enabling cross-organizational collaboration and data-driven innovation. Nevertheless, effective discovery and composition of data services often require deep technical knowledge, limiting the autonomy of domain experts and R&D managers in designing analytics workflows. This paper presents a cooperative approach to data service discovery that combines Large Language Models (LLMs) with Retrieval-Augmented Generation (RAG), leveraging a conceptual model of data services and analytics scenarios. On top of this model, a set of prompting strategies are designed to support different levels of user expertise and interaction goals. These strategies leverage the cooperative nature of the approach, enabling domain experts and R&D managers to incrementally build, extend, and refine analytics data service pipelines through the interaction with LLMs. We describe how these prompting strategies are tightly integrated with the RAG components to inject contextual knowledge derived from a catalog of data services and analytics scenarios. The system is implemented using open-source technologies and evaluated extensively in a real-world smart factory case study. Our evaluation includes both quantitative metrics (precision, recall, faithfulness, factual correctness) and a qualitative user study, demonstrating the effectiveness of prompting strategies and the feasibility of LLM-supported data service discovery in cooperative industrial settings.

Keywords: Large Language Models · Prompt Engineering · Retrieval-Augmented Generation · Data Service Discovery

1 Introduction

Modern cooperative information systems must support intelligent, flexible, and human-in-the-loop mechanisms for designing analytics workflows that span organizational and technological boundaries. In smart manufacturing ecosystems, such as those promoted by the Internet of Production, data services are a key enabler for realizing data-driven collaboration between stakeholders, including

C. Cappiello et al. (Eds.): CoopIS 2025, LNCS 15535, pp. 163–180, 2026.
https://doi.org/10.1007/978-3-032-15538-2_10

domain experts, R&D managers, IT specialists, and system integrators [9]. While domain experts and R&D managers possess deep knowledge of the physical systems and the data required for digital innovation, the responsibility for discovering and composing data services typically falls on IT specialists and system integrators. This separation of concerns can hinder agility and cooperation, especially when analytics pipelines span organizational silos and require fast iterations. Nevertheless, despite the availability of modular and reusable services, the discovery and composition of data services remain a non-trivial task. It often requires technical knowledge on service metadata, composition constraints, and analytical logics, which domain experts may not fully possess. Large Language Models (LLMs) offer a compelling opportunity to reduce this gap, by enabling natural language interaction over service catalogs and supporting human stakeholders in the design of data analytics pipelines [2].

In this work, we propose a cooperative approach to data service discovery based on LLMs. Our key contribution is the design of a set of prompting strategies that build on a conceptual model of data services and analytics scenarios, which explicitly introduces metadata such as service types, data operations, and step/task structures. These prompting strategies support different interaction needs, ranging from initial scenario definition to incremental refinement and service-level suggestions, and are implemented as templates to structure the communication with the LLM. To ensure contextual relevance and precision, these strategies are integrated into a Retrieval-Augmented Generation (RAG) pipeline. This pipeline dynamically injects relevant information, such as service specifications and past analytics scenarios, into the LLM prompts, guiding the model toward grounded and context-aware outputs. Existing approaches in the literature for (data) service discovery based on LLMs and RAG techniques rely on a rather limited service model that does not include analytics scenarios [6,7,13]. The approach has been implemented as an LLM-based system incorporating open-source tools (LangChain, ChromaDB, and IBM Granite LLM), and evaluated in a real-world smart factory domain. We provide an extensive experimental assessment, including: (a) a *quantitative evaluation* of the retrieval and generation components using standard Information Retrieval metrics (top-n precision/recall) and metrics for the assessment of LLM-based applications leveraging RAG (faithfulness, factual correctness); (b) a *qualitative user study* involving domain experts and R&D managers interacting with the system through the designed prompting strategies. Building upon our previous short paper [3], in which we introduced the architecture of the LLM-based system, this work provides a refined set of prompting techniques grounded in cooperation principles and built upon a conceptual model of data services and analytics scenarios, along with a comprehensive experimental validation. In this way, this paper strives to address the following Research Questions (RQs):

RQ1. *How can descriptive metadata of data services and analytics scenarios be leveraged to design prompt templates for the interaction between domain experts, R&D managers and the LLM-based system for data service discovery?*

RQ2. *How can the RAG method be integrated to enhance the contextual knowledge of the LLM-based system, to facilitate the discovery of data services for designing analytics pipelines?*

RQ3. *How effective is the proposed LLM-based approach in the discovery of data services, with reference to a real-world scenario in the Internet of Production context?*

Unlike traditional (data) service discovery based on structured service requests, our approach fosters natural language interaction for supporting service composition, making it accessible to non-technical users and more adaptable to loosely structured or evolving service descriptions. For clarity, in the remainder of this paper, the terms data service discovery and service discovery are used interchangeably. The paper is organised as follows. In Sect. 2 related work is discussed. Section 3 introduces the conceptual model of data services and analytics scenarios. Section 4 provides details on the ingredients for LLM-based service discovery, answering RQ1 and RQ2. In Sect. 5, the preliminary evaluation is discussed, answering RQ3. Finally, Sect. 6 closes the paper.

2   Related Work

In the latest years, different approaches investigated the possibility of employing LLMs for service discovery in several application domains, beyond the smart manufacturing one. Authors in [13] suggest the usage of LLMs for automatic workflow generation, composed of APIs described in a textual manner. Interactions with the LLM are managed through a prompt composed of three parts: contextual information to define the goal of search, available APIs, instructions to generate the code for API composition. Huang et al. [5] employed a LLM to set up an API recommendation system. In their work, a Knowledge Graph is leveraged to overcome limitations such as rigid question templates and out-of-vocabulary failure. Monti et al. [7] propose the NL2ProcessOps approach, which leverages LLMs and RAG for code generation, thus supporting process deployment operations through both human and automated assessments. Li et al. [6] suggest to jointly use a Knowledge Graph (which is called Manufacturing Service Knowledge Graph) and ChatGPT to respond to domain-specific inquiries in the area of manufacturing service discovery.

All the aforementioned studies disregard considerations on how to combine the RAG method with proper prompt templates for service discovery. Indeed, templates employed in [13] do not envisage the presence of placeholders to host inputs from users and their design is targeted mainly to instruct the LLM about the response output style. Even though the approach in [5] focuses on query clarification for improving API recommendation, suggesting five templates (called *AI units*), details about service descriptive metadata and their distinctive features are provided only at a high level of abstraction. The Knowledge Graph model for services provided by Li et al. [6] offers a conceptualisation that is limited to a textual description of the service and its URL, while prompt templates to interact with the LLM are not used. Lastly, despite the approach in [7] is rooted on service discovery, the focus is more on code generation rather than leveraging services metadata to steer the design of LLM prompts.

We close this section by citing the work of Remadi et al. [10], which emphasises the importance of data modelling as a pivotal step of a data integration pipeline, both to improve the responses of their LLM-based system and to generalise the employment of their approach to other use-cases. The intent of our work goes towards a similar direction, in the sense that, with respect to aforementioned research efforts, our LLM-based approach leverages the terminology and concepts descending from analytics scenarios and services descriptive metadata as a cornerstone to design prompt templates. Such templates are used to interact with an LLM-based system for service discovery, fostering the RAG method to enhance LLM contextual knowledge about data services and meaningful analytics pipelines.

3   A Model for Data Services and Analytics Scenarios

3.1   Motivating Example

Let us consider the perspective of an Original Equipment Manufacturer (OEM), aiming to monitor the thermal deformation (*thermal error*) of a five-axis vertical machine used for milling complex three-dimensional parts in steel, aluminium alloys, and composites. In milling machines, the thermal error is one of the most significant factors leading to a structural deformation (observed between the work-piece and the tool acting on the work-piece), influencing the accuracy of the machine tool and decreasing product quality. One of the tests apt to assess the magnitude of thermal error is the *axis-motion test*, separating the contributes of thermal displacement by assuming that each single axis shows a different behaviour and, therefore, has to be moved and tested separately. In this respect, thermal error is ascribable to the displacements $d_{i=1...5}$, where i refers either to a Cartesian or to a rotational axis, measured from the zero-displacement position. Regression models (such as MLRA or LASSO), can be employed to predict displacements $d_{i=1...5}$ as a function of temperatures gauged through sensors mounted by the OEM both internally and externally the machine. In fact, in operational settings, a direct measure of displacements is not feasible, due to the presence of the work-piece and material shavings. The validated prediction model can be employed during daily machine operation.

The data analytics procedure to accomplish displacement predictions is conceivable as a sequence of several atomic tasks (e.g., the measure of temperature through sensors, the selection of train/test data for regression models). These tasks are applicable across different smart manufacturing domains, extending beyond the discussed case study. Examples include quality control, predictive maintenance, process optimization, and supply chain analytics. For the execution of these tasks, according to an Internet of Services (IoS) paradigm, we rely on a catalog of *Atomic Data Services* (or, simply, Data Services, abridged as DS) which, depending on their functionalities, are distinguished amongst: (i) COLLECT services, used by actors within a production network to retrieve data (e.g., from sensors, data stores); (ii) DISPATCH services, to manipulate data and share it across the production network; (iii) MONITOR services, to perform analytics tasks such as prediction or data comparison. Pipelines of DS are constructed to accomplish *Analytics Scenarios* (or, simply, scenarios).

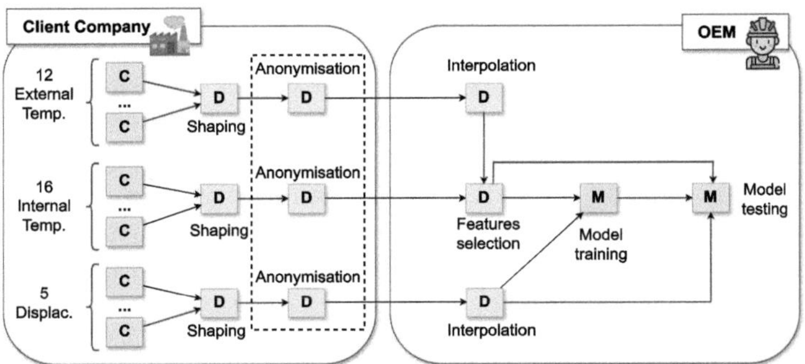

Fig. 1. Pipeline of Data Services (DS) for the example scenario (legend for service types – C: COLLECT, D: DISPATCH, M: MONITOR).

An example of analytics scenario, taken from the considered case study, is when the OEM trains regression models for thermal error prediction based on measures collected from a milling machine hosted by one of his/her clients. The model will be offered as-a-Service to the client after personalised validation on the client data. A pipeline of DS fulfilling this scenario is shown in Fig. 1 and described below.

1. *Collection of measures from the client.* Measures of temperatures are gathered from 28 sensors (12 external, 16 internal), as well as 5 measures of displacements are collected for model validation using COLLECT services. Temperatures and displacements are also referred to as variables or features. Measurements are organised by DISPATCH services into three datasets (data shaping). When preparing data at the client company, DISPATCH services to anonymise data are added before sending data to the OEM.
2. *Interpolation of measures.* Measures of internal temperatures have a higher sampling rate with respect to the other measures. Hence, external temperature and displacement measures are resampled through linear interpolation to align the timestamps, using proper DISPATCH services.
3. *Features selection.* Applied over internal and external temperature features, it aims to remove redundancy and prevent overfitting of certain regression models (e.g., MLRA). To this aim, a DISPATCH service implementing a feature selection method (e.g., hierarchical clustering, Factor Analysis) circumscribes a subset of $m < 28$ temperature features to train a regression model.
4. *Regression model training and testing.* The dataset of m temperature features is split into a train and test dataset. A MONITOR service is used to train a

regression model, thus determining the regression coefficients for each of the m temperature features apt to predict displacements values in the future. Once trained, the regression model is tested over the test dataset through another MONITOR service.

Other scenarios, implemented as pipelines of DS, can be identified in a similar way, in the same smart factory context or in different ones, as well. For example, the OEM may internally handle data preparation and analysis in a lab experiment on a machine that is physically located within the borders of the OEM, without requiring DS for anonymisation of measures collected on one of his/her clients. Furthermore, predictions made with different regression models (e.g., MLRA, LASSO) may be compared using pairs of train-test MONITOR services for each regression model plus an additional MONITOR service to compare the predictions. Finally, multiple client companies may be involved in this kind of experiments, with the aim of exploiting data gathered from similar or different milling machines and engaged in different types of manufacturing operations. All these examples of DS compositions, that represent different analytics scenarios, require IT skills to be designed and implemented. Domain experts and R&D managers, who possess the domain knowledge for creating value-added scenarios, are often hampered in their work by a lack of such IT skills.

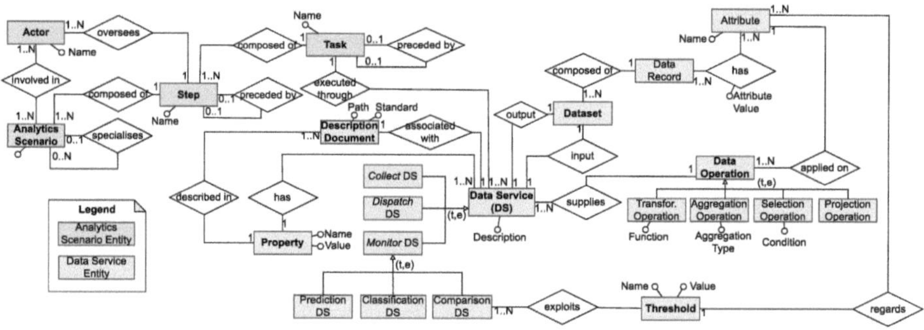

Fig. 2. Data Services and Analytics Scenarios conceptual model (E-R diagram).

3.2   Data Services and Analytics Scenarios Descriptions

In this section, we present the informative elements apt to describe Data Services and Analytics Scenarios introduced above. These elements are represented through the conceptual model illustrated in Fig. 2 as an E-R diagram. DS can be distinguished into COLLECT, DISPATCH and MONITOR services, depending on the provided functionalities. A DS receives as input and produces as output a DATASET, that is, a collection of DATA RECORDs aimed at abstracting data regardless of its type[1]. COLLECT services have an input dataset as well, in the sense that the content of the data source they are meant to read (e.g., a file, a relational database, a sensor) is abstracted through a dataset and then forwarded to other DS within an analytics scenario. For what concerns MONITOR services, they can be in turn categorised into: (i) CLASSIFICATION services, where a classifier model is trained/tested on the input dataset, producing as output a set of class labels; (ii) PREDICTION services, aimed at generating as output continuous values representing predicted values, rather than returning classification labels; (iii) COMPARISON services, where attributes values in the input dataset are compared against reference values (thresholds). Regardless of the type of DS, we model in a declarative way the data operations supplied by a service, thus resembling the primitives of a declarative language (e.g., SQL). Data operations, applied on the input dataset, allow to: (a) select a subset of the attributes in the dataset (PROJECTION); (b) filter data in the dataset (SELECTION); (c) apply an aggregation function (e.g., MIN, MAX, AVG) to the dataset (AGGREGATION); (d) apply a transformation function (e.g., format

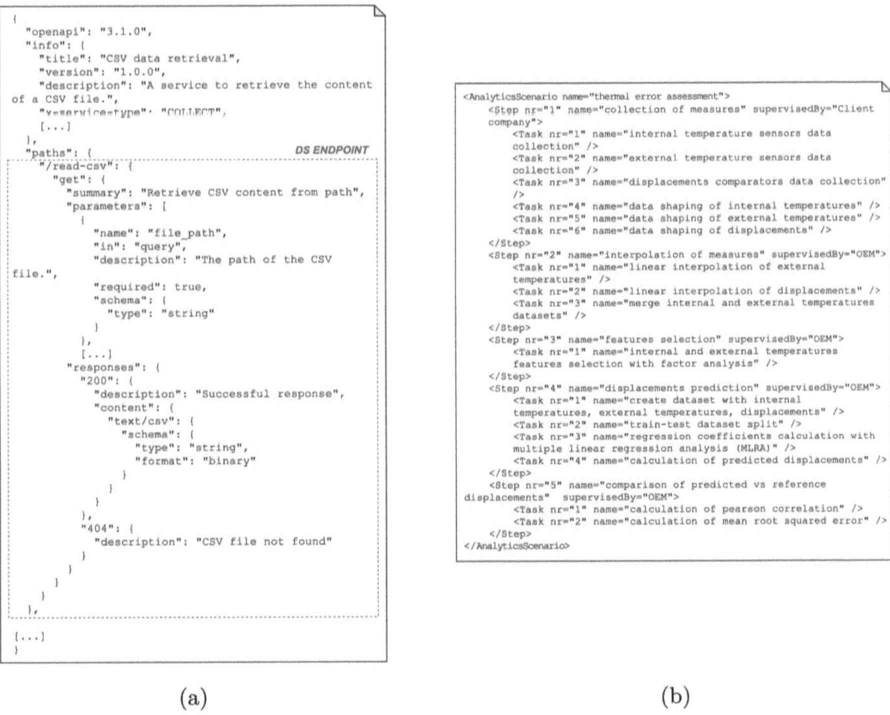

(a)   (b)

Fig. 3. (a) Excerpt of an OpenAPI document (JSON format) of a COLLECT DS (the dashed red line delimits an endpoint). (b) Example of Analytics Scenario document (XML format). The scenario is the one described in Sect. 3.1.

---

[1] For instance, a DATASET may be implemented as a Spark Dataset collection.

conversion, upper/lowercase) over the dataset (TRANSFORMATION). Lastly, each service is associated with a DOCUMENT (complying with standards such as the OpenAPI specification[2]) for the description of additional service metadata PROPERTIES (e.g., endpoints, parameters, request/response formats, authentication methods). Figure 3a reports an example of OpenAPI specification of a COLLECT DS.

Moreover, the model in Fig. 2 gathers all the entities and relationships to conceptualise an ANALYTICS SCENARIO, conceived as a pipeline of Data Services. From a higher abstraction perspective, a scenario involves a sequence of ordered STEPS, each of them supervised by an ACTOR (e.g., client company and OEM), which is in charge of executing the step. In turn, each step is composed of a series of TASKS and a task is accomplished by resorting to a DATA SERVICE. The model allows also for establishing *specialisation* relationships between pairs of analytics scenarios, to highlight that a scenario adds steps/tasks with respect to another one. Figure 3b illustrates an example of XML document representing the Analytics Scenario described in Sect. 3.1.

4   Ingredients for LLM-Based Data Service Discovery

In this section, we introduce the two pivotal elements of our LLM-based system for data service discovery: (i) *prompt templates*, designed leveraging DS and Analytics Scenarios descriptive metadata presented in the previous section, employed by domain experts and R&D managers to discover DS through the LLM and build data analytics pipelines (Sect. 4.1); (ii) the *Retrieval-Augmented Generation* (RAG) *module*, exploited to augment the contextual knowledge of the LLM with data regarding analytics scenarios and DS (Sect. 4.2).

4.1   Prompt Templates to Interact with the LLM-Based System

In the following, we present prompt templates (Fig. 4) designed relying upon the terminology and concepts related to DS and Analytics Scenarios, presented in Sect. 3. Specifically, at this stage of the research, we devised four prompt templates (namely, T1, T2, T3, and T4) pursuing different objectives and built complying with renowned organizational patterns [12]. Instances of such prompts may be chained together to assure a continuous interaction flow, where the output obtained by the LLM-based system exploiting a prompt can be used as (part of) the input for the subsequent one. This technique is denoted as *prompt chaining*[3], and it is useful to relieve the LLM at query time. In fact, if the LLM is prompted with a very detailed user's query, it may struggle answering it. In each template, *placeholders* for the user's input are delimited by curly brackets (e.g., {task}) and derive from the descriptive metadata of DS and Analytics Scenarios, except for the context placeholder. Unlike the others, context is not intended to

---

[2] https://spec.openapis.org/oas/v3.1.0.
[3] https://www.promptingguide.ai/it/techniques/prompt_chaining.

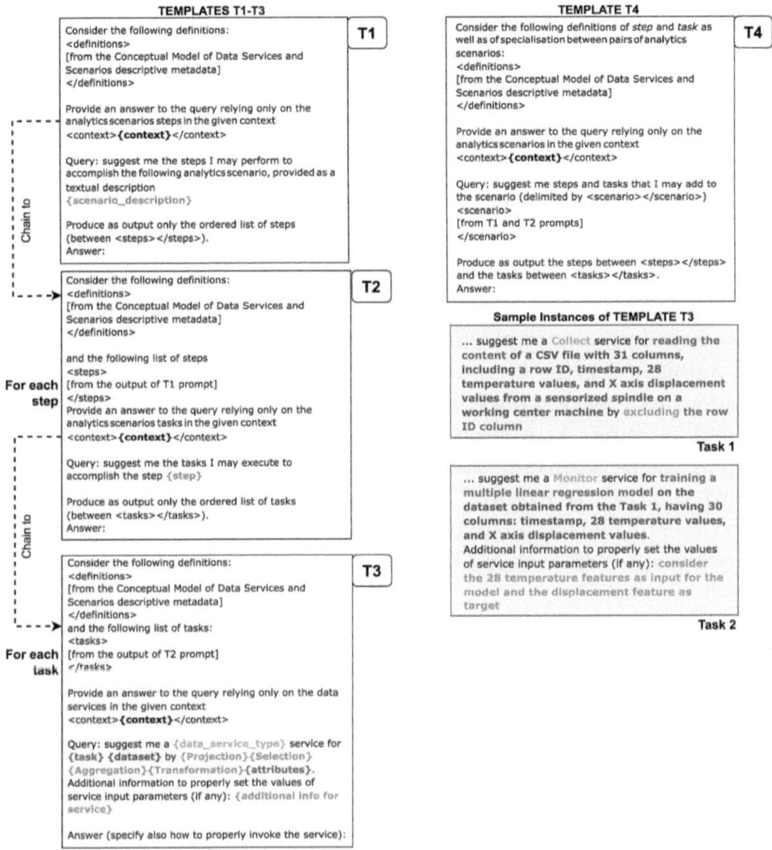

Fig. 4. Prompt templates T1, T2, T3 and T4 (left and top right). Example of instances of template T3 (bottom right).

host any textual input from the user; instead, it serves as a special reference for passing in formatted documents to the prompt. These are retrieved through the RAG module as described in Sect. 4.2. Moreover, *tags* (e.g., `<steps></steps>`) are used within templates to mark relevant text portions that have to be considered by the LLM during the inference process (e.g., definitions or text used to ensure prompt chaining) and to format the response.

Template-Based LLM Interaction Strategies. Prompt templates can be employed to pursue different interaction strategies. At the moment, as anticipated at the beginning of this section, templates and interaction strategies are targeted to domain experts and R&D managers.

1. The first strategy is aimed at supporting users without a clear idea of the structure of the Analytics Scenario (in terms of its inner organisation in steps and tasks), thus expecting a proactive support from the LLM-based system

in both structuring the scenario and finding the DS. In this case, starting from the textual description of an Analytics Scenario, the template T1 is used to obtain a list of the steps to achieve the goal of the scenario. Then the user uses the template T2 for obtaining the tasks to accomplish each step. Lastly, using the template T3 for each task, the user asks for DS suggestion to implement the task.

2. The second strategy is aimed at supporting users possessing a clear idea of the structure of the Analytics Scenario, the order of the steps to perform and, for each step, the tasks to be accomplished. In this respect, as the structure of the scenario has been already defined, the user may interact with the LLM-based system exploiting directly the template T3, possibly specifying the required service type to narrow down the search space through the placeholder `data_service_type` and the data operations, complying with the chosen service type. As a result, the user will be able to discover candidate DS for addressing a specific task.

3. The third strategy is fostered when user's goal is limited to structuring a scenario. As a result, he/she may resort to templates T1-T2 only, while leaving at a later time the discovering of DS apt to fulfil the tasks of the steps of the scenario by using T3.

4. The fourth strategy assumes that the user starts the interaction with the LLM-based system from an already structured scenario (e.g., obtained using T1 and T2 templates) passed as input to the template T4 (between <*scenario*><*/scenario*> tags). The goal of this interaction strategy is to leverage the contextual knowledge provided through the RAG module and the definition of specialisation between scenarios to suggest the user with additional steps/tasks to enrich the given input scenario.

These strategies are particularly valuable when user inputs are expressed in unstructured or partially specified natural language, a common situation when domain experts lack familiarity with technical service specifications.

4.2 Retrieval-Augmented Generation Module

The proposed LLM-based system for DS discovery leverages the Retrieval-Augmented Generation (RAG) module [4] to enhance an LLM with contextual data, thereby improving response coherence and relevance to users' queries. In our case, contextual data has a two-fold nature, as it regards: (i) a catalog of DS, described according to the OpenAPI specification standard, which enables the inclusion of descriptive metadata based on the DS model; (ii) descriptions of available Analytics Scenarios, according to the model. Examples of the two aforementioned contextual data are available at [1]. From a higher viewpoint, RAG is composed of three main macro-phases: (a) *indexing*, gathering the operations required for ingesting data from external data sources (i.e., the so-called contextual data), applying a chunking strategy (to ensure efficient storage and faster retrieval), and an indexing strategy for chunked data, to be stored into a vector database as numeric vectors (exploiting an *embedding model*); (b) *retrieval*, which takes the user's textual query and retrieves the relevant data chunks from the vector database using the query; (c) *generation*, wherein a prompt containing the original user's query and contextual knowledge from the vector database is processed by the LLM to provide an answer to the user.

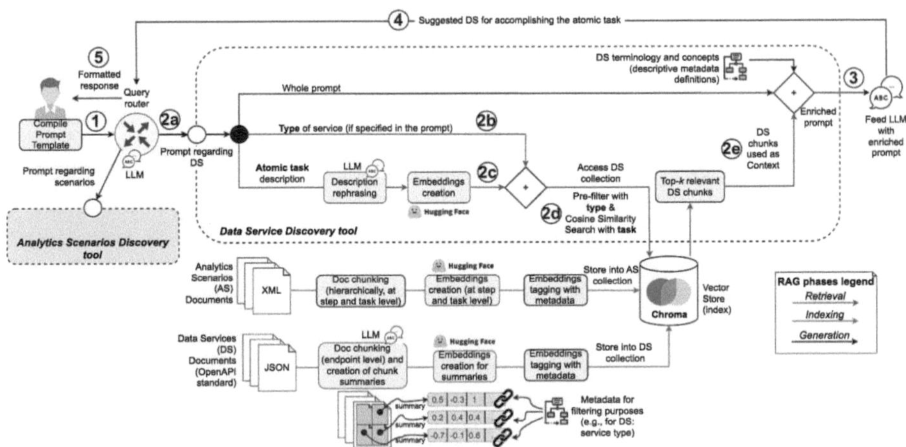

Fig. 5. Overview of Retrieval-Augmented Generation (RAG) module in the LLM-based system (details of the DS discovery process with prompt template T3).

RAG Module Implementation in the LLM-Based System. The architecture implementing the RAG module employed in the LLM-based system for DS discovery is illustrated in Fig. 5. The whole LLM-based system has been implemented relying on LangChain[4], a Python framework for developing LLM-based applications. The source code has been hosted on two Google Colab notebooks available at [1], which have been used to: (i) run the core modules of the LLM (which in our case is the Open Source *granite3-dense-8B*), exploiting the computational resources (in terms of GPUs) offered by the Google Cloud Platform; (ii) implement the RAG module over a dataset of OpenAPI documents of the catalog of DS (serialised in JSON, see example in Fig. 3a) and description of analytics scenarios (serialised in XML, see example in Fig. 3b) and to submit queries to the LLM. Communication between the two notebooks has been established through ngrok tunnelling[5]. Regarding the vector database employed in the Retrieval phase we fostered ChromaDB[6], an Open Source vector database designed for storing and retrieving vector embeddings (generated with the *mixedbread-ai/mxbai-embed-large-v1*[7] model, available within the Hugging-Face platform hub). Within ChromaDB, *collections* serve as the primary organisational unit to group embeddings and associated metadata. Particularly, two

---

different collections have been employed to store the embeddings associated with DS and Analytics Scenarios. User's requests are routed to two LangChain *tools* assisting the discovery process, one dedicated to DS and another to scenarios (an LLM-based routing agent determines which tool to invoke, after inspecting the prompt).

Example of RAG-Based Discovery Workflow. Fig. 5 highlights, for clarity purposes, only the workflow regarding the DS discovery process (which envisages the utilisation of prompt template T3). The information specified by the user in the placeholders of template T3 between curly brackets are employed either during the Retrieval or in the Generation phase of RAG. In the Retrieval phase, the content of {`data_service_type`}, if specified, is used as a filtering key to restrict the cosine similarity search with a rephrased version of {`task`} only over a subset of DS documents chunks. Indeed, ChromaDB, similarly to other vector databases, allows to tag with metadata (e.g., the service type) the vector embeddings, which can be leveraged to pre-filter embeddings, before calculating cosine similarity. Apart from the reasons above, metadata is useful also to tag embeddings of DS chunks with a reference to the DS OpenAPI document they have been generated from. In the Generation phase, the retrieved DS documents chunks are included as part of the prompt in the {`context`} placeholder, and the whole prompt is passed as input to the LLM for the inference process, thus suggesting to the user the DS to accomplish the atomic task (along with the details for DS invocation).

5   Preliminary Evaluation

We conducted both a *quantitative* and a *qualitative* evaluation of the LLM-based system. The *quantitative* evaluation focuses on assessing the performance of the Retrieval (Sect. 5.1) and Generation (Sect. 5.2) phases of the RAG with a dataset D_{eval} composed of: (a) 30 questions related to atomic tasks and Analytics Scenarios (to be submitted to the LLM-based system filling the templates presented in Sect. 4.1); (b) the answer provided by the LLM-based system for each question; (c) the contexts supporting each question (documents chunks retrieved from the vector database and used by the LLM-based system during the inference process to produce the answer returned to the user); (d) the ground truth, the latter corresponding to the expected answer to each question (e.g., the DS to fulfil the atomic task). The content of the dataset reflects the analytical tasks and scenarios accomplished in the real-world smart manufacturing case study presented in Sect. 3. Regarding the *qualitative* evaluation (Sect. 5.3), it aims at assessing the output of the LLM-based system when submitting instances of the prompt templates T1 to T4, to ascertain the effectiveness of the templates to accomplish the interaction strategies presented in Sect. 4.1.

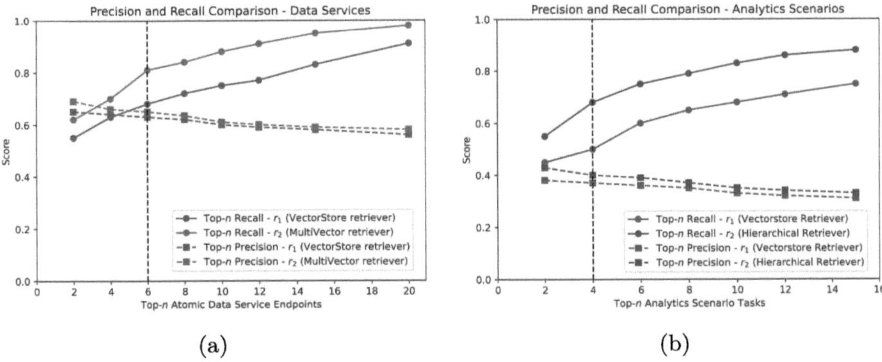

Fig. 6. Average top-n precision and top-n recall for the Retrieval phase of RAG (for DS endpoints retrieval and Analytics Scenarios tasks retrieval) with different types of retriever interfaces.

Table 1. Average values for Faithfulness and Factual Correctness metrics in the quantitative evaluation of the Generation phase of RAG (using the *mixedbread-ai/mxbai-embed-large-v1* embedding model, dimension = 1024).

Search Target	Usage of Templates	Usage of Descriptive Metadata Definitions	granite3–dense–8B Faithf.	Fact. Corr.	Gemma2–27B Faithf.	Fact. Corr.
Data Service	Yes	Yes	0.8901	0.8765	0.9011	0.8867
	No	Yes	0.4892	0.4628	0.5021	0.4781
	Yes	No	0.8123	0.7901	0.8221	0.8023
	No	No	0.4561	0.3895	0.4635	0.3935
Scenarios	Yes	Yes	0.9054	0.8978	0.9162	0.9085
	No	Yes	0.3678	0.3195	0.3735	0.3261
	Yes	No	0.8057	0.7604	0.8129	0.7652
	No	No	0.3021	0.2496	0.3089	0.2531

5.1   Quantitative Evaluation of the Retrieval Phase of RAG

We report the assessment of the effectiveness of the Retrieval phase of RAG constituted by the ChromaDB vector database, as mentioned in Sect. 4.2. The database indexes, in two different collections, the chunks of both the OpenAPI Documents of DS and the Analytics Scenarios description documents. Regarding OpenAPI DS documents, they are chunked at the endpoint level (which corresponds to a specific path that defines how clients may interact with the DS, including supported HTTP methods and responses, see example in Fig. 3a), for the advantages witnessed by this strategy as emphasized in [8]. Instead, regarding analytics scenarios documents, they are chunked firstly at the step level and then at the task level, thus fostering a so-called hierarchical chunking strategy.

As an example, we will focus on the description of the retrieval of DS endpoints using the atomic task description as a query for the vector database. The assessment of the Retrieval phase of RAG has been conducted by calculating the two metrics of top-n precision and top-n recall, as they are the most widely used metrics for the assessment of retrieval systems. Top-n precision metric has been obtained by considering the number of relevant DS endpoints retrieved within the top n results, divided by n, whereas the top-n recall metric has been calculated by dividing the number of relevant DS endpoints among the top n retrieved by the total number of relevant DS endpoints. Figure 6a reports the top-n precision and recall for an increasing maximum number n of DS endpoints retrieved from the vector database (results are averaged over 30 atomic tasks included in the dataset D_{eval}). The metrics have been calculated fostering two different configurations for handling indexing and retrieval of DS endpoints: (i) using the *VectorStore* retriever, a baseline retrieval interface available in the LangChain framework (r_1 in Fig. 6a); (ii) using a *MultiVector* retriever[8], which employs LLM-generated textual summaries of DS endpoints as a way to retrieve original DS endpoints; in this configuration, DS endpoints summaries are embedded and indexed in the vector database in lieu of DS endpoints (r_2 in Fig. 6a). In a similar vein, regarding the retrieval of Analytics Scenarios tasks, Fig. 6b represents top-n precision and top-n recall scores where r_2 is a custom retriever[9] (named *Hierarchical* retriever) which exploits the hierarchical index built upon the chunks of steps and tasks (as introduced above).

Considerations. In Fig. 6, the average top-n recall increases as long as the value of n increases and, for the same value of n, the retrieval strategy r_2 achieves a higher recall with respect to r_1. In particular, the gap in average top-n recall between r_1 and r_2 starts being more pronounced when $n \geq 6$ (for DS) and when $n \geq 4$ (for Analytics Scenarios). These evidences will be further investigated to properly set the k parameter of the LangChain interface for top-k retrieval from the vector database (Fig. 5), taking into account the maximum context length of the LLM and the target of retrieval (i.e., DS or Analytics Scenarios). Hence, indexing summaries of DS endpoints enables a more effective retrieval of relevant DS endpoints (higher top-n recall) as well as when fostering a hierarchical indexing of chunks of steps/tasks. The choice of assessing top-n precision and recall for DS endpoints retrieval in the range $[2, 20]$ was taken considering the total number of DS endpoints present in the vector database (i.e., 40), which are related to the case study presented in Sect. 3. Similar considerations hold also for Analytics Scenarios. We remark that advanced strategies, such as the adoption of custom re-rankers, were not included. The latter will be considered in future research effort, where they will be tested on top of embedding models with different vector size, to further complete and consolidate the experimentation.

5.2   Quantitative Evaluation of the Generation Phase of RAG

The quantitative evaluation of the Generation phase of RAG has been conducted through the so-called *LLM-as-judge evaluation* strategy [14]. This strategy has

---

[8] https://python.langchain.com/docs/how_to/multi_vector/.
[9] https://python.langchain.com/docs/how_to/custom_retriever/.

been recently proposed to enhance the scalability and efficiency of the evaluation process of the output of an LLM (referred to as *evaluated LLM*), adopting an *evaluator LLM* (different from the evaluated one and typically offering superior inference performance), whose aim is to score the output of the evaluated LLM. In these experiments, we evaluated two LLMs (that is *granite3–dense–8B* and *Gemma2–27B*), whereas the evaluator LLM has been *LLama3.1–70B*. All the aforementioned LLMs are Open Source and available within the Ollama models library[10]. The evaluated LLMs are two representatives from the ones having a small (8B) and medium number of parameters (27B). Noteworthy, for the DS and scenarios discovery tasks discussed in this paper, our aim is to: (i) evaluate the impact of using LLMs with different inference capabilities; (ii) determine the extent to which a model with a larger number of parameters (demanding, in exchange, a larger amount of computational resources) delivers enhanced inference performance. The quantitative assessment of the Generation phase has been rooted on two different metrics included in Ragas[11], a Python framework for performance assessment of LLM-based systems fostering RAG: *faithfulness* and *factual correctness*. In particular, *faithfulness* measures the factual consistency of the generated answer against a given context (to identify whether hallucinations occurred), whereas *factual correctness* measures the extent to which the claims in the generated response align with the claims in the ground truth. Both the metrics assume a value in the range $(0, 1)$, the higher the better.

Considerations. The quantitative evaluation of the Generation phase on the dataset D_{eval} provided satisfactory average values for faithfulness and factual correctness with both the two evaluated LLMs. Table 1 reports an overview of average metrics values (using the MultiVector retriever for DS and the Hierarchical retriever for Analytics Scenarios in the Retrieval step). As evidenced from Table 1, when the query submitted to the LLM is formulated adhering to a template, and is enriched with DS and scenarios descriptive metadata definitions (Sect. 3), inserted in the incipit of the prompt, there is an improvement in both the metrics, which is slightly higher for the LLM with 27B parameters. Hence, to contain the usage of computational resources, we opted for *granite3–dense–8B* in the architecture of the LLM-based system (Fig. 5).

5.3   Qualitative Evaluation with the Proposed Prompt Templates

By exploiting prompt templates presented in Sect. 4.1, we performed a qualitative evaluation, thus assessing whether the response obtained from the LLM-based system through an instance of a prompt template fulfils the goal of the request issued by the user. In particular, the qualitative evaluation has been carried out by recruiting a group of seven users from the application context presented in Sect. 3, knowledgeable of LLMs and prompts usage, having the skills of domain experts and R&D managers. When submitting the instances of

---

[10] https://ollama.com/library.
[11] https://docs.ragas.io/en/stable/.

the prompt templates to the LLM-based system, the so-called *In-Context Learning* (ICL) prompt engineering method has been fostered, which strives to control LLM behaviour and the response quality by providing, within the prompt submitted to the LLM, proper demonstrations (e.g., regarding DS to accomplish one or more tasks of a scenario). To this aim, we prepared three groups of prompts and then asked the aforementioned users to submit such prompts to the LLM-based system. The three groups of prompts correspond in turn to three different variants of ICL prompting strategies: (i) *zero-shot* (tested for prompts derived from the templates T1-T2-T3 in Fig. 4), in which no examples are provided to the LLM when submitting the textual prompt; (ii) *one-shot* (tested for prompts derived from the templates T3-T4 in Fig. 4), in which a single DS example is included in the prompt; (iii) *Chain-of-Thought* (tested for prompts derived from the templates T1-T2-T4 in Fig. 4), that essentially involves providing the description of the reasoning steps in the prompt to be submitted to the LLM. The interested reader can find a comprehensive definition and supporting examples for ICL in [11]. For the qualitative evaluation, resembling an ablation study, two different configurations for the LLM-based system have been tested: (i) a full description of OpenAPI documents for DS; (ii) a partial description of OpenAPI documents for DS, where we removed meaningful names (e.g., `summary` and `description` fields).

Considerations. We summarise in the following the outcome of the qualitative evaluation, after collecting and analysing the transcript of the conversations of the users with the LLM-based system. An excerpt of representative conversations with the LLM-based system have been reported in [1].

1. Prompting the LLM-based system with a query not complying with a prompt template (e.g., in the case of template T3, proceeding with a text-free search of DS) required to perform, on average, three interactions to obtain relevant DS for a task (despite relying on a full description of OpenAPI documents).
2. With a full description of OpenAPI documents, zero-shot ICL was already capable of generating the list of steps/tasks of a scenario (when fostering T1 and T2 templates) and of identifying relevant DS for a task (when using template T3).
3. Regardless of the full/partial description of OpenAPI documents for DS, when a prompt built upon templates T1-T2-T3 was provided in bulk (i.e., not leveraging prompt chaining), the LLM spontaneously tried to suggest a pipeline of DS for executing the whole scenario (both for steps and related tasks). However, sometimes the LLM skipped to explicitly associate a task to the invocation of a DS (mainly, DISPATCH DS to perform some intermediate steps of data preparation).
4. Using a partial description of OpenAPI documents, experiments with the template T3 evidenced slight hallucinations in the output of the LLM (e.g., it suggested the name of non-existent services), thus requiring additional interactions to reach the correct answer.

5. Using the template T4, the LLM-based system was capable of suggesting additional steps/tasks to enrich the scenario passed as input through the prompt in at most two-shot.

6 Concluding Remarks

In this paper, we presented a cooperative approach to data service discovery in the Internet of Production. At the core of our contribution is the design of prompting strategies tailored to the interaction needs of domain experts and R&D managers, and grounded in a conceptual model of data services and analytics scenarios. These strategies empower users to incrementally define and refine analytics pipelines through structured, LLM-assisted, dialogues. We demonstrated how these prompting strategies can be effectively integrated with a Retrieval-Augmented Generation (RAG) to enrich LLM prompts with relevant contextual knowledge retrieved from a structured catalog of data services and analytics scenarios. This integration ensures that LLM outputs remain accurate, grounded, and tailored to the user's intent. To validate our approach, we implemented the full system using open-source technologies and conducted an extensive evaluation in a real-world smart manufacturing domain. Our experiments included: (a) a quantitative assessment of the Retrieval and Generation phases using top-n precision, top-n recall, faithfulness, and factual correctness metrics and (b) a qualitative user study, showing that the prompting strategies facilitate cooperative interaction and support effective service discovery even for non-technical users.

Despite the promising results of our current LLM-based system, several limitations remain. For instance, the current quantitative evaluation primarily focuses on the overall effectiveness of the RAG-integrated system, without isolating the contribution of each prompting strategy and architectural module. Additionally, hallucinations were observed in cases of partial metadata, highlighting a need for a more systematic assessment of model behaviour under incomplete information. Introducing more advanced semantics into Analytics Scenarios also poses non-trivial challenges. For example, replicating the semantics of the UML extension relationship requires a thorough understanding of domain-specific constraints and optional behaviours. Capturing these details and guiding the LLM to recognize them reliably will demand careful prompt design and integration of domain knowledge. As a future research effort, we plan to address these limitations by exploring additional relationships between Analytics Scenarios, extending them beyond the current notion of specialization. Inspired by well-established modelling constructs such as UML Use Case relationships, which capture inclusion and extension patterns[12], we aim to investigate how the proposed LLM-based system can assist users in identifying and reasoning over such scenario relationships. Furthermore, future work will aim to

---

[12] https://www.uml-diagrams.org/use-case.html.

isolate and compare the contribution of each prompting strategy and architectural module, providing a more fine-grained understanding of their individual impact on system performance, and to quantify hallucination effects to assess trade-offs between model size, response quality, and computational cost.

Acknowledgements. This study was carried out within the MICS (Made in Italy – Circular and Sustainable) Extended Partnership and received funding from Next-GenerationEU (Italian PNRR – M4 C2, Invest 1.3 – D.D. 1551.11–10-2022, PE00000004).

References

1. Repository with y material for CoopIS (2025). https://tinyurl.com/llm-ds-coopis
2. Aiello, M., Georgievski, I.: Service composition in the ChatGPT era. SOCA **17**(4), 233–238 (2023)
3. Bianchini, D., Garda, M., Melchiori, M., Rula, A.: LLM-driven data service discovery in the internet of production. In: 2025 IEEE 49th Annual Computers, Software, and Applications Conference (COMPSAC). pp. 517–522. IEEE (2025)
4. Gao, Y., et al.: Retrieval-Augmented Generation for Large Language Models: A Survey. arXiv preprint arXiv:2312.10997 (2023)
5. Huang, Q., et al.: Let's chat to find the APIs: connecting human, LLM and knowledge graph through AI chain. In: 2023 38th IEEE/ACM International Conference on Automated Software Engineering (ASE). pp. 471–483 (2023)
6. Li, Y., Starly, B.: Building a knowledge graph to enrich ChatGPT responses in manufacturing service discovery. J. Ind. Inf. Int. **40**, p. 100612 (2024)
7. Monti, F., Leotta, F., Mangler, J., Mecella, M., Rinderle-Ma, S.: NL2ProcessOps: Towards LLM-Guided Code Generation for Process Execution. In: International Conference on Business Process Management. pp. 127–143 (2024)
8. Pesl, R.D., Mathew, J.G., Mecella, M., Aiello, M.: Advanced System Integration: Analyzing OpenAPI Chunking for Retrieval-Augmented Generation. In: Krogstie, J., Rinderle-Ma, S., Kappel, G., Proper, H.A. (eds) Advanced Information Systems Engineering. CAiSE 2025. Lecture Notes in Computer Science, vol 15702. Springer, Cham. pp. 130–148 (2025). https://doi.org/10.1007/978-3-031-94571-7_8
9. Raptis, T.P., Passarella, A., Conti, M.: Data management in industry 4.0: state of the art and open challenges. IEEE Access. **7**, 97052–97093 (2019)
10. Remadi, A., El Hage, K., Hobeika, Y., Bugiotti, F.: To prompt or not to prompt: Navigating the use of Large Language Models for integrating and modeling heterogeneous data. Data & Knowledge Engineering. p. 102313 (2024)
11. Sahoo, P., Singh, A.K., Saha, S., Jain, V., Mondal, S., Chadha, A.: A Systematic Survey of Prompt Engineering in Large Language Models: Techniques and Applications. arXiv:2402.07927 (2024)
12. White, J., et al.: A Prompt Pattern Catalog to Enhance Prompt Engineering with ChatGPT. arXiv preprint arXiv:2302.11382 (2023)
13. Zeng, Z., et al.: FlowMind: Automatic Workflow Generation with LLMs. In: Proceedings of the Fourth ACM International Conference on AI in Finance. pp. 73–81 (2023)
14. Zheng, L., et al.: Judging LLM-as-a-Judge with MT-Bench and Chatbot Arena. Adv. Neu. Inf. Processing Sys. **36**, 46595-46623 (2024)

Process Conformance, Integrity and Compliance

Out of Babylon: Object-Centric Conformance Checking on Graph-Based Abstractions

Erik Wrede[1]([✉]), Jan Niklas van Detten[1,3], Lukas Liss[1],
and Sander J. J. Leemans[1,2]

[1] RWTH Aachen University, Aachen, Germany
erikwrede2@gmail.com
[2] Fraunhofer FIT, Munich, Germany
[3] Celonis, Munich, Germany

Abstract. Process mining employs data-driven techniques to analyse and optimise business processes. An important step in such an analysis is to identify and quantify deviations between the observed and modelled behaviour of a business process using conformance checking techniques. While traditional conformance checking approaches utilise process models that primarily focus on events, recently proposed approaches also consider the involvement of business objects. Those object-centric process models introduce new behavioural deviations due to the involvement of objects in events like missing objects in the execution of an event. However, existing object-centric conformance checking techniques do not precisely detect all these deviations and can only be applied to specific object-centric modelling formalisms. In this paper, we introduce a novel formalism-agnostic object-centric conformance checking approach that presents a common denominator for many object-centric modelling formalisms, enabling comparable conformance checking results. We evaluate our approach on a public object-centric log by demonstrating its ability to detect deviations across multiple modelling formalisms.

Keywords: Process Mining · Conformance Checking · Object-Centric

1 Introduction

Process mining provides techniques to produce data-driven insights into business processes of organisations. These analysis techniques utilize event logs extracted from standard enterprise IT systems, which contain the observed behaviour for individual process executions, called cases [1].

Traditionally, each case describes an isolated business object, like an IT incident. However, business objects in real-life processes are often related to each other. An incident, for example, may require the approval by an employee to be resolved. Process mining techniques that consider cases with multiple business objects are called object-centric. These object-centric process mining techniques

C. Cappiello et al. (Eds.): CoopIS 2025, LNCS 15535, pp. 183–201, 2026.
https://doi.org/10.1007/978-3-032-15538-2_11

analyse the dependencies between objects to generate more realistic insights than traditional event-centric approaches [2].

An important step in that analysis is constructing a process model that describes the observed behaviour. Discovery techniques automatically construct such models from object-centric logs. Alternatively, models can be constructed manually. For that purpose, many object-centric modelling formalisms exist, such as object-centric Petri nets [3], object-centric process trees [8], or object-centric Petri nets with identifiers [12], that all differ in their expressiveness [12]. Substantial differences between these formalisms can, for example, be found in the dynamic generation of objects and the potential synchronisation of objects based on their identity.

Often, the modelled behaviour does not exactly match the behaviour observed in the log. Hence, selecting a suitable process model for further analysis requires understanding how its behaviour differs from the log. Conformance checking techniques are used to identify behavioural deviations between the model and the log and quantify their severity [1].

Such deviations in object-centric models can become increasingly complex, due to the interactions of multiple objects in events. Existing object-centric conformance checking techniques are either insensitive to some deviation types, or do not pinpoint the deviating objects correctly. This way, common object-centric deviations such as missing objects or mismatched object identities are frequently disregarded or hidden inside a generic measure for the deviation severity.

Moreover, existing object-centric conformance checking techniques are specific to individual modelling formalisms, each supporting different levels of expressiveness. A translation between these formalisms for use in conformance checking is not always possible. For example, no current approach can handle both conformance checking of a case on arbitrary object sets as well as a single fixed object set. As a result, existing approaches cannot be used for a cross-formalism comparison between models if they make use of formalism-specific constructs.

In this paper, we propose a novel graph-based conformance checking technique for object-centric process models and event logs. For this purpose, we introduce an abstraction layer for object-centric modelling formalisms called the object-centric state space. Based on this abstraction layer, we formulate the conformance checking problem independent of the utilized modelling formalism. Within the abstraction layer, we are able to detect various types of deviations more precisely than previous techniques. We evaluate our approach on a public object-centric event log and show its compatibility with commonly used modelling formalisms that differ in expressiveness. Our evaluation finds our approach to detect deviations disregarded by existing techniques as they arise from the expressiveness difference across multiple formalisms. However, similar to existing techniques, our approach is limited by the size of the input logs due to its computational complexity.

The paper is organized as follows. Section 2 formalizes object-centric event logs and corresponding modelling formalisms. Section 3 introduces the formalism-independent abstraction layer of an object-centric state space. Subsequently, Sect. 4, describes the conformance checking approach based on that state space. Section 5 evaluates our approach. Section 6 puts our approach in relation to existing work. Finally, Sect. 7 summarizes the paper and future research.

2   Preliminaries

In this section, we introduce object-centric event logs, corresponding graph representations, and modelling formalisms. We use $\{...\}$ to denote sets, $\langle...\rangle$ to denote sequences, and $\mathcal{P}(\{...\})$ to specify a powerset.

2.1   Object-Centric Event Logs

Object-centric event logs contain sets of events, objects and the relations between the two. Each event describes the execution of an activity by a set of business objects. We write $\mathbb{U}_{ev}$, $\mathbb{U}_{act}$, $\mathbb{U}_{obj}$ and $\mathbb{U}_{type}$ for the universe of events, activities, objects and object types respectively. The function $\omega : \mathbb{U}_{obj} \rightarrow \mathbb{U}_{type}$ maps each object to its type, while $\alpha : \mathbb{U}_{ev} \rightarrow \mathbb{U}_{act}$ maps an event to its activity. All events have a timestamp $t(e)$.

Definition 1 (Object-Centric Event Log). *An object-centric event log is a tuple $(\Sigma, \Theta, E2O)$ where $\Sigma \subseteq \mathbb{U}_{ev}$ is a set of events, $\Theta \subseteq \mathbb{U}_{obj}$ is a set of objects and $E2O \subseteq \Sigma \times \Theta$ contains the involvement of each object with events. time is a function mapping each event to a timestamp.*

Object-centric event logs can also be interpreted as labelled graphs. For this purpose, events and objects are represented as nodes. The involvement of an object in the event execution is modelled using edges. Event nodes are labelled with their activity, and object nodes with their object type. Edge labels are inferred from the types and activities of the event and object nodes they connect. $\mathbb{U}_{\lambda}$ is the universe of all labels. We refer to edges and nodes in a graph as elements.

Definition 2 (Log Graph). *A log graph for an object-centric event log $L = (\Sigma, \Theta, E2O)$ is a tuple (N, E, λ) with a set of nodes $N = \{\bullet_e \mid e \in \Sigma\} \cup \{\bullet_o \mid o \in \Theta\}$, a set of directed edges between them $E = \{(\bullet_e, \bullet_o) \mid (e, o) \in E2O\}$ and a labelling function $\lambda : N \cup E \rightarrow \mathbb{U}_{\lambda}$ with $\lambda(\bullet_e) = \alpha(e) \forall_{e \in \Sigma} \wedge \lambda(\bullet_o) = \omega(o) \forall_{o \in \Theta} \wedge \lambda((\bullet_x, \bullet_y)) = (\lambda(\bullet_x), \lambda(\bullet_y))$*

Object-centric event logs can be divided into multiple *cases*, representing individual process executions. Each case contains a subset of objects, events, and the corresponding relations between them. Considering the graph representation of object-centric event logs, a case is a subgraph of a log.

Definition 3 (Case Graph). *For a given log graph $G_L = (N, E, \lambda)$ a case graph is a tuple (N', E', λ) with a subset of nodes $N' \subseteq N$ and the relations between them $E' = E \cap (N' \times N')$. The labelling λ of the nodes is preserved.*

Table 1. Object-centric example log for incident management. Events denoted as activities with the associated objects in the order of their timestamp.

$$\langle\, \texttt{Create}\,\{i_1, e_1\}, \quad \texttt{Create}\,\{i_2, e_3\}, \quad \texttt{Reopen}\,\{i_1\}, \quad \texttt{Resolve}\,\{i_1, e_2\},$$
$$\texttt{Approve}\,\{i_2, e_3\}, \texttt{Approve}\,\{i_1\}, \quad \texttt{Resolve}\,\{i_2, e_3\}, \texttt{Resolve}\,\{i_1, e_2\}\,\rangle$$

A function that maps an object-centric log graph onto a set of case graphs is called a case notion. Various case notions exist, each optimising different quality criteria [4,9].

The events in case graphs can be ordered by their timestamp in the original log. We add corresponding edges between events to represent that order in the graph representation.

Definition 4 (Ordered Case Graph). *An ordered case graph* (N, E, λ) *has edges for the total order between events, i.e.* $\forall_{i,j\in\Sigma} : (t(i) < t(j) \wedge \nexists_{k\in\Sigma} : t(i) < t(k) < t(j)) \implies (\bullet_i, \bullet_j) \in E.$

From now on, we only consider ordered case graphs. Table 1 shows an example object-centric event log with the corresponding log graph in Fig. 1. It describes the handling of incident (i) by employees (e). A case notion based on connected components [4], results in two cases for that log.

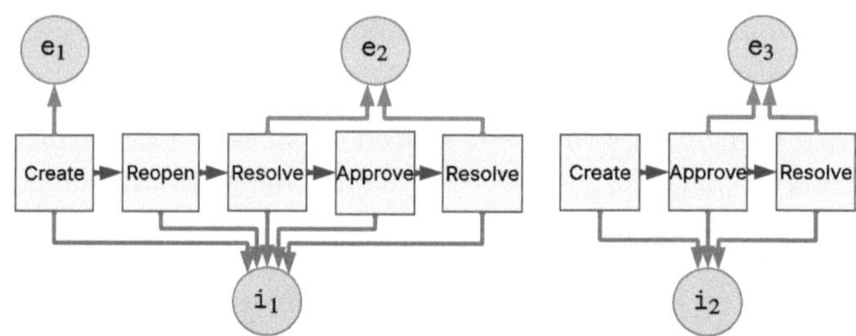

Fig. 1. Two ordered case graphs (left & right) for the log in Table 1.

2.2   Object-Centric Petri Nets

Object-centric Petri nets [3] are bipartite directed graphs, containing two types of nodes: places and transitions. The places of these nets can hold a number of conceptual tokens to represent the current state of each object. Transitions can be used to move these tokens through the places of the net, providing a state-based replay mechanic. Variable arcs indicate the potential involvement of multiple objects of the same type.

Definition 5 (Object-Centric Petri Net). *An object-centric Petri net is a tuple $(P, T, F, l, pt, F_{var})$ with a set of places P, a set of transitions T and a set of directed arcs $F \subseteq (P \times T) \cup (T \times P)$. The labelling function $l : T \to \mathbb{U}_{act} \cup \{\tau\}$ assigns each transition an activity label or the invisible character τ. The function $pt : P \to \mathbb{U}_{type}$ assigns an object type to each place and $F_{var} \subseteq F$ denotes the subset of variable arcs.*

The state of these nets is denoted in a marking $M : P \times \mathbb{U}_{obj}$ that tracks the number of tokens per object and place. Objects can only reside in places of their corresponding type:

$$\forall_{p \in P, o \in \mathbb{U}_{obj}} : M(p, o) > 0 \implies \omega(o) = pt(p)$$

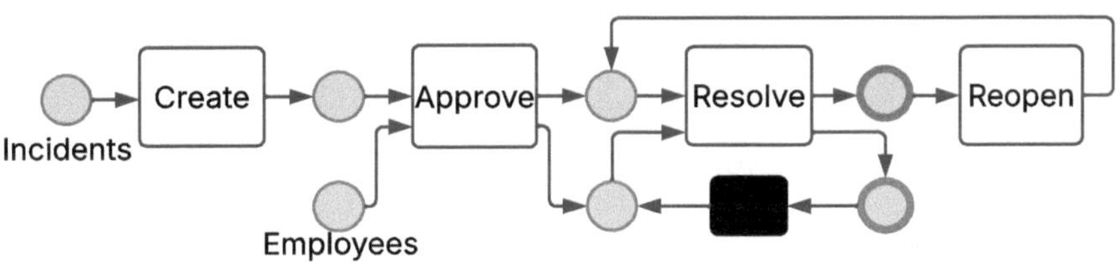

Fig. 2. Object-centric Petri net for the incident management process.

A transition t can be *enabled* in a marking M by an object set $O \subseteq \mathbb{U}_{obj}$. For this purpose, objects from the types of all input places of the transition need to be available (1). Multiple objects of the same type are only allowed if the places of that type are connected by a variable arc (2). Furthermore, all objects in the object set need to actually be available in the respective input places of the matching type (3).

$$(p, t) \in F \iff \exists o \in O : \omega(o) = pt(p) \tag{1}$$

$$(p, t) \in F \setminus F_{var} \implies |\{o \in O \mid \omega(o) = pt(p)\}| = 1 \tag{2}$$

$$o \in O \wedge (p, t) \in F \wedge pt(p) = \omega(o) \implies M(p, o) > 0 \tag{3}$$

A transition t enabled by O can be fired to transfer tokens from the input to output places. This results in the marking:

$$M'(p, o) = M(p, o) - |\{(p, t) \in F\}| + |\{(t, p) \in F\}|$$

We write $M \to^{O,t} M'$ for firing an enabled transition t with the object set O that leads from M to M'. We write $M \to^{O_1, t_1} \ldots \to^{O_n, t_n} M'$ for a firing a sequence of transitions $t_1 \ldots t_n$ with the corresponding object sets $O_1 \ldots O_n$. Given an initial (M_i) and final marking (M_f), an object-centric Petri net defines a language of event sequences:

$$\{\langle (l(t_1), O_1), \ldots, (l(t_n), O_n) \mid l(t_i) \neq \tau \rangle \mid M_i \to^{t_1, O_1} \ldots \to^{t_n, O_n} M_f\}$$

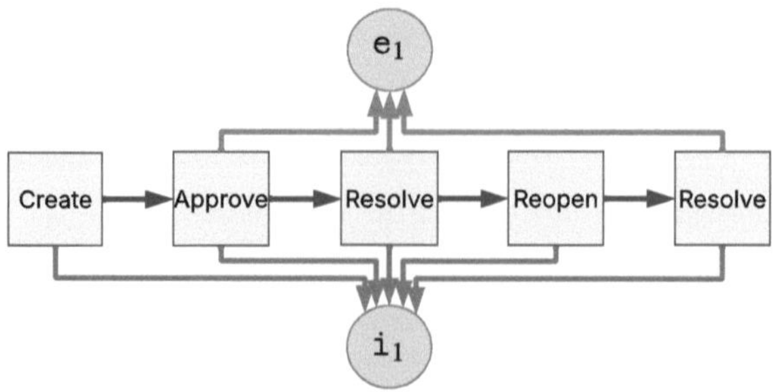

Fig. 3. Replayable case of the object-centric Petri net in Fig. 2.

A case is replayable on a net if any sequence in the language of the net results in the same case graph. Figure 2 shows an object-centric Petri net for our incident management scenario. Figure 3 shows a case that is replayable on the net. Note that the left case from Fig. 1 is not replayable, as the net does not allow an employee to be involved in the incident creation.

2.3   Alternative Modelling Formalisms

Other object-centric formalisms exist that have a deviating expressiveness from standard object-centric Petri nets [12]. Object-centric process trees are an abstraction for an adjusted subclass of object-centric Petri nets with behavioural guarantees, such as the absence of deadlocks [8]. In contrast to standard nets, they allow for tokens to be generated and consumed during the replay, by τ-transitions with only output or input places respectively. SYSSOC nets offer the option to link objects together during the replay of a cases, by using tokens that represent object combinations [10]. Object-centric Petri nets with identifiers (OPIDs) combine these two extensions into a single formalism [12].

3   An Object-Centric State Space

In this section, we define an abstraction layer for cases in object-centric process models, called an object-centric state space. Additionally, we show how existing object-centric formalisms can be abstracted into such a state space.

3.1   State Space Definition

Conceptually, an object-centric state space encodes the replay of cases on a process model into a directed acyclic graph. Each node in the graph represents a case that can be discovered during replay. Starting at an empty case, the replay extends cases with new objects, new events and the relations between them. We capture these case modifications using *actions*. Actions are directed edges that connect states in the state space and represent state changes from one state to another state. The abstraction is completed by a *model state interface* which determines available actions based on each state. The actions are derived from the model state stored in each state as a black box, only accessible by the interface. Algorithms on the OC state space exclusively regard states and actions without looking at the model internals.

We define the universe of all possible states of a model as $\mathbb{U}_I$ and the universe of all cases as $\mathbb{U}_C$. A state then represents a combination of those in $\mathbb{U}_{state} = \mathbb{U}_I \times \mathbb{U}_C$

Definition 6 (State). *A state is a tuple $s = (I, C) \in \mathbb{U}_{state}$ with a black box state I and a case C.*

A state and its case are considered *accepted* if I is an accepting state on the model. Otherwise, we speak of a *partial case*.

Each action in a state space can change the state of the model and the structure of the case. Actions can be differentiated into two types. *OBJ*-actions represent the addition of new objects to the state space. We explicitly model object additions as actions to clearly differentiate between models operating on a fixed object set with a corresponding initial marking and models that can explicitly add new objects. For the following definitions, let $s_1 = (I_1, C_1)$ and $s_2 = (I_2, C_2)$ be states in the state space with $C_1 = (N_1, E_1, \lambda_1), C_2 = (N_2, E_2, \lambda_2)$.

Definition 7. *(OBJ-Action) An OBJ-action $s_1 \Rightarrow^{OBJ,o} s_2$ is available between s_1 and s_2 if the model state can transition from I_1 to I_2 to make o available. This needs to be reflected in the cases with $N_2 = N_1 \cup \{\bullet_o\} \wedge E_2 = E_1$.*

Similarly, *EV*-actions indicate admissible events along with the objects involved in their execution. Each *EV*-action adds a new event along with the edges for object relations and the ordering relation connecting it to the previous event.

Definition 8. *EV-Action) An EV-action $s_1 \Rightarrow^{EV,e,O} s_2$ indicates the execution of an activity $a \in \mathbb{U}_{act}$ with the object set O. Additionally, the change needs to be reflected in the cases with new event node $N_2 = N_1 \cup \{\bullet_e\}, \alpha(e) = a$ and edges $E_2 = E_1 \cup \{(\bullet_e, \bullet_o) \mid o \in O\} \cup \{(\bullet_{e'}\bullet_e)\}$, where $\bullet_{e'} \in N_1 : \nexists_{\bullet_{e''} \in N_1}(e', e'') \in E_1 \wedge e'' \in \mathbb{U}_{ev}$ is the most recently added event without outgoing edges to other events.*

We write $\mathbb{U}_a \subseteq \{EV\} \times \mathbb{U}_{ev} \times \mathcal{P}(\mathbb{U}_{obj}) \cup \{OBJ\} \times \mathbb{U}_{obj}$ for the universe of all possible actions. Since all actions add elements to the cases, the OC state space is acyclic, as looping back to a previous state would require element removals. We use a formalism-specific model state interface to retrieve the set of available actions for any given internal state.

Definition 9 (Model State Interface). *For a state $s = (I, C)$, a model state interface is a function $\mathcal{I} : \mathbb{U}_{state} \rightarrow \mathcal{P}(\mathbb{U}_a \times \mathbb{U}_{state})$, mapping each state to a set of states via actions.*

The *initial state* $s_0 = (I_0, C_0)$ is part of every object-centric state space with C_0 being the empty case and I_0 being the initial state of the underlying model. From s_0, the state space is recursively defined using the model state interface $\mathcal{I}$.

3.2   State Space Construction

We demonstrate how to map models in existing formalisms to a state space. Given an accepting object-centric Petri net $ON = (P, T, F, l, pt, F_{var})$ with initial marking M_i and final marking M_f, the corresponding state space is constructed to contain all cases replayable from the initial marking. The model state interface $\mathcal{I}$ implements the previously defined notion of enabled transitions and corresponding firing sequences.

The initial state s_0 contains an empty marking and an empty case. From s_0, OBJ-actions add tokens of the corresponding object types according to the token counts in the initial marking. This eventually leads to a state s_i representing M_i and a corresponding case containing all objects in the initial marking without any events or relations. For s_i and all subsequent states $s_i \Rightarrow \cdots \Rightarrow s_n$ with marking M, no further OBJ-actions are permitted, and the model state interface $\mathcal{I}$ returns a list of all possible firings $M \rightarrow^{t,O} M'$ from the respective marking that correspond to EV-actions with $s_n \Rightarrow^{EV,t,O} s_n'$.

Note that τ-transitions are internal to the model and are not mapped to separate states. Given a state s, the model state interface recursively expands on all paths of silent transitions $M \rightarrow^{\tau,O} \cdots \rightarrow^{\tau,O'} M'$, collecting all reachable markings with sequences of τ-transitions. We add EV-actions for all $M' \rightarrow^{t,O} M''$ where firing t with O was not enabled in M. We do so without regarding the ordering of τ-transitions, if they lead to the same marking. As such, we avoid symmetries in the state space, as the resulting marking and cases are equivalent. A state with marking M is accepted, if $M = M_f$.

For object-centric process trees, which allow the generation of new objects, we extend the state space by adding OBJ-actions that allow constructing any object set before the first EV-action is executed. Figure 4 shows an state space for the incident management process, with necessary additions to support object-centric process trees highlighted in red. As this formalism allows the addition of new objects during runtime, corresponding branches in which the object sets are expanded are added to the state space. Similarly, we can account for the generation of new objects in other formalisms [12]. Other formalism specific properties, such as the synchronisation of objects, are covered by the model state interface, which restricts the allowed actions accordingly.

4   Conformance Checking on the OC State Space

In this section, we propose an object-centric conformance checking approach for object-centric process models and event logs. Figure 5 provides an overview of the approach. Starting with any OC process model, and a log case, we construct a model state interface to build an OC state space. We then search that state space for accepted cases with minimum distance to the log case. The distance between a log case and an accepted case is determined by the number of necessary element insertions and removals in the accepted case to make both cases isomorph. An assignment showing the insertions and removals to the closest accepted case is then constructed.

This section introduces the distance measure and the search strategy. Finally, we discuss some formalism specific heuristics that can be used to speed up the approach.

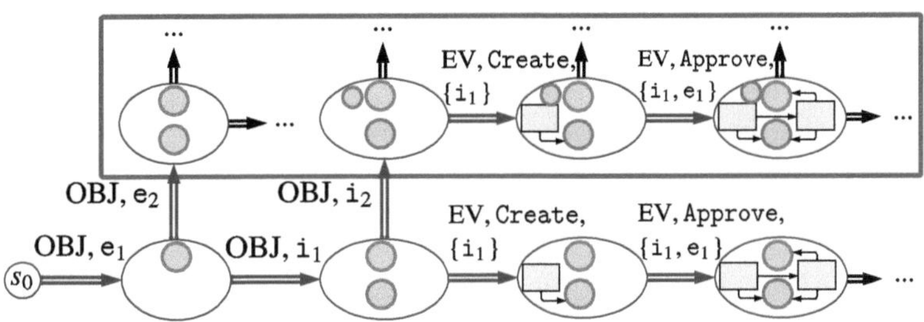

Fig. 4. Excerpt from an example state state, with additional object actions and branches induced by object-centric process trees marked in red. (Color figure online)

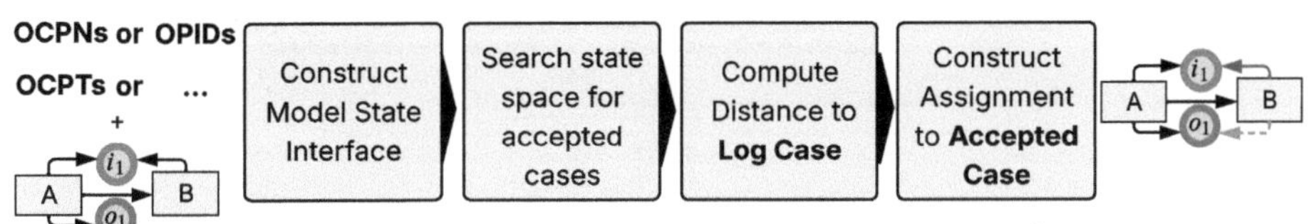

Fig. 5. Overview on Graph-Based Conformance Checking.

4.1   Graph-Based Case Distance

The necessary modifications to the accepted case, along with a labelled graph isomorphism mapping elements from the log case to the modified accepted case are tracked in a *case assignment*.

Definition 10 (Case Assignment). *Given a log case* $C_l = (N_l, E_l, \lambda_l)$ *and an accepted case* $C_a = (N_a, E_a, \lambda_a)$, *a case assignment is a tuple* $\mathcal{A} = (\delta_N, \delta_E, \epsilon_N, \epsilon_E, \lambda_\delta, a_n, a_e)$ *where*

- $\delta_N \subseteq N_l$, $\delta_E \subseteq E_l$ *are sets of missing nodes and edges inserted in the accepted case*

- $\epsilon_N \subseteq N_a$, $\epsilon_E \subseteq E_a$ *are the sets of extra nodes and edges removed from the accepted case*
- λ_δ *is the labelling function for inserted elements*
- $a_n : N_l \rightarrow (N_a \setminus \epsilon_N) \cup \delta_N$, $a_e : E_l \rightarrow (E_a \setminus \epsilon_E) \cup \delta_N$ *are bijective, label-preserving assignment functions for nodes and edges*

Consider the left sample log case in Fig. 1 and the accepted case in Fig. 3. An example for missing elements in the accepted case behaviour is the employee node e_2, along with its edge to `Create`. Additionally, there is an extra edge from `Approved` to e_1, which is not present in the log case. The assignment between the two cases is shown in Fig. 6. Insertions to the accepted case are highlighted with a green border, while removed elements are denoted using grey dotted borders. In addition to the deviations in the object involvement, the total order between the two cases does not match as well. This is again reflected by a sequence of removal and insertion operations of the respective edges, effectively reordering the execution of activities. Since many different assignments exist between two case graphs, we introduce a cost measure based on the number of edit operations to identify optimal assignments.

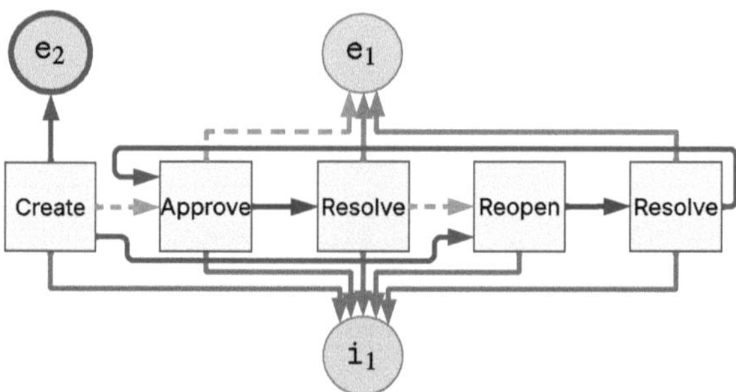

Fig. 6. Optimal assignment from log to accepted case at a cost of 7. Insertions to accepted case marked green. Removals marked using dotted lines. (Color figure online)

The cost of a case assignment $\mathcal{A}$ between two cases C_l and C_a is $c(\mathcal{A}) = |\delta_N| + |\delta_E| + |\epsilon_N| + |\epsilon_E|$. $\mathcal{A}$ is *optimal* if no assignment A' between these cases exists with $c(A') < c(A)$. The cost of an optimal assignment denotes a graph edit distance (GED) from C_l to C_a with removals and insertions. We do not include substitution operations as to force incremental changes, which can be used to visualize the deviations. Several approaches exist to calculate graph edit distances [11], and can be adapted to not take substitutions into account. The function $\text{ASSIGN}(C_l, C_a)$ produces an optimal assignment using a mixed integer linear program with variables representing the possible element assignments, constraints ensuring the validity, and an objective based on cost function introduced above.

The assignment cost is symmetric. Suppose that an optimal assignment $\mathcal{A}'' =$ ASSIGN(C_a, C_l) exists with $c(\mathcal{A}'') < c(\mathcal{A}')$. Reversing $\mathcal{A}''$ by swapping insertions and removals would yield an assignment $\mathcal{A}$ from C_l to C_a with $c(\mathcal{A}''') = c(\mathcal{A}'') < c(\mathcal{A})$. This contradicts the optimality of $\mathcal{A}$. Hence, no such assignment exists, guaranteeing cost function *symmetry*: $c(\text{ASSIGN}(C_l, C_a)) = c(\text{ASSIGN}(C_a, C_l))$.

4.2   Model-Case Conformance

Next, we define the conformance of an individual case to a model. For that purpose, we search the state space of the model for the accepted case with a minimal distance to a given log case $C_l = (N_l, E_l, \lambda_l)$. The search is implemented as a branch-and-bound algorithm, expanding on actions in the state space to discover new accepting states. Cost bounds limit the size of the searchable state, which is potentially infinite given an unbounded number of object sets or loops.

The given problem is a cost minimisation problem. A global upper bound ub tracks the distance of the log case to the best discovered case so far and limits the solution space by excluding all higher-cost states. A lower cost bound $lb(s)$ for each state s estimates the cost of a solution for the current branch and enables selecting the most promising nodes and pruning nodes more expensive than the current upper bound. If the lower bound of a branch in the state space exceeds the upper bound, the branch is pruned. To ensure that no nodes containing promising solutions are falsely pruned, the lower bound must be a monotonous function over the successors of nodes in the state spaces and never overestimate the cost of a branch. Formally, we require for any two states $s \Rightarrow^a s'$ with the corresponding cases C_s and $C_{s'}$ that $lb(s) \leq lb(s')$ and $c(\text{ASSIGN}(C_l, C_{s'})) \geq lb(s')$ if s' is accepting. Given these criteria, these best-first search is guaranteed to yield an optimal solution.

Our lower bound heuristic compares the element counts by label of C_s with the element counts by label in C_l. For a case assignment with a cost of 0, both graphs must have the same number of nodes and edges per label. Therefore, the lower bound to the number of extra elements in C_s is

$$lb(s) = \Sigma(\{\max(0, |(N_s)_l| - |(N_l)_l|) \mid l \in \mathbb{U}_\lambda\}$$
$$\cup \{\max(0, |(E_s)_l| - |(E_l)_l|) \mid l \in \mathbb{U}_\lambda\}).$$

These extra elements will lead to cost in every optimal assignment between the two cases, forming a lower bound to the case assignment cost.

The size of the searchable space is bounded by ub, given a finite number of actions from each state. Any action between two states $s_i \Rightarrow s_n$ leads to a state where $lb(s_n) \geq lb(s_i)$. There are finitely many cases with the same event counts of C_l, hence, the number of paths through the state space without an increase in lb is finite. For other connected states, the lb increases, eventually leading to a node s_n with $lb(s_n) > ub$.

Algorithm 1 depicts the procedure. Starting at s_0, all nodes connected using actions are traversed based on a best-first strategy, prioritizing nodes by their lower cost bounds. If the currently processed node is an accepting state, $\mathcal{A} =$

Algorithm 1. Model-Case Assignment via Branch-and-Bound.

1: **procedure** AssignModelCase(C_l, s_0, $\mathcal{I}$)
2:      **ub** $\leftarrow +\infty$
3:      **bestSolution** $\leftarrow$ null
4:      Open $\leftarrow$ CreateMinHeap
5:      HeapInsert(Open, s_0, $lb(s_0)$)
6:      **while** HeapNotEmpty(Open) **do**
7:          $s \leftarrow$ PopMin(Open)
8:         **if** $lb(s) \geq$ **ub then**
9:            **break**
10:        **if** s is accepting **then**
11:           $\mathcal{A} \leftarrow$ Assign(C_l, C_s)
12:           **if** $cost(\mathcal{A}) <$ **ub then**
13:              **ub** $\leftarrow cost(\mathcal{A})$
14:              **bestSolution** $\leftarrow \mathcal{A}$
15:          **for all** $(a, s') \in \mathcal{I}(s)$ **do**
16:            **if** $lb(s') <$ **ub then**
17:              HeapInsert(Open, s', $lb(s')$)
18:      **return bestSolution**

$assign(C_l, C_s)$ is computed. If $c(\mathcal{A}) < ub$, ub is updated to the cost of the assignment, and the node is saved as the best node, as depicted in lines 10–14. All open nodes s with $lb(s) > ub$ are pruned as shown in lines 9–14.

4.3   Formalism-Specific Heuristics

The previously introduced search strategy can be applied to the state space of any object-centric process model. To further improve the performance of the approach, we specify several optional heuristics to strengthen the lower bound formulated by $lb(s)$. These heuristics can be used to tune the the conformance checking algorithm to the specifics of each individual formalism.

Element Reachability. While our lower bound takes into account extra elements in C_s, missing elements also lead to cost in case assignments. We cannot directly adapt our lower bound heuristic to missing elements in C_s, since a state $s' \in \mathcal{I}(s)$ could add a previously missing node or edge which decreases the cost and violates the monotonicity criterium.

Instead, a model-specific heuristic $reachableFrom(s)$ returns a set of node and edge labels that could be added to the current partial case through actions $s \Rightarrow^a \dots \Rightarrow^{a_i} s_i$ starting from s. The heuristic may never underestimate reachability to preserve cost monotonicity, but may return false positives, resulting in a weaker lower bound. Using $reachabeFrom(s)$, we can add costs for all missing labels that are no longer reachable, as their implied cost will not decrease:

$$\Sigma(\{\max(0, |(N_l)_l| - |(N_s)_l|) + \max(0, |(E_l)_l| - |(E_s)_l|) \mid$$
$$l \in \mathbb{U}_\lambda, l \notin reachableFrom(s)\})$$

Expected Cost. For some modelling formalisms, we can estimate which elements will definitely be added to C_s in the current branch before an accepted state is reached. We can estimate the cost incurred from these elements using a formalism-specific heuristic $futureCost(s)$.

Replay Termination. This heuristic detects if the current branch cannot reach any accepting states and prunes it.

4.4   Implementation of Formalism-Specific Heuristics

We sketch how the formalism-specific heuristics can be integrated into our approach. The heuristics utilise the directed arcs of object-centric Petri nets to find paths between places, while not taking enabled firings into account for performance reasons. Given a net $ON = (P, T, F, l, pt, F_{var})$ and two places p_1, p_n with $pt(p_1) = pt(p_n)$, a path from p_1 to p_n is a sequence of places and transitions $p = \langle p_1, t_1, ..., p_i, t_i, ..., t_{n-1}, p_n \rangle$ where $p_{i+1} \in out(t_i)$ and $p_{i-1} \in in(t)_i$, $pt(p_i) = pt(p_1)$ for all $i < n$. The length of a path is equal to the number of non-silent transitions in the sequence. Shortest paths can be found using depth-first-search.

The heuristic $reachableFrom(s)$ for a state $s = (M_s, C_s)$ first determines the case labels that each transition can produce through the state space action. Then, for each place $p \in P$ and $o \in \mathbb{U}_{obj}$ with $M(p, o) > 0$, it checks if paths to all $p \in P$ exist, and collects all transitions reachable on the paths. For these transitions, the determined labels are returned.

The $futureCost(s)$ heuristic for a state $s = (M_s, C_s)$ determines the shortest path to a final place in a final marking for each place $p \in P$ and $o \in \mathbb{U}_{obj}$ with $M(p, o) > 0$. It then adds cost equal to the number of tokens in the place for each non-silent transition encountered in the path, as at least one additional edge will be added to the ϵ-elements per transition. The heuristic can only be applied to types that do not contribute to the cost derived through the element reachability heuristic. Otherwise, a lower bound cannot be formed, as the choice of a path could influence the number of missing elements in the accepted case.

The replay terminated heuristic is implemented through a check for stuck tokens in places outside the final marking.

For object-centric process trees, we can re-use all heuristics by utilizing the conversion detailed in [8]. The tree-specific traits have an influence on the initial marking of a converted net, but not on the replayable cases from an initial marking onwards. Hence the heuristics explained above are applicable. For formalisms with synchronisations between objects [10, 12], all heuristics explained above are applicable as the synchronisations exclusively restrict model behaviour. As such, the heuristics might be less precise, but still underestimate costs.

5   Evaluation

In this section, we evaluate our object-centric conformance checking approach with regards to its runtime and the detected deviations across two object-centric modelling formalisms.

5.1   Setup

We implemented our approach in Rust for object-centric Petri nets and object-centric process trees. For the calculation of the distance between cases, we used the integer programming solver SCIP [7]. The implementation can be found on GitHub, see https://github.com/erikwrede/ocgraphconf.

In line with previous object-centric conformance checking approaches [12, 16], we evaluate our technique on the BPI Challenge 2017 log [13]. First, we applied an activity filter for the 50% most frequent activities. After the filtering, the object types Offer and Application remained. The processed log has 719 variants, with case sizes ranging from 11 to 90 and object counts ranging from 2 to 11, with a median of 4. The median event count per case is 12 and the median case size is 43. We first evaluated our model-case assignment on the same object-centric Petri net used by previous approaches [12, 16] with a fixed initial marking equal to the object set of the case. Additionally, we created an object-centric process tree with the same control flow, but with variable object sets.

Then, we measured the runtime on a 20-core Intel Xeon Gold 5115 CPU with 500GB of working memory, with each case running on a single thread. We applied a timeout of 45 min to both formalisms. In addition to the runtime, we tracked the completion rate, case assignments, log case properties and checked the resulting assignments for insights.

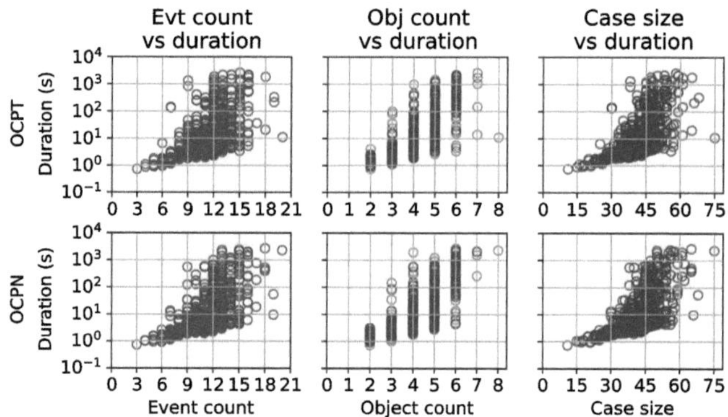

Fig. 7. Evaluation results for the object-centric process trees with variable object sets (top) and object-centric Petri nets (bottom) with static objects.

5.2   Results

The results can be seen in Fig. 7. For the tree, we observed successful completion 88% of cases within the timeout, with an average duration of 99 s. The net evaluation performed better, reaching 90% completion at a 95 s average. The reason for unsuccessful completion was either a timeout, or an out-of-memory error.

The results show an at least exponential runtime complexity of our conformance search for both formalism, with a dependency on the object count. This was to be expected, as more objects in a case increase the state-space exponentially, enabling more possible paths before hitting the cost upper bound. For that reason, most of the cases in the log with 8 or more objects did not complete on both formalisms.

Comparing the results obtained on the net to the tree, the formalism-specific heuristics calculating the lower bound successfully limited additional complexity in most cases with marginal runtime differences. This highlights an advantage of our approach: case conformance for a fixed initial marking can now be compared to the conformance for any object set on the model. Therefore, more insights can be drawn from the results. In our evaluation, 2.5% of all cases achieved a lower-cost assignment with objects differing from the log.

Figure 8 and Fig. 9 shows the assignments for a log case with two offer-objects (o_1 and o_2), but missing activities for the second offer (**Validate, Send**). The net required the accepted case to have the exact same object set and thus required the accepted case to have these activities. Therefore, these activities are removed in the assignment. However, the tree found a different object set that better matches this case. By omitting o_2 from the object set, **Create Offer** and o_2 could be treated as missing nodes in the assignment, highlighted in green. This led to a cost of 4, since less modifications to the accepted case were necessary.

5.3 Discussion

The evaluation results demonstrate a runtime of our approach comparable to existing approaches for most cases [12]. Additionally, we found assignments of different costs between the investigated formalisms, generating novel insights.

Our practical recommendation for cases in which such disagreements are found, is to reflect it back on the underlying process of the input log. In our example, practitioners should use the generated insights to check if adding new object is an option that is supported by the business process or not, as it would change any following analysis based on conformance checking results.

Our approach remains limited due to its complexity, impeding an application of full real-life logs without extensive further research into more precise search heuristics. While this evaluation focused on optimality, the branch-and-bound algorithm is also suitable for approximate conformance checking results. The difference between the upper and lower bounds make it possible to quantify how much current solutions differ from the potentially best solution.

Practitioners should be aware of our decision to use a total order between events, which differs from having individual partial orders per object type, as proposed in [19]. Additionally, we currently do not account for relations between two objects, which are part of the OCEL standard [6]. Reason being, that modelling formalisms discussed in this paper mostly do not explicitly take these properties into account during replay. However, our approach can handle all types of partial event orders and object relations, as long as they can be modelled as elements in case graphs, should future process models require them. To achieve that, the state space could easily be adapted to support them by adding the properties to the case graph and making it available to the model state interface. In principle, it could even account for relation qualifiers, by adding further labels to graph edges. However, we assume such extensions to increase runtime.

It should be noted that the use of a single log for our evaluation, similar to [16], rooted in runtime constraints, poses a threat to the generalizability of the results. Further investigations will be performed in future work.

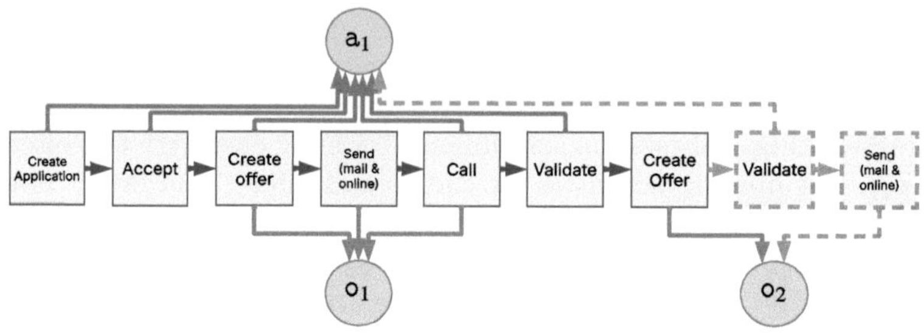

Fig. 8. Optimal assignment for a log case and the OCPN at a cost of 6.

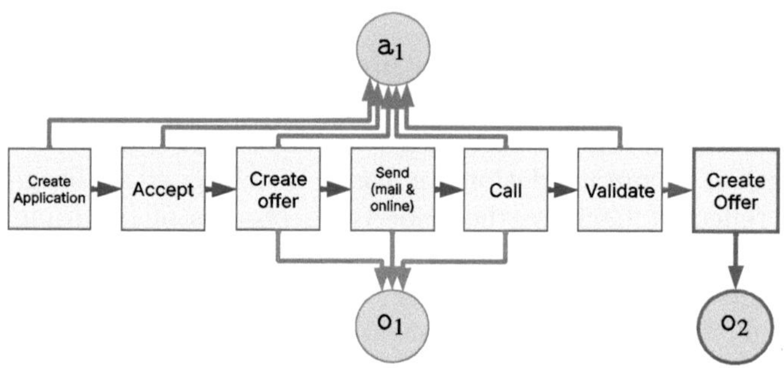

Fig. 9. Optimal assignment for a log case and the OCPT at a cost of 4.

6   Related Work

Various conformance checking approaches exist for event-centric process mining, primarily based on token-based replay [20] and alignments [5]. Alignments detect deviations between observed and modelled behaviour using three types of moves: *synchronous*, *log*, and *model moves*. Synchronous moves happen on both model and log and are free of cost, while model and log moves signal deviating events in the model or case. The alignment yields a number of log and model moves to the event sequence of the case to achieve the sequence accepted by the model. It is similar to our conformance checking approach in that we also define the cost as the number of insertions and removals to a case. However the majority of such approaches are event-centric.

Approaches like data-aware alignments [14], resource-aware alignments [21], or multi-perspective alignments [17] integrate additional dimensions in the alignment computation, which can be used to attribute for object involvements. Mehr et al. [17] introduced *partially synchronous moves* for multi-perspective alignments, representing the same activity in log and model but with different objects involved. However, all partially synchronous moves come with the same static cost, making the approach insensitive to the number of deviating objects per event. These approaches use case notions which might lead to information loss in object-centric logs [2].

Alignment-based conformance checking was applied to the object-centric space in [16]. Compared to event-centric alignments, the cost of a move is set by the number of objects involved. There is no concept of partially synchronous moves. If object sets differ slightly between the log and model move, all objects are counted as costs without identifying the precise deviations. Consequently, a small deviation of one object in a large object set leads to high costs, not precisely identifying deviations in object identity and missing or extra objects as it is the case with our case assignments. Our approach is able to detect the exact event, object, or relationship that lead to each deviation. Additionally, no alignment can be computed for cases with an object set that is not replayable on the model. While our conformance checking approach would not find a solution for this object set either, the approach could be run on an object-centric tree for the same process to find a solution. The approach in [16] shows an exponential runtime complexity dependant on the number of events in a case.

Gianola et al. proposed an object-centric alignment approach using object-centric Petri nets with identifiers (OPIDs), which is able to detect deviations caused by mismatches object identities and can iterate over multiple possible object sets [12]. However, the conformance measure is still unable to identify the precise cause for a deviation, such as a missing object. The OPIDs can also be mapped to the state space we introduced. With our approach, the exact differences in object involvements can be identified by comparing the assignments for the different models that were tested. Gianola et al.'s techinque is slower than the original object-centric alignment approach, again demonstrating the complexity of object-centric conformance checking.

Other techniques focus on checking object-centric data against a set of constraints derived from process models. While also being able to identify object-level deviations, these techniques do not find the closest case accepted by a model and do not specify precise measures [15,18].

To the best of our knowledge, our approach is the only approach supporting arbitrary graph-based structures in object-centric cases, generalizing to any object-centric modelling formalism that can be mapped to a state space.

7   Conclusion

In this paper, we defined an OC state space as a graph-based abstraction of object-centric modelling formalisms. Using this state space, we introduced a novel object-centric conformance checking approach based on the similarity of cases accepted by a model and the cases in a log. We found that our approach successfully checks real-life data, with performance comparable to existing techniques. While, like the other object-centric conformance checking approaches, it is limited by the computational complexity, our approach is the first to successfully provide object-centric conformance checking results across multiple modelling formalisms that cannot be translated into each other without expressiveness differences, such as fixed or dynamic object sets. Additionally, it can detect deviations more precisely than before and its results make comparing the conformance of a case to models of multiple formalisms possible. Further research could focus on finding better heuristics for traversing the state space, leading to improved runtimes and support of larger cases.

Acknowledgment. The project on which this work is based was funded by the German Federal Ministry of Research Technology and Space Travel under grant number 01IS25010. The responsibility for the content lies with the authors.

References

1. van der Aalst, W.M.P.: Process Mining - Data Science in Action, Second Edition. Springer Berlin, Heidelberg (2016). https://doi.org/10.1007/978-3-662-49851-4
2. Aalst, W.M.P.: Object-Centric Process Mining: Dealing with Divergence and Convergence in Event Data. In: Ölveczky, P.C., Salaün, G. (eds.) SEFM 2019. LNCS, vol. 11724, pp. 3–25. Springer, Cham (2019). https://doi.org/10.1007/978-3-030-30446-1_1
3. van der Aalst, W.M.P., Berti, A.: Discov. Object-Centric Petri Nets. Fundam. Informaticae **175**(1–4), 1–40 (2020)
4. Adams, J.N., Schuster, D., Schmitz, S., Schuh, G., van der Aalst, W.M.P.: Defining cases and variants for object-centric event data. In: ICPM 2022. pp. 128–135. IEEE (2022)
5. Adriansyah, A., van Dongen, B.F., van der Aalst, W.M.P.: Conformance checking using cost-based fitness analysis. In: IEEE EDOC 2011. pp. 55–64. IEEE Computer Society (2011)
6. Berti, A., et al.: OCEL (object-centric event log) 2.0 specification. CoRR (2024)
7. Bolusani, S.: The SCIP Optimization Suite 9.0. Technical report, Optimization Online (2024)
8. van Detten, J.N., Schumacher, P., Leemans, S.J.J.: Discovering compact, live and identifier-sound object-centric process models. In: ICPM 2024. pp. 113–120. IEEE (2024)
9. van Detten, J.N., Schumacher, P., Leemans, S.J.J.: A framework for advanced case notions in object-centric process mining. In: ICPM Workshops (2024)

10. van Detten, J.N., Schumacher, P., Leemans, S.J.J.: Object synchronizations and specializations with silent objects in object-centric petri nets. In: Marrella, A., Resinas, M., Jans, M., Rosemann, M. (eds) BPM 2024. LNCS, vol. 14940, pp. 57–74. Springer, Cham (2024). https://doi.org/10.1007/978-3-031-70396-6_4

11. Gao, X., Xiao, B., Tao, D., Li, X.: A survey of graph edit distance. Pattern Anal. Appl. **13**(1), 113–129 (2010)

12. Gianola, A., Montali, M., Winkler, S.: Object-centric conformance alignments with synchronization. In: CAiSE 2024, Proceedings. LNCS, vol. 14663, pp. 3–19. Springer Cham (2024). https://doi.org/10.1007/978-3-031-61057-8_1

13. Khayatbashi, S., Hartig, O., Jalali, A.: Bpi challenge 2017 (ocel) (2023)

14. de Leoni, M., van der Aalst, W.M.P.: Data-aware process mining: discovering decisions in processes using alignments. In: ACM SAC 2023. ACM (2013)

15. Li, T., Park, G., van der Aalst, W.M.P.: Checking constraints for object-centric process executions. In: De Smedt, J., Soffer, P. (eds) ICPM Workshops. LNBIP, vol. 503. Springer, Cham (2023). https://doi.org/10.1007/978-3-031-56107-8_30

16. Liss, L., Adams, J.N., van der Aalst, W.M.P.: Object-centric alignments. In: Almeida, J.P.A., Borbinha, J., Guizzardi, G., Link, S., Zdravkovic, J. (eds) Conceptual Modeling, ER 2023, Proceedings. LNCS, vol. 14320. Springer, Cham (2023). https://doi.org/10.1007/978-3-031-47262-6_11

17. Mehr, A.S.M., de Carvalho, R.M., van Dongen, B.F.: Detecting privacy, data and control-flow deviations in business processes. In: Nurcan, S., Korthaus, A. (eds) CAiSE 2021. LNBIP, vol. 424, pp. 82–91. Springer, Cham (2021). https://doi.org/10.1007/978-3-030-79108-7_10

18. Park, G., van der Aalst, W.M.P.: Monitoring constraints in business processes using object-centric constraint graphs. In: Montali, M., Senderovich, A., Weidlich, M. (eds) ICPM Workshops. LNBIP, vol. 468, pp. 479–492. Springer, Cham (2022). https://doi.org/10.1007/978-3-031-27815-0_35

19. Park, G., Adams, J.N., van der Aalst, W.M.P.: Conformance checking and performance analysis using object-centric directly-follows graphs. In: Marrella, A., Resinas, M., Jans, M., Rosemann, M. (eds) BPM Forum. LNBIP, vol. 526, pp. 179–196. Springer, Cham (2024). https://doi.org/10.1007/978-3-031-70418-5_11

20. Rozinat, A., van der Aalst, W.M.P.: Conformance checking of processes based on monitoring real behavior. Inf. Syst. **33**(1), 64–95 (2008)

21. Sommers, D., Sidorova, N., van Dongen, B.: Aligning event logs to resource-constrained ν-petri nets. In: Bernardinello, L., Petrucci, L. (eds) PETRI. Springer, Cham (2022). https://doi.org/10.1007/978-3-031-06653-5_17

A Framework for Assessing Overcompliance and Undercompliance in Business Processes

Johannes Loebbecke[✉] and Stefanie Rinderle-Ma

TUM School of Computation, Information, and Technology, Technical University of Munich, Garching, Germany
{johannes.loebbecke,stefanie.rinderle-ma}@tum.de

Abstract. Ensuring process compliance is critical for companies and organizations to avoid regulatory penalties, financial losses, and reputational damage. As a result, research has focused on detecting noncompliant instances where processes deviate from rules imposed on their execution and formalizing legal documents to enable automatic compliance verification. However, a crucial but overlooked phenomenon is overcompliance, where processes exceed what is required by regulations or policies, potentially leading to inefficiencies, increased operational costs, or overly rigid processes. While the reasons why companies overcomply with regulations have been extensively analyzed in environmental economics, overcompliance has been largely disregarded in process compliance, where compliance is often categorized as either violated or satisfied, and, at most, the degree of undercompliance is considered. We propose a formal framework for evaluating a degree of compliance, which specifically highlights the differences between perfect compliance, (maximal) undercompliance, and (maximal) overcompliance. Furthermore, we present a technique for estimating the costs associated with over and undercompliance. The approach is prototypically implemented and evaluated using real-world and synthetic event logs.

Keywords: Process Compliance · Compliance Degree · Overcompliance · Undercompliance · Compliance Costs

1 Introduction

Process compliance aims to ensure that processes of companies or organizations adhere to constraints imposed on their execution by legal documents such as laws and contracts [9]. The monetary and reputational threats of noncompliance have led to extensive research on extracting, contextualizing, and formalizing requirements from legal documents [10] as well as verifying compliance of process models [15]. Compliance verification is often based on model-checking and yields a binary result, i.e., either the process model is compliant or not, the latter possibly equipped with a counterexample. It has been acknowledged in literature that more fine-grained diagnostic information might be useful in case of

© The Author(s), under exclusive license to Springer Nature Switzerland AG 2026
C. Cappiello et al. (Eds.): CoopIS 2025, LNCS 15535, pp. 202–220, 2026.
https://doi.org/10.1007/978-3-032-15538-2_12

noncompliance, referring to the *"[a]bility to quantify the degree of compliance"* [17] and [5,12,18], and in particular, to quantify the *undercompliance* of processes. However, there also exists a differentiation in case of compliance, which has been overlooked in process compliance research so far, i.e., *overcompliance*

Overcompliance occurs when organizations implement stricter measures than what is required by regulations [23]. While historically, it was believed that a company would have no reason to overcomply with regulations, companies often see a competitive advantage in overcompliant behavior (e.g., stricter data protection than required, lower emissions than required) [2]. For example, a company can lower costs in the long term by producing goods in a more environmentally friendly way than required if they predict an upcoming change to an environmental regulation [23]. Similarly, many companies see advantages regarding employee agreement and brand name through overcompliance. Accordingly, it is essential for companies to understand over (and under) compliance from a business process perspective, especially as overcompliance can also occur unintended, e.g., as a consequence of regulatory change [24].

Specifically, disregarding overcompliance can lead to processes where (potentially costly) activities are executed (far) more often than required. Furthermore, the recent growth of proposals to extract process and compliance-related information from textual sources necessitate techniques for measuring a complete degree of compliance. We aim to address this gap by answering the following research questions:

RQ1: How to quantify degrees of over/undercompliance in process executions?
RQ2: How to estimate the costs of over/undercompliance in process executions?

We provide a framework for evaluating a quantifiable degree of compliance based on event traces. By modeling laws as normative systems, i.e. as if.. then patterns, we highlight how the antecedent/consequence of a requirement can be used to identify to which degree processes can be over/undercompliant. Furthermore, we present techniques for identifying and estimating the cost of over/undercompliance using event logs. The framework is prototypically implemented and evaluated using real-world and synthetic data. The results show that the proposed undercompliance metric equals the results of existing approaches. The results for overcompliance can be used to evaluate different process implementations and the quality of requirements that are mined from event logs.

The paper is structured as follows: Sect. 2 provides a running example and preliminaries. Section 3 presents the formal definitions and compliance degree calculation algorithm of the framework. Section 4 presents the technique for estimating costs of over/undercompliance, Sect. 5 the evaluation, and Sect. 6 related work. Finally, Sect. 7 concludes with limitations and future work.

2   Running Example and Preliminaries

Running Example: Throughout the paper, we use the example of a simplified loan process, with associated requirements as depicted in Fig. 1. It is inspired by [6] and based on a case study using the Sarbanes-Oxley Act, which mandates certain practices for financial record keeping and a bank's internal policies.

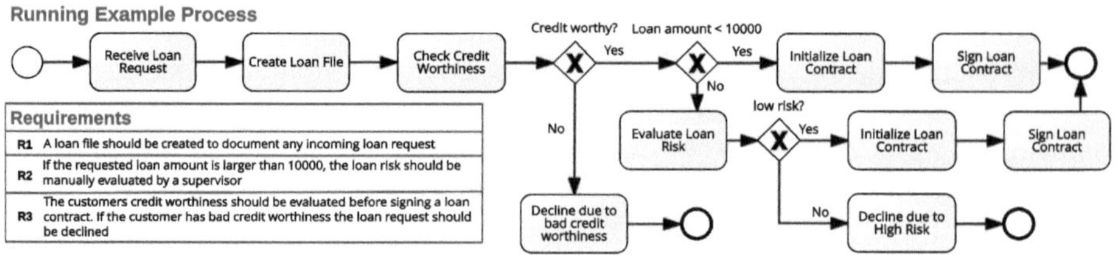

Fig. 1. Running Example: Simplified Loan Request Process and Requirements.

Activity Executions and Process Traces: We provide formal definitions for process activities and their executions stored in traces as this information builds the basis for the subsequent compliance notions [18].

Definition 1 (Activity). *Activity α is defined as a tuple $\alpha := (\lambda, \epsilon, \iota, o)$ with:*

- λ *denotes the activity label*
- ϵ *denotes the service endpoint that is called by α*
- $\iota = \{i_1, i_2, \ldots, i_n\}$ *is the set of input parameters sent towards the endpoint*
- $o = \{o_1, o_2, \ldots, o_m\}$ *is the set of output parameters returned by the endpoint*

Assume that for Fig. 1 activity $\alpha 1 = $ (`Receive Loan Request`, receive, $\emptyset$, {user_id, loan_amount}). During runtime, a process model P is instantiated and executed through a process engine. The activities are executed, i.e., the connected service endpoint is invoked with the specified input parameters to execute the functionality described by the activity label and the output parameters are received from the endpoint at the completion time of the activity, formally:

Definition 2 (Activity Execution). *Let $\alpha = (\lambda, \epsilon, \iota, o)$ be an activity and let $D_1^i, D_2^i, \ldots, D_n^i$ be the domain of the input parameters in ι and $D_1^o, D_2^o, \ldots, D_m^o$ be the domains of the output parameters in o. An activity execution α_{ex} is a tuple $\alpha_{ex} := (\epsilon, \{i_1(x_1), \ldots, i_n(x_n)\}, \{o_1(y_1), \ldots, o_m(y_m)\}\}$ which contains the values of all input and output parameters with: $x_k \in D_k^i \bigcup \{undefined\}, k = 1, \ldots, n$ and $y_l \in D_l^o \bigcup \{undefined\}, l = 1, \ldots, m$*

An example of an activity execution in the running example is $\alpha 5_{ex} = $ (`Evaluate Loan Risk`, `credit_risk_evaluation`, {`user_id(Smith)`, `loan_amount(11000)`}, {`HighRisk(false)`} which represents the execution of activity `Evaluate Loan Risk` where the user id *Smith* and the requested loan amount *11000* is sent to endpoint *credit risk evaluation*, which returns value *false* for the HighRisk output parameter.

The process engine executes the activities in the order specified in the process model. The information about the activity executions for each process instance is stored in process event logs, i.e., for each instance, a trace is logged that reflects the sequential activity executions for that instance. Accordingly, we define an event log $L := \{t_1, \ldots, t_n\}$ consisting of traces $t_i, i = 1, \ldots, n$ where a trace t is defined as a sequence of activity executions, i.e., $t :=< e_1, \ldots, e_m >$ with

$e_j = \alpha_{ex}$ for a corresponding activity α in the underlying process model. For the running example in Fig. 1, one possible trace is $t =< \alpha1_{ex}, \alpha2_{ex}, \alpha3_{ex}, ... >$ with $\alpha1_{ex}$=(Receive Loan Request, receive, undefined, 20000), $\alpha2_{ex} =$ (Create Loan File, $system1, 20000, undefined$), etc.

Requirement Satisfaction: Similar to [10,18], we assume that laws can be modeled as normative systems, where any requirement can be defined as a tuple of a condition (antecedent) and a consequence (deontic effect), i.e., let C be the set of all conditions, and D the set of all consequences, then the set of requirements is $R \subseteq C \times D$. Take R2 in Fig. 1. Here the condition c is requested loan amount > 10000 and the consequence d is loan risk manually evaluated by supervisor. For compliance verification of single traces, it is checked whether requirement $r \in R$ is satisfied for trace $t \in L$. We define auxiliary trace sets:

$$C := \{t \in L | c \text{ holds for t}\}; \ D := \{t \in L | d \text{ holds for t}\} \tag{1}$$

Definition 3 (Trace and process level satisfaction). *Let L be an event log and R the set of all requirements. Then, for trace $t \in L$ and requirement $r = (c, d) \in R$, the trace level requirement satisfaction function $sat(r, t)$ is defined as $sat : R \times L \mapsto \{true, \ false\}$ with*

$$sat((c, d), t) : \begin{cases} true & if \ t \notin C \vee t \in D \\ false & if \ t \in C \wedge l \notin D \end{cases} \tag{2}$$

Trace level satisfaction can be elevated to the process level[1]. Let $\mathcal{L}$ be the set of all event logs. Then: $psat : R \times \mathcal{L} \mapsto \{true, false\}$ with

$$psat(r, L) : \begin{cases} true & \forall t \in L : sat(r, t) = true \\ false & \exists t \in L : sat(r, t) = false \end{cases} \tag{3}$$

Based on Eq. 3, a given set of event logs can be divided into satisfied and violated categories or buckets w.r.t. a given requirement r. However, Eq. 3 does not provide a degree of compliance since it does not differentiate logs in the same bucket. In an extreme case, the violated bucket can contain two logs where, for one log, a single trace violates r, and for the other log, all traces violate r, resulting in different degrees of *undercompliance*. For the satisfied bucket, the differentiation lies in the relation between traces that fulfill the conditions and, hence, the consequence and traces that fulfill the consequence without the condition. Assume two logs, and for both, 10% of the traces fulfill the condition, and for the first log, 10% of the traces also fulfill the consequence, while for the other log, all traces fulfill the consequence. If the consequence is costly, it is worth further examining if the underlying process is potentially *overcompliant*.

---

[1] In the following, we assume that an event log L stores the behavior of a process model P, i.e., the set of all traces that can be generated based on P.

3   Framework for Assessing Overcompliance and Undercompliance

Definition 4 extends the binary classification of Eq. 3 by different levels of over/undercompliance.

Definition 4 (Overcompliance, Undercompliance). *Let L be an event log, $r = (c, d)$ a requirement, and C and D as defined in Eq. 1. Then we define L as*

1. *perfectly compliant iff: $psat(r, L) = true \ \wedge \forall t \in L \setminus C : t \notin D$*
2. *overcompliant iff: $\exists t \in L : t \notin C \wedge t \in D$*
3. *maximally overcompliant iff: $(\exists t \in L : t \notin C) \wedge \forall t \in L \setminus C : t \in D$*
4. *undercompliant iff: $psat(r, L) = false$*
5. *maximally undercompliant iff: $\forall t \in C : t \notin D$*

According to Definition 4, a log (and hence the underlying process) is 1) perfectly compliant iff the consequence is only executed when it is required by the condition, 2) overcompliant iff the consequence is executed in some traces where it is not required, 3) maximally overcompliant iff the consequence is executed in every trace where it is not required, 4) undercompliant iff the consequence is not executed in some of the required traces, and 5) maximally undercompliant iff the consequence is executed in none of the required traces. Figure 2 illustrates the differences between over and undercompliant processes using R2 of the example in Fig. 1. For overcompliance, the condition that defines how often the loan risk evaluation is executed is stricter than required (loan amount < 5,000), while for undercompliance, the condition is less strict than required (loan amount < 50,000). Finally, the loan risk evaluation is always executed in maximally overcompliant and never in maximally undercompliant processes.

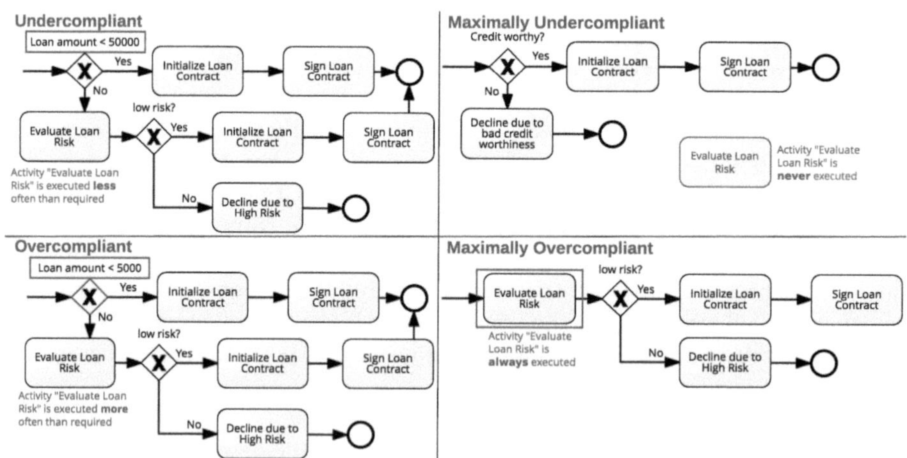

Fig. 2. Over/undercompliant implementations of the running example w.r.t. R3.

Using the compliance notions of Definition 4, we establish a function $csat(r,p)$ for evaluating the compliance degree in Definition 5.

Definition 5 (Compliance Degree). *Assume an event log L and a requirement $r = (c,d)$, with C and D as defined in Eq. 1. Let $Per = D \cap C$ be the set of traces for which d is required and executed. Then the compliance degree function csat is defined as:*

$$csat : R \times \mathcal{L} \to [\text{-}100\%,\, 100\%] \subseteq \mathbb{R} \text{ with} \tag{4}$$

$$csat(r,L) = \begin{cases} \frac{|D|-|Per|}{|L|} & if\ psat(r,L) = true \\ \frac{|Per|-|C|}{|L|} & if\ psat(r,L) = false \end{cases} \tag{5}$$

The formula for csat(r,L) can be specified further:

$$if\ psat(r,L) = true: \begin{cases} csat(r,L) = 1 - \frac{|C|}{|L|} \implies maximal\ overcompliance \\ 0 < csat(r,L) \le 1 - \frac{|C|}{|L|} \implies overcompliance \\ csat(r,L) = 0 \implies perfect\ compliance \end{cases}$$

$$\tag{6}$$

$$if\ psat(r,L) = false: \begin{cases} 0 > csat(r,L) \ge -\frac{|C|}{|L|} \implies undercompliance \\ csat(r,L) = -\frac{|C|}{|L|} \implies maximal\ undercompliance \end{cases}$$

$$\tag{7}$$

Definition 5 does not allow an event log to be considered both under and overcompliant at the same time. However, consider some trace $t \in L : t \in C \wedge t \notin D$. By definition, this trace would cause L to be undercompliant. However, assume another trace $t^* \in L : t^* \notin C \wedge t^* \in D$, i.e., an overcompliant trace. In this case, it could be argued that we need independent degrees of undercompliance and overcompliance, defined as follows:

Definition 6 (Over and Undercompliance Degrees). *Let assumptions be as in Definition 5. We define the degrees of overcompliance o and undercompliance u:*

$$o = \frac{|D|-|Per|}{|L|} \qquad u = \frac{|Per|-|C|}{|L|}$$

From these definitions, we can infer statements about potential compliance degrees a process can take w.r.t. specific requirements:

Theorem 1. *Let $\mathcal{P}$ be the set of all process models and let $P \in \mathcal{P}$ be behaviorally represented by log L. Let further $r = (c,d) \in \mathcal{R}$ be a requirement. Then the following statements hold:*
Statement 1: If $\neg c \implies \neg d$, then P cannot be overcompliant w.r.t. r.
Statement 2: If $\neg c \implies d$ and $\exists t \in L : t \notin C$, then P is maximally overcompliant w.r.t. r.

Proof. We prove both statements by contradiction.

Statement 1: Assume, P which is overcompliant w.r.t. requirement $r = (c, d)$, where $\neg c \implies \neg d$. According to Definition 4 $\exists t \in L : t \notin C \wedge t \in D$. Through Eq. 1 we define $t \in C$ as c is satisfied for t and $t \in D$ as d is satisfied for t. Accordingly, t does not satisfy c, but does satisfy d, which contradicts with $\neg c \implies \neg d$. By contradiction we have proven that no t can exist in L, so no process can be overcompliant w.r.t. to any requirement $r = (c, d)$ where $\neg c \implies \neg d$.

Statement 2: Assume, P is not maximally overcompliant w.r.t requirement $r = (c, d)$, where $\neg c \implies d$ and $\exists t \in L : t \notin C$. According to Definition 4 a process is not maximally overcompliant iff $\neg(\exists t \in L : t \notin C) \vee \neg \forall t \in L \setminus C : t \in D$. Per assumption $\neg(\exists t \in L : t \notin C)$ is false, so P is not maximally overcompliant iff $\exists t \in L \setminus C : t \notin D$. However, due to $\neg c \implies d$, $\forall t \in L \setminus C : t \in D$, so P has to be maximally overcompliant.

Applying the framework, the first step in event-log-based identification is to evaluate the compliance of all traces. By definition, for the undercompliance degree, we then divide the amount of traces where the consequence is correctly executed $|Per|$, minus the amount of traces where the consequence is required $|C|$, by the total number of traces $|L|$. Meanwhile, for the overcompliance degree we divide the number of traces where the consequence is currently executed $|D|$ minus $|Per|$ by $|L|$. The complete algorithm is illustrated in Algorithm 1

Algorithm 1. Compliance Degrees.

Require: Requirement $r = (c, d)$, Process $L = \{t_1, \ldots, t_n\}$
Ensure: overcompliance degree o, undercompliance degree u
  Initialize Set C, D by evaluating c, d
  Initialize Sets $Compliant, Per \leftarrow [\,]$
  for all $t \in L$ **do**
    if $t \in C$ **then**
      if $t \in D$ **then**
        Append t to $Compliant,\ Per$
      end if
    else
      Append t to $Compliant$
    end if
  end for
  $o = \frac{|D| - |Per|}{|L|}$
  $u = \frac{|Per| - |C|}{|L|}$
  return (o, u)

Storing sets using universal hashing with length operation worst case time complexity O(1), average lookup time complexity of O(1), and lookup expected worst case time complexity of O(1) [11], the degree calculation itself also has average and expected worst case time complexity of O(1). Due to the `for all` iteration, which equals the evaluation of $psat(r, p)$, the complete computational complexity of Algorithm 1 is $O(|L|)$. Notably, the degree calculation is independent of the verification technique as long as the required sets of traces are established, so the complete computational complexity can potentially be further reduced through abstraction techniques such as [7].

4   Costs and Gains for Different Compliance Degrees

Undercompliance with laws is not an option for companies and organizations. Undercompliance with other rules, such as guidelines, may still lead to undesired consequences, but can be subject to compliance risk management [9], i.e., if the costs of (perfect) compliance exceed the costs of being fined for undercompliance, then undercompliance might become tolerable in certain cases. Overcompliance can likewise result in increased costs, but may also be a voluntary decision for reasons such as maintaining a good reputation [2]. Hence, an assessment of the over/undercompliance degrees (cf. Definition 6) combined with costs can be a vital instrument for compliance risk management. Thus, we propose a technique for estimating the cost of over/undercompliance based on the following key values:

- $p = \frac{|C|}{|L|}$: % of traces where the consequence has to be executed for perfect compliance
- $c = \frac{|D|}{|L|}$: % of traces where the consequence is *currently* executed
- u (c.f. Definition 6): % of undercompliant traces
- C_{viol}: The estimated cost of an undercompliant execution per trace, e.g., cost of compensation when a single process execution violates a contract
- C_{con}: The estimated cost of executing the consequence in a single trace, e.g., the work time required by an employee to conduct a risk assessment
- G_{over}: Estimated gains of executing an overcompliant process per trace

Instead of focusing on the cost of specific past executions, we aim to estimate the cost of upcoming executions. Predicting exact costs is challenging and highly domain specific, since over/undercompliance costs may stem from quantifiable factors such as energy consumption, qualitative factors such as brand reputation, and probabilistic factors that capture the risk of undesired outcomes. We therefore regard the following formulas as an estimation technique that can be used alongside other risk management techniques which approximate values for C_{con} and C_{viol}. Accordingly, the simplest estimate of upcoming costs of compliance per trace, multiplies the respective costs with the trace percentages.

Definition 7 (Simplified Compliance Costs per Trace). *Let u be defined as in Defintion 6. Then the simplified cost of compliance per trace C_{trace} can be calculated as $C_{trace} := |u| * C_{viol} + c * C_{con}$.*

While, Defintion 7 provides an assessment of compliance costs, it disregards potential cost reductions (*gains*) through undercompliance. The gain of undercompliance can be seen as the value gained from not executing the consequence when it would be required, i.e., the cost of a perfectly compliant implementation.

Definition 8 (Compliance Costs per Trace Adjusted by Undercompliance Gain). *Let the assumptions be as in Defintion 7. The compliance costs per trace $C_{trace}^{adj\_u}$ adjusted by the gain of being undercompliant can be calculated as $C_{trace}^{adj\_u} := |u| * C_{viol} + (c - p) * C_{con}$.*

As motivated in the introduction, there are also cases when overcompliance provides a competitive advantage. These gains of overcompliance (G_{over}) can be challenging to estimate, as advantages like brand name are highly dynamic, difficult to quantify, and may scale with the degree of overcompliance, leading to a gains function. However, assuming that a fixed gain of overcompliance can be calculated at a per trace level, it can be assessed as follows:

Definition 9 (Compliance Costs per trace Adjusted by Gains). *Let the assumptions be as in Defintion 7. The compliance costs per trace adjusted by the gains of being undercompliant and overcompliant can be calculated as $C_{trace}^{adj} := |u| * C_{viol} + (c - p) * C_{con} - (c - p) * G_{over}$.*

One special case to simplify the calculation is that if a process is compliant, then $|Per| = |C|$ and $u = 0$ since every trace required by C was also implemented, which leads to $o = \frac{|D| - |Per|}{|L|} = \frac{|D| - |C|}{|L|} = \frac{|D|}{|L|} - \frac{|C|}{|L|} = c - p$ (cf. Defintion 6). This means that the cost of overcompliance can then be calculated as $o * (C_{con} - G_{over})$. We illustrate potential costs using R2 and a synthetic event log in Sect. 5.3.

5   Evaluation

We evaluate the proposed framework for assessing over/undercompliance using real-world event logs[2] and synthetic event logs of the running example process w.r.t. a) feasibility and b) alignment with existing undercompliance metrics [4]. By verifying that other researchers use the same metric for undercompliance, and defining overcompliance in accordance, we aim to propose metrics that fit with practitioners' intuitive understanding of the underlying concepts. Furthermore, we illustrate the assessment of overcompliance costs using the running example and a synthetic event log. While the over/undercompliance metric and cost calculations are novel, the custom-created, verification techniques required for the metric calculation do not utilize any novel concepts and could be replaced with different verification techniques. Accordingly, performance is not evaluated, as the expected worst-case computational complexity of the metric calculation is $O(1)$ (cf. Section 3), so performance depends almost entirely on the verification techniques. All code and the synthetic datasets are available on GitHub[3].

5.1   Real World Event Log Evaluation

To verify that the measures calculated using our framework align with the intuitive interpretations of practitioners, we verify alignment of the undercompliance

---

[2] all available at https://data.4tu.nl.

[3] https://github.com/JohannesLbck/OverCompliance accessed 2025-06-09.

degree with results calculated in related work [3–5]. We used the BPIC2012 and the Sepsis201 event logs, with associated requirement B1 derived from the analysis report submitted to the BPI challenge [4] and S1 and S2 extracted from medical guidelines for treating sepsis patients [3]. All three requirements require the eventual execution of an activity B within a time x after an activity A was executed. To model these requirements as a norm using the condition/consequence pattern, each requirement is split into two, where the first requirement enforces $A \implies B$ while, when defining $A \to B$ as A appearing before B in a trace, the second states that $A \to B \wedge B.time - A.time > x \implies false$, i.e. R1.1 states that if A, then (eventually follows) B while R1.2 states that if A leads to B and the time between the two is higher than x, compliance is violated. While there are other ways to model the original requirements, in practice, R1.2 would likely define an alternative activity that must be executed in case the time requirement is violated, i.e., a compensatory action [9] and/or a process termination would replace the $false$ consequence. An overview of the evaluation results using the BPIC2012 and Sepsis201 event logs is in Table 1. For example, for B1.1, the requirement, initially proposed as a conformance constraint by [4], verifies how many submitted proposals are finally accepted. Treating this as a compliance requirement, we identify that 60.93% of proposals are not accepted, leading to an undercompliance degree of -60.93% percent, aligning with the result in [4].

Table 1. Real-world datasets evaluations results. Requirements are verified on the event logs, the degree is calculated according to Algorithm 1 and compared to the degrees found in [3,4]. Since all logs are undercompliant, the compliance degrees result in negative values. The values are equal for Algorithm 1 and [3,4].

ID	Formalized Compliance Requirement	Event Log	Compliance Degree	
			Alg. 1	[3,4]
B1.1	A_SUBMITTED $\implies$ A_ACCEPTED	BPIC12	-60.93%	-60.93%
B1.2	$S1.1 \wedge$ A_SUBMITTED.t $-$ A_ACCEPTED.t $> 86400 \implies false$	BPIC12	-8.11%	-8.11%
S1.1	Triage $\implies$ Antibiotics	Sepsis	-9.28%	-9.28%
S1.2	$S1.1 \wedge$ Triage.t $-$ Antibiotics.t $> 3600 \implies false$	Sepsis	-57.29%	-57.29%
S2.1	Triage $\implies$ LacticAcid	Sepsis	-26.32%	-26.32%
S2.2	$S1.1 \wedge$ Triage.t $-$ LacticAcid.t $> 10800 \implies false$	Sepsis	-3.51%	-3.51%

For the real-world examples in Table 1, all compliance degree values are equal for Algorithm 1 and [3,4]. This confirms that the proposed undercompliance metric aligns with practitioners' understanding of the concept. The various degrees of undercompliance for B1, S1, and S2 reflect the different frequency of violations. Here, we can identify a potential reason why overcompliance has been largely disregarded so far. Any requirement where the condition enforces a consequence on every single trace (i.e., it is globally enforced), has $\neg c \implies \neg d$, since, if a trace is not satisfied it also doesn't exist in the process. Thus, according to Statement 1 of Theorem 1, a process cannot be overcompliant w.r.t. global requirements. Since A_SUBMITTED appears in every trace in BPIC12 and Triage appears in every trace in Sepsis, B1.1, S1.1 and S2.1 are global requirements. Furthermore, any formula of style $A \implies false$ can be seen as $true \implies \neg A$, so B1.2, S1.2, and S2.2 also enforce a consequence on every trace.

Similarly, Statement 1 of Theorem 1 shows that processes can also not be overcompliant w.r.t. the widely used *followed by* and *precedence* requirement patterns [20,21]. Consider a requirement R stating that if `A occurs, then B must occur after` A. If the condition is not satisfied, i.e., A does not occur in a trace t, then the requirement as a whole is (vacuously) satisfied. However, the consequence is not satisfied, since B occurring after A is impossible without A, i.e., the existence of A is a necessary condition for the consequence to be true. As these simple patterns are common, many requirements in related work cannot be overcompliant. Thus, we additionally evaluate over- and undercompliance of the BPIC11 log w.r.t. B2–B5 proposed by [17] and of the BPIC17 log w.r.t. a set of artificial requirements, B6–B9. Formal representations of requirements B2–B9 (with simplified activity and data object labels) and the identified over- and undercompliance degrees are shown in Table 2.

Table 2. BPIC11 and BPIC17 dataset evaluations results. Requirements are verified on the event logs, and the degrees are calculated according to Algorithm 1. Activity and data object identifiers are simplified for space. Full Identifiers available on GitHub.

ID	Formal	Event Log	Compliance	
			Under	Over
B2	tarief ∨ consult $\implies$ (tarief ∧ consult) ∨ (¬tarief ∧ ¬consult)	BPIC11	-16.8%	1.1%
B3	hemoglobine ∧ Treatment ID $= 495326 \implies$ hemoglobine → ureum	BPIC11	0.0%	9.4%
B4	formula is in footnote[a]	BPIC11	-10.2%	44.5%
B5	teleconsult ∧ (Tcode $= 101$ ∧ (Pcode $= SGAL\|\|SGNA$))) $\implies$ ¬fostatase	BPIC11	-1.8%	39.5%
B6	CreditScore < 100 ∧ loan_amount $> 40000 \implies$ Assess fraud	BPIC17	-4.6%	0.9%
B7	A_Submitted $\implies$ W_Complete application	BPIC17	0.0%	35.1%
B8	A_Submitted $\implies$ O_Sent (mail and online)	BPIC17	0.0%	1.5%
B9	LoanGoal $= Home\_improvement \implies$ loan_amount < 10000	BPIC17	-17.5%	28.9%

a natrium ∧ ((Age > 70 ∧ Tcode > 802 ∧ Treatment ID < 394725) ∨ Tcode $= 803$ ∨ Tcode $= 703$) $\implies$ ¬(natrium → calcium)

B2–B5 are requirements mined by [17] out of a 50/50 train/test split of the BPIC11 dataset using the *Declare Miner* component of the process mining tool ProM [1]. From 16 mined requirements covering various process perspectives, we select four that permit overcompliance, i.e., the consequence can be satisfied, while the condition is not satisfied (cf. Theorem 1). Verifying and calculating over- and undercompliance degrees shows that, the process is overcompliant with respect to all selected requirements.

Here, B2, which maps to R2 in [17], is suitable for illustrating both statements of Theorem 1. B2 states that if one of `administratief tarief - eerste pol` (abbreviated as A) or `vervolgcon- sult poliklinisch` (abbreviated as B) occurs in a trace, then either both or neither must occur. From an undercompliance perspective, this is equivalent to: if A or B occurs, then both A and B

must occur, since A or B implies that $\neg A$ and $\neg B$ is false. Considering over-compliance, Statement 1 of Theorem 1 applies to this reformulation, since the condition is also a necessary condition for the satisfaction of the consequence, i.e., it cannot be overcompliant. However Statement 2 applies to the original requirement B2 and accordingly BPIC11 is maximally overcompliant w.r.t. B2, since the condition being false implies the consequence being true. In the case of B2, the (maximal) overcompliance results in 1.1%: A or B occurs in 1130 out of 1143 traces, while the remaining 13 traces are overcompliant.

B3, corresponding to R10 in [17], requires that if `hemoglobine foto-elektrisch` occurs in a trace and the data object `case:diagnosis treatment combination ID` equals 495326, then it must eventually be followed by `ureum`. While this requirement is never violated, there is only one trace where the ID equals 495326, but in 109 traces `ureum` eventually follows `hemoglobine foto-elektrisch`, resulting in 9.4% overcompliance.

Overall, the evaluation of BPIC11 with mined requirements B2–5 suggests that overcompliance provides a useful signal for evaluating mined requirements. Specifically, overcompliance can complement existing evaluation methods used in rule mining approaches [13,14], as they use support and confidence level to evaluate the correctness of rule mining approaches while considering vacuous satisfaction [19]. Considering overcompliance can help practitioners determine whether mined rules reflect a causal relationship or are just accidentally satisfied, which is likely in case of low support and high overcompliance.

The requirements B6–B9 for the BPIC17 dataset are artificially created to highlight overcompliance identification while also allowing undercompliance. For example, B6 states that if the credit score of the applicant is below 100 and the requested loan amount is larger than 40000, potential fraud should be assessed. Testing this requirement, reveals that in 4.6% of traces where the condition holds, the fraud assessment is not executed (i.e., 4.6% undercompliance), while in 0.9% of all traces the fraud assessment is executed, while it is not required according to the (artificial) requirement (i.e., 0.9% overcompliance). These results highlight, how over-compliance can be identified in real world event logs. To further highlight how different models, when executed with a process execution engine, lead to over- and undercompliant logs, we also verify the requirements of the running example on three synthetic event logs.

5.2 Synthetic Event Log Evaluation

The synthetic event logs were created using the Cloud Process Execution Engine (CPEE)[4] by simulating the execution of the running example process (Fig. 1), the four different implementations of the running example process seen in Fig. 2, and versions of the running example that are undercompliant w.r.t. R1, R3.1, and R3.2. For the simulation, we replaced activity behavior with timeouts to create logs that directly represent the process execution. Additionally, we utilized a time dilation feature to generate more realistic logs with irregular differences

---

[4] https://cpee.org/.

between start and end events. In total, we created three different synthetic event logs: *Synthetic O*, *Synthetic U*, and *Synthetic M*, where O represents an overcompliant process containing only compliant and overcompliant traces, U represents an undercompliant process, without overcompliant traces, while M is an undercompliant process, that also contains overcompliant traces. O and U contain 50 traces each, while M contains 100 traces, and for all traces, the `loan amounts` were sampled between 500 and 100000, while the `credit worthiness` and `loan risk` were sampled with an 80/20 and a 75/25 distribution for true/false respectively. The evaluation results using the synthetic event logs are in Table 3. Using R2 as an example, if the loan amount is larger than 10000, the risk evaluation should be executed before a contract is signed. Verifying this requirement on the overcompliant process described by O, the resulting degree is 22.0% since all traces are compliant, but there are 11 out of 50 traces that execute the consequence even when it is not required. Verifying the same requirement on U reveals an undercompliance level of -46%. Finally, since M contains both undercompliant, compliant, and overcompliant traces w.r.t all requirements, it has a smaller undercompliance level w.r.t R2 of -17%. Meanwhile, O and U are perfectly compliant w.r.t. R3.2 since the underlying processes were over/undercompliant w.r.t R2 but perfectly compliant w.r.t. R3.2. Finally, M contains undercompliant traces for all requirements but also overcompliant and perfectly compliant traces. These results highlight the connection between the process model executed with a process execution engine and the over- and undercompliance metrics: If a model was executed by a execution engine and the model did not change, then the process can only be either over or undercompliant. If the executed model changed, then the process can be both over- and undercompliant.

Table 3. Synthetic datasets evaluations results. Requirements are verified on the event logs, and the degrees are calculated according to Algorithm 1.

ID	Formal	Event Log	Compliance	
			Under	Over
R1	`Receive_Request` → `Create_File`	Synth. M	-11.0%	0.0%
R2	`Sign.loan_amount` > 10000 $\implies$ `Evaluate_Risk` → `Sign`	Synth. O	0.0%	22.0%
R2	`Sign.loan_amount` > 10000 $\implies$ `Evaluate_Risk` → `Sign`	Synth. U	-46.0%	0.0%
R2	`Sign.loan_amount` > 10000 $\implies$ `Evaluate_Risk` → `Sign`	Synth. M	-17.0%	11.0%
R3.1	`Check_Credit` → `Sign`	Synth. M	-6.0%	28.9%
R3.2	`Check_Credit.worthiness` = *false* $\implies$ `Decline`	Synth. O	0.0%	0.0%
R3.2	`Check_Credit.worthiness` = *false* $\implies$ `Decline`	Synth. U	0.0%	0.0%
R3.2	`Check_Credit.worthiness` = *false* $\implies$ `Decline`	Synth. M	-3.0%	0.0%

In general, overcompliant processes are correctly identified from event logs, and the degree of overcompliance correctly scales with the amount of overcompliant traces. The performance is not evaluated since calculating the degree takes

$O(1)$, i.e., the performance depends almost entirely on the verification technique, which is not the focus of this paper.

5.3   Overcompliance Cost Calculation

We illustrate the costs of over/undercompliance using M by comparing potential implementations w.r.t. R2 and assuming values for C_{con} and C_{viol}. We assume that the risk assessment takes 3 h at 40 per hour, i.e., $C_{con} = 120$, and that, if not reviewed, every second loan above 10000 results in losses of 3000, leading to a per-trace cost of $C_{viol} = 1500$. For this example, gains of overcompliance could arise by rejecting risky loan requests with a loan amount below 10000. However, this would likely be a cost function, so we assume $G_{over} = 0$ for simplicity.

Assuming the traces given by M, if the risk assessment is always executed (i.e., by a maximally overcompliant process), the cost per trace can be calculated as $0 * 1500 + (1 - 0.47) * 120 = 63.6$. If the process were perfectly compliant, the risk assessment would be executed exactly when required ($|Per| = |C| = 47$), and the cost would be $0 * 1500 + (0.47 - 0.47) * 120 = 0$. M actually describes an undercompliant process with some overcompliant traces, with costs $0.17 * 1500 + (0.41 - 0.47) * 120 = 247.8$. Finally, if the risk assessment is never executed, the process is maximally undercompliant, and the cost can be calculated as $0.47 * 1500 + (0 - 0.47) * 120 = 648.6$.

For these calculations, we assumed that C_{viol}, C_{con}, and G_{over} are known and independent of the degree of compliance. In practice, they may be challenging to quantify and depend on u and o, leading to a more complex estimation problem. Generally, we believe that cost estimates are often only feasible for discrete compliance levels. For example, suppose that analysis has shown that executing a risk assessment for loan amounts between 5000 and 10000 saves $G_{over} = 200$ on average per trace by avoiding risky loans. Given the trace distribution M where for 57% of traces the loan amount exceeds 5000 and for 47% of traces it exceeds 10000, the perfectly compliant process costs $0 * 1500 + (0.47 - 0.47) * 120 + 0 * 200 = 0$, while the overcompliance process with a 5000 threshold results in $0 * 1500 + (0.57 - 0.47) * 120 - 0.1 * 200 = -8$, making the overcompliant process more profitable.

6   Related Work

We first review the state of the art concerning over/undercompliance in business process research and then highlight contributions from other fields addressing overcompliance.

Overcompliance in Business Process Compliance, Compliance Degrees: No existing BPC surveys [9,15,27] consider overcompliance. Lopez and Hildebrand [15] find that formal verification techniques are mature, while integration with Business Process Management Systems and the ability to handle regulatory changes are areas for improvement. Hashmi et al. [9] highlight existing challenges in requirements extraction and synthesis of different compliance approaches towards a complete BPC solution. We mention overcompliance in our previous work [24] in the context of assessing compliance between legal documents and company internal realizations to identify deviations. One type of deviation is the *severity deviation*, which is defined as a form of overcompliance that occurs when a realization is stricter about aspects of requirements or includes constraints that are not required by the legal document. However, no quantification of different degrees of undercompliance and overcompliance is provided that can be directly evaluated from event logs. Several approaches present degrees of compliance [5,12,16,25] and formal, behavioral frameworks for compliance verification [10,18]. Lu et al. [16] propose an approach for measuring the degree of compliance based on the difference between the desired process state and the actual process state while only considering *ideal*, *sub-ideal*, and *non-ideal* states, which map to perfect compliance and undercompliance, but disregard overcompliance. Similarly [12] highlight that binary compliance results (violated/satisfied) are insufficient, but only consider the addition of *partial compliance* mapping to undercompliance. Shamsaei [25] proposes using the User Requirements Notation (URN) to combine goal-oriented requirement modeling with scenario modeling to define sets of KPIs for each process, which are defined as linear functions between the targets and the worst values, i.e., between perfect compliance and undercompliance. Finally, our approach in [5] considers the magnitude of a violation, i.e., of undercompliance, in a predictive compliance approach. Hashmi et al. [10] present an abstract formal framework that can be used for evaluating verification approaches. They specifically focus on the different types of conditions, consequences, and the temporal validity of requirements, while we highlight overcompliance and establish a degree of compliance. In our previous work [18], verification results are divided into satisfied, violated, and violable (partial traces, for which the full trace could still violate compliance) instead of considering a quantifiable compliance degree that spans over/undercompliance.

There are also connections between the presented work, and work discussing declarative process mining. Maggi et al. [19], discuss *semantic vacuity detection*, highlighting that requirements that are satisfied while its condition is satisfied (activated) have more semantic value, compared to requirements that are satisfied *vacuosly*, i.e., because the condition is not satisfied. Overcompliance occurs when the consequence of a requirement is satisfied, while the requirement itself is vacuously satisfied. Accordingly, the techniques by [19] for determining whether the condition of a requirement is satisfied or not enable overcompliance identification. Other declarative mining approaches [13,14] also detect vacuous requirement satisfaction, without considering overcompliance.

Overcompliance in Environmental Economics: While BPC has yet to analyze overcompliance, it has been extensively researched in the field of environmental economics [2,8,22,23,26]. Rorie [23] presents an integrated theory of corporate environmental offending and overcompliance by extending the framework presented by [8] with a focus on explaining overcompliance. They identify that rational firm-level factors, such as costs, and multiple individual-level factors, including perceived morality and potential benefits, affect the degree of compliance. In contrast, individual-level social sanctions and benefits seem to be unrelated. Similarly, [26] attempt to explain overcompliance by analyzing how the degree of enforcement affects the degree of compliance, specifically highlighting that increasing fines for undercompliance does not only affect undercompliant corporations but also increases the overcompliance level of overcompliant companies. An interesting point is discussed by [22], who differentiate between overcompliance resulting from technological indivisibilities and companies adopting uniform technologies across facilities that face varying regulations, as well as "intentional overcompliance", highlighting that individual level and company internal factors have a substantial effect on the degree of intentional overcompliance. For this paper, we do not differentiate different forms of overcompliance by their reason but instead focus on the degree of over/undercompliance. An older contribution [2] attempts to explain overcompliance using a simple model to argue that consumers preferring environmentally friendly products directly leads to companies implementing overcompliant measures.

In general, it can be said that related (environmental) economics contributions focus on explaining why (employees in) companies over or undercomply with regulations, while our work proposes a framework for evaluating the degree of over/undercompliance from a business process perspective.

7   Conclusion

Conclusion: While the motivation of companies to overcomply with regulations has been extensively studied in environmental economics [23], business process compliance research has largely overlooked this phenomenon. Typically, existing approaches classify compliance into binary compliant/violated results or, at most, consider partial compliance [5]. In contrast, we present a trace-based framework for quantifying over/undercompliance in business processes and estimating associated costs. The framework has been prototypically implemented and evaluated using real-world and synthetic event logs.

Limitations and Future Work: A limitation of our framework is the need for preprocessing in case of interdependent rules. Consider a process described by traces t_1, t_2 subject to requirements $r_1 = (c_1, d_1)$ and $r_2 = (c_2, d_2)$ where $c_1 \neq c_2$, $d_1 \equiv d_2$, c_1 holds in t_1, c_2 holds in t_2, and d_1 and d_2 hold in t_1 and t_2. According to our framework, this would cause the process to be maximally overcompliant, while intuitively, the model is perfectly compliant. To address this problem, if two rules have equivalent consequences, the rules can be combined into a single rule by connecting the conditions with a logical *or* (e.g., $r_1 \wedge r_2$ become $r_* = (c_1 \vee c_2, d_1)$. More challenging are partial overlaps in the consequences through $\vee$ connectors (and the equivalent $\neg((\neg d_1) \wedge (\neg d_2))$. Such rules, while rare, require complex preprocessing to identify and resolve overlaps before the framework can be applied. Furthermore, our framework uses a behavioral perspective, where a process is defined by its set of traces. While this directly enables ex-post, event log-based analysis, it is more challenging to apply it to design/run time verification, where predicting all possible traces that a model can create is not always feasible, since loops and data conditions can lead to infinite traces and state explosion, which requires abstraction techniques for performant verification [7]. By contrast, ex-post approaches can only provide empirical predictions for future executions due to their reliance on past data. We plan to evaluate design and runtime verification approaches using real-world datasets regarding over/undercompliance identification in the future. The antecedent/consequence model of requirements used throughout this paper is based on related work [10,18] and compatible with various formalizations (e.g.,MTL, LTL, or CTL). However, we do not evaluate whether different formalizations are more or less suited for evaluating over/undercompliance. The cost estimation technique is straightforward, but requires the trace distribution and associated costs, which, as discussed, can be challenging to predict. However, as illustrated in the evaluation, the method is practical for estimating costs at discrete compliance levels using event logs in combination with other risk assessment activities.

Acknowledgments. This study was funded as part of the TRPro project by the German Research Association (Deutsche Forschungsgemeinschaft) as "Sachbeihilfe" under the project number 514769482. We further acknowledge the excellent reviewer input.

References

1. van der Aalst, W.M., van Dongen, B.F., Günther, C.W., Rozinat, A., Verbeek, H., Weijters, A.: Prom: The process mining toolkit. In: BPM Demos, pp. 1–4. CEUR-WS. org (2009)
2. Arora, S., Gangopadhyay, S.: Toward a theoretical model of voluntary overcompliance. J. Econ. Behav. Org. **28**(3), 289–309 (1995)
3. Bakhshi, A., Hassannayebi, E., Sadeghi, A.H.: Optimizing sepsis care through heuristics methods in process mining: A trajectory analysis. Healthcare Anal. **3**, pp. 100–187 (2023)
4. Burattin, A., Maggi, F.M., Sperduti, A.: Conformance checking based on multi-perspective declarative process models. Expert Sys. Appl. **65**, pp. 194–211 (2016)
5. Chen, Q., Rinderle-Ma, S., Wen, L.: Beyond yes or no: Predictive compliance monitoring approaches for quantifying the magnitude of compliance violations. arXiv preprint arXiv:2502.01141 (2025)
6. Elgammal, A., Turetken, O., van den Heuvel, W.J., Papazoglou, M.: Formalizing and appling compliance patterns for business process compliance. Soft. Sys. Model. **15**(1), pp. 119–146 (2016)
7. Groefsema, H., van Beest, N.R.T.P., Armas-Cervantes, A.: Efficient conditional compliance checking of business process models. Comput. Ind. **115**, p. 103181 (2020)

8. Gunningham, N., Kagan, R.A., Thornton, D.: Shades of Green: Business, Regulation, and Environment. Stanford University Press (2003)

9. Hashmi, M., Governatori, G., Lam, H.P., Wynn, M.T.: Are we done with business process compliance: state of the art and challenges ahead. Knowl. Inf. Sys. **57**, pp. 79–133 (2018). https://doi.org/10.1007/s10115-017-1142-1

10. Hashmi, M., Governatori, G., Wynn, M.T.: Normative requirements for regulatory compliance: An abstract formal framework. Inf. Syst. Frontiers **18**(3), 429–455 (2016)

11. Knuth, D.E.: The Art of Computer Programming: Sorting and Searching, volume 3. Addison-Wesley Professional (1998)

12. Lam, H.P., Hashmi, M., Kumar, A.: Towards a formal framework for partial compliance of business processes. In: Rodríguez-Doncel, V., Palmirani, M., Araszkiewicz, M., Casanovas, P., Pagallo, U., Sartor, G. (eds) International Workshop on AI Approaches to the Complexity of Legal Systems. pp. 90–105. Springer Cham (2018). https://doi.org/10.1007/978-3-030-89811-3_7

13. Leno, V., Dumas, M., Maggi, F.M.: Correlating activation and target conditions in data-aware declarative process discovery. In: Business Process Management. pp. 176–193 (2018)

14. Leno, V., Dumas, M., Maggi, F.M., La Rosa, M., Polyvyanyy, A.: Automated discovery of declarative process models with correlated data conditions. Inf. Syst. **89**, 101482 (2020)

15. López, H.A., Hildebrandt, T.T.: Three Decades of Formal Methods in Business Process Compliance: A systematic Literature Review. arXiv preprint arXiv:2410.10906 (2024)

16. Lu, R., Sadiq, S., Governatori, G.: Measurement of compliance distance in business processes. Inf. Sys. Manag. **25**(4), pp. 344–355 (2008)

17. Ly, L.T., Maggi, F.M., Montali, M., Rinderle-Ma, S., van der Aalst, W.M.P.: Compliance monitoring in business processes: Functionalities, application, and tool-support. Inf. Syst. **54**, 209–234 (2015)

18. Ly, L.T., Rinderle-Ma, S., Göser, K., Dadam, P.: On enabling integrated process compliance with semantic constraints in process management systems - requirements, challenges, solutions. Inf. Syst. Frontiers **14**(2), 195–219 (2012)

19. Maggi, F.M., Montali, M., Di Ciccio, C., Mendling, J.: Semantic Vacuity Detection in Declarative Process Mining. In: La Rosa, M., Loos, P., Pastor, O. (eds.) BPM 2016. LNCS, vol. 9850, pp. 158–175. Springer, Cham (2016). https://doi.org/10.1007/978-3-319-45348-4_10

20. Montali, M., Pesic, M., Aalst, W.M.v.d., Chesani, F., Mello, P., Storari, S.: Declarative specification and verification of service choreographiess. ACM Trans. Web (TWEB) **4**(1), 1–62 (2010)

21. Pesic, M., Schonenberg, H., Van der Aalst, W.M.: Declare: Full support for loosely-structured processes. In: 11th IEEE international enterprise distributed object computing conference (EDOC 2007). pp. 287–287. IEEE (2007)

22. Prakash, A.: Why do firms adopt 'beyond-compliance' environmental policies? Bus. Strateg. Environ. **10**(5), 286–299 (2001)

23. Rorie, M.: An integrated theory of corporate environmental compliance and over-compliance. Crime Law Soc. Chang. (3), 65–101 (2015). https://doi.org/10.1007/s10611-015-9571-9

24. Sai, C., Winter, K., Fernanda, E., Rinderle-Ma, S.: Detecting deviations between external and internal regulatory requirements for improved process compliance assessment. In: Advanced Information Systems Engineering. pp. 401–416 (2023)

25. Shamsaei, A.: Indicator-based policy compliance of business processes. Ph.D. thesis, Citeseer (2012)
26. Shimshack, J.P., Ward, M.B.: Enforcement and over-compliance. J. Environ. Econ. Manag. **55**(1), 90–105 (2008)
27. Zasada, A., Hashmi, M., Fellmann, M., Knuplesch, D.: Evaluation of compliance rule languages for modelling regulatory compliance requirements. Soft. **2**(1), pp. 71–120 (2023)

Data Integrity-by-Design: Combining Declarative Object-Centric Choreographies and Entity Relationship Models

Tilman Zuckmantel[1], Hugo A. López[2], Yongluan Zhou[1], Boris Düdder[1], and Thomas T. Hildebrandt[1(✉)]

[1] University of Copenhagen, Copenhagen, Denmark
`hilde@di.ku.dk`
[2] Technical University of Denmark, Lyngby, Denmark

Abstract. This work proposes a novel technique to align Object-Centric Process models and data integrity constraints from Entity-Relationship (ER) Diagrams, supporting data-dependent access control and guaranteeing data-integrity-by-design in the execution of a business process. Recent developments in process modelling and mining notations have highlighted how critical data objects affect the evolution of process models. Yet, few works have considered the integration of data relationships between data objects in object-centric modelling notations. As a consequence, object-centric process models (OCPM) may violate data-integrity and existential dependency constraints that are necessary for the deployment of models in information systems. We examine how OCPM can integrate access control, cardinality constraints, existential dependency, total participation, and structural integrity. In particular, we extend the semantics of one OCPM language, the Object-Centric Condition Response Choreographies (OC-DCR choreographies), to include explicit identities of actors and object deletion and extend the execution semantics to respect the ER model constraints. We illustrate the idea with a running example of an OC-DCR graph and an ER model for a small healthcare process.

1 Introduction

The definition of an Enterprise Architecture typically requires the representation of the basic layout and connectivity of dimensions in an enterprise (such as data, information, systems, technologies, data, people, and business processes) [11]. Yet, the integration across dimensions is often not easy. For example, well-established architectural methods such as Zachman's EA framework [23] limit their considerations to identifying the relation between multiple organizational views, leaving the integration between the data (*what*) and the process (*how*) outside their scope. This is not particular to a single EA framework, and modelling notations supporting the definition of enterprise architectures have kept separate concerns. This is the case with business processes and data models. For instance, the BPMN standard allows the introduction of data objects that can be created and updated, but the omission of an optional activity may violate data integrity constraints. These constraints are normally not expressed in a business

C. Cappiello et al. (Eds.): CoopIS 2025, LNCS 15535, pp. 221–238, 2026.
https://doi.org/10.1007/978-3-032-15538-2_13

process model, but they live in the definition of a database schema that is not accessible by a process modeler.

A recent trend in process modelling and mining fields has shed light on the inter-relationship between data and processes. Object-Centric Process Models (OCPMs) incorporate objects and their interactions into a business process execution semantics [1,2,5,24]. In particular, these notations allow the creation, modification, and deletion of objects within a process model execution [19]. However, except for [2], they are not tied to a data model, and the work in [2] does not consider distributed processes and role-based access control. Manipulation of objects in the evolution of these processes can lead to undetected structural inconsistencies [13] due to a poor alignment between data, people, and process dimensions. We propose to integrate the data integrity constraints of a data model into the behavior of a distributed process model to remediate this gap. In particular, we aim to combine one OCPM notation with the data integrity constraints of an ER Model. We will use the Object-Centric Dynamic Condition Response (OC-DCR) Choreography [24] notation, extending its execution semantics with ER models. The DCR process language was introduced in [12] as a declarative process language for knowledge work processes, where correct executions are defined as those that satisfy a set of behavioral constraints. After 15 years of research, the notation has been extended with e.g., data, time constraints, and choreographic roles and supported by mature cloud-based design and execution tools[1] used in industrial enterprise information management systems[2]. The result is a combined model of Object-centric Entity Relationship (OCER) DCR Choreographies. By combining the constraints of the two models, the execution of OCER-DCR Choreographies ensures the structural integrity, cardinality, and total participation constraints provided by the ER models, as well as the access control and behavioral constraints of the processes, particularly the existential dependencies of objects. Note that even though the choreographies are global models, the described behavior can be deployed in a distributed system.

To exemplify the integration between processes and data, we use a running example of a prescription workflow shown in Fig. 1 represented as an OC-DCR Choreography. We briefly describe its components, while its formalization is given in Sect. 2. The process supports iterative agreement on a prescription: the nurse may reject a doctor's proposal, prompting revision and re-signing, until the prescription is mutually agreed upon. Once trusted, the medication is administered. At any point, the doctor may cancel the prescription. A prescription is modeled as a *class* (denoted as a rectangle labeled with "C"). Classes can be instantiated as *objects*, and have *activities* (e.g., *Give medicine*) determining their life cycle. The data model is presented in Fig. 2. It specifies data integrity constraints for the entities. For example, a *Prescription* is always assigned to exactly one *Patient*, via a total participation (double line) of *Prescription* in the *For* relationship, and the cardinality 1 for the *Patient* and the *For* relationship. Finally, the double lines of the *Needs* relationship show that an *Order* entity can only coexist with *Prescription*. When a doctor creates or cancels a prescription, the execution must follow these data integrity constraints. This means that it must be ensured when a *Prescription*

---

¹ Create a free academic account at DCRSolutions.net.

² www.kmd.net/insights/using-the-capabilities-of-case-activities-to-automate-case-handling exemplifies the use of DCR Graphs in the NEC WorkZone EIM system.

is created that it refers to exactly one *Patient*, and one kind of *Medicine*. Dually, deletion of a *Prescription* also leads to the deletion of the coexisting *Order* entity, if present.

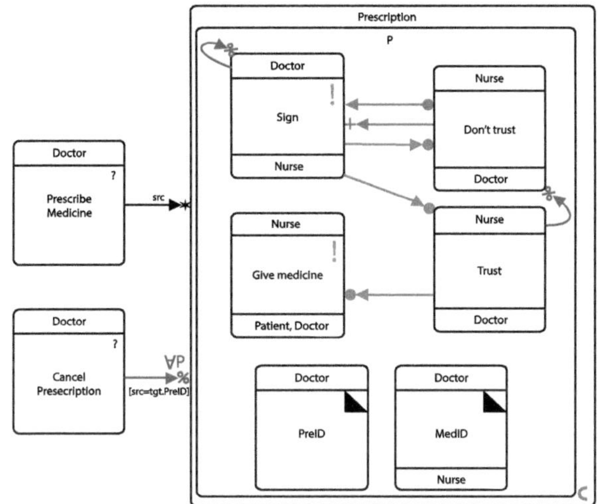

Fig. 1. Running example of healthcare OC-DCR choreography.

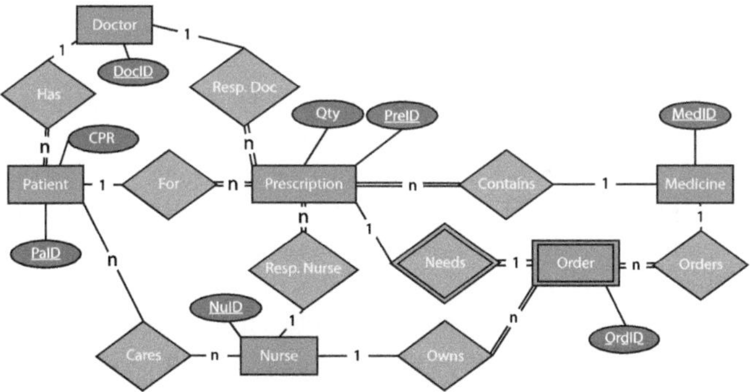

Fig. 2. ER diagram showing the underlying data model for our running example.

While the OC-DCR choreographies and ER models are expressive on their own, some constraints and behaviour depend on both models. For instance, when a prescription is created, we want to restrict access to the data and actions in the prescription to a particular Nurse, Patient, and Doctor. Also, there is no support for permanently deleting data in OC-DCR graphs, only the weaker notion of exclusion. In this paper, we address these shortcomings by combining the OC-DCR graph language with ER models, thereby ensuring that the data model underlying the process remains consistent when executing activities that modify objects. In particular, we present the following contributions:

1. We formally define OCER-DCR Choreographies, combining OC-DCR Choreographies and ER models, by integrating ER data integrity requirements into the semantics of OC-DCR graphs, ensuring that processes run in conformance with structural integrity constraints.
2. We extend OCER-DCR Choreographies with a delete operation and explicit data-dependent identities for roles.
3. We propose a novel visual notation for representing objects and classes within OC-DCR graphs that utilizes the ER model, thereby enhancing the readability and conceptual clarity of OC-DCR graphs.

The structure of this paper follows: Sect. 2 introduces OC-DCR graphs and ER Models. In Sect. 3, we introduce OCER-DCR Choreographies as a way to integrate both models. Section 4 compares related work, and finally Sect. 5 concludes the paper and discusses future work.

2   Preliminaries

To integrate OC-DCR choreographies with ER models, we first provide formal definitions of both frameworks.

2.1   Object-Centric DCR Graphs and Choreographies

In the following, we recall the formal definition of Object-Centric Dynamic Condition Response Graphs (OC-DCR graphs) as originally presented in [5] and extended to choreographies with data in [24].

We first review in definition 1 the notion of a DCR graph with data and nested activity groups on which OC-DCR graphs are based.

A DCR Graph with data and nested groups of activities is a directed graph. The nodes of the graph is a set $A = \mathcal{A} \uplus \mathcal{G}$ of activities ($\mathcal{A}$) and activity groups ($\mathcal{G}$). The edges (E) are relations of different types (R) that define conditions for and effects of executing activities. We assume a set of data values V (including the null value $\perp$) and record keys $\mathcal{K}$. The types of values can be integers, strings, or finite records $[K \to V]$, where $K \subset \mathcal{K}$ is a finite set of record keys. Records are written $\{(k_1, v_1), \ldots, (k_n, v_n)\}$ with keys $k_i \in K$ and values $v_i \in V$. We also assume a set $\mathrm{Exp}_\mathcal{A}$ of well-typed expressions evaluating values in V, including each activity $\alpha \in \mathcal{A}$ as an atomic expression α that evaluates to the current value of the activity, which is recorded in a value map Va assigning the current value to each activity, as elaborated below. We let expressions $\mathrm{BExp}_\mathcal{A} \subset \mathrm{Exp}_\mathcal{A}$ denote boolean expressions and $\mathrm{RExp}_\mathcal{A}^K \subset \mathrm{Exp}_\mathcal{A}$ record expressions of type $[K \to V]$.

Expressions are always attached to an edge of the graph with a source node s and a target node t, and their evaluation is written $[[\exp]]_{\mathrm{Va},s,t}$. Finally, we assume special expressions src and tgt evaluating to the value of the source and target node of the edge to which the expression is attached, i.e. $[[src]]_{\mathrm{Va},s,t} = \mathrm{Va}(s)$ and $[[tgt]]_{\mathrm{Va},s,t} = \mathrm{Va}(t)$, respectively.

Definition 1. *A DCR Graph G with data and nested groups of activities is given by a tuple $(\mathcal{A}, dom, \mathcal{A}^i, \mathcal{A}^p, \mathcal{A}^d, \mathcal{G}, \triangleright, R, E, L, l, M)$ where*

1. *$\mathcal{A}$ is a set of activities ranged over by α,*
2. *dom is the domain function $dom : \mathcal{A} \to \mathcal{D}$ assigning a data type in the set of domains $\mathcal{D}$ to each activity,*
3. *$\mathcal{A}^i \subseteq \mathcal{A}$ is the input activities,*
4. *$\mathcal{A}^p \subseteq \mathcal{A}$ is the parameter activities,*
5. *$\mathcal{A}^d \subseteq \mathcal{A}$ is the pure data activities,*
6. *$\mathcal{G}$ is a set of activity groups ranged over by γ,*
7. *$\triangleright \subseteq A \times \mathcal{G}$ is a grouping relation, where $a \triangleright \gamma$ reads a is member of γ,*
8. *$R = \{\xrightarrow{g}\bullet, \bullet\xrightarrow{g}, \xrightarrow{g}+, \xrightarrow{g}\%, \xrightarrow{g}=_e\}$ are the relation types, for $g \in \mathsf{BExp}_{\mathcal{A}}$ and $e \in \mathsf{Exp}_{\mathcal{A}}$*
9. *$E \subseteq A \times R \times A$ is the relations,*
10. *L is the set of labels,*
11. *$l : \mathcal{A} \to L$ is a labelling function between activities and labels,*
12. *$M = (\mathsf{Ex}, \mathsf{Re}, \mathsf{In}, \mathsf{Va}) \in \mathcal{P}(\mathcal{A}) \times \mathcal{P}(\mathcal{A}) \times \mathcal{P}(\mathcal{A}) \times [\mathcal{A} \to V]$ is the marking,*

where $A = \mathcal{A} \uplus \mathcal{G}$ is the disjoint union of activities and activity groups. We write $>$ for $\triangleright^+$ (the transitive closure of $\triangleright$) and require that it is irreflexive. We write $\geq$ for reflexive closure of $>$ and $\leq$ for the inverse of $\geq$. We write $a\phi a'$ for $\phi \in R$, if $(a'', \phi, a''') \in E, a \geq a'' \wedge a''' < a'$.

The marking $M = (\mathsf{Ex}, \mathsf{Re}, \mathsf{In}, \mathsf{Va})$ defines the current state of the process. The set Ex is the activities that have been **ex**ecuted at least once. The set Re is the activities that are so-called pending **re**sponses, meaning that they must be executed (or become not included) before the process can terminate. The set In defines the set of activities that are currently said to be **in**cluded in the graph. Finally, each activity is further assigned a value given by the map $\mathsf{Va} : \mathcal{A} \to V$.

Input activities ($\alpha \in \mathcal{A}^i$) receive a data value from the environment when executed, which is then recorded in the value map as the new value of α. Parameter activities ($\mathcal{A}^p$) are used when objects are instantiated from graphs, to allow passing the initial values of the activities as a record value $\bar{p} \in \mathsf{RExp}_{\mathcal{A}}^{\mathcal{A}^p}$. We write $G[\bar{p}]$ for the graph that has the same structure as G but a modified value map $\mathsf{Va}[\bar{p}]$ in which $\mathsf{Va}[\bar{p}](\alpha) = v$ if $\bar{p}(\alpha) = v$, and $\mathsf{Va}(\alpha)$ otherwise. The pure data activities ($\mathcal{A}^d$) are used to store data values and cannot be executed independently.

The set of relation types R defines how activities in a DCR graph interact. Each relation is guarded by a boolean expression $g \in \mathsf{BExp}_{\mathcal{A}}$, and is only considered when this guard evaluates to true. The relation $a\xrightarrow{g}\bullet a'$ is a condition relation, denoting that if g evaluates to true, then activity a' may only be executed, if a has previously been executed. The relation $a\bullet\xrightarrow{g}a'$ represents a response, denoting that a' must eventually be executed after a is executed, if g evaluates to true at the time a is executed. The inclusion and exclusion relations, $a\xrightarrow{g}+a'$ and $a\xrightarrow{g}\%a'$, dynamically respectively add or remove a' from the set of included activities when executing a in a state where g evaluates to true. Finally, the value assignment relation $a\xrightarrow{g}=_e a'$ assigns a new value to activity a' based on evaluating the expression e if a is executed and g evaluates to true.

The label of an activity defines the visible action when the activity is executed. We also use it to assign roles to activities, determining which participants initiate/write data to the activity and who (besides the initiator) receives/reads the data. Concretely, we assume a set of roles $\mathcal{R}$, and labels as interactions, which consist of an activity name, an initiator role, and a (possibly empty) set of receiver roles.

Definition 2. *An* interaction *label is written as* $(a, r \to R)$, *in which the action* $a \in \mathsf{Act}$ *is* initiated *by the role* $r \in \mathsf{Roles}$ *and* received *by the roles* $R \subset \mathsf{Roles}\backslash\{r\}$, *We denote by* $\mathsf{Int}_{\mathsf{Act}}$ *the set of all interactions over action names* Act.

We now define DCR Choreographies as DCR Graphs extended with a set of roles, labels being interactions over these roles. The definition extends the one in [24] to include an explicit assignment of roles to identities.

Definition 3. *A triple* $(G, \mathcal{R}, Id)$ *is a DCR Choreography when* G *is a DCR graph with data and nested groups of activities and labels a set of interactions, i.e.* $L = \mathsf{Int}_{\mathsf{Act}}$, $\mathcal{R}$ *is a finite set of roles, and* $Id : \mathcal{R} \to V$ *is a record, assigning participant identities to roles. For* $Id' : \mathcal{R} \to V$ *a record assigning participant identities to roles, write* $G^{[Id']}$ *for the DCR Choreography* $(G, \mathcal{R}, Id')$, *i.e., the choreography obtained from* G *by updating the assignment of participant identities to roles.*

Before we continue to define what it means to execute an activity, we define When an activity is enabled, it can potentially be executed.

Definition 4. *Let* G *be a DCR graph with data and groups of activities, having the set of activities* $\mathcal{A}$ *and marking* $M = (\mathsf{Ex}, \mathsf{Re}, \mathsf{In}, \mathsf{Va})$. *An activity* α *is* enabled, *which we will write* $\mathsf{enabled}(G, \alpha)$, *iff:*

$$1.\ \alpha \in \mathsf{In}\backslash\mathcal{A}^d \qquad 2.\ \forall \alpha' \in \mathsf{In}.\ \alpha' \xrightarrow{g} \bullet \alpha \wedge [[g]]_{M,\alpha',\alpha} \implies \alpha' \in \mathsf{Ex}$$

The first condition states that for an activity α to be enabled, it must not be a data activity, i.e. $\alpha \notin \mathcal{A}^d$, and it is included in the current marking, i.e. $\alpha \in \mathsf{In}$. The second condition states that, if there are currently included activities $\alpha' \in \mathsf{In}$ that are current conditions for α, they must have been executed, that is $\alpha' \in \mathsf{Ex}$.

We now define the semantics for the execution of an activity in a DCR graph.

Definition 5. *Let* $G = (\mathcal{A}, dom, \mathcal{A}^i, \mathcal{A}^p, \mathcal{A}^d, \mathcal{G}, \rhd, R, E, L, l, M)$ *be a DCR graph with data and groups of activities, with* $M = (\mathsf{Ex}, \mathsf{Re}, \mathsf{In}, \mathsf{Va})$. *We define* $M[\alpha \mapsto v] = (\mathsf{Ex}, \mathsf{Re}, \mathsf{In}, \mathsf{Va}_v)$ *with* $\mathsf{Va}_v(\alpha) = v$ *and* $\mathsf{Va}_v(\alpha') = \mathsf{Va}(\alpha')$ *for* $\alpha' \neq \alpha$. *For a value* v, *let* $\mathsf{Execute}(M, \alpha, v) = (\mathsf{Ex}', \mathsf{Re}', \mathsf{In}', \mathsf{Va}')$ *for*

1. $\mathsf{Ex}' = \mathsf{Ex} \cup \{\alpha\}$
2. $\mathsf{Re}' = (\mathsf{Re}\backslash\{\alpha\}) \cup \{\alpha' \mid \alpha \bullet \xrightarrow{g} \alpha' \wedge [[g]]_{\mathsf{Va}_v,\alpha,\alpha'}\}$
3. $\mathsf{In}' = (\mathsf{In}\backslash\{\alpha' \mid \alpha \xrightarrow{g} \% \alpha' \wedge [[g]]_{\mathsf{Va}_v,\alpha,\alpha'}\}) \cup \{\alpha' \mid \alpha \xrightarrow{g} + \alpha' \wedge [[g]]_{\mathsf{Va}_v,\alpha,\alpha'}\}$
4. $\mathsf{Va}'(\alpha') = [[e]]_{\mathsf{Va}_v,\alpha,\alpha'} \ if\ \alpha \xrightarrow{g} =_e \alpha' \wedge [[g]]_{\mathsf{Va}_v,\alpha,\alpha'}$
5. $\mathsf{Va}'(\alpha') = \mathsf{Va}_v(\alpha') \ if\ \alpha \xrightarrow{g} =_e \alpha' \wedge \neg([[g]]_{\mathsf{Va}_v,\alpha,\alpha'})$

The effect of executing α is then the graph $G' = (\mathcal{A}, \mathcal{A}^i, \mathcal{A}^p, \mathcal{A}^d \mathcal{G}, \rhd, R, E, L, l, M')$, where $M' = \mathsf{Execute}(M, \alpha, v)$ if $\alpha \in \mathcal{A}^i$ and v is the input value provided by the environment, and $M' = \mathsf{Execute}(M, \alpha, \mathsf{Va}(\alpha))$ if $\alpha \notin \mathcal{A}^i$. In the first case we write $G \xrightarrow{\alpha, v} G'$ and in the latter we write $G \xrightarrow{\alpha} G'$.

To capture the influence of input data, an intermediate marking $M_v = (\mathsf{Ex}, \mathsf{Re}, \mathsf{In}, \mathsf{Va}_v)$ is introduced, where $\mathsf{Va}_v(\alpha) = v$ reflects a value v provided by the environment, while all other activity values remain unchanged. Based on this, the execution proceeds through a sequence of updates. First, α is added to the set of executed activities Ex. The response set Re is then extended to include every activity α' such that $\alpha \bullet\!\xrightarrow{g} \alpha'$ and the guard g evaluates to true under Va_v. The inclusion set is modified by removing all α' for which $\alpha \xrightarrow{g}\%\alpha'$, and adding those where $\alpha \xrightarrow{g}+\alpha'$, again subject to the guard evaluation. Value assignments are handled conditionally. If α is related to α' via a value assignment relation $\alpha \xrightarrow{g}_{exp} \alpha'$ and g holds, then the value of α' is updated to the evaluation result of exp. Otherwise, it retains its value from Va_v. Together, these updates define the new marking resulting from executing α, either with an externally supplied value if α is an input activity (for $\alpha \in \mathcal{A}^i$) or without if α is not an input activity (if $\alpha \notin \mathcal{A}^i$).

We now define an Object-Centric DCR Choreography as a DCR Choreography that has been extended with a new spawn relation (for spawning objects), a set of class names, and a class definition, mapping each class to a DCR Choreography (extended with a spawn relation). The definition extends the one in [24] to include assignment of role identities to roles when an object is created.

Definition 6. *An Object-centric DCR (OC-DCR) Choreography is a tuple*

$$((G_\top, \mathcal{R}_\top, Id_\top), \to\!*_\top, Oid, C, \psi, \phi),$$

where Oid is a finite set of object identities, C is a finite set of classes, $\psi : Oid \to C$ is a mapping of object identities to classes, and ϕ is the class definition function, assigning to each class in C a pair $((G_c, \mathcal{R}_c, Id_c), \to\!*_c)$ consisting of a class choreography and a spawn relation, where for $\zeta \in C \uplus \{\top\}$

1. *$G_\zeta = (\mathcal{A}_\zeta, dom_\zeta, \mathcal{A}^i_\zeta, \mathcal{A}^p_\zeta, \mathcal{A}^d_\zeta, \mathcal{G}_\zeta, \rhd_\zeta, R, E_\zeta, L_\zeta, l_\zeta, M_\zeta)$, are DCR graphs with data and nested groups of activities and $\mathcal{A}_\zeta \cap \mathcal{A}_{\zeta'} = \emptyset$ for $\zeta \neq \zeta'$*
2. *$\to\!*_\zeta \subseteq \mathcal{A}_\zeta \times \mathsf{BExp}_{\mathcal{A}_\zeta} \times \bigcup_{c \in C}(\mathsf{RExp}^{\mathcal{A}^p_c}_{\mathcal{A}_\zeta} \times \mathsf{RExp}^{\mathcal{R}_c}_{\mathcal{A}_\zeta} \times \{c\})$ are the* instantiation *relations, where we write $\alpha \xrightarrow{g}\!*_\zeta (\bar{p}, \bar{r})c'$ for $(\alpha, g, (\bar{p}, \bar{r}, c')) \in \to\!*_\zeta$,*
3. *$\mathcal{G}_\top = \mathcal{A}_\forall \uplus \mathcal{G}$, where $\mathcal{A}_\forall = \bigcup_{c \in C}\{\alpha_\forall \mid \alpha \in \mathcal{A}_c\}$*
4. *$\mathcal{A}_\top = \{\alpha@i \mid i \in Oid, \alpha \in \mathcal{A}_{\psi(i)}\} \cup \{\alpha@\top \mid \alpha \in \mathcal{A}\}$*
5. *$\mathcal{R}_\top = \{r@i \mid i \in Oid, r \in \mathcal{R}_{\psi(i)}\} \cup \{\alpha@\top \mid r \in \mathcal{R}\}$*

Part (1.) of the definition requires that every class graph G_ζ is itself a DCR graph with data and nested groups of activities. The activity sets $\mathcal{A}_\zeta$ are pairwise disjoint so that object instances do not clash during execution. Part (2.) defines dynamic object creation by a spawning relation written $\to\!*$. Whenever activity a gets executed and the guard g evaluates to true, a new object of class c' is instantiated. The parameter records

$\bar{p}$ and $\bar{r}$ play the role of a constructor in object creation, assigning initial values to the parameter activities and role identities in $G_{c'}$. Part (3.) introduces activity groups $\alpha_\forall$ for each activity α in the class graphs. These groups are used to store the activities that spawn during object instantiation.

We now define the semantics of spawning objects. For simplicity, we assume each activity spawns at most one class of objects. We write $G \cup G'$ for the component-wise union of two DCR Graphs G and G'.

Definition 7. *Let $G_{oc} = ((G, \mathcal{R}, Id), \to*, Oid, C, \psi, \phi)$ be an OC-DCR Choreography with marking $M = (\mathsf{Ex}, \mathsf{Re}, \mathsf{In}, \mathsf{Va})$ and class choreographies $((G_c, \mathcal{R}_c, Id_c),$ $\to*_c)$ for $c \in C$. Assume $\alpha \xrightarrow{g}* (\bar{p}, \bar{r})c$ and $\bar{v} = [[\bar{p}]]_{\mathsf{Va},\alpha,c}$ and $\bar{i} = [[\bar{r}]]_{\mathsf{Va},\alpha,c}$. For $id \notin Oid$ a fresh object identifier, let $G_{c\#id}$ denote the OC-DCR graph obtained from $G_c[\bar{v}]$ by renaming each activity/activity group α and role r of $G_c[\bar{v}]$ to $\alpha@id$ and $r@id$ respectively, but keeping all relations and value assignments. Let $G \cup G_{c\#id} = (\mathcal{A}', dom', \mathcal{A}'^i, \mathcal{A}'^p, \mathcal{A}'^d, \mathcal{G}', \triangleright', R', E', L', l', M')$. Executing α in G_{oc} then results in the OC-DCR Choreography*

$$G^*_{oc} = ((G^*, \mathcal{R}^*, Id^*), \to*, Oid \cup \{id\}, C, \psi[id \mapsto c], \phi),$$

where $\mathcal{R}^* = \mathcal{R} \cup \{r@id \mid r \in \mathcal{R}_c\}$, $Id^* = Id \cup \{(r@id, \bar{i}(r)) \mid r \in \mathcal{R}_c\}$ and $G^* = (\mathcal{A}', dom', \mathcal{A}'^i, \mathcal{A}'^p, \mathcal{A}'^d, \mathcal{G}', \triangleright^*, R', E', L', l', M^*)$, where $\triangleright^* = \triangleright' \cup \{(\alpha, \alpha_\forall) \mid \alpha \in \mathcal{A}_{c\#id}\}$ and $M^* = \mathsf{Execute}(M', \alpha, v)$ if $\alpha \in \mathcal{A}^i_\top$ and v is the input value provided by the environment and $M^* = \mathsf{Execute}(M', \alpha, \mathsf{Va}(\alpha))$ otherwise. In the first case we write $G_{oc} \xrightarrow{\alpha,v} G^*_{oc}$ and in the latter we write $G_{oc} \xrightarrow{\alpha} G^*_{oc}$.

In words, if $\alpha \xrightarrow{g}* (\bar{p}, \bar{r})c$ and $\bar{v}$ is the record values obtained by evaluating the parameter $\bar{p}$ expression in the marking M, then the first thing that happens when α is executed (if the guard g evaluates to true), the creation of a new graph $G_{c\#id}$ obtained from the class graph $G_c[\bar{v}]$ with parameter activities instantiated according to $\bar{v}$ by renaming all activities, groups and roles to include a fresh object identifier id. This graph is then added to the top-level graph, and we add the roles of the spawned object (extended with the object identifier) and the role mapping given by the record $\bar{i}$ obtained from evaluating the role mapping expression $\bar{p}$. Finally, we nest all the new activities in the corresponding $\forall$-groups and update the marking according to the definition of execution given for the underlying DCR Graph.

As introduced earlier, Fig. 1 provides an example of an OC-DCR graph modeling a hospital scenario. The central component is the class `Prescription`, shown as a nested DCR graph containing activities such as `Sign`, `Give medicine`, `Trust`, and `Don't trust`, and a data activity `PreID` that carries the primary key of the object and can be instantiated via a parameter record. The class is instantiated via the `Prescribe Medicine` activity, connected by a spawn relation, and includes a parameter record for the prescription ID that is passed via the keyword *src*. Internally, the class graph defines conditions, responses, and inclusions to declare the order of actions. For example, a nurse may only give medicine after the doctor has signed. Additionally, a doctor can at any time cancel the prescription. This is formally realized by wrapping the prescription class in an additional group that the exclude relation targets. Since semantically, activities from classes are lifted to the top-level graph into the corresponding ∀-groups, a direct relation from the `Cancel Prescription` activity to the class is not sufficient.

2.2   Entity Relationship Model

The Entity-Relationship (ER) model is a widely used approach for modeling data by representing objects as entities and their associations between them as relationships [4,18]. The model is grounded in set-theoretical constructs to formally define entities and their relationships. Based on this formal definition, ER diagrams are used in practice to specify ER models graphically. Here we provide a formal definition of ER diagrams closely following the foundational work of Thalheim [21,22]. To keep the exposition simple, we restrict our ER model fragment to binary relationships and exclude ER model extensions such as generalization and specialization.

Fundamentally, formalizations of the ER model distinguish between two levels: The schema level defines entity types and relationship types. Based on the types, the instance level defines an ER instance as a set of entities and a set of relationship instances, which represent the data that exists at a certain point in time of execution [4,9,22].

Attributes are the basic descriptive elements of entities and relationships. Formally, we follow [21] and assume a set of attributes $\mathcal{U}$ and a set of domains of values $\mathcal{D}$. We further assume that each attribute is assigned a domain (or type) via a function $dom : \mathcal{U} \rightarrow \mathcal{D}$, specifying the type of values it can hold. In Fig. 2 `PatID,PreID`, etc. are all examples of attributes. While they are formally mapped to a domain, in the diagram, we don't explicitly show the domain.

Attributes are associated with entities, formally defined in Definition 8 inspired by [21]. We distinguish between entity types, which are categories of objects, and entity instances, which are concrete instantiations of the types within a particular data model state. Although ER diagrams often refer to "entities", they depict entity types. An entity type $\mathbb{E}$ is defined as a pair $(A(\mathbb{E}), key(\mathbb{E}))$, where $A(\mathbb{E})$ is a set of attributes and $key(\mathbb{E}) \in A(\mathbb{E})$ is An attribute that serves as the primary key. A subset of entity types is the so-called weak entity types that are existentially dependent on another entity. In Fig. 2, the entity type `Prescription` is defined as (`Prescription`, {`PreID, Qnt`}, `PreID`), where `PreID` is its primary key, and `Qnt` is an attribute holding the quantity of the medicine. The type `Order` is a weak entity type existentially dependent on `Prescription` with no attributes except for the weak key.

Definition 8 (Entity Types and Instances). *An **entity type** $\mathbb{E}$ is a tuple $\langle name(\mathbb{E}), A(\mathbb{E}), key(\mathbb{E})\rangle$ where $name(\mathbb{E})$ is the name of the type, $A(\mathbb{E})$ is a set of attributes and $key(\mathbb{E}) \in A(\mathbb{E})$ In any ER model, we assume that no two entity types have the same name. An instance $e = \langle name(\mathbb{E}), \{(a_1, v_1), \ldots, (a_n, v_n)\}\rangle$ of the type $\mathbb{E}$ is called an **entity** or **entity instance**.*

We now define binary relationship types, which express associations between two entity types. A binary relationship type connects exactly two entity types. Formally, it is represented as a pair, consisting of the name of the relationship and a set of the two participating entity types. In general, relationships may also have a set of attributes, but we omit this for simplicity. In the healthcare ER diagram (Fig. 2), `For` is a binary relationship type defined as $(\text{For}, \{\texttt{Patient}, \texttt{Prescription}\})$ between `Patient` and `Prescription`.

Each relationship type is instantiated in a particular state σ of the data model as a set of binary relationship instances, each linking one entity from the first type to one from the second.

Definition 9 (Binary Relationship Types and Instances). *Let $\mathbb{E}_1, \mathbb{E}_2$ be two distinct entity types. A **binary relationship type** $\mathbb{R} = (name(\mathbb{R}), \{\mathbb{E}_1, \mathbb{E}_2\})$ consists of its name and the two entity types, which we say **participates** in $\mathbb{R}$. Let E_1^S, E_2^S be sets of entities of respectively entity type $\mathbb{E}_1$ and $\mathbb{E}_2$. In any ER-model, we assume that no two relation types between the same two entity-types have the same name. An instance r of the relationship type $\mathbb{R}$ is called **binary relationship**, or **binary relationship instance** and is a pair $\langle name(\mathbb{R}), \{e_1, e_2\} \rangle$, where $(e1, e2) \in E_1^S \times E_2^S$.*

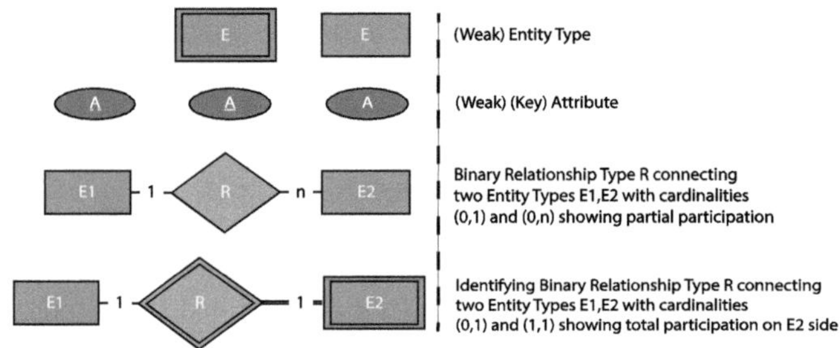

Fig. 3. Visual Representation of core ER modeling concepts used in this paper.

Figure 3 provides an overview of the graphical notation used in our ER diagrams. Moreover, Cardinality constraints as defined in Definition 10 below, again following [21], further refine how entities participate in relationships. They are specified per entity type and relationship and indicate how often an entity instance may or must participate in a relationship. In the ER diagram, these are shown as either a 1 or an n on the edges, where the 1 denotes at most one, and n denotes no upper limit. For the lower bound, a double line means 1 and a single line means 0. For example, the `For` relationship between `Patient` and `Prescription` in Fig. 2, the constraint $comp(\text{For}, \texttt{Patient}) = (0, n)$ expresses that a patient can have zero or more prescriptions.

Definition 10 (Cardinality Constraint). *Let $\mathbb{R}(\mathbb{E}_1, \mathbb{E}_2)$ be a binary relationship type. A **cardinality constraint***

$$comp(\mathbb{R}, \mathbb{E}_i) \in \{(0, 1), (1, 1), (0, n), (1, n)\}, i \in \{1, 2\}$$

for the relationship type $\mathbb{R}$ and entity type $\mathbb{E}_i$ provides a pair (min, max). The number min is the least number of relationship instances that must exist involving any entity e

*of $\mathbb{E}_i$ and the relationship type $\mathbb{R}$. If $min = 1$, we say that $\mathbb{E}_i$ has **total participation** in $\mathbb{R}$, and otherwise, if $min = 0$, we say it has **partial participation**. Dually, if $max = 1$ then there must be at most one participation, and $max = n$ means that there is no upper bound.*

The lower bound of a cardinality constraint distinguishes between total and partial participation. An entity type participates totally in a relationship if every instance appears in at least one relationship instance. Otherwise, the participation is partial. For example, the constraint $comp(\texttt{Needs}, \texttt{Order}) = (1, 1)$ expresses total participation of Order in the Needs relationship, indicating that every order must be linked to a prescription (and exactly one). Some relationships also play a role in identifying weak entity types. A weak entity type depends on another type for identification and must participate totally in a specific relationship to be identifiable. In our example, Order is a weak entity type and participates totally in the Needs relationship with Prescription.

Definition 11 (Identifiying Relationship Type). *Let $\mathbb{R} = (\mathbb{E}_1, \mathbb{E}_2)$ be a binary relationship type. We call $\mathbb{R}$ a **candidate identifying relationship type**, if either $\mathbb{E}_1$ or $\mathbb{E}_2$ is a weak entity type and participates totally in $\mathbb{R}$, and the other is not a weak entity type.*

We can now define a complete ER model in Definition 12. The model encompasses the global set of attributes and domains, entity types, binary relationship types, identifying relationship markings, and cardinality constraints. Additionally, it includes a state that captures the actual instances of entities and relationships at a given point in time.

Definition 12 (ER Model). *An ER model $\mathcal{ER} = (\mathcal{U}, \mathcal{D}, \mathcal{E}, \mathcal{E}_w, \mathcal{R}, \mathcal{I}, comp, S)$ is a tuple consisting of a set of attributes $\mathcal{U}$, a set of domains $\mathcal{D}$, a set of entity types $\mathcal{E}$, a set $\mathcal{E}_w \subseteq \mathcal{E}$ of weak entity types, a set of binary relationship types $\mathcal{R}$, a set of identifying relationship types $\mathcal{I} \subseteq \mathcal{R}$ (which must be candidate identifying relationship types), a cardinality constraints assignment, comp, and a state S that contains a set of entities E for each entity type $\mathbb{E} \in \mathcal{E}$ and a set R for each binary relationship type $\mathbb{R} \in \mathcal{R}$. $S[\mathbb{E}], S[\mathbb{R}]$ for $\mathbb{E} \in \mathcal{E} \wedge \mathbb{R} \in \mathcal{R}$ then denote the entity set and relationship set for entity type $\mathbb{E}$, and relationship type $\mathbb{R}$, respectively, and let $\mathcal{R}[\mathbb{E}]$ and $\mathcal{R}[[\mathbb{E}]]$ denote the relationship types that $\mathbb{E}$ participates in and has total participation in, respectively. For entity sets $S[\mathbb{E}]$ we let $S[\mathbb{E}](k)$ denote the entity e in entity set $S[\mathbb{E}]$ with primary key k. Finally, let $S[\mathcal{E}]$ denote the set of all entities and $S[\mathcal{R}]$ the set of all relationships.*

Now that we have defined an ER model, we can specify in Definition 13 which properties determine the structural consistency of an ER model. We specify that an ER model is structurally consistent if (1) every key in each entity set is unique, (2) each weak entity type is connected via at least one identifying relation to an entity on which it is existentially dependent, and (3) the cardinalities within the diagram are respected for all relation instances, including total and partial participation. These integrity constraints are well-established in conceptual data modeling [9, 21, 22].

Definition 13 (Structural Consistency). *Let $\mathcal{ER} = (\mathcal{U}, \mathcal{D}, \mathcal{E}, \mathcal{E}_w, \mathcal{R}, \mathcal{I}, comp, S)$ be an ER model. We call $\mathcal{ER}$ **structurally consistent**, iff*

1. $\forall \mathbb{E} \in \mathcal{E}.e, e' \in S[\mathbb{E}]. \; key(e) = key(e') \Rightarrow e = e'.$

2. $\forall \mathbb{E}_1 \in \mathcal{E}_w.\ (\exists \mathbb{E}_2 \in \mathcal{E} \backslash \mathcal{E}_w.\mathbb{E}_1 \neq \mathbb{E}_2\ .$
   $\exists(name(\mathbb{R}), \{\mathbb{E}_2, \mathbb{E}_1\}) \in \mathcal{I} \cap \mathcal{R}[[\mathbb{E}_1]],$
3. $\forall (name(\mathbb{R}), \{\mathbb{E}_1, \mathbb{E}_2\}) \in \mathcal{R}.\ \textsc{Card}(\mathbb{R}, \mathbb{E}_1) \wedge \textsc{Card}(\mathbb{R}, \mathbb{E}_2).$

where for $\mathbb{R}(name(\mathbb{R}), \{\mathbb{E}, _\}) \in \mathcal{R}$*,* $min \in \{0, 1\}$*, and* $max \in \{1, n\}$*,* $\textsc{Card}(\mathbb{R}, \mathbb{E})$ *is defined as:*

$$
\begin{aligned}
&comp(\mathbb{R}, \mathbb{E}) = (1, max) \Rightarrow \forall e \in S[\mathbb{E}].\exists \langle n, Ent\rangle \in S[\mathbb{R}].e \in Ent) \wedge \\
&(comp(\mathbb{R}, \mathbb{E}) = (min, 1) \Rightarrow \forall e \in S[\mathbb{E}]. \\
&\quad (\exists \langle n_1, Ent_1\rangle, \langle n_2, Ent_2\rangle \in S[\mathbb{R}] \wedge e \in Ent_1 \cap Ent_2) \\
&\quad\quad \Rightarrow \langle n_1, Ent_1\rangle = \langle n_2, Ent_2\rangle).
\end{aligned}
$$

3 OCER-DCR: Combining OC-DCR Choreographies and ER Models

Below, we define OCER-DCR Choreographies, which combine ER models and OC-DCR Choreographies, and also add an operation for the deletion of objects to be able to capture all CRUD operations. Intuitively, the classes and roles in an OCER-DCR Graph each have a corresponding entity type in the ER model, and each data activity of a class either has a corresponding attribute of the entity corresponding to the class or it is the name of a relationship to another entity.

Figure 4 shows the resulting OCER-DCR Choreography after executing Prescribe Medicine. The model showcases all the new features. Firstly, we now have an explicit delete relation from the Cancel Prescription activity to the Prescription class (indicated with a bin symbol). It receives the prescription ID as input, and utilizes the data model to know which data activity inside the class holds the key. Second, the roles of the spawned object are explicitly assigned identities in the spawn relation (provided as input values to Prescribe Medicine), and the data activities inside the class directly correspond to attributes and relationships for Prescription in the data model. This allows us to dynamically create entities and relationships in the ER model and use it to record the state of dynamically spawned objects, as visualized in the top.

We first extend OC-DCR choreographies with deletion.

Definition 14 (OC-DCR Choreography with Deletion). *An OC-DCR choreography with deletion is a tuple* $((G_\top, \mathcal{R}_\top, Id_\top) \rightarrow\!\!*_\top, \rightarrow 🗑_\top, \psi, C, \phi)$*, where*

1. $((G_\top, \mathcal{R}_\top, Id_\top) \rightarrow\!\!*_\top, \psi, C, \phi')$ *is an OC-DCR choreography and for all* $c \in C$*,* $\phi(c) = ((G_c, \mathcal{R}_c, Id_c), \rightarrow\!\!*_c, \rightarrow 🗑_c)$*, for* $\phi'(c) = ((G_c, \mathcal{R}_c, Id_c), \rightarrow\!\!*_c)$
2. $\rightarrow 🗑_\zeta \subseteq A_\zeta \times \mathsf{BExp}_{A_\zeta} \times \mathsf{Exp}_{A_\zeta} \times C$ *for* $\zeta \in C \uplus \{\top\}$ *are the deletion relations, where we write* $\alpha \overset{g}{\rightarrow 🗑_c} ec'$ *for* $(\alpha, g, e, c') \in \rightarrow 🗑_c$

We then define OCER-DCR Choreographies, which combine the two types of models by gluing them together based on the names of the data activities and roles in the DCR model, as well as the corresponding entities and relationships in the ER model.

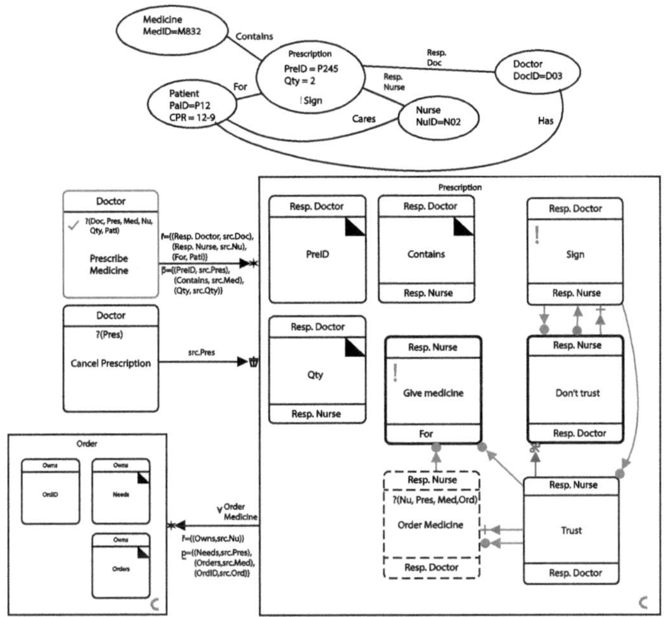

Fig. 4. OCER-DCR Choreography after executing Prescribe Medicine.

Definition 15 (OCER-DCR Choreography). *An Object-centric Entity Relationship (OCER-)DCR choreography is a pair* $(\mathcal{ER}, \mathcal{G})$ *where* $\mathcal{ER} = (\mathcal{U}, \mathcal{D}, \mathcal{E}, \mathcal{E}_w$ $\mathcal{R}, \mathcal{I}, comp, S)$ *is a structurally consistent ER model and* $\mathcal{G} = ((G, \mathcal{R}, Id) \rightarrow *, \rightarrow \textrm{⛟}, Oid, C, \psi, \phi)$ *is an OC-DCR choreography with deletion, such that*

1. $\forall c \in C. \exists \mathbb{E} \in \mathcal{E}.c = name(\mathbb{E}) \wedge \{l(\alpha) \mid \alpha \in \mathcal{A}_c^d\} \cup \mathcal{R}_c \subseteq \mathcal{R}[\mathbb{E}] \cup A(\mathbb{E}) \wedge$
   $\mathcal{R}[[\mathbb{E}]] \cup A(\mathbb{E}) \subseteq \{l(\alpha) \mid \alpha \in \mathcal{A}_c^d\} \cup \mathcal{R}_c$
2. $\forall \mathbb{E} \in \mathcal{E}. \exists c \in C.c = name(\mathbb{E}) \Rightarrow \exists \alpha \in \mathcal{A}_c^d.l(\alpha) = key(\mathbb{E}) \wedge \forall e \in S[\mathbb{E}]. \exists id \in Oid.Va(\alpha@id) = key(e).$
3. $\forall id \in Oid, \exists \mathbb{E} \in \mathcal{E}. \exists e \in S[\mathbb{E}].l(\alpha) = key(\mathbb{E}) \wedge Va(\alpha) = key(e).$

For $e \in \mathbb{E}$ *define* OBJID$(e) = id$ *if* $\psi(id) = name(\mathbb{E}) = c$ *and* $\alpha \in \mathcal{A}_c^d.l(\alpha) = key(\mathbb{E})$ *and* $Va(\alpha) = key(e)$. *For* $id \in Oid$ *define* ENT$(id) = e$, *if* $e \in S[\mathbb{E}]$ *and* $\exists c \in C.\exists \alpha \in \mathcal{A}_c^d.l(\alpha) = key(\mathbb{E}) \wedge Va(\alpha@id) = key(e)$.

(1) For each class, there is an entity type $\mathbb{E}$ named as the class, such that each name of a data activity and role is either an attribute of the entity $\mathbb{E}$ or a name of a relationship in which $\mathbb{E}$ participates in, and the other way, every relationship type that $\mathbb{E}$ participates totally in and attribute name must be either a role or the name of a data activity. (2) For each entity in the state that is represented as a class in the OC-DCR graph, there exists an object in the OC-DCR graph. (3) For each object in the OC-DCR graph, there

exists an entity. We now extend the semantics for the spawn relationship to update the ER model.

Definition 16 (Spawn update of ER model). *Let $(\mathcal{ER}, \mathcal{G})$ be an OCER-DCR Choreography, where $\mathcal{ER} = (\mathcal{U}, \mathcal{D}, \mathcal{E}, \mathcal{E}_w, \mathcal{R}, \mathcal{I}, \mathcal{C}, S)$ and $\mathcal{G} = ((G, \mathcal{R}, Id), \to*, \to \overline{\mathbf{w}}, \psi, C, \phi)$ and G has marking $M = (\text{Ex}, \text{Re}, \text{In}, \text{Va})$ and class graphs $((G_c, \mathcal{R}_c, Id_c), \to*_c, \to \overline{\mathbf{w}}_c)$ for $c \in C$. Assume $\alpha \xrightarrow{g}* (\bar{p}, \bar{r})c$ and $\bar{v} = [[\bar{p}]]_{\text{Va}, \alpha, c}$ and $\bar{i} = [[\bar{r}]]_{\text{Va}, \alpha, c}$. Then the effect of executing α is defined on the graph similar to how is defined in Definition 7 and the effect on the ER-model is the updated ER model $\mathcal{ER}' = (\mathcal{U}, \mathcal{D}, \mathcal{E}, \mathcal{E}_w, \mathcal{R}, \mathcal{I}, \mathcal{C}, S')$, where $S' = S \cup \{e_{id}\} \cup \{\langle r, \{e_{id}, e_r\}\rangle \mid r \in \mathcal{R}_c \wedge \exists \mathbb{E}.name(\mathbb{E}) = r \wedge e_r = S[\mathbb{E}](\bar{i}(r))\} \cup \{\langle d, \{e_{id}, e_d\}\rangle \mid d \in l(\mathcal{A}_c^d) \cap name(\mathcal{R}[\mathbb{E}_c]).\exists \mathbb{E}.name(\mathbb{E}) = d.\exists \alpha \in \mathcal{A}_c^d.e_d = S[\mathbb{E}](\text{Va}(\alpha)) \wedge l(\alpha) = d\}$, where $e_{id} = \langle c, A_c\rangle$, $A_c : (l(\mathcal{A}_c^d)\backslash name(\mathcal{R}[\mathbb{E}_c])) \to V$ is defined as $A_c(a) = \text{Va}(\alpha)$ if $a \in l(\mathcal{A}_c^d)\backslash name(\mathcal{R}[\mathbb{E}_c])$ and $l(\alpha) = a$ and $l(\mathcal{A}_c^d) = \{l(\alpha) \mid \alpha \in \mathcal{A}_c^d\}$ and $name(\mathbb{E}_c) = c$.*

To implement the deletion as an OCER-DCR Choreography relation, we define the scope of the deletion of an entity. Intuitively, for a given entity that is to be deleted, all relations that refer to this entity must be deleted. In addition, all existentially dependent entities and their relations must also be deleted. Since we do not allow a chain of existential dependencies in our ER model, we do not have to look further than the direct neighbors. The following definitions characterize the set DELSET, and the set of objects corresponding to the deletes of an entity.

Definition 17 (DELETESET). *Let $\mathcal{ER} = (\mathcal{U}, \mathcal{D}, \mathcal{E}, \mathcal{E}_w, \mathcal{R}, \mathcal{I}, comp, S)$ be a structurally consistent ER model. Let $e_1 = \langle name, attrs\rangle \in S[\mathbb{E}_1]$ for $\mathbb{E}_1 \in \mathcal{E}$. Define $\text{ExDep}(e_1)$, the set of all existentially dependent entities on e_1, as*

$$\text{ExDep}(e_1) = \{e_2 \mid \exists(name(\mathbb{R}), \{\mathbb{E}_1, \mathbb{E}_2\}) \in \mathcal{I}.comp(\mathbb{E}_2, \mathbb{R}) = (1, max)$$
$$\wedge (\exists\langle n, \{e_1, e_2\}\rangle \in S[\mathbb{R}].\mathbb{E}_2 \in \mathcal{E}_w\}.$$

We then let

$$\text{DelSet}(e_1) = \{e_1\} \cup \text{ExDep}(e_1) \cup \{r \in S[\mathcal{R}] \mid r = \langle n, \{e_1, e_2\}\rangle\} \cup$$
$$\{r \in S[\mathcal{R}] \mid \exists e_2 \in \text{ExDep}(e_1).r = \langle n, \{e_2, e_3\}\rangle\}$$

denote the set of entities and relationships to delete for the deletion of entity e_1.

Definition 18 (DeleteObjects). *Let $(\mathcal{ER}, \mathcal{G})$ be an OCER-DCR Choreography. We define $\text{OcDelSet}(e) = \{\text{ObjId}(e') \mid e' \in \text{DelSet}(e)\}$.*

The set OCDELSET contains all object IDs for which the corresponding activities within the OC-DCR choreography need to be deleted. We can now formally define the semantics of the deletion of an object. For simplicity, we assume that each activity deletes at most one class of objects, and the same activity does not spawn and delete objects.

Definition 19 (OCER-DCR Delete Semantics). *Let $(\mathcal{ER}, \mathcal{G})$ be an OCER-DCR Choreography, where $\mathcal{ER} = (\mathcal{U}, \mathcal{D}, \mathcal{E}, \mathcal{E}_w, \mathcal{R}, \mathcal{I}, \mathcal{C}, S)$ and $\mathcal{G} = ((G, \mathcal{R}, Id), \to*, \to \text{🗑}, \psi, C, \phi)$ and G has marking $M = (\mathsf{Ex}, \mathsf{Re}, \mathsf{In}, \mathsf{Va})$ and class graphs $((G_c, \mathcal{R}_c, Id_c), \to*_c, \to \text{🗑}_c)$ for $c \in C$. Assume $\alpha \overset{g}{\to} \text{🗑} e_k c$ and $k = [[e_k]]_{\mathsf{Va},\alpha,c}$ is the value obtained by evaluating the parameter expression e_k in the marking M. This value should be the key of an entity $S[\mathbb{E}](k)$. representing class c, i.e. $name(\mathbb{E}) = c$. The result of executing α is then the OCER-DCR Choreography $(\mathcal{ER}', \mathcal{G}')$ obtained from $(\mathcal{ER}, \mathcal{G})$ by letting $\mathcal{ER}'$ be the ER model obtained by deleting all entities and relationships in $\mathrm{DELSET}(e)$ from $\mathcal{ER}$ and $\mathcal{G}'$ be the graph obtained from $\mathcal{G}$ by deleting all activities $\alpha@id$ for $id \in \mathrm{OCDELSET}(e)$, and all relations involving these activities removed as well, and with marking $M' = \mathsf{Execute}(M, \alpha, v)$ if $\alpha \in \mathcal{A}_\top^i$ and v is the input value provided by the environment and $M' = \mathsf{Execute}(M', \alpha, \mathsf{Va}(\alpha))$ otherwise.*

We have now defined the changes to the ER model for the spawning and deletion of objects. However, not all insertions or deletions are safe. An inserted entity may violate the cardinality constraints and Some entities from the deleted set may be related to other entities that are not weak entity types, but are totally participating in a relationship with them. We therefore extend the enabledness relation for activities in the OC-DCR graph so that we only enable spawns and deletions that are safe to perform. This can be derived from the ER model.

Definition 20 (Enabledness with ER Model). *Let $(\mathcal{ER}, \mathcal{G})$ be an OCER-DCR Choreography, where $\mathcal{ER} = (\mathcal{U}, \mathcal{D}, \mathcal{E}, \mathcal{E}_w, \mathcal{R}, \mathcal{I}, \mathcal{C}, S)$ and $\mathcal{G} = ((G, \mathcal{R}, Id), \to*, \to \text{🗑}, \psi, C, \phi)$ and G has activities $\mathcal{A}$ and marking $M = (\mathsf{Ex}, \mathsf{Re}, \mathsf{In}, \mathsf{Va})$. An activity $\alpha \in \mathcal{A}$ is enabled iff*

1. α is enabled according to Definition 4.
2. $\mathcal{ER}'$ is structurally consistent according to Definition 13.

where $\mathcal{ER}'$ is the ER Model resulting from executing α as defined in Definition 16 and Definition 19.

To show why we have introduced a new delete operation in definition 19 and 20, we would like to refer to our initial running example in Fig. 1. Here we have simulated the deletion of the prescription object using an $\forall$-exclude ($\to\%$) relation. This relation also requires a group nesting within the class to remove all activities of the spawned object. On the contrary, the new delete ($\to \text{🗑}$) relation can delete an object within the OC-DCR choreography directly using its primary key, as shown in Fig. 4. In addition, definition 20 allows us to express that we only enable activities originating a deletion if the data model resulting from the deletion is structurally consistent.

fig:oc-dcr-presecription-after-ordinate

4   Related Work

Recently, various contributions on integrating data and processes have led to so-called data-aware processes [2,8,20]. Probably the closest related work is the one in [2] that formalizes the combination of data constraints and declarative process constraints in the context of the OCBC approach. Two extensions for the BPMN language introduce support for SQL queries on a relational data model. [3,8]. De Giacomo et al. integrate a UML class diagram with a BPMN model. Here, activities refer to a class diagram via OCL constructs. This yields an executable system that couples data and process [7]. Moreover, DCR graphs have been extended to include simple data types into activities [6]. At the same time, object-centricity grew as a concept for process models in the field of process mining [1]. In this paradigm, process models also need to express the semantics of many coexisting objects. For this purpose, Ghilardi et al. propose COA-nets [10]. COA-nets are an extension of Colored Petri nets for multi-object scenarios. Similarly, Christfort et al. introduce Object-Centric DCR Graphs to model multi-object scenarios in a declarative process model [5]. Initially, OC-DCR Graphs only support many-to-many updates of objects. An extension by Zuckmantel et al. also allows for the update of single objects [24]. Several works show that BPMN lacks expressiveness for such multi-object interactions. As a consequence, Seidel et al. propose OC-BPMN, a graphical language that splits a BPMN model into fragments linked by a data model [16]. OC-BPMN enriches BPMN with the ability to create, reference, and correlate objects via a shared schema. Yet, its semantics are given informally. The view of the data model for the objects also plays a role in object-centred models. König et al. have outlined that many of the recent works are giving a means to object state [13]. But the question arises if such a state is unifiable. Finally, Lichtenstein et al. also reason about consistency properties when combining data model and process model [14].

In summary, except [2], the presented approaches either enrich processes with data semantics or declarative constraints. In the present work, we focused as in [2] on the inclusion of the data model together with its data integrity constraints, but also added explicit support for data-dependent access control.

5   Conclusion and Future Work

In this work, we combine OC-DCR Choreographies, an Object-Centric Process Model (OCPM) with role-based access constraints, with an ER model. We embed the semantics of ER models into the execution semantics of OC-DCR choreographies. This allows for the explicit assignment of data-dependent identities to roles that can access objects, ensuring that objects respect data integrity constraints on insertion and deletion during process execution. These data constraints are cardinalities, key uniqueness, referential integrity, and existential dependency.

This work currently supports only a fragment of ER modeling, focusing on binary relationships and restricted cardinalities (1:1, 1:n, n:m). We do not yet model attributes in relationships, and recursive relationships remain future work. Smith et al.'s work on generalization and aggregation [17] suggests promising directions for extending object notions in process models.

ER models relate closely to UML class diagrams [15], which include features like directed relationships, inheritance, and aggregation. With Object Constraint Language (OCL), UML also supports customized data integrity constraints. We plan to explore how these features align with object-centric requirements.

Furthermore, this work presents a global model of choreography involving multiple participants. In our choreography, the ER model is centralized, and therefore, it can be an interesting future work to investigate a notion of endpoint projection for OCER-DCR Choreographies.

Last, we introduce insertion and deletion into the semantics of OC-DCR in a way that allows for deadlocks. If these operations do not maintain structural integrity, the spawning or deleting activity is not enabled. Dependent on the state of the ER model, this may block process execution entirely. An interesting future work is to investigate deadlock detection and prevention for OCER-DCR Choreographies. Finally, it would be interesting to explore how the ideas in the present paper can be applied to other approaches, in particular the one in [2].

References

1. van der Aalst, W.M.P.: Object-Centric Process Mining: Dealing with Divergence and Convergence in Event Data, pp. 3–25. Springer International Publishing (2019)
2. Artale, A., Kovtunova, A., Montali, M., van der Aalst, W.M.P.: Modeling and Reasoning over Declarative Data-Aware Processes with Object-Centric Behavioral Constraints, pp. 139–156. Springer International Publishing (2019)
3. Calvanese, D., Montali, M., Patrizi, F., Rivkin, A.: Modeling and In-Database Management of Relational, Data-Aware Processes, pp. 328–345. Springer International Publishing (2019)
4. Chen, P.P.S.: The entity-relationship model–toward a unified view of data. ACM Trans. Database Syst. **1**(1), 9–36 (1976)
5. Christfort, A.K., Rivkin, A., Fahland, D., Hildebrandt, T.T., Slaats, T.: Discovery of object-centric declarative models. In: 2024 6th International Conference on Process Mining (ICPM), pp. 121–128. IEEE (Oct 2024)
6. Costa Seco, J., Debois, S., Hildebrandt, T., Slaats, T.: Reseda: declaring live event-driven computations as reactive semi-structured data. In: EDOC, pp. 75–84. IEEE (Oct 2018)
7. De Giacomo, G., Oriol, X., Estañol, M., Teniente, E.: Linking data and bpmn processes to achieve executable models, pp. 612–628 (2017)
8. Di Ciccio, C., Marrella, A., Russo, A.: Knowledge-intensive processes: characteristics, requirements and analysis of contemporary approaches. J. Data Semantics **4**(1), 29–57 (2014). https://doi.org/10.1007/s13740-014-0038-4
9. Elmasri, R., Navathe, S.: Fundamentals of database systems. Addison-Wesley, Boston [u.a.], 6. ed. edn. (2011), literaturverz. S. 1099 - 1132
10. Ghilardi, S., Gianola, A., Montali, M., Rivkin, A.: Petri net-based object-centric processes with read-only data. Inf. Syst. **107**, 102011 (2022). https://doi.org/10.1016/j.is.2022.102011
11. Gregor, S., Hart, D., Martin, N.: Enterprise architectures: enablers of business strategy and is/it alignment in government. Inform. Technol. People **20**(2), 96–120 (2007)
12. Hildebrandt, T.T., Mukkamala, R.R.: Declarative event-based workflow as distributed dynamic condition response graphs. arXiv preprint arXiv:1110.4161 (2011)
13. König, M., Gießler, R., Brandt, W., Seidel, A., Weske, M.: A Unified View on Data Object States, pp. 259–276. Springer Nature Switzerland (2025). https://doi.org/10.1007/978-3-031-94571-7_15
14. Lichtenstein, T., Weske, M.: Data consistency as a criterion for process choreography design. In: Link, S., Reinhartz-Berger, I., Zdravkovic, J., Bork, D., Srinivasa, S. (eds.) ER Forum. CEUR Workshop Proceedings, vol. 3211. CEUR-WS.org (2022). https://ceur-ws.org/Vol-3211/CR_095.pdf

15. Rumbaugh, J.: Er is uml. J. Inform. Syst. Educ. **17**(1), 21–25 (Spring 2006). https://www.proquest.com/scholarly-journals/er-is-uml/docview/200130685/se-2

16. Seidel, A., König, M., Weske, M.: Towards object-centric BPMN process models. In: del-Río-Ortega et al., A. (ed.) Proceedings of the Best Dissertation Award, Doctoral Consortium, and Demonstration & Resources Forum at BPM 2024. CEUR Workshop Proceedings, vol. 3758, pp. 176–182. CEUR-WS.org (2024). https://ceur-ws.org/Vol-3758/paper-32.pdf

17. Smith, J.M., Smith, D.C.P.: Database abstractions: aggregation and generalization. ACM Trans. Database Syst. **2**(2), 105–133 (1977). https://doi.org/10.1145/320544.320546

18. Song, I.Y., Chen, P.P.: Entity Relationship Model, pp. 1003–1009. Springer US (2009). https://doi.org/10.1007/978-0-387-39940-9_148

19. Steinau, S., Andrews, K., Reichert, M.: Executing Lifecycle Processes in Object-Aware Process Management, pp. 25–44. Springer International Publishing (2019). https://doi.org/10.1007/978-3-030-11638-5_2

20. Steinau, S., Marrella, A., Andrews, K., Leotta, F., Mecella, M., Reichert, M.: DALEC: a framework for the systematic evaluation of data-centric approaches to process management software. Softw. Syst. Model. **18**(4), 2679–2716 (2018). https://doi.org/10.1007/s10270-018-0695-0

21. Thalheim, B.: Fundamentals of cardinality constraints, pp. 7–23. Springer Berlin Heidelberg (1992). https://doi.org/10.1007/3-540-56023-8_3

22. Thalheim, B.: Entity-Relationship Modeling. Springer Berlin Heidelberg (2000). https://doi.org/10.1007/978-3-662-04058-4

23. Zachman, J.A.: The zachman framework for enterprise architecture. Primer for Enterprise Engineering and Manufacturing.[si]: Zachman International, pp. 3283–3290 (2003)

24. Zuckmantel, T., Zhou, Y., Düdder, B., Hildebrandt, T.: DACEO: Declarative Asynchronous Choreographies with General Data-Dependent Event-Ordering and Objects, pp. 197–216. Springer Nature Switzerland (2025). https://doi.org/10.1007/978-3-031-95589-1_10

Incremental Synchronization of BPMN Models and Documentations by Leveraging Structural Algorithms and LLMs

David Cremer[1], Benjamin Dalmas[2], Quentin Nivon[1], and Gwen Salaün[1(✉)]

[1] Univ. Grenoble Alpes, CNRS, Grenoble INP, Inria, LIG, 38000 Grenoble, France
{david.cremer,quentin.nivon,gwen.salaun}@inria.fr
[2] iGrafx, 35510 Cesson-Sévigné, France
benjamin.dalmas@igrafx.com

Abstract. Maintaining consistency between business process models and their textual descriptions is critical for operational clarity, compliance, and communication. However, as process models evolve, updating documentation remains costly and error-prone. Existing methods often require manual rewriting or full text regeneration, discarding valuable domain-specific language. This paper presents an edit-based synchronization approach that incrementally updates textual descriptions to reflect changes in Business Process Model and Notation (BPMN) diagrams while preserving unaffected content. We propose two complementary algorithms: the Longest Common Execution Subsequence (LCES) approach for balanced acyclic models, and a heuristic beam search for more complex structures with loops and unbalanced gateways. The resulting transformation steps are translated into structured prompts guiding a large language model to produce minimal, style-consistent revisions. A prototype system demonstrates high semantic accuracy and stylistic coherence across diverse process evolution scenarios.

Keywords: Process Modeling · Business Process Management (BPM) · Text Synchronization · Large Language Models (LLMs)

1 Introduction

Business processes prescribe how work unfolds within and across organizational boundaries. Expressed in tasks, decisions, and control-flow dependencies, they encode operational intent, compliance obligations, and institutional knowledge that guide day-to-day execution. Making these processes explicit and comprehensible is therefore vital for optimisation, regulatory assurance, and cross-functional alignment.

Organizations typically capture a process in two complementary ways: (i) a *graphical model* such as a Business Process Model and Notation (BPMN) diagram, which lends itself to simulation and automated execution [4,9], and (ii) a *textual description* that narrates procedures, exceptions, and rationale in natural language, which remains indispensable for non-technical stakeholders [6,16]. Maintaining both artifacts in lock-step is notoriously difficult. Models evolve quickly as regulations or business needs

C. Cappiello et al. (Eds.): CoopIS 2025, LNCS 15535, pp. 239–256, 2026.
https://doi.org/10.1007/978-3-032-15538-2_14

change, while the accompanying text lags behind, leading to inconsistencies that cause errors and erode trust [1, 11].

Current practices rely on analysts manually updating the prose whenever a model changes—a costly and error-prone activity that does not scale to repositories with hundreds of processes [25]. Full regeneration of the text with natural language generation techniques is a tempting alternative, but tends to discard domain-specific phrasing and validated narrative that users value [10]. We argue that *synchronization rather than regeneration* is the more effective paradigm: update only the fragments of prose affected by structural edits in the BPMN while preserving everything else. Realizing this vision poses two technical challenges: (1) detecting and representing model edits in a suitable form allowing textual revision, and (2) mapping those edits to minimal, stylistically coherent changes in the documentation.

To tackle these challenges, we present an automated approach that treats process-text consistency as an *edit-based* synchronization problem. Specifically, we combine graph-based model differencing with prompt-guided editing by large language models (LLMs). For balanced acyclic models, we introduce the *Longest Common Execution Subsequence* (LCES) algorithm to isolate shared control-flow, while for processes containing loops or unbalanced gateways, we employ a custom beam-search heuristic that explores plausible sequences of insertions, deletions, and refinements. The detected edits are then translated into structured prompts that steer an LLM to revise only the relevant sentences, thus preserving validated language and narrative voice. Experiments indicate that this approach can produce text that remains semantically aligned with updated processes and stylistically consistent with original descriptions.

Contributions and Paper Outline. The contribution of this paper is threefold: (i) it proposes an edit-based synchronization approach for aligning BPMN models with their textual descriptions, (ii) it introduces algorithms for structured differencing, specifically the Longest Common Execution Subsequence algorithm and a beam search heuristic, and (iii) it develops a prompt design strategy that enables minimal, style-preserving edits using large language models.

The paper is structured as follows. Section 2 reviews BPMN and language models. Section 3 overviews the approach. Section 4 details the algorithms and the prompting. Section 5 describes the implementation and experiments. Section 6 discusses related work, and Sect. 7 concludes the paper.

2   Preliminaries

BPMN and Graph Representation. Business Process Model and Notation 2.0 (BPMN) [13] is a widely used standard for modeling business processes. This work focuses on activity diagrams that describe control flow through a combination of events, tasks, gateways, and sequence flows. Specifically, the node types *start event* and *end event* delimit the execution, *tasks* represent atomic activities that have exactly one incoming and one outgoing flow, and *gateways* define branching and merging points in the process. Gateways with one incoming flow and multiple outgoing flows are called *splits*, for example a split parallel gateway that initiates concurrent branches. Gateways with multiple incoming flows and one outgoing flow are called *merges*, which synchronize or join parallel or alternative paths. A *sequence flow* connects two nodes that are executed one after the other in a specific order.

To support analysis and transformation, BPMN models are often represented as directed, vertex-labeled graphs that capture structural and control-flow relationships between process elements. Formally, a process is modeled as a graph $G = (V, E, \lambda, \theta, v_{\text{start}}, v_{\text{end}})$, where V denotes the set of nodes, E the set of directed edges corresponding to sequence flows, λ assigns a unique name label to each node, and θ specifies the node type (start, end, task, exclusive gateway, or parallel gateway). Each process is assumed to have exactly one start event v_{start} and one end event v_{end}, forming a single-entry, single-exit structure. While BPMN permits multiple start or end events, these can be normalized by introducing synthetic gateways without affecting the semantics.

A BPMN process is considered *balanced* when all branches that split at a gateway rejoin at a single, unique merge point. This allows for clear sequencing and nesting of control flow. In contrast, an *unbalanced* process allows branches to merge at different points, lacking a unique correspondence between splits and merges.

Large Language Models. Large Language Models (LLMs) are pre-trained neural networks capable of understanding and generating human-like text. They are widely used in natural language processing tasks such as summarization, question answering, text classification, and structured data extraction. In this work, we rely on the GPT-4.1 model—developed by OpenAI—as an example of a state-of-the-art LLM. GPT, which stands for *Generative Pre-trained Transformer*, is based on a transformer architecture and operates through prompt-based interactions, where natural language prompts specify the task or question to be addressed. The model generates coherent and contextually appropriate text completions by predicting the most likely continuation of a prompt.

3   Approach Overview

Our method incrementally updates textual process descriptions to reflect changes in BPMN models while preserving the original wording and structure as much as possible. The *key idea* is to avoid regenerating the entire description from scratch. Instead, we progressively transform the initial BPMN model into the modified version through a sequence of *small, structured steps*. Each step captures a localized change—such as adding or removing a task, changing a gateway, or reordering elements—and directly guides how the text is revised.

This approach addresses two core challenges. The first is to decompose the overall model change into an *ordered sequence of discrete edits* that can be applied incrementally. Rather than computing a flat diff, we construct a transformation path that starts from the initial model and progressively produces the target model. The second challenge is to ensure that each transformation step leads to a *local, targeted update of the text*. After each model edit, we prompt the language model to revise only the relevant part of the description, preserving the rest and maintaining stylistic consistency. The overall pipeline consists of three stages, recalled in Fig. 1.

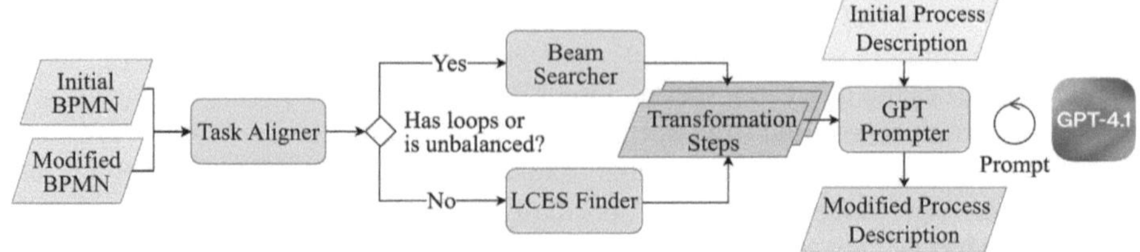

Fig. 1. High level overview of the pipeline.

Stage 1: Identifying Additions and Deletions. We first detect tasks that have been added or removed between the initial and modified BPMN models. These are recorded explicitly as transformation steps and separated from structural changes affecting shared tasks. This ensures that later alignment focuses only on comparable parts of the model.

Stage 2: Computing a Transformation Sequence. For the remaining structure, where the set of tasks is shared between both models and only the control flow differs, we derive a sequence of edits needed to convert the initial model into the modified one. If the models are acyclic and balanced, we apply a *Longest Common Execution Subsequence (LCES)* algorithm that generalizes sequence alignment to process graphs and produces efficient, deterministic edit sequences. If the models are more complex—containing loops or unbalanced control flow—we instead use a *heuristic beam search* that explores alternative edit sequences and selects promising candidates based on structural similarity. In both cases, the output is an ordered list of transformation steps.

Stage 3: Incremental Text Update. Finally, each transformation step is applied in order. For each step, a targeted prompt is generated to guide the language model in revising only the corresponding part of the text. Because each prompt is limited in scope, the process achieves *edit-based textual synchronization*: it updates what has changed while preserving the rest. This stepwise, localized approach enables minimal, structure-aware revisions that maintain clarity and continuity in process documentation.

4   Process Model Differencing and Text Revision

4.1   Task Alignment

The first stage of the approach establishes a correspondence between the tasks of the initial and the modified BPMN models. This step isolates changes to the set of tasks themselves, separately from changes in how the tasks are connected or ordered. Specifically, we compare the set of tasks in each model by their labels: tasks that appear only in the modified model are marked as *insertions*, while tasks that appear only in the initial model are marked as *deletions*. This interpretation is natural, since any task present in one version but absent in the other must have been added or removed during modification. After identifying these differences, we produce reduced models that retain only the shared tasks. This allows the following steps to focus exclusively on how the order and connections between tasks have changed, without being affected by tasks that no longer exist or have newly appeared.

4.2   Longest Common Execution Subsequence Approach

The first component of our approach for computing transformation steps is the *Longest Common Execution Subsequence* (LCES). This stage operates on the reduced versions of the models that include only the tasks present in both process definitions. The main goal of LCES is to systematically derive the edits needed to transform the reduced initial model into the reduced modified model. It does so by identifying a shared intermediate model that captures the parts of the process remaining unchanged in their relative order. From this common structure, the necessary deletions, insertions, and control-flow adjustments can be precisely determined.

More precisely, the LCES captures the largest subsequence of tasks and gateways that appear in the same relative order in both models and can be obtained by only deleting elements. When both BPMN models are *acyclic* and *balanced*, this approach yields a well-defined, terminating sequence of edits that incrementally transforms the initial model into the modified one. From this shared core, the remaining edits can be precisely determined: deletions of elements unique to the initial model, additions of elements unique to the modified model, and any necessary adjustments to gateway types to preserve structural consistency.

A key property of this approach is that all intermediate models produced during the transformation remain semantically correct and connected. This ensures that each step corresponds to a coherent and interpretable change, supporting clear and localized updates of the textual description. LCES requires that each split gateway has a corresponding merge, which is why we can only apply it to balanced models.

To increase the amount of elements in the LCES, we also apply a reduction step that removes structurally redundant gateways, such as nested splits of the same type or gateways without any branching behavior. While optional, this preprocessing often increases the number of the shared elements in the intermediate model and simplifies the resulting transformation sequence.

Common Execution Subsequence. A *common execution subsequence* (CES) is a set of elements occurring in both models in the same relative order, even if other elements are interleaved. In a sequential process, this corresponds to the longest list of tasks appearing in the same order. In models with branching and parallel flows, a CES must also respect partial orders and structural constraints.

Formally, a CES is a set of matched pairs of semantically equivalent nodes that preserve execution order and control-flow consistency. Two nodes are equivalent if they represent the same process role (start or end event), tasks with identical labels, or gateways with the same control-flow function (i.e., both splits or both merges). A CES aligns such nodes so that each node is matched at most once, the execution order remains consistent without introducing reversals, all control-flow relationships are respected, and all matched elements belong to corresponding branches in both models. This means that whenever a region of parallel or alternative paths is encountered, either the entire region is matched—including the split and merge gateways—or any matched nodes inside it must all come from a single branch. In other words, a CES never mixes elements from different branches within the same split-merge block.

LCES Computation. The Longest Common Execution Sequence (LCES) algorithm computes the CES containing the largest number of matched elements. It generalizes the classical longest common subsequence problem [12] to process models represented as directed acyclic graphs (DAGs).

At each pair of nodes, the algorithm explores three possibilities: (1) match the nodes if they are semantically equivalent (line 2), (2) advance in the first model by skipping the current node (line 8), or (3) advance in the second model (line 9). If the nodes are not equivalent, the algorithm simply skips one of them; if they do match, it considers both matching and skipping to find the longest possible alignment. In the matching case, it either continues the LCES computation recursively with the successor nodes in both models (line 3), or, if both nodes are split gateways, it applies a specialized flattening procedure to align their outgoing branches (lines 5–6).

In this case, the algorithm recursively computes an LCES for each pair of outgoing branches—one from each model—resulting in a set of candidate branch alignments. However, these alignments cannot be merged naively for two reasons. First, alignments that do not include the corresponding merge gateway are discarded, as they match elements that remain within the split-merge region in only one of the models. Second, combining alignments that reuse the same branch multiple times would mix activities from distinct paths and violate the control-flow structure. To prevent this, the algorithm selects a subset of branch alignments that are *pairwise disjoint*, meaning that each branch from each model is used at most once. These selected alignments are then concatenated into a single coherent, *flattened* region that provides a semantically consistent and non-overlapping correspondence between the matched split gateways and their respective merge gateways.

Including a matched pair does not always yield the longest sequence. Sometimes, it is better to skip a potential match at the current position in order to align more structurally significant elements further downstream. For instance, the algorithm may choose to skip matching a split gateway now so that it can be aligned with a more appropriate corresponding split gateway later in the other model—resulting in a longer common execution sequence. To account for such cases, the recurrence always considers all three possibilities at each step and retains only those continuations that achieve maximal length (lines 11–12). Algorithm 1 illustrates how the LCES is computed recursively over pairs of nodes:

Example. To illustrate the computation, we consider the two BPMN models shown in Fig. 2. The algorithm starts by matching the end events (O) and the tasks H and G. After that, the models diverge: the initial model continues with task F, while the modified model reaches a merge gateway (◈). Since these elements do not match, the algorithm explores both options—skipping ahead in either model—to find the next possible alignment. In both cases, it arrives at a point where the control flow diverges, making linear continuation impossible. As a result, the algorithm enumerates all feasible combinations of branches between the corresponding split and merge gateways in the two models. Stopping at the split gateway, this yields the following six candidate execution subsequences:

Algorithm 1: $\text{LCES}(v, v')$.

1:   $C_1 \leftarrow \emptyset$
2:   **if** $\text{MATCH}(v, v')$ **then** $\triangleright$ Option 1: match nodes
3:       $R \leftarrow \{\text{LCES}(u, u') \mid u \in \text{SUCC}(v),\ u' \in \text{SUCC}(v')\}$ $\triangleright$ Recursively extend match
4:       $C_1 \leftarrow \{[(v, v')] \cup A \mid A \in R\}$ $\triangleright$ Non-flattened alignments
5:       **if** $\text{ISSPLIT}(v)$ **and** $\text{ISSPLIT}(v')$ **then**
6:           $C_1 \leftarrow C_1 \cup \{[(v, v')] \cup A \mid A \in \text{FLATTEN}(R)\}$ $\triangleright$ Flattened alignments
7:       **end if**
8:   **end if**
9:   $C_2 \leftarrow \{\text{LCES}(u, v') \mid u \in \text{SUCC}(v)\}$ $\triangleright$ Option 2: skip v
10: $C_3 \leftarrow \{\text{LCES}(v, u') \mid u' \in \text{SUCC}(v')\}$ $\triangleright$ Option 3: skip v'
11: $C \leftarrow C_1 \cup C_2 \cup C_3$
12: **return** sequences in C with maximal length

$$\pi_{11} = \langle (A, A), (B, B), (\diamond, \diamond), (G, G), (H, H), (\bigcirc, \bigcirc) \rangle$$

$$\pi_{12} = \langle (\diamond, \diamond), (G, G), (H, H), (\bigcirc, \bigcirc) \rangle$$

$$\pi_{13} = \{\langle (F, F), (G, G), (H, H), (\bigcirc, \bigcirc) \rangle, \langle (\diamond, \diamond), (G, G), (H, H), (\bigcirc, \bigcirc) \rangle\}.$$

$$\pi_{21} = \langle (C, C), (E, E), (\diamond, \diamond), (G, G), (H, H), (\bigcirc, \bigcirc) \rangle$$

$$\pi_{22} = \langle (D, D), (\diamond, \diamond), (G, G), (H, H), (\bigcirc, \bigcirc) \rangle$$

$$\pi_{23} = \{\langle (F, F), (G, G), (H, H), (\bigcirc, \bigcirc) \rangle, \langle (\diamond, \diamond), (G, G), (H, H), (\bigcirc, \bigcirc) \rangle\}.$$

Once all candidate subsequences are collected, the algorithm attempts to flatten them. Among the candidates, π_{13} and π_{23} each contain two alternative subsequences. One of these includes a match for task F but omits the corresponding merge gateway. This indicates that task F lies within the split-merge region in one model but outside of it in the other. Since flattening only applies to matches fully enclosed by corresponding split and merge gateways in both models, these subsequences are excluded. Each of the valid candidate sequences is split into a prefix (before the merge) and a suffix (after the merge). Naively combining all prefixes would yield the union of tasks A, B, C, D, and E. However, this combination is structurally invalid: in the upper model, A and B belong to one branch, while C and E belong to another; in the lower model, all four tasks appear in the same branch. Simply deleting tasks from either model would not produce a con-

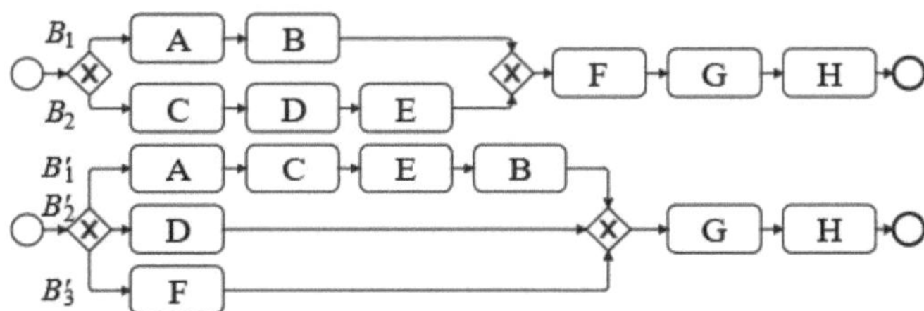

Fig. 2. Initial (top) and modified (bottom) BPMN models.

sistent shared structure. Including all these tasks would require matching branch B_1 in the upper model to branch B_1' (to align A and B) and also matching branch B_2 to the same branch B_1' (to align C and E)—violating the constraint that each branch may only be used once. To resolve this, the algorithm selects the largest subset of matches that satisfies this restriction. The largest valid combination pairs branch B_1 with B_1', contributing A and B, and branch B_2 with B_2', contributing D. This defines the flattened region of consistently aligned tasks inside the split-merge block. From the merge gateway onward, the algorithm resumes linear matching, appending the suffix that includes G, H, and the end event. The resulting Longest Common Execution Subsequence is:

$$\langle (\bigcirc, \bigcirc), (\diamondsuit, \diamondsuit), (A, A), (B, B), (D, D), (\diamondsuit, \diamondsuit), (G, G), (H, H), (\mathbf{O}, \mathbf{O}) \rangle$$

As a consequence, tasks C, E, and F are excluded from the shared sequence. They must be deleted from their original positions and re-inserted at their new locations to transform the initial model into the modified one. This example shows how the algorithm maximizes alignment while preserving control-flow consistency and avoiding structurally invalid branch combinations.

4.3 Beam Search Approach

Beam search is used when BPMN models contain loops or unbalanced control-flow structures where split gateways no longer have a unique corresponding merge. In such cases, cycles and asymmetric flows require a more flexible search that incrementally explores alternative transformation paths without exhaustively enumerating all possibilities. Instead, beam search maintains a bounded set of promising candidates in parallel, extending each by applying domain-specific edit operations.

Each candidate represents a partial transformation path incrementally extended by applying domain-specific edit operations. Candidates are evaluated using a cost function that estimates how closely their control-flow structure matches the target. Only the most promising candidates are retained and further expanded, ensuring that the search remains computationally feasible while progressively approaching the target model. If no valid transformation path is found within a predefined time or resource budget, the system falls back to regenerating the process description from scratch, guaranteeing a usable result in all cases.

Unlike in the LCES approach, intermediate models produced by beam search are not guaranteed to be semantically correct BPMN models at every step. Structurally relaxed constructs—such as gateways with only one incoming and one outgoing flow, or inconsistently nested branches—are temporarily permitted to increase flexibility. These inconsistencies are corrected by the end of the transformation sequence.

Edit Operations. Beam search explores alternative models by applying domain-specific edit operations. The primary operation is *task movement*, which implicitly covers both removal and reinsertion. To move a task, the algorithm either bypasses it—connecting its predecessor and successor—or, if it lies between gateways, removes it with adjacent flows while preserving connectivity. The task is then reinserted either along any sequence flow or between a gateway (not a merge) and another gateway (not a split), ensuring clear and unambiguous control flow. Beyond task movement, sequence flows can be inserted between gateways, provided that each retains a consistent role as a split or a merge. Flows may be deleted if all nodes remain reachable from the start event. Gateways can also be added along sequence flows or removed when they act as structural pass-throughs (i.e., with exactly one incoming and one outgoing flow).

Cost Model. At each iteration, candidates are evaluated using a cost function that combines the cumulative cost of edits applied so far with a heuristic estimate of the remaining difference to the target BPMN model. The search strategy uses a classical formulation:

$$f(n) = g(n) + h(n)$$

where $f(n)$ is the estimated total cost of transforming candidate n. The term $g(n)$ denotes the cumulative cost of applied edits, and $h(n)$ is the heuristic component that guides the search toward the target model. This work adopts a uniform cost model for $g(n)$, where each operation contributes the same fixed cost. Although weighting edits differently could reflect their semantic impact, experiments showed that such weighting often distorts the search (for instance, heavily penalizing task movement can lead to excessive gateway insertions).

Structural Edge Abstraction and Heuristic. To robustly compare candidates, each sequence flow is abstracted as a *Structural Edge* that encodes the role and local structure of its source and target nodes. For tasks and events, this abstraction combines their type and label (e.g., distinguishing task `Approve Request` from task `Review Application`). For gateways, which often lack unique labels, it includes the gateway's type and a canonical hash summarizing its adjacent incoming and outgoing flows. Two Structural Edges are considered equal if both their source and target representations match exactly, ensuring that only flows occupying comparable positions in the process are treated as equivalent. The heuristic $h(n)$ quantifies the remaining difference between a candidate and the target model:

$$h(n) = |E_T| + 0.5 \cdot |E_n \setminus E_T| - |E_n \cap E_T|$$

where E_n and E_T are the sets of Structural Edges in the candidate and target, respectively. This scoring rewards matching edges, penalizes extra edges moderately, and penalizes missing edges more strongly. The asymmetry reflects that surplus edges often arise as temporary artifacts during construction and can be removed later, whereas missing edges indicate that parts of the target process are still absent. Although the heuristic is not necessarily admissible, beam search does not require admissibility and instead prioritizes efficient exploration. By comparing control flow at the level of individual edges and their local context, this approach provides fine-grained, practical guidance without relying on global graph similarity measures.

Practical Considerations. While beam search effectively captures a wide range of structural edits and produces good results in most cases, its performance can be less responsive when building deeply nested gateway structures. The structural-edge heuristic provides strong guidance for localized changes and incremental refinements but may only recognize progress in complex regions once sufficient surrounding context has been assembled. To maintain tractability, the search operates within configurable time-outs. If no valid transformation is identified within the allotted time, the method reliably falls back to generating a new process description, ensuring that an updated result is always produced. Finally, the beam width governs the balance between completeness and computational cost: wider beams can improve reconstruction success rates while requiring additional resources. In this work, the beam width is selected empirically.

4.4   GPT-Based Prompting Strategy

After computing a transformation path between the initial and modified BPMN models—using either the LCES approach or the beam search heuristic—the final step is to update the corresponding process description. Rather than regenerating the entire text, the method applies targeted, incremental edits that preserve the original wording, tone, and structure. Each structural change—such as inserting, removing, or reordering a task—is treated as a self-contained transformation. For each change, a prompt is constructed comprising several well-defined components:

Role Framing. The prompt begins by instructing the model to act as a BPMN process modeling expert. Research has shown that role-based prompting can improve the relevance and task alignment of large language model outputs [14]. In this context, the role is intended to steer the model toward domain-appropriate language and interpretations.

Change Description. Each prompt includes a short natural language sentence specifying the structural modification applied to the process model. This contextualizes the transformation for the language model, allowing it to focus on the relevant part of the process without relying solely on structural inference from the graphs.

Update Instructions. The model is instructed to revise the process description precisely and minimally, based on the structural change and adjacency lists. It is guided to reason about the main flow using forward adjacency, and about prerequisites using backward adjacency. The style of the original text should be preserved, with each change integrated naturally and without redundancy. The output must consist only of the updated full description.

Full-Context Editing. The full process description is provided in each prompt to convey the original writing style and structure, allowing the model to locate and revise the relevant section implicitly without explicit extraction or annotation.

Graph Inputs and Format. To limit prompt size and reduce irrelevant context, we extract a localized subgraph centered around the changed node rather than using the full BPMN model. This subgraph is defined through a two-phase traversal: a forward search from the changed node, its immediate predecessor, and its successor, stopping at task nodes or start/end events; and a backward search from each of these, again terminating at task or event nodes. A symmetric backward-then-forward traversal is also performed to capture additional dependencies. The union of all reachable task and event nodes defines the subgraph focus. From this set, we construct forward and backward adjacency lists that preserve the actual control-flow structure, including links to gateways even if those were not reached during traversal. Gateways are represented using structured objects that encode their control-flow semantics (e.g., parallel or exclusive branching), preserving the executable logic of the process model. The resulting structure is encoded as JSON and introduced to the model through an accompanying textual explanation of the format. This enables the model to interpret the control-flow graph consistently and reason over its structure in relation to the description.

Example. To illustrate this approach, we use a simplified university enrollment process where a new task, `Assign Case Officer`, is inserted after the application review. Figure 3 shows the BPMN models before and after this change.

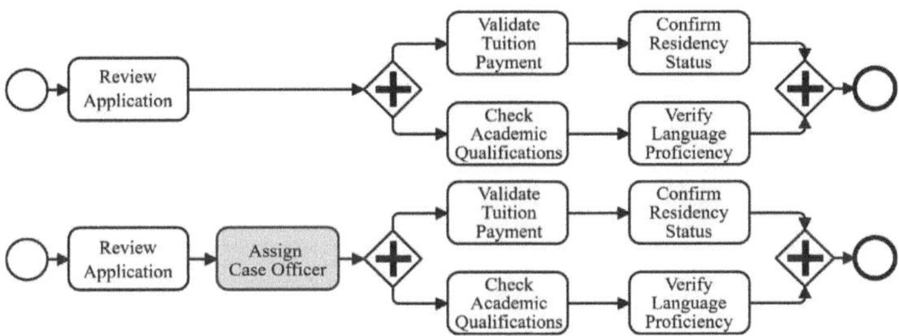

Fig. 3. BPMN models before and after inserting the `Assign Case Officer` task.

The complete prompt for this transformation is shown in Table 1, illustrating all components of the prompting strategy.

Applying the prompt yields the following output:

```
The process begins when the university reviews a student's
application. Next, a case officer is assigned to the
application. The workflow then proceeds in parallel along
two branches. [...]
```

5   Tool and Experiments

5.1   Tool

To validate the proposed approach, we developed a prototype system that automatically updates textual process descriptions when a BPMN model changes. The tool takes two BPMN 2.0 XML models (original and modified) together with the initial description, and produces an updated text reflecting the structural differences. The transformation pipeline combines model parsing, structural comparison, and prompt-based text rewriting using GPT-4.1. Depending on the models' properties, it selects either a Longest Common Execution Subsequence algorithm or a beam search strategy to compute the transformation path. Each step generates a targeted prompt to ensure minimal deviation from the original wording unless structural edits are necessary.

The implementation comprises approximately 7k lines of Java code. The tool is available both as a standalone command-line application and as an integrated module within an existing web platform for BPMN generation from natural language descriptions [20]. The web interface, built with HTML, CSS, JavaScript, and `bpmn.io`, allows users to edit diagrams interactively and triggers updates with a single action. A Node.js backend relays the models and description to the Java engine, which returns the revised text for display.

The current prototype requires semantically valid BPMN models that include parallel and exclusive gateways, loops, a single start and end event, and uniquely named tasks.

Table 1. Prompt for inserting the task `Assign Case Officer`.

Component	Prompt Content
Role Framing	You are an expert in BPMN process modeling.
Change Description	In the modified version, the new task 'Assign Case Officer' has been added.
Graph Format	The process flow graphs are provided as JSON adjacency lists in two forms: - Forward adjacency: each node lists its possible next steps (successors). - Backward adjacency: each node lists its prerequisites (predecessors). Nodes may be connected by direct task names, or by objects indicating gateways or control flow, e.g.: { "type": "parallel", "branches": [...] } for parallel execution, { "type": "exclusive", "branches": [...] } for exclusive (XOR) choices. Interpret these structures according to their BPMN semantics.
Update Instructions	You are provided with: - An initial process description. - Two versions of the process flow graph (original and modified), each encoded as both a forward adjacency list and a backward adjacency list. Your task: - Update the process description so that it accurately and naturally reflects the addition and integration of the new task. - Carefully analyze the adjacency lists to determine how the new task affects the sequence, available choices, conditions, or outcomes in the process. - Use the forward adjacency lists to understand and describe the main process flow. - Use the backward adjacency lists to check prerequisites and ensure consistency. - Adapt the description in the style of the given process description, making the change as precise, short, and minimal as possible. - Ensure each dependency, condition, or sequence is described only once, and avoid repeating the same requirement in different ways. Combine all prerequisites for each step into a single statement. Answer only with the full, updated process description.

(continued)

Table 1. (*continued*)

Full-Context Editing	The original description is: The process begins when the university reviews a student's application. The workflow then proceeds in parallel along two branches. In one branch, the student's academic qualifications are checked and their language proficiency is verified. In the other branch, the tuition payment is validated and the student's residency status is confirmed.
Graph Inputs	The initial process flow graph (forward adjacency): { 'Review Application': [{ 'type': 'parallel', 'branches': ['Check Academic Qualifications', 'Validate Tuition Payment'] }], 'Check Academic Qualifications': ['Verify Language Proficiency'], ...} The initial process flow graph (backward adjacency): { 'Review Application': ['Start Event'], 'Check Academic Qualifications': ['Review Application'], ...} The new process flow graph (forward adjacency): { 'Review Application': ['Assign Case Officer'], 'Assign Case Officer': [{ 'type': 'parallel', 'branches': ['Check Academic Qualifications', 'Validate Tuition Payment'] }], ...} The new process flow graph (backward adjacency): { 'Assign Case Officer': ['Review Application'], 'Validate Tuition Payment': ['Assign Case Officer'], ...}

5.2   Experiments

We evaluated our approach on a total of 50 BPMN models, derived from two representative base processes: one *unbalanced* and one *balanced*. Both models were adapted from existing processes in the literature [5, 11] and slightly modified for evaluation. The unbalanced model contains 16 tasks, 3 parallel gateways with nesting, and 2 exclusive gateways with nesting, while the balanced model contains 18 tasks, 1 parallel gateways, and 3 exclusive gateways with nesting. For each, we applied five structural transformations at each transformation length (from one to five edits), resulting in 25 test cases per category.

Transformations included task, sequence flow, and gateway additions or deletions, as well as task movements and gateway type changes. Each modified BPMN was paired with its original textual description to serve as input for the update task. We compared our method to a baseline using direct prompting with GPT-4.1. In the baseline, the model was given the role of a BPMN expert, and asked to revise the original description based on the modified and original BPMN models (provided in XML), making only minimal, style-preserving changes.

Output quality was evaluated manually along two dimensions. Semantic correctness was assessed by verifying whether the updated description accurately reflected the modified control flow; scores were binary (1 for correct, 0 for incorrect). Stylistic consistency was rated on a 0–2 scale, based on how well the output matched the tone, phrasing, and structure of the original text, where higher values indicate better alignment. Because both methods rely on GPT and generally produce fluent text, we applied a deliberately critical lens to judge whether edits were minimal and stylistically coherent. For each transformation length (1 to 5), scores were averaged across all corresponding test cases in both the balanced and unbalanced categories. Since semantic correctness reflects whether the generated description remains faithful to the process logic, it is considered the primary evaluation criterion.

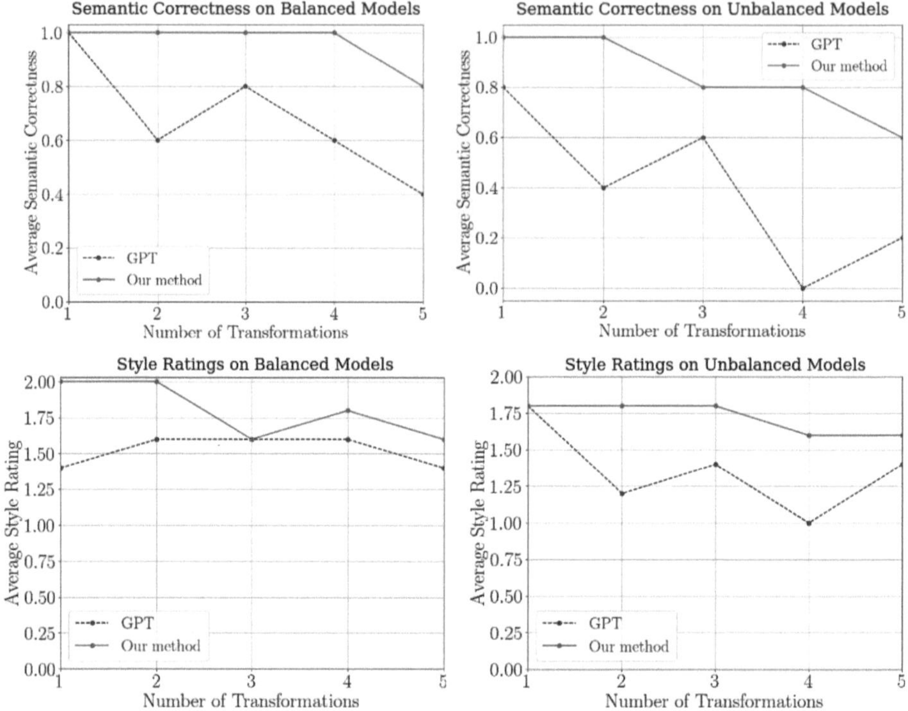

Fig. 4. Average semantic and stylistic scores by number of transformations.

Results and Discussion. Figure 4 shows average semantic and stylistic scores across transformation lengths for both model categories. Overall, our method consistently outperformed the GPT baseline in both metrics. In terms of semantic correctness, our method maintained high scores across all settings, with only a modest decline as the number of edits increased. For balanced models, performance remained particularly strong, likely due to their regular structure and clearer execution semantics. Unbalanced models showed slightly lower accuracy, but our method remained efficient even under more complex transformations.

In contrast, the GPT baseline degraded noticeably as transformations accumulated, especially for unbalanced models. Without intermediate guidance or structure-aware prompting, GPT frequently overlooked changes or misinterpreted updated control flow, resulting in omissions, misplaced tasks, or semantically incorrect descriptions. These issues became more common with larger edits. Our incremental synchronization strategy avoided such drift by isolating and addressing each structural change in sequence.

Stylistic consistency scores were generally high for both methods, as expected from GPT-based generation. However, our method achieved slightly higher ratings overall. The baseline more often introduced stylistic shifts not present in the original text, such as inserting generic phrases like "then the process branches" or adopting a more explanatory tone. Our method more reliably preserved the original style, although occasional artifacts appeared when the same task was revised multiple times, sometimes leading to repetition or awkward reordering. These differences, while subtle, were observed consistently and contributed to the improved stylistic performance of our approach.

Finally, it is worth noticing that GPT was used with its *temperature* parameter set to 0, ensuring determinism between identical runs.

Execution Time Analysis. To assess practical viability, we measured execution times across all test cases, distinguishing between the *search time* (i.e., model differencing), *prompting time* (LLM invocation), and the overall *total time*. Figure 5 presents the average execution times for balanced and unbalanced models, grouped by transformation length.

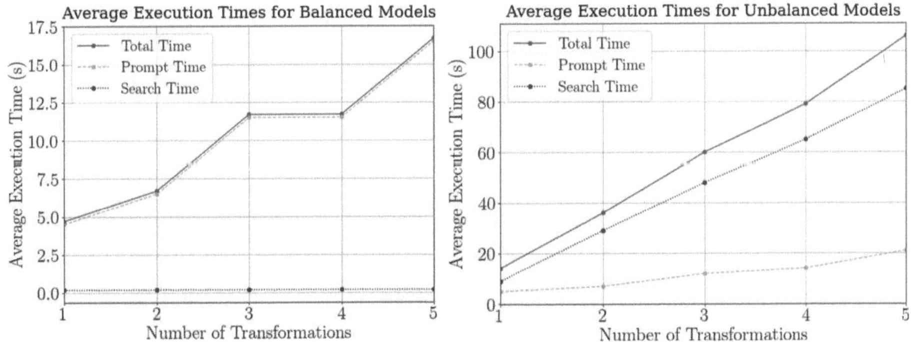

Fig. 5. Average Execution Times by Number of Transformations.

For balanced models, search times remained negligible across all transformation lengths, as expected from the deterministic LCES algorithm. Most of the total time was spent on prompting, which grew roughly linearly with the number of transformations—an intuitive result given that each transformation triggers a separate prompt. In contrast, unbalanced models showed significantly higher execution times overall. Here, the search time (due to beam search) clearly dominated the total runtime and increased steadily with transformation length. Nevertheless, growth remained approximately linear, and even the most complex scenarios (involving five transformations) were completed in under 120 s on average. These results highlight two key findings: (1) the LCES-based synchronization for balanced processes is extremely efficient, and (2) while beam search for unbalanced models is computationally more expensive, it consistently converges and remains tractable even for complex updates. This confirms the approach's feasibility for interactive settings and its efficiency under structural variability.

Threats to Validity. Although our evaluation setup is systematic and representative, it is not exhaustive. The selected base processes and transformation types capture a broad range of realistic structural edits, but do not cover all possible combinations. Moreover, the effectiveness of both our method and the baseline depend on the clarity and specificity of the original descriptions. Ambiguous or underspecified input may reduce output quality, particularly with regard to semantic correctness. That said, the test cases were carefully designed to reflect typical evolution scenarios, and the consistency of results across both balanced and unbalanced models supports the general usability of the findings.

6   Related Work

Several works aim at measuring the degree of similarity of business process models [7, 8, 18, 21]. [8] uses causal footprints as an abstract representation of the behaviour captured by a process model. Then, given two footprints, the similarity is computed using the vector space model approach from information filtering and retrieval. [18] relies on Petri nets and propose to compare process models by analysing event logs with typical execution sequences. [7] tackles the problem of retrieving process models from a repository that most closely resemble a given process model. [21] propose two measures of similarity between two versions of a BPMN process. The first one relies on the syntactic descriptions of the processes considered as input, whereas the second one focuses on their semantic models.

Prompt-based strategies have become increasingly central for adapting large language models (LLMs) to structured inputs such as code, tables, and diagrams. Approaches like Code2Seq [2] encode abstract syntax trees as paths for neural summarization, while few-shot prompting [17] shows that pretrained LLMs can generalize over knowledge graphs using carefully crafted textual prompts. More recently, multimodal pipelines such as GenFlowchart [3] have combined OCR-derived structure with prompt engineering to generate fluent descriptions of visual diagrams. These systems are typically optimized for single-pass generation over static inputs.

Graph-to-text generation produces fluent descriptions from structured graphs such as knowledge bases. Structure-aware Transformers [24] incorporate relative positional encodings to improve relational coherence but assume that the complete graph is available at generation time. Few-shot prompting [17] and instruction-tuned models like GraphGPT [22] demonstrate that LLMs can generalize structural knowledge in zero-shot settings. Surveys by Yuan and Färber [23] highlight that most systems focus on producing new text from scratch rather than maintaining continuity across revisions.

More domain-specific work has addressed BPMN and UML verbalization. For BPMN, Leopold et al. [15, 16] pioneered pipelines translating process fragments into sentences, while Azevedo et al. [4] proposed synchronisation frameworks linking diagrams and text but still regenerating full descriptions after each change. The Process-to-Text framework [10] produces high-level summaries of mined processes but does not aim for maintainable documentation. In UML, the authors of [6, 19] developed grammar-driven approaches that ensure traceability but rely on controlled vocabularies and lack support for incremental updates.

Work explicitly addressing incremental updates is limited. Zhu et al. [25] generate abstract Business Process Text Sketches from Conditional Process Trees using large language models, primarily to bootstrap datasets rather than maintain authored documentation; each change yields a new summary without preserving prior phrasing or structure. Azevedo et al.'s bidirectional framework [4] allows incremental edits from text to model but regenerates full descriptions when models change, limiting continuity. The Process-to-Text framework [10] supports time-sensitive summarization of evolving process logs but does not track sentence-level alignment in curated documentation.

Incremental, style-preserving documentation thus remains an open challenge. This paper addresses it by combining symbolic diffs with targeted LLM prompts to enable minimal, localized revisions to maintain coherence as models evolve.

7 Conclusion and Future Work

This work addressed the challenge of maintaining alignment between textual process descriptions and evolving BPMN models. As business processes change through insertions, deletions, or structural refinements, updating documentation accurately while preserving style and validated language becomes critical. We introduced a structured methodology for deriving transformation steps—a minimal sequence of edits mapping the differences between process models—and developed two complementary strategies to compute them: the Longest Common Execution Subsequence (LCES) for balanced acyclic models and a heuristic Beam Search approach for more complex structures. A GPT-based prompting framework incrementally applies each edit, enabling targeted updates rather than wholesale regeneration. Experiments showed that this approach produces semantically correct, stylistically coherent updates while significantly reducing manual effort.

Future work could enhance the system along several dimensions. Fine-tuning the language model on real-world process documentation may improve fluency, terminology, and the ability to accurately reflect control-flow semantics. Richer heuristics—such as graph embeddings or BPMN-specific similarity measures—could help the Beam Search to more effectively identify meaningful transformations. Additionally, supporting group-level edits over entire branches or subprocesses and recognizing common BPMN patterns like loops and decision points could enable more concise transformation sequences and tailored prompting strategies.

References

1. Van der Aa, H., Leopold, H., Reijers, H.A.: Detecting inconsistencies between process models and textual descriptions. In: Proceeding of BPM'15 (2015)
2. Alon, U., Brody, S., Levy, O., Yahav, E.: code2seq: Generating sequences from structured representations of code (2019)
3. Arbaz, A., Fan, H., Ding, J., Qiu, M., Feng, Y.: Genflowchart: parsing and understanding flowchart using generative AI. In: Knowlege Science, Engineering Management (2024)
4. Azevedo, L.G., de Almeida Rodrigues, R., Revoredo, K.: BPMN model and text instructions automatic synchronization. In: Proceedings of ICEIS'18 (2018)

5. Bellan, P., et al.: Pet: An annotated dataset for process extraction from natural language text tasks. In: Business Process Management Workshops (2023)
6. Burden, H., Heldal, R.: Natural language generation from class diagrams. In: Proceedings of MoDeVVa'11 (2011)
7. Dijkman, R.M., Dumas, M., van Dongen, B.F., Käärik, R., Mendling, J.: Similarity of business process models: metrics and evaluation. Inf. Syst. **36**(2), 498–516 (2011)
8. van Dongen, B.F., Dijkman, R.M., Mendling, J.: Measuring similarity between business process models. In: Proceedings of CAISE'08, pp. 450–464 (2008)
9. Dumas, M., La Rosa, M., Mendling, J., Reijers, H.A., et al.: Fundamentals of business process management. Springer (2013)
10. Fontenla-Seco, Y., Lama, M., Bugarín, A.: Process-to-text: a framework for the quantitative description of processes in natural language. In: Proceedings of TAILOR'20
11. Friedrich, F.: Automated Generation of Business Process Models from Natural Language Input. Master's thesis (2010)
12. Hirschberg, D.S.: A linear space algorithm for computing maximal common subsequences. In: Communications of the ACM (1975)
13. ISO/IEC: International Standard 19510, Information technology – Business Process Model and Notation (2013)
14. Kong, A., et al.: Better zero-shot reasoning with role-play prompting (2024)
15. Leopold, H., Mendling, J., Polyvyanyy, A.: Generating natural language texts from business process models. In: Advanced Information Systems Engineering (2012)
16. Leopold, H., Mendling, J., Polyvyanyy, A.: Supporting process model validation through natural language generation. Transactions on Software Engineering (2014)
17. Li, J., Tang, T., Zhao, W.X., Wei, Z., Yuan, N.J., Wen, J.R.: Few-shot knowledge graph-to-text generation with pretrained language models (2021)
18. de Medeiros, A.K.A., van der Aalst, W.M.P., Weijters, A.J.M.M.: Quantifying Process Equivalence Based on Observed Behavior. Data Knowl, Eng (2008)
19. Meziane, F., Athanasakis, N., Ananiadou, S.: Generating natural language specifications from UML class diagrams. Requirements Engineering (2008)
20. Nivon, Q., Salaün, G.: Automated generation of BPMN processes from textual requirements. In: Proceedings of ICSOC'24 (2024)
21. Salaün, G.: Quantifying the Similarity of BPMN Processes. In: Proc. of APSEC'22, pp. 377–386. IEEE (2022)
22. Tang, J., et al.: Graphgpt: graph instruction tuning for large language models. In: Proceedings of SIGIR'24 (2024)
23. Yuan, S., Färber, M.: Evaluating generative models for graph-to-text generation (2023)
24. Zhao, F., Zou, H., Yan, C.: Structure-aware knowledge graph-to-text generation with planning selection and similarity distinction. In: Proceedings of EMNLP'23 (2023)
25. Zhu, R., Hu, Q., Li, W., Xiao, H., Wang, C., Zhou, Z.: Business process text sketch automation generation using large language model (2023)

Intelligent and Secure Connected Systems

Impact-Sensitive Conflict Management in Smart IoT-Based Systems Using Attention Networks

Christson Awanyo[✉], Nawal Guermouche, and Morel Kouhossounon Vianney

LAAS-CNRS, University of Toulouse, INSA, Toulouse, France
{kjbcawanyo,nguermou,mdkouhossounon}@laas.fr

Abstract. Modern IoT environments are increasingly evolving into system-of-systems, where independently managed subsystems interconnect and operate over shared IoT devices and infrastructures. As these heterogeneous systems evolve autonomously, the potential for IoT conflicts rises, particularly when they issue overlapping or competing control requests. This growing complexity underscores the need for a robust, dynamic, and real-time conflict management framework that can adapt to changing contexts and system behaviors. Traditional resolution strategies, such as fixed priorities or first-come-first-served, often fail to consider contextual factors and the effective impact of decisions, resulting in degraded non-functional properties.

To address these challenges, we propose an impact-aware, attention-based conflict management framework. Our approach resolves conflicts by jointly considering request importance and their predicted system-level consequences. By leveraging real-time contextual data and historical conflict patterns, the model dynamically selects resolution actions that minimize negative impacts. We demonstrate the effectiveness of this framework through extensive evaluations in a smart transportation scenario, using energy consumption and CO_2 emissions as key non-functional metrics.

Keywords: IoT · Conflict Resolution · Non Functional Properties · Impact · Attention Model · Dynamic Systems · Large Scale IoT Systems · Smart City

1 Introduction

The rapid growth of the Internet of Things (IoT), driven by advances in Artificial Intelligence (AI), is transforming urban infrastructure and service delivery. Smart cities exemplify this shift, connecting vast networks of sensors, devices, and systems across domains like transportation, energy, health, and governance. This interconnectivity enables more efficient, data-driven decision-making. However, as IoT systems grow in scale and complexity, managing their interactions becomes increasingly challenging. These systems typically operate autonomously,

C. Cappiello et al. (Eds.): CoopIS 2025, LNCS 15535, pp. 259–276, 2026.
https://doi.org/10.1007/978-3-032-15538-2_15

each pursuing distinct and potentially conflicting objectives. This can lead to what we refer to as *IoT conflicts*. An IoT conflict occurs when simultaneous IoT invocations result in undesirable outcomes [16].

While conflict detection has been extensively studied in the literature [9,17, 18], conflict resolution remains a critical challenge. Effectively resolving conflicts is essential to ensure operational efficiency, safety, and system-wide consistency in dynamic and interconnected IoT environments. Conflict resolution in IoT systems generally follows two main approaches. The first category encompasses static approaches, which aim to detect and resolve potential conflicts during the system's design phase through formal or heuristic static analysis techniques [3,5, 8,9]. These methods enable the detection of conflicts before system deployment, ensuring that issues are managed early on. Once potential conflicts are identified, they are resolved by modifying the system's operational policy logic. This process may involve reconfiguring rules, adjusting parameters, or altering workflows to ensure smooth, conflict-free operation. By addressing conflicts at this early stage, the system can operate more efficiently and reliably, significantly reducing the likelihood of issues arising during execution. However, static resolution faces important limitations. It must exhaustively consider all possible interactions to detect potential conflicts, a task that is highly complex and often unfeasible in dynamic and constantly evolving IoT environments.

In contrast, the second category consists of dynamic, runtime conflict resolution approaches [1,11,19], which detect and resolve conflicts on the fly. These methods rely on reactive mechanisms based on predefined rules [17], ontological reasoning [4], or data-driven techniques such as matrix factorization [6]. They enable the system to adapt to changing conditions and resolve conflicts as they arise, ensuring continuity of service even in the presence of conflicting events or objectives. However, these approaches often remain rigid and insufficiently responsive in complex, open, and continuously evolving environments. They typically lack real-time, context-aware adaptability and fail to consider the broader impact of resolution decisions on system-wide non-functional properties such as energy efficiency, latency, or environmental sustainability. Consequently, while they may resolve immediate conflicts, they often fail to optimize long-term system performance or support strategic operational objectives.

To overcome these limitations, we propose a conflict resolution framework that integrates contextual awareness and impact-sensitive decision making. Our approach leverages the prioritization capabilities of attention mechanisms in conjunction with a predictive model that estimates the impact on non-functional metrics of each incoming request. These impact scores are integrated into a utility-based optimization model, enabling the selection of resolution actions that not only resolve conflicts but also promote overall system efficiency and alignment with high-level performance goals.

The contribution of this paper can be summarized as follows:

- We introduce an impact-sensitive, context-aware conflict resolution framework for IoT systems that jointly considers request priorities, contextual factors, and predicted system-level consequences on non-functional metrics.

- We formulate conflict resolution as a utility-driven optimization problem, where the selected set of non-conflicting actions maximizes overall system utility by balancing importance and impact under conflict constraints.
- We design a hybrid model that combines attention mechanisms with a predictive impact estimation model, enabling the framework to dynamically focus on relevant contextual features while forecasting the effects of potential actions.
- We conducted extensive experiments in a smart transportation scenario and demonstrated improvements in responsiveness, efficiency, and non-functional properties alignment.

The remainder of this paper is structured as follows. Section 2 introduces a motivation use case. Section 3 provides a comprehensive review of related works. In Section 4.1, we formalize the problem we address. Section 4 presents the proposed impact-sensitive conflict management approach. Section 5 presents the experimental setup, performance evaluation, and analysis of results. Finally, Section 6 concludes the paper.

2   Motivation Scenario

In the context of modern smart cities, connected vehicles act as intelligent agents within a complex IoT-driven ecosystem, interacting with systems for traffic control, emergency response, environmental monitoring, and navigation. Continuously exchanging contextual data (e.g., speed, position, acceleration), they receive real-time instructions, such as accelerate, decelerate, or stop. In this context, consider a connected vehicle approaching an urban intersection when it receives requests from several independent systems:

- The *traffic management system* requests acceleration to alleviate downstream congestion.
- The *Emergency response system* issues an urgent stop request to clear the way for an approaching ambulance.
- The *safety monitoring system* requests a gradual deceleration due to detected slippery road conditions ahead.
- The *navigation assistance system* asks to slow down and make a right turn to avoid an upcoming obstacle.

In addition to responding to external directives, the vehicle must consider the driver's goals, reaching the destination safely, comfortably, and efficiently, alongside its own internal objectives related to non-functional properties. In this example, we focus on two key parameters: minimizing energy consumption and reducing CO_2 emissions, both essential for economic efficiency and environmental sustainability.

The convergence of external requests and internally driven objectives often leads to conflicts, especially when their underlying goals are misaligned. To tackle this challenge, the vehicle's system must continuously and adaptively balance the

competing demands of diverse stakeholders against its own operational impera-
tives. Effective conflict resolution entails more than simply accepting or rejecting
requests, it requires managing the complexity of real-time decision-making in
dynamic environments. Moreover, this process must be impact-aware, rigorously
assessing the implications of each decision on critical non-functional system-level
metrics, such as energy efficiency and environmental sustainability.

3   Related Work

Conflicts in IoT systems have been extensively investigated and are commonly classified into three main categories: *Rule-based*, *Application-based*, and
Ontology-based [16]. Rule-based conflicts occur when automation rules impose
contradictory actions on the same device [15,17]. Application-based conflicts
emerge from incompatible interactions between multiple applications and a
shared device or its surrounding environment [10,12,14]. Ontology-based conflicts, on the other hand, are detected through semantic reasoning over structured models that capture relationships and constraints among system entities
[4,7].

Conflict resolution is critical to ensuring the reliable and efficient operation
of IoT systems. Static approaches like SOTERIA [5] use formal verification techniques by translating IoT code into an intermediate representation, deriving state
models, and applying model checking to identify and correct conflicts. HOME-
GUARD [8] targets Cross-App Interference (CAI) by analyzing the automation semantics of multiple applications and assessing their combined behavior
to identify potential conflicts. Similarly, IoTMon [9] captures physical interactions between applications by generating interaction chains and evaluating risks
through a three-phase process: application analysis, interaction discovery, and
mitigation. Although effective in controlled settings, these static methods struggle to handle the complexity and dynamism of real-world IoT ecosystems.

Various on-the-fly approaches have been developed to complement static
methods and better accommodate the dynamic nature of IoT systems. [2] defined
a real-time smart home analysis approach that allows users to specify their privacy preferences. Using a Natural Language Processing (NLP) model, the approach analyzes the actions of various services to ensure they align with the user's
specifications. Any actions that conflict with these preferences are automatically
blocked to maintain privacy. [13] presented a dynamic conflict resolution approach that leverages Integer Linear Programming (ILP) and Signal Temporal
Logic (STL). In this approach, a watchdog continuously monitors the system's
state to detect conflicts in real time. This approach provides effective real-time
resolution across various conflict types by abstracting the nature of the conflict.
However, this approach presents significant limitations: the resolution process
can experience a combinatorial explosion within huge and complex systems, and
it does not consider the contextual factors surrounding conflicts.

[6] presented a conflict resolution framework related to preferences for IoT
services in multi-resident smart homes that rely on the use of a temporal proximity strategy for preference extraction over time and matrix factorization via

Singular Value Decomposition (SVD) for preference aggregation. This approach enhances contextual relevance by integrating both current and ideal resident preferences. However, this work focuses mainly on conflicts related to preferences, and the resolution consists of satisfying residents according to their current and past preferences. The resolution consists of changing for instance the preferences of users. This approach cannot be applied in scenarios related to conflicts related to critical requests, where executing alternative actions cannot be accepted. Moreover, it faces several limitations, including the computational complexity of matrix factorization, which hampers its scalability. Additionally, it struggles to adapt to sudden changes in user preferences and exhibits variable effectiveness across different smart home scenarios. These issues negatively impact the framework's performance and adaptability in dynamic and open environments. In [1], we proposed a conflict resolution approach based on a deep learning model to dynamically prioritize incoming IoT requests based on contextual and historical data. While this method effectively ensures non-conflicting decision-making, it overlooks the context-awareness and impact of requests on key non-functional parameters. Consequently, although the selected actions avoid conflicts, they may violate the overall system constraints.

To address the limitations of existing conflict resolution approaches, we introduce a novel runtime framework that integrates attention mechanisms, adaptive learning, and impact-aware reasoning.

4   Impact-Sensitive Conflict Resolution Framework

4.1   Problem Formulation

Let an IoT system $\mathcal{S}$ be capable of performing a set of actions $A = \{a_1, a_2, \ldots, a_n\}$. This system receives requests from external systems $\{SR_1, SR_2, \ldots, SR_m\}$, where each request r_j is defined as:

$$r_j = [a_j, w_j, st_j, et_j, t_j, lon_i, lat_i]$$

where a_j denotes the action requested, $w_j \in [0, 1]$, $\sum_j^m w_j = 1$ represents the weight preference for the request of the jth system SR_j, st_j, et_j indicate the desired execution window defined by a starting time st_j and end time et_j, t_j is the submission time of the request, lon_i, lat_i represent the geographical coordinates (longitude lon_i and latitude lon_i) specifying the location where the action i is intended to be executed.

A conflict occurs when two or more requests, such as $r_j = [a_j, w_j, st_j, et_j, t_j, lon_j, lat_j]$ and $r_k = [a_k, w_k, st_k, et_k, t_k, lon_k, lat_k]$, specify different actions and share overlapping execution intervals, denoted $C(r_j, r_k)$:

$$C(r_j, r_k) = \begin{cases} 1 & \text{if } a_j \neq a_k \text{ and } [st_j, et_j] \cap [st_k, et_k] \neq \emptyset \\ 0 & \text{otherwise} \end{cases}$$

The objective is to dynamically resolve conflicts by jointly considering the context of each request and its potential impact on key non-functional parameters.

Conflict Resolution Optimization: In conflict resolution, the objective is to select and prioritize a subset of actions for immediate execution while deferring or rejecting others, with the aim of maximizing overall system utility and minimizing adverse effects on critical non-functional metrics.

Consider a binary variable $x_i \in \{0, 1\}$ for each request r_i, where $x_i = 1$ indicates that the request is selected for execution, and $x_i = 0$ otherwise. The objective is to maximize the total utility by integrating both the request priority and its estimated impact on non-functional metrics:

$$\max \left(\sum_{i=1}^{n} w_i x_i + \lambda \sum_{i=1}^{n} x_i \cdot \left(\sum_{j=1}^{m} \beta_j q_{ij} \right) \right)$$

Where w_i denotes the intrinsic priority weight of request r_i, q_{ij} represents the predicted impact of request r_i on the jth non-functional metric, β_j represents the weight or importance coefficient associated with the jth non-functional metric, λ is a tunable trade-off parameter that balances priority-driven and impact-aware decision-making.

4.2   Impact-Sensitive Attention-Based Conflict Resolution

Algorithm 1 outlines the proposed *impact-sensitive attention-based conflict resolution approach.*

Given a set of incoming requests $\boldsymbol{R}$, the objective is to identify a conflict-free subset $S \subseteq R$ that maximizes overall utility while minimizing the anticipated negative impact on the system's non-functional metrics.

The algorithm operates in two main stages: **impact prediction** and **conflict resolution**.

1. **Impact Prediction:** For each incoming request, the system predicts its expected influence on key non-functional metrics using contextual attributes and historical data. This step enriches each request with impact-aware features that guide the subsequent resolution process.
2. **Conflict Resolution:** Based on the enriched request representations, the resolution process proceeds through the following three steps:
   (a) **Contextual Encoding:** An attention mechanism encodes each request in relation to the entire request set, capturing interdependencies, contextual relevance, and relative priorities to form globally informed representations.
   (b) **Utility Scoring:** These contextual representations are passed through dense neural layers to compute utility scores that integrate both the request's functional priority and its predicted non-functional impact. A softmax function is applied to normalize the scores, enabling effective comparison and ranking.
   (c) **Conflict-Aware Selection and Filtering:** Leveraging learned resolution patterns and real-time conflict detection logic, the algorithm

---

Algorithm 1. Impact-Sensitive Attention-based Conflict Resolution.

Require: Set of requests $R = \{r_1, r_2, \ldots, r_n\}$
$\qquad$ Conflict function $C(r_i, r_j)$
$\qquad$ QoS weights $\beta = [\beta_1, \ldots, \beta_m]$
$\qquad$ Trade-off factor $\lambda \in \mathbb{R}^+$
Ensure: Selected subset $S \subseteq R$ with no conflicts
1:　　**Impact Prediction:**
2: **for** each $r_i \in R$ **do**
3:　$q_i \leftarrow \text{PredictQoSImpact}(r_i)$
4:　$r_i \leftarrow r_i \cup q_i$ $\qquad\qquad\qquad\qquad$ // Augment request with QoS impact
5: **end for**
6:　　**Request Selection:**
7: **for** each $r_i \in R$ **do**
8:　$e_i \leftarrow \text{Embed}(r_i)$ $\qquad\qquad\qquad\qquad$ //Request Encoding
9: **end for**
10: $q \leftarrow \text{ComputeGlobalContext}(R)$ $\qquad\qquad$ //Attention Encoding
11: **for** each e_i **do**
12:　$\alpha_i \leftarrow \text{AttentionScore}(e_i, q)$
13:　$h_i \leftarrow \alpha_i \cdot e_i$
14: **end for**
15: **for** each r_i **do**
16:　$z_i \leftarrow \text{DenseLayers}(h_i)$ $\qquad\qquad\qquad$ //Request Scoring
17: **end for**
18: **for** each r_i **do**
19:　$x_i \leftarrow \text{Softmax}(z_i)$ $\qquad\qquad\qquad\qquad$ //Softmax Step
20: **end for**
21: Iterative Selection:
22: $S \leftarrow \emptyset, \quad R_{\text{remain}} \leftarrow R$
23: **while** $R_{\text{remain}} \neq \emptyset$ **do**
24:　$r^* \leftarrow \arg\max_{r \in R_{\text{remain}}} U_r$
25:　$S \leftarrow S \cup \{r^*\}$
26:　$R_{\text{remain}} \leftarrow R_{\text{remain}} \setminus \{r^*\}$
27:　Filter R_{remain} to keep only requests non-conflicting with S
28: **end while**
29: **return** S

---

iteratively selects the highest-scoring requests. The final selection optimally balances functional requirements with system-wide non-functional impact.

Each of these stages is detailed below.

1. Impact Prediction. The objective is to estimate the potential impact of executing a given request r_i on the system's internal objectives. This process is carried out using the model illustrated in Fig. 1.

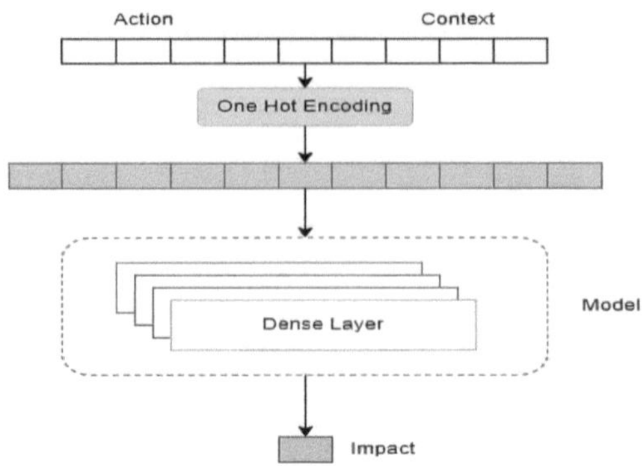

Fig. 1. Impact Prediction.

Particularly, the model comprises the following components:

- **One-Hot Encoding Layer:** Transforms categorical attributes (e.g., `type`) into a binary vector representation suitable for neural processing;
- **Stack of Fully Connected Dense Layers:** Learns complex, non-linear interactions among input features to produce a latent representation.

The final output is a scalar value that quantifies the predicted impact of executing request r_i on a targeted system-level non-functional objective.

Example 1. Let us consider the use case previously introduced in Section 2, involving a connected vehicle receiving multiple requests. Each request is characterized by an action, a priority weight, a time window (start and end), a timestamp of issuance, and a target location specified by longitude and latitude respectively:

- $r_1 = [Accelerate, 0.4, 08:30, 08:34, 08:29, lon_1, lat_1]$
- $r_2 = [Stop, 0.6, 08:31, 08:35, 08:36, lon_2, lat_2]$
- $r_3 = [Decelerate, 0.5, 08:30, 08:34, 08:30, lon_3, lat_3]$
- $r_4 = [Decelerate, 0.5, 08:35, 08:37, 08:30, lon_4, lat_4]$

In this scenario, we consider the two non-functional impact metrics: *energy consumption* and *CO_2 emissions*. Using the model we propose, the predicted impact of each request r_i is represented by a vector q_i :

- $q_1 = [energy\_impact(r_1), emission\_impact(r_1)]$
- $q_2 = [energy\_impact(r_2), emission\_impact(r_2)]$
- $q_3 = [energy\_impact(r_3), emission\_impact(r_3)]$
- $q_4 = [energy\_impact(r_4), emission\_impact(r_4)]$

For illustration, the predicted values (normalized between 0 and 1) are as follows:

- $q_1 = [0.78, 0.85]$ (High energy and emission impact due to acceleration)

- $q_2 = [0.20,\ 0.15]$ (Low energy and emission impact for stopping)
- $q_3 = [0.35,\ 0.30]$ (Moderate impact from deceleration)
- $q_4 = [0.38,\ 0.33]$ (Similar deceleration impact in a later time window)

These impact vectors serve as inputs to the conflict resolution process, enabling the system to assess the trade-offs between functional priorities and non-functional consequences. The goal is to prioritize requests that align with system objectives while minimizing overall energy use and environmental footprint.

2. Conflict Resolution. Once the list of candidate requests has been enriched with their corresponding predicted impact values, it is forwarded to the decision-making module responsible for determining which requests to accept or reject. This selection process is conducted iteratively, evaluating one request at a time while dynamically updating the set of accepted requests to ensure that no conflicts are introduced.

During each iteration, the system jointly considers the priority weight and the predicted impact of each request on the system's non-functional objectives. The decision process aims to maximize overall utility while maintaining conflict-free execution. This utility-driven selection enables the system to make informed trade-offs between functional demands and non-functional constraints. The architecture of the selection model is depicted in Fig. 2.

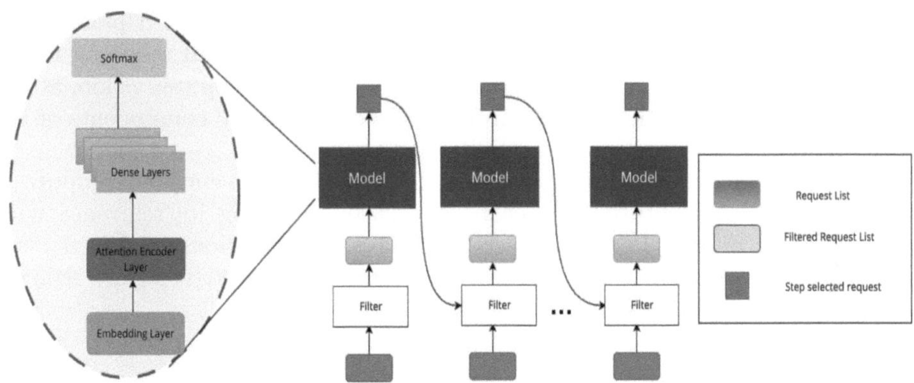

Fig. 2. Architecture of the request's selection.

(a) Contextual Encoding. This step focuses on constructing a structured and informative representation of each request, which is essential for effective downstream processing. Following the impact prediction phase, each request $r_j = [a_j, w_j, st_j, et_j, t_j, lon_j, lat_j, q_j]$ is encoded as a comprehensive feature vector that integrates both semantic and contextual attributes. This vector encapsulates key dimensions including the intended action (a_j), priority weight (w_j), timing constraints $(st_j,\ et_j,\ t_j)$, location features (lon_j, lat_j), as well as the predicted non-functional impact (q_j).

To enhance its expressiveness, this representation is passed through an embedding layer, which projects the input into a higher-dimensional latent space. This transformation enables the model to capture intricate patterns, correlations, and dependencies between various request components. By leveraging the contextual and sequential characteristics of the data, the embedding process produces a richer and more discriminative encoding, better suited for subsequent attention-based reasoning. This refined representation facilitates more accurate prioritization, contextual understanding, and ultimately, more effective conflict detection and resolution within the system.

Example 2. Consider the four requests r_1, r_2, r_3, and r_4, previously described and augmented with their predicted impact vectors. Each of these requests is now transformed into its corresponding embedding representation using the learned embedding function. We denote the resulting encoded vectors as:

$$e_1 = \text{Embed}(r_1), \quad e_2 = \text{Embed}(r_2), \quad e_3 = \text{Embed}(r_3), \quad e_4 = \text{Embed}(r_4).$$

These embeddings serve as compact, high-dimensional representations that preserve both the structural and semantic properties of the original requests, enabling subsequent attention-based processing and utility scoring.

Attention Encoder. In our impact-sensitive conflict resolution setting, each request is represented by an embedding that integrates both its contextual attributes and predicted impacts. The attention encoder leverages these enriched embeddings to model inter-request relationships, uncover latent dependencies, and highlight potential conflicts among concurrently submitted requests. Originating from advances in natural language processing and computer vision, attention mechanisms allow models to selectively focus on critical components of the input, thereby enhancing interpretability and performance.

Given a set of input vectors $\{e_1, e_2, e_3, e_4\}$, the attention encoder computes a context-aware representation for each request by weighing its relevance with respect to the others. For each encoded vector e_i, attention weights α_{ij} are computed with respect to every other vector e_j in the set, typically using a scaled dot-product attention mechanism:

$$\alpha_i = \frac{e^{q \cdot k_i}}{\sum_{j=1}^{n} e^{q \cdot k_j}}$$

where $q = W_Q e_i$ is the query vector for request r_i, and $k_j = W_K e_j$ is the key vector for each other request r_j. W_Q and W_K are learnable projection matrices that map the input embeddings into a common query-key space. The attention weight α_i reflects how relevant request r_j is to r_i, based on the similarity of their representations.

The final context-aware representation $\tilde{e}_i$ of request r_i is obtained by computing a weighted sum over the value-transformed embeddings:

$$\tilde{e}_i = \sum_{j=1}^{n} \alpha_{ij} \cdot v_j,$$

where $v_j = W_V e_j$ and W_V is the value projection matrix.

This context-aware encoding $\tilde{e}_i$ captures not only the intrinsic features of r_i, but also its relationship to other concurrent requests. These enriched representations are subsequently used for utility scoring and conflict resolution decisions.

Example 3. Building upon the embedded vectors e_1, e_2, e_3, e_4 from Example 2, the attention encoder processes these representations to model contextual dependencies between the requests. The mechanism computes attention scores α_i for each request by evaluating its relevance with respect to the others in the set. The result is a set of attention-informed embeddings, where each updated representation incorporates both the intrinsic characteristics of the request and its relationships with other concurrent requests. This enriched encoding is subsequently used to guide the scoring and selection processes.

(b) Utility Scoring. In this phase, each request undergoes a sequence of transformations designed to extract and refine the most informative features for decision-making. The attention-informed embeddings are first passed through a stack of fully connected (dense) layers, which capture complex, non-linear interactions among contextual attributes such as action type, timing, priority, and predicted impact. This process results in enriched representations that emphasize decision-critical patterns across the request set.

These refined representations are then used to compute utility scores, which are then normalized through a softmax function to derive selection probabilities:

$$P(r_i) = \frac{e^{z_i}}{\sum_{j=1}^{n} e^{z_j}}$$

where z_i denotes the utility score assigned to request r_i, computed from its context-aware representation $\tilde{e}_i$. These utility scores encapsulate both the functional relevance (e.g., action type, timing constraints) and the anticipated non-functional impact (e.g., energy usage, CO_2 emission) of each request.

The softmax layer normalizes these utility scores into a probability distribution over all candidate requests, allowing the model to compare and rank them effectively. Requests with higher selection probabilities are more likely to be included in the final conflict-free execution plan. Higher probabilities indicate a stronger alignment with the system's decision criteria, thereby guiding the construction of a conflict-free execution plan that optimally balances operational goals with system-wide impact.

Example 4. The vectors obtained from the attention encoder are passed through a series of dense layers to produce refined feature representations. Let us denote the attention-informed embeddings of the four requests as $\tilde{e}_1, \tilde{e}_2, \tilde{e}_3, \tilde{e}_4$. Each vector $\tilde{e}_i$ is processed to compute a utility score z_i, which reflects the overall relevance of executing request r_i based on its contextual relevance and predicted impact.

These utility scores are then normalized using the softmax function to obtain selection probabilities:

$$P(r_i) = \frac{e^{z_i}}{\sum_{j=1}^{4} e^{z_j}}$$

Suppose the computed utility scores for the four requests are as follows:

$$z_1 = 3.5, \quad z_2 = 0.25, \quad z_3 = 1.4, \quad z_4 = 2.1$$

Applying the softmax yields:

$$P(r_1) \approx 0.710, \quad P(r_2) \approx 0.0275, \quad P(r_3) \approx 0.087, \quad P(r_4) \approx 0.175$$

These probabilities guide the conflict-aware selection module, which iteratively selects the highest-ranked non-conflicting requests (e.g., r_3 followed by r_1), thereby forming an optimized execution plan that balances functionality and non-functional impact.

(c) Conflict-Aware Selection and Filtering. In this final stage, the algorithm constructs a conflict-free execution plan by selecting requests based on their softmax-derived utility scores, while rigorously enforcing conflict-avoidance constraints. The goal is to maximize the overall utility of the selected set while ensuring that no two selected requests conflict in terms of timing or action compatibility. In this context, request filtering plays an important role in the iterative conflict resolution process. Since the model selects one request at a time, it is essential to prevent newly selected requests from conflicting with those already accepted. To achieve this, a dynamic filtering mechanism is employed after each selection step to eliminate potential conflicts from the remaining candidate pool.

Specifically, once a subset of requests $\mathcal{R}$ has been selected, the model constructs a binary mask that excludes any incoming request r_i that conflicts with any request of $\mathcal{R}$. This ensures that only conflict-free requests are eligible for selection in subsequent iterations.

The mask M for a given request r_i is defined as follows:

$$M(r_i) = \begin{cases} 0 & \text{if } \exists\, r_j \in \mathcal{R} \text{ such that } C(r_i, r_j) = 1 \\ 1 & \text{otherwise} \end{cases}$$

Here, $C(r_i, r_j) = 1$ denotes a conflict between requests r_i and r_j. The mask effectively removes any conflicting requests from consideration, allowing the system to focus only on candidates that maintain global consistency.

Example 5. Consider the set of requests previously introduced in Example 1:

- $r_1 = [\text{Accelerate}, 0.4, 08{:}30, 08{:}34, 08{:}29, \text{lon}_1, \text{lat}_1]$
- $r_2 = [\text{Stop}, 0.6, 08{:}31, 08{:}35, 08{:}36, \text{lon}_2, \text{lat}_2]$
- $r_3 = [\text{Decelerate}, 0.5, 08{:}30, 08{:}34, 08{:}30, \text{lon}_3, \text{lat}_3]$
- $r_4 = [\text{Decelerate}, 0.5, 08{:}35, 08{:}37, 08{:}30, \text{lon}_4, \text{lat}_4]$

Assume that request r_1 is selected in the first iteration due to its highest selection probability. The conflict-aware filtering mechanism must now exclude any request that conflicts with r_1 based on overlapping execution time and incompatible action semantics.

Requests r_2 and r_3 overlap in time with r_1 (08:30âĂŞ08:34 vs. 08:31âĂŞ08:35 and 08:30âĂŞ08:34, respectively) and involve conflicting actions (**Stop** and **Decelerate** vs. **Accelerate**). As a result, they are excluded from the candidate pool.

Request r_4, however, starts after r_1 ends (from 08:35 to 08:37), and does not conflict temporally or functionally with r_1, so it remains eligible.

The resulting binary mask M after the first iteration is:

$$M = [1, 0, 0, 1]$$

indicating that only r_1 and r_4 are valid for selection. In the next iteration, a new softmax is computed over the remaining unmasked request r_4, and the selection process continues. This dynamic filtering ensures that the final execution plan remains conflict-free while maximizing utility.

5   Experimental Evaluation

5.1   Experimental Setup

The proposed approach has been implemented and evaluated using Python 3.11. The experiments have been conducted on Windows 10 64-bit with a 2.4 Ghz Intel(R) I7 processor and 16GB RAM.

Dataset

We built a dataset to simulate and capture conflicts in realistic urban traffic settings using the *Simulation of Urban Mobility* (SUMO)[1] , an open-source microscopic traffic simulator for large-scale, intermodal systems involving vehicles and pedestrians. SUMO offers tools for scenario creation, behavior modeling, routing, and signal control, making it ideal for generating high-fidelity datasets that reflect real-world mobility dynamics.

For our experiments, we used SUMO version 1.20.0 and extracted a road network segment in Toulouse, France, via the *OSMWebWizard* tool, which integrates OpenStreetMap (OSM) data. Traffic routes were auto-generated to reflect plausible urban flows. During simulation, we monitored a specific vehicle and recorded its fuel consumption and CO_2 emissions, key non-functional metrics for evaluating the environmental and operational impact of individual request resolutions in our conflict resolution framework.

The resulting dataset includes detailed vehicle trajectories, time-sensitive control requests, and labeled conflict instances. It forms a robust foundation

---

[1] https://sumo.dlr.de

for training and evaluating our impact-aware, attention-based decision-making model. It is publicly accessible via GitHub (https://github.com/cawanyo/data.git), enabling reproducibility and facilitating further research in conflict resolution for smart mobility systems.

Simulations were conducted in two distinct phases to evaluate the impact of control requests on traffic performance:

- **Baseline Phase:** Multiple simulations were executed under standard conditions using the initially generated road network, without any external interventions. This phase served as a control scenario. Observations revealed that traffic metrics, specifically fuel consumption and CO_2 emissions, remained relatively stable across runs, establishing a consistent performance baseline.
- **Perturbation Phase:** In this phase, we introduced a series of simulated control requests, at randomly selected times and locations. These interventions aimed to mimic dynamic interactions and potential conflicts. As in the baseline phase, we monitored the vehicle and recorded its fuel consumption and CO_2 emissions at the end of each trip. The comparison between both phases enabled us to assess the non-functional impact of the introduced requests on overall system behavior.

Optimization

To train our model to select the optimal request at each step, we use *Cross-Entropy Loss*, suitable for multi-class classification with softmax outputs. Since the model selects one request at a time, the target is an integer index of the correct request. The loss penalizes low predicted probabilities for the correct request, encouraging higher attention to relevant inputs.

Formally, given a set of n candidate requests with model-predicted scores $\hat{\mathbf{z}} = [\hat{z}_1, \hat{z}_2, \ldots, \hat{z}_n]$ (logits before softmax), and a ground truth label $z \in \{1, 2, \ldots, n\}$, the loss is:

$$\mathcal{L}_{\text{CE}} = -\log \left(\frac{e^{\hat{z}_z}}{\sum_{j=1}^{n} e^{\hat{z}_j}} \right)$$

This is minimized when the model assigns the highest probability to the correct request.

For optimization, we use *Adam*, which adaptively adjusts each parameter's learning rate using estimates of the first and second moments of gradients. Adam is known for its efficiency and stability, especially with noisy or sparse gradients. Its fast convergence and minimal tuning requirements make it well-suited to our attention-based framework, which must learn dynamic feature relevance and complex contextual interactions across concurrent requests.

5.2   Evaluation

Each conflict resolution in the training set was constructed by exhaustively exploring all valid combinations of non-conflicting requests and selecting the combination that maximizes the overall utility function (brute force). This ensures that the training labels represent optimal decisions. Fig. 3 and 4 show the evolution of the training loss and the model's accuracy, respectively. These results confirm the convergence and learning stability of the model, providing a solid foundation for evaluation on unseen data.

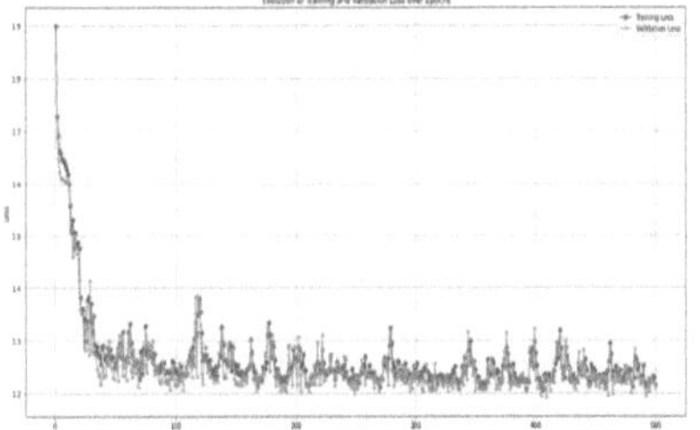

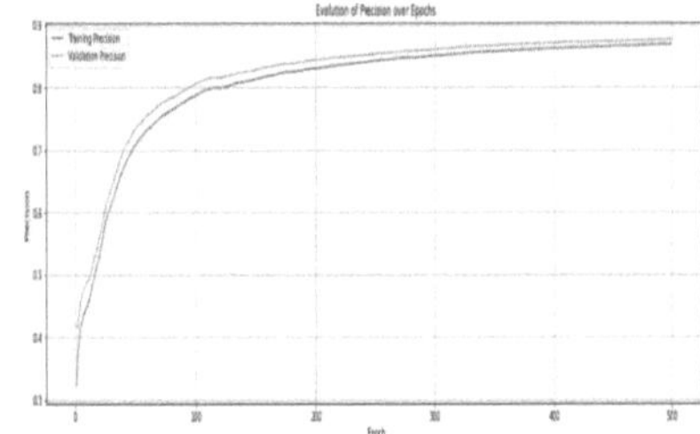

Fig. 3. Evolution of the loss during the training.

Fig. 4. Evolution of the precision during the training.

The execution time of our approach, compared to the brute-force method, is illustrated in Fig. 5. While the brute-force approach guarantees optimality by exhaustively exploring all possible request combinations, its computational cost escalates rapidly with the number of concurrent requests, rendering it impractical for real-time or large-scale deployments. In contrast, our proposed method demonstrates a substantial reduction in execution time, maintaining scalability and responsiveness even as the request volume increases. This efficiency gain becomes increasingly pronounced with larger input sizes, as illustrated in Fig. 6, where execution times are plotted on a logarithmic scale to emphasize the widening performance gap.

The results highlight the scalability of our approach and its practical relevance to real-world scenarios, where efficient conflict resolution among numerous concurrent requests is essential for maintaining system responsiveness and operational effectiveness.

Moreover, we assessed the accuracy of the prediction model by comparing the global utility of predicted combinations to those of the best real combinations observed across different sets of requests. This evaluation is essential for measuring the performance of the model and identifying both its strengths and potential areas for refinement. The results, depicted in Fig. 7, provide a clear visual comparison between predicted and optimal utilities, enabling an intuitive analysis of consistency, deviations, and performance trends across combinations of varying sizes.

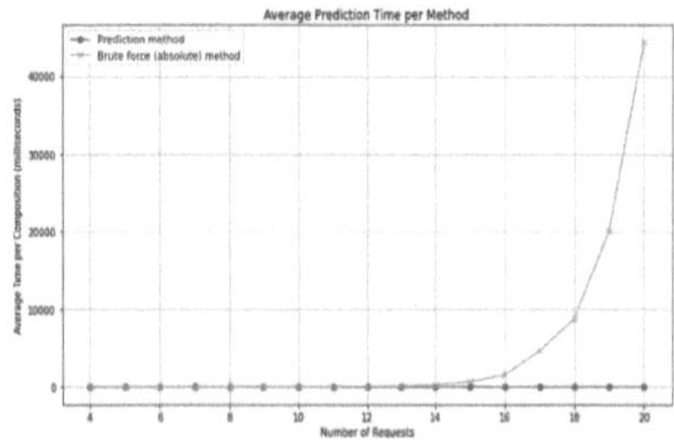

Fig. 5. Evolution of the execution time.

Fig. 6. Log scale of the execution time.

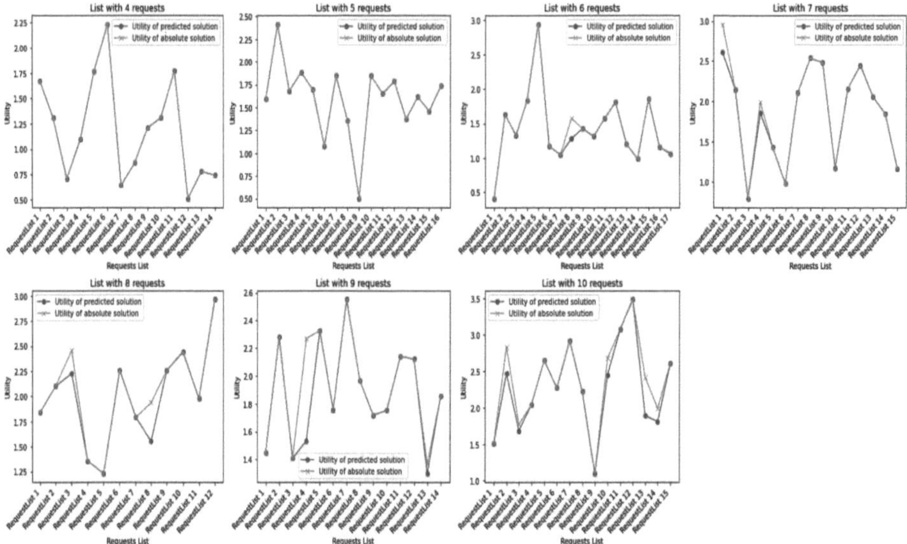

Fig. 7. Comparison between predicted and real objective function scores across different numbers of requests.

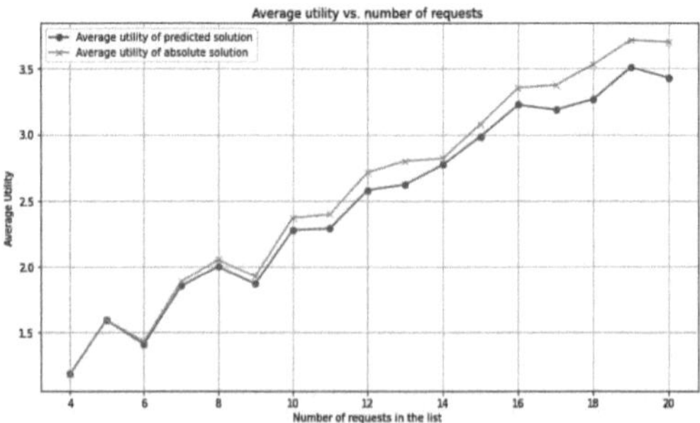

Fig. 8. Evolution of the average utility according to the number of requests.

In addition, Fig. 8 shows that the prediction model generally yields accurate utility estimates across various request list sizes.

The overall alignment between predicted and actual utility values indicates that the model effectively captures the underlying decision patterns. However, as the number of concurrent requests increases, slightly larger deviations begin to emerge. These discrepancies suggest that while the model scales well, its predictive reliability may be challenged in more complex scenarios involving higher request density or increased conflict potential. This highlights the need for further refinement in handling intricate interdependencies, particularly under high-load conditions.

6   Conclusion

In this paper, we proposed an impact-sensitive, attention-based framework for conflict resolution in IoT systems that jointly considers request importance, contextual relevance, and the non-functional impact of resolution decisions. Unlike prior models focused mainly on priority, our approach integrates predictive capabilities to estimate the effect of each request on multiple non-functional metrics, enabling more informed, utility-driven decisions.

In this context, we formalized conflict resolution as a utility maximization problem, selecting requests that optimize overall system benefit while meeting action compatibility constraints. The model uses attention mechanisms to dynamically focus on relevant context and employs an iterative strategy to resolve conflicts in real time. Evaluations show that our model effectively identifies high-utility request combinations and adapts to varying request densities. Crucially, incorporating impact predictions significantly improves decision quality, especially in complex, multi-objective scenarios.

As part of future work, we plan to extend our framework toward multi-agent coordination, where distributed systems must collaboratively negotiate and reconcile conflicting objectives in real time, further advancing the scalability and robustness of conflict resolution across both local and global smart IoT ecosystems. In addition, we aim to expand our experimental evaluation to include more concrete and large-scale scenarios, allowing us to assess the practical applicability and performance of our approach in more realistic and diverse environments.

References

1. Awanyo, C., Guermouche, N.: Attention-driven conflict management in smart Iot-based systems. In: Service-Oriented Computing - 22nd International Conference, ICSOC 2024. https://doi.org/10.1007/978-981-96-0805-8_10
2. Babun, L., Celik, Z.B., McDaniel, P., Uluagac, S.: real-time analysis of privacy-(un)aware Iot applications. In: Proceedings on Privacy Enhancing Technologies **2021**, 145–166 (01 2021). https://doi.org/10.2478/popets-2021-0009
3. Bastys, I., Balliu, M., Sabelfeld, A.: If this then what? controlling flows in Iot apps. In: Proceedings of the 2018 ACM SIGSAC Conference on Computer and Communications Security (2018). https://doi.org/10.1145/3243734.3243841

4. Camacho, R., Carreira, P., Lynce, I., R., S.: An ontology-based approach to conflict resolution in home and building automation systems. Expert Syst. Appl. **41**, 6161–6173 (10 2014). https://doi.org/10.1016/j.eswa.2014.04.017

5. Celik, Z.B., McDaniel, P., Tan, G.: Soteria: automated IoT safety and security analysis. In: 2018 USENIX Annual Technical Conference (USENIX ATC 18), pp. 147–158. USENIX Association, Boston, MA (Jul 2018). https://www.usenix.org/conference/atc18/presentation/celik

6. Chaki, D., Bouguettaya, A.: Dynamic conflict resolution of iot services in smart homes. In: Hacid, H., Kao, O., Mecella, M., Moha, N., Paik, H. (eds.) ICSOC 2021. LNCS, vol. 13121, pp. 368–384. Springer, Cham (2021). https://doi.org/10.1007/978-3-030-91431-8_23

7. Chaki, D., Bouguettaya, A., Mistry, S.: A conflict detection framework for Iot services in multi-resident smart homes, pp. 224–231 (10 2020). https://doi.org/10.1109/ICWS49710.2020.00036

8. Chi, H., Zeng, Q., Du, X., Yu, J.: Cross-app interference threats in smart homes: categorization, detection and handling. In: Proceedings - 50th Annual IEEE/IFIP International Conference on Dependable Systems and Networks, DSN 2020 (June 2020). https://doi.org/10.1109/DSN48063.2020.00056

9. Ding, W., Hu, H.: On the safety of Iot device physical interaction control, pp. 832–846 (10 2018). https://doi.org/10.1145/3243734.3243865

10. Igaki, H., Nakamura, M.: Modeling and detecting feature interactions among integrated services of home network systems. IEICE Trans. **93-D**, 822–833 (04 2010). https://doi.org/10.1587/transinf.E93.D.822

11. Jia, Y., et al.: Contexiot: towards providing contextual integrity to applied Iot platforms (01 2017). https://doi.org/10.14722/ndss.2017.23051

12. Leelaprute, P., Takafumi, M., Tsuchiya, T., Kikuno, T.: Detecting feature interactions in home appliance networks, pp. 895–903 (01 2008). https://doi.org/10.1109/SNPD.2008.158

13. Ma, M., Stankovic, J., Feng, L.: Cityresolver: a decision support system for conflict resolution in smart cities, pp. 55–64 (04 2018). https://doi.org/10.1109/ICCPS.2018.00014

14. Nakamura, M., Igaki, H., Matsumoto, K.i.: Feature interactions in integrated services of networked home appliances (07 2005)

15. Perumal, T., Sulaiman, M., Datta, S.K., Ramachandran, T., Leong, C.: Rule-based conflict resolution framework for internet of things device management in smart home environment, pp. 1–2 (10 2016). https://doi.org/10.1109/GCCE.2016.7800444

16. Pradeep, P., Kant, K.: Conflict detection and resolution in iot systems: a survey. IoT **3**(1), 191–218 (2022). https://www.mdpi.com/2624-831X/3/1/12

17. Pradeep Kumar, P., Pal, A., Kant, K.: Automating conflict detection and mitigation in large-scale Iot systems (04 2021). https://doi.org/10.1109/CCGrid51090.2021.00063

18. Sun, Y., Wang, X., Luo, H., Li, X.: Conflict detection scheme based on formal rule model for smart building systems. IEEE Trans. Human-Mach. Syst. **45**, 1–13 (11 2014). https://doi.org/10.1109/THMS.2014.2364613

19. Wang, Q., Hassan, W., Bates, A., Gunter, C.: Fear and logging in the internet of things (01 2018). https://doi.org/10.14722/ndss.2018.23291

Digital Twin Narratives: Framework
for Clear Communication

Faten El Outa[(✉)], Hugo Breuillard, and Guillaume Dechambenoit

French Geological Survey (BRGM), Orléans, France
`f.elouta@brgm.fr`

Abstract. Digital Twin (DT) systems are increasingly applied in environmental contexts to support real-time monitoring, forecasting, and decision-making. While technically advanced, many DT implementations fall short in communicating insights in ways that are accessible, interpretable, and actionable for diverse audiences. This paper introduces a user-centered framework that enhances the communicative power of environmental DTs through the integration of data storytelling techniques. The proposed approach is structured around five components: (i) a four-phase data storytelling process, (ii) a user-system interaction model driven by user intent, (iii) progressive levels of knowledge formalization, (iv) a workflow that adapts key data storytelling activities to generate DT outputs that are both analytically robust and communication-ready, and (v) a semantic mapping table that links analytical operations to narrative and visual outputs. Together, these components enable DT systems to transform analytical results into meaningful, audience-adapted stories. The framework is illustrated through an environmental prediction use case, demonstrating its potential to enhance interpretability, increase user engagement, and support more informed decision-making.

Keywords: Environmental Digital Twins · Data Storytelling · Narrative Visualization · Human-Centered Communication · IA

1 Introduction

Context. Digital Twin (DT) systems are gaining widespread adoption across various sectors, particularly in industrial, urban, and environmental contexts [8,9,11,15,24]. These systems are designed to monitor, simulate, and predict complex phenomena such as groundwater behavior, flood risks, and climate-related hazards. These systems combine real-time sensor data, simulation models, and Artificial Intelligence (AI) techniques to generate predictive and actionable insights. While their technical capabilities are well established, their core purpose lies in supporting data-informed decision-making by diverse users, including experts, policymakers, and the general public. As such, DT systems must be designed not solely around technical feasibility but also around their communicative function—that is, their ability to effectively deliver insights in forms that users can interpret, understand, and act upon [20]. In environmental contexts especially, where urgent decisions are often required, this communicative role becomes essential for early warning systems, sustainability planning, and public policy development.

Problem. Despite their analytical and technological sophistication, most existing DT implementations emphasize data integration, algorithmic performance, and system responsiveness—while giving comparatively little attention to how outputs are structured, interpreted, or communicated to end users [2,7,16,21]. In practice, DT results are often delivered through dashboards or static visualizations that lack contextual framing and are not tailored to users information needs or levels of expertise. This is particularly problematic in environmental contexts, where outputs must often reach heterogeneous audiences, including domain experts, decision-makers, journalists, and the general public. When findings are presented in generic or overly technical formats, they risk being misunderstood, overlooked, or excluded from important decisions.

Need. To overcome these limitations, there is a pressing need to enhance the communicative dimension of environmental DTs. Specifically, DT systems should incorporate mechanisms that support not only accurate computation but also meaningful, user-centered communication.

Brainstorming. Narratives are powerful cognitive tools for organizing information, evoking emotion, and shaping human understanding. Data storytelling, in particular, provides a structured framework for translating analytical results into coherent, goal-driven messages through the use of narrative techniques, visualizations, and audience-aware framing [4,19,20]. This approach has been widely adopted in journalism, public health, and civic communication, yet it remains largely underexplored in the design of DTs. Given the interpretive challenges and public facing role of environmental DTs, we argue that storytelling techniques are not merely complementary but essential for ensuring that DT outputs are understandable, contextually relevant, and aligned with user intent.

Contribution. In this paper, we introduce a user-centered framework for environmental DTs that operationalizes data storytelling principles to support interpretability and audience adaptation within DT context. Our contribution is structured around five interrelated components:

(i) A general data storytelling process [18] organized into four phases covering activities from data exploration until the final communication of structured narratives.

(ii) A user-system interaction model where user intent guides the generation of tailored DT outputs, integrating both analytical processing and communicative delivery.

(iii) Three progressive levels of knowledge formalization—*personal, interpersonal,* and *community*—that guide the refinement of insights throughout the process.

(iv) A workflow that reuses the core activities of the data storytelling process [18] to construct DT outputs that are both analytically sound and communicatively tailored;

(v) A semantic mapping table constitutes a foundational technical aspect that enables the potential automation of data storytelling within DT systems.

An earlier version of our data-storytelling workflow for digital twins was accepted as a short paper at DEXA 2025. This article extends our DEXA 2025 short paper by presenting a unified framework, detailing a three-level communication workflow and a comprehensive technical blueprint with semantic mapping tables for real-world deployment, and validating everything with a Python prototype that offers an interactive interface from raw sensor data to narrative insights.

The remainder of this paper is organized as follows. Section 2 reviews related work in the areas of DTs and data storytelling. Section 3 introduces the proposed framework, detailing its core components: the data storytelling process, user-system interaction model, levels of knowledge formalization, layered workflow, and semantic mapping table. Section 4 and 5 demonstrate the applicability of this framework through environmental forecasting scenario. Finally, Sect. 6 concludes the paper and discusses future research directions.

2   Related Work

Understanding how DT systems can better serve decision-making requires looking beyond their technical architecture and into their communicative functions. This section reviews two key areas of related work that collectively motivate our approach: (i) the development and limitations of current DT systems in delivering interpretable insights, and (ii) research in data storytelling that aims to make data outputs more interpretable, engaging, and actionable.

DT Systems. DT systems [1] are increasingly recognized as powerful decision-support tools capable of simulating, monitoring, and forecasting complex phenomena in real time. Their adoption spans a wide range of domains, including manufacturing [13], urban analytics [5], and environmental monitoring [6]. More recently, the concept has been extended to business operations through Business Process DTs (BPDT), which synchronize organizational workflows and enable predictive decision-making [12]. Despite these advances, most DT frameworks remain primarily focused on technical dimensions such as data integration, system architecture, and AI-based modeling. As a result, the communicative function of DTs—their ability to adapt outputs to user needs, knowledge levels, and decision contexts—remains underdeveloped. For instance, Kang and Mo [21] emphasize real-time AI-driven data exchange in the AEC sector, while Osama [16] outlines a structured pipeline from data capture to decision-making. Yet, both approaches prioritize technical efficiency over human-centered interpretation. This gap is particularly limiting for non-technical stakeholders, as existing

DT implementations often fail to provide outputs that are meaningfully structured, interpretable, and actionable across diverse audiences.

Approach to Human-Centered Communication. In contrast to traditional DT implementations, data storytelling explicitly prioritizes structuring and narrating data-driven insights to enhance user comprehension. Segel and Heer [20] introduced foundational narrative visualization principles designed to support communication beyond conventional charts. Expanding upon this, Vassiliadis et al. [23] proposed intentional operators, shifting analytical queries from purely technical data retrieval to explicit expressions of user intent, captured through high-level analytical goals such as Describe, Assess, Explain, Predict, and Suggest. These intentional operators facilitate mapping user intent directly to corresponding analytical methods and data models. Further refining this narrative focus, Bach et al. [4] identified 18 design patterns for systematically crafting data narratives, while El Outa [19] emphasized intentionality as crucial for aligning narrative structures with users' analytical goals. Nevertheless, such storytelling frameworks have yet to be systematically integrated into DT architectures. Consequently, existing DT implementations seldom leverage structured narrative methodologies or audience-adaptive messaging strategies, leaving significant gaps between complex analytical outputs and user understanding [1].

3   Towards a Framework for Environmental DT

To enhance the communicative capacity of DT systems, this work proposes a user-centric framework grounded in data storytelling. The contribution is built upon five interrelated pillars: (i) a data storytelling process [18] which provides the narrative backbone for transforming data into meaningful insights; (ii) a model of user-system interaction in which user intent actively drives both analytical computation and the generation of communicative outputs tailored to audience needs; (iii) a progressive model of insight formalization across three levels supports the gradual refinement of outputs from exploration to public dissemination; (iv) a workflow that reuses data storytelling activities to guide the construction of DT; and (v) a semantic mapping table that serves as the operational core of this framework, linking intentional operators to relevant datasets, algorithms, result types, narrative patterns, and visualization formats.

3.1   A Process for Data Storytelling

Data storytelling, the art of crafting coherent narratives from data, sits at the intersection of multiple domains, notably data processing, analysis, visualization, and communication (Fig. 1).

At the heart of our framework lies the data storytelling process introduced by El Outa et al. [17,19], which offers a structured methodology for transforming complex data into clear, engaging, and user-centric narratives. This process covers the complete narrative cycle, from initial exploration of datasets to the final visual communication of insights, through four distinct and iterative phases:

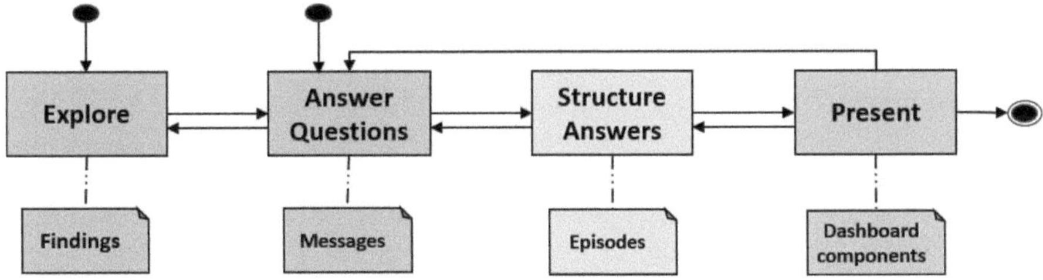

Fig. 1. The four-phase data storytelling process [17, 19].

1. **Explore** focuses on collecting, integrating, and preprocessing data, using analytical tools and visualizations to extract findings. Findings are then formulated and validated, potentially triggering further analysis or data collection.
2. **Answer Questions** guides the formulation of analytical goals and questions, and the derivation of messages from findings. Messages express insights aligned with user intent, transforming data patterns into interpretable responses.
3. **Structure Answers** organizes selected messages into narrative units, acts and episodes, tailored to the target audience and structured according to a chosen storytelling plot, thus shaping a coherent and interpretable data narrative.
4. **Present** involves designing visual narratives and dashboards that present acts and episodes. It includes defining interactivity modes and assembling visual components (e.g., charts, text, graphics) to communicate the story effectively to the audience.

Together, these four phases form the DT engine ensuring that system outputs remain aligned with user needs. For a more detailed account of the activities and their methodological grounding, we refer the reader to [18].

3.2 Modeling User Intent in DT Communication

A key contribution of this work lies in structuring the user-system interaction as a bidirectional communication model that integrates user intent into the narrative generation process, an aspect largely overlooked in prior DT and data storytelling literature [19]. Our approach addresses this gap by explicitly modeling both User and System interaction as illustrated in Fig. 2:

1. **User:** This component captures user intent [19], which we define as the high-level analytical goal [23] (e.g., to explore, assess, predict, or suggest). Unlike most data systems that treat users as passive recipients of output, our process acknowledges users as active contributors who initiate and shape the communication workflow. It supports a wide range of user profiles, including domain experts, policymakers, journalists, and citizens, each with varying analytical needs and communicative expectations. To ensure effective communication,

we distinguish between two key audience types—public and expert—based on their familiarity with data, interpretive skills, and information needs. This distinction allows the system to adapt visual and narrative outputs accordingly. An intuitive user interface (UI) enables these users to specify their intent through the selection of predefined intentional operators, configure environmental contexts (e.g., drought, flood), and define spatiotemporal parameters. For example, an environmental expert may request short-term flood predictions for a specific region and target audience, prompting the system to adapt the analytical model, visualization, and narrative structure accordingly.

2. **System:** The system component is responsible for executing data processing, analysis, and visualization in response to the user's declared intent. To operationalize this intent into communicative outputs, the system relies on a semantic mapping table detailed in Subsect. 3.5 that links each analytical goal to suitable datasets, algorithms, narrative patterns, and visualizations.

3.3   Structuring Knowledge for Communication

To support meaningful communication in DT systems, we propose a model that structures how knowledge evolves during user-system interaction. Drawing on communication theory [10], particularly Bateson and Ruech's levels of interaction (intrapersonal, interpersonal, cultural), we adapt this logic to describe how data transforms into communicable knowledge. In our framework, this progression is captured through three levels of formalization:

- **Personal Circle:** This involves preliminary and informal exploration, where knowledge remains primarily implicit or minimally structured. For example, a domain expert exploring preliminary environmental data might simply take personal notes or create basic visualizations without explicit context or annotations.
- **Interpersonal Circle:** At this level, knowledge is more explicitly structured for clarity, precision, and collaborative interaction. For instance, two researchers or a journalist and an expert might create annotated visualizations or structured bullet points clearly outlining key findings, making it easy for collaborators to discuss, refine, and build upon the shared understanding.
- **Community Circle:** This represents the highest level of formalization, designed for wide dissemination, requiring fully structured, clear, and accessible communication. For example, journalists publishing a detailed data-driven news article or policymakers sharing official environmental dashboards with comprehensive explanatory texts, detailed visual captions, and context-sensitive narratives.

3.4   Integrating Storytelling Into DT Pipelines

While the previous subsection described the conceptual levels of knowledge formalization, this Subsection details how these levels are operationalized within

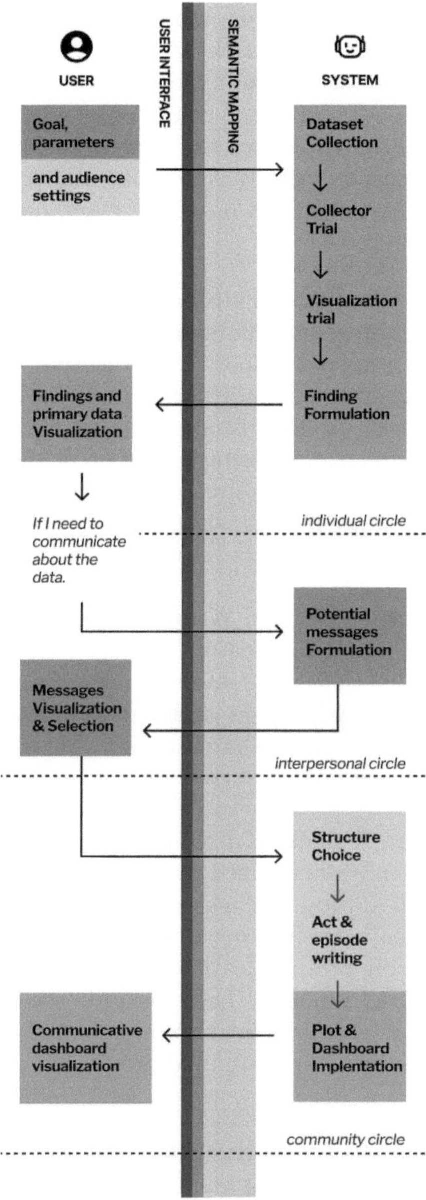

Fig. 2. User-System Communication Workflow for Digital Twins.

a structured storytelling workflow. The goal is to transform analytical outputs into narratives that are progressively refined and adapted to different audience needs. Figure 2 presents a layered communication workflow that integrates the four-phase data storytelling process (see Subsect. 3.1) with the levels of formalization (Personal, Interpersonal, Community) along interaction bewteen user and system DT. The color scheme reflects the four phases of the data storytelling process: Explore (pink), Answer Questions (purple), Structure Answers (yellow), and Present (blue), with each color corresponding to its respective set of activities. This workflow structures the generation of DT outputs, ensuring that insights are not only analytically sound but also progressively shaped into communicative formats aligned with user intent and audience expectations. In more detail:

- **Individual Circle – Preliminary Knowledge Exploration:** In this initial circle, knowledge is largely unstructured and meant for individual interpretation. Guided by user-specified analytical objectives and parameters such as complement of goal and type of audience, the system selects relevant datasets and algorithms, trials them, and visualizes preliminary results such as trends, distributions, or risk zones, without applying predefined narrative structures. At this exploratory stage, a finding emerges from the exploration phase, understood as a combination of the dataset used, the algorithm applied, and the resulting output, providing the user a basis for reflection and informal sense-making.
- **Interpersonal Circle – Shared Knowledge Structuring:** At this level, knowledge begins to take on a clearer form for collaborative interpretation. The system develop potential messages interpreting the finding retrieved, selecting appropriate visualizations and applying narrative design patterns (e.g. *Call-to-Action*) to support shared review. Messages are framed to support collaborative review and dialogue such as experts, journalists, or analysts.
- **Community Circle – Public Knowledge Communication:** In this final circle, knowledge is fully formalized and prepared for wide dissemination. The system selects an appropriate narrative structure—such as a plot type— followed by the development of storytelling acts, which are then translated into visual formats using communicative templates (e.g., dashboards, episodic narratives, or structured reports). These outputs are tailored to the intended audience (e.g., general public, policymakers), ensuring that the final communication is accessible, context-aware, and actionable across diverse communities.

This workflow constitutes a core contribution of our work, proposing a novel integration of storytelling into DT communication pipelines. By operationalizing the four phases of data storytelling within each circle of formalization, we enable DT systems to generate outputs that are not only technically sound, but also semantically structured, intentional, and accessible across varied audiences.

3.5 Semantic Mapping: From User Intent to Communication

DT systems often integrate complex, heterogeneous data pipelines to serve diverse user objectives, yet they frequently fail to translate high-level intent into coherent, audience-tailored narratives. To bridge this gap, we draw on established data-storytelling techniques [4,20,22], which offer formalized methods for turning analytical outputs into structured messages through narrative templates, visual encodings, and audience-aware framing.

To make this actionable, we introduce semantic mapping tables, a structured artifact in which each row defines a complete mapping from a specific user intent (e.g., Describe, Predict, Assess, Suggest [23]) to its requisite datasets, analytical algorithms, result types, narrative patterns, visualization formats, and target audience profile. This explicit linkage enables DT systems to dynamically configure their analytics and presentation layers in accordance with both communicative goals and stakeholder needs. Although presented here as a unified concept, the mapping table is instantiated differently across our three communication layers: the *Individual Circle* emphasizes precise data transformations and algorithmic parameters; the *Interpersonal Circle* tailors narrative structures and simplified visuals for peer collaboration; and the *Community Circle* prioritizes high-level overviews, contextual framing, and accessible language for broader stakeholder engagement. These layer-specific operationalizations are detailed in the following sections.

Individual Circle: Analytical Mapping Based on User Intent. Table 1 presents the association between each intentional operator and the analytical layer of the workflow. It provides a structured overview of the relationship between various user operators, the types of datasets they interact with, the algorithms employed, and the nature of the results produced. The "Describe" operator is associated with unstructured or unknown data and utilizes clustering or dimensionality reduction algorithms to generate distributions and projections. The "Assess" operator deals with known categories, employing classification models to produce predicted class probabilities. For known or historical data, regression models are used to forecast or predict values. Lastly, the "Suggest" operator is involved in scenario or decision-making processes, leveraging recommendation or reinforcement learning algorithms to provide sequential recommendations. This mapping showcases the different machine learning-based methods designed to meet specific user requirements and data types, and it automatically guides the selection of the most suitable algorithm internally. This mapping is grounded in practical experience in an environmental DT which analyzes regional emissions, risk assessments, and forecasting tasks.

Interpersonal–Community Circle: Communicative Strategies. Table 2 complements the analytical mapping by aligning each operator with its recommended narrative message patterns [4], storytelling structures [14], and suitable chart types differentiated by audience (e.g., public vs. expert). Chart types were selected based on the taxonomy of visualization techniques described in Srinivas et al. [22], which aligns visual forms with analytical purposes such as distribution analysis, trend detection, relationship mapping, and decision support. For each user intent, charts were mapped to the most cognitively accessible formats

Table 1. Individual Circle: Mapping between User Operators and Analytical Components.

Operator	Dataset	Algorithm	Result Type
Describe	Unstructured/unknown data	Clustering or dimensionality reduction	Distributions, projections
Assess	Known categories	Classification models	Predicted Classes Probabilities
Predict	Known/historical data	Regression models	Predicted/forecast values
Suggest	Scenario/Decision making process	Recommendation/ Reinforcement learning	Sequential recommendations

for public audiences and to more complex, data-dense representations for expert users, ensuring alignment with both communicative clarity and analytical depth.

Below is a concise overview:

– **Describe:** When users need to explore new or unfamiliar information, *Familiarization* (linking data to everyday concepts) and *Concretize* (using tangible icons for abstract figures) ground the audience. The *Stack of Blocks* structure helps organize details in straightforward sections. For a **public audience**, basic visuals like bar or pie charts deliver an immediate overview. In contrast, an **expert audience** may rely on histograms or box plots for more advanced statistical insights. The visualization types differ by audience to balance accessibility and depth: for the public, simple and familiar charts (e.g., bar, pie, or line charts) are selected to ease comprehension and highlight key messages, while for experts, more detailed analytical visualizations (e.g., box plots, scatter plots, or heatmaps) are used to enable precise exploration and technical interpretation.
– **Assess:** Evaluating performance or making comparisons benefits from *Rhetorical Question* (promoting reflection) and *Defamiliarization* (encouraging fresh perspectives). The *Freytag Pyramid* introduces a narrative arc, leading from setup to a resolution of findings. For a **public audience**, stacked bar charts or line charts highlight basic trends and proportions. An **expert audience** benefits from scatter plots and correlation heatmaps, uncovering multi-dimensional relationships. Public-facing visuals like stacked bar charts or line charts reveal immediate performance trends, while experts can leverage scatter plots and correlation heatmaps to detect multi-dimensional relationships.
– **Predict:** For forecasting or forward-looking analyses, *Gradual Reveal* (progressive insight) and *Call-to-Action* (highlighting urgency) keep participants engaged. The *Water Tower* structure launches with a strong opening and expands in accessible segments. A **public audience** typically grasps future

Table 2. Community Circle: Message Patterns, Plot Structures, and Recommended Visualizations by Operator and Audience.

Operator	Message Pattern(s)	Plot Structure	Visualization Type	
			Public	**Expert**
Describe	Familiarization, Concretize	Stack of Blocks	– Bar Chart – Pie Chart	– Histogram – Box Plot
Assess	Rhetorical Question, Defamiliarization	Freytag Pyramid	– Stacked Bar Chart – Line Chart	– Scatter Plot – Correlation Heatmap
Predict	Gradual Reveal, Call-to-Action	Water Tower	– Line Chart – Area Chart	– Box Plot – Density Plot
Suggest	Comparison, Call-to-Action	Three-Act Structure	– Stacked Bar Chart – Pie Chart	– Tree Map – Sunburst Chart

trends through line and area charts, while an **expert audience** requires box plots or density plots to assess variability and probability distributions.

– **Suggest:** When the goal is to guide decisions or highlight possible options, *Compare* (placing outcomes side by side) and a *Call-to-Action* (prompting a specific response) underscore the urgency. Drawing on the *Three-Act Structure*, the story sets the context, explores conflicts (trade-offs), and ends with a recommended path. A **public audience** finds stacked bar charts or pie charts most useful for a straightforward breakdown of options. An **expert audience** can dive deeper into hierarchical solutions using tree maps or sunburst charts.

Overall, this mapping combines machine learning outputs (*Describe, Assess, Predict, Suggest*) with recognized storytelling frameworks [4, 14] to guide DT systems in automatically selecting the most appropriate narrative approach and visualization style for each audience. By integrating narrative theory with data analysis, we ensure outputs are both informative and engaging, advancing more human-centered AI applications in areas like environmental modeling and risk assessment.

4   Case Study: Predicting Groundwater Levels

Table 3. Groundwater level forecast scenario in Digital Twin for Piezometer 03266X0009/P for the year 2019.

Element	Description
Intentional Operator	*Predict* — Used to anticipate environmental conditions and guide preventive actions.
Parameters	Groundwater Level, Location (Piezometer 03266X0009/P), Date (2019-01-01), Forecast Horizon (12 months).
Dataset	Historical time series: weekly groundwater levels, local rainfall, and evapotranspiration from past years.
Algorithm	Random Forest Regression — Applied to model complex, non-linear interactions between inputs (e.g., rainfall, evapotranspiration) and outputs (e.g., groundwater levels).
Type of Result	Numerical values — Predicted weekly groundwater levels for 2019 (in meters).
Narrative Pattern	Gradual Reveal + Call-to-Action — Forecast results are progressively unveiled to build audience engagement, followed by a clear directive. Example: "Week by week, groundwater levels have steadily dropped. By July, projections indicate values falling below 113.5 meters, the drought alert threshold. To prevent water shortages, initiate conservation efforts before the end of spring."
Plot Structure	Water Tower — Begins with an impactful introduction and sequentially delivers accessible insights.
Visualization	Line Chart + Area Chart with Threshold Marker — Tracks changes over time and flags critical levels intuitively.

Groundwater levels are declining in many regions, increasing the risks of drought and water shortages. Anticipating future trends is therefore essential not only for timely management decisions, but also for communicating risks clearly and fostering a shared understanding among stakeholders (Table 3).

This scenario illustrates how the model functions through user-system interaction across the three communication circles. A Figma-based dashboard prototype was also developed but is not shown due to space limitations.

- **User Component:** The process begins with a non-expert user (e.g., a concerned citizen or local community stakeholder) interacting with the DT through a user friendly interface. The user specifies their analytical goal, to *Predict* future (forecast) groundwater levels—along with relevant environmental parameters such as location (Piezometer 03266X0009/P), temporal scope (year 2019), and thematic context (potential drought risk). This declaration of intent activates the system's communication pipeline.

- **System Component:** In response, the system selects relevant datasets, including historical time series of groundwater levels, rainfall, and evapotranspiration, and applies a suitable algorithm—Random Forest Regression, to model and forecast aquifer behavior. The system also uses a semantically grounded mapping table to identify the appropriate message patterns, visual representations, and narrative structures aligned with the user's intent and target audience.
- **Individual Circle – Preliminary Knowledge Exploration:** At this stage, the user is presented with raw data outputs such as historical and predicted groundwater trends, allowing for informal, individual sense-making. The system surfaces unstructured visual cues—such as line charts showing rainfall and aquifer level correlations, without imposing a specific narrative. These early visuals help the user explore patterns and reflect on recent environmental changes, laying the groundwork for further interpretation.
- **Interpersonal Circle – Shared Knowledge Structuring:** As engagement deepens, the system translates the explored data into potential communicative messages using predefined narrative patterns. Here, the "Gradual Reveal" pattern is applied to disclose forecast information incrementally, enhancing user curiosity and involvement. This is paired with a "Call-to-Action" to emphasize the urgency of the situation and prompt behavioral response. For example, "Week by week, groundwater levels have steadily dropped. By July, projections indicate values falling below 113.5 m, the drought alert threshold. To prevent water shortages, initiate conservation efforts before the end of spring." This structured narrative supports interpersonal discussion among stakeholders (e.g., local experts, journalists, or environmental communicators), guiding collaborative understanding of the forecasted risk.
- **Community Circle – Public Knowledge Communication:** In the final stage, the knowledge is formalized into a cohesive story tailored for public dissemination. The system applies the "Water Tower" plot structure, which begins with a strong contextual opening, such as a headline metric on aquifer depletion, and then reveals supporting insights in logically stacked segments. Each segment adds value without overwhelming the audience, maintaining clarity and flow. Visually, this is implemented through a combination of a line chart (showing weekly level trends) and an area chart (highlighting cumulative decline), overlaid with a threshold marker at 113.5 m to signify the drought risk boundary. This layered design ensures that the message remains accessible and visually intuitive to non-expert audiences. The final output ends with a clear directive, encouraging water conservation measures during spring, transforming data into action and promoting community preparedness.

This example demonstrates how the proposed framework increases interpretability of complex forecasts, sustains user engagement through progressive storytelling, and ultimately supports timely and informed decision-making in environmental risk contexts.

5 Audience-Aware Interface: Proof-of-Concept Implementation

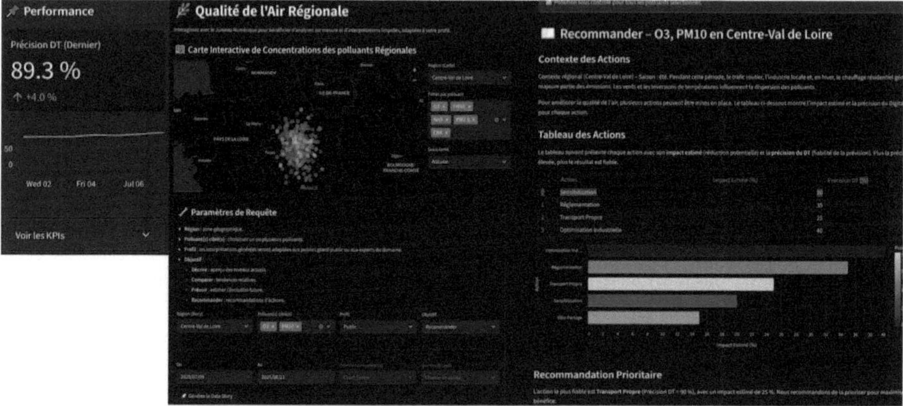

Fig. 3. Proof-of-concept interface for an air-quality Digital Twin.

A lightweight prototype[1] developed in Google Colab demonstrates that the proposed framework can be implemented with modest effort, using simulated data and standard machine learning libraries. As illustrated in Fig. 3, the left-hand panel demonstrates how the user interacts with the DT translating intent into a system readable query, while also displaying overall KPIs that track the DT's performance over time; the right-hand panel presents the complete data story: ranked action items, color-coded bar charts, interpretive text following a call-to-action pattern, and KPI badges. The interface couples three functional elements that mirror the pillars of our storytelling framework:

i) **Explorable Digital-Twin Data.** An interactive map presents current pollutant concentrations for the chosen region, supplying the empirical basis for exploration and for the *Explore* phase.

ii) **Audience-Informed Intent Capture.** A unified control panel asks the user to (a) indicate their profile (*novice* or *expert*) and (b) select a high-level analytical goal—*Describe, Assess, Predict* or *Suggest/Recommend*. This

---

[1] https://github.com/faten-elouta/Digital-twins.

single step fixes the vocabulary, visual granularity and chart types suggested later on by the semantic mapping tables (Tables 1–2) and converts a vague question into a well-formed request that can traverse the four storytelling phases.

iii) **KPI Metrics.** Dedicated badges display key performance indicators—e.g. the current precision of the Digital-Twin forecasts and the trend of that precision over time—offering an immediate, quantitative view of model evolution and reliability. These metrics provide users with confidence in the results delivered during the *Answer* phase and act as credibility cues in the final *Present* stage.

When the form is submitted, the prototype first consults the **analytical mapping tables** to select the datasets, algorithms, and output formats that match the user's intent. It then refers to the **narrative mapping table** to determine the message pattern (e.g., rhetorical question, comparative statement), plot structure (e.g., inverted pyramid), and visual encoding best suited to both the operator's role and the target audience. ChatGPT is used to generate the resulting data story in accordance with these mappings. Under the hood, mapping configurations are loaded into `pandas` DataFrames, `scikit-learn`'s `LinearRegression` module powers the forecasting engine, and all interactive charts are rendered via `Altair` (with geospatial layers from `pydeck`) within a `Streamlit` app. Streamlit's `@st.cache_data` decorator ensures efficient data handling, and the `openai` Python client library drives the narrative generation. This design executes the *Explore, Answer, Structure,* and *Present* phases in a unified, audience-aware flow that transforms raw DT data into actionable insights.

6   Conclusion and Discussion

This paper proposed a user-centered framework for enhancing Digital Twin communication through data storytelling. Grounded in a four-phase narrative process, the framework integrates user intent, levels of knowledge formalization, and a semantic mapping table to support the generation of communicative and audience specific outputs. We demonstrated the framework using an environmental prediction use case involving groundwater forecasts.

At the core of this approach lies a semantic mapping table that links user intent to datasets, algorithms, message patterns, narrative structures, and visualization formats. This mapping can serve as a foundation for ontology-driven communication components in DT systems. Formalizing this mapping into an ontology [3] would not only standardize communication processes but also support intelligent reasoning, content adaptation, and interoperability across different environmental applications.

The layered storytelling workflow—structured around increasing levels of formalization (Personal, Interpersonal, Community), ensures flexibility in tailoring outputs based on audience complexity and intent. Moreover, modeling this workflow using Business Process Model and Notation (BPMN) facilitates its integration into existing system architectures, enabling semi-automated storytelling pipelines within DT platforms [12].

The presented use case highlights how user intent—expressed via high-level analytical operators—can drive the entire pipeline from data processing to narrative generation. Future work will focus on evaluating the proposed framework in operational settings across audience groups (experts, decision-makers, and the general public), assessing the impact of different message strategies on comprehension, trust, and decision-making. Additional research will also explore integrating large language models (LLMs) to dynamically translate analytical results into narratives aligned with our ontology-based mappings, opening pathways for scalable, adaptive, and participatory DT communication.

Acknowledgments. This work has been realized within the JUNON Program of Environmental Digital Twin creation and has received financial support under the Ambition Recherche et Développement JUNON Program, funded by the Région Centre-Val de Loire (France).

Disclosure of Interests. The authors declare that they have no competing interests relevant to the content of this article.

References

1. Digital twins: State of the art theory and practice, challenges, and open research questions. J. Ind. Inf. Integr. **30**, 100383 (2022). https://doi.org/10.1016/j.jii.2022.100383
2. Digital twins for cities: Analyzing the gap between concepts and current implementations with a specific focus on data integration. Int. J. Appl. Earth Obs. Geoinf. **122** (2023)
3. Ontologies in digital twins: A systematic literature review. Futur. Gener. Comput. Syst. **153**, 442–456 (2024)
4. Bach, B., Kerracher, N., Hall, K., Kennedy, J., Riche, N.H., Carpendale, S.: Narrative design patterns for data-driven storytelling. In: Proceedings of the 2018 CHI Conference on Human Factors in Computing Systems. ACM (2018)
5. Batty, M.: Digital twins. Environ. Plann. B **45**(5) (2018)
6. Benetton, M., et al.: Developing digital twins for environmental monitoring and management. Environ. Model. Softw. **143**, 105090 (2021)
7. Cimino, C., Negri, E., Fumagalli, L.: Review of digital twin applications: communication and usability perspectives. Comput. Ind. **113**, 103130 (2019)
8. Climate-ADAPT: Coupling high-resolution flood modelling and 3D digital twins (2023). https://climate-adapt.eea.europa.eu/en/mission/solutions/mission-stories/coupling-high-resolution-flood-modelling-story34. European Climate Adaptation Platform. Accessed 9 Apr 2025
9. Digital Twin Earth Hydrology Group: Digital twin earth: Hydrology and the water cycle (2023). https://www.frontiersin.org/journals/science/article-hubs/digital-twin-earth-dte-hydrology-water-cycle. Frontiers in Earth Science. Accessed 9 Apr 2025

10. Espuny, C.P.: Chapitre 3. les théories de la communication. In: Communication: L'ouvrage de toutes les communications, pp. 83–106. Vuibert (2018). https://shs.cairn.info/communication--9782311405033-page-83?lang=fr
11. FloodDAM-DT Consortium: Flooddam-dt completes its flood risk digital twin prototype (2023). https://www.spaceclimateobservatory.org/flooddam-dt-completes-its-flood-risk-digital-twin-prototype. Space Climate Observatory. Accessed 9 Apr 2025
12. Fornari, L., Rossi, M., Del Fiore, G.: Business process digital twins: a framework for real-time predictive process management. Inf. Syst. **110** (2025)
13. Grieves, M.: Digital twin: Manufacturing excellence through virtual factory replication (2015)
14. Heravi, B.: Storytelling structures in data journalism: introducing the water tower structure (2022)
15. Liu, Y., et al.: Multi-scale digital twin with physics-informed ml for groundwater contamination (2022). arXiv preprint. https://arxiv.org/abs/2211.10884
16. Osama, H.: From photogrammetry to real-time decision: the digital twin pipeline in smart environments. Elsevier Smart Cities (2024)
17. Outa, F.E., Francia, M., Marcel, P., Peralta, V., Vassiliadis, P.: Towards a conceptual model for data narratives. In: ER (2020)
18. Outa, F.E., Marcel, P., Peralta, V., da Silva, R., Chagnoux, M., Vassiliadis, P.: Data narrative crafting via a comprehensive and well-founded process. In: ADBIS. Lecture Notes in Computer Science, vol. 13389. Springer (2022)
19. Outa, F.E., Marcel, P., Peralta, V,, Vassiliadis, P.: Highlighting the importance of intentional aspects in data narrative crafting processes. Inf. Syst. Front. **26** (2024)
20. Segel, J., Heer, J.: Narrative visualization: telling stories with data. IEEE Trans. Visual Comput. Graphics **16**(6), 1139–1148 (2010)
21. Skoury, L., Leder, S., Menges, A., Wortmann, T.: Digital twin architecture for the AEC industry: a case study in collective robotic construction (2024)
22. Srinivas, T.A.S., Sravanthi, Y., Vinod Kumar, Y., Dwaraka Srihith, I.V.: From charts to dashboards: an overview of data visualization methods. Adv. Comput. Technol. Appl. **7**(1), 1–14 (2024). https://doi.org/10.5281/zenodo.10060647
23. Vassiliadis, P., Marcel, P., Rizzi, S.: Beyond roll-up's and drill-down's: an intentional analytics model to reinvent OLAP. Inf. Syst. (2019)
24. World Economic Forum: Why digital twins might transform the world of water management (2023). https://www.weforum.org/stories/2024/11/why-digital-twins-might-transform-the-world-of-water-management. World Economic Forum. Accessed 9 Apr 2025

Towards User-Centric Authorization
for Data Access, Sharing and Control

Florian Weingartshofer[ID], Aya Mohamed[(✉)][ID], and Marc Kurz[ID]

Department of Smart and Interconnected Living (SAIL), University of Applied
Sciences Upper Austria, Hagenberg, Austria
{florian.weingartshofer,aya.mohamed,marc.kurz}@fh-hagenberg.at

Abstract. With the increasing demand and interest in users' data in
various domains like energy and Internet of Things (IoT), access to these
data should be protected, but also controlled by the user for transparent data access and sharing. Currently, there is no standard for user-
centric authorization as in typical authorization and access control models due to challenges related to the different authorization processes and
entities involved, which vary for each domain and use case. First, we
explain user-centric authorization compared to traditional authorization
and user consent along with related work. We propose a user-centric
authorization approach to involve users in the authorization process to
decide about access to their private data by requesters, share specific
data with interested parties, and control even after granting the permission. Actors (e.g., user, requester, and data provider), resources (i.e.,
request and data), general states, and request structure are defined for
the permission request, data access, and revoke processes. Our approach
is implemented and applied within the *European Distributed Data Infrastructure for Energy (EDDIE)* project to access and share energy data.
We provide a demo case, including implementation of the model and
detailed steps from creating a permission request until getting a decision
from the end-customer and receiving the requested energy consumption
data. Finally, we discuss characteristics of our approach, such as multi-
transparency, permission revocation, access audit, data granularity, and
external termination.

Keywords: User-Centric Authorization · Access Control · Data
Sharing

1   Introduction

Active participation of users when granting access and sharing of their private
data is increasingly required nowadays for better engagement and sense of ownership instead of having a passive role like in traditional access control systems.
However, there is no standard model for user-centric authorization, which relies
on user decision rather than evaluation of authorization policies in traditional

authorization models. Furthermore, there is no single process for user-centric authorization, making it harder to apply the concept in different scenarios.

Our work contributes to defining and applying a user-centric authorization approach for data access, sharing, and control. We propose a general process for authorization request, data access, and revoke of permission that can be adapted according to permission procedure requirements. Our authorization model relies on real-time decisions by users on access requests for interactive control and transparent sharing of their private data. Thus, we define the following research questions to address user-centric authorization theoretically and technically.

RQ1. What is user-centric authorization compared to traditional authorization and user consent?

RQ2. What are the challenges and suitable concepts to define a user-centric authorization model for data access and sharing?

RQ3. How is the proposed approach implemented and applied to real cases?

This work is implemented and demonstrated in the context of the *European Distributed Data Infrastructure for Energy (EDDIE)*[1] project as a proof of concept. This project aims to develop a framework for sharing energy data between customers and third parties. Data are retrieved from different national and regional data providers, which have complex legal, regulatory, and infrastructural procedures. Hence, our approach introduces an authorization model that addresses these challenges and involves the user in the permission request process. Although EDDIE focuses on energy data, the approach can be applied to other data access/sharing scenarios and domains (e.g., health and IoT).

The rest of the paper is structured as follows. In Sect. 2, we provide an overview of user-centric authorization concepts, including related work. In Sect. 3, we define our user-centric authorization model and explain the process of permission request, data access, and revoke. We present the implementation details along with a demonstration case in the context of EDDIE in Sects. 4 and 5 respectively. We discuss the characteristics of our approach in Sect. 6, concluding with a summary and an outlook for future work in Sect. 7.

2   State of the Art

User-centricity provides stronger user control and privacy [2]. Aspects related to user-centric security and privacy have been addressed, such as identity management in Bhargav-Spantzel et al. [2], Personally Identifiable Information (PII) management in Marillonnet et al. [4], and privacy-preserving models in Rivadeneira et al. [9]. However, user-centricity in the context of authorization and access control has been considered only for operating systems and smart domain. Martínez et al. [5] address security and privacy for data dissemination in a smart-city context, integrating policy-based authorization with an encryption mechanism. This work aims to protect access to smart meter data by allowing users to define their own access control preferences through the *extensible*

---

[1] https://eddie.energy/.

access control markup language (XACML). While the approach is related to access control at the network edge, specifically IoT devices, in terms of defining fine-grained authorization policy and who can or cannot access devices' data, we focus on the data access and sharing aspect, involving different actors and domains. Roesner et al. [10] propose a user-driven access control approach for users to grant and control access by applications to user-owned resources on modern client platforms. They introduce *access control gadgets (ACGs)* as an operating system technique implemented at the kernel level for a least privilege, in-context, and non-disruptive permission granting. The ACG mechanism enables users to grant permissions at the time of use and implicitly extracts users' access control intentions from their in-application actions and tasks.

Concerning authorization and access control, only authorized individuals should access sensitive information and resources. Traditional authorization models represent authorization policies specifying the subject requesting access, the resource that needs to be protected, and the action performed. The authorization model is enforced by the access control model, and the defined authorization policies are enforced by the access control mechanism that implements the access control model [6]. Currently, various user data are collected, such as energy consumption data and health data from wearable devices. Thus, parties interested in such data should be authorized by the user, even if the data are collected and stored remotely by a data provider. Hence, transparent mechanisms and systems are needed to allow users to regain control over their information [9].

Although user consent and user-centric authorization aim to empower users with control over their data, they differ conceptually. Both can be time-limited and revoked at anytime by the user. User consent refers to explicit permission given by users for processing or sharing their personal data. It is usually given once and has no granularity. Mechanisms for specifying and enforcing consents are necessary to actually protect user data. For instance, Tokas and Owe [11] propose a framework for consent management in terms of policy and consent specification language, as well as a run-time system for dynamic checking of privacy compliance. In addition, the work in [4] introduces a PII manager to enforce user consent and keep track of user authorizations.

User-centric (also referred to as user-driven) authorization enables users to control who can access what data, when and how (e.g., frequency, action, and purpose). User-centric authorization and access control models are not based on the definition and enforcement of authorization policies since the user is involved in the access decision process. In authorization models, a request has to be initiated to access any data even when the same subject accesses the same resource, but this is not the case for user consent. The authorization request is part of the traditional and user-centric authorization models as a formal way for the subject to request permission to access specific resource(s), including data granularity and time scope. For example, XACML defines the element *Request* as an abstraction layer used by the policy language [7]. In traditional access control models, the runtime values in the request related to the subject and resource are used to evaluate the policy, whereas the request in user-centric authorization is relevant for both users to decide about access and data providers to retrieve the requested data upon user permission.

3   Approach

With the increasing amount and sensitivity of data, not only authorization and access control needed to protect private data, but the user should also be involved in deciding who can access or with whom they share which data. In the energy domain, for example, users can share their consumption data with third parties, controlling the time range, interval, and type (e.g., validated historical data or near real-time data), regardless of where the data are stored, whether locally on the user side or managed by a central authority. Accordingly, we consider the following challenges in this work:

- User involved in the decision process.
- Different entities involved in data access and sharing.
- Different authorization processes.
- Transparent data access and sharing.

We introduce an approach to *user-centric authorization for data access, sharing, and control (UADSC)*. Our proposed model is user-centric, as users decide about access in the process of requesting permission. It also includes the different entities involved in data access and sharing, such as the user, data provider, and requester. Furthermore, we consider not only different general phases in terms of permission request, data access, and permission revoke, but also different states for each process that can be adapted based on the use case and authorization process. The UADSC model allows for monitoring the request state and transparent data access and sharing, since the user is informed about the details of requested data. Let the model be defined as a tuple:

$$\text{UADSC} = (S, A, R, \delta, F)$$

S $= S_{\text{request}} \cup S_{\text{access}} \cup S_{\text{revoke}}$

S_{request} = {CREATED, VALIDATED, SENT, UNABLE_TO_SEND, TIMED_OUT, REJECTED, INVALID, ACCEPTED, MALFORMED}

S_{access} = {FULFILLED, UNFULFILLABLE}

S_{revoke} = {REVOKED, TERMINATED, REQUIRES_EXTERNAL_TERMINATION, EXTERNALLY_TERMINATED, FAILED_TO_TERMINATE}

A = {user, requester, data_provider, system}

R = {request, data}

F = {REJECTED, TIMED_OUT, INVALID, FULFILLED, UNFULFILLABLE, REVOKED, TERMINATED, EXTERNALLY_TERMINATED, MALFORMED}

where S is a set of states, A is a set of actors, R is a set of resources, δ is the transition function ($\delta : S \times A \times R \rightarrow S$) summarized in Table 1 (e.g., $\delta(\text{CREATED}, \text{requester}, \text{request}) \rightarrow \{\text{VALIDATED}, \text{MALFORMED}\}$), and F is a set of final states. The states are classified into request, access, and revoke categories. The initial state is CREATED. The FULFILLED, UNFULFILLABLE and TERMINATED states are only considered final when no external termination is required.

The *request* is the resource for the request permission phase, while *data* is the resource when accessing the data and revoking the permission. The actors represent the different roles in this model, which are *user* controlling access to private data, the party providing the data, and *requester* initiating the permission request. Users are involved in the permission request process to decide about accessing and sharing their private data. The *data provider* is responsible for forwarding the request to the user, sending data, and external termination (if required). The revoke can be triggered by the users to stop sharing their data, or the requester can terminate the permission. Furthermore, we define *system* as an actor for validation and retry purposes.

Table 1. UADSC states transition in terms of actors and resources.

Resource	Actor	Current State	Next State
Request	Requester	CREATED	VALIDATED, MALFORMED
	System	VALIDATED	SENT, UNABLE_TO_SEND
	User	SENT	ACCEPTED, REJECTED
	System	SENT	TIMED_OUT, INVALID
	System	UNABLE_TO_SEND	VALIDATED
Data	Data provider	ACCEPTED	FULFILLED, UNFULFILLABLE
	User	ACCEPTED	REVOKED
	Requester	ACCEPTED	TERMINATED
	System	TERMINATED, FULFILLED, UNFULFILLABLE	REQUIRES_EXTERNAL_TERMINATION
	Data provider	REQUIRES_EXTERNAL_TERMINATION	EXTERNALLY_TERMINATED, FAILED_TO_TERMINATE
	System	FAILED_TO_TERMINATE	REQUIRES_EXTERNAL_TERMINATION

Figure 1 depicts the detailed process for permission request, data access, and permission termination and revoke. First, a permission request for accessing specific data is **CREATED** upon receiving a permission request from the requester. Then, the request is validated syntactically and semantically (e.g., the start date being not after the end date) before sending the request to the data provider. If the request validation is not successful, the transition to **MALFORMED** state occurs. From the **VALIDATED** state, the system attempts to send the request to the user through the data provider. If the request cannot be sent to the data provider for reasons not related to the validity of the request, e.g., the data provider's system is not available, transition to **UNABLE_TO_SEND** occurs. Transition to the **VALIDATED** state again is performed by the system to allow the requester to resend the request. The option to retry sending the request and the number of attempts is implementation-specific.

After successfully sending the request to the data provider, the response could be from the user or the system. The system response indicates a server-side error and the request is considered to be **INVALID**. Upon receiving a response from the user, the process proceeds with the data access phase when the authorization request is **ACCEPTED** or ends when **REJECTED** from the user. If no response is received, the request state will be **TIMED_OUT** after some time depending on the implementation. When the request is **ACCEPTED**, the data provider can start the *data access* process by sending the requested data. If the data received satisfy the request conditions (e.g., granularity and time-frame), transition to **FULFILLED**

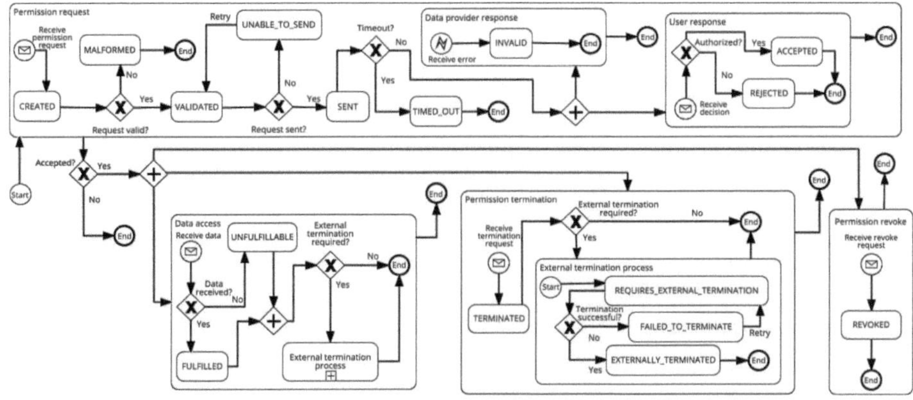

Fig. 1. The UADSC model processes and states.

occurs. Otherwise, the data is considered UNFULFILLABLE. At the end of this phase, the system checks whether an external termination by the data provider is required or not.

Revocation and termination are independent of data access. However, both processes can only be initiated after accepting the authorization request. The user can revoke the granted access or the requester can terminate the given permission before it is fulfilled. If the user revokes the request, the data provider informs the requester about the revocation and invalidates credentials (if any) used by the requester to access the user data. The request state is then transitioned to REVOKED, which is a final state. Thus, a new request has to be created in case of sharing the data again. The request can be TERMINATED when the requester no longer needs access to the user's data. If the data provider implements a mechanism (e.g., RFC 7009 [3]) to revoke the permission from the requester, the request is transitioned to the REQUIRES_EXTERNAL_TERMINATION state. Otherwise, the TERMINATED state is a final state. If the termination request cannot be sent to the data provider, it will be marked as FAILED_TO_TERMINATE. In this step, resending the termination request can be done by transitioning to the previous state. The number of attempts is left open to implementation. The request is EXTERNALLY_TERMINATED when the termination request is successfully sent to the data provider.

In traditional authorization models, access requests are defined in terms of subject, resource, and conditions to be evaluated and used to retrieve the relevant data if authorized [12]. In the context of our UADSC model, the user decides on access requests instead of authorization policy-based evaluation. However, permission requests include details related to the requester and resource to inform the user what data are requested, by whom, and why access is needed (e.g., GDPR purpose). We provide an XML schema definition (XSD) for the permission request in Listing 1 to elaborate the core structure of the request. However, it can be extended upon need and property names can be adapted to domain-specific ones for more flexibility to the UADSC model implementation.

Listing 1. XSD for the permission request.

```
<xs:complexType name="PermissionRequest">
  <xs:sequence>
    <xs:element name="permissionId" type="xs:string"/>
    <xs:element name="connectionId" type="xs:string" minOccurs="0"/>
    <xs:element name="created" type="xs:dateTime"/>
    <xs:element name="status" type="PermissionProcessState"/>
    <xs:element name="start" type="xs:date" minOccurs="0"/>
    <xs:element name="end" type="xs:date" minOccurs="0"/>
    <xs:element name="requestedData" type="RequestedData"/>
    <xs:element name="requesterInformation" type="Requester"
        minOccurs="0"/>
    <xs:element name="dataProviderInformation" type="DataProvider"/>
  </xs:sequence>
</xs:complexType>
```

The *permissionId* is a unique identifier that is generated when a permission request is CREATED to be used as a reference throughout its lifecycle. The request *status* can be monitored by relating the current state as defined in the UADSC model and the *created* timestamp to this identifier. The permission request optionally includes *connectionId* as another identifier for grouping multiple permission requests, e.g. requests of a user on the requester's system. Concerning the time frame of the requested data, the current date is the default, unless specified in the permission request using a *start* and *end* date. Requester-specific information is not defined as part of the request, but rather as configuration data associated with the request to identify the requester, unless requester-related details (e.g., metering points) are required as input. *DataProvider* and *RequestedData*, including purpose, are defined based on the domain. In the energy domain, information related to the data provider includes metered data administrator and permission administrator, whereas the requested data have properties like energy type (e.g., electricity, natural gas, etc.) and granularity representing resolution of the data. The information required to revoke or terminate a permission is based on the data provider. Thus, there is no formal definition for the revocation or termination request. However, we update the permission request in our implementation with the current state for logging and processing purposes.

We defined the actors of the UADSC model to deal with different scenarios and use cases. Depending on the domain and the use case, entities associated with these actors are defined. For example, users can share their data with a third party by initiating a request and approving it. Consequently, the *requester* for the *permission request* phase is the same as the *user*, but for the *permission revoke* the requester is the third party, who receives the data and can accordingly terminate the granted permission. The same applies to the data provider. In some cases, the data are available on the user side (e.g., local storage of real-time data) rather than being centrally managed. Thus, the entities *user* and *data provider* would be the same.

In summary, we discussed the challenges to define a general user-centric authorization model for data access and sharing. We explained the components of the UADSC model in terms of the actors involved in one or more states for the resources (i.e., request and data) in addition to the flow of each process (i.e., request, access and revoke) to address RQ2. We provide the implementation details of our approach in the upcoming section (refer to RQ3).

4   Implementation

Our UADSC model is applied in the context of a real project in the energy domain to allow users to share their private data with third-parties. Although this model is implemented in different ways in the EDDIE project for data sharing, it can be used in other domains to request specific data from users (e.g., health data).

Our implementation is based on the event sourcing pattern [1]. The event sourcing pattern depicts each change in a domain object as an event. In the context of the UADSC, when a permission request is created, a new event is created with the initial information. Therefore, each state transition is an event. Each event must include the attributes defined in Listing 2, but can have additional optional attributes. The first attribute is an aggregate identifier, called *permissionId*, which relates all events to a single permission request. The *created* timestamp allows events sorting and recreate the timeline of changes for a single permission request. The *status* of the event is the same as defined in the UADSC model. Events are persisted in an append-only store using PostgreSQL, where events are saved to an event table that is write and read only (i.e., no update or delete operations are permitted). This table represents all the attributes of different events as columns.

Listing 2. XSD for the permission event.

```
<xs:complexType name="PermissionEvent">
  <xs:sequence>
    <xs:element name="permissionId" type="xs:string"/>
    <xs:element name="status" type="PermissionProcessState"/>
    <xs:element name="created" type="xs:dateTime"/>
  </xs:sequence>
</xs:complexType>
```

The collection of all events related to one permission request is called an aggregate. The aggregate is created via a PostgreSQL view. It is created using a window function, the permission ID to create partitions, and the created timestamp to sort the events in a partition. Each column of the event table is aggregated through an aggregate function. In many cases, the aggregate function calculates the latest non-null value, but it can be freely chosen for each column of the event table. For example, a sum aggregate function can be used to get the sum of all values in a specific column. The aggregates are constructed using a PostgreSQL view (see Listing 3).

Listing 3. Permission event aggregate.

```
CREATE FUNCTION coalesce2(anyelement, anyelement)
RETURNS anyelement LANGUAGE sql AS 'SELECT coalesce($1, $2)';

CREATE AGGREGATE firstval_agg(anyelement)
    (sfunc = coalesce2, stype =anyelement);
```

```
CREATE VIEW request AS
SELECT DISTINCT ON (permission_id) permission_id,
                   firstval_agg(status) OVER w AS status,
                   MIN(event_created) OVER w AS created
FROM permission_event
WINDOW w AS (PARTITION BY permission_id ORDER BY event_created DESC)
ORDER BY permission_id, event_created;
```

The event sourcing pattern has been selected because it offers flexibility in terms of including new attributes and updating old ones. This can be done by adding a new column to the event table or setting a new value for a column without including values that do not need to be updated. Each event for a specific state in the UADSC model can include different attributes. For example, the CREATED event might include a user identifier and the ACCEPTED event includes an access token. Different states can also update the value of existing attributes, such as the status attribute which is updated with each event. Events are emitted via an internal *eventbus*, to which components can subscribe. Subscribers then take actions based on the events received from the eventbus. Furthermore, events have to be persisted to the event store using the outbox pattern [8]. The outbox pattern guarantees that only events that are successfully persisted to the event store are sent to the eventbus. This is done by first persisting the event to the database and checking if the operation was successful. In this case, the event is propagated to the event bus. Furthermore, this guarantees that events are always available via the event store and subscribers of the event bus get the newest version of the aggregate whenever required.

For our implementation, we used Java 21, Spring Boot and PostgreSQL. There are several implementations of eventbus for Java, including those provided by Project Reactor[2] and Google Guava[3]. However, both of these options are deprecated. Therefore, we use Project Reactor Sinks[4] for our implementation. Subscribers can subscribe to events using either the type of event or the status of the event. This simple approach allows for flexible filtering for subscribers. In the context of the EDDIE project, the code should be open source but not yet public since it is still a work in progress. However, our implementation of the UADSC model is documented[5].

5   Demonstration Case

We applied our UADSC model to many data access and sharing scenarios in the energy domain between customers, third parties, as well as national and regional data providers, each having a different authorization process for requesting, revoking, and terminating permissions. For this demo case, we implement the UADSC model to create permission requests and receive data from EDA[6], the platform for energy data exchange in Austria.

---

[2] https://github.com/spring-attic/reactor-bus.

[3] https://github.com/google/guava/wiki/EventBusExplained.

[4] https://projectreactor.io/docs/core/release/reference/coreFeatures/sinks.html.

[5] https://architecture.eddie.energy/framework/2-integrating/integrating.html.

[6] https://www.eda.at/portal.

Concerning the actors in the context of the UADSC, they can be flexibly defined according to whether the data is requested for access or shared by the user. Let us apply both scenarios to our demo case. In the data request case, the permission request is initiated by the eligible party, while the end customer must be the entity initiating the process to share their data. However, the requester for the data access phase is the eligible party that receives the customer (i.e., user) data from EDA (i.e., data provider). The user and data provider are the same in both data request and sharing in all UADSC processes, which are permission request, data access, and revoke. In our implementation, we act as an eligible party and end customers share their energy consumption data. Therefore, the customer is the user and requester only in the permission request phase.

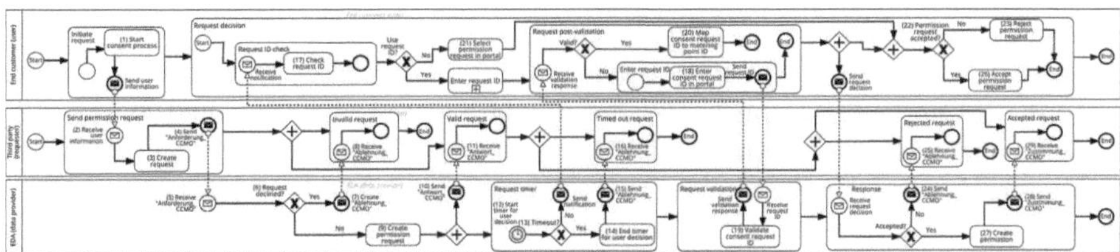

Fig. 2. Permission request process between users, requesters and EDA (data provider).

EDA implements their own permission process (see Fig. 2), which is built on top of the AS4 protocol. In step (1), the end customer creates a permission request with the third party, also referred to as *eligible party*. The request is created in step (3), which is the **CREATED** status in the UADSC model and a created event is emitted after receiving user information (2), such as the distribution system operator (DSO) of the customer and an optional metering point identifier. If the metering point ID is included here, the customer is informed of the permission request directly in the DSO portal of the customer. Otherwise, they would need to use the request ID to find the request. The request is validated in step (3) to verify that the requested timeframe and resolution are supported by EDA. If it is successfully validated, an event with the **VALIDATED** status is emitted. This event additionally contains a generated identifier for the request and a conversation ID. The request ID is used to identify a request on EDA's side, and the conversation ID identifies messages related to a specific process. Furthermore, the validated event contains information about the kind of data requested, a timeframe of the requested data, and resolution of the timeseries data. If validated, the permission request is sent to EDA in step (4). Otherwise, another event is emitted with the **MALFORMED** status, which is a final status and cannot be recovered.

After receiving the request (5), EDA validates the permission request in step (6). If it is invalid, the eligible party is informed about it in step (8), triggering an event with the **SENT** status, since the requester now knows that the request was sent to EDA, and another one with the INVALID status. If it is valid, a timer in step (12) is started and EDA shows the request to the customer. If the customer does nothing until the timer runs out (13), the request is automatically rejected by EDA (14), and the eligible party is informed about it in step (16). This triggers an event with the status TIMED_OUT. If the request is valid, it is made available to the user. If the user informed the eligible party about their metering point ID, it would automatically be shown to the end user on their portal (22). Otherwise, the user has to enter the consent request ID (18), which is generated by the eligible party. EDA verifies that the consent request ID exists and is valid (19) and shows the consent request to the user (20).

In step (22), users decide whether to accept or reject the permission request. If the permission request is rejected (23), the requester is informed of the decision in step (25) after being sent by EDA in step (24). Consequently, an event with the status REJECTED is triggered. In the case of accepting the request (26), the permission is created and the notification is sent by EDA to the eligible party in steps (27) and (28) respectively. Then, the requester is informed in step (29) and an event with the status ACCEPTED is emitted. The accepted event contains the metering point ID for which the request was accepted, which is the same as the one provided (if any) in the created event. In addition, it contains a consent ID, which can be used to manage the request on EDA's side.

Only at this point will EDA send the requested data to the requester. The end customer can revoke the request after granting permission. For the revocation process, the customer has to revoke the permission in the DSO portal. Accordingly, the permission of the eligible party is removed for that customer. The eligible party is then informed about the revocation, and an event with the REVOKED status is emitted. Alternatively, the eligible party can terminate a request if the data is no longer needed. Figure 3 shows this process. First, a request needs to be marked as TERMINATED, which means, no data concerning the request should be forwarded anymore. Then, an event with the status REQUIRES_EXTERNAL_TERMINATION is emitted. The termination document is prepared and sent to EDA in step (1), which is validated in step (2). If the document is invalid, EDA will send a response in step (3). After receiving the response at the eligible party in step (4), an event with the status FAILED_TO_TERMINATE is emitted and the external termination can be tried again. If the termination with EDA is successful, the data access is terminated and an acknowledgment is sent in steps (5) and (6) respectively. The requester is informed about the result in step (7) and an event with the status EXTERNALLY_TERMINATED is emitted.

We now present the sequence of events in our implementation for the permission request phase, from initiating a request to receiving the user decision. Each time the status of the permission request is changed, the eligible party is informed about the change. The message contains the connection ID, the permission ID, current status, and the timestamp when the message was created as defined in the permission request (recall Listing 1). Furthermore, it contains some domain-specific properties, such as the data need ID and the data source information, which are equivalent to the requested data and the data provider

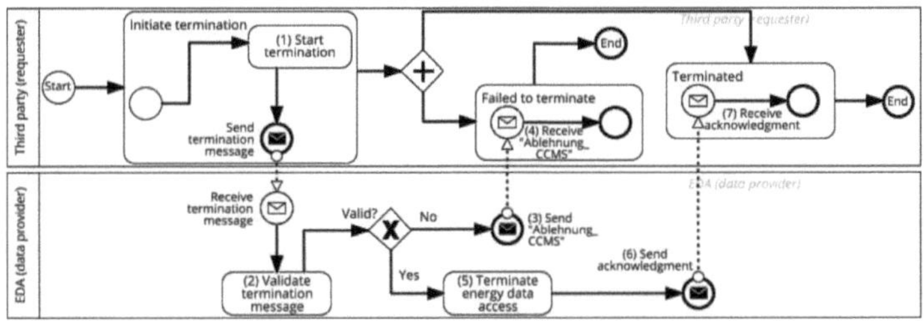

Fig. 3. Termination process by the requester in EDA.

information, respectively. A permission request is created to get the validated historical data for a specific meter. The eligible party is notified of the new permission request via a created message as shown in Listing 4.

Listing 4. Permission request with status CREATED.

```
<ConnectionStatusMessage>
  <connectionId>0636908d-f3da-43dd-98d8-53fa74d3c4b9</connectionId>
  <permissionId>a13c4b7b-a10d-4e9c-8243-5009fb5245d8</permissionId>
  <dataNeedId>bcfa426c-dfc2-4fae-be68-6d460a1f5630</dataNeedId>
  <dataSourceInformation>
      <countryCode>AT</countryCode>
      <meteredDataAdministratorId>AT001000</meteredDataAdministratorId>
      <permissionAdministratorId>AT001000</permissionAdministratorId>
      <regionConnectorId>at-eda</regionConnectorId>
  </dataSourceInformation>
  <created>2025-07-11T09:12:47.210845497Z</created>
  <status>CREATED</status>
</ConnectionStatusMessage>
```

The permission request is validated and the eligible party is notified about the validity (see Listing 5).

Listing 5. Permission request with status VALIDATED.

```
<ConnectionStatusMessage>
  <connectionId>0636908d-f3da-43dd-98d8-53fa74d3c4b9</connectionId>
  <permissionId>a13c4b7b-a10d-4e9c-8243-5009fb5245d8</permissionId>
  <dataNeedId>bcfa426c-dfc2-4fae-be68-6d460a1f5630</dataNeedId>
  <dataSourceInformation>...</dataSourceInformation>
  <created>2025-07-11T09:12:47.222985108Z</created>
  <status>VALIDATED</status>
</ConnectionStatusMessage>
```

The permission request is then translated into an EDA compatible format and transmitted to them. Upon receiving the request, they notify the eligible party and the **SENT** message is emitted. As depicted in Listing 6, the message also contains a CM request ID, which can be used by the eligible party and the end customer to identify a consent request on the EDA's side.

Listing 6. Permission request with status SENT.

```
<ConnectionStatusMessage>
  <connectionId>0636908d-f3da-43dd-98d8-53fa74d3c4b9</connectionId>
  <permissionId>a13c4b7b-a10d-4e9c-8243-5009fb5245d8</permissionId>
  <dataNeedId>bcfa426c-dfc2-4fae-be68-6d460a1f5630</dataNeedId>
  <dataSourceInformation>...</dataSourceInformation>
  <created>2025-07-11T09:12:50.742024086Z</created>
  <status>SENT</status>
  <message>Message received (response code 99)</message>
```

```
<additionalInformation>
  <cmRequestId>MPB403Y4</cmRequestId>
</additionalInformation>
</ConnectionStatusMessage>
```

When the end customer accepts the consent request, the eligible party is notified and a message with the same structure and status ACCEPTED is emitted. When all data are received from EDA, the eligible party is notified of the fulfilled permission request by a FULFILLED message as in Listing 7.

Listing 7. Permission request with status FULFILLED.

```
<ConnectionStatusMessage>
  <connectionId>0636908d-f3da-43dd-98d8-53fa74d3c4b9</connectionId>
  <permissionId>a13c4b7b-a10d-4e9c-8243-5009fb5245d8</permissionId>
  <dataNeedId>bcfa426c-dfc2-4fae-be68-6d460a1f5630</dataNeedId>
  <dataSourceInformation>...</dataSourceInformation>
  <created>2025-07-11T09:48:20.40408245Z</created>
  <status>FULFILLED</status>
  <message>Customer accepted the request (response code 175)</message>
  <additionalInformation>
    <cmRequestId>MPB403Y4</cmRequestId>
  </additionalInformation>
</ConnectionStatusMessage>
```

The time difference between the first message and the SENT message shows that the duration of the entire permission request process for this scenario is approximately 3 s. The created and validated messages are sent in the same second, showing the responsiveness of our implementation of the UADSC model to the requester. The time is mostly taken until the message confirming that the request is successfully sent to the data provider, which is EDA in this demo case. At this point, the request appears on their portal for the user to decide about the data access, ending this phase to start retrieving the requested data. We provide a screenshot of the message exchange between the requester and EDA in Fig. 4. The Time column shows when the messages were received by the implementation, the Message ID is a unique identifier for each message, and the Type describes the response defined according to the communication flow previously described in Fig. 2.

Time ↑	Message ID ↑↓	Type ↑↓
Enter Time	Enter Message ID	Enter Type
11.07.2025 11:12:47.256	EP100129T1752225167213@EDDIE.FH	ANFORDERUNG_CCMO
11.07.2025 11:12:50.586	AT001000202507111112480332179177921@wn.wienit.at	ANTWORT_CCMO
11.07.2025 11:21:27.769	AT001000202507111112480332179179832@wn.wienit.at	ZUSTIMMUNG_CCMO
11.07.2025 11:48:18.765	AT001000202507111148161992179187034@wn.wienit.at	DATEN_CRMSG

Fig. 4. Message exchange between the requester and EDA.

The AS4 message in the first row is the request from the eligible party to EDA, whereas the second is the acknowledgment that the request was received by EDA, which triggers the SENT status update in Listing 6. The ANFORDERUNG_CCMO is sent by the requester to EDA as represented in Fig. 2 step (4), while the flow is reversed for the `ANTWORT_CCMO` in step (10). The user decision is shown in the third message, which has type `ZUSTIMMUNG_CCMO` sent to the requester by EDA in step (28) and triggers the `ACCEPTED` status update. The message called `DATEN_CRMSG` contains the requested data. After receiving all requested data, the eligible party is notified via the `FULFILLED` status update in Listing 7.

Our implementation for this demo case currently has more than 2300 users and 12,800 requests in one year. Besides the demo case for EDA as a data provider in Austria, the UADSC model is applied in the EDDIE project for data providers in different countries, including Belgium, Denmark, Finland, France, Netherlands, Spain and the United States. Thus, we prove the feasibility and applicability of the UADSC in real use cases with different authorization processes and entities, involving users in permission request and revoke. In addition to the preliminary performance-related observations provided in this demo case from the timestamp of each permission request, we consider extensive evaluation of the UADSC model and our implementation as future work.

6   Discussion

In this section, we discuss the characteristics considered as goals of this work in defining and implementing the UADSC model, highlighting implementation- and model-specific improvements. We classify the characteristics according to their priority and relevance to *critical*, *optional* and *supplemental*. Table 2 summarizes the characteristics and whether they are supported in the model and/or the implementation.

Table 2. Characteristics and their priority for the UADSC model and implementation.

Characteristics	Priority	Supported
Multi-transparency	Critical	✓
Permission revocation	Critical	✓
Access audit	Critical	✓
Requester notification before user decision	Critical	✗
Data granularity	Optional	✓
External termination	Optional	✓
Conditional access	Optional	✗
Intervals for data access	Optional	✗
Permission granularity	Supplemental	✗

Multi-transparency is one of the main objectives of this work, such that the user is clearly informed who is accessing what, as well as keeping the third party (i.e., requester) updated with the state of their request(s), since they are also part of the authorization process. The permission request structure (refer to Listing 1) includes details of the sender, receiver, and data (e.g., type and start/end date). In addition, there are states defined in the UADSC model that can be used to inform the requester if the request is created, sent, or authorized, and whether the user responded or an error/timeout occurred.

Permission revocation refers to revoking the granted access by the user. As discussed in Sect. 3, both the revocation and termination processes are part of our proposed model. The granted permission can be revoked anytime by the user, even before the data are received by the requester. This is handled in the UADSC by enabling data access and permission revoke processes to take place upon user acceptance of the permission request. The permission revoke phase also includes the case in which the requester terminates the permission.

Access audit is related to logging the access actions. This is supported not only in our model definition using different states for request, access, revoke and termination, but also in our implementation by storing decisions and changes for all requests to be viewed by users or analyzed by parties requesting access. We implemented a simulation tool and an admin console for request status auditing purposes, verifying our implementation of the UADSC model by checking the sequence of states for different defined scenarios.

In our current implementation, requesters are only informed about the status of their requests after receiving a decision from the user. To address *requester notification before user decision*, an implementation-specific extension would be informing the requester that the request has been successfully sent to the data provider. This can be done using pushed authorization requests (PAR)[7]. For PARs, the requester can send the request to the data provider, which validates the request and returns a reference to the request that can be used in the redirect URI. We consider this characteristic to be critical only for the data request scenario, but not for data sharing.

Data granularity in our context is the option to request specific data in terms of resolution, type, dates, etc. Data granularity is supported not only in the permission request, but also in data fulfillment by checking and filtering the data received from the data provider to match the requested one. We consider data granularity to be optional, as it is not the main purpose of the UADSC model, unlike other access control models that focus more on granularity, such as *attribute-based access control (ABAC)*.

External termination in our context is to terminate the permissions granted for data access on the data provider side. This is because even if the requester does not need access to the data anymore and already terminated the permission, the data provider should be informed in order not to keep sending the requested data. In the external termination process, the requester sends a termination request to the data provider (refer to Fig. 3 as an example). Although this sub-process is included in the UADSC model, it is optional because not all data providers support termination by external parties.

---

[7] https://datatracker.ietf.org/doc/html/rfc9126.

We identify *conditional access* to be addressed in future work. The user can optionally define temporary or condition-based access rules instead of manually managing each request. This feature requires extending the model to define and enforce authorization policies for handling the step in which the user response is required. In our case, we implement the data sharing scenario of the UADSC model. Therefore, users only receive the requests they initiated. For access request scenarios, the UADSC should be extended or integrated with user-defined policy approaches to reduce the burden on users to evaluate every request.

Furthermore, the UADSC focuses more on the permission request details than the data access phase. We defined only two states, indicating whether the data is successfully retrieved by the data provider and received by the requester (`FULFILLED`) or not (`UNFULFILLABLE`). A model-specific improvement could be defining additional states and sub-processes to indicate that part of the data are already retrieved from the data provider, but not yet fulfilled. This would further improve multi-transparency by informing the user and the requester which data is requested and when. For example, in the energy domain, validated historical data are only available after being processed by the data provider. For the requester to get the latest data, it needs to be requested from the data provider in regular intervals.

Permission granularity allows the user to control which parts of the data can be accessed. However, this depends on the resources to be accessed. In our implementation, the user either permits or denies access to the requested data for specific dates as a whole. This is because the energy metering data cannot be segmented to avoid missing context.

7   Conclusion

Access and sharing of user private data have recently increased significantly in various sectors. Although benefits are offered to both users and parties interested in these data, user-centricity in the context of authorization and access control should be considered. Traditional authorization and access control models rely on the definition and enforcement of authorization policies, which are not sufficient to enable users to decide who can access their data or with whom they can share their data. Thus, we focus on user control over data access for transparent sharing of private data.

In this work, we first provide an overview of user-centric authorization compared to traditional authorization and user consent. User-centric authorization and user consent have similarities with respect to revocation by users and limiting access in terms of time and accessing parties. However, user-centric authorization further controls the granularity of requested data. Furthermore, users are informed for each data access request instead of collecting their consent once without knowing what data is accessed or shared. Unlike the passive role of users in traditional access control models, they can actively participate in the permission process.

Based on the results of the first research question (RQ1), we identify challenges related to data access and sharing to be addressed in our proposed approach in terms of involving users in the authorization decision, taking into consideration different entities and authorization processes. Accordingly, we introduce a user-centric authorization model for data access, sharing, and control (UADSC). It includes the user, requester, and data provider in the permission request, data access, and permission revoke processes. The user decides on the access requests and can revoke the permission at any point after being accepted, whereas the requester initiates permission requests and can terminate given access. The data provider is responsible for forwarding requests to the user and retrieving the requested data upon granting the permission. We provide an XSD for the permission request and define general states for the UADSC model, including creating, validating, and sending requests in addition to user decision, termination, revoke, and (un)fulfilled data access. Some of these states are considered final and cannot be reverted (e.g., `TIMED_OUT` and `REJECTED`). The UADSC permission request, entities, and states can be defined and adapted depending on the domain and use case.

Regarding the last research question (RQ3), our UADSC model is implemented and applied in different use cases, one of which is discussed in this paper. In this demo case, energy data can be requested or shared between customers and third parties, where the data are provided by an energy data exchange platform called *EDA*. Furthermore, we discuss the UADSC model as a user-centric authorization approach, such as multi-transparency for both users and requesters, permission revocation, access audit, data granularity, and external termination. Aspects related to requester notification before user decision, conditional access, data access in intervals, and permission granularity are not currently supported, but are feasible to apply.

In addition to implementing the UADSC model in the *EDDIE* project, we plan to extend the approach for a *Common European Energy Data Space (CEEDS)* project called *INSIEME*[8]. For this, different aspects of user-centric authorization for data spaces are taken into account to fit the requirements of this big project. In future work, we also consider integrating policy-based and user-centric approaches for advanced authorization and access control, as well as the general applicability of the UADSC model.

Acknowledgments. This work is conducted under the ambit of EDDIE—'European Distributed Data Infrastructure for Energy', co-funded by the European Union's Horizon Innovation Actions under grant agreement No. 101069510. Funded by the European Union. Views and opinions expressed are however those of the author(s) only and do not necessarily reflect those of the European Union or CINEA. Neither the European Union nor the granting authority can be held responsible for them.

---

[8] https://insieme.energy/.

Disclosure of Interest. The authors have no competing interests to declare that are relevant to the content of this article.

References

1. Azure: Event sourcing pattern. https://learn.microsoft.com/en-us/azure/architecture/patterns/event-sourcing
2. Bhargav-Spantzel, A., Camenisch, J., Gross, T., Sommer, D.: User centricity: a taxonomy and open issues. In: Proceedings of the Second ACM Workshop on Digital Identity Management, DIM 2006, pp. 1–10. Association for Computing Machinery, New York (2006). https://doi.org/10.1145/1179529.1179531
3. Lodderstedt, T., Dronia, S., Scurtescu, M.: Oauth 2.0 token revocation. RFC 7009 (2013). https://doi.org/10.17487/RFC7009
4. Marillonnet, P., Ates, M., Laurent, M., Kaaniche, N.: An efficient user-centric consent management design for multiservices platforms. Secur. Commun. Netw. **2021**(1), 5512075 (2021). https://doi.org/10.1155/2021/5512075
5. Martínez, J.A., Hernández-Ramos, J.L., Beltrán, V., Skarmeta, A., Ruiz, P.M.: A user-centric internet of things platform to empower users for managing security and privacy concerns in the internet of energy. Int. J. Distrib. Sens. Netw. **13**(8), 1550147717727974 (2017). https://doi.org/10.1177/1550147717727974
6. Mohamed, A., Auer, D., Hofer, D., Küng, J.: A systematic literature review for authorization and access control: definitions, strategies and models. Int. J. Web Inf. Syst. **18** (2022). https://doi.org/10.1108/IJWIS-04-2022-0077
7. Oasis, O.: eXtensible Access Control Markup Language (XACML) Version 3.0 (2013). http://docs.oasis-open.org/xacml/3.0/xacml-3.0-core-spec-os-en.html
8. Richardson, C.: Microservices Patterns: With examples in Java. Manning Publications (2018). https://www.manning.com/books/microservices-patterns
9. Rivadeneira, J.E., Sá Silva, J., Colomo-Palacios, R., Rodrigues, A., Boavida, F.: User-centric privacy preserving models for a new era of the internet of things. J. Netw. Comput. Appl. **217**, 103695 (2023). https://doi.org/10.1016/j.jnca.2023.103695
10. Roesner, F., Kohno, T., Moshchuk, A., Parno, B., Wang, H.J., Cowan, C.: User-driven access control: rethinking permission granting in modern operating systems. In: 2012 IEEE Symposium on Security and Privacy, pp. 224–238 (2012). https://doi.org/10.1109/SP.2012.24
11. Tokas, S., Owe, O.: A formal framework for consent management. In: Gotsman, A., Sokolova, A. (eds.) FORTE 2020. LNCS, vol. 12136, pp. 169–186. Springer, Cham (2020). https://doi.org/10.1007/978-3-030-50086-3_10
12. di Vimercati, S.D.C., Paraboschi, S., Samarati, P.: Access control: principles and solutions. Softw. Pract. Exper. **33**(5), 397–421 (2003). https://doi.org/10.1002/spe.513

RDF Query Answering in the Presence of Access Restrictions

Maxime Buron[1] , Hritika Kathuria[2(✉)] , Ioana Manolescu[2] ,
and George Siachamis[2]

[1] Université de Clermont Auvergne, Clermont-Ferrand, France
`maxime.buron@uca.fr`
[2] Inria & Institut Polytechnique de Paris, Palaiseau, France
`{hritika.kathuria,ioana.manolescu,george.siachamis}@inria.fr`

Abstract. In this work, we explore algorithms for answering conjunctive RDF queries in the presence of RDFS ontologies and access control. We consider an access control setting where by default all users have access to the complete graph, and a *restriction* can forbid user a user's access to specific IRIs. Here, restricting for user u the access to an IRI i entails that: no answer to a query by u may contain the IRI i; no triple containing i can be used to compute an answer for a query by i, nor to entail such a triple via reasoning with the ontology. We present a set of query answering algorithms for this novel context, and prove that five among them are correct, i.e., sound and complete, with respect to both the ontology and the access restrictions in place. We have implemented all our algorithms and present experiments comparing their performance.

Keywords: Semantic Web · Access Control · Query Answering

1 Introduction

Knowledge graphs, especially RDF graphs standardized by the World Wide Web Consortium, are a simple, flexible and powerful format for heterogeneous data. In RDF (Resource Description Framework), *resources*, identified by *International Resource Identifiers* (IRIs) are described by their *properties*, which have *values*. A (subject, property, value) combination is called a *triple*. A value can itself be a resource, e.g., a company as a person's employer; both can be described further. A value can also be a *literal* (constants with optional types). A literal has no further properties. RDF also supports *blank nodes*, anonymous resources, modeling partial knowledge. For instance, an RDF graph may state that the group to which employee Alice belongs is _:g, where _:g is a blank node; we know that the group exists, even if we do not know a full IRI for it. RDF resources and blank nodes can be assigned *types* (or classes), e.g., Alice may be described in a graph as being of type Employee. We denote the *special RDF property* used to attach types to resources by $\boxed{\tau}$.

A key RDF feature is support for *ontologies*, which enrich data understanding and exploitation. Ontologies can be specified in languages of varying expressive power. Among these, RDF Schema (RDFS, in short) [28] provides properties allowing to state

C. Cappiello et al. (Eds.): CoopIS 2025, LNCS 15535, pp. 312–330, 2026.
https://doi.org/10.1007/978-3-032-15538-2_18

relationships between classes and/or properties. For instance, we can specify that Clerk is a subclass of Employee, or that anyone having a paysheet is an Employee. In the presence of an ontology, *inference* (also called *entailment*) may lead to some triples being *implicitly* part of an RDF graph, even if not explicitly stated. For instance, if an RDF graph contains the triples (Alice, τ, Clerk) and (Clerk, subclassOf, Employee), the triple (Alice, τ, Employee) is also implicitly part of the graph. The presence of implicit triples requires special care when answering queries over a graph, in order for the answer to correctly reflect all the triples. For RDFS, polynomial-time algorithms for query answering in the presence of ontologies exist [9,15], while OWL dialects have significantly higher complexity [4]. For this reason, in this work, we consider RDFS ontologies.

In a multi-user setting, a user's access to an RDF graph may be limited (*restricted*). Accordingly, many RDF data access control proposals have been made in the literature (see Sect. 9). They may differ on the *scope* of an access right, e.g., a node, a triple, or a set of triples; they consider *positive* privileges, in the sense of SQL's GRANT, and/or *negative* ones, which restrict (or hide) parts of the graph to a user. However, most methods *do not account for ontologies*. Some works partially support RDFS [17,22] without full query answering; others use OWL [14,20] but with high reasoning costs.

To our knowledge, this is the first work thoroughly exploring *algorithms for answering conjunctive RDF queries in the presence of RDFS ontologies and access control*. We consider that by default all users have access to the complete graph, and a *restriction* can forbid user u's access to specific IRIs. Restricting the access of user u to IRI i entails that: no answer for u may contain i; no triple containing i can be used to compute an answer for a query, nor to entail such a triple via reasoning with the ontology. We present a *set of novel query answering algorithms for this context*, with respect to both the ontology and the access restrictions.

Below, we recall RDF preliminaries in Sect. 2 and state our problem in Sect. 3. Section 4, 5, 6 and 7 describe our algorithms, leveraging multiple techniques: materialization of entailed triples, query reformulation, and triple provenance. Section 8 covers experiments, followed by related work and conclusion. The extended version [2] contains all formal proofs and the set of experimental queries.

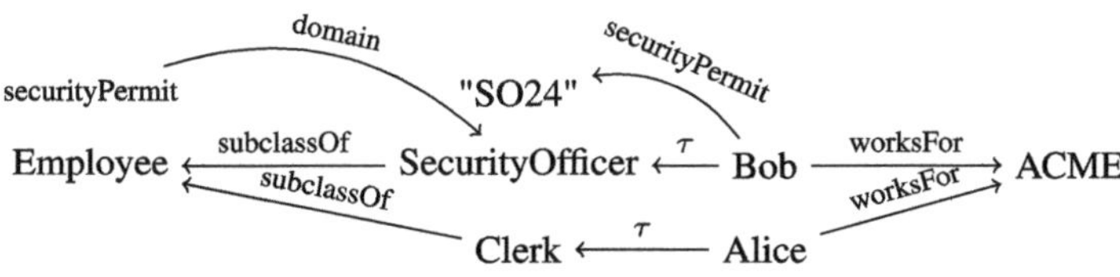

Fig. 1. Sample RDF graph.

2 Preliminaries

We recall the core concepts and terminology describing RDF graphs in (Sect. 2.1), RDF queries and query answering (Sect. 2.2).

2.1 RDF Graphs, Entailment and Saturation

We consider given a set $\mathcal{I}$ of International Resource Identifiers (IRIs, in short), a set $\mathcal{L}$ of literals and a set of blank nodes $\mathcal{B}$ that are pairwise disjoint. A triple is an element in $(\mathcal{I} \cup \mathcal{B}) \times \mathcal{I} \times (\mathcal{I} \cup \mathcal{B} \cup \mathcal{L})$; its elements are called the subject, property, and object (or value). Among the IRIs $\mathcal{I}$, the special IRI rdf:type, denoted τ, in short, is part of the RDF standard itself; it characterizes subjects by associating them various *classes*, or types. For instance, the triple (Alice, τ, Clerk) states that the resource identified by the IRI Alice is of the type having for IRI Clerk.

An RDF graph $\mathcal{G}$ is a set of triples. In particular, $\mathcal{G}$ may contain RDF Schema [28] (**RDFS**, in short) ontology triples, whose property is one among the four **RDFS properties**: subclassOf, subpropertyOf, domain and range. Intuitively, $(c_1, \text{subclassOf}, c_2)$ states that the type (or class) c_1 is a specialization (subclass) of c_2, e.g., Clerk subclassOf Employee; $(p_1, \text{subpropertyOf}, p_2)$ specifies that p_1 is a more specific property than p_2, e.g., isDirectorOf is a subproperty of worksFor; (p, domain, c) means that any subject having property p is of type c, e.g., anyone having a studentCardNumber is a Student, and, symetrically, (p, range, c) means that any value of property p is of class c, e.g., the value of a birthPlace is a GeographicLocation. We denote by $\text{Val}(\mathcal{G})$ the set of IRIs, blank nodes and literals used in $\mathcal{G}$ and by $\mathcal{O}_\mathcal{G}$ (or simply $\mathcal{O}$ when this does not cause any confusion) the set of ontology triples in $\mathcal{G}$. We define:

Definition 1 (Class and property positions). *Given an (s, p, o) triple, we say the object position is a* class position *if p is τ. Further, if p is* subclassOf, *we say the subject and object positions of the triple are* class position. *Finally, if p is* domain, *respectively,* range, *then the object position is also called* class position. *In a triple (s, p, o), we say p is a* data property position *if p is neither τ, nor* subclassOf, subpropertyOf, domain *or* range.

Note that we define data property positions slightly differently from class positions, based on their actual use in the graph. That is: if a property appears only in an ontology triple, but its value is not defined for any subject IRI, we do not consider it a data property.

Definition 2 (Classes and data properties). *A class present in $\mathcal{G}$ is an IRI appearing in a class position in some triple of $\mathcal{G}$. A data property in $\mathcal{G}$ is an IRI appearing in a property position in a triple of $\mathcal{G}$.*

Figure 1 illustrates a sample graph. Labels such as Alice, Bob, etc. designate IRIs, and quoted strings such as "SO24" denote literals. Properties are shown as labels on edges; RDFS properties are shown in blue. The classes present in this graph are: Employee, SecurityOfficer, and Clerk, whereas the data properties are worksFor and securityPermit.

If $\mathcal{G}$ contains ontology triples, this may lead to the presence of *entailed* triples, that hold in $\mathcal{G}$ even though they are not explicitly part of it. The RDFS entailment process is defined by a set of entailment rules [1]. In this work, we only consider *the four rules that infer type and data triples*. We leave out rules that also infer schema triples mainly to simplify the presentation of our algorithms, and also because they do not entail data or type triples, that is the reason why they are rarely considered in the literature.

We say that there is an *entailment step* $(t_1, t_2) \xrightarrow{r} t$ from $\mathcal{G}$, when two triples t_1 and t_2 in $\mathcal{G}$ trigger a rule r to entail a triple t. For instance, in our sample graph, the triples (Alice, τ, Clerk) and (Clerk, subclassOf, Employee) lead to the implicit triple (Alice, τ, Employee). Further, the triple (hasSecurityPermit, domain, SecurityOfficer) means that any resource that is the subject of the property securityPermit, is of type SecurityOfficer. This triple, together with (Bob, securityPermit, "SO24"), entail that (Bob, τ, SecurityOfficer). As this example illustrates, *an entailed triple may also be explicitly present in $\mathcal{G}$.*

As shown above, a given graph may entail different triples. In turn, any entailed triple, together with an ontology triple, may lead to more entailed triples. The **saturation** of $\mathcal{G}$, denoted $\mathcal{G}^+$, is the graph to which we add all the triples it entails directly or indirectly. It is known that the saturation of an RDF graph w.r.t. an RDFS ontology can be computed in polynomial time, is finite, and its size is polynomial in the size of the original graph $\mathcal{G}$ [15]. In our example, $\mathcal{G}^+ = \mathcal{G} \cup \{$(Alice, τ, Employee), (Bob, τ, Employee)$\}$.

2.2   RDF Queries and Query Answering

We consider available a set $\mathcal{V}$ of variables. A *triple pattern* is of the form (s, p, o) that belongs to $(\mathcal{I} \cup \mathcal{V}) \times (\mathcal{I} \cup \mathcal{V}) \times (\mathcal{I} \cup \mathcal{L} \cup \mathcal{V})$. A **Basic Graph Pattern (BGP, in short) query** q is of the form: $q(\bar{x}) :\text{-} t_1, t_2, \ldots, t_k$, where the t_i, $1 \leq i \leq k$, are triple patterns, the right-hand part is called the body of the query, while the head $\bar{x}$ denotes a list of variables, all of which must appear in the body. We denote by $\text{Var}(q)$ the set of variables that appear in the body of q. For instance, the query $q_1(x, y) :\text{-} (x, \tau, y), (x, \text{worksFor}, \text{ACME})$ asks for all the employees of ACME, together with their types.

The **evaluation of a BGP query** q **over an RDF graph** $\mathcal{G}$, denoted $q^0(\mathcal{G})$, is defined as follows:

- An *homomorphism* from q to $\mathcal{G}$ is a function ϕ from $\text{Var}(q)$ to $\text{Val}(\mathcal{G})$ such that for each triple pattern t_i in the body of q, the triple $\phi(t_i)$ (obtained from the substitution of the variables in t_i by their image by ϕ) belongs to $\mathcal{G}$.
- For each homomorphism ϕ from q to $\mathcal{G}$ as above, we denote by $\phi(\bar{x})$ the tuple of IRIs, blank nodes and literals to which the variables $\bar{x}$ are mapped by ϕ.
- The evaluation $q^0(\mathcal{G})$ is defined as: $\{\phi(\bar{x}) \mid \phi$ is an homomorphism from q to $\mathcal{G}\}$. In our example, $q_1^0(\mathcal{G}) = \{\phi_1(\bar{x}), \phi_2(\bar{x})\} = \{$(Bob, SecurityOfficer), (Alice, Clerk)$\}$.

The **answer of a BGP query** q **over a graph** $\mathcal{G}$ is defined as the evaluation of q over the saturated graph $\mathcal{G}^+$: $q(\mathcal{G}) = q^0(\mathcal{G}^+)$.

As a consequence, computing the query answer $q(\mathcal{G})$ requires to follow one of the following two strategies:

- *Materialize* $\mathcal{G}^+$, i.e., compute all the triples it entails and add them explicitly to the graph. Then, evaluating q on $\mathcal{G}^+$ produces all the desired results.
- *Reformulate* the query using the ontology triples $\mathcal{O}$, into an expanded query q^{ref}, so that evaluating q^{ref} over $\mathcal{G}$ produces the full answer to q over $\mathcal{G}$.

On the graph $\mathcal{G}$ in Fig. 1, consider the query $q_2(x)$:- $(x, \tau, \text{Employee})$. To answer it via materialization, it suffices to evaluate it on the saturation $\mathcal{G}^+$ (Sect. 2.1). Thanks to the two extra triples in $\mathcal{G}^+$, this leads to the answer $q_2(\mathcal{G}) = \{(\text{Alice}), (\text{Bob})\}$. Observe that simply *evaluating* q_2 against $\mathcal{G}$ lead to the empty answer, because in $\mathcal{G}$, no resource is declared to be of type Employee.

Polynomial-time algorithms for query reformulation have been described e.g. in [9, 15]; the latter extends the former to RDF reasoning that also produces new ontology triples, and queries that carry also over the ontology. Because of its generality, we rely on [9] for this work. We illustrate it via **two reformulation examples**, while delegating the algorithmic details to [9].

First, the reformulation of query q_2 above: $q_2^{\text{ref}} = q_2 \cup q_2^1 \cup q_2^2 \cup q_2^3$, where $q_2^1(x)$:- (x, τ, Clerk), $q_2^2(x)$:- $(x, \tau, \text{SecurityOfficer})$, $q_2^3(x)$:- $(x, \text{securityPermit}, y)$. An answer to q_2^1 is an answer to q_2, because any Clerk is an Employee, and similarly any answer to q_2^2 is also an Employee. Finally, the domain constraint on the securityPermit property ensures that an answer to q_2^3 is also an employee. Our sample graph does not support any other answers for q_2. As this example demonstrates, reformulation may lead to a *union* of BGP queries.

To see a more elaborate example, consider the query: $q_3(y, z)$:- (x, y, ACME), (x, τ, z), $(z, \text{subclassOf}, u)$, asking for all the relationships that a subject x may have with ACME, and the type z attached to x, such that z has a known supertype. The reformulated q^3 is: $q_3^{\text{ref}} = q_3^1 \cup q_3^2$, where $q_3^1(y, \text{Clerk})$:- (x, y, ACME), (x, τ, Clerk) and $q_3^2(y, \text{SecurityOfficer})$:- (x, y, ACME), $(x, \tau, \text{SecurityOfficer})$. Note that q_3^1 and q_3^2 only have two triples, whereas q_3 had three. The last q_3 triple carries over the ontology; it is *evaluated* by the reformulation algorithm, and its results injected into the remaining triples during the reformulation. Also note that because q_3 requires returning types, the type IRIs are present in the heads of q_3^1 and q_3^2, which are thus not BGPs as defined (but are a small generalization thereof).

The trade-offs between materialization and reformulation are as follows. Materialization takes some time to compute and space to store, however, it simplifies query evaluation. When the data and/or ontology triples change, the materialized graph may need to be updated to reflect these changes, which may be costly. Reformulation-based query answering does not require any upfront cost nor maintenance; however, the reformulated query evaluation may be costly.

We will also need to refer to a restriction of the BGP query language, considered in many RDF data management works:

Definition 3 (Relational BGP). *We call* relational BGP *a BGP satisfying:*

1. *No variable appears in class or property position (Definition 1) in a BGP triple;*
2. *Explicitly querying the ontology is not allowed, i.e.,* subclassOf, subpropertyOf, domain, range *do not appear in a property position in the BGP.*

The term "relational" captures the fact that relational BGPs only carry over the data (the facts) present in RDF graphs, not over the ontology. The BGP q_2 above is relational, whereas q_1 is not, because y appears in a class position. In the sequel, unless otherwise specified, our discussion carries over all BGPs (not just the relational ones).

3   Problem Statement

We now introduce the problem we consider. Section 3.1 describes our notion of access control in RDF graphs, while Sect. 3.2 defines the problem of restriction-aware query answering on RDF graphs.

3.1   Restriction-Based Access Control

Users. We consider available a set $\mathcal{U}$ of users.

Definition 4 (Restriction). *An* access restriction *is a pair of the form* (u, r) *where* $u \in \mathcal{U}$ *is a user and* r *is an IRI, different from* subclassOf, subpropertyOf, domain, range *and* τ.

We exclude the τ property, as well as the standard RDFS properties, from the restrictions, in order to preserve the core features of RDF and RDFS, respectively. Let us fix a user $u \in \mathcal{U}$ and let AR be a set of access restrictions whose user is u; let A be the set of IRIs appearing in AR. Without loss of generality, we assume that all the IRIs in A appear in $\mathcal{G}$ i.e. $A \subseteq Val(\mathcal{G})$.

Definition 5 (Restricted graph). *We define the* restriction of a graph $\mathcal{G}$ based on A as
$$\mathcal{G}_A = \mathcal{G} \setminus (\bigcup_{a \in A} \{(s, p, o) | (s, p, o) \in \mathcal{G} \text{ and } s - a \vee p - a \vee o = a\})$$

Intuitively, $\mathcal{G}_A$ contains the triples in $\mathcal{G}$ without the ones featuring one of the restricted IRIs. For example, consider the restriction set $AR = \{(u, \text{SecurityOfficer}), (u, \text{securityPermit})\}$ and our sample graph in Fig. 1. The restricted graph $\mathcal{G}_A$ consists of the triples: $\mathcal{G}_A = \{(\text{Alice}, \tau, \text{Clerk}), (\text{Clerk}, \text{subclassOf}, \text{Employee}), (\text{Alice}, \text{worksFor}, \text{ACME}), (\text{Bob}, \text{worksFor}, \text{ACME})\}$ Four $\mathcal{G}$ triples are absent from $\mathcal{G}_A$ (two ontology, and two data triples): the three in which SecurityOfficer appears, as well as (Bob, securityPermit, "SO24").

A set of properties hold concerning $\mathcal{G}_A$. First:

Property 1. Applying entailment on an RDF graph $\mathcal{G}_A$ which does not contain a specific set of IRIs cannot to lead to triples that contain a restricted IRI.

Property 2 (Inclusion). This inclusion holds: $(\mathcal{G}_A)^+ \subseteq (\mathcal{G}^+)_A$. In general, the opposite inclusion does not hold.

For our sample graph, we obtain: $(\mathcal{G}_A)^+ = \{(\text{Alice}, \tau, \text{Clerk}), (\text{Clerk}, \text{subclassOf}, \text{Employee}), (\text{Alice}, \text{worksFor}, \text{ACME}), (\text{Bob}, \text{worksFor}, \text{ACME}), (\text{Alice}, \tau, \text{Employee})\}$ One additional triple is introduced in $(\mathcal{G}^+)_A$: (Bob, τ, Employee). This exemplifies that in general, the opposite inclusion in Property 2 does not hold.

3.2   Answering RDF Queries in the Presence of Access Restrictions

The problem we consider in this work is: answering queries over RDF graphs in the presence of access restrictions (Definition 4).

Intuitively, if the access of a user u to some IRIs, and thus to all triples where these IRIs appear, is restricted, then no homomorphism ϕ can map a triple pattern in the body of q, into a restricted $\mathcal{G}^+$ triple. This may disable some homomorphisms that exist in the absence of access restrictions, and thus, lead to some answers not being found any more.

Note that a given answer may be due to some homomorphism ϕ' invalidated by the restrictions, and simultaneously due to some other homomorphism ϕ'' that is not impacted by the restrictions. In this case, we consider that the answer is available. This is coherent with the natural query evaluation semantics, stating that each homomorphism leads to an answer. Our choice corresponds to a default "allow" (positive) policy; opting instead for a "deny" default policy would require a different set of algorithms.

Definition 6 (Query answer in the presence of access restrictions). *Given a graph $\mathcal{G}$, the set of restricted IRIs A for a user $u \in \mathcal{U}$ as above, and a query q, the answer to q based on $\mathcal{G}$ and A, denoted $q(\mathcal{G}, A)$, is the answer to q over the restricted $\mathcal{G}$:* $q(\mathcal{G}, A) = q((\mathcal{G}_A)^+).$

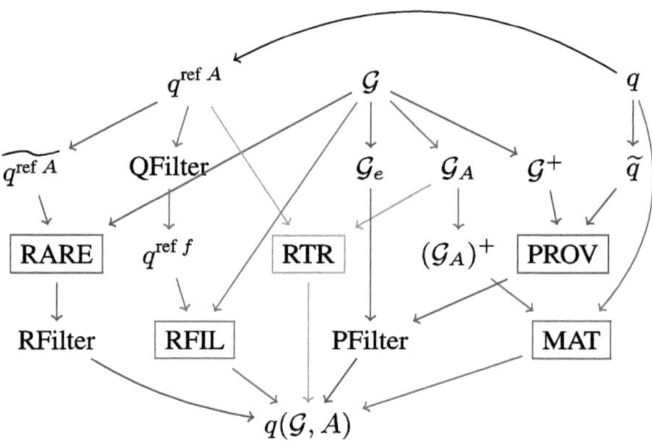

Fig. 2. Overview of our algorithms.

Roadmap. In the sequel, we discuss multiple algorithms for the above problem. These algorithms rely on a set of individual steps applied to the graph and/or the query; Fig. 2 traces the main steps of our *correct* (sound and complete) algorithms. A few alternative methods that may fail to compute the correct results, are not included in the Figure. We assign a different color to each algorithm, and leave in black elements shared by multiple algorithms. Each box labeled with an algorithm name, e.g., $\boxed{\text{MAT}}$, designates the *query evaluation* step of that algorithm, where results are actually computed from a graph.

Restriction Check. A simple check can be made on a BGP query prior to evaluation: if at least one query triple involves a restricted IRI, the query has empty results (because any result would require an homomorphism, and no such homomorphism exists). Such queries are immediately returned an empty answer. Below, we consider answering queries not determined to have an empty answer.

4   Baseline Algorithms

We now present algorithms for our problem, obtained with minimal modifications to materialization and reformulation algorithms.

4.1   Materialization-Based Algorithms (MAT)

The algorithm $\boxed{\text{MAT}}$ follows directly from Definition 6:

1. Restrict the graph, i.e., compute $\mathcal{G}_A$.
2. Saturate it, i.e., build $(\mathcal{G}_A)^+$.
3. Evaluate q over the resulting graph i.e., $q^0((\mathcal{G}_A)^+)$.

For example, evaluating our query $q_1(x) :\text{-} (x, \tau, y), (x, \text{worksFor}, \text{ACME})$ on the graph $(\mathcal{G}_A)^+$ shown in Sect. 3.1 only returns (Alice).

Algorithm MAT is clearly correct (it is both sound and complete w.r.t. Definition 6), since it computes the query answers, i.e., $q(\mathcal{G}_A)$.

4.2   Restrict-Then-Reformulate (RTR)

A direct reformulation-based algorithm $\boxed{\text{RTR}}$ can also be devised:

1. Restrict $\mathcal{G}$ using A, that is, compute $\mathcal{G}_A$.
2. Compute the reformulation of q using the restricted ontology, denoted $q^{\text{ref}\,A}$.
3. Evaluate $q^{\text{ref}\,A}$ over $\mathcal{G}_A$.

One major drawback of MAT and RTR algorithm is that on a single input graph, one graph per user need to be build and queried. In the following sections, we investigate more sophisticated algorithms avoiding this drawback.

5   Provenance-Based Result Pruning (PROV)

We now present a new materialization-based algorithm PROV. As shown in Property 2, a query answering algorithm that evaluates the query over the restriction of the saturated graph may to lead to unsound results from $(\mathcal{G}^+)_A$. To avoid it, PROV tracks restricted IRIs throughout inference and query evaluation, to output only allowed answers. We start by introducing a few helper notions.

Definition 7 (Query extension). *Given a BGP query q, the extension of q, denoted $\widetilde{q}$, is a BGP whose head contains all the variables in q, and having the same body as q.*

For our sample BGP query $q_1(x) :\text{-} (x, \tau, y)$, $(x, \text{worksFor}, \text{ACME})$ (Sect. 2.2), the extension is $\widetilde{q_1}(x, y) :\text{-} (x, \tau, y)$, $(x, \text{worksFor}, \text{ACME})$. Observe that *each extended query result is due to exactly one homomorphism into* $\mathcal{G}^+$ whereas the result of an arbitrary BGPQ could be due to several. Based on this observation, we define:

Definition 8 (Triples leading to an extended query answer). *For a given result* $r \in \widetilde{q}(G^+)$, *we call **triples leading to** r, denoted T_r, the set of triples obained by replacing, in each triple in the body of $\widetilde{q}$, each variable with the IRI, blank nodes or literal to which the variable is bound in r.*

For instance, recall the query $\widetilde{q_1}(x, y)$ and consider the result $r = (\text{Alice}, \text{Clerk})$ to $\widetilde{q_1}$. Then, T_r is $\{(\text{Alice}, \tau, \text{Clerk}), (\text{Alice}, \text{worksFor}, \text{ACME})\}$. *Extending the query guarantees that we can compute T_r directly from each answer.* In contrast, the result of a non-extended query may be due to several (alternative) triple sets; further, retrieving these sets requires a query evaluation engine specifically designed, e.g., [26]; in this work, instead, we rely on standard conjunctive query engines. Note that $\widetilde{q}$ has at least as many results as q, and its evaluation could be more costly.

Definition 9 (Entailment graph). *The entailment graph of an RDF graph $\mathcal{G}$ is a directed graph $\mathcal{G}_e$ obtained as follows. $\mathcal{G}_e$ contains a node for each triple in $\mathcal{G}$. Further, for each possible entailment step (Sect. 2.1) of the form $(t_1, t_2) \xrightarrow{r} t$ that can apply based on $\mathcal{G}$, and possibly triples previously entailed from $\mathcal{G}$, where t_1, t_2, t are triples and r is an entailment rule, $\mathcal{G}_e$ contains:*

- *One node for each of the triples t_1, t_2, t, such that $\mathcal{G}_e$ contains at most one node for any triple from $\mathcal{G}^+$. For each triple, $\mathcal{G}_e$ also stores whether it was explicitly present in $\mathcal{G}$;*
- *One node labeled r; we denote this node by n_r;*
- *Edges from the nodes corresponding to t_1 and t_2 to n_r;*
- *An edge from n_r to the node corresponding to t. Node n_r only has this outgoing edge, and only has the two incoming edges described above (in other words, there is exactly one node for each rule application).*

In our example, assigning to each triple in $\mathcal{G}$ (Fig. 1) a node identifier, as shown in Table 1 (ignore for now the last line in blue), the entailment graph appears in Fig. 3, with a node name shown in a box, e.g., $\boxed{n_{\text{Aw}}}$, $\boxed{n_{\text{B}\tau\text{S}}}$, etc. if the node is explicitly present in the graph. Again, ignore for now the blue nodes and edges. We say **a triple is permitted** if it does not contain any restricted IRI. In Table 1 and Fig. 3, the non-permitted triples are shown in red; they contain the restricted IRI SecurityOfficer or securityPermit.

Cycles in Entailment Graphs. Cycles in the entailment graphs are unlikely: it is not common for a triple to (directly, or transitively) entail itself. This may still happen, *only* when the ontology implies that a class (resp. a property) is a subclass (resp. subproperty) of itself, i.e., there is a cycle in the class (resp. property) hierarchy. Below, we assume there are no such cycles. If it does exist, it can be eliminated without loss of expressivity by merging all the classes (resp. properties) involved in the cycle into a single one. With the above notions, we can define:

Table 1. Triple identifiers for the sample entailment graph.

Triple	ID	Triple	ID
(Alice, worksFor, ACME)	n_{Aw}	(Clerk, subclassOf, Employee)	n_{subC}
(Bob, worksFor, Acme)	n_{Bw}	(SecurityOfficer, subclassOf, Employee)	n_{subS}
(Alice, τ, Clerk)	$n_{\mathrm{A\tau C}}$	(Bob, securityPermit, "SO24")	n_{sp}
(Bob, τ, SecurityOfficer)	$n_{\mathrm{B\tau S}}$	(securityPermit, domain, SecurityOfficer)	n_{sdS}
(Alice, τ, Employee)	$n_{\mathrm{A\tau E}}$	(Bob, τ, Employee)	$n_{\mathrm{B\tau E}}$
(worksFor, domain, Employee)	n_{wdE}		

Definition 10 (Entailment and entailment provenance (EP)). *Let t be a triple represented by a node n_t in the entailment graph $\mathcal{G}_e$. An* entailment *of t is a subtree of $\mathcal{G}_e$, such that all the tree leaves are explicit triples. The* entailment provenance *of t, denoted $EP(t)$, is the sub-DAG of $\mathcal{G}_e$ containing all the entailments of t.*

For instance, assume that $\mathcal{G}$ contains also the extra triple in blue in Table 1. This, together with the triple (Alice, worksFor, ACME), would lead to another entailment for n_{ArE}; this is shown by blue nodes and edges in Fig. 3. Similarly, $EP(n_{\mathrm{B\tau E}})$ contains three entailments: (i) the lowest subtree (in blue); (ii) the subtree consisting of $n_{\mathrm{B\tau S}}$, n_{subS} (these are both explicit triples) and $n^2_{\mathrm{subclassOf}}$; ($ii$) the subtree that starts from n_{sp} and n_{sdS} and *derives* $n_{\mathrm{B\tau S}}$, instead of using the explicit triple. As the examples illustrate, an entailment provenance encodes the set of alternative ways why t may hold.

We say an **entailment is permitted** if it contains no restricted triples. For example, both entailments of $n_{\mathrm{A\tau E}}$ are permitted; only the entailment denoted (i) above for $n_{\mathrm{B\tau E}}$, consisting of blue nodes and edges, is permitted.

Entailment Graphs Are Complete: By definition of $\mathcal{G}_e$, for each entailed triple t, all the entailments of t are subtrees of $\mathcal{G}_e$.

We can now describe the complete $\boxed{\text{PROV}}$ algorithm:

1. **Saturation with provenance**: Saturate $\mathcal{G}$, and, while doing so, build the entailment provenance $\mathcal{G}_e$.
2. **Query extension**: Let $\widetilde{q}$ be the extension of q.
3. **Query evaluation and result construction**:
   (a) Compute $R = \widetilde{q}^{0}(\mathcal{G}^{+})$, the evaluation of $\widetilde{q}$ over the saturated graph.
   (b) For each result $r \in R$:
       i. If every triple leading to r (Definition 8) has atleast one permitted entailment provenance in $\mathcal{G}_e$, then the projection $\pi_q(r)$, that retains from r only the variables from the head of q, is a result of $q(\mathcal{G}_A)$.

Following the evaluation of the extended $\widetilde{q_1}$ from the beginning of this section, its result $r' = (\mathrm{Bob}, \mathrm{Employee})$ has $T_{r'} = \{(\mathrm{Bob}, \tau, \mathrm{Employee}), (\mathrm{Bob}, \mathrm{worksFor}, \mathrm{ACME})\}$. The first triple in $T_{r'}$ has a permitted entailment only if the blue triple is part of the graph, in which case (Bob) is returned as an answer for q_1 by algorithm PROV. Observe that both triples in $T_{r'}$ are themselves permitted; we need their entailments to judge whether an answer can be returned based on r', or not.

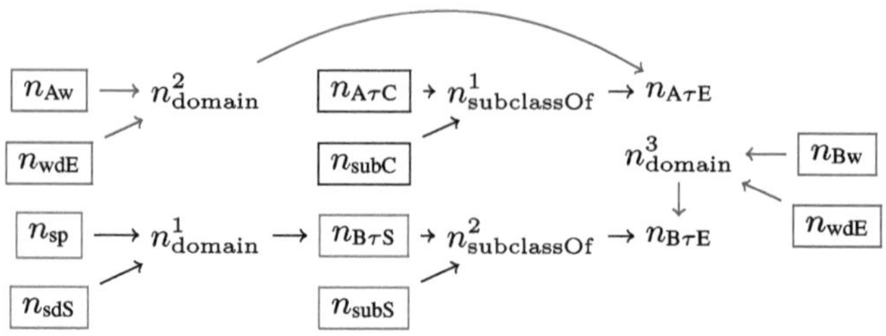

Fig. 3. Entailment graph for the sample graph in Fig. 1.

Reduced Provenance. The entailment graph $\mathcal{G}_e$ represents every triple in $\mathcal{G}^+$. The reason why we represent even explicit triples, even if not involved in any entailment, is step (3(b)i) of the PROV algorithm: this checks every $\mathcal{G}^+$ triple that may have served to build an answer, whether it is implicit and/or explicit. A $\mathcal{G}$ triple is by definition explicit in $\mathcal{G}^+$ (being in $\mathcal{G}$ counts as one provenance), and the triple may have others due to entailment. Each of these provenances suffices for a triple to satisfy the check. However, the provenance graph is quite large (at least as large as $\mathcal{G}^+$), which makes its processing cumbersome.

As an optimization, instead of storing $\mathcal{G}_e$, we store a *reduced* version thereof, obtained by *removing from $\mathcal{G}_e$ any entailment chain leading to a triple that is (also) explicit*. We do keep the triple itself, but remove the node(s) corresponding to each rule application that entails the triple (denoted n_r in Definition 9), together with their adjacent edges. For example, in Fig. 3, the node n^1_{domain} and its adjacent edges are not present in the reduced $\mathcal{G}_e$.

Property 3. Algorithm PROV is also correct on the <u>reduced</u> entailment graph.

6 Restriction-Aware Reformulation (RAR and RARE)

In this section, we seek to avoid expensive computations on the graph, and capturing entailment provenance, and instead, attempt to take in account the access restrictions in the query reformulation process. Algorithm $\boxed{\text{RAR}}$ (Restriction-Aware Reformulation) proceeds as follows:

1. Reformulate q into $q^{\mathrm{ref}\,A}$ taking the set of restricted IRIs into account:
    - While reformulating a query triple t_q using a $\mathcal{O}$ rule, if the rule uses a restricted IRI, ignore that reformulation.
    Note that this is the same reformulated query as in RTR (Sect. 4.2).
2. Evaluate $q^{\mathrm{ref}\,A}$ on $\mathcal{G}$.

For instance, on the query $q_2(x) \text{:-}\, (x, \tau, \text{Employee})$, the restricted reformulation $q_2^{\text{ref } A}$ is: $q_2 \cup q_2^1$, where $q_2^1(x) \text{:-}\, (x, \tau, \text{Clerk})$. Comparing this with the full reformulation of q_2 (Sect. 2.2), we can see that the reformulations q_2^2 and q_2^3, resulting (also) from non-permitted $\mathcal{G}$ triples, specifically (SecurityOfficer, subclassOf, Employee) and (securityPermit, domain, SecurityOfficer) are omitted in $q_2^{\text{ref } A}$.

While algorithm RAR is complete, it is **unsound** in some cases:

1. For instance, consider that we restrict the IRI Bob, and the simple query $q_4(x) \text{:-}\, (x, \text{worksFor}, \text{ACME})$: reformulation leaves q_4 unchanged, and evaluation returns $\{(\text{Alice}), (\text{Bob})\}$. Intuitively, this is because *RAR only restricts the ontology, and not the graph $\mathcal{G}$.*
2. Now consider that we restrict property p_1 in a simple graph $\mathcal{G}_5 = \{(i_1, p_1, i_2), (i_2, p_2, i_3)\}$, and the query $q_5(x, w) \text{:-}\, (x, y, z), (z, u, w)$. Lacking an ontology, reformulation leaves q_5 unchanged; evaluation returns (i_1, i_3) which is not a valid answer, because it relies on the restricted p_1. Here, the problem is due to *the variables in property positions*, which (restriction-unaware) evaluation binds to the restricted p_1.

Based on these observations, we describe Algorithm $\boxed{\text{RARE}}$ (Restriction-Aware Reformulation and Extension):

1. (As in RAR) Reformulate q with the restricted ontology, leading to $q^{\text{ref } A}$.
2. Extend each conjunctive query in $q^{\text{ref } A}$; we denote by $\widetilde{q^{\text{ref } A}}$ the union of these extended BGPs (recall Definition 7).
3. For each $\widetilde{q}_i$ that is a union term in $\widetilde{q^{\text{ref } A}}$:
   (a) Evaluate $\widetilde{q}_i$ over $\mathcal{G}$. *If $\widetilde{q}_i$ has variables in class or property positions, evaluation may bind them to restricted IRIs!*
   (b) For each $r \in \widetilde{q_i^0}(\mathcal{G})$: if all the triples in T_r are permitted, then the projection $\pi_{q_i}(r)$ is returned as an answer to q. This step is denoted RFilter in Fig. 2.

It is easy to see that the completeness of RAR extends also to RARE, because every RAR answer is also returned by RARE. Further, we define:

Definition 11 (CP restrictions). *We say a set AR of access restrictions are class-property restrictions (CP, in short), if every restricted IRI is a class or a data property in $\mathcal{G}$ (recall Definition 1).*

Property 4 (Soundness for CP restrictions only). Let AR be a set of CP restrictions. (i) For relational BGPs (Definition 3), Algorithm RAR is sound. (ii) Algorithm RARE is sound for general BGPs.

7 Algorithms Based on Filtering (MFIL and RFIL)

So far, the queries which we relied upon were conjunctive (BGPs), or (after reformulation), unions of such queries. In the spirit of [21], we can also slightly extend conjunctive queries with inequality predicates, as follows:

Definition 12 (BGP query with filters). *A BGP query with filters (**BGPf**, in short) q^f consists of: a conjunctive query q, together with a set of inequality predicates, each of the form $v \neq a$, where v is a variable from the body of q, and $a \in A$, the restriction set for user u. The result of evaluating a BGPf q^f over $\mathcal{G}$ is the set of results derived from at least one homomorphism from q to $\mathcal{G}$ that satisfies all the inequality predicates.*

Given a conjunctive query q and a set of access restrictions AR for user u, with the restricted IRI set A, Algorithm $\boxed{\text{QFilter}}$ builds a BGPf q^f based on q, if one exists, or returns an empty query:

1. Let I be a set of inequality predicates, initially empty, and $\mathcal{G}^+$ is the saturated graph.
2. For each triple t in the body of q:
   (a) If t's subject, respectively, predicate or object is an URI:
       – If the IRI is an $a \in A$, return an empty query.
   (b) If t's subject, predicate or object is a variable v:
       – For each $a \in A$, add to I the predicate $v \neq a$.

Filtered queries can be used in more query answering algorithms. First, we consider a **materialization-based algorithm with filtering**, named $\boxed{\text{MFIL}}$:

1. Saturate $\mathcal{G}$.
2. Filter q with the restrictions, leading to a filtered q^f.
3. Evaluate q^f over $\mathcal{G}^+$.

Algorithm $\boxed{\text{MFIL}}$ is not sound. To see that, assume a graph of two triples: (SecurityOfficer, subclassOf, Employee) and (Bob, τ, SecurityOfficer), and assume as before that SecurityOfficer is restricted. Saturation adds (Bob, τ, Employee). Given the query $q_6(x) :\text{-} (x, \tau, \text{Employee})$, the filtered query q_6^f is: $q_6^f(x) :\text{-} (x, \tau, \text{Employee}) \wedge (x \neq \text{SecurityOfficer})$. Evaluating this over $\mathcal{G}^+$ returns Bob, even though the correct answer is empty. The problem is that filtering acts on the consequences of inference and can no longer discern that some results are due to restricted IRIs.

Next, we present a **reformulation-based algorithm with filtering**, or $\boxed{\text{RFIL}}$, in short.

1. (As in RAR and RARE) Reformulate q on the restricted ontology, leading to a union of sub-queries q^{ref}.
2. For each sub-query q_i of q^{ref}, apply Algorithm QFilter to filter q_i. Gather the resulting non-empty queries into a union, denoted $q^{\text{ref } f}$.
3. Evaluate $q^{\text{ref } f}$ over $\mathcal{G}$.

Considering the latest example, $q_6^{\text{ref}}(x) = q_6(x) \cup q_6^1(x)$ where $q_6^1(x) :\text{-} (x, \tau, \text{SecurityOfficer})$. Therefore, $q_6^{\text{ref } f}(x) :\text{-} (x, \tau, Employee) \wedge (x \neq \text{SecurityOfficer})$, which has no results evaluated over $\mathcal{G}$.

8   Experiments

We detail the settings in Sect. 8.1 and our result analysis in Sect. 8.2.

Table 2. Query characteristics on the 1M (top) and 10M (bottom) datasets.

Metric	q_1	q_2	q_3	q_4	q_5	q_6	q_7	q_8	q_9	q_{10}	q_{11}	q_{12}
$\|q(1M)\|$	1 133 860	1 522	70 827	151	224 573	288 500	2 138 212	56 200	19 731	28 100	37 224	84 300
$\|q^{ref}\|$	509	11	5	1	25	493	509	1	1	215	2545	9671
$\|q(1M, A_1)\|$	1 069 047	1 522	70 827	0	224 558	218 698	2 069 328	56 199	19 717	28 084	0	84 251
ARR_{A_1}	0.943	1.000	1.000	**0.000**	1.000	0.759	0.968	1.000	1.000	0.999	**0.000**	0.999
$\|q^{ref\,A_1}\|$	315	7	5	0	25	299	315	1	1	188	315	5985
$\|q(1M, A_2)\|$	470 184	1 521	0	108	0	0	777 837	53 781	0	28 100	35 710	84 300
ARR_{A_2}	**0.415**	0.999	**0.000**	0.715	**0.000**	**0.000**	**0.364**	0.957	**0.000**	1.000	0.959	1.000
$\|q^{ref\,A_2}\|$	336	5	0	1	0	0	336	1	0	147	1008	6048
$\|q(1M, A_3)\|$	1 121 954	1 522	70 827	0	0	58 220	1 913 882	56 200	19 731	28 100	37 224	84 300
ARR_{A_3}	0.989	1.000	1.000	**0.000**	**0.000**	**0.202**	0.895	1.000	1.000	1.000	1.000	1.000
$\|q^{ref\,A_3}\|$	122	11	5	0	0	106	122	1	1	68	610	2318
$\|q(10M)\|$	11 958 511	16 236	755 971	585	2 145 750	3 182 610	23 219 926	600 000	210 336	600 000	573 483	900 000
$\|q^{ref}\|$	1791	11	5	1	73	1775	1791	1	1	649	8955	34029
$\|q(10M, A_1)\|$	11 302 423	16 236	755 971	0	2 145 729	2 452 499	22 528 719	599 999	210 334	299 995	0	899 987
ARR_{A_1}	0.945	1.000	1.000	**0.000**	1.000	0.771	0.970	1.000	1.000	**0.500**	**0.000**	0.999
$\|q^{ref\,A_1}\|$	1100	7	5	0	73	1084	1100	1	1	612	1100	20900
$\|q(10M, A_2)\|$	5 037 030	16 235	0	542	0	0	9 522 562	597 581	0	300 000	571 189	900 000
ARR_{A_2}	**0.421**	0.999	**0.000**	0.926	**0.000**	**0.000**	**0.410**	0.996	**0.000**	**0.5000**	0.997	1.000
$\|q^{ref\,A_2}\|$	1204	5	0	1	0	0	1204	1	0	437	3612	21672
$\|q(10M, A_3)\|$	11 879 546	16 236	755 971	0	0	1 527 609	21 665 733	600 000	210 336	300 000	573 483	900 000
ARR_{A_3}	0.993	1.000	1.000	**0.000**	**0.000**	**0.480**	0.933	1.000	1.000	**0.500**	1.000	1.000
$\|q^{ref\,A_3}\|$	414	11	5	0	0	398	414	1	1	360	2070	7866

8.1 Experimental Settings

We implemented our algorithms in OntoSQL, a Java-based platform (https://ontosql.inria.fr), providing RDF storage, saturation [15], BGP query answering via evaluation or reformulation as in [9], atop Postgres 12.4. Experiments ran on CentOS Linux 7.5, 2.7 GHz Intel Core i7, 160 GB RAM.

Implementation. OntoSQL *optionally* saturates graphs upon loading. Given a graph $\mathcal{G}$ and a set A of access restrictions, we *restrict* $\mathcal{G}$'s triples directly upon loading, thus, we load only $\mathcal{G}_A$ and we can saturate it leading to $(\mathcal{G}_A)^+$. For *entailment provenances* (Sect. 5), we modified OntoSQL's saturation algorithm [15], as described in Sect. 5; we build directly the *reduced* entailment graph $\mathcal{G}_e$. We serialize it JSON and bring it in memory when needed by an algorithm. We extended OntoSQL's BGPs to support *BGPQs with filters*, translating them into SQL by adding v <> IRI predicates for each restricted IRI in A, to the WHERE clause.

Graphs. We used BSBM [6] graphs of 1M and 10M triples, having: 44 properties; 177 (respectively, 611) classes; 215 (respectively, 649) ontology triples using domain, range, subclass, and subproperty in this (decreasing) frequency order.

Restrictions. Lacking a standard benchmark, we built three access restrictions sets A_1, A_2, A_3 to simulate varied scenarii. A_1 (**10 IRIs**) class IRIs such as vocab:Offer (56,208 mentions in 1M), rev:Review (28,106), vocab:ProductFeature (4,746), and vocab:Product (2,816). A_2 (**60 IRIs**) mixes classes (vocab:Offer, vocab:Producer, and foaf:Person), and properties (productFeature, rating1-4, reviewDate, and dc:title). A_3 (**100 IRIs**) is a narrow, instance-level restriction containing: 3 ProductFeatures, 3 Products, 19 Reviews and 75 Offers. IRIs in A_1, A_2 span diverse frequencies (11–56k mentions on 1M). Their *impact*: on

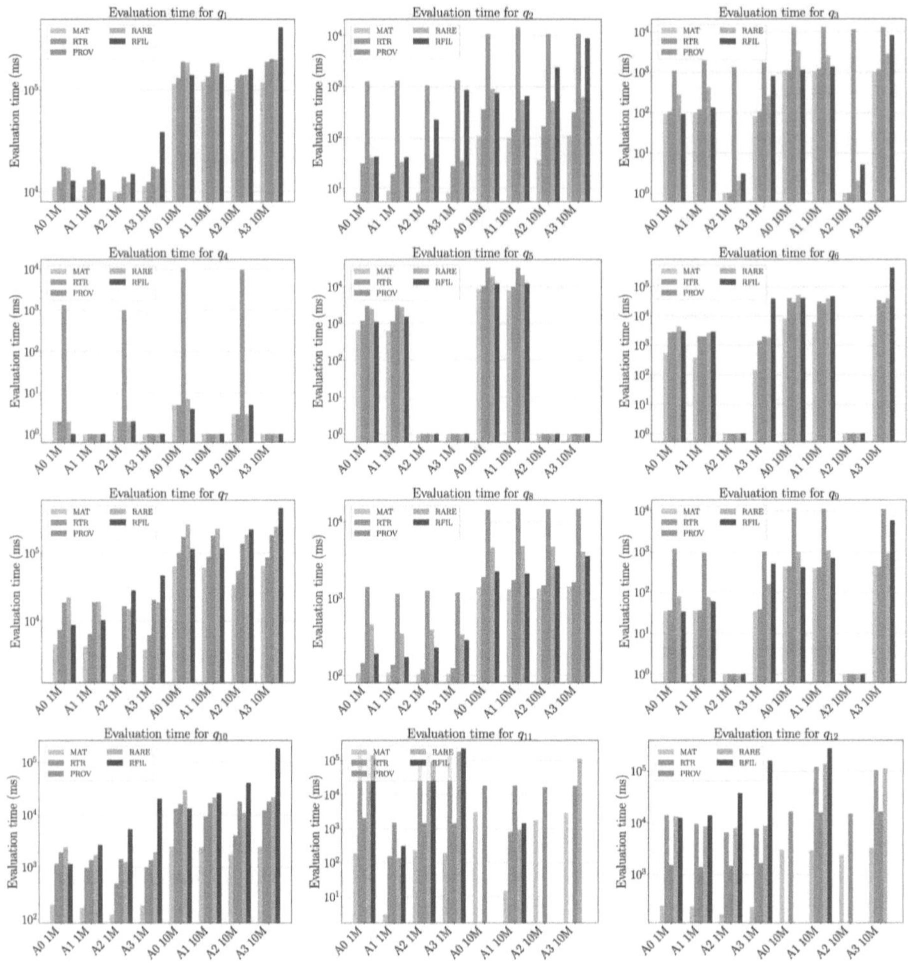

Fig. 4. Per-query answering times.

1M, A_2 removes 58.5% triples, while A_1 6% and A_3 only 1%; on 10M, A_2 restricts 58% triples, A_1 5.7% and A_3 only 0.07%. Clearly, A_2 restricts the graph the most. For comparison, we use A_0, the empty restriction set.

Queries. Our queries have 1 to 7 triples, returning from 0 to 22M results. Basic queries like q_1 (return all triples) and q_2 (find all foaf:Agents) test saturation overhead and filtering. q_3 retrieves ratings subjects; q_4 instances of ProductType (blocked under A_1 and A_3). Relational BGPs (q_5-q_8) join triples about, respectively: offers, product features, prices, and vendors (impacted by foaf:homepage in A_2). q_9, q_{10} combine ontological and instance triples. q_{11}, q_{12} trigger large reformulations. q_{12} asks for any subject pointing to a Product.

Table 3. Data loading times (ms) for 10M dataset and restriction set (A_k).

Dataset (10M)	MAT	RTR	PROV	RARE	RFIL
A_1	1 129 007	689 086	1 272 307	731 955	751 715
A_2	564 633	368 054	1 257 329	747 226	764 277
A_3	931 294	544 101	1 270 806	749 371	750 916

8.2   Results

Loading Data with(out) Restrictions. Table 3 shows loading and pre-processing times for the 10M dataset across restriction sets. PROV is slowest, followed by MAT. It comes from the fact that MAT saturates $\mathcal{G}_A$, while PROV saturates $\mathcal{G}$ entirely and builds the entailment graph $\mathcal{G}_e$. RARE and RFIL are faster, as they just load $\mathcal{G}$. RTR is fastest, filtering triples upon ingestion, so the restricted triples never make it into the database. We measure **query sensitivity to restrictions** first **syntactically** via $|q^{ref\,A_k}|$, the number of reformulation (BGPQs in the union) in case of restriction set A_k, and **semantically** via ARR_{A_k} the *Answer Retention Ratio*: the fraction of query answers without restrictions that are returned under A_k. Table 2 show $|q^{ref\,A_k}|$ and ARR_{A_k} per query, highlighting strong (**bold**), moderate (*italics*), or no impact (normal). For example, q_6, is fully blocked under A_2 (ARR 0.00), but retains 75% answers under A_1, and 20% under A_3.

Query answering times appear in Fig. 4 for both datasets (logarithmic y-axis). Missing bars indicate runs exceeding a 20-minute timeout. Queries rejected by the simple IRI check (Sect. 3.1) are plotted at 1ms, even when they took less, for distinction from timeout. **Simple queries** q_1 and q_2 show small runtime differences across restriction sets. q_1 consistently takes longer due to its large result set, especially in PROV. RFIL exhibits slight overhead due to high reformulation size. q_2 has minimal reformulation overhead. **Mildly restricted queries** q_3, q_4, q_8 and q_9 are blocked or moderately impacted under A_k. They have small reformulation sizes, therefore, while PROV takes the longest (particularly in A_2), the reformulation based algorithms, like RARE, are fast. q_4 is rejected outright under A_1 and A_3. q_8 and q_9 maintain stable runtimes across algorithms, with PROV slower by at least a factor of 2. **Joins with moderate to large reformulations** (q_5, q_6, q_{10}): q_5 and q_6 are blocked under A_2/A_3, stopping early, but under A_1 runtimes mirror unrestricted performance (A_0). q_{10} with its many reformulations in all A_k, shows PROV's advantage over RFIL/RARE. **Complex reformulations** q_7, q_{11} and q_{12} show high cost and timeouts for reformulation-based methods ($|q^{ref\,A_k}|$ reaching 6 000+ for q_{12}), while PROV performs better.

Discussion. In practice, multiple users may operate over a single graph, each with their own restriction set A_u. This raises questions about the best query answering strategy when balancing *loading time*, *query time*, and *disk usage*. Baseline algorithms MAT and RTR perform well in query evaluation but require storing a distinct graph for each user. This may lead to large disk consumption and high loading times. MAT further amplifies this by storing fully materialized graphs. In contrast, RFIL, RARE and PROV avoid per-user copies by operating on the original graph or it saturation. However, RARE suffers in complex reformulation cases, while RFIL when restriction sets are big. PROV is a robust solution, but it is frequently 10 times slower, especially with large answer sets.

Takeaway. The optimal strategy depends on many characteristics: for few users or highly static graphs, MAT and RTR may be acceptable despite storage costs. As user count grows, reformulation or filtering strategies become preferable. Among these, PROV is robust for complex queries; RFIL and RARE handle most workloads efficiently.

9 Related Work

The classical *role-based access control (RBAC)* involves *users*, *roles* (operational needs), and *privileges* associating a role to (data object, access mode), e.g., the data object may be a table, or a query over it, and the access mode could be *read* or *write*. Since user-role separation is useful but straightforward, we omit it for clarity and discuss privileges given to users directly. More recent research works on access control in relational databases introduce predicate-level access control [11], leverage encryption, e.g., [25], middleware architectures [23], etc.

Early **policy-based frameworks for RDF stores** treat triples and their insertion/deletion as controlled actions with explicit rules. [16] presents an access control model for OWL ontologies, but do not provide query evaluation or answering methods. Privileges in [17] are triple patterns, positive (permitting) or negative (forbidding); this may cause conflicts. The authors consider a limited form of RDFS reasoning, propagating privileges along subclassOf and subpropertyOf hierarchies and determine whether a triple is permitted or forbidden for a user, but query answering is not studied. RDF access privileges in [24] permit or prohibit users to insert, delete, or read triples matching specific patterns; privileges can be conditioned by predicates over the user and/or the triples, such as "only the creator of class C may add (x, τ, C)". A prototype implementation using Jena checks triple-level actions with RDFS reasoning. However, it requires maintaining per-triple "access labels" which is costly (no experiments are provided). Queries with multi-triple bodies are not supported.

Focusing on **query (read)** access control, several works enforce it by **rewriting SPARQL queries** before evaluation. They specify positive and negative access policies as queries and *add them to user queries to exclude unauthorized results*—some using MINUS [3], others using FILTER. Reasoning is often not considered. Our MFIL algorithm is very similar (but as we have shown, incomplete in the presence of ontologies). In [19], privileges grant or restrict access over relational BGP results. User queries are then *rewritten over the set of privileges seen as materialized views*, for two semantics (considering that data not covered by the policies is permitted, respectively, is restricted). Reasoning is not considered; the method remains unimplemented. The fQuery approach [21] defines an access control policy as a set of positive and negative filters on query results, attached to a user; ontologies or reasoning are not considered. A user's SPARQL query is rewritten by *injecting FILTER clauses reflecting the access control policies*; this corresponds to our MFIL algorithm. Similarly, [8] rewrites queries to restrict visible graphs. Authorization ontologies (permissive policies) are used to define graph-level visibility, and rewritten queries derive only accessible graphs.

Some techniques store **accessibility labels** for each triple. In [13], triples are *annotated with labels ("accessible"/"inaccessible")* conditioned by conjunctive RDF queries. This raises efficiency issues when policies change, as labels must be recomputed. This is impractical for multi-user scenarios, reasoning is also not considered. In [22], *triple access labels are logical formulas* that may involve labels of other triples. Policies restrict some triples, and RDFS reasoning (e.g., via subclassOf relationships) propagates restrictions. Labels are dynamically (re-)evaluated upon access requests. However, only certain policies is studied experimentally, and generalizing to multi-user settings would require RDF store modifications impacting performance.

Efficient provenance capture is the topic of [5]. Our provenance gathering (Sect. 5) aligns with their semi-naïve one; their more efficient method assumes that the original graph is saturated, an assumption which, for full generality, we do not make.

RDF access control based on OWL (not RDFS) ontologies has also been investigated. In [10], OWL is used to specify restrictions and policies, while a query can only request one resource. OWL defines classes by expressive logical formulas (intersection, existential/universal quantifiers, etc.). This is leveraged in [14,20], where *access restrictions define classes* such that determining whether an IRI is accessible reduces to an OWL inference task. In [20], a dedicated OWL ontology is introduced for access restrictions, including property reification, while [14] defines one class per authorization: restricting C denies access to any IRI of type C and its subclasses. These flexible approaches incur high OWL inference costs [14]. Unlike our BGPs (Sect. 2.2), these works support relational BGP triple patterns. A survey [18] focuses on positive and negative privileges (grant/restrict), conflict resolution, and highlights the lack of reasoning support in most prior solutions. Departing from RBAC models, a **cryptography-based** RDF access control approach is presented in [12]. A data owner encrypt each triple (or a part of it) and shares decryption keys tied to query patterns. A user may decrypt data if their keys satisfy the relevant predicate, enabling fine-grained access at the triple level.

Privacy in Graph Data Sharing. Beyond access restrictions, recent works [7,27] explore *transforming* RDF graphs, i.e., anonymizing nodes, or modifying sensitive graph portions. These works ignore ontologies; combining them with ours is an interesting area of future work.

Acknowledgements. This work is funded by the France 2030 investment plan, supporting the DXP project as part of the IPCEI-CIS European initiative.

References

1. RDF 1.1 Semantics (2014). https://www.w3.org/TR/rdf11-mt/#rdfs-entailment
2. Extended version of this work (2025). https://hal.science/view/index/docid/5250941
3. Abel, F., Coi, J.L.D., Henze, N., et al.: Enabling advanced and context-dependent access control in RDF stores. In: The Semantic Web (2007)
4. Artale, A., Calvanese, D., Kontchakov, R., Zakharyaschev, M.: The dl-lite family and relations. J. Artif. Intell. Res. **36** (2009)
5. Belhajjame, K., Mejri, M.Y.: Online maintenance of evolving graphs with RDFS-based saturation and why-provenance support. J. Web Semant. **78** (2023)

6. Bizer, C., Schultz, A.: The berlin SPARQL benchmark. IJSWIS **5**(2) (2009)
7. Boiret, A., Eichler, C., Nguyen, B., Taki, S.: Graph rewriting primitives for semantic graph databases sanitization. Comput. Sci. Inf. Syst. **21**(3) (2024)
8. Brunk, C., Sigg, L., Harth, A.: Enforcing scalable authorization on SPARQL queries. In: SEMANTiCS (2016)
9. Buron, M., Goasdoué, F., Manolescu, I., Mugnier, M.L.: Reformulation-based query answering for RDF graphs with RDFS ontologies. In: ESWC (2019)
10. Carminati, B., Ferrari, E., Heatherly, R., et al.: A semantic web based framework for social network access control. In: SACMAT (2009)
11. Chaudhuri, S., Dutta, T., Sudarshan, S.: Fine grained authorization through predicated grants. In: ICDE (2007)
12. Fernández, J.D., Kirrane, S., Polleres, A., Steyskal, S.: Self-enforcing access control for encrypted RDF. In: ESWC (2017)
13. Flouris, G., Fundulaki, I., Michou, M., Antoniou, G.: Controlling access to RDF graphs. In: FIS (2010)
14. Fornara, N., Marfia, F.: Modeling and enforcing access control obligations for SPARQL-DL queries. In: SEMANTiCS (2016)
15. Goasdoué, F., Manolescu, I., Roatis, A.: Efficient query answering against dynamic RDF databases. In: EDBT/ICDT (2013)
16. Ionita, C.M., Osborn, S.L.: Specifying an access control model for ontologies for the semantic web. In: SDM (2005)
17. Jain, A., Farkas, C.: Secure resource description framework: an access control model. In: SACMAT (2006)
18. Kirrane, S., Mileo, A., Decker, S.: Access control and the resource description framework: a survey. Semantic Web **8**(2) (2017)
19. Li, J., Cheung, W.K.: Query rewriting for access control on semantic web. In: Secure Data Management (2008)
20. Masoumzadeh, A., Joshi, J.: Osnac: an ontology-based access control model for social networking systems. In: SocialCom (2010)
21. Oulmakhzoune, S., Cuppens-Boulahia, N., Cuppens, F., et al.: fQuery: SPARQL query rewriting to enforce data confidentiality. In: DBSec, vol. 6377 (2010)
22. Papakonstantinou, V., Michou, M., Fundulaki, I., et al.: Access control for RDF graphs using abstract models. In: SACMAT (2012)
23. Pappachan, P., Yus, R., Mehrotra, S., Freytag, J.C.: Sieve: a middleware approach to scalable access control for database management systems. PVLDB **13**(11) (2020)
24. Reddivari, P., Finin, T., Joshi, A.: Policy-based access control for an RDF store. In: IJCAI Workshop: Semantic Web for Collaborative Knowledge Acquisition (2007)
25. Sarfraz, M.I., Nabeel, M., Cao, J., Bertino, E.: Dbmask: fine-grained access control on encrypted relational databases. In: CODASPY (2015)
26. Senellart, P., Jachiet, L., Maniu, S., Ramusat, Y.: ProvSQL: provenance and probability management in PostgreSQL. PVLDB **11**(12) (2018)
27. Taki, S., Boiret, A., Eichler, C., Nguyen, B.: Cohesive database neighborhoods for differential privacy: mapping relational databases to RDF. In: WISE (2024)
28. RDF Schema. https://www.w3.org/TR/rdf12-schema/

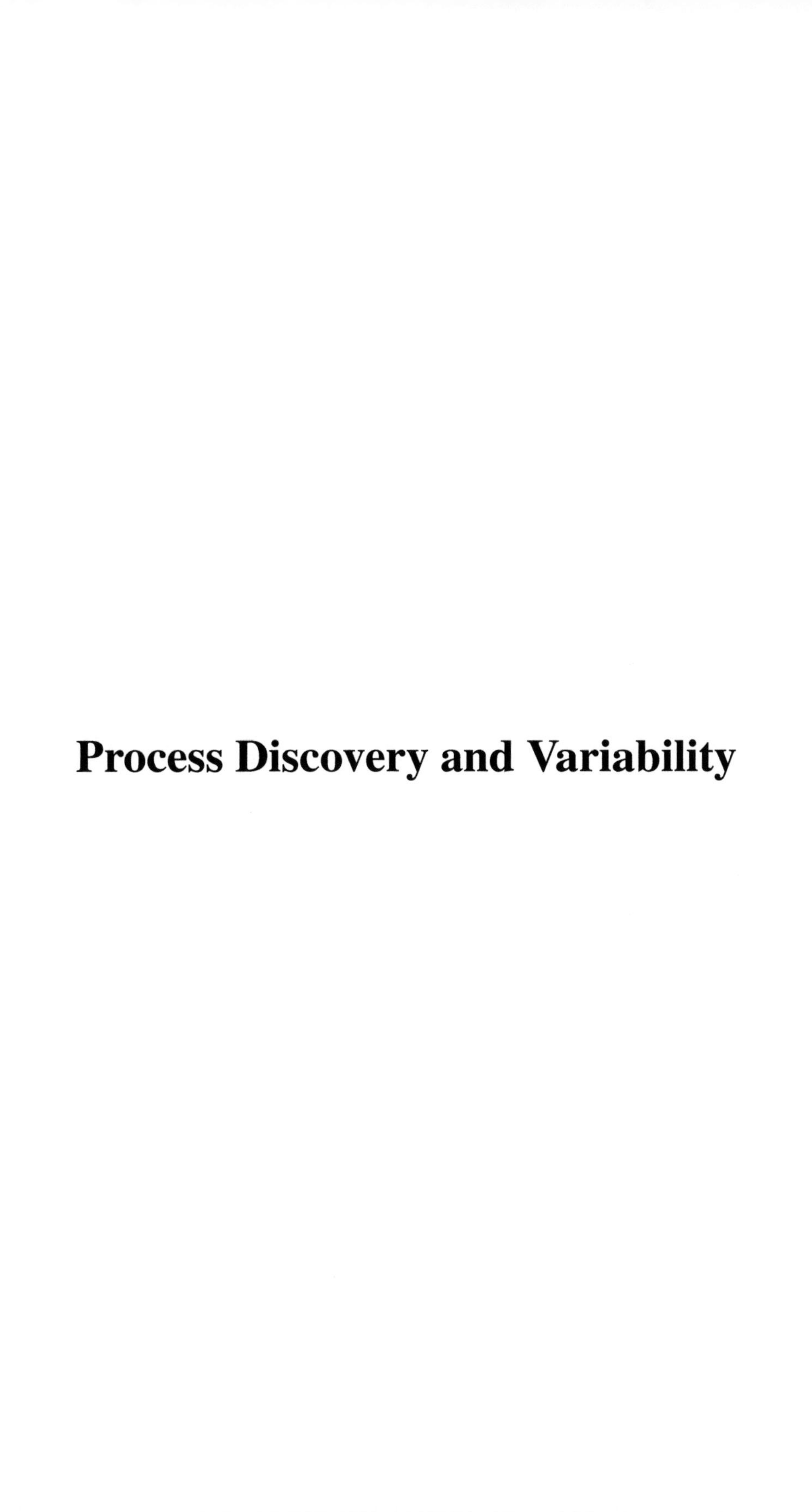

Process Discovery and Variability

Unsupervised Hierarchical Process Mining
with the Process Fragment Miner

Joern Tobis[(✉)] [iD], Felix Schumann [iD], Juergen Mangler [iD], and Stefanie Rinderle-Ma [iD]

TUM School of Computation, Information and Technology, Technical University of Munich,
Garching, Germany
`{joern.tobis,felix.schumann,juergen.mangler,`
`stefanie.rinderle-ma}@tum.de`

Abstract. Abstracting processes into a hierarchical structure of subprocesses helps to improve the understandability and readability of process models. Mining such hierarchical process models from event logs is an active subfield in process mining research. Existing approaches often require activities to be labeled with a hierarchy notion or context data to identify hierarchies. In this work, we propose the ProcessFragmentMiner (PFM) to fragment an event log into subprocesses that represent the root process. PFM harnesses the dependency matrix generated by the heuristics miner in combination with different fragment ranking mechanisms. This work uses the inductive and split miner to mine the resulting process models for each fragment. PFM is evaluated against a supervised and an unsupervised hierarchical process mining approach from the literature. We find that PFM works best in combination with the presented Bigram ranking method and can match supervised approaches for some data sets. The proposed PFM approach enables hierarchical process mining on any event log without the need for any preprocessing steps.

Keywords: Process Mining · Automated Process Discovery · Hierarchical Process Discovery · Event Abstraction · Model Abstraction · Unsupervised Process Mining

1 Introduction

Structuring a process into subprocesses can increase the understandability of a process model [12] and is well established and supported by many modeling approaches, modeling tools, and execution engines, e.g., BPMN, Signavio, or CPEE [11]. Automatically discovering subprocesses and hierarchical structures from event logs is considered one approach to finding the right abstraction level for a process, which is an important problem in BPM [3]. The abstraction level at which events are reported is, in many cases, much lower than what a user actually requires from a process model [16]. Especially when dealing with larger processes in terms of tasks and process participants, finding a reasonable abstraction level to create a top-level representation of what is happening creates better understandability. Typical use cases span from automated production

C. Cappiello et al. (Eds.): CoopIS 2025, LNCS 15535, pp. 333–350, 2026.
https://doi.org/10.1007/978-3-032-15538-2_19

processes in manufacturing to more knowledge-driven processes, such as clinical processes. Solving this granularity problem can further foster the application of process mining, especially in knowledge-intensive processes [3].

Process mining approaches that deal with different abstraction levels are categorized by the taxonomy provided in [16]. A core distinction is the supervision strategy. Most approaches rely on a supervised approach, which either has a direct labeling of hierarchies, such as [10], or uses context data to identify labels, such as [9]. To overcome the need for a pre-labeled event log, we propose an unsupervised hierarchical mining approach called ProcessFragmentMiner (PFM). PFM enables an automatic organization of process activities into subprocesses. As input, the approach requires an event log, which is considered discrete event data. The unsupervised PFM approach brings multiple benefits to users of hierarchical process mining techniques. Being based purely on an event log, no additional labeling or preprocessing of events is needed. Since the process discovery part is only addressed in the last part of the pipeline, different discovery algorithms can be used.

The PFM approach can be understood as one step towards advancing process mining by "bridging the preprocessing (specifically, the event abstraction) and the Mining & Analysis phases of typical process mining workflows" [3]. The result of PFM is an initial hierarchical process model with a single hierarchy level that structures the process. Based on this, domain experts obtain an overview of the process at first sight and can take further refinement actions.

PFM is implemented as a five-step approach to mine hierarchical process models from an event log. The core of the approach is a dependency matrix as used by the HeuristicsMiner [15]. This dependency matrix is then used to calculate possible process subtraces. We propose three different ranking methods to rank subtraces before recombining them into a full process model. For each identified subprocess fragment, specific subprocess models are mined. Additionally, the process model between those fragments is mined. We evaluate the processes discovered by our approach based on established evaluation methods as presented in [2, 10] and compare them with the supervised domain knowledge approach and unsupervised random approach presented in [10].

The remainder of this article is structured as follows. In Sect. 2, we provide an overview of other approaches for hierarchical process mining. Section 3 describes the details of the unsupervised hierarchical process mining approach PFM. In Sect. 4, we evaluate the performance of the overall approach and the different ranking approaches based on benchmarks known from the literature. Section 5 discusses the results, and Sect. 6 concludes the paper.

2   Related Work

Discovering process hierarchies from an event log requires the abstraction of events to higher-level events or the clustering of tasks into subprocesses. [16] presents a literature review on event abstraction in process mining. The authors present a taxonomy containing multiple dimensions to analyze different event abstraction methods. With regard to this work, the most important dimension is the supervision strategy, which describes whether the abstraction is done in a supervised or unsupervised manner. Supervised approaches require additional information on a hierarchy between events. According to [16], most approaches use some form of supervision. Meanwhile, the PFM approach proposed in this work is fully unsupervised.

The FlexHMiner presented in [10] uses the notion of *activity trees* to discover process hierarchy within an event log. The authors propose a fully supervised approach based on the task labels, as well as an unsupervised approach. The unsupervised approach uses random clustering to identify hierarchies. Measured by *fitness, precision, F1-Score, complexity,* and *size,* the authors find that the supervised approach outperforms the unsupervised approach, and both approaches outperform a flat process mining approach on said measures.

Besides supervised approaches based on task labels [9, 10] proposes the use of multi-level event information to identify the hierarchy, called Multi-Level Miner (MLM). For MLM, multi-layer classifiers are chosen based on domain knowledge as well as by the analysis of short loops for attributes. The authors argue that the discovered process models are easier to understand than flat process models for users. In comparison, we aim for a purely unsupervised methodology that is applied to an event log before user interaction. The goal is to provide an understandable process model to the user, which can then be further refined by a domain expert.

Local Process Model (LPM) Discovery is described in [13, 14] as the only approach to mine local process models with formal semantics. For each subprocess fragment, a process tree is created, which holds information on formal semantics. PFM adds the semantics to each subprocess fragment after having built a full process model from the subprocesses. To identify these process models, any mining approach can be used.

3   Methodology

The PFM approach uses an event log L as input. L comprises multiple events, each of which is associated with a unique case identifier of the associated activity and belongs to one process instance. A timestamp indicates when the event occurred, and a label identifies an event, formally: Let $\mathcal{A}$ be the set of all process activities, and TS be the set of all timestamps. The set of events $E{:}\subseteq \mathcal{A} \times \mathcal{TS}$ describes all events e=(a,ts) that reflect the execution of activity $a \in A$ at time $ts \in TS$. A trace $t :-< e_1, ..., e_n >$ is defined as a sequence of events that describe the execution of a sequence of activities for an underlying process. An event log L is a multiset of traces, $\mathcal{L}$ the set of all logs, $A_L : \mathcal{L} \mapsto \mathcal{A}$ determines the set of activities for which corresponding events are present in L.

PFM follows a structured, sequential, multi-stage processing pipeline. With the event log as input, this pipeline consists of the steps:

Step 1: Calculate the dependency matrix
Step 2: Calculate possible subprocess fragments
Step 3: Rank all fragments using one of three methods: Heuristic-Ranking (HR), Bigram-Ranking (BR), and Similarity-Ranking (SR).
Step 4: Find a disjoint set of fragments to build the full process model
Step 5: Discover the root process model and fragment process models

3.1 Step 1: Calculate Dependency Matrix with HeuristicsMiner

We calculate a dependency matrix M as it is used by the HeuristicsMiner [15], i.e. for log L, i.e., a quadratic matrix with row and columns determined by the set of activities A_L (see Table 1). The entries m_{ij} are determined based on the *strength of dependency* $Dep(a_i, a_j)$ between activities a_i and a_j which is calculated following the HeuristicsMiner formula:

$$\mathrm{Dep}(a_i, a_j) = \frac{|a_i \to a_j| - |a_j \to a_i|}{|a_i \to a_j| + |a_j \to a_i| + 1} \quad \text{with} \tag{1}$$

$|a_i \to a_j| := |\{t \in L \mid \exists e = (a_i, ts_{a_i}), e' = (a_j, ts_{a_j}) \in t \wedge e \text{ directly followed by } e'\}|$

This formula yields a value in a range of $[-1, 1]$ that describes the sequential relationship between activity a_i and activity a_j. Following this, values close to 1 indicate a strong dependency from a_i towards a_j, i.e., a_i almost always leads to a_j. Values close to -1 indicate a strong inverse relationship, i.e., a_j more often leads to a_i. Values close to 0 do not indicate a clear dependency between activities (activities may occur independently or in parallel). Table 1 shows an exemplary dependency matrix derived from the event log. Each row holds the dependencies between a_i (row identifier) to all dependent tasks a_j (column identifier).

Table 1. Example event log (left) and its corresponding dependency matrix (right), mined using the HeuristicsMiner.

instance	event	timestamp
7ad	C_4	16:03:01
7ad	C_1	16:04:07
...	...	...
04c	A_2	16:04:52
04c	A_1	16:04:58
04c	A_1	16:05:14
...	...	...
c80	B_5	15:48:59
c80	B_5	15:49:10
c80	B_4	15:50:00

	A_1	A_2	B_1	B_2	B_3	B_4	B_5	B_6	C_1	C_2	C_3	C_4	C_5
A_1	0.99	0.79	–	–	–	–	–	–	–	–	–	–	–
A_2	-0.79	0.99	–	–	–	0.97	–	–	–	–	–	0.97	–
B_1	0.95	–	–	–	-0.57	–	–	–	–	–	–	0.97	–
B_2	–	–	–	–	–	–	–	1.00	–	–	–	–	–
B_3	–	–	–	–	–	–	–	1.00	–	–	–	–	–
B_4	0.88	-0.57	–	–	–	0.99	0.99	-0.59	–	–	–	–	–
B_5	–	–	-1.00	1.00	–	-1.00	–	–	–	–	–	–	–
B_6	–	-0.83	–	–	–	0.59	1.00	1.00	–	–	–	–	–
C_1	0.96	–	–	–	–	0.96	–	–	–	–	–	-0.58	–
C_2	–	–	–	–	–	–	–	–	-0.99	–	–	–	–
C_3	–	–	–	–	–	–	–	–	–	-0.99	–	–	–
C_4	0.92	–	–	–	–	–	–	–	-0.58	–	–	0.99	–
C_5	–	–	–	–	–	–	–	–	–	–	–	–	-1.00

Intuitively, to find traces in the matrix, a threshold could be defined that sets an acceptance level for a relationship between two tasks. Without a threshold, process traces can be found with an *all-activities-connected heuristic*, which always chooses the best candidate from the possible related candidates [15].

3.2 Step 2: Calculate Possible Subtraces

In contrast to the *all-activities-connected heuristic* [15], PFM finds a subtrace t^* by performing a depth-first search starting from every activity $a \in M$. A subtrace is represented as an ordered list of activities. Figure 1 shows how the traces are derived from the matrix. The universe of subtraces contains every possible subtrace starting from each activity in M. A subtrace t^* is not necessarily a subset of a trace $t \in L$. Since it is created from the dependency matrix M, additional subtraces are possible.

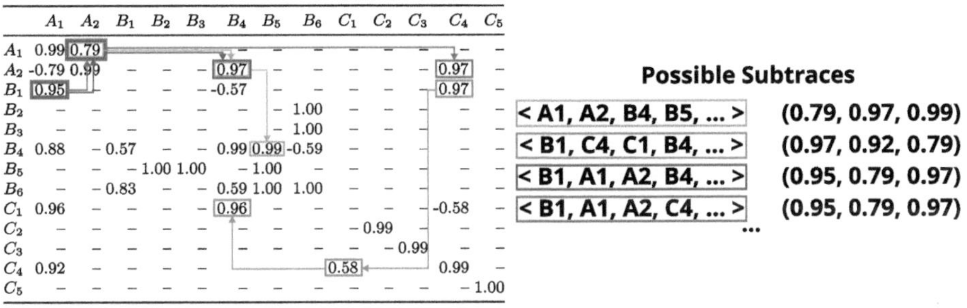

	A_1	A_2	B_1	B_2	B_3	B_4	B_5	B_6	C_1	C_2	C_3	C_4	C_5
A_1	0.99	0.79	–	–	–	–	–	–	–	–	–	–	–
A_2	-0.79	0.99	–	–	–	0.97	–	–	–	–	–	0.97	–
B_1	0.95	–	–	–	–	-0.57	–	–	–	–	–	0.97	–
B_2	–	–	–	–	–	–	–	1.00	–	–	–	–	–
B_3	–	–	–	–	–	–	–	1.00	–	–	–	–	–
B_4	0.88	–	0.57	–	–	0.99	0.99	-0.59	–	–	–	–	–
B_5	–	–	–	1.00	1.00	–	1.00	–	–	–	–	–	–
B_6	–	–	0.83	–	–	0.59	1.00	1.00	–	–	–	–	–
C_1	0.96	–	–	–	–	0.96	–	–	–	–	–	-0.58	–
C_2	–	–	–	–	–	–	–	–	–	0.99	–	–	–
C_3	–	–	–	–	–	–	–	–	–	–	0.99	–	–
C_4	0.92	–	–	–	–	–	–	0.58	–	–	–	0.99	–
C_5	–	–	–	–	–	–	–	–	–	–	–	–	1.00

Possible Subtraces

< A1, A2, B4, B5, ... >	(0.79, 0.97, 0.99)
< B1, C4, C1, B4, ... >	(0.97, 0.92, 0.79)
< B1, A1, A2, B4, ... >	(0.95, 0.79, 0.97)
< B1, A1, A2, C4, ... >	(0.95, 0.79, 0.97)
...	

Fig. 1. Deriving possible subtraces from a dependency matrix M starting at dependency (a_1, a_2).

Algorithm 1 describes how all subtraces are created from the dependency matrix M. It performs a depth-first search over the matrix and returns all possible subtraces by exploring all valid activity sequences. By setting a `threshold`, it can be specified which next activities are accepted to be added to a subtrace. The default for this `threshold` is 0. By setting `min_depth` and `max_depth`, a minimum and maximum size for subtraces can be set. In an unconstrained setting, finding all possible subtraces can lead to high computational complexity. Specifying minimum and maximum depth parameters for a subtrace or a high threshold can be used to constrain this step.

A found subtrace represents one candidate of a subprocess to hierarchically structure the process model of the event log. Resulting from the full set of subtraces, the goal is to find a combination of n subtraces that represent the root process in the best way with respect to some quality measure (see detailed explanation in Sect. 3.4).

3.3 Step 3: Ranking of Subtraces

Different approaches to measure the quality of a subtrace can be used to rank the identified subtraces. The quality of a subtrace describes how unambiguous the dependencies within a subtrace are. The ranking of subtraces is necessary for the recombination of the subtraces to the full process in the following step (see Sect. 3.4). We present three approaches that use the given dependency matrix M and the set of found subtraces. The three approaches span from a heuristic ranking approach, over the bigram ranking with interpretable co-occurrence features, to the Word2Vec-based ranking, which

---

Algorithm 1. Calculate all subtraces from the dependency matrix.

Require: dependencies (dictionary), threshold, max_depth, min_depth
Ensure: all_subtraces (list of traces)
1: all_subtraces ← empty list
2: **procedure** DFS(trace, depth)
3:      current ← last element of trace
4:      **if** depth ≥ max_depth **then**
5:          Append copy of trace to all_subtraces
6:          **return**
7:      **end if**
8:      next_nodes ← dependencies[current] (default empty dictionary)
9:      extended ← **false**
10:     **for all** (next_act, strength) in next_nodes **do**
11:         **if** strength ≥ threshold **and** next_act ∉ trace **then**
12:             Append next_act to trace
13:             DFS(trace, depth +1)
14:             Remove last element from trace
15:             extended ← **true**
16:         **end if**
17:     **end for**
18:     **if** not extended **and** depth ≥ min_depth **then**
19:         Append copy of trace to all_subtraces
20:     **end if**
21: **end procedure**
22: **for all** start_node in dependencies **do**
23:     DFS([start_node], 1)
24: **end for**
25: **return** all_subtraces

---

behaves more like a 'black box' due to its opaque vector representations and lack of interpretable features. Each of the ranking approaches creates a ranked list of possible subtraces as output.

Heuristic Ranking (HR). Given the dependency matrix M (see Eq. (1)), where m_{ij} represents the strength of a dependency from activity a_i to activity a_j, the heuristic ranking for a subtrace $t^* =< a_1, \ldots, a_n >$ is defined as the product of the dependency strengths Dep along the trace t^*:

$$\mathrm{HR}(t^*) = \prod_{l=1}^{k-1} Dep_{a_l a_{l+1}} \tag{2}$$

This ranking approach uses the dependency matrix to assign higher rankings to variants with stronger cumulative dependencies. It is computationally inexpensive to calculate.

Bigram Ranking (BR). Bigram Ranking evaluates the likelihood of a trace based on bigram probabilities derived from the event log. A bigram matrix is constructed by counting transitions between pairs of activities in the log. To account for data sparsity and unseen transitions, smoothing is applied to the matrix M. We define the smoothed bigram probability of transitioning from activity a_i to activity a_j as:

$$P(a_j \mid a_i) = \frac{C(a_i, a_j) + \alpha}{C(a_i) + \alpha \cdot |A|} \tag{3}$$

where:

- $C(a_i, a_j)$ is the count of transitions from a_i to a_j in the log,
- $C(a_i) = \sum_{j=1}^{k} C(a_i, a)$ is the total number of times a_i is followed by any activity,
- $|A|$ is the number of unique activities,
- α is a smoothing parameter (e.g., $\alpha = 1$ for Laplace smoothing).

The resulting *bigram probability matrix* $P \in \mathbb{R}^{k \times k}$ is defined as:

$$P = \begin{bmatrix} P(a_1 \mid a_1) & P(a_2 \mid a_1) & \cdots & P(a_k \mid a_1) \\ P(a_1 \mid a_2) & P(a_2 \mid a_2) & \cdots & P(a_k \mid a_2) \\ \vdots & \vdots & \ddots & \vdots \\ P(a_1 \mid a_k) & P(a_2 \mid a_k) & \cdots & P(a_k \mid a_k) \end{bmatrix}$$

Each row of the matrix corresponds to a source activity a_i, and each column corresponds to a target activity a_j. The matrix is row-normalized and reflects the smoothed probabilities of transitions observed in the event log.

The overall likelihood of a trace $t^* = < a_1, a_2, \ldots, a_n >$ is computed as the product of the *unigram probability* of the initial activity and the sequence of bigram transition probabilities between successive activities:

$$P(t^*) = P(a_1) \cdot \prod_{i=2}^{n} P(a_i \mid a_{i-1}) \tag{4}$$

Here, $P(a_1)$ denotes the *unigram probability* of starting with activity a_1, while each $P(a_i \mid a_{i-1})$ represents a *bigram probability*, i.e., the conditional probability of activity a_i given the preceding activity a_{i-1}. These bigram probabilities are obtained from the *bigram probability matrix*.

Traces are then ranked based on their computed likelihood $P(t^*)$, with higher-probability traces being ranked higher.

Similarity Ranking (SR). As proposed in [8], we capture semantic similarity with a model trained on event log L. We leverage the functionality of the Python package Word2Vec to score the similarity of every task, which we then interpret as our ranking. Word2Vec directly computes a similarity score based on semantic similarity. Word2Vec is a neural embedding model that learns dense vector representations for words based on their distributional context. Similarity is measured by the cosine similarity in the embedding space. In accordance with [8], we embed traces as sentences and events as words. With the derived model from the event log, we compute the cosine similarity of an activity and its successor activity. Once the scores for all $n - 1$ consecutive activity pairs in a subtrace of length n have been computed, their mean is used as the ranking score for the subtrace. This process is repeated for each subtrace.

3.4   Step 4: Selection of a Disjoint Fragment Set Covering All Events

After identifying and ranking the subtraces, a strategy must be found to combine corresponding process fragments into a new process model. Let t^* be a subtrace. Then the corresponding process fragment $f_t := \{a \in \mathcal{A} \mid \exists\, e = (a, t_a) \in t\}$ is defined as the set of all activities with corresponding events in t^*. The problem of finding such a disjoint set corresponds to an instance of the Maximum-Weight Independent Set (MWIS) problem, which is known to be NP-hard [6]. In some special cases, the MWIS problem can be solved using a dynamic programming approach similar to the Knapsack problem [7]. This reduces the storage requirement from $\mathcal{O}\,(b \times n^*)$ to $\mathcal{O}(b)$ [5]. While optimizing storage constraints, runtime-wise, the completeness of the NP-hard problem makes it impossible to solve it optimally in a reasonable time for lots of possible combinations, e.g., a large number of small subtraces. To enable calculation within a reasonable runtime even for larger instances, we implemented a beam search strategy that reduces computational complexity by limiting the number of partial solutions explored at each step. This allows for a broader search space than pure greedy selection, while still maintaining practical efficiency. In addition, we further elaborated on the greedy approach to make it more comprehensive and interpretable, for instance, by explicitly enforcing disjointness and guaranteeing full event coverage. Together, these enhancements strike a balance between solution quality and runtime scalability.

Algorithm 2 describes a greedy approach to identify a disjoint set of fragments that collectively cover all events in the log. First, the best following trace is selected until no trace can be added further. If any events remain uncovered, meaning they are not part of any fragment and no suitable fragment can represent them, they are grouped into a final fragment to ensure complete log coverage.

Algorithm 2 iterates over the list of `ranked_fragments`, which is sorted in descending order based on the ranking described in Sect. 3.2. For each candidate fragment, the algorithm checks whether it overlaps with any previously selected fragment by performing a bitwise intersection between its mask and the accumulated mask of already used events. If the candidate does not share any events with the selected fragments, it is added to the result. After all candidates have been considered, the algorithm identifies any remaining uncovered events and groups them into a final fragment. This guarantees that the returned fragments are non-overlapping and collectively cover all events in the log.

The greedy approach offers favorable computational and memory complexity, as it processes each fragment in a single pass while maintaining a minimal state. However, further improvements have been proposed within the implementation of PFM to enhance the quality of the resulting scores while still ensuring reasonable runtime. These include techniques such as beam search and dynamic programming, which explore a broader space of candidate fragment combinations and can yield better overall solutions at the cost of increased, but still manageable, computational effort.

3.5   Step 5: Discover Root Process Model and Fragments Process Models

After identifying a final set of fragments, process models for each fragment and a full process can be mined. The top-level process model created from the identified frag-

---

Algorithm 2. Greedy Candidate State from Ranked Fragments.

Require:

      `ranked_fragments`: list of $(score, trace, trace\_mask)$ sorted descending

      `reconstruct_trace(mask)`   ▷ build a trace fragment from a given mask

Ensure: A disjoint set of fragments whose union covers all events

 1: $used\_mask \leftarrow 0$

 2: $trace\_list \leftarrow [\,]$

 3: $score\_list \leftarrow [\,]$

 4: $total\_score \leftarrow 0$

 5: **for all** $(score, trace, trace\_mask) \in ranked\_fragments$ **do**

 6:      **if** $used\_mask \,\&\, trace\_mask \neq 0$ **then**

 7:          **continue**   ▷ Skip overlapping

 8:      **end if**

 9:      $used\_mask \leftarrow used\_mask \mid trace\_mask$

10:      append $trace$ **to** $trace\_list$

11:      append $score$ **to** $score\_list$

12:      $total\_score \leftarrow total\_score + score$

13: **end for**

14:                         ▷ Add leftover events to ensure full coverage

15: $all\_mask \leftarrow$ mask of all events

16: **if** $used\_mask \neq all\_mask$ **then**

17:      $leftover\_mask \leftarrow all\_mask \,\&\, \sim used\_mask$

18:      $leftover\_trace \leftarrow$ `reconstruct_trace`$(leftover\_mask)$

19:      append $leftover\_trace$ **to** $trace\_list$ ▷ No change to total_score (no scoring for leftover)

20: **end if**

21: **return** $(used\_mask, total\_score, trace\_list, score\_list)$

---

ments is called the *root* model. The *root* model represents an abstracted version of the process itself. It shows the interaction of the found fragments for the given event log.

Within each of the found fragments, the process must also be mined. We call these models the *subprocess* models. A subprocess represents traces equivalent to the events in a fragment f in the event log L. Any miner could be used for this step. For PFM, we use the inductive miner [15] and the split miner [1] to mine both the *root* model and *subprocess* models. According to [2], the inductive miner and the split miner outperform other miners in quality and execution time.

Mining the Subprocess Models. To mine the *subprocess* models, the event log L is reduced for each fragment identified in Step 4 by a projection function $sp(L)$. The subprocess event log L_{sp} is created by keeping the events that correspond to an activity that is part of the selected fragment f. For each fragment in the set of selected fragments, L_{sp} is generated. This follows the projection function specified in [10]. The *subprocess* model can then be mined from this subprocess event log L_{sp} by applying a discovery algorithm.

Mining the Root Model. To generate the *root* model, an abstraction of the found fragments is needed. To do so, we use the abstraction function $f \uparrow$ described in [10] to abstract the log. For each trace in L, a single start event x^s and a single end event x^e are identified for each subprocess trace. Since we allow for fragments of size one, it is possible that a subprocess consists of one or multiple events for the same activity, i.e., a loop. If a subprocess consists of one single event, the timestamps for x^s and x^e are the same. If a subprocess consists of more than one event, i.e., a loop, x^s has the timestamp of the first occurrence, and x^e has the timestamp of the last occurrence. The resulting abstracted log $f \uparrow (L)$ consists only of these events and is then again mined with a discovery algorithm.

4   Evaluation

To evaluate PFM, we have prototypically implemented the approach (see Sect. 4.1). Moreover, we conduct several experiments (see Sect. 4.2–4.5) where we follow the quality measures proposed in [2] and compare the PFM approach with the findings of [10]. To run the experiments, we use the *cpd_benchmark* repository,[1] which implements the benchmarks proposed in [2].

4.1   Implementation of the Approach

PFM is implemented in python and is publicly available.[2] PFM uses the process discovery algorithms provided by ProM accessed through cpd_benchmark. To calculate the dependency matrix, PM4Py is used [4]. Creating and ranking all possible fragments for an event log is computationally highly expensive. For event logs with a large number of events, this calculation becomes intractable on standard machines. By setting reasonable values for the `maximum_depth` parameter and `threshold`, this calculation can be constrained in order to ensure reasonable computing times. Since the maximum depth parameter directly constrains the size that a fragment can take, the quality of the resulting hierarchical process models is affected by setting a low value.

The computationally hardest part is the combination of disjoint sets to rebuild the full process. It is an instance of the maximum-weight independent set problem and, therefore, NP-hard. In the implementation, finding a good solution to the problem is approached by allowing for two approaches to solve this. For smaller datasets, dynamic programming can be used. This approach finds qualitatively better solutions but is not recommended for event logs that lead to a large dependency matrix. In this case, beam search should be used.

4.2   Experimental Setups

For the evaluation, we compare the performance of the PFM approach and the different Ranking methods. Since the initial ranking of fragments has a big impact on the resulting hierarchical process model, the different ranking methods lead to process models of different quality. We evaluate the quality of each ranking method, namely Heuristic

---

[1] https://gitlab.com/janikbenzin/cpd_benchmark.

[2] https://github.com/jhtobis/process-fragment-miner.

Ranking (HR), Bigram Ranking (BR) and Similarity Ranking (SR) in two ways. Once for the resulting root model (Root) and once as proposed in [10] by averaging over the found fragments. We compare the quality scores with the reported scores for DK-FH* (Domain Knowledge approach) and RC-FH* (random clustering approach) [10]. Since [10] does not report quality measures for the resulting root model, the DK-FH and RC-FH approaches have been re-implemented and re-measured to enable a comparison (see DK, RC in Table 2).

To get a selection of disjoint fragment sets (Step 4), the DP approach is used for the datasets BPIC12, BPIC17_f, BPIC15_1f, ChessPiece. For the other datasets (BPIC15_{2-5}), beam search is used, due to the high number of activities present in the event logs. As described in [10], we employ the Inductive Miner with 0.2 path filtering (IMf) and the Split Miner (SM) with standard settings.

4.3   Data Sets

As in [10], we evaluate the PFM approach using publicly available real-life event logs from the BPIC Challenges, including BPIC12, a filtered collection of BPIC15, and a filtered version of BPIC17. The BPIC12 and BPIC17 Datasets have 36 and 18 unique activities. Meanwhile, the BPIC15 Log is split into five sublogs, which comprise 70, 82, 62, 65, and 74 activities. The BPIC15 sets allow for a much higher number of possible subprocess fragment candidates. The logs used for this study are the filtered logs as used in [2, 10]. In addition to these logs, we add one event log "ChessPiece" which was produced with the process engine CPEE [11] and taken from a production use case. For this event log the hierarchical order was also known, to enable the use of DK-FH

4.4   Model Quality Measures

In accordance with [10], we use the five quality measures *fitness*, *precision*, *F1-Score*, *complexity*, and *size* to quantify the quality of the found process models. These measures have been proposed in [2]. To measure the quality of the root model, the abstraction function $f \uparrow$ is applied to the resulting event log, and the quality measures are calculated on the resulting event log. For the subprocess models, for each subprocess event log, the measures are calculated and then averaged.

The quality metrics of the derived subprocess models must also be interpreted in conjunction with those of the corresponding root models, as their performance and significance are contextually interdependent.

4.5   Results of Empirical Study

The findings of the experimental study are shown in Table 2. We compare our approach with the two approaches described in [10], namely RC as an unsupervised approach and DK as a supervised Domain Knowledge approach. DK and RC represent the results we achieved through a re-implementation of both approaches; RC-FH* and DK-FH* represent the results as reported in [10]. Instead of relying on a single execution as done in [10] for RC, we use the mean of 10 executions. The reason for this is the goal of better comparability by smoothing outliers, since RC is a fully randomized approach. For RC-FH*, the authors report a maximum fragment size of 10. The row labeled *IMF* reports the scores using the inductive miner [15], *SM* for the split miner [1]. *HR* describes Heuristic Ranking method, *BR* the Bigram Ranking method, and *SR* the Similarity ranking method.

Inductive and Split Miner. In combination with PFM, the IMF generally performs better than SM for the *fitness* metric. Conversely, the *precision* measure is higher for SM. The same accounts for the *F1-score*. For both root and mean metrics, the *F1-score* is higher when applying SM.

In terms of model size and complexity, SM generates smaller and less complex process models for both the root and the subprocess models. This effect is stronger for PMF than for the random clustering.

Comparison of Subprocess Means. When looking at the mean metrics over the subprocesses, the PFM approach achieves better results than RC when using SM. For BPIC12, PFM with SM matches or outperforms RC-FH* in all measures and RC in all measures but for *precision* with BR. With IMF for BPIC12, the HR and SR perform better than RC (RC-FH*). For the BPIC15_{1-5}f PFM achieves similar outcomes as RC, and in many cases achieves a better score than RC & RC-FH*.

Interestingly, for the "ChessPiece" event log generated with a process engine, PFM outperforms RC consistently. Also, the scores for the DK approach can be reached. For all other approaches, the supervised Domain Knowledge approach remains the best possible solution in terms of the quality measures.

Comparison of Root Model. When looking at the root model, PFM generally matches or improves the scores of RC, especially when using SM. For all BPIC15 sets, RC performs badly for precision when using IMF. The PFM approaches are more stable in that regard, except for SR for the Dataset BPIC15_3f. While RC underperforms for the

Table 2. Evaluation results.

Log	Alg	DAlg	Root Metrics					Mean Metrics					#SPs
			Fi	Pr	$F1$	CFC	$Size$	$\overline{Fi}$	$\overline{Pr}$	$\overline{F1}$	$\overline{CFC}$	$\overline{Size}$	
BPIC12	HR		**1.00**	0.64	0.78	10.00	24.00	**0.97**	**0.82**	**0.88**	8.00	15.00	5
	BR		**1.00**	0.75	0.86	10.00	27.00	0.94	0.78	0.84	7.83	14.17	6
	SR	IMf	0.99	0.65	0.79	11.00	24.00	0.96	**0.82**	**0.88**	**7.20**	**13.80**	5
	RC-FH*		–	–	–	–	–	**0.97**	0.78	0.86	20.00	35.00	4
	RC		0.99	**0.81**	**0.89**	**4.00**	**13.60**	0.96	0.73	0.82	15.67	25.53	3
	DK-FH*		–	–	–	–	–	0.96	0.78	0.86	20.00	36.00	4
	DK		1.00	0.82	0.90	8.00	18.00	0.98	0.76	0.85	16.33	26.67	–
	HR		0.94	0.87	0.90	10.00	22.00	0.92	**0.97**	0.94	8.00	14.40	5
	BR		0.94	0.88	0.91	16.00	30.00	0.94	0.93	0.93	**5.67**	**11.33**	6
	SR	SM	**0.95**	**1.00**	**0.98**	4.00	16.00	**0.95**	0.96	**0.95**	8.80	15.00	5
	RC-FH*		–	–	–	–	–	0.92	0.90	0.90	14.00	28.00	3
	RC		0.86	0.98	0.92	**3.50**	**11.60**	0.92	0.94	0.93	14.47	23.87	3
	DK-FH*		–	–	–	–	–	0.89	0.94	0.91	10.00	22.00	4
	DK		0.88	1.00	0.94	4.00	12.00	0.87	0.95	0.91	11.33	21.00	–

(continued)

Table 2. (*continued*)

Log	Alg	DAlg	*Fi*	*Pr*	*F1*	*CFC*	*Size*	$\overline{Fi}$	$\overline{Pr}$	$\overline{F1}$	$\overline{CFC}$	$\overline{Size}$	#*SPs*
BPIC15_1f	HR		0.95	**0.87**	**0.91**	**10.00**	**23.00**	**0.99**	0.77	0.86	20.60	34.60	5
	BR		0.95	**0.87**	**0.91**	**10.00**	**23.00**	**0.99**	0.77	0.86	20.60	34.60	5
	SR	IMf	0.97	0.80	0.87	13.00	29.00	0.98	0.77	0.86	20.00	34.00	5
	RC-FH*		–	–	–	–	–	0.97	0.84	0.88	16.00	29.00	9
	RC		**0.99**	0.35	0.52	18.30	38.00	0.96	**0.88**	**0.92**	**13.56**	**23.48**	8
	DK-FH*		–	–	–	–	–	**0.99**	0.87	0.91	9.00	19.00	15
	DK		0.99	0.73	0.84	18.00	38.00	0.99	0.92	0.95	11.75	20.12	–
	HR		0.78	**1.00**	0.88	**2.00**	**16.00**	0.91	0.98	**0.94**	9.60	24.80	5
	BR		0.78	**1.00**	0.88	**2.00**	**16.00**	0.91	0.98	**0.94**	9.60	24.80	5
	SR	SM	**0.89**	**1.00**	**0.94**	6.00	20.00	0.89	**0.99**	0.93	9.40	24.80	5
	RC-FH*		–	–	–	–	–	0.88	**0.99**	0.93	**8.00**	22.00	9
	RC		0.75	0.94	0.84	14.80	35.20	0.86	0.98	0.92	8.86	**19.36**	8
	DK-FH*		–	–	–	–	–	0.96	0.98	0.97	4.00	14.00	15
	DK		0.91	1.00	0.95	8.00	28.00	0.98	0.99	0.98	5.25	15.75	–
BPIC15_2f	HR		**0.98**	0.55	0.70	23.00	45.00	**0.97**	0.78	0.86	16.00	27.00	8
	BR		0.86	**0.81**	**0.83**	**9.00**	**32.00**	**0.97**	0.80	0.87	15.38	26.12	8
	SR	IMf	**0.98**	0.63	0.77	22.00	39.00	**0.97**	0.75	0.84	23.00	36.50	6
	RC-FH*		–	–	–	–	–	0.95	0.85	0.89	16.00	33.00	10
	RC		**0.98**	0.28	0.44	19.20	42.60	0.94	**0.89**	**0.92**	**14.34**	**25.31**	9
	DK-FH*		–	–	–	–	–	**0.97**	0.91	0.93	7.00	16.00	21
	DK		0.98	0.77	0.87	29.00	58.00	0.99	0.96	0.97	7.92	15.38	–
	HR		0.80	**1.00**	0.89	**2.00**	22.00	0.84	**0.98**	0.90	7.00	19.00	8
	BR		0.79	**1.00**	0.88	**2.00**	22.00	0.85	**0.98**	0.91	**5.75**	**17.75**	8
	SR	SM	**0.83**	**1.00**	**0.91**	**2.00**	18.00	**0.86**	**0.98**	**0.92**	9.67	24.67	6
	RC-FH*		–	–	–	–	–	0.83	0.96	0.89	11.00	26.00	10
	RC		0.70	0.97	0.81	10.80	33.40	0.80	0.97	0.87	9.28	20.21	9
	DK-FH*		–	–	–	–	–	0.94	0.99	0.97	4.00	13.00	21
	DK		0.72	0.97	0.83	12.00	42.00	0.97	0.99	0.98	3.69	11.77	–
BPIC15_3f	HR		0.97	0.66	0.78	18.00	40.00	0.95	0.83	0.88	13.29	**22.57**	7
	BR		0.93	**0.81**	**0.87**	6.00	**26.00**	0.97	0.83	0.89	13.57	22.71	7
	SR	IMf	**1.00**	0.47	0.63	29.00	52.00	**0.99**	0.76	0.86	14.71	23.29	7
	RC-FH*		–	–	–	–	–	0.94	0.87	**0.90**	16.00	33.00	8
	RC		0.98	0.59	0.73	**5.50**	**26.00**	0.93	**0.88**	**0.90**	**12.79**	23.63	7
	DK-FH*		–	–	–	–	–	0.97	0.94	0.95	6.00	15.00	17
	DK		0.99	0.64	0.78	22.00	43.00	0.99	0.96	0.97	8.80	15.90	–
	HR		0.85	**1.00**	0.92	**2.00**	**20.00**	**0.87**	**0.99**	**0.92**	5.71	**16.29**	7
	BR		**0.87**	**1.00**	**0.93**	4.00	22.00	0.85	0.98	0.91	6.57	17.14	7
	SR	SM	0.81	**1.00**	0.90	3.00	22.00	0.82	**0.99**	0.89	6.00	16.57	7
	RC-FH*		–	–	–	–	–	**0.87**	0.98	**0.92**	10.00	23.00	7
	RC		0.79	0.95	0.86	6.30	25.00	0.81	0.97	0.88	7.23	18.02	7
	DK-FH*		–	–	–	–	–	0.95	**0.99**	0.97	3.00	12.00	17
	DK		0.83	1.00	0.91	8.00	32.00	0.98	0.99	0.98	3.00	10.90	–
BPIC15_4f	HR		0.97	0.72	0.83	8.00	**26.00**	**0.97**	0.75	0.84	18.80	31.80	5
	BR		0.91	**0.88**	0.90	**5.00**	**26.00**	0.94	0.82	0.87	15.33	26.83	6
	SR	IMf	0.98	0.87	**0.92**	11.00	27.00	0.96	0.79	0.86	20.00	32.40	5
	RC-FH*		–	–	–	–	–	**0.97**	0.81	0.87	18.00	35.00	8
	RC		**0.99**	0.39	0.56	17.60	37.60	0.94	**0.86**	**0.90**	**14.44**	**25.43**	7
	DK-FH*		–	–	–	–	–	0.98	0.96	0.97	5.00	13.00	21
	DK		0.97	0.62	0.76	34.00	62.00	0.99	0.97	0.98	5.69	11.85	–
	HR		0.85	**1.00**	0.92	**0.00**	**14.00**	0.82	0.95	0.88	7.20	21.80	5
	BR		0.87	**1.00**	0.93	3.00	20.00	**0.83**	**0.99**	**0.90**	**5.17**	**17.83**	6
	SR	SM	**0.93**	0.99	**0.96**	5.00	20.00	**0.83**	0.97	0.89	7.20	21.80	5
	RC-FH*		–	–	–	–	–	**0.83**	0.98	**0.90**	8.00	24.00	8
	RC		0.80	0.98	0.88	6.10	24.30	0.80	0.97	0.87	7.06	18.38	7
	DK-FH*		–	–	–	–	–	0.95	**0.99**	0.97	2.00	11.00	21
	DK		0.72	0.98	0.83	8.00	38.00	0.96	0.99	0.98	2.00	8.85	–

(*continued*)

Table 2. (*continued*)

Log	Alg	DAlg	Fi	Pr	$F1$	CFC	$Size$	$\overline{Fi}$	$\overline{Pr}$	$\overline{F1}$	$\overline{CFC}$	$\overline{Size}$	$\#SPs$
BPIC15_1f	HR		0.95	**0.87**	**0.91**	**10.00**	**23.00**	**0.99**	0.77	0.86	20.60	34.60	5
	BR		0.95	**0.87**	**0.91**	**10.00**	**23.00**	**0.99**	0.77	0.86	20.60	34.60	5
	SR	IMf	0.97	0.80	0.87	13.00	29.00	0.98	0.77	0.86	20.00	34.00	5
	RC-FH*		–	–	–	–	–	0.97	0.84	0.88	16.00	29.00	9
	RC		**0.99**	0.35	0.52	18.30	38.00	0.96	**0.88**	**0.92**	**13.56**	**23.48**	8
	DK-FH*		–	–	–	–	–	**0.99**	0.87	0.91	9.00	19.00	15
	DK		0.99	0.73	0.84	18.00	38.00	0.99	0.92	0.95	11.75	20.12	–
	HR		0.78	**1.00**	0.88	**2.00**	**16.00**	**0.91**	0.98	**0.94**	9.60	24.80	5
	BR		0.78	**1.00**	0.88	**2.00**	**16.00**	**0.91**	0.98	**0.94**	9.60	24.80	5
	SR	SM	**0.89**	**1.00**	**0.94**	6.00	20.00	0.89	**0.99**	0.93	9.40	24.80	5
	RC-FH*		–	–	–	–	–	0.88	**0.99**	0.93	**8.00**	22.00	9
	RC		0.75	0.94	0.84	14.80	35.20	0.86	0.98	0.92	8.86	**19.36**	8
	DK-FH*		–	–	–	–	–	0.96	0.98	0.97	4.00	14.00	15
	DK		0.91	1.00	0.95	8.00	28.00	0.98	0.99	0.98	5.25	15.75	–
BPIC15_2f	HR		**0.98**	0.55	0.70	23.00	45.00	**0.97**	0.78	0.86	16.00	27.00	8
	BR		0.86	**0.81**	**0.83**	**9.00**	**32.00**	**0.97**	0.80	0.87	15.38	26.12	8
	SR	IMf	**0.98**	0.63	0.77	22.00	39.00	**0.97**	0.75	0.84	23.00	36.50	6
	RC-FH*		–	–	–	–	–	0.95	0.85	0.89	16.00	33.00	10
	RC		**0.98**	0.28	0.44	19.20	42.60	0.94	**0.89**	**0.92**	**14.34**	**25.31**	9
	DK-FH*		–	–	–	–	–	**0.97**	0.91	0.93	7.00	16.00	21
	DK		0.98	0.77	0.87	29.00	58.00	0.99	0.96	0.97	7.92	15.38	–
	HR		0.80	**1.00**	0.89	**2.00**	22.00	0.84	**0.98**	0.90	7.00	19.00	8
	BR		0.79	**1.00**	0.88	**2.00**	22.00	0.85	**0.98**	0.91	**5.75**	**17.75**	8
	SR	SM	**0.83**	**1.00**	**0.91**	**2.00**	18.00	0.86	**0.98**	**0.92**	9.67	24.67	6
	RC-FH*		–	–	–	–	–	0.83	0.96	0.89	11.00	26.00	10
	RC		0.70	0.97	0.81	10.80	33.40	0.80	0.97	0.87	9.28	20.21	9
	DK-FH*		–	–	–	–	–	0.94	0.99	0.97	4.00	13.00	21
	DK		0.72	0.97	0.83	12.00	42.00	0.97	0.99	0.98	3.69	11.77	–
BPIC15_3f	HR		0.97	0.66	0.78	18.00	40.00	0.95	0.83	0.88	13.29	**22.57**	7
	BR		0.93	**0.81**	**0.87**	6.00	**26.00**	0.97	0.83	0.89	13.57	22.71	7
	SR	IMf	**1.00**	0.47	0.63	29.00	52.00	**0.99**	0.76	0.86	14.71	23.29	7
	RC-FH*		–	–	–	–	–	0.94	0.87	**0.90**	16.00	33.00	8
	RC		0.98	0.59	0.73	**5.50**	**26.00**	0.93	**0.88**	**0.90**	**12.79**	23.63	7
	DK-FH*		–	–	–	–	–	0.97	0.94	0.95	6.00	15.00	17
	DK		0.99	0.64	0.78	22.00	43.00	0.99	0.96	0.97	8.80	15.90	–
	HR		0.85	**1.00**	0.92	**2.00**	**20.00**	0.87	**0.99**	0.92	**5.71**	**16.29**	7
	BR		**0.87**	**1.00**	**0.93**	4.00	22.00	0.85	0.98	0.91	6.57	17.14	7
	SR	SM	0.81	**1.00**	0.90	3.00	22.00	0.82	**0.99**	0.89	6.00	16.57	7
	RC-FH*		–	–	–	–	–	**0.87**	0.98	**0.92**	10.00	23.00	7
	RC		0.79	0.95	0.86	6.30	25.00	0.81	0.97	0.88	7.23	18.02	7
	DK-FH*		–	–	–	–	–	0.95	**0.99**	0.97	3.00	12.00	17
	DK		0.83	1.00	0.91	8.00	32.00	0.98	0.99	0.98	3.00	10.90	–
BPIC15_4f	HR		0.97	0.72	0.83	8.00	**26.00**	**0.97**	0.75	0.84	18.80	31.80	5
	BR		0.91	**0.88**	0.90	**5.00**	**26.00**	0.94	0.82	0.87	15.33	26.83	6
	SR	IMf	0.98	0.87	**0.92**	11.00	27.00	0.96	0.79	0.86	20.00	32.40	5
	RC-FH*		–	–	–	–	–	**0.97**	0.81	0.87	18.00	35.00	8
	RC		**0.99**	0.39	0.56	17.60	37.60	0.94	**0.86**	**0.90**	**14.44**	**25.43**	7
	DK-FH*		–	–	–	–	–	0.98	0.96	0.97	5.00	13.00	21
	DK		0.97	0.62	0.76	34.00	62.00	0.99	0.97	0.98	5.69	11.85	–
	HR		0.85	**1.00**	0.92	**0.00**	14.00	0.82	0.95	0.88	7.20	21.80	5
	BR		0.87	**1.00**	0.93	3.00	20.00	**0.83**	**0.99**	0.90	**5.17**	**17.83**	6
	SR	SM	**0.93**	0.99	**0.96**	5.00	20.00	**0.83**	0.97	0.89	7.20	21.80	5
	RC-FH*		–	–	–	–	–	**0.83**	0.98	**0.90**	8.00	24.00	8
	RC		0.80	0.98	0.88	6.10	24.30	0.80	0.97	0.87	7.06	18.38	7
	DK-FH*		–	–	–	–	–	0.95	**0.99**	0.97	2.00	11.00	21
	DK		0.72	0.98	0.83	8.00	38.00	0.96	0.99	0.98	2.00	8.85	–

BPIC datasets, it performs very well on the ChessPiece dataset. For the Root Metrics, DK is often outperformed. Only in a few cases, such as for BPIC15_1f, DK strikes the best Fitness score alone.

Comparison of Different Ranking Models. Considering the different ranking methods, HR, BR, and SR, no clear-cut best approach can be identified. SR performs very well, yet has certain steep drops in precision, e.g., for the "ChessPiece" dataset. Among all datasets and both root and mean metric, the BR approach is the most stable and reaches the best values the most. It additionally does not underperform for any of the datasets. The risk of harsh outliers for BR is smaller than for the other two ranking approaches. Most importantly, the BR performs consistently well for both root and mean metrics on the same dataset.

Table 2 shows that the PFM approach can achieve good outcomes in mining hierarchical process models. Looking at the root and mean metrics together, we can see that the PFM approaches perform more uniformly for the two metrics than the random approach. Especially for the larger Datasets BPIC15_{1-5}f in combination with IMF, the RC approach drops in performance for *precision*. Meanwhile, the PFM approach with the BR ranking method and SM performs stable on both performance metrics and is the most consistent of the unsupervised approaches. While the supervised approach DK often performs best, in certain settings, e.g., for the "ChessPiece" dataset, it can be outperformed by the unsupervised PFM approach. DK also reaches comparably low scores for the root model on the BPIC15_{1-5}f datasets. Here, the PFM shows its strength for *precision* in combination with SM.

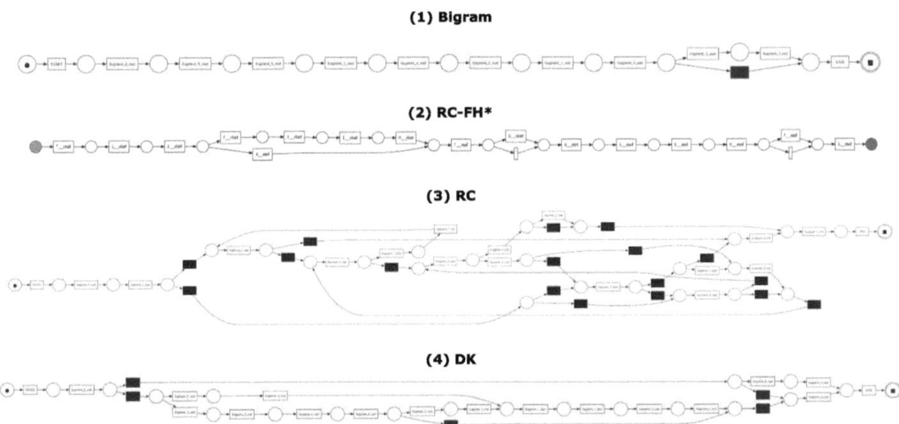

Fig. 2. Comparison of bigram (1), RC-FH* (2), RC (3), and DK (4) on BPIC15_1f data set with SM, where (2) is taken from [10].

5   Discussion

Abstracting flat event logs into more hierarchical ones brings positive effects in terms of understandability for a user. Yet, it is unclear how the simplification achieved through a hierarchical process model can be measured best, or how hierarchical process models could be compared to flat ones [9]. While the measures defined in [2] mark important quality benchmarks for process mining, it can be seen that they are not well suited for hierarchical process mining. As shown in [10], comparing flat approaches with a hierarchical modeling approach can lead to big improvements for these quality measures, even when using random clustering (RC). The measures *fitness*, *precision*, and *F1-score* disregard the semantics in the abstracted process models. While this is acceptable for flat process models mined on complete event logs, for subsets of an event log, this measure leads to confusion. The mean metric on subprocesses can give no good insight into the found process model since noisy events are discarded; therefore, we also measured the root metric in this work and consider root and mean metrics both separately, and interdependently. To this end, an approach to measure the simplicity and understandability of a hierarchical process model is both missing and needed. It cannot be quantified by the current quality measures whether the hierarchical process models found by any approach are better understood by domain experts than flat approaches. Figure 2 presents the found root models for BPIC15_1f with Bigram Ranking (1), RC-FH*(2), RC(3), and DK(4). We can see that PFM with the Bigram Ranking (1) leads to a clean, sequential process model, which allows for the exclusion of Fragment_3. Meanwhile, the random approaches RC-FH* and RC lead to process models in which the subprocesses are heavily interlinked and no structure can be identified. Yet, RC performs similarly well on the quality measures for this data set, as the other approaches (see Table 2). The DK approach and the Bigram ranking provide both good and well-structured root models.

Future work on hierarchical process models should focus on finding appropriate quality measures to compare the found models for both the root and the subprocess models in combination. These measures should also strive to consider the semantics of a process model.

6   Conclusion and Outlook

In this work, we presented PFM, an unsupervised hierarchical process mining approach based on the dependency matrix generated by the HeuristicsMiner [15]. At the core of the approach is the creation and ranking of subtraces from an event log. We developed and tested three different ranking methods for subtraces. We show that the identification of hierarchical models without any additional information, such as context data or labeling, is possible and can lead to comparable outcomes as supervised approaches. To do so, the PFM approach was evaluated against existing supervised and unsupervised approaches by applying known process mining quality metrics on the mined subprocess models and the identified root models. We find that PFM works best and most consistently over different datasets when using it in combination with the Split Miner and the Bigram Ranking method. The source code for PFM is available.

In future work, the PFM approach should be integrated into a software tool, which enables users and domain experts to iteratively analyse and define hierarchies in processes in an intertwined way. This will help bridge the typical process mining workflow from preprocessing to mining & analysis [3]. This work offers different directions to further improve the performance of PFM. Through a more intertwined approach of building subprocess fragments and ranking them, the computational overhead could be reduced by focusing on only computing higher-ranked fragments. Formulating the recombination problem as a combinatorial optimization problem is also an interesting research direction. With PFM, we present an unsupervised hierarchical process mining approach, which can be applied to any event log without the need for specific log pre-processing. It can be used to create a meaningful overview of a process at the beginning of a process mining and optimization project. PFM enables domain experts to quickly get a concise overview of a process.

Acknowledgments. This work was funded by the Deutsche Forschungsgemeinschaft (DFG, German Research Foundation) – GRK2201 – Projektnummer - 277991500.

Disclosure of Interests. The authors have no competing interests to declare that are relevant to the content of this article.

References

1. Augusto, A., Conforti, R., Dumas, M., La Rosa, M., Polyvyanyy, A.: Split miner: automated discovery of accurate and simple business process models from event logs. Knowl. Inf. Syst. **59**(2), 251–284 (2019)
2. Augusto, A., et al.: Automated discovery of process models from event logs: review and benchmark. IEEE Trans. Knowl. Data Eng. **31**(4), 686–705 (2019)
3. Beerepoot, I., et al.: The biggest business process management problems to solve before we die. Comput. Ind. **146**, 103837 (2023)
4. Berti, A., van Zelst, S., Schuster, D.: Pm4py: a process mining library for python. Softw. Impacts **17**, 100556 (2023)
5. Chebil, K., Khemakhem, M.: A dynamic programming algorithm for the knapsack problem with setup. Comput. Oper. Res. **64**, 40–50 (2015)
6. Garey, M.R., Johnson, D.S.: Computers and Intractability: A Guide to the Theory of NP-Completeness. W.H. Freeman and Company (1979)
7. Kellerer, H., Pferschy, U., Pisinger, D.: Knapsack Problems. Springer (2004)
8. Koninck, P.D., vanden Broucke, S., Weerdt, J.D.: act2vec, trace2vec, log2vec, and model2vec: representation learning for business processes. In: Business Process Management, pp. 305–321 (2018)
9. Leemans, S.J., Goel, K., Van Zelst, S.J.: Using multi-level information in hierarchical process mining: balancing behavioural quality and model complexity. In: Process, pp. 137–144 (2020)
10. Lu, X., Gal, A., Reijers, H.A.: Discovering hierarchical processes using flexible activity trees for event abstraction. In: Process Mining, pp. 145–152 (2020)
11. Mangler, J., Rinderle-Ma, S.: CPEE-cloud process exection engine. In: Business Process Management Demos, pp. 51–55 (2014)
12. Mendling, J., Reijers, H.A., van der Aalst, W.M.P.: Seven process modeling guidelines (7PMG). Inf. Softw. Technol. **52**(2), 127–136 (2010)
13. Tax, N., Dalmas, B., Sidorova, N., van der Aalst, W.M.P., Norre, S.: Interest-driven discovery of local process models. Inf. Syst. **77**, 105–117 (2018)

14. Tax, N., Sidorova, N., Haakma, R., van der Aalst, W.M.P.: Mining local process models. J. Innov. Digit. Ecosyst. **3**(2), 183–196 (2016)
15. Weijters, A.J., van Der Aalst, W.M., De Medeiros, A.A.: Process mining with the HeuristicsMiner algorithm. Technische Universiteit Eindhoven (2006)
16. van Zelst, S.J., Mannhardt, F., de Leoni, M., Koschmider, A.: Event abstraction in process mining: literature review and taxonomy. Granular Comput. **6**(3), 719–736 (2021)

BPMN Patterns for Process Variability

Philipp Hehnle[(✉)][iD] and Manfred Reichert[iD]

Institute of Databases and Information Systems, Ulm University, Ulm, Germany
`{philipp.hehnle,manfred.reichert}@uni-ulm.de`

Abstract. Frequently, variants of the same business process are run in different organisations. Approaches have been proposed that allow managing process variants and reusing process models, i.e. changes can be applied centrally instead of applying them to each process variant. However, these approaches often extend modelling notations requiring proprietary tools. Therefore, we present modelling patterns for different types of variability in processes as solutions for this recurring problem by solely relying on standard BPMN 2.0, i.e. common BPMN 2.0 modelling tools and process engines can be used. As part of the evaluation, two processes encompassing variability were implemented and executed on two process engines demonstrating the technical soundness of the patterns. In addition, results from expert interviews indicate that the patterns are useful, relevant, and easy to use.

Keywords: Business Process Management · Process Configuration · Process Variability · Software Reuse · Process Family

1 Introduction

Municipalities frequently operate similar business processes with slight differences, resulting in variants of a business process [14, 19, 20]. When maintaining each process variant separately and requirements change (e.g. due to legal requirements), the changes need to be applied to each process variant, which is time-consuming and error-prone [17]. In contrast, capturing all process variants in one process model by connecting the variants using gateways results in large process models, which are hard to understand and maintain [17]. Therefore, the approaches of *customisable process models* have emerged [20]. Applying transformations to a customisable process model and thereby creating a process variant is referred to as *deriving* a process variant [14, 15, 20]. The approaches of customisable process models often use special elements or symbols to express variability, which requires proprietary modelling tools and tools to derive process variants.

Patterns are reusable solutions to frequently recurring problems [1]. As with object-oriented software engineering, where a variety of design patterns can be adopted to reuse successful software architectures [11], we propose modelling patterns to allow for process variability based on the BPMN 2.0 modelling notation [24]. BPMN 2.0 is chosen as basis for our patterns as we agree with other researchers that BPMN is the de-facto industry standard [8, 9, 33]. As the proposed modelling patterns solely rely on BPMN, common BPMN-based Workflow Management Systems (WfMS) can be used to run the derived process variants.

© The Author(s), under exclusive license to Springer Nature Switzerland AG 2026
C. Cappiello et al. (Eds.): CoopIS 2025, LNCS 15535, pp. 351–369, 2026.
https://doi.org/10.1007/978-3-032-15538-2_20

1.1 Problem Statement

Previous approaches of customisable process models [20] extend process modelling notations to express variability, which prevents the use of common modelling tools. Furthermore, special tools to derive process variants and/or special WfMSs are required to execute process variants. In addition, some approaches present concepts only and do not provide any tools, which entails that process variants cannot be automatically derived or executed.

1.2 Contribution

As opposed to the approaches of customisable process models [20], this paper allows for process variability by relying only on standard elements of BPMN 2.0. BPMN elements are identified whose behaviour varies in different organisations resulting in process variants. Then, modelling patterns are presented describing how to model processes to enable variability for the identified BPMN elements, which allows employing common modelling tools for process design and common WfMS for process execution.

1.3 Outline

Section 2 provides an overview about approaches dealing with process variability and presents process patterns for common modelling challenges. In Sect. 3, the research method is outlined. The patterns for process variability are introduced in Sect. 4. In Sect. 5, the patterns are evaluated. In a case study, two business processes are implemented and executed in two WfMSs demonstrating the technical practicability of the patterns. Furthermore, the results of expert interviews indicate that the patterns are useful, relevant, and easy to use. Section 6 concludes the paper with a summary and an outlook.

2 Related Work

This section presents approaches for process variant management and process patterns providing solutions to recurring challenges of business processes.

2.1 Process Variability

The location in a customisable process model at which elements are added or removed is called *variation point* [20].

The authors in [29] apply the concept of *Hiding and Blocking* to customisable process models. When deriving process variants, activities may be blocked, i.e. the path cannot be taken any more at runtime, or may be hidden, i.e. at runtime they are skipped. New languages were designed applying Hiding and Blocking. Configurable EPC (C-EPC) is an extension of EPC and Configurable YAWL (C-YAWL) is an extension of YAWL [13,29]. Furthermore, splits (AND/OR) may be restricted, e.g. an OR-split can be restricted to an AND-split. There is also an extension for BPMN called *C-BPMN* applying Hiding and Blocking [33].

Besides removing elements, *Provop* [15–17] allows adding, moving, and modifying elements in a process model. In a base process model, adjustment points (i.e. variation points) are specified at which change operations can be applied.

Similar to Provop, the approach *ABIS* defines variable regions (i.e. variation points) in a process model at which process fragments can be inserted [31]. As opposed to Provop, deleting elements of a process model is not supported.

In *Variant-rich business processes*, stereotypes known from UML are used to identify variable elements (i.e. variation points) in BPMN 1.0 process models [26]. As BPMN 1.0 is used, the process models are not executable and need to be implemented in Java. The variation points can be resolved exploiting mechanisms for Java known from software product line engineering, e.g. gateways and events can be configured via parameters read by Java from configuration files.

The *BPMN** [28] approach also extends BPMN to mark variation points (e.g. an activity). To derive a process variant the tool presented in [10] can be used. During derivation, one or more implementations may be selected for a variation point. When selecting multiple implementations, a gateway is used to join them.

The *ADOM* approach uses reference process models containing variation points (e.g. activities, events, and gateways), which are annotated with cardinalities (i.e. lower and upper boundary) [3]. During derivation, a variation point element can be instantiated as often as the corresponding cardinalities allow. If an element is instantiated multiple times, the resulting instances are connected via gateways and configured/specialised accordingly. Due to extensive manual work (i.e. configuration), this approach is not suitable for automatic derivation.

BPMNext [7] is an approach that uses BPMN to create process models in which elements can be marked as variation points (e.g. activities). Implementations of these variation points are modelled as own process models and replace the variation points elements during process variant derivation.

To enable process variability on the implementation level, i.e. allow for the selection of implementations for an activity (e.g. user task or service task), tools and concepts from software product line engineering can be adopted [18, 19].

In summary, there are approaches for control flow variability and implementation variability of processes. However, the approaches require proprietary tools. This work aims at providing BPMN process patterns for variability, which allow for the use of common modelling tools and unmodified WfMS for execution.

2.2 Process Patterns

While the approaches in Sect. 2.1 aim for reusability of process models by making them customisable, the approach presented in [22] introduces quality process fragments (which might also be considered process patterns), which can be reused, i.e. the fragments can be combined and included at arbitrary positions in process models to check the quality of information before processing them.

In [21], time patterns are presented. Using these patterns, it becomes possible to specify minimal and maximal time intervals between activities, durations for a set of activities or an entire business process, and earliest and latest start and completion dates of activities or business processes to name a few examples. Furthermore, a pattern is presented that introduces variability in business processes based on time. For instance, a special time-dependent gateway can be used to determine the outgoing branch based on the current time.

In [30], process patterns are deduced as solutions for recurring challenges in evolving and adapting process models at runtime. Two kinds of patterns are distinguished. 1) *Adaption patterns* apply changes to process models and transform the process model to a variant. 2) *Patterns for changes in predefined regions* allow deferring decisions from build time to runtime by specifying variable regions at build time whose implementation may be determined at runtime. Examples for the first kind of patterns are inserting, deleting, and moving process fragments in a process model. An example for the second kind of pattern is a placeholder activity, which may be substituted at runtime by a concrete implementation.

In [34], process patterns including the ones from [30] are consolidated and put into a hierarchy depicting the relations between the patterns, e.g. which pattern reuses another pattern. The approach proposes to use rules at runtime to automatically select a specific adaption pattern for a variable region based on context information. However, the approach also allows users to select the adaption pattern.

The authors in [4] investigated to what extent process modelling tools can detect process anti-patterns in terms of comprehensibility, semantics, and the misuse of BPMN elements.

To mitigate the environmental impact of business processes, green business process patterns are presented [2,23] including compensation activities (e.g. donation for an environmental organisation) and outsourcing (i.e. performing an activity more efficiently by a specialised organisation). Finally, a method is presented to deduce green business process patterns from existing patterns [23].

BPMN process models may be unnecessary complex when there are redundant or repetitive paths. In [25], an algorithm and a process pattern repository are presented which allow automatically finding and replacing complex patterns with simple behaviour-preserving patterns from the repository.

3   Research Method

Goal of this paper is to provide BPMN modelling patterns for a set of variation points enabling variability in process models. In the following, it is described how the BPMN elements are identified that may constitute a variation point and for which a modelling pattern is introduced.

3.1   Selection Criteria

This paper considers elements of BPMN 2.0 as variation points whose behaviour may be changed, i.e. the implementation is selectable. Removing paths of a process (i.e. sequence flows) as proposed in [13,29] constitutes complementary work and is out of scope of this paper.

3.2 Sources of Data and Data Collection

Expert interviews with German municipalities, in which we discussed variations in municipal business processes [19], and literature serve as sources for variation point identification. The interview notes can be found on GitHub[1].

3.3 Variation Point Identification Procedure

In order to identify elements that may constitute a variation point, the business processes are analysed that have been discussed during our interviews with German municipalities. Then, literature is reviewed to confirm that the selected elements act as variation points in other contexts as well. As patterns are reusable solutions to frequently recurring problems [1], patterns are only deduced for elements that are identified as variation points by at least three other researchers.

4 Process Variability Patterns

First, this section identifies the elements of BPMN 2.0 that may constitute a variation point. Then, modelling patterns are collected and described that serve as a blueprint for modelling variability for the identified variation points. While [30] proposes patterns and features to also enable process variability at runtime, which requires WfMSs to support the former, this work aims at enabling variability at deployment time by relying solely on BPMN 2.0 and therefore allowing for the use of common unmodified WfMSs. When deriving a process variant, for each variation point a behaviour can be selected to which we refer as *implementation* (e.g. type of an event).

4.1 Variation Point Identification

Figure 1 depicts the BPMN elements as legend that are used throughout this work to illustrate processes. Furthermore, three dots represent a placeholder for an arbitrary number of elements that are omitted for clarity, whereas a question mark denotes a BPMN element as a variation point.

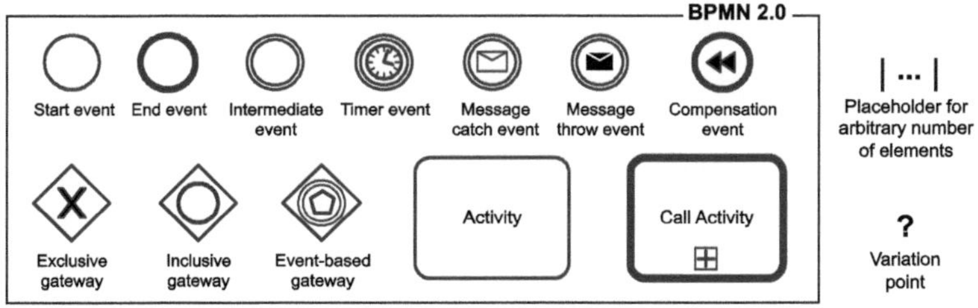

Fig. 1. Process Model Legend.

---

[1] https://github.com/hehnle/interviews-digitisation-in-german-municipalities.

During the interviews, the experts described Examples 1 and 2 as illustrations for business processes that vary among municipalities. Based on these processes, BPMN elements that may constitute variation points are deduced.

> **Example 1** In many German municipalities, for a fee, craftspersons are entitled to apply for a special parking permit, which grants them the right to park their vehicle in the urban area without having to pay for each stop, which is useful as they often visit multiple customers a day carrying heavy tools. This parking permit is valid for a specific period of time after which the craftsperson is required to pay the fee again. In some municipalities, the parking permit is a subscription model, i.e. when the parking permit expires the fee is automatically collected and the new parking permit is reissued. In other municipalities, the craftsperson needs to request a new the parking permit. Furthermore, in some municipalities the craftsperson gets reminded before the parking permit expires, whereas others do not send notifications. Figure 2 shows the *parking permit renewal* process.

In Fig. 2, Activity `Remind of renewal` (labelled with a question mark) is a variation point as there are different implementations (e.g. e-mail reminder, no reminder). Furthermore, in a subscription model, Event `Parking permit renewed` is a timer, whereas Event `Parking permit renewal declined` is a message event (both labelled with a question mark), i.e. after the parking permit expires the timer event is triggered and a new parking permit is issued if the craftsperson does not send a message before expiration. In contrast, when the applicant needs to actively request the renewal of the parking permit, the event types are reversed. Thus, activities and events may constitute variation points.

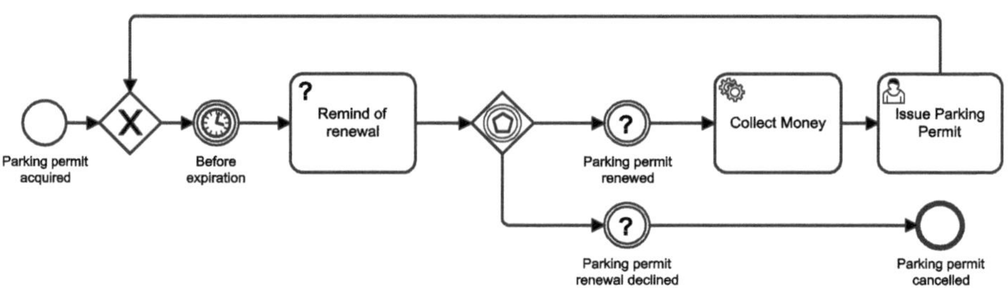

Fig. 2. Parking Permit Renewal Business Process.

> **Example 2** While generally in municipalities the direct supervisor of the employee needs to approve a travel request, in some municipalities another manager/mayor needs to approve the travel if an overnight stay is included or the travel destination is outside the state. Figure 3 shows an extract of the *travel request* process. At the start, it is determined whether the direct supervisor and/or another manager need to check the travel request.

As Example 2 outlines, gateway Check type can have different implementations (labelled with a question mark), e.g. a regular check is always required (i.e. by supervisor) and depending on the travel destination and the number of overnight stays a special check (i.e. another manager or mayor) is required.

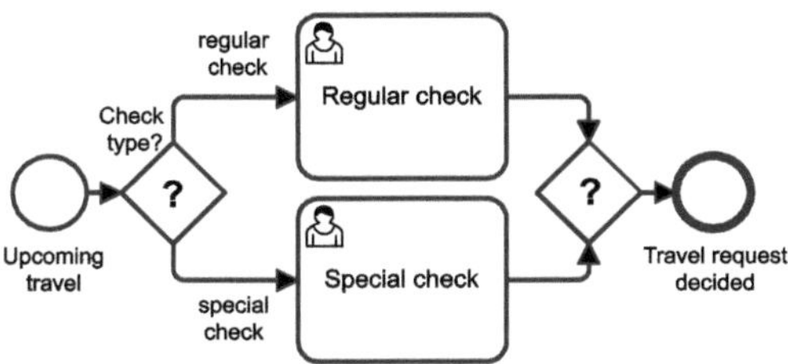

Fig. 3. Travel Request Business Process.

Investigating Examples 1 and 2, the following three BPMN elements have been identified as possible variation points: events, activities, and gateways. Reviewing literature revealed that other researcher also identified activities [7,26,28], events [3,26,31] and gateways [3,13,26,33] as variation points. As opposed to related work, events shall not only be configured, e.g. the duration of a timer event is configured, but also the type of the event shall be specified, e.g. timer event, message event. Pools and Lanes (i.e. roles) are identified as variation points in literature as well [7,31]. However, during our research we could not confirm the need for variable roles. Consequently, the aforementioned elements of BPMN 2.0 (events, activities, gateways) are selected as variation points for which modelling patterns are described.

4.2   BPMN Patterns to Model Process Variability

In the following, five patterns for process variability are described supporting the identified variation points. Three patterns cover events as one pattern cannot introduce variability to start events, intermediate events, and end events. In line with [2,30], each pattern has a name, a description, and a scenario describing a use case of the pattern. Furthermore, for each pattern the problem is stated, the solution is sketched, and related patterns are named. Besides, for each pattern, the literature referencing the corresponding variation point on which the pattern is based is cited. Each solution has the same structure. A process model containing an element that shall constitute a variation point is considered the *Core Process (CP)* which is transformed to *CP'*. In addition, for each implementation of the variation point a *supporting process model (SP)* is created. Depending on the selected implementation (i.e. desired behaviour), the corresponding supporting process together with the transformed *CP'* is deployed to a WfMS.

Note that the presented approach assumes that the respective processes have been modelled and their variation points have been identified, e.g. by conducting collaborative modelling workshops. Variation points may be marked with question marks (as

Table 1. Variability Pattern VP1: Variable Start Event Type

Variability Pattern VP1: Variable Start Event Type
Description The start event is a variation point in that its type is variable. The type of the start event can be selected at deployment time.
Scenario A newsletter process of a company (including drafting, proofreading, and sending the newsletter) might be started regularly (i.e. timer event) or on demand (i.e. message event).
Problem There are multiple variants of the same process which have different types of start events.
Solution The core process CP whose start event shall be a variation point (labelled with a question mark) is transformed to CP' by replacing the start event with a message catch event. Note that the core process may have an arbitrary number of further process elements (e.g. activities, gateways, events) depicted as three dots, which remain as they are during the transformation. For each process variant, a supporting process (cf. SP1 and SP2) is created comprising a start and an end event. The start event has the desired implementation of the variation point for this specific process variant, i.e. the desired start event type (e.g. timer event). The end event of the supporting process is a message throw event that correlates with the start event of the CP'. The transformed core process CP' and the supporting process are deployed together. They can be started by triggering the start event of the supporting process which, in turn, starts CP'. Two examples are shown. SP1 has a message catch start event. SP2 has a timer start event. Depending on what implementation for the variation point is chosen (i.e. timer or message), CP' is deployed together with either SP1 or SP2. 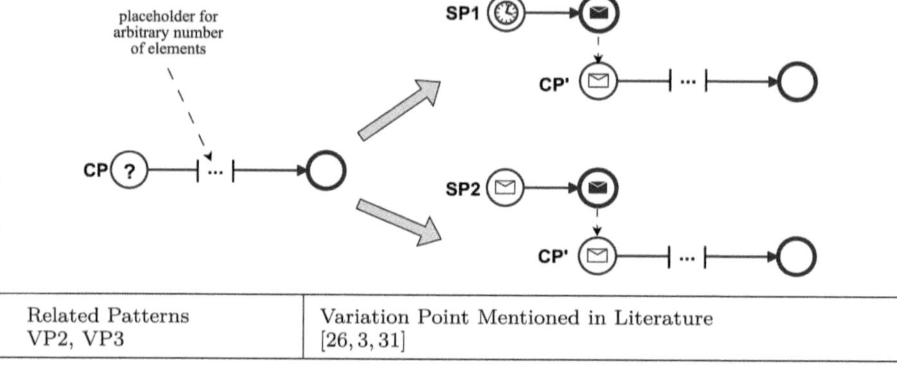

Related Patterns VP2, VP3	Variation Point Mentioned in Literature [26, 3, 31]

suggested in this work) in the process models, which serve as a starting point for applying the proposed patterns. While the question marks are not part of the BPMN standard, after applying the proposed patterns, the process models are schema-compliant, which allows them to be executed.

Variability Pattern VP1 is described by Table 1 and is applied when the type of the start event of a process is variable. A process might be triggered, for example, by a timer or by a message. To apply the pattern, the core process *CP* which contains a variable start event is transformed to *CP'* by replacing the variation point start event with a message start event. Furthermore, for each process variant, a supporting process is modelled containing a start event of the type which is desired for this variant. To trigger the *CP'*, the start event of the supporting process is triggered according to its type. Then the supporting process correlates the message start event of *CP'*. Variability Pattern VP1 is related to patterns VP2 and VP3 covering variable intermediate/end events.

Table 2 shows Variability Pattern VP2. A process may have an intermediate event which constitutes a variation point. The variable intermediate event may, for example, be a timer event or a message catch event. To apply the pattern, the core process *CP* which contains a variable intermediate event is transformed to *CP'* by replacing the latter with a message throw and a message catch event. For each process variant, a supporting process is created which is triggered by the message throw event of CP' and which contains an intermediate event of the type which is desired for this specific process variant. Afterwards, the supporting process correlates the message catch event of *CP'* to resume *CP'*.

Variability Pattern VP3 is introduced in Table 3. An end event of a process may be variable. The end event may, for example, be a message throw event or a compensate event. To apply the pattern, the core process *CP* containing a variable end event is transformed to *CP'* by replacing the end event with a message end event. For each process variant, a supporting process is created that has a message start event, which is correlated by the message end event of *CP'* and has an end event of the desired type of this specific process variant.

Variability Pattern VP4 is illustrated in Table 4. The type of an activity may be variable, e.g. a user task or a service task. To apply the pattern, the core process *CP* containing the variable activity is transformed to *CP'* by replacing the variable activity with a call activity. For each process variant, a supporting process is created which is called by the call activity of *CP'*. The supporting process contains an activity with the desired type of the process variant, e.g. user task or service task. After the supporting process has completed, *CP'* resumes.

Table 2. Variability Pattern VP2: Variable Intermediate Event Type

Variability Pattern VP2: Variable Intermediate Event Type
Description An intermediate event is a variation point in that its type is variable. The type of the intermediate event can be selected at deployment time.
Scenario On the one hand, the special parking permit for craftspersons can be a subscription model. When the parking permit expires, a timer event triggers the renewal process which collects the money and issues a new parking permit. On the other hand, when a parking permit expires, the craftsperson may have to send a message to initiate the renewal.
Problem There are multiple variants of the same process having varying intermediate event types.
Solution The core process CP whose intermediate event shall be a variation point (labelled with a question mark) is transformed to CP' by replacing the intermediate event with a message throw event and a message catch event. For each process variant, a supporting process is created comprising a message start, an intermediate event with the desired type of the variation point for this specific process variant, and a message end event. The start event of the supporting process is triggered by CP'. The supporting process pauses until the intermediate event is triggered. Then the end event triggers CP' so that the latter continues. The core process and the supporting process are deployed together. In the following, two examples are shown. Supporting process SP1 has an intermediate timer event. Supporting process SP2 has an intermediate message catch event. Depending on what implementation for the variation point is chosen (i.e. timer or message), CP' is deployed together with either SP1 or SP2. 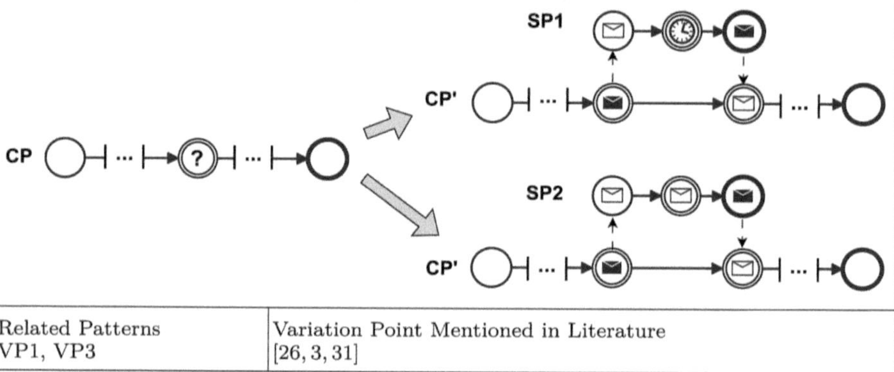

| Related Patterns
VP1, VP3 | Variation Point Mentioned in Literature
[26, 3, 31] |

Table 5 shows Variability Pattern VP5. The type of a gateway in a process may be variable, i.e. the gateway may be inclusive, exclusive, or parallel. To apply the pattern, the core process *CP* containing the variable gateway is transformed to *CP'* by replacing the variable gateway with a call activity and an inclusive gateway. For each process variant, a supporting process is created that can be invoked by the call activity of *CP'* and that contains a service task whose output data is used by the gateway of *CP'* to determine the outgoing sequence flows. Depending on the implementation of the service task, one, multiple, or all sequence flows can be taken equating to an exclusive, inclusive, and parallel gateway, respectively. VP5 uses VP4 as it exploits a call activity to exchange the implementation logic determining the outgoing sequence flow.

Table 3. Variability Pattern VP3: Variable End Event Type

Variability Pattern VP3: Variable End Event Type
Description The end event is a variation point in that its type is variable. The type of the end event can be selected at deployment time.
Scenario Consider the example of the special parking permit for craftspersons process. The craftsperson applies for a parking permit. In one variant of the process, the applicant pays the fee immediately after applying. When the application is checked and rejected the end event needs to be a compensation event that reimburses the fee to the applicant. In another variant of the process in which the applicant does not pay the fee immediately, the end event after rejecting the application may simply be a message event notifying the applicant of the rejection.
Problem There are multiple variants of the same process that have an end event whose type can differ.
Solution The core process CP whose end event shall be a variation point (labelled with a question mark) is transformed to CP' by replacing the end event with a message end event. For each process variant, a supporting process is created comprising a message start event and an end event with the desired type of the variation point for this specific process variant. When a process instance of CP' reaches the end event the supporting process is triggered via message correlation. Then, the supporting process ends with the desired end event type of the process variant. The core process and the supporting process are deployed together. In the following, two examples are shown. Supporting process SP1 has a message end event. Supporting process SP2 has a compensation end event. Depending on what implementation for the variation point is chosen (i.e. message or compensation), CP' is deployed together with either SP1 or SP2.

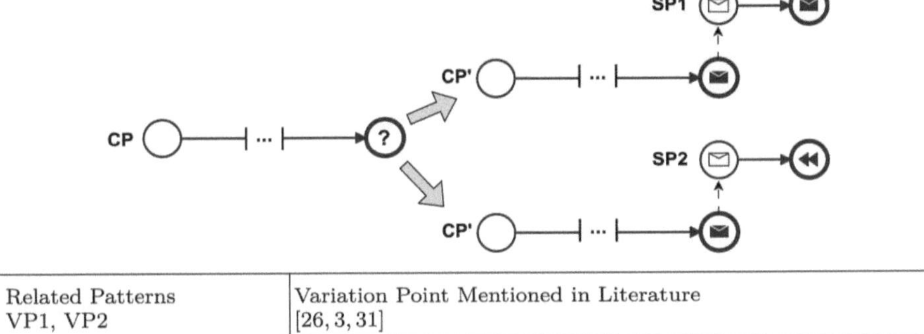

Related Patterns	Variation Point Mentioned in Literature
VP1, VP2	[26, 3, 31]

5   Evaluation

This section discloses limitations of the presented patterns, evaluates them in a case study and in expert interviews, and discusses threats to validity.

5.1   Limitations

There are mainly four limitations: *L1)* Monitoring business processes using the presented patterns might be impacted as multiple processes need to be monitored (i.e. core process plus supporting processes). Furthermore, *L2)* the expressiveness of the process models might be reduced, when parts of the process are contained in supporting

Table 4. Variability Pattern VP4: Variable Activity Type

Variability Pattern VP4: Variable Activity Type
Description The type of an activity in a process is a variation point. At deployment time the type of the activity is specified, e.g. user task, service task.
Scenario Consider the example of the special parking permit for craftsperson process. After a craftsperson has applied for a parking permit, the application needs to be checked. In one process variant, the application is checked automatically, i.e. a service task is used. In another process variant, the application is checked by a municipal clerk, i.e. a user task is used.
Problem There are multiple variants of the same process that have an activity whose type can differ.
Solution The core process CP containing an activity which is a variation point (labelled with a question mark) is transformed to CP' by replacing the variation point activity with a call activity. For each process variant, a supporting process is created comprising an activity with the desired type of the variation point for this specific process variant (e.g. user task, service task). When a process instance of CP' reaches the call activity the supporting process is called. Then, the supporting process executes the activity that implements the variation point. In the following, one examples is shown. Supporting process SP1 contains a user task. There can be further supporting processes containing service tasks. If the variation point activity of CP shall be implemented as a user task, CP' and SP1 are deployed together. Otherwise, CP' is deployed with a different supporting process. 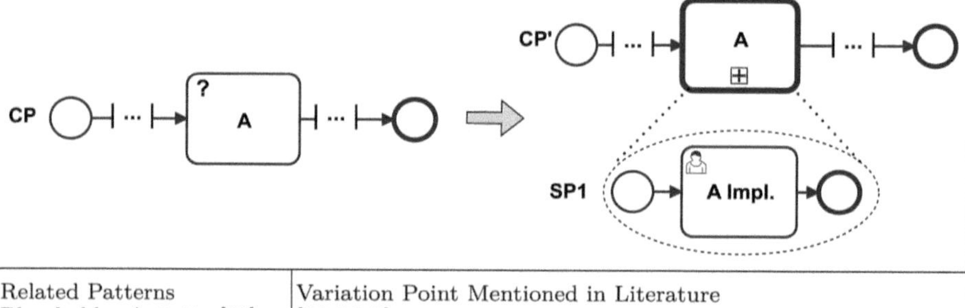

Related Patterns	Variation Point Mentioned in Literature
Placeholder Activity [30]	[26, 28, 7]

processes instead of in the core process. Besides, *L3)* business logic implementing process activities (i.e. code) needs to be contained in the process model, which makes the code hard to maintain. Otherwise, concepts and tools need to be adopted to manage the code and decide which code needs to be deployed alongside what process model variant [19], which contradicts the goal of the presented patterns to avoid introducing new tools. Finally, *L4)* using the presented patterns variability can only be resolved at deployment time (i.e. at deployment time, supporting processes are chosen determining the behaviour).

5.2 Case Study

To demonstrate that the presented patterns can be used in process models executed on WfMSs and show the implications, the business processes described by Examples 1 and

Table 5. Variability Pattern VP5: Variable Gateway Type

Variability Pattern VP5: Variable Gateway Type
Description The gateway of a process is a variation point. The type of gateway and the conditions of the outgoing sequence flows can be selected at deployment time.
Scenario Consider the travel request process of German municipalities. Depending on the municipality, there are different variables (i.e. number of overnight stays, travel destination) that are evaluated at the gateway to determine who needs to approve the request.
Problem There are multiple variants of the same process that have a gateway whose type can differ.
Solution The core process CP whose gateway shall be a variation point (labelled with a question mark) is transformed to CP' by replacing the gateway with a call activity and an inclusive gateway. For each process variant, a supporting process is created comprising a service task, which itself contains logic producing output data based on which the outgoing sequence flows are determined. Depending on the implementation of the service task, one, several, or all sequence flows can be taken which equates to exclusive, inclusive, and parallel gateway behaviour. Consider the following example: Supporting process SP1 has a service task that implements the logic for choosing the outgoing sequence flows. Depending on the desired gateway type of a process variant, CP' is deployed together with the corresponding supporting process that implements the desired gateway type. 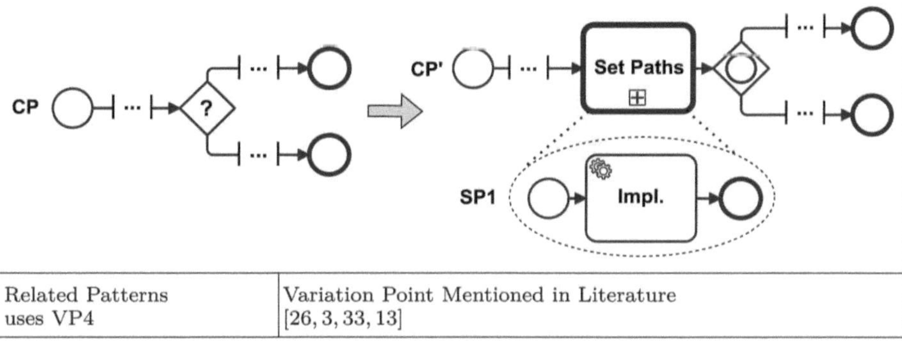

Related Patterns uses VP4	Variation Point Mentioned in Literature [26, 3, 33, 13]

2 are implemented and executed in a case study. In the following, the setup is described and results are discussed.

Setup. Various WfMSs have been evaluated with respect to conformance of BPMN [12] and performance [27]. Compared to other WfMSs, Camunda 7 has performed well. While Camunda 7 is still maintained, its end of life has been announced. Note that opposed to what the names suggests, Camunda 8 is not a new Version but rather an entire new WfMS. Consequently, we implemented the processes in the case study for both Camunda 7 (v7.23.0) and 8 (v8.7). The process models can be found on GitHub[2]. While the visual representation of the BPMN process models are almost identical, tech-

---

[2] https://github.com/hehnle/BPMN-Patterns-for-Process-Variability.

nical properties need to be set to allow for the execution of the process models by Camunda 7[3] and 8[4].

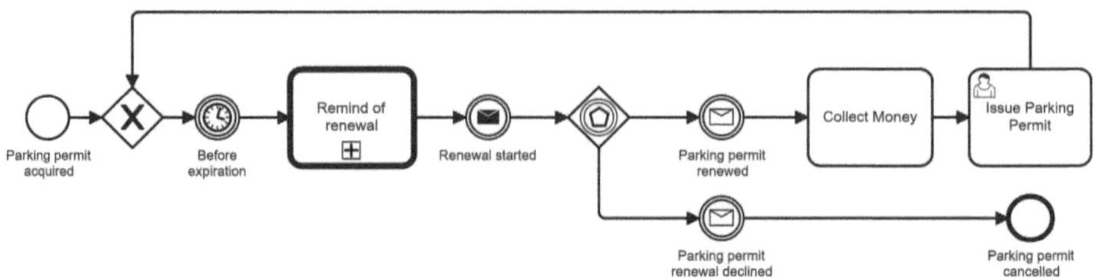

Fig. 4. Patterns 2 and 4 Applied to *Parking Permit Renewal* Business Process.

In Fig. 4, Patterns 2 and 4 were applied to the *parking permit renewal* process. Activity `Remind of renewal` is a variation point and implemented as call activity (i.e. Pattern 4). Different subprocesses are available that may be called to remind the craftsperson. While Fig. 5 shows a subprocess consisting solely of a start/end event (i.e. no reminder is sent), Activity `Send mail` in Fig. 6 reminds the craftsperson via e-mail by exploiting Camunda 8's low-code capabilities (i.e. solely a configuration is required) recognisable by the symbol in the upper left corner. Furthermore, in Fig. 4, Events `Parking permit renewed` and `Parking permit renewal declined` are variation points. Although each of the two events constitutes a variation point, they depend on each other, i.e. one event is always a timer event and the other one is a message event. Therefore, Pattern 2 is slightly adapted to treat both events as one variation point. As it is not possible to place a message throw event right in front of both events due to the event-based gateway, the message throw event is placed before the event-based gateway. Figure 7 shows a supporting process, which is started before the event-based gateways in Fig. 2 is reached. Figure 7 represents the active renewal behaviour, i.e. the craftsperson needs to actively start the renewal of the parking permit or otherwise after some time the process is cancelled. On GitHub, further supporting processes implementing other behaviours can be found as well as the *travel request* process, which is omitted due to page limitations.

Result. The case study could demonstrate that business processes using the presented patterns can be executed on BPMN-compliant WfMSs. Furthermore, the presented patterns can be adapted and combined to satisfy multiple variation points in one process model, e.g. Patterns 2 and 4 are combined in process model *parking permit renewal*. Finally, WfMSs supporting low-code features, such as Camunda 8, mitigate limitation *L3* as only the configuration (e.g. for e-mail) needs to be stored in the process model.

5.3 Expert Interviews

To get feedback with respect to usefulness, relevance, and ease of use of the presented patterns we conducted 12 expert interviews (cf. Table 6). To get profound and valid

---

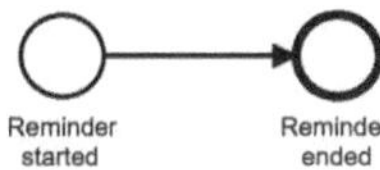

Fig. 5. Supporting Process: No Reminder.

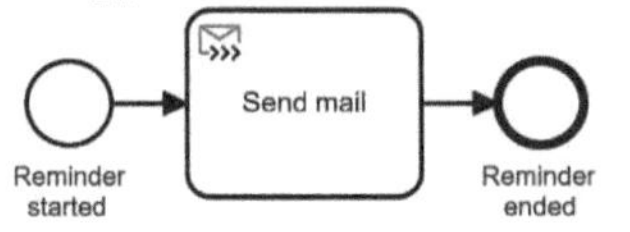

Fig. 6. Supporting Process: E-Mail Reminder (Camunda 8).

Fig. 7. Supporting Process: Active Renewal Mode.

feedback, we interviewed experts with hands-on experience with BPMN and at least some years of professional experience of which some bring up to two decades of total professional experience. While we also conducted an interview with an intern, we did not include their feedback in the evaluation.

Table 6. Expert Panel Overview.

ID	Job Title	YoE*		ID	Job Title	YoE*
A	IT Consultant	10 (10) G		G	BPM Consultant	10 (10) G
B	Practice Lead BPM	20 (25) G		H	BPM Consultant	6 (6) G
C	BPM Consultant	3 (5) G		I	CEO	15 (17) G
D	BPM Consultant	4 (4) G		J	BPM Freelancer	14 (20) G
E	Practice Lead BPM	8 (25) G		K	Process Analyst	5 (8) C
F	BPM Consultant	10 (10) G		L	Professor	15 (25) B

* Years of professional experience with BPMN (total)
G: located in Germany, C: located in Canada, B: located in Brazil

In the interview, we explained the challenge of process variability and other approaches (cf. Sect. 2) and finally presented *VP1-VP5* (including the case study) as an alternative solely relying on BPMN as the main advantage. In line with the Technology Acceptance Model [5,6], we provided the experts with two statements about the perceived usefulness and ease of use for each pattern to which they could express their degree of agreement, i.e. from *strongly disagree* to *strongly agree*. Furthermore, the experts were asked to express their degree of agreement with respect to whether, despite the limitations, the modelling patterns are a good alternative to other process variability approaches that use proprietary modelling languages and tools. The answers and comments of the experts are contained in the aforementioned GitHub repository as well.

The results of the interviews are summarised in Table 7. Excluding the neutral answers, a majority of the experts finds the patterns useful and relevant, and easy to use. While Pattern 4 is best perceived, i.e. none of experts disagrees that Pattern 4 is useful, relevant, and easy to use, only a narrow majority of four experts (strongly) agrees and five experts are undecided whether Pattern 5 is easy to use. The most critical participant is Expert J who strongly disagrees with all statements except with the ones for Pattern 4 due to a variety of reasons. According to Expert J business processes should have fixed start and end events, i.e. if the start and end event differs, it is not the same process, which is violated by Pattern 1 and 3. Furthermore, Expert J emphasises the advantage of BPMN to represent business requirements in a notation that is mutually understood by domain and IT experts, which is impacted by the patterns. Therefore, he strongly disagrees that the patterns are a good alternative to model variability. Instead, he recommends modelling process variants separately or use notations that allow explicitly representing variability. While Experts D, G and H and agree that the introduced BPMN patterns are a good alternative to other approaches for process variability, the three experts also highlight the impact on comprehensibility. During the discussion, some experts point out that the patterns may be used interchangeably. Instead of making the type of an activity variable with Pattern 4 and the type of an event with Pattern 2, both Patterns 2 and 4 can be used to make entire process fragments variable including activities, events, and gateways. Expert L asks how to choose the right pattern if several patterns can be used for a variation point and whether a catalogue could help. While Expert A likes both Pattern 2 and 4, Experts H and J favour Pattern 4.

Table 7. Results of the Conducted Expert Interviews.

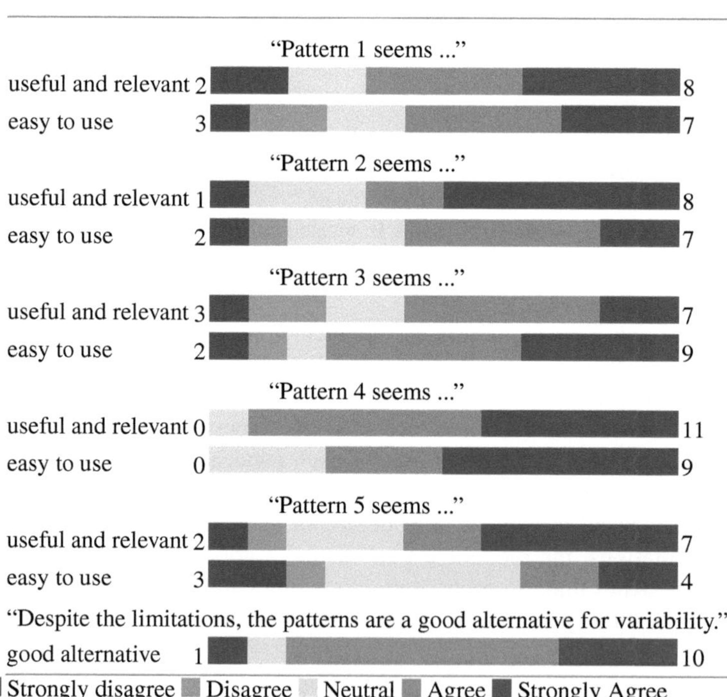

In conclusion, in general the patterns were perceived useful and easy to use, whereby there are differences due to personal modelling preferences, which is consistent with our intent to provide a collection of patterns from which some can be picked, combined, and extended according to preferences. Finally, a majority of experts (strongly) agrees that the patterns are a good alternative to existing approaches as no proprietary modelling language and tool is required.

5.4   Threats to Validity

We mitigated common *threats to validity* [32]: To avoid drawing false conclusions (i.e. *threats to internal validity*), we discussed the answers with the experts to get a better understanding. An *external threat to validity* is the lack of generalisability. While 12 experts is a rather small group, we strongly believe that due to their rich experience their feedback is profound and valid. Although most of the experts are located in Germany, we cover three countries proving that the challenge is not limited to Germany. Finally, the introduced patterns may not be suitable for each digitalisation project realising process variability due to the listed limitations. However, according to the experts the patterns are a good alternative to existing approaches. *Threats to construct validity*: In contrast to anonymous surveys, participants' questions could be answered and their backgrounds be verified, ensuring the answers are valid and based on professional experience outweighing the disadvantage of any perceived pressure to agree.

6   Conclusion

Based on literature and interviews with German municipalities, BPMN 2.0 elements were identified that may constitute variations points resulting in process variants. These elements include events, activities, and gateways. Then, five modelling patterns were presented to allow for variability in process models by solely relying on BPMN 2.0. The variable behaviour is modelled in separate process models. Depending on the deployed process models, the behaviours of the variation points are determined. Common modelling tools and unmodified WfMSs can be used, which was demonstrated in a case study during the evaluation. Furthermore, the results of expert interviews indicate that the patterns are useful, relevant, easy to use, and pose a good alternative to approaches from literature.

Future work shall investigate whether resolving process variability at runtime is also possible by solely relying on modelling patterns. In addition, the presented patterns shall be generalised such that they are notation-independent.

Disclosure of Interests. Philipp Hehnle reports a relationship with Camunda Services GmbH that includes: travel reimbursement.

References

1. Alexander, C., Ishikawa, S., Silverstein, M.: A Pattern Language: Towns, Buildings, Construction. Oxford University Press, New York (1977)

2. Nowak, A., Leymann, F., Schleicher, D., Schumm, D., Wagner, S.: Green business process patterns. In: Proceedings of the 18th Conference on Pattern Languages of Programs, pp. 1–10. ACM (2011)

3. Berger, I.R., Soffer, P., Sturm, A.: Organisational reference models: supporting an adequate design of local business processes. Int. J. Bus. Process. Integr. Manag. 4(2), 134–149 (2009)

4. de Brito Dias, C.L., Stein Dani, V., Mendling, J., Thom, L.H.: Anti-patterns for process modeling problems: an analysis of BPMN 2.0-based tools behavior. In: Di Francescomarino, C., Dijkman, R., Zdun, U. (eds.) BPM 2019. LNBIP, vol. 362, pp. 745–757. Springer, Cham (2019). https://doi.org/10.1007/978-3-030-37453-2_59

5. Davis, F.D.: A technology acceptance model for empirically testing new end-user information systems : theory and results. Doctoral dissertation, Massachusetts Institute of Technology, Sloan School of Management, Cambridge (1986)

6. Davis, F.D.: Perceived usefulness, perceived ease of use, and user acceptance of information technology. MIS Q. 13(3), 319 (1989)

7. Delgado, A., Calegari, D.: BPMN 2.0 based modeling and customization of variants in business process families. In: Latin American Computer Conference, pp. 1–9 (2017)

8. Delgado, A., Calegari, D., García, F., Weber, B.: Model-driven management of BPMN-based business process families. Softw. Syst. Model. 21(6), 2517–2553 (2022)

9. Döhring, M., Zimmermann, B.: vBPMN: event-aware workflow variants by weaving BPMN2 and business rules. In: Halpin, T., et al. (eds.) BPMDS/EMMSAD -2011. LNBIP, vol. 81, pp. 332–341. Springer, Heidelberg (2011). https://doi.org/10.1007/978-3-642-21759-3_24

10. Ferreira, D.A.M., Paiva, D.M.B., Cagnin, M.I.: BPL-framework 2.0: support tool for creation and instantiation of business process lines. In: International Conference on Software Engineering and Knowledge Engineering, pp. 81–84 (2017)

11. Gamma, E.: Design Patterns: Elements of Reusable Object-Oriented Software. Addison-Wesley Professional Computing Series. Addison-Wesley, Reading (1995)

12. Geiger, M., Harrer, S., Lenhard, J., Wirtz, G.: BPMN 2.0: the state of support and implementation. Future Gener. Comput. Syst. 80, 250–262 (2018)

13. Gottschalk, F., van der Aalst, W.M.P., Jansen-Vullers, M.H., La Rosa, M.: Configurable workflow models. Int. J. Cooperative Inf. Syst. 17(02), 177–221 (2008)

14. Gottschalk, F., Wagemakers, T.A.C., Jansen-Vullers, M.H., van der Aalst, W.M.P., La Rosa, M.: Configurable process models: experiences from a municipality case study. In: van Eck, P., Gordijn, J., Wieringa, R. (eds.) CAiSE 2009. LNCS, vol. 5565, pp. 486–500. Springer, Heidelberg (2009). https://doi.org/10.1007/978-3-642-02144-2_38

15. Hallerbach, A., Bauer, T., Reichert, M.: Managing process variants in the process lifecycle. In: International Conference on Enterprise Information Systems, pp. 154–161 (2008)

16. Hallerbach, A., Bauer, T., Reichert, M.: Capturing variability in business process models: the Provop approach. J. Softw. Maint. Evol. Res. Pract. 22(6-7), 519–546 (2010)

17. Hallerbach, A., Bauer, T., Reichert, M.: Configuration and management of process variants. In: Handbook on BPM, pp. 237–255. Springer (2010)

18. Hehnle, P., Reichert, M.: Handling process variants in information systems with software product line engineering. In: IEEE Conference on Business Informatics, pp. 1–10 (2023)

19. Hehnle, P., Reichert, M.: Flexible process variant binding in information systems with software product line engineering. J. Syst. Softw. 230, 112530 (2025)

20. La Rosa, M., van der Aalst, W.M.P., Dumas, M., Milani, F.P.: Business process variability modeling: a survey. ACM Comput. Surv. 50(1), 1–45 (2017)

21. Lanz, A., Weber, B., Reichert, M.: Time patterns for process-aware information systems. Requirements Eng. 19(2), 113–141 (2014)

22. Lopes, C.S., Da Silveira, D.S., Araujo, J.: Business processes fragments to promote information quality. Int. J. Qual. Reliab. Manage. 38(9), 1880–1901 (2021)

23. Nowak, A., Leymann, F.: Green business process patterns – Part II (short paper). In: International Conference on Service-Oriented Computing and Applications, pp. 168–173 (2013)
24. Object Management Group: Business Process Model and Notation (BPMN): Version 2.0.2 (2013). https://www.omg.org/spec/BPMN/2.0.2/PDF
25. Ramos-Merino, M., Álvarez-Sabucedo, L.M., Santos-Gago, J.M., de Arriba-Pérez, F.: A pattern based method for simplifying a BPMN process model. Appl. Sci. **9**(11), 2322 (2019)
26. Schnieders, A., Puhlmann, F.: Variability mechanisms in e-business process families. In: International Conference on Business Information Systems (2006)
27. Skouradaki, M., Ferme, V., Pautasso, C., Leymann, F., van Hoorn, A.: Micro-benchmarking BPMN 2.0 workflow management systems with workflow patterns. In: Nurcan, S., Soffer, P., Bajec, M., Eder, J. (eds.) CAiSE 2016. LNCS, vol. 9694, pp. 67–82. Springer, Cham (2016). https://doi.org/10.1007/978-3-319-39696-5_5
28. Terenciani, M., Paiva, D., Landre, G., Cagnin, M.I.: BPMN* - a notation for representation of variability in business process towards supporting business process line modeling. In: International Conference on Software Engineering and Knowledge Engineering, pp. 227–230. KSI Research Inc. and Knowledge Systems Institute Graduate School (2015)
29. van der Aalst, W.M.P., Dreiling, A., Gottschalk, F., Rosemann, M., Jansen-Vullers, M.H.: Configurable process models as a basis for reference modeling. In: Bussler, C.J., Haller, A. (eds.) BPM 2005. LNCS, vol. 3812, pp. 512–518. Springer, Heidelberg (2006). https://doi.org/10.1007/11678564_47
30. Weber, B., Reichert, M., Rinderle-Ma, S.: Change patterns and change support features - enhancing flexibility in process-aware information systems. Data Knowl. Eng. **66**(3), 438–466 (2008)
31. Weidmann, M., Koetter, F., Kintz, M., Schleicher, D., Mietzner, R.: Adaptive business process modeling in the internet of services (ABIS). In: International Conference on Internet and Web Applications and Services (2011)
32. Wohlin, C., Runeson, P., Höst, M., Ohlsson, M.C., Regnell, B., Wesslén, A.: Experimentation in Software Engineering, 2nd edn. Springer, Heidelberg (2024)
33. Zhang, H., Han, W., Ouyang, C.: Extending BPMN for configurable process modeling. In: ISPE Inc. International Conference on Concurrent Engineering, pp. 317–330. IOS Press (2014)
34. Zimmermann, B., Doehring, M.: Patterns for flexible BPMN workflows. In: European Conference on Pattern Languages of Programs, pp. 1–9. ACM (2011)

Agentic Generation of Process Models
from Regulatory Texts

Catherine Sai[✉][iD] and Stefanie Rinderle-Ma[✉][iD]

Technical University of Munich, TUM School of Computation, Information and Technology,
Garching, Germany
{catherine.sai,stefanie.rinderle-ma}@tum.de

Abstract. Process model generation is still mostly a manual task. A vast amount
of process-relevant information is captured in textual sources such as regulatory
documents and process descriptions. Hence, (semi-) automatic extraction of process model information from textual sources and translation into process models
based on graphical notations such as BPMN are ongoing and, with the advent of
generative AI, increasingly performant. However, existing approaches for process
model generation from text are often limited to control flow aspects and require
precise process descriptions as input. Regulatory documents describing processes
pose different challenges than process descriptions and are widespread, highly
relevant and of increasing volume in organizations. In this work, we exploit a
generative AI architecture to present an approach that can automatically generate BPMN 2.0 process models from regulatory texts such as the GDPR. The
approach is evaluated on five use cases with regulatory text and corresponding
process models from different domains and with different challenges. This way,
we can demonstrate that the proposed approach can automatically generate reference models from regulatory requirement documentations. When compared to
existing approaches, the proposed approach results in an improvement of both,
syntactic and semantic process model quality.

Keywords: Process Model Generation · Regulatory Process Description ·
Natural Language Processing · BPMN · LLM · Multi-Agent

1   Introduction

Visual process models are widely recognized for their role in helping employees understand, correctly execute, and improve business processes [7,18]. Their value is particularly evident when navigating changes, such as onboarding new staff or adapting
processes to new requirements. The absence of clear process visibility can lead to significant operational inefficiencies and high costs, as noted by industry analysts who
state, "The lack of visibility and understanding of company-wide and locally defined
processes [...] can generate high costs [...]"[1]. Despite this proven need, many business

---

[1] https://blogs.sap.com/2022/08/10/5-reasons-why-process-modeling-is-the-operational-
backbone-of-your-journey-to-process-analytics-initiatives/.

C. Cappiello et al. (Eds.): CoopIS 2025, LNCS 15535, pp. 370–387, 2026.
https://doi.org/10.1007/978-3-032-15538-2_21

processes still lack a formal visual representation. The primary bottleneck is the manual creation process, which is time-consuming and requires significant domain knowledge and specialized modeling skills. This "lack of qualified modelers" [24] is compounded by the fact that manual modeling is susceptible to errors, with industry model collections exhibiting "high error rates (between 10% and 20%)" [17]. Consequently, researchers have increasingly turned to automating the generation of process models from existing business resources, most notably textual descriptions [1, 13].

By contrast, this paper focuses on a particularly challenging, yet crucial source for process model generation, i.e., regulatory documents [28]. These documents, such as company regulations, legal statutes, or compliance rules, dictate what must be done, by whom, and under what conditions. However, they are typically written in natural language that is inherently ambiguous, complex, and not directly executable by IT systems [12]. In particular, a significant gap exists between these policy documents and the formal, structured process models required for effective business operations. Manually bridging this gap is a slow, expensive, and highly error-prone task that demands dual expertise in both the legal domain and process modeling. The challenges are amplified by the specific characteristics of legal texts, which often feature long, complex sentence structures, a high proportion of words irrelevant to the process flow, passive voice with implicit actors, and numerous cross-references to other paragraphs or documents [26]. Nevertheless, the utility of process modeling in this domain is clear; for instance, studies have shown that legal stakeholders can effectively understand BPMN models of legal processes, highlighting both the need and the feasibility of representing legal knowledge as formal processes [7].

Existing approaches to automated process discovery from text, whether based on traditional NLP or modern Large Language Models (LLMs), often fall short when confronted with the unique complexities of regulatory documents. Traditional rule-based methods may lack the flexibility to interpret ambiguous legal language, while LLM-based approaches (e.g., simple one-shot queries) can struggle to produce structurally complete and precise BPMN models. In particular, no existing work fully supports the automatic transformation of regulatory texts into BPMN 2.0 models with actor-responsibilities modeled as pools/lanes. This is a critical gap, particularly as the representation of roles and responsibilities is essential in regulatory contexts, especially for cooperative aspects in processes.

To address these limitations, this paper introduces a novel approach for generating comprehensive BPMN models from complex regulatory texts. The core contributions of this work are as follows:

- A **multi-agent** reasoning and refinement **architecture** that reflects on its own performance and iteratively improves its own results - completely automated.
- An **extended applicability** specifically tailored to handle the complexities of **regulatory documents**, capable of generating rich reference models that include key BPMN elements such as actor roles within pools.
- A **new benchmark dataset** consisting of five regulatory text-model pairs from diverse domains and complexity levels, released as an open-source resource to facilitate future research and comparative analysis in this area.

- An **automated evaluation framework** that provides objective and multi-faceted metrics for comparing generated process models, enabling a transparent assessment of an approach's capabilities and remaining challenges.

The remainder of this paper is structured as follows. Section 2 discusses related work in automated process model generation. The proposed approach, its novel components, and the analyzed aspects are presented in Sect. 3. This is followed by Sect. 5, which provides a comprehensive evaluation of our approach against existing work and on novel use cases. Finally, a discussion of the limitations and the conclusion are presented in Sect. 6 and Sect. 7, respectively.

2 Preliminaries and Related Work

This work is concerned with imperative process modeling, defining process control flows (and roles) explicitly, as exemplified by BPMN[2]. We adopt this focus because imperative models provide a visual representation of the process that is readily understood by diverse stakeholders, while the explicit assignment of roles and responsibilities is essential for effective organizational coordination. This combination of procedural clarity and defined responsibilities serves as a stable foundation for both, straightforward automation and seamless integration into operational workflows, which are the primary goals of this research. Therefore, we do not consider declarative approaches. To provide a structured overview, we differentiate prior work on information extraction and process model generation from text based on three key dimensions (cf. Table 1):

1. **Input Texts:** i) Process descriptions vs. ii) regulatory documents
2. **Method:** i) (partly) manual ii) rule-based NLP, iii) conversational LLM-based generation, iv) automated, single-turn interaction (one-shot, few-shot, agentic) LLM approaches
3. **Output Format:** i) (mapped) relevant text fragments, ii) (various) process models without roles/organizational structure (e.g. Mermaid) and iii) process model beyond control flow (e.g. BPMN with pools/lanes)

Early foundational efforts [10,26] show the feasibility of text-to-process modeling with classical NLP. The work by [26] is not fully automated and is based on formalization in addition to NLP techniques to create structured process models, aiming at the creation of reference models from regulatory texts. In contrast, the framework by Friedrich et al. [10] is automated and systematically addresses several key NLP challenges. However, despite its significance, this approach presents two limitations. Firstly, the method is based on fixed rules and not designed to handle regulatory documents. Secondly, from a technical perspective, its implementation poses limitations regarding reuse, adaptation, and extension. These limitations in both domain applicability and technical accessibility highlight the need for a more modern and flexible approach incorporating current state-of-the-art reasoning solutions like LLMs.

---

[2] Business Process Modeling and Notation, https://www.bpmn.org.

Table 1. Comparison of Related Work on Information Extraction and Process Generation from Text.

1. Input Text	2. Method	3. Output Format	Reference
i) Process desc.	ii) (rule-based) NLP	iii) process model with pools	[9,10]
i) Process desc.	iii) conversational LLM	ii) process model w/o pools	[13,14]
i) Process desc.	iv) automated LLM	i) (mapped) rel. text fragments	[5,11,21,22]
i) Process desc.	iv) automated LLM	ii) process model w/o pools	[15]
ii) Reg. doc.	i) (partly) manual	ii) process model w/o pools	[8,26]
ii) Reg. doc.	i) (partly) manual	iii) process model with pools	[3]
ii) Reg. doc.	ii) (rule-based) NLP	i) (mapped) rel. text fragments	[16,19,20,25,28]
ii) Reg. doc.	iv) automated LLM	iii) process model with pools	our approach

Dimyadi et al. [8] use BPMN as part of an auditing system and Audrito and Ferraris [3] explore BPMN for legal education. The goal of both works aligns with ours (modeling regulatory text as BPMN), though their methods are human-driven; this shows the value of BPMN for legal compliance and the need for automation in the creation (which our LLM approach seeks to provide). Further regulatory compliance research such as [16,19,20,25,28] utilizes traditional NLP techniques to demonstrate use-cases of turning regulatory texts into process logic. They share the task of identifying and extracting relevant text fragments and either map these to process elements [19,28] or other textual fragments [20,25], or store the extracted requirements in knowledge graphs [16]. Their research highlights the challenges of regulatory texts and the importance of structuring regulatory text for automated compliance.

Leaving the regulatory application area, Bellan et al. [5] investigate GPT-3 as a large pre-trained LLM to automate the extraction of process elements from textual process descriptions. Neuberger et al. [21,22] extract process information from text through trained (machine learning) models, targeting enriched process model construction, but without generating executable models. In [21], the authors aim at process information extraction through LLMs, with focus on a guide for structured prompting, analysis which aspects of a prompt improve the results and which do not. We incorporate their findings in our prompt design as detailed in Sect. 3. Using GPT-4 with one initial prompt, [11] examines its capabilities to generate BPMN models from textual process descriptions. However, the output of their LLM approach is not a BPMN model, but BPMN element pairs, e.g., `XOR (Proposal accepted)` $\implies$ `Task1`. Furthermore, the evaluation is based on a manual mapping "between the entities identified in the dataset and the ones produced by GPT4" and restricted to identify the pair of their defined gold standard in the LLM output as well as actor activity pairs.

Our previous work investigates conversational process modeling to support iterative process model design and redesign with LLMs: [13] analyzes the ability of LLMs to create BPMN process models from process descriptions. In [14], we propose a method for process model redesign with iterative user feedback. This work differs from previous work regarding input (regulatory documents instead of process descriptions) and output (pools and lanes in addition to control flow). Moreover, this work furthers the KPIs for assessing the output of created process models proposed in [13] into a novel evaluation metric.

The LLM-based approach ProMoAI [15] aims at generating BPMN models from text, but currently lacks full BPMN feature support for, e.g., pools and lanes, simplify gateways, are not designed for regulatory documents and lack functionalities like document upload. Despite these drawbacks, it is the most comparable solution to our approach, thus we will use [15] as a base model in the evaluation to compare the results of the approach proposed in this work. The emergence of generative AI has led to various (non-scientific) tools that aim to convert natural language directly into BPMN 2.0 models, seemingly offering functionality comparable to ProMoAi [15]. Examples include BPMN Sketch Miner[3] and BPMN GPT[4]. However, an initial evaluation reveals significant limitations when these tools are applied to regulatory documents, often resulting in invalid BPMN models.

3   CARB: Collaborative Agents for Regulatory BPMN

Figure 1 illustrates the **C**ollaborative **A**gents for **R**egulatory **B**PMN (CARB) generation approach proposed in this work. Input to CARB is a regulatory text that contains process-related information (cf. Figure 1, I.). All instructions and queries to the LLM agents are generic, i.e., use case independent. The length of the input text is variable, it can span from a paragraph to a multi-page section of a regulatory document (cf. Table 2 for token size and other statistics of our tested use cases). The processing framework (cf. Figure 1, II.) comprises a supervisor agent, coordinating four specialized worker agents, and a set of foundational tools for file system interaction and BPMN validation. The agents are set-up with the Gemini 2.5 Pro LLM, but this could be changed to another model in the future without further adjustments to the approach. Gemini 2.5 Pro is chosen because it has a big context window necessary for BPMN creation and shows strong reasoning and coding capabilities[5], consistently ranking high on benchmarks such as GPQA Diamond[6].

Architecture: The architecture of our approach is based on a hierarchical multi-agent system[7] designed to automate the generation and iterative refinement of process models from regulatory text in Business Process Model and Notation (BPMN) 2.0 format. For this a supervisor Large Language Model (LLM) agent acts as central orchestrator who manages a team of specialized LLM agents. Each agent is an LLM instance (Gemini 2.5 Pro) given a specific system prompt that defines its role, constraints, and objectives. Through this separation of concerns, the complex task of BPMN creation from a regulatory text, is separated into a series of smaller, manageable problems. At the same time this architecture offers modularity which is advantageous for debugging, adjustments/extensions and is more robust, as e.g. the failure of one agent to perform his task does not lead to the failure of the whole approach.

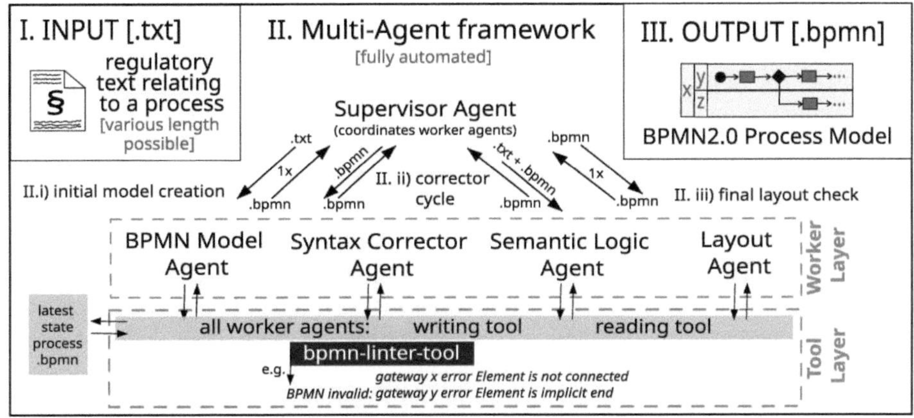

Fig. 1. CARB: Collaborative Agents for Regulatory BPMN generation.

Tool Layer: All agents have access to the read- and write-file-tools, which offer standard functions for operations on text and BPMN/XML files. The Syntax Corrector Agent additionally uses the bpmn-linter-tool, which checks the BPMN file against the formal BPMN 2.0 specification. In order to automatically use the bpmnlint program as a tool, we wrap the bpmnlint command-line interface using a Python script.

Worker Layer: The **BPMN Modeler Agent** receives the regulatory text from the supervisor and creates the initial BPMN 2.0 XML structure. Its prompt mandates the creation of all necessary process elements (pools, tasks, gateways, events) and, critically, the corresponding visual layout information with *bpmndi*. It is designed to run only as initial step of the framework to deliver a *.bpmn* version that can be iteratively improved by the other worker agents. After the initial creation of the BPMN 2.0 model from the regulatory text, the **Syntax Corrector Agent** uses the bpmn-linter-tool to inspect the model. The tool delivers feedback on the structure and components of the model, assessing its syntactic validity. In case of an invalid result from the tool, the Syntax Corrector Agent is supplied with error insights, e.g. *Start Event x having an incoming sequence flow*. The Syntax Corrector Agent then takes these insights as input for its own reasoning, utilizing the reading and writing tool to correct the current process model XML file concerning syntactic validity. After correcting the XML, it re-runs the bpmn-linter-tool validation in a self-correction loop, if errors are reported (both new or persisting), it re-enters the self-correction loop until the BPMN is syntactically valid. Following the syntactic validation check, the **Semantic Logic Agent** proceeds to analyze the model's logic against the source text. It compares the BPMN file against the original text, specifically verifying the implementation of conditional logic (gateways), obligations (must), permissions (may), and other business rules. If discrepancies are found, the Semantic Logic Agent corrects these, utilizing the reading and writing tools to modify the process model XML file. Finally, the **Layout Agent** is designed to inspect the visual representation of the syntactically and semantically improved BPMN process model. The aim of this agents is i.e. to eliminate element overlaps (especially labels), enforcing orthogonal (horizontal/vertical) sequence flows or ensuring elements are contained within their parent pools. In order to improve these elements, the agent utilizes the reading and writing tools to modify the coordinates within the *bpmndi* element of the XML file.

Supervisor: The Supervisor Agent coordinates the workflow with a combination of predefined sequence and execution-dependent routing. This control flow ensures that corrections are made in a logical order, preventing cascading errors. The process begins with the Supervisor invoking the BPMN Modeler Agent to produce the initial draft of the model. The supervisor is setup to only call the modeler once, which is strongly enforced in the execution script as otherwise the BPMN generation would start from an initial state and all previous correction effort would be lost. Following the initial BPMN creation, the supervisor initiates an iterative refinement cycle designed to achieve both syntactic and semantic correctness. First, the Supervisor calls the Syntax Corrector Agent, and after the syntax is validated, it calls the Semantic Logic Agent. If the Semantic agent makes a change to the file, the Supervisor restarts the loop by calling the Syntax Corrector Agent again. This ensures that any semantic modification has not inadvertently violated BPMN syntax rules. Similarly, if the Syntax agent identifies that the semantic corrected file is invalid and adjusts it, the resulting BPMN is sent again to the Semantic Logic Agent for reevaluation, ensuring that the conditions described in the text are still represented correctly in the XML file. This correction loop repeats until both Agents assess validity without corrections. Once the model passes through the primary correction loop without any further modifications (i.e., it is both syntactically and semantically sound), the Supervisor calls the Layout Corrector Agent for a single pass to clean up the visual diagram. As a final safety measure, the Supervisor invokes the Syntax Corrector Agent one last time to confirm that the layout adjustments did not corrupt the XML structure. The process terminates successfully when the final syntax check passes. To prevent infinite loops (e.g., if an agent repeatedly fails to fix an error), the Supervisor maintains an attempt counter for each agent and will halt the process if a predefined limit is reached, preserving the last working version of the model.

The final output (cf. Figure 1, III.) is a syntactically and semantically improved BPMN 2.0 process model with specific emphasis on (regulatory) conditional modeling and actor responsibility inclusion.

4   Evaluation Metric

LLMs offer new opportunities in the automated creation of process models [14] and thus significantly reduce manual effort and improve consistency. However, an ongoing challenge is the holistic and objective evaluation of their results. To close this gap we propose a holistic evaluation metric, incorporating existing evaluation techniques and explaining their limitations. In order to access the quality of an LLM generated model, we identified 4 core aspects:

A. **Syntactic Quality** [17,27]: Is the generated model compliant with the BPMN 2.0 standard?
B. **Semantic Quality** [13,28]: Does the model accurately represent the meaning, logic, and normative constraints of the source legal text?

C. **Layout:** How good is the Layout of the resulting BPMN visualization (Adherance to BPMN 2.0 Guidelines[8])? Are there flow or even task overlaps? Is the flow from left to right etc.?

D. **Stability of Results** [21]**:** How consistent are the generated models across multiple runs, given the non-deterministic nature of LLMs?

Although cost is also a known challenge for LLM-based approaches [21], continuous advances in model efficiency are rapidly lowering this barrier. Therefore, this work focuses on the three mentioned quality dimensions.

A. Syntactic Quality. A generated process model must first be syntactically valid, adhering to the BPMN 2.0 modeling standards. For this validation, we leverage the Free Online BPMN Quality Analysis Service[9]. For this assessment, the generated .bpmn models are uploaded to the online service, which offers a visualization of the process, identifies modeling mistakes and checks the BPMN 2.0 Notation compliance. Examples of errors that are assessed include missing incoming/outgoing flows, gateways that are neither splits nor joins, or warnings like the information that a task label doesn't start with a verb. We deselect the consideration of multiple end events as warnings, but aside from that, keep all the checks they offer in the demo. The metrics we use from the BPMN Quality Analysis Service are the number of errors and warnings.

B. Semantic Quality. Ensuring a model is syntactically correct is necessary, but insufficient. The ultimate measure of value is semantic correctness, i.e., how well a model represents the meaning of the source text. The core challenge in evaluating semantic correctness for process models generated from text, stems from a dual ambiguity. On the one hand, the inherent ambiguity of natural language means that the same (regulatory) text can be interpreted differently by various audiences. On the other hand, the representational freedom in process modeling allows for the same process being modeled in different ways. For regulatory documents these ambiguity challenges are even greater due to the interpretable legal language being used and the complexity of the contained topics.

Our approach builds upon foundational research in automated BPMN generation, compliance checking and LLM evaluation. [10], used *Graph Edit Distance (GED)* for measuring process model similarity. GED calculates the minimum-cost transformation of one graph into another, considering node/edge insertions, deletions, and substitutions. Friedrich's enhanced this by incorporating the semantic similarity of element labels for the matching. There are two main reasons why GED is not suitable for our approach. Firstly, it heavily depends on a gold standard model and views this as the only truth. Hence, GED is incapable to verify that a model is a faithful representation of a regulatory text, calculating the models similarity, but not the link between the model element and the specific legal clause that justifies it. Secondly, even if a gold standard model exists, GED cannot validate if an activity is obligatory or permitted

---

[8] https://www.bpmnquickguide.com/view-bpmn-quick-guide/.

[9] https://freebpmnquality.github.io/.

(e.g., with GED two element pairs can seem a perfect match, even if the text required one to be mandatory and the other optional). While our framework also uses a gold standard for the comparison of BPMN element existence (e.g., actors, activities, event. etc.) and placement (e.g., activity placed in correct actor pool), we additionally include the regulatory source text for the semantic evaluation as the ultimate ground truth fro complex conditional requirements. Our previous work in [13] provides KPIs for task extraction from text. In [28], we provide a fitness score to quantify the relevance of text to a model and a cost score to penalize three specific violations, namely (1) missing obligatory activities, (2) wrong order of activities and (3) wrong resource allocation of activities. We adapt and extend this prior metrics, introducing the Regulatory Semantics Score (RSS), which is comprised of three components, where we explicitly distinguish between the *completeness* covering the existence of an element, its *correctness*, i.e., position/relations, and *traceability* measuring the percentage of generated elements that are present in the gold standard in order to asses the grounding of elements in the source text to prevent hallucination and over-compliance (cf. [25]). This differentiation transparently identifies whether an error in the generated model is caused by missing information retrieval from the text (completeness, i.e., element not existent in model) or due to its processing in relation to the other elements (correctness) or created by the LLM as, e.g., a cause of too much creativity (traceability).

Completeness checks if all elements that should exist actually exist in the generated model. This can be done via the *recall* for the following elements:

(i)   % of **actors [AR]** that correctly exist in the model (e.g. as BPMN Pools or Lanes)
(ii) % of **activities [AY]** that correctly exist in the model (cf. [13], only obligatory activities: [28])
(iii) % of **events [EV]** that correctly exist in the model (e.g. start, end, intermediate events)
(iv) % of **AND gateways [AG]** that correctly exist in the model
(v)   % of **XOR gateways [XG]** that correctly exist in the model
(vi) % of **data objects [DO]** that correctly exist in the model

The completeness check is automated through a semantic similarity score with a threshold to define if, e.g., a role name in the generated model is semantically similar to the desired label in the gold standard model or not. Using Sentence Transformer [23] embeddings and cosine similarity, for each element-type (i, ii, etc.) in the gold standard, the best-matching element (with a score above the element-types similarity threshold) in the generated model is identified. This label similarity check is performed for elements (i)-(iii) and (vi). For the gateways we use a count at this point, as gateways (with the exception of XOR-splits) are not required to have a label and thus cannot be distinguished from one another. Thus, here we only verify the number of AND and XOR gateways that exist in the model. Their correct placement is checked in the next step.

Correctness checks the following aspects in the resulting process model:

(i)   % of activities with correct **actor assignment [AA]**

(ii) % **control flow [CF]** (are activities, gateways, events and objects connected in the correct sequence?)

(iii) % of correct **decision logic [DL]** elements (meaning the conditions on the outgoing paths of XOR split)

(iv) % **conditional logic [CL]** (specification correctly modeled?, here we pay special attention to regulatory specifications like obligations)

    (a) % of **temporal** constraints correctly translated into gateway logic and event triggers

    (b) % of **obligatory** actions (e.g. shall, should, must, has to [4]) modeled as part of a non-optional execution path

    (c) % of **prohibited** actions (e.g. must not) correctly modeled as impossible paths or explicit exception flows

    (d) % of **permitted** actions (e.g. can, may) correctly modeled as optional paths (e.g. following a choice gateway)

For the correctness evaluation, we compare the generated model against both, the gold-standard reference model and the original regulatory text. The methodology involves two primary stages: structural comparison of relational pairs (i-iii) and logical validation (iv). For i), we compare actor-activity-pairs extracted from the gold standard to semantically similar actor-activity-pairs in the generated model. Both elements of the pair have to be semantically similar to their counterpart in a comparison pair in order to be considered correct. We again use sentence-embeddings and cosine similarity (with static element thresholds) to assess the semantic similarity between element labels. Similarly for ii) we extract the labels of all direct connections between elements (tasks, events, gateways) as (source, target) pairs. The pairs are checked the same way as described for the i) pairs, based on semantic similarity. This evaluation relies on the elements being named. If e.g., a gateway in the model does not have a label, it cannot be included as a source or target in a control flow pair. For iii), the approach checks if XOR-gateway-split labels are semantically similar and if that is the case if the outgoing sequence flows are also semantically similar. So for this decision logic check, the pair that is compared between gold standard and generated model consists of the gateway label and the sequence flows that exit the gateway. Note that especially (i)-(iii) depend on the existence of the elements. If e.g., an actor was not identified at all this will not only affect the completeness score, but also the correctness score as there can be no actor-activity assignment for the missing actor. Aspect (iv), is evaluated differently. Here, we leverage an LLM for its reasoning capabilities in assessing the conditional logic modeling. The LLM is designed to identify business rules and constraints from the source text and analyze them against the generated model to verify if those rules are implemented logically and correctly.

Traceability checks the following numbers:

(i) % of **activities [AI]** that correctly exist in the model vs. all activities that exist in the model

(ii) % of **actors [AP]** that correctly exist in the model vs. all actors that exist in the model

This dimension ensures auditability by verifying that model elements are explicitly grounded in the source text, preventing models to rank high that contain unnecessary elements (e.g. hallucinations by the LLM). The most suitable metric is *precision* as it measures the percentage of correct elements (that should exists in the model) over all the elements generated. To keep the evaluation concise we limit this check to the actor and activity elements, as they usually contain the most essential information of a process.

Calculating an Overall Regulatory Semantics Score. The overall RSS score is a weighted average of the scores from each dimension:

$$\mathbf{RSS} = \mathrm{Score}_{\mathrm{Completeness}} \cdot w_c + \mathrm{Score}_{\mathrm{Correctness}} \cdot w_r$$

$$+ \mathrm{Score}_{\mathrm{Traceability}} \cdot w_t \quad \text{where} \quad \sum w_i = 1 \quad (1)$$

The weights (w_i) can be adjusted based on the evaluation's focus. We recommend a focus on correctness, as this contains the most advanced aspects (e.g., conditional logic). This score provides a quantitative measure of similarity between the legal text semantics and the generated model.

C. Layout. To assess the Layout of the resulting BPMN visualization, we use the generated BPMN as input for a LLM (Gemini 2.5 Pro), designed to identify and count defined criteria of the BPMN 2.0 Layout Guidelines[10] (e.g. flow, label or element overlaps, non-orthogonal flows, etc.).

D. Stability of Results. LLMs are known for their non-deterministic output, which raises concerns about the stability of results. To address this, we adopt a methodology analogous to [21]. We run the model generation process multiple times (we chose three iterations) for the same input setup (text and prompt). By calculating the standard deviation of the semantic evaluation results, we can quantify the variance of the generated models. A low standard deviation indicates the stability of the generation process and its results.

The proposed multi-criteria evaluation systematically assesses syntactic correctness, semantic fidelity (via the RSS score), layout of the resulting visualization, and result stability. It aims at providing a holistic, quantitative understanding of the utility of a process model created from legal text. The evaluation metric integrates established methods with novel, text-grounded semantic checks, paving the way for the trustworthy application of LLMs in the legal domain.

5 Evaluation

The CARB approach is implemented in Python using the LangChain[11] framework. It is publicly available at https://github.com/CatherineSaiTUM/RegText2BPMN, and can be run through a simple google colab setup. In the following, we evaluate CARB based on different data sets.

---

[10] https://www.bpmnquickguide.com/view-bpmn-quick-guide/.
[11] https://www.langchain.com/.

5.1 Data Sets, Gold Standard Creation, and Base Models

We use gold standard process models created from texts as the comparison between model and model is more objectifiable than from text to model [10]. The data set consists of five BPMN process models and their corresponding texts from five different regulatory documents of various domains. For two processes, the regulatory text and corresponding process model exist, but are adjusted by us for higher consistency with the BPMN 2.0 standard and better representation of the given information. The two adjusted models are taken from [2,28] (GDPR) and [6,28] (Smart Meter). To validate the necessity for adjustment of the models, we check the original models for syntax quality (cf. Sect. 4) using the Free BPMN Quality tool. In both cases, errors are detected such as missing connection to sequence flow and modeling organizational aspects as task labels instead of using pools or lanes. The adapted process models are checked without any errors or warnings by the Free BPMN Quality tool. For the three other use cases, we create text-process model pairs without an existing process model from the regulatory text. In detail, we first identify text passages in regulatory documents (like laws, regulations, and enactments) that include the description of a process. The texts are then manually annotated into categories actor, action, condition/ process relevant information, and process irrelevant information. Parallel to this, the texts are provided to an LLM (Gemini 2.5 Pro Chat) to create an initial BPMN model. Subsequently, the initial BPMN model and the annotated information are manually combined to improve the BPMN model and ensure its adequate representation of the all relevant information. Finally, the five resulting process models are quantitatively evaluated by the automated syntax quality metric as described in Sect. 4. Furthermore, the authors reviewed the semantical fit and layout of the resulting models as a qualitative assessment, since an automated analysis of these aspects is only possible when a gold standard model already exists, and in this case such models were being created.

An overview of the use cases with information on the textual and model data is displayed in Tab. 2. As mentioned in [9] the performance an approach depends on the number of sentences or average sentence length contained in the input text. Thus, we show statistics on the input complexity of each use case through the number of sentences n and the average length of sentences measured in number of tokens l. For the assessment of gold standard (GS) model complexity, we extend the measures provided in [9] by roles, resulting in 4 values: the size of the models in terms of nodes N (activities and events), gateways G, edges E, and roles R. Use case III. (Blood Donor Selection) is by far the longest input text as a whole section of a regulation concerned with the details of the corresponding process. the manually created process model has 39 nodes, 14 gateways, and 54 edges. Use case V. (Customer Due Diligence) is the shortest in terms of number of sentences, but the sentences are long with on average 34.5 tokens, which makes it very challenging to extract information.

We compare CARB to two existing solutions as base models, i.e., 1) ProMoAi [15] and 2) Gemini 2.5 Pro Chat with the prompt design from [21]. The LLM chosen for processing within ProMoAi is also Gemini 2.5 Pro for comparability reasons. For base model 1) *ProMoAi*, it should be noted that the resulting process models are focused on control flow, neglecting actors, gateway labels and events (except start and end event) and thus create more simplistic process models. For the base model 2), we incorporate

Table 2. Input text and gold standard model characteristics for the 5 use cases.

Use Cases			Text Input		GS Model			
name	domain	source model	n	l	N	G	E	R
I. Smart Meter	energy mgmt.	adj. from [6,28]	14	25.9	28	9	36	4
II. GDPR	data privacy	adj. from [2,28]	23	28.1	21	13	38	4
III. Blood Donor Selection	medical procedure	newly created	524	22.1	39	14	54	4
IV. Health Data Exchange	medical data	newly created	19	24.9	19	3	19	4
V. Customer Due Diligence	finance	newly created	12	34.5	24	5	28	3

the prompt designed by [21], using the sections that are identified as 'useful' in their prompt evaluation and adjust what is necessary for BPMN model creation (as their prompt aims at a textual output/ process information extraction). The adjusted prompt is used in the Gemini 2.5 Pro Chat resulting in .bpmn output.

5.2   A. Syntactic Quality

Concerning the syntactic evaluation results (cf. Table 3) CARB outperforms Gemini Chat. Compared to ProMoAi CARB has less warnings, but leads to some errors. These errors marked for 4 out of the 15 runs with CARB (resulting in the overall average errors of 0.4), occur due to multiple start events within a pool, e.g., 2 errors for one run of the GDPR are caused by two intermediate message events wrongly being modeled as start message events. However, ProMoAI does not run into errors as their detected process logic is rather simplistic, i.e., there are no events and pools in the models.

Table 3. Syntactic Evaluation.

Use Case	GeminiChat		ProMoAi		CARB	
	Avg. Errors	Avg. Warn.	Avg. Errors	Avg. Warn.	Avg. Errors	Avg. Warn.
I. Smart M.	14.00	0.33	0.00	1.67	0.00	0.33
II. GDPR	22.67	0.00	0.00	4.33	0.67	0.33
III. Blood D.	17.33	0.33	0.00	1.67	0.67	0.00
IV. Health D.	20.67	0.00	0.00	1.33	0.00	0.67
V. CDD	7.33	0.67	0.00	3.00	0.67	1.67
Overall	**16.40**	**0.27**	**0.00**	**2.40**	**0.40**	**0.60**

5.3   B. Semantic Quality

The %-values shown in Table 4 are the average for all 3 runs per use case for each of the evaluation aspects introduced in Sect. 4. The results per execution run as well as the absolute values and the automated evaluation script are included in the code repository. As correctness is the core of the semantic evaluation, it is weighted with 0.6 in the RSS score, while completeness is weighted with 0.3 and traceability with 0.1.

Table 4. Semantic Evaluation [average values for 3 executions].

	Use Case	completeness						correctness				trace.		RSS
		AR	AY	EV	DO	AG	XG	AA	CF	DL	CL	AP	AI	
Gemini	I. Smart Meter	0.83	0.24	**0.36**	N/A	0.33	0.33	0.20	**0.05**	0.07	0.59	0.92	**0.64**	**0.34**
	II. GDPR	**1.00**	0.50	0.27	N/A	0.00	0.47	0.50	0.07	0.33	0.60	**1.00**	0.63	0.44
	III. Blood D.	0.33	0.22	0.22	N/A	N/A	0.11	0.07	0.10	0.14	0.35	0.36	0.46	0.21
	IV. Health D.	**1.00**	0.75	0.27	0.00	N/A	0.00	0.63	0.21	0.00	0.48	0.78	**0.95**	0.41
	V. CDD	**0.78**	0.24	0.07	0.00	N/A	0.20	0.19	0.05	0.17	0.29	**0.78**	0.54	0.25
ProMoAi	I. Smart Meter	0.00	0.27	0.15	N/A	**0.67**	**0.57**	0.00	0.00	0.00	0.61	0.00	0.48	0.22
	II. GDPR	0.00	0.47	0.09	N/A	**1.00**	**1.00**	0.00	0.03	0.00	0.72	0.00	0.26	0.28
	III. Blood D.	0.00	0.27	0.00	N/A	N/A	**0.61**	0.00	0.06	0.00	0.49	0.00	0.28	0.16
	IV. Health D.	0.00	0.58	0.00	0.00	N/A	**1.00**	0.00	0.04	0.00	0.74	0.00	0.72	0.25
	V. CDD	0.00	0.36	0.00	0.00	N/A	**1.00**	0.00	0.00	0.00	0.62	0.00	0.26	0.19
CARB	I. Smart Meter	**0.92**	**0.33**	0.23	N/A	0.00	**0.57**	**0.29**	0.04	**0.20**	**0.86**	**1.00**	0.51	**0.34**
	II. GDPR	**1.00**	**0.63**	**0.55**	N/A	0.67	0.83	**0.63**	**0.14**	**0.48**	**0.71**	**1.00**	**0.65**	**0.56**
	III. Blood D.	**0.42**	**0.48**	**0.36**	N/A	N/A	0.33	**0.11**	**0.18**	**0.29**	**0.71**	**0.61**	**0.47**	**0.31**
	IV. Health D.	**1.00**	**0.79**	**0.52**	0.00	N/A	0.56	**0.75**	**0.48**	**0.33**	**0.80**	**0.82**	0.85	**0.58**
	V. CDD	0.67	**0.43**	**0.19**	0.00	N/A	0.93	**0.33**	**0.08**	**0.33**	**0.86**	0.56	**0.65**	**0.38**

For *completeness* scores, CARB performs clearly better than base models in generating necessary activities (AY) and events (EV). For actor (AR) identification it is slightly better than Gemini Chat (superior in 2 use cases, inferior in one), but here the results are comparable with the Gemini Chat approach. None of the models created data objects (DO). For gateways (AG) and (XG), CARB performs better than Gemini Chat, but ProMoAi seems superior to both. However, for the interpretation of these results it is important to note, that ProMoAi only includes activities, (unlabeled) gateways and start- and end event in their process models, thus it is to be expected to generate many gateways as they do not include other modeling options. The completeness is only a simplistic existence check, counting the number of gateways per type existing in the model. The check concerning correct decision logic is evaluated in correctness.

The evaluation of *correctness* demonstrates that CARB achieves the highest performance scores across all four tested aspects and five use cases (with exception of one CF value). As all three compared approaches incorporate LLM-based reasoning, they each demonstrate satisfactory performance for the conditional logic (CL). Nevertheless, CARB's specific architecture ensures its superior performance in this category as well.

The *Traceability* metric measures how well generated actors and activities are grounded in the source text; low scores indicate potential hallucinations or an incorrect level of detail. While CARB again achieves the best results, its performance is more comparable to Gemini Chat on this metric, showing a smaller advantage than was observed for completeness and correctness.

The *RSS* offers an overall performance indicator per use case. It clearly supports the expectation that the blood donor use case III was the most difficult to model due to its extensive input text. All 3 approaches perform worst on this use case. Use case V (CDD) was the second most challenging, likely due to the length of its sentences.

5.4   C. Layout

Table 5. Layout Evaluation Scores.

Use Case	Gemini	ProMoAi	CARB
I. Smart M.	0.70	0.20	0.50
II. GDPR	0.20	0.10	0.30
III. Blood D.	0.40	0.10	0.20
IV. Health D.	0.90	0.15	0.65
V. CDD	0.65	0.10	0.33
Avg. Score	**0.57**	**0.13**	**0.40**

The layout quality of the generated process models is evaluated based on their visual representation (.png). For each use case, only the first generated model is considered. An overall layout score (cf. Table 5), ranging from 0.0 (very poor) to 1.0 (perfect), is assigned by an LLM (Gemini 2.5 Pro) according to specified quality criteria (cf. Section 4). In terms of layout, CARB does not outperform the baseline methods. It scores higher than ProMoAi and lower than Gemini. One potential reason for CARB's lower performance is the increased complexity and element count in its generated models, which introduces more opportunities for layout errors. However, the layout agent itself yields only marginal improvements, suggesting an inherent difficulty in using a reasoning agent to interpret positional information from an XML source. Therefore, a deterministic, rule-based approach may be more suitable for this task.

5.5   D. Stability of Results

To assess the stability of the generated outputs, we execute the five use cases three times with each approach. Table 6 presents the resulting average standard deviation for the 12 semantic evaluation results. Overall, the models demonstrate high stability, evidenced by low standard deviations. The primary source of instability is the existence of AND-Gateways (AG), which shows the highest standard deviation. This occurs because in most runs no gateways are generated, but in rare instances, the models includes two, creating the variance.

Table 6. Average Standard Deviation Across All Use Cases.

Approach	completeness						correctness				trace	
	AR	AY	EV	DO	AG	XG	AA	CF	DL	CL	AP	AI
Gemini	0.07	0.08	0.11	0.00	0.29	0.09	0.05	0.07	0.08	0.06	0.17	0.15
ProMoAi	0.00	0.09	0.00	0.00	0.29	0.08	0.00	0.03	0.00	0.20	0.00	0.08
CARB	0.12	0.10	0.10	0.00	0.29	0.16	0.05	0.07	0.22	0.09	0.11	0.15

6   Discussion

A primary limitation concerns the *applicability* of our approach to different types of input texts. CARB is specifically designed for regulatory documents that contain procedural logic, such as sequences, and conditional rules. For texts that are purely declarative and lack such procedural information, our method is less suitable. In these cases, alternative approaches like declarative process model extraction, as proposed by van der Aa et al. [1], would likely yield more appropriate results. Furthermore, while we expect that CARB's dynamic architecture could model non-regulatory texts by simply omitting unneeded components like conditional logic, this was not verified. The applicability of our approach to non-regulatory documents was outside the scope of our evaluation and remains an area for future work.

Another consideration is the *intended usage* of the results. The models generated by CARB should not be viewed as final, fully legally compliant representations of the text. As discussed in Sect. 4, the inherent ambiguity in natural language makes it unreasonable to expect a generated model to be a 100% perfect match to a human-created gold standard. Instead, they are designed to serve as initial reference models. Their primary purpose is to aid stakeholders with a foundational, procedural understanding of complex regulations and to act as an aid in the manual modeling of regulatory process logic. We strongly recommend that any generated model undergoes a thorough review by both a legal expert and a process modeling expert before it is considered a ground truth or integrated into business operations.

Finally, a challenge in our evaluation is the subjective nature of *process granularity*. The level of detail captured in a process model can vary between modelers, and our system may make different choices than a human expert. For instance, a single, high-level activity in the gold standard, such as 'Forward request to system', is represented by a generated model in a finer granularity, splitting the 'request' into two distinct activities 'Initiate Activation' and 'Initiate Deactivation'. This discrepancy is not an error, but a difference in the level of abstraction.

7   Conclusion

This work introduces CARB, a novel approach to automatically generate BPMN process models from regulatory texts. The novel contributions of this work are twofold. First, CARB is designed to interpret modalities, such as obligations and permissions, inherent in legal documents. Second, it utilizes a Supervisor Multi-Agent framework that decomposes the complex task of process model generation with layout information into specialized sub-tasks for individual agents. This architecture enables iterative quality checks and self-correction, significantly improving the final output. The evaluation demonstrates that CARB outperforms existing methods in extracting model information beyond control flow, e.g., pools and lanes, and at the same time offers comparable or even superior performance w.r.t. syntactic correctness and semantic quality. For future work, we plan to engage legal experts to further validate the semantic accuracy of both, the gold standard and the generated models. Furthermore, we will enhance the layout agent by developing a rule-based tool to address the persistent challenge of automated process model visualization without flaws.

References

1. van der Aa, H., Di Ciccio, C., Leopold, H., Reijers, H.A.: Extracting declarative process models from natural language. In: Advanced Information Systems Engineering, pp. 365–382 (2019)
2. Agostinelli, S., Maggi, F.M., Marrella, A., Sapio, F.: Achieving GDPR compliance of BPMN process models. In: CAiSE Forum, pp. 10–22 (2019)
3. Audrito, D., Ferraris, A.F.: Legal design through business process model and notation (BPMN): a digital services act case-study. In: Joint Ontology Workshops (2023)
4. Bellan, P., Dragoni, M., Ghidini, C.: Combining natural language processing approaches for rule extraction from legal documents. In: AI Approaches to the Complexity of Legal Systems Workshops, pp. 287–300 (2017)
5. Bellan, P., Dragoni, M., Ghidini, C.: Extracting business process entities and relations from text using pre-trained LMS. In: Enterprise Distributed Object Computing Conference, pp. 182–199 (2022)
6. Böhmer, K., et al.: Application and testing of business processes in the energy domain. In: BTW, pp. 25–32 (2017)
7. Capuzzimati, F., Violato, A., Baldoni, M., Boella, G.: Business process management for legal domains: Supporting execution and management of preliminary injunctions. In: Legal Knowledge and Information Systems, pp. 149–152 (2015)
8. Dimyadi, J., Clifton, C., Spearpoint, M., Amor, R.: Computerising regulatory knowledge for building engineering design. J. Comput. Civil Eng. (2024)
9. Friedrich, F.: Automated generation of business process models from natural language input (2010)
10. Friedrich, F., Mendling, J., Puhlmann, F.: Process model generation from natural language text. In: Advanced Information Systems Engineering, pp. 482–496 (2011)
11. Grohs, M., Abb, L., Elsayed, N., Rehse, J.: Large language models can accomplish business process management tasks. In: Business Process Management Workshops, pp. 453–465 (2023)
12. Hashmi, M., Governatori, G., Lam, H.-P., Wynn, M.T.: Are we done with business process compliance: state of the art and challenges ahead. Knowl. Inf. Syst. **57**(1), 79–133 (2018). https://doi.org/10.1007/s10115-017-1142-1
13. Klievtsova, N., Benzin, J., Kampik, T., Mangler, J., Rinderle-Ma, S.: Conversational process modelling: State of the art, applications, and implications in practice. In: BPM Forum, pp. 319–336 (2023)
14. Klievtsova, N., Kampik, T., Mangler, J., Rinderle-Ma, S.: Conversationally actionable process model creation. In: Cooperative Information System, pp. 39–55 (2024)

15. Kourani, H., Berti, A., Schuster, D., van der Aalst, W.M.P.: Promoai: process modeling with generative ai. In: IJCAI Demo Track, pp. 8708–8712 (2024)
16. Kruiper, R., Kumar, B., Watson, R., Sadeghineko, F., Gray, A.J.G., Konstas, I.: A platform-based natural language processing-driven strategy for digitalising regulatory compliance processes for the built environment. Adv. Eng. Informatics 102653 (2024)
17. Mendling, J.: Metrics for Process Models: Empirical Foundations of Verification, Error Prediction, and Guidelines for Correctness. Springer (2008)
18. Mendling, J., Reijers, H.A., van der Aalst, W.M.P.: Seven process modeling guidelines (7PMG). Inf. Softw. Technol, pp. 127–136 (2010)
19. Muram, F.U., Javed, M.A., Kanwal, S.: Facilitating compliance of process models with critical system standards using NLP. In: Evaluation of Novel Approaches to Software Engineering, pp. 306–313 (2021)
20. Nake, L., Kuehnel, S., Bauer, L., Sackmann, S.: Towards identifying gdpr-critical tasks in textual business process descriptions. In: GI Jahrestagung, pp. 1895–1908 (2023)
21. Neuberger, J., Ackermann, L., van der Aa, H., Jablonski, S.: A universal prompting strategy for extracting process model information. In: Conceptual Modeling, pp. 38–55 (2024)
22. Neuberger, J., Ackermann, L., Jablonski, S.: Beyond rule-based named entity recognition and relation extraction for process model generation from natural language text. In: Cooperative Information Systems, pp. 179–197 (2023)
23. Reimers, N., Gurevych, I.: Sentence-bert: Sentence embeddings using siamese bert-networks. In: Empirical Methods in Natural Language Processing, EMNLP (2019)
24. Rosemann, M.: Potential pitfalls of process modeling: part A. Bus. Process. Manag. J. 249–254 (2006)
25. Sai, C., Winter, K., Rinderle-Ma, S.: Detecting deviations between external and internal regulatory requirements for improved process compliance assessment. In: Advanced Information Systems Engineering, pp. 401–416 (2023)
26. Wang, H.J., Zhao, J.L., Zhang, L.: Policy-driven process mapping (PDPM): discovering process models from business policies. Decis. Support Syst. **48**(1), 267–281 (2009)
27. Weske, M.: Business Process Management: Concepts, Languages. Springer, Architectures (2007)
28. Winter, K., van der Aa, H., Rinderle-Ma, S., Weidlich, M.: Assessing the compliance of business process models with regulatory documents. In: Conceptual Modeling, pp. 189–203 (2020)

Architecture, Engineering and Governance of Information Systems

A Method for Automated Deployment Architecture Reconstruction from Heterogeneously Nested Deployment Models

Marcel Weller[1]([✉]) [ID], Uwe Breitenbücher[2] [ID], and Steffen Becker[1] [ID]

[1] University of Stuttgart, 70569 Stuttgart, Germany
{Marcel.Weller,Steffen.Becker}@informatik.uni-stuttgart.de
[2] Reutlingen University, 72762 Reutlingen, Germany
uwe.breitenbuecher@reutlingen-university.de

Abstract. Deploying large-scale software systems often requires combining multiple different deployment technologies by creating heterogeneously nested deployment models, for example, using Kubernetes manifests within a Terraform configuration file. If such nested models need to be manually analyzed regarding the architecture of the final deployment, immense technical expertise in different technologies is required. Moreover, current automated architecture reconstruction approaches do not consider such heterogeneously nested deployment models. Therefore, we present a rule-based method that automatically transforms a given deployment model into a technology-agnostic, graph-based architecture model while considering heterogeneously nested deployment models. We applied the method in a case study to reconstruct the deployment architectures from six deployment models of three reference applications using different combinations of the technologies Ansible, Kubernetes, Terraform, Helm, Bash, and Docker. The case study shows that many architectural aspects can be reconstructed generically, but some parts need custom or semantic analysis transformation rules.

Keywords: Software Architecture · Deployment Models · Architecture Reconstruction · Model-Driven Software Engineering

1 Introduction

Large-scale applications rely on *deployment technologies* to automate complex deployments based on deployment models, which describe the components to be deployed, their configurations, relations, and the mapping to the infrastructure. We conducted expert interviews, showing that in practice, several deployment technologies must be combined to achieve complete deployment automation. This results in *heterogeneously nested deployment models*, such as Ansible playbooks used in a Terraform configuration file, which are typically split across multiple files and are written in different Domain Specific Languages (DSLs).

Therefore, the reconstruction of the *deployment architecture* [19] from deployment models is a major challenge: Architects must have in-depth technical expertise

C. Cappiello et al. (Eds.): CoopIS 2025, LNCS 15535, pp. 391–409, 2026.
https://doi.org/10.1007/978-3-032-15538-2_22

about each DSL and technology to understand the deployment models, e.g., to assess architecture conformance to best practices [22] or to tackle architectural drift. Thus, architects would benefit from an automated reconstruction of the deployment architecture. However, handling heterogeneous technologies is considered a general challenge of Software Architecture Reconstruction (SAR) approaches [7], and current SAR approaches do not support heterogeneously nested deployment models. In a demonstration paper [34], we presented a first prototype of the Deployment Model Abstraction Framework (DeMAF), to create a technology-agnostic deployment model from a heterogeneous deployment model. However, the version of the DeMAF at that time could not support arbitrary models and technologies and did not focus on architectural information.

Therefore, we formulate the following research question for this paper:

> **Research Question:** How can the deployment architecture be automatically reconstructed from technology-specific deployment models that include deployment models of other technologies?

We address this question by introducing a model-driven method to automatically transform a given deployment model into a technology-agnostic, graph-based architecture model. Our method employs transformation rules and recursively applies itself to each nested model to tackle heterogeneity and enable extensibility. We implement our method in a new version of the DeMAF and run a case study on two reference applications with a total of six deployment models of different technologies and sizes. The case study shows the capability of our method to reconstruct deployment architectures, while the limits are shown where the analysis of further artifacts, for example, Docker images or application source code, is needed to reconstruct more detailed architectural information.

The paper is structured as follows: Sect. 2 describes fundamentals. Section 3 presents our expert interviews and Sect. 4 introduces a motivating example. We present our method in Sect. 5. Section 6 describes the new DeMAF we use for the evaluation in Sect. 7. We discuss related work in Sect. 8 and present conclusions in Sect. 9.

2   Fundamentals

This section introduces the basics of deployment technologies and overviews how common architectural methods integrate the deployment architecture.

2.1   Deployment Technologies and Deployment Models

Manually deploying large-scale software systems that consist of many components having non-trivial configurations and dependencies among each other is considered error-prone and time-consuming [9]. Therefore, *deployment technologies* have been developed to automatically execute so-called *deployment models*, which describe how the software system has to be deployed. Deployment models are written in a certain *DSL* and typically support either *declarative modeling*, to describe what has to be deployed in the form of a desired state, or *imperative modeling,* to precisely describe all tasks and their order of the deployment process [9]. In practice, often multiple deployment technologies have to be combined to automate the orchestrated deployment of all system parts completely.

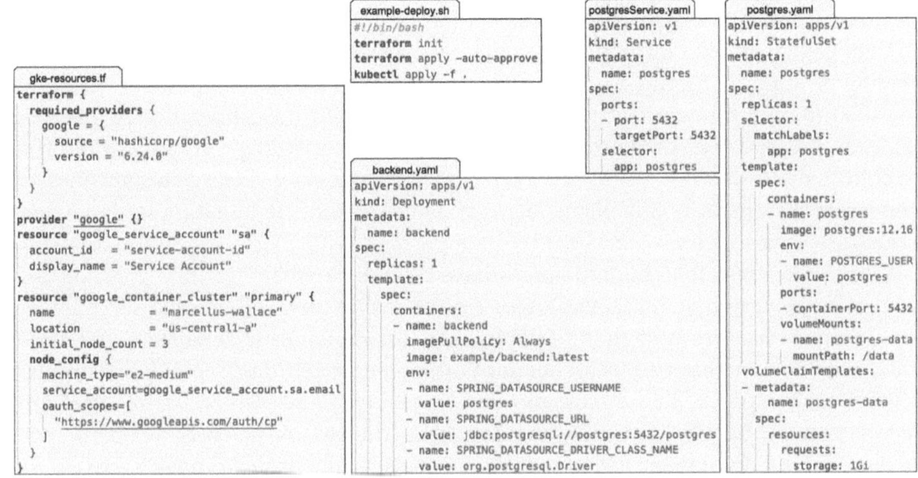

Fig. 1. Motivating example of a heterogeneously nested deployment model.

2.2   Deployment Architecture

Many architectural standards and languages enable modeling the *deployment architecture* of a system, e.g., the 4+1 View Model defines the physical view (also called *deployment view*) that describes the mappings of the software to the hardware [17]. Similarly, the *arc42 deployment view* describes how software artifacts are mapped to the technical infrastructure [15]. *UML* models the deployment of software artifacts to deployment targets in a deployment diagram [23]. The *C4 model* provides deployment diagrams to supplement a core set of four static structure diagrams to model software systems [5]. The *Language Ecosystem for Modeling Microservice Architecture (LEMMA)* models the assignment of microservices to computing nodes in operation models [27]. Thus, architecture models focus on a higher-level, abstract deployment view than deployment models. As a result, architecture models make it easier for people to understand the architecture of a system since technical details are abstracted. This is particularly important for the deployment of complex software systems because, as we will see in Sect. 3, they often require a combination of multiple deployment technologies. However, combining deployment technologies spreads information about the deployment architecture to multiple deployment models of different technologies, which makes it difficult to understand the overall deployment architecture of the entire system.

3 Problem Analysis

In order to analyze the combination of deployment technologies in more detail, we conducted interviews with ten experts in deployment technologies. Each interview took around 15 min and was conducted online with Microsoft Teams using audio recording and automated text transcription. During the interview, we first asked for demographic information, including age, gender, current job title, and years of industry experience. We then gave a general introduction to the interview topic to ensure a common understanding of important terms, such as software system or deployment model. After that, we asked the main interview questions. We anonymized the automatically generated text transcript and corrected errors based on the audio recording. From the transcripts, we collect the interview results for each interview question. For open questions, we summarized the main points of the answers and used inductive coding to derive categories.

The results show that all participants have used deployment technologies and combined different deployment technologies for the deployment of a single software system. The most used combination of deployment technologies is *Terraform and Kubernetes*, which was mentioned by all but one participant. Regarding combinations of three or more technologies, the combination of *Terraform, Kubernetes, Helm, and Ansible* was mentioned the most (5/10 participants). The reason given by all participants for combining deployment technologies is that deployment technologies usually fulfill different use cases and must be combined to cover all system aspects. Half of the participants also combine deployment technologies because of the cooperation with other people or teams. Common problems when combining deployment technologies are integrating the configuration (mentioned by 80%) and coordinating the execution (mentioned by 60%) of the deployment models of different deployment technologies. Examples of these categories are configuring application connections across different technologies and abstraction levels, and determining the correct execution order in the imperative modeling of Bash scripts or CI/CD pipelines. In addition, four participants mentioned problems in learning or teaching deployment technologies. When asked how easy or difficult it is to keep an overview of the deployment, answers differ. Two participants state it to be rather easy because each deployment technology has a specific responsibility. The majority of the participants (60%), however, rate it rather hard because of the complex technology stack or the high complexity of the software system. Finally, we asked the participants if they would use a tool that can visualize a comprehensive overview of the deployment of a software system, including information from the artifacts of all deployment technologies involved. Only one participant was unsure if they would use such a tool, while all other participants would use it or at least evaluate it (one participant), either for communication (8/10 participants) or their own understanding (8/10 participants). The participants described various ways of utilizing the tool for communication, e.g., for onboarding new team members, in decision boards, customer meetings, or for exchanging information with other experts working on the deployment model. We provide the interview questions, anonymized transcripts, and all interview results in the supplemental material [33].

Our interviews show that a tool that analyzes all deployment models of a single software system to reconstruct the deployment architecture of the entire system would be used by most interviewees for communication and understanding purposes. In addition to these interviews, Sect. 4 analyzes a small deployment example to emphasize the technical complexity of deployment architecture reconstruction from deployment models and why automation is essential.

4   Motivating Example

We introduce a motivating example to demonstrate the typical challenges of analyzing deployment models in terms of deployment architecture. Figure 1 shows five files written in the DSLsof Terraform, Kubernetes, and Bash, which are linked with each other and, therefore, form a single overall deployment model that can be executed. To analyze the deployment architecture of the system that gets deployed by this deployment model, we need to analyze all these files in detail. The Bash script is the main entry point of the overall deployment model and orchestrates the execution of the Terraform and Kubernetes files. The Terraform file deploys a Kubernetes cluster on the Google Cloud Platform (GCP). The three files of the Kubernetes deployment model describe the deployment of a Java Spring Boot application called *backend* and a PostgreSQL database called *postgres* on the Kubernetes cluster. The backend application connects to the postgres database through the postgres service. Figure 2 shows the analyzed deployment architecture.

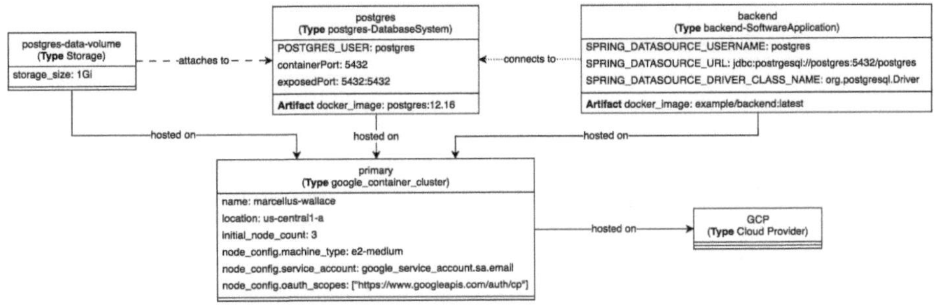

Fig. 2. Reconstructed deployment architecture of the motivating example.

Even analyzing this simplified deployment model with its five small files is a real challenge that requires immense expertise: three different DSLs need to be understood, the dependencies in the models need to be recognized, and technical configurations must be abstracted to architectural, technology-independent information. Thus, for large-scale systems, a deployment model quickly contains or invokes many other deployment models of different technologies that have to work together, which requires a huge effort to analyze the deployment architecture hidden in all these technical files. Therefore, a manual deployment architecture reconstruction is not efficient, especially since it has to be repeated every time the deployment needs to be adapted.

5   Automated Deployment Architecture Reconstruction from Heterogeneously Nested Deployment Models

To tackle the challenges motivated in Sect. 4, we present a method for automatically reconstructing the deployment architecture from deployment models.

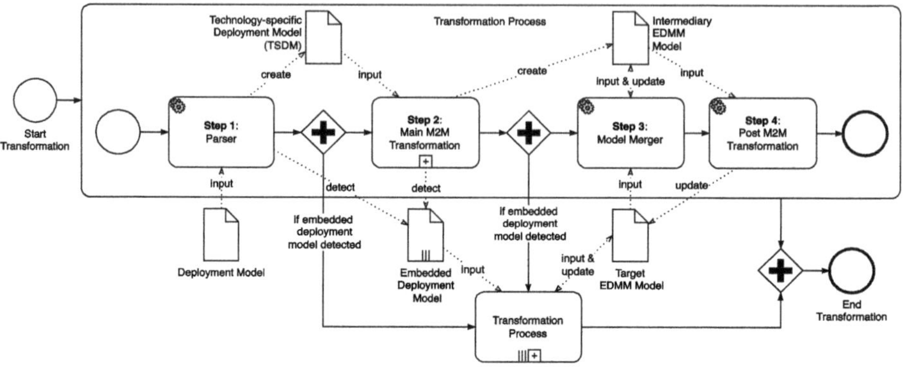

Fig. 3. Conceptual overview of the method.

5.1   Overview of the Method

We present an overview of our method in Fig. 3, which is realized as a transformation process that consists of four steps. The method is designed to run completely automated without requiring any manual input or intervention apart from the initial input of the deployment model. In the first step, the *deployment model parser* parses the input deployment model into an abstract representation called *technology-specific deployment model (TSDM)..* The second step executes the *main model-to-model (M2M) transformation* that transforms the TSDM into an Essential Deployment Metamodel (EDMM) model called the *intermediary EDMM model.* EDMM is a metamodel to express deployment models in a technology-agnostic way and was created by analyzing the 13 most prominent deployment technologies and combining their commonalities into one metamodel [35]. Therefore, we use EDMM to describe the deployment architecture. The first two steps may detect embedded deployment models that are contained in or invoked by the input deployment model. If so, the steps automatically extract the embedded deployment model and start an additional transformation process for the corresponding deployment technology. This new transformation process executes the same steps but may provide different technology-specific implementations. Thus, our method is technology-agnostic and extensible to arbitrary deployment technologies. In the third step, the *model merger* merges the output of previous transformation processes (called *Target EDMM Model* in Fig. 3) into the intermediary EDMM model. The *post M2M transformation* step is another model transformation to find architectural information spanning several embedded deployment models by analyzing the intermediary

EDMM model and finally updating the target EDMM model. After all transformations, the target EDMM model is the result.

The creation of the target EDMM model from several source models in separate transformations conforms to the *model merging* pattern [18]. The benefit of this split is that the transformation is divided into smaller and more modular parts, and the size of the source model is decreased. Therefore, we can deal with deployment models of any complexity regarding the nesting of embedded deployment models. However, the scheduling of the transformation processes and the management of the models become more complex compared to a single transformation that takes all embedded deployment models as input at once.

Step 1: Deployment Model Parser. Transformation rules should not be specified on the DSL as it makes the rules unnecessarily complex and invalid when the DSL evolves [30]. Therefore, the first step parses the deployment model represented in the concrete syntax of the deployment technologies DSL to the TSDM.. The TSDM. represents the deployment model in the abstract syntax of the deployment technology metamodel (see the left side of Fig. 4). However, most deployment technologies do not define such a metamodel, so we must define it from the DSL specification. This has the advantage of applying the *filter before processing* pattern [18] by only including the constructs of the DSL that are relevant for the transformation in the metamodel and parser. This way, we can filter out technology-specific information from the deployment models and reduce the transformation processing costs. Because some deployment technologies provide extensive DSLs with many different constructs, we can focus on selected parts of the DSL relevant for reconstructing the deployment architecture.

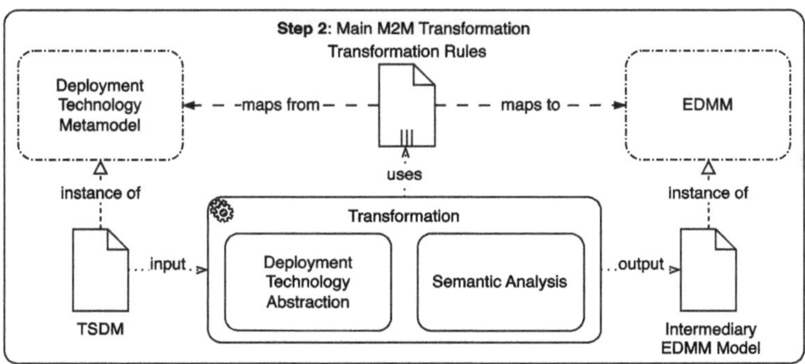

Fig. 4. Concept of Step 2: Main Model-to-Model Transformation.

Step 2: Main M2M Transformation. Figure 4 details the concept of Step 2. The TSDM is transformed into the intermediary EDMM model based on a set of transformation rules that map the deployment technology metamodel to the EDMM. The transformation rules use predefined relation types and may define a set of component types to detect. The transformation processes information in two different ways. The *deployment technology abstraction* executes rules to map the constructs of the deployment technology metamodel to the constructs of the EDMM. With the *semantic analysis*, the transformation interprets semantics in the TSDM that go beyond the semantics defined by the deployment technologies DSL. For example, Terraform relies on custom modules called providers, such as the *google* provider in Fig. 1, which facilitates the specification of various GCP resources. The semantics of these resources are defined by the provider implementation and not by the Terraform DSL.. Another example is a Bash script that orchestrates the execution of embedded deployment models as shown in Fig. 1. The commands are provided by external CLI tools such as kubectl for deploying Kubernetes deployment models. For each CLI tool, a custom rule must be defined to detect the embedded deployment model, including its location and configuration parameters. The rules for the deployment technology abstraction and the semantic analysis are detailed in Sect. 5.2 for each deployment technology.

Step 3: Model Merger. After Step 2, the model merger step merges the target EDMM model into the newly created intermediary EDMM model. The model merger adds the existing model entities to the newly created model entities of the intermediary EDMM model. However, when merging the transformation results, we must ensure the absence or resolution of conflicts resulting from different transformation processes. Therefore, the model merger checks for components or relations with the same name and associated type, and for component types or relation types with the same name. In these cases, the duplicate model entities are merged into one model entity that contains all information while further resolving possible duplicate properties, operations, and artifacts.

Step 4: Post M2M Transformation. Until now, the transformation process has transformed the input deployment model into the EDMM model without taking into account results from the previous transformation processes stored in the target EDMM model. Therefore, Step 4 is an optional step to post-process the intermediary EDMM model, which now contains the merged information from the target EDMM model. The Post M2M Transformation is an endogenous model-to-model transformation that takes the intermediary EDMM model as input and, as an output, updates the target EDMM model. In an endogenous transformation, the target and source metamodels are the same [18]. This allows for finding architectural information that spans the transformation results of multiple embedded deployment models, e.g., relations between newly created and existing components. In the case of Kubernetes, the Post M2M Transformation creates hosted-on relations to an existing Kubernetes cluster component.

5.2 Mappings

In this section, we present the application of our method to the deployment technologies Ansible, Terraform, and Kubernetes. We explain the mappings of technology-specific constructs to EDMM and where we apply semantic analysis.

Ansible. Ansible enables deploying software to local or remote host systems through desired state management [2]. A deployment is described in YAML-based *playbooks*, which can be distributed across several files. Playbooks contain *plays* that each define a set of *tasks* to be executed in the given order on one or more *hosts*. Hosts are infrastructure nodes and serve as the deployment target. Each task contains one *module* that defines the code to execute. Ansible supports providing custom modules, often organized in collections, for executing all kinds of tasks. For example, the Docker collection provides modules for building Docker images, starting Docker containers, and more. Furthermore, collections for Kubernetes, Helm, and other deployment technologies exist to **embed deployment models** of other languages. In addition to tasks, plays can define *roles*. Roles contain a set of tasks, variables, or *dependencies* to other roles organized in a predefined file structure that can be loaded by a play.

Table 1. Mapping of Ansible Constructs to EDMM.

Ansible Construct	EDMM Construct
Host	Component & Component Type
Role	Component & Component Type
Roles and Hosts in the same Play	hosted-on Relation
Variable	Property
Task	Operation
File	Artifact
Dependency	connects-to Relation
Module	Artifact

We define the rules shown in Table 1 for the deployment technology abstraction from Ansible to EDMM. We map each host and role to a component and respective component type. For components that result from roles, we create a hosted-on relation to the components that result from hosts in the same play. Variables contained in the role are transformed into component properties. For each task in the role, we create an operation. If the task references a file, the file is mapped to an artifact that implements the operation. Dependencies of roles are transformed into connects-to relations between the corresponding components.

The **semantic analysis** of Ansible is challenging due to its expandability: Separate rules must be defined for each module. We can generally map modules to artifacts, but often more specific information about a module is needed. For example, the aforementioned Docker container module should be transformed into an artifact representing the referenced Docker image and another artifact that contains the command to run the Docker container.

Terraform. Terraform provides the JSON-based Terraform language to create *configuration files*, in which the deployment of infrastructure resources, such as compute or networking, as well as software components, can be described [13]. Terraform models mainly contain *resource*, *variable*, and *provider* definitions. A resource describes a component that should be deployed and is of a specific *resource type*. The resource types are provided by the definition of a provider, which also enables Terraform to access specific APIs of services or platforms to deploy the respective resources. For example, the Google provider of the motivating example in Fig. 1 enables the deployment of resources on GCP.

Table 2. Mapping of Terraform Resources to EDMM.

Terraform Construct	EDMM Construct
Resource	Component & Component Type
Resource Argument & (Variable)	Component Property
depends_on Meta-Argument	depends-on Relation (refined to concrete type)
Provider	Component & hosted-on Relations

Table 2 shows the mapping of Terraform to EDMM. We map resources to EDMM components and component types. The name of the resource is mapped to the name of the component. From the resource type, we infer the name of the component type. In case there are several resources with the same resource type, the resulting components share the same component type. As a result, the transformation creates the component types based on the available resource definitions in the input Terraform model and, therefore, supports arbitrary providers.

In Terraform models, resources are configured through arguments, which we map to component properties while resolving variable references. Arguments can be defined in nested blocks inside the resource definition (e.g. *node_config* block in Fig. 1). Accordingly, we resolve the blocks and nested blocks to the contained arguments. The *depends_on* meta-argument of a resource expresses dependencies on other resources. Consequently, we map each dependency to a generic EDMM depends-on relation between the corresponding components. Lastly, we map specific providers to a component and the corresponding component type to express cloud providers. We currently support the mapping of Azure, AWS, and GCP to a component with the component type *Cloud Provider*. The providers are identified by the *source* keyword in the *required providers* block of the Terraform model. For all components originating from resource types of the cloud provider, a hosted-on relation is created to the cloud provider component. The motivating example in Fig. 1 uses the Google provider from which the *GCP* component in Fig. 2 is created, which hosts the *Google container cluster*.

For **semantic analysis**, we define resource type-specific transformation rules, e.g., to detect a database. In addition, components are removed if they describe logical resources such as the *Google service account* resource in Fig. 1. Lastly, we refine generic depends-on relations into concrete relation types, such as connects-to, based on the provider and resource type of the source and target components.

Terraform providers allow the **embedding of deployment models** of other deployment technologies, such as Kubernetes or Helm. The Helm provider allows the definition of Helm Charts as Terraform resources. Therefore, the Terraform transformation process extracts the embedded Helm chart from the Terraform resource and passes it to the Helm transformation process. Due to the large number of available Terraform providers, covering all possible cases requires substantial implementation and maintenance effort. Therefore, we currently focus on Azure, AWS, GCP, Kubernetes, Helm, and Docker providers.

Kubernetes and Helm. Kubernetes is a technology for orchestrating Containers, which are deployed as *pods* on a Kubernetes Cluster [32]. The deployment is described in declarative configuration files in the *Kubernetes language*, which defines various *Kubernetes objects*. Helm builds on Kubernetes by providing reusable and templated Kubernetes deployment models called Helm *charts* [14]. As a result, every Helm chart contains an embedded Kubernetes deployment model. To transform Helm charts, we extract the embedded Kubernetes deployment model and resolve the templated values from the given configuration.

Table 3. Mapping of Kubernetes Objects to EDMM.

Kubernetes Object	EDMM Construct
Pod (in Deployment / Stateful Set)	Component
Container Port	Component Property
Environment Variable	Component Property & connects-to Relation
Container Image	Component Artifact & Component Type
Service Port	Component Property
PVC & Volume & Volume Mount	Component & attaches-to Relation

Table 3 shows the transformation rules between Kubernetes objects relevant for deployment architecture and EDMM constructs. The *deployment* and *stateful set* objects specify the workload in the form of a *pod* to run on the Kubernetes cluster for describing stateless and stateful applications. Thus, we map them to components. The component's name is set from the deployment or stateful set name. From the pod specification, we define the properties and artifacts of the component and derive the component type. Pods specify one or more *containers* consisting of *container ports*, *environment variables*, and *container image*. We map each container port and environment variable to a component property, and the container image to a component artifact of type *docker image*. In addition to the artifact, we map Docker images to component types, so that components using the same Docker image have the same component type. This allows the detection of system software such as DBMSs or message brokers through semantic analysis of Docker image names. Similar to approaches described by [1, 29], we define a list of the Docker image names of commonly used system software, e.g., PostgreSQL or MySQL to create *database system* component types (see the *postgres* component in Fig. 2 which has the type *postgres-DatabaseSystem*).

Service objects enable access to pods from inside and outside the cluster. A service defines the endpoints to expose through a *service port* that maps to one or more container ports of a pod. We transform service ports to component properties. Kubernetes provides objects to deploy persistent storage for containers, namely *Persistent Volume Claim (PVC)*, *volume*, and *volume mount*. We match these objects to create a component of type *Storage*. An *attaches-to* relation is created from the storage component to the component created from the pod that contains the volume (see the *postgres-data-volume* component in Fig. 2).

Kubernetes allows the implicit configuration of pod connections in environment variables that reference the name of a Kubernetes service object. For example, the *SPRING_DATASOURCE_URL* variable of the *backend.yaml* in Fig. 1 configures the connection of the backend to the postgres database by referencing the postgres service name. Therefore, we define **semantic analysis** rules to map environment variables that define a connection string to connects-to relations. Semantic analysis is needed because the software running in the container defines the environment variable key and value naming scheme. To define a generic transformation rule, we filter environment variable keys for keywords such as *connect*, *url*, or *server*, and check the environment variable value for the name of a service object to create a connects-to relation. Lastly, the Post M2M Transformation creates hosted-on relations from all created components to a Kubernetes cluster component. As shown in Fig. 2, the *primary* component was recognized as a Kubernetes cluster.

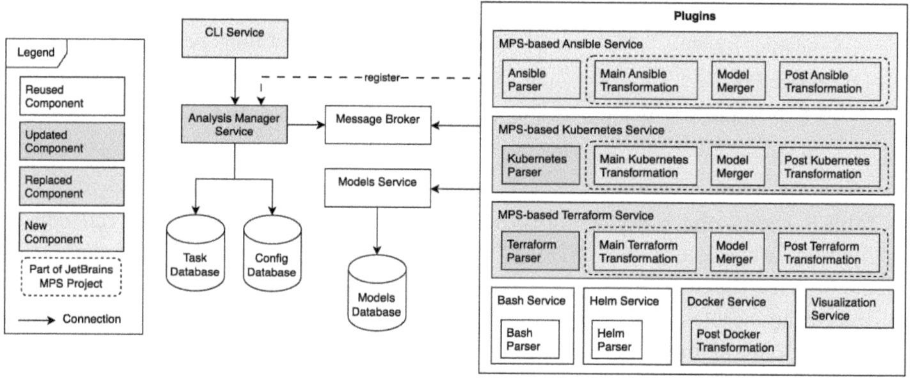

Fig. 5. Architecture overview of the new DeMAF (reuses and extends [34]).

6   Prototypical Implementation

We provide a new version of the DeMAF that implements the presented method.

The old version of the DeMAF [34] consists of several independent services for creating an EDMM model from technology-specific deployment models: *Plugin services* implement the logic to support a specific deployment technology, and the *analysis manager service* orchestrates the transformation over the plugins [34]. The old DeMAF provided plugins for Bash, Kubernetes, Helm, and Terraform.

Figure 5 shows the architecture of the new DeMAF, highlighting the most important changes. The new DeMAF adds three new MPS-based plugin services for Ansible, Kubernetes, and Terraform that implement the transformation process according to our model-driven method, replacing the existing Kubernetes and Terraform plugins of the old DeMAF. For this, each new plugin service encapsulates a JetBrains MPS project executable to implement steps 2, 3, and 4 of our method. We add the Docker plugin to the new DeMAF, which implements component type detection from Docker image names as outlined in Sect. 5.2 as part of Step 4. This allows reuse for other deployment technologies that use Docker containers, e.g., the Ansible Docker collection or the Terraform Docker provider. The old DeMAF outputs the EDMM model in YAML syntax. In addition to this textual representation, the new DeMAF also offers a graphical representation of the deployment architecture using the new *visualization service*. Lastly, the new DeMAF adds the *CLI Service* that was formerly integrated into the analysis manager in the old DeMAF.

7 Evaluation of the Method

Table 4. Deployment Models used for the evaluation.

Deployment Model	Used Deployment Technologies	#Files	LOC
OTEL Ans	Ansible, Docker	82	10361
OTEL Kube	Kubernetes, Docker	1	10942
OTEL TF	Terraform, Docker	14	9978
T2 MS	Bash, Helm, Kubernetes, Terraform, Docker	16	703
T2 Mod	Bash, Helm, Kubernetes, Terraform, Docker	7	337
Meitrex	Terraform, Helm, Kubernetes, Docker	16	1858

To evaluate our method, we conducted a case study based on a Goal Question Metric (GQM) model with the goal to *evaluate the ability to reconstruct the deployment architecture from technology-specific deployment models*. We applied our method to 6 deployment model cases of different sizes and deployment technologies by transforming them with our extended DeMAF prototype into EDMM models that represent the reconstructed deployment architectures. Afterward, we compared these models with the expected ground truth deployment architecture, which we reconstructed manually based on the original deployment models, documentation, and the deployed applications. We define four GQM questions: (**Q1**) *Does the generated model contain all expected components?*, (**Q2**) *Does the generated model contain incorrect component type assignments?*, (**Q3**) *Does the generated model contain all expected relations?*, and (**Q4**) *Does the generated model contain incorrect relation type assignments?*. Q2 and Q4 are measured by calculating the number and percentage of incorrectly assigned types. Similar to the case study performed by Alshuqayran [1], we use the metrics *precision*, *recall*, and *F1 score* for Q1 and Q3 as follows:

$$Precision = \frac{TP}{TP + FP} \quad Recall = \frac{TP}{TP + FN} \quad F1 = \frac{2 * TP}{2 * TP + FP + FN} \quad (1)$$

TP (True Positives) Components/relations present in both models
FP (False Positives) Components/relations present in the actual EDMM model but missing in the expected EDMM model
FN (False Negatives) Components/relations missing in the actual EDMM model but present in the expected EDMM model

Table 4 lists the 6 deployment model cases, the used technologies, the number of files, and lines of code (LOC).. The deployment models are based on three reference applications, the *OpenTelemetry Astronomy Shop Demo (OTEL)* [25], the *T2Store (T2)* [31], and *Meitrex* [20]. OTEL provides 3 deployment models that describe the same application using the technologies Ansible (OTEL Ans), Kubernetes (OTEL Kube), and Terraform (OTEL TF). T2 is implemented in two applications of different architectural styles (T2 MS, T2 Mod). The Zenodo repository provides all evaluation files, including deployment models, documentation, expected and actual EDMM models, and the new DeMAF [33].

7.1 Results and Discussion

Table 5 shows our results (also provided in [33]).

All expected components were found in every case, and no incorrect relation types were assigned. The main differences are incorrectly assigned component types (Q2) and missing connects-to relations (Q3). The incorrectly assigned component types in the OTEL cases are due to unconventional naming of the OTEL Docker images, which distinguish the OTEL microservices based on the image tag and not on the image name. As a result, 17 components of the OTEL share the same component type, which accounts for 65% of all assignments being incorrect in each case. Thus, our method depends

Table 5. Measured metrics of the GQM per deployment model.

Deployment Model	Q1	Q2		Q3						Q4
	F1	#	%	P	R	F1	TP	FP	FN	#
OTEL Ans	100%	17	65%	100%	88%	94%	79	0	11	0
OTEL Kube	100%	17	65%	100%	88%	94%	79	0	11	0
OTEL TF	100%	17	65%	100%	87%	93%	78	0	12	0
T2 MS	100%	2	9%	100%	100%	100%	52	0	0	0
T2 Mod	100%	0	0%	100%	100%	100%	12	0	0	0
Meitrex	100%	0	0%	90%	80%	85%	80	9	20	0

on best practices regarding image naming, which helps to detect such violations. In future work, we may support custom naming conventions through external configuration. In the T2 MS case, the two PostgreSQL database components were not identified as database system types because a custom Docker image was used instead of the official one. Detecting types from custom images requires analysis of the Docker image layers, which is part of future work.

Regarding the expected relations, the OTEL cases did not find 11 (OTEL Ans, OTEL Kube) and 12 (OTEL TF) relations, the T2 cases found all relations. The missing relations are connects-to relations between monitoring services, e.g., Grafana or the OTEL Collector, which are configured in external configuration files. In particular, the Grafana component must connect to the Jaeger, Prometheus, and OpenSearch components. This is configured in external YAML files in the OTEL Ans and OTEL TF cases and embedded in a ConfigMap in the OTEL Kube case. Thus, such configuration files need to be considered, too. However, the mentioned files are not written in the DSL of the deployment technology, but in a custom, application-specific format. This is similar to the Meitrex case, where the actual model missed 20 relations, while it found 9 unexpected relations. Meitrex uses the distributed application runtime *Dapr*, which introduces custom Kubernetes objects to configure Pod communication. Thus, for detecting such relations, special transformation rules need to be defined for specific applications or runtimes, which is not efficient and should be solved by generically analyzing network traffic, etc. This is part of our future work.

The results show that deployment architectures could be reconstructed from all deployment models. The aspects of the deployment architecture associated with the 4+1 deployment view (components and hosted-on relations) could be reconstructed completely. However, architectural information associated with the 4+1 development view is sometimes lacking, especially regarding the connects-to relations. Another challenge is detecting meaningful component types, as deployment technologies often do not distinguish between different deployment entities.

7.2 Threats to Validity

We identify threats to validity of our evaluation based on the categories by [28]. A threat to internal validity is the creation of a ground truth deployment architecture that does not contain any false information. To counter this, we applied peer debriefing through an expert group, including the authors and an external researcher. Still, more independent people could have been included to strengthen the validity. We selected cases based on reference applications that vary in the used deployment technologies, size of the deployment model, and architectural styles. The cases represent different domains (learning management system and web shop applications) but are all based on containerized workloads, posing a threat to external validity. Our method is extensible with rules based on deployment artifacts such as Java JARs that are similar to the Docker image rules. To increase the reliability of the evaluation, we provide a repository that describes how to conduct the study, including scripts for measuring the metrics [33].

8   Previous and Related Work

In previous work [34], we presented the old DeMAF as a first prototype to create technology-agnostic deployment models from heterogeneous deployment models. Although possible, the extensibility of the old DeMAF is limited due to a missing overarching method and the use of custom code for transforming the deployment models. Accordingly, we highlighted the need for a general method and a standardized and verifiable transformation process for future work. Therefore, in this paper, we presented a method based on a standardized transformation process and general mapping rules from several deployment technologies to the EDMM.

Related SAR approaches exist that involve deployment models. SAR is a process for obtaining the architecture of an implemented system from the existing system [24]. Categories of SAR approaches are *static*, *dynamic*, and *manual*, which reconstruct the architecture from static artifacts, the deployed system, or expert knowledge, respectively [6]. *Hybrid* SAR approaches combine categories.

Bakhtin et al. [4] overview 37 SAR approaches for microservice architecture reconstruction [4]. The distributed nature of microservices and the use of Docker often require using deployment technologies. Despite this, only four of the 37 approaches take deployment models as input [12,16,21,29]

MicroART [12], Infragenie [3], and the attack-graph-generator [16] are static or hybrid SAR approaches that analyze Docker Compose files to identify microservices, configurations, and relations. An extension to Infragenie supports Terraform deployment models but not in combination with Docker Compose [11]. Other approaches focus on the application source code and include Docker Compose files to enrich information, while extensibility to other deployment technologies is often mentioned but not demonstrated or evaluated [1,22,26,27].

Fekete et al. [10] use static analysis to identify microservices from Helm charts [10]. Each Helm chart is mapped to a microservice, and relations are obtained by analyzing the contained Kubernetes template. The resulting visualization still contains technology-specific information about Kubernetes objects, e.g., ConfigMaps used by a microservice. μMiner [21] and μTOM [29] employ static analysis to map Kubernetes deployment models to μTOSCA. μMiner leverages dynamic analysis of the deployed application to detect relations [21]. μTOM infers relations from static analysis of the Kiali graph, which shows microservice interactions obtained from application monitoring [29]. Endres et al. [8] create reusable TOSCA components from Chef or Juju deployment models [8].

To conclude, only a few SAR approaches focus on or include deployment models. Many of these approaches focus on Docker Compose, a deployment technology primarily used for local deployment or testing, but considered unsuitable for large production systems. Furthermore, several approaches involve manual tasks and do not provide a complete automatic reconstruction [1,22,26,27]. Most importantly, none of these approaches considers heterogeneous deployment models, especially regarding nested deployment models of other deployment technologies.

9   Conclusion and Future Work

Leveraging model transformation rules and detecting embedded deployment models enables the reconstruction of architectural information across technologies such as Kubernetes, Terraform, and Ansible. However, some architectural information, particularly connects-to relations, often must be determined based on semantic analysis. Moreover, covering all features and edge cases of the deployment technologies remains a challenge, especially when including community-provided extensions. In this regard and for including new technologies, the modularity of our method proves essential for the maintainability and evolvability.

In future work, we plan to integrate our method into automated processes, e.g., for evolution tracking. Moreover, it would be interesting to combine our approach with dynamic SAR approaches to either confirm the reconstructed architecture or enhance it with information gathered from the running system. The combination with other static SAR approaches that focus on different static artifacts than deployment models, for example, source code files, would allow for the reconstruction of more architectural views. Finally, we plan to implement our method in DevOps teams to evaluate how to adopt it in practice.

References

1. Alshuqayran, N.: Static Microservice Architecture Recovery Using Model-Driven Engineering. Ph.D. thesis, University of Brighton (May 2020)
2. Ansible project contributors: Ansible Documentation (Feb 2025). https://docs.ansible.com/ansible/latest/index.html. Accessed 11 Mar 2025
3. de Araújo Ferreira, R.J.: Recovery of Software and Architecture from Code Repositories. Master's thesis, University of Porto (2022)
4. Bakhtin, A., et al.: Tools reconstructing microservice architecture: a systematic mapping study. In: Software Architecture. ECSA 2023 Tracks, Workshops, and Doctoral Symposium, pp. 3–18 (2024)
5. Brown, S.: The C4 model for visualising software architecture. Leanpub (Feb 2023)
6. Cerny, T., et al.: Microservice architecture reconstruction and visualization techniques: a review. In: 2022 IEEE International Conference on Service-Oriented System Engineering (SOSE), pp. 39–48 (2022)
7. Ducasse, S., Pollet, D.: Software architecture reconstruction: a process-oriented taxonomy. IEEE Trans. Software Eng. **35**(4), 573–591 (2009)
8. Endres, C., Breitenbücher, U., Leymann, F., Wettinger, J.: Anything to topology - a method and system architecture to topologize technology-specific application deployment artifacts. In: Proceedings of the 7th International Conference on Cloud Computing and Services Science (CLOSER 2017), pp. 180–190. SciTePress (2017)
9. Endres, C., et al.: Declarative vs. imperative: two modeling patterns for the automated deployment of applications. In: Proceedings of the 9th International Conference on Pervasive Patterns and Applications, pp. 22–27. XPS (2017)
10. Fekete, A., et al.: Automatic dependency tracking in microservice-based systems using static analysis in helm charts. In: 2023 International Conference on Software, Telecommunications and Computer Networks (SoftCOM), pp. 1–7 (2023)
11. Figueiredo, D.J.G.O.D.: Recovery of Software and Architecture and Models from Infrastructure-as-Code. Master's thesis, University of Porto (2024)

12. Granchelli, G., et al.: Towards recovering the software architecture of microservice-based systems. In: 2017 IEEE International Conference on Software Architecture Workshops (ICSAW), pp. 46–53 (2017)
13. HashiCorp, Inc.: Terraform Documentation (Mar 2025). https://developer.hashicorp.com/terraform/docs. Accessed 23 Mar 2025
14. Helm Authors: Helm Architecture (2025).https://helm.sh/docs/topics/architecture. Accessed 11 Mar 2025
15. Hruschka, P., Starke, G.: arc42 Template Overview (Mar 2025). https://arc42.org/overview. Accessed 7 Mar 2025
16. Ibrahim, A., et al.: Attack graph generation for microservice architecture. In: Proceedings of the 34th ACM/SIGAPP Symposium on Applied Computing, pp. 1235–1242 (2019)
17. Kruchten, P.: Architectural Blueprints—The "4+1" ViewModel of Software Architecture. IEEE Softw. **12**(6), 42–50 (1995)
18. Lano, K., Kolahdouz-Rahimi, S.: Model-transformation design patterns. IEEE Trans. Softw. Eng. **40**(12), 1224–1259 (2014)
19. Medvidovic, N., Malek, S.: Software deployment architecture and quality-of-service in pervasive environments. In: International Workshop on Engineering of Software Services for Pervasive Environments: In Conjunction with the 6th ESEC/FSE Joint Meeting, pp. 47–51 (2007)
20. Meißner, N.: MEITREX - gamified and adaptive intelligent tutoring in software engineering education. In: Proceedings of the 2024 IEEE/ACM 46th International Conference on Software Engineering: Companion Proceedings, pp. 198–200 (2024)
21. Muntoni, G., Soldani, J., Brogi, A.: Mining the architecture of microservice-based applications from their kubernetes deployment. In: Advances in Service-Oriented and Cloud Computing, pp. 103–115. Springer International Publishing (2021)
22. Ntentos, E.: Supporting Architecture Evolution in Microservice-Based Systems and Infrastructure-as-Code Based Deployments. Ph.D. thesis, Universität Wien (2023)
23. Object Management Group, Inc. (OMG): OMG® Unified Modeling Language® (OMG UML®) Version 2.5.1 (2017). https://www.omg.org/spec/UML/2.5.1/
24. O'Brien, L., et al.: Software Architecture Reconstruction: Practice Needs and Current Approaches. Carnegie Mellon University, Tech. rep. (2002)
25. OpenTelemetry Authors: OpenTelemetry Demo Docs (Feb 2025). https://opentelemetry.io/docs/demo. Accessed 9 Mar 2025
26. Quéval, P.J., Zdun, U.: Extracting the architecture of microservices: an approach for explainability and traceability. In: Software Architecture, pp. 346–353. Springer Nature Switzerland (2023)
27. Rademacher, F.: A Language Ecosystem for Modeling Microservice Architecture. Ph.D. thesis, Universität Kassel (2022)
28. Runeson, P., et al.: Case Study Research in Software Engineering. John Wiley & Sons, Ltd (2012)
29. Soldani, J., Khalili, J., Brogi, A.: Offline mining of microservice-based architectures (extended version). SN Comput. Sci. **4**(3), 304 (2023)
30. Stahl, T., Völter, M., Czarnecki, K.: Model-Driven Software Development: Technology, Engineering. Inc, Management. John Wiley & Sons (2006)
31. Stieß, S.S., Kopp, D.: T2-Project Documentation (2024). https://t2-documentation.readthedocs.io. Accessed 09 Mar 2025
32. The Kubernetes Authors: Kubernetes Documentation (Mar 2025). https://kubernetes.io/docs/home. Accessed 23 Mar 2025
33. Weller, M.: A Method for Automated Deployment Architecture Reconstruction from Heterogeneously Nested Deployment Models - Supplemental Material (2025). https://doi.org/10.5281/zenodo.15882026

34. Weller, M., et al.: The deployment model abstraction framework. In: Enterprise Design, Operations, and Computing. EDOC 2022 Workshops, pp. 319–325 (2023)
35. Wurster, M., et al.: The essential deployment metamodel: a systematic review of deployment automation technologies. SICS Softw.-Intensive Cyber-Phys. Syst. **35**, 63–75 (2019)

Automated Synthesis of Kubernetes Variability from OpenAPI Schemas

Brian Flores[(✉)] [iD], Jose-Miguel Horcas [iD], Mercedes Amor [iD], and Lidia Fuentes [iD]

ITIS Software, Universidad de Málaga, Málaga, Spain
`{bfl699,horcas,map,lfuentes}@uma.es`

Abstract. Kubernetes (K8s) has emerged as the de facto standard for orchestrating containerized applications, offering extensive configurability to meet diverse deployment needs. However, this flexibility introduces significant complexity, leading to steep learning curves and a high propensity for configuration errors due to the manual navigation of vast documentation. While variability modeling techniques has proven successful in software product lines (SPLs) to manage such configuration complexity, its application in infrastructure systems such as K8s remains limited. This paper presents an automated approach for synthesizing a comprehensive K8s variability model directly from its official OpenAPI schemas. We demonstrate that this automatically generated model offers broader coverage of the configuration space than a manually constructed model previously developed from the API documentation. Furthermore, we evaluate the model's effectiveness in configuration validation against 250,000 real-world K8s configurations, comparing it with existing K8s validation tools. Our approach achieves 94.8% configuration validity, offering comprehensive structural and semantic checks that go beyond schema compliance or policy enforcement provided by other tools.

Keywords: Configuration · Feature Model · Kubernetes · Manifest Files · Software Product Line · Variability Modeling · YAML

1 Introduction

Kubernetes (K8s) [7,27] has become de facto standard for orchestrating containerized applications in most of computing environments [8], from centralized clouds to edge devices [11]. Having become one of the fastest-growing project in the history of open-source software. Recent statistics show that 60% of organizations have adopted K8s, and more companies are planning to do so. Leading cloud providers such as AWS, Microsoft Azure, Google Cloud, and VMware significantly facilitate K8s adoption by offering fully managed services [1,2].

K8s is designed as a flexible, modular, and declarative platform for managing containerized applications [7,27]. At the core of this design is the use of resource manifests (i.e., typically YAML files [22]) that declare the desired state of system components such as pods, deployments, services, and volumes. Each resource type comes with its own set of parameters, default values, and constraints, all of which are described in the official K8s API specification [32].

© The Author(s), under exclusive license to Springer Nature Switzerland AG 2026
C. Cappiello et al. (Eds.): CoopIS 2025, LNCS 15535, pp. 410–428, 2026.
https://doi.org/10.1007/978-3-032-15538-2_23

Its flexibility and extensibility allow developers and system administrators to finely tune deployment parameters to meet a wide variety of requirements. However, this high degree of configurability also introduces significant complexity when managing, validating, and maintaining K8s configurations [31]. K8s now supports hundreds of resource types and thousands of configuration options, many of which interact in subtle and non-obvious ways. Although these options are documented in natural language and partially structured through the K8s API, users must manually navigate extensive documentation to determine what is configurable, which parameters are required or optional, which values are valid, and how different options interact. This results in a steep learning curve and a high likelihood of configuration errors, particularly in complex deployments. Then misconfigurations are common, often resulting in unstable deployments, performance issues, or unexpected behavior [28].

In recent years, variability modeling, particularly in the form of *feature models* [12], has been widely used to manage configuration complexity in software product lines (SPLs) [3]. Feature models provide a structured representation of configurable options and their constraints, allowing users to analyze the configuration space, identify valid configurations, and generate instances automatically. Despite their success in domains such as the Linux kernel [20] or automotive software [26], feature models have not yet seen widespread application in DevOps and infrastructure systems and platforms such as K8s (see Sect. 2). In a previous work [18], we manually constructed a feature model of K8s based on its official API documentation, aiming to capture its configuration space in a formal, explainable way. Although effective, the manual process was time consuming, required extensive domain knowledge and iterative refinement, and ultimately only captured an infinitesimal fraction of the K8s configuration space (see Sect. 5).

In this paper, we advance towards a complete and replicable feature model by presenting an automated approach to synthesize the variability of K8s directly from its official OpenAPI schemas [24] (see Sect. 3). This approach not only reduces manual effort, but also ensures greater alignment with the actual API definitions. By parsing types, default values, value restrictions, and hierarchical relationships from the schema, we can generate an up-to-date, consistent, and expressive model of the K8s configuration space (Sect. 4). Our motivation is twofold: (1) we aim to demonstrate that effective automated variability extraction is feasible for a complex and rapidly evolving system such as K8s; (2) we argue that having such a model is not only useful for SPL research, but also brings practical benefits to the K8s ecosystem, including configuration validation, documentation, and reasoning [25]. The resulting feature model, specified in the Universal Variability Language (UVL) [6], enables advanced modeling constructs required to specify the variability of K8s and the usage of a rich tool ecosystem [14]. We validate the automatically synthesized model using a large corpus of over 250,000 real-world K8s configurations, comparing it with existing K8s validation tools. Furthermore, we compare this automatically extracted model with a manually curated model previously built from the official documentation, assessing their coverage, structure, and complexity (Sect. 5). Beyond their utility as an abstraction, these models enable: the validation of existing configurations, the automatic generation of valid manifests, the production of human-readable documentation, and reasoning over the configuration space, such as identifying all valid variants or common misconfigurations. Our contributions aim to bridge the gap between formal variability modeling and the real-world needs of K8s users, by showing how an automated, up-to-date, and explainable variability model can enhance configuration management, deployment reliability, and developer productivity. By bridging formal modeling with practical DevOps concerns, we hope to make variability models a valuable tool in infrastructure and cloud-native engineering.

2 Background and Related Work

2.1 Kubernetes

Kubernetes (K8s) [7,27] is a widely adopted open-source platform for automating the deployment and management of containerized applications. Its architecture is built around configurable resources such as pods, services, and deployments, defined declaratively through manifest files, written in YAML [22]. Listing 1.1 shows an example of YAML file configuring a service. The structure and semantics of these resources are formally described in two main sources of API documentation: the K8s API reference documentation and the OpenAPI schemas.

Listing 1.1. YAML manifest file for configuring a Service in K8s.

```
1  apiVersion: v1
2  kind: Service
3  metadata:
4    name: my-service
5  spec:
6    selector:
7      app: my-app
8    ports:
9      - protocol: TCP
10       port: 80
11       targetPort: 8080
```

K8s API Reference Documentation. The K8s API reference [32] provides a human-readable, web-based guide to all K8s resource types. It describes the hierarchical structure of the API, the available fields and types for each resource, and how these elements interact. This documentation is primarily intended for developers and operators writing YAML manifests or interacting with the cluster.

OpenAPI Schemas. In parallel, K8s exposes a machine-readable specification of its API based on the OpenAPI standard [24]. These OpenAPI schemas define the formal structure, types, default values, enumerations, and validation rules of all K8s resources. Listing 1.2 shows the main JSON schema definition of a Service which defines its most abstract properties (i.e., apiVersion, kind, metadata, and spec). Some of these properties (e.g., metadata, spec) are further refined in other linked schemas (see lines 14 and 18). Existing tools, IDE extensions, and configuration validators use this schema to verify manifest correctness, provide autocompletion, and generate client libraries.

Although both forms describe the same underlying API and are derived form the same source, their purposes differ: The API reference documentation is optimized for human consumption and learning, whereas the OpenAPI schemas are consumed by tools and automation pipelines. Then the reference documentation includes additional explanations, usage notes, and examples. In contrast, the OpenAPI schemas provide strict, canonical definitions required for programmatic validation and generation tasks.

Listing 1.2. JSON schema for defining the top properties of a Service in K8s.

```
1  "io.k8s.api.core.v1.Service": {
2    "description": "Represents a network service abstraction with a name, port,
   ↪  and selector.",
3    "properties": {
4      "apiVersion": {
5        "description": "Specifies the API version of the object.",
6        "type": "string"
7      },
8      "kind": {
9        "description": "Indicates the REST resource type of this object.",
10       "type": "string",
11       "enum": ["Service"]
12     },
13     "metadata": {
14       "$ref": "#/definitions/io.k8s.apimachinery.pkg.apis.meta.v1.ObjectMeta",
15       "description": "Standard metadata for the object."
16     },
17     "spec": {
18       "$ref": "#/definitions/io.k8s.api.core.v1.ServiceSpec",
19       "description": "Defines the desired behavior of the service."
20  }}}
```

2.2 Feature Modeling and Software Product Lines

Feature models [12] are a well-established formalism for representing variability in Software Product Lines (SPLs) [3]. A feature model encodes a hierarchy of *features*, which represent system capabilities or configuration options, and a set of constraints that define valid combinations. Features can be mandatory, optional, or part of alternative or inclusive-or groups. Cross-tree constraints in form of complex logical formulas further refine the configuration space.

Feature modeling enables advanced configuration analysis, including detection of invalid configurations, automatic instance generation, and consistency checking. Recent efforts have extended the classical feature modeling formalism to support richer types of variability, such as numerical features, attributes, string-typed values, and clonable features, through the new Universal Variability Language (UVL) [6]. UVL is supported by an emerging tool ecosystem [14] that enables automated reasoning tasks [13], including feature model validation, configuration space exploration, and integration with DevOps workflows, making it suitable for large-scale and evolving systems such as K8s.

2.3 Related Work on Configuration and Variability in Kubernetes

Several recent studies have addressed the growing complexity and misconfiguration risks in K8s deployments. Misconfiguration is recognized as one of the most prevalent sources of failures and vulnerabilities in K8s-based systems [28]. To tackle this, a variety of tools and empirical analyses have emerged.

Validation and Analysis Tools for K8s Configurations. A rich ecosystem of practical tools exists to validate K8s manifests and configurations, targeting security, best practices, schema compliance, and policy enforcement [10]. Examples include static analyzers such as *KubeLinter* and *kube-score*, policy engines like *OPA Gatekeeper* and *Kyverno*, as well as schema validation utilities such as *kubeconform*. Some tools rely on K8s OpenAPI schemas to verify manifest correctness and flag deprecated or removed API fields, while others apply customizable policy rules or perform security scans. Table 1 summarizes the main tools currently available, highlighting their validation focus and maintenance status. Diarra et al. [10] evaluated these tools using 13 key criteria (e.g., schema validation, verification types) in the context of cloud-native network functions. Although these tools provide valuable checks at different abstraction levels (e.g., misconfigurations and security risks), they generally do not provide higher-level analysis of feature interactions or comprehensive modeling of the configuration space, underscoring the need for approaches like ours that synthesize formal feature models from K8s specifications.

Table 1. Overview of Kubernetes validation tools.

Tool	Last update[+]	Validation type[*]
Copper	Jun 2020[U]	Validates RBAC configurations (obsolete)
Datree	Aug 2023[D]	Static rule-based misconfiguration checker (obsolete)
KubeLinter	Jun 2025	YAML linter with security and best-practice checks
kube-score	Apr 2025	Static analysis with reliability and security advice
Polaris CLI	Jun 2025	Static validation with CLI and dashboard (paid features)
Config-lint	Jun 2020[U]	Limited static rule validation (obsolete)
Conftest	Jun 2025	Custom policy validation using OPA engine
Terrascan	May 2025	Configurable IaC and K8s security scanner
Trivy	Jun 2025	Versatile scanner for security, IaC, and CVEs
kubeconform	May 2025	OpenAPI schema validation, CI-friendly

+ D: Deprecated, U: Unmaintained.
* RBAC: Role-Based Access Control. IaC: Infrastructure as Code. OPA: Open Policy Agent. CVE: Common Vulnerabilities and Exposures.

Empirical Studies and Configuration Mining. Other works have studied common usage patterns to detect anti-patterns or vulnerabilities mining public K8s configurations from open-source repositories and container images [28,33,35]. These studies provide insights into how K8s resources are used in practice, but they focus on concrete configurations rather than abstracting the underlying variability space. Some efforts, such as *Columbo* [19], attempt to extract configuration models or mine constraints, but they typically rely on statistical inference or heuristics, and are not aligned with SPL methodologies. Several performance and tuning frameworks have been proposed to analyze and optimize container configurations in K8s [9]. Other works analyze the evolution and change patterns of K8s configuration scripts to understand maintenance challenges [30].

Variability Modeling Approaches. While feature modeling has been widely adopted in SPL research, its application to DevOps platforms, such as K8s, still remains limited. Stötzner et al. [31] highlighted the lack of formal variability representations in deployment technologies and advocated for incorporating SPL techniques in infrastructure configuration. Deployment automation tools such as *Helm charts* [16] or *FOCloud* [21]. facilitate configuration management and modularization in K8s deployments. However, to our knowledge, no prior work has proposed a systematic method for synthesizing feature models of K8s from its official specifications.

Reverse engineering of feature models is a common SPL technique, extracting variability from configurations [5], constraints [29], or code [4]. Approaches based on feature graphs [29], evolutionary algorithms [23], or Monte Carlo simulations [17] have shown success, though they often suffer from poor interpretability [34]. However, no such techniques have yet been applied to K8s.

Manual synthesis of models from documentation is less common but has been applied in domains such as mobile applications [15]. Our previous work [18] presented a manually curated feature model of K8s derived from its API reference documentation. While it demonstrated the feasibility and utility of feature models in this context, it required significant manual effort and was difficult to maintain as K8s evolved.

3   Automated Synthesis of Kubernetes Variability Model

Figure 1 provides a global view of our approach for the automatic synthesis of the K8s variability model, covering three interconnected capabilities: (i) extracting a formal feature model from the official OpenAPI schemas; (ii) validating existing configurations using the generated model; and (iii) supporting configuration generation and exploration.

The process is organized into a pipeline that begins with the retrieval and analysis of the OpenAPI schemas and ends with the construction and exploitation of a feature model. The workflow comprises the following main phases:

1. **Schema Retrieval and Feature Identification.** We first retrieve the OpenAPI-based JSON schemas of a given K8s version. Once downloaded, the definitions are parsed to identify potential features and their hierarchical relationships. Each top-level resource (e.g., pod, service, deployment) is treated as a candidate root-level feature. Properties within each resource are extracted and analyzed as potential sub-features or attributes, preserving the structure declared in the schemas.
2. **Variability Mapping and Feature Construction.** The extracted elements are mapped to variability constructs in UVL using a set of mapping rules. For instance, the presence of a required field marks a feature as mandatory, while other fields are treated as optional by default. Data types are mapped to typed features in UVL (e.g.,

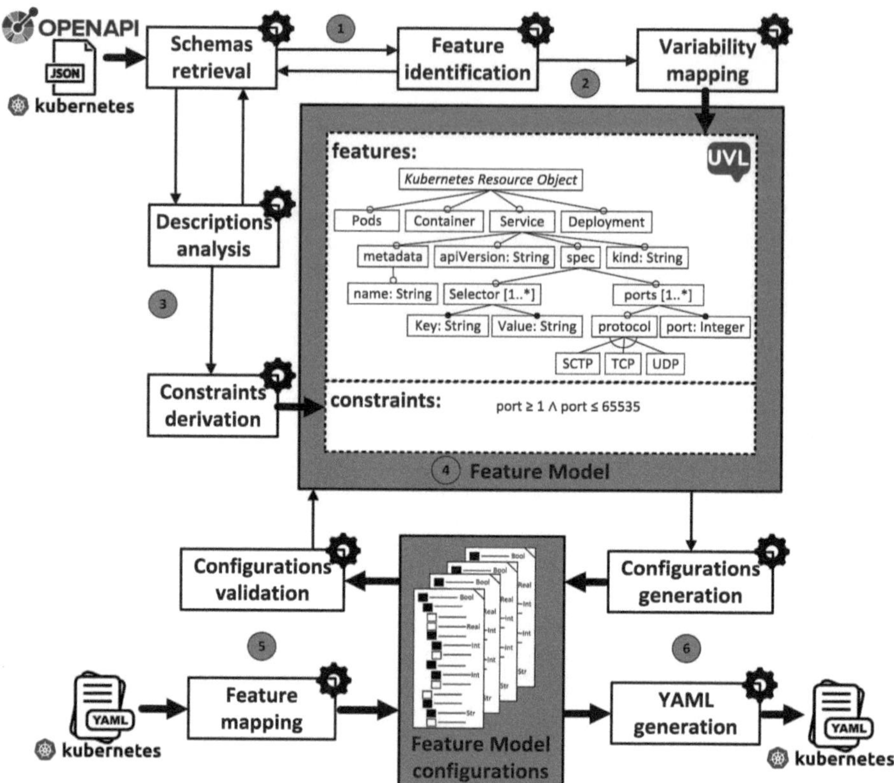

Fig. 1. Our approach for automatic synthesizing the K8s feature model from the OpenAPI schemas, validating YAML files and generating new configurations.

integer, string, boolean, real). Arrays are translated into clonable features with cardinality constraints (e.g., `ports [1..*]`), and enumerations are used to derive alternative feature groups.

3. **Description Analysis and Constraint Derivation.** Descriptions associated with schema fields are mined to enrich the feature model. These natural-language fragments are used to extract default values, identify enumerated domains not formalized in the schema, and infer additional constraints such as numeric ranges, mutual exclusions, or conditional requirements. This step significantly increases the expressiveness and precision of the resulting model. For instance, a constraint such as $port \geq 1 \land port \leq 65535$ can be inferred from the description of a field in the Service's `port` object.

4. **Feature Model Generation in UVL.** All extracted information is synthesized into a UVL-compliant feature model. The model includes the features, their types and attributes (e.g., default values, documentation), and the derived constraints. The use of UVL enables advanced modeling constructs and compatibility with modern variability analysis tools.

5. **Model-Based Validation of Real Configurations.** The resulting feature model is used to validate existing K8s YAML configurations. By mapping each manifest to a partial configuration and checking it against the constraints of the model, we can automatically detect misconfigurations, missing mandatory fields, or invalid value combinations.
6. **Configuration Generation and Exploration.** Finally, the feature model can be used to generate valid YAML configurations, either from complete or partial configurations, or to explore the configuration space for documentation, testing, or reasoning purposes. The UVL model supports reasoning tasks such as identifying all valid variants, computing common configurations, or explaining invalid ones.

4   Technical Decisions of the Synthesis Process

This section provides a comprehensive and in-depth description of the automated methodology for synthesizing the K8s variability model.

4.1   Schema Retrieval and Feature Identification

The initial phase of the automated synthesis process involves the robust and systematic acquisition of K8s OpenAPI JSON schemas. These schemas are available in code repositories which organizes the schemas by the K8s version, with each directory containing numerous files representing distinct K8s objects (e.g., the schema for a Service in Listing 1.2). A crucial consolidated file, `definitions.json`, is present within each version, acting as a central reference point for all schema definitions. To ensure accessibility and reproducibility, a dedicated bash script was developed to automate the download of any specified K8s schema version.

Table 2. Mapping between data types of K8s properties to UVL features.

K8s type	UVL feature type
boolean	Booolean
integer	Integer
number	Real
string	String
object	Boolean with sub-features
array	Boolean with cardinality $[1..*]$

Once the relevant K8s JSON schemas are retrieved, the next step involves their systematic exploration to identify key elements such as object definitions, properties, data types, and inter-schema references. Each top-level schema definition, typically representing a K8s kind (e.g., pod, deployment, service), is initially recognized as a top-feature and a significant branch in the variability model. Sub-properties within these definitions are then identified as candidate sub-features or feature attributes (e.g., default values or documentation). This step focuses on extracting the raw structural data, which will subsequently be transformed into a UVL model, establishing the basic hierarchical relationships inherent in the K8s API.

Feature Naming Convention. To ensure uniqueness and clarity within the feature model, a consistent naming convention was devised. Schema names, which inherently contain information about their version and group (e.g., `io.k8s.api. admissionregistration.v1.AuditAnnotation` indicates the group `admissionregistration` and version `v1` for the `AuditAnnotation` kind), are fully integrated into the model representation. Invalid UVL syntax characters (e.g., dots) are replaced with underscores (e.g., `io_k8s_api_admissionregistration_ v1_Audit_Annotation`). Furthermore, when adding sub-features, the property's name is concatenated with the main schema's name, thereby generating a hierarchical and ordered nomenclature.

4.2   Variability Mapping and Feature Construction

The in-depth schema exploration leds to several design decisions regarding the automated mapping.

Root of the Feature Model. The feature model is rooted by a conceptual *Kubernetes Resource Object* (KRO) representing the overarching configurable entity within K8s (i.e., pods, containers, services, deployments,...). Given the absence of explicit declarations regarding mandatory or required usage for top-level properties within the schemas, we consider all top-level features directly under this root as optional features, establishing the initial hierarchy of the UVL model.

Mapping Schema Fields to Features. The most frequently encountered fields within the object schemas are `properties`, `$ref`, and `required`.

- `properties`: This field contains the schema properties, each typically accompanied by a description and a data type. These properties are directly translated into sub-features of the main feature, with their respective data types (string, integer, boolean, number, object, array) determining their format in the UVL model (which only support Boolean, Integer, Real, and String). Notably, Table 2 shows the mapping from the K8s data types of KROs' properties to UVL features.
- `$ref`: This field provides a reference (URL) to other schemas. For instance, the `Service` schema shown in Listing 1.2 contains two inter-schema references: one for the `metadata` (line 14), and other for `specification` (line 18) of the Service. Each reference leds to the corresponding schemas. For instance, Listing 1.3 shows the schema for the `ServicePort` definition. These referenced schemas are incorporated into the feature model as sub-trees.

Listing 1.3. JSON schema property of ServicePorts extension in K8s.

```
1  "io.k8s.api.core.v1.ServicePort": {
2    "description": "Defines port details for a service.",
3    "properties": {
4      "port": {
5        "description": "Port exposed by the service.",
6        "format": "int32",
7        "type": "integer"
8      },
9      "protocol": {
10       "description": "IP protocol used (TCP, UDP, or SCTP).",
11       "type": "string"
12     },
13     "targetPort": {
14       "$ref": "#/definitions/io.k8s.apimachinery.pkg.util.intstr.IntOrString",
15       "description": "Port on the target pod receiving traffic."
16     }},
17   "required": ["port"],
18   "type": "object"
19 }
```

- `required`: This field explicitly lists sub-features that are mandatory, while all other properties are `optional`. For instance, the `ServicePort` definition (Listing 1.3) declares that `port` is mandatory (line 18), and thus, must be present in all configurations where the `ServicePort` is selected.

Handling `enum` Properties. The `enum` property, typically found within the `kind` property of fields, is interpreted to define default values (see lines 8–11 in Listing 1.2). In such cases, the `enum` value directly corresponds to the `kind` of the feature name and is captured in the model using a `default` attribute.

4.3   Description Analysis and Constraint Derivation

Beyond the structural elements explicitly defined in the OpenAPI schemas, the `description` fields provide valuable natural language information that often encodes hidden variability aspects, constraints, default values, and valid options. We implemented a rule-based mechanism to extract such information and enrich the feature model with additional semantics.

Default Value Extraction. Many features include informal declarations of default values within their descriptions, particularly for `boolean` and `integer` types. For instance, the sentence *"Default to false"* in a field description is parsed to associate a `{default false}` attribute with the corresponding feature. Our approach uses regular expressions to detect these patterns, including numeric defaults (e.g., *default to 644*) while handling special cases such as octal literals (e.g., `0644`) that are invalid in UVL.

Inference of Valid Values. Descriptions often informally enumerate possible values for a field without using the `enum` construct. Phrases such as *"valid options are"*, *"can be"*, or *"status may be"* introduce categorical domains. These inferred domains are then encoded as alternative sub-features under the corresponding group feature.

Implicit Hierarchy and Mandatoriness. In some cases, the schema structure does not include certain constraints that are nevertheless described informally. For example, a field not listed in the `required` list may have a description ending with the word *"Required"*. We scan such cases and promote the corresponding feature to `mandatory` status in the model.

Automated Constraint Generation. Each field's description is parsed using a modular pipeline of regular-expression-based extractors that specialize in detecting different types of constraints, summarized in Table 3.

Table 3. Constraint types and number of instances automatically extracted (#).

Restriction Type	Description	#
OS-based exclusion	Enables/disables features based on the selected operating system	1247
Numeric ranges I	Captures expressions with bounded intervals or range indications	+700
Numeric ranges II	Handles "greater than", "less than", and textual values ("zero")	+400
Mutual exclusion	Ensures that two features cannot be selected simultaneously	12
Conditional inclusion	Selects a feature only if another takes a specific value (e.g., type)	+300
Required-When	A feature must be selected only when another takes a specific value	8
Operator dependency	A feature is conditioned on the value of an operator (e.g., In, NotIn)	701
At least one	At least one among a group of features must be enabled	+450
Implicit OR relations	Extracts relations from higher-level descriptions (e.g., A or B)	56
Complex logic	Captures logical conditions involving multiple interrelated features	25
String-based values	Applies when string fields constrain selection (e.g., kind field)	10
RestartPolicy	Restricts allowed values for template.spec.restartPolicy	19
Minimum values	Captures lower bounds like min seconds, repetitions, ranges	1426
Total		**5364**

4.4 Feature Model Generation in UVL

After extracting structural elements, mapping variability constructs, and enriching the model with constraints and semantics, the final step of our pipeline is the generation of a formal feature model using UVL [6].

Listing 1.4 shows an excerpt of the UVL model automatically synthesized for the `Service` resource, based on the OpenAPI schemas presented in Listings 1.2–1.3. This example illustrates how our methodology translates schema content into a structured, annotated, and typed variability model.

- The `Service` feature (line 3) corresponds to the top-level KRO of this branch.
- String fields such as `apiVersion` and `kind` are modeled as typed subfeatures (lines 6 and 7). The field `kind` includes a default value `"Service"`, extracted from the `enum` field in the schema.

- References to nested objects, such as `metadata` (line 8) and `spec` (line 12), are expanded recursively, with subtrees preserving the original schema hierarchy.
- Feature cardinalities (aka multi-features), such as `selector [1..*]` (line 15) and `ports [1..*]` (line 19), reflect array-valued fields in the schema, ensuring that the model captures the multiplicity of these properties. A multi-feature allows configuring its subtree multiple times.
- Each feature includes a `doc` attribute, containing natural-language documentation automatically extracted from the schema's `description` field.
- The `protocol` field is modeled as an optional feature with an `alternative` group, capturing the enumerated domain `TCP`, `UDP`, and `SCTP`, with `TCP` marked as the default (lines 24–28).
- Fields like `targetPort`, which accept multiple data types (e.g., string or integer), are modeled as `alternative` groups with typed subfeatures, preserving the semantics of the OpenAPI union type (lines 29–32).
- Cross-tree constraints are expressed as logical boolean formulas and arithmetic expressions using the UVL syntax (line 35).

4.5 Model-Based Validation of Real Configurations

Once the feature model is synthesized, we leverage it to validate real K8s configurations (e.g., YAML manifests) by checking whether they constitute valid configurations conform to the model. The validation process operates as follows: (1) Given a YAML file, it is parsed into a structured configuration tree, matching the hierarchical structure of the feature model. String fields, nested objects, and arrays are mapped to their corresponding features, preserving types and cardinalities; (2) the resulting configuration is interpreted as a partial feature selection, where mapped features from the YAML file are selected, while the others feature from the UVL model are undecided; and (3) the configuration is then evaluated against the feature model constraints using SAT solvers [13], which performs satisfiability checking, constraint propagation, and structural validation.

This process allows detecting a wide range of misconfigurations, including: missing mandatory fields not declared in the YAML; invalid combinations of feature values that violate constraints (e.g., out-of-range integers, mutually exclusive options); or incorrect nesting or cardinality, such as empty arrays where at least one element is required. Unlike schema-based tools (e.g., *kubeconform*), our model supports semantic constraints and cross-tree logic, enabling detection of errors that go beyond structural validation.

4.6 Configuration Generation and Exploration

The feature model not only supports validation, but also enables automated configuration generation and exploration. Given the formal definition of valid configurations, our system provides the following capabilities:

- **Full Configuration Generation:** A SAT-based reasoning engine can compute one or more complete configurations that satisfy all constraints of the model. These are

Listing 1.4. Excerpt of the feature model in UVL for the Service KRO.

```
1  features
2    ...
3    Service {doc 'Represents a network service abstraction with a name, port, and selector.'}
4      optional
5        String Service_apiVersion {doc 'Specifies the API version of the object.'}
6        String Service_kind {default 'Service', doc 'The REST resource type of this object.'}
7        Service_metadata {doc 'Standard metadata for the object.'}
8          optional
9            String Service_metadata_name {doc 'Unique name of the object in its namespace.'}
10       Service_spec {doc 'Defines the desired behavior of the service.'}
11         optional
12           Service_spec_selector cardinality [1..*] {doc 'Labels to select target pods for routing.'}
13             mandatory
14               String Service_spec_selector_KeyMap {doc 'Key in the selector map for pods.'}
15               String Service_spec_selector_ValueMap {doc 'Value in the selector map for pods.'}
16           Service_spec_ports cardinality [1..*] {doc 'Ports exposed by the service.'}
17             mandatory
18               Integer Service_spec_ports_port {doc 'Port exposed by the service.'}
19             optional
20               Service_spec_ports_protocol {doc 'IP protocol used (TCP, UDP, or SCTP).'}
21                 alternative
22                   io_k8s_api_core_v1_Service_spec_ports_protocol_SCTP
23                   io_k8s_api_core_v1_Service_spec_ports_protocol_TCP {default}
24                   io_k8s_api_core_v1_Service_spec_ports_protocol_UDP
25               Service_spec_ports_targetPort {doc 'Port on the target pod receiving traffic.'}
26                 alternative
27                   String Service_spec_ports_targetPort_asString
28                   Integer Service_spec_ports_targetPort_asInteger
29       ...
30  constraints
31    port >= 1 & port <= 65535
32    ...
```

guaranteed to be valid, and can be automatically serialized into syntactically correct and semantically valid YAML manifests.

- **Partial Configuration Completion:** Users can specify a partial configuration (e.g., selected container type, service kind, or specific port), and the generator will complete the remaining feature selections while ensuring model validity.
- **Exploration of the Configuration Space:** The feature model can be queried to compute statistics (e.g., number of valid configurations), identify dead features (i.e., features that never appear in a configuration) or core features (i.e., features present in all configurations), analyze variability hotspots, or explore constrained subspaces (e.g., all valid configurations with `protocol=UDP`).

Generated configurations can serve different purposes such as documentation (e.g., showing prototypical examples of valid manifests), testing (e.g., generating diverse deployment variants to validate infrastructure robustness), and diagnosis (e.g., explaining why a given configuration is invalid, by tracing the violated constraints or unsatisfied dependencies). These capabilities are made possible by the expressiveness and analyzability of the feature model, turning the traditionally informal and error-prone process of writing manifests into a structured, analyzable, and automatable task.

5   Evaluation

To guide our evaluation we formulate the following research questions (RQ).

RQ1: *How do the characteristics of the automatically synthesized K8s variability model compare to a manually generated one? Rationale:* This question aims to characterize the properties of the automatically generated variability model and compare it against a manually crafted model, such as the one presented in our prior work [18]. It allows us to discuss key metrics and analyze how automation impacts these properties versus a human-driven effort.

RQ2: *How effective is the automatically synthesized K8s variability model for configuration validation compared to existing tools? Rationale:* This question focuses on the practical applicability and utility of our model. It investigates its effectiveness in validating real-world K8s configurations and positions its capabilities against widely used, specialized tools within the K8s ecosystem.

5.1   Experimental Setup

Open Science Data and Reproducibility. In the spirit of open science and to ensure the full reproducibility of our results, both the automatically synthesized K8s variability model and all related artifacts, including the scripts used for its generation and the configurations validation, are made publicly available[1].

Configuration Validation Dataset. The K8s OpenAPI schemas were programmatically retrieved from a specialized repository[2], which provides a well-instrumented and regularly updated forks of the official K8s API definitions. We used the `v1.30.2` version of the schemas. For configuration validation, we used a dataset of 250,000 K8s configurations. These configurations were systematically extracted from the dataset described in our previous work [18], which provides a diverse and representative collection of real-world K8s deployments.

Comparative Tools. The tools included in our comparison were those discussed in detail in Sect. 2 (Table 1). These tools were chosen to represent various validation strategies within the K8s ecosystem, including schema validation, policy enforcement, and best practice checks.

5.2   Results

RQ1: How do the Characteristics of the Automatically Synthesized K8s Variability Model Compare to a Manually Generated One? The automatically synthesized K8s variability model presents a significantly more extensive and complex representation of K8s configurability when compared to a manually generated model [18]. This difference is evident in the following key metrics (see the characterization of both K8s feature models in Fig. 2).

---

[1] K8s variability model: https://github.com/CAOSD-group/fm-json-kubernetes.

[2] OpenAPI schemas repository: https://github.com/yannh/kubernetes-json-schema.

- **Scale and Scope:** The automatically synthesized model is substantially larger, with 66,242 features and 5,364 constraints, drastically contrasting with the manual model's 738 features and 93 constraints. In fact, our model contains up to 626 top features each of them corresponding with a different K8s resource object (e.g., pod, service, deployment) in contrast to only 11 top features (KROs) from the manual counterpart. This leads to a vastly expanded configuration space: approximately $8.06 \times 10^{10,457}$ configurations for the automated model compared to 5.73×10^{77} for the manual one.

- **Feature Richness:** The automated model demonstrates a greater density of advanced variability concepts. While both models incorporate typed features (non-Boolean), the automatically synthesized model has a significantly higher absolute number, with 31,626 typed features compared to 319 in the manual model. This increase is consistent across specific typed features, with the automatic model containing 6,111 numerical features (versus 57 in the manual model) and 25,515 string features (versus 262 in the manual model). The ability to configure multiple instances of a resource or parameter is also more prevalent in the automated model, with 7,921 multi-features compared to 61 in the manual counterpart.

- **Constraint Complexity:** The automatically synthesized model captures a much higher volume of intricate relationships and rules: a notable 53% (2,817 constraints) of the automatic model's constraints are arithmetic, involving numerical features. This is significantly higher than the 37% (34 constraints) observed in the manual model. While the manual model has a slightly higher percentage of features involved in constraints (23% vs. 17%), the sheer number of features and constraints in the automatic model means a far greater absolute quantity of features are subject to formal rules.

- **Attributes and Explicability:** The automatic model excels in incorporating metadata and documentation, with 99% of its features including at least one attribute. This is higher than the 73% in the manual model. The prevalence of the `{doc «string»}` attribute enhances the features' explicability.

In summary, the automatically synthesized K8s feature model provides a far more comprehensive, detailed, and complex representation of K8s' configurable aspects, capturing nuances and relationships that would be extremely challenging to synthesize manually.

RQ2: How Effective Is the Automatically Synthesized K8s Variability Model for Configuration Validation Compared to Existing Tools? Our automatically synthesized K8s variability model demonstrates superior effectiveness in configuration validation compared to most existing tools, as depicted in Fig. 3. While the `Kubeconform` tool excels at validating against JSON schemas, providing 98.3% validity by ensuring structural correctness, they do not assess semantic validity or constraints satisfaction. Similarly, `Terrascan` and `Trivy` focus on policy enforcement, which, while crucial, represents a different aspect of validation. Other tools show significantly lower percentages of valid configurations, indicating their specific focus on best practices, security, or predefined policy checks rather than comprehensive structural and semantic validity based on the full variability model. Our approach, leveraging a SAT solver, achieves 94.8% valid configurations. This high percentage, second only to `Kubeconform` (which only

Manual K8s FM	
Features	738
Top features	11 (1%)
Typed features	319 (43%)
Numerical features	57 (8%)
String features	262 (36%)
Multi-features	61 (8%)
Tree relationships	569
Mandatory features	194 (36%)
Optional features	337 (63%)
Feature groups	38 (7%)
Depth of tree	8
Branching factor	3.92
Cross-tree constraints	93
Logical constraints	59 (63%)
Arithmetic constraints	34 (37%)
Features in constraints	172 (23%)
Attributes	5
Features with attributes	538 (73%)
Satisfiable (valid)	Yes
Core features	27 (4%)
Dead features	207 (28%)
Variant features	504 (68%)
Configurations	5.73e77

(a) Manually synthesized K8s FM [18].

Automated K8s FM	
Features	66242
Top features	626 (1%)
Typed features	31626 (48%)
Numerical features	6111 (9%)
String features	25515 (39%)
Multi-features	7921 (12%)
Tree relationships	58740
Mandatory features	15799 (29%)
Optional features	38726 (71%)
Feature groups	4215 (7%)
Depth of tree	15
Branching factor	3.02
Cross-tree constraints	5364
Logical constraints	2547 (47%)
Arithmetic constraints	2817 (53%)
Features in constraints	11150 (17%)
Attributes	3
Features with attributes	65767 (99%)
Satisfiable (valid)	Yes
Core features	1 (0%)
Dead features	914 (1%)
Variant features	65327 (99%)
Configurations	8.06e10457

(b) Automatically synthesized K8s FM.

Fig. 2. Comparison of the K8s feature models (FM) characteristics.

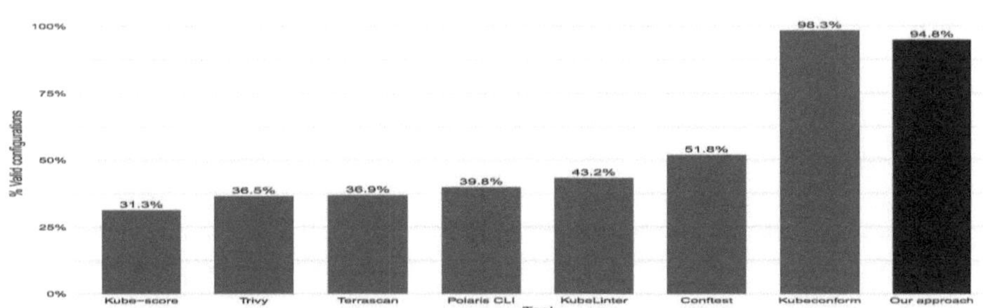

Fig. 3. Configuration validity: Comparison of existing K8s tools.

validates schema), indicates that our model provides a more holistic and accurate validation of K8s configurations against its inherent variability, encompassing structural and semantic constraints beyond mere schema compliance or policy checks (see also Table 1). The trade-off for this comprehensive validation is a higher computational cost due to the use of a SAT solver. For instance, the median validation time for a configuration is 3.5 s, a comprehensible delay for a user. As future work, we aim to significantly reduce these times to be more comparable with other tools, such as Kube-conform, which operates in approximately 1.5 ms.

6 Conclusions and Future Work

This paper has introduced an automated, schema-driven process to synthesize a formal and expressive variability model of K8s. Our approach successfully bridges the gap between DevOps configurations and SPL engineering, yielding a scalable and explainable representation of K8s variability with real-world validation power and integration potential into modern toolchains.

In future work, we plan to enhance performance by reducing SAT validation times, support incremental model updates as new API versions are released, and investigate the application of our approach to other configurable platforms beyond K8s. Additionally, we aim to explore the integration of the model into CI/CD pipelines to support live validation and configuration assistance during development.

Acknowledgments. Work supported by the projects *IRIS* PID2021-122812OB-I00 and *SAVIA* PID2024-159945NB-I00 (co-financed by FEDER funds); *DUNE* DGP_PIDI_2024_00092; and by ITIS/Universidad de Málaga.

Disclosure of Interests. The authors have no competing interests to declare that are relevant to the content of this article.

References

1. Guide latest Kubernetes adoption statistics: Global insights and analysis for 2025. https://edgedelta.com/company/blog/kubernetes-adoption-statistics. Accessed 01 June 2025
2. Statista Kubernetes - statistics & facts. https://www.statista.com/topics/8409/kubernetes/. Accessed 01 June 2025
3. Apel, S., Batory, D.S., Kästner, C., Saake, G.: Feature-Oriented Software Product Lines - Concepts and Implementation. Springer, Heidelberg (2013). https://doi.org/10.1007/978-3-642-37521-7
4. Assunção, W.K.G., Lopez-Herrejon, R.E., Linsbauer, L., Vergilio, S.R., Egyed, A.: Multi-objective reverse engineering of variability-safe feature models based on code dependencies of system variants. Empir. Softw. Eng. **22**(4), 1763–1794 (2017). https://doi.org/10.1007/S10664-016-9462-4
5. Assunção, W.K.G., Vergilio, S.R., Lopez-Herrejon, R.E., Linsbauer, L.: Search-based variability model synthesis from variant configurations. In: Handbook of Re-Engineering Software Intensive Systems into Software Product Lines, pp. 115–141 (2023). https://doi.org/10.1007/978-3-031-11686-5_5
6. Benavides, D., Sundermann, C., Feichtinger, K., Galindo, J.A., Rabiser, R., Thüm, T.: UVL: feature modelling with the universal variability language. J. Syst. Softw. **225**, 112326 (2025). https://doi.org/10.1016/j.jss.2024.112326
7. Burns, B., Beda, J., Hightower, K., Evenson, L.: Kubernetes: up and running (2022)
8. Casalicchio, E., Iannucci, S.: The state-of-the-art in container technologies: application, orchestration and security. Concurr. Comput. Pract. Exp. **32**(17) (2020). https://doi.org/10.1002/CPE.5668

9. Chiba, T., Nakazawa, R., Horii, H., Suneja, S., Seelam, S.: Confadvisor: A performance-centric configuration tuning framework for containers on Kubernetes. In: IEEE International Conference on Cloud Engineering (IC2E), pp. 168–178 (2019). https://doi.org/10.1109/IC2E.2019.00031

10. Diarra, B., Guillouard, K., Ouzzif, M., Merle, P., Stefani, J.B.: In-depth analysis of Kubernetes manifest verification tools for robust CNF deployment. In: 27th Conference on Innovation in Clouds, Internet and Networks (ICIN), pp. 17–24 (2024). https://doi.org/10.1109/ICIN60470.2024.10494445

11. Faria, B., Abreu, D.P., Velasquez, K., Curado, M.: Self-organising approach to anomaly mitigation in the cloud-to-edge continuum. In: 30th International Conference on Cooperative Information Systems (CoopIS). LNCS, vol. 15506, pp. 263–279. Springer, Heidelberg (2024). https://doi.org/10.1007/978-3-031-81375-7_15

12. Felfernig, A., Falkner, A.A., Benavides, D.: Feature Models - AI-Driven Design, Analysis and Applications. Springer Briefs in Computer Science. Springer, Heidelberg (2024). https://doi.org/10.1007/978-3-031-61874-1

13. Galindo, J.A., Horcas, J.M., Felfernig, A., Fernández-Amorós, D., Benavides, D.: FLAMA: A collaborative effort to build a new framework for the automated analysis of feature models. In: 27th ACM International Systems and Software Product Line Conference (SPLC) (2023). https://doi.org/10.1145/3579028.3609008

14. Galindo, J.A., Romero-Organvidez, D., Bhushan, M., Aguilera, J.M.H., Benavides, D.: Open Science principles in software product lines: the case of the UVL ecosystem. In: 28th ACM International Systems and Software Product Line Conference (SPLC), vol. A, p. 223. ACM (2024). https://doi.org/10.1145/3646548.3674550

15. Galindo, J.A., Turner, H.A., Benavides, D., White, J.: Testing variability-intensive systems using automated analysis: an application to Android. Softw. Qual. J. **24**(2), 365–405 (2016). https://doi.org/10.1007/S11219-014-9258-Y

16. Gokhale, S., et al.: Creating helm charts to ease deployment of enterprise application and its related services in Kubernetes. In: International Conference on Computing, Communication and Green Engineering (CCGE), pp. 1–5 (2021). https://doi.org/10.1109/CCGE50943.2021.9776450

17. Horcas, J.M., Galindo, J.A., Heradio, R., Fernández-Amorós, D., Benavides, D.: A monte carlo tree search conceptual framework for feature model analyses. J. Syst. Softw. **195**, 111551 (2023). https://doi.org/10.1016/J.JSS.2022.111551

18. Horcas, J.M., Pinilla, M.A., Fuentes, L.: The Kubernetes variability model: synthesizing variability from the k8s API documentation: a case study. In: 19th International Working Conference on Variability Modelling of Software-Intensive Systems (VaMoS), pp. 58–67. ACM (2025). https://doi.org/10.1145/3715340.3715440

19. Jansen, M., Talluri, S., Doekemeijer, K., Tehrany, N., Iosup, A., Trivedi, A.: Columbo: a reasoning framework for Kubernetes' configuration space. In: 16th ACM/SPEC International Conference on Performance Engineering (ICPE), pp. 45–57. ACM (2025). https://doi.org/10.1145/3676151.3719374

20. Kuiter, E., Sundermann, C., Thüm, T., Hess, T., Krieter, S., Saake, G.: How configurable is the Linux kernel? Analyzing two decades of feature-model history. ACM Trans. Softw. Eng. Methodol. (2025). https://doi.org/10.1145/3729423

21. Kumara, I., Ariz, M.H., Chhetri, M.B., Mohammadi, M., Heuvel, W.J.V.D., Tamburri, D.A.: Focloud: feature model guided performance prediction and explanation for deployment configurable cloud applications. IEEE Trans. Serv. Comput. **16**(1), 302–314 (2023). https://doi.org/10.1109/TSC.2022.3142853

22. Le, V.C., Yoo, M.: Application for managing YAML template for Kubernetes. J. Kor. Inst. Commun. Inf. Sci. **46**(11), 1950–1957 (2021). https://doi.org/10.7840/kics.2021.46.11.1950

23. Lopez-Herrejon, R.E., et al.: An assessment of search-based techniques for reverse engineering feature models. J. Syst. Softw. **103**, 353–369 (2015). https://doi.org/10.1016/J.JSS.2014.10.037
24. Martin, P.: Extending Kubernetes API with Custom Resources Definitions, pp. 193–207. Apress (2023). https://doi.org/10.1007/978-1-4842-9026-2_8
25. Munoz, D.J., Pinto, M., Fuentes, L.: Detecting feature influences to quality attributes in large and partially measured spaces using smart sampling and dynamic learning. Knowl.-Based Syst. **270**, 110558 (2023). https://doi.org/10.1016/j.knosys.2023.110558
26. Oliinyk, O., Petersen, K., Schoelzke, M., Becker, M., Schneickert, S.: Structuring automotive product lines and feature models: an exploratory study at Opel. Requir. Eng. **22**(1), 105–135 (2017)
27. Poulton, N.: The kubernetes book. NIGEL POULTON LTD (2023)
28. Rahman, A., Shamim, S.I., Bose, D.B., Pandita, R.: Security misconfigurations in open source Kubernetes manifests: an empirical study. ACM Trans. Softw. Eng. Methodol. **32**(4) (2023). https://doi.org/10.1145/3579639
29. She, S., Ryssel, U., Andersen, N., Wasowski, A., Czarnecki, K.: Efficient synthesis of feature models. Inf. Softw. Technol. **56**(9), 1122–1143 (2014). https://doi.org/10.1016/J.INFSOF.2014.01.012
30. Singh, A.: Configuration Changes in Kubernetes Configuration Scripts. Master's thesis, Auburn University (2025). https://etd.auburn.edu/handle/10415/9682
31. Stötzner, M., Breitenbücher, U., Pesl, R.D., Becker, S.: Managing the variability of component implementations and their deployment configurations across heterogeneous deployment technologies. In: 29th International Conference on Cooperative Information Systems (CoopIS), vol. 14353, pp. 61–78 (2023). https://doi.org/10.1007/978-3-031-46846-9_4
32. The Kubernetes Authors: Kubernetes API documentation (2025). https://kubernetes.io/docs/reference/generated/kubernetes-api/v1.30/#api-overview, v1.30
33. Xu, Q., Gao, Y., Wei, J.: An empirical study on Kubernetes operator bugs. In: 33rd ACM SIGSOFT International Symposium on Software Testing and Analysis (ISSTA), pp. 1746–1758. ACM (2024). https://doi.org/10.1145/3650212.3680396
34. Zednik, C., Boelsen, H.: Scientific exploration and explainable artificial intelligence. Minds Mach. **32**(1), 219–239 (2022). https://doi.org/10.1007/S11023-021-09583-6
35. Zhang, Y., Meredith, R., Reeves, W., Coriolano, J., Babar, M.A., Rahman, A.: Does generative AI generate smells related to container orchestration?: An exploratory study with Kubernetes manifests. In: 21st International Conference on Mining Software Repositories (MSR), pp. 192–196. ACM (2024). https://doi.org/10.1145/3643991.3645079

A Maturity Model for Blockchain Adoption in the Banking Industry

Faruk Hasić[✉], Amalia Morel de Westgaver, and Johannes De Smedt

Leuven Institute for Research on Information Systems (LIRIS), KU Leuven, Leuven, Belgium
`faruk.hasic@kuleuven.be`

Abstract. Blockchain is an emerging technology that facilitates the elimination of intermediaries or third parties, thereby reducing costs and enhancing efficiency. Over the past decade, blockchain has been integrated across various industries, yet its wide-scale adoption within the financial industry remains uncertain. This paper seeks to aid financial institutions in adopting blockchain technology by developing a maturity model. This model is intended to assist organisations in assessing their current maturity level and charting a way forward towards a more enhanced adoption of the technology. We construct an initial model based on literature on existing maturity models in other fields of study. Subsequently, we refine the model through the Delphi approach which is a qualitative, systematic, and iterative panel method. We conduct the Delphi method in three rounds with experts in the field, yielding a final maturity model and a corresponding questionnaire which allows financial institutions to conduct a self-assessment of their blockchain adoption capabilities. We discuss the validity of the model and provide a proof of concept through a self-assessment exercise by a participating institution. The panel participants and contributing institutions concurred that the resulting maturity model and the corresponding self-assessment questionnaire are relevant and useful tools for the purpose of assessing their current maturity and informing future actions to enhance their blockchain adoption capabilities.

Keywords: Maturity Models · Distributed Ledger Technology · Blockchain · FinTech · Delphi Method

1 Introduction

Technological disruptions profoundly influence daily life. In finance, technology continuously redefines customer interactions and expectations, driven by a growing digital client base and data proliferation. Customers now demand instant, accessible, and efficient financial services, such as remote account opening and real-time transfers, facilitated by fintech innovations [13]. Financial institutions must adopt these technologies

---

This paper is largely based on the master's thesis by A. Morel de Westgaver. The authors used Artificial Intelligence (AI) tools as aid in the writing process. ChatGPT was used to condense the introduction and conclusion sections of the thesis for the purpose of this paper. All outputs were verified and if needed amended by the authors. Additionally, the authors used Overleaf AI Assist for language suggestions.

© The Author(s), under exclusive license to Springer Nature Switzerland AG 2026
C. Cappiello et al. (Eds.): CoopIS 2025, LNCS 15535, pp. 429–446, 2026.
https://doi.org/10.1007/978-3-032-15538-2_24

to remain competitive, benefiting from automation and other advancements such as machine learning and cloud computing [9].

Blockchain technology, applicable in various sectors, offers a decentralized database that enables secure information transfer without intermediaries. In finance, it has the potential to facilitate international transfers, reduce costs, and improve security [34]. However, the wide-scale adoption of blockchain technologies by financial institutions is uncertain. Financial institutions should assess their readiness for blockchain adoption, also in light of oncoming Central Bank Digital Currencies (CBDC). However, banks lack solid tools to assess their maturity and chart a way forward to enhance their capabilities. This paper proposes a maturity model (MM) for blockchain technology in finance, addressing this gap in the academic literature. Existing models in other sectors and for related technologies, such as AI and Industry 4.0, offer a foundation. The paper is organised as follows. Section 2 covers key background concepts, Sect. 3 details the methodology, and Sect. 4 outlines the development of the maturity model. In Sect. 5 we discuss the validity of the maturity model and the corresponding self-assessment tool. Section 6 discusses the limitations. Finally, Sect. 7 provides the conclusions.

2 Background Information

This section focuses on a general overview of blockchain technology in the financial industry and introduces the concept of maturity models.

2.1 Blockchain Technology in the Financial Industry

The financial sector fundamentally relies on trust, and blockchain technology aims to enhance this by fostering trust mechanisms within its framework [37]. Blockchain addresses certain flaws in the financial industry, where intermediaries such as banks and service providers hold significant power, while individuals have little influence [37]. By replacing third-party dependency with blockchain systems, a more equitable power distribution is achieved, allowing greater participation in financial networks. Traditional banking faces challenges such as uniform service offerings, inefficient processes due to multiple intermediaries, and centralized data storage, which increase security risks. Blockchain offers solutions by enabling personalized services, streamlining transactions, and decentralizing data with robust encryption, thus enhancing security and reducing costs [13,40]. This technology also fosters financial inclusion by lowering operational costs, allowing banks to serve previously inaccessible markets, particularly in emerging economies [13].

Traditional cross-border payments are often slow and expensive, with bank-imposed fees adding 10–15% to the cost and processing times ranging from 2–7 days due to intermediaries. Blockchain technology addresses these inefficiencies by eliminating intermediaries, thus reducing transfer costs and accelerating transactions to mere seconds [13,31].

Also other areas of finance face challenges from blockchain adoption [40]. In trade finance, blockchain technology improves the sector by digitizing and automating processes, thus reducing errors, fraud, and costs while improving efficiency and transparency. Traditional lending could also face challenges as blockchain technology facilitates direct negotiations between borrowers and lenders, automating processes through smart contracts and enhancing efficiency. Similarly, in the insurance sector, blockchain enables the use of smart contracts to manage claims, automating processes and enhancing data security. The Know Your Customer (KYC) process benefits from blockchain by streamlining data verification, reducing time and costs, and improving efficiency and security [19].

While blockchain technology poses challenges to traditional finance, the technology itself, despite its many advantages, faces challenges on its own as well, including scalability issues, high energy consumption, vulnerability to cybercrime, and privacy concerns [6]. Although blockchain has potential to transform the financial sector, its adoption is still in the early stages and requires regulatory adaptation [13].

Organizations must critically evaluate blockchain's maturity and strategic value, ensuring it addresses genuine needs rather than implementing costly solutions for non-existent problems. Financial institutions are encouraged to adopt a disruptive mindset, focusing on innovative business models and engaging stakeholders to facilitate blockchain integration effectively. As blockchain continues to evolve, it is crucial for the financial industry to invest in this technology and enhance its understanding [6].

2.2 Maturity Models

The Software Engineering Institute (SEI), functioning as a research and development center under the auspices of the U.S. Department of Defense, initially devised a maturity questionnaire alongside two distinct methodologies aimed at evaluating software-process maturity: software-process assessment and software-capability evaluation. Subsequently, four years later, the SEI evolved this questionnaire into the Capability Maturity Model (CMM) in 1991, which delineates best practices across various domains to enhance software development [22]. Within the organizational framework, five distinct degrees of maturity were established, each characterized by unique attributes. This model subsequently transitioned into the Capability Maturity Model Integration (CMMI), which retains the original stages while emphasizing five critical factors: goals, commitment, ability, measurement, and verification.

Maturity models serve as abstract representations that enable organizations to pinpoint areas for potential enhancement, assessing an organization's resource or disciplinary maturity level. Typically, these models incorporate qualitative data to evaluate entities such as individuals, groups, processes, institutions, physical items, and technology and posit that as organizations evolve over time, they will achieve a defined "final" level of development [38]. Consequently, these models can function as managerial tools facilitating the growth of the entities under investigation. Additionally, these models outline a developmental trajectory, with stages that underscore the prospective benefits arising from advancement. Generally, maturity models encompass five levels, ranging from the lowest to the highest, commonly identified as Initial, Managed, Defined, Quantitatively Managed, and Optimizing. However, the number of levels varies across different maturity models. Each level comprises distinct criteria requisite for progression to the subsequent stage [24]. Each stage signifies a new echelon of maturity, and

Table 1. Maturity levels and their descriptions [28,38].

Maturity Level	Level Description
Level 1: Initial	The organization lacks structure and relies on employee skills rather than established procedures to be successful. However, products and services are working, they are frequently over budget and delivered late
Level 2: Managed	While projects are planned and managed according to defined standards, leadership support is typically insufficient, and the processes are typically limited to a single department or unit
Level 3: Defined	The organization has clear, documented procedures that are followed consistently all across the organization. Although there are no official metrics in place to impose them, the processes are handled with a knowledge of how they relate to one another
Level 4: Quantitatively Managed	Performance is monitored continuously, and sub-processes are managed using statistical and quantitative methods. The identification and correction of variations results in predictable and controllable performance
Level 5: Optimizing	Quantitative measurements are used to continuously improve processes, with a focus on both incremental and innovative changes. The employees are given the authority to carry out improvements, and role-based continuous improvement is integrated

each level should articulate the advancement of a sub-dimension. Table 1 describes a summary of the levels of a five levels model [16].

In summary, the main goals of maturity models are to assess the current level of maturity of a specific process, to compare the maturity of an organization with that of other organizations and with industry best practices, and to provide a framework for continuous improvement of the maturity level [25].

3   Methodology

This paper seeks to develop a maturity model for the adoption of blockchain technology within the financial industry, structured through a three staged methodology. The first stage aims at developing a preliminary maturity model based on a review of existing publications on blockchain, particularly focusing on its applications in the financial sector, and existing maturity models in adjacent fields. This maturity model will contain dimensions, sub-dimensions, and levels based on existing literature. In the second phase, expert interviews are conducted within the financial and blockchain sectors. These semi-structured interviews facilitate the refinement and validation of the model, culminating in a finalized maturity model. This model is subsequently converted into a self-assessment survey. Finally, the model is applied which can be applied to a financial organization as a proof of concept and a practical implementation example. The methodology is grounded in the Delphi method which is further developed below. Figure 1 illustrates the research methodology employed in this study [15,30].

The Delphi method is used to finalise and/or refine the maturity model. The Delphi method is a structured method that enables experts in an area of study to offer their opin-

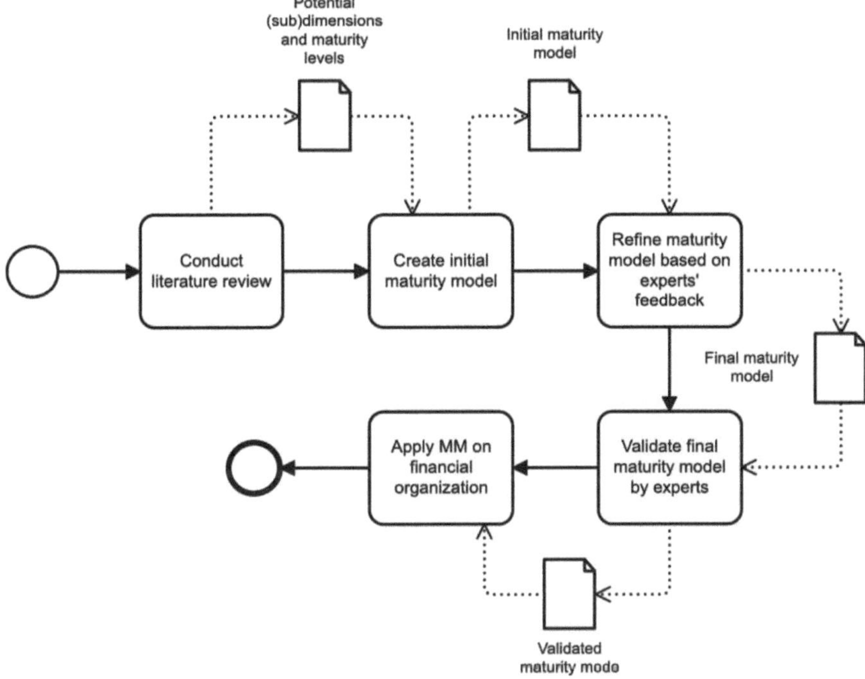

Fig. 1. Methodology to develop a maturity model.

ions on a particular subject. The Delphi technique makes sure that the participants are not influenced by the opinions of others through multiple sequential rounds of anonymous questionnaires. With the end goal of reaching a consensus on the chosen subject. Additionally, participants are chosen based on their expertise [23]. Although the number of rounds may vary, Delphi studies are often conducted in three rounds to ensure consensus.

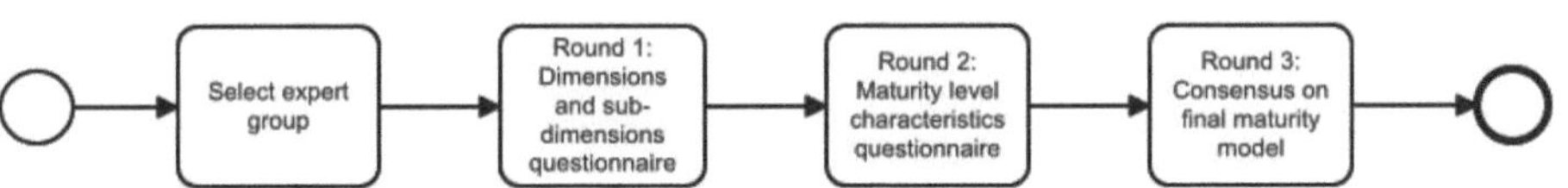

Fig. 2. Delphi method in three rounds to refine the maturity model based on experts' feedback.

The researcher should collect and summarise all the opinions after the questionnaires. By the third interview round, every expert can agree or disagree with the summary made by the researcher based on all experts' opinions [39]. Figure 2 explains the steps of a Delphi study used for this paper based on an article on Corporate Finance Institute (2022).

For the purpose of this study, the three Delphi rounds were conducted over a period of seven weeks. For the first round, the participants were provided with the dimensions and sub-dimensions of the initial model developed from literature and were asked to rate each dimension as stay, change, delete, or blank in case of no opinion. If change was chosen, participants could provide feedback or suggestions on the changes they deem necessary. The results of the first round were used to adapt the model, this adapted model will be presented to the experts to start the second round. In the second round, the participants should evaluate the maturity levels and the definitions per level. Here, the experts could choose stay, change, or blank. Again, an enhanced and adapted maturity model will be generated. Finally, in the third round, the participants were asked to validate the model as a whole. Consensus for round one was determined by computing the percentage of votes for each dimension and sub-dimension to stay, change, or delete. In the second round, participants can rate each definition per level as stay, change, or blank. In round three, participants received the final and adapted maturity model. This round is needed to validate the whole model one last time, participants may give additional feedback if deemed relevant. Figure 3 illustrates the steps to reach a consensus based on the percentage of votes by the experts.

In other words, changes to the maturity model will be determined based on the percentage of votes for each option (stay, change, delete):

- A dimension or subdimension will be removed if more than (or equal to) 50% of votes are for deletion.
- If the percentage of votes to stay is greater than or equal to 60%, minor or no changes will be made.
- If the percentage of votes to stay is between 40% and 60%, medium changes will be made.
- If the percentage of votes to change is 50% or higher, large changes will be made.
- If there is a lack of consensus or if a dimension or subdimension is unclear, a second iteration may be needed.

After the changes, the model is again presented to the experts in order to confirm the consensus.

4   Constructing the Maturity Model

This section details the construction of the initial maturity model based on literature and the refinements of the model through expert feedback via the Delphi method.

4.1   Initial Maturity Model Development

From relevant and frequently occurring themes in existing literature, three dimensions and 14 sub-dimensions have been chosen to create the initial maturity model[1]. The first

---

[1] The literature review was conducted by querying the Scopus and Web of Science databases for maturity model research in modern technologies, such as advanced information systems, smart process management systems, smart supply chains, online payment systems, Artificial Intelligence (AI), Blockchain, and Internet of Things (IoT). Subsequently, forward and backward snowballing was applied to broaden the search. Papers were assessed manually for their relevance and usefulness for the definition of maturity model dimensions.

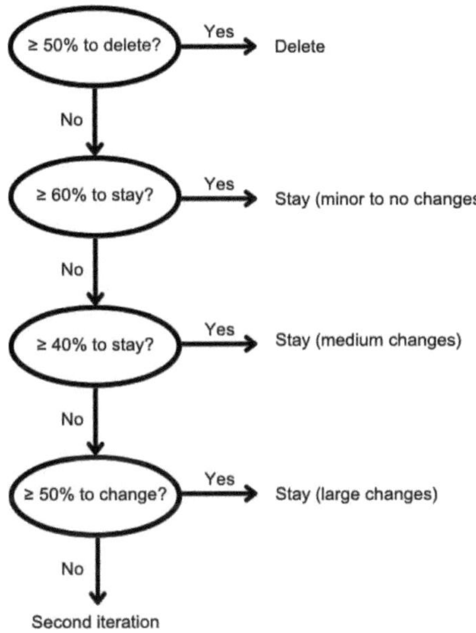

Fig. 3. Delphi consensus mechanism.

dimension People relates to the level of competency, skills, and engagement of individuals within and external to an organization, as well as the overall culture and leadership that supports blockchain technology. The second dimension Technology refers to the level of efficiency of an organization's technological systems, processes, and infrastructure. The sub-dimensions (Infrastructure, Data management, Integration with existing systems, Performance and scalability, Security, and Network) are all key components that contribute to the overall maturity of the technology dimension. The last dimension Organization and strategy assesses the level of effectiveness and alignment of an organization's objectives with its overall strategy.

Table 2 lists the definitions of the chosen (sub)dimensions and relates these to sources in literature to create the initial maturity model. The sources used for the initial maturity model consisted of a combination of published academic papers and articles from reputable organizations or firms.

Each sub-dimension has five levels with given definitions [26]:

Level 0 (None): The financial institution is not mature and doesn't implement blockchain to improve business and doesn't offer blockchain-based products and services.

Level 1 (Defining): The financial institution knows about blockchain applications improving business and is defining it, however, is not using the technology.

Level 2 (Adopting): The financial institution implements some blockchain applications.

Table 2. Dimensions and sub-dimensions of the initial maturity model constructed from literature.

Dimension	Sub-dimension	Definition (initial MM)	Source
People	Skills & training	The ability to effectively train their staff on the use of its blockchain implementation and to enrich their knowledge	[3,20,25,26,33], [8,12,14,21,35], [2,18]
People	External stakeholders (customers, partners. . .)	The ability to collaborate with other organizations, build relationships within the larger blockchain ecosystem, and deliver a positive user experience for the customers	[12,25,26,28], [2,18,21,27]
People	Support management/employees towards blockchain	The ability to foster a culture that supports and encourages the adoption of blockchain technology (leadership, top management, employees,. . .)	[20,25,26,28], [?] [8,14,35]
Technology	Infrastructure (hardware & software)	The quality of the infrastructure supporting the organization's blockchain implementation	[8,10,14,35]
Technology	Data management	The ability to effectively manage and secure the data stored on the blockchain system	[8,10,12,14]
Technology	Integration with existing systems	The ability to integrate its blockchain implementation with its existing IT systems and processes	[11]
Technology	Performance and scalability	The ability to ensure that its blockchain technology can handle the required level of transactions and data volume	[7,10,27,41,42]
Technology	Security	The ability to secure its blockchain system against cyber threats and vulnerabilities	[1,12,27,33,36], [10]
Technology	Network	The ability to build and maintain a strong, secure, and scalable blockchain network. Records of transactions cannot be altered and are permanent	[27,33,36]
Organization & strategy	Governance, regulation & compliance	The understanding of compliance with relevant laws, regulations, and industry standards related to its blockchain technology	[3,20,25,26,28], [8,12,14,21], [2,10,27]
Organization & strategy	Strategy	The overall goals and objectives for its blockchain implementation, as well as the alignment of those goals with its broader business strategy	[3,12,20,26,28], [2,8,14,27,35]
Organization & strategy	Research and development	The investment and commitment to research and development (innovation) activities related to blockchain technology	[4]
Organization & strategy	Sustainability	The ability to ensure that its blockchain implementation is environmentally sustainable and energy efficient	[1,18,29,32]
Organization & strategy	Products & services	The ability to design, develop, and deliver high-quality products and services that leverage blockchain technology	[2,26–28]

Level 3 (Managing): The financial institution implements many blockchain applications.

Level 4 (Integrated): The financial institution is mature and implements all possible blockchain applications to improve business.

The initial version of the maturity model is based on existing literature in adjacent fields of study and needs practical feedback from field experts to further specify and enhance the model. The Delphi method is used to direct expert feedback towards a consensus and a refined maturity model. The composition of the expert panel can be found in Table 3.

For confidential reasons, the names of the participants stay anonymous. Job titles include *Senior consultant, Innovation manager, Owner, Head of FinTech.*

4.2 First Delphi Round: Reaching Consensus on the Dimensions and Sub-dimensions

Based on the expert feedback in the first round, adjustments to the model were carried out. As a reminder, according to the consensus mechanism, each (sub-)dimension can undergo minor to no changes, medium changes, large changes, or even deletion. The

Table 3. Expert Panel Composition (n = 7).

Characteristic	n
Role purely in blockchain	2
Role is a combination of finance and blockchain	5
Years of experience in finance and/or blockchain	
[2–5[years	2
[5–10[years	2
10+ years	3

three dimensions received positive feedback and could stay. Experts also indicated that most the sub-dimensions could stay without any changes. The sub-dimension "Sustainability" is eliminated based on consensus rules, as 50% of participants advocated for its removal, deeming it not yet a critical pillar despite its increasing importance. For minor modifications, the sub-dimension "Strategy" is renamed "Strategy and Vision," reflecting feedback that both elements are crucial for successful innovation. Vision is a future-oriented goal that inspires and motivates, while strategy is a plan of action to achieve specific objectives [17]. The "Products & Services" sub-dimension remains largely unchanged, emphasising the importance of aligning blockchain implementation with existing offerings to ensure they remain user-friendly. For medium changes, the "External Stakeholders" sub-dimension is expanded to "All Stakeholders," incorporating both internal and external parties, including investors, owners, and boards of directors, per feedback from various experts. Education and skill development for partners using blockchain applications are also highlighted as crucial [5]. Ultimately, the revised maturity model consists of three dimensions and 13 sub-dimensions. The updated model after the first round is detailed online, with applied changes highlighted in the model[2].

4.3 Second Delphi Round: Reaching Consensus on the Maturity Level Characteristics

The revised maturity model from the first round served as the foundation for the second round of evaluation. Initially, participants were asked to review the first-round outcomes to ensure a shared understanding. Consensus was reached on the adapted model from the first round. Subsequently, participants assessed the maturity levels for each sub-dimension. Most sub-dimensions required no modifications, while a few warranted minor adjustments. The collected feedback was used to refine and finalize the maturity model following the second round, the results of which are available online, with the adjusted model after round where the carried out changes were highlighted[3].

---

[2] See the template used for Round 1 and the results of Round 1.
[3] See the template used for Round 2 and the results of Round 2.

4.4   Third Delphi Round: Reaching Consensus on the Final Maturity Model

Round three is used to validate the adapted model that was developed as a result of the expert interactions in round two. The participants all agreed on the adapted maturity model after the second round, indicating that the maturity model as a whole was consistent and sound. Thus, this adapted maturity model is considered as the final maturity model on which the questionnaire will be built to assess the blockchain maturity of financial institutions. The full final maturity model is available online[4], and is also depicted in Figs. 4, 5 and 6.

5   Validity

In this section, we investigate and discuss the validity of the model.

5.1   Internal Validity

Ensuring internal validity is essential in any research study. In this work, internal validity was addressed through the application of triangulation. As described by Patton (1999), triangulation refers to the use of multiple methods or data sources in qualitative research to develop a comprehensive understanding of a phenomenon. It is commonly employed to enhance validity by corroborating findings across different types of evidence. In this study, triangulation was achieved by integrating data from three primary sources: (1) a scientific literature review, (2) expert interviews conducted using the Delphi method, and (3) the application of the developed maturity model to a real-world use case through self-assessment. Note that in the case of this paper, the maturity model development process represents sequential phases rather than multiple data sources to corroborate a single finding as is the case in the classical triangulation method.

The primary data collection method consisted of semi-structured interviews, selected to facilitate in-depth exploration and gather expert insights from professionals in both the finance and blockchain domains. This approach was chosen to ground the development of the maturity model in practical, domain-specific knowledge. Contributions from both finance and blockchain experts were considered critical to ensure the model's relevance and applicability.

5.2   External Validity

Following the development of the initial maturity model based on a comprehensive literature review, expert feedback was solicited and used to refine and enhance the model. The final version of the maturity model was subsequently operationalised into a questionnaire banks can use to carry out a self-assessment of their blockchain adoption maturity[5].

---

[4] See the template used for Round 3 and the resulting final maturity model after Round 3, which is contained within the self-assessment questionnaire.

[5] Self-assessment tool for blockchain adoption maturity in the financial industry.

Sub-Dimension	Definition	Level 0 - None	Level 1 - Defining	Level 2 - Adopting	Level 3 - Managing	Level 4 - Integrated
Skills & Training	The ability to effectively train their staff on the use of its blockchain implementation and to enrich their knowledge.	The organization has not recognised the need for its employees to receive training and skills in blockchain technology. There are no employee training programmes.	The organization is beginning to understand how important training and skills are and is searching for training programs. (Higher) management goes to conferences and talks to blockchain experts to learn more about the technology themselves.	The organization has started to adopt training programs for their employees. Employees are actively participating to extend their skills and knowledge.	The organization has a well-defined training program in place. Employees are encouraged to stay up-to-date with the latest developments in blockchain technology.	Employees (who works with blockchain) have a strong knowledge and expertise of blockchain technology and its potential applications.
All stakeholders (internal & external)	The ability to collaborate with other organisations, build relationships within the larger blockchain ecosystem, and deliver a positive user experience for the customers.	The organization has not yet identified any potential partners, customers or other relevant stakeholders.	The organization has identified potential partners, customers or other stakeholders, but has not yet engaged with them.	The organization has started to engage with partners and customers to explore their potential blockchain technology. The organization provides a "proof-of-concept", they listen to the needs of their stakeholders and test some concepts on a smaller scale.	The organization is managing partnerships with stakeholders. The organisation ensures a positive user experience for customers.	The organization is working closely with its stakeholders to create a blockchain-based ecosystem. The organisation delivers excellent user experience. The organization create feedback mechanisms that are available for all stakeholders. There is a clear structure and guidance to follow-up and implement the feedback where it's useful.
Support management/employees towards blockchain	The ability to foster a culture that supports and encourages the adoption of blockchain technology (leadership, top management, employees,...)	There is no support from employees or top management towards the adoption of blockchain.	There is limited support from employees and top management. The organization may create a channel (e.g. Slack) dedicated to blockchain where employees/management can add/share information related to blockchain and educate each other or keep each other updated about the latest trends in the industry.	There is growing support from employees and top management. The organization may reimburse costs to its employees if they voluntarily choose to take some classes/trainings/events about blockchain.	There is strong support from employees and top management. Promoting conferences/ education platforms/ courses to the employees, but should still be voluntarily.	There is a strong culture of support and encouragement towards the adoption of blockchain. Employees and management are fully commited to blockchain technology. Management needs basic understanding of blockchain-concepts.

Fig. 4. Final maturity model - *People* dimension.

Sub-Dimesion	Definition	Level 0 - None	Level 1 - Defining	Level 2 - Adopting	Level 3 - Managing	Level 4 - Integrated
Infrastructure (hardware & software)	The quality of the infrastructure supporting the organization's blockchain implementation.	There is no infrastructure in place to support the blockchain system. There is no hardware or software specifically designed for blockchain.	The organization is defining its infrastructure needs for blockchain.	The organization has invested in hardware and software.	The organization is responsible for managing the infrastructure, and is continuously optimizing it to ensure the best performance.	The infrastructure is capable of handling complex blockchain transactions, handling scalability, and is completely integrated with the organization's broader IT architecture.
Data management	The ability to effectively manage and secure the data stored on the blockchain system.	No data is being managed on the blockchain.	The organization starts to develop a data management strategy.	The organization has developed a data management strategy. Security measures are implemented to protect the data.	A mature data management strategy has been established.	The organization has an advanced data management strategy.
Integration with existing systems	The ability to integrate its blockchain implementation with its existing IT systems and processes.	No integration with existing IT systems and processes.	The organization is defining how it can integrate blockchain technology with its existing IT systems and processes.	The organization is starting to integrate blockchain with some existing IT systems and processes.	The organization has successfully integrated blockchain with some existing IT systems and processes.	The organization has fully integrated blockchain with its existing IT systems and processes.
Performance and scalability	The ability to ensure that its blockchain technology can handle the required level of transactions and data volume.	Performance is not optimal and there are scalability issues. There is no blockchain adoption yet, there is no related KPI to measure.	Performance and scalability requirements are being defined.	Performance and scalability targets are established.	The organization is starting to find areas for optimization and improvement in order to ensure that its blockchain system can fulfil performance and scalability needs as usage will increase.	The organization is using modern technology and best practices to ensure that its blockchain implementation can handle even the most complex use cases.
Security	The ability to secure its blockchain system against cyber threats and vulnerabilities.	The organization does not have any security measures in place.	A security strategy is defined. This may include identifying potential threats, determining risk levels, and creating security policies and procedures.	The organization has started to adopt security measures to protect their system.	The organization has developed a complete security program and is actively managing the system for potential threats and vulnerabilities.	Security is fully integrated into the organization's blockchain system and is able to quickly detect and respond to potential security incidents.
Network	The ability to build and maintain a strong, secure, and scalable blockchain network.	There is no blockchain network in place.	The organization is defining their blockchain network's requirements, such as the types of nodes that will be used, the consensus algorithm that will be used to validate transactions,...	A basic blockchain network has been implemented. This level is the trial-and-error phase that helps the organization making adjustments (technical and non-technical).	The organization has developed a complete blockchain network and is actively managing it.	The organization has implemented a mature blockchain network and is continuously improving it with its related stakeholders and/or users. They have achieved high levels of scalability, security, and reliability.

Fig. 5. Final maturity model - *Technology* dimension.

Sub-Dimesion	Definition	Level 0 - None	Level 1 - Defining	Level 2 - Adopting	Level 3 - Managing	Level 4 - Integrated
Governance, regulation & compliance	The understanding of compliance with relevant laws, regulations, and industry standards related to its blockchain technology.	The organization does not have any compliance measures in place for relevant laws, regulations, and industry standards.	The organization is starting to define the compliance measures for relevant laws, regulations, and industry standards.	The organization has adopted measures to ensure compliance with relevant laws, regulations, and industry standards.	A complete governance, regulation, and compliance program is in place and the organization is actively managing it.	Governance, regulation, and compliance is fully integrated into the organization's blockchain system. They are able to quickly detect and respond to compliance issues. Mechanisms or monthly updates are used to check if they are still compliant with the latest regulations. The organization is thus well-prepared by the time it needs to comply with the new regulations or laws that may impact business.
Strategy and vision	The overall goals and objectives for its blockchain implementation, as well as the alignment of those goals with its broader business strategy and vision.	No overall goals or objectives for their blockchain implementation is set.	Overall goals and objectives are being defined, as well as how these goals align with their broader business strategy. KPIs are defined.	The blockchain implementation strategy is being adopted and is aligned with business strategy. The organization is collecting feedback to know wether or not the goals and objectives are aligned with its business objectives.	The organization has developed a complete strategy for their blockchain implementation that aligns with their business strategy.	The organization has fully integrated their blockchain implementation strategy and vision into their business strategy. They are measuring KPIs to track progress. A feedback system is implemented that results of KPIs, the organization can react quickly if needed.
Research and development	The investment and commitment to research and development (innovation) activities related to blockchain technology.	The organization has not yet invested in any research or development activities related to blockchain technology.	Research about blockchain is starting to be conducted by the organization.	The organization is actively conducting and investing in research.	The organization has a well-established research and development program.	The organization has strong focus on research and development. They are actively investing in innovation to improve their blockchain solutions.
Products & Services	The ability to design, develop, and deliver high-quality products and services that leverage blockchain technology.	The organization has not yet considered using blockchain technology in its products or services.	The organization conducts market research to understand customer needs.	Blockchain technology is being adopted in their products and services.	The organization has developed a strategy for managing the integration of blockchain technology into its products and services.	The organization has fully integrated blockchain technology into their products and services to deliver unique value to their customers. Implementation of feedback systems to know what the customers thinks about the UX/UI and being sure that a summary of the feedback will reach management so the organization can adopt it.

Fig. 6. Final maturity model - *Organisation & Strategy* dimension.

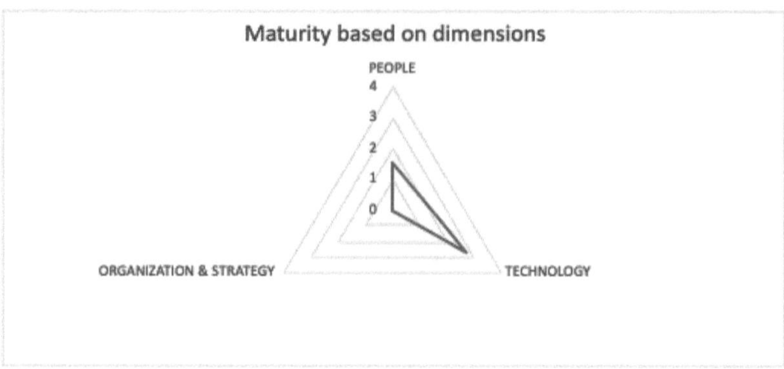

Fig. 7. Maturity assessment on dimensions.

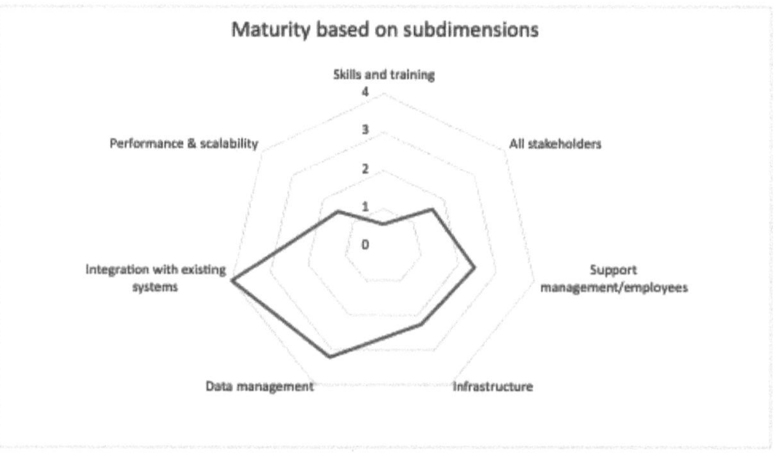

Fig. 8. Maturity assessment on sub-dimensions.

The self-assessment was subsequently carried out by a participating institution. Maturity is assessed based on averages of the self-assessment survey, which results in two radar charts as illustrated in Fig. 7 and Fig. 8. Due to confidentiality reasons, not all sub-dimensions were answered, hence the zero for dimension *Organization & Strategy*. Additionally, for the dimension *Technology*, the sub-dimensions *Network* and *Security* were not included. To preserve confidentiality, the participating institution will remain unnamed.

The participants agreed that the self-assessment questionnaire was easy to use, and that the maturity model gives interesting insights that help chart a course to achieve higher levels of maturity on the assessed sub-dimensions. However, they suggest that the evaluation would ideally be conducted by someone with advanced knowledge of blockchain technology, rather than by a manager.

6   Limitations

The approach followed in this paper has limitations. Firstly, the number of participants in the conducted Delphi study is limited and a larger expert panel would be beneficial for future studies. Additionally, the study is geographically concentrated as all participating institutions and experts are based in Belgium. Broadening the study to other geographical areas would enhance the validity of the model. Moreover, more institutions should apply and evaluate the resulting self-assessment tool. Finally, the inputs provided in the self-assessment should ideally be challenged by experienced outsiders.

7   Conclusion

Blockchain technology has introduced significant benefits and opportunities across various sectors. Among its advantages are increased efficiency, enhanced trust and transparency, and reduced operational costs, primarily achieved by eliminating the need for intermediaries. In this evolving landscape, financial institutions must remain informed about technological advancements and evaluate their readiness to adopt blockchain solutions. However, assessing their current level of maturity in blockchain implementation remains a challenge, largely due to the absence of a comprehensive maturity model tailored to the specific needs of financial institutions. To address this gap, we developed a maturity model for blockchain adoption in the financial industry.

The development of the maturity model followed a three-phase methodology. First, a literature review was conducted to establish a foundational understanding of the subject and to identify existing frameworks. Based on this review, an initial maturity model was constructed, comprising three dimensions, 14 sub-dimensions, and five maturity levels. In the second phase, the model was refined through expert input using the Delphi method. Experts were selected based on their professional roles and years of experience, ensuring representation from both the finance and blockchain domains. Over the course of three Delphi rounds conducted over seven weeks, the model was iteratively refined. The final version consisted of three dimensions, 13 sub-dimensions, and five maturity levels.

Following the finalisation of the model, a self-assessment was conducted by a participating institution. The self-assessment tool was deemed both accessible and informative for assessing blockchain maturity and informing future capability developments.

In conclusion, the developed maturity model effectively addresses a gap in literature by providing a framework for organizations to assess their current level of maturity in blockchain implementation. Each maturity level is defined by specific criteria, offering structured guidance to support institutional decision-making and capability development planning.

Acknowledgements. This study was financed by the Research Foundation Flanders under grant number G039923N and by KU Leuven, Belgium under project 3H200414, and Internal Funds KU Leuven under grant number C14/23/031.

References

1. Bamakan, S.M.H., Motavali, A., Babaei Bondarti, A.: A survey of blockchain consensus algorithms performance evaluation criteria. Expert Syst. Appl. **154**, 113385 (2020). https://doi.org/10.1016/j.eswa.2020.113385
2. Bandara, O., Vidanagamachchi, K., Wickramarachchi, R.: A model for assessing maturity of industry 4.0 in the banking sector. In: Proceedings of the International Conference on Industrial Engineering and Operations Management, vol. 2019 (2019)
3. Bankole, F., Taiwo, A., Claims, I.: An extended digital forensic readiness and maturity model. Forensic Sci. Int. Digit. Invest. **40**, 301348 (2022). https://doi.org/10.1016/j.fsidi.2022.301348
4. Brennan, T., Ernst, P., Katz, J., Roth, E.: Building an R&D strategy for modern times. McKinsey & Company (2020). https://www.mckinsey.com/capabilities/strategy-and-corporate-finance/ourinsights/building-an-r-and-d-strategy-for-modern-times
5. Cardwell, L.A., Williams, S., Pyle, A.: Corporate public relations dynamics: internal vs. external stakeholders and the role of the practitioner. Pub. Relat. Rev. **43**(1), 152–162 (2017)
6. Chang, V., Baudier, P., Zhang, H., Xu, Q., Zhang, J., Arami, M.: How blockchain can impact financial services – the overview, challenges and recommendations from expert interviewees. Technol. Forecast. Soc. Change **158**, 120166 (2020). https://doi.org/10.1016/j.techfore.2020.120166
7. Chauhan, A., Malviya, O.P., Verma, M., Mor, T.S.: Blockchain and scalability. In: 2018 IEEE International Conference on Software Quality, Reliability and Security Companion (QRS-C) (2018). https://doi.org/10.1109/qrs-c.2018.00034
8. Comuzzi, M., Patel, A.: How organisations leverage big data: a maturity model. Ind. Manag. Data Syst. **116**(8), 1468–1492 (2016). https://doi.org/10.1108/imds-12-2015-0495
9. Das, S.R.: The future of fintech. Financ. Manage. **48**(4), 981–1007 (2019). https://doi.org/10.1111/fima.12297
10. Garg, P., Gupta, B., Chauhan, A.K., Sivarajah, U., Gupta, S., Modgil, S.: Measuring the perceived benefits of implementing blockchain technology in the banking sector. Technol. Forecast. Soc. Change **163**, 120407 (2021). https://doi.org/10.1016/j.techfore.2020.120407
11. Gordon, W.J., Catalini, C.: Blockchain technology for healthcare: facilitating the transition to patient-driven interoperability. Comput. Struct. Biotechnol. J. **16**, 224–230 (2018). https://doi.org/10.1016/j.csbj.2018.06.003
12. Goumeh, F., Barforoush, A.A.: A digital maturity model for digital banking revolution for Iranian banks. In: 2021 26th International Computer Conference, Computer Society of Iran (CSICC) (2021). https://doi.org/10.1109/csicc52343.2021.9420566
13. Gupta, P., Tham, M.T.: Fintech: The New DNA of Financial Services. De Gruyter Press (2018)
14. Hansen, H.F., Lillesund, E., Mikalef, P., Altwaijry, N.: Understanding artificial intelligence diffusion through an ai capability maturity model. Inf. Syst. Front., 1–17 (2024)
15. Hasić, F., Beirens, B., Serral, E.: Maturity model for IoT adoption in hospitals. Comput. Inf. **41**(1), 213–232 (2022). https://doi.org/10.31577/cai_2022_1_213
16. Heller, A., Varney, J.: Using process management maturity models: a path to attaining process management excellence. APQC Rep. K **4419** (2013)
17. Hofstrand, D.: Vision and mission statements–a roadmap of where you want to go and how to get there. Ag Decision Maker, pp. 1–4 (2016). https://www.extension.iastate.edu/agdm/wholefarm/html/c5-09.html
18. Hong, L., Hales, D.N.: Blockchain performance in supply chain management: application in blockchain integration companies. Ind. Manag. Data Syst. **121**(9), 1969–1996 (2021). https://doi.org/10.1108/imds-10-2020-0598

19. Malhotra, D., Saini, P., Singh, A.K.: How blockchain can automate KYC: systematic review. Wireless Pers. Commun. **122**(2), 1987–2021 (2021). https://doi.org/10.1007/s11277-021-08977-0
20. Mendling, J., et al.: Blockchains for business process management - challenges and opportunities. ACM Trans. Manag. Inf. Syst. **9**(1), 1–16 (2018). https://doi.org/10.1145/3183367
21. Okuyucu, A., Yavuz, N.: Big data maturity models for the public sector: a review of state and organizational level models. Transforming Gov. People Process Policy **14**(4), 681–699 (2020). https://doi.org/10.1108/tg-09-2019-0085
22. Paulk, M., Curtis, B., Chrissis, M., Weber, C.: Capability maturity model, version 1.1. IEEE Softw. **10**(4), 18–27 (1993). https://doi.org/10.1109/52.219617
23. Powell, C.E.: The Delphi technique: myths and realities. J. Adv. Nurs. **41**(4), 376–382 (2003). https://doi.org/10.1046/j.1365-2648.2003.02537.x
24. Proença, D., Borbinha, J.: Maturity models for information systems - a state of the art. Procedia Comput. Sci. **100**, 1042–1049 (2016). https://doi.org/10.1016/j.procs.2016.09.279
25. Randeree, K., Mahal, A., Narwani, A.: A business continuity management maturity model for the UAE banking sector. Bus. Process. Manag. J. **18**(3), 472–492 (2012). https://doi.org/10.1108/14637151211232650
26. Ronaghi, M.H.: A blockchain maturity model in agricultural supply chain. Inf. Process. Agricult. **8**(3), 398–408 (2021). https://doi.org/10.1016/j.inpa.2020.10.004
27. Saheb, T., Mamaghani, F.H.: Exploring the barriers and organizational values of blockchain adoption in the banking industry. J. High Technol. Managem. Res. **32**(2), 100417 (2021). https://doi.org/10.1016/j.hitech.2021.100417
28. Schumacher, A., Erol, S., Sihn, W.: A maturity model for assessing industry 4.0 readiness and maturity of manufacturing enterprises. Procedia CIRP **52**, 161–166 (2016). https://doi.org/10.1016/j.procir.2016.07.040
29. Sedlmeir, J., Buhl, H.U., Fridgen, G., Keller, R.: The energy consumption of blockchain technology: beyond myth. Bus. Inf. Syst. Eng. **62**(6), 599–608 (2020). https://doi.org/10.1007/s12599-020-00656-x
30. Serral, E., Vander Stede, C., Hasić, F.: Leveraging IoT in retail industry: a maturity model. In: 2020 IEEE 22nd Conference on Business Informatics (CBI), vol. 1, pp. 114–123. IEEE (2020)
31. Thanapal, K., Mehta, D., Mudaliar, K., Shaikh, B.: Online payment using blockchain. In: ITM Web of Conferences, vol. 32, p. 03007 (2020). https://doi.org/10.1051/itmconf/20203203007
32. United Nations Environment Programme: In battle against climate crisis, don't overlook the blockchain (2022). https://www.unep.org/news-and-stories/story/battle-against-climate-crisis-dont-overlook-blockchain
33. Unny, R.B., Lal, B.: Blockchain in supply chain management: a review of the capability maturity model. In: Re-Imagining Diffusion and Adoption of Information Technology and Systems: A Continuing Conversation, pp. 149–158 (2020). https://doi.org/10.1007/978-3-030-64849-7_14
34. Vivekanadam, B.: Analysis of recent trend and applications in block chain technology. J. Innov. Sustain. Manag. Appl. Comput. Sci. **2**(4), 200–206 (2020). https://doi.org/10.36548/jismac.2020.4.003
35. Von Solms, J., Langerman, J.: Digital technology adoption in a bank treasury and performing a digital maturity assessment. Afr. J. Sci. Technol. Innov. Dev. **14**(2), 302–315 (2021). https://doi.org/10.1080/20421338.2020.1857519
36. Wang, H., Chen, K., Xu, D.: A maturity model for blockchain adoption. Financ. Innov. **2**(1) (2016). https://doi.org/10.1186/s40854-016-0031-z

37. Wang, Y., Kim, D., Jeong, D.: A survey of the application of blockchain in multiple fields of financial services. J. Inf. Process. Syst. **16**(4), 935–958 (2020). https://doi.org/10.3745/jips.04.0185
38. Wendler, R.: The maturity of maturity model research: a systematic mapping study. Inf. Softw. Technol. **54**(12), 1317–1339 (2012). https://doi.org/10.1016/j.infsof.2012.07.007
39. Williamson, K., Johanson, G.: Research Methods: Information, Systems, and Contexts. Chandos Publishing (2017)
40. Wu, H., et al.: Blockchain for finance: a survey. IET Blockchain **4**(2), 101–123 (2024)
41. Xie, J., Yu, F.R., Huang, T., Xie, R., Liu, J., Liu, Y.: A survey on the scalability of blockchain systems. IEEE Netw. **33**(5), 166–173 (2019). https://doi.org/10.1109/mnet.001.1800290
42. Zhou, Q., Huang, H., Zheng, Z., Bian, J.: Solutions to scalability of blockchain: a survey. IEEE Access **8**, 16440–16455 (2020). https://doi.org/10.1109/access.2020.2967218

Fed-DL: Federated Learning with Distributed Ledger for Social Demographic Equality

Jaya Pathak[1(✉)], Yash Pandey[1], Jagat Sesh Challa[1], and Amitesh Singh Rajput[2]

[1] Department of Computer Science and Information Systems, Birla Institute of Technology and Science Pilani, Pilani, India
{p20200412,f20210661,jagatsesh}@pilani.bits-pilani.ac.in
[2] Rajiv Gandhi National Cyber Law Centre, National Law Institute University, Bhopal, India
amiteshrajput@nliu.ac.in

Abstract. Federated Learning has become a viable solution to train machine learning models on decentralized data without sharing sensitive information. Meanwhile, Blockchain ensures data integrity and transparency. In this work, we utilize the best of both worlds by implementing a distributed blockchain ledger within a federated learning system, named Fed-DL. Due to aggregation of non-IID data within federated setup, the model favors over-represented groups within clients. This introduces inequality in model's predictive performance across different demographics, resulting in bias within the system. The proposed federated learning framework based on smart contract filters irregular or false updates from clients that negatively impact predictive analysis within demographic groups. This framework is also effective in reducing the server traffic by allowing limited updates which are validated through consensus for model aggregation at the server. Fed-DL not only helps in protecting sensitive client's information but also fosters trust and equality among participants through transparency and record (updates) traceability. This approach enhances the overall quality of machine learning models while adhering to data protection laws and prompts fair and ethical practice. Results indicate that the proposed framework performs well in non-IID data scenarios and is also robust against poisoning attacks.

Keywords: Federated Machine Learning · Blockchain · Secure Distributed Systems · Predictive Fairness · Access Control

1 Introduction

In today's rapidly evolving digital landscape, data is being increasingly generated at an alarming rate, requiring need for efficient data processing methods to deliver meaningful predictions. Machine Learning (ML) algorithms are becoming popular for handling sensitive decision making across various sectors. However, data regulation like EU's General Data Protection Regulation (GDPR) [16], California Consumer Privacy Act (CCPA) [19] in United Sates poses significant challenges for organizations that indulgences in predictions through client's personal data. These regulations often lead to insufficient data collection, affecting accuracy of predictions.

C. Cappiello et al. (Eds.): CoopIS 2025, LNCS 15535, pp. 447–462, 2026.
https://doi.org/10.1007/978-3-032-15538-2_25

Imposing privacy-preserving regulations limits the ability for models to perform effective data analytics. For effective data utilization, Federated Learning (FL) has emerged as a viable solution, by training ML models in a decentralized-collaborative way without the need for data sharing [14]. Here, clients process their personal data independently with the model provided to them and shares an update parameter (gradient) with a central server. The server aggregates the updates received from the clients to built global model, which would be shared to the available clients during the next round model training. This setup trains models across several decentralized locations without the need to store sensitive data centrally. It also ensures information security and adheres to the regulations and policies for data sovereignty [18].

Machine learning algorithms mostly rely on the data provided for processing and decision-making. A notable challenge arises when the training data contains inherent biases against specific groups, leading to major impact on the predictive outcome. In decision-making context, fairness is defined as the absence of prejudice or preference towards any specific group [8]. However, ML models tend to discriminate as the data provided to them exhibit biases with respect to features related to sensitive attributes like gender, race, age, sexual orientation, etc. Therefore, the presence of bias in training data not only undermines accuracy of the model but also raises ethical concerns regarding fairness and inclusion.

To overcome the above challenge, this work proposes a novel approach - Federated learning with Distributed Ledger (Fed-DL) integrating a distributed blockchain ledger into federated learning system where, FL provides secure collaborative environment, blockchain's smart contract automates fairness check within clients. This enables collaborative data training while maintaining data privacy and client updates traceability. The main motivation of this work is to encourage specific client updates that help in increasing predictive accuracy for under-represented minority groups based on demographic information. This new architecture combining federated learning with blockchain provides a comprehensive, trusted and secure solution for a large-scale decentralized data processing. We achieve this by utilizing consensus mechanism to limit the communication frequency by filtering client's update. By setting an immutable distributed ledger with an automated smart contract before model aggregation at the server, the proposed framework is able to identify and filter updates that negatively impact accuracy for specific groups.

The main contribution of this paper are provided below:

1. To the best of our knowledge, this is among the few works combining federated learning and blockchain for a collaborative training and trustworthy environment for social demographic equitability.
2. An architecture for Fed-DL: Federated Learning with Distributed Ledger is proposed that provides a distributed, multi-party collaborative environment, while ensuring trust and equality through consensus mechanism.
3. The proposed system is studied for its robustness under various attack scenarios in case of non-IID data setting.

The remainder of this paper is organized as follows: Sect. 2 illustrates background about federated learning, blockchain and recent work integrating them for various applications. Section 3 details the proposed Fed-DL architecture and operational aspect of equality through smart contracts. Section 4 presents experimental analysis to understand the impact of data distribution within clients. This section also presents attack scenario to test the robustness of the proposed architecture. Section 5 provides a comparative analysis between the proposed technique and previous state-of-the-art distribute learning systems. Finally, Sect. 6 concludes the paper.

2   Background and Related Work

We review topics that include - federated learning, blockchain technology, social predictive equality among clients. We also discuss recent distributed systems that leverage blockchain mechanisms.

2.1   Federated Learning

Federated learning is a decentralized collaborative learning system where each n client works with their local data D, and a server $\mathbb{S}$ that provides an initial global model $\mathbb{G}^r$ to clients and aggregates the updates received at the end of each training rounds [14].

After the server broadcasts the initial model $\mathbb{G}^r$ to n clients, each client trains it locally and sends only the model updates (Δw_i) back to the server for aggregation. Once the server receives updates from enough clients, it aggregates received model updates to prepare the next global model $\mathbb{G}^{r+1}$ and again broadcasts it, this continues till model convergence. In FedAvg [14], local model updates (Δw_i) are combined through weighted averaging to create global model, based on amount of data within each client, mathematically represented with Eq. 1. However, since FL operates on decentralized data that may inherently contain biases favoring specific demographic groups with larger datasets, there is a risk that the global model could become biased toward those groups [9]. To overcome this, we propose a blockchain enabled federated learning system that enables fair predictions and equality across demographic groups, detailed discussion in Sect. 3.

$$\mathbb{G}^{r+1} = \frac{1}{n} \sum_{i=1}^{n} (\frac{d_i}{D} \Delta w_i) \tag{1}$$

Here, d_i is the local data within each client i, n number of clients and r number of training rounds.

2.2   Blockchain and Smart Contract

Blockchain is a distributed ledger system that stores records of data blocks, maintained by node clients in a network. This architecture allows storage of immutable transactional records in blocks, which are linked together using a cryptographic mechanism to form a chain like structure. Within this system, only trusted transactional records are validated by peers [25]. These validations are essential for maintaining the integrity of the blockchain, as they ensure that only legitimate transactions are included in the ledger. Participants who perform the validation of transactions are called as miners and are rewarded for their computational work. Since miners cannot be fully trusted to include a transactional update, blockchain network employ a consensus mechanism to reach agreement on the validity of transactions.

Smart Contracts (SC) are set of programs with predefined conditions that are stored on the blockchain [4]. SC automates processes like access control management for model updates thereby enhancing system efficiency and transparency. Whenever these conditions are satisfied, smart contracts are executed and verified by miners through a consensus mechanism. After verification, if the transaction (model update) is passed by $\geq 50\%$ clients in the system, the transaction is accepted and flagged as "accepted: True" and is stored as a block within the blockchain. Similarly, a rejected transaction is stored with a flag "accepted: False". These transactions are then immutably stored within the ledger, ensuring transparency and accountability.

In this work, we utilize immutable record-keeping capabilities of blockchain to enhance the predictive equality among diversed demographics clients by identifying anomalous or suspicious updates received from clients prior to global model aggregation in a federated learning framework. Blockchain also ensure decentralized trust building in a network of mutually distrusted participants. The utilization of a blockchain ledger is crucial to maintain traceability as well as in ensuring tamper-resistance in case of any infiltration.

2.3 Social Equality

In terms of social justice within a federation, discrimination is mostly caused due to one or many reasons like, heterogeneous and non-independent and identically distributed (non-IID) data across clients [9], or due to data imbalance within classes, or due to inherent prejudices within the client's data. The use of sensitive attributes like gender, race and age during model training lead to social discrimination [8]. Discrimination are mostly intentional and are explicitly based on these sensitive attributes, hence are easily identifiable. Studies also suggest due to factors like data imbalance and bias exhibit lower accuracy for minority groups. This discrimination could lead to distrust in ML based intelligent system and could also lead to ethical implications. To overcome the discrimination based on predictive accuracy for minority groups, we propose a framework based on blockchain's distributed ledger within a heterogeneous federated system.

2.4 Blockchain Based Decentralized Distributed Learning

The integration of FL with blockchain is an emerging field that combines strengths of both technologies to enhance data privacy, security and efficiency. Recent studies [5,12,13,15,18,20–22] have proposed frameworks that utilize this integration and are useful in various applications. A significant distinction between the existing frameworks and our proposed one is the absence of a central server for model aggregation.

The Biscotti framework [18] was an early effort to combine blockchain with federated learning, introducing Proof-of-Federation (PoF) to improve FL robustness. BLADE-FL [13] uses Proof-of-Work (PoW) to distribute both training and mining tasks among clients, promoting trusted cooperative ML. Security in decentralized FL is addressed in SPDL [21] using Byzantine Fault Tolerance (BFT) to coordinate learning while preserving privacy through blockchain. Similarly, B-FL [22] applies BFT to prevent model tampering and enhance trust in FL systems.

Fair incentive mechanisms in blockchain-based federated learning are explored in FairReward [5] based on equity theory [1] to ensure transparent and equitable reward distribution via blockchain. BFLC [12] maintains an immutable ledger of updates and consensus decisions, rewarding valuable contributions and penalizing malicious ones. Similarly, InFEDge [20] tackles incentives in hierarchical FL using smart contracts to automate rewards based on data quality and volume. Furthermore, LBFL [15] introduces Proof-of-Contribution (PoC), forming client committees based on contributions to reduce selection latency, prevent congestion, and ensure legitimate participation.

Although, all above mentioned frameworks ensures data integrity and trusted coordination among peers, they do not guarantee equitable and secure learning across the system, highlighting an area for further development in ensuring fairness and security in FL environment. Motivated by the above, this paper proposes Fed-DL framework that integrates a distributed ledger within a federated system and utilizes consensus algorithm to ensure demographic predictive equality and trust within the peers in a distributed framework.

3   Fed-DL

This section provides the system architecture for the proposed Fed-DL framework. The proposed architecture consists of three module: a central server, for model aggregation; decentralized clients, containing personal and sensitive data; and a distributed blockchain ledger, for validating clients update through smart contract.

3.1   System Architecture

The system architecture for Fed-DL is provided in Fig. 1, each components are discussed below:

1. Decentralized Clients: Set of participating clients that train model on their local data and share only model updates (gradients).
2. A Distributed Blockchain Ledger with Smart Contract: To store model updates (gradients) received from clients. Whenever SC is triggered, each transaction is verified through consensus by miners, if a transaction is passed by $\geq 50\%$ clients in the system, it is flagged as "True" else the transaction is flagged as "False". All these transactions are then stored immutably as blocks in the blockchain.
3. A Central Server: To aggregate the validated updates received from distributed ledger to form global model for the next round. Then, broadcasts the aggregated global model back to clients for next round model training.

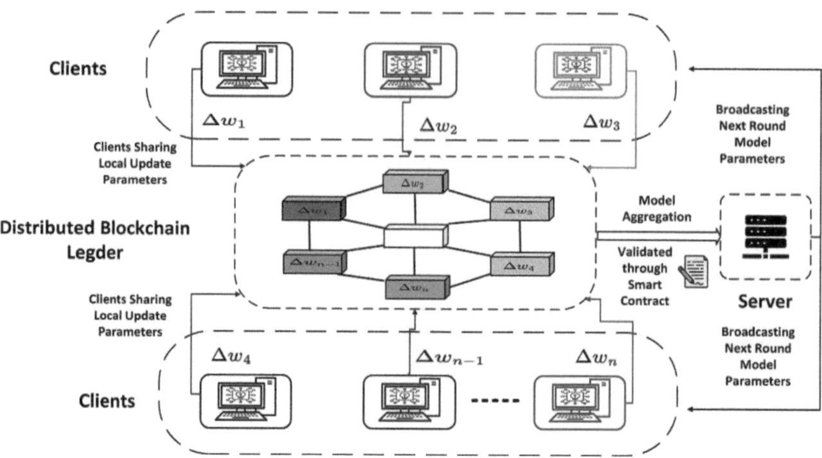

Fig. 1. System Architecture: Federated Learning with Distributed Ledger (Fed-DL).

3.2 Working of Fed-DL

The overall architecture and functioning of the proposed Fed-DL is presented in Fig. 1. A step-wise working is provided below.

1. Each client processes their personal data locally and share model updates with the distributed ledger.
2. The blockchain ledger contains smart contract that validates the incoming model updates from clients. All the transactions are stored as blocks with a flag either True or False, depending upon the condition as per Eq. 3.
3. Once an update is received in blockchain ledger, the records received from client are immutably maintained in the distributed ledger in the form of blocks. This component is essential to monitor and regulate participants behavior through smart contracts. The objective is to identify any inconsistency in local updates and exclude it from global model aggregation.
4. Smart contracts utilize a consensus mechanism for validating transactions (model updates) submitted by clients. Transactions that satisfy the condition, are shared using InterPlanetary File Systems (IPFS) with the server for model aggregation. All the accepted updates are used during aggregation, such that the overall performance is not affected.
5. The above steps are repeated till model convergence.

The detailed step are provided using Algorithm 1. Before the local updates are received by server for global aggregation, each update is passed through a screening procedure via smart contract. If an update is accepted via smart contract, it is flagged as TRUE. Each update either flagged or not are stored within distributed ledger L as blocks B_i. This is done for each client at each iteration. At the end of each iteration, the

---

Algorithm 1. Working of the Fed-DL framework.

    Input: Client list N, Global model update w_G^r, local client update list $\{w_1^r, w_2^r,...,w_n^r\}$,
            number of rounds r
    Output: A Distributed Ledger with accepted blocks of client's update
            $L = \{B_0, B_1, ..., B_n\}$

1 **for** *each training round* $r = 1, 2, ..$ **do**
2   **for** *each client* $n = 1, 2, ..., N$ **do**
        /* Smart Contract   */
3   **if** $(G_{Acc_{min}}^r - w_{Acc_{min}}^{r+1}) <= \tau$ **then**
            /* Accept update and do flag == True   */
4             $B_i \leftarrow w_i^r$
5   **else**
            /* Accept update and do flag == False   */
6             $B_i \leftarrow w_i^r$
        /* Store accepted updates in ledger   */
7     $L \leftarrow B_i$
        /* Aggregate validated updates (flag == True) makes next
            round global model   */
8     $\mathbb{G}^{r+1} = \frac{1}{N} \sum_{i=1}^{N} d_i L$
    /* Broadcast $\mathbb{G}^{r+1}$ for next round training   */

---

server aggregates all updates that are flagged in ledger, represented as:

$$\mathbb{G}^{r+1} = \frac{1}{n} \sum_{i=1}^{n} d_i L \tag{2}$$

The major motivation is to enhance client's updates that helps in increasing the prediction accuracy for social demographic minority groups. This is achieved by limiting model updates from clients that reduces the overall accuracy for these underrepresented groups. Additionally, by utilizing all the accepted updates in previous communication rounds helps in improving the global accuracy of model, even when clients updates are significantly reduced during upcoming rounds of training.

3.3 Equality Through Consensus

In a FL system, discrimination occurs when the data used to train machine learning model is biased against specific groups [8]. For instance, if a system is trained on decentralized data that predominantly represents majority demographic groups (e.g. males), the resulting model may perform well for that group while exhibiting significantly lower accuracy for minority groups (e.g. females). To overcome this discrimination, we propose a framework leveraging FL system with a distributed blockchain ledger to reduce predictive bias against demographic minority groups.

The proposed Fed-DL addresses issues of data bias by ensuring that ML models are trained on diversed and representative datasets. This setup utilizes blockchain's distributed ledger to maintain equality based on predictive model accuracy for different population represented in training data. Before client's updates are received by the server for the next round model aggregation, the updates are passed to a distributed ledger that stores model updates received from clients. This ledger validates the updates submitted by clients. The updates from clients are accepted based on:

$$(G^r_{Acc_{min}} - w^{r+1}_{Acc_{min}}) <= \tau \tag{3}$$

here, $G^r_{Acc_{min}}$ represents the accuracy received on minority class based on the current global model, and $w^{r+1}_{Acc_{min}}$ is the accuracy on minority class based on the updated local model. The maximum accuracy threshold that client's need to maintain to get their update accepted during consensus is denoted using τ. This serves as a tunable hyperparameter that controls the performance degradation on the minority class. Lower values of τ impose stricter fairness conditions, resulting in fewer acceptance updates. Conversely, higher values allow more updates but may reduce fairness guarantee. The optimal choice of τ depends on the desired trade-off between fairness and system efficiency. The proposed framework also increases the accuracy for both demographic groups by selecting those updates which increases the overall accuracy and maintains equality between demographic groups. Although, it is well-established that selective update aggregation can lead to model convergence [14]. Assuming sufficient client diversity in each round, the system continues to aggregate set of updates, which supports convergence.

3.4 Security and Privacy Threats

In federated learning, clients participate in a collaborative model training process while maintaining their data locally. However, there are significant concerns regarding trust among clients. Any adversary may act as a genuine client and attempt poisoning attack by sharing malicious update with the server, that aims to degrade the performance of the global model. We assume that an adversary may control multiple clients within the federated network, thereby increasing the potential impact of their attacks [2].

Prior work uses various gradient aggregation rules (GARs) like krum, multi-krum aggregation, trimmed mean, median based algorithm [23] to protect against any poisoning attacks in a multi-party federated system. However, they are not effective against every classes of attacks. Additionally, in case of non-IID data, unique and outlier data are considered as malicious and are removed at model aggregation [18], which could lead to further discrimination.

Previous privacy-preserving distributed systems does not address the demographic fairness point of view [5,13,18,21], that are also robust against poisoning attacks. The proposed framework, Fed-DL is robust against such poisoning attack that aims to degrade the performance of specific demographic groups. Our framework employs a filtering mechanism that evaluates updates received from clients before model aggregation. Consequently, such attacks intended to lower accuracy for specific group are easily detected and mitigated using this approach.

4   Evaluations

In this section, experiment results are provided to evaluate the robustness against non-IID data and poisoning attacks within the distributed system.

4.1   Design Overview and Assumptions

Each client trains a model locally by performing a standard optimization algorithm, Stochastic Gradient Descent [3]. After this the participants contribute to training by sharing model updates. These updates are stored within the distributed ledger in the form of update blocks at each training round. At each iteration, only the validated updates (that balances accuracies among demographic groups) are selected from the ledger for the next round model aggregation.

Attacker's Assumptions: Adversaries may perform a poisoning attack by sharing malicious updates during model aggregation. The main goal of these attackers is to divert the global model from convergence. We assume that not more than 30% of the contributors are adversaries. For simulation, the data of these adversaries are mislabeled to a different class, causing increase in model misclassification. Note that, we do not assume any attacks such as information leakage that aims to learn the sensitive information or client's data.

4.2   Experiment Setup

The distributed federated network is implemented using the tensorflow federated framework, integrated with Hyperledger fabric for blockchain operations, and employed IPFS for data storage and retrieval. To demonstrate the effectiveness of the proposed framework, we choose two dataset for salary prediction task widely used in fairness studies: ADULT Income [7] and ACS-PUMS Income Dataset [6] with approximately 48,000 and 1,664,500 data entries respectively. The evaluations are based on sensitive attributes such as gender and race, assessing each individually, to address the bias originating from these attributes.

The dataset is divided into training and testing in $80 : 20$ ratio. The training data is divided among N clients to simulate real-world scenario, where the data practically vary with respect to the distribution and volume across devices. The result for ADULT dataset is based on 5 clients, and ACS-PUMS under 10 clients. During training, each client performs 10 local epochs with a batch size of 64 before sharing updates to the distributed ledger. A 1-D convolution neural network (CNN) is used as the base model at both server and clients, for both datasets. Adam is used as an optimizer and ReLU as the activation function at each client, with a learning rate of 0.01 and FedAvg [14] as the default aggregation algorithm at the server.

4.3   Statistical Metrics

The effectiveness of the proposed framework in minimizing disparity based on predictive accuracy on sensitive attributes has been assessed in this section. We employ statistical metrics to quantify accuracy differences between majority and minority demographic groups like average difference (Avg), maximum difference (Max), minimum difference (Min) and geometric mean (GM) difference of accuracy for both groups at each round. These values indicates the average, maximum, minimum and geometric mean difference in predictive accuracy for majority and minority groups. A reduction in these metrics signifies an improved equality between the groups.

Table 1 demonstrates effectiveness of the proposed Fed-DL framework based on measures related to accuracy difference between demographic majority and minority group. By limiting client updates aggregated at server, this framework effectively reduces the volume of updates that server needs to process. Additionally, Fig. 2 provides accuracy graphs for majority and minority demographics for the ADULT and ACS-PUMS datasets, comparing the accuracy difference between the federated baseline [14] and the proposed Fed-DL framework. Results demonstrate a notable reduction in accuracy differences as well as higher accuracy for all the demographic groups. Furthermore, the proposed framework significantly reduces the communication overhead associated with transmitting client updates for aggregation. By selectively sharing updates validated via consensus mechanism, the cost of communication is minimized while maintaining demographic equality with respect to predictive accuracy. Comparing the results in sub-figure 2a and 2c showcase that *having biased data could be worse than less data*, as it can reinforce generalization. By rejecting updates that disrupts the predictions, Fed-DL filters updates that propagates biased correlations, resulting in more robust global model. The improvement in overall global accuracy suggests that bias in traditional FL have data utility issue.

Table 1. Comparison with various statistical metrics on accuracy difference between demographic majority and minority.

	Statistical Metrics				Accepted list of clients updates
	Avg	Max	Min	GM	
Fed-Baseline [14]	12.67	23.89	7.80	12.30	All updates at every round
Fed-DL	6.05	22.15	0.49	3.82	[1,2,4],[1,2],[2],[0,1],[2],[2],[],[2],[0,1],[0,1], [0,1,2,4],[0],[1,2,4],[],[1],[0],[1,2],[2],[1,2]

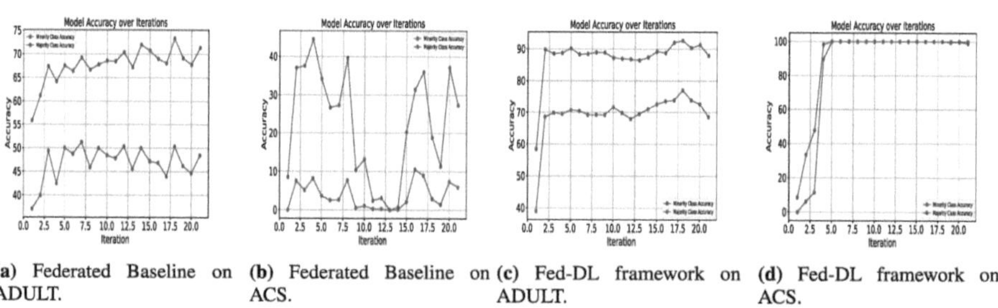

(a) Federated Baseline on ADULT. (b) Federated Baseline on ACS. (c) Fed-DL framework on ADULT. (d) Fed-DL framework on ACS.

Fig. 2. Predictive accuracy disparities between demographic groups: Fed-DL vs Federated Baseline [14] on ADULT and ACS-PUMS datasets.

Table 2. Statistical metrics of accuracy differences between majority and minority demographics across τ, analyzed with different levels of non-IID data based on sensitive attributes for federated baseline [14] and proposed framework.

Attribute	Dataset	Metric	$\beta = 0.1$				$\beta = 0.5$				$\beta = 1.0$			
			FL	Fed-DL			FL	Fed-DL			FL	Fed-DL		
				$\tau = 4$	$\tau = 8$	$\tau = 10$		$\tau = 4$	$\tau = 8$	$\tau = 10$		$\tau = 4$	$\tau = 8$	$\tau = 10$
Gender	**ADULT**	**Avg**	13.19	0.79	1.10	1.41	22.24	13.59	16.14	12.13	13.48	10.24	11.88	10.84
		Max	22.14	16.71	19.37	22.14	26.95	19.52	20.15	22.72	27.85	17.77	27.85	17.40
		Min	9.83	−0.04	−0.04	0.0	16.54	10.17	14.02	8.83	7.11	6.73	7.16	8.26
		GM	12.93	0.0	0.0	0.0	22.13	13.33	16.04	11.74	12.92	9.96	11.45	10.68
	ACS	**Avg**	19.28	1.29	30.3	1.97	32.59	1.84	1.70	2.04	23.45	7.51	11.49	14.39
		Max	30.20	26.28	22.33	30.23	43.21	29.38	16.67	23.99	35.35	29.70	30.34	31.57
		Min	6.68	−0.03	0.0	0.0	4.52	0.0	0.0	0.0	12.93	2.23	4.36	5.32
		GM	19.25	0.0	0.0	0.0	30.06	0.0	0.0	0.0	22.96	6.07	9.55	12.42
Race	**ADULT**	**Avg**	2.80	−0.24	−0.20	−0.45	3.98	1.26	0.59	1.66	8.77	1.36	−0.79	1.07
		Max	6.92	0	0.0	0.39	7.62	3.04	1.89	5.32	11.79	4.57	2.93	5.89
		Min	−0.83	−3.92	−0.83	−9.63	−5.32	−5.32	−2.78	−4.95	2.71	−1.94	−3.07	−1.43
		GM	0.0	0	0.0	0.0	0.0	0.0	0.0	0.0	8.42	0.0	0.0	0.0
	ACS	**Avg**	1.94	−0.02	0.34	0.45	19.24	0.41	1.23	0.91	9.63	2.87	1.31	1.78
		Max	10.91	1.61	3.28	10.91	24.17	6.90	20.39	14.61	16.72	12.23	3.92	16.72
		Min	0.22	−0.26	−0.14	−0.23	3.28	−0.11	−0.11	−0.05	6.73	0.13	−0.02	0.48
		GM	1.24	0.0	0.0	0.0	18.24	0.0	0.0	0.0	9.27	1.85	0.0	0.0

4.4 Non-IID Robustness Analysis

In this section, we present the analysis aimed at evaluating the performance of the proposed methodology under various experimental conditions. The analysis focuses on examining parameters such as the Dirichlet parameter β and accuracy threshold τ, their impact on the effectiveness of the proposed framework. By varying these parameters across datasets (ADULT and ACS-PUMS), we highlight the robustness of Fed-DL framework in case of non-IID data. Table 2 presents the results on both ADULT and ACS-PUMS dataset based on gender and racial demographics with varying accuracy threshold over non-IID data.

Results are based on varying client data sizes using the Dirichlet parameter β, where smaller values indicate more non-IID data and larger values yield IID distributions. We also examined the effect of different accuracy thresholds τ, for conditional update acceptance. Results demonstrate a significant reduction in predictive accuracy difference between demographic groups based on statistical metrics observed across all experimental variations. As stated earlier, lower values for these metrics indicate enhanced equality between demographic groups. This is achieved by segregating updates that fail to meet the condition mentioned in smart contract, thereby preventing them from participation during global model aggregation. This condition ensures that only reliable and unbiased updates comprises the global model.

The proposed approach utilizes FL system with a distributed blockchain ledger to reduce predictive bias against demographic minorities. The server acts as a conduit, allowing only updates that ensure predictive equality. Client updates are immutably stored on the ledger, ensuring traceability and tamper-resistance. Only updates flagged as TRUE are used in global aggregation, preserving accuracy for both minority and majority groups.

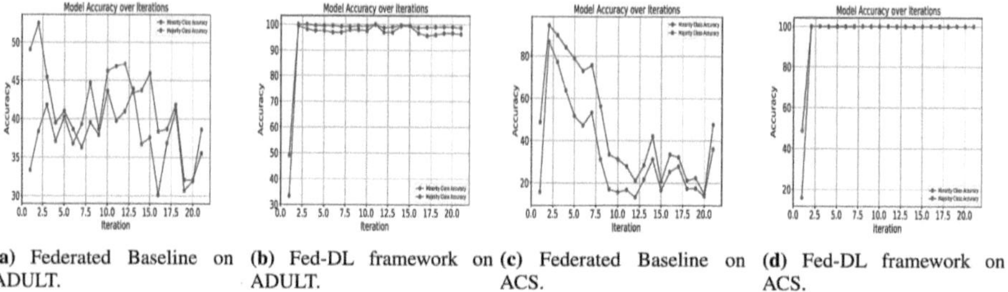

(a) Federated Baseline on ADULT.   (b) Fed-DL framework on ADULT.   (c) Federated Baseline on ACS.   (d) Fed-DL framework on ACS.

Fig. 3. Predictive accuracy disparities across demographic groups under a 30% label-flipping attack: Fed-DL vs Federated Baseline [14] on ADULT and ACS-PUMS datasets.

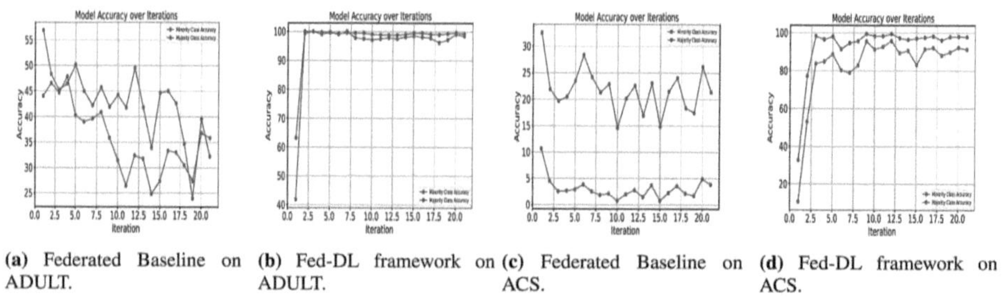

(a) Federated Baseline on ADULT.   (b) Fed-DL framework on ADULT.   (c) Federated Baseline on ACS.   (d) Fed-DL framework on ACS.

Fig. 4. Predictive accuracy disparities across demographic groups under 30% Gaussian noise attack: Fed-DL vs Federated Baseline [14] on ADULT and ACS-PUMS datasets.

4.5   Sybil Attack Analysis: Fed-DL Robustness

This section analyze robustness of Fed-DL in case of poisoning attacks. We assume adversaries might perform poisoning attack by sharing malicious updates during model aggregation. Attackers main goal is to harm global model by targeting minorities data within clients. Note that we do not assume any information leakage attack on the ledger, that aims to learn the sensitive information or properties of client's data. Due to the inherent correlation between output labels and sensitive attributes (e.g., race, gender), any injected noise or distortion might affect client accuracy associated with those attributes [10]. The proposed framework also reduces communication overhead related to update sharing during attacks. SC filters any malicious updates prior to their propagation to the server for aggregation, thereby enhancing system resilience against adversarial attack.

Two types of poisoning attacks have been analyzed: targeted label-flipping attack [11] that targets positive outcome class and a Gaussian poisoning attack that involves injecting random noise into client's update [24]. Figure 3 compares the accuracy over majority and minority demographic groups on federated baseline vs proposed Fed-DL approach in a highly non-IID data setup in case of targeted label flipping attack. Similarly, Fig. 4 presents accuracy results for demographic groups in case of a Gaussian data poisoning attack for federated baseline vs proposed Fed-DL approach in highly

Table 3. Fed-DL framework surviving 30% coordinated sybil poisoning attacks: a targeted sign-flipping and a Gaussian noise attack (with $\mu = 0$ and $\sigma = 0.5$) on the ADULT [7] and ACS-PUMS dataset [6].

Attack	Dataset	Attacker	Test acc&loss	Accepted updates
Sign Flipping	ADULT	Client 1	0.83, 0.11	[[0,3,4][0,4][0,4][0,4][0,4][0,4][4][0,4][0,4][4][0,4][0,4][0,4][0,4][0,4][0,4][0,4][0,4][0,4][0,4]]
	ACS	Client 1, 2, 4	0.94, 0.04	[[0,1,3,4,5,7,9][3,5,7,9][5,7,9][3,5,7,9][5,7,9][5,7,9][5,7,9][5,7,9][3,5,7,9][5,7,9][5,7,9][5,7,9][5,7,9][5,7,9][5,7,9][5,7,9][5,7,9][5,7,9][5,7,9]]
Gaussian Noise	ADULT	Client 3	0.84, 0.10	[[0,3,4][0,4][0,4][4][0,4][0,4][0,4][0,4][0,4][0,4][0,4][0,4][0,4][0,4][0,4][0,4][0,4][0,4][0,4][4]]
	ACS	Client 1, 3, 4	0.94, 0.03	[[0,4,5,6,7,8][4,5][5][0,5][5][0,4,5][0,5][5][5][5][5][5][5][0,5][5][5][5][0,5][5][5]]

Table 4. Comparative Analysis of proposed Fed-DL framework and previous state-of-the-art methods [13,18,21].

Features	Proposed Method	Biscotti [18]	Blade-FL [13]	SPDL [21]
Blockchain Usage	To restrict false/unfair updates from aggregation	For privacy and security in FL	For improving decentralization and security	For maintaining secure framework for decentralized learning
Functioning	Enhance fairness across demographics and lowers communication overhead	Focuses on ensuring privacy and security in FL	Overcomes single point failure problem	Efficiently coordinates the decentralized learning process
Consensus Mechanism	Utilizes Proof-of-Stake (PoS)	Uses Proof-of-Federation (PoF)	Uses Proof of Work (PoW)	Utilizes Byzantine Fault Tolerance (BFT)
Data Handling	Segregates unreliable updates based on consensus validation	Ensures encrypted updates are shared	Decentralized data handling through blockchain	Securely aggregate clients gradients without exposing data
Data Security	Ensures only reliable updates are considered	Ensures only encrypted model updates are shared	Ensures secure communication between clients and blockchain	Utilizes consensus to ensure data integrity and security during training
Gradient Aggregation Rule	FedAvg	Multi-krum	FedAvg	Krum

non-IID data. Results demonstrate that the Fed-DL approach is able to tolerate any feasible infiltration up to a realistic attack strength of 30% sybil coordination in the system [17]. Conversely, the proposed framework not only maintains the accuracy levels between demographic groups but also helps enhancing their predictive accuracy. Table 3 presents the list of accepted client updates in case of a sign-flipping attack, targeted on positive class and a Gaussian noise attack on the ADULT and ACS-PUMS dataset on 30% sybil coordination.

5   Comparison with State-of-the-Art Methods

A comparative analysis between the proposed Fed-DL and other existing blockchain based decentralized learning systems [13, 18, 21] is presented in Table 4. The aim is to highlight the dissimilarity among these approaches for data protection, data handling, data security and other aspects. While Biscotti [18] lays the foundational framework of decentralized multi-party machine learning approach, the proposed Fed-DL framework ensures demographic fairness in model performance across groups. Meanwhile, client management frameworks like Blade-FL [13] advocates for decentralized data handling through blockchain to enhance security while maintaining data privacy. On the other hand, security issues are addressed in frameworks like BFL [22], SPDL [21] which are based on the BFT consensus that implements secure gradient aggregation to prevent exposing clients sensitive data. Fair incentive mechanism like FairReward [5], BFLC [12] and InFEDge [20] ensures equitable reward distribution in a blockchain based federated learning system. The proposed Fed-DL framework aims at providing enhanced demographic fairness within the groups and prevents from various forms of poisoning attacks, utilizing blockchain's capabilities of immutability and traceability for promoting fair decentralized learning.

6   Conclusion and Future Work

This work proposes Fed-DL, a decentralized federated learning framework utilizing blockchain technology to ensure data integrity. The system comprise of clients, central server and a distributed ledger with smart contract between clients and server. The ledger stores all updates received from clients and forwards updates validated through the consensus. The framework addresses the issues of data imbalance and bias within a collaborative federated learning paradigm. By utilizing blockchain's distributed ledger to store and validate updates from clients, we ensure that ML models are trained on diverse and heterogeneous data without being partial against any particular demographic group. This not only ensures demographic equality based on predictive performance among clients but also reduces communication overhead related to update sharing. Furthermore, the framework demonstrates robustness against poisoning and up to 30% coordinated Sybil attacks, preserving model integrity and performance under adversarial conditions.

While the current validation rule in the smart contract is based on fixed threshold value τ, it simply guarantees fairness posing a limit on the system's flexibility. In future, an adaptive thresholding strategy could be utilized to dynamically tune τ according to system performance, data heterogeneity or fairness-utility trade-offs. Moreover, this work could also be extended to include a client reputation system based on consistently validated updates to incentivize trustworthy behavior.

Acknowledgements. The authors acknowledge the use of ChatGPT for sentence rephrasing and language refinement to enhance clarity and readability of the manuscript.

References

1. Adams, J.S.: Inequity in social exchange. In: Advances in Experimental Social Psychology, vol. 2, pp. 267–299. Elsevier (1965)
2. Bagdasaryan, E., Veit, A., Hua, Y., Estrin, D., Shmatikov, V.: How to backdoor federated learning. In: International Conference on Artificial Intelligence and Statistics, pp. 2938–2948. PMLR (2020)
3. Bottou, L.: Stochastic gradient descent tricks. In: Montavon, G., Orr, G.B., Müller, K.-R. (eds.) Neural Networks: Tricks of the Trade. LNCS, vol. 7700, pp. 421–436. Springer, Heidelberg (2012). https://doi.org/10.1007/978-3-642-35289-8_25
4. Buterin, V., et al.: A next-generation smart contract and decentralized application platform. In: White Paper, vol. 3, pp. 2–1 (2014)
5. Chen, G., et al.: Fairreward: towards fair reward distribution using equity theory in blockchain-based federated learning. IEEE Trans. Depend. Secure Comput. **22**, 1612–1626 (2024)
6. Ding, F., Hardt, M., Miller, J., Schmidt, L.: Retiring adult: new datasets for fair machine learning. In: Advances in Neural Information Processing Systems, vol. 34, pp. 6478–6490 (2021)
7. Dua, D., Graff, C.: UCI machine learning repository (2017). http://archive.ics.uci.edu/ml/datasets/Adult
8. Dwork, C., Hardt, M., Pitassi, T., Reingold, O., Zemel, R.: Fairness through awareness. In: Proceedings of the 3rd Innovations in Theoretical Computer Science Conference, pp. 214–226 (2012)
9. Ezzeldin, Y.H., Yan, S., He, C., Ferrara, E., Avestimehr, A.S.: Fairfed: enabling group fairness in federated learning. In: Proceedings of the AAAI Conference on Artificial Intelligence, vol. 37, pp. 7494–7502 (2023)
10. Hardt, M., Price, E., Srebro, N.: Equality of opportunity in supervised learning. In: Advances in Neural Information Processing Systems, vol. 29 (2016)
11. Huang, L., Joseph, A.D., Nelson, B., Rubinstein, B.I., Tygar, J.D.: Adversarial machine learning. In: Proceedings of the 4th ACM Workshop on Security and Artificial Intelligence, pp. 43–58 (2011)
12. Li, Y., Chen, C., Liu, N., Huang, H., Zheng, Z., Yan, Q.: A blockchain-based decentralized federated learning framework with committee consensus. IEEE Netw. **35**, 234–241 (2020)
13. Ma, C., et al.: When federated learning meets blockchain: a new distributed learning paradigm. IEEE Comput. Intell. Maga. **17**, 26–33 (2022)
14. McMahan, B., Moore, E., Ramage, D., Hampson, S., Arcas, B.A.: Communication-efficient learning of deep networks from decentralized data. In: Artificial Intelligence and Statistics, pp. 1273–1282. Proceedings of Machine Learning Research (PMLR) (2017)
15. Qiao, S., et al.: LBFL: a lightweight blockchain-based federated learning framework with proof-of-contribution committee consensus. IEEE Trans. Big Data **11**, 1745–1759 (2024)

16. Regulation, P.: Regulation (eu) 2016/679 of the European parliament and of the council. In: Regulation (eu), vol. 679 (2016)
17. Sagar, S., Li, C.S., Loke, S.W., Choi, J.: Poisoning attacks and defenses in federated learning: a survey. arXiv preprint arXiv:2301.05795 (2023)
18. Shayan, M., Fung, C., Yoon, C.J., Beschastnikh, I.: Biscotti: a blockchain system for private and secure federated learning. IEEE Trans. Parallel Distrib. Syst. **32**, 1513–1525 (2020)
19. de la Torre, L.: A guide to the california consumer privacy act of 2018. SSRN 3275571 (2018)
20. Wang, X., Zhao, Y., Qiu, C., Liu, Z., Nie, J., Leung, V.C.: Infedge: a blockchain-based incentive mechanism in hierarchical federated learning for end-edge-cloud communications. IEEE J. Selected Areas Commun. **40**, 3325–3342 (2022)
21. Xu, M., Zou, Z., Cheng, Y., Hu, Q., Yu, D., Cheng, X.: SPDL: a blockchain-enabled secure and privacy-preserving decentralized learning system. IEEE Trans. Comput. **72**, 548–558 (2022)
22. Yang, Z., Shi, Y., Zhou, Y., Wang, Z., Yang, K.: Trustworthy federated learning via blockchain. IEEE Internet Things J. **10**, 92–109 (2023)
23. Yin, D., Chen, Y., Kannan, R., Bartlett, P.: Byzantine-robust distributed learning: towards optimal statistical rates. In: International Conference on Machine Learning, pp. 5650–5659. Proceedings of Machine Learning Research (PMLR) (2018)
24. Zhang, S., Pan, Y., Liu, Q., Yan, Z., Choo, K.K.R., Wang, G.: Backdoor attacks and defenses targeting multi-domain AI models: a comprehensive review. ACM Comput. Surv. **57**, 1–35 (2024)
25. Zheng, Z., Xie, S., Dai, H.N., Chen, X., Wang, H.: Blockchain challenges and opportunities: a survey. Int. J. Web Grid Serv. **14**, 352–375 (2018)

Short Papers

Accurate and Noise-Tolerant Extraction of Routine Logs in Robotic Process Automation

Massimiliano de Leoni[1(✉)], Faizan Ahmed Khan[1], and Simone Agostinelli[2]

[1] Department of Mathematics, University of Padua, Padua, Italy
`massimiliano.deleoni@unipd.it`, `faizanahmed.khan@phd.unipd.it`
[2] Department of Engineering and Science, Universitas Mercatorum of Rome, Rome, Italy
`simone.agostinelli@unimercatorum.it`

Abstract. Robotic Process Mining focuses on the identification of the routine types performed by human resources through a User Interface. The ultimate goal is to discover routine-type models to enable robotic process automation. The discovery of routine-type models requires the provision of a routine log. Unfortunately, the vast majority of existing works do not directly focus on enabling the model discovery, limiting themselves to extracting the set of actions that are part of the routines. They were also not evaluated in scenarios characterized by inconsistent routine execution, hereafter referred to as noise, which reflects natural variability and occasional errors in human performance. This paper presents a clustering-based technique that aims to extract routine logs. Experiments were conducted on nine UI logs from the literature with different levels of injected noise. Our technique was compared with existing techniques, most of which are not meant to discover routine logs but were adapted for the purpose. The results were evaluated through standard state-of-the-art metrics, showing that we can extract more accurate routine logs than what the state of the art could, especially in the presence of noise.

Keywords: Routine Log · Routine Identification · Robotic Process Automation · Routine-Type Model Discovery · Robotic Process Mining

1 Introduction

Robotic Process Automation (RPA) is a maturing technology [2] that creates software (SW) robots to partially or fully automate rule-based and repetitive *routines* performed by human users in their applications' user interfaces (UIs) [11].

Jimenez et al. [9] put forward a methodology to automate the routines and replace them with SW robots, which consists of three steps: *(i)* identify the candidate routine types to automate by means of interviews and observation of workers conducting their daily work, *(ii)* record the interactions that take place during routines' enactment on the UI of software applications into dedicated UI logs, and *(iii)* specify their conceptual and technical structure for defining the behavior of SW robots in the form of routine-type models. Once these models have been defined, commercial RPA tools allow SW robots to automate a wide range of routines in a record-and-replay fashion.

© The Author(s), under exclusive license to Springer Nature Switzerland AG 2026
C. Cappiello et al. (Eds.): CoopIS 2025, LNCS 15535, pp. 465–475, 2026.
https://doi.org/10.1007/978-3-032-15538-2_26

The third step of the methodology, namely the definition of the routine-type model, can be easily achieved through the application of process discovery techniques [1]. However, traditional process discovery techniques require the event log to record a set of executions of one process type. This is achieved by associating a case identifier to each event, which enables grouping events into traces, each of which represents one execution of the process that is aimed to be discovered. UI logs cannot be directly employed by traditional process discovery techniques because they do not follow the assumptions mentioned above: firstly, UI-log events do not have case identifiers that allow grouping events into individual routine executions; secondly, UI logs contain executions of different routine types, instead of one single routine type.

It follows that the automatic discovery of routine-type models requires transforming UI logs into a set of routine logs, one per routine type. Subsequently, the events - in fact, UI events - of the routine log related to a certain type T must be assigned identifiers that enable grouping the events into individual executions of T. In the remainder, we refer to UI events of routine logs as actions, to differentiate them from the events of traditional event logs. Our proposal shares commonalities with techniques for event-log trace clustering, such as [14]. However, they require event logs with case identifiers as input, which differs from the structure of UI logs. While this limitation might possibly be lifted, their applicability to UI logs and RPA has so far remained an unexplored area.

The literature largely proposes techniques that can allocate UI actions to routine types, without attempting to create routine logs [5, 10], [6], with the notable exception of Rebmann et al. [12] and Abb et al. [3]. Unfortunately, identifying the actions of different routine types is unsatisfactory, because the creation of SW robots requires modeling how these actions must be ordered. We thus attempted to adapt existing techniques to discover routine logs, but the results were not as satisfactory as we aimed at. Our goal would also have been to compare with Abb et al. [3], which enables direct extraction of routine logs. Unfortunately, the lack of a public reference implementation prevented us from carrying out the comparison.

Furthermore, these techniques were designed and assessed in scenarios where humans always work consistently, and thus all routine executions of a certain type were somewhat always executed in the same manner. This scenario is not realistic because humans naturally perform different executions of the same routine type in a slightly different manner and, additionally, they can make mistakes, which requires corrective actions, such as undoing mistakes and redoing the right actions. For instance, humans may copy and paste the wrong cells of an Excel file, possibly realizing their mistakes and trying to fix them through additional actions. This lack of consistency and outlier behavior is hereafter referred to as noise. If the techniques to extract routine logs are not robust against noise, routine logs are mistakenly created. As a consequence, when applying discovery techniques onto these erroneous UI logs, the resulting routine-type models may be inaccurate and imprecise.

This paper proposes a new technique that is able to extract routine logs from UI logs and is noise-tolerant. The validity of the proposal was evaluated on nine different UI logs with varying levels of injected noise, and compared against state-of-the-art techniques, which were adapted for the purpose but, unfortunately, without achieving the same result quality as that of our proposal. The assessment of the accuracy in extracting routine logs has been based on the two different state-of-the-art criteria: *Jaccard Coefficient (JC)* and *fitness*.

The rest of the paper is structured as follows. Section 2 introduces the background required to understand the entire paper. Section 3 presents the three-step technique to the discovery of routine logs, while Sect. 4 compares it with existing techniques against standard metrics. Finally, Sect. 5 concludes the paper.

2 Preliminary Concepts

Here we introduce the basic concepts related to Robotic Process Mining (RPM). We aim to discover the types of routines that users perform. Each routine execution is composed of a sequence of UI actions (e.g., copying and pasting cells, clicking buttons). In this paper, we aim to discover the models of routine types from a UI log, which records the actions performed by users through the UI:

Definition 1 (UI Log). *Let $\mathcal{A}$ be the set of UI actions of interest. A UI Log Σ is a sequence of actions, namely $\Sigma \in \mathcal{A}^*$.*

Note that UI logs can generally be richer than simply containing the names of the activities; for instance, the UI log could record the timestamps, the user names, etc. However, these concepts are abstracted here because they are irrelevant for the remainder of the paper.

We denote the length of the sequence Σ by $|\Sigma|$, i.e., the number of actions it contains. For each index i with $1 \leq i \leq |\Sigma|$, $\Sigma(i)$ denotes the i-th action in the sequence Σ.

The identification of the routine types requires the identification of routine executions from UI logs and their subsequent clustering: every cluster contains the execution of routines of the same type. Each **routine execution** λ consists of actions performed by one single user, which is recorded as a sequence of execution of actions of a routine, namely $\lambda \in \mathcal{A}^*$. The clustering of the routine executions is defined as follows:[1]

Definition 2 (The Problem of Clustering Routine Executions). *Let $\mathcal{A}$ be the set of UI actions of interest. Let $\Sigma \in \mathcal{A}^*$ be a UI Log. The problem of clustering routine executions from Σ consists in:*

1. *Extracting the multiset $W \in \mathcal{B}(\mathcal{A}^*)$ of routine executions from Σ,*
2. *Clustering W in a set $\{C_1, \ldots, C_n\} \subset \mathcal{B}(\mathcal{A}^*)$ such that $W = \biguplus_{i=1}^{n} C_i$, where n is the number of routine types and C_i is the routine log related to the i-th routine type.*

The extraction of routine executions is often referred to in the literature as **segmentation** [4]. Each identified cluster at point 2 is a **routine log**, which contains the executions of routines in the UI log that are of the same type. Note the use of multisets for the identified routines and routine logs. Since routines are abstracted out as actions,

---

[1] Given a set X, $\mathcal{B}(X)$ indicates the set of all multisets with elements in X. Given two multisets Y and Z, $Y \uplus Z$ indicates the union of Y and Z, namely the multiset of the elements in Y combined with those in Z, each with a cardinality that is the sum of its cardinality in Y and in Z.

the same routine is likely going to occur multiple times. In fact, each routine type is expected to be independently automated through RPA Tools (e.g., the automation of the reimbursement procedure or student enrollment).

For each routine log $C = \{\sigma_1, \ldots, \sigma_n\}$ associated with some routine type T, a model of T can be discovered, using existing process-discovery techniques on C [1]. The goal of this paper is to discover routine logs by addressing the problem outlined in Definition 2. *These routine logs are naturally used to discover models of routine types, but this paper does not provide a contribution in this respect. However, the assessment is also based on the fitness metric, which enables determining whether an extracted routine log is able to be used as input to discover an accordant routine type* (cf. Definition 4 in Sect. 4.1).

In this paper, UI logs are modeled without considering the resources that execute the routines. This simplification is not restrictive. If UI log events were defined as pairs of actions and resources, one could easily derive a sub-log for each resource r by retaining only the actions performed by r. By subsequently concatenating the sub-UI logs of all resources and projecting solely on the actions, one would obtain a UI log that aligns with Definition 1. Note that each execution of any routine type is naturally carried out by the same resource. Moreover, timestamps are irrelevant to the proposed technique, as will become clear in the remainder of this paper.

3   A Technique for Discovering Routine Logs

The starting point of the technique is a UI log $\Sigma \in \mathcal{A}^*$ (cf. Definition 1). The UI log Σ contains different routine executions $\lambda \in \mathcal{A}^*$. The proposed work aims to discover routine logs (namely, a multiset of routine executions) that can later be used to discover routine-type models.

Extraction of the Multiset of Routine Executions. The extraction of routine executions requires one to define the set $\mathcal{A}_F \subset \mathcal{A}$ of actions that mark the completion of a routine execution.

Given the UI log $\Sigma \in \mathcal{A}^*$, we identify the multiset $W \in \mathcal{B}(\mathcal{A}^*)$ of routine executions by segmenting Σ at occurrences of actions from $\mathcal{A}_F$. The log is split into subsequences $\mathcal{F}(\Sigma) = \{t_1, t_2, \ldots, t_p\}$ such that: $t_j \in \mathcal{A}^*, \quad \forall j \in [1, p], \quad \Sigma = \bigoplus_{k=1}^{p} t_k$, where the symbol $\bigoplus$ denotes sequence concatenation, and each t_j contains exactly one action from $\mathcal{A}_F$, appearing only as its final element. The resulting multiset of routine executions is as follows $W = \biguplus_{t_j \in \mathcal{F}(\Sigma)} t_j$

Encoding of the Routine Executions. Following the extraction of the multiset of routine executions W, we transform all routine executions $[\lambda_1, \lambda_2, \ldots, \lambda_p] \in W$ into a multiset of feature vectors, which are subsequently clustered.

Let $\langle a_1, \ldots, a_n \rangle$ be any ordering of the activities in $\mathcal{A}$, namely $\mathcal{A} = \cup_{i=1}^{n} a_i$. Each routine execution $\lambda \in W$ is encoded into a vector $(v_1, \ldots, v_n)$ where, for all $1 \leq i \leq n$, v_i is equal to the number of executions of actions a_i in λ. For example, consider three routine executions: $\lambda_1 = \langle a, b \rangle, \quad \lambda_2 = \langle a, c, c \rangle, \quad \lambda_3 = \langle b, c \rangle$. When encoded, their corresponding vectors are: $\lambda_1 \rightarrow (1, 1, 0), \quad \lambda_2 \rightarrow (1, 0, 2), \quad \lambda_3 \rightarrow (0, 1, 1)$.

Clustering. Once the different routine executions are encoded as vectors with dimensions related to the actions of the UI logs, these vectors and consequently the routine executions are clustered. Each cluster C_i is associated with one routine type T and becomes one routine log C. For each vector in C_i, the corresponding routine execution is added to C_i. The proposed technique is independent of the specific clustering method employed. However, we have equipped our implementation with three clustering methods: K-Means [8], DBSCAN [7], and HDBSCAN [13]. We use the default distance metric, i.e., the Euclidean distance, provided by each algorithm in their standard configurations.

4 Experiments

To validate the effectiveness of our proposed technique, we conducted a series of experiments using the synthetic UI logs that were generated and employed by Leno et al. [10]. The goal was to assess how well our technique discovers routine execution models compared to existing state-of-the-art techniques. These experiments focus on evaluating routine log extraction, conformance checking, and robustness to noise. The implementation and evaluation of the proposed technique, along with its comparison to state-of-the art techniques in Python, are available at https://github.com/Faizanunipd/Routine-Model-Discovery-by-Extracting-Routine-Logs-in-RPA.git. Section 4.1 discusses the data sets and evaluation methodology, and Sect. 4.2 provides a detailed analysis of the comparative results.

4.1 Data Sets and Evaluation Methodology

For the evaluation, we used the nine UI logs that Leno et al. [10] synthetically generated and employed in the experiments for their technique. These UI logs were chosen because they were provided with ground-truth models of the routines, which are supplied as Colour Petri nets in CPN-Tools format [6]. These UI logs did not contain noise; a perfect clustering would guarantee that each routine execution in each log of any routine type r is perfectly fitting with the ground-truth model of r. As indicated in Sect. 1, we also aim to assess how our technique compares with those from the state of the art when humans are not consistent in executing instances of the same routine type (e.g., because of mistaken actions). This means that UI logs contain inconsistencies. This type of analysis of UI logs with inconsistencies was not considered in previous research works on routine-type discovery, neither when developing the techniques nor when assessing them.

Algorithm 1 shows the pseudocode to add noise to a UI log Σ, so as to finally return a UI log Σ'. The algorithm requires a noise level $l \in [0, 1]$, and builds Σ' by subsequently concatenating events. The algorithm iterates over the action index $i \in [1, |\Sigma|]$: action $\Sigma(i)$ is concatenated to Σ' with probability $(1 - l)$, while it is removed with probability $0.5 \cdot l$ (lines 4–5). With the remaining probability of $0.5 \cdot l$, a new action is created for a random activity and concatenated to Σ': however, the index i is not increased, which means that $\Sigma(i)$ might still be concatenated at the next iteration cycle.

Algorithm 1. Noise Injection in a UI log segment

Input: A UI log segment $\Sigma \in \mathcal{A}^*$, Noise Level $l \in [0, 1]$
Output: A noisy UI log segment $\Sigma' \in \mathcal{A}^*$

```
1  Σ' ← ⟨⟩ ;                                        // Initialize output log
2  i ← 1;
3  while i ≤ |Σ| do
       /* random(0, 1) generates a random number according to a uniform
          distribution in [0, 1]                                          */
4      if random(0, 1) ≤ l then
5          if random(0, 1) ≤ 0.5 then
6              |   i ← i + 1;                        // Simulate missing action by skipping
7          end
8          else
9              |   ē ← createAction(A);  // Create an action for a random activity in
                      A
10             |   Σ' ← Σ' ⊕ ⟨ē⟩ ;                   // Concatenate random action
11         end
12     end
13     else
14         |   e ← Σ(i) ;                            // Access current action
15         |   Σ' ← Σ' ⊕ ⟨e⟩ ;                      // Concatenate current action to output
16         |   i ← i + 1;
17     end
18  end
19  return Σ';
```

The clustering obtained by our technique and by the state-of-the-art techniques has initially been assessed using the Jaccard coefficient (JC), as in Leno et al. [10]. Specifically, given a set $\overline{C} = \{C_1, \ldots, C_n\}$ of routine logs, the metric computes the average over every routine $C_j \in \overline{C}$ of how well the set of actions in C_j matches the most similar reference set G_i, which represents the set of actions in the ith ground-truth routine type:

Definition 3 (Jaccard Coefficient). *Let* $\overline{C} = \{C_1, \ldots, C_n\} \subset \mathcal{B}(\mathcal{A}^*)$ *be the set of routine logs discovered from a UI log. Let* $\mathcal{A}_{C_i} = \bigcup_{a \in C_i}(a)$ *be the set of actions in* C_i. *Let* $\mathcal{G} = \{G_1, \ldots, G_n\}$ *be the set of ground-truth actions for each of the n routine types, namely* $G_i \subseteq \mathcal{A}$ *for any* $1 \leq i \leq n$. *The Jaccard Coefficient is computed as follows:*

$$JC(\overline{C}, \mathcal{G}) = \text{avg}_{C \in \overline{C}} \left(\max_{G_i \in \mathcal{G}} \frac{|\mathcal{A}_C \cap G_i|}{|\mathcal{A}_C \cup G_i|} \right)$$

However, Jaccard Coefficient (JC) only considers which activities are performed within routines, ignoring the order of the constituent actions. Since we know the exact model m of each routine type, we can compute $LogModelFitness(C, m)$ between a routine log C and a routine model m using traditional process-mining fitness calculation [1]. Then, adapting Definition 3 to this context, we compute the average over all routine logs that contain traces (i.e., $|C| > 0$) of the maximum log-model fitness value with respect to each ground-truth model.

Definition 4 (Fitness). *Let* $\overline{C} = \{C_1, \ldots, C_n\} \subset \mathcal{B}(\mathcal{A}^*)$ *be the set of routine logs discovered from a UI log. Let C be a routine log. Let* $\mathcal{M} = \{m_1, \ldots, m_n\}$ *be the set of ground-truth routine models. The fitness between the set of* $\overline{C}$ *of routine logs and the* *set of $\mathcal{M}$ models is defined as follows:*

$$Fitness(\overline{\mathcal{C}}, \mathcal{M}) = \text{avg}_{C \in \overline{\mathcal{C}} \ s.t. \ |C|>0} \left(\max_{m_j \in \mathcal{M}} LogModelFitness(C, m_j) \right)$$

Routine models for the nine UI logs are provided in the form of Petri nets, and we compute the alignment-based fitness [1] of the routine logs against every routine-type model.

For each UI log discussed in Sect. 4.1, we extracted the set of routine logs, using our technique and other techniques from the literature, and compared the results in terms of Jaccard Coefficient (JC) and fitness. As mentioned above, we also introduced noise with levels $0.1, 0.2, 0.3$ and 0.4 (cf. Algorithm 1) to assess the robustness of the various techniques with increasing levels of noise. For each noise level larger than zero, noise was introduced 10 times per UI log. This iterative process mitigates bias from a single instance of noise and ensures a more reliable performance evaluation. The final results were obtained by averaging scores over multiple repetitions, accounting for variability due to stochastic factors in the noise injection during experimentation.

To illustrate the superiority of the results obtained by our technique, we also computed the Jaccard coefficients and the fitness values for three techniques from the state-of-the-art, namely by Leno et al. [10], Agostinelli et al. [5], and Rebmann et al. [12]. Leno et al. [10] proposed four different variants based on length-based routine extraction, frequency-based routine extraction, cohesion-based routine extraction, and coverage-based routine extraction.

Both Leno et al. [10] and Agostinelli et al. [5] only allow extracting the set of routine actions for each routine type, without extracting the routine logs. As mentioned, this would not enable the discovery of routine models. For the evaluation discussion in this section, it would not be possible to compute the fitness metrics in Definition 4. With the goal in mind to extract the routine logs, each set S_i of routine actions, which identifies a routine type T_i, is transformed into a vector V_i of as many dimensions as the number of actions in the UI log. Each dimension is associated with an action, and takes the value 0 or 1 depending on whether or not the action is part of S. For example: Given a UI log with actions $\{A, B, C, D, E\}$, the action set for routine type T_1, denoted as $S_1 = \{A, C, D\}$, is represented by the binary vector $V_1 = (1, 0, 1, 1, 0)$. In this vector, each position corresponds to an action from the UI log, where 1 indicates that the action is part of V_i and 0 indicates that it is not. Each routine execution is also converted into a vector, analogously to what is discussed in Sect. 3, and assigned to the routine type T_i so that V_i is the closest.

4.2   Evaluation Results

As discussed above, we evaluated the techniques from the state of the art by Leno et al. [10], Agostinelli et al. [5], and Rebmann et al. [12] and compared with our technique. For Leno et al. [10], we evaluated the four variants. Our technique was evaluated in three configurations where K-Means, DBSCAN and HDBSCAN were employed as clustering methods (cf. Sect. 3).

The results of our experiments are reported in Figs. 1a and 1b, in terms of values of JC and fitness, respectively. Each line refers to a different technique or variant.

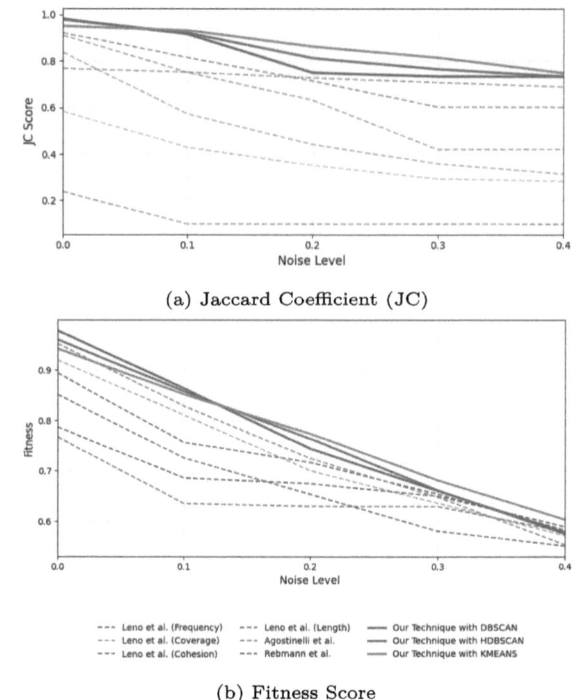

(a) Jaccard Coefficient (JC)

(b) Fitness Score

Fig. 1. Trend of the JC and fitness values for the different techniques evaluated, under varying noise levels. The dotted lines represent state-of-the-art techniques, while the solid lines correspond to our techniques using different clustering methods.

The x-axis indicates the noise level, and the y-axis refers to the JC or fitness value for every technique and noise level, namely 0 (i.e., no noise), 0.1, 0.2, 0.3 and 0.4. The points referring to each technique and noise level are the average over the nine UI logs employed in the experiments, where each experiment was run ten times for each log, technique and noise level.

The comparison of JC metric in Fig. 1a shows that our technique achieves higher values of the metric, consistently for all clustering techniques and noise levels.

The fitness computation excludes the routine logs that are generated without traces. In fact, this situation occurs when our technique is compared with Leno et al. [10] and Agostinelli et al. [5]. As a consequence, some routine types are assigned a set of actions that is a subset of those assigned to a different routine type. When routine executions are then assigned to routine types they are often associated to the routine type with the largest set of actions. This ultimately means that no routine associated with the routine types has a smaller set of actions. As indicated in Definition 4, we exclude the empty routine logs, i.e., routine logs without traces, from the fitness computation because fitness cannot formally be computed on an empty log.

Table 1 illustrates the percentage of empty routine logs for each technique and noise level. It highlights a significant drawback of certain routine discovery techniques: the generation of empty routine logs. The method by Agostinelli et al. [5] consistently produces a high percentage of empty logs, over 75% against all noise levels, indicating that many of its discovered routines fail to attract any traces. Similarly, the frequency and coverage variants of Leno et al. [10] also yield substantial portions of empty logs, particularly under no noise conditions (e.g., 70% and 51% at noise level 0.0, respectively). In contrast, our technique and that by Rebmann et al. [12] do not produce empty routine logs, demonstrating stronger alignment between discovered routines and observed behavior.

Table 1. Percentage of empty routine logs for different techniques and noise levels. We do not report on Rebmann et al. [12] and our technique because the empty-log percentage is always 0%.

Noise Level	Leno et al. [10]				Agostinelli et al. [5]
	Frequency	Coverage	Cohesion	Length	
0.0	70%	51%	13%	14%	89%
0.1	0%	23%	25%	13%	79%
0.2	0%	13%	12%	10%	79%
0.3	0%	8%	3%	0%	78%
0.4	0%	5%	3%	0%	76%

Figure 1b shows that our technique generally achieves higher fitness scores than what state-of-the-art techniques do, for every noise level. While the K-Means variant performs slightly worse than Agostinelli et al. for noise level 0.0, both DBSCAN and HDBSCAN consistently outperform existing methods. However, the margin of improvement admittedly narrows progressively with increasingly higher noise levels. This is also partly due to the fact that, even in case of perfect creation of routine logs, the fitness decreases when the noise increases: for larger noise levels, there is a clear lower maximum in the fitness values that can be achieved, even in presence of a perfect assignment of routine executions to routine logs. Note that noise levels of 0.3 and 0.4 refer to UI logs with an extremely large variability of behavior of humans and a large extent of their mistakes. There is also an increased risk of misclassification. Specifically, when routines share overlapping actions, traces with higher levels of noise may be incorrectly clustered with a different routine type. This behavior is reflected in the observed decline in fitness at high noise levels. The analysis of the results in Figs. 1a and 1b illustrates that, on average, our technique outperforms the state of the art for every noise level.

In conclusion, the findings confirm our initial hypothesis that the main benefit of our technique is to generate the routine logs, compared with the state-of-the-art techniques, which conversely only assign actions to routine types and do not generate routine logs. The results indicate that further extensions of state-of-the-art techniques, when applied as a post hoc approach to generating routine logs, do not reach the same level of quality in terms of Jaccard Coefficient (JC) and fitness metrics.

Lastly, if we compare the performance of our technique for different clustering methods that are supported (cf. Sect. 3), K-Means achieved the highest performance.

K-Means assigns all points to clusters, which leads to higher fitness and JC scores, especially under noisy conditions. HDBSCAN and DBSCAN perform better on cleaner data but degrade more under noise. Overall, K-Means is more robust to noise, while HDBSCAN and DBSCAN are preferable for clean, well-separated data.

5   Conclusion

This paper starts from the belief that RPA require models of the types of routines that are targeted. RPA tools indeed requires a formal model of how the routines should be executed. Although these models can be designed manually by experts, the risk is high that these hand-made models reflect the experts' perceptions, which might not accurately match how the routines are actually performed. It is thus imperative to try to discover the models of the different routine types from the so-called UI logs, which record how human actors perform the routine actions via information systems and software. As UI logs contain executions of different routine types, we need to split them into distinct routine logs, one per routine type, which can then be used as input for model discovery of each routine type. This is far from being trivial: we do not know in advance the actions that belong to each routine type, and the same action can also be shared among multiple routine types.

Current literature predominantly focuses on techniques that use UI logs to solely assign human actions to routine types, but neglects the creation of routine logs, which are an essential input for discovering routine-type models. Moreover, existing approaches overlook the fact that humans often act inconsistently or make errors, referred to as noise, such as copying the wrong cells in a spreadsheet and correcting them through additional actions. If techniques for extracting routine logs are not robust to noise, the resulting routine logs may be flawed, which lead to inaccurate and imprecise routine-type models when used as input to discovery techniques.

The above consideration motivated us to propose a technique that paves the way for improved routine-type model discovery that enhances process discovery in RPM. In particular, the technique is able to extract routine logs from UI logs, even in the presence of noise. Our technique leverages cluster methods while being independent of the peculiarities of any of them, and its implementation supports K-Means, DBSCAN, and HDBSCAN.

Extensive experimentation was conducted on nine UI logs with varying levels of noise induced up to 0.4 using a bootstrap technique. The assessment was based on state-of-the-art evaluation metrics, namely the JC and fitness score. The results showed that our technique produces more accurate routine logs, and is consistently more resilient to noise. Our experimental results also indicate that the technique is computationally efficient across UI logs of varying sizes, demonstrating practical scalability.

We conclude by highlighting some threat of validity and directions for future work. First, our technique requires a user-defined set of completion actions to perform segmentation: While this assumption typically holds in practice (e.g., routines terminate after pressing a button, saving a file, sending an email), we acknowledge that this requires the provision of domain knowledge, which might sometimes not be present.

Importantly, the assessment was conducted using synthetic data, the same data sets employed by Leno et al. [10] in their evaluation. This choice is motivated by the need for ground-truth models of the different routine types, which are essential for calculating the fitness and JC scores. While evaluating with real-world UI logs would be a valuable complementary analysis, it would not offer a concrete basis for assessing the quality of routine log identification, neither for our approach nor for existing methods in the literature.

References

1. van der Aalst, W.: Process Mining: Data Science in Action. Springer, Berlin Heidelberg (2016)
2. Van der Aalst, W.M., Bichler, M., Heinzl, A.: Robotic process automation (2018)
3. Abb, L., Bormann, C., van der Aa, H., Rehse, J.R.: Trace clustering for user behavior mining. In: ECIS (2022)
4. Agostinelli, S.: Generating Executable Robotic Process Automation Scripts from Unsegmented User Interface Logs. LNBIP, vol. 522. Springer (2024). https://doi.org/10.1007/978-3-031-61368-5
5. Agostinelli, S., Leotta, F., Marrella, A.: Interactive segmentation of user interface logs. In: Hacid, H., Kao, O., Mecella, M., Moha, N., Paik, H. (eds.) ICSOC 2021. LNCS, vol. 13121, pp. 65–80. Springer, Cham (2021). https://doi.org/10.1007/978-3-030-91431-8_5
6. Bosco, A., Augusto, A., Dumas, M., La Rosa, M., Fortino, G.: Discovering automatable routines from user interaction logs. In: Hildebrandt, T., van Dongen, B.F., Röglinger, M., Mendling, J. (eds.) BPM 2019. LNBIP, vol. 360, pp. 144–162. Springer, Cham (2019). https://doi.org/10.1007/978-3-030-26643-1_9
7. Deng, D.: Dbscan clustering algorithm based on density. In: 7th International Forum on Electrical Engineering and Automation (IFEEA), pp. 949–953. IEEE (2020)
8. Hartigan, J.A., Wong, M.A.: Algorithm as 136: a k-means clustering algorithm. J. Royal Stat. Society. Series C (Appli. Statist.) **28**(1), 100–108 (1979)
9. Jimenez-Ramirez, A., Reijers, H.A., Barba, I., Del Valle, C.: A method to improve the early stages of the robotic process automation lifecycle. In: Giorgini, P., Weber, B. (eds.) CAiSE 2019. LNCS, vol. 11483, pp. 446–461. Springer, Cham (2019). https://doi.org/10.1007/978-3-030-21290-2_28
10. Leno, V., Augusto, A., Dumas, M., Rosa, M.L., Maggi, F.M., Polyvyanyy, A.: Identifying candidate routines for robotic process automation from unsegmented UI logs. In: van Dongen, B.F., Montali, M., Wynn, M.T. (eds.) 2nd International Conference on Process Mining, ICPM 2020, Padua, Italy, 4-9 October 2020. pp. 153–160. IEEE (2020)
11. Plattfaut, R., Borghoff, V.: Robotic process automation: a literature-based research agenda. J. Inf. Syst. **36**(2), 173–191 (2022)
12. Rebmann, A., van der Aa, H.: Unsupervised task recognition from user interaction streams. In: Indulska, M., Reinhartz-Berger, I., Cetina, C., Pastor, O. (eds.) CAiSE 2023. LNCS, vol. 13901, pp. 141–157. Springer, Cham (2023). https://doi.org/10.1007/978-3-031-34560-9_9
13. Stewart, G., Al-Khassaweneh, M.: An implementation of the hdbscan* clustering algorithm. Appl. Sci. **12**(5), 2405 (2022)
14. Zandkarimi, F., Rehse, J.R., Soudmand, P., Hoehle, H.: A generic framework for trace clustering in process mining. In: 2020 2nd International Conference on Process Mining (ICPM), pp. 177–184. IEEE (2020)

Enhancing Suitable Tasks Selection for RPA Through Fuzzy AHP and AI Methods

Imen Korâani[1,2(✉)], Wiem Chebil[1,3], and Sonia Ayachi Ghannouchi[1,4]

[1] RIADI Laboratory LR99ES26, National School of Computer Science, University of Manouba, Manouba University Campus, Manouba 2010, Tunisia
[2] Higher Institute of Computer Science and Telecommunications of Hammam Sousse, University of Sousse, Sousse 4002, Tunisia
imenekoraani@gmail.com
[3] Higher Institute of Computer Sciences of Mahdia, University of Monastir, Monastir 5000, Tunisia
[4] Higher Institute of Management of Sousse, University of Sousse, Sousse 4002, Tunisia

Abstract. Currently, increasing attention is devoted to the digitization of operations and business processes in companies to provide more value to their customers. Organizations have started to adopt technological advancements, such as Robotic Process Automation (RPA), to optimize their operations and reduce the burden of repetitive, low-value tasks. RPA improves productivity by automating structured processes. To harness these benefits, organizations face the challenge of identifying process activities that are viable automation candidates. The goal of this work is to propose a richer RPA lifecycle by integrating Multi-Criteria Decision Analysis (MCDA) and Artificial Intelligence (AI). MCDA, and more specifically the fuzzy analytical hierarchy process (Fuzzy AHP), offers a structured method for prioritizing automation candidates while handling uncertainty in expert evaluations. AI further extends RPA's capabilities to more complex and unstructured tasks, enabling intelligent, adaptive automation. By combining these three approaches, we propose a smarter, data-informed framework to guide automation strategies and maximize the impact of RPA within organizations.

Keywords: Robotic Process Automation RPA · Fuzzy Analytic Hierarchy Process (Fuzzy AHP) · Muti-Criteria Decision Analysis MCDA · Artificial Intelligence (AI)

1 Introduction

RPA offers significant potential to improve efficiency by automating repetitive and well-structured business tasks [12]. RPA can function as standalone applications or be integrated into larger systems, enhancing productivity, reducing execution time, and minimizing human errors. However, its success depends on selecting suitable processes, as automating inappropriate tasks may not yield the expected benefits. To support informed process selection, Multi-Criteria Decision Analysis (MCDA) provides a structured framework to evaluate and prioritize tasks based on criteria such as frequency,

C. Cappiello et al. (Eds.): CoopIS 2025, LNCS 15535, pp. 476–486, 2026.
https://doi.org/10.1007/978-3-032-15538-2_27

standardization, complexity, and expected return on investment. Artificial Intelligence (AI) further enhances RPA by enabling automation of complex, decision-driven tasks involving unstructured data and predictive analytics [19]. By combining MCDA and AI, organizations can move from automating simple tasks to more strategic and cognitively demanding activities. This research aims to improve the analysis phase of the RPA lifecycle, supporting more efficient and accurate decision-making. It addresses the following key questions:

RQ1: How can organizations identify the most suitable candidates for RPA automation ?

RQ2: Which AI techniques and MCDA methods can be applied in the analysis phase, and how can they be effectively integrated ?

This paper is organized as follows. In Sect. 2, a theoretical background with information related to the topics of RPA, MCDA and AI methods is provided. In Sect. 3, we present a literature review on the crucial factors for identifying suitable automation candidates. Section 4 presents a discussion of current approaches, identifies their limitations, and highlights the motivation behind our proposed solution. In Sect. 5, the proposed method is explained in detail. Section 6 presents the experimental evaluation and results of applying the method on real-world data. Finally, Sect. 7 concludes the paper and outlining possible directions for future work.

2   Background

2.1   Robotic Process Automation

Robotic Process Automation refers to the use of software robots to automate routine, structured, and rules-based tasks traditionally performed by humans. Although definitions vary, RPA generally replicates human interactions with user interfaces and executes processes autonomously according to predefined business rules [10]. The RPA lifecycle typically includes four phases: (1) Analysis: identifying tasks suitable for automation, (2) Development: designing and coding bots, (3) Testing: verifying performance, and (4) Deployment and Maintenance: implementing bots and ensuring long-term functionality [16]. A critical factor for successful RPA implementation is task selection. Key criteria include repetitiveness, rule-based and standardized nature, stability of the environment, minimal exception handling, significant manual effort, degree of digitization, low complexity, and long execution time [8,17]. Tasks meeting these conditions are considered strong candidates for automation.

2.2   Multi-Criteria Decision Analysis

Multi-Criteria Decision Analysis (MCDA) is a decision-support tool that allows for the evaluation and prioritization of alternatives by considering multiple, sometimes conflicting criteria [14]. In the field of Robotic Process Automation (RPA), it helps identify the processes most suitable for automation based on factors such as frequency, standardization, complexity, or maturity. Among the most commonly used techniques is the Analytic Hierarchy Process (AHP), which structures the decision problem hierarchically and relies on pairwise comparisons to establish priorities [11]. However, traditional AHP assumes precise and consistent judgments, which is often unrealistic. To address this limitation, the Fuzzy AHP approach incorporates fuzzy logic, allowing uncertain or subjective judgments to be expressed using linguistic variables [18]. This makes the evaluation more reflective of reality, especially when decisions are based on intuition or expert opinion. Fuzzy AHP has proven effective in various fields such as supply chain management, healthcare decision-making, and project prioritization, where uncertainty and imprecise information are common [5].

2.3 Artificial Intelligence

The combination of AI and RPA often referred to as Intelligent Process Automation (IPA) enables organizations to automate end-to-end processes with greater flexibility and autonomy [2]. This integration allows bots not only to execute tasks but also to adapt and improve their performance over time. In the RPA lifecycle, AI can contribute particularly to the analysis and decision phases. It supports better identification of automation candidates by uncovering hidden patterns and correlations in process execution logs. This complements approaches like MCDA by adding predictive and adaptive layers to the decision-making process, making it more robust and forward-looking.

3 Related Work

Wanner J et al. [20] proposed a selection method using quantifiable measures that can be extracted from software event logs. They extract information like execution frequency, execution time, standardization, and stability from event logs, and combine it into a quantifiable measurement system. This system of indicators provides decision support for companies seeking to better prioritize their RPA activities and maximize their return on investment. Another approach proposed by Choi D. et al. [6] consists of the following four steps: *i)* Generation of the user interface (UI) log; *ii)* Transformation of the UI log into a log format supported by Process Mining techniques, including defining transformation rules to enrich action names and filtering irrelevant actions; *iii)* Discovery of tasks from the transformed UI log using process discovery techniques, producing a complete process model; *iv)* Selection of candidate tasks for automation, based on Frequency, Periodicity, and Duration. Viehhauser J and Doerr M [19] proposed a structured, quantifiable method to identify and prioritize candidates for RPA automation. The approach consists of three main steps: defining strategic and operational automation objectives, identifying and prioritizing processes using a mathematical model, and selecting the most promising processes for implementation. The study highlights that the most critical selection criteria are process standardization, transaction volume, process and application maturity, manual effort, data quality, and failure rate. Evaluation on real-world management accounting data confirms the method's applicability and effectiveness. Axmann B et al. [3] presented a simple approach to select the appropriate RPA software. The criteria selection and evaluation were done with the Pairwise Comparison and Benefit Value Analysis method. The pairwise method is used to weigh the criteria. While the benefit value analysis is carried out to select the alternative solution such as the best process to be automated or the best software. Mohammadi et al. [13] proposed an approach to identify process variants suitable for RPA automation. The model relies on four key factors drawn from the literature: transaction volume, standardization, maturity, and complexity, all of which can be quantified using process mining techniques. K-means clustering is employed to group the data and highlight automatable processes. The effectiveness of the model is demonstrated through an evaluation compared to two benchmark models. Silva Costa D et al. [7] presented method for selecting processes for automation combining two multi-criteria decision-making techniques, 'Analytic Hierarchy Process (AHP) and Technique for Order of Preference by Similarity to Ideal Solution (TOPSIS), was proposed, demonstrated, and evaluated. This study follows the Design Science Research Methodology (DSRM) and applies the proposed method for selecting processes for automation to a real-life scenario. The result will be a method to support the proper selection of business processes for automation, increasing the success of implementing RPA tools in an organization.

4   Discussion and Contribution

Existing studies supporting the analysis phase of the RPA lifecycle exhibit various limitations, such as reliance on structured logs, sensitivity to noisy or interleaved data, limited adaptability, and narrow evaluation domains. These approaches address isolated aspects without offering a comprehensive, integrated, and context-sensitive framework for selecting automation candidates. In contrast, our work proposes a hybrid framework that combines Multi-Criteria Decision Analysis (MCDA) and Artificial Intelligence (AI) to enhance the analysis phase of the RPA lifecycle. Fuzzy AHP is employed to capture vagueness in expert judgments, while clustering (K-Means) and classification (Random Forest) automate task prioritization. This integration leverages MCDA's structured evaluation with AI's adaptive and predictive capabilities, enabling scalable, transparent, and robust decision-making [13]. By unifying complementary techniques, our approach addresses previous limitations and supports more efficient, consistent, and goal-driven automation strategies.

5   Proposed Approach

The architecture Fig. 1 includes 3 interconnected steps: (1) Data Pre-processing using Pandas, (2) Multi-criteria Evaluation using Fuzzy AHP, (3) Hybrid Task Classification via Pseudo-Labeling and Supervised Learning.

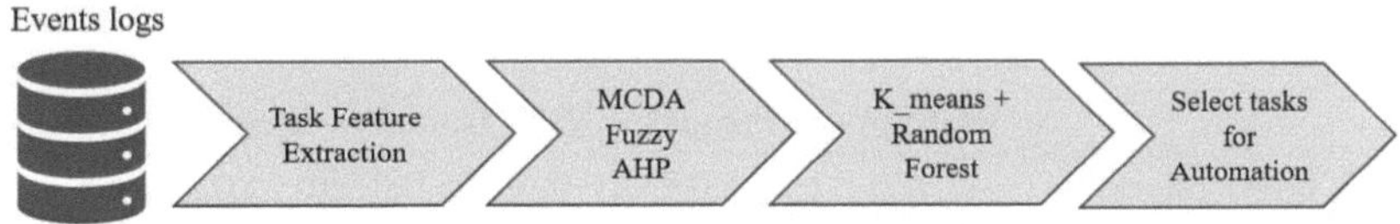

Fig. 1. Overview of the proposed architecture.

5.1 Feature Extraction for Automation Assessment

A crucial step in implementing Robotic Process Automation (RPA) is identifying tasks suitable for automation. Several studies have proposed key attributes for assessing automation potential [15]. **Standardization** measures the repetitiveness and consistency of a process. Highly standardized processes, following a predefined sequence with minimal variations, are easier to automate [1]. **Execution volume** and **frequency** indicate how often a task occurs. Tasks with high frequency or volume generally have a greater operational impact and return on investment (ROI), making them prime candidates for automation [9]. **Complexity** reflects the presence of branches, exceptions, conditional logic, or human intervention. Processes with low complexity, requiring minimal human judgment, are more amenable to automation [15]. **Execution time** refers to the duration required to complete a task and helps prioritize tasks with significant potential time savings [17]. The `Pandas` library is extensively used to extract these features from event logs. These extracted features provide the basis for applying the Fuzzy Analytic Hierarchy Process (Fuzzy AHP) to prioritize tasks for automation.

5.2 Fuzzy AHP Methodology

The Fuzzy Analytic Hierarchy Process (Fuzzy AHP) enables the prioritization of alternatives while accounting for uncertainty in expert judgments by using *Triangular Fuzzy Numbers* (TFNs). The following steps follow Chang's extent analysis method [4].

Definition of Criteria. The relevant evaluation criteria for RPA task automation are defined based on existing literature and validated by domain experts. The selected criteria are: Standardisation, Frequency, Average Duration, and Complexity.

Construction of the Fuzzy Pairwise Comparison Matrix. Fuzzy pairwise comparisons are represented using *Triangular Fuzzy Numbers* (TFNs) [18], which allow a flexible modeling of expert judgments under uncertainty. Each element of the matrix is defined as:

$$\tilde{a}_{ij} = (l_{ij}, m_{ij}, u_{ij}) \tag{1}$$

where l_{ij} denotes the lower bound of the judgment, m_{ij} is the most probable value (central estimate), and u_{ij} represents the upper bound of the judgment.

Table 1. Fuzzy pairwise comparison matrix.

	Standardisation	Frequency	Avg_Duration	Complexity
Standardisation	(1,1,1)	(0.5,0.75,1)	(0.33,0.5,0.67)	(0.25,0.33,0.5)
Frequency	(1,1.33,2)	(1,1,1)	(0.5,0.75,1)	(0.33,0.5,0.67)
Avg_Duration	(1.5,2,3)	(1,1.33,2)	(1,1,1)	(0.5,0.75,1)
Complexity	(2,3,4)	(1.5,2,3)	(1,1.33,2)	(1,1,1)

The fuzzy pairwise comparison matrix (Table 1) uses Triangular Fuzzy Numbers (TFNs) to flexibly represent expert judgments on the relative importance of evaluation criteria [18].

Computation of Fuzzy Weights (Chang's Method)

Fuzzy Synthetic Extent for each Criterion.

$$S_i = \tilde{M}_i \otimes \left(\sum_{i=1}^{n} \tilde{M}_i \right)^{-1}, \quad \text{where} \tilde{M}_i = \sum_{j=1}^{n} \tilde{a}_{ij} \tag{2}$$

Degree of Possibility that $\tilde{S}_i \geq \tilde{S}_j$. To compare two fuzzy synthetic extents $\tilde{S}_i = (l_i, m_i, u_i)$ and $\tilde{S}_j = (l_j, m_j, u_j)$, the degree of possibility that $\tilde{S}_i \geq \tilde{S}_j$ is defined as [4]:

$$V(\tilde{S}_i \geq \tilde{S}_j) = \begin{cases} 1, & \text{if } m_i \geq m_j \\ 0, & \text{if } l_j \geq u_i \\ \frac{l_j - u_i}{(m_i - u_i) - (m_j - l_j)}, & \text{otherwise} \end{cases} \tag{3}$$

This function evaluates the extent to which $\tilde{S}_i$ is greater than or equal to $\tilde{S}_j$, taking into account the overlap of their respective membership functions.

Fuzzy Priority Vector. After computing all degrees of possibility $V(\tilde{S}_i \geq \tilde{S}_j)$, the final fuzzy priority weight for each criterion is obtained by taking the minimum degree of possibility of $\tilde{S}_i$ over all $\tilde{S}_j$, where $i \neq j$. This defines the fuzzy priority vector w', expressed as:

$$w'_i = \min_{j \neq i} V(\tilde{S}_i \geq \tilde{S}_j) \tag{4}$$

The resulting vector is then normalized to obtain the final weight vector $w = (w_1, w_2, \ldots, w_n)$, which reflects the relative importance of each criterion in a crisp form.

Defuzzification and Normalization. Each fuzzy weight $\tilde{w}_i = (l_i, m_i, u_i)$ is defuzzified using the centroid (COG) method to obtain a crisp representative value:

$$w_i = \frac{l_i + m_i + u_i}{3} \tag{5}$$

The resulting crisp weights are normalized to ensure their sum equals 1:

$$w_i^* = \frac{w_i}{\sum_{k=1}^{n} w_k} \tag{6}$$

The normalized weights w_i^* form the final priority vector used for decision-making. Table 2 presents the resulting weights for each evaluation criterion after applying Fuzzy AHP.

Table 2. Final weights of evaluation criteria using Fuzzy AHP.

Criterion	Weight
Standardisation	0.346
Frequency	0.277
Avg_Duration	0.202
Complexity	0.175

Evaluation of Alternatives (e.g., Tasks). Each alternative T_k is evaluated based on the selected criteria. Let x_{kj} represent the raw performance of task T_k on criterion C_j. To ensure comparability across different scales, values are normalized using min-max scaling as follows:

$$x_{kj}^{\text{norm}} = \frac{x_{kj} - \min(x_j)}{\max(x_j) - \min(x_j)} \tag{7}$$

For cost-type or negative criteria (such as complexity or average duration), the normalized values are inverted to maintain a consistent "higher-is-better" interpretation:

$$x_{kj}^{\text{inv}} = 1 - x_{kj}^{\text{norm}} \tag{8}$$

This preprocessing step ensures that all evaluation scores are on a common scale $[0, 1]$ and aligned in terms of preference direction.

Weighted Scoring of Tasks. The final weighted score for each task is computed as:

$$\text{Score}(T_k) = \sum_{j=1}^{n} w_j^* \cdot x_{kj}^{\text{norm}}$$

Each task was then scored using a weighted sum of its normalized values for the criteria. The result, called the fuzzy AHP score, represents the global automation priority of the task. Table 3 presents a sample of the computed task scores, highlighting the variability in task characteristics and their respective automation potential.

Table 3. Sample of hospital tasks with key features and Fuzzy AHP scores.

Task	Frequency	Avg Duration	Standardisation	Complexity	Fuzzy AHP Score
Task1	1.00	0.0021	0.70	0.83	0.67
Task2	1.00	0.0033	0.27	1.00	0.52
Task3	0.03	0.0024	1.00	0.33	0.45
Task4	0.31	0.0017	0.62	0.83	0.44
Task5	0.40	0.0027	0.59	0.67	0.43

Task1: Choose COVID-19 procedure, Task2: Check progress after treatment, Task3: Orient to/Keep in intensive care, Task4: Check for disease, Task5: Conduct/Retrieve PCR.

5.3 Hybrid Classification Approach

The proposed methodology introduces a hybrid framework to identify tasks suitable for RPA automation. Tasks are first evaluated with Fuzzy AHP, producing global automation priority scores that account for uncertainty in expert judgments. These scores are then clustered using K-Means ($k = 2$) to separate tasks into likely automatable and non-automatable groups, with the highest-score cluster providing pseudolabels that bridge MCDA prioritization and supervised learning. Pseudolabels are combined with operational features of event logs: execution frequency, standardization, process complexity, and average duration to form an enriched training data set for a Random Forest classifier. This algorithm handles heterogeneous features, models non-linear relationships, resists overfitting, and offers interpretability via feature importance. Overall, this hybrid approach integrates expert-driven MCDA and AI techniques, combining fuzzy prioritization, clustering, and supervised learning to produce a structured, scalable, and generalizable method for task selection. It improves the accuracy, reliability, and strategic guidance of automation initiatives in organizations.

6 Experimental Evaluation and Results

6.1 Experimental Pipeline

The validation of the proposed approach relied on hospital event logs collected at Farhat Hached during the COVID-19 pandemic. Each log entry contained the task name, start and end timestamps, and the role responsible for execution. Using Pandas, we derived four task-level features: execution frequency, degree of standardization, task complexity, and average execution duration, which capture the main dimensions influencing automation potential. Expert pairwise comparisons were then converted into fuzzy numbers, and weights were calculated through fuzzy AHP: Standardization (0.346), Frequency (0.277), Duration (0.202), and Complexity (0.175). These weights were used to compute a global automation score for each task. To distinguish automatable from non-automatable tasks, K-Means ($k=2$) was applied to the dataset combining Fuzzy AHP scores and task features. The resulting clusters served as pseudo-labels for training a Random Forest classifier, enabling prediction of automation suitability from event log data. This hybrid methodology synergizes the strengths of MCDA for systematic prioritization and machine learning for predictive automation classification, thus offering a scalable and interpretable framework to support RPA initiatives in healthcare.

6.2 Performance Evaluation

Table 4 presents a sample of the computed task scores, showing the variability in task characteristics and their automation potential.

Table 4. Excerpt of hospital tasks with Fuzzy AHP scores and K-Means cluster assignments.

Task	Fuzzy AHP Score	Cluster
Choose COVID-19 procedure	0.6693	0
Check progress after treatment	0.5193	0
Orient to/Keep in intensive care unit	0.4479	1
Check for disease	0.4449	0
Conduct / Retrieve PCR	0.4337	0
Retrieve PCR result	0.3920	1
Conduct COVID-19 treatment	0.3644	0
Decide on diagnostic protocol/procedure	0.3606	1

The Random Forest model was trained on the enriched dataset, achieving an overall accuracy of 83%. Weighted recall also reached 83%, reflecting the model's strong ability to identify automatable tasks. The weighted F1-score was 0.76, while precision was slightly lower at 69%, mainly due to class imbalance: the minority class (non-automatable tasks) was underrepresented, leading to missed predictions and reduced precision. To further validate robustness, we applied the approach to a second dataset, a publicly available hospital event logs.[1] This dataset contains richer traces and a more balanced class distribution. Results are compared in Table 5.

Table 5. Classification performance comparison of Random Forest on two hospital datasets.

Metric	Dataset1 (Farhat Hached)	Dataset2 (Public Logs)
Accuracy	0.83	0.98
Precision (weighted)	0.69	0.98
Recall (weighted)	0.83	0.98
F1-score (weighted)	0.76	0.98

As shown, performance was substantially higher on Dataset 2 (98% across all metrics) compared to Dataset 1, largely due to larger sample size and better class balance. In contrast, Dataset 1 suffered from severe imbalance, leading to lower precision despite good recall. These findings confirm that combining Fuzzy AHP with machine learning provides a robust and generalizable approach for identifying automation opportunities, while also highlighting the importance of dataset characteristics in predictive performance.

7 Conclusion and Future Work

In this paper, we propose an enhanced RPA lifecycle that integrates fuzzy multi-criteria evaluation, clustering, and supervised learning to systematically support task selection.

---

[1] https://raw.githubusercontent.com/jibreelaziz/Hospital-dataset/main/Hospital_Dataset.csv.

Applied to two hospital event log datasets, the approach demonstrated promising results in identifying tasks with high automation potential. Nevertheless, current limitations include the reliance on Pandas, which constrains deeper process-level analysis, and the relatively small number of datasets, which may limit the generalizability of the findings across different domains. Future work will focus on integrating process mining techniques to enrich preprocessing with contextual and sequence-aware features, implementing a prototype of the proposed lifecycle for real-world deployment, and extending the experiments to multiple datasets from different domains to strengthen robustness and general applicability.

References

1. Agostinelli, S., Marrella, A., Mecella, M.: Exploring the challenge of automated segmentation in robotic process automation. In: Cherfi, S., Perini, A., Nurcan, S. (eds.) RCIS 2021. LNBIP, vol. 415, pp. 38–54. Springer, Cham (2021). https://doi.org/10.1007/978-3-030-75018-3_3
2. Asadov, R.: Intelligent process automation: Streamlining operations and enhancing efficiency in management. SSRN (2023). https://doi.org/10.2139/ssrn.4495188
3. Axmann, B., Harmoko, H.: Process & software selection for robotic process automation (rpa). Tehnički glasnik **16**(3), 412–419 (2022)
4. Chang, D.: Applications of the extent analysis method on fuzzy ahp. Eur. J. Oper. Res. **95**(3), 649–655 (1996). https://doi.org/10.1016/0377-2217(95)00300-2
5. Chebil, W., Soualmia, L.F., Omri, M.N., Darmoni, S.J.: Indexing biomedical documents with a possibilistic network. J. Am. Soc. Inf. Sci. **67**(4), 928–941 (2016)
6. Choi, D., R'bigui, H., Cho, C.: Candidate digital tasks selection methodology for automation with robotic process automation. Sustainability **13**(16), 8980 (2021)
7. Costa, D.S., Mamede, H.S., Da Silva, M.M.: A method for selecting processes for automation with AHP and TOPSIS. Heliyon **9**(3) (2023)
8. Elsayed, N.S.S., Kassem, G.: Assessing process suitability for robotic process automation: A process mining approach. In: Wirtschaftsinformatik 2022 Proceedings, Student Track. p. 18. AIS Electronic Library (AISeL), Nuremberg, Germany (2022). https://aisel.aisnet.org/wi2022/student_track/student_track/18/
9. Hallikainen, P., Bekkhus, A., Pan, T.: Decision criteria for rpa adoption: a qualitative study. Inform. Technol. People **35**(4), 1159–1184 (2022)
10. IEEE Corporate Advisory Group: Robotic process automation (rpa) white paper, p. 11 (2017)
11. Kahraman, C., Cebeci, U., Ruan, D.: Multi-criteria supplier selection using fuzzy ahp. Int. J. Prod. Econ. **87**(3), 171–184 (2004)
12. Kumar, K., Shah, R., Kumar, N., Singh, R.P.: Application of robotic process automation. In: Gao, X.-Z., Kumar, R., Srivastava, S., Soni, B.P. (eds.) Applications of Artificial Intelligence in Engineering. AIS, pp. 929–937. Springer, Singapore (2021). https://doi.org/10.1007/978-981-33-4604-8_75
13. Mohammadi, F., Vanani, I.: A model for optimizing the identification of process variants in robotic process automation. In: Proceedings of the 2023 Tenth International Conference on Social Networks Analysis, Management and Security (SNAMS), pp. 1–7. IEEE (2023). https://doi.org/10.1109/SNAMS57568.2023.10298579
14. Munda, G.: Multiple criteria decision analysis: principles and practice. Environ. Sci. Policy for Sustainable Develop. **46**(5), 23–31 (2004)
15. Rozario, D., Venkatagiri, S.: Prioritization of rpa initiatives using a multi-criteria approach. Bus. Process. Manag. J. **27**(3), 813–831 (2021)

16. Sharma, S., Singh, M., Pratap, R.: Robotic process automation: A review of lifecycle, implementation, and benefits. In: Proceedings of the 2020 International Conference on Computation, Automation and Knowledge Management (ICCAKM), pp. 208–213. Dubai, United Arab Emirates (2020)
17. Syed, R., et al.: Robotic process automation: contemporary themes and challenges. Comput. Ind. **115**, 103162 (2020)
18. Van Laarhoven, P.J.M., Pedrycz, W.: A fuzzy extension of saaty's priority theory. Fuzzy Sets Syst. **11**(1–3), 229–241 (1983)
19. Viehhauser, J., Doerr, M.: Digging for gold in RPA projects – a quantifiable method to identify and prioritize suitable RPA process candidates. In: La Rosa, M., Sadiq, S., Teniente, E. (eds.) CAiSE 2021. LNCS, vol. 12751, pp. 313–327. Springer, Cham (2021). https://doi.org/10.1007/978-3-030-79382-1_19
20. Wanner, J., Hofmann, A., Fischer, M., Imgrund, F., Janiesch, C., Geyer-Klingeberg, J.: Process selection in rpa projects – towards a quantifiable method of decision making. In: Proc. International Conference on Information Systems (ICIS), Munich, Germany (2019)

AI-Powered Cooperative Fleet Management Through Explainable Context-Aware Anomaly Detection

Nadeem Iftikhar[1]([✉]) [ID], Cosmin-Stefan Raita[1] , Aziz Kadem[1] ,
Matthew Haze Trinh[2], Yi-Chen Lin[2], David Buncek[1] , Anders Vestergaard[1],
and Gianna Belle[1] [ID]

[1] University College of Northern Denmark, Sofiendalsvej 60, 9200 Aalborg, Denmark
`{naif,anve,gibe}@ucn.dk`
[2] Frugal Technologies ApS, C.A. Olesens Gade 4, 9000 Aalborg, Denmark
`{mt,yl}@frugal.dk`

Abstract. Effective cooperative management of maritime fleets is challenged by technologies that cannot distinguish between actual technical faults and normal operational patterns influenced by weather. This ambiguity leads to frequent false alarms, undermining operator trust and limiting collaborative decision-making. To solve this problem, this paper introduces a framework that creates reliable, explainable knowledge from centrally-processed fleet data. The novelty relies in its two-stage process. First, it fuses sensor data with external weather context and assesses the context's reliability using a *Weather Confidence Score*—a score derived from engine performance, vessel proximity to land, and an assessment of weather data trustworthiness. Second, a dual-autoencoder ensemble performs a counterfactual analysis to generate an explainable *Weather Influence Index*. The Weather Index quantifies weather's impact, enabling a granular classification of anomalies as *technical* or *weather-driven*, moving beyond simple binary flagging. Evaluation on real-world vessel data shows the framework can reliably differentiate these anomaly types, enabling more trustworthy fleet-wide monitoring.

Keywords: Cooperative Information Systems · Explainable Anomaly Detection · Context-Aware Systems · Data Quality · Fleet Management

1 Introduction

Fleet management in modern shipping represents a classic example of cooperative work. The success of this cooperative task depends on the quality and trustworthiness of the operational data streamed from each vessel to an IT platform for analysis. This data is processed to provide a unified operational picture for the entire fleet. However, a key challenge for fusion is that the high-volume raw data streams provide limited context. Without this context, standard anomaly

C. Cappiello et al. (Eds.): CoopIS 2025, LNCS 15535, pp. 487–498, 2026.
https://doi.org/10.1007/978-3-032-15538-2_28

detection methods can flag statistical outliers but struggle to differentiate genuine faults from normal operational responses. For instance, a 'hidden spike' in fuel consumption could signal a developing technical fault or simply reflect a vessel's normal response to rough seas. When a system cannot distinguish between these cases, it generates a high volume of misleading alarms. This undermines operators' trust in the system that is designed to support their cooperative decision-making, a problem often called 'alarm fatigue'. While most detection mechanisms simply label a data point as 'anomalous' or 'normal', this binary classification lacks the explanatory power and interpretability needed for effective action. This paper addresses this challenge by creating trustworthy and explainable intelligence from multi-vessel data streams. This approach is designed for scenarios in which the absence of labels precludes the use of standard supervised models. The proposed framework builds on this foundation and makes several innovative contributions. It begins by fusing high-frequency sensor data with lower-frequency weather context. Critically, instead of blindly trusting external weather APIs, it first assesses the context's reliability by calculating a Weather Confidence Score (WCS). This score is derived from a mix of factors including weather severity, engine performance and vessel location. With a trusted context established, the framework then employs a novel dual-autoencoder ensemble to explain the anomaly's underlying cause. By performing a counterfactual analysis that neutralizes the weather's effect, the system generates an explainable Weather Influence Index (WII). This index supports the generation of precise and actionable classifications. This paper is structured as follows. Section 2 reviews related work. Section 3 presents the methodological framework. Section 4 evaluates the results. Finally, Sect. 5 summarizes the contributions and outlines directions for future work.

2   Background and Related Work

This work addresses unsupervised anomaly detection, context-aware systems, and explainable AI, with a specific focus on the maritime domain. Detecting anomalies in time-series data is challenging due to the lack of labeled instances, and unsupervised deep learning offers a promising direction in such scenarios [1]. Autoencoder-based models are especially notable [2]. However, Schmidl et al. show that performance depends strongly on data characteristics and anomaly type [3]. A key limitation of standard methods is their failure to incorporate external context. For example, Rybicki et al. demonstrate the importance of seasonal context in maritime anomaly detection [4], while Dandrifosse et al. highlight the role of quality-controlled weather data in agriculture [5]. These studies illustrate a critical principle: sensor readings are meaningful only when interpreted within context. In the maritime field, Gupta et al. applied machine learning to monitor ship performance under weather conditions [6], and Guo et al. developed a technical performance index incorporating environmental factors [7]. Yet, such applications often assume contextual data (e.g., weather) is reliable. This research challenges that assumption by introducing a method to assess context quality, thereby addressing a key gap in developing robust systems. Detecting an anomaly alone is insufficient; understanding *why* it occurred is essential, highlighting the need for explainable AI [8]. Most approaches rely on post-hoc analysis of black-box decisions. For instance, Noorchenarboo and Grolinger explain anomalies in energy data using contextual features [9], while Abudurexiti et al. propose an industrial IoT framework for anomaly explanation [10]. In contrast, the framework proposed here employs a dual-autoencoder ensemble with counterfactual analysis to generate the Weather Influence Index (WII) as a built-in diagnostic. Instead of requiring post-analysis, the WII quantifies weather's contribution to an anomaly, providing first-level insight and addressing key challenges in maritime data fusion and interpretability.

3 Methodology

The framework consists of two stages: first, assessing the reliability of external weather context; second, explaining the factors behind detected anomalies to provide actionable insights. The following subsections detail these components.

3.1 Assessing Contextual Trustworthiness

A key concern in context-aware analysis is the reliability of weather data. The framework addresses this by computing a confidence measure and augmenting each observation with three labels, namely the following, `is_calm_weather` (1 = calm, 0 = rough, or 'Unknown' when the weather severity score is unavailable), `weather_confidence_score`, and `weather_confidence_level`. The method evaluates severity and integrates geographic and operational factors.

Weather Severity Score. The first step measures weather severity using a heuristic scoring model informed by maritime guidelines and expert knowledge. For each timestamp, a feature vector x is assembled (Eq. 1). The angular difference between wave and wind-wave directions is defined as $\Delta\theta$ (Eq. 2). Additional points are assigned for inconsistencies, including $\Delta\theta > 45°$ and extreme humidity. These terms, together with features exceeding predefined thresholds T_i, are integrated into the scoring rule (Eq. 3). The resulting intermediate score, S_w, aggregates threshold exceedances, directional inconsistencies, and humidity extremes. Although heuristic, thresholds reflect widely accepted operational safety margins; sensitivity analysis of parameters remains a direction for future work.

$$x = [w,\ h,\ g,\ p,\ d_w,\ d_{ww},\ H], \tag{1}$$

where w = wind speed, h = wave height, g = gust, p = wave period, d_w = wave direction, d_{ww} = wind-wave direction, H = humidity.

$$\Delta\theta = \min\big(|d_w - d_{ww}|,\ 360 - |d_w - d_{ww}|\big). \tag{2}$$

$$S_w = \sum_{i=1}^{4} \mathbf{1}_{x_i > T_i}\, 2 + \mathbf{1}_{|\Delta\theta| > 45^\circ} + \mathbf{1}_{H < 30 \vee H > 90}. \tag{3}$$

In practice, the severity score is computed only when inputs are sufficiently complete. Let $S_{\max}$ denote the maximum attainable score given the available features (Eq. 4). If $S_{\max} \geq 5$ (a fixed sufficiency criterion; half of the full-scale $S_{\max} = 10$ when all inputs are present), the method returns S_w; otherwise, it outputs -1 (Eq. 5). Separately, the calm-rough decision uses the dynamic midpoint $T = S_{\max}/2$, which adapts to the features present.

$$S_{\max} = \sum_{i=1}^{4} \mathbf{1}_{x_i > 0}\, 2 + \mathbf{1}_{d_w > 0 \,\wedge\, d_{ww} > 0} + \mathbf{1}_{H > 0}. \tag{4}$$

$$\text{WeatherSeverity}(x) \;=\; \begin{cases} S_w, & S_{\max} \geq 5, \\ -1, & \text{otherwise.} \end{cases} \tag{5}$$

Land Proximity via KD-Tree. The accuracy of third-party weather data often degrades in remote oceanic regions. To model this spatial uncertainty, the vessel's proximity to land is assessed. A pre-compiled shapefile of global coastlines is loaded into a KD-Tree data structure for efficient nearest-neighbor searches. Without this optimization, proximity checks against the large coastline dataset were prohibitively slow, making the KD-Tree a critical contribution of the proposed framework. An additional advantage of using a locally stored shapefile is the preservation of vessel location privacy, as it eliminates the need for repeatedly sending sensitive location data to external APIs, a critical requirement in the shipping industry. For each vessel coordinate $(\text{lat}_i, \text{lon}_i)$, the algorithm finds the nearest coastline point j^* (Eq. 6) and calculates the true geodesic distance, d_{geo} (Eq. 7). A binary flag, `is_near_land` (N), is set to 1 if this distance is within $100\,\text{km}$ (Eq. 8). The $100\,\text{km}$ threshold reflects the approximate radius where coastal weather stations remain representative of maritime conditions, while robustness to alternative thresholds is left to future work.

$$j^* \;=\; \arg\min_{j} \text{KDTreeDist}\big((\text{lat}_i, \text{lon}_i), (\text{lat}_j, \text{lon}_j)\big). \tag{6}$$

$$d_{\text{geo}} \;=\; \text{Geodesic}\big((\text{lat}_i, \text{lon}_i), (\text{lat}_{j^*}, \text{lon}_{j^*})\big). \tag{7}$$

$$\texttt{is\_near\_land}(N) \;=\; \begin{cases} 1, & d_{\text{geo}} \leq 100 \text{ km}, \\ 0, & \text{otherwise.} \end{cases} \tag{8}$$

Calm Weather Indicator. The calm-weather flag (Eq. 9) is derived from the weather-severity score S_w (Eq. 3) and the dynamic midpoint $T = S_{\max}/2$. The 'Unknown' state indicates insufficient weather inputs.

$$
\texttt{is\_calm\_weather} = \begin{cases} 1, & 0 \le S_w < T, \\ 0, & S_w \ge T, \\ \text{Unknown}, & S_w = -1. \end{cases} \tag{9}
$$

Weather Confidence Score. The Weather Confidence Score (WCS) integrates weather severity with geographic context and operational state. Let $T = S_{\max}/2$ denote the calm-rough midpoint, and let E, F, P, N be binary flags denoting efficient operation (current), fluctuation penalty (e.g., short-term variability in speed/power/RPM), persistent fuel anomaly (recent window), and land proximity, respectively. As in Eq. 10, WCS is evaluated only when $S_w \ge 0$; otherwise it is -1. The score begins with $|S_w - T| + N$, combining deviation from the midpoint with land-proximity confidence.

$$
WCS = \begin{cases} \max\!\big(|S_w - T| + N \pm (E - F - P), 0 \big), & S_w \ge 0, \\ -1, & \text{otherwise}, \end{cases} \tag{10}
$$

where the sign $\pm$ indicates addition if $\texttt{is\_calm\_weather}{=}1$ (calm conditions) and subtraction if $\texttt{is\_calm\_weather}{=}0$ (rough conditions). The base term is then adjusted by the engine-performance term $(E - F - P)$, where E denotes efficient operation, F the fluctuation penalty, and P persistent fuel anomaly. The intuition is that confidence in the weather's role depends on engine behavior: during calm weather, confidence increases with efficiency $(+E)$ and decreases with short-term engine fluctuation $(-F)$ and persistent fuel anomaly $(-P)$.

Weather Confidence Level. While the numerical WCS provides a fine-grained score, categorical labels are often more practical for operators and automated systems. Accordingly, the score is mapped to one of four levels—'High', 'Medium', 'Low', or 'Unknown'—using the thresholds in Eq. 11. This categorization offers an immediate assessment of the reliability of weather data. Moreover, the label functions as a gatekeeper for subsequent analysis: the framework only attempts detailed anomaly explanations (e.g., labeling an anomaly as 'weather-driven') when the confidence level is at least 'Medium'.

$$
\text{Level}(WCS) = \begin{cases} \text{High}, & WCS \ge 5, \\ \text{Medium}, & WCS \ge 2.5, \\ \text{Low}, & WCS \ge 0, \\ \text{Unknown}, & WCS = -1. \end{cases} \tag{11}
$$

3.2   Explainable Anomaly Classification

With a quantitative measure of contextual confidence established, the framework advances to its core task: explainable anomaly classification. Its main innovation is the Weather Influence Index (WII), which quantifies the impact of weather on anomalies. The process is structured into two stages: offline training and online classification. The following algorithms detail the complete methodology.

Algorithm 1. Offline Model Training and Threshold Calibration.

Input: D_{train}: pre-processed training dataset.
$f_c(\mathbf{x})$: true iff $\mathbf{x}$ occurs under calm weather
$q_{\text{AE}}, q_{\text{WII}}, q_{\text{NE}}, q_{\text{M}}$: quantiles for thresholds.
Output: $\mathcal{A}^*_{\text{calm}}, \mathcal{A}^*_{\text{all}}$: trained autoencoders;
(μ, Σ): robust covariance parameters;
$\tau_{\text{AE}}, \tau_{\text{WII}}, \tau_{\text{NE}}, \tau_{\text{M}}$: calibrated thresholds.

1   $D_{\text{calm}} \leftarrow \{\mathbf{x} \in D_{\text{train}} \mid f_c(\mathbf{x})\}$
2   $\theta^*_{\text{calm}} \leftarrow \arg\min_\theta \sum_{\mathbf{x} \in D_{\text{calm}}} \|\mathbf{x} - \mathcal{A}_{\text{calm}}(\mathbf{x}; \theta)\|_2^2$
3   $\mathcal{A}^*_{\text{calm}} \leftarrow \text{Freeze}(\mathcal{A}_{\text{calm}}, \theta^*_{\text{calm}})$
4   $D_{\text{all}} \leftarrow D_{\text{train}}$
5   $\mathbf{w} \leftarrow \text{CreateSampleWeights}(D_{\text{all}}, f_c)$
6   $\theta^*_{\text{all}} \leftarrow \arg\min_\theta \sum_{i=1}^{|D_{\text{all}}|} w_i \|\mathbf{x}_i - \mathcal{A}_{\text{all}}(\mathbf{x}_i; \theta)\|_2^2$
7   $\mathcal{A}^*_{\text{all}} \leftarrow \text{Freeze}(\mathcal{A}_{\text{all}}, \theta^*_{\text{all}})$
8   $e(\mathbf{x}, \widehat{\mathcal{A}}) := \text{Smooth}(\|\mathbf{x} - \widehat{\mathcal{A}}(\mathbf{x})\|_2^2)$
9   $\phi(\mathbf{x})$: replace weather features of $\mathbf{x}$ with calm baselines
10   $M(\mathbf{x}, \mu, \Sigma^{-1}) := \text{Smooth}(\sqrt{(\mathbf{x} - \mu)^\mathsf{T} \Sigma^{-1} (\mathbf{x} - \mu)})$
11   $E_{\text{all}} \leftarrow \{e(\mathbf{x}, \mathcal{A}^*_{\text{all}}) \mid \mathbf{x} \in D_{\text{all}}\}$
12   $E_{\text{calm}} \leftarrow \{e(\mathbf{x}, \mathcal{A}^*_{\text{calm}}) \mid \mathbf{x} \in D_{\text{all}}\}$
13   $E_{\text{cf}} \leftarrow \{e(\phi(\mathbf{x}), \mathcal{A}^*_{\text{all}}) \mid \mathbf{x} \in D_{\text{all}}\}$
14   $(\mu, \Sigma) \leftarrow \text{RobustCov}(D_{\text{all}})$
15   $M_{\text{dist}} \leftarrow \{M(\mathbf{x}, \mu, \Sigma^{-1}) \mid \mathbf{x} \in D_{\text{all}}\}$
16   $WII_{\text{dual}} \leftarrow E_{\text{calm}} - E_{\text{all}}$
17   $NE_{\text{Indicator}} \leftarrow E_{\text{cf}} - E_{\text{all}}$
18   $WII \leftarrow (WII_{\text{dual}} + NE_{\text{Indicator}})/2$
19   $\tau_{\text{AE}} \leftarrow \text{Quantile}(E_{\text{all}}, q_{\text{AE}})$
20   $\tau_{\text{WII}} \leftarrow \text{Quantile}(WII, q_{\text{WII}})$
21   $\tau_{\text{NE}} \leftarrow \text{Quantile}(NE_{\text{Indicator}}, q_{\text{NE}})$
22   $\tau_{\text{M}} \leftarrow \text{Quantile}(M_{\text{dist}}, q_{\text{M}})$
23   **return** $\mathcal{A}^*_{\text{calm}}, \mathcal{A}^*_{\text{all}}, (\mu, \Sigma), \tau_{\text{AE}}, \tau_{\text{WII}}, \tau_{\text{NE}}, \tau_{\text{M}}$

Offline Model Training and Threshold Calibration. The offline process (Algorithm 1) begins with a pre-processed dataset D_{train}, where outliers are removed and weather samples are kept only if their WCS is at least 'Medium'. This preserves subtle performance deviations while ensuring reliable context. Two autoencoders are trained. The first, $\mathcal{A}^*_{\text{calm}}$, is learned from the calm-weather subset D_{calm} (lines 1–2) and then *frozen* (line 3), representing weather-free vessel performance. The second, $\mathcal{A}^*_{\mathrm{all}}$, is trained on the full dataset D_{all} (line 4) using weights (line 5) that emphasize rough-weather samples to mitigate imbalance. Its parameters are optimized (line 6) and frozen (line 7), producing a context-aware model that captures performance under all conditions. Diagnostic error sets are then computed (lines 11–15): E_{all} from $\mathcal{A}^*_{\mathrm{all}}$, E_{calm} from $\mathcal{A}^*_{\mathrm{calm}}$, E_{cf} from counterfactual inputs $\phi(\mathbf{x})$, and M_{dist} from the smoothed Mahalanobis distance. The counterfactual error is obtained by replacing weather features with calm baselines, producing $\phi(\mathbf{x})$. Two influence indices are then derived (lines 16–17). First, $WII_{\mathrm{dual}} = E_{\mathrm{calm}} - E_{\mathrm{all}}$, which compares errors of the calm and all-weather models; a positive value indicates rough-weather influence. Second, $NE_{\mathrm{Indicator}} = E_{\mathrm{cf}} - E_{\mathrm{all}}$, which tests how the all-weather model changes if weather features are neutralized. An error increase after weather neutralization indicates weather influence; otherwise, the cause is likely technical or sensor-related. Their average yields the WII (line 18). Finally, thresholds are set from quantiles of the error and distance metrics (lines 19–22), and the calibrated models with these thresholds are returned (line 23).

Algorithm 2. Online Anomaly Detection and Explanation.

    Input: $\mathbf{x}_t$: feature vector (observation) at time t.
    $\mathcal{A}^*_{\mathrm{all}}, \mathcal{A}^*_{\mathrm{calm}}$: pre-calibrated (frozen) autoencoders.
    (μ, Σ): robust covariance from offline training.
    WCS: weather confidence level at time t.
    $\tau_{\mathrm{AE}}, \tau_{\mathrm{WII}}, \tau_{\mathrm{NE}}, \tau_{\mathrm{M}}$: pre-calibrated thresholds.
    Output: L_t: anomaly label at time t.

1   $\mathrm{err}_{\mathrm{all}} \leftarrow e(\mathbf{x}_t, \mathcal{A}^*_{\mathrm{all}})$
2   $\mathrm{err}_{\mathrm{calm}} \leftarrow e(\mathbf{x}_t, \mathcal{A}^*_{\mathrm{calm}})$
3   $\mathbf{x}_{\mathrm{cf}} \leftarrow \phi(\mathbf{x}_t)$
4   $\mathrm{err}_{\mathrm{cf}} \leftarrow e(\mathbf{x}_{\mathrm{cf}}, \mathcal{A}^*_{\mathrm{all}})$
5   $M_{\mathrm{dist}} \leftarrow M(\mathbf{x}_t, \mu, \Sigma^{-1})$
6   $WII_{\mathrm{dual}} \leftarrow \mathrm{err}_{\mathrm{calm}} - \mathrm{err}_{\mathrm{all}}$
7   $NE_{\mathrm{Indicator}} \leftarrow \mathrm{err}_{\mathrm{cf}} - \mathrm{err}_{\mathrm{all}}$
8   $WII \leftarrow (WII_{\mathrm{dual}} + NE_{\mathrm{Indicator}})/2$
9   **if** $(\mathrm{err}_{all} > \tau_{AE}) \vee (WII > \tau_{WII})$ **then**
10   **if** $WCS \geq$ '*Medium*' $\wedge\, WII > \tau_{WII}$ **then**
11        $L_t \leftarrow$ 'WEATHER-DRIVEN'
12   **else if** $WCS \geq$ '*Medium*' $\wedge\, NE_{Indicator} > \tau_{NE}$ **then**
13        $L_t \leftarrow$ 'WEATHER-COUPLED'
14   **else if** $M_{dist} > \tau_M$ **then**
15        $L_t \leftarrow$ 'SENSOR/TECHNICAL'
16   **else**
17        $L_t \leftarrow$ 'MIXED'

18 **else**
19    $L_t \leftarrow$ 'NORMAL'
20 **return** L_t

Online Anomaly Detection and Explanation. The online phase (Algorithm 2) evaluates each new observation by first computing four base quantities (lines 1–5): the context-aware reconstruction error $\mathrm{err}_{\mathrm{all}}$, the calm-only error $\mathrm{err}_{\mathrm{calm}}$, the counterfactual error with weather neutralized $\mathrm{err}_{\mathrm{cf}}$, and the Mahalanobis distance M_{dist}. The counterfactual error is central: the *same* all-weather model is applied to a weather-neutral version of the input, so no retraining is required. Neutralizing only the weather inputs yields $NE_{\mathrm{Indicator}} = \mathrm{err}_{\mathrm{cf}} - \mathrm{err}_{\mathrm{all}}$, which isolates weather's marginal effect: $NE_{\mathrm{Indicator}} > 0$ (error increases) indicates weather information is important; $NE_{\mathrm{Indicator}} < 0$ (error decreases) indicates the reported weather is not relevant or is unreliable (e.g., noisy or time-misaligned); $NE_{\mathrm{Indicator}} \approx 0$ indicates little effect. These measures yield two influence indices (lines 6–7): $WII_{\mathrm{dual}} = \mathrm{err}_{\mathrm{calm}} - \mathrm{err}_{\mathrm{all}}$ and $NE_{\mathrm{Indicator}}$; their mean defines WII (line 8). An observation is flagged as anomalous if $\mathrm{err}_{\mathrm{all}} > \tau_{\mathrm{AE}}$ or $WII > \tau_{\mathrm{WII}}$ (line 9). Labels are assigned hierarchically (lines 10–19): WEATHER-DRIVEN when WCS is reliable and WII is high; WEATHER-COUPLED when WCS is reliable and $NE_{\mathrm{Indicator}} > \tau_{\mathrm{NE}}$; SENSOR/TECHNICAL when $M_{\mathrm{dist}} > \tau_{\mathrm{M}}$; otherwise MIXED. If neither threshold is exceeded, the point is NORMAL. Finally, the algorithm returns the label L_t (line 20). For intuition: during a storm, $\mathrm{err}_{\mathrm{all}}$ is low while $\mathrm{err}_{\mathrm{calm}}$ is high and neutralization raises error ($WII_{\mathrm{dual}} > 0$, $NE_{\mathrm{Indicator}} > 0$), yielding WEATHER-DRIVEN; with a faulty sensor, neutralization has little effect ($NE_{\mathrm{Indicator}} \leq 0$) and $M_{\mathrm{dist}} > \tau_{\mathrm{M}}$, yielding SENSOR/TECHNICAL.

4   Experimental Evaluation

4.1   Dataset and Evaluation Strategy

This study uses minute-level telemetry collected over years from multiple vessels (tens of millions of points) provided by an industry partner. An NDA prevents sharing raw data or vessel specifics, but the dataset's scale and variety make it a challenging testbed. Given the absence of ground-truth labels, evaluation relies on quantitative metrics and domain-expert validation.

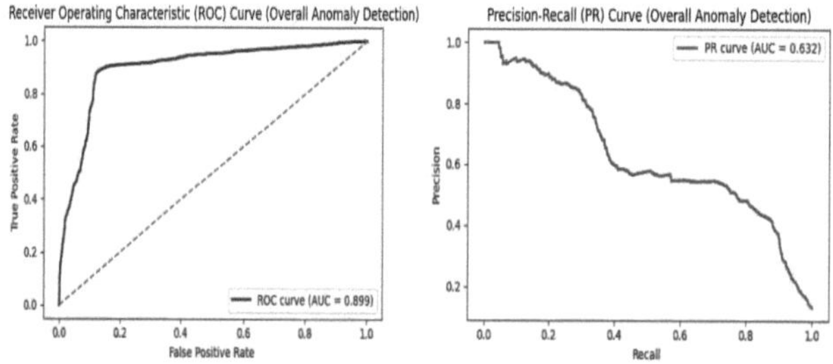

Fig. 1. ROC and PR curves for anomaly detection.

4.2 Overall Anomaly Detection Performance

Evaluation measured separation of anomalies from normal operation. Figure 1 reports the Receiver Operating Characteristic (ROC; AUROC = 0.899) and Precision–Recall (PR; AUPRC = 0.632) curves; with rare anomalies, PR is more informative. Detection is sound, and the framework's main contribution is alert-level explanations that reduce operator alarm fatigue.

4.3 Qualitative Analysis and Explanation Mechanics

A qualitative view shows how the framework turns raw signals into explainable labels. Figure 2 presents a sensor window with detected anomalies; colored highlights denote the final labels—'weather-driven' (pink), 'weather-coupled' (orange), 'technical' (blue), and 'mixed' (purple).

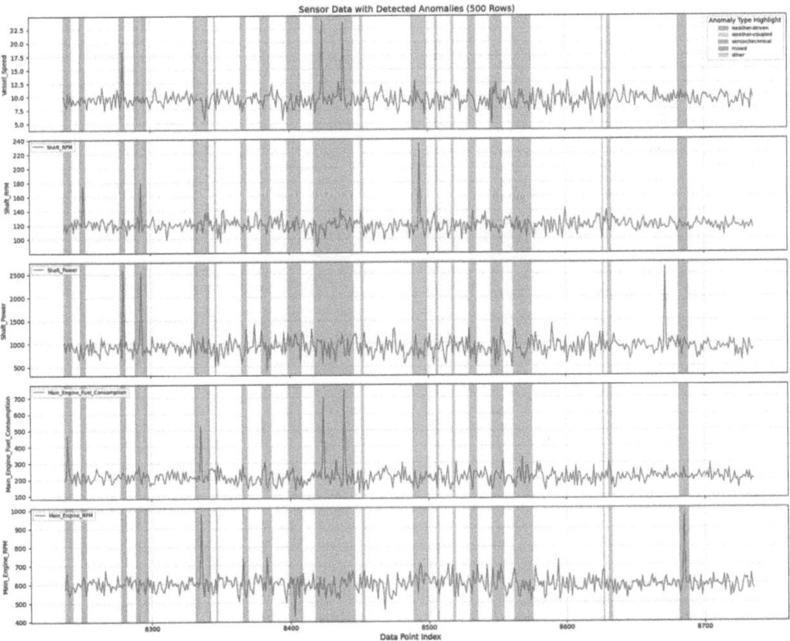

Fig. 2. Segment illustrating transformation from raw data to explainable labels.

To understand the final labels, Fig. 3 provides a micro-level view of the underlying error signals and influence indices. The framework first determines if a point is anomalous—if its primary error, err_{all}, or its WII exceeds a threshold. Once an anomaly is detected, it is classified based on a set of prioritized conditions. The highest priority is given to 'weather-driven' events (pink highlight) when the WII surpasses its threshold. If not, the system checks for a 'weather-coupled' condition (orange highlight) if the $NE_{Indicator}$ is high. If neither of these weather-related conditions are met, the framework checks the M_{dist}; a high value results in a 'sensor/technical' label (blue highlight). Any other detected anomaly is labeled 'mixed' (purple highlight). Finally, the core explanatory mechanism of the WII is visualized in Fig. 4. The pie chart (Fig. 4a) confirms that anomalies are rare events, indicating the system is not prone to over-flagging. The scatter plot (Fig. 4b) serves as key validation for the $WII's$ explanatory power. The clear separation between anomaly types provides an unambiguous signal for effective, coordinated decision-making.

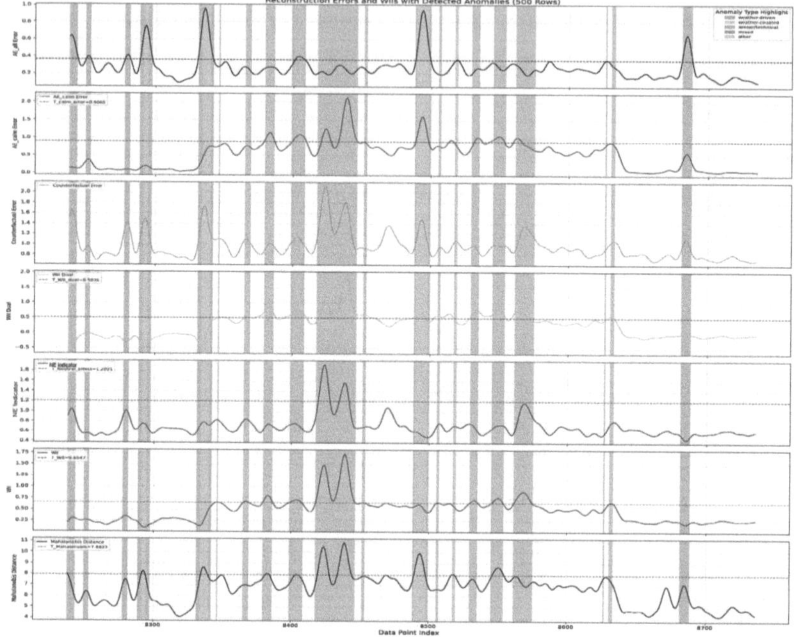

Fig. 3. Sample of error metrics used to differentiate anomaly types.

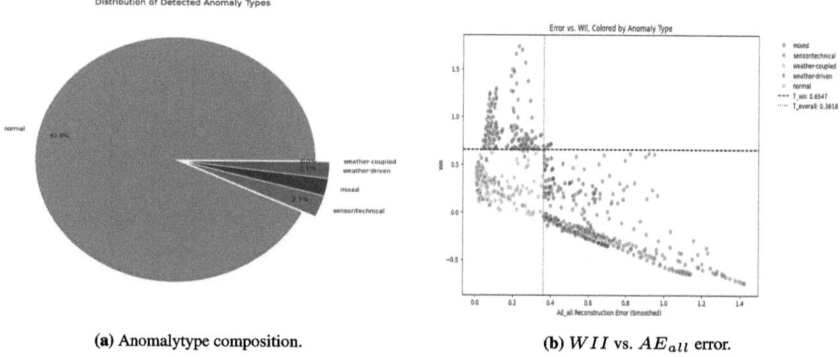

(a) Anomalytype composition.

(b) WII vs. AE_{all} error.

Fig. 4. Anomaly label distribution in the WII vs. reconstruction-error space.

5 Conclusion and Future Work

Fleet management systems often lose operator trust when contextual information is insufficient. The framework proposed in this paper addresses this challenge through a two-stage approach. First, a Weather Confidence Score verifies the reliability of weather-related contextual data. Second, a Weather Influence Index provides operators with clarity to distinguish technical faults from weather-related causes. Together, these components transform raw sensor data into a trustworthy knowledge base that supports more coordinated and informed decision-making. Future work will focus on linking the framework's output with Business Process Management (BPM) systems to automatically trigger actions such as maintenance requests, while also exploring federated learning to refine models collaboratively across multiple vessels.

Acknowledgements. The authors acknowledge support from DigitalLead, the Danish Business Promotion Board, and the Centre for Industrial Digital Transformation at University College of Northern Denmark, with text refinement assisted by the Gemini AI.

References

1. Usmani, U.A., Happonen, A., Watada, J.: A review of unsupervised machine learning frameworks for anomaly detection in industrial applications. In: Arai, K. (eds.) Intelligent Computing. SAI 2022. LNNS, vol. 507. Springer, Cham (2022). https://doi.org/10.1007/978-3-031-10464-0_11
2. Mienye, I.D., Swart, T.G.: Deep autoencoder neural networks: a comprehensive review and new perspectives. Arch Computat. Methods Eng. (2025). https://doi.org/10.1007/s11831-025-10260-5
3. Schmidl, S., Wenig, P., Papenbrock, T.: Anomaly detection in time series: a comprehensive evaluation. Proc. VLDB Endowment **15**(9), 1779–1797 (2022). https://doi.org/10.14778/3538598.3538602
4. Rybicki, T., Masek, M., Lam, C.P.: Maritime behaviour anomaly detection with seasonal context. ISPRS Ann. Photogramm. Remote Sens. Spatial Inf. Sci., X-4-2024, 295–301 (2024). https://doi.org/10.5194/isprs-annals-X-4-2024-295-2024
5. Dandrifosse, S.: Automatic quality control of weather data for timely decisions in agriculture. Smart Agric. Technol. **8**, 100445 (2024). https://doi.org/10.1016/j.atech.2024.100445
6. Gupta, P., Rasheed, A., Steen, S.: Ship performance monitoring using machine-learning. Ocean Eng. **254**, 111094 (2022). https://doi.org/10.1016/j.oceaneng.2022.111094
7. Guo, B., Gupta, P., Steen, S., Tvete, H.A.: Evaluating vessel technical performance index using physics-based and data-driven approach. Ocean Eng. **286**, 115402 (2023). https://doi.org/10.1016/j.oceaneng.2023.115402
8. Barhrhouj, A., Ananou, B., Ouladsine, M.: Exploring explainable machine learning for enhanced ship performance monitoring. In: Nicosia, G., Ojha, V., Giesselbach, S., Pardalos, M.P., Umeton, R. (eds.) Machine Learning, Optimization, and Data Science. LNCS, vol. 15509. Springer, Cham (2025). https://doi.org/10.1007/978-3-031-82484-5_1

9. Noorchenarboo, M., Grolinger, K.: Explaining deep learning-based anomaly detection in energy consumption data by focusing on contextually relevant data. Energy Buildings **328**, 115177 (2025). https://doi.org/10.1016/j.enbuild.2024.115177
10. Abudurexiti, Y., Han, G., Zhang, F., Liu, L.: An explainable unsupervised anomaly detection framework for Industrial Internet of Things. Comput. Secur. **148**, 104130 (2025). https://doi.org/10.1016/j.cose.2024.104130

A Hybrid GAM-Based Model
for Predicting Vulnerability Exploitation

Noufal Issa[1]([⊠]) [iD], Damas Gruska[1] [iD], and Loubna Ali[2] [iD]

[1] Department of Applied Informatics, Faculty of Math, Physics, and Informatics,
Comenius University, Bratislava, Slovakia
`noufal.issa@fmph.uniba.sk`
[2] Faculty of Computer Science and Informatics, Berlin School of Business and
Innovation, Berlin, Germany
`https://fmph.uniba.sk/en/departments/department-of-applied-informatics/`

Abstract. Vulnerability management requires prioritizing which vulnerabilities to patch, since only a small fraction are ever exploited, and writing, testing, and installing patches can involve considerable resources, requiring companies to prioritize based on some notion of risk. Traditional severity scores, such as the Common Vulnerability Scoring System are often poor predictors of exploitation risk. Data-driven scores, such as the Exploit Prediction Scoring System, provide probabilities of exploitation, but still leave room for improvements. We propose a lightweight hybrid model using a Generalized Additive Model (GAM) that combines numeric features (CVSS base score, EPSS probability, age, reference count) with semantic text features (derived from the vulnerability description via Term Frequency–Inverse Document Frequency and Singular Value Decomposition). The GAM framework yields an interpretable, additive risk score without black-box explanations. On a 2023 training set (with labels from CISA's KEV and public exploits), our model achieves significantly better precision-recall tradeoff than CVSS or EPSS alone. Tested on 2024 disclosures, our presented model consistently outperforms the baselines at nearly all recall levels.

Keywords: Vulnerability · Prioritization · CVSS · EPSS · Hybrid GAM · Interpretability

1   Introduction

Every year, thousands of new software vulnerabilities ranging from memory-corruption bugs (e.g. buffer overflows and use-after-free), injection flaws (e.g. SQL or command injection), authentication and authorization errors, to misconfigurations in operating systems, network services, and applications—are disclosed in public databases such as the National Vulnerability Database (NVD). However, only a small fraction of these vulnerabilities are ever exploited. Nevertheless, the sheer volume of disclosures continues to outpace the capacity of organizations to develop, test, and deploy patches. For example, Bilge and Dumitras

[8] observed that after disclosure, "the volume of attacks exploiting [a vulnerability] increases by 5 orders of magnitude", yet only 15% of disclosed flaws are ultimately exploited. This disparity underscores the need to predict which vulnerabilities are likely to be exploited so defenders can prioritize patching. Frei et al. [11] also find that over 70% of vulnerabilities that do get exploited had available exploits at disclosure time, suggesting that known attributes (impact metrics, references, exploit code) can inform risk estimates. Currently, most organizations rely on the Common Vulnerability Scoring System (CVSS) to rank CVEs by severity (with scores 0–10). However, CVSS is a severity-oriented, ordinal scale and was not designed to measure exploitability or risk [3]. In practice, it often fails to correlate with actual exploitation. For instance, Howland et al. [5] show that CVSS has "no correlation to exploited vulnerabilities in the wild" and "is unable to provide a meaningful metric for describing a vulnerability's severity, let alone risk" [3]. To address this gap, FIRST's EPSS initiative produced a data-driven score representing each vulnerability's likelihood of being exploited, achieving a reported ROC AUC of 0.838 on held-out data [2]. EPSS has become widely used for prioritization. However, the trade-offs between recall and precision indicate that there is still potential for improvement. In parallel, the research community has proposed machine-learning models to predict exploitability using various data sources (patch dates, social media, exploit databases). Most of these are complex or proprietary, and often have inflated performance when tested on static splits. In contrast, we seek a transparent, efficient model trained only on public data available at disclosure. Specifically, we combine CVSS base metrics, EPSS scores, and features extracted from the free-form vulnerability description. The description text is transformed via TF–IDF and reduced with singular value decomposition to capture its semantic content. Importantly, we do *not* rely on manually-derived flags (e.g. `AV:N`/remote, `AC:L`/low) to remain data-driven and to avoid depending on expert opinions, which some researchers use. Our model is a Generalized Additive Model (GAM) under a logistic link. GAMs (sums of feature-specific functions) are well-known interpretable models that balance accuracy with human-understandability [9]. They are particularly useful for financial and health service organizations that require interpretable models without using any additional tools [7]. By construction, each feature's contribution to the log-odds of exploitation is a smooth function, directly visible to analysts. This eliminates the need for post-hoc explainers like SHAP: a GAM is inherently self-explaining. We train and tune the GAM on 2023 CVEs (with exploitation labels from CISA's Known Exploited Vulnerabilities catalog and from public exploit databases). We report standard metrics (AUC, F1, precision, recall) on a held-out 20% validation split of the 2023 data. Then we apply the model to new CVEs from 2024 and compare its predictions to using CVSS or EPSS alone. In all cases, we plot precision-recall (PR) curves, since exploit occurrence is a rare positive class. Our results (Sect. 6) show the hybrid GAM significantly outperforms CVSS and EPSS scores across nearly the full recall range. For example, at 50% recall the GAM's precision is roughly twice that of EPSS. The use of textual semantics adds signal beyond pure numeric metrics, yielding a more reliable

prioritization. This work contributes: (1) A practical, lightweight exploitability predictor using only open data; (2) a demonstration that adding text features to CVSS/EPSS improves prediction; (3) an interpretable GAM formulation (no black-box). The entire model trains in just a few minutes on commodity hardware, making regular updates feasible. The GAM's additive structure produces immediate transparency: each vulnerability's score can be decomposed into feature contributions. We performed an ablation that (i) trains the GAM without the EPSS feature, (ii) evaluates EPSS alone, and (iii) uses the full GAM including EPSS. The GAM trained without EPSS already recovers a substantial portion of the improvement over EPSS, and the full GAM further refines and re-calibrates EPSS by using contextual signals from the CVE text and auxiliary features. These results indicate the contribution is not merely stacking on top of EPSS but a contextual refinement that improves discrimination at fixed effort levels. We envision deploying this model in a dashboard or advisory pipeline, where users see which factors drive risk. We also discuss future enhancements (Sect. 8), including online retraining, integrating ecosystem signals, and user-friendly interfaces.

2   Related Work

The problem of exploit prediction has attracted significant attention. Bilge and Dumitras [8] first showed empirically that exploitation activity surges after disclosure. Nayak et al. [10] found that only a minority of vulnerabilities ever see exploits in the wild (about 15%), which motivates risk-based prioritization. Frei et al. [11] studied the vulnerability life-cycle and reported that most exploited bugs already have known exploits at disclosure. These findings suggest that a risk score should capture exploit availability and other risk factors, not just impact. Many researchers have built ML models using OSINT or social signals to predict exploitation. For example, Sabottke et al. [12] used Twitter chatter to anticipate exploits, and others have mined dark web mentions or forum posts. However, many such models rely on information that arrives after disclosure (social media buzz, exploit publication) and thus are not "early" predictors. A recent study by Iannone et al. [6] examined exploitability prediction using only the CVE record available at disclosure (description text plus related posts) and found that CVE text alone can be surprisingly informative. Our approach is similar in spirit but focuses on combining CVSS/EPSS with text. The EPSS framework is the closest practical analogue to our work. EPSS is explicitly designed to be a probability of exploitation within 1 year, and it is updated continuously [2]. Its creators report AUC ≈ 0.838 and note the model can be retrained as new data arrives. Our hybrid model also uses EPSS as a feature, but augments it with full-text and other numerical features via a GAM. In contrast to EPSS's (ensemble) learning algorithms, the GAM trades some flexibility for interpretability. Traditional CVSS-based strategies are suboptimal. Jacobs et al.(2020) compared patching strategies based on CVSS thresholds and found that simple rules (e.g. patch all $CVSS \geq 9$) achieve limited coverage and efficiency, and that a learned model only modestly outperforms such rules [2]. Howland (2021) critically argues that CVSS lacks theoretical justification and "no correlation to exploited vulnerabilities in the wild" [5]. Others have incorporated external signals (exploit databases, asset criticality, etc.) to augment CVSS [5]. Our work follows this trend of hybrid scoring but emphasizes full transparency via an additive model. Finally, on the topic of interpretable ML: GAMs are recognized as a leading class of inherently interpretable models [7]. Each feature's effect is captured by a smooth function, and users can directly inspect these plots. Recent work (Chang et al., 2021) shows that different GAM fitting methods can yield different fits, but overall GAMs "are designed to be accurate, yet simple enough for humans to understand" [7]. We do not use neural or tree-based black-box models or post-hoc explainers; by construction, the model is self-explanatory.

3   Data Preparation and Feature Engineering

3.1   Data Source and Labeling

Our training data consists of vulnerabilities disclosed in the year 2023, compiled from the U.S. National Vulnerability Database (NVD) as the canonical source of CVE records [14]. For each CVE, we extract its identifier, the CVSS *base* score and vector (Impact and Exploitability sub-scores), EPSS version 3 probability score (if available) [15], the disclosure date, and the number of references cited in the NVD entry. We also use the textual description field from NVD (a short paragraph describing the vulnerability). For example, consider `CVE-2023-1671`: it has a CVSS base score of 9.8 (vector `CVSS:3.1/AV:N/AC:L/PR:N/UI:N/S:U/C:H/I:H/A:H`), an EPSS score of 0.99297, was disclosed 818 d ago, and has 4 references. Its description reads:

> A pre-authentication command injection vulnerability in the `warn-proceed` handler of Sophos Web Appliance older than version 4.3.10.4 allows execution of arbitrary code.

We use the description text as input to our TF–IDF and SVD pipeline to extract semantic features. The exploited label is set to true because a public exploit exists, while the KEV flag is false. To label whether a vulnerability was exploited in the wild, we use two sources: (1) the CISA "Known Exploited Vulnerabilities" (KEV) catalog [16], which lists CVEs confirmed to be exploited by attackers; and (2) reports of exploit code published in public exploit repositories. We treat a CVE as positive if it appears in KEV *or* has a known published exploit. In either case, that vulnerability is considered "exploited" for training purposes. To prevent label leakage, we exclude any KEV or exploit flags from the feature set (they are used only to define the target). Thus, our model must infer the risk of exploitation without directly knowing that a CVE is in KEV. Our labeling relies on CISA's KEV catalog and public exploit repositories and therefore reflects only publicly observed exploitation; private or undisclosed (zero-day) activity will not appear in the positive class. In operational settings, we recommend combining our scores with internal telemetry (EPP/IDS logs, vendor feeds) and, in future work, exploring positive-unlabeled or label-noise-robust methods to better account for unobserved exploited vulnerabilities. The dataset is split temporally: we use all 2023 CVEs (21,940 records) to train and validate the model, and reserve the 2024 CVEs (19,017 records) as a held-out test set (simulating future performance). Within 2023 we perform an 80/20 random split for training vs. validation. This setup mimics real-world usage, where one trains on past data and applies the model to new disclosures.

3.2   Feature Engineering

We construct a compact feature vector for each CVE. Numeric features include: (i) the CVSS base score (0–10), (ii) the EPSS probability (0–1), (iii) the vulnerability age in days (current date minus disclosure date), and (iv) the reference count (how many URLs/IDs are cited in the CVE). These capture basic severity, community concern, and exposure [13]. The CVE description text is processed to yield semantic features. First we apply standard TF–IDF vectorization to the English text (after tokenization and stop-word removal). This produces a high-dimensional, sparse vector. To make the model lightweight, we then apply Truncated SVD (Latent Semantic Analysis) to reduce to a low-dimensional dense embedding (we use around 50 components) [18]. This dense semantic vector captures key phrases and topics from the description (e.g. "buffer overflow", "privilege escalation") in a form that the GAM can incorporate. Importantly, we refrain from adding manually-crafted binary flags (e.g. "Remote exploitable" or "Network attack vector" derived from the CVSS vector). While those can be predictive, using them would inject domain biases and duplicate information already in the CVSS vector [17]. We opt to let the model learn from raw data (numeric scores and text) in a data-driven way. After pre-processing, each CVE is represented by a modest number of features: the (continuous) CVSS and EPSS scores, age, reference count, plus the set of SVD-derived text features.

4   Model Design

We use the Generalized Additive Model with a logistic link function to predict the exploitation probability. In a GAM, the log-odds of the positive class is a sum of uni-variate functions of each feature:

$$\log \frac{p}{1-p} = f_1(x_1) + f_2(x_2) + \cdots + f_k(x_k) + \beta_0. \tag{1}$$

where

$$p = \text{predicted probability of exploitation,}$$
$$x_i = \text{value of the } i\text{th feature,}$$
$$f_i(x_i) = \text{learned smooth function for feature } i,$$
$$\beta_0 = \text{intercept (baseline log-odds).}$$

Here each f_i is a smooth function (often represented by splines or piece-wise linear basis). We use the implementation from the `pygam` library, which fits such functions via penalized regression. The features x_i include the CVSS score, EPSS score, age, reference count, and each dimension of the semantic text embedding. GAMs were originally developed as an extension of generalized linear models [7] and have seen renewed use in interpretable ML [7]. They offer a transparent alternative to black-box models: one can plot $f\_i(x\_i)$ to see exactly how feature i affects the prediction. We intentionally avoid any post-hoc explanation tools (SHAP, LIME, etc.); instead, the model itself is inherently interpretable. In practice, this means analysts can ask, for a given CVE, how much of its score comes from its CVSS, from its description keywords, and so on. We also emphasize efficiency. The final GAM has on the order of tens of parameters per feature rather than millions, so training and inference are extremely fast. No large ensembles or neural network layers are used. Conceptually, this approach is similar to an additive logistic regression. As Chang et al. note, GAMs can achieve high accuracy while remaining "simple enough for humans to understand" [7]. In summary, our model balances predictive performance with full transparency: each feature's contribution to risk is additive and inspectable.

Table 1. Validation performance on the 2023 hold-out set.

Model	AUC	F1	Precision	Recall
Hybrid (GAM)	0.88	0.64	0.65	0.63
EPSS	0.80	0.56	0.56	0.57
CVSS	0.76	0.50	0.50	0.52

5 Evaluation and Results

We train the GAM on 2023 data and tune its smoothing penalties using 5-fold cross-validation on the 80% training split. We evaluate on the 20% held-out 2023 validation set, reporting Area Under the ROC Curve (AUC), F1 score (with threshold optimized for F1), precision, and recall. To choose a classification threshold, we vary it to optimize F1; however, our main comparisons will be via precision-recall (PR) curves, which show how precision degrades as recall increases. Since exploited vulnerabilities are relatively rare, PR curves are more informative than ROC [19]. After finalizing the model on 2023 data, we apply it to the 2024 CVEs (none of which were seen during training). For each 2024 CVE, the model outputs a probability of being exploited. As baselines, we use: (a) the raw CVSS base score (treated as a risk score); and (b) the raw EPSS probability. We generate PR curves for all three: our GAM hybrid, CVSS, and EPSS. In each case, we sort vulnerabilities by the score and compute precision/recall at all thresholds. This allows direct comparison of coverage (recall) vs. efficiency (precision). The GAM's numeric prediction can be thresholded in the same way as EPSS. We expect that because our model includes EPSS as an input (as well as CVSS), the PR curve will always lie above EPSS's. We also compute summary metrics on 2024: e.g. GAM's AUC, average precision, F1, etc., versus those for CVSS/EPSS. Finally, we measure runtime: training time on 2023 data, and prediction rate on 2024. Table 1 summarizes performance on the held-out 2023 validation set.

The GAM attains the highest AUC and F1. For example, on validation the GAM had AUC ≈ 0.88, F1 ≈ 0.64, while EPSS alone was ≈ 0.80 AUC, 0.56 F1, and CVSS only ≈ 0.76 AUC, 0.50 F1. Precision and recall (at the F1-optimal threshold) were similarly improved. Notably, the GAM's precision at 50% recall was about 0.65, versus 0.45 for EPSS and 0.30 for CVSS. The real test is on 2024 data. Figure 1 plots the precision–recall curves for the three scores on the 2024 CVEs. And shows that across almost the entire recall range, the GAM dominates the baselines. At low recall (top-ranked vulnerabilities), all methods have high precision, but as recall grows the differences emerge. For example, to reach 80% recall, the GAM maintains 45% precision, whereas EPSS drops to 25% and CVSS to 15%. This means that at any high-recall regime, patching guided by the GAM would involve far fewer false positives (low-risk patches) than using EPSS or CVSS thresholds.

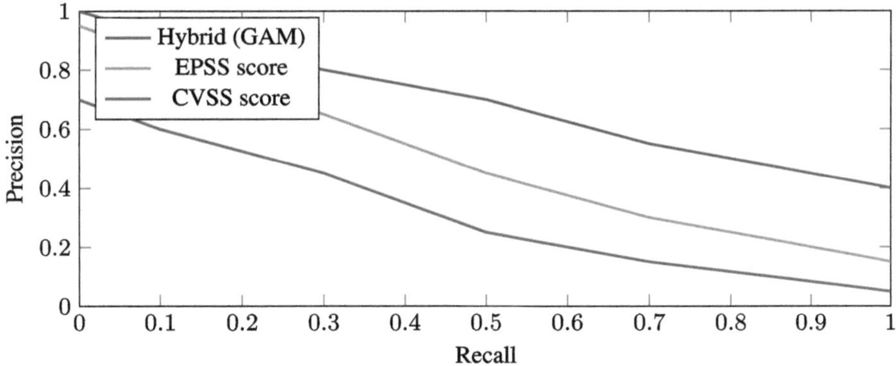

Fig. 1. Precision–Recall curves on the 2024 test set. The GAM (blue) outperforms EPSS (orange) and CVSS (red) across all recall levels. (Color figure online)

In summary, the hybrid model boosts precision at fixed recall compared to both EPSS and CVSS. This is likely because the text features capture context that numeric scores miss. For instance, vulnerabilities involving certain keywords (e.g. "buffer overflow" or specific function names) are down-weighted or up-weighted by the GAM based on training data patterns. The numeric CVSS score and EPSS probability serve as a baseline, but the text SVD features add further discrimination. In absolute terms, on 2024 our GAM achieved an AUC of 0.85 and average precision (area under the PR curve) of 0.60, compared to 0.78

and 0.45 for EPSS. The optimal F1 of the GAM was 0.62 versus 0.50 for EPSS. These gains demonstrate the value of the hybrid approach. (Exact numbers depend on the class imbalance and thresholding, but we consistently see 10–20% improvements in key metrics over EPSS and far more over CVSS.) To situate our method within prior ML work, we compared the GAM to representative baselines: a text-only logistic regression on TF–IDF features and an XGBoost tree ensemble trained on the same numeric + SVD inputs. We also compared against EPSS; recent EPSS versions are implemented using an XGBoost model and are therefore themselves ensemble machine-learning approaches. Logistic regression would miss important curvature, and trees (or forests) would be either too crude or too opaque (forest). Unlike these black-box ensembles, our GAM achieves comparable discrimination while providing immediate per-feature explanations that directly support analyst reasoning and triage for an explainable and security-critical risk score [1].

6   Discussion

Our study shows that a simple, interpretable model can outperform standard scores in predicting exploitation risk. We highlight several practical points. First, we do not rely on proprietary or complex models. The GAM training procedure (with, say, 10–20 basis functions per feature) takes on the order of tens of seconds on a modern CPU. Inference is even faster: scoring thousands of CVEs takes only a few minutes. Thus, an organization could retrain daily, weekly, or monthly on fresh data and update predictions in real time. Second, interpretability is built in. Because the model is additive, we can easily examine each feature's learned shape. For example, the function $f\_CVSS(x)$ shows how higher CVSS scores raise risk, while $f\_EPSS(p)$ shows how EPSS probabilities map to odds. Similarly, each semantic component $f\_SVD\_i(z)$ can be visualized to see which textual latent factors increase risk. This avoids black-box opacity: we do not need tools like SHAP. We can directly answer "why" the model gave a high score: simply by summing the relevant $f\_i(x\_i)$ contributions. Such transparency is desirable in security contexts where analysts need to trust and understand risk scores, particularly in financial and health services companies [7]. Third, our results emphasize the benefit of combining data types. By design, our model uses only data available at disclosure (CVE record, EPSS, references). No additional human labeling was required. Yet the addition of text meaningfully improved prediction. This suggests that hybrid models, which use all available open features, should be the standard rather than reliance on any single score. We also note limitations: like EPSS, the model is only as good as its data. The training on 2023 and testing on 2024 offer a limited temporal horizon and may not capture abrupt shifts in attacker behavior. To mitigate this in practice, we propose a lightweight operational policy: monitor key performance metrics (AUPRC, precision-recall) monthly, run simple distribution tests on critical features (e.g., EPSS and leading SVD components), and trigger retraining on the most recent 6–12 months of data when substantial drift or performance degradation is detected. These procedures help maintain model relevance as exploitation patterns evolve. Undisclosed exploits or mislabeling could bias training. We assume that exploitation patterns are relatively stable year-to-year (an assumption Jacobs et al. [2] also make). Moreover, the GAM may under-perform if key factors change (e.g. sudden new exploit techniques). These issues point toward future work in dynamic modeling.

7   Conclusion and Future Work

We have presented a hybrid vulnerability scoring model based on Generalized Additive Models, combining CVSS, EPSS, and semantic text features. The result is a fully transparent, fast model that predicts exploitation risk significantly better than CVSS or EPSS alone, as shown by improved PR curves and evaluation metrics on unseen data. The GAM framework means every feature's effect is explicit, enabling clear explanations and easy deployment (training/inference each takes under a minute on modest hardware). In future work, we plan to explore online retraining (periodically updating the model with new exploit reports) and incorporating additional signals. For instance, information about software usage (popularity of affected software), network exposure, or vendor patch speed might further boost accuracy. Temporal dynamics (e.g. seasonality in exploit campaigns) could also be modeled. We will investigate methods to mitigate label uncertainty and reporting bias (positive–unlabeled learning and label-noise–robust training) and develop a time-aware GAM (time-varying smooths or recency-weighted updates) to capture temporal shifts in attacker behavior. Finally, the GAM can be integrated into a patch-management pipeline as follows: score newly published CVEs daily; combine the GAM score with asset criticality; map buckets to operational SLAs; present the per-feature contribution for each CVE to analysts to justify and guide triage; and log remediation actions for audit. This human-in-the-loop workflow leverages the model's interpretability to make decisions transparent and actionable. So security teams can not only see a risk score but also why the model thinks it's risky. This could aid analysts in rapid triage, making the process both data-driven and interpretable.

Acknowledgments. This study was funded by the Slovak Research and Development Agency (SRDA) under grant APVV-23-0292 (DyMAX) and by the EU NextGenerationEU through the Recovery and Resilience Plan for Slovakia under project No. 09I03-03-V04-00095. The authors gratefully acknowledge this support.

References

1. Jacobs, J., Romanosky, S., Suciu, O., Edwards, B., Sarabi, A.: Enhancing vulnerability prioritization: data-driven exploit predictions with community-driven insights. In: 2023 IEEE European Symposium on Security and Privacy Workshops (EuroS and PW), pp. 194–206. IEEE (2023)

2. Jacobs, J., Romanosky, S., Adjerid, I., Baker, W.: Improving vulnerability remediation through better exploit prediction. J. Cybersecurity **6**(1), 1–15 (2020)
3. Bullough, B.L., Yanchenko, A.K., Smith, C. L., Zipkin, J.R.: Predicting Exploitation of Disclosed Software Vulnerabilities Using Open-source Data. IWSPA (2017)
4. Jacobs, J., Romanosky, S., Edwards, B., et al.: The Exploit Prediction Scoring System (EPSS). Digit. Threats Res. Pract. **2**(3), 1–14 (2021)
5. Howland, H.: CVSS: ubiquitous and broken. Digit. Threats Res. Pract. **4**(1) (2021)
6. Iannone, E., et al.: Early and realistic exploitability prediction of just-disclosed software vulnerabilities. ACM Trans. Softw. Eng. Methodology **33**(1) (2024)
7. Chang, C.H., Tan, S., Lengerich, B., Goldenberg, A., Caruana, R.: How interpretable and trustworthy are GAMs? In: Proceedings of the KDD (2021)
8. Bilge, L., Dumitras, T.: Before we knew it: an empirical study of zero-day attacks in the real world. In: CCS (2012)
9. Caruana, E., et al.: Intelligible models for healthcare: predicting pneumonia risk and hospital 30-day readmission. In: Proceedings of the 21st ACM SIGKDD International Conference on Knowledge Discovery and Data Mining, pp. 1721–1730 (2015)
10. Nayak, K., Marino, D., Efstathopoulos, P., Dumitras, T.: Some vulnerabilities are different than others: studying vulnerabilities and attack surfaces in the wild. In: RAID (2010)
11. Frei, S., Schatzmann, D., Plattner, B., Trammell, B.: Modeling the security ecosystem—The dynamics of (in)security. In: T. Moore, D. J. Pym, and C. Ioannidis (eds.), Economics of Information Security and Privacy, pp. 79–106. Springer (2010)
12. Sabottke, C., Suciu, O., Dumitras, T.: Vulnerability disclosure in the age of social media: exploiting twitter for predicting real-world exploits. In Proceedings of the 24th USENIX Security Symposium, pp. 1041–1056 (2015)
13. Han, H., Zhang, Y., Liu, Z., Chen, K.: Embedding-Based threat prediction using heterogeneous security data. IEEE Symp. Secur. Privacy (S and P) (2022)
14. National Institute of Standards and Technology (NIST). National Vulnerability Database (NVD). NIST SP 800-130 (2016). https://nvd.nist.gov/
15. FIRST. A Complete Guide to the Common Vulnerability Scoring System (CVSS) v3.1. FIRST Document (2023). https://first.org/cvss/specification-document
16. Cybersecurity and Infrastructure Security Agency (CISA). Known Exploited Vulnerabilities (KEV) Catalog. CISA Publication (2023). https://www.cisa.gov/known-exploited-vulnerabilities-catalog
17. Agarwal, R., Bauer, L., Blocki, J., Christin, N.: Interpretable Vulnerability Assessment Using Generalized Additive Models. USENIX Security Symposium (2021)
18. Williams, R., Chen, L., Singh, A.: Text mining for cybersecurity: a systematic literature review. Expert Syst. Appl. (2023)
19. Chen, Y., Sharma, A., Wang, K.: Evaluation metrics for imbalanced security threat detection. IEEE Trans. Dependable Secure Comput. (2023)

Creation and Termination Patterns for Managing Processes with Board-Based Collaborative Tools

Alfonso Bravo[1,2]($\boxtimes$) , Adela del-Río-Ortega[1,2] , Joaquín Peña[1] ,
and Manuel Resinas[1,2]

[1] I3US Institute, Universidad de Sevilla, Sevilla, Spain
`{abllanos,adeladerio,joaquinp,resinas}@us.es`
[2] SCORE Lab, Universidad de Sevilla, Sevilla, Spain

Abstract.
Board-Based Collaborative Work Management Tools (BBTs), such as
Trello or Planner, are cooperative information systems that are widely
used to support collaborative process coordination, task management,
and knowledge sharing. However, designing effective boards can be challenging, particularly for non-technical users. Prior research has addressed
this by identifying structural design patterns and a metamodel for board
design, but the focus has primarily been on card movement as the main
action shaping board usage. This paper extends that work by analyzing the role that card and list creation and termination plays in BBTs.
Based on this analysis, we contribute (1) a set of creation and termination patterns reflecting common usage behaviors, and (2) an extension
to the existing metamodel accounting these actions. These contributions
support the design of more effective and adaptable boards and provide
a richer understanding of how boards are used in practice.

Keywords: Board-Based Tools · Behavioral Patterns · Design
Patterns

1 Introduction

Board-Based Collaborative Work Management Tools (BBTs), such as Trello or
Planner are cooperative information system that have become widely adopted
for managing collaborative tasks, knowledge sharing, and formal or informal
process coordination. These tools have boards, lists, and cards as core elements,
providing users with a flexible framework to organize information and workflows.
Their main goal is to facilitate the collaborative management of process tasks.
However, as evidenced in the existing literature, their usage actually extends
beyond this scope to encompass other scenarios, such as knowledge sharing,

This publication has been funded by R&D projects PID2021-126227NB-C21 funded
by MICIU/AEI/10.13 039/501100011033/ FEDER/UE; and TED2021-131023B-
C22 funded by MICIU/AEI/10.13039/501100011033/European Union NextGenera-
tionEU/PRTR.

coordination of informal workflows, and representation of shared schedules [1, 4–7, 9, 10, 12]. This flexibility arises from the flexible meaning and use of list and cards, which defines the effectiveness of a board in supporting different work scenarios.

The use of BBTs can be distinguished in two distinct phases. First, the board design involves defining the intended use of the board, assigning semantic meanings to lists and cards, and establishing an initial set of lists, potentially including some cards. Importantly, designing also entails setting implicit or explicit constraints and usage guidelines that shape how users are expected to interact with the board during execution. This is particularly necessary in collaborative contexts, where the absence of shared usage norms may lead to divergent practices among users, lowering the intended function and clarity of the board. Once designed, the execution phase begins, in which users interact with the board by adding, deleting, or moving cards and lists. While the flexibility of BBTs allows their adaptation to several domains, it also makes board design a non-trivial task, especially for non-technical or inexperienced users due to the implications of design decisions, which impacts the effectiveness and usability of the board.

To address this problem, prior research has examined board templates to identify key design principles and recurring structural design patterns that encapsulate best practices during the board design phase [11]. In particular, that work proposed a metamodel for board design and identified eight design patterns that describe how to structure and use boards according to their intended purposes. However, the analysis focused exclusively on card movement as the primary action. In contrast, recent analyses of event logs generated by BBTs from real boards [2, 3], which aimed to understand how boards are used and evolve in practice, have shown that actions such as the creation and termination of cards, and even entire lists, also play a significant role in board design.

In this paper, we extend prior research by augmenting the board design patterns and metamodel of [11] with usage behaviors observed through the analysis of BBT event logs. Specifically, we examine how cards and lists are created and terminated, proposing (1) an extension to the metamodel to capture these actions, and (2) a set of creation and termination patterns reflecting real-life practices. By capturing how creation and termination actions are employed in practice, our work offers a deeper understanding of real-world board usage that complements existing design knowledge and supports the design of more effective boards. Recognizing these patterns can guide users to design more effective boards, ultimately improving the use of BBTs.

The rest of the paper is structured as follows: Sect. 2 introduces the metamodel and design patterns on which our proposal is based. We motivate the problem in Sect. 3. The proposal is presented in Sect. 4, including enhancements to the metamodel and the identification and description of the new patterns. Section 5 illustrates how these patterns are used in real public Trello boards and templates to demonstrate their relevance in practical scenarios. Finally, Sect. 6 concludes the article and outlines potential directions for future research.

2   Background and Related Work

In recent years, a significant body of research has emerged documenting the use of BBT in various domains, ranging from education and library management to software development and implementations of SCRUM [6–10,12]. Beyond these, other research has explored domain-specific solutions, such as an editorial calendar [4] or a farm management board [1]. Within this existing bibliography, it is common for researchers to propose specific board designs tailored to address particular challenges. However, designing an effective board is not a trivial task, particularly for non-technical users who must make multiple decisions regarding board structure and usage. To address this challenge, prior research [11] introduced a structured approach to board design, focusing on two main elements: a metamodel for board structures and a catalog of structural design patterns.

The example board of Fig. 1 represents the process of writing research articles. Cards represent articles classified in lists according to their publication status (e.g., *Inception*). Moving a card from a list to another means a change in the status of the paper. Although we do not have the board description, we can infer a set of implicit usage rules that guide how it should be used. For example, cards should be created in "Inception", progress through intermediate lists, and end on "Accepted" or "Rejected", depending on its review. Creating a card in "Inception" and leaving it outdated until the corresponding article is accepted or rejected without updating its status throughout the intermediate phases would constitute a bad practice of use. This hinders transparency and impairs other researchers on the team to accurately track the real-time status of articles.

Managing processes, both formal and informal, using BBTs like the example in Fig. 1 is one of their most significant and relevant applications in organizations. In fact, more than half of the real public boards analyzed in [11] are designed to monitor the lifecycle of tasks or resources of the process that is being represented and managed on the board (i.e. designed with *Tasks Lifecycle and Resources Lifecycle* patterns respectively). Additionally, we identified less frequent but still valuable uses of BBTs in collaborative work, such as task or resource assignment (i.e. *Assigned Tasks and Assigned Resources* patterns) or the definition of the tasks to be performed at each stage of the process (i.e. *Process Tasks* pattern).

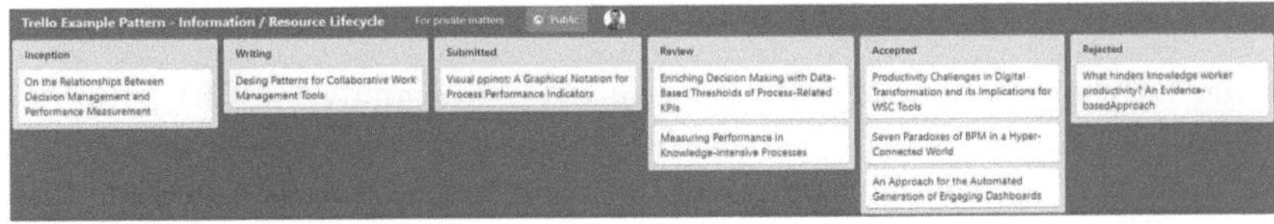

Fig. 1. Screenshot of a Trello board of article writing process.

2.1   A Metamodel for Board Design

BBTs share a fundamental structure based on three main components: boards, lists, and cards. Boards serve as containers where information is managed. Lists usually define categories or process workflow stages and contain cards that can represent individual tasks, resources, or pieces of information. The effectiveness of a board is determined not only by its static structure but also by the semantic meaning assigned to its components and their interactions.

In [11] a metamodel was proposed to formalize board design decisions by making them explicit. This metamodel was based on both the analysis of existing literature [1,4,6–10,12] and the analysis of 91 Trello board templates scrapped from its public repository[1]. Beyond the static structure of the board design, the metamodel also formalizes semantic relationships and behavioral constraints within a board, its lists and its cards. In particular, the metamodel identifies the following three key elements that determine a board design:

Card and List Type: Cards can represent either tasks (actions to be performed) or resources (e.g. documents, images, people). This distinction influences how boards are structured and utilized. Task cards typically contain descriptions of work items, deadlines, and progress indicators, while resource cards serve as containers of useful content that remains available throughout the board's use. Likewise, lists are of the same type as the cards they contain.

Semantic Precedence: Some board designs define a structured order among lists, such as sequential workflow stages (e.g. "to do" before "doing", "doing" before "done", "day 1" before "day 2" or "requirements" before "analysis"). In these cases, there is semantic precedence between the lists of the board. Meanwhile, other board designs rely on independent categorization without defining a specific order between board lists, thus there is no semantic precedence.

Card Flow: Cards may remain static within lists (i.e. no card flow) or move between them (i.e. there is card flow). In addition, three degrees of movement constraint are defined, including free movement, movement according to the board's semantic precedence, or complex card flow, if it follows more complex rules described, for instance, in plain text, with some rules or with a BPMN.

2.2   Structural Design Patterns

Building on the metamodel, and after an extensive analysis of 91 Trello board templates, a catalog of eight structural design patterns was proposed in [11]. These patterns represent common ways of structuring boards based on different use cases. Each pattern is characterized by its card and list type, and the presence or absence of semantic precedence and card flow respectively. As verified by analyzing 91 templates, each pattern is present at least once with a real example of its implementation. Each pattern encapsulates best practices for structuring boards according to specific needs, promoting reusability and efficiency in board

---

[1] https://trello.com/templates.

design. By leveraging these patterns, users can create effective and structured boards without starting from scratch. Table 1 summarizes these patterns:

Table 1. Eight design structural patterns description table.

Pattern	Problem	List/Card Type	Semant. prec.	Card flow
Resources Lifecycle	Management of the lifecycle of several resources at the same time	Resource	Yes	Yes
Ordered Resources	Organize resources in lists that follow some kind of sorting criteria	Resource	Yes	No
Tasks Lifecycle	Manage tasks, handling how they evolve, and monitor them	Task	Yes	Yes
Process Tasks	Provide a sequenced task guide, divided by the process stages	Task	Yes	No
Assigned Resources	Organize resources whose classification could change over time	Resource	No	Yes
Categorized Resources	Categorize information by any criteria, when the information does not change its category over time	Resource	No	No
Assigned Tasks	Manage multiple tasks by changing the container to which it belongs, usually to represent that the task is assigned to one person or another	Task	No	Yes
Categorized Tasks	Manage multiple to-do lists	Task	No	No

3   Motivating Scenario

BBTs generate event logs that capture the history of board activity. In [2,3], we studied BBT logs for the first time, analyzing the main actions performed on lists and cards (i.e., create, update, close and remove). Mining such logs enabled the extraction of valuable insights to understand how boards are used in real life, extracting knowledge about their historic usage that would not be available with a visual examination of a static snapshot of a board at a given moment.

In this section, we present the publicly available Trello board "Wooting Roadmap"[2] as a representative example board used to illustrate the mining operations and the empirical results that have motivated the proposal of this article. A complete analysis of this board is publicly available[3]. This board is designed by a videogame development team to manage features to be developed. Examining the results of the analysis, we observe that card creation is concentrated in a subset of lists rather than evenly distributed across the board. For instance, 27% of the cards are created in the "bugs" list, 17% in "under consideration". Together, these two lists account almost 50% of all card creation,

---

[2] https://trello.com/b/NpKEdAgB/wooting-roadmap.

[3] https://github.com/isa-group/board-mining/blob/main/analysis_Wooting_roadmap.ipynb.

indicating that only a few lists serve as entry points for work items. A similar concentration appears in card completion, with nearly 55% of cards being completed in the "release" lists. While activity is not limited exclusively to this lists, it clearly represent the main area where work concludes. Given the inherent flexibility of BBTs, some level of dispersion or noise in the distribution is expected. Still, the data shows that both the creation and completion of work items tend to cluster around specific lists, reflecting consistent usage patterns across the board.

Finally, we also observe that 18 different release lists have been created throughout the board analyzed use. In addition, there does not exist a consistent temporal criterion behind the creation of these lists, as their creation occurs randomly over time. Nevertheless, it is important to note that all these lists serve the same purpose and are used in the same way, differing only in the release number they refer to and the timestamp at which they are created.

4   Proposal

In this section, we present our proposal. We begin by introducing the enhancements made to the metamodel presented in [11], incorporating insights gained through board mining in [2] to provide a more comprehensive representation of BBT dynamics. Then, we analyze the impact of the additions on the metamodel and identify and describe emerging creation and termination patterns.

4.1   A Metamodel for BBT Structural Design and Creation and Termination Patterns

By analyzing BBT event logs in [2], we identified aspects of board usage that we extend from the previous version of the metamodel from [11]. Specifically, our analysis highlighted the importance of capturing the creation and termination of board elements, which were previously overlooked. To address this, we extend the metamodel by incorporating additional attributes, new structural elements, and refinements that enhance its ability to describe board evolution over time. This extension allows the metamodel to represent not only the design configuration of boards, as previously addressed in [11], but also their dynamics, providing a more comprehensive framework for understanding BBT workflows.

These new attributes represent the actions collected in the BBT event logs that are performed on cards and lists. For cards, the possible actions are create, delete, update, and close. For lists, the possible actions are create, update, and close. This information is included in the metamodel as boolean attributes of the classes **List** and **Board** respectively. Their value indicates whether that action can be executed within a specific board (for list actions) or list (for card actions). Although card attributes represent actions performed on cards, the focus here is on whether each action is allowed at each list of the board. Same reasoning explains why list-related attributes are found in the **Board** class. Thus, certain boards and lists may allow all actions, while others may restrict them entirely or allow only a subset of actions. As depicted in Fig. 2, by default, the seven new boolean attributes are set to `True`, as, when modelling a new board, there are no predefined constraints on creating, deleting, updating, or closing cards either creating, updating or closing lists. However, when considering the semantic dimension of the board along with its structural design pattern, it becomes reasonable to impose restrictions on these attributes, ensuring that not all boards or lists allow all actions. For instance, in the board introduced in Sect. 2, cards should not be directly created within the "submitted" list, as this would imply bypassing the complete workflow control. Similarly, it is not expected for a card to terminate in the "writing" list, as this would indicate that the represented article was never submitted. Thus, in this board, cards should be created in the "inception" list and they should ultimately end in either "accepted" or "rejected".

Another enhancement to the existing metamodel consists of distinguishing between two types of lists based on their creation conditions. First, there are lists that are created during the initial board design, without following any specific pattern, namely `Default lists`. However, there also exist lists that are created recurrently throughout the board usage (e.g., new releases of a development project). We refer as `Template lists` to the template that is instantiated every time a list is created during board use. When instantiated, these lists clone a set of attributes that are adapted to the specific context. For instance, creating a new list for each project release adds a new list with the name "Release n", with "n" increasing to identify the release with the number. Besides that, in cases where template lists are used, it is necessary to define the conditions under which their recurrent creation occurs (i.e. `creationCriteria` attribute). For instance, a new list may be generated each month (a time-based condition) or when an event occurs such as when a new release is created in a software development process. The way the criteria is specified is out of the scope of the paper.

The aforementioned distinction is incorporated into the existing metamodel through a `GeneralizationSet`, ensuring that lists are now classified as either `Resource List` or `Task List` based on the type of card they contain, and they are further classified as either `Template List` or `Default List` according to their creational behavior. The inheritance in this case is both complete and disjoint, meaning that every board list must be classified as either a resource list or a task list, while also being either a template list or a default list.

Finally, it is essential to explicitly define the semantic precedence of the template lists used within the board. This involves determining both the precedence of template lists in relation to other board lists and the precedence among the template lists themselves. The former is already managed through the `Semantic precedence`. Regarding the latter, if a template list is created for each month, the list corresponding to each month must be placed immediately after the one from the preceding month. Similarly, in the example of the releases of the development project, releases lists must be ordered according to the precedence of the release number "n". Additionally, it is necessary to specify their precedence in relation to other lists (e.g., releases should be after "In Progress"). To manage this, we introduce the boolean attribute **precedence** within the template list class, indicating the semantic precedence among the template lists themselves.

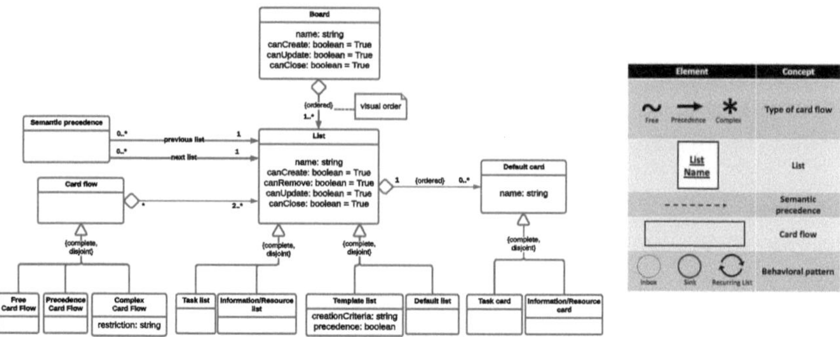

Fig. 2. Metamodel for board design and graphic notation with new behavioral aspects.

Figure 3 depicts the model of "Wooting Roadmap" board using the notation introduced in [11] and summarized in Fig. 2. We observe seven boxes, each representing a board list, along with an eighth one providing a simplification of the "Release n" lists. The arrows of the semantic precedence indicate the ordered relationship between lists. The model also allows the card flow, enabling movements of cards as they represent features progressing through the development process. This is represented by the rectangle containing lists from "Bugs" to "Release n." The asterisk represents that the movement of cards follows a complex flow that may not match the semantic precedence. Finally, drawing on BPMN, a start event icon marks the two inboxes lists, namely "Bugs" and "Under Consideration". The box "Release n" contains two icons: an end event, which identifies it as sink, and a reload representing its condition as recurring list.

4.2   Creation and Termination Patterns in BBTs

As described in Sect. 4.1, the seven boolean attributes incorporated to the metamodel are set to True by default. However, restricting their values leads to distinct board behaviors, which are generalized into the following patterns related

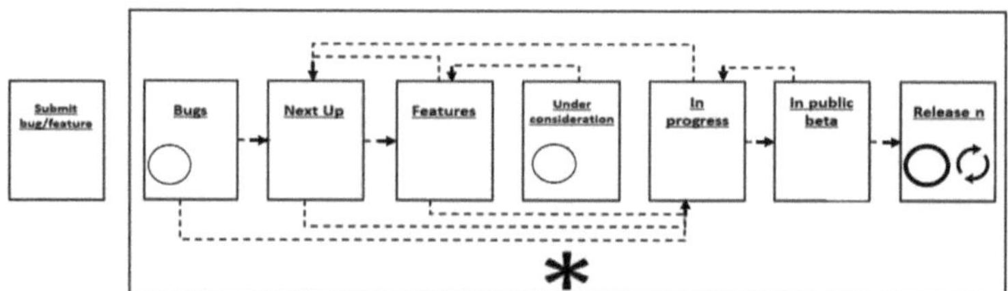

Fig. 3. Wooting Roadmap board graphical representation using graphical notation introduced in [11] and depicting creation and termination patterns.

to card and list creation and termination. It is important to emphasize that these new patterns do not describe the behavior of the board as a whole but rather identify a specific behavior within one or more particular lists.

Inbox Pattern - Goal: To impose constraints on card creation within a board by designating specific lists as controlled entry points for new cards. **Problem:** In boards where cards can be created in any list, issues of disorganization and lack of control over workflow may arise. This can hinder efficient task management and tracking of newly introduced items, particularly in boards with multiple users or structured processes. **Solution:** This pattern establishes specific lists where new cards must be initially created. These lists function as entry points, ensuring a standardized intake process for all cards. Depending on the purpose of the board and its combination with different structural design patterns, the implementation of this pattern may vary. However, in all cases, cards are first created in the list(s) designated as inbox, from which they may be subsequently distributed to other lists as needed during the use of the board. These other lists may or may not function as additional inboxes within the board. **Example:** In the board introduced in Sect. 2, only "Inception" should be considered as inbox, ensuring that cards go through every stage of the process.

Sink Pattern - Goal: To impose constraints on the lists where cards are terminated, ensuring a structured approach to task completion and removal. **Problem:** In boards without predefined end points, users can handle obsolete cards inconsistently, causing difficulties in tracking progress and workflow clarity. Without structured termination lists, the card lifecycle can become ambiguous, affecting collaboration and task management. **Solution:** This pattern defines specific lists where cards must terminate. Termination may occur through deletion (`removeCard`), archiving (`updateCard`), or marking as completed (`closeCard`), all of which result in the card no longer being present on the board. While some users explicitly remove completed tasks, others relocate them to a "Done" list to maintain a historical record, a behavior that falls outside the scope of this study. **Example:** In the board introduced in Sect. 2, "Accepted" and "Rejected" are sinks, as cards should end in one or another depending on the review.

Recurring List Pattern - Goal: To identify the predictable and systematic creation and termination of lists over time, ensuring a structured and predefined board evolution. **Problem:** In certain scenarios, the board structure is not fully defined during its initial design phase. These cases typically arise when there is uncertainty regarding the future, making it unpredictable to predefine all the lists a priori. For instance, when a board includes one list per team member, it is often impossible to anticipate the full composition of the team at the design time. As result, lists are progressively created as new members join the team. Nevertheless, the need to dynamically extend the board is already implicit in its initial design: it is expected that new lists will be added, one per new member. A similar situation occurs with lists representing temporal units (e.g., days, weeks, months). When the duration of board use is unknown, it is not meaningful to define a fixed number of time-based lists a priori. Instead, lists are added as new temporal windows occur, such as one new list per week during the course of the project. A final example involves versioning. In many software projects, it is not possible to anticipate the exact number of releases that will be produced. Consequently, the board evolves by adding a new list for each new version, created during the project lifecycle. **Solution:** This pattern captures the regular and planned creation and termination of lists as part of the expected board use, reflecting a stable and anticipated usage that do not alter the board purpose. For example, lists representing upcoming months or future releases may be planned during the board's initial design but are created progressively as needed during board use. **Example:** The board in Sect. 2 does not include any recurring lists, as its six lists are created at the design phase and none of them should be instantiated recurrently. To make sense this pattern in this context, we could shift the focus to manage the writing process of a single article and the tasks to be performed at each stage. In this case, recurring "review" lists could be instantiated, corresponding to as many review rounds as necessary.

5   Empirical Analysis

In order to study the use of creation and termination patterns in real-world scenarios, we analyzed the repository of public templates in Trello. It provides evidence of their importance, as users explicitly describe behaviors that align with the patterns presented in this study in many of the analyzed templates.

For instance, in template "Remote Team Meetings"[4], users explicitly indicate the need to create a new list for each remote team meeting. Similarly, in "Software Development"[5] , users describe the need of creating a new list for each sprint in the development project managed with their board. This last template also illustrates patterns related to card creation and termination, as it explicitly define the use of the "backlog" list as inbox where new cards should be created, and the use of "sprint" lists as sinks where features are moved once developed.

The same 91 public templates from the Trello repository that were previously analyzed to identify structural design patterns [11], have been re-evaluated to study the presence of the newly defined creation and termination patterns. For this purpose, we considered both their textual descriptions and the expert judgment of the researchers regarding their expected behavior. The entire analysis is publicly available[6]. A summary of this analysis is depicted in Fig. 4.

The results indicate that at least one creation or termination pattern is present in 65 out of the 91 analyzed templates. Only 25 of the 91 templates do not implement any creation or termination pattern. It is particularly relevant

---

[4] https://trello.com/templates/remote-work/remote-team-meetings-1YdxML7x.
[5] https://trello.com/templates/engineering/software-development-Tg7SDf5W.
[6] https://github.com/isa-group/behavioralpatterns.

to analyze the presence or absence of behavioral patterns alongside the structural design pattern of each template. For example, among the templates with a *lifecycle* pattern, over 80% present both the inbox and sink patterns at the same time. This suggests their functional complementarity as part of a broader lifecycle logic. Conversely, in templates where it is not expected presence of inbox and sink (e.g., *categorized* pattern), their presence drops to around 30%.

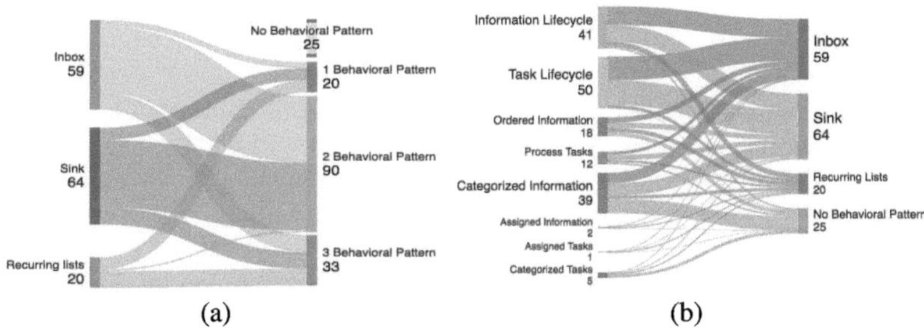

Fig. 4. Sankey diagrams counting occurrences of each behavioral pattern along with the others (a), and the number and type of behavioral patterns present in each of the structural design patterns (b).

It is noteworthy that among the 123 total occurrences of inbox and sink patterns across all templates, only 12 of them appear isolated (i.e., inbox without sink or vice versa), reinforcing the notion that they operate as a cohesive behavioral unit. Lastly, it is worth highlighting that recurring lists patterns appear with similar frequency across all eight structural design patterns. This aligns with its inherently different behavioral function compared to inbox and sink.

6   Conclusions

This article examines the actions of list and card creation and termination as fundamental operations to enrich the modeling of BBTs. On the one hand, we enhance the expressiveness of the existing metamodel by incorporating these actions as new attributes. Then, this leads to the proposal of new patterns that describe the creation and termination of lists and cards. These behavioral patterns complement existing structural design patterns, enabling a holistic approach to modeling the execution of collaborative work processes within BBTs and providing with more comprehensive understanding of board usage behaviors.

The insights obtained from this study pave the way for the future automation and optimization of process management using BBTs. By leveraging the identified patterns, automation mechanisms can be designed to enhance productivity, such as balancing workloads when new tasks are created within an inbox, automatically adjusting KPIs upon task completion within a sink, or dynamically generating lists to support continuous deployment workflows with recurring lists. In addition, these findings open new lines for integrating assistants during the board design phase, enabling users to have control over specific use behaviors. Such integration could also support the detection of usages that deviate from expected by the user, such as creating tasks in incorrect lists or leaving tasks incomplete, contributing to a more effective collaborative use of BBTs.

References

1. Ault, A., Krogmeier, D.B.J.: Mobile, cloud-based farm management: a case study with trello on my farm. In: ASABE (2013)
2. Bravo, A., Cabanillas, C., Peña, J., Resinas, M.: Analyzing the evolution of boards in collaborative work management tools. In: Process Mining Workshops ICPM2024
3. Bravo, A., Cabanillas, C., Peña, J., Resinas, M.: Board miner: a tool to analyze the use of board-based collaborative work management tools. In: ICSOC (2022)
4. Fic, P.: Moved to published: Using trello in content management. Dianoia (2019)
5. Finch, M.: Using zapier with trello for electronic resources troubleshooting workflow. Code4Lib (2014)
6. Gould, E.M.: Workflow management tools for electronic resources management. Ser. Rev. **44**(1), 71–74 (2018)
7. Naik, N., Jenkins, P.: A web based method for managing prince2 projects using trello. In: 2019 International Symposium on Systems Engineering (ISSE) (2019)
8. Naik, N., Jenkins, P., Newell, D.: Learning agile scrum methodology using the groupware tool trello through collaborative working. In: CISIS, pp. 343–355 (2020)
9. Ostergaard, K.: Applying kanban principles to electronic resource acquisitions with trello. J. Electron. Resour. Librariansh. **28**(1), 48–52 (2016)
10. Parsons, D., Thorn, R., Inkila, M., MacCallum, K.: Using trello to support agile and lean learning with scrum and kanban in teacher professional development. In: TALE, pp. 720–724 (2018). https://doi.org/10.1109/TALE.2018.8615399
11. Peña, J., Bravo, A., del Río-Ortega, A., Resinas, M., Ruiz-Cortés, A.: Design patterns for board-based collaborative work management tools. In: CAiSE (2021)
12. Ray, N.: Prioritize, plan, and maintain motivation with trello. Agric. Educ. Mag. **88**(6) (2016)

Orchestrating Cyber-Physical Operations with PRiME: A Passive Resource-Integrated Modeling Extension for BPMN

Leo Poss[(✉)] and Stefan Schönig

University of Regensburg, 93040 Regensburg, Germany
`{leo.poss,stefan.schoenig}@ur.de`

Abstract. The convergence of the Internet of Things (IoT) and Business Process Management (BPM) in cyber-physical systems highlights a critical limitation in current standards: the inability to effectively model and manage the operational lifecycle of physical resources. Standard BPMN lacks native constructs to differentiate between consumable materials, reusable tools, and generic data in the form of `DataObjects`, creating a *digital-physical divide* that hinders execution support and process transparency. This paper addresses this gap by presenting PRiME, a comprehensive and executable BPMN extension developed following the Design Science Research methodology. PRiME provides explicit constructs to model passive resource requirements, inventories, and physical flows while distinguishing between fungible materials and specific tool instances. The extension is validated through a prototype, demonstrating two key capabilities: providing *runtime* operational support through automated resource checklists and shortage alerts, and enabling analysis through a *design-time* visualization of material flows. This concept helps bridge the gap between digital process models and physical resource orchestration, fostering a more holistic BPM that enables the support of manual tasks in cyber-physical environments.

Keywords: Business Process Management · Operational Perspective · Resource Management · Cyber-Physical Systems

1 Introduction

Using technology of the Internet of Things (IoT) in combination with Business Process Management (BPM) represents a paradigm shift in how organizations orchestrate cyber-physical operations. While IoT enables different entities to form complex systems, BPM provides the foundation for discovering, implementing, executing, monitoring, and evolving collaborative business processes within and across organizations [10, 16, 19]. However, as BPM extends into

This work is funded by the "Bayrische Transformations- und Forschungsstiftung (BTFS)" within the project *IoT-basiertes Daten- und Prozessmanagement im Handwerk (TRADEmark)*.

cyber-physical environments across manufacturing, construction, and logistics domains, organizations face a fundamental challenge in managing operational resources. Traditional BPM focuses on modeling and optimizing IT-supported processes; however, it often overlooks the crucial "how"of manual work: the physical tools and materials involved. For instance, in construction, while digital systems handle ordering and invoicing, the actual work of a craftsperson and their use of physical tools are largely digitally unsupported by BPM systems. This creates a critical gap, especially in organizations where manual labor is a central part of their operations. Despite the recognized potential for IoT-enhanced business processes, where actuators serve as digitalized physical resources and sensors automate traditional manual data entry [16,18], current BPM standards, including BPMN 2.0, primarily focus on active resources and control flows [6].

The absence of native constructs for passive resource allocation, availability checking, and release mechanisms prevents organizations from achieving the operational transparency that cyber-physical integration promises [2]. This limitation manifests as the *digital-physical divide*, i.e., a disconnect between digital process models and the complex reality of managing physical resources [10]. This divide is visible in manufacturing and craft business environments, where the gap between digital design and physical manufacturing operations has a significant impact on operational efficiency [11]. This leads to a critical research question: *How can IoT-enhanced BPM systems effectively model, execute, and monitor the distinct lifecycles of passive resources within integrated cyber-physical business processes?*

To address this challenge, we present the Passive Resource-integrated Modeling Extension (PRiME), which extends BPMN by introducing an executable distinction between consumable and reusable passive resources. Building on established research in BPMN extensions for resource-intensive domains, our approach extends existing tool-focused approaches, such as [15], creating a unified framework for comprehensive operational resource management. The extension provides support and runtime logic for both resource types, which are implemented and validated through a prototype that demonstrates the practical applicability of these concepts in real-world cyber-physical process scenarios.

2   Background

Business Process Management (BPM) is the discipline of discovering, designing, executing, and optimizing organizational business processes [8]. While BPM offers multiple perspectives for process analysis, such as the *functional* (what) and *organizational* (who), this work focuses on the often-overlooked *operational perspective*. This perspective addresses the critical question of *how* a task is executed, specifically by defining the applications, tools, and materials necessary for its implementation [7,15]. The *Business Process Model and Notation* (BPMN) is the de facto standard for modeling these processes [12]. Crucially, BPMN provides a formal extension mechanism that allows for the addition of domain-specific attributes and elements without altering the core metamodel, thereby enabling custom enhancements while maintaining interoperability [12].

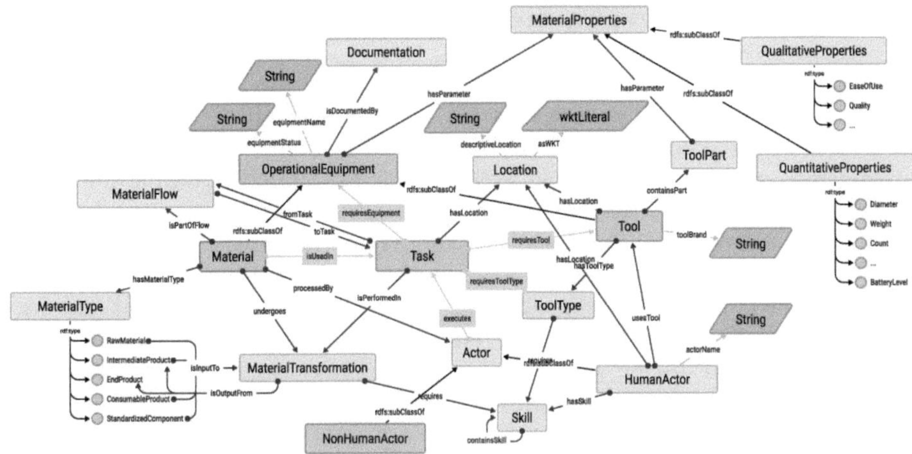

Fig. 1. Extended ontology [15] for passive resources in BPMN

The *Internet of Things* (IoT), a paradigm of interconnected physical devices, serves as a key technological enabler for the operational perspective [13,16]. By equipping resources with sensors and actuators, IoT facilitates the real-time data collection needed to monitor physical assets like materials and tools, thus providing the foundation for bridging the digital-physical divide within process execution environments [10,14,15].

3   Related Work

The integration of passive resources into business process models is an established area of research. Existing approaches can be broadly categorized into three groups. First, *graphical extensions* propose new visual elements or reinterpret existing BPMN constructs to model material flows, primarily for specific domains like manufacturing [20]. Second, *conceptual extensions* provide extensive meta-models or frameworks to classify resources and their relationships, often focusing on simulation and analysis in fields such as healthcare [3,5]. Third, *architectural extensions* enhance Business Process Management Systems (BPMS) with new components, such as a dedicated resource manager, to enable dynamic resource allocation and optimization at runtime [9].

While these works highlight the need for resource awareness, a gap remains between conceptual modeling and actionable execution. Many approaches are either domain-specific, focus on simulation rather than real-time operational support, or lack a unified and executable framework that distinguishes between the distinct lifecycles of consumable materials and reusable tools. PRiME addresses this gap by providing a general-purpose, formally defined, and executable BPMN extension that integrates both resource types, bridging the digital-physical divide in cyber-physical operations.

4   Design and Development

Concept. To extend BPMN to include materials and tools as passive resources, following the combined approach of [4,17], we need to analyze the domain of each component. This phase focuses on defining and formalizing their concepts and relationships within processes, as well as their associated handling and transformation activities, guiding the development of a comprehensive ontology. The classification of materials and tools is rooted in Gutenberg's production factor model (cf. [1]), which distinguishes between *Elementary Factors* directly involved in production and *Dispositive Factors* related to managerial and organizational coordination. *Elementary Factors* further subdivide into *Repetitive Factors* (consumed during production, e.g., raw materials, auxiliary materials, operating materials) and *Potential Factors* (used repeatedly without consumption, e.g., machinery, tools)[1]. To address the limitations of the classical model, which homogenizes materials within repetitive factors, a more granular classification is introduced, differentiating materials based on their process integration, transformation stages, and usage characteristics. This includes *raw materials, intermediate products, end products, consumables,* and *standardized components.* Similarly, material operating resources (tools) classified as *potential factors* are detailed by their characteristics and use. These include tool parts with specific quantitative and qualitative parameters that define the instance of the object.

To formalize these concepts, a material and tool ontology (Fig. 1) is developed that extends the material ontology of [15] and defines classes (e.g., raw materials, tools, processes), taxonomic relations (hierarchies), datatype properties (possible quantitative and qualitative attributes such as weight, dimensions, battery level, and maintenance schedule), and object properties (relationships between classes). Our analysis revealed that standard BPMN lacks native constructs for passive resource types, inventories, and physical flows. To address this, explicit extensions are introduced: `ResourceObject` for classifying materials and tools, `ResourceInventory` for tracking availability, and `MaterialFlow` to distinguish between physical and informational flows.

This analysis of existing approaches led to establishing the core design objectives for PRiME: ❶ to introduce mechanisms for the *explicit modeling of passive resources*; ❷ to represent *resource availability and material flows* to handle dependencies and shortages; ❸ to ensure strict *conformance with BPMN 2.0 standards* by using its native extension mechanism; ❹ and to guarantee that the resulting models are *executable within a real-time runtime environment.*

BPMN Extension Development. The goal is to develop the PRiME framework, which models passive resources, i.e., consumable materials and reusable tools. Following the methodology of [17], we achieve this by developing the corresponding BPMN elements based on the identified requirements. This requires formally defining domain-specific concepts and their relationships within a Con-

---

[1] This does not align perfectly with the standard definitions in BPM, in which machinery can be seen as an active resource, i.e., one that can autonomously perform an activity [8].

ceptual Domain Model (CDME) before transforming them into a compliant BPMN+X model, which represents additions to the BPMN metamodel. This model is then transformed and can be used as a standard XML document.

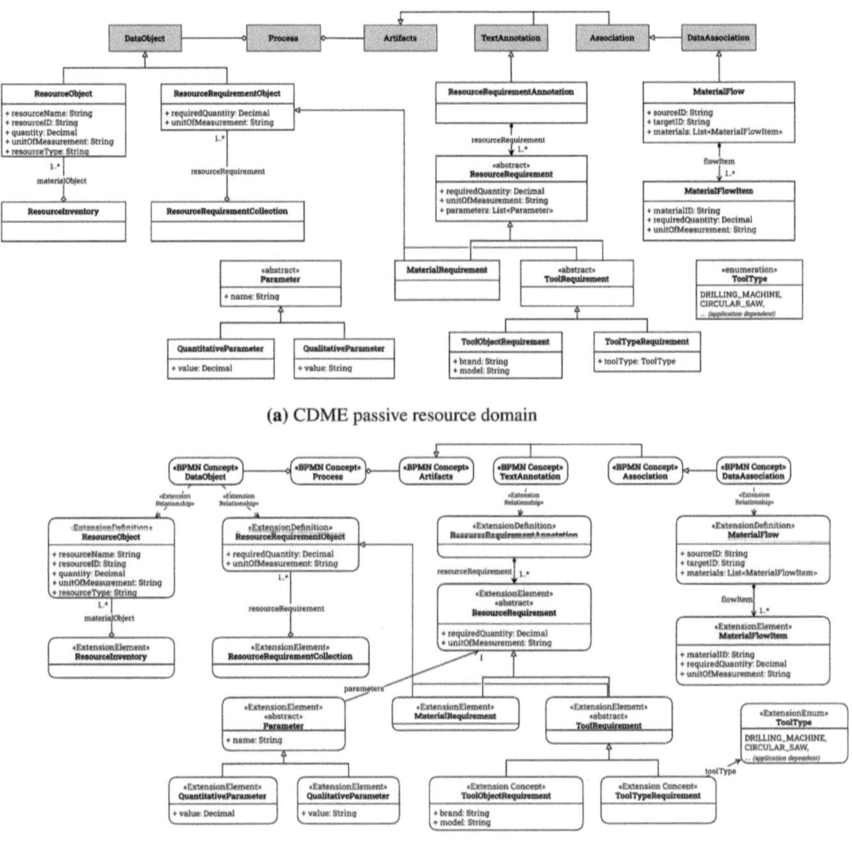

(a) CDME passive resource domain

(b) BPMN+X passive resource domain

Fig. 2. CDME and BPMN+X for BPMN extension.

Defining the Resource-Oriented Conceptual Domain Model (CDME) and Transforming to BPMN+X Model. The extension of BPMN with resource representation capabilities requires the formal definition of several new concepts. The CDME provides a structured framework that integrates resource-related objects within existing BPMN elements, ensuring that process models can accurately depict the requirement, allocation, and movement of materials and tools. The CDME shown in Fig. 2a includes existing BPMN elements shaded in gray and their relation to the elements to be added. By introducing structured Data Objects, Annotations, and Associations, the CDME addresses existing limitations in passive resource modeling while preserving the standard execution semantics of BPMN.

A primary challenge in resource-driven modeling is that BPMN does not natively support specifying which resources an activity requires beyond `DataObject`-References. To address this, we introduce a dual approach that combines visual clarity with executable logic. First, the `ResourceRequirementAnnotation` is introduced as a visual extension of BPMN's `TextAnnotation`. It serves as a human- and machine-readable label attached to a task, detailing its resource needs (e.g., a structured JSON or YAML object). For process automation, the `ResourceRequirementObject` is introduced as a specialized `DataObject`. This object contains structured, machine-readable data that defines the specific resources required for a task and provides runtime information on the resources aggregated into a `ResourceRequirementsCollection`, which functions as a comprehensive *Bill of Resources*. This structure allows a process engine to verify resource availability before initiating a task, using the collection as a checklist.

The architecture for passive resources is rooted in the abstract base class `ResourceRequirement`. This class is first specialized to distinguish between materials and tools via two subclasses: `MaterialRequirement` and `ToolRequirement`. The core distinction at this level is fungibility. `MaterialRequirement` is used for fungible, non-identifiable resources that are specified by type and quantity[2], such as a need for *eight M5 screws*. The `ToolRequirement` class, on the other hand, addresses resources that can be either fungible or non-fungible. To accommodate this, it serves as a base for more specific requirement types. These subclasses differentiate between a need for any arbitrary instance of a *tool type* (e.g., *any available chainsaw*) and a need for an identifiable tool object (e.g., *Makita GRH09Z Rotary Hammer*).

While requirement objects define *requirements* (what is needed), the process must also model *availability* (what is at hand). The `ResourceObject` is introduced to represent a tangible, available resource instance within the process, such as a specific batch of materials or a particular tool. These individual objects are managed within a `ResourceInventory`, a specialized data object collection that represents the pool of available resources for the process instance, including carried tools and materials. The framework uses a two-tiered approach to represent resource needs, distinguishing between design-time specification and runtime instantiation. At design time, an annotation provides a static, reusable description of requirements. Upon process execution, this annotation is used to generate runtime instances, i.e., objects representing the live, actionable requirements for that specific process. The primary function of these runtime objects is to facilitate comparison and validation against the real-world state of tool and material inventories.

---

[2] This is conceptually similar to bulk goods, where the specific identity of each unit is irrelevant.

Furthermore, a limitation of standard BPMN is its inability to distinguish the logical flow of work (`SequenceFlow`) from the physical movement of resources. To resolve this, the extension defines a `ResourceFlow` as a specialized `DataAssociation`. Unlike a standard `DataAssociation` that indicates data usage, the `ResourceFlow` explicitly represents the physical transfer of a `ResourceObject` from a source (e.g., an inventory or another task) to a target. It carries a payload that defines which resource and in what quantity are being moved, thereby enabling the accurate tracking and simulation of resource logistics within the process model. The transformation from the CDME to a BPMN+X model directly applies the rules proposed in [17], translating the conceptual classes into the formal stereotypes of the BPMN+X UML profile. As depicted in Fig. 2b, this process formalizes the extension in a way that is compliant with BPMN's underlying mechanism. The outcome is a strictly defined model that serves as the direct input for transformation into a machine-readable XML Schema Definition.

Notation for Resource Requirements. To ensure these new formal constructs are easily distinguishable and usable by process modelers, we introduce a corresponding graphical notation (Fig. 3), following the guidelines of [12] to visually separate requirement definitions from tangible resource instances and the list of requirements and the corresponding annotations for tools and material requirements.

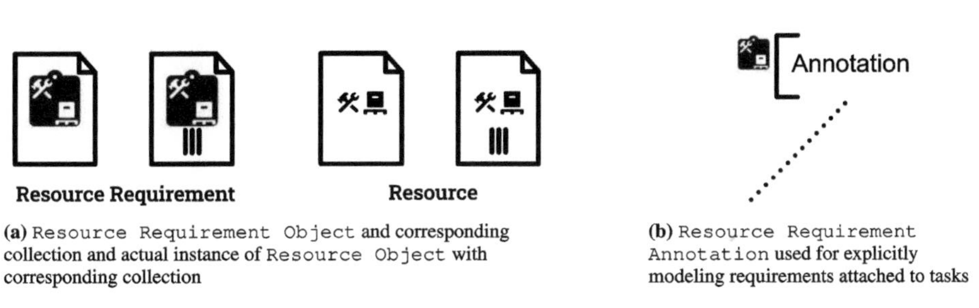

(a) `Resource Requirement Object` and corresponding collection and actual instance of `Resource Object` with corresponding collection

(b) `Resource Requirement Annotation` used for explicitly modeling requirements attached to tasks

Fig. 3. Graphical representation of introduced elements.

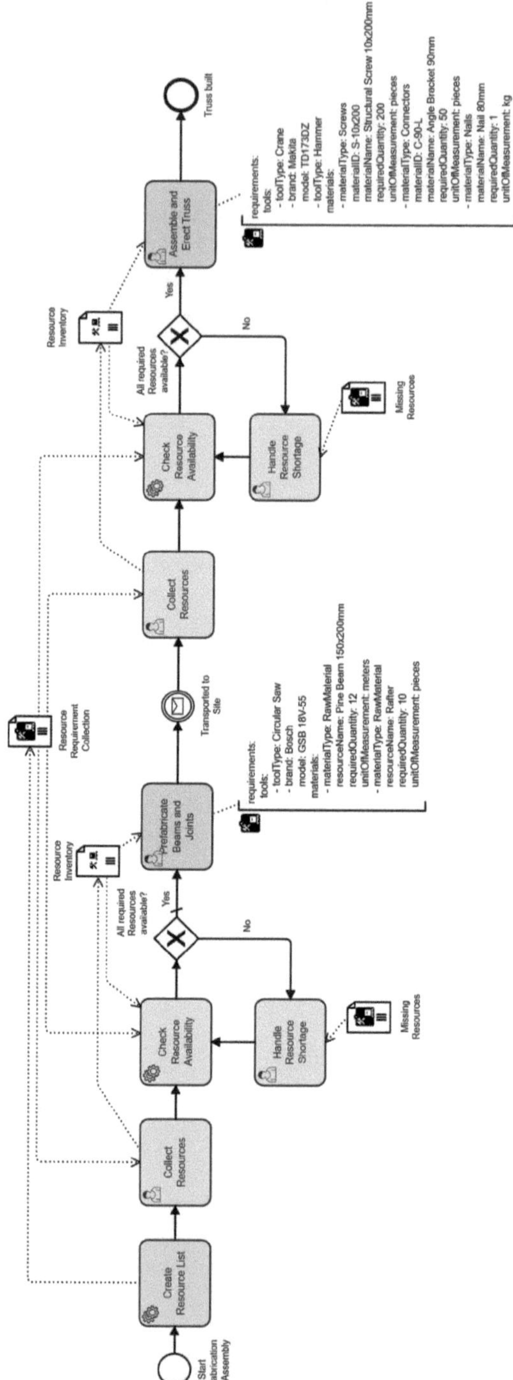

Fig. 4. Process model from an ongoing research project enhanced with PRiME elements.

5   Demonstration and Evaluation

To demonstrate and evaluate the new elements, we will present two distinct examples based on real-world requirements identified in collaboration with actors from the craft business sector. One is similar to the example in [15], where additional information on requirements is directly attached to the tasks within the process model, accessed during process *runtime* to automatically provide information on required and possibly missing tools (and material) in the task list. The second example takes a step further by introducing a novel way to statically parse and provide relevant information about resource requirements in the form of a Sankey diagram, which serves as an overlay to the process model, displaying the flow of materials through each step during *design-time.*

Runtime Support: Monitoring Required and Carried Resources During Process Execution To demonstrate the practical utility of our approach, we apply the concept from [15] to provide runtime support for monitoring the tools and materials required for manual tasks. The process in Fig. 4 describes a carpenter building a wooden roof truss. It involves two main tasks (*Prefabricate Beams and Joints* and *Assemble and Erect Truss*), each with distinct material and tool requirements specified via annotations. The model explicitly shows the verification of these requirements and the handling of potential material shortages.

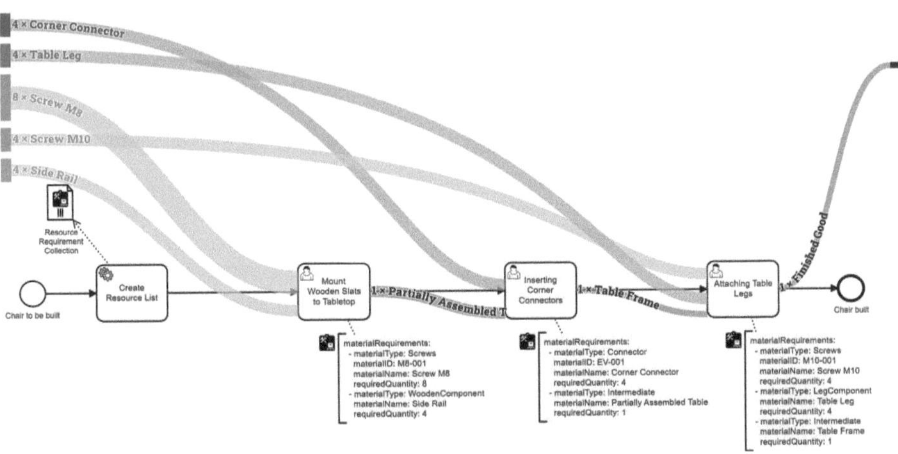

Fig. 5. Visualization of material flow added to process model.

The technical implementation involves several key steps: We first iterate through all annotations in the process model to compile a comprehensive Bill of Resources, which lists all requirements for a single process instance in the *Create Resource List* service task (marked in green, modeled as *Resource Requirement Collection*). Concurrently, we parse the requirements for individual tasks to make them accessible during execution. When a new process instance is initiated, the system automatically generates a list of resources needed for each task. If we then detect a mismatch between required (*Resource Requirement Collection*) and actually carried or prepared resources (*Resource Inventory*), which are tracked automatically using IoT devices and sensors in our project, we can directly intervene and highlight any missing resources. This proactive verification mechanism ensures that operators are adequately equipped before starting a task, reducing errors and improving workflow efficiency.

Design-Time Visualization: Displaying Material Flow on a Process Model. Beyond execution support, the extracted material requirements can be used to visualize the material flow directly on the process model at design time[3]. This visualization is achieved by a prototype that parses the structured material annotations from the process model's XML. It then renders them as a Sankey diagram overlay, where materials are categorized and color-coded to enhance visual clarity. Figure 5 illustrates the material flow for assembling a wooden table by showing the required raw materials (left) that flow into sequential tasks, where they are consumed. It also visualizes the creation of intermediate products (e.g., *Partially Assembled Table*) that are then utilized in a downstream task, culminating in the *Finished Good*.

6 Discussion

This work successfully developed and demonstrated PRiME, a comprehensive framework that addresses the digital-physical divide in cyber-physical systems. PRiME successfully met its design objectives by introducing a dual-artifact approach for ❶ explicit resource modeling, ❷ incorporating `ResourceInventory` and `ResourceFlow` constructs for tracking availability and physical movement, ❸ ensuring conformance through the official BPMN extension mechanism, and ❹ proving its practical applicability via executable Camunda prototypes. By meeting these objectives, PRiME synthesizes and improves upon the three categories of related work. It incorporates *graphical* elements through new icons and a novel Sankey-based visualization, providing the intuitive modeling clarity that purely *architectural* solutions often lack. Its *conceptual* foundation, based on a formal ontology and CDME, is designed for general applicability, unlike more domain-specific models. Most importantly, the extension is *executable*, overcoming the primary limitation of conceptual and simulation-focused approaches that neglect direct operational applicability.

The use of DSRM, integrated with the extension development process of [4,17], ensures the artifact is well-founded and systematically designed. The dual approach of using a human-readable and machine-readable `ResourceRequirementAnnotation` for modeling clarity process automation effectively connects the design-time needs of process modelers with the runtime requirements of a process engine. This is demonstrated through two separate use

---

[3] See https://github.com/LeoPoss/PRiME_MaterialFlow for the accompanying repository.

cases: providing *runtime* resource checklists and shortage alerts to operational workers, and offering a *design-time* visualization of material flows for process analysts. The practical implications of PRiME are twofold: *(i)* for process participants, it provides real-time operational guidance that reduces cognitive load and prevents errors caused by missing equipment and *(ii)* for process designers and managers, the explicit modeling of physical resources enables new forms of analysis, such as bottleneck detection in material flows or simulation of resource costs, creating a more holistic view of operational efficiency.

Despite these contributions, our current work has limitations. The Sankey-based visualization may face scalability challenges with complex, non-linear processes; the runtime mechanism could introduce performance overhead in large-scale deployments; and the framework's accuracy depends on the quality of manual annotations. In terms of validity, the external validity is currently limited to the craft business sector, and further studies are needed to assess PRIME's generalizability. Construct validity is supported by grounding our extension in established production theory and the formal BPMN extension mechanism, ensuring our constructs accurately represent the intended real-world concepts.

7   Conclusion

This paper addresses the critical gap between digital process models and physical reality in cyber-physical systems, where standard BPMN fails to adequately represent the distinct operational lifecycles of materials and tools. We presented the Passive Resource-integrated Modeling Extension (PRiME), a formally defined and executable framework that resolves this challenge. By introducing an ontology that differentiates between consumable and reusable passive resources, PRiME provides the first BPMN extension validated to enable real-time operational guidance through resource checks and strategic design-time analysis via material flow visualization. PRiME establishes the integration of the operational perspective as an achievable and valuable enhancement for modern BPM. The primary implication is that process models can now serve as a more faithful and executable blueprint for orchestrating complex physical work.

To build upon this foundation, future work should focus on two key areas that can expand the scope and capabilities of the framework. First, the development of a dynamic resource management component is necessary to move from simple availability checks to optimized scheduling and contention resolution for shared, reusable tools. Second, the current material flow visualization should be extended into a fully interactive process digital twin, enabling real-time simulation and predictive analysis of resource consumption within complex, non-linear workflows. Integrating the operational perspective directly into executable models is a critical step toward a holistic BPM, where the orchestration of physical assets is no longer an afterthought but a first-class citizen alongside digital control flow.

References

1. Albach, H., Brockhoff, K.K.L., Eymann, E., Jungen, P., Steven, M., Luhmer, A.: Theory of the Firm. Erich Gutenberg's Foundations and Further Developments. Springer, Berlin Heidelberg (2000). https://doi.org/10.1007/978-3-642-59661-2
2. Beverungen, D., Buijs, J.C.A.M., Becker, J., et al.: Seven paradoxes of business process management in a hyper-connected world. Bus. Inf. Sys. Eng. **63**(2), 145–156 (2020)
3. Bocciarelli, P., D'Ambrogio, A., Giglio, A., et al.: A BPMN Extension to Enable the Explicit Modeling of Task Resources. In: 2nd INCOSE Italia Conference on Systems Engineering, CIISE 2016, pp. 40–47 (2016)
4. Braun, R., Esswein, W.: Extending bpmn for modeling resource aspects in the domain of machine tools. In: Advanced Materials and Information Technology Processing. AMITP13. WIT Trans. on Eng. Sci. **1**(87), pp. 449–458. WIT Press (2014)
5. Braun, R., Burwitz, M., Schlieter, H., et al.: Clinical processes from various angles - amplifying bpmn for integrated hospital management. In: 2015 IEEE International Conference on Bioinformatics and Biomedicine (BIBM). pp. 837–845. IEEE (2015)
6. Cabanillas, C., Resinas, M., del Río-Ortega, A., et al.: Specification and automated design-time analysis of the business process human resource perspective. Inform. Syst. **52**, 55–82 (2015)
7. Curtis, B., Kellner, M.I., Over, J.: Process modeling. Commun. ACM **35**(9), 75–90 (1992)
8. Marlon, D., Marcello, L.R., Jan, M., Hajo, A.R.: Fundamentals of Business Process Management. MSE, Springer, Heidelberg (2018). https://doi.org/10.1007/978-3-662-56509-4_9
9. Ihde, S., Pufahl, L., Lin, M.B., et al.: Optimized Resource Allocations in Business Process Models. In: Hildebrandt, T., van Dongen, B., Röglinger, M., Mendling, J. (eds) Business Process Management Forum. BPM 2019. pp. 55–71. Springer, Cham (2019). https://doi.org/10.1007/978-3-030-26643-1_4
10. Janiesch, C., Koschmider, A., Mecella, M., et al.: The internet of things meets business process management: A manifesto. IEEE Sys. Man Cybern. Mag. **6**(4), 34–44 (2020)
11. Lee, J., Bagheri, B., Kao, H.A.: A cyber-physical systems architecture for industry 4.0-based manufacturing systems. Manufact. Letters **3**, 18–23 (2015)
12. OMG: Business Process Model and Notation (BPMN), Version 2.0.2 (2011)
13. Poss, L., Dietz, L., Schönig, S.: Labpmn: Location-aware business process modeling and notation. In: Proceedings of the International Conference on Cooperative Information Systems (CoopIS) 2023 (2023)
14. Poss, L., Schönig, S.: Location-aware business process modeling and execution. Softw. Syst. Model. **24**(1), 37–67 (2024)
15. Poss, L., Schönig, S.: Formalizing the operational perspective in bpm: an ontology-based approach for tool integration. Business Process Management Journal (2025)
16. Schönig, S., Ackermann, L., Jablonski, S., Ermer, A.: IoT meets BPM: a bidirectional communication architecture for IoT-aware process execution. Softw. Syst. Model. **19**(6), 1443–1459 (2020). https://doi.org/10.1007/s10270-020-00785-7
17. Stroppi, L.J.R., Chiotti, O., Villarreal, P.D.: Extending BPMN 2.0: Method and tool support. In: Dijkman, R., Hofstetter, J., Koehler, J. (eds) Business Process Model and Notation. Lecture Notes in Business Information Processing, pp. 59–73. Springer Berlin Heidelberg (2011). https://doi.org/10.1007/978-3-642-25160-3_5

18. Valderas, P., Torres, V., Serral, E.: Towards an interdisciplinary development of IoT-enhanced business processes. Bus. Inf. Sys. Eng. **65**(1), 25–48 (2022)
19. Weske, M.: Business Process Management. Concepts, Languages, Architectures. Springer, Berlin Heidelberg (2019). https://doi.org/10.1007/978-3-662-69518-0
20. Zor, S., Görlach, K., Leymann, F.: Using Bpmn for Modeling Manufacturing Processes (2010)

Automated Interoperability with ML/AI: A Survey of Model/Schema Approaches

Joshua Tetteh Ocansey[1](✉) , Yngve Lamo[1] , Adrian Rutle[1] ,
Fazle Rabbi[2] , and Bahareh Fatemi[2]

[1] Western Norway University of Applied Science, Bergen, Norway
`jtoc@hvl.no`
[2] University of Bergen, Bergen, Norway

Abstract. Automated interoperability plays a pivotal role in managing heterogeneous artefacts across software engineering and data-intensive domains. While conventional approaches often depend on manual or rule-based methods, recent advances in machine learning (ML) and artificial intelligence (AI) present promising avenues for automating interoperability tasks such as matching, mapping, and alignment. However, existing surveys rarely provide a systematic account of how ML/AI techniques address structural and semantic heterogeneity. This paper presents a tertiary study and a critical synthesis of recent developments in AI-driven model interoperability. From a corpus of 82 contributions identified in 19 secondary studies, we selected and classified 19 primary papers that explicitly apply ML/AI methods. Using an extended feature model, we analyze these works along multiple dimensions, including artefact management, execution context, and learning techniques. We also identify key research challenges in explainability, generalization, transformation semantics, and conformance validation, offering a foundation for future research and tool development.

Keywords: Model · Schema · Interoperability · ML · AI · Matching · Mapping · Alignment

1 Introduction

The growing complexity and heterogeneity of structured data across domains have intensified the need for intelligent and automated solutions to ensure model and schema interoperability and reuse. These challenges arise not only from structural differences, such as varying formats, naming conventions, and organizational hierarchies, but also from semantic heterogeneity, where conceptually equivalent entities may differ in terminology (synonyms) or share the same name with divergent meanings (homonyms) [12].

In the domain of software engineering, data management, and system integration, the terms *model* and *schema* are often used interchangeably, although they denote distinct concepts with specific roles. In this survey, we collectively classify them as *artefacts* of interoperability, while for simplicity, both schema and model types are referred to as *models* throughout the article.

A model is an abstract representation that captures key aspects of a system, supporting design, analysis, and communication in Model-Driven Engineering (MDE) [29]. For example, UML class diagrams model the software structure, while mathematical models describe physical behavior.

A schema is a data model that provides a structured representation of information defining the organization, structure, and constraints of information within a system [7,19]. Represented through ER models or hierarchical trees, schemas enable data validation, consistency, and interoperability [1,18].

Despite differences in abstraction and tooling, both domains converge on a common challenge: achieving effective mapping and alignment of artefacts in dynamic and heterogeneous environments. Previous surveys on schema matching and model comparison, such as those of Sutanta et al. [30], Stephan and Cordy [27], and El Haddadi et al. [10] primarily emphasize rule-based, manual, or domain-specific techniques. However, they provide limited insight into recent ML/AI-driven approaches or cross-domain interoperability challenges.

A key contribution of this work is the introduction of an extended feature model to classify model interoperability approaches, building on and refining the frameworks proposed by Stunkel et al. [28,29]. Unlike traditional taxonomy-based or lattice-oriented classification schemes, which often impose rigid hierarchies or assume mutually exclusive categories, the feature model offers a more expressive and flexible framework. It enables the representation of overlapping, multi-dimensional, and interrelated characteristics of interoperability techniques, which is essential given the diversity of approaches in the ML/AI landscape. Moreover, the feature model supports composition and modularity, allowing new techniques or attributes to be integrated without re-engineering the classification structure.

Building on previous secondary studies on schema matching, model comparison, and interoperability frameworks, this work conducts a tertiary level analysis by systematically synthesizing primary articles that apply ML/AI techniques to interoperability tasks. The need for such a tertiary study arises from the rapid evolution of intelligent methods, which are often underrepresented in traditional surveys focused on manual or rule-based approaches.

This survey examines how recent AI/ML-driven approaches address structural, semantic, and similarity-based heterogeneity in model and schema interoperability. It identifies key research gaps, including limited support for model consistency, transformation semantics, and conformance checking. By synthesizing research from the past decade, the survey provides an up-to-date perspective aimed at guiding multidisciplinary efforts toward developing scalable, explainable, and domain-adaptive interoperability frameworks.

2 Background

2.1 Model Management and Interoperability

Model Management (MoM) focuses on creating, transforming, and integrating models as first-class entities to support consistency and interoperability across heterogeneous systems [5,29]. It encompasses operations such as transformation [8], verification [28], and repair, all aimed at ensuring the correctness and reusability of models in different domains.

Interoperability typically involves three core operations: *matching, mapping, and alignment* [31]. Matching identifies semantic correspondences between elements in different models or schemas using linguistic, structural, or instance-based strategies [9]. This foundational step informs subsequent transformation tasks.

Mapping specifies how the elements matched are related, including transformation rules and constraints such as privacy or security policies [8]. These mappings vary in granularity and often handle complex conversions such as nested elements or unit reconciliation [16]. Alignment then integrates these mappings into a unified, consistent representation while resolving semantic and structural inconsistencies. It supports conformance checking and change propagation, often involving iterative refinement through feedback loops [31].

2.2   Feature Models

Feature models are abstract representations widely used in software engineering to capture and manage the variability and commonality of software product lines (SPLs) [8]. Over time, feature models have become a de facto standard for presenting the results of literature studies, particularly in the software engineering domain [28]. They provide a structured and hierarchical way to classify and organize approaches, as demonstrated by their recent use in classifying model federation approaches [3]. Given their effectiveness in organizing and analyzing state-of-the-art techniques, feature models are well-suited for our survey.

Rather than developing a classification framework from the ground up, we adopt and extend the feature model originally proposed by Stünkel et al. [29] and the refined version in Stünkel's dissertation [28]. The original model, developed in the context of multi-model evolution and model repair, offers a structured basis for representing artefact relationships, consistency, and transformation, concepts that align well with our focus on interoperability.

We incorporate core concepts from their model related to the multi-artefact perspective, including `Artefact`, `Correspondence`, and `Execution_Context`. We further extend the `Operation` dimension by introducing the sub-features `Mapping` and `Alignment`, which are essential for capturing the full scope of interoperability processes beyond mere matching. Furthermore, we introduce a new dimension, `Approaches`. This characterizes the use of ML / AI techniques in the reviewed studies.

The resulting feature model is structured into abstract and concrete features, following the formalization in [28]. Abstract features, represented with a light blue background, can consist of other abstract or concrete features. They serve as high-level categories that group related concepts. Concrete features, represented with a deep blue background, are Boolean variables that indicate whether a particular study or approach considers that feature. Abstract features can also represent groups of concrete features, which may be organized as inclusive (or-group) or exclusive (xor-group) enumerations, depending on the context.

3   Survey Methodology

Conducting a literature review in software engineering requires a systematic and unbiased approach to ensure the reproducibility, comprehensiveness, and reliability of results [15].

Our methodology adopts the established structure of secondary and tertiary studies. A *secondary study* refers to a systematic review that synthesizes the findings of primary research articles. In contrast, a *tertiary study* such as the present survey builds on these secondary studies by analyzing and comparing them to uncover broader trends, gaps, and methodological patterns relevant to model interoperability.

As illustrated in the PRISMA flow diagram[1] in Fig. 1, the initial step of our search and classification process was the identification of relevant secondary studies. To this end, we conducted a structured search using the *Semantic Scholar* database. Semantic Scholar is an AI-powered academic search engine that indexes millions of peer-reviewed articles across scientific disciplines. Its semantic indexing capabilities and metadata classification make it particularly suitable for systematic literature searches in computer science and engineering.

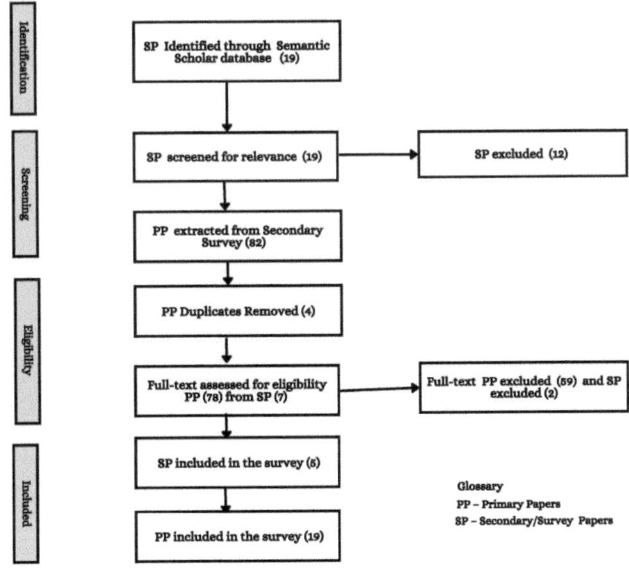

Fig. 1. Survey Methodology.

---

[1] https://www.prisma-statement.org/prisma-2020-flow-diagram.

We used the following keyword query:

("Survey" OR "Literature Review" OR "Feature-based" OR
"Overview" OR "Taxonomy")
AND ("Model" OR "Schema" OR "Ontology"))
AND ("Matching" OR "Mapping" OR "Comparison" OR
"Alignment")000000

The search was filtered by the following.

- **Fields of Study**: Computer Science and Engineering
- **Publication Date Range**: 2015 to 2025
- **Document Type**: Peer-reviewed, nonpreprint

This initial query returned 19 secondary studies, which were then screened using the following inclusion and exclusion criteria:

- The study focuses on model interoperability, particularly matching, mapping, or alignment.
- The study is based on primary articles that employ ML/AI/NLP techniques.
- The article is published in a peer-reviewed venue (not a pre-print).
- The domain of application includes data management, model-driven engineering (MDE), software engineering, or ontology/knowledge representation.

A total of 82 primary articles were initially identified from 7 secondary surveys. These were screened using the following criteria:

- The article addresses the model interoperability as a core contribution.
- It applies machine learning, artificial intelligence, or NLP techniques.
- It was published in or after 2015.
- It is a final publication (not a pre-print or white paper).

To ensure quality and uniqueness, a deduplication process was applied, removing 4 duplicate articles. After the initial screening process, 7 secondary studies were retained, collectively referencing 78 primary papers. These papers were subjected to a full-text eligibility assessment.

From five secondary studies, we selected 19 distinct primary articles that form the basis of our classification using the extended feature model. Table 1 summarizes the secondary sources and the number of articles extracted from each.

4   Classification

The root of our classification is the feature model `Multi-Artefact Management`, which organises the surveyed contributions into two complementary views: (i) the `Multi-Artefact` view, focusing on the management, structure and relationships of models and schemas, and (ii) the ML/AI `Approaches` view, which captures the range of machine learning and artificial intelligence methods applied in automated model and schema interoperability. Together, these views, as illustrated

Table 1. Summary of Secondary Studies and Selected Primary Articles.

Study Title	Citation #	Primary Studies #	Selected
Overview on Data Ingestion and Schema Matching	[10]	10	6
Semantic Text Matching Using Intelligent Methods: A Survey	[2]	15	2
Model Merging in LLMs, MLLMs, and Beyond: Methods, Theories, Applications and Opportunities	[34]	12	2
Neural Networks for Entity Matching: A Survey	[4]	18	8
A Review of Machine Learning Approaches for Semantics-Based String Matching	[26]	8	1
Total	–	**63**	**19**

in Fig. 2, represent the various strategies used to automate interoperability tasks such as `matching`, `mapping`, and `alignment` across heterogeneous systems. The complete classification feature model is available on GitHub[2], developed using the FeatureIDE framework[3].

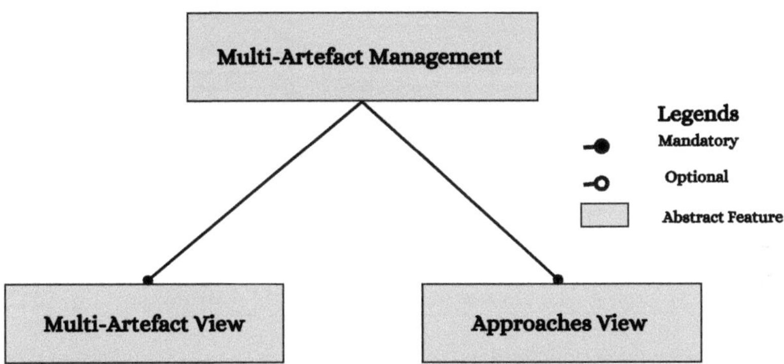

Fig. 2. High-level Feature.

4.1   Multi-Artefacts Feature

The `Multi-Artefact` dimension captures the foundational characteristics of models and schemas as interoperable artefacts situated in distinct technical environments. This classification considers the types of artefacts (e.g., models,

---

[2] https://github.com/Joshocan/Schema.Comparison.Feature-Models.
[3] https://www.featureide.de/.

schemas), their formalism (e.g., graphs, logic) and the technical space in which they operate (e.g., XML, UML). The `Abstraction Level` differentiates between the instance, model and metamodel layers, ensuring that alignment processes occur at appropriate levels of abstraction.

The core operations in interoperability; `matching`, `mapping`, and `alignment`. Matching identifies correspondences across artefact elements using structural, syntactic, semantic, or similarity-based strategies. Mapping defines the transformation logic between matched elements, often incorporating constraints and data translation rules. Alignment consolidates mappings to resolve inconsistencies and maintain conformance between models and their instances, typically in an iterative feedback loop.

The execution and management aspects are also crucial. The execution context includes whether tasks are performed once or repeatedly and how results are stored (transient vs. persistent). Management encompasses correspondence constraints, transformation paradigms (e.g., model-driven, operator-based), and consistency assurance techniques such as verification and change propagation. A complete breakdown of these features is available in the GitHub repository's image folder.

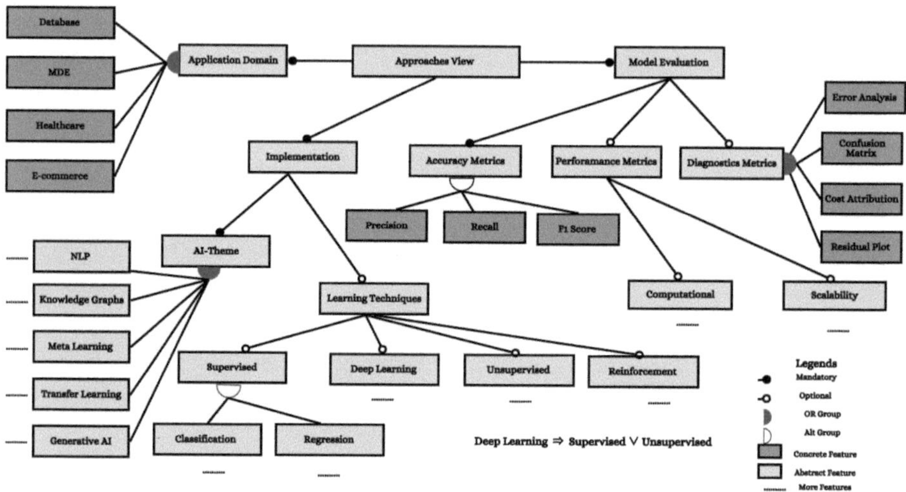

Fig. 3. Approaches Feature – Complete version is available on GitHub(https://github.com/Joshocan/Schema.Comparison.Feature-Models/images.)

4.2 Approaches Feature

The `Approaches` feature describes the strategies and techniques used to automate the interoperability process using artificial intelligence and machine learning methods. It provides a structured view of how various problems are addressed, the domains of application, the scale of data handled, the implementation themes adopted, and how the resulting models are evaluated.

The `Application_domain` sub-feature captures the target domain of the interoperability approach. Common domains include `database` systems, where schema integration and data migration are key. Other domains, such as the semantic web, healthcare informatics, MDE etc.

The `Implementation` sub-feature characterizes the AI and learning methods applied. The `AI_theme` dimension includes approaches such as NLP-based techniques such as leveraging language models for label similarity, `knowledge graph`-based strategies, `meta_learning` for adapting matching models to new domains, `transfer_learning` for reusing learned features across domains, and `generative_AI` for producing synthetic correspondences or mappings.

The `learning_techniques` dimension includes `supervised_learning` where models are trained on labeled correspondences, `unsupervised_learning` which discovering patterns without labeled data, `deep_learning`, and `reinforcement_learning` (where strategies are optimised through iterative feedback).

The `Model_Evaluation` sub-feature outlines how approaches assess the quality of their ML/AI models. `Accuracy_metrics` include standard measures such as `precision`, `recall`, and `F-score` for evaluating correspondence detection. `Performance_metrics` capture computational efficiency, such as runtime or memory usage.

5   Survey Findings

5.1   Classification of Articles

To structure the diverse contributions reviewed in this study, we categorize them along two complementary classification dimensions: the `Multi-Artefact Feature View` and the `Approaches Feature View`. These dimensions capture the semantic complexity, technical challenges, and methodological variations present in the interoperability of automated models and schemas, particularly across heterogeneous artefacts. Table 2 presents a sample of tools categorized using selected key features of our feature model. The complete classification for all selected articles is publicly available via GitHub [2]

Multi-Artefact Feature View. Among the reviewed contributions, the most prevalent level of abstraction occurs at the model level, where artefacts frequently recur in the form of schemas. Graph-based formalisms are dominant, particularly RDF triples [6] and property graphs hMatcher [35], due to their ability to uniformly represent diverse structural and semantic elements across heterogeneous artefacts. These abstractions support flexible integration of data models, entity relationships, and ontologies.

The choice of serialization formats varies widely across studies. Common approaches include JSON-LD, as used in Auto-EM [39] and Mudgal et al. [21],

Table 2. Excerpt of ML/AI tools for model interoperability.

FEATURES	ADnEV [25]	EmbDI [6]	hMatcher [35]	SMAT [37]
Artefact				
Type	Model and Schema	Model and Schema	Schema	Schema
Techspace	n/a	Relational Database	n/a	n/a
Formalism	Schemata, OWL	Graph-based	Graph-based	n/a
Operations	Matching	Matching, Mapping	Matching	Matching
Abstraction Level	Model Level	Instance Level	Model Level	Model level
Matching Strategies				
Structural	Graph	Graph	n/a	n/a
Similarity	n/a	Entity resolution, Token Matching	Element	Named (equality of synonyms)
Semantic	Ontology-based	Instance-based	Context-based Similarity Measure (CSSM)	Linguistic Context-based
Execution Context				
Invocation	Once	Repeated	Repeated	Once
Storage	Cloud Storage	Transient (In memory)	Cloud Storage	Cloud Storage
Management				
Correspondence:				
Constraints	Binary Arity	n/a		
Authority	Centralised, Symmetric	Centralised, Symmetric	Decentralised, Symmetric	Decentralised, Symmetric
Commonality	Implicit	Implicit	Implicit	Implicit
Consistency:				
Verification Scope	Inter-artefacts	Inter-artefacts	Inter-artefacts	Inter-artefacts
Technique	Dynamic validation	Static Analysis, Theory proving	Static Analysis, Dynamic Validation	Dynamic Validation
Transformation:				
Paradigm	Operator-based	Model-driven	Model-driven	Model-driven
Direction	Multi-directional	Bi-directional	Bi-directional	Uni-directional
Architecture Type	Local view	Local view	Global	Local
Technique	Incremental transformation	Heterogeneous Transformation	Merging	Attention over attention Mechanism
Application Domain	Databases, E-commerce	Databases	Bioinformatics, Data Warehousing	Healthcare
AI Theme	Meta-Learning	Knowledge Graph	NLP	NLP
Learning Techniques				
Supervised	CNN, RNN, CRNN	DeepER	n/a	DNN, BiLSTM, GloVe
Unsupervised	n/a	Random Walks, TF-IDF FastText	n/a	
Reinforcement	n/a	n/a	n/a	n/a
Model Evaluation				
Performance	Cosine Similarity, Similarity Metrics	Efficiency of entity embeddings	Runtime, Scalability	Precision, Recall, F1 Score
Accuracy	Precision, Recall, F1 Score, Cosine Similarity	Precision, Recall, F1 Score	Precision, Recall, F1 Score	
Diagnostics	Predictor Functions	n/a	n/a	n/a

XML formats in Nozaki et al. [22], and *custom domain-specific languages* such as ML-Schema [23], which captures metadata for machine learning pipelines. Despite this diversity, many systems introduce a canonical intermediate representation to bridge semantic mismatches between artefacts. However, such representations are notably lacking in healthcare-oriented models, such as SMAT [37], where domain-specific semantics remain less interoperable.

Although less common, metamodel-level abstractions are also employed, particularly in scenarios involving alignment or validation tasks governed by metamodel constraints. For instance, Publio et al. [23] leverage ML-Schema not only as a serialization format but also as a *meta-level schema definition*—effectively serving as a "schema of schemas" to guide the structuring and evolution of domain-specific models.

Matching serves as the foundational operation in most interoperability workflows, underpinning the more complex tasks of mapping and alignment. It is frequently operationalized on three levels, structural, semantic, and similarity-based, reflecting its central role in identifying correspondences between heterogeneous artefacts. ADnEV [25], for example, addresses cross-domain schema matching by refining similarity matrices, while Cappuzzo et al. [6] extend matching to mapping and alignment through the use of tripartite graph embeddings and optimization techniques. Similarly, hMatcher [35] and SMAT [37] integrate semantic strategies such as context-aware similarity and attention mechanisms, respectively, to enhance the fidelity of matching operations.

Structural matching approaches are exemplified by tools such as AIMatch [13], which align tables and attributes using syntactic schema patterns. Semantic techniques are employed in systems such as Ditto [17], which utilizes fine-tuned pre-trained language models to resolve ambiguities in entity relationships. Similarity-based approaches, including Semantic Schema Matching by Nozaki et al. [22], apply word vector representations such as Word2Vec and cosine similarity metrics to align attribute-level elements.

Mapping operations often build on these correspondences using rule-based mechanisms, as seen in Seeping Semantics [11] with SPARQL rules, or model-driven transformations, as in Auto-EM [39]. Finally, alignment seeks to ensure global consistency across artefacts. Vitruvius [14] implements bidirectional transformations to synchronize UML and Java artefacts, while KCMF [33] leverages knowledge fusion techniques to aggregate and reconcile outputs from large language models, reducing semantic drift and hallucination in schema integration tasks.

Approaches Feature View The majority of the approaches surveyed are designed for conventional domains, particularly databases and information systems. Notable examples in this category include *it's AI Match* [13], *ADnEV* [25], *EmbDI* [6], *Auto-EM* [39], and *Ditto* [17], all of which focus on structured data integration and schema interoperability. A smaller number of tools are tailored for specialized domains; for instance, *SMAT* [37] and *SEMPROP* [11] address interoperability challenges within healthcare contexts. Niche applications are also represented, such as *Ensemble BERT* [36] for patent document analysis and *hMatcher* [35] for e-commerce schema alignment. A few systems such as *STMAP* [32] and *FEBRL* [24]exhibit cross-domain capabilities, indicating their potential applicability across diverse sectors beyond their original intended use cases.

Within the broader landscape of AI-based interoperability solutions, Knowledge Graphs (KGs) and Natural Language Processing (NLP) emerge as the dominant technological paradigms. Several systems harness KGs to support relational reasoning; for instance, *EmbDI* [6] encodes table and attribute relationships through graph embeddings, while *Seeping Semantics* [11] constructs enterprise-level KGs to enhance data discovery. NLP techniques, particularly those based on transformer architectures such as BERT and its variants, are widely adopted for semantic alignment tasks. Prominent examples include *Ditto* [17] and *SMAT* [37], which utilize contextual embeddings to disambiguate entity and schema elements. Although generative AI is still underutilized in current schema matching frameworks, *KCMF* [33] demonstrates its feasibility by employing LLMs to generate matching logic without requiring model fine-tuning. Furthermore, the use of transfer learning and meta-learning is exemplified by *Auto-EM* [39], which allows flexible adaptation across schema types with minimal reliance on task-specific training data.

An analysis of learning techniques reveals a clear dominance of *supervised deep learning*, especially through the use of pre-trained language models (PLMs) such as BERT, which are extensively employed for schema matching and entity resolution tasks, as seen in systems like *Ditto* [17] and *SMAT* [37]. *Transfer learning* further enhances these models by enabling effective adaptation to new domains with limited training data, exemplified by tools such as *Auto-EM* [39] and *Low-resource Deep ER* [14]. On the other hand, *unsupervised learning* approaches such as those based on word embeddings, are employed in systems like *EmbDI*

Evaluation practices in model interoperability predominantly focus on *accuracy metrics*, with precision, recall, and F1-score being the most widely used; appearing in more 70% of the approaches surveyed. Tools such as *Ditto* [17] and *SMAT* [37] exemplify this trend employing these metrics to evaluate supervised matching tasks.

Beyond accuracy, *performance metrics* such as execution time and scalability, are increasingly reported to capture the operational trade-offs of the systems. For instance, *EmbDI* [6] achieves scalable integration through distributed embeddings, while *It's AI Match* [13] utilizes GPU acceleration to complete matching operations in under three minutes.

However, the use of *diagnostic metrics* including error analysis, cost attribution, and failure mode inspection, remains limited. Only a few contributions, such as *DeepMatcher* [21] and *KCMF* [33], provide detailed information on failure cases or computational costs, such as token-level usage in LLM inference.

5.2   Threats to Validity

This tertiary survey, while carefully designed, faces several limitations. First, it is not fully systematic, since it builds on existing secondary surveys rather than a direct, exhaustive review of the primary literature. This may omit recent or domain-specific works not covered in those sources. Additionally, relying solely on Semantic Scholar may introduce selection bias, as key studies indexed in other databases (e.g., Scopus, IEEE Xplore, ACM DL) could be missed.

Secondly, our classification is based on an extended version of a feature model from previous work [28,29], adapted to explicitly include models and schemas, and a new ML/AI Approaches dimension. While this improves relevance, not all features were traceable in the reviewed studies due to inconsistent terminology and limited detail. Some features remained unclassified or inferred. This highlights the need for standardised vocabularies and automated feature extraction, which we identify as areas for future work in Sect. 5.3.

5.3   Related and Future Works

While previous surveys have examined schema matching, model federation, and semantic integration, they mostly emphasize rule-based or domain-specific methods. Few offer a comprehensive view of ML/AI-driven automation for matching, mapping, and alignment across heterogeneous artefacts. This survey fills that gap by synthesizing recent advances in AI-powered interoperability.

Sutanta et al. [30] present a foundational overview of schema matching prototypes, classifying techniques into schema-based, instance-based, and hybrid models. While this historical perspective is valuable, their analysis is largely confined to traditional and manual approaches, offering limited insights into modern AI-driven or cross-domain solutions. In a more recent contribution, El Haddadi et al. [10] examine schema matching within the context of data ingestion pipelines. Their work offers a detailed classification of ingestion strategies and integration challenges, but only touches lightly on the depth of ML techniques and lacks analysis of model generalisation or explainability.

Stephan and Cordy [27] survey model comparison approaches within the domain of Model-Driven Engineering (MDE), focusing on static ID-based, similarity-based, and signature-based techniques. While their work is highly relevant to intra-model analysis, it does not extend to AI-powered matching across diverse schema types. Similarly, Amrani et al. [3] conduct a survey on federative model management strategies in Model-Based Systems Engineering (MBSE), introducing a manually developed feature model to classify federated approaches. However, this manual classification approach carries the risk of misclassifying contributions due to its limited automation and subjectivity. Furthermore, their work primarily emphasizes tool integration and consistency management across models, rather than focusing on schema-level interoperability or leveraging intelligent AI-driven methods for matching and alignment.

From this review, several key research gaps emerge. First, while large language models (LLMs) show strong potential for feature extraction from unstructured text, their application to feature model generation and evolution remains underdeveloped. Ensuring correctness, completeness, and structural integrity in generated models is crucial for domains such as Model-Driven Engineering (MDE) and Software Product Line Engineering (SPLE), where poor model quality can compromise downstream processes. Second, most existing tools for feature modeling, such as FeatureIDE, SPLOT [20] lack formal mechanisms to explain why features are included, excluded, or refined. Future research must integrate structured argumentation frameworks [38] to support transparent, traceable, and justifiable modeling decisions.

Moreover, the prevalence of pairwise comparison techniques [35] restricts scalability and semantic coherence when handling multiple artefacts simultaneously. This highlights the need for n-ary and collective matching strategies that can perform global alignment. Similarly, many ML-based solutions are tightly coupled to specific datasets and domains, limiting their generalisability. Incorporating domain-adaptive methods, transfer learning, or meta-learning approaches could significantly enhance their robustness and reuse across various contexts.

Another major concern lies in the lack of explainability in deep learning-based interoperability tools. Most act as black boxes, offering little to no insight into why certain correspondences are made. This is particularly problematic in safety-critical domains such as healthcare and other safety-sensitive systems. Future tools must integrate explainable ML techniques [24] or formal justification methods such as argumentation-based frameworks capable of producing traceable justifications for each decision, thus supporting model governance, accountability.

6   Conclusion

This survey has reviewed and synthesized recent advances in machine learning (ML) and artificial intelligence (AI) techniques applied to model and schema interoperability tasks, including matching, mapping, and alignment. By classifying 19 representative primary studies into two complementary points of view, multi-artifact features, and implementation approaches, we highlighted key trends, capabilities, and limitations of existing solutions. The review reveals a growing reliance on deep learning, knowledge graphs, and transfer learning, along with persistent challenges related to explainability, generalizability, and consistency management. Our analysis also identifies significant gaps in end-to-end interpretability.

Future research should explore integrative frameworks that combine formal reasoning, adaptive learning, and transparent decision making to address the evolving complexity of heterogeneous artefact interoperability.

References

1. Algergawy, A.: Management of Xml Data by Means of Schema Matching (2010)
2. Alqasemi, F., Ahmed, Y.K., Aldafer, M.F., Assarwie, N.F.: Semantic text matching using intelligent methods: A Survey. pp. 1–8 (2024). https://doi.org/10.1109/eSmarTA62850.2024.10638873, https://doi.org/10.1109/eSmarTA62850.2024.10638873
3. Amrani, M., Mittal, R., Goulão, M., Amaral, V., Guérin, S., Martínez, S., Blouin, D., Bhobe, A., Hallak, Y.: A Sur. Fed. Approaches Model Manag. Mbse **10**(1145/3652620), 3688221 (2024)
4. Barlaug, N., Gulla, J.A.: Neural networks for entity matching: A survey. ACM Trans. Knowl. Discov. Data. **15**(3), 52:1–52:37 (2021). https://doi.org/10.1145/3442200, https://doi.org/10.1145/3442200
5. Bernstein, P.A., Ho, H.: Model management and schema mappings: theory and practice. In: Proceedings of the 33rd International Conference on Very Large Data Bases (VLDB '07). pp. 1439–1440 (2007)
6. Cappuzzo, R., Papotti, P., Thirumuruganathan, S.: Creating embeddings of heterogeneous relational datasets for data integration tasks. In: 2020 ACM SIGMOD International Conference on Management of Data (2020)
7. Carvalho, M., Lopes, D., Abdelouahab, Z.: A Framework Based on Model Driven Engineering to Support Schema Merging in Database Systems (2015)
8. Czarnecki, K., Helsen, S.: Classification of Model Transformation Approaches (2003)
9. Do, H.H., Melnik, S., Rahm, E.: Comparison of schema matching evaluations. In: Chaudhri, A.B., Jeckle, M., Rahm, E., Unland, R. (eds) Web, Web-Services, and Database Systems. vol 2593, pp. 221–237. Springer, Berlin, Heidelberg (2002). https://doi.org/10.1007/3-540-36560-5_17
10. El Haddadi, O., Chevalier, M., Dousset, B., El Allaoui, A.: Overview on data ingestion and schema matching. Data Metadata. **3**, 219 (2024).https://doi.org/10.56294/dm2024219, https://doi.org/10.56294/dm2024219
11. Fernandez, R.C., Mansour, E., Qahtan, A.A., Elmagarmid, A., Ilyas, I., Madden, S., et al.: Seeping semantics: Linking datasets using word embeddings for data discovery. In: 2018 IEEE 34th International Conference on Data Engineering. IEEE (2018)
12. Hakimpour, F., Geppert, A.: Resolving semantic heterogeneity in schema integration. pp. 297–308 (2001). https://doi.org/10.1145/505168.505196
13. Hättasch, B., Truong-Ngoc, M., Schmidt, A., Binnig, C.: It's ai match: A two-step approach for schema matching using embeddings (2022). https://arxiv.org/abs/2203.04366
14. Kasai, J., Qian, K., Gurajada, S., Li, Y., Popa, L.: Low-resource deep entity resolution with transfer and active learning. In: Proceedings of the 57th Annual Meeting of the Association for Computational Linguistics. pp. 5851–5861. Association for Computational Linguistics, Stroudsburg, PA, USA (2019)
15. Kitchenham, B., et al.: Guidelines for performing systematic literature reviews in software engineering. Tech. Rep. 1, Software Engineering Group, School of Computer Science and Mathematics, Keele University, Keele, Staffs ST5 5BG, UK (2007). https://www.elsevier.com/__data/promis_misc/525444systematicreviewsguide.pdf
16. Legler, F., Naumann, F.: A Classification of Schema Mappings and Analysis of Mapping Tools (2007)

17. Li, Y., Li, J., Suhara, Y., Doan, A., Tan, W.C.: Deep entity matching with pre-trained language models. Proc. VLDB Endowment **14**(1), 50–60 (2020)
18. Lóscio, B.F., Salgado, A.C., do Rêgo Galvão, L.: Conceptual Modeling of Xml Schemas (2003)
19. Mani, M., Muntz, R.R.: Data Modeling Using Xml Schemas (2003)
20. Mendonça, M., Branco, M., Cowan, D.D.: S.P.L.O.T. - software product lines online tools. pp. 761–762. ACM, Orlando, Florida, USA (Oct 2009). https://doi.org/10.1145/1639950.1640002, https://doi.org/10.1145/1639950.1640002
21. Mudgal, S., et al.: Deep learning for entity matching: A design space exploration. In: Proceedings of the 2018 International Conference on Management of Data. pp. 19–34. ACM, New York, NY, USA (2018)
22. Nozaki, K., Hochin, T., Nomiya, H.: Semantic schema matching for string attribute with word vectors. In: Proceedings of the 2019 6th International Conference on Computational Science/Intelligence and Applied Informatics. pp. 25–30 (2019)
23. Publio, G.C., et al.: Ml-schema: Exposing the semantics of machine learning with schemas and ontologies (2018). https://arxiv.org/abs/1807.05351
24. Reyes-Galaviz, O.F., Pedrycz, W., He, Z., Pizzi, N.J.: A supervised gradient-based learning algorithm for optimized entity resolution **112**(C) (2017). https://doi.org/10.1016/j.datak.2017.10.004, https://doi.org/10.1016/j.datak.2017.10.004
25. Shraga, R., Gal, A., Roitman, H.: ADnEV: cross-domain schema matching using deep similarity matrix adjustment and evaluation. Proc. VLDB Endowment **13**(9), 1401–1415 (2020)
26. Srivatsana Kala, K.U.: A review of machine learning approaches for semantics-based string matching. Gengpi (2024).https://doi.org/10.55248/gengpi.5.0624.1451, https://doi.org/10.55248/gengpi.5.0624.1451
27. Stephan, M., Cordy, J.R.: A Survey of Model Comparison Approaches and Applications (2013)
28. Stünkel, P.: A Framework for Multi-model Consistency Management. Ph.D. Thesis, Western Norway University of Applied Sciences (2022)
29. Stünkel, P., König, H., Rutle, A., Lamo, Y.: Multi-model evolution through model repair. J. Obj. Tech. **20**(1), 1:1–25 (2021).https://doi.org/10.5381/jot.2021.20.1.a2
30. Sutanta, E., Wardoyo, R., Mustofa, K., Winarko, E.: Survey: Models and prototypes of schema matching. Int. J. Elect. Comp. Eng. (IJECE). **6**(3), 1011–1022 (2016). https://doi.org/10.11591/ijece.v6i3.9789, http://iaesjournal.com/online/index.php/IJECE
31. Teran-Somohano, A., Smith, A., Yilmaz, L.: Model Alignment Using Optimization and Design of Experiments. pp. 1288–1299 (2017)
32. Wang, Y., Zhang, B., Liu, W., Cai, J., Zhang, H.: STMAP: A novel semantic text matching model augmented with embedding perturbations. Inf. Proc. Manag. **61**(1), 103576 (2024)
33. Xu, Y., Li, H., Chen, K., Shou, L.: Kcmf: A Knowledge-Compliant Framework for Schema and Entity Matching with Fine-Tuning-Free Llms (2025). https://arxiv.org/abs/2410.12480
34. Yang, E., et al.: Model Merging in llms, mllms, and Beyond: Methods, Theories, Applications and Opportunities. arXiv preprint arXiv:2408.07666 (2024), https://doi.org/10.48550/arXiv.2408.07666
35. Yousfi, A., Yazidi, M.H.E., Zellou, A.: hmatcher: Matching schemas holistically. Int. J. Intell. Eng. Sys. (2020). https://doi.org/10.22266/ijies2020.1031.43
36. Yu, L., Liu, B., Lin, Q., Zhao, X., Che, C.: Semantic Similarity Matching for Patent Documents Using Ensemble BERT-Related Model and Novel Text Processing Method (2024)

37. Zhang, J., Shin, B., Choi, J.D., Ho, J.C.: SMAT: an attention-based deep learning solution to the automation of schema matching. In: Bellatreche, L., Dumas, M., Karras, P., Matulevičius, R. (eds) Advances in Databases and Information Systems. pp. 260–274. Springer International Publishing (2021). https://doi.org/10.1007/978-3-030-82472-3_19

38. Zhang, Y., Li, P., Lai, Y., Zhou, D., He, Y.: Large, small or both: A novel data augmentation framework based on language models for debiasing opinion summarization. arXiv preprint (2024), https://arxiv.org/abs/2403.07693, submitted on 12 Mar 2024 (v1). Last revised 19 Mar 2024

39. Zhao, C., He, Y.: Auto-EM: End-to-end fuzzy entity-matching using pre-trained deep models and transfer learning. In: Proceedings of the World Wide Web Conference. pp. 2413–2424. ACM, New York, NY, USA (2019)

Boosting the Entity-Relationship Model for Document-Oriented Databases

Andrea Avignone[1]([envelope]) [ORCID], Silvia Chiusano[1] [ORCID], Alessandro Fiori[1] [ORCID],
and Riccardo Torlone[2] [ORCID]

[1] Department of Control and Computer Engineering, Politecnico di Torino, Turin,
Italy
andrea.avignone@polito.it, silvia.chiusano@polito.it,
alessandro.fiori@polito.it
[2] Department of Computer Science and Automation Engineering, Università Roma
Tre, Rome, Italy
riccardo.torlone@uniroma3.it

Abstract. The growing adoption of NoSQL document-oriented
databases, such as MongoDB, has introduced new paradigms for managing data with flexibility and scalability. These characteristics make document models suitable for applications that involve heterogeneous data sources and evolving information needs. Current design methodologies often lack formal support, covering only a subset of Entity-Relationship (ER) constructs or relying on general-purpose notations like UML, which are not optimized for database design. In this work, we propose ER_d, a revised version of the ER model to support the conceptual design of document-oriented databases. ER_d extends the classical ER framework to capture the hierarchical and flexible nature of document structures, enabling a more accurate and semantically rich representation of data. We define a set of translation rules that map conceptual constructs into typical document patterns like embedding, referencing, and polymorphism.

Keywords: Document Database · Data Modeling ·
Entity-Relationship

1 Introduction

The emergence of NoSQL databases, particularly document-oriented systems such as MongoDB, has introduced new challenges and opportunities in database design [11]. These systems offer advantages in scalability, performance and flexibility over strict schema constraints and referential integrity [3]. Document databases typically rely on JSON-like formats, enhancing interoperability and integration across heterogeneous components, services, and organizations.

Despite their advantages, NoSQL databases lack established methodologies for conceptual modeling, a crucial step in database design that provides an high-level representation of data. To address these challenges, [13] proposed an

C. Cappiello et al. (Eds.): CoopIS 2025, LNCS 15535, pp. 550–561, 2026.
https://doi.org/10.1007/978-3-032-15538-2_33

abstract model capturing commonalities across NoSQL systems. Complementary research adapted UML to NoSQL design: [14] introduced a model-driven transformation to graph databases, [10] derived physical NoSQL models from UML class diagrams without design guidance, and [5] proposed a UML-like Generic Data Metamodel unifying conceptual information and access patterns across paradigms. While UML remains general-purpose, the Entity-Relationship (ER) model was conceived specifically for conceptual database design, now being a reference to represent real-world entities and their relationships in an intuitive, yet formal manner. Its application to NoSQL remains limited: existing studies only explore preliminary mappings to document-oriented databases, covering a restricted set of design patterns and lacking a solid formalization. [15] combined the ER model with ERQL queries to guide the design of Cassandra databases, demonstrating the impact of conceptual modeling on physical design. This idea was further extended in [12,16], where the Enhanced Entity-Relationship (EER) model was enriched with NoSQL-specific constructs and workload information to optimize the logical design.

Existing approaches lack formality or alignment with the distinctive features of document models, making it difficult to ensure semantic consistency and maintainability in collaborative settings. This paper addresses this methodological gap by proposing a revised version of the ER model, denoted ER_d, to support the conceptual design of a document database. The main contributions are: (i) **A boosted ER conceptual model** designed for the flexibility and hierarchical nature of document databases; (ii) **Formalized translation rules for document-based data**, mapping traditional ER constructs to document structures, as embedding, referencing, and polymorphism, while relaxing certain relational constraints to leverage the flexible schema capabilities of document databases; (iii) **Support for practical adoption:** compatibility with traditional ER modeling, taking advantage of the conceptual clarity of ER modeling while fully exploiting the performance and flexibility of document-oriented systems, easing its use for designers comfortable with relational systems to produce the final JSON schema.

2   Using ER_d for Document-Based Data Modeling

Document-oriented databases adopt a modeling approach distinct from traditional relational design. Instead of emphasizing normalization, the schema is shaped around application-specific access patterns, as exemplified by the widely adopted MongoDB. They generally favor embedding related data that is frequently accessed (avoiding joins), denormalizing to improve performance or simplify queries, referencing large or independently accessed entities, and leveraging polymorphism for heterogeneous or hierarchical structures (documents with varying fields or nested compositions within the same collection).

We propose a methodology for conceptual design of document-oriented databases using ER_d: (i) *Requirement Analysis*, to identify entities, relationships, attributes, and constraints; (ii) *Conceptual Design*, to create an ER_d schema representing the domain; (iii) *Translation to Logical Model,* to select appropriate modeling strategies based on schema and access patterns, and apply translation rules.

2.1   Constructs of the ER$_d$ Model

Table 1 shows the main ER$_d$ constructs and Fig. 1 the corresponding symbols.

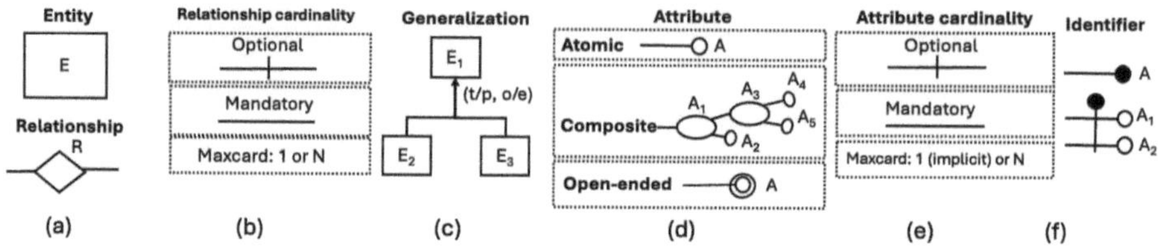

Fig. 1. Constructs of the ER$_d$ model and their graphical representation.

Table 1. Summary of ER$_d$ constructs and corresponding translation patterns.

Construct	Description	Translation Pattern
Entity	Representation of a real-world object, concept or time-based record.	Standard Entity: Document or embedded object, depending on relationships; Time-based entity: Bucket Pattern.
Relationship	Association between two or more entities.	Embedded document, referencing, extended referencing or subset pattern.
Attribute	Property of an entity/relationship, atomic or a structure.	Direct field in document, nested fields or sub-documents.
Identifier	Uniquely identifies entity occurrences.	Mapped to _id or preserved as attribute.
Generalization	Hierarchy linking a parent entity to specialized child entities.	Polymorphic documents into parent (flat or nested with discriminator) or collection per child.

Entities represent classes of objects with an autonomous existence; an occurrence of an entity represents an object of this class. To preserve the peculiarity of flexible-schema documents, differently from *ER*, occurrences in ER$_d$ are *partly homogeneous*: they are characterized by some common properties, but each of them may also have some specific properties.

Relationships represent logic links between two or more entities, where each occurrence is a n-tuple of occurrences of entities, one from each participating entity. The participation of an entity E_i in a relationship R is defined by minimum and maximum cardinalities $(m_i..n_i)$. In the ER semantics, $n_i \in \{1, N\}$ specifies whether each E_i occurrence is associated with at most one occurrence of R (1) or an unbounded number (N), while m_i denotes mandatory or optional participation. In the ER$_d$ schema, when the participation of E_i in R is optional, the two constructs are linked by an *optional arc* (i.e., an arch with a dash); a non-dashed arc is used when the participation is mandatory. The connecting arc is labeled with the maximum cardinality of E_i in R (1 or N) (see Fig. 1b).

Generalizations distinguish between subsets of occurrences (child entities) within a given entity (parent entity). Child entities have their own specific properties while inheriting all properties of the parent. As in ER, generalizations are characterized by *covering*—whether all occurrences of the parent must belong to at least one child (total (t) vs. partial (p)), and *overlap*—whether an occurrence may belong to multiple children (overlapping (o) vs. exclusive (e)).

Attributes represent the properties that characterize entities and relationships. In the ER_d model, the traditional ER constructs are extended to capture the hierarchical organization of real-world data and the flexibility of document-oriented schemas. Attributes can be *atomic*, representing single properties, or *composite*, grouping related sub-attributes. Unlike ER, composite attributes in ER_d are recursive, allowing the construction of *hierarchical trees* that combine both atomic and composite sub-attributes (Fig. 1d). To accommodate evolving schemas and avoid over-specification, ER_d also supports *open-ended attributes*: partially specified properties at conceptual level, whose structure may vary because information is not yet available or may be introduced later.

The *Cardinality* specifies the minimum and maximum number of values an attribute can take for each occurrence of the linked entity (relationship). The `maxcard` indicates whether an occurrence is associated with at most one value or with many; unlike traditional ER, in ER_d unbounded cardinality can also apply to composite attributes, resulting in *multivalued* and *multivalued composite* attributes. The `mincard` indicates if the association is optional (0) or mandatory (1). Optionality is reinterpreted: in ER it denotes a possible *missing value*, while in ER_d it denotes a *missing field*, which may be absent in some occurrences. In hierarchical trees, optionality propagates to all descendants, whereas mandatory presence and `maxcard` apply locally. Optionality is indicated by a dashed arc (solid if mandatory, Fig. 1e), labeled with the maximum cardinality ('N' if unbounded, omitted for single-valued). In a hierarchical attribute tree, the optional arc is shown only for the first optional attribute. Formally, an attribute A is defined as $A(O : m..n, \tau)$, where O is the owning construct, $m..n$ its cardinality, and τ its type (`atomic` or `composite`).

Identifiers are attributes that uniquely distinguish instances of an entity. Following the common ER approach, an entity E is associated with one or more identifying attributes $K = A_1, \ldots, A_k$ such that no two instances of E share the same combination of values. Identifiers can consist of atomic attributes.

Temporal Information allow the modeling of *time-stamped* fine-grained events (e.g., measurements). It can be typically represented through the conventional entity type or as attributes annotated with timestamps, associated with a primary entity which gives the event *context* (e.g., a device, user, sensor). Events are *homogeneous* and *repeated* over time. The entity with time role T is linked to a context entity E through a relationship R, typically a many-to-many relationship in which entity E can also optionally participate. Each instance of T corresponds to a specific point or interval in time. The occurrences of the relationship R are the time series data. This provides a semantic basis for translation strategies suited to document-oriented systems, such as the bucket pattern.

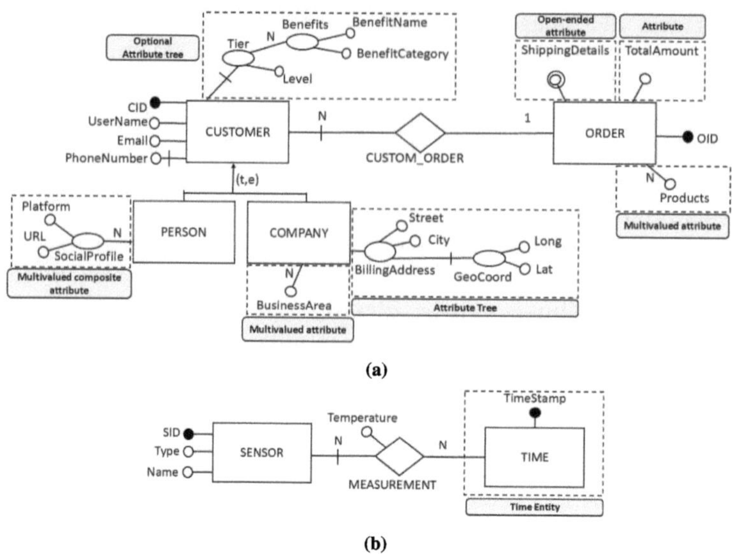

Fig. 2. Example of ER$_d$ schema: (a) e-commerce platform for managing orders by customers; (b) temperature sensor collecting time-based measures.

2.2   Case Study

To show the proposed conceptual data model and the design method we present two examples: an e-commerce platform and a sensor system recording temperature measurements over time, as reported with the ER$_d$ schema in Fig. 2.

Product Orders. Figure 2a models product orders made by customers on an e-commerce platform. The schema includes entities CUSTOMER and ORDER linked by a one-to-many binary relationship with optional participation of the CUSTOMER entity (optional arc). The generalization highlights two distinct sub-categories of customers: PERSON and COMPANY. The CUSTOMER entity is characterized, among others, by properties UserName (atomic attribute), CID (identifier), and Tier (composite attribute). This is the root of a hierarchical data structure grouping attributes Level and Benefits, including BenefitName and BenefitCategory. Since Tier is an optional attribute, all attributes included in the associated hierarchy are optional. The child entities are further characterized, among others, by SocialProfile for PERSON and BillingAddress for COMPANY, including the optional GeoCoord attribute. ORDER includes the atomic attribute TotalAmount, the multivalued Products and the open-ended attribute ShippingDetails (working as a placeholder for information that can be specified later).

Temperature Monitoring. Fig. 2b models a sensor collecting temperature measurements based on time. It is modeled using the entity SENSOR with its attributes, and a binary relationship with the time-based entity TIME. This highlights that a new measure is tracked at each distinct timestamp.

3 Translation of ER_d Constructs Into Documents

This section presents the patterns for translating the ER_d constructs into document-oriented databases, using the JSON Schema representation, a common format used to describe and validate the structure of documents. When an ER_d schema is provided, these patterns are applied as follows. First, the translation of entities, taking into account the types of associated attributes and possible involvement in generalization. Then, the translation of relationships that link entities.

Entities represent collections, and entity occurrences are documents of the collection. They are represented as JSON-based documents, composed of field-value pairs. The value associated with a field can be a variety of data types. It is defined by the attributes that characterize the entity and the relationships in which the entity is involved.

Attributes represent specific properties. In ER_d they are extended with optionality, composition, maximum cardinality, and hierarchical structure. The *open-ended* attributes are not translated in this phase.

Optional and mandatory attributes are modeled using the `required` and `properties` keywords in the JSON Schema. The `required` array lists the names of mandatory attributes, while `properties` defines all the expected attributes and their types. Optional attributes are simply not listed in `required`.

Composite attributes are modeled as structured sub-attributes using *nested subdocuments*. Each sub-attribute is encoded as a field within a structured object, preserving logical grouping and supporting efficient access.

Multivalued attributes are translated into fields with an `array` structure. The same concept stands for the composite attribute, in which a *multivalued composite attribute* is translated as an array of nested subdocuments. For *Hierarchical attributes*, the same translation rules apply by visiting the tree and representing each attribute with the corresponding data structure.

Example 1. Figure 3 shows the obtained JSON schema of the conceptual attributes of the `CUSTOMER` entity (Fig. 2a), along with a portion of an example instance, highlighting the distinction between optional and mandatory attributes.

```
{  required: [ "username", "email" ],
   properties: {
      username: {type: ... },  // required
      email: {type: ... },     // required
      phone: {type: ... },     // optional
   }}
```

(a)

```
{  username: "user1188",
   email: "customer@mail.com" }
```

(b)

Fig. 3. Attributes translation distinguishing optional and mandatory fields: (a) JSON Schema and (b) Example of a single instance.

Example 2. COMPANY (Fig. 2a) includes a composite attribute and a multivalued attribute: `BillingAddress(Street,City,GeoCoord)` and `BusinessArea`. In ER_d, the composite attribute is translated into a nested document, with `GeoCoord` represented as an additional level of nesting, while the multivalued attribute becomes an array of values. Figure 4 shows a corresponding pseudo-JSON Schema and a focused instance illustrating these attributes.

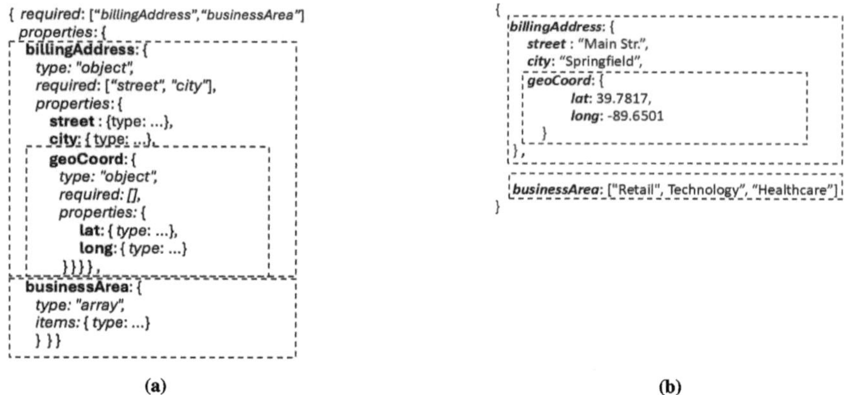

(a)   (b)

Fig. 4. Conceptual translation of composite and multivalued attributes: (a) JSON Schema and (b) Example of a single instance.

Identifiers are required for each document. In the translation phase, two options are available for document identification. (i) *Preserve the conceptual identifier* as the document's `_id`, ensuring semantic continuity and query clarity; (ii) *Use the default _ id field* automatically generated. In MongoDB, the system assigns the `ObjectId` to `_id`. The conceptual identifier, if present, is translated into one or more (mandatory) attributes.

Generalizations can be translated following different strategies depending on the structural characteristics of the hierarchy, similar to the standard ER model with customization for document-oriented databases.

Single Collection Inheritance (collapse child into parent). All child entities are stored in the same collection as the parent entity using the inheritance pattern based on polymorphism. Attributes specific to a child entity become optional in the parent structure. A type discriminator field (e.g., "`typ`") is used to distinguish among child entities. If the generalization is overlapped, the discriminator field is mapped to an array of values. Two structural variants can be used: *flat* and *nested polymorphic structures*. Figure 5 illustrates both strategies with the parent CUSTOMER and the child COMPANY. In the flat variant, both parent and child attributes appear at the root level of the document. In the nested variant, common attributes remain at the root, while child-specific properties are

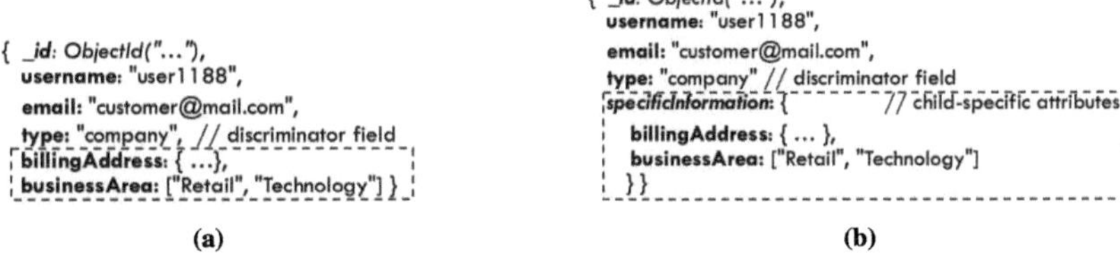

Fig. 5. Polymorphic modeling in document databases: comparison between (a) Flat polymorphic structure and (b) Nested polymorphic structure.

grouped in a dedicated subdocument (e.g., `specificInformation`), providing clearer separation and better support for complex subtype data.

Relationships linked to child entities are reassigned to the parent, with optional participation to reflect that only instances of specific subtypes are involved. The relationships are then translated with the standard rules.

Multiple Collections (collapse parent into child entities). Each child entity is stored in its own collection, inheriting the parent attributes. This pattern improves write performance and simplifies type-specific queries but may introduce redundancy. The generalization in Fig. 2a generates two collections, **Person** and **Company**, each containing both the parent attributes (e.g., **username**) and subtype-specific ones. This translation is possible only if the generalization is total; otherwise, the parent occurrences not covered by child would not be represented. The relationships connected to the parent entity are inherited by all child entities and then translated following the standard rules.

In a hybrid solution, child documents reference the parent to avoid redundancy, but this is generally discouraged in MongoDB due to extra lookups.

Relationships. We define four patterns for translating binary relationships between entities E_1, E_2, each one with trade-offs regarding data redundancy, query performance, and consistency maintenance [4] [7] [8]: embedding, referencing, extended referencing, and subset. The implementation can be in either E_1, E_2, or bidirectionally, depending on access patterns and performance requirements. For ternary relationships, apply these patterns by considering each entity occurrence associated with a pair from the other two linked entities.

Embedding Pattern. This strategy incorporates related entity instances directly within another entity's documents, eliminating the need for a separate collection. In **1:1** relationships, a single related instance is nested as an object, while in **1:N** or **N:N** relationships, multiple related instances are embedded as an array of subdocuments. This pattern reduces the need for join-like operations and improves read performance but may introduce redundancy and a denormalized model. It is recommended for relationships where the embedded data is tightly coupled and frequently accessed together. In **1:1** relationships, embedding depends on **mincard**: optional entities are generally embedded into mandatory ones to avoid data loss, while embedding between two mandatory entities can be decided based on access frequency, favoring embedding the less-accessed entity into the more-accessed one.

Example 3. Figure 6a illustrates how the CUSTOM_ORDER relationship (Fig. 2a) can be translated using the *Embedding Pattern*. Documents of the ORDER entity are embedded directly within the Customer collection (orders sub-document), allowing each customer document to contain its associated orders as nested sub-documents. This design enables efficient retrieval of related data in a single query, as customer and corresponding orders information are stored together in the same document. It improves read performance, but may lead to document growth concerns when the number of embedded orders becomes large.

Referencing Pattern. Entities remain in separate documents, connected through identifiers of related instances. For example, an occurrence $e_1 \in E_1$ may store a set of references $id_{e_2^1}, id_{e_2^2}, \ldots, id_{e_2^n}$ to instances of E_2. This approach is suitable for many-to-many (N:N) relationships or when entities need to be accessed independently, as it preserves normalization and avoids redundancy, though at the cost of additional read operations to resolve references.

Example 4. Figure 6b shows the application of the *Referencing Pattern* to model the CUSTOM_ORDER. The Customer documents do not contain the full Order data but instead include references (i.e., oid) to separate documents in the Order collection. This allows separate management and access to related orders.

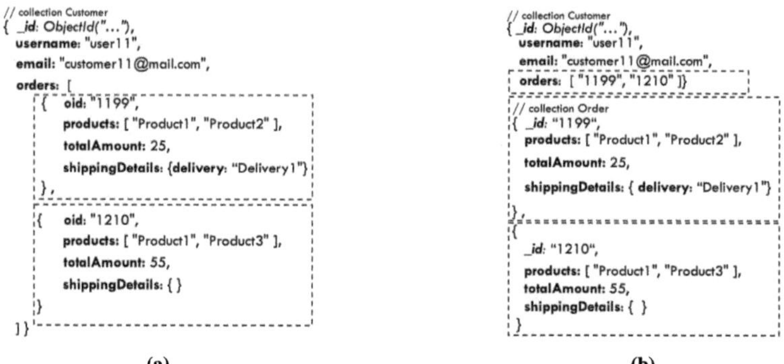

(a)   (b)

Fig. 6. Modeling relationships: comparison between (a) Embedding related data within a document and (b) Referencing related documents via IDs.

Extended Referencing Pattern. This extends basic referencing by including, besides identifiers, a projection of selected attributes from the referenced entity. For instance, an occurrence $e_1 \in E_1$ may store pairs $(id_{e_2^i}, \pi(e_2^i))$ referencing instances $e_2^i \in E_2$, where $\pi(e_2^i)$ denotes the chosen attributes. This partial denormalization improves query performance by avoiding additional join for frequently accessed fields, while the full document remains separate and accessible when needed. This pattern is suitable when embedding the full document is not practical due to size and when some fields of the referenced document are frequently accessed together with the referencing document.

Subset Pattern. This embeds only a subset of the instances of a related entity based on defined selection criteria, suitable for high-cardinality relationships where full embedding would be inefficient. An occurrence $e_1 \in E_1$ may include $\pi(e_2) \mid e_2 \in E_2 \wedge \sigma(e_2)$, where $\sigma(e_2)$ selects the filtered instances (e.g., the last 5 sessions) and $\pi(e_2)$ projects only the relevant attributes. This pattern naturally supports *extended referencing*, as it allows embedding not only references (identifiers) but also a reduced set of attributes for each selected instance.

Bucket Pattern groups homogeneous, fine-grained data into aggregate documents called *buckets*, instead of storing each record separately. It is applied to entities with a temporal role and their associated relationship-entity (Fig. 2b). Given a set of homogeneous occurrences $\{r_1, r_2, \ldots, r_n\}$ of a relationship R, a bucket document B_b is defined as an object with a field `bucket_id` set to b and a field `records` containing an array of $m \leq n$ relationship instances, $[r_1, r_2, \ldots, r_m]$. A grouping function $\beta : r_i \mapsto b$ assigns each record to a bucket based on a chosen criterion (e.g., time window, user ID). This pattern is recommended with large volumes of time-based records, when queries typically target groups of records and reducing write operations is crucial. A practical constraint is the maximum document size (e.g., 16MB in MongoDB), which may require splitting buckets once the limit is exceeded.

Example 5. Considering Fig. 2b, we can imagine a sensor generating temperature readings every minute might aggregate one day's worth of data as follows:

$$B_{2024\text{-}01\text{-}01} = \{date : \text{"2024-01-01"}, readings : [r_1, r_2, \ldots, r_m]\} \qquad (1)$$

4 Conclusions

This paper presented ER_d, a revised ER model for the conceptual design of document-oriented databases. ER_d extends traditional ER constructs to capture the hierarchical and flexible nature of document data structures. By incorporating document-native design patterns, the methodology combines conceptual rigor with the flexibility of NoSQL databases. It allows designers to model document databases using the familiar ER paradigm, with a structured and nearly automatic transformation from conceptual specifications to document schemas. Future work will focus on comparing JSON schemas derived from ER specifications against real implementations, and the integration of workload considerations.

Acknowledgments. This study was partially carried out within the FAIR - Future Artificial Intelligence Research - and received funding from the European Union Next-GenerationEU (PNRR - MISSIONE 4 COMPONENTE 2, INVESTIMENTO

1.3 D.D. 1555 11/10/2022, PE00000013) and the PRIN-MUR project 2022XERWK9-S-PIC4CHU, and was partially supported by the SmartData@PoliTO center. This manuscript reflects only the authors' views and opinions, neither the EU nor the EC can be considered responsible for them. The authors would like to thank Santa Panduri for supporting the model definition.

Disclosure of Interests. The authors have no competing interests to declare that are relevant to the content of this article.

References

1. Chen, P.P.-S.: The entity-relationship model–toward a unified view of data. ACM Trans. Database Syst. **1**(1), 9–36 (1976). https://doi.org/10.1145/320434.320440
2. Batini, C., Ceri, S., Navathe, S.B.: Conceptual Database Design: An Entity-Relationship Approach. Benjamin-Cummings, USA (1991)
3. Cattell, R.: Scalable SQL and NoSQL data stores. SIGMOD Rec. **39**(4), 12–27 (2010). https://doi.org/10.1145/1978915.1978919
4. Varga, V., Andor, C. F., Săcărea, C.: Conceptual graphs based modeling of MongoDB data structure and query. In: Endres, D., Alam, M., Şotropa, D. (eds)Graph-Based Representation and Reasoning. International Conference on Conceptual Structures, Springer, Cham, pp. 262–270 (2019). https://doi.org/10.1007/978-3-030-23182-8_21
5. de la Vega, A., García-Saiz, D., Blanco, C., Zorrilla, M., Sánchez, P.: Mortadelo: Automatic generation of NoSQL stores from platform-independent data models. Future Gener. Comput. Syst. **105**, 455–474 (2020). https://doi.org/10.1016/j.future.2019.11.032
6. Varga, V., Jánosi-Rancz, K.T., Kálmán, B.: Conceptual design of document NoSQL database with formal concept analysis. Acta Polytech. Hung. **13**(2), 229–248 (2016)
7. Roy-Hubara, N., Sturm, A., Shoval, P.: Designing NoSQL databases based on multiple requirement views. Data Knowl. Eng. **145**, 102149 (2023). https://doi.org/10.1016/j.datak.2023.102149
8. Imam, A. A., Basri, S., Ahmad, R., Aziz, N., Gonzâlez-Aparicio, M. T.: New cardinality notations and styles for modeling NoSQL document-store databases. In: TENCON 2017 - IEEE Region 10 Conference, IEEE, pp. 2765–2770 (2017)
9. Herrero, V., Abelló, A., Romero, O.: NOSQL design for analytical workloads: variability matters. In: Comyn-Wattiau, I., Tanaka, K., Song, I.Y., Yamamoto, S., Saeki, M. (eds) Conceptual Modeling. ER 2016 International Conference on Conceptual Modeling. Vol. 9974, Springer Cham, pp. 50–64 (2016). https://doi.org/10.1007/978-3-319-46397-1_4
10. Abdelhedi, F., Brahim, A. A., Atigui, F., Zurfluh, G.: UMLtoNoSQL: Automatic transformation of conceptual schema to NoSQL databases. In: IEEE/ACS 14th International Conference on Computer Systems and Applications (AICCSA), pp. 272–279 (2017). https://doi.org/10.1109/AICCSA.2017.76
11. Vera-Olivera, H., Guo, R., Huacarpuma, R. C., Da Silva, A. P. B., Mariano, A. M., Holanda, M.: Data Modeling and NoSQL Databases: A Systematic Mapping Review. ACM Comput. Surv. **54**(6), Article 116 (2022). https://doi.org/10.1145/3457608
12. Lima, C., Mello, R.S.: On proposing and evaluating a NoSQL document database logical approach. Int. J. Web Inf. Syst. **12**(4), 398–417 (2016). https://doi.org/10.1108/IJWIS-04-2016-0018

13. Atzeni, P., Bugiotti, F., Cabibbo, L., Torlone, R.: Data modeling in the NoSQL world. Comput. Stand. Interfaces **67**, 1–16 (2020)
14. Daniel, G., Gómez, A., Cabot, J.: UMLto[No]SQL: Mapping conceptual schemas to heterogeneous datastores. In: 13th International Conference on Research Challenges in Information Science (RCIS), pp. 1–13 (2019). https://doi.org/10.1109/RCIS.2019.8877094
15. Chebotko, A., Kashlev, A., Lu, S.: A Big Data modeling methodology for Apache Cassandra. In: IEEE International Congress on Big Data, pp. 238–245 (2015). https://doi.org/10.1109/BigDataCongress.2015.41
16. Bansal, N., Sachdeva, S., Awasthi, L.K.: Schema generation for document stores using workload-driven approach. J. Supercomput. **80**(3), 4000–4048 (2024)

Ontology-Guided Chain-of-Thought Reasoning for Knowledge Graph Construction with Large Language Model

Gang Xiao, Wenhui Li, Jiawei Lu (✉), and Siyu Chen

China Jiliang University, Hangzhou 310018, China
viivan@cjlu.edu.cn

Abstract. To address the challenges of traditional knowledge graph construction (KGC) methods, this paper proposes a framework AdaOntoKG that combines ontology-driven and adaptive chain-of-thought reasoning (Adaptive CoT). The framework builds and expands domain ontologies with LLMs, and guides triple extraction through Zero-Shot-CoT and Few-Shot-CoT, with ontology constraints ensuring semantic consistency and structural validity. Experiments on multiple benchmarks show that AdaOntoKG outperforms mainstream baselines in F1 and AUC, while achieving high ontology conformance. Overall, AdaOntoKG enhances accuracy, controllability, and domain adaptability, providing a scalable solution for constructing high-quality knowledge graphs.

Keywords: Knowledge Graph Construction · Ontology · Large Language · Models · Chain-of-Thought Reasoning

1 Introduction

Knowledge Graph (KG) is widely used in domains such as aerospace [1], industry [2] and product interaction [3]. Essentially, a KG is a directed, labeled graph consisting of entities and their semantic relations, typically represented as triples [4].

Current Knowledge Graph Construction (KGC) methods fall into two main categories: rule-based and deep learning-based approaches. Rule-based methods rely on manually defined rules but suffer from high labor costs and poor scalability [5]. Deep learning-based methods, applied to tasks like named entity recognition (NER) [6], entity classification [7] and relation extraction [8]. However, these methods still rely heavily on labor-intensive annotations. Thus, reducing manual dependence while maintaining accuracy and generalization remains a key challenge in KGC.

The emergence of large language models (LLMs) brings new opportunities for automated KGC [9]. LLMs excel in zero-shot and few-shot learning [10]. However, they still face challenges in domain-specific KGC: often producing redundant or irrelevant triples, which reduces interpretability and credibility [11].

To address the above issues, this paper proposes the AdaOntoKG framework, which integrates ontology construction with adaptive chain-of-thought (Adaptive CoT) reasoning. Specifically, our method constructs the initial ontology through a series of steps

C. Cappiello et al. (Eds.): CoopIS 2025, LNCS 15535, pp. 562–572, 2026.
https://doi.org/10.1007/978-3-032-15538-2_34

and then employs LLMs to expand it under domain-specific rules. During the extraction process, a feedback mechanism between Zero-Shot-CoT and Few-Shot-CoT is introduced to iteratively refine candidate triples. The ontology structure serves as a semantic constraint throughout the process, ensuring consistency and accuracy through semantic validation and iterative refinement. Our method effectively reduces the need for manually crafted examples and expert involvement, significantly improving the efficiency and quality of KGC.

1.1 Related Work

Ontologies have long been used to provide structured guidance in KGC, ensuring semantic consistency and reducing the complexity of integrating heterogeneous sources. For instance, Suchanek et al. [12] integrated WordNet with Wikipedia to build YAGO, while Jia et al. [13] employed predefined ontologies to support automated extraction in cybersecurity. These works have confirmed the value of ontological constraints, yet still suffer from limited flexibility, reducing adaptability in dynamic domains.

LLMs have demonstrated excellent performance across various NLP tasks, including those related to KGC. For example, in NER, researchers [14] have used pre-trained language models like BERT to effectively improve entity recognition accuracy on large-scale corpora. In addition, The LLM-TIKG system [15] combined contrastive learning with LLMs to construct threat intelligence knowledge graphs, thereby further improving the efficiency and quality of event extraction. While these studies have improved KGC by flexibly utilizing LLMs to extract implicit knowledge and complex relations, the relation generation remains opaque, limiting interpretability and hindering error analysis.

Prompt engineering further enhances the reasoning capability of LLMs by guiding their outputs through prompts. Kojima et al. [16] showed that zero-shot prompting can elicit stepwise reasoning, and Li et al. [17] employed LLMs with CoT to extract knowledge from unstructured technical documents and build a structured KG. Nevertheless, existing CoT-based prompting still faces a trade-off: zero-shot offers high automation but unstable quality, while few-shot improves accuracy but requires costly manual examples.

2 Methods

2.1 Framework

This paper proposes a knowledge graph construction framework, AdaOntoKG (as illustrated in Fig. 1). The framework aims to support the automated construction of a normalized knowledge graph from heterogeneous data. This is achieved by applying unified semantic constraints and a multi-path knowledge extraction mechanism.

During the data input and processing stage, the framework sequentially handles four types of input: ontologies, unstructured, semi-structured and structured data. First, ontology data undergoes requirement analysis and related steps to form an initial ontology. It is then expanded with the assistance of LLMs to generate a more comprehensive ontology structure, which is used for subsequent knowledge alignment and semantic constraint.

For unstructured textual data, the framework introduces a reasoning process that combines LLMs with Adaptive CoT. This mechanism consists of two stages: an initial

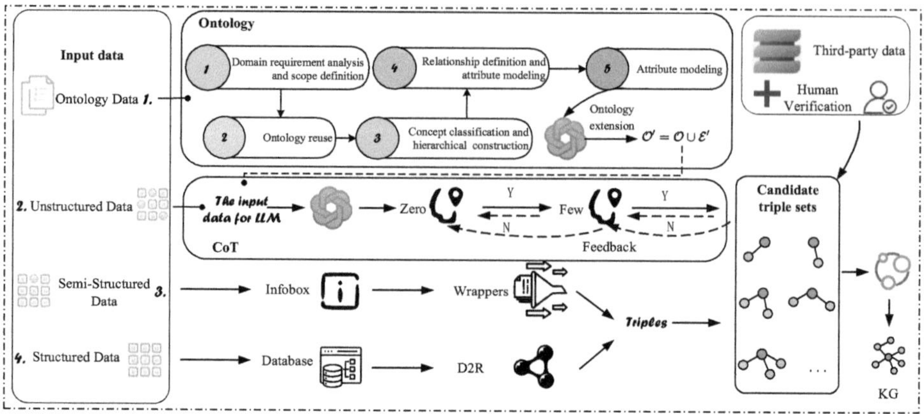

Fig. 1. AdaOntoKG Framework.

candidate triple generation in the Zero-Shot-CoT phase, and refined extraction in the Few-Shot-CoT phase. Throughout the process, ontology rules are embedded to provide continuous validation and feedback, ensuring the semantic consistency and structural completeness of the extracted results. With respect to semi-structured and structured data, the framework uses a template-driven method and an automatic mapping mechanism to extract triples. After generating candidate triples, the system performs ontology-driven validation and cross-validation against external knowledge bases, with a human-in-the-loop mechanism to correct anomalies. Then, the validated triples can be used to construct a knowledge graph that supports diverse applications.

2.2 Ontology

Traditional ontology construction methods mainly focus on defining concepts and relations, while often overlooking the need for dynamic supplementation and evolution. To address this, we propose a staged strategy. The detailed design is presented in the following subsections.

Domain Requirement Analysis and Scope Definition. Domain requirement analysis serves as the starting point of ontology construction, aiming to clarify its applicable domain, knowledge boundaries, and application scenarios.

Based on this, the domain scope in this study is formally defined as follows:

$$Scope = (Domain, Purpose, Boundary) \tag{1}$$

Here, Domain refers to the knowledge domain or subject area, Purpose denotes the specific application objectives of the target ontology, and Boundary defines the limits of knowledge coverage.

Ontology Reuse. To improve construction efficiency, existing ontologies should be assessed for potential reuse based on their coverage, adaptability, and granularity. When no ontology is directly reusable, draw on authoritative related-domain ontologies and standards, extracting core terms, relations, and design principles to facilitate reuse in the target ontology.

Concept Categorization and Hierarchy Construction. The concept system, as the core of the ontology, organizes domain knowledge and ensures semantic precision. Core concepts are extracted, and an inheritance hierarchy ConceptHierarchy$_{isA}$ is then constructed.

Relationship Definition and Attribute Modeling. Relational modeling defines the multi-dimensional semantic associations between conceptual entities, with a focus on constructing object properties (*ObjectProperty*). Each property is modeled based on domain data structures and industry standards, and must specify a clear domain and range.

In order to enhance the semantic expression ability of object attributes, the ontology further introduces a constraint type set (*SemanticConstraintSet*) to standardize the logical properties, including symmetry, transitivity, reflexivity, antisymmetry, and functionality.

Attribute System Design. The attribute system AttributeSet defines the key characteristics of conceptual entities, including attribute types, constraints, and value ranges.

LLM-Based Ontology Extension. After the initial ontology construction, this study proposes an LLM-assisted extension method to accommodate the continuous evolution of domain knowledge. Based on the existing ontology, the method generates new concepts, attributes, and relations using LLMs, with domain rules introduced as a constraint framework to ensure logical consistency and domain adaptability.

The construction of domain rules is grounded in the conceptual structure, relational network, and attribute characteristics of the initial ontology. It systematically organizes semantic constraints, inference patterns, and value assignment specifications between entities, and generalizes them into a rule set $\mathcal{R}$.

During the extension process, let the current ontology be defined as $\mathcal{O}$. Then, the LLM first infers potential extension directions based on the existing ontology structure and generates a set of candidate extensions:

$$\mathcal{E} = \{e_1, e_2, \ldots, e_m\} \tag{2}$$

Each item e_i represents a potential new concept, attribute, or relation. To ensure the quality of the extensions, a domain rule consistency verification mechanism is introduced, with a validation function defined as:

$$\text{Verify} : \mathcal{E} \times \mathcal{R} \rightarrow \{0,1\} \tag{3}$$

That is, for each extension candidate e_i, if it satisfies all relevant domain rules, its value is 0; otherwise, it is 1. Through this verification process, only high-quality extensions $\mathcal{E}'$ that conform to the rules are retained.

Finally, the filtered extension content is integrated into the original ontology to form the updated ontology:

$$\mathcal{O}' = \mathcal{O} \cup \mathcal{E}' \tag{4}$$

In summary, the proposed ontology construction method ensures adaptive evolution, providing strong extensibility for continuous domain knowledge development.

2.3 CoT

In recent years, CoT methods have shown strong potential in enhancing LLM reasoning. The current key challenge is to reduce manual dependency while ensuring extraction accuracy.

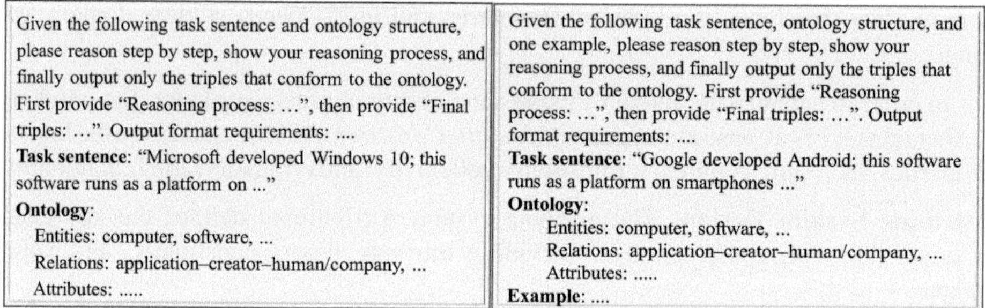

Fig. 2. Illustrative Prompt Example (Zero-Shot-CoT Stage on the Left, Few-Shot-CoT Stage on the Right).

To address this issue, we propose an Adaptive CoT approach that combines Zero-Shot-CoT for generating initial reasoning chains with Few-Shot-CoT for iterative refinement. One illustrative example is shown in Fig. 2. The method establishes a closed-loop optimization process through a Forward Pass and Backward Refinement mechanism, ensuring that the extracted triples conform to ontology constraints and exhibit high semantic consistency.

In the Adaptive CoT method, we first employ Zero-Shot-CoT to directly extract an initial set of triples from the text T, aiming to capture both relational and attribute information. For entity–relation–entity triples, the candidate set is defined as:

$$S_0^r = \{(h, r, t)|h, t \in E, r \in R\} \tag{5}$$

Here, h, r, and t represent the head entity, relation, and tail entity, respectively; E denotes the set of possible entities, and R the set of possible relations. Meanwhile, we also extract a candidate set of entity–attribute–value triples from the text:

$$S_0^a = \{(e, a, v)|e \in E, a \in A, v \in V\} \tag{6}$$

Here, e denotes the entity, a the attribute, and v the attribute value; A represents the set of candidate attributes, and V denotes the possible value range for attributes.

The objective of this stage is to broadly explore potential semantic relations within the text, providing a comprehensive foundation for subsequent optimization.

Ontology Constraint Matching. The knowledge graph ontology constraints are defined, and relation triples and attribute triples that satisfy the following conditions are retained:

$$S_1^r = \left\{(h, r, t) \in S_0^r | h, t \in E_{ontology}, r \in R_{ontology}\right\} \tag{7}$$

$$S_1^a = \left\{(e, a, v) \in S_0^a | e \in E_{ontology}, a \in A_{ontology}, v \in V_{ontology}\right\} \tag{8}$$

Here, $E_{ontology}$, $R_{ontology}$, $A_{ontology}$, and $V_{ontology}$ represent the sets of entities, relations, attributes, and attribute values defined in the ontology, respectively, ensuring that the candidate results conform to the predefined ontology constraints.

Confidence Scoring. Each triple is assigned a confidence function $P(\bullet)$ based on the output of the LLM, and a threshold τ is set to filter high-confidence candidates, which are denoted as S_2^r and S_2^a. The confidence score can be obtained either through LLM self-evaluation or multi-turn reasoning-based estimation.

Knowledge Base Cross-Validation. If a high-quality external knowledge base exists in the target domain, it is further used to verify the factual correctness of the triples:

$$S_3^r = \left\{(h, r, t) \in S_2^r | verify(h, r, t) = 1\right\} \tag{9}$$

$$S_3^a = \left\{(e, a, v) \in S_2^a | verify(e, a, v) = 1\right\} \tag{10}$$

Here, $verify(\bullet)$ is a binary function that returns 1 if the triple is validated by the knowledge base, and 0 otherwise.

The filtered set of high-quality triples is automatically constructed into Few-Shot examples to guide the next round of reasoning. In the final Few-Shot-CoT iterative reasoning stage, these examples are used to perform second-stage reasoning on the target text $T\prime$, generating a new set of knowledge triples S_4.

In addition, we introduce an error feedback mechanism that combines both ontology-based and human verification. If certain triples in S_4 violate ontology rules, they are sent back to the previous stage for correction, with human validation further ensuring the effectiveness of the revisions.

The final high-quality triples refined through the two-stage process serve as the final output for KGC and are also fed back into the preceding Zero-Shot-CoT and Few-Shot-CoT stages to enhance reasoning quality. By establishing a cyclic feedback mechanism between semantic coverage and inference accuracy, our method significantly improves extraction consistency and stability while maintaining strong automation and cross-domain adaptability.

3 Experiments

To systematically validate the effectiveness and stability of the proposed AdaOntoKG method in KGC tasks, three types of experiments are designed.

3.1 Experiment Setup

We run all experiments on a single NVIDIA A100 GPU, using GPT-4 Turbo for ontology-guided, CoT-based triple extraction with low-temperature decoding (T = 0.1). Evaluation covers four OpenIE benchmarks: OIE2016, WEB, NYT, PENN [18–21] with F1 score and AUC, and additionally reports Ontology Conformance (OC) together with precision and recall on Wikidata-TekGen [22].

3.2 Baseline Comparison

Table 1. Performance comparison between AdaOntoKG and baseline models (F1/AUC). **Bold** values indicate the best performance among all models.

Model	OIE2016		WEB		NYT		PENN	
	F1	AUC	F1	AUC	F1	AUC	F1	AUC
OpenIE 6(2020)	55.3	61.1	61.1	64.9	30.7	55.2	54.2	63.1
Stanford OIE(2023)	59.3	65.1	63.3	69.3	31.1	56.9	56.8	67.1
DeepEx(2021)	72.6	58.6	91.2	82.4	85.5	72.5	88.5	81.5
PIVE(2023)	70.4	71.1	89.8	86.0	83.5	77.9	86.0	81.2
SAC-KG(2024)	74.7	73.2	**96.6**	95.7	88.8	87.3	91.1	90.1
AdaOntoKG(Ours)	**76.1**	**74.3**	96.0	**96.1**	**89.1**	**88.1**	**92.5**	**91.2**

We compare AdaOntoKG with current state-of-the-art methods to evaluate its practical performance in the OpenIE task. The compared methods include rule-based extractors OpenIE 6 [23] and Stanford OIE [24], as well as language model-based approaches such as DeepEx [25], PIVE [26], and SAC-KG [27].

As shown in Table 1, AdaOntoKG achieves performance that matches or surpasses the current state-of-the-art methods overall. On the OIE2016, NYT, and PENN datasets, it outperforms SAC-KG in F1 score by 1.4, 0.3, and 1.4 percentage points, and in AUC by 1.1, 0.8, and 1.1, respectively, with more notable improvements on NYT and PENN due to their higher semantic complexity and structural diversity. Although its F1 score on the WEB dataset is slightly lower, AdaOntoKG still achieves a marginal gain in AUC, demonstrating robustness in confidence ranking. By integrating ontology knowledge with CoT reasoning, AdaOntoKG significantly reduces ambiguity in relation and entity identification, and thus performs particularly well on complex textual data. In summary, the results confirm the overall effectiveness of AdaOntoKG and provide evidence that ontology constraints and the CoT mechanism contribute to better generalization in open-domain scenarios with complex semantics and diverse relational structures.

3.3 Ablation Study

To evaluate the contribution of each module, we construct three ablated variants of AdaOntoKG: (1) w/o Few-Shot-CoT: removes the Few-Shot stage and retains only Zero-Shot-CoT; (2) w/o Ontology Validation: disables the ontology-based triple structure validation mechanism; (3) w/o CoT: removes the entire Chain-of-Thought reasoning process and performs extraction using only simple prompting.

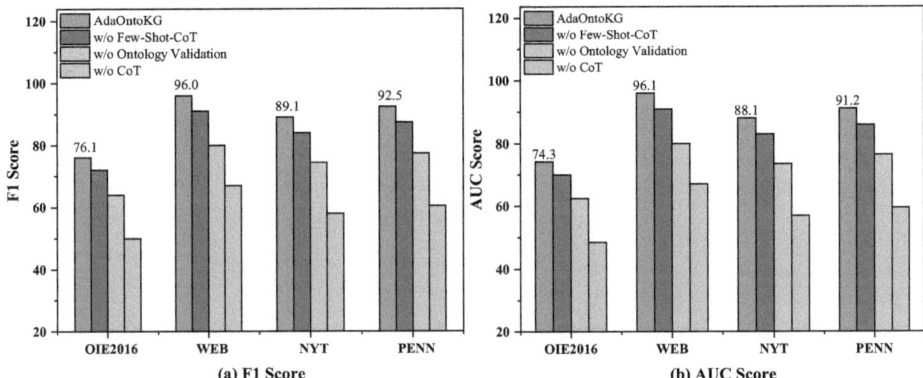

Fig. 3. Ablation study results of different model variations across datasets. (a) F1 Score comparison; (b) AUC Score comparison.

As shown in Fig. 3, the full model achieves an F1 score of 76.1 and an AUC of 74.3 on the OIE2016 dataset, outperforming all variants. Performance drops by 4 points without Few-Shot-CoT, further reduces performance to around 64/62.5 when the ontology validation module is removed, and shows the most severe degradation (50.0/48.5) under the exclusion of CoT. Similar trends appear on NYT, WEB, and PENN. In conclusion, Few-Shot-CoT improves semantic precision, ontology validation enforces structural constraints, and CoT is central to reasoning, together ensuring the quality and stability of AdaOntoKG.

3.4 OC Evaluation

We evaluate the proposed AdaOntoKG method using the OC metric on the Wikidata-TekGen dataset. This dataset covers ten subdomains, each associated with a corresponding set of ontology relations. For clarity of presentation, the ten ontologies are divided into two groups and listed in Table 2 as Type A and Type B, respectively.

The results show that AdaOntoKG produces highly consistent outputs across all domains, with OC scores above 90% for most ontology types. This indicates the model can effectively follow ontology constraints to generate valid triples. In well-structured domains like Book and Sport, scores reach 0.95 or higher. In more ambiguous domains such as Culture and Nature, where ontology coverage is limited, scores slightly drop but remain within a reasonable range, showing the model's robustness in handling complex knowledge structures.

Table 2. OC Value Statistics of different ontologies.

Type A	OC Value	Type B	OC Value
Movie Ontology	0.93	Computer Ontology	0.92
Music Ontology	0.94	Space Ontology	0.81
Sport Ontology	0.96	Politics Ontology	0.92
Book Ontology	0.95	Nature Ontology	0.85
Military Ontology	0.93	Culture Ontology	0.69

Overall, AdaOntoKG demonstrates strong structural generalization and relation generation consistency across different ontological domains by incorporating explicit ontology validation and CoT reasoning.

4 Conclusion

This study proposes AdaOntoKG, a framework that integrates ontology rules with LLM-based reasoning to reduce the cost and instability of knowledge graph construction. By employing an Adaptive CoT mechanism, the method generates and filters triples without extensive manual examples, while ontologies enforce structural constraints and semantic validation. Experiments show superior extraction accuracy, ontology conformance, and cross-domain generalization, highlighting its potential for practical deployment. Although AdaOntoKG can in principle be extended to semi-structured or structured inputs, our focus is on unstructured text where semantic ambiguity is most challenging. Future work will investigate self-correcting reasoning chains and multimodal knowledge extraction to further improve semantic understanding and real-world applicability.

Acknowledgments. This work is supported by the "Pioneer" and "Leading Goose" R&D Program of Zhejiang Province, China (No. 2025C01022, No. 2023C01022), the LingYan Planning Project of Zhejiang Province, China (No. 2023C01215) and the Science and Technology Key Research Planning Project of HuZhou city, China (NO.2022ZD2019).

Disclosure of Interests. The authors declare no competing interests.

References

1. Zhou, B., Li, X., Liu, T., et al.: CausalKGPT: industrial structure causal knowledge-enhanced large language model for cause analysis of quality problems in aerospace product manufacturing. Adv. Eng. Inf. **59**, 102333 (2024)
2. Wan, Y., Chen, Z., Liu, Y., et al.: Empowering LLMs by hybrid retrieval-augmented generation for domain-centric Q&A in smart manufacturing. Adv. Eng. Inf. **65**, 103212 (2025)
3. Vizcarra, J., Haruta, S., Kurokawa, M.: Representing the interaction between users and products via LLM-assisted knowledge graph construction. In: Proceedings of the 2024 IEEE 18th International Conference on Semantic Computing (ICSC), pp. 231–232. IEEE (2024)

4. Hao, X., Ji, Z., Li, X., et al.: Construction and application of a knowledge graph. Remote Sens. **13**(13), 2511 (2021)
5. Hofer, M., Obraczka, D., Saeedi, A., Köpcke, H., Rahm, E.: Construction of knowledge graphs: current state and challenges. Information **15**, 509 (2024)
6. Ehrmann, M., Hamdi, A., Pontes, E.L., et al.: Named entity recognition and classification in historical documents: a survey. ACM Comput. Surv. **56**(2), 1–47 (2023)
7. Zhao, Y., Zhou, H., Zhang, A., et al.: Connecting embeddings based on multiplex relational graph attention networks for knowledge graph entity typing. IEEE Trans. Knowl. Data Eng. **35**(5), 4608–4620 (2022)
8. Xishuo, Z., Liu, L., Wang, H., et al.: Survey of entity relationship extraction methods in knowledge graphs. J. Front. Comput. Sci. Technol. **18**(3), 574 (2024)
9. Zhu, Y., Wang, X., Chen, J., et al.: LLMs for knowledge graph construction and reasoning: recent capabilities and future opportunities. World Wide Web **27**(5), 58 (2024)
10. Zhang, B., Soh, H.: Extract, Define, Canonicalize: an LLM-based framework for knowledge graph construction. In: Proceedings of the 2024 Conference on Empirical Methods in Natural Language Processing (EMNLP), pp. 9820–9836. ACL, Miami (2024)
11. Nie, J., Hou, X., Song, W., et al.: Knowledge graph efficient construction: embedding chain-of-thought into LLMs. Proc. VLDB Endow. **15**(2150), 8097 (2024)
12. Suchanek, F.M., Kasneci, G., Weikum, G.: Yago: a core of semantic knowledge. In: Proceedings of the International Conference on World Wide Web (WWW), pp. 697–706 (2007)
13. Jia, Y., Qi, Y., Shang, H., et al.: A practical approach to constructing a knowledge graph for cybersecurity. Eng. **4**(1), 53–60 (2018)
14. Zhang, H., Liu, X., Pan, H., et al.: ASER: towards large-scale commonsense knowledge acquisition via higher-order selectional preference over eventualities. Artif. Intell. **309**, 103740 (2022)
15. Hu, Y., Zou, F., Han, J., et al.: LLM-TIKG: threat intelligence knowledge graph construction utilizing large language model. Comput. Secur. **145**, 103999 (2024)
16. Kojima, T., Gu, S.S., Reid, M., et al.: Large language models are zero-shot reasoners. Adv. Neural. Inf. Process. Syst. **35**, 22199–22213 (2022)
17. Li, X., Zheng, J., Su, Z., et al.: Construction of knowledge graph of substation main equipment based on LLM. In: 2024 3rd Asia Power and Electrical Technology Conference (APET), pp. 746–750. IEEE (2024)
18. Stanovsky, G., Dagan, I.: Creating a large benchmark for open information extraction. In: Proceedings of the 2016 Conference on Empirical Methods in Natural Language Processing, pp. 2300–2305 (2016)
19. Mesquita, F., Schmidek, J., Barbosa, D.: Effectiveness and efficiency of open relation extraction. In: Proceedings of the 2013 Conference on Empirical Methods in Natural Language Processing, pp. 447–457 (2013)
20. Riedel, S., Yao, L., McCallum, A.: Modeling relations and their mentions without labeled text. In: Balcázar, J.L., Bonchi, F., Gionis, A., Sebag, M. (eds.) Machine Learning and Knowledge Discovery in Databases. ECML PKDD 2010. Lecture Notes in Computer Science, vol. 6323, pp. 148–163. Springer, Heidelberg (2010)
21. Radford, A., et al.: Learning transferable visual models from natural language supervision. In: International Conference on Machine Learning, pp. 8748–8763. PMLR (2021)
22. Mihindukulasooriya, N., Tiwari, S., Enguix, C.F., et al.: Text2KGBench: a benchmark for ontology-driven knowledge graph generation from text. In: International Semantic Web Conference, pp. 247–265. Springer, Cham (2023)
23. Kolluru, K., Adlakha, V., Aggarwal, S., Chakrabarti, S., et al.: OpenIE6: iterative grid labeling and coordination analysis for open information extraction. arXiv preprint arXiv:2010.03147 (2020)

24. Angeli, G., Premkumar, M.J.J., Manning, C.D.: Leveraging linguistic structure for open domain information extraction. In: Proceedings of the 53rd Annual Meeting of the Association for Computational Linguistics and the 7th International Joint Conference on Natural Language Processing, vol. 1: Long Papers, pp. 344–354 (2015)
25. Wang, C., Liu, X., Chen, Z., Hong, H., Tang, J., Song, D.: Zero-shot information extraction as a unified text-to-triple translation. arXiv preprint arXiv:2109.11171 (2021)
26. Han, J., Collier, N., Buntine, W., Shareghi, E.: PIVE: prompting with iterative verification improving graph-based generative capability of LLMs. arXiv preprint arXiv:2305.12392 (2023)
27. Chen, H., Shen, X., Lv, Q., Wang, J., Ni, X., Ye, J.: SAC-KG: exploiting large language models as skilled automatic constructors for domain knowledge graph. In: Proceedings of the 62nd Annual Meeting of the Association for Computational Linguistics, volume 1: Long Papers, pp. 4345–4360. Association for Computational Linguistics, Bangkok (2024)

Embedding-Based Ontology Term Recommendation System for FAIR Data Publishing Workflows

Nan Liu[✉][iD], Mohamed-Anis Koubaa[iD], Andreas Schmidt[iD], Karl-Uwe Stucky[iD], Wolfgang Suess[iD], and Veit Hagenmeyer[iD]

Karlsruhe Institute of Technology, Karlsruhe , Germany
{nan.liu,mohamed.koubaa,andreas.schmidt,karl-uwe.stucky,
wolfgang.suess,veit.hagenmeyer}@kit.edu

Abstract. FAIR (Findable, Accessible, Interoperable, and Reusable) data publications are important for enabling open energy research across interdisciplinary domains. The realization of the FAIR principle for data still faces many challenges, such as the diversity of data formats, semantic heterogeneity, lack of formalized ontologies, and error-prone manual annotation of data. These challenges impede the effective sharing and integration of energy data. To address these issues, we propose an automated ontology term recommendation system based on ontology embedding and semantic similarity, aiming to facilitate FAIR data publication in energy research. Our recommendation system utilizes contextual embeddings to automate semantic annotation of heterogeneous energy datasets by linking data elements to predefined energy-specific ontologies and referring to the top-K most relevant ontology concepts. The proposed system is designed to significantly streamline the semantic annotation process for energy researchers, thereby accelerating the process of open energy research. For evaluation, we test our system on the SemTab Challenge 2024 dataset provided by the Ontology Alignment Evaluation Initiative (OAEI). The experimental results show that our system improves the matching accuracy significantly compared to the baseline system.

Keywords: Energy Data Management · FAIR Principles · Large Language Model · Ontology Embeddings · Ontology Alignment · Recommendation System

1 Introduction

Energy systems are becoming increasingly complex as they interconnect and integrate multiple energy sources (such as energy storage systems, smart grids, etc.). The operation and optimization of such systems not only rely on a large amount of structured data, but also continuously generate extensive data resources. How to effectively share and reuse these data is important for open science research and data-driven energy management. However, there are still many challenges in real-world applications. For example, different energy systems and research projects often use their own terminology and

C. Cappiello et al. (Eds.): CoopIS 2025, LNCS 15535, pp. 573–583, 2026.
https://doi.org/10.1007/978-3-032-15538-2_35

nomenclature, due to the lack of unified semantic standards, the same concept will have different field names in different datasets, which thereby limits the reusability of the data for semantic search, automated reasoning, and cross-system integration. To achieve efficient reuse of energy data, semantic annotation is considered a core technology following the FAIR principles [20]. After the semantic annotation, the data has a clear semantic definition and can be released to an open data platform or knowledge graphs. However, manual semantic annotation is extremely difficult and error-prone. First, researchers or data providers may not be familiar with the structure of the ontology. Many researchers are familiar with their own domain knowledge but lack the background knowledge of the semantic web technologies to understand the inheritance relationships or subclass relations between ontology terms. Secondly, the same terminology varies in different domains or standards. Terminology in the energy domain often has multiple meanings. The definitions and structure of the same term may also differ from one ontology to another. Manual determination of the differences between these terms requires reviewing a large number of documents, which is time-consuming and challenging. Finally, the manual annotation process is difficult to maintain consistently. Without assistive tools, researchers need to perform term-by-term terminology queries and comparisons, and manually map them to the target ontology. Different people may have different understandings of the terminology, which may have inconsistent results. This semantic inconsistency will directly affect the subsequent data integration, information retrieval, and knowledge reasoning tasks.

With the extensive use of Natural Language Processing (NLP), especially pre-trained language models, more and more language understanding and semantic reasoning tasks can be automated by NLP models. Semantic annotation maps the natural language descriptions to formalized domain ontologies and can also be improved with the help of NLP. The main contribution of this paper is the development of an ontology term recommendation system to assist or partially replace the manual semantic annotation process. The system automatically extracts descriptive information from energy-related tabular (meta)data sets and then uses a large language model to automatically enrich the data descriptions. By calculating the semantic similarity, the system will generate the top-K most relevant recommendation results. Through the proposed system, users can quickly select appropriate ontology terms for their data, thereby reducing annotation barriers and improving the accuracy and consistency of semantic annotation. The following sections are organized as follows: In Sect. 2 and 3, we review the existing work and background knowledge related to this research. Section 4 presents the overall system architecture. Section 5 shows the experimental setup, and Sect. 6 shows and analyzes the results. And finally, we conclude the paper in Sect. 7.

2   Related Work

Semantic annotation is a crucial step towards semantic interoperability of data, which aims to semantically link data to ontology terms. Early semantic annotation methods mostly relied on manual or rule-based methods, for instance, in [15], which provides an overview of traditional approaches, such as rule-based methods [11–13]. Some machine learning-based methods [4,6,10] were also used for semantic annotation. However, these methods are less efficient with large-scale datasets and require more ontological knowledge from the users. In recent years, some research has encoded ontology terms as vector embeddings (aka ontology embedding). By representing the labels, definitions, and the structural relationships of ontology terms in the vector space, it is possible to match data fields with ontology terms. In [2], Chen et al. comprehensively classified and analyzed ontology embedding methods. For instance, geometric modeling methods [16,21], sequence modeling methods [1], and graph propagation methods [9].

3   Background

3.1   Semantic Annotation

The aim of the semantic annotation is to enrich datasets with machine-readable, structured metadata, which enables better data integration, aggregation, search, and reuse. In practice, this is achieved by connecting the entities within datasets from controlled vocabularies. These vocabularies are usually characterized by clear definitions and uniform terminology. Currently, there are two main approaches for semantic annotation. The first is that data providers manually annotate their datasets by selecting terms from established domain-specific vocabularies. The second is that metadata registries empower the community to register metadata that describes existing datasets or their variations. In both contexts, the level of semantic control of the descriptive vocabularies employed directly impacts the findability and interoperability of datasets. Moreover, semantic annotation can also help the knowledge extraction process because the use of unique identifiers within given ontologies or thesauri for concepts enables precise linking across datasets and applications.

3.2   Embedding Selection

Word embedding is an important and widely used technique in NLP and has achieved significant results in many tasks such as text classification [18], information retrieval [7,8], and question answering systems [5,14]. Word embedding can capture hidden semantic and syntactic information [19] at the word-level. The most popular word embedding technique is BERT [3]. BERT is a pre-trained language model based on the encoder-only transformer. The pre-training phase of BERT includes two unsupervised tasks, first, Masked Language Model (MLM), where 15% of the input words are randomly masked and subsequently predicted. The second task is Next Sentence Prediction (NSP), which aims to understand the relationship between two sentences, in other words, to determine whether two sentences are consecutive.

In addition to word embedding, sentence embedding has also become a prominent area of research in recent years. The goal of sentence embedding is to encode the whole sentence as a dense fixed-length vector to capture the overall semantic information of the sentence, which can be used for semantic matching and retrieval. Among many sentence embedding methods, Sentence-Bidirectional Encoder Representations from Transformer (SBERT) [17] has received much attention as an important model.

4   Recommendation System Design

Based on the FAIR principles, we outline a data publication workflow, as shown in Fig. 1. First, Energy Data Orchestrator (EDO) collects and organizes information from the Research Data Management Organizer (RDMO)[1] and other organizations (such as the sensor management system, knowledge graphs, and electronic lab notebooks). EDO compiles this information into structured metadata and provides a user interface where data providers can edit (meta)data descriptions. To ensure that data are FAIRly published, we design an ontology term recommendation system that achieves automatic annotation. After annotation, datasets can be published to open data platforms or integrated into knowledge graphs with standardized ontology terms. In the following, we detail the design and implementation of the recommendation system.

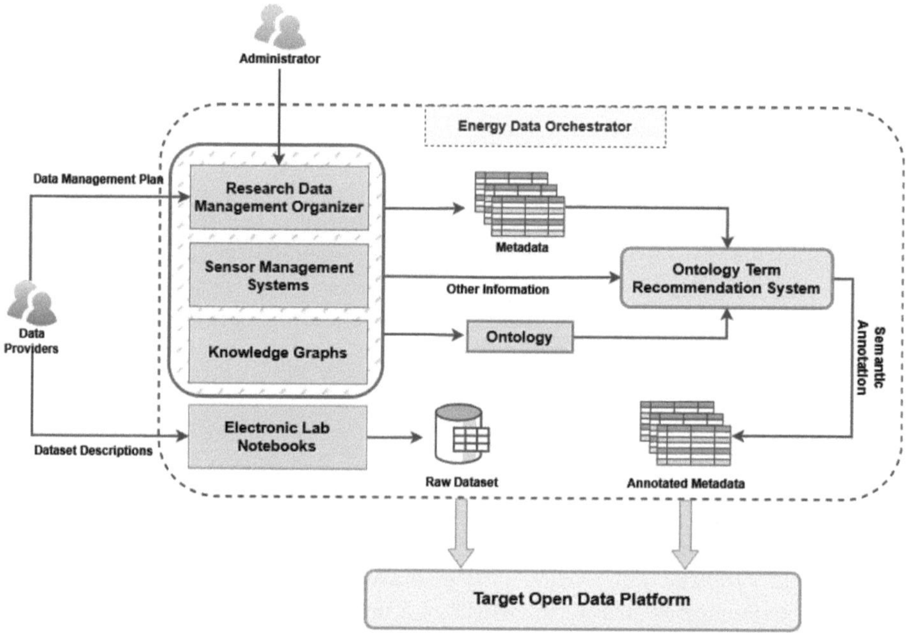

Fig. 1. FAIR Energy Data Publication Pipeline with EDO.

4.1   Tabular Data Extraction and Enrichment

After the EDO has collected the metadata, the system first performs entity-level extraction of the metadata. The data extraction and enrichment workflow is shown in Fig. 2. The system first automatically identifies each column of the table and extracts its header, data type, and units. However, the row metadata alone may lack semantic diversity,

---

[1] https://rdmorganiser.github.io/.

especially when column names are abbreviated, ambiguous, or domain-specific. Since most embedding models (e.g., SBERT) are not pre-trained on such domain-specific corpora, the resulting embeddings may fail to capture useful semantic information from them. To address this problem, we introduce large language models (LLMs) to enhance the expression of metadata descriptions. Given the extracted column name and contextual information, an LLM is prompted to generate a clean natural language description that captures the domain-specific semantics. To implement this, we develop an effective prompt template for LLM-enriched metadata descriptions. The prompt structure is shown in Listing 1.1.

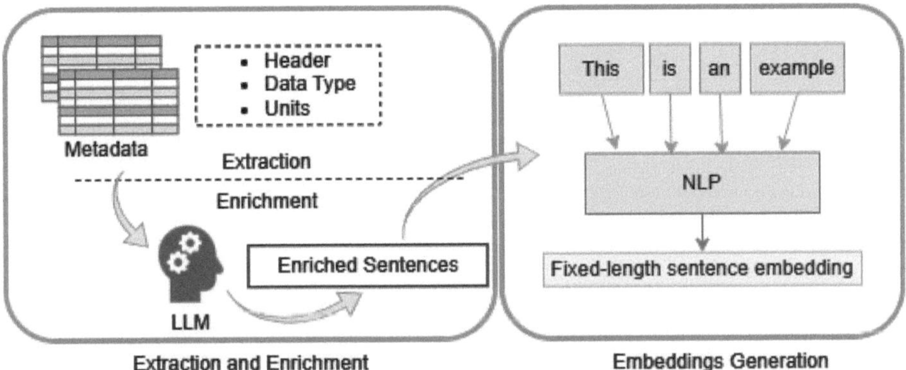

Fig. 2. Tabular Data Extraction and Enrichment workflow.

In addition, to avoid semantic ambiguities in the embedding due to excessive information or lengthy descriptions, we use weighted concatenation methods. The labels of data fields are embedded separately from their descriptions (LLM-generated descriptions), and the label is given a higher weight. The reason for this is that we are able to focus on the core semantics of the metadata while using the contextual richness offered by their descriptions. The mathematical formulation can be expressed as follows:

$$\mathbf{E}_{\text{final}} = \lambda \cdot \mathbf{E}_{\text{label}} \, \| \, (1 - \lambda) \cdot \mathbf{E}_{\text{desc}} \tag{1}$$

where $\lambda \in [0, 1]$ is a weighting hyperparameter and in our case λ is 0.6. $\|$ denotes a vector concatenation operation.

4.2 Ontology Embeddings

In our recommendation system, textual semantic information of ontologies are used as the core information. As shown in Algorithm 1, we first extract all classes and individuals in the ontology as the nodes of the graph, and the relation between them as the edges of the graph. The graph can be represented as $G = (N, E)$. Then, we extract all textual attributes for each node $n \in N$, including `rdfs:label`, `rdfs:comment`, and available synonyms from WordNet[2], and splice them into natural language sentences. We encode these sentences using a pre-trained Sentence-BERT[3] model from the Hugging Face library to generate a sentence-level embedding E_n^{text} for each node.

Algorithm 1. Ontology Embedding Construction.

Require: Ontology file O (e.g., OWL), pretrained SBERT model, RGCN model (optional)
Ensure: Ontology embeddings E
    Step 1: Ontology Parsing
1: Extract all **classes** C and **individuals** I from O
2: $N \leftarrow C \cup I$
    Step 2: Relation Graph Construction
3: Initialize edge set $E \leftarrow \{\}$
4: Build graph $G = (N, E)$ with typed edges
    Step 3: Textual Embedding via SBERT
5: **for** each node $n \in N$ **do**
6:    Retrieve `rdfs:label`, `rdfs:comment`, and synonyms from `WordNet`
7:    Concatenate as: $t_n \leftarrow$ `label [SEP] comment [SEP] synonyms`
8:    $Emb_n^{\text{text}} \leftarrow \text{SBERT}(t_n)$
9: **end for**
10: **return** Final ontology embeddings Emb

4.3 Recommendation Strategies

We use a recommendation strategy based on semantic embedding similarity retrieval, which is shown in Algorithm 2. We calculate the similarity score between the embeddings of metadata descriptions and the embedding of a pre-calculated ontology. Specifically, we use a pre-trained Sentence-BERT to encode the metadata field descriptions as a normalized embedding $\mathbf{v}_x \in \mathbb{R}^d$, and ontology embedding $\{\mathbf{e}_1, \mathbf{e}_2, \ldots, \mathbf{e}_i\}$, $\mathbf{e}_i \in \mathbb{R}^d$. The similarity score between $\mathbf{v}_x$ and $\mathbf{e}_i$ can be calculated using cosine similarity:

$$s_i = \cos(\mathbf{v}_x, \mathbf{e}_i) = \frac{\mathbf{v}_x \cdot \mathbf{e}_i}{\|\mathbf{v}_x\| \cdot \|\mathbf{e}_i\|} \tag{2}$$

We rank all similarity scores $\mathbf{s}_i$, and return the first top-K terms with the highest scores as the recommendation results.

---

[2] https://wordnet.princeton.edu/.
[3] https://huggingface.co/sentence-transformers/all-MiniLM-L6-v2.

Algorithm 2. Ontology Term Recommendation with Embedding Similarity.

Require: Input text x (e.g., field description), ontology embeddings E^{comb}, corresponding concept IDs

Ensure: Top-k recommended ontology terms

 1: **function** RECOMMENDCONCEPTS(x, E^{comb}, k)
 2:     $q \leftarrow$ GetCombinedEmbedding(x)
 3:     Normalize q and E^{comb}
 4:     Compute cosine similarities between q and all E^{comb}
 5:     Retrieve top-k concepts with highest scores
 6:     **return** Recommended term list with labels, scores, and URIs
 7: **end function**
 8: **Main execution:**
 9: **for** each input description x_i in dataset **do**
10:     $R_i \leftarrow$ RECOMMENDCONCEPTS(x_i, E^{comb}, k)
11:     Save R_i to output
12: **end for**

Listing 1.1. Prompt Template

```
You are a scientific assistant. Based on the metadata below,
    generate one concise but informative sentence to describe a
    dataset column. If a unit symbol is given, convert it into
    natural language (for example, kWh to kilowatt hours) and
    explain it in context.
-Column name: {name}
-Description: {desc}
-Unit symbol: {unit}
-Data type: {dtype}
```

5   Experiments

5.1   Data Set

We evaluate our system using the OAEI SemTab 2024 Challenge dataset, focusing on the Metadata to Knowledge Graph round 1 task. Due to the limited contextual information of the provided metadata files, this task is very challenging and requires a higher level of semantic understanding from the recommendation system. The data set is available on the GitHub repository[4]. This task contains a collection of metadata tables extracted from web tables, the DBpedia ontology, and a ground truth dataset for evaluation. The metadata file consists of 141 columns. Each column includes column IDs, labels, table IDs, table names and a list of all column labels in the same table, which aims to provide contextual information. The DBpedia Ontology contains 2881 properties. Each property includes a unique identifier, a property label, and a textual description. The ground truth assigns the most semantically matched DBpedia property for each column, which enables a standard evaluation of ontology term recommendation systems.

---

[4] https://github.com/sem-tab-challenge/2024/tree/main/data/metadata2kg/round1.

5.2 Experiment Setups

We conduct several comparison experiments to evaluate the impact of the richness of metadata descriptions and different embedding fusion methods on the performance of our recommendation system. To ensure a fair comparison, all the experiments use the same ontology embeddings. We splice the label, definition, and synonyms from Word-Net for each ontology term and encode them using SBERT to generate the ontology embeddings.

We use SBERT (all-mpnet-base-v2) to generate embeddings for both metadata information and ontology terms, and compute cosine similarity to rank the top 5 candidate ontology terms. All experiments are performed on the HAICORE@KIT[5] high-performance computing platform equipped with Intel Xeon Platinum 8368 CPUs and an NVIDIA A100-40 GPU.

5.3 Evaluation Metrics

To evaluate the performance of our recommendation system, we use the Python evaluation script provided by the OAEI SemTab 2024 Challenge, which is available in the GitHub repository. The Python script can evaluate the accuracy of the mapping between the given metadata file and the ground truth file. It contains two metrics, Hit@1 and Hit@5. A Hit@k metric is used to measure the proportion of the top-K terms in the recommendation list that contain the correct term. Specifically, Hit@1 indicates whether the correct recommendation is ranked at the top of the recommendation list, while Hit@5 checks if it appears within the top five.

6 Results

6.1 Experimental Results

The results of the experiments described in Sect. 5 are shown in Table 1. Different metadata information and embedding fusion methods can directly affect the experiment results. The baseline method (Label only) achieves 28% and 45% on Hit@1 and Hit@5. With the addition of the table name, Hit@1 improves to 33%, which shows that contextual information is helpful in understanding the semantics of columns. Both Hit@1 and Hit@5 decrease with the weighted fusion. One possible reason is that directly using the table name may introduce semantic ambiguity. This could reduce the overall quality of the metadata representation. Thus, we introduce the LLM-enriched metadata descriptions. With these enriched descriptions, our system achieves a Hit@1 of 35% and Hit@5 of 59% using the vector concatenation method. Furthermore, by applying a weighted fusion method, the Hit@1 increases to 47% and Hit@5 to 61%. These results demonstrate the effectiveness of using LLM to enrich the semantic representation of metadata, as well as the weighted embedding fusion method.

---

[5] https://www.nhr.kit.edu/userdocs/haicore/.

Table 1. Experiment Results.

Metadata Embeddings	Hit@1	Hit@5
SBERT(label)	28%	45%
SBERT(label+table name)	33%	44%
SBERT(label)+SBERT(table name)	22%	44%
SBERT(label+gpt-4o-mini enriched description)	35%	59%
SBERT(label)+SBERT(gpt-4o-mini enriched description)	47%	61%

7 Conclusion

In this paper, we propose an ontology term recommendation system that aims to help researchers reduce the semantic annotation barriers that they face during the FAIR data publication process. The goal of the proposed system is to minimize the misannotation by users due to a lack of ontology knowledge, thereby enhancing the interoperability and reusability of the energy research data, which supports open science research. Semantic similarity is used to match the tabular metadata field name with respective ontology terms and recommend the top-K most relevant ontology terms to users. In our recommendation system, we design an optional structural information enhancement module to consider the structural features of complex ontologies. The system uses graph-based embedding to enrich the semantic diversity. We also enrich and complete the metadata of energy data using a large language model. The code of the recommendation system can be found in a GitHub repository[6]. Experimental results show that the system can provide accurate ontology term recommendations without relying on the users' deep understanding of the target ontology. This approach effectively simplifies the data publishing process.

However, the system still has some limitations. For example, it may still have some errors when dealing with semantic ambiguity. In future work, we will introduce a user feedback mechanism to make the recommendation process more interactive and accurate. Besides, we will consider adding an ontology matching module to the system to support cross-ontology term recommendation and annotation, which can enhance the data interoperability and better meet the goal of FAIR data management.

Acknowledgements. The authors would like to thank the German Federal Government, the German State Governments, and the Joint Science Conference (GWK) for their funding and support as part of the NFDI4Energy consortium. The work was funded by the German Research Foundation (DFG) – 501865131 within the German National Research Data Infrastructure (NFDI, www.nfdi.de).

This work is supported by the Helmholtz Association Initiative and Networking Fund on the HAICORE@KIT partition and the Helmholtz Metadata Collaboration (HMC).

---

[6] https://github.com/nnliu1/sem_annotation.

References

1. Chen, J., Hu, P., Jimenez-Ruiz, E., Holter, O.M., Antonyrajah, D., Horrocks, I.: Owl2vec*: embedding of owl ontologies. Mach. Learn. **110**(7), 1813–1845 (2021)
2. Chen, J., Mashkova, O., Zhapa-Camacho, F., Hoehndorf, R., He, Y., Horrocks, I.: Ontology embedding: a survey of methods, applications and resources. IEEE Trans. Knowl. Data Eng. (2025)
3. Devlin, J., Chang, M.W., Lee, K., Toutanova, K.: BERT: pre-training of deep bidirectional transformers for language understanding. In: Burstein, J., Doran, C., Solorio, T. (eds.) Proceedings of the 2019 Conference of the North American Chapter of the Association for Computational Linguistics: Human Language Technologies, Volume 1 (Long and Short Papers). pp. 4171–4186. Association for Computational Linguistics, Minneapolis, Minnesota (Jun 2019). https://doi.org/10.18653/v1/N19-1423, https://aclanthology.org/N19-1423/
4. Dingli, A., Ciravegna, F., Wilks, Y.: Automatic semantic annotation using unsupervised information extraction and integration. In: Workshop on Knowledge Markup and Semantic Annotation (2003)
5. Esposito, M., Damiano, E., Minutolo, A., De Pietro, G., Fujita, H.: Hybrid query expansion using lexical resources and word embeddings for sentence retrieval in question answering. Inf. Sci. **514**, 88–105 (2020)
6. Etzioni, O., et al.: Unsupervised named-entity extraction from the web: An experimental study. Artif. Intell. **165**(1), 91–134 (2005)
7. Ganguly, D., Roy, D., Mitra, M., Jones, G.J.: Word embedding based generalized language model for information retrieval. In: Proceedings of the 38th International ACM SIGIR Conference on Research and Development in Information Retrieval, pp. 795–798 (2015)
8. Hambarde, K.A., Proenca, H.: Information retrieval: recent advances and beyond. IEEE Access **11**, 76581–76604 (2023)
9. Hao, Z., Mayer, W., Xia, J., Li, G., Qin, L., Feng, Z.: Ontology alignment with semantic and structural embeddings. J. Web Semant. **78**, 100798 (2023)
10. Kiyavitskaya, N., Zeni, N., Cordy, J.R., Mich, L., Mylopoulos, J.: Cerno: light-weight tool support for semantic annotation of textual documents. Data Knowl. Eng. **68**(12), 1470–1492 (2009)
11. Kogut, P.A., Holmes III, W.S.: Aerodaml: applying information extraction to generate daml annotations from web pages. In: Semannot@ K-CAP 2001 (2001)
12. Krötzsch, M., Vrandečić, D., Völkel, M.: Semantic mediawiki. In: International Semantic Web Conference, pp. 935–942. Springer (2006)
13. Malik, S.K., Prakash, N., Rizvi, S.: Semantic annotation framework for intelligent information retrieval using kim architecture. Inter. J. Web Semantic Technol. (IJWest) **1**(4), 12–26 (2010)
14. Nassiri, K., Akhloufi, M.: Transformer models used for text-based question answering systems. Appl. Intell. **53**(9), 10602–10635 (2023)
15. Oliveira, P., Rocha, J.: Semantic annotation tools survey. In: 2013 IEEE Symposium on Computational Intelligence and Data Mining (CIDM), pp. 301–307 (2013). https://doi.org/10.1109/CIDM.2013.6597251
16. Peng, X., Tang, Z., Kulmanov, M., Niu, K., Hoehndorf, R.: Description logic el++ embeddings with intersectional closure. ArXiv abs/ arxiv: 2202.14018 (2022), https://api.semanticscholar.org/CorpusID:247158730

17. Reimers, N., Gurevych, I.: Sentence-BERT: Sentence embeddings using Siamese BERT-networks. In: Inui, K., Jiang, J., Ng, V., Wan, X. (eds.) Proceedings of the 2019 Conference on Empirical Methods in Natural Language Processing and the 9th International Joint Conference on Natural Language Processing (EMNLP-IJCNLP), pp. 3982–3992. Association for Computational Linguistics, Hong Kong, China (Nov 2019). https://doi.org/10.18653/v1/D19-1410, https://aclanthology.org/D19-1410/
18. Selva Birunda, S., Kanniga Devi, R.: A review on word embedding techniques for text classification. In: Raj, J.S., Iliyasu, A.M., Bestak, R., Baig, Z.A. (eds.) Innovative Data Communication Technologies and Application. LNDECT, vol. 59, pp. 267–281. Springer, Singapore (2021). https://doi.org/10.1007/978-981-15-9651-3_23
19. Wang, B., Wang, A., Chen, F., Wang, Y., Kuo, C.C.J.: Evaluating word embedding models: methods and experimental results. APSIPA Trans. Signal Inform. Process. **8**, e19 (2019)
20. Wilkinson, M.D., et al.: The fair guiding principles for scientific data management and stewardship. Scientific Data **3**(1), 1–9 (2016)
21. Xiong, B., Potyka, N., Tran, T.K., Nayyeri, M., Staab, S.: Faithful embeddings for el++ knowledge bases. In: International Semantic Web Conference, pp. 22–38. Springer (2022). https://doi.org/10.1007/978-3-031-19433-7_2

Path-Based Explanations for Knowledge Graph-Driven Course Recommendation

Nadia Ben Hadj Boubaker[1]([✉])(iD), Zahra Kodia[1](iD), and Nadia Yacoubi Ayadi[2](iD)

[1] University of Tunis, ISG Tunis, SMART-LAB, Tunis, Tunisia
{nadia.benhadjboubaker,zahra.kodia}@isg.rnu.tn
[2] Université Claude Bernard Lyon 1, CNRS, LIRIS (UMR 5205), Lyon, France
nadia.yacoubi-ayadi@univ-lyon1.fr

Abstract. Recommendation systems (RS) play a key role in e-learning by guiding learners toward relevant educational resources. Yet, the integration of domain knowledge to enhance both accuracy and explainability remains underexplored. This paper presents an explainable e-learning RS grounded in an educational Knowledge Graph (KG). The KG is constructed by extracting and linking key course concepts, and leveraged through embedding techniques to improve recommendation quality. To ensure transparency, we propose a path-based explanation mechanism that identifies and ranks user–course connections using a scoring function combining similarity measures and random walk probabilities. A case study demonstrates that the approach not only improves recommendation accuracy but also generates diverse, interpretable explanations, contributing to more transparent and trustworthy systems.

Keywords: Recommendation Systems · Knowledge Graphs · Explainability · E-Learning

1 Introduction

Explainable Artificial Intelligence (XAI) has become essential need towards increasing trust and transparency in machine learning models, especially in domains where decision-making impacts users directly. Knowledge Graphs (KG) offer a promising solution by representing entities and their relationships in a structured, semantically rich form. The dual capability of supporting machine reasoning and enabling human-understandable explanations makes KG a natural fit for XAI [16]. In the context of recommender systems (RS), explainability can be achieved either through intrinsically transparent models or via post-hoc methods designed to justify system outputs [23]. Increasingly, KGs have been integrated into RS to address the limitations of conventional approaches by unifying preference propagation with KG embedding regularization [6,21]. Explanations are typically generated by tracking semantic paths from user interactions to recommended items, thereby improving acceptance, satisfaction, and trust. Nevertheless, most existing approaches rely on open-domain KGs such as DBpedia or Freebase [3]. While these resources offer broad coverage, they often lack the

C. Cappiello et al. (Eds.): CoopIS 2025, LNCS 15535, pp. 584–595, 2026.
https://doi.org/10.1007/978-3-032-15538-2_36

domain-specific granularity required for precise and reliable explanations in specialized contexts such as education. To address this gap, we propose a post-hoc explainable framework for educational recommender systems. In this paper, we introduce EduKA, a domain-specific knowledge graph that integrates user interactions with detailed metadata about learning materials. We compare multiple Knowledge Graph Embedding (KGE) methods to evaluate their impact on recommendation performance and present a case study illustrating how EduKA supports interpretable reasoning chains. Our findings demonstrate that domain-specific KGs can enhance both transparency and trustworthiness in educational recommendations.

The paper is structured as follows: Sect. 2 reviews related work on knowledge graph construction in e-learning contexts and their use in explainable recommender systems. In Sect. 3, we present our proposed approach, detailing the EduKA knowledge graph construction pipeline and comparing different knowledge graph embedding techniques to evaluate their effect on recommendation performance. Section 4 introduces a path-based post-hoc explainability method that leverages the structural richness of EduKA to generate interpretable recommendations. Finally, Sect. 5 summarizes our contributions and outlines our future work.

2   Related Works

Recent advances in Machine Learning (ML) and Natural Language Processing (NLP) have stimulated growing interest in the automatic construction of KG [8]. In the educational domain, this task remains particularly challenging due to the difficulty of extracting core pedagogical elements such as learning outcomes, prerequisite relations, and domain-specific concepts [1]. To address these challenges, Lu et al. [12] introduced DS-MOCE, which combines pre-trained language models with domain-specific embeddings to extract course concepts from MOOCs, thereby mitigating issues of noisy or incomplete annotations. Similarly, Reales et al. [17] leveraged large language models (LLMs) to construct semantic KGs using pipelines that integrate zero-shot triple extraction with DBpedia-based enrichment.

Beyond their construction, KG have also been increasingly applied in e-learning recommender systems to improve both personalization and interpretability [7]. Ain et al. [2] modeled learner knowledge through personal KGs enriched with SBERT embeddings, while Boubaker et al. [4] proposed KA-ERN, which combines KG embeddings with ensemble deep learning for personalized recommendations. Troussas et al. [20] designed a path-based system linking students and activities through relations such as difficulty or cognitive level, with recommendations generated via meta-paths and pattern mining. While these approaches demonstrate high recommendation accuracy, they often lack explainability, which remains essential for fostering user trust and understanding.

To address this limitation, post-hoc explanation techniques such as LIME [18] and SHAP [13] have been applied to clarify recommendation processes. Nevertheless, these approaches often struggle to provide explanations that are both intuitive and aligned with domain knowledge, particularly when neural networks are employed in complex domains such as healthcare [23] and education [15]. In this context, our work contributes to the growing research on explainable educational recommender systems. We introduce EduKA, a purpose-built educational knowledge graph that captures rich semantic relationships among users, courses, and domain concepts. Leveraging EduKA, we generate post-hoc explanations in the form of ranked paths, enabling learners to trace and better comprehend the reasoning behind recommendations.

3   Proposed Approach

In this section, we introduce the pipeline of the proposed approach which comprises three main phases: (1) the EduKA (Educational Knowledge GrAph) modeling and construction, (2) the recommendation generation, and (3) the explainability generation. Figure 1 illustrates the overall workflow of the proposed approach.

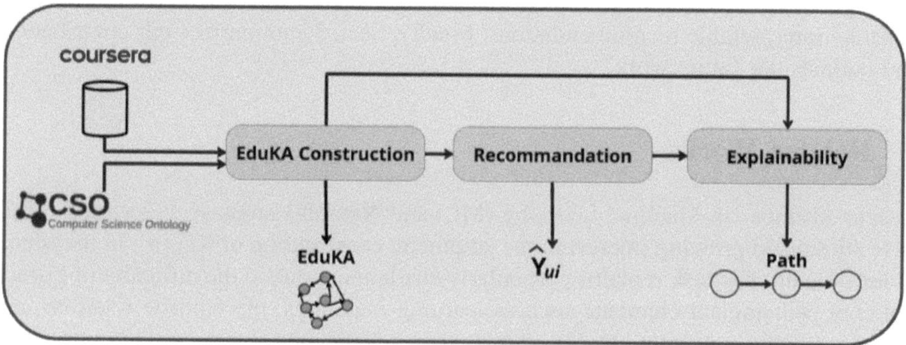

Fig. 1. The workflow of our approach.

3.1   EduKA Graph Modeling and Construction

The EduKA knowledge graph[1] has been developed as part of this research to support explainable recommendations in educational contexts. It is modeled as an RDF graph that integrates both user–item interaction data and structured domain knowledge considering a Coursera dataset[2] (Fig. 2).

The graph construction process is based on a multi-stage pipeline that combines state-of-the-art Natural Language Processing (NLP) and knowledge modeling. It includes automated concept extraction, entity linking, and semantic graph construction, enabling the transformation of unstructured textual data into a structured knowledge representation. The key components of this process are described in detail in following.

---

[1] The RDF version of EduKA is available at https://zenodo.org/records/15804872.
[2] https://www.kaggle.com/datasets/khusheekapoor/coursera-courses-dataset-2021.

Course Concept (CC) Extraction. To identify course-related concepts, we adopt a dual strategy leveraging two complementary methods. First, we apply a keyphrase extraction approach based on the KBIR framework [9], which combines contextual semantic understanding and candidate ranking. The model, built upon a RoBERTa encoder [11] and trained on the Inspec benchmark, achieves state-of-the-art performance in extracting domain-relevant keyphrases. This makes it particularly suitable for capturing the core educational topics expressed in course descriptions.

In parallel, we employ the DBpedia Spotlight API[3] to detect and link named entities present in both course titles and descriptions. A confidence threshold of 0.8 is applied to ensure precision and contextual relevance in the entity recognition process. This ensures that a subset of extracted entities are reliably aligned with concepts in the DBpedia knowledge base, thereby facilitating semantic grounding within a structured RDF graph.

Entity Disambiguation and Linking. Entity linking (EL) involves the task of mapping course keyphrases extracted in the first step of the pipeline to structured domain knowledge formalized in domain ontologies. Specifically, we leverage the Computer Science Ontology (CSO)[4] to support domain-specific entity linking, as the majority of courses in our dataset fall within the computer science field. In order to disambiguate the outputs of CC extraction step, we go through a two-fold process:

- **Ontology-Based Entity Linking:** The CSO provides a comprehensive and hierarchically structured vocabulary for computer science topics. To operationalize its use, we transform the ontology into a dictionary-based representation, enabling efficient matching and grouping of semantically equivalent or related terms under unified labels. Additionally, a curated subset of the CSO was developed to reduce redundancy and ensure consistency in concept mapping across all educational resources within the graph.
- **Fuzzy String for Approximate Matching:** In cases where exact string matching with CSO concepts fail, we integrate the FuzzyWuzzy library[5] which performs approximate string matching using the Levenshtein distance metric. It is particularly well-suited for identifying approximate matches and effectively handling minor variations in word order, spelling, and structure. In our work, FuzzyWuzzy was integrated to handle cases where course keywords did not directly match any concept in the CSO or Basic Concepts List. By applying a high similarity threshold of 0.9, we ensured that only relevant and semantically meaningful matches were accepted, reducing false positives.

KG Modeling and Generation. The RDFLib Python library is used to construct the RDF graph, structuring course metadata (e.g., title, difficulty level) according to open vocabularies such as Schema.org[6] and Dublin Core standards. In EduKA, each

---

[3] https://www.dbpedia-spotlight.org/api.

[4] https://cso.kmi.open.ac.uk/home.

[5] https://pypi.org/project/fuzzywuzzy/.

[6] https://schema.org/.

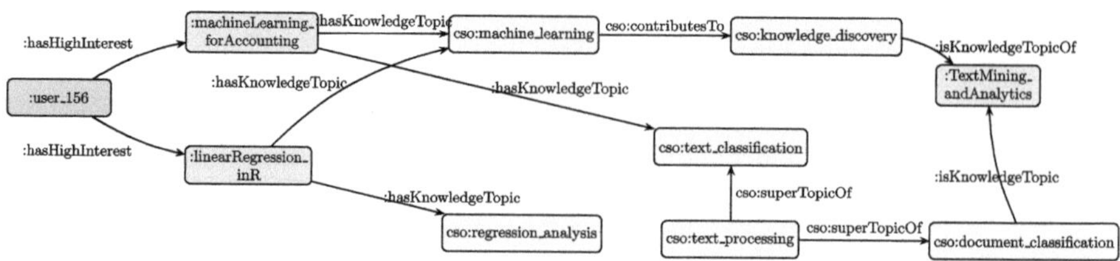

Fig. 2. An EduKA sub-graph illustrating user-item interactions, CSO course concepts and their inter-links.

course is semantically linked to CSO topics using the *eduka:hasKnowledgeTopic* property. Additionally, user-item interactions are integrated into the graph, categorized into three levels—*eduka:smallInterest, eduka:mediumInterest,* and *eduka:highInterest*—to capture varying user engagement levels with courses. Table 1 provides an overview of the statistics of the EduKA knowledge graph, including user-item interactions and the structural properties of the underlying knowledge graph.

Table 1. Graph Statistics.

User-Item dataset	# of Users: 1,000
	# of Items: 3,533
	# of Interactions: 68,801
EduKA Knowledge graph	# of Entities: 15,300
	# of Entity Types: 3
	# of Relation Types: 11
	# of Triplets: 111,304

3.2 Recommendation Generation

In this section, we present a comprehensive evaluation designed to assess the performance of several KGE techniques in the context of recommendation systems. The embeddings generated by different approaches were used as input features for multiple classification models, enabling us to evaluate their predictive capacity in identifying relevant user-item interactions. The goal of this phase is not to introduce a new recommendation model, but rather to assess the suitability of various knowledge graph embedding techniques in supporting effective recommendations. We explore how different embeddings capture well the relational and semantic structure of the graph and support the recommendation task.

Thus, we have investigated five embedding methods that represent diverse approaches to graph representation learning: DistMult [22], TransR [10], Node2Vec [5], DeepWalk [14], and RDF2Vec [19]. These techniques were selected to cover both translational distance models (e.g., TransR), bilinear semantic models (e.g., DistMult), and path-based or random-walk strategies (e.g., Node2Vec, DeepWalk, RDF2Vec), thereby enabling a comparative analysis from topological and semantic perspectives.

Each embedding method was first used to generate vector representations for all entities in the EduKA knowledge graph. For every user-course pair, the embeddings of the user and the course were concatenated into a single feature vector $[f(u) \parallel f(i)]$, capturing both user interests and course characteristics. These vectors were then used as input to three classifiers: Multi-Layer Perceptron (MLP), Random Forest (RF), and XGBoost in order to predict the relevance of each user-course interaction. The resulting predictions were treated as recommendations, and model performance was evaluated using Precision, Recall, and F1-score metrics providing a quantitative evaluation of how well the embeddings supported accurate recommendations.

Table 2. Recommendation experiments: performance of different embedding methods and classifiers.

Embedding	Classifier	Precision	Recall	F1
DistMult	MLP	0.420	0.322	0.364
	RF	0.436	**0.990**	0.131
	XGBoost	**0.943**	0.986	**0.964**
Node2Vec	MLP	0.828	**0.815**	**0.821**
	RF	**0.945**	0.412	0.574
	XGBoost	0.839	0.669	0.745
DeepWalk	MLP	0.750	**0.857**	0.800
	RF	0.714	0.833	**0.769**
	XGBoost	**0.944**	0.586	0.723
RDF2Vec	MLP	0.771	0.900	**0.985**
	RF	0.769	0.269	0.399
	XGBoost	**0.846**	**0.919**	0.881
TransR	MLP	**0.908**	**0.944**	**0.926**
	RF	0.836	0.880	0.834
	XGBoost	0.876	0.880	0.878

As presented in Table 2, RDF2Vec and TransR combined with MLP deliver the best overall performance, with F1-scores of 0.985 and 0.926, respectively, indicating an excellent balance between precision and recall. DistMult performs well only when paired with XGBoost but shows very low performance with other classifiers, highlighting its strong dependence on the classification model. Random-walk-based methods, such as Node2Vec and DeepWalk, achieve intermediate performance. Among the classifiers, MLP consistently yields the best results, while RF favors high recall at the expense of precision, leading to lower F1-scores.

These findings contribute directly to the selection of embedding techniques for the KG-based recommendation framework. They demonstrate that certain models, particularly TransR and RDF2Vec, support accurate classification. In Sect. 4, we demonstrate how they also preserve semantic signals that can support post-hoc interpretability.

4   Explainibility Generation

While KGE-based methods capture relational patterns effectively, their latent representations remain opaque, limiting transparency in recommendation predictions. In educational settings, where trust and accountability are critical, explainability is essential to reveal which semantic and structural elements of the graph drive user–course recommendations. To address this, we introduce an explanation approach that exploits the semantic and structural richness of the EduKA knowledge graph. Our method generates path-level post-hoc explanations by exploring all user–item paths and presenting them as interpretable evidence chains. These chains leverage the explicitly defined semantics of nodes (e.g., topics, sub-topics, related topics) and edges (e.g., hasInterestIn, isKnowledgeTopicOf) to provide human-understandable justifications for recommendations. The underlying intuition is that considering multiple alternative paths highlights the diversity and robustness of the recommendation, showing not only why a course is relevant from one perspective but also reinforcing its validity through different semantic connections. Therefore, we propose a Path Ranking Approach (PRA), which systematically scores and ranks candidate paths based on their semantic coherence and structural plausibility. As illustrated in Table 3, the candidate paths may vary considerably in terms of length, informativeness, and clarity. Through a case study analysis, we show that PRA enables the selection of the most salient explanation paths, ensuring both relevance and interpretability in the context of user-centered educational recommendations.

4.1   Path Ranking Approach

Given a knowledge graph be denoted by $\mathcal{G} = (\mathcal{E}, \mathcal{R})$, where $\mathcal{E}$ is the set of entities (e.g., learners, courses, concepts) and $\mathcal{R}$ is the set of directed relations (e.g., eduka:highInterest, eduka:hasKnowledgeTopic, cso:ContributesTo). Let a set of paths $\mathcal{P} = \{p_1, p_2, \ldots, p_N\}$ such as each path p_i is defined as follows:

$$p_i = (v_0 = u, v_1, v_2, \ldots, v_L = i)$$

connecting the learner node u to a recommended course i. We assign to each path p_i a ranking score $S(p_i)$ defined as:

$$S(p_i) = \alpha \cdot \tilde{S}_{\mathrm{jac}}(p_i) + \beta \cdot \tilde{S}_{\mathrm{rw}}(p_i) \tag{1}$$

where:

- $\tilde{S}_{\mathrm{jac}}(p_i)$ is the normalized semantic similarity score based on jaccard index,
- $\tilde{S}_{\mathrm{rw}}(p_i)$ is the normalized relevance score based on random walk probability,
- $\alpha, \beta \in [0, 1]$ are weighting parameters satisfying $\alpha + \beta = 1$, controlling the influence of each component.

Path Similarity via Jaccard Index. Each path p_i is first transformed into a token set $T(p_i)$ containing the normalized labels of all nodes and edges along the path. This representation captures the key semantic and ontological elements involved in the explanation.

$$S_{\text{jac}}(p_i) = \frac{1}{N} \sum_{j=1}^{N} \frac{|T(p_i) \cap T(p_j)|}{|T(p_i) \cup T(p_j)|} \tag{2}$$

This formulation favors paths that exhibit greater lexical overlap with others, highlighting recurring semantic patterns in the explanation space. For comparability across paths, the raw Jaccard scores are normalized via min-max scaling:

$$\tilde{S}_{\text{jac}}(p_i) = \frac{S_{\text{jac}}(p_i) - \min_k S_{\text{jac}}(p_k)}{\max_k S_{\text{jac}}(p_k) - \min_k S_{\text{jac}}(p_k)} \tag{3}$$

Random Walk-Based Path Scoring. To capture both structural accessibility and semantic relevance of path-level explanations, we propose an improved scoring mechanism that integrates transition probabilities, relation semantics, and length normalization. The score of the path p_i is calculated as:

$$S_{\text{rw}}(p_i) = \left(\prod_{\ell=0}^{L-1} \mathbb{P}(v_{\ell+1} \mid v_\ell) \cdot w(e_{\ell,\ell+1}) \right)^{\frac{1}{L}} \tag{4}$$

where:

- $\mathbb{P}(v_{\ell+1} \mid v_\ell)$ is the transition probability from node v_ℓ to $v_{\ell+1}$, typically defined as:

$$\mathbb{P}(v_{\ell+1} \mid v_\ell) = \frac{1}{\deg^+(v_\ell)}$$

with $\deg^+(v_\ell)$ being the out-degree of node v_ℓ.
- $w(e_{\ell,\ell+1}) \in \mathbb{R}^+$ is an edge importance weight reflecting the semantic contribution of relation $e_{\ell,\ell+1}$ to the path's value.
- The exponent $\frac{1}{L}$ ensures geometric mean normalization, mitigating the penalization of longer paths.

After computing $S_{\text{rw}}(p_i)$ for all candidate paths, scores are normalized using min-max scaling:

$$\tilde{S}_{\text{rw}}(p_i) = \frac{S_{\text{rw}}(p_i) - \min_k S_{\text{rw}}(p_k)}{\max_k S_{\text{rw}}(p_k) - \min_k S_{\text{rw}}(p_k)} \tag{5}$$

The final path ranking score is a weighted combination of these two components, balancing semantic coherence with graph connectivity. To confirm the effectiveness and interpretability of this approach, we present a case study that illustrates how highly ranked paths are both meaningful and informative, providing transparent, interpretable explanations for recommended courses while emphasizing patterns common across learners' interactions.

4.2 Case Study Analysis

In order to evaluate the PRA approach, we design a case study that illustrates its effectiveness in providing and ranking explanation paths. Specifically, we consider a scenario where the course *Text Mining and Analytics* is recommended to a given user ($user_{156}$). For this user–item pair, we systematically extract all possible paths within the EduKA knowledge graph that connect the user to the recommended course.

In total, we identified 10 distinct paths and grouped them according to their structural patterns. Four main path patterns were distinguished, as illustrated in Table 3. The reported frequency indicates how many explanation paths of a given pattern were found in our running example. These patterns highlight both the diversity and richness of the explanations, as well as the system's ability to uncover various meaningful connections that justify the recommendation. Each pattern reflects a specific way in which the user's prior learning history is semantically connected to the recommended course.

Table 3. Frequent explanation path patterns observed in the knowledge graph.

Path pattern	Frequency
$u \xrightarrow{\text{hasInterest}} c \xrightarrow{\text{hasKnowledgeTopic}} t_1 \xrightarrow{\text{contributesTo}} t_2 \xrightarrow{\text{isKnowledgeTopicOf}} c_{\text{rec}}$	5
$u \xrightarrow{\text{hasInterest}} c \xrightarrow{\text{hasKnowledgeTopic}} t \xrightarrow{\text{isKnowledgeTopicOf}} c_{\text{rec}}$	3
$u \xrightarrow{\text{hasInterest}} c \xrightarrow{\text{hasKnowledgeTopic}} t_1 \xrightarrow{\text{superTopicOf}} t_2 \xrightarrow{\text{isKnowledgeTopicOf}} c_{\text{rec}}$	1
$u \xrightarrow{\text{hasInterest}} c \xrightarrow{\text{hasKnowledgeTopic}} t_1 \xrightarrow{\text{superTopicOf}^{-1}} t_2 \xrightarrow{\text{superTopicOf}} t_3 \xrightarrow{\text{isKnowledgeTopicOf}} c_{\text{rec}}$	1

Once the candidate paths are extracted, we apply the Path Ranking Algorithm (PRA) to assign scores and rank them. Table 4 presents the results, showing the normalized Jaccard similarity, the normalized random walk probability, and the final aggregated score computed using a weighted combination of both values. In our experiments, we set $\alpha = 0.3$ and $\beta = 0.7$, assigning more importance to Jaccard similarity. This configuration yielded the best performance.

According to this ranking, the top-scored paths were P_2, P_3, and P_1. Their detailed structures are shown below:

```
P1 : user_156 --[hasHighInterest]--> Machine Learning for
     Accounting
            --[hasKnowledgeTopic]--> data_analytics
            --[ContributesTo]--> knowledge_discovery
            --[isKnowledgeTopicOf]--> Text Mining and Analytics
```

```
P2: user_156 --[hasHighInterest]--> Machine Learning for
     Accounting
            --[hasKnowledgeTopic]--> machine-learning
            --[ContributesTo]--> knowledge_discovery
            --[isKnowledgeTopicOf]--> Text Mining and Analytics
```

```
P3: user_156 --[hasHighInterest]--> Building and analyzing LR
    model in R
            --[hasKnowledgeTopic]--> machine-learning
            --[ContributesTo]--> knowledge_discovery
            --[isKnowledgeTopicOf]--> Text Mining and Analytics
```

Table 4. List of paths and their corresponding scores ($\alpha = 0.3$, $\beta = 0.7$).

Path ID	Nor. Jac. Sim.	Nor. RW Prob.	Final Score
p_2	0.589	0.472	0.804
p_3	0.558	0.562	0.772
p_1	0.573	0.472	0.740
p_9	0.545	0.562	0.720
p_5	0.563	0.368	0.596
p_4	0.516	0.464	0.508
p_7	0.512	0.472	0.501
p_6	0.468	0.562	0.418
p_8	0.411	0.668	0.300
p_{10}	0.413	0.584	0.225

Overall, this case study underscores several strengths of the proposed approach. First, it enables multi-hop reasoning, allowing the system to move beyond direct user–item interactions and uncover deeper semantic connections across multiple levels of the knowledge graph (Table 3). Second, the diversity of the extracted paths enriches the explanations and ensures they capture multiple facets of user interests. In summary, the qualitative analysis demonstrates that our method produces human-understandable, diverse, and meaningful explanations by effectively leveraging the structural and semantic richness of the educational knowledge graph.

5 Conclusions and Future Works

In this paper, we introduced an explainable recommender system specifically designed for the e-learning domain. Our work explored the potential of leveraging an educational knowledge graph, EduKA, to enhance both the accuracy of course recommendations and the transparency of their underlying rationale. By integrating knowledge graph embeddings with a path-ranking explanation mechanism, we demonstrated how recommendation accuracy can be improved while also providing diverse and semantically meaningful justifications. Beyond the technical contributions, this work highlights the importance of explainability in fostering trust and adoption of recommender systems in education. Explanations that are grounded in domain concepts not only help learners understand why a course is suggested, but also support metacognitive processes such as reflecting on one's prior knowledge and planning learning trajectories.

As future work, we aim to conduct a comprehensive user study to evaluate the usefulness, clarity, and perceived fairness of the generated explanations. Such a study will provide insights into how learners with different backgrounds and goals interpret the explanations, and whether these explanations effectively support decision-making in practice. Ultimately, this research contributes to the growing field of explainable educational recommender systems and provides a groundwork for building user-centric, transparent, and pedagogically aligned recommendation technologies.

References

1. Ain, Q.U., Chatti, M.A., Bakar, K.G.C., Joarder, S., Alatrash, R.: Automatic construction of educational knowledge graphs: a word embedding-based approach. Information **14**(10), 526 (2023)
2. Ain, Q.U., Chatti, M.A., Meteng Kamdem, P.A., Alatrash, R., Joarder, S., Siepmann, C.: Learner modeling and recommendation of learning resources using personal knowledge graphs. In: Proceedings of the 14th Learning Analytics and Knowledge Conference, pp. 273–283 (2024)
3. Alnahhas, A., Alkhatib, B.: Augmented context-based conceptual user modeling for personalized recommendation system in online social networks. Inter. J. Cognitive Inform. Nat. Intell. (IJCINI) **14**(3), 1–19 (2020)
4. Boubaker, N.B.H., Kodia, Z., Ayadi, N.Y.: Personalized e-learning knowledge graph-based recommender system using ensemble attention networks. In: 16th International Conference on Management of Digital EcoSystems (MEDES 2024) (2024)
5. Grover, A., Leskovec, J.: node2vec: scalable feature learning for networks. InLProceedings of the 22nd ACM SIGKDD International Conference on Knowledge Discovery and Data Mining, pp. 855–864 (2016)
6. Huang, Y., Zhao, F., Gui, X., Jin, H.: Path-enhanced explainable recommendation with knowledge graphs. World Wide Web **24**(5), 1769–1789 (2021)
7. Hubert, N., Brun, A., Monticolo, D.: Vers un système de recommandation explicable pour l'orientation scolaire. In: Workshop EXPLAIN'AI-EGC Blois 2022 (2022)
8. Ji, S., Pan, S., Cambria, E., Marttinen, P., Yu, P.S.: A survey on knowledge graphs: Representation, acquisition, and applications. IEEE Trans. Neural Netw. Lear. Sys/ **33**(2), 494–514 (2021)
9. Kulkarni, M., Mahata, D., Arora, R., Bhowmik, R.: Learning rich representation of keyphrases from text. arXiv:2112.08547 (2021)
10. Lin, Y., Liu, Z., Sun, M., Liu, Y., Zhu, X.: Learning entity and relation embeddings for knowledge graph completion. In: Proceedings of the AAAI Conference on Artificial Intelligence, vol. 29 (2015)
11. Liu, Y., et al.: Roberta: A robustly optimized BERT pretraining approach. arXiv:1907.11692 (2019)
12. Lu, M., Wang, Y., Yu, J., Du, Y., Hou, L., Li, J.: Distantly supervised course concept extraction in moocs with academic discipline. In: Proceedings of the 61st Annual Meeting of the Association for Computational Linguistics (Volume 1: Long Papers), pp. 13044–13059 (2023)
13. Mosca, E., Szigeti, F., Tragianni, S., Gallagher, D., Groh, G.: Shap-based explanation methods: a review for nlp interpretability. In: Proceedings of the 29th International Conference on Computational Linguistics (2022), pp. 4593–4603

14. Perozzi, B., Al-Rfou, R., Skiena, S.: Deepwalk: online learning of social representations. In Proceedings of the 20th ACM SIGKDD International Conference on Knowledge Discovery and Data Mining, pp. 701–710 (2014)
15. Praseptiawan, M., Putri, N.M., Muchtarom, M.F.D., Zakaria, M.H., Pee, A. N.C.: Application of collaborative filtering and explainable ai methods in recommendation system modeling to predict mooc course preferences. In: 2024 2nd International Symposium on Information Technology and Digital Innovation (ISITDI, pp. 228–233. IEEE (2024)
16. Rajabi, E., Etminani, K.: Knowledge-graph-based explainable AI: A systematic review. J. Inf. Sci. **50**(4), 1019–1029 (2024)
17. Reales, D., Manrique, R., Grévisse, C.: Core concept identification in educational resources via knowledge graphs and large language models. SN Comput. Sci. **5**(8), 1029 (2024)
18. Ribeiro, M.T., Singh, S., Guestrin, C.: why should i trust you?" explaining the predictions of any classifier. In: Proceedings of the 22nd ACM SIGKDD International Conference on Knowledge Discovery and Data Mining, pp. 1135–1144 (2016)
19. Ristoski, P., Paulheim, H.: RDF2Vec: RDF graph embeddings for data mining. In: Groth, P., et al. (eds.) ISWC 2016. LNCS, vol. 9981, pp. 498–514. Springer, Cham (2016). https://doi. org/10.1007/978-3-319-46523-4_30
20. Troussas, C., Krouska, A.: Path-based recommender system for learning activities using knowledge graphs. Information **14**(1), 9 (2022)
21. Wang, H., et alRipplenet: Propagating user preferences on the knowledge graph for recommender systems. In: Proceedings of the 27th ACM International Conference on Information and Knowledge Management, pp. 417–426 (2018)
22. Yang, B., Yih, W.-t., He, X., Gao, J., Deng, L.: Embedding entities and relations for learning and inference in knowledge bases. arXiv:1412.6575 (2014)
23. Zhang, Y., Chen, X., et al.: Explainable recommendation: a survey and new perspectives. Found. Trends Inf. Retr. **14**(1), 1–101 (2020)

Lazy Prediction in Querying Graph Databases

Jacques Chabin[1], Cristina D. Aguiar[2], Mirian Halfeld-Ferrari[1],

Martin A. Musicante[3], and Lingchen Wang[1(✉)]

[1] Université d'Orléans, INSA CVL, LIFO, UR 4022, Orléans, France
{jacques.chabin,mirian,lingchen.wang}@univ-orleans.fr
[2] Department of Computer Science, University of São Paulo (USP), São Paulo, Brazil
cdac@icmc.usp.br
[3] DIMAp, Computer Science Department, UFRN, Natal, Brazil
martin.musicante@ufrn.br

Abstract. This work focuses on querying incomplete data graphs using a hybrid, query-driven approach. The method combines the certainty of known paths with the flexibility of on-the-fly embedding-based link prediction guided by the query structure. A lazy-prediction strategy is used to improve relevance while limiting unnecessary inference. We evaluate our method on two embedding-based models and datasets, and test predictive strategies with different search space reductions.

Keywords: Incomplete Graph Database · Link Prediction · Regular Path Query

1 Introduction

Graph databases represent entities as nodes and relationships as edges, but are often incomplete due to real-world complexity and evolving data. We study regular path queries, expressed as regular expressions, over such data. Given start nodes W, the goal is to find paths matching a regular expression R, with their endpoints as answers. To handle missing information, we enhance querying with link prediction.

Key Challenges

(1) *Deferred Prediction on Query Demand.* Unlike conventional approaches that proactively enrich the graph beforehand [11], this method postpones predictions until a query is issued, thus avoiding unnecessary or irrelevant additions. How can we establish a framework that delays the generation of predicted links until they are actually needed?

(2) *Enhancing Query Precision.* Predicted edges introduce uncertainty, which can undermine the reliability of query results [1]. Some methods address this by embedding nodes and processing entire queries in geometric space [17]. However, uncertainty tends to accumulate with each additional operation, potentially degrading the final outcome. Can we improve query accuracy by combining the known graph structure with selectively inferred connections?

Authors listed in alphabetical order. The work is part of Wang's PhD thesis.

C. Cappiello et al. (Eds.): CoopIS 2025, LNCS 15535, pp. 596–606, 2026.
https://doi.org/10.1007/978-3-032-15538-2_37

This paper explores querying incomplete data graphs using ML(Machine Learning) to predict missing links while limiting error propagation. The **main contributions** of this work are as follows:

(1) A **hybrid approach** mixing certainties (following exactly the paths that exist in a graph) and probabilities (taking into account edges that might exist).
(2) A **lazy-prediction querying strategy**, inspired by demand-driven computation, which performs predictions on-the-fly, guided by the query.
(3) An **experimental evaluation** combining different prediction strategies (based on top-k ranking or thresholding) with standard search space reduction techniques.

Related Work. Incomplete data is a well-known challenge, less studied in graph databases [8,9,27] than in relational models [16,20]. Traditional solutions rely on logical rules, either via materialization or query rewriting, with inference supported by rule chasing or dynamic inference [10,14,23]. Lazy evaluation improves scalability by avoiding unnecessary computation and limiting non-termination risks in recursive settings [5,15]. It aligns well with hybrid approaches combining symbolic reasoning with statistical predictions [29]. As modern data graphs from multiple sources are often incomplete [7,19,24], predictive models are increasingly used to provide approximate answers without assuming full expert knowledge.

In [12], approximate query answering approaches are classified into three main groups: approaches based on pre-trained embeddings such as [3], projection-based query embeddings such as [17,25,26], and message-passing neural networks as in [2, 13]. Our approach, which uses TransR or RESCAL embeddings, falls into the first category: it scores query atoms with link prediction models and aggregates them using t-norms and t-conorms, i.e., continuous relaxations of conjunction and disjunction. Link predictors estimate the plausibility of triples (h, r, t) via geometric or neural scoring functions over embeddings. Our method uses embeddings only to estimate individual links when required by the query process, reducing the propagation of uncertainty.

Paper Organization: Section 2 introduces key concepts. Our lazy predictive query method is detailed in Sect. 3, with experimental results in Sect. 4. Section 5 concludes the paper.

2 Preliminaries

We introduce concepts necessary to understand our approach.

Definition 1 (Fuzzy Data Graphs). *Given $\Sigma = \{l_1, \ldots, l_n\}$, a finite set of labels, we define a **Fuzzy Data Graph** (or just data graph) as a triple $\mathbb{G} = (\mathbb{V}, \mathbb{E}, \mu)$, where $\mathbb{V}$ is a finite set of vertices, $\mathbb{E}$ is a set of directed edges, $\mathbb{E} = \{(x, l, y) \mid x, y \in \mathbb{V}, l \in \Sigma\}$ and $\mu : \mathbb{E} \to [0, 1]$ is a function associating a value in $[0, 1]$ to each edge. An edge $(x, l, y) \in \mathbb{E}$ can also be noted as $l(x, y)$.* $\square$

This kind of fuzzy data graph is also called a data graph with crisp nodes and fuzzy edges [18]. Notice that a (crisp) data graph is a fuzzy data graph where all the edges are associated with the value 1.

Definition 2 (Regular Path Query). *A **Regular Path Query** $Q = (R, W)$ on a (fuzzy or crisp) data graph $\mathbb{G}$ is defined by a regular expression R over Σ and a set of nodes $W \subseteq \mathbb{V}$.* $\qquad\square$

The evaluation of a regular path query $Q = (R, W)$ over a graph will identify those nodes of the graph that are reachable from nodes in W by a path defined by a string in the language denoted by the regular expression R.

Definition 3 (Query evaluation). *Given the set of labels Σ, a new label $l_Q \notin \Sigma$, and a fuzzy data graph $\mathbb{G} = (\mathbb{V}, \mathbb{E}, \mu)$, the evaluation of $Q = (R, W)$ on $\mathbb{G}$ results in a new graph $\mathbb{G}' = (\mathbb{V}, \mathbb{E}', \mu')$ where:*

- *$\mathbb{E}' = \mathbb{E} \cup \{(a, l_Q, b)\}$ such that, for each edge (a, l_Q, b), we have $a \in W$ and there exists a path $l_1(a, a_1)\, l_2(a_1, a_2) \ldots l_n(a_n, b)$ from a to b in $\mathbb{G}$;*
- *The string $l_1 \ldots l_n$ is in the language denoted by the regular expression R;*
- *The function μ' is defined as:*

$$\mu'(e) = \begin{cases} \mu(e) & e \in \mathbb{E} \\ \mu(l_1(a, a_1)) \circledast \mu(l_2(a_1, a_2)) \circledast \cdots \circledast \mu(l_n(a_n, b)) & \text{otherwise.} \end{cases}$$

Where the function $\circledast : [0, 1] \times [0, 1] \to [0, 1]$. $\qquad\square$

The function $\circledast$ is defined for each application and is intended to calculate a value associated with a path. This function is expected to respect the properties of a t-norm operator [4], *i.e.*, the function $\circledast$ should be commutative, monotonic, and associative, with the number 1 being its identity element.

Evaluating a query $Q = (R, W)$ on graph $\mathbb{G}$ requires traversing $\mathbb{G}$ starting at a node $a \in W$. This traversal is guided by a finite state automaton M_R, derived from R. We denote $M_R = (\mathsf{St}, \Sigma, \delta, s_0, \mathsf{F})$ where St is a finite set of states, $s_0 \in \mathsf{St}$ is the initial state, $\mathsf{F} \subseteq \mathsf{St}$ is the set of final states and δ is a transition relation.

3 Predictive Querying on Graphs

Our query-answering method combines traditional regular path query answering with link prediction. The method corresponds to a traversal of the product graph between the data graph and a finite automaton for the regular expression in the query, where a link prediction phase can be triggered at each step. Algorithm 1 describes the process in detail and takes three parameters: (1) A fuzzy data graph $\mathbb{G} = (\mathbb{V}, \mathbb{E}, \mu)$, (2) A query $Q = (R, W)$ over $\mathbb{G}$, where R is a regular expression over Σ, such that $l_Q \notin \Sigma$ is a new label, and $W \subseteq \mathbb{V}$ is the set of initial nodes for the path query, and (3) *max* is a natural number defining the maximum number of inferred edges for each path in the solution.

Algorithm 1. Evaluation of Regular Path Queries with Prediction.

Input: - $\mathbb{G} = (\mathbb{V}, \mathbb{E}, \mu)$ is a fuzzy data graph
       - $Q = (R, W)$, where R is a regular expression over Σ, and $W \subseteq \mathbb{V}$
       - $max \in \mathbb{N}$, the maximum number of inferred edges in each solution path.
Output: - $\mathbb{G}' = (\mathbb{V}, \mathbb{E}', \mu')$, such that:
       - $l_Q(a, b) \in \mathbb{G}'$ iff $\forall a \in W$, there is a R-defined path from a to b in $\mathbb{G}'$.

1   **function** *eval(Q,* $\mathbb{G}$*, max)*
2     $\mathbb{G}' \leftarrow \mathbb{G}$, (where $\mathbb{E}' = \mathbb{E}$ and $\mu' = \mu$)
3     $(s_0, \Sigma, \delta, \mathsf{F}) \leftarrow \text{BuildAutomaton}(R)$
4     $Frontier = \{(s_0, n, n, 1, 0) \mid n \in W\}$
5   **while** *there are unvisited tuples in* $Frontier$ **do**
6   Choose an unvisited tuple $t = (s, n_0, n, \gamma, i) \in Frontier$
7   Mark t as visited
8   **if** $s \in \mathsf{F}$ **then**
9           $\mathbb{E}' \leftarrow \mathbb{E}' \cup \{l_Q(n_0, n)\}$;   // Add edge $l_Q(n_0, n)$ to $\mathbb{E}'$,
10           $\mu' \leftarrow \mu' \cup \{(l_Q(n_0, n), \gamma)\}$;   // with truth-value γ.
11   **if** $i < max$ **then**
12   **foreach** l *such that* $\exists s'.(s, l, s') \in \delta$ **do**
13              $(\mathbb{E}'', \mu'') = \text{Predict}(\mathbb{G}', l, n)$;   // the pair $(\mathbb{E}'', \mu'')$ contains
14              $\mathbb{E}' \leftarrow \mathbb{E}' \cup \mathbb{E}''$;   // new predicted edges $l(n, x)$,
15              $\mu' \leftarrow \mu' \cup \mu''$;   // with truth-values in μ'.
16   **foreach** $n' \in \mathbb{V}$ *such that* $l(n, n') \in \mathbb{E}'$ **do**
17   **if** $\mu'(l(n, n')) = 1$ **then**
18              $Frontier \leftarrow Frontier \uplus (s', n_o, n', \gamma \circledast \mu'(l(n, n')), i)$
19   **else if** $i < max \wedge \mu'(l(n, n')) < 1$ **then**
20              $Frontier \leftarrow Frontier \uplus (s', n_o, n', \gamma \circledast \mu'(l(n, n')), i+1)$
21   **return** $\mathbb{G}'$

The goal of Algorithm 1 is to process Q and return a new version of $\mathbb{G}$ with new edges representing the paths that are answers for Q. Edges predicted by the algorithm are also added to the answer graph.

In the first part of Algorithm 1 (line 3), given the regular expression R, the automaton M_R is built (Sect. 2). The set $Frontier$ (line 4) stores 5-tuples, which represent traces on the (virtual) product automaton of $\mathbb{G}$ and M_R. Each tuple in $Frontier$ has the format $(s', n_0, n_{curr}, \gamma, i)$ where (1) s' is the state in M_R we are currently considering, (2) n_0 denotes an initial node of the query, *i.e.*, $n_0 \in W$, (3) n_{curr} is the current node being processed in the query, (4) $\gamma \in [0, 1]$ is the fuzzy truth value associated with a potential edge from n_0 to n_{curr}. (5) i is the number of inferred edges used to reach n_{curr} from n_0.

On line 4, the $Frontier$ set is initialized: for each node $n \in W$ of query Q, a tuple $(s_0, n, n, 1, 0)$ is added to $Frontier$, indicating a path from a node to itself. All initial tuples in $Frontier$ are marked as *unvisited*.

The loop on line 5 begins by chosing an unvisited tuple $t = (s, n_0, n, \gamma, i)$ from $Frontier$. In this tuple, if s is a final state of the automaton M_R (line 8), a new edge connecting node n_0 to n is added to the graph $\mathbb{G}'$. This new edge, labeled l_Q, represents an answer for Q.

Algorithm 1 then examines all possible outcome transitions from s in the automaton M_R. Recall that transition symbols of the automaton M_R correspond to relationships (edges) in our graph $\mathbb{G}$. Let l be a possible output transition from state s to state s'. Thus, being at node n of $\mathbb{G}'$, we consider all nodes n' which are neighbors of n by l.

The commands at lines 13-15 aim to predict new l-relationships from the current node n and add them to $\mathbb{G}'$. The prediction will be made if the maximum number of predicted edges on the path has not been reached. The prediction function is called at line 13. This function uses the embedded graph to obtain new l-labeled edges departing from node n. The details of the prediction mechanism are given in Predicting Links Between Nodes .

Then, in the loop beginning on line 16, for each node n' for which there is an l-edge (predicted or already existing) from n, we create a new 5-tuple to indicate a step forward in our traversal (thus, advancing the frontier). Notice that the function $\uplus$ adds an unvisited tuple t to the set *Frontier*, provided that one of the following conditions is satisfied: (i) there is no other tuple in *Frontier* with the same automaton state, departure node, and current node, or (ii) if such a tuple exists, the weight (truth value) of the tuple already in *Frontier* is less than the weight of t.

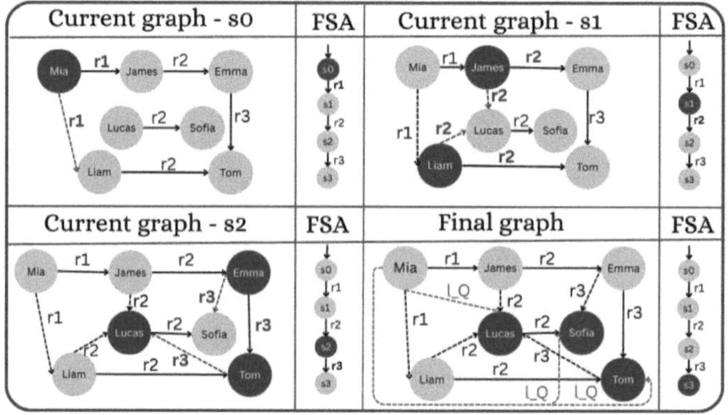

Fig. 1. Lazy - Prediction Querying on Graphs. Dashed arrows represent predicted links, while solid arrows represent real edges.

Example 1. Figure 1 illustrates the evaluation of query $Q = (r_1.r_2.r_3, \{Mia\})$ over a graph database using a finite state automaton (FSA)-guided search. Starting from the source node *Mia*, the FSA begins in state s_0 expecting an r_1 transition. From *Mia*, there is a real r_1 edge to *James*, and a predicted r_1 edge to *Liam*. In state s_1, which expects a r_2 relation, *James* leads via a real r_2 edge to *Emma* and a predicted r_2 edge to *Lucas*, *Liam* has a real r_2 edge to *Tom* and a predicted r_2 edge also to *Lucas*. In state s_2, the FSA seeks an r_3 edge, *Emma* has a real r_3 edge to *Tom* and a predicted r_3 edge to *Sofia*, while a predicted r_3 edge exists from *Tom* to *Lucas*, there exist no real or predicted r_3 edges from *Lucas*. This completes the accepted paths, and the FSA reaches the final state s_3. Let us consider two of all valid solutions obtained: by the path $Mia \xrightarrow{r_1} James \xrightarrow{r_2} Emma \xrightarrow{r_3} Tom$ (without predictions) or by the path $Mia \xrightarrow{r_1} Liam$

$\xrightarrow{r_2}$ *Tom* $\xrightarrow{r_3}$ *Lucas* (with two predictions). The final graph consolidates both real and predicted transitions that satisfy the regular expression query. $\square$

Predicting Links Between Nodes. We explore two graph embedding methods from distinct families [6], each offering explicit representations of nodes and relations while effectively capturing both structural and semantic patterns:

- *TransR* [21] uses separate embedding spaces for entities and relations. For each triple (h, r, t), entities embeddings are vectors $\mathbf{h}, \mathbf{t} \in \mathbb{R}^k$, while a relation embedding is $\mathbf{r} \in \mathbb{R}^d$, where k and d may be different. Each relation r has a matrix $\mathbf{M}_r \in \mathbb{R}^{k \times d}$ projecting entities from entity space to relation space. The projected entity vectors are defined as $\mathbf{h_r} = \mathbf{h} \cdot \mathbf{M}_r$ and $\mathbf{t_r} = \mathbf{t} \cdot \mathbf{M}r$. The score function is defined as $score_{transR}(h, r, t) = ||\mathbf{h}_r + \mathbf{r} - \mathbf{t}_r||$.

- *RESCAL* [22] models latent interactions via tensor decomposition. Each triple (h, r, t) is scored by $score_{rescal}(h, r, t) = \mathbf{h}^T \mathbf{R}_r \mathbf{t}$, where $\mathbf{h}, \mathbf{t}$ are entity vectors and $\mathbf{R}_r$ is a relation-specific matrix.

When a prediction step occurs, the main embedding operation is applied to compute the vector representation of the target node. For TransR, given a node n with embedding $\mathbf{v}_n$ and relation r with embedding $\mathbf{r}$, we compute $score_{transR}(h, r, t) = ||\mathbf{h}_r + \mathbf{r} - \mathbf{t}_r||$, where $\mathbf{h}_r = \mathbf{v}_n \cdot \mathbf{M}_r$ and $\mathbf{t}_r = \mathbf{v}_i \cdot \mathbf{M}_r$ for every node $v_i \in \mathbb{V}$. Strategies like Top-k select nodes with best scores. RESCAL follows the same logic but uses its own scoring function.

4   Experimental Results

Our experimental process incorporates various prediction variations for comparative analysis across diverse datasets and queries. Additionally, we explore strategies to streamline research, such as clustering and limiting the number of prediction-based answers. This section outlines our experimental methodology.

Queries. For each scenario (presented below), we use an initial graph named G_0 as our ground truth to evaluate our system. From the initial graph G_0, represented as a set of triples, we randomly generate a set of queries of length 1–3: $Q_1(X, Y) : -P_1(X, Y)$; $Q_2(X, Y) : -P_1(X, X_1) \wedge P_2(X_1, Y)$ and $Q_3(X, Y) : -P_1(X, X_1) \wedge P_2(X_1, X_2) \wedge P_3(X_2, Y)$; where each P_i is a relationship (edge label) existing in G_0 and X is the query's starting node. All queries are guaranteed to have at least one answer in G_0.

To simulate incompleteness, we construct G_1 by randomly removing one triple per path supporting a query answer in G_0, making all queries unanswerable in G_1. Similarly, G_2 and G_3 are obtained by deleting one triple from 50% and 20% of such paths in G_0, respectively, leading to more than 50% and 20% answer loss due to overlap across answers.

We also generate star-queries by applying Kleene star to one predicate, *e.g.*, $Q_{3*}(X, Y) : -P_1(X, X_1) \wedge P_2(X_1, X_2)^* \wedge P_3(X_2, Y)$.

Predictive Strategies. The predictive step of our approach can be summarized as follows: given a node n and a relationship r, we predict a next node t using four methods: (1) **RRand**: from node n, randomly select at most k nodes t among triples (n, r, t) whose score meets a given threshold. This strategy serves as our baseline. (2) **RScore**: from node n, select all nodes t such that the score of triples (n, r, t) meets a given threshold. (3) **Top-k**: from node n, select the k nodes t corresponding to the triples (n, r, t) with the highest scores. (4) **Top-k+**: from node n, select the top k nodes t such that the triples (n, r, t) both have the highest scores and satisfy a score threshold.

Techniques. We investigate if it is possible to maintain accurate predictions while reducing their quantity. In this context, we consider the following four techniques, that are applied in conjunction with the four strategies described above and compare their outcomes: (1) **Initial Technique**: After performing graph embedding, given a node and a relation, the score function is used to compute scores between the given node-relation pair and all other nodes in the graph. (2) **Cluster-Based Technique**: We first cluster the nodes based on their embeddings. Given a source node h and a relation r (and their embeddings), we compute $score(h, r, c_i)$ for each cluster centroid c_i, to identify the nearest cluster c_{near}. We then compute $score(h, r, v_j)$ for all nodes v_j within c_{near} and select the top-scoring nodes. (3) **Max-Based Technique**: To limit the number of predictions in an answer path on the graph, we introduce the parameter Max, defining the maximum number of predicted edges permitted in any answer. (4) **Cluster and Max-Based Technique**: To combine the principles of both the Cluster-Based and Max-Based approaches.

Implementation. We used Python for computing embeddings via the PyKEEN library ([28] for details on these parameters), running on JupyterHub with an NVIDIA Quadro RTX 6000 GPU, 2 x Intel(R) Xeon(R) Gold 5220R CPU 2.20 GHz/48 CPU cores, 64GB/DIMM DDR4/3200MHz, MIREV server. Query evaluation was implemented in Elixir and executed via Visual Studio on an Intel Core i7 machine.

Analysing Results. We now discuss the results obtained when running the tests. Due to space limits, not all our results are shown here; they are available at [28]. Our tests obtained similar results for the Kinships and UMLS datasets. We also noted that RESCAL and TransR yield similar performance and behave comparably across both datasets. Also, **Top-5+** and **RScore** yield similar outcomes. Thus, we detail here TransR on UMLS results, for **Top-5** and **RScore**.

Figures 2, 3, 4 and 5 show bar charts for our different query types. Recall, Precision, and F_1 scores are shown in blue, green, and orange, respectively. Each query set is represented by four groups of three bars: the first group corresponds to the strategy with Initial technique, followed by groups using Cluster-based, Max-based, and Cluster- and Max-based. These appear in order, with fading colors to distinguish each technique (as in Fig. 2). To interpret the results, we focus on the F_1 score, which reflects the balance between Recall and Precision.

Non-Star Queries. On G_1, **Top-5** outperforms **RScore** for length-1 and length-2 queries, whereas **RScore** performs better for length-3 queries (Fig. 2). Using the Max-based technique, **RScore** achieves ≈ 0.75 Recall, ≈ 0.97 Precision, and an F_1 score rising to ≈ 0.82. The use of the cluster (with or without the Max-based one) results in

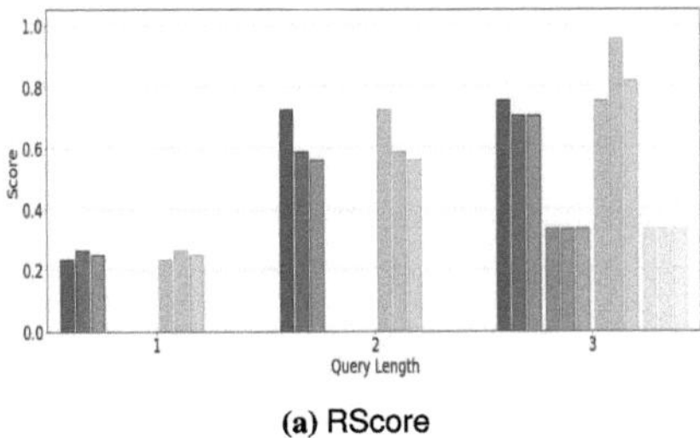

(a) RScore

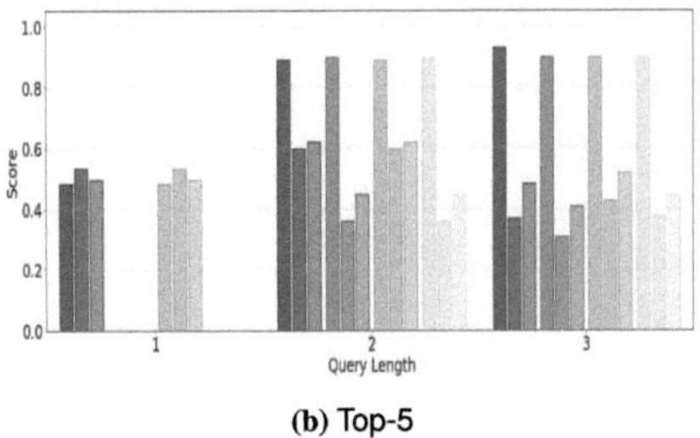

(b) Top-5

Fig. 2. Metrics (recall, precision, F_1) by query length on G_1 (UMLS dataset, TransR). Each group of three bars represents a strategyâĂŞtechnique combination.

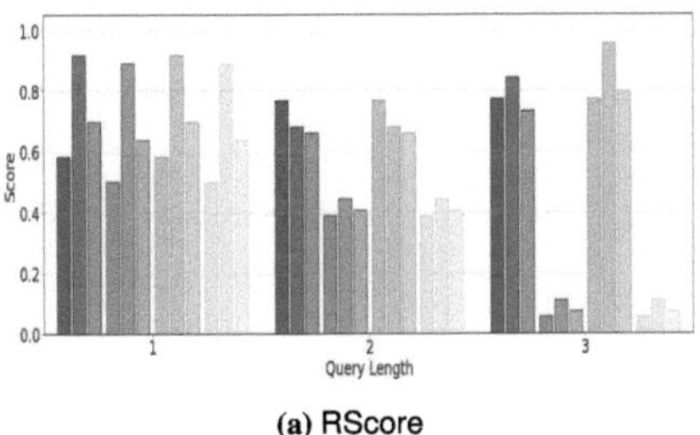

(a) RScore

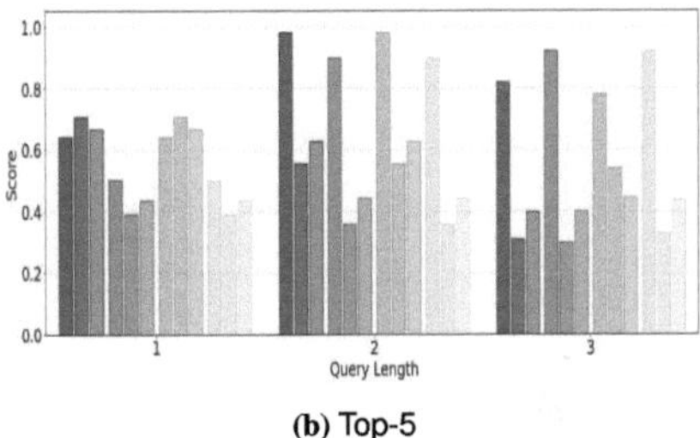

(b) Top-5

Fig. 3. Metrics (recall, precision, F_1) by query length on G_2 (UMLS dataset, TransR). Each group of three bars represents a strategyâĂŞtechnique combination.

consistently low F_1 scores across all strategies. This is particularly evident for **Rscore** and **Top5+**, with no answers for length-1 and length-2 queries.

On G_2, strategies combined with non-clustered techniques perform better (Fig. 3). Considering only strategies without added techniques, **Top-5** shows higher Recall (≈ 1) but lower Precision; its F_1 score declines with longer queries, while **RScore** (with Precision close to 0.9) and **Top-5+** improve and outperform it on length-3 queries.

Results on G_3 are similar. As the most complete graph, all non-clustered strategies (except **Top-5+**) retrieve over 90% of answers for no-star queries. **RScore** and **Top-5+** offer higher Precision than **Top-5**, with **RScore** being more stable (around 0.8) and achieving the best F_1 score, retrieving all answers for length-2 and 3 queries.

Star queries. Star queries maintain high Recall across strategies. On G_1, **RScore** offers strong Precision (up to 0.98) and high F_1 scores (up to 0.88), with recall improving as queries get longer. However, Cluster- and Max-based techniques reduce their Recall. On G_2 (Fig. 4), **RScore** and **Top-5+** yield similar results across all metrics, consistently achieving the higher performance with F_1 scores around 0.8 in all configurations. In contrast, **Top-5** shows high Recall but lower Precision and F_1 scores, around 0.6. On G_3 (Fig. 5), star queries yield high F_1 scores with both **RScore** and **Top-5**. Cluster- and Max-based techniques have little effect on the results.

In summary, based on F_1 scores, the ranking of the four strategies is: **RScore** performs best with higher Precision but lower Recall; followed by **Top-5** with higher

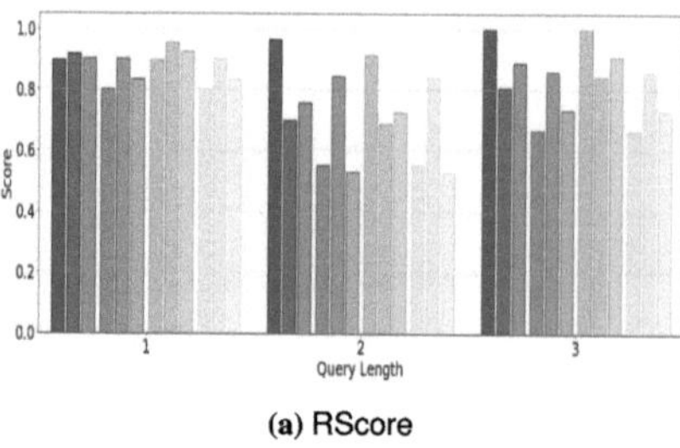

(a) RScore

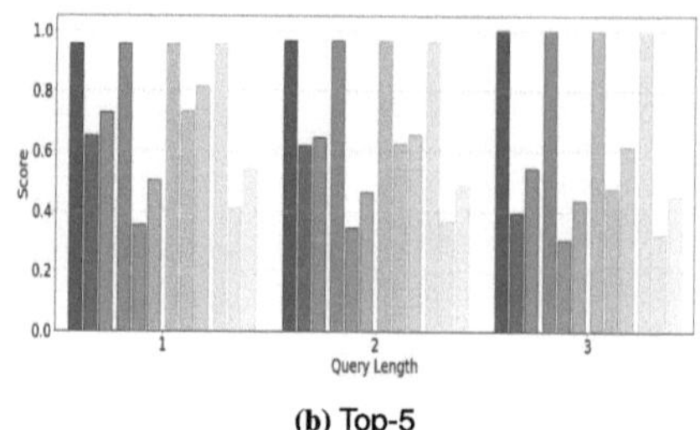

(b) Top-5

Fig. 4. Metrics (recall, precision, F_1) by query length on G_2^* (UMLS dataset, TransR). Each group of three bars represents a strategyâĂŞtechnique combination.

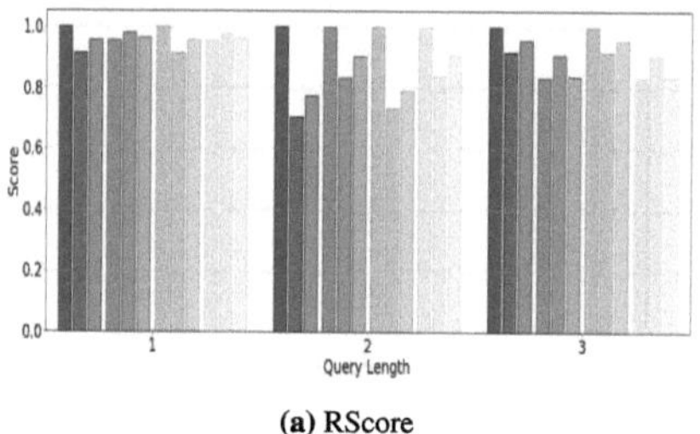

(a) RScore

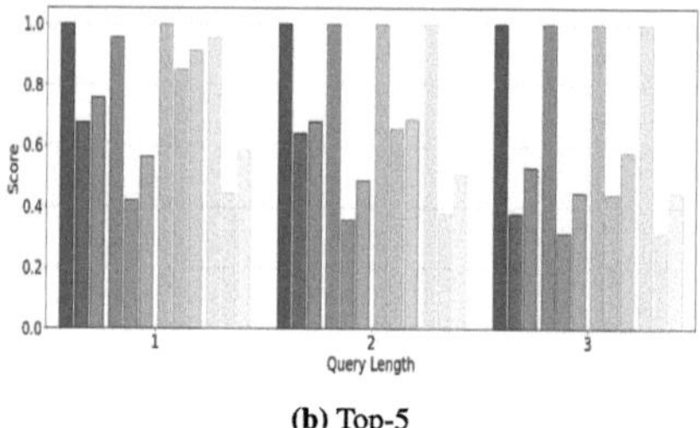

(b) Top-5

Fig. 5. Metrics (recall, precision, F_1) by query length on G_3^* (UMLS dataset, TransR). Each group of three bars represents a strategyâĂŞtechnique combination.

Recall but lower Precision; then **Top-5+**; and lastly, the baseline **RRand**. Strategies combined with Cluster-based techniques reduce computation time but at a significant F_1 score cost. The Max parameter has a little effect on non-star queries and only occasionally reduces results for star queries, which mostly remain comparable to non-clustered approaches. Finally, star queries take much longer to evaluate (4 to 280 s) than non-star queries (0.05 to 18 s).

Evaluating Our Approach Against the Initial Challenges. We provide a preliminary assessment of how our approach addresses the challenges outlined in Sect. 1: (1) Our lazy-prediction strategy offers clear efficiency benefits. Let C be the fixed cost of computing the score for a predicted triple (a, l, b), given a chosen embedding and prediction method. If all scores are precomputed before query execution, the total cost is: $|V| \cdot |\Sigma| \cdot |V| \cdot$ C, as every possible triple over all nodes and labels must be evaluated. In contrast, our lazy approach computes predictions only when required during query execution. For a query $Q = (R, W)$, the prediction cost is: $\sum_{i=1}^{|R|} (N_{i-1} \cdot |V| \cdot$ C) where $N_0 = |W|$ and N_i is the number of intermediate results after processing the first i symbols of the regular expression R. This cost can be further reduced by strategies that limit the number of predictions per query. Once the maximum is reached, no further predictions are made. (2) A direct comparison with [17] is not feasible due to significant differences in dataset formats and query execution models (due to their one-answer-per-step constraint versus our multi-answer setting), our results show that accuracy improves when using the crisp edges of the graph, instead the embedded ones. Specifically, F_1 scores are consistently higher on G_3 than on G_1 or G_2 for most queries, supporting our hypothesis that uncertainty accumulates with each additional prediction step.

5   Concluding Remarks

We address regular path queries over incomplete graphs by combining observed and predicted edges through a lazy-prediction strategy, which triggers predictions only when needed, reducing cost while preserving accuracy. Experiments show that F_1 improves with graph completeness and that RScore with lazy prediction yields the best precisionâĂŞrecall trade-off, unlike exhaustive prediction, which increases cost without clear gains. Future work will extend to richer query languages, enhance prediction via graph pre-analysis, and explore comparisons with methods like [17], requiring harmonized protocols or adapted implementations.

Acknowledgments. This work is partly funded by ARD-JUNON DATA. We sporadically used ChatGPT, Mistral, Grammarly, and DeepL to refine the text.

References

1. Adlakha, V., Shah, P., Bedathur, S.J., Mausam: Regex queries over incomplete knowledge bases. In: 3rd Conf. on Automated Knowledge Base Construction (2021)
2. Alivanistos, D., Berrendorf, M., Cochez, M., Niepert, M.: Query embedding on hyper-relational knowledge graphs. In: ICLR (2022)
3. Arakelyan, E., Daza, D., Minervini, P., Cochez, M.: Complex query answering with neural link predictors. arXiv preprint arXiv:2011.03459 (2020)
4. Boixader, D., Recasens, J.: Vague and fuzzy t-norms and t-conorms. Fuzzy Sets and Systems **433**, 156–175 (2022), aggregation Operations
5. Calì, A., Gottlob, G., Lukasiewicz, T.: A general datalog-based framework for tractable query answering over ontologies. J. Web Sem. **14**, 57–83 (2012)
6. Cao, J., Fang, J., Meng, Z., Liang, S.: Knowledge graph embedding: a survey from the perspective of representation spaces. ACM Comp. Surveys **56**(6), 1–42 (2024)
7. Chabin, J., Halfeld-Ferrari, M., Hiot, N.: From Text to Databases: Attribute grammar as database meta-model, October 2024
8. Chabin, J., Halfeld Ferrari, M., Hiot, N., Laurent, D.: Managing linked nulls in property graphs: Tools to ensure consistency and reduce redundancy. In: ADBIS. LNCS, vol. 13985, pp. 180–194. Springer (2023)
9. Chabin, J., Halfeld Ferrari, M., Laurent, D.: Consistent updating of databases with marked nulls. Knowl. Inf. Syst. **62**(4), 1571–1609 (2020)
10. Chabin, J., Halfeld Ferrari, M., Markhoff, B., Nguyen, T.B.: Validating data from semantic web providers. In: SOFSEM. LNCS, vol. 10706, pp. 682–695 (2018)
11. Chen, Z., Wang, Y., Zhao, B., Cheng, J., Zhao, X., Duan, Z.: Knowledge graph completion: a review. IEEE Access **8**, 192435–192456 (2020)
12. Cochez, M., et al.: Approximate answering of graph queries. In: Compendium of Neurosymbolic Artificial Intelligence, pp. 373–386 (2023)

13. Daza, D., Cochez, M.: Message passing query embedding. In: ICML Workshop on Graph Representation Learning and Beyond (2020)
14. Deutsch, A., Popa, L., Tannen, V.: Query reformulation with constraints. SIGMOD Record **35**(1), 65–73 (2006)
15. Gottlob, G., Orsi, G., Pieris, A.: Ontological queries: Rewriting and optimization. In: Proc. 27th ICDE, Germany, pp. 2–13 (2011)
16. Grahne, G.: The Problem of Incomplete Information in Relational Databases, Lecture Notes in Computer Science, vol. 554. Springer (1991)
17. Hamilton, W.L., Bajaj, P., Zitnik, M., Jurafsky, D., Leskovec, J.: Embedding logical queries on knowledge graphs. In: Proc. Int. Conf. on Neural Information Processing Syst., pp. 2030–2041. NIPS'18 (2018)
18. Hassan, N., Ahmad, T.: A review on taxonomy of fuzzy graph. Malaysian Journal of Fundamental and Applied Sciences **13** (04 2017)
19. Hogan, A., et al.: Knowledge graphs. ACM Comput. Surv. **54**(4) (2022)
20. Imielinski, T., Lipski, W., Jr.: Incomplete information in relational databases. J. ACM **31**(4), 761–791 (1984)
21. Lin, Y., Liu, Z., Sun, M., Liu, Y., Zhu, X.: Learning entity and relation embeddings for knowledge graph completion. In: AAAI, pp. 2181–2187 (2015)
22. Nickel, M., Tresp, V., Kriegel, H.: A three-way model for collective learning on multi-relational data. In: ICML, pp. 809–816. Omnipress (2011)
23. Onet, A.: The chase procedure and its applications in data exchange. In: Data Exchange, Integration, and Streams, pp. 1–37 (2013)
24. Paulheim, H.: Knowledge graph refinement: a survey of approaches and evaluation methods. Semantic Web **8**(3), 489–508 (2017)
25. Ren, H., Hu, W., Leskovec, J.: Query2box: Reasoning over knowledge graphs in vector space using box embeddings. In: ICLR (2020)
26. Ren, H., Leskovec, J.: Beta embeddings for multi-hop logical reasoning in knowledge graphs. Adv. in Neural Information Processing Systems **33** (2020)
27. Sirangelo, C.: Representing and Querying Incomplete Information: a Data Interoperability Perspective (2014). https://tel.archives-ouvertes.fr/tel-01092547
28. Wang, L.: (2025). https://gitlab.com/bardeee/lqp.git
29. West, R., Gabrilovich, E., Murphy, K., Sun, S., Gupta, R., Lin, D.: Knowledge base completion via search-based question answering. In: WWW, pp. 515–526 (2014)

Performance Improvement for an Intensive SPARQL-Based Application: The ERA Route Compatibility Check Tool

Daniel Doña[ID], Oscar Corcho[ID], and Edna Ruckhaus[✉][ID]

Universidad Politénica de Madrid, Madrid, Spain
{daniel.dona,o.corcho,e.ruckhaus}@upm.es
http://www.upm.es

Abstract. This paper addresses performance challenges in the European Union Agency for Railways (ERA) Route Compatibility Check (RCC) tool, a system that intensively uses SPARQL to query a large-scale knowledge graph. The application determines if a vehicle type is compatible with a railway route's characteristics, but a naïve approach of checking all route tracks leads to poor performance. To resolve this, we implemented and evaluated two performance improvement strategies: track aggregation and query parallelization. Track aggregation groups tracks with identical technical parameters to drastically reduce the number of evaluations during query execution, while parallel execution maximizes the throughput of the SPARQL endpoint. Our evaluation, comparing the optimised strategy against the naïve baseline, demonstrates a significant, approximately five-fold improvement in execution time for long routes. This work shows that combining data summarization with parallel execution is an effective approach for making SPARQL-intensive applications on large knowledge graphs performant and responsive.

Keywords: SPARQL · RDF · Query Performance

1 Introduction

This paper presents the work done to improve the performance of SPARQL query evaluation in an application that uses SPARQL intensively: the Route Compatibility Check (RCC) application[1] maintained by the European Union Agency for Railways (ERA). Its objective is to determine whether a vehicle is compatible with the characteristics of the railway tracks in a given route.

The initial steps of the transformation of ERA registries (more specifically the railway infrastructure and vehicle registries) from a more traditional to a data-centric approach supported by knowledge graphs were described in [2]. A semantic layer was created for data integration across the base registries maintained by the agency. The main use case that demonstrated the usefulness of such an approach was the RCC application. This application uses data from the European Register of Authorized Vehicle Types

---

[1] https://data-interop.era.europa.eu/route-compatibility.

C. Cappiello et al. (Eds.): CoopIS 2025, LNCS 15535, pp. 607–617, 2026.
https://doi.org/10.1007/978-3-032-15538-2_38

(ERATV) and the Register of Infrastructure (RINF), so as to allow checking whether a vehicle type is compatible with a certain railway route according to certain technical parameters. Potential routes between two operational points (e.g. train stations) are calculated using information on the network topology, and then compatibility checks for these characteristics are evaluated.

In the following years, the work evolved from this initial version into a richer and well-governed semantic layer with additional resources and functionalities, as described in [3]. The RINF System, now in production at https://data-interop.era.europa.eu/, enables the search of information regarding the characteristics and capabilities of operational points (OPs) and sections of line (SoLs) that belong to the static rail network, includes a map-based representation of all these resources and also a completely refactored version of the RCC application.

RINF data in the ERA Knowledge Graph (ERA KG) is generated from data sources that are provided by each EU member state via their Infrastructure Managers (IMs) or National Registration Entities (NREs) using the ERA ontology in its version $3.0.1^2$. ERATV data is generated from a relational database, which is populated using a Web application. The ontology is conceptualized as a layered model where a distinction is made among the functional (physical infrastructure) concepts present in RINF (e.g., OPs, SoLs, tracks, tunnels) and the topological concepts in the network (e.g., net elements, net relations, navigability) that are necessary for route calculation. The magnitude of the ERA KG is in the order of 39 million triples that include the description of 364K track segments, 65K stations, 63K georeferenced objects, and 2K vehicle types.

Given the magnitude of the ERA KG, performance issues emerged in most of RINF system's functionalities (for the creation of the KG and for its exploitation). In the specific case of RCC, compatibility checks between the technical characteristics of tracks and vehicle types are done using declarative SPARQL queries posed against the knowledge graph. The performance of these checks is related to the complexity of the queries that need to be executed, the length of the route (number of tracks) and the number of parameter compatibility checks that are defined. In a naïve approach, given the SPARQL query that has been defined for a compatibility check, the computation for a vehicle type over a route consisting of 50 tracks and 32 compatibility checks, involves executing the query 1,600 times, with a total of approximately 56,000 evaluations according to the SPARQL operators and functions used. In practice, the performance for the end-user was not acceptable with this approach and thus, the improvement of the behaviour of this functionality was necessary.

Following, we will describe the RCC application using a running example of a route that crosses borders among two EU member states.

1.1   RCC Running Example

The RCC application and service checks if a certain railway vehicle (e.g. as a locomotive unit, passenger car, wagon) of an authorized type of vehicle (hence available in ERATV) can travel the route from operational point (OP) A to OP B. Each route is

---

² https://data-interop.era.europa.eu/era-vocabulary/v3-20240618/.

composed of a sequence of SoLs (tracks) with potentially different technical parameters. Each track goes between two OPs.

Figure 1 shows the shortest route between `Rotterdam Centraal - NLRtd` and `Antwerpen - Centraal BEDFN`. This route consists of 19 tracks, and passes through a border point named `Meer-Grens` in Belgium and `HSL Breda grens` in The Netherlands (OP ID `EU00089`) The vehicle type chosen is `TGV Thalys PBKA RubY (13-018-0006-4-001-001)`, a type of vehicle that is auhorized to run in The Netherlands and in Belgium.

The summarized RCC results are displayed. For each track, the results show the number of *Compatible* check results, `10`, between the track and the vehicle type, according to the RCC checks procedures that have been defined, e.g. the minimum wheel diameter for fixed obtuse crossings for the vehicle type (ERATV index 4.8.2) must be greater or equal than the corresponding RINF parameter for the running track (RINF index 1.1.1.1.5.2).

In addition, the application presents the parameters that *Need manual check*, i.e., those parameters that are taxonomies in both registries, RINF and ERATV, but do not have identical values, i.e., there may be a degree of compatibility; in this example there are no parameters in this case. Also, it presents parameters that are *Not compatible*, i.e. do not satisfy the compatibility check, and those *Unknown*, i.e., where there are no data in at least one of the registries.

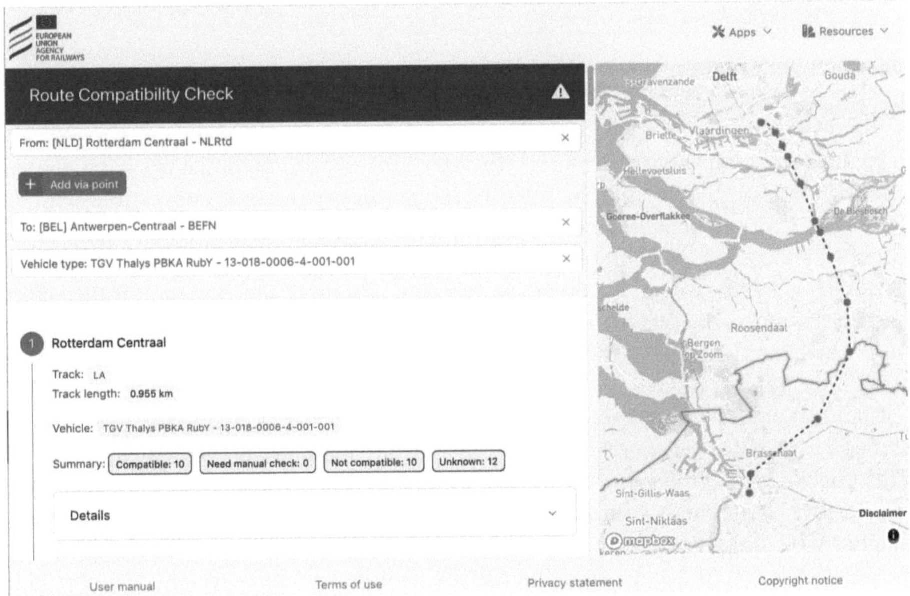

Fig. 1. RCC. Summary of the compatibility check for the route between `Rotterdam Centraal` and `Antwerpen Centraal` stations for vehicle type `TGV Thalys PBKA RubY`.

The user can see the details of the RCC check for each track, such as the portion shown in Fig. 2.

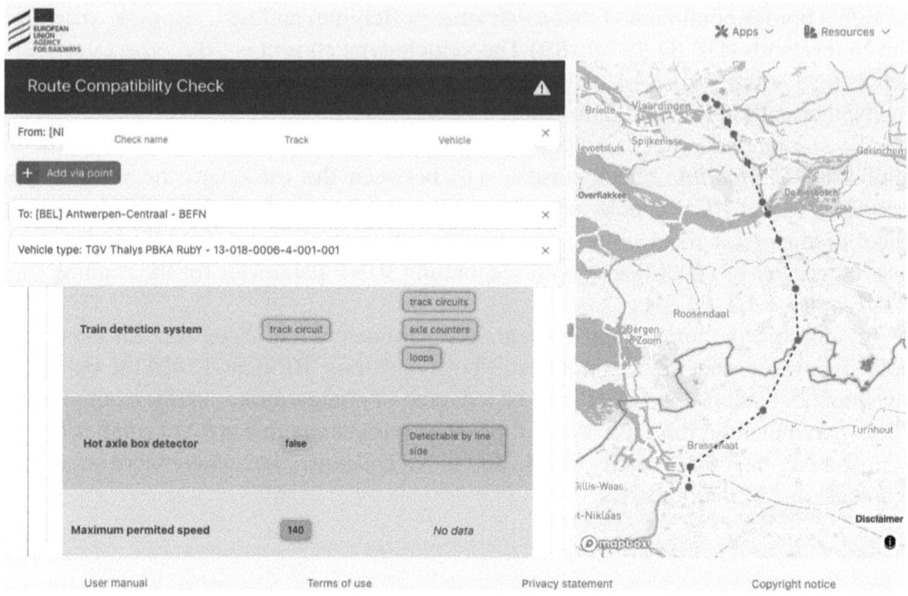

Fig. 2. RCC. Details of parameter compatibility results.

In this result, the value of `Train detection system` for the track, i.e. the system used to detect the position of vehicles in the railway track, is compatible with one of the values for the vehicle type ("track circuits"), whereas the values for `Hot axle box detector` are not compatible because the RINF value is "false", i.e. there is no trackside hot axle box detector, and there is a value for this characteristic for the vehicle type. Furthermore, the parameter `Maximum permitted speed`, i.e. nominal maximum operational speed on the line, has a "No data" value for the maximum design speed of the vehicle type.

The challenge for this application was to have the checks defined in a declarative manner, i.e. as SPARQL queries, to facilitate the creation and maintenance of compatibility checks, and at the same time make these queries performant for routes that may scale to several hundreds of tracks. We applied two techniques: (i) A domain-specific heuristic which aggregates the parameter checks that throw identical results, and (ii) The parallelization of query execution using a well-known concurrency design pattern, i.e. a *worker pool*. The performance of these optimal execution strategies was compared with the performance of naïve execution, where results show a significant improvement.

In the next section we will describe the content of the ERA KG referring to both RINF and ERATV data. Next, we explain the parameter compatibility checks and the implementation of an improved SPARQL query execution strategy. Following, the evaluation of this improved execution vs the naïve execution is presented. Finally, the limitations of the RCC implementation are described.

2   The ERA KG

The ERA KG[3] is an RDF dataset composed of four graphs.

1. RINF graph (http://data.europa.eu/949/graph/rinf). The graph contains data that represent the physical railway network: operational points (OPs) connected with sections of line (SoLs) that in turn contain tracks. There are also data on tunnels, platforms, and sidings, among others. These elements of the railway network are described by their generic properties such as name, ID and validity dates, and by their technical parameters. e.g. `Energy supply system`, `Acceleration allowed near level crossing`.
   Data are transformed from XML files or uploaded directly as RDF datasets. Data provided as XML are mapped into RDF using a declarative set of transformation rules developed with the RDF Mapping Language (RML). In this transformation process, the topology data is generated from the infrastructure elements. Potential routes between two OPs are calculated using information on the network topology.
2. ERATV graph ((http://data.europa.eu/949/graph/eratv). It contains the generic attributes (e.g., `Authorized country`) and technical parameters of vehicle types. This data is mapped from a relational database into RDF using RML mappings. Examples of technical parameters are `Emergency braking` and `Parkingbrake maximum gradient`. Some of the vehicle type parameters are used to check the technical compatibility between a type of vehicle and a route, e.g. `Energy supply system`, `Gauging`, `Maximum contact wire height`.
3. SKOS graph ((http://data.europa.eu/949/graph/skos). Taxonomies are annotated with terms using the Simple Knowledge Organization System (SKOS) vocabulary [4]. Concepts are organized in concept schemes and preferred and alternative labels are defined (`skos:prefLabel` and `skos:altLabel`).
4. Ontology graph (http://data.europa.eu/949/graph/ontology). It contains the ERA ontology, used to represent data in the three previous graphs.

Next, we will describe some specifics on the integration of data sources and on the treatment of missing data in the ERA KG.

2.1   Different Values for the Same Parameters in the RINF and ERATV Data Sources

It should be noted that the process of producing a compatibility report compares data in the RINF and ERATV graphs. On the one hand, RINF data comes mostly from XML datasets built by each member state according to the RINF Application Guide [1] and following a strict validation process (based on a combination of XML Schema and

---

[3] https://zenodo.org/records/15513855.

SHACL). This ensures data correctness and consistency among the different member states. On the other hand, the ERATV graph is built from a relational database whose data follows a less strict validation process.

Thus, for the same technical parameter, data from both graphs are in some cases incorrect or inconsistent (e.g., use of abbreviations, use of upper and lower case, same instances represented differently by different member states). This problem becomes especially evident in SKOS taxonomies that represent a concept in both RINF and ERATV, e.g. `Energy supply system`. As a result, it was necessary to harmonize RINF and ERATV values through a cleaning process to define URIs, labels and alternative labels. Relationships between RINF and ERATV concepts were added through the `skos:exactMatch` and `skos:closeMatch` annotations according to their similarity. These annotations are used for RCC checks. An example of a portion of the Energy Supply Systems taxonomy follows.

```
era-ess-eratv:1-5kv-specific-case-ie a skos:Concept;
   skos:inScheme era-ess:EnergySupplySystems;
   skos:prefLabel "1.5kV (Specific Case IE)";
   skos:altLabel "1.5kV Specific Case IE";
   skos:closeMatch era-ess-rinf:DC40.
era-ess-rinf:DC40 a skos:Concept;
   skos:inScheme era-ess:EnergySupplySystems;
   skos:prefLabel "DC 1.5kV" .
```

The ERATV concept has a preferred label and an alternative label (without parentheses) that was generated after the cleaning process. It is a close match with the RINF concept `era-ess-rinf:DC40`.

2.2 Missing Data

Missing data must be taken into account for compatibility checks. There are several cases of missing data in RINF data provision:

- `Not applicable` - NA value, when the parameter is not mandatory and there is no value.
- `Not provided` - NYA value, when the data is not available.
- Cases when there is no value and none of the previous two cases are specified.

Note that in ERATV, missing values are not standardized, there may be specified in different forms, e.g. `N`, `None`, `none`, or simply no value is provided.

3   RCC Implementation

Each compatibility check[4] has been implemented as a Yet Another Markup Language (YAML) file that is configurable with metadata, e.g. `id`, `name`, `enabled`, and three groups of SPARQL CONSTRUCT queries to generate the check report that is output to users: (i) Generates metadata for the check report, (ii) Checks preconditions and does the check if preconditions are satisfied, (iii) Retrieves additional information for the report such as SKOS labels for property values.

---

[4] https://doi.org/10.5281/zenodo.17098118.

3.1 Types of Compatibility Checks

Checks can be categorized into four groups:

1. Boolean-based. Checks that are based on checking that both RINF and ERATV values are "true". This is the case of parameter `GSM-R use of group 555`.
2. Numeric-based. Checks that are based on arithmetic comparisons such as the `Maximum speed` check where ERATV parameter `Vehicle type maximum speed <=` RINF parameter `Maximum permitted speed`.
3. SKOS-based. Checks that involve properties that point to the same SKOS concept scheme. For example the `Energy supply system` check that verifies that the parameter used for both ERATV and RINF must match. When there is at least one pair of values that are exact matches, then the check will output a *Compatible* result, if there are no exact matches and at least one close match, the output will be *Need manual check* (illustrated in Sect. 2.1); otherwise it will give a *Not compatible* result.
4. Hybrid. This is the case of checks where the datatypes for RINF and ERATV are different. For example `Hot Axle Box detection` is compatible if the track value of parameter `Existence of trackside hot axle box detector (HABD)` is "true" and the value of the vehicle type parameter `Axle bearing condition monitoring` is one of the taxonomy values (the parameter points to a SKOS concept scheme).

Following we will describe the treatment of missing data during checks, the parallelization of queries and the grouping of tracks with the same parameter values.

3.2 Treatment of Missing Data

For each compatibility check, the preconditions for their execution is that data in both RINF and ERATV must exist. That is: (i) There are no triples `?track era:notYetAvailable ?p` or `?track era:notApplicable ?p`, (ii) There is at least one value for both track and vehicle type.

If both preconditions are satisfied then the results are bound, if not satisfied the `result:unableToCheck` metadata is produced for the output report. These preconditions are necessary in order to detect missing data in advance. Without preconditions, missing data would always yield incompatible results.

3.3 Optimisations in the RCC Implementation

The evaluation at once of all the SPARQL queries that would be required to produce a compatibility report in a medium or large route would result in a poor performance of the application, due to the congestion of the SPARQL endpoint. Therefore, different types of optimisations have been implemented.

Optimisation 1. Query Parallelism. We leverage the triplestore's ability to execute queries concurrently. A typical check definition consists of three independent `CONSTRUCT` queries that generate different parts of the data contained in the final report. Since the queries are not interdependent, execution order is not a limiting factor and we can execute them in parallel.

We implement a worker pool to handle the query execution, ensuring that as soon as a query finishes, the next one is sent to the SPARQL endpoint. In this way, we can keep a constant processing load in the triplestore, establishing a consistent performance but also limiting congestion, adjusting the number of workers if required. We scaled the number of workers in the pool to fit the particular triplestore deployment of ERA, taking into account the number of CPUs available and its performance with the different workload configurations.

Optimisation 2. Track Aggregation. In general, adjacent tracks in a route share the same values of technical parameters. Therefore, we found an optimisation opportunity grouping tracks by their parameter values.

Groups of tracks are precomputed (for each checked property) and used to transform the whole list of tracks for a route into sets of group representatives. Compatibility is then calculated only for unique values. This approach reduces the load and improves the performance of the RCC application, especially in the case of long routes. It consists of the following execution steps:

1. Within each **defined check**, properties required are **retrieved** for each track.
   - Each track's **hash** is computed from the **property's value**.
   - When multiple values exist for a track, they are **concatenated**.
2. Pairs of calculated (`track, hash`) values are **stored for the generation of groupings** on requested routes.

3.4   Report Generation

The generation of the compatibility report follows several stages.

Data Collection. Data collection is executed for each check, using the query execution worker pool.

1. Using the structure described in Sect. 3.3, **tracks are grouped based on equal property values**.
2. A **sample track from each generated grouping is taken** and replaced on the check queries. Queries are designed to take multiple values for vehicles and tracks parameters.
3. The compatibility result is **retrieved in the form of a subgraph** for the particular check. The subgraph contains the results ID, the compatibility verdict, and additional metadata related to the comparison of property values.
4. With the resulting values, the initial grouping is undone and **the results extrapolated** to all the requested tracks.

Report Serialization. Once all the required information is collected as a report graph, the RDF graph is transformed into a JSON object to be sent back to the RCC user interface.

4   Evaluation

The purpose of this evaluation is to analyse the impact of the optimisations described in Sect. 3, parallelization and track aggregation, on the reduction of the time needed to obtain the report. To test this optimisation, we compare the results against a baseline, which we call the naïve execution strategy.

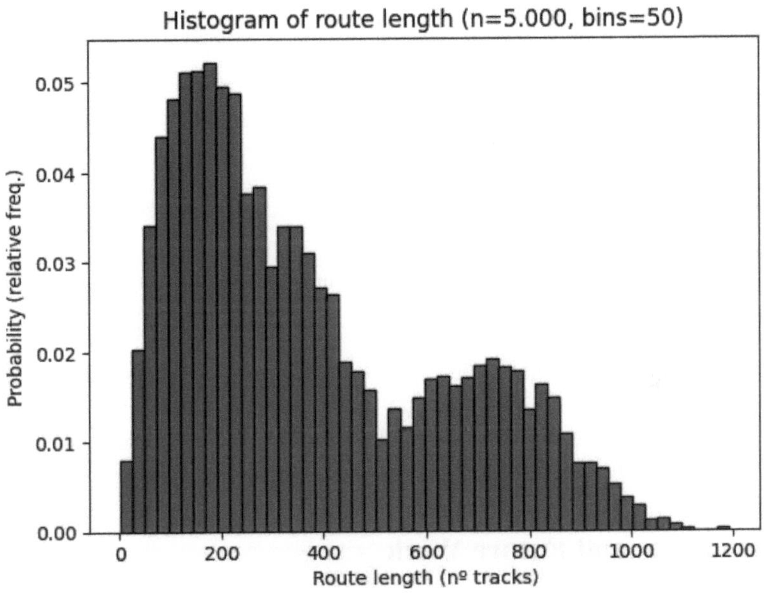

Fig. 3. Histogram depicting the length distribution of routes based on randomly picked Operational Points.

Two distinct virtual machines were used in the experimental setup. The first housed the Virtuoso triplestore, akin to the ERA production system, with 32 GiB RAM and 4 vCPUs allocated. ERA had already opted for Virtuoso following preliminary tests of various triple stores. The second machine, equipped with 8 GiB RAM and 4 vCPUs, deployed the RCC backend Docker container. A set of routes with assorted lengths was generated by picking operational points randomly over the EU member states. Figure 3 shows the length frequency distribution of these routes.

With these routes, the optimised execution approach was evaluated against the baseline naïve approach. The results, which plot execution time against route length, are presented in Fig. 4.

The results demonstrate a significant reduction in the time required to execute all checks, achieving approximately a five-fold improvement on the tested routes. Notably, this performance gain was not observed for extremely short routes. We attribute this enhancement to two main factors: the use of more lightweight SPARQL queries that involve fewer tracks, and the resulting decrease in data traffic from the triplestore.

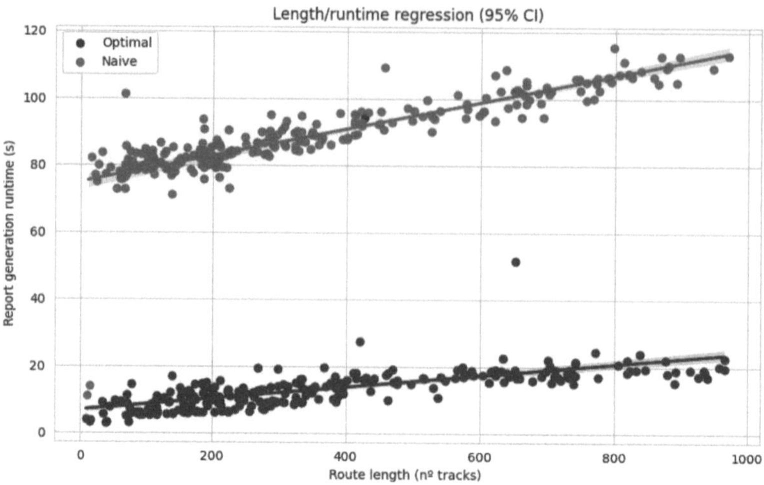

Fig. 4. Comparison of optimal execution vs. naïve execution.

Additionally, we found that under optimal conditions, query execution parallelism can boost performance by as much as 3.5 times (using 4 threads on a system with 4 vCPUs), but, since the triple store is shared with other applications, real-world performance will likely be lower.

5　Conclusions and Future Work

Our experimental results show that in the specific case of long routes, the naïve approach, i.e. executing the query defined in the check without any pre-processing, requires a large number of computations and is not performant.

Additionally, having a set of declarative SPARQL queries that implement RCC checks, contained in YAML files that are easy to comprehend, create, and update, is an advantage from the software maintenance point of view. However, the downside is that SPARQL's expressivity is not geared for checks that consist mostly of conditional expressions. This work on the improvement of SPARQL performance for RCC checks is aimed at compensating for this disadvantage with techniques such as aggregation of results and parallelization of queries.

It should be noted that the RCC checks implemented in the pilot version described in [2] are procedural in nature and are executed on the client side. This approach has the advantage of saving resources on the server side. However, it does not allow for the improvements that were required to have an acceptable response time for users. Therefore, the RCC logic was moved to the server side, where checks are declarative and easier to maintain.

Additionally, the efficiency of some of the proposed improvements may be dependent on the specific triplestore used and its optimisation techniques.

Acknowledgements. We would like to thank Julián Rojas from Ghent University for his contribution to the initial development of the ERA RCC application, and Marina Aguado, Dragos Patru, Ghislain Atemezing, and Polymnia Vasilopoulou from the European Union Agency for Railways (ERA) for their participation in the ERA RCC development.

References

1. European Union Agency for Railways: Registers of Infrastructure (RINF) (2025). https://www.era.europa.eu/domains/registers/rinf_en
2. Rojas Meléndez, J., Aguado, M., Vasilopoulou, P., Velitchkov, I., Van Assche, D., Colpaert, P., Verborgh, R.: Leveraging Semantic Web technologies for digital interoperability in the railway domain. In: Proceedings of the 20th International Semantic Web Conference. Lecture Notes in Computer Science, vol. 12851, pp. 648–664. Springer (2021). https://doi.org/10.1007/978-3-030-88361-4_38
3. Toledo, J., et al.: Using semantic technologies in the railway domain: the Register of Infrastructure (RINF) System. In: Proceedings of the 24th International Semantic Web Conference (2025)
4. World Wide Web Consortium (W3C): SKOS Core Vocabulary Specification (2005). https://www.w3.org/TR/swbp-skos-core-spec/

Adaptive by Design: Rethinking the MLOC Architecture for Learning Systems

Marco Hüller[✉] [iD], Roman Küble [iD], and Jörg Hähner [iD]

Organic Computing Group, University of Augsburg, Am Technologiezentrum 8,
Augsburg, Germany
marco.hueller@uni-a.de

Abstract. Adaptive cyber-physical systems must cope with changing environments while guaranteeing reliable operation. The Multi-Layered Observer/Controller (MLOC) architecture provides a well-established blueprint for such self-organising systems, yet broader adoption is constrained by two key shortcomings: (i) a static, rule-based decision layer that scales poorly with state-space complexity and (ii) a fixed simulator that cannot model unforeseen dynamics. This paper proposes a lightweight redesign of MLOC's operational and adaptive layers. First, we propose replacing the XCS Classifier System (XCS) in Layer 1 with reinforcement learning agents, which reduces configuration effort and enables continuous control in high-dimensional domains. Second, we suggest a dynamic Layer 2 simulator that is fine-tuned or fully exchanged whenever an anomaly detector signals model drift. The detector differentiates between simulation mismatch and agent uncertainty, triggering simulator updates or focused agent fine-tuning without breaching MLOC's safety principle of avoiding exploratory actions in the real system. All components are lightweight, making them suitable for platforms with limited resources. Furthermore, depending on the chosen methods, the models may remain interpretable—preserving one of the key advantages of the original XCS. The redesign preserves MLOC's hierarchical structure and unifies reactive control, long-term learning, and model maintenance, substantially widening its applicability to complex and uncertain environments.

Keywords: MLOC · Organic Computing · Reinforcement Learning · XCS

1 Introduction

The increasing complexity of modern computing systems has created a demand for architectures that can autonomously handle environmental changes. Organic Computing (OC) [11,12,20] addresses this challenge by designing systems with inherent self-organization, self-optimization, and adaptability. The Multi-Layered Observer/Controller (MLOC) architecture [12] is a prominent methodology in the field of OC. It employs a hierarchical control structure, enabling individual layers to specialize in distinct levels of decision-making and learning.

At its core, the MLOC architecture divides control mechanisms into multiple levels. These include a reactive layer responsible for immediate operational decisions, an

C. Cappiello et al. (Eds.): CoopIS 2025, LNCS 15535, pp. 618–628, 2026.
https://doi.org/10.1007/978-3-032-15538-2_39

adaptive layer for long-term strategy refinement, and an optional top-level layer for managing system goals and priorities. This layered structure is designed to facilitate flexibility, resilience and long-term adaptability. A key advantage of MLOC over traditional monolithic systems is its integration of simulation and learning: new strategies can be evaluated in a model (i.e., internal simulator) of the environment before being applied, enabling safe exploration and more robust decision-making in complex or safety-critical scenarios.

However, practical implementations of MLOC reveal several critical limitations that hinder its broader adoption, particularly in highly uncertain or complex environments. One major limitation arises from the static nature of decision-making in existing MLOC implementations, which heavily relies on the XCS Classifier System (XCS) [24]. This reliance is problematic, as inherent challenges of XCS, including its significant configuration complexity and predominantly reactive learning behavior, have been recognized as key research issues that limit its broader applicability for adaptive agents [16]. Additionally, current MLOC systems often lack continuous self-optimization and adaptability, particularly in the interaction between short-term operational control and long-term learning processes.

We focus on architectural modifications to Layer 1 and Layer 2, which form the core feedback loop responsible for runtime decisions and learning. We propose the integration of reinforcement learning (RL) [18] to replace traditional rule-based decision mechanisms and introduce methods to improve the adaptivity of internal simulation components for more context-sensitive, robust behavior. The full MLOC architecture includes a higher-level organizational layer (Layer 3) responsible for goal management, which also offers potential for improvement. However, an analysis of this layer is beyond the scope of this work and briefly addressed in the discussion of future research.

The remainder of this paper is organized as follows: Sect. 2 explains the theoretical background of the MLOC architecture and discusses related work. Section 3 analyzes the key limitations of the current MLOC approach. Building upon these insights, Sect. 4 presents targeted architectural modifications for Layer 1 and Layer 2. Section 5 concludes the paper and outlines potential directions for future research.

2 Background and Related Work

The Multi-Layered Observer/Controller architecture [12] is a reference architecture from the field of OC that aims to design complex, self-organizing and adaptive systems in a structured and controllable way. This section provides an overview of the fundamental concepts underlying MLOC, reviews existing application scenarios, and explores related architectural paradigms.

2.1 Fundamental Concepts of MLOC

MLOC is based on a multi-layered structure (see Fig. 1) in which each layer takes on specific roles:

- **Layer 0** describes the System under Observation and Control (SuOC), e.g. a software service or a cyber-physical system. This forms the basis for all higher-level observation and control processes.

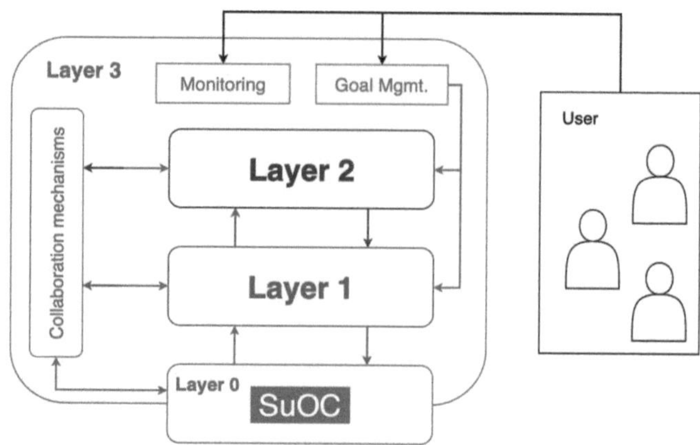

Fig. 1. The MLOC architecture with its hierarchically organised layers.

- **Layer 1** is responsible for operational control based on current sensor data. Decisions are typically reactive and usually supported by simple learning procedures (the standard is a modified XCS version). The aim of this layer is to enable a robust, immediate response to environmental changes.
- **Layer 2** implements adaptive control processes. Based on long-term observations, it analyses system behaviour, identifies optimisation potential, and adapts the strategies of Layer 1 if necessary. Simulation-based approaches are often used to enable evaluation-based decision-making.
- **Layer 3** forms an optional organisational level that deals with the higher-level objectives and long-term system strategy. It can be used to resolve conflicting objectives, rebalance priorities and adapt the overall system to changing framework conditions.

Through the functional separation into several observation and control levels, the MLOC architecture supports structured self-organisation and at the same time enables controllable and transparent system development. The interaction of the layers creates the basis for technical systems that are both responsive in the short term and capable of learning and adapting in the long term.

2.2 Applications

The MLOC architecture has been used in various application areas to implement adaptive, self-optimising systems.

One example was provided by Sommer et al. [15] with the Organic Traffic Control System, which used MLOC for decentralised control of urban traffic nodes. This system used Layer 1 to process traffic data with the help of learning-based methods, while Layer 2 performed simulation-based optimisation and Layer 3 coordinated strategic objectives—resulting in significantly reduced waiting times and emissions.

MLOC was also used successfully in the field of robotic swarms: Von Mammen et al. [21] showed how autonomous drone systems could navigate and coordinate themselves while also being able to adaptively fulfil long-term tasks. In this case, Layer 1 was responsible for local control, Layer 2 for optimising behaviour and Layer 3 for formulating or adapting global goals.

Another use case involved network communication. Tomforde et al. [19] used MLOC to optimise protocol parameters dynamically at runtime. While Layer 1 reacted to current network conditions, Layer 2 used genetic algorithms to identify more efficient configurations.

2.3 Alternative Approaches

In addition to the MLOC architecture, there are several approaches that pursue similar goals and address key aspects such as adaptability, modularisation and context sensitivity. They can be broadly distinguished into fundamental control patterns and other architectural blueprints.

Among the most influential control patterns are the MAPE-K loop [6] and the LRA-M pattern [7]. MLOC can be seen as a concrete instantiation of these patterns: the Observer handles monitoring, analysis, and learning, while the Controller performs planning and execution. The main architectural difference lies in their organization. MLOC arranges multiple Observer/Controller pairs—each analogous to a single MAPE-K or LRA-M loop—in a prescriptive, multi-layer hierarchy with distinct layers for different time scales and scopes. This contrasts with decentralized systems of equivalent MAPE-K or LRA-M loops, where global behavior emerges from local interactions.

A related concept is Anytime Learning by Zilberstein [26], which partitions systems into a learning component (akin to the Observer) and an execution component (akin to the Controller and SuOC). Unlike MLOC, it defines only two components. MLOC refines this structure by introducing a hierarchical layering of observer and controller roles operating at different time scales.

With LifeLong Computing (LLC), Weyns et al. [23] proposed a concept that enabled systems to develop autonomously over their lifetime. It integrated online experiments, modular expandability and empirical knowledge. Compared to MLOC, LLC focusses more on long-term evolutionary adaptation.

Petrovska et al. [14] presented a theoretical framework with a formal definition of adaptive systems based on a quality function. This enables a system to evaluate its behaviour and to independently initiate adaptation measures if it misses the target. Rather than building on structural layering as in MLOC, their approach introduces a complementary, quality-driven notion of adaptation grounded in formal semantics.

A framework for modelling adaptive requirements based on proven design patterns has been developed by Silva et al. [4]. It primarily supports the conceptual phase of system development and is also aimed at non-experts. Compared to MLOC, the focus here remains on the model-based preparation of system adaptation.

Bruni et al. [3] proposed a formal concept for adaptivity that is based on the explicit separation of application logic and control data. Adaptivity is achieved through the targeted modification of this data at runtime. The approach is structurally similar to MLOC, but is based on a more in-depth formal foundation.

While all of these approaches share conceptual similarities with MLOC, none of them fully replicate the integrated, hierarchical control and simulation structure that characterizes it.

3   Limitations of the Current MLOC Architecture

Although the MLOC architecture is designed to support adaptivity by separating operational control (Layer 1) from long-term learning mechanisms (Layer 2), practical implementations reveal important limitations, especially in dynamic or uncertain environments [17]. We argue that its broader applicability is constrained by two key factors: static decision-making and a lack of effective self-optimization.

Static Decision Mechanisms. In current research, MLOC is typically combined with the XCS, which uses rule-based learning for decision making [12]. While XCS performs well in simple and stable environments, it reaches computational and structural limits as complexity increases [17]. The number of rules grows exponentially with the size of the state space, making learning inefficient and computationally prohibitive.

Another drawback of XCS is its extensive parameter space of 24 variables, which complicates configuration [12]. Moreover, unmodified XCS focuses on short-term rewards, neglecting strategic long-term decisions [17]. Extensions like XCSCR [25] address this issue, but have not yet been applied within the MLOC context.

Although MLOC allows for alternative decision mechanisms such as RL, this potential remains underexplored due to the architecture's strong historical focus on XCS. A more flexible design could significantly enhance adaptability.[1]

Absence of Adaptivity and Self-Optimization. A key limitation of the current MLOC implementation is the weak interaction between Layer 1 and Layer 2. While Layer 1 makes real-time decisions, this information is not continuously integrated into the simulation models or control strategies of Layer 2. As a result, decision-making remains reactive, long-term patterns are overlooked, and true self-optimization is not achieved.

Although reflection layers have been proposed for XCS agents [16], they remain tightly coupled to XCS and fail to address the architectural separation inherent in MLOC, which highlights the need for alternative mechanisms.

Additionally, learning in Layer 2 depends on a static simulation model and cannot adapt to unanticipated scenarios. In practice, constructing models that capture the full range of possible situations is often infeasible, which limits MLOC's use to idealized settings with near-perfect assumptions.

In summary, the current MLOC architecture suffers from limited adaptability and fragmented feedback. While conceptually robust, its practical use in dynamic environments remains constrained.

---

[1] There has been some consideration of exchanging XCS with RL algorithms, e.g., by Breitsameter [2], but these ideas have not been further developed.

4   Modifications

As outlined in the previous section, the classical MLOC architecture suffers from two key limitations: its reliance on static, rule-based decision mechanisms and the weak coupling between operational and adaptive layers. To address these issues, we propose a set of complementary modifications targeting Layer 1 and Layer 2. The core idea is to replace the XCS-based logic in Layer 1 with more scalable RL algorithms. In parallel, we improve the adaptivity of Layer 2 through anomaly detection and flexible simulation handling.

Unlike prior work that focuses on internal XCS extensions, such as reflective meta-learning [16], our approach introduces a structural redesign of the control and learning flow.

4.1   Overview of Structural Changes

Figure 2 contrasts Layers 1 and 2 of the original MLOC architecture (a) with the proposed modifications (b). In the original design, Layer 1 uses a modified XCS classifier for decision-making, while Layer 2 relies on a static simulator for offline learning and strategy refinement.

In the revised version, XCS is replaced by a RL agent in Layer 1, enabling more flexible and scalable decisions, especially in high-dimensional or continuous environments. Simultaneously, the simulator in Layer 2 becomes dynamic, meaning it is no longer fixed but adapts to observed data to better capture changing conditions. These changes establish tighter coupling between the layers: uncertainty or degraded performance in Layer 1 can now trigger model updates or retraining in Layer 2, strengthening feedback and improving self-optimization.

The improvements are modular: using an RL agent can improve scalability, support faster convergence, and simplify configuration. Similarly, introducing a dynamic model in Layer 2 without changing Layer 1 supports adaptability by enabling internal models to evolve with the environment.

The full potential of the revised architecture unfolds when both enhancements are combined, but each can also be applied independently, depending on system context and requirements.

4.2   Anomaly Detection

Various types of anomalies can arise within the MLOC framework, each indicating a mismatch between internal assumptions and the external environment. Here, anomalies refer to persistent or acute discrepancies, whether structural or behavioral, between internal models and real-world observations.

Two categories of anomalies are particularly relevant in our setting: (i) *simulation mismatch*, where the internal simulator no longer reflects actual system dynamics, and (ii) *agent uncertainty*, which indicates that the policy in Layer 1 lacks sufficient confidence for reliable decision-making. Additional signals—such as unexpected state transitions, implausible action sequences, or deviant reward signals—may also serve as indicators but are not explicitly addressed in this work.

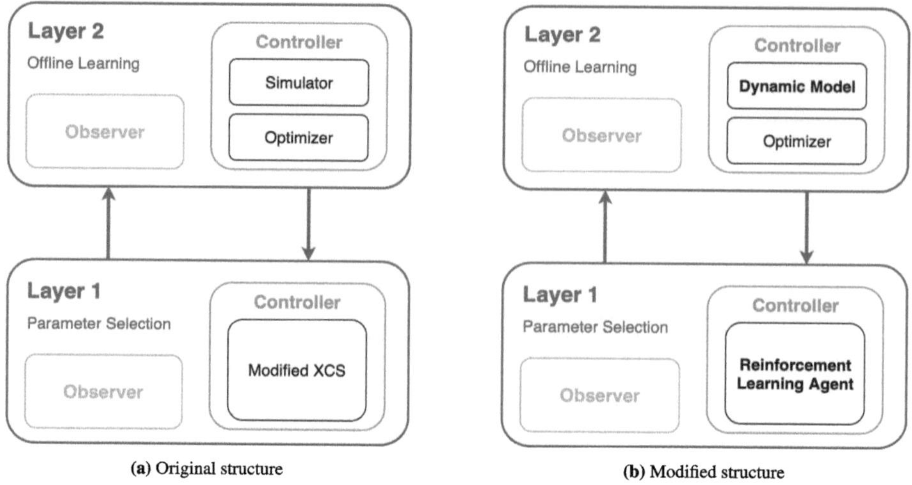

Fig. 2. Comparison of the original (a) and modified (b) Layer 1 and Layer 2 of the MLOC architecture.

Identifying such anomalies is crucial for enabling the adaptive mechanisms, which will be proposed in Sect. 4.3. Depending on the case, the system may retrain the agent, adjust learning priorities, or update the simulation model. Anomaly detection thus becomes the entry point for controlled adaptation.

Simulation Mismatch. In adaptive systems, internal simulators must accurately reflect the real environment to support effective learning and decision-making. However, real-world dynamics often change over time, which can lead to a mismatch between simulated and actual behavior. A misaligned simulator can lead to ineffective or even harmful strategies. Without mechanisms to detect drift or degradation, the architecture cannot maintain alignment with the real system. This is particularly critical in MLOC, where real-time exploration is intentionally avoided, and simulation becomes the primary means for safe adaptation.

To identify these mismatches, the simulator can be executed in parallel to the real system, using identical input sequences. Deviations between predicted and observed outcomes are continuously monitored, and statistically significant differences are flagged as indicators of simulation invalidity.

To respond without violating MLOC's safety principles, which prohibit unsafe exploration in the real environment, only passive, offline adaptation is permitted. A promising approach is *Offline RL*, such as Conservative Q-Learning (CQL) [8] or Behaviour Cloning [1], which use historical data to update the simulator. Alternatively, an *ensemble simulator approach* maintains several pre-trained models and selects the one most consistent with observations. However, this approach may struggle in previously unseen scenarios, where none of the available models is sufficiently accurate. In such cases, the system can fall back to robust, predefined actions until a better model is available.

Agent Uncertainty. In the original MLOC architecture with XCS, uncertainty is implicitly encoded in the performance values of its rules, which serve as a measure of confidence. However, when replacing XCS with a RL agent, an explicit mechanism for uncertainty estimation becomes necessary.

Such uncertainty can be assessed through internal metrics that vary depending on the learning algorithm. For both value-based methods (e.g., DQN [9]) and policy-based methods (e.g., A3C [10]), entropy of the action distribution or policy can be used to estimate confidence [5]. Additionally, ensemble methods—where multiple agents or networks are trained in parallel—capture uncertainty via variance in their predictions [13]. Another popular technique is Monte Carlo dropout, which approximates Bayesian inference by sampling different dropout masks during inference [5].

These metrics help identify states or transitions where the agent lacks confidence, often due to insufficient or unrepresentative training data in specific regions of the state space.

In response, the agent can be selectively fine-tuned in Layer 2 with a focus on these identified regions, thereby enhancing decision quality. This closed-loop interaction between Layer 1 and Layer 2 enables the architecture to continuously adapt to evolving conditions.

4.3   Enhancements

Building on the previously discussed anomaly detection mechanisms, we identify three complementary strategies for improving MLOC's adaptivity: (i) replacing the rule-based XCS system in Layer 1 with a model-free RL agent, (ii) introducing a dynamic simulation model in Layer 2, and (iii) combining both to enable tightly integrated learning and control.

The applicability of each strategy depends on system-specific constraints. Safety-critical applications typically require a fixed, verifiable simulation model to ensure predictable behavior. In contrast, less restrictive systems may benefit from adaptive simulation components that evolve over time and enhance long-term flexibility.

Dynamic Simulation. A dynamic simulation model in Layer 2 can be applied independently of changes in Layer 1. Here, only the simulation component is adapted to reflect changing system behavior based on observed data. This setup improves long-term adaptability without altering the decision-making logic.

A dynamic model enables Layer 2 to respond more flexibly to deviations between predictions and real-world outcomes, as detected by the anomaly mechanisms. Rather than relying on a static model that may become outdated, the system continuously refines its simulation logic, for example through offline RL or model ensemble selection, as discussed in the previous section.

Exchanging XCS with RL. Replacing the XCS in Layer 1 with RL agents offers a more scalable and easier-to-configure decision layer, particularly in dynamic or high-dimensional settings. We consider two RL categories: tabular methods such as Q-learning [22] and deep RL methods such as DQN [9] or A3C [10].

Tabular RL is attractive for low-dimensional tasks: it is easy to tune, interpretable, and requires fewer parameters than XCS. Its weakness is poor scalability, as continuous or large state spaces require manual discretisation.

Deep RL removes this limitation by learning directly from high-dimensional, continuous inputs, making it suitable for multimodal or noisy domains. The trade-off is higher computational cost and reduced transparency, in contrast to XCS and tabular RL methods, which offers rule-based, interpretable decision logic. This loss of explainability may be problematic in safety-critical or regulated applications.

As discussed, XCS offers implicit confidence estimation via performance values. When replaced by RL agents, explicit uncertainty measures are needed to decide when control should escalate to Layer 2. In this setting, Layer 2 no longer synthesises new rules but fine-tunes the agent in uncertain regions.

Combined Approach. This variant combines both enhancements: a learning agent in Layer 1 and a dynamic simulator in Layer 2. The simulator adapts to observed data and fine-tunes the agent in uncertain situations, while the agent continues to make real-time decisions. The approach is agnostic to the specific RL algorithm used; any method that supports uncertainty estimation and targeted refinement can be applied.

Model-based RL emerges as a natural implementation of this setup. Here, the learned model in Layer 2 serves as an internal simulator, enabling offline updates in regions where the agent lacks confidence. However, model learning typically requires exploratory interaction with the real environment to collect informative data—especially in underexplored areas. This contradicts one of MLOC's core principles: avoiding real-world exploration to ensure safety.

Nevertheless, in non-safety-critical domains, this trade-off may be acceptable. Model-based RL can then fully leverage the combined structure to achieve a more adaptive and self-optimising MLOC architecture.

5   Conclusion

This paper has identified key limitations of the classical Multi-Layered Observer/Controller (MLOC) architecture in the context of adaptive and learning systems. In particular, we highlighted the static nature of decision mechanisms and the insufficient self-optimization capabilities as major barriers to practical applicability in complex environments. To address these challenges, we proposed several architectural modifications, including the integration of RL algorithms (both tabular and deep), the introduction of a dynamic simulation model, and mechanisms for anomaly detection. These enhancements allow MLOC to operate more flexibly and robustly, enabling continuous learning and improved decision-making under uncertainty. By aligning the architecture more closely with Organic Computing principles, its applicability broadens to a wider range of real-world domains.

Despite improving adaptability and learning, the proposed modifications introduce new challenges. Reinforcement learning methods can suffer from instability, data inefficiency, and tuning complexity. Dynamic simulators depend on high-quality historical data, which may be limited or biased. The approach also assumes a clean separation of layers, which is not always realistic. Finally, while real-world exploration is avoided, the effectiveness in rapidly changing environments still requires empirical validation.

Future work will focus on empirical validation of the proposed concepts, with particular emphasis on evaluating long-term system behaviour and the interplay between learning, simulation, and anomaly detection in dynamic environments. Additionally, extending the current enhancements to include dynamic goal management in Layer 3 represents a promising direction for further increasing system autonomy and contextual awareness. This could enable systems to adjust not only their behaviour but also their objectives in response to changing user requirements or environmental conditions, further strengthening the adaptability envisioned by the MLOC architecture.

References

1. Bain, M., et al.: A framework for behavioural cloning. In: Sloman, A., Hogg, D., Humphreys, G., Partridge, D., Howe, A. (eds.) Machine Intelligence 15, pp. 103–129. Oxford University Press (2000). https://doi.org/10.1093/oso/9780198538677.003.0006
2. Breitsameter, L.: Anytime Learning - The next Step in Organic Computing? (2018). https://doi.org/10.48550/arXiv.1808.07590
3. Bruni, R., et al.: A conceptual framework for adaptation. In: Fundamental Approaches to Software Engineering (2012)
4. Da Silva, J.P.S., et al.: Towards a framework for self-adaptive systems conceptual modeling. In: Proceedings of the XIX Brazilian Symposium on Information Systems (2023). https://doi.org/10.1145/3592813.3592921
5. Gal, Y., et al.: Dropout as a Bayesian approximation: representing model uncertainty in deep learning. In: International Conference on Machine Learning, pp. 1050–1059. PMLR (2016)
6. Kephart, J., et al.: The vision of autonomic computing. Computer **36**(1), 41–50 (2003)
7. Kounev, S., et al.: The notion of self-aware computing. In: Kounev, S., Kephart, J.O., Milenkoski, A., Zhu, X. (eds.) Self-Aware Computing Systems, pp. 3–16. Springer, Cham (2017)
8. Kumar, A., , et al.: Conservative Q-Learning for Offline Reinforcement Learning (2020). https://doi.org/10.48550/arXiv.2006.04779
9. Mnih, V., et al.: Playing Atari with Deep Reinforcement Learning (2013). https://doi.org/10.48550/arXiv.1312.5602
10. Mnih, V., et al.: Asynchronous methods for deep reinforcement learning. In: International Conference on Machine Learning, pp. 1928–1937. PmLR (2016)
11. Müller-Schloer, C., et al.: Organic Computing–A Paradigm Shift for Complex Systems. Springer, Basel (2011). https://doi.org/10.1007/978-3-0348-0130-0
12. Müller-Schloer, C., Tomforde, S.: Organic Computing – Technical Systems for Survival in the Real World. AS, Springer, Cham (2017). https://doi.org/10.1007/978-3-319-68477-2
13. Osband, I., et al.: Deep exploration via bootstrapped DQN. Adv. Neural Inf. Process. Syst. **29** (2016)
14. Petrovska, A., et al.: A theoretical framework for self-adaptive systems: specifications, formalisation, and architectural implications. In: Proceedings of the 38th ACM/SIGAPP Symposium on Applied Computing (2023). https://doi.org/10.1145/3555776.3577665
15. Sommer, M., Tomforde, S., Hähner, J.: An organic computing approach to resilient traffic management. In: McCluskey, T.L., Kotsialos, A., Müller, J.P., Klügl, F., Rana, O., Schumann, R. (eds.) Autonomic Road Transport Support Systems. AS, chap 7, pp. 113–130. Springer, Cham (2016). https://doi.org/10.1007/978-3-319-25808-9_7

16. Stein, A., et al.: Reflective learning classifier systems for self-adaptive and self-organising agents. In: 2021 IEEE International Conference on Autonomic Computing and Self-Organizing Systems Companion (ACSOS-C), pp. 139–145. IEEE (2021)
17. Steinberger, M., et al.: Evaluating adaptive systems: a comparative study of XCS and established reinforcement learning algorithms in noisy multi-step environments. In: Architecture of Computing Systems. Springer, Cham (2025, to appear). Presented at the International Conference on Architecture of Computing Systems 2025, April 2025
18. Sutton, R.S.: Reinforcement Learning: An Introduction. A Bradford Book (2018)
19. Tomforde, S., et al.: Cooperative self-optimisation of network protocol parameters at run-time. In: 2015 12th International Conference on Informatics in Control, Automation and Robotics (ICINCO) (2015)
20. Tomforde, S., et al.: Organic computing in the spotlight. CoRR (2017)
21. Von Mammen, S., et al.: An organic computing approach to self-organizing robot ensembles. Front. Robot. AI **3** (2016)
22. Watkins, C.J., et al.: Q-learning. Mach. Learn. (1992). https://doi.org/10.1007/BF00992698
23. Weyns, D., et al.: Lifelong computing (2021)
24. Wilson, S.W.: Classifier fitness based on accuracy. Evolutionary computation (1995)
25. Zhang, Z., et al.: XCS with combined reward method (XCSCR) for policy search in multistep problems. In: 2019 IEEE Congress on Evolutionary Computation (CEC) (2019). https://doi.org/10.1109/CEC.2019.8790115
26. Zilberstein, S.: Using anytime algorithms in intelligent systems. AI Mag. **17**(3), 73 (1996)

MuC: A Multi-core Tucker Model with Core Attention

Yanhui Zhang[✉], Dong Zhu, and Aiping Li

National University of Defense Technology, Changsha, Hunan, China
{zhangyh,zhud,liaiping}@nudt.edu.cn

Abstract. Knowledge graph completion (KGC) aims to infer missing triples from existing data. While tensor decomposition-based models offer strong expressiveness, their large core tensors often cause overfitting. We propose **MuC**, a multi-core tensor model that factorizes the core tensor into several smaller cores and introduces a *core attention mechanism* to dynamically select relevant cores based on entity-relation input. To encourage diversity among cores, we design a *geometric consistency constraint*, and to stabilize multi-path interactions, we generalize embedding norm regularization into *channel regularization*. Experiments show that MuC improves MRR by **22.83%** on FB15k-237 and **21.51%** on YAGO3-10 compared to strong baselines. Further analysis of core attention weights and dataset characteristics demonstrates the effectiveness of MuC's dynamic core selection in enhancing adaptability and expressiveness.

Keywords: Knowledge Graph Completion · Tensor Decomposition · Multi-Core Structure · Attention Mechanism

1 Introduction

Knowledge graphs (KGs) represent structured information as triples (h, r, t), where h and t denote head and tail entities and r represents the relation between them. KGs power a wide range of applications such as recommendation [6], question answering [3], and information retrieval [24]. However, real-world KGs are inherently incomplete, motivating the task of knowledge graph completion (KGC)—inferring missing links by learning meaningful representations of entities and relations.

Among existing approaches, tensor decomposition-based (TDB) models have shown strong expressiveness and theoretical grounding. In particular, TuckER [1] uses Tucker decomposition [19] to model interactions via a global core tensor $\mathcal{W}$. Despite its effectiveness, the single-core design poses scalability issues, as the core tensor grows cubically with embedding size and is shared across all triples, making it prone to overfitting and limited in modeling relation diversity [23].

To address these limitations, we introduce **MuC**, a **multi-core** tensor model with dynamic core selection. MuC replaces the monolithic core with multiple smaller ones

---

D. Zhu and A. Li—Co-corresponding authors.

C. Cappiello et al. (Eds.): CoopIS 2025, LNCS 15535, pp. 629–639, 2026.
https://doi.org/10.1007/978-3-032-15538-2_40

and incorporates a *core attention mechanism* to select relevant cores based on entity-relation input. To further stabilize training and encourage functional diversity, we propose two regularization strategies: *channel regularization* to constrain multi-path outputs, and a *geometric consistency constraint* to encourage separation between core functionalities.

Recent KGC models often enhance generalization by incorporating auxiliary information via two main paradigms: structure-enhanced and semantic-enhanced modeling. The former uses graph structures like neighbors or paths (e.g., NBFNet [28], MoCoKGC [10], MEIM [17]), while the latter leverages textual descriptions with pre-trained language models (e.g., KG-BERT [26], SimKGC [21], CoLE [12]).

Despite these trends, our experiments show that MuC, without leveraging any external textual or structural information beyond the raw triples, achieves improvement in MRR (Mean Reciprocal Rank) on both FB15k-237 and YAGO3-10. This underscores the effectiveness of purely structural modeling approaches, especially in scenarios where semantic resources are scarce or relational patterns are complex. Our findings reaffirm the potential of efficient, purely structural solutions for KGC.

The main contributions of this paper are summarized as follows:

- **MuC Model:** We propose a multi-core tensor decomposition framework with a core attention mechanism, enabling dynamic core selection while maintaining parameter efficiency;
- **Multi-Core Regularization:** We design two tailored regularization strategies, geometric consistency and channel regularization to promote functional diversity and stabilize multi-path interactions;
- **Empirical Gains:** MuC achieves significant improvements over strong baselines on FB15k-237 and YAGO3-10, demonstrating the effectiveness of purely structural modeling in complex relational settings.

Our code and implementation details are publicly available at GitHub[1].

2   Related Work

2.1   Link Prediction

A knowledge graph is formally defined as a set of factual triples $\mathcal{S} = \{(h, r, t)\} \subseteq \mathcal{E} \times \mathcal{R} \times \mathcal{E}$, where $\mathcal{E}$ denotes the set of entities and $\mathcal{R}$ denotes the set of relations. Each triple (h, r, t) represents a directed link from the head entity $h \in \mathcal{E}$ to the tail entity $t \in \mathcal{E}$ via relation $r \in \mathcal{R}$. The task of link prediction, or knowledge graph completion, involves estimating the plausibility of unseen triples, i.e., determining whether a candidate triple (h, r, t) is likely to be valid. This task can be represented as a third-order binary tensor $\mathcal{X} \in \{0, 1\}^{|\mathcal{E}| \times |\mathcal{R}| \times |\mathcal{E}|}$, where $\mathcal{X}_{hrt} = 1$ if and only if $(h, r, t) \in \mathcal{S}$.

Numerous approaches have been proposed for the task, broadly falling into three categories: translation-based models, tensor decomposition-based models, and neural network-based models [27]. Translation-based methods, such as TransE [2] and

---

[1] https://github.com/Mirroraaa/Paper-MuC.

TransH [22], interpret relations as translation vectors operating in the entity embedding space. These models are computationally efficient and intuitively interpretable. TDB models, including RESCAL [13], DistMult [25], and TuckER [1], leverage multilinear algebra techniques to model interactions between entities and relations, offering strong expressiveness through structured decompositions. And MuC is a Tucker-style model. Neural models, such as ConvE [4] and R-GCN [14], incorporate convolutional and graph neural networks to capture complex local structures and contextual information, often yielding strong empirical performance.

2.2 TuckER: Tucker Decomposition for KGC

TuckER [1] factorizes the binary indicator tensor $\mathcal{X} \in \{0, 1\}^{|\mathcal{E}| \times |\mathcal{R}| \times |\mathcal{E}|}$ using Tucker decomposition:

$$\mathcal{X} \approx \mathcal{W} \times_1 H \times_2 R \times_3 T, \tag{1}$$

where $\mathcal{W} \in \mathbb{R}^{D \times D \times D}$ is a shared core tensor that captures entity-relation interactions. $\mathbf{H}, \mathbf{T} \in \mathbb{R}^{|\mathcal{E}| \times D}$ are the embedding matrices for head and tail entities, and $\mathbf{R} \in \mathbb{R}^{|\mathcal{R}| \times D}$ is the embedding matrix for relations. Each head entity h is represented by an embedding vector $\mathbf{h} \in \mathbb{R}^D$, tail entity t by $\mathbf{t} \in \mathbb{R}^D$, and relation r by $\mathbf{r} \in \mathbb{R}^D$. The operator $\times_n$ denotes the n-mode tensor product [8].

The scoring function for a triple (h, r, t) is computed by projecting the embeddings into the core tensor:

$$\phi(h, r, t) = \mathcal{W} \times_1 \mathbf{r} \times_2 \mathbf{h} \times_3 \mathbf{t}. \tag{2}$$

TuckER provides a unified framework that subsumes several prior tensor decomposition models as special cases, including RESCAL [13], DistMult [25], ComplEx [18], and SimplE [7]. While TuckER decouples core tensor size from the number of entities and relations, the core still contains D^3 parameters, leading to high computational cost and overfitting risk, especially under limited supervision.

2.3 Intermediate Variables Regularization

Traditional regularization methods typically apply ℓ_2 regularization to entity and relation embeddings [13], while N3 regularization [9] penalizes higher-order norms to suppress spiky activations. However, these approaches only constrain input embeddings, ignoring internal variables generated during scoring.

To address this, *Intermediate Variables Regularization* (IVR) [23] introduces explicit penalties on both embeddings and intermediate tensors computed during forward passes. By splitting the embedding dimension into multiple parts, IVR applies regularization not just to embeddings but also to first- and second-order tensor interactions. This fine-grained control improves model robustness and has shown consistent gains across various TDB models.

Theoretically, IVR approximates an upper bound of the overlapping trace norm [15], promoting low-rank structure in the scoring tensor and further mitigating overfitting.

3   Method

3.1   MuC Model

To avoid redundancy and better capture relation-specific features, we replace the single core tensor with a set of C smaller cores $\mathcal{W}^{(i)}{}_{i=1}^{C}$, each $\in \mathbb{R}^{P\times P\times P}$, as shown in Fig. 1. These cores share dimensions but learn distinct semantic patterns.

To adaptively select among them, we introduce a core attention mechanism that assigns dynamic weights based on the head entity and relation. A feed-forward network $\mathcal{A}(\cdot)$ takes the concatenated embedding $[\mathbf{h};\mathbf{r}] \in \mathbb{R}^{2D}$ and outputs a softmax distribution over the C cores:

$$\boldsymbol{\alpha}(h, r) = \mathrm{softmax}\left(\mathcal{A}([\mathbf{h};\mathbf{r}])\right), \quad \boldsymbol{\alpha} \in \mathbb{R}^{C}. \tag{3}$$

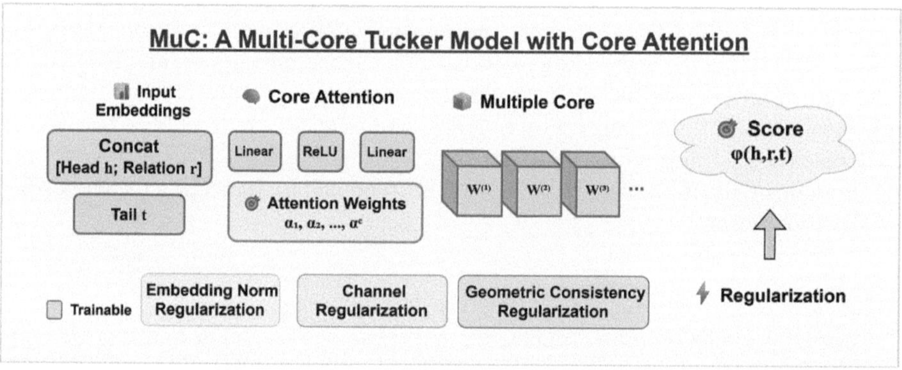

Fig. 1. Architecture of the proposed MuC model. The model employs core attention over multiple core tensors to compute scores $\varphi(h, r, t)$ from head, relation, and tail embeddings, with regularization components improving training stability and embedding diversity.

The attention network $\mathcal{A}(\cdot)$ is implemented as a three-layer multilayer perceptron (MLP) with ReLU activations:

$$\mathcal{A}([\mathbf{h};\mathbf{r}]) = \mathbf{W}_3 \cdot \mathrm{ReLU}\left(\mathbf{W}_2 \cdot \mathrm{ReLU}(\mathbf{W}_1 \cdot [\mathbf{h};\mathbf{r}])\right). \tag{4}$$

Importantly, instead of first aggregating the core tensors, MuC performs the full interaction path independently for each core. This design choice prevents premature mixing of signals and allows each core $\mathcal{W}^{(i)}$ to specialize during training. The final scoring function for a triple (h, r, t) is defined as the weighted sum over the outputs of each core tensor:

$$\phi(h, r, t) = \sum_{i=1}^{C} \alpha_i(h, r) \cdot \left(\mathcal{W}^{(i)} \times_1 \mathbf{r} \times_2 \mathbf{h} \times_3 \mathbf{t}\right), \tag{5}$$

where $\alpha_i(h, r)$ denotes the attention weight assigned to the i-th core tensor for the given (h, r) pair.

The model is trained using the standard cross-entropy loss over the predicted tail entity distribution:

$$\mathcal{L}_{\mathrm{main}} = -\log\left(\frac{\exp(\phi(h, r, t))}{\sum_{j=1}^{|\mathcal{E}|} \exp(\phi(h, r, j))}\right). \tag{6}$$

3.2 Geometric Consistency Constraint

We define *geometric consistency* as the property that the core tensors occupy spatially distinct regions in the latent interaction space. This is measured by the Euclidean distances between their activation centroids.

Centroid Estimation. For each core tensor $\mathcal{W}^{(i)} \in \mathbb{R}^{P \times P \times P}$, we compute its activation centroid along each axis by taking a weighted average based on the absolute activation values. The centroid along the x-axis is given by:

$$\mu_x^{(i)} = \frac{\sum\limits_{x=1}^{P} x \cdot \sum\limits_{y=1}^{P} \sum\limits_{z=1}^{P} |\mathcal{W}_{x,y,z}^{(i)}|}{\sum\limits_{x,y,z} |\mathcal{W}_{x,y,z}^{(i)}|}. \tag{7}$$

The centroids along the y- and z-axes are computed analogously. The centroid of the i-th core tensor is represented as a 3D coordinate vector:

$$\mathbf{c}^{(i)} = [\mu_x^{(i)}, \mu_y^{(i)}, \mu_z^{(i)}] \in \mathbb{R}^3, \tag{8}$$

and the centroids for all C core tensors are stacked into a matrix $\mathbf{C} \in \mathbb{R}^{C \times 3}$.

Collapse Penalty. To prevent the centroids of different cores from collapsing to similar regions, we compute pairwise Euclidean distances between core centroids:

$$\mathcal{D}_{ij} = \|\mathbf{c}^{(i)} - \mathbf{c}^{(j)}\|_2. \tag{9}$$

For each core tensor, we identify the nearest neighboring core and use the corresponding distance as an indicator of collapse risk:

$$d_{\mathrm{min}}^{(i)} = \min_{j \neq i} \mathcal{D}_{ij}. \tag{10}$$

The geometric consistency loss is then defined as the average negative log-distance between each core and its closest neighbor:

$$\mathcal{L}_{\mathrm{geo}} = -\frac{1}{C} \sum_{i=1}^{C} \log\left(d_{\mathrm{min}}^{(i)} + \epsilon\right), \tag{11}$$

where ϵ is a small constant (set to 10^{-6}) added for numerical stability. This regularization penalizes close centroid placements and encourages each core to occupy a distinct activation region in the latent interaction space.

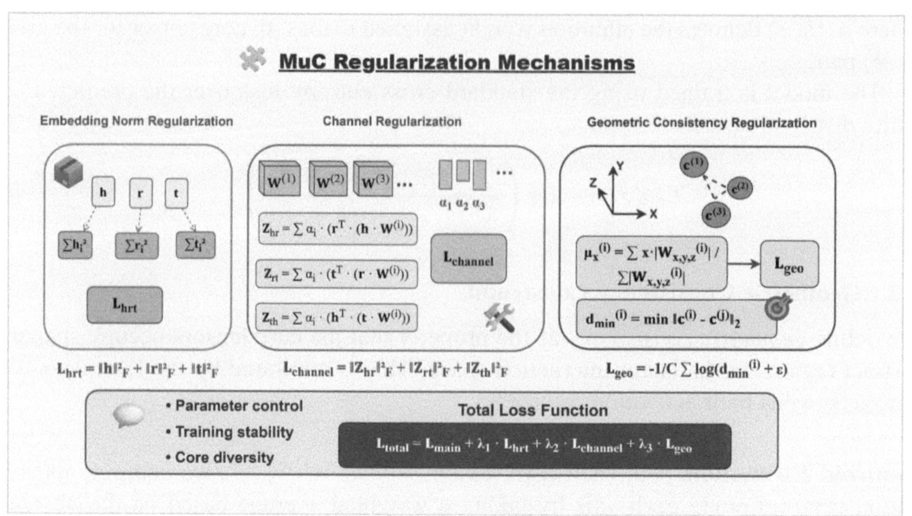

Fig. 2. Overview of MuC regularization. Three loss terms (L_{hrt}, L_{channel}, L_{geo}) improve embedding control, channel stability, and geometric consistency.

3.3 Channel Regularization for Multi-core Interactions

The multi-core design introduces several interaction paths between entity and relation embeddings. We denote the attention-weighted outputs from these paths as $\mathbf{Z}_{hr}$, $\mathbf{Z}_{rt}$, and $\mathbf{Z}_{th}$ as illustrated in Fig. 2.

While such paths improve expressiveness, they can cause skewed attention and overfitting. To address this, we introduce *Channel Regularization*, which penalizes the overall activation magnitude of these outputs:

$$\mathcal{L}_{\mathrm{channel}} = \left\|\mathbf{Z}_{hr}\right\|_F^2 + \left\|\mathbf{Z}_{rt}\right\|_F^2 + \left\|\mathbf{Z}_{th}\right\|_F^2. \tag{12}$$

This encourages balanced core usage and stabilizes learning.

3.4 Loss Function

MuC combines core attention, geometric consistency, and channel regularization to improve multi-core learning. The attention mechanism enables dynamic core selection, while $\mathcal{L}$geo encourages spatial separation and $\mathcal{L}$channel stabilizes multi-path activations.

The overall training objective is defined as:

$$\mathcal{L}_{\mathrm{total}} = \mathcal{L}_{\mathrm{main}} + \lambda_1 \cdot \mathcal{L}_{\mathrm{hrt}} + \lambda_2 \cdot \mathcal{L}_{\mathrm{channel}} + \lambda_3 \cdot \mathcal{L}_{\mathrm{geo}}, \tag{13}$$

where $\mathcal{L}_{\mathrm{main}}$ denotes the cross-entropy loss for link prediction, and the remaining terms are regularization components.

Specifically, $\mathcal{L}_{\text{hrt}}$ applies ℓ_2 norm regularization to the embeddings of the head, relation, and tail, defined as:

$$\mathcal{L}_{\text{hrt}} = \|\mathbf{h}\|_F^2 + \|\mathbf{r}\|_F^2 + \|\mathbf{t}\|_F^2. \tag{14}$$

$\mathcal{L}$channel limits the scale of attention-weighted outputs to prevent core dominance, while $\mathcal{L}$geo promotes core diversity by penalizing centroid collapse.

4 Experiments

4.1 Experiment Setting

We evaluate MuC on WN18RR [4], FB15k-237 [16], and YAGO3-10 [4] (see Table 1). Models are trained using Adagrad [5] with learning rate 0.1, batch size 256, and embedding dimension $D = 200$. Each core tensor has size $P = 100$, and the number of cores $C \in 1, 3, 5, 7$. We report filtered MRR, Hits@1, and Hits@10, and also analyze average and maximum core attention weights to examine how MuC distributes importance across cores.

Table 1. Statistics of WN18RR, FB15k-237, and YAGO3-10 datasets.

Dataset	#Entities	#Relations	#Train Triples	#(h, r) Pairs
WN18RR	40,943	11	86,835	66,166
FB15k-237	14,541	237	272,115	102,188
YAGO3-10	123,182	37	1,079,040	307,973

4.2 Experiment Results

We compare the performance of **MuC** against a range of strong baseline models, including classical tensor decomposition methods, IVR-regularized variants, as well as structure-enhanced and semantics-enhanced approaches. The results are presented in Table 2.

Compared to TuckER, MuC achieves substantial improvements in both prediction accuracy and generalization ability, particularly on FB15k-237 and YAGO3-10. When benchmarked against TuckER-IVR, MuC obtains comparable performance on WN18RR, but yields significant gains on FB15k-237 and YAGO3-10, with relative improvements of **22.83%** and **21.51%** in MRR respectively. These results validate the effectiveness of the proposed multi-core architecture in capturing diverse interaction patterns across datasets.

MuC also outperforms several recent models that leverage additional structural or semantic signals. On FB15k-237, it surpasses NBFNet by **8.92%** in MRR, and on YAGO3-10, it outperforms MEIM by a margin of **20.68%**. Notably, these methods incorporate neighborhood-aware aggregation or pre-trained textual embeddings, while MuC relies solely on triple-level modeling.

Overall, MuC establishes a new state of the art among purely structural knowledge graph completion models.

Table 2. Comparison of model performance (MRR and Hits@k) on three benchmark datasets.

Model	WN18RR			FB15k-237			YAGO3-10		
	MRR	H@1	H@10	MRR	H@1	H@10	MRR	H@1	H@10
Pure structural Models									
TransE [2]	0.225	0.016	0.521	0.312	0.212	0.510			
TuckER [1]	0.446	0.423	0.490	0.321	0.233	0.498	0.551	0.476	0.689
TuckER-IVR [23]	0.501	0.460	0.579	0.368	0.274	0.555	0.581	0.508	0.712
Structure-enhanced Models									
MoCoKGC [10]	**0.742**	**0.665**	**0.881**	0.391	0.296	0.580			
NBFNet [28]	0.551	0.497	0.666	0.415	0.321	0.599	0.563	0.480	0.708
MEIM [17]	0.499	0.458	0.577	0.369	0.274	0.557	0.585	0.514	0.716
Semantics-enhanced Models									
KG-BERT [26]	0.216	0.041	0.524			0.420			
StAR [20]	0.551	0.459	0.732	0.365	0.266	0.562			
SimKGC [21]	0.671	0.595	0.802	0.338	0.252	0.511			
CoLE [12]	0.593	0.538	0.701	0.389	0.294	0.572			
Our Multi-Core Model									
MuC (no reg)	0.442	0.423	0.473	0.420	0.330	0.601	0.697	0.646	0.787
MuC	0.507	0.469	0.576	**0.452**	**0.357**	**0.641**	**0.706**	**0.648**	**0.801**

4.3   Result Analysis

To evaluate the multi-core mechanism, we analyze attention weights at the best epoch with and without regularization (Table 3). Regularization promotes more balanced core usage, supporting functional diversity.

Dataset characteristics influence attention patterns. WN18RR, with symmetric and hierarchical relations [11], sees limited benefit from multiple cores. In contrast, FB15k-237 and YAGO3-10, which have more complex relations [16], benefit more from core diversity.

Notably, YAGO3-10 achieves strong results with attention concentrated on a single core, suggesting specialization suffices in entity-rich, relation-sparse settings. FB15k-237 shows broader attention, reflecting relational diversity but risking under-trained paths.

These patterns imply a link between dataset structure and core attention, though further quantitative validation is needed.

4.4   Ablation Study

We assess each regularization term by removing it individually (Table 4). Channel regularization stabilizes training by constraining intermediate activations, while geometric consistency enhances core diversity, especially on complex datasets like YAGO3-

Table 3. Average and maximum attention weights of core tensors in MuC, with and without Geometric Consistency Regularization.Values less than 0.001 are recorded as 0.

Dataset	Reg.	Type	Core 1	Core 2	Core 3	Core 4	Core 5
WN18RR	No	Avg	0.000	0.000	0.000	0.000	0.999
WN18RR	No	Max	0.008	0.000	0.000	0.000	1.000
WN18RR	Yes	Avg	0.014	0.026	0.009	0.011	0.939
WN18RR	Yes	Max	0.024	0.038	0.016	0.018	0.965
FB15k-237	No	Avg	0.038	0.419	0.115	0.412	0.016
FB15k-237	No	Max	0.047	0.468	0.135	0.475	0.024
FB15k-237	Yes	Avg	0.095	0.140	0.056	0.560	0.148
FB15k-237	Yes	Max	0.113	0.170	0.074	0.613	0.175
YAGO3-10	No	Avg	0.000	0.999	0.000	—	
YAGO3-10	No	Max	0.004	1.000	0.000	—	
YAGO3-10	Yes	Avg	0.999	0.000	0.000	—	
YAGO3-10	Yes	Max	1.000	0.004	0.004	—	

Table 4. Effect of removing different components on MRR across datasets.

Configuration	WN18RR	FB15k-237	YAGO3-10
w/o Embedding Norm Regularization	0.479	0.436	0.701
w/o Channel Regularization	0.443	0.420	0.693
w/o Geometric Consistency	0.489	0.449	0.704

10 (Table 3). These components are complementary, jointly improving generalization through stability and specialization.

5   Conclusion

We propose MuC, a multi-core tensor model for knowledge graph completion that improves expressiveness and adaptability via dynamic core selection. It leverages lightweight core tensors with attention, along with two regularizers: channel regularization for stability and a geometric consistency constraint for diversity.

MuC achieves strong results without external information, outperforming TuckER and recent enhanced models, validating its effectiveness in structural modeling.

Future work includes integrating MuC with LLMs to incorporate semantic priors and evaluating its scalability to larger graphs with more entities and relations.

References

1. Balažević, I., Allen, C., Hospedales, T.M.: Tucker: tensor factorization for knowledge graph completion. arXiv preprint arXiv:1901.09590 (2019)
2. Bordes, A., Usunier, N., Garcia-Duran, A., Weston, J., Yakhnenko, O.: Translating embeddings for modeling multi-relational data. Adv. Neural Inf. Process. Syst. **26** (2013)
3. Chen, Z., et al.: Knowledge graphs meet multi-modal learning: a comprehensive survey. arXiv preprint arXiv:2402.05391 (2024)
4. Dettmers, T., Minervini, P., Stenetorp, P., Riedel, S.: Convolutional 2d knowledge graph embeddings. In: Proceedings of the AAAI Conference on Artificial Intelligence, vol. 32 (2018)
5. Duchi, J., Hazan, E., Singer, Y.: Adaptive subgradient methods for online learning and stochastic optimization. J. Mach. Learn. Res. **12**(7) (2011)
6. Jiang, Y., Yang, Y., Xia, L., Huang, C.: DiffKG: knowledge graph diffusion model for recommendation. In: Proceedings of the 17th ACM International Conference on Web Search and Data Mining, pp. 313–321 (2024)
7. Kazemi, S.M., Poole, D.: Simple embedding for link prediction in knowledge graphs. Adv. Neural Inf. Process. Syst. **31** (2018)
8. Kolda, T.G., Bader, B.W.: Tensor decompositions and applications. SIAM Rev. **51**(3), 455–500 (2009)
9. Lacroix, T., Usunier, N., Obozinski, G.: Canonical tensor decomposition for knowledge base completion. In: International Conference on Machine Learning, pp. 2863–2872. PMLR (2018)
10. Li, Q., Zhong, Y., Qin, Y.: MoCoKGC: momentum contrast entity encoding for knowledge graph completion. In: Proceedings of the 2024 Conference on Empirical Methods in Natural Language Processing, pp. 14940–14952 (2024)
11. Liu, S., Qin, Y., Xu, M., Kolmanič, S.: Knowledge graph completion with triple structure and text representation. Int. J. Comput. Intell. Syst. **16**(1), 95 (2023)
12. Liu, Y., Sun, Z., Li, G., Hu, W.: I know what you do not know: knowledge graph embedding via co-distillation learning. In: Proceedings of the 31st ACM International Conference on Information & Knowledge Management, pp. 1329–1338 (2022)
13. Nickel, M., Tresp, V., Kriegel, H.P., et al.: A three-way model for collective learning on multi-relational data. In: ICML, vol. 11, pp. 3104482–3104584 (2011)
14. Schlichtkrull, M., Kipf, T.N., Bloem, P., van den Berg, R., Titov, I., Welling, M.: Modeling relational data with graph convolutional networks. In: Gangemi, A., et al. (eds.) ESWC 2018. LNCS, vol. 10843, pp. 593–607. Springer, Cham (2018). https://doi.org/10.1007/978-3-319-93417-4_38
15. Tomioka, R., Suzuki, T., Hayashi, K., Kashima, H.: Statistical performance of convex tensor decomposition. Adv. Neural Inf. Process. Syst. **24** (2011)
16. Toutanova, K., Chen, D., Pantel, P., Poon, H., Choudhury, P., Gamon, M.: Representing text for joint embedding of text and knowledge bases. In: Proceedings of the 2015 Conference on Empirical Methods in Natural Language Processing, pp. 1499–1509 (2015)
17. Tran, H.N., Takasu, A.: MEIM: multi-partition embedding interaction beyond block term format for efficient and expressive link prediction. arXiv preprint arXiv:2209.15597 (2022)
18. Trouillon, T., Dance, C.R., Gaussier, É., Welbl, J., Riedel, S., Bouchard, G.: Knowledge graph completion via complex tensor factorization. J. Mach. Learn. Res. **18**(130), 1–38 (2017)
19. Tucker, L.R.: Some mathematical notes on three-mode factor analysis. Psychometrika **31**(3), 279–311 (1966)

20. Wang, B., Shen, T., Long, G., Zhou, T., Wang, Y., Chang, Y.: Structure-augmented text representation learning for efficient knowledge graph completion. In: Proceedings of the Web Conference 2021, pp. 1737–1748 (2021)
21. Wang, L., Zhao, W., Wei, Z., Liu, J.: SimKGC: simple contrastive knowledge graph completion with pre-trained language models. arXiv preprint arXiv:2203.02167 (2022)
22. Wang, Z., Zhang, J., Feng, J., Chen, Z.: Knowledge graph embedding by translating on hyperplanes. In: Proceedings of the AAAI Conference on Artificial Intelligence, vol. 28 (2014)
23. Xiao, C., Cao, Y.: Knowledge graph completion by intermediate variables regularization. Adv. Neural. Inf. Process. Syst. 37, 110218–110245 (2024)
24. Xiong, C., Power, R., Callan, J.: Explicit semantic ranking for academic search via knowledge graph embedding. In: Proceedings of the 26th International Conference on World Wide Web, pp. 1271–1279 (2017)
25. Yang, B., Yih, W.t., He, X., Gao, J., Deng, L.: Embedding entities and relations for learning and inference in knowledge bases. arXiv preprint arXiv:1412.6575 (2014)
26. Yao, L., Mao, C., Luo, Y.: KG-BERT: BERT for knowledge graph completion. arXiv preprint arXiv:1909.03193 (2019)
27. Zhang, J., Chen, B., Zhang, L., Ke, X., Ding, H.: Neural, symbolic and neural-symbolic reasoning on knowledge graphs. AI Open 2, 14–35 (2021)
28. Zhu, Z., Zhang, Z., Xhonneux, L.P., Tang, J.: Neural bellman-ford networks: a general graph neural network framework for link prediction. Adv. Neural. Inf. Process. Syst. 34, 29476–29490 (2021)

A Systematic Literature Review on Software Visualization Tools for Program Comprehension

Stefan-Octavian Custura^(✉)

Faculty of Mathematics and Computer Science, Babeş-Bolyai University, Cluj-Napoca, Romania
stefan.custura@ubbcluj.ro

Abstract. As software systems are continuously being developed and more and more programmers are working on a project, program comprehension is a topic that should be analyzed thoroughly to help the industry accommodate changes for engineers, regardless of experience or age. This way, we tackled the field of Software Visualization and analysed its characteristics in the recent literature through a Systematic Literature Review, where we investigated what and how software is visualized, and how such tools can be empirically validated. Our study notes a mass use of three different approaches for software visualization, while also discovering representations in both graphical and numerical forms. This study also gathers information and views on where software visualization can expand with the current use of artificial intelligence in the day-to-day processes of industry software engineering. Our research shows that current software visualization tools are mainly based on the same three topics, *Code Metrics*, *Dependencies*, and *Code Changes*, but are starting to expand in different directions, tackling more specific issues as the software development field is quickly growing, offering a development perspective towards new or combined approaches of how can program comprehension be enhanced.

1 Introduction

"In the ever-evolving landscape of technology, the cultivation of emerging talent is crucial to the sustained growth and innovation of organizations" [17]. As software systems expand and become more complex, software engineers face increasing challenges in maintaining and integrating into such projects. With modern artificial intelligence aiding code development, adequate program comprehension has become even more critical for engineers in their daily work.

Our goal is to examine current findings and experimental results in software visualization, with a particular emphasis on how these approaches support program comprehension in diverse software development environments.

Consequently, this study reviews the present state of program comprehension research, especially regarding software visualization techniques, to highlight existing gaps and suggest improvements that could enhance the work of software engineers globally.

To accomplish this, we performed a Systematic Literature Review (SLR) following the methodology proposed by Kitchenham et al. [11].

C. Cappiello et al. (Eds.): CoopIS 2025, LNCS 15535, pp. 640–650, 2026.
https://doi.org/10.1007/978-3-032-15538-2_41

The contributions made in this paper are composed of:

- Conducting an SLR on Software Visualization approaches currently existing in the recent literature,
- Analyzing findings based on three research questions related to software visualization modes, visualized parameters, and possible evaluations of researched tools,
- Offering directions for the future development of the software visualization field, given the use of Artificial Intelligence tools in software development
- Approaching the possibility of collaboration between approaches so that software engineers can benefit more from fewer tools.

The rest of the paper is organized as follows: Sect. 2 outlines background elements related to software visualization and the methodology for our systematic literature review. Section 3 displays the study's design by presenting the definition of the research questions in the process, while Sect. 4 offers a grasp of the process of conducting this systematic literature review. Section 5 provides an overview of the answers to our research questions, which are discussed in Sect. 6. The threats to the study's validity are presented in Sect. 7, and Sect. 8 concludes our work.

2 Background: Theoretical Concepts

This section presents the theoretical background for program comprehension and software visualization tools.

Program Comprehension. Program Comprehension [27] is a field in Computer Science that is constantly growing, given that both technologies and the developers change frequently. This way, there have been several branches growing from this core concept, with tools that are now widely used in the field of software engineering. For example, such tools can analyze the quality of the code, offering maintainability metrics, as SonarQube does (https://www.sonarsource.com/), or help in the process of reviewing code, a tool integrated nowadays in most of the Version Control applications that are used in the industry, such as GitHub (https://github.com/).

Use of Artificial Intelligence in Software Development. Given the latest development in Large Language Models (LLMs) [19], a plethora of development tools have shifted towards the use of Artificial Intelligence (AI) to help the programmer write, debug, and understand software systems more easily. This way, several tools are currently in use in the industry, such as Github Copilot (https://github.com/copilot), Cursor https://www.cursor.com/, or Claude (https://claude.ai/). These tools help in the development of software. Still, they can sometimes make mistakes or create unintelligible code, increasing the need for a strict and clear program comprehension process in the software system [8].

Software Visualization. Software visualization tools [14] are currently used in software engineering to help project participants understand the system they are working on. In this direction, the tools can be used by technical persons, such as software engineers, to quickly understand the complexity of specific parts of the code as well as find refactoring opportunities and discover parts of the code that are prone to bugs (https:// github.com/), or by non-technical participants, such as project managers, to understand how complex would a specific feature be and how much time it would require to implement, at least as a brief idea [4].

Furthermore, our work focuses on analyzing the current visualization techniques available, tackling different approaches that might be useful to software developers working in the industry, practitioners starting their careers in the field, and practitioners trying to understand large software systems to increase their chances of joining a project.

3   Systematic Literature Review: Study Design

This section presents the design of our Systematic Literature Review (SLR), including the steps of the study, the research questions, and the protocol used.

To analyze the current literature on the usage of Software Visualization tools towards program comprehension, we follow the methodologies [10, 11] regarding Systematic Literature Review (SLR). The work of Kitchenham et al. [11] presents the guidelines for performing the SLR in software engineering, which should consist of three main phases, as follows: (1) A SLR starts with the planning phase, which describes the motivation for the study, specifies the research questions (RQs) to be answered, and develops the rules for conducting the SLR. (2) The second phase is represented by collecting the primary studies and extracting information, following the rules from the first step. (3) The latter phase is represented by the report of the information gathered throughout the whole SLR process, from motivation to data synthesis and RQs.

Research Questions Definition. Towards reaching the goal of the current systematic literature review, the following three research questions are defined:

RQ1: *What are the existing software visualization manners?* This question aims to analyze the existing ways in which software can be represented and in which manner this is done, either through diagrams, graphs, or other visualization methods.

RQ2: *What are existing software visualization tools analyzing?* This question aims to cover the parts that the literature has considered essential to be visualized in the software visualization tools, and what thresholds are defined for those analyzed components.

RQ3: *How are software visualization tools and program comprehension enhancements validated?* This question is aimed towards the experimental part of the studies, as program comprehension tends toward the cognitive aspects of the human brain, and proper validation may require different approaches.

4   Conducting the SLR

This section presents the process of the SLR, from the search and selection process of the papers to the synthesis of the data from the primary studies.

Search and Selection Process. The search and selection process aims to identify articles that can answer our previously stated research questions.

Database Search. The search was carried out on five indexing systems and databases: IEEE Explore, ACM Digital Library, SCOPUS, Springer, and ScienceDirect. Considering the three research questions that we want to address, a set of keywords was defined such that we can obtain relevant primary studies, as follows: Keywords *Program Comprehension*, *Software Metric*, and *Code Quality* were used as search criteria in all scopes, and *Testing* was used as exclusion criteria if present in Title & Abstracts.

We combine these keywords in our search query in a way that they could provide relevant primary studies for our current systematic literature review. In this way, we defined a set of relevant keywords for our review, which we combined using the *AND* operator. On the other hand, we aim to filter the found studies to ensure our research focuses on software visualization and program comprehension in the context of software development, excluding tests, which are included in the filtering criteria. In this context, the result string is presented in Eq. 1. In some cases, the search string was manually adapted for each source.

$$Crt_1 \text{ AND } Crt_2 \text{ AND } Crt_3 \text{ AND } Crt_4 \text{ NOT } ExCrt_1 \qquad (1)$$

The number of selected papers from the previously stated databases was distributed as follows: 30 from IEEE-Explorer, 40 from ACM-DL, 20 from Scopus, 25 from Springer, and 100 from ScienceDirect.

Furthermore, given that the field of software visualization is continuously growing, we decided to apply our criteria to studies performed after the year 2010.

After applying other activities for augmenting the list of papers (merging, duplicates and impurity removal, inclusion and exclusion criteria, snowballing) we obtained a set of 206 studies.

Data Extraction. The total number of studies relevant for this work is 49, presented in [5]. The articles have a unique identifier (that is, from S1 to S49). The data extraction process is performed manually to collect data from the selected primary studies, considering their different characteristics.

Data Synthesis. During this activity, the information gathered in the previous steps [5] is analyzed and summarized. The narrative synthesis techniques [23] are used to explain and interpret the results found from the analysis.

The Research Rabbit (https://www.researchrabbit.ai/) tool was used to get other insights about the selected articles, as all of the investigated papers were added to the collection. An essential view towards improving the investigation can be provided by a perspective on the authors' network. It can be observed that there are relatively few networks, with only two networks of three authors and two networks of two authors. The general topic of software visualization is still evolving in various directions, with researchers exploring these areas independently until collaborations and merged ideas can emerge.

To properly synthesize our data, we investigated different aspects of the selected studies that can be relevant to one another.

Firstly, we analyzed the number of visualization tools that were presented, how many of the studies present an actual visualization method, and how many present other program comprehension tools that just help in cognitively visualizing the software. We noticed that 12% of the studies do not present actual visualization tools in their implementation, but they do present other tools that help towards program comprehension and display various information. For example, the works of Widyasari et al. [29] (S24) and Nam et al. [18] (S20) present tools that use Artificial Intelligence and Large Language Model tools and that can present and localize errors directly during the development process.

Moreover, if we want to go deeper into the visualization modes, we tried to observe the way in which the visualization tools work, and specifically the way in which the software system is represented. This way, Fig. 1a presents the approaches that were present in the studies regarding the visualization method. We notice that half of the studies are displaying the system through graphs and diagrams(e.g., S2, S3, S6, S19, S25, S31, S32), but there are also different available options, such as using a metaphor(e.g., S27, S38, S39), an animation (S11), or just classical statistics (e.g., S4, S12, S18) and highlighting (e.g., S1, S7, S8, S10).

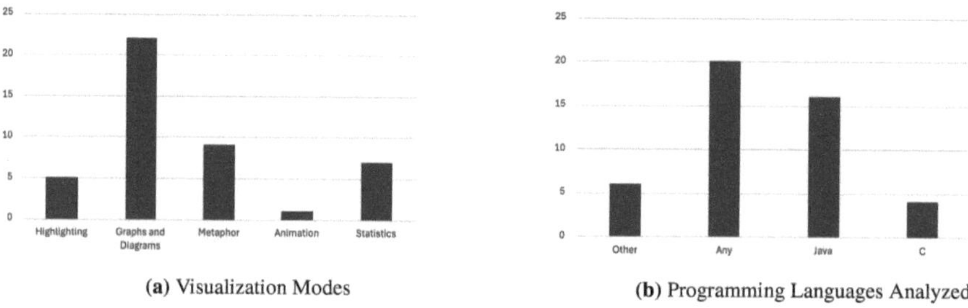

(a) Visualization Modes   (b) Programming Languages Analyzed

Fig. 1. Visualization Modes and Visualized Languages.

Although the approaches in visualizations created by Moreno et al. [15] (S19) and Romano et al. [24] (S33) fit in the above-presented classification, their work is worth mentioning as they tried to upgrade the process of program comprehension by introducing a different technology in the field: *Virtual Reality* (VR). This approach enables their work to focus on displaying specific visualizations in both VR and 2D.

Secondly, we observed what programming languages are considered while implementing such program comprehension tools, and checked if a large number of software engineers around the world can use those tools. This way, we noticed in Fig. 1b that a great number of tools are able to analyze any programming language, as they are implemented to analyze the Abstract Syntax Tree (AST) of the software system. However, we also notice that a large number of studies are focusing on an Object-Oriented programming language, mainly Java (e.g., S5, S10, S16), while some studies are focusing on C (e.g., S28, S40) and other programming languages, such as Haskell (S8), COBOL (S37) or Python (S23).

Furthermore, our study takes a deeper look at what exactly is analyzed when creating such software of visualization, and we noticed in Fig. 2a a distribution of present approaches. We notice that there are some specific issues tackled in some of the tools, such as *Annotations* (S13), *SQL Traces* (S4), or *Preprocessor* (S14), while the three main approaches are based on *Code Metrics* (e.g., S12, S16, S19), *Dependencies* (e.g., S27, S30, S35) or *Code Changes* (e.g., S1, S7, S48), these having the most usages in the existing literature and being also the topics that can be present in any programming language. The *Dependencies* can be analyzed in different ways, as some studies perform a static analysis to obtain the dependencies in the source code, while other studies observe and perform such computations at runtime, creating a structured view of the dependencies that are used during the use of a feature.

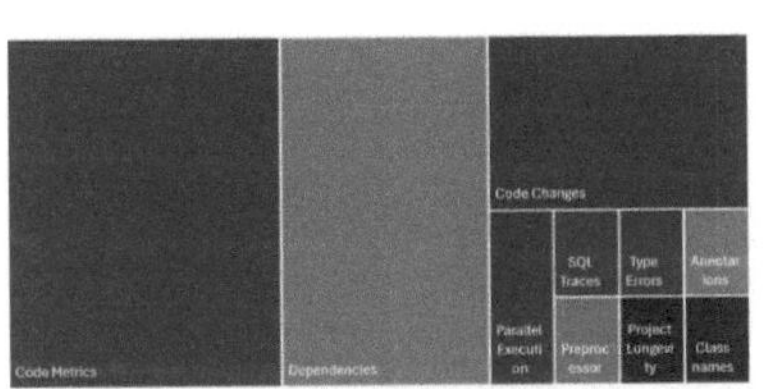

(a) What is analyzed in the tool's implementation

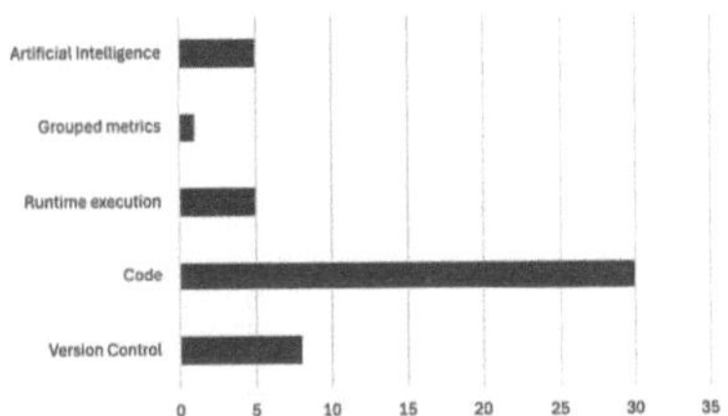

(b) Approaches used in obtaining information to be visualized

Fig. 2. Approaches and Usages.

Additionally, we studied which methods were considered in analyzing the above criteria for visualization. In this way, our observations are presented in Fig. 2b, where we can notice that a vast majority of the studies are based on static analysis of the code (e.g., S13, S14, S15). However, some studies perform their program comprehension tasks based on Version Control information (e.g., git, svn), while others analyze the execution at runtime (e.g., S40, S44), performing tasks based on the live execution, and five studies are creating their comprehension approaches based on results obtained by artificial intelligence, such as LLMs.

Lastly, our focus was also on the experimental side of the studies, analyzing the types of evaluations that were carried out to ensure the quality of the work. Given that, for a program comprehension study, we need to analyze cognitive processes as well as other tools [12], we wanted to observe the introduction of different participants in the selected studies.

Though it seems like external participants' involvement would be necessary for a program comprehension study, we noticed that about 24.5% of the analyzed studies are not evaluating their tools in any way that includes participants.

In the same manner, by analyzing how these experiments were performed, we noticed that most of the studies with participants were conducted via the Questionnaire Method, with variations in some works by including focus groups, expert discussions, or interviews. Also, regarding the studies that were not performed with participants, the experimental process may vary depending on the approach used toward software visualization. The tools utilizing artificial intelligence were primarily evaluated using pre-labeled data sets. In contrast, other tools that created visualizations assessed their understanding of a piece of software, as well as the quality and speed of structure generation.

5   Results

In this section, we will answer the research questions presented in Sect. 3 based on the information collected in the performed SLR.

Results on RQ1: *What Are the Existing Software Visualization Manners?*
We noticed that there are several visualization modes available that can help improve program comprehension, including, but not limited to, statistics, graphs and diagrams, metaphors, and highlighting.

By diving deeper into this topic, we observed what is defined explicitly in each of these methods. Firstly, the topic of statistics is represented by different tables and charts that can help in offering a good overview of the system. The work of Noughi et al. [20] (S4) qualitatively presents the usefulness of such visualizations, as they offer statistical views of SQL Traces during the runtime execution of the program.

By the manner considered as graphs and diagrams, we believe any visualization that can be created using standard geometrical forms (e.g., Graphs [3] (S3), [7] (S29)), or UML Diagrams [30] (32), which help in discovering and analyzing risk zones in the software system.

The metaphor visualization is a topic that can offer different views on the topic, as they are currently represented in different manners that can be more or less complicated. For example, the work of Balogh et al. [2] (S5) presents an outstanding manner of visualizing a software system by using the city metaphor in a video game, Minecraft. However, the representation of the clothing metaphor can also be observed in the works of Romano et al. [24] (S33), Mortara et al. [16] (S16), and Dashuber et al. [6] (S27), each of them using the city metaphor in different approaches: Virtual Reality, with an emphasis on code metrics and, respectively, with an emphasis on dependencies.

Answer of RQ1: Various visualization modes can enhance understandability for both junior and senior individuals, depending on their methods. However, there remains room for further discoveries, given the diverse preferences of individuals worldwide.

Results on RQ2: *What Are Existing Software Visualization Tools Analyzing?*
We observe that the distribution of analyzed parts in Fig. 2a is uneven in some parts, offering a clear argument regarding the majority of the performed analysis: *Code Metrics* (e.g., [2] (S5)), *Dependencies* (e.g., [25] (S9)), and *Code Changes* (e.g., [21] (S48)). However, we notice that some works are starting in other directions, such as *Parallel Execution* (e.g. [28] (S44)), which tries to visualize how threads are working and communicating with each other, *SQL Traces* (S4), which wants to outline the requests to the database in a software system, and going more and more specific depending on the needs of software engineers.

Answer of RQ2: The most concrete focus is done on *Code Metrics*, *Dependencies*, and *Code Changes*, but some areas are under development and can be offered attention in future work of software visualization tools.

Results on RQ3: *How Are Software Visualization Tools and Program Comprehension Enhancements Validated?*

The selected studies offered various experimental techniques, with a vast majority of the studies being performed with external participants. This way, we noticed various empirical validation techniques done with these participants, such as questionnaires (e.g., the work of Porkolab et al. [22] (S17)), expert focus groups (e.g., the work of Schuur et al. [26] (S6)), or interviews (e.g., the work of Lima et al. [13] (S13)). Moreover, we noticed that some studies were conducted without participants and also offered different perspectives on empirical validations of such software tools. For example, the work of Armenti et al. [1] (S11) offers a good overview of how comparisons between commit animations and commit messages can be performed.

Answer of RQ3: The core part in the validation of software visualization tools lies in the inclusion of external participants, as different psychological characteristics of the program comprehension domain remain to be understood, how various individuals observe components.

6   Findings and Discussions

Discussions of Results. We observe, based on the performed investigation, that the field of software visualization is continuously developing, as research also tends to turn to the use of artificial intelligence or the addition of new technologies. Moreover, as time and technology progress, the software development industry is growing larger and larger, and there appear to be multiple new areas that would benefit from work in terms of program comprehension and visualization of software.

Gaps, Challenges, Open Issues. Currently, an essential challenge for software visualization tools is to be able to properly validate them with external participants, as we need to have a sample as varied as possible, with biases as small as possible, so that we can minimize the threats to the validity of our studies.

Another challenge that might arise in the future regarding program comprehension would be the use of artificial intelligence in software development. Although LLMs are capable of passing the Turing test [9], we cannot yet have a proper overview of the quality of code written by an LLM. This way, program comprehension should focus on integrating such information as future developments, such that we can keep creating maintainable software systems together with new tools and technologies.

Opportunities and Recommendations. After our study, we found different opportunities for development in the area of software visualization.

Firstly, there is a pressing need for the creation of integrated tools that combine multiple visualization techniques into a single platform. This would allow software engineers to switch between different visualization modes depending on their specific needs during program comprehension.

Secondly, future research should focus on user-centered design principles to ensure that visualization tools are tailored to the specific needs of software engineers. Conducting usability studies can provide valuable insight into how these tools can be improved to enhance user experience.

7   Threats to Validity

The validity threats addressed in this study pertain to construction, historical records, and bias concerns. We mitigate the first two threats by employing established systematic methods throughout our research process and carefully documenting each step in our research protocol. Furthermore, by offering a detailed protocol, we allow other researchers in the field to replicate our study or use the study design framework as a foundational reference for new literature reviews. Another factor that may threaten the validity of the study is the human factor and the concern of possible biases, which we tried to reduce by performing the same content analysis process for each of the selected studies, focusing on the same key aspect in each work.

8   Conclusions

This study aimed to observe the current state-of-the-art regarding software visualization tools, in order to provide future perspectives regarding the development of the field, and to discover in what directions the current scientific research is growing. We acquire various insights on what and how components are visualized, and how such tools and studies can be validated.

We provide a better overview of the current topics that are mainly used for software visualization (*Code metrics*, *Dependencies*, and *Code changes*), while also being able to gather the current visualization techniques considered by different researchers (based on *Graphs and Diagrams* and *Metaphor Representations*). Moreover, we outlined different development possibilities for this field, including the use of artificial intelligence, as well as the need to analyze code written by artificial intelligence.

Acknowledgements. I want to express my gratitude to my Ph.D. coordinator for the invaluable guidance and support in the verification and validation of this work.

References

1. Armenti, C., Lanza, M.: Using animations to understand commits. In: 2024 IEEE International Conference on Software Maintenance and Evolution (ICSME), pp. 660–665. IEEE (2024)
2. Balogh, G., Szabolics, A., Beszédes, A.: Codemetropolis: eclipse over the city of source code. In: 2015 IEEE 15th International Working Conference on Source Code Analysis and Manipulation (SCAM), pp. 271–276. IEEE (2015)
3. Borowski, K., Balis, B., Orzechowski, T.: Semantic code graph-an information model to facilitate software comprehension. IEEE Access **12**, 27279–27310 (2024)
4. Couto, J.M.C., Kroll, J., Ruiz, D.D., Prikladnicki, R.: A PMBoK extension proposal for data visualization in software project management. In: ICEIS (2), pp. 54–65 (2021)
5. Custura, O.: A systematic literature review on software visualization tools for program comprehension. https://doi.org/10.6084/m9.figshare.28784069.v2. Accessed Apr 2025
6. Dashuber, V., Philippsen, M.: Trace visualization within the software city metaphor: controlled experiments on program comprehension. Inf. Softw. Technol. **150**, 106989 (2022)

7. Fregnan, E., Fröhlich, J., Spadini, D., Bacchelli, A.: Graph-based visualization of merge requests for code review. J. Syst. Softw. **195**, 111506 (2023)

8. Javaid, M., Haleem, A., Khan, I.H., Suman, R.: Understanding the potential applications of artificial intelligence in agriculture sector. Adv. Agrochem **2**(1), 15–30 (2023)

9. Jones, C.R., Bergen, B.K.: Large language models pass the turing test. arXiv preprint arXiv:2503.23674 (2025)

10. Kitchenham, B.: Procedures for performing systematic reviews. Keele UK Keele Univ. **33** (2004)

11. Kitchenham, B., Charters, S.: Guidelines for performing systematic literature reviews in software engineering **2** (2007)

12. Letovsky, S.: Cognitive processes in program comprehension. J. Syst. Softw. **7**(4), 325–339 (1987)

13. Lima, P., Melegati, J., Gomes, E., Pereira, N.S., Guerra, E., Meirelles, P.: CADV: a software visualization approach for code annotations distribution. Inf. Softw. Technol. **154**, 107089 (2023)

14. Maruyama, K., Omori, T., Hayashi, S., Hayashi, S.: A visualization tool recording historical data of program comprehension tasks. In: IEEE International Conference on Program Comprehension (2014). https://doi.org/10.1145/2597008.2597802

15. Moreno-Lumbreras, D., Robles, G., Izquierdo-Cortázar, D., Gonzalez-Barahona, J.M.: Software development metrics: to VR or not to VR. Empir. Softw. Eng. **29**(2), 42 (2024)

16. Mortara, J., Collet, P., Dery-Pinna, A.M.: Visualization of object-oriented software in a city metaphor: comprehending the implemented variability and its technical debt. J. Syst. Softw. **208**, 111876 (2024)

17. Muscalagiu, A.I., Custura, S.O., Ioan, B.M.: Developing interns into full-fledged software engineers. In: 2024 IEEE International Conference on Software Analysis, Evolution and Reengineering-Companion (SANER-C), pp. 84–92. IEEE (2024)

18. Nam, D., Macvean, A., Hellendoorn, V., Vasilescu, B., Myers, B.: Using an LLM to help with code understanding. In: Proceedings of the IEEE/ACM 46th International Conference on Software Engineering, pp. 1–13 (2024)

19. Naveed, H., et al.: A comprehensive overview of large language models. arXiv preprint arXiv:2307.06435 (2023)

20. Noughi, N., Hanenberg, S., Cleve, A.: An empirical study on the usage of SQL execution traces for program comprehension. In: 2017 IEEE International Conference on Software Quality, Reliability and Security Companion (QRS-C), pp. 47–54. IEEE (2017)

21. Occhipinti, G., Nagy, C., Minelli, R., Lanza, M.: Syn: ultra-scale software evolution comprehension. In: 2023 IEEE/ACM 31st International Conference on Program Comprehension (ICPC), pp. 69–73. IEEE (2023)

22. Porkoláb, Z., Brunner, T., Krupp, D., Csordás, M.: Codecompass: an open software comprehension framework for industrial usage. In: Proceedings of the 26th Conference on Program Comprehension, pp. 361–369 (2018)

23. Rodgers, M., et al.: Testing methodological guidance on the conduct of narrative synthesis in systematic reviews: effectiveness of interventions to promote smoke alarm ownership and function. Evaluation **15**(1), 49–73 (2009)

24. Romano, S., Capece, N., Erra, U., Scanniello, G., Lanza, M.: On the use of virtual reality in software visualization: the case of the city metaphor. Inf. Softw. Technol. **114**, 92–106 (2019)

25. Schneider, T., Tymchuk, Y., Salgado, R., Bergel, A.: CuboidMatrix: exploring dynamic structural connections in software components using space-time cube. In: 2016 IEEE working conference on software visualization (VISSOFT), pp. 116–125. IEEE (2016)

26. van der Schuur, H., Jansen, S., Brinkkemper, S.: Reducing maintenance effort through software operation knowledge: an eclectic empirical evaluation. In: 2011 15th European Conference on Software Maintenance and Reengineering, pp. 201–210. IEEE (2011)
27. Siegmund, J.: Program comprehension: past, present, and future. In: 2016 IEEE 23rd International Conference on Software Analysis, Evolution, and Reengineering (SANER), vol. 5, pp. 13–20. IEEE (2016)
28. Trümper, J., Bohnet, J., Voigt, S., Döllner, J.: Visualization of multithreaded behavior to facilitate maintenance of complex software systems. In: 2010 Seventh International Conference on the Quality of Information and Communications Technology, pp. 325–330. IEEE (2010)
29. Widyasari, R., Ang, J.W., Nguyen, T.G., Sharma, N., Lo, D.: Demystifying faulty code: step-by-step reasoning for explainable fault localization. In: 2024 IEEE International Conference on Software Analysis, Evolution and Reengineering (SANER), pp. 568–579. IEEE (2024)
30. Yang, J., Lee, Y., Chang, K.H.: Evaluations of Jaguarcode: a web-based object-oriented programming environment with static and dynamic visualization. J. Syst. Softw. **145**, 147–163 (2018)

CodeASG: An Approach for Extracting Code Embeddings from Abstract Syntax Graphs

Alexandru-Gabriel Sîrbu[(✉)][ID] and Gabriela Czibula[ID]

Babeş-Bolyai University, Cluj-Napoca, Romania
`{alexandru.sirbu,gabriela.czibula}@ubbcluj.ro`

Abstract. In programming languages, learning models often treat code as a natural language, causing them to learn syntax and semantics implicitly. The paper proposes, as a proof of concept, a new approach to generate source code embeddings based on Abstract Syntax Graphs, a more compact and less redundant representation than traditional ASTs, particularly at the leaf node level. Thus, a Graph Attention Network model is employed for learning to reconstruct ASGs and internalize structural information. To evaluate the quality of the resulting embeddings, the embedded data is clustered using k-means, DBSCAN, and Spectral Clustering, using the cosine similarity distance metric. Performance is assessed using silhouette scores, outperforming those achieved by state-of-the-art models such as `CodeBERT` and `CodeT5` on the same task.

Keywords: Code Embedding · Abstract Syntax Graph · Deep Learning · Graph Neural Network · Clustering

1 Introduction

Embeddings are dense vector representations of data designed to capture essential features, relationships, and contextual information in a compact and numerical format. Embeddings are particularly useful for a wide range of tasks by enabling models to understand the underlying structure and semantics of the data more effectively. For example, in natural language processing, word embeddings like those generated by Doc2Vec, Word2Vec, GloVe, or transformer-based models such as BERT (*Bidirectional Encoder Representations from Transformers*) [2] encode words and phrases based on their contextual relationships, facilitating tasks such as sentiment analysis, translation, and question answering. The utility of embeddings extends far beyond text processing. In the domain of software engineering, embeddings can represent code snippets, enabling models to understand their syntactic and semantic properties. These embeddings are instrumental in tasks such as code search, software defect detection, code summarization, and clone detection, where identifying similarities or meaningful patterns is crucial.

This paper introduces, as a proof of concept, a new approach (`CodeASG`) to code representation that addresses the redundancies commonly found in the Abstract Syntax Tree (AST). We have introduced ASGs in a previous work [9] as an extension to

C. Cappiello et al. (Eds.): CoopIS 2025, LNCS 15535, pp. 651–661, 2026.
https://doi.org/10.1007/978-3-032-15538-2_42

ASTs to provide a more compact and semantically rich structure, capturing the essential relationships and dependencies within the code while reducing the repetitive information found in the leaf nodes. By leveraging this improved representation, the proposed methodology aims to generate embeddings that encapsulate both the syntactic and semantic properties of code more effectively. The model is pre-trained on the task of next node and edge prediction within the ASG, allowing it to learn the sequential and structural transitions inherent in code graphs. This pre-training step enables the model to develop a deep understanding of the code's hierarchical and relational structure, which is crucial for downstream tasks. When represented in adjacency matrix format, ASTs present a significant challenge for generative models due to their inherent sparsity. In the adjacency matrix, the vast majority of entries correspond to non-edges, making the matrix extremely sparse. For generative models trained on such representations, this sparsity creates a bias, effectively treating true edges as noise and defaulting to predicting no edges at all.

The experiments conducted further aim to evaluate the extent to which the embeddings generated using `CodeASG` are more qualitative than those generated using state-of-the-art models such as `CodeBERT` and `CodeT5` on the same task. With this aim, the proof of concept considers a single dataset containing Python sections of code. If this stands, the study can be further extended on a larger scale by considering multiple datasets and more baselines for code embeddings generation and by assessing the utility of `CodeASG` embeddings in downstream tasks. To validate the quality of the generated embeddings, the study employs clustering techniques, applying algorithms such as k-means, DBSCAN, and `Spectral Clustering`. The clustering performance is evaluated using the silhouette score, a metric that measures cohesion and separation of clusters. The work presented in this paper is new, as there is no similar work using ASGs for extracting source code embeddings. In particular, the paper aims to answer the following research questions: **RQ1.** *What strategies can be used to effectively handle the sparsity of edges in graph representations to improve the models' accuracy and robustness?*; **RQ2.** *How does a structure-based code embedding compare to a non-structure-based code embedding in terms of grouping similar structures together?*

The rest of the paper is organized as follows. Section 2 outlines some related works in the field. Section 3 presents the methodology for designing and evaluating the `CodeASG` model, while Sect. 4 analyzes the results obtained and highlights the strengths, weaknesses, opportunities, and threats of the proposed approach. The conclusions of the study and directions for future work are outlined in Sect. 5.

2   Background

CodeBERT [3] is a bimodal pre-trained model designed to handle both natural language and programming language data. It innovates with BERT [2], which is focused solely on natural language text, extending its applicability from natural language to the domain of programming languages. The pre-training of CodeBERT was conducted on a dataset comprising of both bimodal natural language and programming language pairs, and unimodal code samples across six programming languages: Python, Java, JavaScript, PHP, Ruby and Go. `CodeT5` [11] advances beyond `CodeBERT` by introducing a unified encoder-decoder architecture optimized for code understanding and generation tasks, utilizing the T5 framework [5]. While `CodeBERT` focuses on bidirectional encoder representations for bimodal tasks, `CodeT5` innovates by addressing the specific structural characteristics of programming languages. `CodeT5` uses a dataset larger than `CodeBERT`, handling in addition to the original six programming languages, C and C#.

Pre-trained embedding models bring significant practical advantages by encoding complex semantic and contextual patterns into fixed-length vectors, thereby enabling downstream tasks such as clustering, classification, and retrieval to be performed more effectively and with far less task-specific data. To ensure these embeddings truly capture meaningful relationships, it is common to validate them through clustering analyses, and by measuring how well the resulting clusters align with known categories. Scott et al. [7] investigate the performance of clustering methods on pre-trained embedding, comparing shallow unsupervised and deep supervised techniques across diverse datasets. The embeddings are derived from a ResNet50 backbone trained on datasets such as Cars196, Stanford Online Products, and a private dataset. The study evaluates clustering methods to assess cluster coherence and alignment with ground truth. For clustering, both shallow unsupervised methods, such as k-means, hierarchical agglomerative clustering, and spectral clustering, and deep supervised methods, such as GCN-VE and STR-FC are tested, demonstrating that shallow methods like hierarchical clustering often outperform deep methods on embeddings with lower discriminability, as measured by Recall.

Yeasmin et al. [13] evaluate clustering performance on a dataset created by scraping news articles from The Daily Star, whose content is categorized into seven domains. The embeddings are generated using a pre-trained BERT model, which maps text documents to 768-dimensional vectors that encapsulate both syntactic and semantic information. To compare clustering methods, the authors applied both distance-based and density-based algorithms. The clustering performance is assessed using evaluation metrics like the Dunn index and the Silhouette coefficient, which measure cluster compactness and separation.

3   Methodology

For answering **RQ1**, this section introduces the methodology employed for pre-training the model, as well as presenting the method used for validating its resulting embeddings. Although ASTs have long been used to represent the structure of code, they often suffer from redundancy, as entities of the same name can be stored in two or more different leaves in the original tree, as shown in the image on the left side of Fig. 1. The ASG is an extension of the AST, which addresses the redundancy issue by merging identical entities, introducing loops that transform the original tree into a graph [9]. Figure 1 shows the differences between an AST and an ASG, reducing its redundancy. Besides the addressed redundancy, the ASG is inherently structured, which allows it to be easily serialized and deserialized from code, thus being able to be constructed incrementally, allowing for a flexible and controlled generation process. To overcome the sparsity of the edges in the original AST, edges between nodes of the same level have been introduced. Such edges can also serve as an ordering mechanism that allows the reconstruction of the original code from the ASG. Thus, the ASG provides a more compact and efficient representation as compared to AST, which directly enhances generative capabilities. As detailed in the experimental part, on average, ASGs contain significantly fewer nodes than ASTs, reducing the length of sequences that must be generated and thus simplifying the task for generative models. At the same time, ASGs exhibit a higher degree of connectivity, leading to an edge-to-node-squared ratio denser than that of ASTs, which allows ASGs to capture dependencies more effectively.

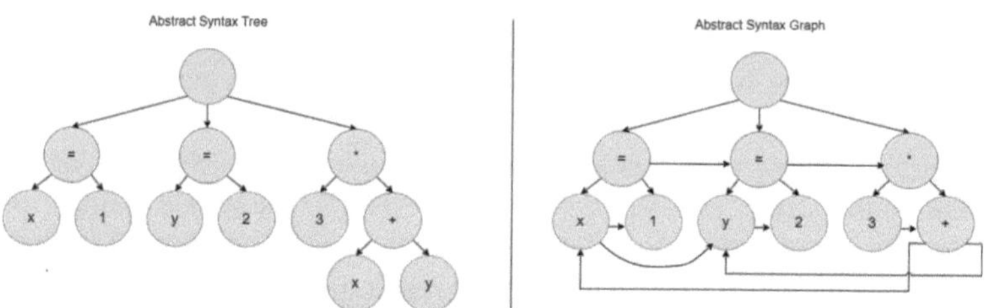

Fig. 1. Comparison between an AST (left) and an ASG (right).

3.1 Formalisation

The task of creating embeddings for a section of code using its ASG representation involves processing the ASG as input and predicting the next node and edge in the graph as output. Thus, we can represent the original graph as $G = (\mathcal{V}, E)$, where $\mathcal{V} = \{v_1, v_2, ..., v_n\}$ is the set of nodes and $E \subseteq \mathcal{V} \times \mathcal{V}$ is the set of edges between nodes. At each step t, the task is to predict the next node $v_{t+1} \in \mathcal{V}$ and the edges $\tilde{E}_{t+1} = \{(v_{t+1}, v_i) \mid v_i \in \mathcal{V} \wedge (v_{t+1}, v_i) \in E\}$. Then, the input at step t will be

$$G_t = (\mathcal{V}_t, E_t), \text{ where } \mathcal{V}_t \subseteq \mathcal{V} \text{ and } E_t = \bigcup_{k=0}^{t} \tilde{E}_k, \quad E_t \subseteq E \text{ (in particular, } \mathcal{V}_0 = \tilde{E}_0 = \tilde{E}_1 = \emptyset).$$

For the task of the next node prediction, the model will learn the conditional probability distribution $P(v_{t+1}|G_t, \theta)$, representing the probability of generating the next node given the graph at step t and the hyperparameters θ. Formally, the best hyperparameters $\tilde{\theta}$ of the model are tho that minimize (a regularized) loss function, i.e., $\tilde{\theta} = \arg\min_{\theta} \sum_{t \in \mathbb{N}} \mathcal{L}(G_t, \theta)$, where $\mathcal{L}(G_t, \theta) = \mathcal{L}_{nodes}(G_t, \theta) + \mathcal{L}_{edges}(G_t, \theta)$. Thus, for the

nodes, the loss function can be written as $\mathcal{L}_{nodes}(G_t, \theta) = -\sum_{k=1}^{t} log P(v_k|G_{k-1}, \theta)$.

In parallel with the generation of the next node, the model also predicts the edges of the new node with pre-existing nodes, which are based on the probability distribution $P(E_{t+1}|v_{t+1}, G_t, \theta) = \prod_{v_t \in \mathcal{V}_t} P((v_{t+1}, v_i) \in E_{t+1}|G_t, \theta)$. Thus, the edge loss function

can be written as $\mathcal{L}_{edges}(G_t,\theta) = -\sum\limits_{k=1}^{t} \sum\limits_{v_i \in \mathcal{V}_k} (y_{k,i} \cdot log\,P((v_k, v_i) \in E_k | G_{k-1}, \theta) +$
$(1 - y_{k,i}) \cdot log(1 - P((v_k, v_i) \in E_k | G_{k-1}, \theta)))$, where $y_{k,i} \in \{0, 1\}$ indicates whether there is an edge between v_k and v_i.

3.2   The CodeASG Learning Model

The proposed CodeASG model will be pretrained for the task of next-node and edge prediction, building the graph incrementally, one node at a time, along with its edges, with the previously generated nodes [4]. To achieve this, Graph Neural Networks are used, which represent a type of neural network specifically designed to work with data-structured graphs, where data are represented as nodes connected by edges, which reflect more complex and irregular relationships as compared to traditional neural networks.

The architecture of the proposed deep learning model CodeASG consists of three main components: the *Backbone*, the *Node Predictor*, and the *Edge Predictor*, which can be seen in Fig. 2.

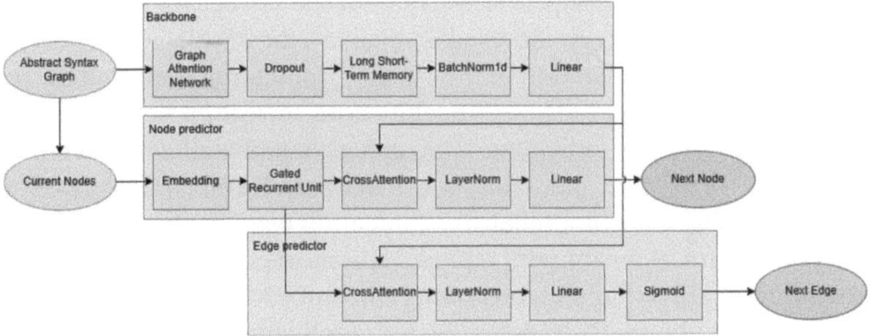

Fig. 2. CodeASG model architecture.

The ***Backbone*** processes the full ASG using a Graph Attention Network, which highlights the importance of neighboring nodes and extracts both structural and semantic features. To avoid overfitting, a Dropout layer randomly deactivates neurons during training and passes the extracted features through a Long Short-Term Memory network, which captures sequential dependencies within the graph. Batch normalization ensures stable training by keeping feature scales consistent, before a Linear layer summarizes the global graph context into an embedding representation. The ***Node Predictor*** embeds the current ASG nodes into dense vectors and processes them with a Gated Recurrent Unit, generating a context vector that captures the sequence's local information. A Cross-Attention mechanism aligns this local context with the Backbone's global graph features, enabling the predictor to attend to relevant regions of the ASG. The features are normalized with LayerNorm, and passed through a Linear layer to predict the next node. The ***Edge Predictor*** reuses the GRU's context, but applies a separate

Cross-Attention layer, focusing on edge-specific relationships. LayerNorm ensures stability, and a Linear layer followed by a Sigmoid activation outputs edge probabilities, effectively modeling edge presence as a binary classification.

The `CodeASG` model is evaluated using metrics such as *accuracy*, *precision*, and *recall*, with particular attention to *recall* for edge prediction, as edges are typically sparse in the ASG, and therefore are harder to predict. High recall for edges indicates the model's ability to detect true positive connections, which is crucial for maintaining the graph's structural integrity. The employed attention-based model and the metrics used during the training prevent dealing with the issue of sparsity of the edges, which answers **RQ1**. Once the model is trained, its backbone is employed to generate embeddings for the entire code section.

3.3   Performance Evaluation

To evaluate the quality of the embeddings, clustering algorithms [1] such as k-means, DBSCAN, and `Spectral clustering` are applied. These algorithms group the code representations based on similarity, with the cosine distance serving as the metric for clustering. *Cosine distance* is particularly effective for high-dimensional embeddings, as it measures the angular similarity between vectors and ensures robustness to scale differences. Given the unsupervised nature of the clustering task, evaluation metrics such as the *Silhouette score* are used to analyze the results. The silhouette score assesses the cohesion and separation of the clusters, indicating how well the data points fit into their assigned clusters. The silhouette score measures how well samples are clustered, with higher values indicating more cohesive and well-separated clusters.

By combining predictive modeling for ASG-based embedding generation with unsupervised clustering and comprehensive evaluation metrics, the proposed `CodeASG` approach not only extracts meaningful representations of code but also provides insights into its structural organization, demonstrating the embeddings' ability to capture code semantics and highlighting their potential for applications like code classification, retrieval, and defect detection.

4   Experimental Results

This section presents implementation details that facilitate the replication of this study, as well as the results obtained after applying several clustering algorithms on the embedded data entries, with the scope of answering **RQ2**. To facilitate the replication of our findings, the source code is made public [10].

The dataset used for this study is the same as the one employed by `CodeBERT` [3], specifically focusing on the Python sections of code, comprising a total of 824,342 samples. Each code section in the dataset was represented as an ASG, capturing its structural and semantic relationships. To train the model, ASGs were decomposed into triplets of the current graph, next node, and next edge, providing fine-grained transitions for learning. Due to the size of the dataset, only 10% of the sequences were used for training, while another 2% was allocated for validation and testing. To prevent data leakage, it was ensured that subgraphs in the validation and testing sets originated from code sections that did not contribute any subgraphs to the training set, thus preserving diversity and robust generalization. As mentioned in Sect. 1, the adjacency matrix of the AST is extremely sparse, as the vast majority of entries correspond to non-edges. In our dataset, the average number of nodes is 166.79, and the number of edges is 165.79. However, when normalized against the total possible connections (computed as the squared number of nodes), the ratio of edges to potential edges is only 0.0094. We note that on average ASGs contain 90.54 nodes, significantly fewer than ASTs, thus providing a more compact and efficient representation and enhancing generative capabilities. Moreover, ASGs have an average of 256.1 edges, which leads to an edge-to-node-squared ratio of 0.036 (almost four times denser than that of ASTs). This allows ASGs to capture dependencies more effectively than ASTs.

Furthermore, by employing the same dataset used in CodeBERT, the study ensures compatibility and comparability with existing state-of-the-art methods, facilitating a robust evaluation of the proposed approach. The dataset's breadth and depth, covering diverse Python code samples, provide an excellent foundation for training and testing the model, enabling it to generate embeddings that are both syntactically and semantically rich.

4.1 Hyperparameters Settings and Model Training

The CodeASG model, consisting of the three modules described in Sect. 3.2, is composed of 4,129,802 parameters. In the following, details about the model architecture and the hyperparameter setting are presented for each module.

The Graph Attention Network of the *Backbone* has 160 input features, 256 output features per layer, and 4 layers. A probability of 0.05 is used for the Dropout layer, while the bidirectional LSTM has 4 layers, an input size of 256, and a hidden size of 128. The bidirectional configuration allows LSTM to process information in both forward and backward directions, improving the representation of graph sequences. The 256-dimensional output vector of the final Linear Layer serves as the global representation of the ASG. The Embedding layer of the *Node Predictor* maps the 262 possible node types into a 256-dimensional embedding space, using padding index 0 to handle variable-length sequences. The GRU has 4-layers with a hidden size of 256. The final Linear layer has 262 output features, corresponding to the vocabulary size. Regarding the *Edge Predictor* module, the Cross-Attention output is normalized using LayerNorm and adaptively pooled with AdaptiveAvgPool1d. The Linear layer has 4 output features, representing the possible edge types in the graph.

To train the CodeASG model, the criterion for the *nodes prediction* uses Cross Entropy Loss for multi-class classification of nodes, while the criterion for the *edges prediction* employs Binary Cross-Entropy Loss. The performance od the model is evaluated using metrics like Multiclass Accuracy for nodes and Binary Accuracy, Binary Precision, Binary Recall, and Binary F1 Score for edges, which can be seen in Fig. 3, having all an upward trend with minimal overfitting since training and validation trends have close values. These metrics ensure a comprehensive evaluation, particularly for sparse edge predictions where precision and recall are critical. The losses achieved during training and validation can be seen in Fig. 4, showing a steady decrease, even with the spike at epoch 40 for the node prediction model, with a minimal divergence between training and validation, thus showing a strong sign of stable learning.

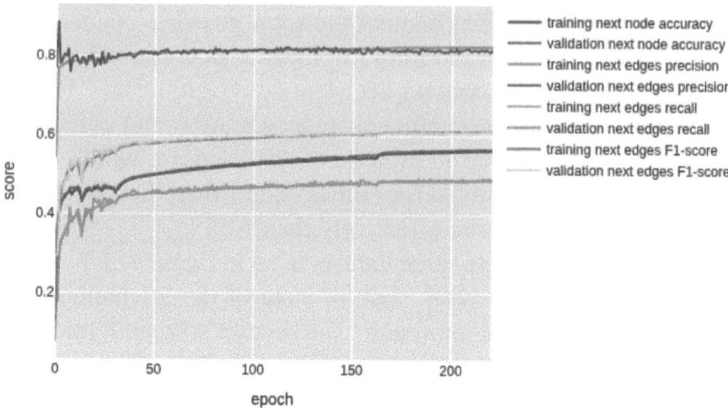

Fig. 3. Training and validation metrics.

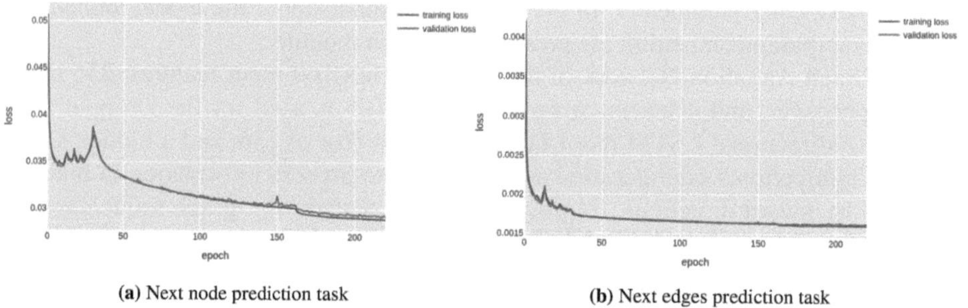

(a) Next node prediction task

(b) Next edges prediction task

Fig. 4. Training and validation losses for the prediction tasks.

4.2   Results and Discussion

For assessing the quality of the embeddings generated by our `CodeASG` model, Table 1 presents the silhouette scores for clustering the embeddings provided by our model `CodeASG` and two state-of-the-art models for generating embeddings for a section of code, namely `CodeBERT` and `CodeT5`.

The optimal number k of clusters for clustering with k-means and `Spectral Clustering` was determined by applying the Elbow method. The within-cluster sum of squares is plotted against varying values of k, and the point where the curve begins to flatten, indicating diminishing returns in clustering compactness, is selected (as it can be

Table 1. Silhouette scores for clustering the embeddings obtained using `CodeASG`, `CodeBERT` and `CodeT5`.

Model	k-means	DBSCAN	Spectral clustering
`CodeBERT`	0.0598	0.1936	0.2615
`CodeT5`	0.0606	0.1975	0.2663
Our `CodeASG` model	**0.0626**	**0.2001**	**0.2694**

seen in Fig. 5a). This Elbow point was used to guide our selection and to ensure robustness. We also computed Silhouette scores across multiple values of k, thus selecting the value that yielded the highest average score. For DBSCAN, the *eps* parameter was determined using the Elbow method on sorted k-Nearest Neighbor distances [6], whose values can be visualized in Fig. 5b, where $k = 2 \times N - 1$, with N being the embedding dimensionality, which helps identify the threshold that separates dense regions from outliers. The *min_samples* parameter was set to $2 \times N$ to balance sensitivity to small clusters while minimizing noise. These choices were applied separately to each embedding type, i.e., CodeBERT, CodeT5, and CodeASG, allowing for fair and adaptive evaluation of the clustering performance. The results shown in Table 1 demonstrate the effectiveness of the proposed `CodeASG` model for generating embeddings from the ASG representation of code.

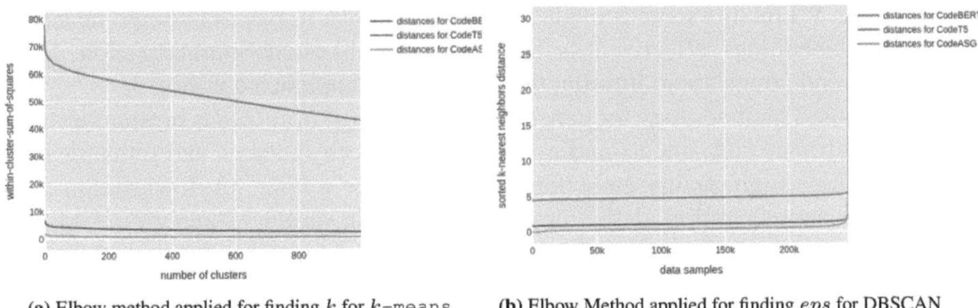

(a) Elbow method applied for finding k for k-means   (b) Elbow Method applied for finding *eps* for DBSCAN

Fig. 5. Elbow method applied to finding the optimal hyperparameters.

Compared to `CodeBERT` and `CodeT5`, the proposed model consistently outperforms across all three clustering algorithms, the most significant improvement being observed in `Spectral Clustering`. Spectral clustering leverages graph-based representations, suggesting that the embeddings generated by the proposed model are particularly suited for capturing structural and semantic nuances of ASGs. To determine if the improvement achieved using `CodeASG` over `CodeBERT` and `CodeT5` is statistically significant, a one-tailed paired Wilcoxon signed-rank test [8, 12] was applied. The improvement achieved using `CodeASG` was proven to be statistically significant, at a significance level of $alpha = 0.05$.

The proposed `CodeASG` approach offers several significant strengths, particularly in its focus on improving performance through the efficient use of tokens and its emphasis on sparsity and scalability. ASGs capture the structural and semantic relationships within the code more compactly, allowing the model to process less redundant information while retaining the richness of the code's semantics. This reduced token count improves the computational efficiency of the model, enabling faster training and inference without sacrificing representational quality. Additionally, the approach places a strong emphasis on sparsity, particularly in how it predicts edges within the ASG. Since edges of these graphs are often sparse, the model is specifically designed to handle this aspect effectively. By utilizing a combination of Graph Attention Networks and attention-driven predictors, the approach ensures that only the most relevant graph relationships are learned, minimizing noise and focusing on critical dependencies.

While the proposed approach offers numerous strengths, it also has specific weaknesses that could impact its performance and applicability. One of the primary limitations lies in its reliance on a subset of the dataset for training due to the computational cost of processing its entirety. Although selecting 10% of the sequences helps manage scalability, it may result in a loss of diversity in the training data, potentially limiting the model's ability to generalize to unseen or more complex code structures. Another notable weakness is its reliance on a parser to transform the original code into its AST representation, which will later be transformed into the ASG representation. The need for a parser restricts the approach to programming languages with well-defined parsers, limiting its flexibility and cross-language applicability compared to parser-independent models. Lastly, the evaluation focuses primarily on clustering metrics such as the Silhouette score. While this score provides valuable insights, it may not comprehensively capture the embeddings' effectiveness for broader tasks like code summarization, defect detection, or code translation, limiting the scope of the approach's utility.

The proposed methodology for generating embeddings from ASGs presents a strong potential to advance code understanding by capturing both syntactic and semantic code structures. These high-quality embeddings can enhance a range of downstream tasks such as code summarization, defect detection, and code similarity analysis. Additionally, the inherent flexibility of ASGs makes this method adaptable for multi-language support, enabling language-agnostic embeddings that are useful in cross-language scenarios, such as legacy code migration or translation. However, the approach also faces notable challenges. Its reliance on parsers to generate ASTs, which are then transformed into ASGs, introduces dependency on parser accuracy and availability, limiting applicability in languages lacking mature parsing tools. Moreover, further evaluation on predefined tasks, such as code summarization or defect prediction, is required for assessing the quality of the ASG-based embeddings, as clustering metrics, although they provide some insights, they do not fully evaluate the practicability of the obtained embeddings.

5   Conclusions and Future Work

The paper introduced, as a proof of concept, the `CodeASG` approach, which uses the ASG representation of the code to generate more meaningful embeddings, which was later validated against `CodeBERT` and `CodeT5`. Thus, the proposed methodology outperformed in terms of clusters' silhouette score both `CodeBERT` and `CodeT5` when applying k-means, DBSCAN, and Spectral clustering. The research questions formulated in Sect. 1 have been answered. As an answer to RQ1, the CodeASG approach was introduced to model the sequential and structural dependencies in the source code's syntax and handle the sparsity of edges in the ASG representation of the code. RQ2 was answered in Sect. 4.2, by highlighting a statistically significant performance improvement achieved when clustering embeddings generated using CodeASG over CodeBERT and CodeT5.

For future work, the proposed methodology requires further validation of the quality of the generated embeddings, which can be achieved by applying them to supervised tasks and comparing their performance against embeddings from other models, such as CodeBERT, considering even AST-based models. Tasks like code classification, defect detection, or function similarity prediction will provide additional insights into the embeddings' ability to capture both syntactic and semantic features. Another promising direction is the development of methods to automatically parse code into ASGs without relying on external parsers, thus eliminating the dependency on language-specific parsers, addressing a significant limitation of CodeASG.

Acknowledgments. This work was supported by a grant of the Ministry of Research, Innovation and Digitization, CCCDI-UEFISCDI, project number PN-IV-P7-7.1-PED-2024-0121, within PNCDI IV.

References

1. Chaudhry, M., et al.: A systematic literature review on identifying patterns using unsupervised clustering algorithms: a DM perspective. Symmetry **15**(9) (2023)
2. Devlin, J., Chang, M., Lee, K., Toutanova, K.: BERT: Pre-training of Deep Bidirectional Transformers for Language Understanding, pp. 4171–4186 (2019)
3. Feng, Z., Guo, D., et al.: CodeBERT: a pre-trained model for programming and natural languages. In: EMNLP, pp. 1536–1547. ACM (2020)
4. Liao, R., Li, Y., et al.: Efficient graph generation with graph recurrent attention networks. In: NeurIPS, pp. 4257–4267 (2019)
5. Raffel, C., Shazeer, N., et al.: Exploring the limits of transfer learning with a unified text-to-text transformer. JMLR **21**(140), 1–67 (2020)
6. Schubert, E., Sander, J., et al.: DBSCAN revisited, revisited: why and how you should (still) use DBSCAN. TODS **42**(3), 1–21 (2017)
7. Scott, T.R., Liu, T., et al.: An empirical study on clustering pretrained embeddings: is deep strictly better? NeurIPS Workshop **poster** (2022)
8. Siegel, S., Castellan, N.: Nonparametric Statistics for the Behavioral Sciences, 2nd edn. McGraw–Hill, Inc. (1988)
9. Sîrbu, A.G., Czibula, G.: Automatic code generation based on Abstract Syntax-based encoding. ESWA **264**, 125821 (2025)
10. Sîrbu, A.G.: CodeASG GitHub repository (2024). https://github.com/sirbualexandrugabriel/code_asg. Accessed 11 Sept 2025
11. Wang, Y., et al.: CodeT5: identifier-aware unified pre-trained encoder-decoder models for code understanding and generation. In: EMNLP, pp. 8696–8708 (2021)
12. Social Science Statistics (2024). http://www.socscistatistics.com/tests/. Accessed 15 May 2025
13. Yeasmin, S., Afrin, N., Huq, M.R.: Transformer-based text clustering for newspaper articles. In: MIET, vol. 490, pp. 443–457. Springer (2022)

A Hybrid Query Language for Digital Twins

Philipp Zech[1]([⊠])(iD), Manuel Burger[1], Linus Wald[1], Philipp Pobitzer[1],
Sascha Hammes[2](iD), and Judith Michael[3](iD)

[1] Department of Computer Science, University of Innsbruck, Innsbruck, Austria
{philipp.zech,manuel.burger,linus.wald,
philipp.pobitzer}@uibk.ac.at
[2] Unit of Energy Efficient Building, University of Innsbruck, Innsbruck, Austria
[3] Programming and Software Engineering, University of Regensburg, Regensburg, Germany
judith.michael@ur.de

Abstract. The full potential of Digital Twins (DTs) is hindered by the challenge of integrating complex engineering models with high-frequency runtime data from disparate sources. Existing approaches lack a unified mechanism to query across the boundary of static models and dynamic data, leading to fragmented and inconsistent DT systems. We introduce a hybrid query language that unifies model and data retrieval, translating queries into SPARQL for model access and SQL for data access within a single declarative statement. Our evaluation demonstrates that this approach overcomes the models-meet-data challenge by enabling scalable, near real-time queries, thereby paving the way for more robust and integrated DT applications.

Keyword: Digital Twins, Models-Meet-Data, Domain-Specific Language, Query Language, Data Integration.

1 Introduction

Existing Digital Twin (DT) solutions generally fail to adequately address the *models-meet-data* challenge [17], which involves synchronizing models and data across heterogeneous sources, managing their co-evolution, and providing unified access. Current approaches largely capitalize on manual integration efforts [21] which yields error-prone solutions that lack interoperability and mechanisms for efficient synchronization, leading to fragmented and disharmonized DT systems. The disconnect between models and operational data remains one of the primary obstacles to full-scale DT implementation [8,15]. This challenge is further complicated by the inherent heterogeneity of DT ecosystems, where cyber-physical systems operate across multiple abstraction levels and temporal scales [4,24]. Commensurate with this, the central question of our work arises, viz., *how can we develop a unified mechanism to enable seamless integration, management, and provisioning of heterogeneous models and data for DT engineering while ensuring scalability and interoperability?*

To this end, we propose a hybrid query language atop a repository for DTs [22,23] for integrated model and data retrieval, to resolve the models-meet-data challenge. Our

C. Cappiello et al. (Eds.): CoopIS 2025, LNCS 15535, pp. 662–672, 2026.
https://doi.org/10.1007/978-3-032-15538-2_43

approach enables efficient aggregation of models and runtime data with unified access, fostering interoperability and operational efficiency in DT systems. Our solution builds upon established information integration principles from cooperative information systems, including schema integration, distributed query processing, semantic interoperability, and data fusion [7, 19], to address the models-meet-data challenge in DT engineering.

Organization. Section 2 outlines the context of our work, followed by Sect. 3 where we outline our challenges and contributions. Section 4 discusses our contributions in detail. We evaluate our proposal in Sect. 5 and discuss our results in Sect. 6. We conclude in Sect. 7.

2   Background and Related Work

The effective implementation of DTs is hindered by a fundamental challenge: the seamless integration of heterogeneous engineering models with dynamic runtime data, known as the *models-meet-data* challenge [17]. This problem stems from the historical separation between model-driven engineering (MDE) and data management technologies [9, 22, 23], which has led to fragmented tools and manual integration efforts that lack scalability [21]. Consequently, models are managed in specialized repositories with distinct query languages while runtime data resides in separate databases. This fragmentation creates significant barriers to DT operations by impeding the co-evolution of models and data [10], preventing unified data access, and complicating the execution of hybrid queries essential for consistency checking and comprehensive analysis.

Recent work in DT data management consistently highlights the unresolved challenge of integrated model-data access [14]. While semantic approaches [13], multi-scale modeling [24], and data-level integration using GraphQL [5] have been explored, they lack a unified mechanism for querying across both engineering models and runtime data. Our approach builds on foundational data integration principles [7, 19] to provide a concrete solution to the *models-meet-data* challenge articulated by van den Brand et al. [17]. To the best of our knowledge, no hybrid query language targeting both models and data in DTs currently exists; existing solutions rely on manual, non-scalable integration techniques [2, 21], reinforcing the novelty of our unified query interface.

Our work extends the DAIRY repository for DT engineering [22, 23] in the construction domain by introducing a unified *models-meet-data* representation via knowledge graphs, and a Domain-Specific Language (DSL) with a query generator and executor to enable hybrid querying across versioned models and runtime data.

3   Challenges and Contributions

We aim to fill the research gap of seamlessly integrating models and data for DT engineering with our proposed hybrid query language. It builds upon established information integration principles while addressing the specific challenges of DT environments, viz.,

1. the integration of heterogeneous data sources,
2. the dynamic evolution of models and data, and
3. a lack of unified access mechanisms to models-and-data.

In resolving these challenges, we deliver the following contributions

1. advancing the DAIRY repository to support model-data integration,
2. a hybrid query language for integrated model and data retrieval, and
3. a prototype addressing the models-meet-data challenge.

thereby investigating the following research questions:

RQ1: What mechanisms need to be implemented within the DAIRY repository to ensure seamless synchronization between evolving models and dynamic data sources in DT systems?

RQ2: How can a hybrid query language be designed to effectively integrate and retrieve heterogeneous model and runtime data in DT environments?

Our work is grounded in Design Science Research (DSR) [20] where the central contribution is a hybrid query language embedded in a repository for DTs. Our artifact evolved through multiple iterative cycles, each responding to insights from the problem space, system feedback, and user trials [22, 23], and is implemented as a solution to the following design science problem [20]:

Improve *DT engineering* (context)
by designing *a hybrid query language for models and data* (artifact)
that satisfies *the models-meet-challenge* (requirement)
to deliver *a unified representation on a physical twin.* (goal)

# 4	A Hybrid Query Language for Digital Twin Engineering

Our solution capitalizes on a global-as-a-view (cf. unified schema, local views) [16] approach where a global data model for building runtime data (cf. Sect. 4.1) is defined in terms of local data sources (e.g., devices in a building). This data model is linked to a building model which establishes a knowledge graph and lays the foundation for our hybrid query language (cf. Sect. 4.2).

## 4.1	Data Modeling

We link a static, ifcOWL-based building model (persisted in DAIRY) with a manually defined dynamic data model following the star schema [3]. This integration is achieved by generating a semantic data model using the SOSA/SSN ontology from the dynamic data model, which creates a unified knowledge graph representing the building's structure and its corresponding data schemas. Runtime data is persisted in a dedicated relational database, to avoid the computational overhead and scalability issues associated with frequent, high-volume data ingestion in a knowledge graph. This design enables a *lazy-linking* approach, inspired by lazy evaluation [6], where combined model-data queries leverage the knowledge graph and redirect data retrieval to the appropriate SQL tables. This design ensures that models and data can be queried independently without performance degradation while allowing for their efficient, on-demand combination.

4.2   A Hybrid Query Language for Models and Data BSQL

Our Basic Sensor Query Language (BSQL) is designed to retrieve both model and runtime data by providing a simple and intuitive way to specify the information to retrieve. BSQL queries are structured into two main components, viz., the SENSOR part and the DATA part. Consequently, queries are executed in a two-step process:

(1) The SENSOR part is translated into SPARQL and executed against the model store. It filters specified sensors and their associated static information from the models (contained in IfcPropertySets at every sensor).
(2) The DATA part is translated into SQL and is executed against the data warehouse to retrieve runtime data for each sensor retrieved in (1).

BSQL's novelty lies in unifying querying across structured model repositories and runtime data stores using a lightweight, composable syntax with lazy evaluation semantics [6]. BSQL is implemented using Xtext [1] for developing the query language and Xtend [1] for query generation.

```
1   <Statement> ::= 'SENSOR_SELECT' <PropertySelectType>
2                   ['WHERE' '{' <PropertyConditions> '}' ]
3                   ['ORDER_BY' <PSID_PID> [<Order>] {',' <PSID_PID> [<Order>]}]
4                   ['LIMIT' <INT>]
5   <PropertySelectType> ::= 'BASIC' | '(' <Clause> {',' <Clause>} ')'
6   <Clause> ::= 'PROPERTY_SET' <PSID> 'PROPERTIES' '(' <PID> {',' <PID>} ')'
7   <PropertyConditions> ::= ['NOT'] <PropCond> {('AND' | 'OR') ['NOT']
     ↪    <PropCond>}
8   <PropCond> ::= <PSID_PID> <PropertyComparison> | '(' <PropertyConditions> ')'
9   <PropertyComparison> ::= (* comparison against a value that the property holds
     ↪    *)
10  <PSID_PID> ::= <PSID> '.' <PID> | 'Sensor.Id'
11  <PSID> ::= <String>
12  <PID> ::= <String>
13  <Order> ::= 'ASC' | 'DESC'
```

Listing 1. Simplified syntax of the SENSOR part of our DSL (in EBNF) for querying models-and-data. <String> denotes any valid UTF-8 strings, <INT> denotes an integer, <PSID> a property set ID and <PID> a property ID. <PropertyComparison> allow for detailed comparison and filtering of retrieved data. Best viewed on a computer screen.

Sensor Queries. Listing 1 shows the grammar of the SENSOR part of queries formulated using our hybrid models-meet-data query language. The SENSOR part of our queries is initiated with the keyword SENSOR_SELECT (Listing 1 , line 1), followed by optional clauses that specify property sets, each associated with one or more properties of a sensor (l.5-6). The query can be refined using a WHERE clause (l.2), which includes conditions that filter sensors based on whether certain properties fall within specified sets of values, which then can also be logically connected using AND, OR, and NOT (l.7-9). Additionally, the results can be ordered using the ORDER_BY clause (l.3), which sorts the data in ascending (ASC) or descending (DESC) order (l.13). The number of returned results can be controlled using the LIMIT clause (l.4) followed by an integer. This enables the construction of flexible and powerful queries to retrieve sensors from building models based on various criteria. <PSID> (l.11) denotes a property set ID and <PID> (l.12) a property ID, respectively.

```
1   <Statement> ::= 'DATA_SELECT' <DataSelectType>
2                   ['WHERE' '{' <DataCondition> '}']
3                   ['GROUP' 'receiveTime' <GroupByTime>]
4                   ['ORDER_BY' 'receiveTime' ['ASC' | 'DESC']]
5                   ['LIMIT' <INT>]
6   <DataSelectType> ::= '*' | <AggregationType> {',' <AggregationType>}
7   <AggregationType> ::= 'MAX' | 'MIN' | 'AVG' | 'COUNT' | 'SUM'
8   <DataCondition> ::= [<AllSensorsConditions>] ['[' <SensorSpecificConditions>
     ↪   ']' ]
9   <AllSensorsConditions> ::= ['NOT'] <AllCond> {('AND' | 'OR') ['NOT']
     ↪   <AllCond>}
10  <AllCond> ::= <ReceiveTimeCond> | '(' <AllSensorsConditions> ')'
11  <ReceiveTimeCond> ::= 'receiveTime' <ReceiveTimeComparison>
12  <ReceiveTimeComparison> ::= (* comparison against the receive_time path *)
13  <SensorSpecificConditions> ::= <SensorCondition> {',' <SensorCondition>}
14  <SensorCondition> ::= <PayloadCondition> 'ON_SENSOR_WITH_ID' <String>
15  <PayloadCondition> ::= ['NOT'] <PathCond> {('AND' | 'OR') ['NOT'] <PathCond>}
16  <PathCond> ::= <Path> <PathComparison>
17  <PathComparison> ::= (* comparison against a path of modeled sensor *)
18  <GroupByTime> ::= 'PER_YEAR' | 'PER_MONTH' | 'PER_DAY' | 'PER_HOUR' |
     ↪   'PER_MINUTE'
19  <Path> ::= ':' <String> {':' <String>}
```

Listing 2. Simplified syntax of the DATA part of our DSL (in EBNF) for querying models-and-data. <String> denotes any valid UTF-8 string and <INT> an integer. <ReceiveTimeComparison> and <PathComparison> allow for detailed comparison and filtering of retrieved data. Best viewed on a computer screen.

Data Queries. Data queries complement sensor queries by enabling the retrieval of runtime data to combine static model information with dynamic runtime data. Listing 2 outlines the grammar of the DATA part of our hybrid query language for selecting and filtering sensor data. The DATA_SELECT statement (Listing 2 , line 1) is the core construct, allowing users to select data using either predefined types or custom selections (l.6-7). The query can include a WHERE clause (l.2) to filter data based on conditions, which can be logically connected using AND, OR, and NOT operators (l.8–17). These conditions can pertain to the receiveTime or specific measurements associated with sensors. The GROUP clause (l.3) allows data to be aggregated by time intervals such as year, month, or day (l.18), while the ORDER_BY clause (l.4) specifies the sorting order of the results, e.g., based on the receiveTime, or aggregations. Additionally, the LIMIT clause (l.5) restricts the number of results returned.

Our hybrid query language for models-meet-data offers a powerful framework for precise sensor and data selection and analysis. It allows users to define complex queries with conditions, aggregations, and temporal groupings, enabling targeted and efficient data retrieval from DTs via DAIRY. BSQL supports advanced filtering, sorting, and limiting of results, making it ideal for efficient operational monitoring as showcased in Sect. 5.

5   Evaluation

We evaluated our approach using a real-world setting: a Living Lab at the University of Innsbruck, equipped with a heterogeneous network of 32 sensors measuring environmental conditions (e.g., temperature, CO2, air quality), occupancy (PIR, radar), and imaging data (thermal array). The evaluation focuses on two aspects: (i) the performance and scalability of query execution (cf. Sect. 5.1), and (ii) a practical use case from building management, identifying rooms where temperature exceeds a predefined threshold (cf. Sect. 5.2). Following the star schema (cf. Sect. 4.1), his scenario utilized a data model with one dimension table for the sensors (`devices`), and two fact tables for both room conditions (`room_conditions`) and occupancy (`occupant_data`), respectively.

5.1   Technical Evaluation

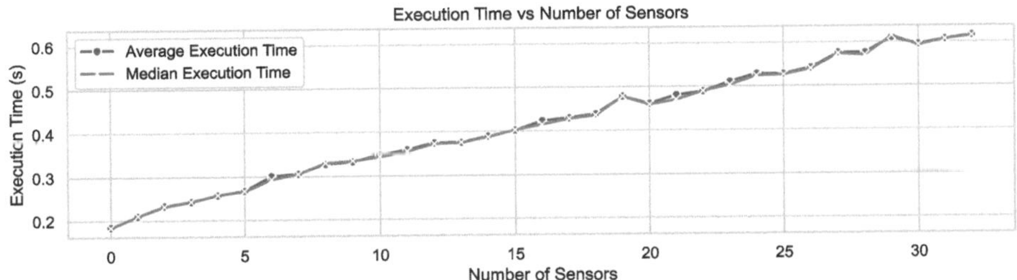

Fig. 1. Summary of query execution times.

To evaluate query efficacy, we benchmarked a hybrid query retrieving static model data (room location) and the most recent dynamic sensor payload for a variable number of sensors, from N=0 to 32. The primary execution overhead stems not from the delegated SQL and SPARQL queries, but from the preceding code generation and validation phase. This phase performs essential syntactic and semantic checks (e.g., verifying property IDs against the model) and incorporates optimizations such as reduced knowledge graph traversal and placeholder replacement for efficient SQL generation [18]. As confirmed by the results shown in Fig. 1, the total execution time exhibits efficient linear scaling, validating the scalability of our architecture.

5.2   Operational Runtime Monitoring

Our use case in a larger context addresses occupant comfort and safety [2] by querying the DT for rooms which temperature is not within a specified range (e.g., due to a broken heater). Doing so allows to adapt building operations continuously to better meet occupant comfort [2]. Specifically, we (i) check the model of the aforesaid Living Lab into DAIRY [23], (ii) create the relevant data model (cf. Sect. 4.1), and (iii) automatically collect data from the Living Lab in DAIRY [23]. Observe that for this the sensors in the Living Lab are configured to send data to the repository via MQTT. This establishes the foundational infrastructure of a DT of the building which subsequently can be used for operational runtime monitoring.

We employ our DT to identify rooms which temperature falls outside a specified range (observe that in our example we only have one room which however does not negatively impact the correctness of our results and later conclusions in Sect. 6). Given BSQL, we next formulated a query that allows to identify sensors in a building model and subsequently filter for those, whose temperature readings fall outside a specified range. By being located inside a room in the building model we can further extract room information via the sensor. This results in a list of sensors alongside their location (e.g., the room) in the building whose temperature readings fall outside the specified temperature range. Listing 3 (see p. 7) shows the corresponding query. First, in the SENSOR_SELECT part we extract relevant temperature sensors from the building model using family and type; in the subsequent DATA_SELECT part we then query for those sensors whose temperature measurements fall outside a specific range (e.g., $20°C - 22°C$).

```
1   SENSOR_SELECT (
2       PROPERTY_SET 'Allgemein' PROPERTIES ('Room'),
3       PROPERTY_SET 'Andere' PROPERTIES ('Familie und Typ')
4   )
5   WHERE {
6       Sensor.Id IN ('41','42','43') AND
7       'Andere'.'Familie und Typ' = 'Temperature_Sensor_Surface: XENSIV PAS CO2 -
    ↪   Temperature'
8   }
9   DATA_SELECT * WHERE {
10      receiveTime BETWEEN '2024-12-30 23:00:00' AND '2024-12-31 00:00:00'
11          [
12                  :'temperature' NOT_BETWEEN 20 AND 22 ON_SENSOR_WITH_ID '41',
13                  :'temperature' NOT_BETWEEN 20 AND 22 ON_SENSOR_WITH_ID '42',
14                  :'temperature' NOT_BETWEEN 20 AND 22 ON_SENSOR_WITH_ID '43'
15          ]
16  }
17  ORDER_BY receiveTime DESC LIMIT 1
```

Listing 3. Hybrid query for retrieving all rooms whose current temperature readings fall outside specified ranges.

Listing 4 (see p. 7) shows the raw JSON reply as a list of sensors and their locations, cf. the rooms they are located in, falling outside the specified temperature range. In our example, Room A needs attention. Facility managers thus using a few known relevant sensors IDs can easily check and identify anomalies, and react appropriately (e.g., by fixing a broken heater). The total execution time of the query was ~0.235 s once again showcasing the performance of our proposal in that it allows to establish near real-time monitoring cycles (ignoring any latency related to the retrieval of building data which is outside our control).

```
1  {"bsql_response":{"sensors":[{"static_dimension":{"Andere":{"Familie und
↪   Typ":"Temperature_Sensor_Surface: XENSIV PAS CO2 - Temperature"},"Allgemein":{"Room":"Room
↪   A"}},"dynamic_dimension":{"reading_count":1,"metadata":{"temperature":"DOUBLE","receive_time":
↪   "TIMESTAMP"},"sensor_readings":[{"temperature":17.74743080882481,"receive_time":"2024-12-31
↪   00:00:00.0"}]},"sensor_id":"42"},{"static_dimension":{"Andere":{"Familie und
↪   Typ":"Temperature_Sensor_Surface: XENSIV PAS CO2 - Temperature"},"Allgemein":{"Room":"Room
↪   A"}},"dynamic_dimension":{"reading_count":1,"metadata":{"temperature":"DOUBLE","receive_time":
↪   "TIMESTAMP"},"sensor_readings":[{"temperature":17.59644148648948,"receive_time":"2024-12-31
↪   00:00:00.0"}]},"sensor_id":"43"},{"static_dimension":{"Andere":{"Familie und
↪   Typ":"Temperature_Sensor_Surface: XENSIV PAS CO2 - Temperature"},"Allgemein":{"Room":"Room
↪   A"}},"dynamic_dimension":{"reading_count":1,"metadata":{"temperature":"DOUBLE","receive_time":
↪   "TIMESTAMP"},"sensor_readings":[{"temperature":17.598542091060978,"receive_time":"2024-12-31
↪   00:00:00.0"}]},"sensor_id":"41"}],"sensor_count":3},"execution_time":"PT0.235859844S"}
```

Listing 4. Raw JSON response to our query for operational runtime monitoring of room temperatures, showing rooms where sensor readings fall outside the specified range (cf. Listing 3). Room A is falling outside the range.

```
1  SENSOR_SELECT (
2      PROPERTY_SET 'Allgemein' PROPERTIES ('Room'),
3      PROPERTY_SET 'Andere' PROPERTIES ('Familie und Typ')
4  )
5  WHERE {
6      (Sensor.Id IN ('41','42','43') AND 'Andere'.'Familie und Typ' =
↪       'Temperature_Sensor_Surface: XENSIV PAS CO2 - Temperature') OR
7      (Sensor.Id IN ('55','56') AND 'Andere'.'Familie und Typ' =
↪       'PIR_Sensor_Surface: HC-SR501')
8  }
9  DATA_SELECT * WHERE {
10     receiveTime BETWEEN '2024-12-30 23:00:00' AND '2024-12-31 00:00:00'
11         [
12             :'temperature' > 30 ON_SENSOR_WITH_ID '41',
13             :'temperature' > 30 ON_SENSOR_WITH_ID '42',
14             :'temperature' > 30 ON_SENSOR_WITH_ID '43',
15             :'occupant' = TRUE ON_SENSOR_WITH_ID '55',
16             :'occupant' = TRUE ON_SENSOR_WITH_ID '56'
17         ]
18 }
19 ORDER_BY receiveTime DESC LIMIT 1
```

Listing 5. Adapted query from Listing 3 to check from occupied rooms with a critical temperature level.

The query from Listing 3 readily can be adapted to other use cases, e.g., querying for occupied rooms where the temperature level reaches a critical threshold that could negatively affect an occupant's health, depending on the available sensors. As an example, Listing 5 (see p. 8) shows a query for identifying occupied rooms whose temperatures exceed a threshold of 30°C.

6 Discussion

Our work provides a concrete solution to the models-meet-data challenge [17] by introducing a hybrid query language that unifies static model representations with dynamic runtime data. In contrast to existing DT solutions that maintain separate infrastructures and rely on ad-hoc integration [2,21], our approach is grounded in established data integration principles [7]. By linking an ifcOWL-based building model with a SOSA/SSN-based data model, we establish a unified semantic framework that enables a single declarative language, BSQL, to retrieve data across these distinct paradigms using SPARQL and SQL.

In answering our research questions, we extended the DAIRY repository with two key design strategies: a clear architectural demarcation between model and data stores (cf. RQ1), and a lazy-linking mechanism for on-demand data fusion (cf. RQ2). Our evaluation demonstrates that this approach not only maintains consistency and operational efficiency but also ensures scalable query performance. The ability to handle advanced scenarios, such as temporal and semantic filtering, through a single interface simplifies the analytical processes for practitioners. This work therefore represents a significant step toward overcoming the fragmented data representations and synchronization challenges that have hindered the development of robust, integrated DT applications.

In direct contrast to related work (cf. Sect. 2), our approach establishes a unified semantic framework by linking an ifcOWL-based model with a SOSA/SSN-based data model. This enables a single declarative query language, BSQL, that applies formal schema integration principles rather than relying on ad-hoc mediation. By embedding this language within the DAIRY repository, our solution overcomes the limitations of fragmented data representations and inconsistent model-data synchronization seen in previous work. The key architectural decisions—separating model and data stores while enabling on-demand fusion via lazy-linking—ensure both scalability and practical applicability in resolving model and data integration in DTs.

6.1 Limitations and Future Work

Future work will address three key limitations. First, the expressiveness of BSQL is currently limited to properties directly defined via `IfcRelDefinesByProperties`; we plan to investigate property inference through path traversal [11] and OWL reasoning [12]. Second, we will work to mitigate the initial query compilation latency (cf. Sect. 5.1) by optimizing the query planning and code generation pipeline to better support highly dynamic settings. Finally, the generalizability of our approach will be assessed by extending our evaluation to other domains, such as industrial automation and healthcare, which is facilitated by the repository's underlying RDF-based architecture [22,23].

7   Conclusion

In our work, we presented a hybrid query language designed to address the challenge of integrating heterogeneous models with dynamic runtime data in DT engineering. We developed our approach within the context of the DAIRY repository, where static building models represented in ifcOWL are seamlessly connected to runtime data stored in a relational database through a unified semantic framework. By mapping static model information to SPARQL queries and runtime data to SQL queries within a single declarative query language, cf. BSQL, our solution not only simplifies access but also enhances consistency across different data sources.

Our evaluation, conducted in the context of building operations, revealed that the proposed hybrid query language is capable of efficiently retrieving and aggregating sensor data while maintaining scalable performance as the number of sensors increases. Overall, our contribution presents a solution to resolving the models-meet-data challenge in DTs. The unified querying approach developed in our work paves the way for more reliable and efficient integration of diverse data sources, facilitating real-time monitoring and comprehensive analysis without imposing the complexity of multiple, disjointed query interfaces.

Acknowledgments. This research has received funding from the Austrian Research Promotion Agency (FFG) under Grant Agreements No.: 910225, BOREALIS, and 898708, TwinLight.

References

1. Bettini, L.: Implementing Domain-specific Languages With Xtext and Xtend. Packt Publishing Ltd (2016)
2. Hauer, M., et al.: Integrating digital twins with BIM for enhanced building control strategies: a systematic literature review focusing on daylight and artificial lighting systems. Buildings **14**(3), 805 (2024)
3. Iqbal, M.Z., Mustafa, G., Sarwar, N., Wajid, S.H., Nasir, J., Siddque, S.: A review of star schema and snowflakes schema. In: Bajwa, I.S., Sibalija, T., Jawawi, D.N.A. (eds.) INTAP 2019. CCIS, vol. 1198, pp. 129–140. Springer, Singapore (2020). https://doi.org/10.1007/978-981-15-5232-8_12
4. Jia, W., Wang, W., Zhang, Z.: From simple digital twin to complex digital twin Part I: a novel modeling method for multi-scale and multi-scenario digital twin. Adv. Eng. Inform. **53**, 101706 (2022)
5. Koren, I., Jansen, N., Michael, J., Rumpe, B., Böse, E.: A low-code approach for data view extraction from engineering models with GraphQL. In: International Conference on Model Driven Engineering Languages and Systems Companion (MODELS-C). ACM/IEEE (2023)
6. Launchbury, J.: A natural semantics for lazy evaluation. In: 20th ACM SIGPLAN-SIGACT symposium on Principles of programming languages, pp. 144–154 (1993)
7. Lenzerini, M.: Data integration: a theoretical perspective. In: 21st ACM SIGMOD-SIGACT-SIGART Symposium on Principles of Database Systems, pp. 233–246 (2002)
8. Liu, X., et al.: A systematic review of digital twin about physical entities, virtual models, twin data, and applications. Adv. Eng. Inform. **55**, 101876 (2023)
9. Michael, J., Bork, D., Wimmer, M., Mayr, H.: Quo Vadis modeling? Findings of a community survey, an Ad-hoc bibliometric analysis, and expert interviews on data, process, and software modeling. J. Softw. Syst. Model. (SoSyM) **23**(1), 7–28 (2024)
10. Michael, J., David, I., Bork, D.: Digital twin evolution for sustainable smart ecosystems. In: MODELS Companion 2024: International Conference on Model Driven Engineering Languages and Systems, pp. 1061–1065. ACM (2024)
11. Mojžiš, J., Laclavík, M.: SRelation: fast RDF graph traversal. In: Klinov, P., Mouromtsev, D. (eds.) KESW 2013. CCIS, vol. 394, pp. 69–82. Springer, Heidelberg (2013). https://doi.org/10.1007/978-3-642-41360-5_6
12. Polleres, A., Hogan, A., Delbru, R., Umbrich, J.: RDFS and OWL reasoning for linked data. In: Rudolph, S., Gottlob, G., Horrocks, I., van Harmelen, F. (eds.) Reasoning Web 2013. LNCS, vol. 8067, pp. 91–149. Springer, Heidelberg (2013). https://doi.org/10.1007/978-3-642-39784-4_2

13. Qiang, Z., et al.: A systematic comparison and evaluation of building ontologies for deploying data-driven analytics in smart buildings. Energy Build. **292**, 113054 (2023)
14. Tao, F., Xiao, B., Qi, Q., Cheng, J., Ji, P.: Digital twin modeling. J. Manuf. Syst. **64**, 372–389 (2022)
15. Tao, F., Zhang, H., Zhang, C.: Advancements and challenges of digital twins in industry. Nat. Comput. Sci. **4**(3), 169–177 (2024)
16. Ullman, J.D.: Information integration using logical views. In: Afrati, F., Kolaitis, P. (eds.) ICDT 1997. LNCS, vol. 1186, pp. 19–40. Springer, Heidelberg (1997). https://doi.org/10.1007/3-540-62222-5_34
17. Van Den Brand, M., Cleophas, L., Gunasekaran, R., Haverkort, B., Negrin, D.A.M., Muctadir, H.M.: Models meet data: challenges to create virtual entities for digital twins. In: 2021 ACM/IEEE International Conference on Model Driven Engineering Languages and Systems Companion (MODELS-C), pp. 225–228 (2021)
18. Wang, P., Shi, T., Reddy, C.K.: Text-to-SQL generation for question answering on electronic medical records. In: Web Conference 2020, pp. 350–361 (2020)
19. Wiederhold, G.: Mediators in the architecture of future information systems. Computer **25**(3), 38–49 (1992)
20. Wieringa, R.J.: Statistical difference-making experiments. In: Design Science Methodology for Information Systems and Software Engineering, pp. 295–317. Springer, Heidelberg (2014). https://doi.org/10.1007/978-3-662-43839-8_20
21. Zech, P., Clark, T., Breu, R.: An empirical analysis of digital twin adoption. In: 58th Hawaiin International Conference on System Sciences (HICSS'58), pp. 6253–6262 (2025)
22. Zech, P., Fröch, G., Breu, R.: A requirements study on model repositories for digital twins in construction engineering. In: International Conference on Cooperative Information Systems, pp. 459–469. Springer, Cham (2023)
23. Zech, P., Pobitzer, P., Fröch, G., Breu, R.: A proposal for a models-meet-data repository for digital twins in construction engineering. In: IEEE 21st International Conference on Software Architecture Companion (ICSA-C), pp. 111–118. IEEE (2024)
24. Zhang, H., Qi, Q., Tao, F.: A multi-scale modeling method for digital twin shop-floor. J. Manuf. Syst. **62**, 417–428 (2022)

Trial by Twin: Behavior-Predictive Trust in Autonomous Drone Swarms

Danish Iqbal[✉][iD], Hind Bangui[iD], and Bruno Rossi[iD]

Faculty of Informatics, Masaryk University, Brno, Czech Republic
{danish,hind.bangui,brossi}@mail.muni.cz

Abstract. To achieve future autonomous mobility for Unmanned Aerial Vehicles (UAVs), reliable runtime trust assurance is crucial. This paper presents a trust-assurance method for autonomous drones utilizing runtime compliance checking via a Digital Twin (DT). The DT incorporates drone-specific metrics from AirSim simulations, including sensors' health and network centrality for real-time behavior analysis. Drones collaborate in swarms, sharing predictive and actual behaviors for trust assessment. The model uses Random Forest (RF), Support Vector Regression (SVR), and Convolutional Neural Network (CNN) to estimate swarm coordination rates as trust indicators, with each iteration classifying drones as Trusted or Malicious. The model was tested in an autonomous drone delivery system against various trust-related attacks, demonstrating SVR's effectiveness in estimating coordination rates and RF and SVM's role in trust classification.

Keywords: Trust · Modeling · Autonomous Drones · Digital Twin · Run-Time Compliance Checking · Attacks · Trust-Assurance

1 Introduction

In recent years, the autonomous drones industry has been the focus of rapid achievements in terms of automation [3]. This evolution of automation extended the influence beyond ground vehicles as Unmanned Aerial Vehicles (UAVs), including autonomous drones [1], significantly expanding the role of intelligent systems in domains such as defense, surveillance, and autonomous logistics. With the widespread adoption of drones in different application domains, trust assurance has acquired great importance [5]. Trust can be described as the attitude or belief of an agent to achieve a specific goal in interaction with another agent in the presence of uncertainty and vulnerability [10].

In swarms of autonomous drones, the accurate detection of malicious intent injected by external actors becomes critical [4,9,11]. Current studies on trust building and malicious intent detection are primarily based on traditional methods such as rule-based systems [13], which operate on fixed logic and static behavior models that fail to adequately address the complex communication features of drone swarms in dynamic environment.

Trust assurance in autonomous ecosystems remains a significant challenge for both industry and academia [2]. To address these trust-building challenges in constantly

C. Cappiello et al. (Eds.): CoopIS 2025, LNCS 15535, pp. 673–683, 2026.
https://doi.org/10.1007/978-3-032-15538-2_44

evolving environments, a quick decision about trust within drone-to-drone communication is explored during swarm collaboration in autonomous ecosystems [6,7]. However, we envision employing the transmission of digital information between drones to communicate mutual behavior that becomes the baseline to build trust between them [5]. Furthermore, the role of Artificial Intelligence (AI), encompassing machine learning (ML) and deep learning (DL), has become increasingly vital in strengthening autonomous drones' trustworthiness. Advanced classification through the DL model is instrumental in analyzing complex data patterns, playing a pivotal role in anomaly detection and the prevention of unsafe operation in ecosystems [1].

In this paper, we examine the role of a model for behavior-predictive trust based on DTs that model in real-time the drones' communication. We have three main contributions: i) *Dynamic Trust Quantification*: we propose a novel mechanism for real-time trust evaluation in autonomous drone networks by integrating several metrics computed from drones behavior-predicted social behavior; ii) *Run-Time Compliance Checking via DT Integration*: our framework incorporates a DT design for information exchange at runtime; iii) *Experimental evaluation based on Trust-related attacks*: we apply the proposed solution in a swarm simulation environment, to see the impact of different trust attacks.

2 System Model

A model-based approach [5] serves as a foundation concept for trust assurance among collaborating autonomous drones. Furthermore, it introduces the concept of DT design [6] as a communication pattern of drone-predicted behavior within the autonomous ecosystem. The approach comprises a two-stage ML framework designed to improve trust assessment in drone swarms. In the first stage, a regression model is trained to estimate the swarm coordination rate, capturing social behavioral consistency as a quantitative trust indicator. The estimated coordination rate, along with performance-related features such as latency, packet loss, and mobility, is then used to compute a trust score that reflects the drone's consistency (among predicted and actual behavior) during swarm operations. In the second stage, a classification model utilizes the predicted coordination rate, trust score, and other features (including social centrality measures) to assign discrete trust labels: Trusted or Malicious.

2.1 Problem Formulation

The social network arising from the interaction among collaborating autonomous drones is characterized as an undirected graph denoted by $\mathcal{G} = \{V, E\}$, where V represents the set of drones and E represents the communication or social interaction links between them.

Each drone $d_i \in V$ interacts with a subset of peers $s \in S$, identifying a potential cluster $D_s \subset D$ within the swarm. The trustworthiness of a drone $d_j \in D_s$, from the perspective of its collaborating peer drone d_i, is represented as a binary-valued trust score $Ts_{d_i,d_j} \in [0, 1]$. This score encapsulates a multi-dimensional evaluation based on behavioral, social, and centrality metrics. The set D_s thus includes those drones with which drone d_i has established a valid social relationship.

The identification of the trustworthy peer in the cluster, the drone d_i selects the drone $d_j^* \in D_s$ with the highest trust score: $d_j^* = \max_{d_j \in D_s} Ts_{d_i,d_j}$

2.2 Drone Communication Network Model

The proposed approach conceptualizes drone swarms into four distinct areas: simulation of drone behavior and communication, information exchange and compliance checking through a DT representation, coordination and trust score estimation using regression models, and classification of drone behavior to detect malicious activity within the autonomous swarm ecosystem (Fig. 1).

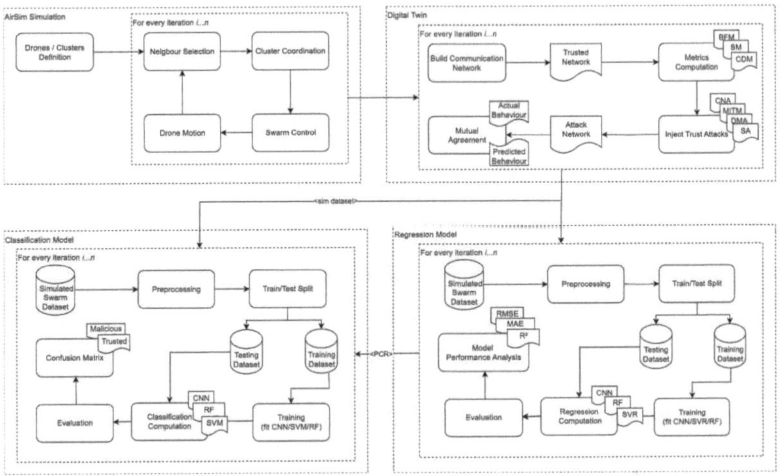

Fig. 1. Swarm Simulation Workflow Framework.

The swarm network structure is made of the following components:

Drone: The drone class comprises three layers: behavior, social, and centrality metrics. The drone behavior class scripts the parameters for a single drone and environment. The state of the drone is presented by an equation at time t. where $d_i(t)$ denotes the state of drone i at time t.

$$D(t) = \sum_{i=1}^{N} d_i(t)$$

Swarm: The swarm behavior relies on individual drone actions and pairwise influence with neighbors. The rules for the swarm are defined as a repulsion force to avoid collision and velocity alignment of the drones in the cluster. This is mathematically represented as:

$$S(t) = \sum_{i=1}^{N} \left(d_i(t) + \sum_{j \in N_i(t)} \phi_{ij}(t) \right)$$

where, $S(t)$ is the swarm state at time t, $d_i(t)$ is the state of drone i, $N_i(t)$ is the set of its neighbors, and $\phi_{ij}(t)$ models the interaction (e.g., acceptance or repulsion) between drone i and neighbor j.

Neighbor Selection. The selection allows a drone to communicate with nearby drones within a proximity for critical task mission completion. It is defined as:

$$N_i(t) = \{d_j \in D \setminus \{d_i\} \mid \|p_j(t) - p_i(t)\| \leq r_c\}$$

In this equation, $N_i(t)$ is the neighbor set of drone i at time t, $p_i(t)$ is the position of drone i, and r_c is the communication range threshold.

2.3   Trust Evaluation Metrics

The examination of existing literature [5] on trust-building among autonomous collaborating drones, along with the use of DT design as a communication pattern, was proposed in our previous study [6]. Based on existing studies [1,15], the important metrics for establishing trust in terms of various drone interactions in swarm networks are defined below.

Behavior Functionality Metric (BFM). The Behavioral Functionality Metric utilizes the behavior properties of autonomous drones, as described in [6], to assess the drone's health, such as sensor functionality and battery status, before permitting it to join the swarm network. A health score is generated based on the performance of its physical component's functionality. A higher BFM score indicates optimal battery life and sensor functionality and is deemed reliable enough to join the network. Conversely, drones with a lower BFM score are flagged for additional monitoring or excluded from the network. This procedure ensures that fully functional drones can join the network, reducing the risk to the overall network posed by malfunctioning drones. The BFM is defined as:

$$BFM = F_i, \quad \text{where } F_i \in [0, 1] \tag{1}$$

Values are based on diagnostics and reflect the reliability of the drone's sensors

Social Metric (SM). The Social Metric (SM) employs the social features described in [6] as predictive indicators for trust evaluation. The SM evaluates a drone's actual trajectory against its predicted behavior using protocol-defined operational parameters such as speed, position, altitude, inter-drone distance, and location. It ensures that each drone maintains its predicted and actual social agreement in operation.

$$SM = 1 - \frac{\left| n_i^{SM} - \widehat{n}_i^{SM} \right|}{\max\left(n_i^{SM}, \widehat{n}_i^{SM}\right) + \varepsilon} \tag{2}$$

where ϵ is a small constant to prevent division by zero. $SM \in [0, 1]$, with values closer to 1 indicating high behavioral alignment.

Centrality Deviation Metric (CDM). The Centrality Deviation Metric [15] is designed to evaluate a drone's centrality within the network, based on its positional attributes and influence over other drones. Similar to that of humans, the interaction of two or more drones with each other allows the formation of a social relationship. The metric requires drones to maintain expected centrality levels to ensure proper network functioning. Any divergence from the expected centrality may signal disruptions or malicious activities, such as attempts to interfere with communication or gain control over other drones. This metric captures the deviation in network influence:

$$CDM = 1 - \frac{|c_i - \hat{c}_i|}{\max(c_i, \hat{c}_i) + \epsilon} \tag{3}$$

where c_i is the observed actual centrality and $\hat{c}_i$ is the predicted centrality from the DT pattern of the drone.

Reliability Impact (RI). Communication risk is the combination of latency and packet loss in a swarm network:

$$RI = \frac{L_i + PL_i}{2} \tag{4}$$

2.4   Trust Evaluation Algorithm

The algorithm is applied in an operational environment within the simulation. It first calculates the Behavior Functionality Metric (BFM), Social Metric (SM), and Centrality Deviation Metric (CDM). For every drone, these metrics are aggregated to calculate the Behavioral Assessment (BA). Afterwards, latency and packet loss metrics are used to calculate the Reliability Impact (RI).

Subsequently, the algorithm computes the actual coordination rate (cr) based on matches in speed (SPT), sensors (SMT), centrality (CMT), and packet loss. A regression model, trained on simulated swarm data, uses the RF, SVR, and CNN to predict the coordination rate. The Trust Score (TS) is then calculated as the product of BA, RI, and predicted coordination rate (cr). Furthermore, drones are classified as Trusted or Malicious using ML models (RF, SVM, CNN) based on TS, coordination rate, and telemetry data under various attacks (e.g., SA, MITM). This classification considers the computed TS, predicted coordination rate, and actual coordination rate from the simulated environment.

Algorithm 1. Malicious Drone Detection.

1: **procedure** TRUST SCORE CALCULATION
2:     **Input:** Dataset $\mathcal{D}$ (Predicted and observed metrics for each drone)
3:     **Output:** TS (Trust scores), L_{mal} (List of malicious drones), $L_{Trusted}$ (List of trustworthy drones)

4:     **Step 1: Initialization**
5:     Initialize $TS \leftarrow []$, $L_{mal} \leftarrow []$, $L_{Trusted} \leftarrow []$

6:     **Step 2: Trust Score and Coordination Prediction**
7:     **for** each drone d_i in $\mathcal{D}$ **do**
8:         Compute BFM using Equation (1)
9:         Compute SM using Equation (2)
10:         Compute CDM using Equation (3)
11:         $BA \leftarrow \dfrac{SM + CDM + BFM}{3}$
12:         Compute RI using Equation (4)
13:         Compute SPT, SMT, CMT
14:         $cr(\text{actual}) \leftarrow SPT + SMT + CMT + (1 - \text{PacketLoss})$
15:         Predict cr using a regression model based on historical swarm data
16:         $ts \leftarrow BA \times RI \times cr(\text{actual})$
17:         Append ts to TS

18:         **Step 3: ML-based Classification**
19:         Input features: Features $\leftarrow (ts, cr, SM, CDM, BFM)$
20:         Predicted label $\leftarrow$ *Trusted* or *Malicious*
21:         **if** Predicted label is *Malicious* **then**
22:             Add d_i to L_{mal} $\triangleright$ Label is Malicious âĂŞ isolate and report
23:         **else if** Predicted label is *Trusted* **then**
24: $\triangleright$ Label is Trusted âĂŞ drone is safe
25:         **end if**
26:     **end for**
27:     **Step 4: Return Results**
28:     **return** TS, L_{mal}
29: **end procedure**

2.5 Machine Learning-Based Model

To overcome the limitations of traditional trust assessment methods, such as linear weighted models that lack adaptability to dynamic and nonlinear swarm behavior [8]. We adopt an ML-based framework with separate regression and classification stages [14]. In the regression stage, SVR, RF, and CNN are used to estimate the swarm coordination rate as a continuous trust metric. These models were selected for their robustness to noise (RF), ability to capture nonlinear relationships (SVR), and capability to learn complex temporal-spatial patterns (CNN). In the classification stage, RF, SVM, and CNN are used to assign trust labels. SVM was chosen for its margin-maximizing properties, while RF and CNN handle diverse, high-dimensional features effectively.

Each drone mutually checks its predicted behavior with the actual behavior of the drone in a swarm network. The DT-based Trust System creates a DT pattern for information exchange for each drone to predict expected behavior in real-time. Trust is calculated by comparing predicted and observed metrics such as social, centrality, and sensor health. This enables dynamic, data-driven trust evaluation and detection of malicious behavior using ML models like RF, SVM, and CNN in swarm networks.

3 Experimental Evaluation

To evaluate the trust prediction capabilities of our proposed framework, we applied the proposed approach in a controlled swarm simulation environment. The algorithm integrates a two-stage ML process, combining regression and classification. In the regression stage, SVR, RF, and CNN are used to estimate the swarm coordination rate as a continuous trust indicator. A more detailed description of the experimental design is provided in Section VI of the paper [6].

3.1 Experimentation Setup

We conducted our experiments on a 64-bit Windows 10 system equipped with an 11th Gen Intel Core i7-1165G7, 2.80GHz CPU with 16 GB RAM, using Python version 3.12.6. The drone simulation environment was developed using Unreal Engine integrated with Microsoft's AirSim plugin [12]. Each simulation iteration involved three clusters of three autonomous drones each. During 15 iterations, more than 100 drones were simulated in various dynamic cluster configurations. A custom-built DT plugin was implemented in Python. The dataset generated from these simulations was analyzed using TensorFlow-based ML and DL models within a Jupyter Notebook environment configured via Anaconda[1].

3.2 Result Analysis

The results of malicious drone detection are analyzed using various attacks, including Sybil, MITM, critical node and data manipulation attacks. A range of ML and DL models, such as RF, SVR and CNN are employed to check the consistency between the drone's actual and declared behavior, and classify them as malicious or trustworthy.

3.3 Threat Model Analysis

Trust management in drone swarms is vulnerable to attacks such as impersonation, data manipulation, and communication disruption [1]. We simulated four common attack types to evaluate the resilience of our trust model. Trusted drones maintained high and stable coordination, while malicious drones showed low and fluctuating coordination, especially under manipulation attacks (Fig. 2).

---

[1] Source code and replication package: https://github.com/danish745/AIRism-Attack-Evaluation-Trial-by-Twin-Replication.

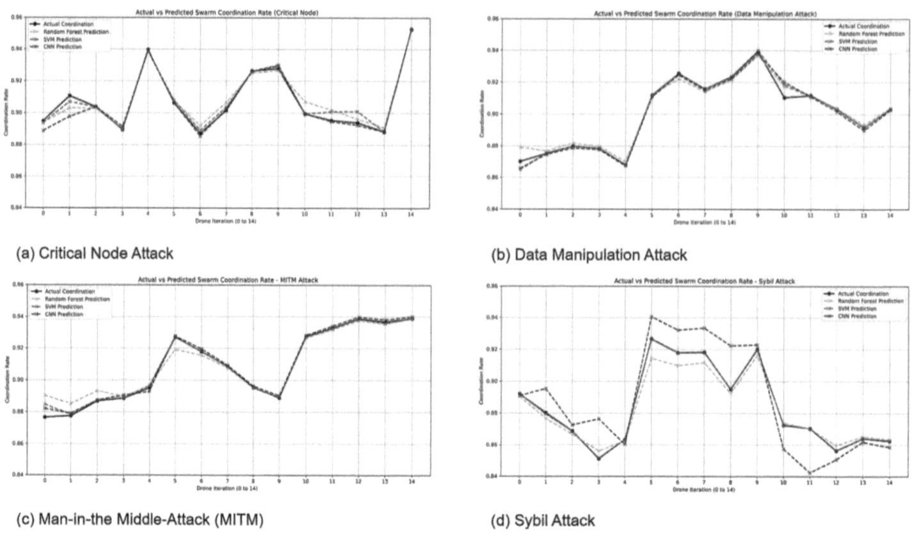

(a) Critical Node Attack

(b) Data Manipulation Attack

(c) Man-in-the Middle-Attack (MITM)

(d) Sybil Attack

Fig. 2. Injected Trust Attacks Result.

1. **Critical Node Attack (CNA):** This attack targeted drones that serve a pivotal role in network topology within the swarm network, possessing more weight and a high centrality (Fig. 2a). A malicious node either impersonates or disables such a critical node, causing a significant disturbance in the network structure.
2. **Data Manipulation Attack (DMA):** In this attack, a malicious drone manipulated its telemetry data, including behavioral and social metrics such as speed, location, and sensor health (Fig. 2b). The manipulated values deviated from the predicted metrics generated by its internal model, resulting in inconsistencies between declared and actual behavior.
3. **Man-in-the-Middle Attack (MITM):** In a MITM Attack, malicious drones intercept and delay communication among other drones in the swarm (Fig. 2c). By injecting artificial latency and causing packet loss, the attacker impaired message reliability and increased communication risk.
4. **Sybil Attack (SA):** In the execution of this attack, we injected multiple fake drone identities or replicated the behavior of trusted drones in the swarm (Fig. 2d). These fake drones are utilized to interfere in swarm networks by emulating communication patterns and creating deceptive topologies.

3.4 Model Evaluation and Results

MAE, RMSE, and R^2 are used to measure prediction performance. Table 1 summarizes the regression results and demonstrates a reliable approximation of the swarm's behavioral consistency under adversarial attack scenarios. This output provides a consistency check to improve trustworthiness in dynamic autonomous ecosystems in the classification stage.

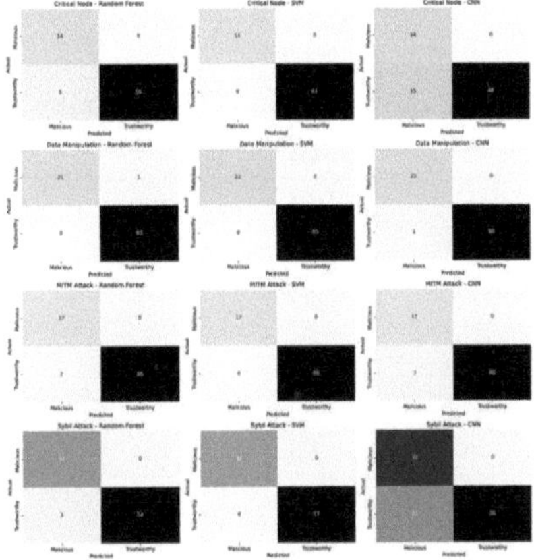

Fig. 3. Confusion Matrices by type of attack.

Table 1. Model performance across different attacks.

Attack	Model	MAE	RMSE	$R^2 Score$
Critical Node	SVR	0.002757	0.007296	0.9835
Critical Node	RF	0.006880	0.010678	0.9647
Critical Node	CNN	0.020762	0.030069	0.7201
Data Manipulation	SVR	0.001655	0.008511	0.9774
Data Manipulation	RF	0.004029	0.010209	0.9674
Data Manipulation	CNN	0.010640	0.018910	0.8883
MITM Attack	SVR	0.001429	0.006591	0.9838
MITM Attack	RF	0.004963	0.011097	0.9539
MITM Attack	CNN	0.014636	0.018688	0.8694
Sybil Attack	SVR	0.000634	0.000920	0.9998
Sybil Attack	RF	0.007965	0.013264	0.9512
Sybil Attack	CNN	0.032741	0.039606	0.5652

SVR and RF models yield the most reliable predictions across all attack types, with notably high R^2 scores and minimal error metrics (Table 1). These models effectively handle DMA and MITM attacks, showing strong predictive performance. In contrast, CNN performs poorly, particularly under SA and CNA, with significantly higher error rates and lower R^2 scores. Based on the results on the experiment, SVR can be used for the evaluation of the attacks in the first step of the proposed method to estimate the coordination rate under adversial trust attacks.

The confusion matrices (Fig. 3) illustrate the classification performance of three models, RF, SVM, and CNN, under various trust-related attack scenarios, including Critical Node, Data Manipulation, MITM, and Sybil attacks. The x-axis of each matrix represents predicted labels (Malicious or Trustworthy), while the y-axis denotes the actual labels. RF and SVM demonstrate superior classification performance across most attacks, particularly in the MITM and DMA cases, where the predictions closely align with actual behavior. CNN shows moderate effectiveness but suffers noticeable misclassifications, especially in the SA and CNA, where several trustworthy drones are incorrectly labeled as malicious.

These patterns are quantitatively supported by the classification metrics summarized in Table 2, which reports precision, recall, F1-score, and accuracy for each model-attack combination. As shown, SA and CNA tend to have higher misclassification rates, indicating a greater disruption to behavioral patterns and trust inference. In contrast, MITM and DMA yield clearer class separation, resulting in higher reliability across models.

The evaluation results demonstrate the level of accuracy of the proposed approach to assess the dynamic behavior of autonomous drone swarms within autonomous ecosystems. Particularly, the regression stage estimated low prediction errors across various attack scenarios to estimate the coordination rate as a consistency feature among actual and predicted behavior during the collaboration of autonomous drones in a swarm network. The subsequent classification stage helped in achieving distinct classification

Table 2. Classification metrics across various attack scenarios.

Attack	Model	Accuracy	Precision	Recall	F1 Score	Support (Malicious)	Support (Trustworthy)
CNA	RF	0.9333	1.0000	0.9180	0.9573	14	61
CNA	SVM	1.0000	1.0000	1.0000	1.0000	14	61
CNA	CNN	0.7867	1.0000	0.7377	0.8491	14	61
DMA	RF	0.9905	0.9881	1.0000	0.9940	22	83
DMA	SVM	1.0000	1.0000	1.0000	1.0000	22	83
DMa	CNN	0.9429	1.0000	0.9277	0.9625	22	83
MITM	RF	0.9810	1.0000	0.9773	0.9885	17	88
MITM	SVM	1.0000	1.0000	1.0000	1.0000	17	88
MITM	CNN	0.9048	1.0000	0.8864	0.9398	17	88
SA	RF	0.9462	1.0000	0.9359	0.9669	15	78
SA	SVM	1.0000	1.0000	1.0000	1.0000	15	78
SA	CNN	0.8387	0.9846	0.8205	0.8951	15	78

between trust states to be run in every iteration in real-time to identify the trustworthiness of drones.

4   Conclusion

This paper presented a behavior-predictive trust assessment approach through runtime compliance checking by leveraging predictive behavior modeled via a DT for autonomous drone swarms. Functional, social, and centrality metrics were used to represent predicted behavior during swarm collaboration and evaluated under various trust-related attacks, including Critical Node, Data Manipulation, MITM, and SA. To identify the level of trust in a swarm within autonomous ecosystems, we proposed a two-stage approach with regression to calculate the predicted coordination rate of the swarm of drones followed by classification stage for the trustworthiness of the drones. Finally, the proposed behavior-predictive trust framework using DT offers an effective mechanism for identifying and isolating malicious drones in real-time, ensuring safer swarm coordination in autonomous drone ecosystems. In future work, we plan to enhance the framework with additional metrics, scale it to larger swarms, and implement real-time DT integration in more dynamic and realistic environments.

Acknowledgment. The work was supported by GAMU project "Forensic Support for Building Trust in Smart Software Ecosystems" (no. MUNI/G/1142/2022).

References

1. Akram, J., Anaissi, A., Rathore, R.S., Jhaveri, R.H., Akram, A.: Digital twin-driven trust management in open ran-based spatial crowdsourcing drone services. IEEE Trans. Green Commun. Networking (2024)
2. Cioroaica, E., Chren, S., Buhnova, B., Kuhn, T., Dimitrov, D.: Reference architecture for trust-based digital ecosystems. In: 2020 IEEE International Conference on Software Architecture Companion (ICSA-C), pp. 266–273. IEEE (2020)
3. Conti, F.C., Santoro, C., Santoro, F.F.: Twinflie: a digital twin uav orchestrator and simulator. In: 2023 IEEE Intl Conf on Dependable, Autonomic and Secure Computing, International Conference on Pervasive Intelligence and Computing, International Conference on Cloud and Big Data Computing, Intl Conf on Cyber Science and Technology Congress (DASC/PiCom/CBDCom/CyberSciTech), pp. 0258–0263. IEEE (2023)
4. Gupta, L., Jain, R., Vaszkun, G.: Survey of important issues in uav communication networks. IEEE Commun. Surv. Tutorials $18(2)$, 1123–1152 (2015)
5. Iqbal, D., Buhnova, B.: Model-based approach for building trust in autonomous drones through digital twins. In: 2022 IEEE International Conference on Systems, Man, and Cybernetics (SMC), pp. 656–662 (2022). https://doi.org/10.1109/SMC53654.2022.9945227
6. Iqbal, D., Buhnova, B.: Digital twin design for autonomous drones. In: 2024 19th Conference on Computer Science and Intelligence Systems (FedCSIS), pp. 119–130 (2024). https://doi.org/10.15439/2024F6765
7. Iqbal., D., Buhnova., B., Cioroaica., E.: Digital twins for trust building in autonomous drones through dynamic safety evaluation. In: Proceedings of the 18th International Conference on Evaluation of Novel Approaches to Software Engineering - ENASE, pp. 629–639. INSTICC, SciTePress (2023)
8. Jayasinghe, U., Lee, G.M., Um, T.W., Shi, Q.: Machine learning based trust computational model for iot services. IEEE Trans. Sustain. Comput. $4(1)$, 39–52 (2018)
9. Khan, N.A., Brohi, S.N., Jhanjhi, N.: Uav s applications, architecture, security issues and attack scenarios: a survey. In: Intelligent Computing and Innovation on Data Science: Proceedings of ICTIDS 2019, pp. 753–760. Springer (2020)
10. Lee, J.D., See, K.A.: Trust in automation: designing for appropriate reliance. Hum. Factors $46(1)$, 50–80 (2004)
11. Rahimzadagan, N., Vahs, M., Leite, I., Stower, R.: Drone fail me now: how drone failures affect trust and risk-taking decisions. In: Companion of the 2024 ACM/IEEE International Conference on Human-Robot Interaction (2024)
12. Shah, S., Dey, D., Lovett, C., Kapoor, A.: Airsim: high-fidelity visual and physical simulation for autonomous vehicles. In: Field and Service Robotics (2017). https://arxiv.org/abs/1705.05065
13. Skopik, F., Schall, D., Dustdar, S.: Modeling and mining of dynamic trust in complex service-oriented systems. Springer (2011)
14. Tangade, S., Kumaar, R.A., Azam, F., et al.: Detection of malicious nodes in flying ad-hoc network with supervised machine learning. In: 2022 Third International Conference on Smart Technologies in Computing, Electrical and Electronics (ICSTCEE), pp. 1–5. IEEE (2022)
15. Teng, M., Gao, C., Wang, Z., Li, X.: A communication-based identification of critical drones in malicious drone swarm networks. Complex Intell. Syst. $10(3)$, 3197–3211 (2024)

Inferring a Hierarchical Input Type for Plug-and-Play SQL

Santosh Aryal[1], Shubham Swami[1], Curtis Dyreson[1(✉)] [ID],
and Sourav S. Bhowmick[2] [ID]

[1] Department of Computer Science, Utah State University, Logan, UT, USA
{a02345936,curtis.dyreson}@usu.edu
[2] Nanyang Technological University, Singapore, Singapore
assourav@ntu.edu.sg
https://www.usu.edu/cs/people/CurtisDyreson/ ,
https://personal.ntu.edu.sg/assourav/

Abstract. Plug-and-play queries simplify the process of writing SQL queries. In plug-and-play SQL a programmer uses a query guard to specify a query's input type. The input type is the shape of the data needed by a query. The input type can be matched to a database's schema to determine whether the query can be safely evaluated. Plug-and-play queries are portable, easier to write, and are type safe. But plug-and-play queries depend on the programmer to provide an input type. Since the programmer could err in sketching the input type this paper shows how to *infer* the input type from the query itself, thereby removing the need for manual construction. We consider two cases for inferring the input type: with and without knowledge of the database's schema. Knowing the schema can help to prune the input type, making it smaller and more flexible. This paper describes the inference algorithm.

Keywords: Plug-and-Play · SQL · Query Guards · Guard Inference

1 Introduction

A database query has an input type and an output type; the query transforms data from the input to the output type. For database query languages there are two kinds of input type, 1) either a generic type, *e.g., Any*, or 2) (a subset of) a database's schema. In languages for schemaless databases, like XQuery and Cypher, the input type is generic. There is no compiler type check for the input type, instead a query will evaluate on any data collection, producing an empty result if a path expression in the query fails to navigate to desired data. In languages for databases that have a schema, such as SQL, the input type is the names of tables and columns that appear in the query, which is a subset of a schema. The compiler checks the input type and generates an error if there is a mismatch.

In plug-and-play SQL, instead of a generic type or a subset of the schema, a *query guard* is used as the input type [5]. The query guard is a conceptual

C. Cappiello et al. (Eds.): CoopIS 2025, LNCS 15535, pp. 684–695, 2026.
https://doi.org/10.1007/978-3-032-15538-2_45

model that succinctly describes the necessary *miniworld* for query evaluation. A query together with the conceptual model of the data needed by the query is type matched to the schema of the database. The match produces a transformed query that is executable against the schema as well as a report on type errors or potential information loss in the transformation. Using a conceptual model as the input type makes a query type safe, portable, easier to code, and more resilient to schema changes.

In this paper we extend our previous work to show how to automatically *infer* a hierarchical input type for an SQL query. One potential problem with query guards is that the guard and the query are specified in separate clauses, so the two parts of a plug-and-play query could be out of sync. The guard may mention names not present in the query, or vice-versa. Additionally a manually constructed query guard may not best express the input type for the query. Finally, information on the input type could help a query writer to craft a query in, for instance, a query integrated development environment (IDE). To address these shortcomings, this paper presents an algorithm to infer an input type for an SQL query. The algorithm parses a query and constructs a query guard that represents the input type. We show how the input type can be pruned to make it smaller and more flexible. The inference algorithm is possible to run without knowledge of the schema though the schema helps, in particular, in pruning an inferred input type.

The primary contribution of this paper is this guard inference algorithm for plug-and-play SQL (Sect. 3). This paper is organized as follows. The next section reviews and motivates query guards for plug-and-play SQL. Section 3 gives an algorithm for inferring a query guard from an SQL query. The paper concludes with a short summary and gives some avenues for continuing the research in the future.

2 Motivating Plug-and-Play Queries

In this section we review the motivation for plug-and-play queries described in more detail elsewhere [5].

In his seminal paper on the relational model, E. F. Codd identified *access path dependence* as one of the drawbacks of the hierarchical model [2]. Codd pointed out that queries in a hierarchical (or network) model necessarily have to use access paths ("dot" operators) to navigate to desired data. The access paths tightly couple the query to a specific hierarchy, which is problematic since the same data could be organized in different hierarchies, so a query written for one hierarchy would fail if the same data were organized differently. Access path dependence decreases query portability and increases the brittleness of queries to changes in the structure of the data.

But hierarchical data also makes some aspects of querying potentially easier. First, access paths in hierarchical queries are simpler and more straightforward to express than joins in a relational database, an advantage also present in graph queries in languages such as Cypher and GQL, and in SQL for SurrealDB, which uses a RELATE clause to build relationships between tables that can be navigated by path expressions. Joins are implicitly embedded in a hierarchical data structure, performed when creating the data model, and these embedded joins in the data are easily navigated with a path expression. Second, grouping and aggregation can be more naturally expressed in hierarchical data. Their expression in SQL has been shown to be cognitively challenging for many users, especially programmers learning SQL [1,4,6]. Third, Codd's critique of access path dependence applies only to *stored* hierarchies. Hierarchies computed when a query is evaluated, which we call *virtual hierarchies* [3], have no such dependence.

We leveraged virtual hierarchies to support plug-and-play SQL. Plug-and-play SQL pairs a query to a hierarchical specification of its input type, we call the specification a *query guard*, to create a plug-and-play query. We motivate the utility of query guards with an example. Suppose that we have a relational database with data about biological specimens collected in the field. A user could query the database using the query in Fig. 1 to retrieve the names of botanists who collected *Asteraceae* (plants in the Daisy family) specimens in 2023. The query joins the `taxa`, `occurrences`, and `collectors` tables, applies the appropriate selection conditions, and projects the name of the botanist. The query explicitly uses logical pointers (foreign key to key associations) from the `taxa` table to the `occurrences` and `collectors` tables. We can rewrite the query as a plug-and-play SQL query using a query guard as shown in Fig. 2. The guard specifies the *shape* or type of the *input* to the query. The guard stipulates that the query can be evaluated on any data collection that has this hierarchy, or that can be converted or transformed to the desired shape (within information loss guarantees).

```
SELECT collectors.name
FROM taxa, occurrences, collectors
WHERE taxa.tid = occurrences.tid AND collectors.id = occurrences.collid
  AND taxa.family = 'Asteraceae' AND occurrences.year = 2023
```

Fig. 1. Retrieve the names of botanists who collected *Asteraceae* specimens in 2023.

One big advantage of plug-and-play SQL queries is that they are *portable.* The query in Fig. 2 is portable to data collections that have different shapes (*i.e.,* we do not care how many steps are involved in "joining" the tables to construct the hierarchy). A second advantage is that the hierarchy naturally *groups* the data, and the grouping can be exploited in a query for aggregation. Suppose for instance we only wanted those collectors who collected more than 40 specimens then we could modify the query as shown in Fig. 3. Querying against a hierarchy simplifies grouping and aggregation (as in XQuery and Cypher).

```
GUARD {
   collectors {
       name,
       occurrences {
           family,
           year
           }
       }
   }
SELECT name
WHERE family = 'Asteraceae'
       AND year = 2023
```

Fig. 2. Retrieve the names of those who collected *Asteraceae* specimens in 2023.

```
GUARD {
   collectors {
       name,
       occurrences {
           family,
           year
           }
       }
   }
SELECT name
WHERE family = 'Asteraceae'
       AND year = 2023 AND COUNT(*) > 40
```

Fig. 3. Who collected more than 40 *Asteraceae* specimens in 2023.

```
SELECT A.name
FROM (SELECT name, count(*) as C
      FROM collectors
              LEFT OUTER JOIN occurrences ON collectors.id = occurrences.collid
              LEFT OUTER JOIN taxa ON occurrences.'taxon ID' = taxa.'taxon ID'
      WHERE family = 'Asteraceae' AND year = 2023
      GROUP BY name
      HAVING count(*) > 40
      ) A
```

Fig. 4. SQL for retrieving who collected *Asteraceae* specimens in 2023.

Elsewhere we describe how to match the guard to the database's schema and generate an SQL query [5]. The matching and generation process produces the query given in Fig. 4 for the plug-and-play query of Fig. 3. The code for the project is open-source and available from https://github.com/cdyreson/PlugAndPlaySQL.

3 Guard Inference

In this section we consider the problem of inferring a query guard from an SQL query. Guard inference will help to convert existing SQL queries into plug-and-play queries. Inference will also aid in writing queries by helping query writers create a guard and by generating a guard as feedback for a user in, for instance, an integrated development environment; the guard could be generated in a side panel to aid in query construction and modification.

In general the problem is given an SQL query to generate a query guard. We first consider query guard generation with knowledge of the schema. Knowledge of the schema helps to both infer the guard and to *prune* or refine the guard, making it more general and smaller. Typically queries are constructed with respect to a given schema, but plug-and-play queries are designed to be portable so we would anticipate schema-less construction is possible.

This section is divided into four parts. First, we describe overall design goals for the inference algorithm. Next, we introduce the algorithm, called the Guard Generation Algorithm, which is a detailed guide for building the guard for an SQL query. We focus on the common subset of SQL, namely, SPJ (select-project-join) queries [8]. We also discuss pruning techniques to reduce the size of the guard. Finally, we analyze the complexity of the algorithm.

3.1   Design Goals

The process of inferring a hierarchical input type has several goals that should be observed to produce a "good" hierarchy.

- **Accuracy:** The inferred hierarchy must accurately mirror the query's structural demands, reflecting the precise relationships between the tables involved in the query.
- **Declarative and Reusable:** The hierarchy should maintain a standard form, free from specific data dependencies, enabling its reuse across multiple queries with similar structural demands.
- **Concise:** The hierarchy should eliminate all non-essential elements, promoting ease of interpretation and modification.
- **Completeness:** The input type should include (at a minimum), all of the names necessary to produce the output type. The query maps an input type to an output type and if the input type fails to include a name in the output type, the query result will necessarily be incomplete.

3.2   Example Inference

As an example, consider the query given in Fig. 4. There are nine names in the query: `taxa`, `occurrences`, `collectors.name`, `taxa.tid`, `occurrences.tid`, `collectors.id`, `occurrences.collid`, `taxa.family`, and `occurrences.year` that should be arranged in a hierarchy.

We observe that there is a natural parent to child relationship between table and column names. The "dot" operator shows which column names can be naturally placed as children of table names. We will call each constructed tree a *table tree*. The table trees for the query given in Fig. 4 are shown in Fig. 5.

The next step is to organize the table trees in a hierarchy. We observe that there are certain column names that must be in the result, in particular, columns named in a GROUP BY are important since the data is grouped using those columns. Second, columns that appear in the SELECT clause are a key part of the input type. In the inferred hierarchy these important columns should be closer to the top of the tree. Each column name is assigned a weight to signify its importance in the input type, with GROUP BY and SELECT column names given the highest weight. The weight of a table tree is the sum of the weights of its

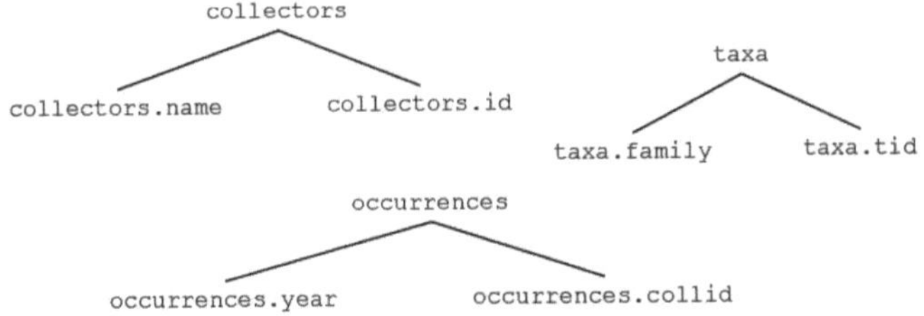

Fig. 5. The table trees for the query given in Fig. 4.

column names. Table trees are then placed in a hierarchy based on their weight, the highest being selected first, the next highest second, etc. Table trees that are not related (through some association, *e.g.,* a join on foreign keys, between the tables) can be made siblings since the tables are orthogonal. For the query given in Fig. 4 the table trees are organized in the hierarchy given in Fig. 6. First, **taxa** or **collectors** could be selected since they each have exactly one column that appears in the SELECT clause; they are not siblings since they are related through **occurrences**. Then **occurrences** is placed at the bottom since it has no columns in the SELECT clause.

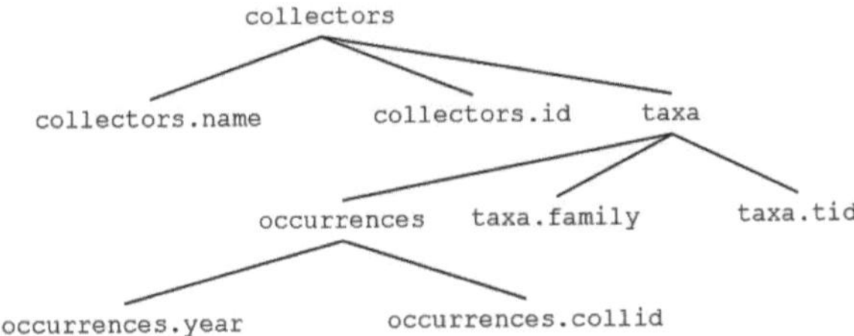

Fig. 6. The table trees organized in a hierarchy.

Finally schema knowledge helps us prune column and table names, and sometimes table trees. Some of the column names are unique in the schema so the table name can be removed. Note also that the **occurrences** table name is related (in the WHERE clause) to both the **taxa** and **collectors** names, through a join on foreign keys. These joins are generated by the evaluation of the guard so do not need to be present in the guard. Both optimizations are illustrated in Fig. 7 that result in the hierarchy shown in Fig. 8.

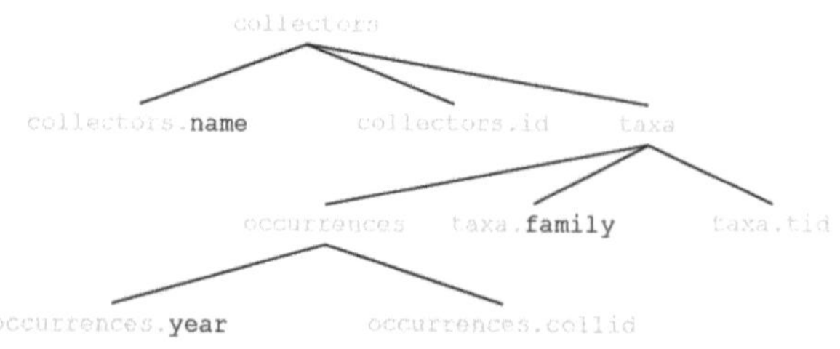

Fig. 8. The hierarchy after optimization.

Fig. 7. The optimizations applied to the hierarchy of Fig. 6. Names that are shaded can be pruned.

Input Type Modifications. In general an SQL query, Q, maps an input type, I, to an output type, T. I is a set of table names, $t_1, \ldots, t_n$, and column names that are unambiguously associated with a specific table, $t_1.c_1, \ldots, t_k.c_m$. The input type is strict in the sense that if one of the column or table names present in the query is absent in the schema, the query will not compile. Let $\mathcal{S}_I$ be the set of schemas for which Q will compile. Q trivially has the following "flat hierarchy" guard, which naturally expresses the FROM clause in Q (essentially just a list of the table trees).

```
GUARD {
    t₁ { t₁.c₁,... all columns associated with t₁ },
    ...
    tₙ { tₙ.c₁,... all columns associated with tₙ }
}
```

Building the hierarchy creates relationships among the table trees and so a guard with a non-flat hierarchy will *narrow* the input type I. Suppose input type I' places t_1 as a child of t_2 in the guard, then $\mathcal{S}_{I'} \subseteq \mathcal{S}_I$.

Narrowing type conversions in programming languages, *e.g.*, from a float to an integer, are information conserving. *Widening* conversions however, potentially lose information. If we remove the name $t_i.c_x$ from the guard G yielding G' then the set of schemas for which the plug-and-play query with guard G' is larger than that with guard G, *i.e.*, $\mathcal{S}_G \subseteq \mathcal{S}_{G'}$. Moreover, there is the potential to further widen the input type by removing table names, at the smallest yielding a guard just built from the names that must be present in the output type, $c_1, \ldots, c_m$. Each nane removed from the queries widens the set of potential schemas that match the reduced input type.

So a plug-and-play query can be made more flexible through *pruning*, but may be widened to types match input types very different from the schema for which the query was originally crafted. Hence, we see the pruning as creating a range of potential guards from which a query writer can select a guard to pair with the query.

3.3   Algorithm

The guard generation algorithm is given in Algorithm 1.

We make two assumptions. First that the schema is available to disambiguate column names (determining which table each column belongs to) and to help determine which tables are related through joins on foreign keys. Second that a query, Q, is parsed to produce the following.

- A set of subqueries, Q_s, in the WHERE or HAVING clauses.
- A set of queries, Q_f, that construct tables in the FROM clause.
- A set of table names, T, and a set of column names, C, where T and C are names from the parts of Q not in Q_s or Q_f.
- A set of undirected edges, J, from table $x \in T$ to table $y \in T$ if x is *related* to y by an inner or left outer join on some association (foreign key).

The algorithm starts by initializing dictionaries to map a column to the table to which it belongs and to record the column weight. The next step parses the query. Parsing identifies the output columns, the tables involved, conditions linked to these tables, and the weight of each column. The guard is recursively constructed, with each subquery and query in the FROM clause generating a guard that will be incorporated into the query. Table trees are then formed and assigned weights. The guard is then formed by selecting the table trees, from the tree with the highest weight to that with the lowest weight.

After a guard is constructed it can be, if desired, pruned. The pruning process eliminates the specification of table names from the guard as well as joins on foreign keys since those are reconstructed in the plug-and-play evaluation of the guard.

Example 1 (Subquery - schema is available). The second example is for a query with a subquery. This query given below performs a semi-join between two tables.

```
SELECT name
FROM collectors
WHERE ID IN (
    SELECT "collector id"
    FROM occurrences
    WHERE locale LIKE "Utah"
)
```

The inferred guard is shown below.

```
GUARD {
    collectors {
        name,
        occurrences {
          "collector id",
          locale
        }
    }
}
```

To infer the guard, the algorithm goes through the following steps.

Algorithm 1. Guard Inference with Schema Knowledge.

Input: SQL query Q

Output: Guard G representing the hierarchical input type

   /* Initialize global variables   */

```
 1  ColumnWeightsMap ← new Map()
 2  RelatedMap ← new Map()
    /* Generate guard, use an initial weight of 1                          */
 3  return computeGuard(Q, 1)
 4
 5  Function computeGuard(Q, w)
 6  |   TableTreesList ← []
 7  |   TreesPriorityQueue ← new Priority Queue() /* Parse Q, see the algorithm
    |       description for details of the parse results                    */
 8  |   (Q_s, Q_f, T, C, R) ← parse(Q)
 9  |   for each column, c ∈ C do
10  |   |   currentWeight ← ColumnWeightsMap.get(c)? ColumnWeightsMap.get(c) : 0
11  |   |   if c appears in the SELECT or GROUP BY then
12  |   |   |   ColumnWeightsMap.put(c, currentWeight + w)
13  |   |   end
14  |   end
    |   /* Recursively process subqueries in Q_s, decrease column weight in
    |       subquery                                                        */
15  |   for each subquery q ∈ Q_s do
16  |   |   TableTreesList.pushAll(computeGuard(q, w * 0.1))
17  |   end
    |   /* Recursively process tables constructed by SELECTs in the FROM clause,
    |       Q_f                                                             */
18  |   for each SELECT query q ∈ Q_f do
19  |   |   TableTreesList.pushAll(computeGuard(q, w))
20  |   end
    |   /* Calculate the weight of each tree, sum, is a function that sums the
    |       values of all columns in the tree, and place the tree in a priority
    |       queue based (prioritize by lowest to highest)                  */
21  |   for each t in TableTreesList do
22  |   |   TreesPriorityQueue.add(t, sum(t)
23  |   end
    |   /* Build the hierarchy                                             */
24  |   G ← {}
25  |   while TreesPriorityQueue.notEmpty() do
    |   |   /* Get the next tree from the priority queue                   */
26  |   |   t ← TreesPriorityQueue.poll()
    |   |   /* Look for a related tree, root is a function that gets the root
    |   |       table name in the tree                                     */
27  |   |   for each root(t), v ∈ J do
28  |   |   |   if ∃r[r ∈ G ∧ v = root(r)] then
29  |   |   |   |   t.addChild(r)
30  |   |   |   |   G.remove(r)
31  |   |   |   end
32  |   |   end
33  |   |   G.add(t)
34  |   end
35  |   return G
```

---

1. **Weight Columns:** The SELECT clause specifies `name` as the output column in the outer query, so it is given a higher weight.
2. **Form Table Trees:** The outer query has one table tree and the inner query also contributes a table tree. The weight of the outer table tree is higher than that of the inner query table tree.
3. **Generate Hierarchy:** The outer query table tree is chosen as the root, with the inner query table tree placed as its child.
4. **Pruning:** The guard could be further simplified by promoting one of the highest weighted columns to be the root of the table tree and reasoning about the foreign key to eliminate the join on the tables as given below.

```
GUARD {
    name {
        locale
    }
}
```

3.4 When the Schema Is Not Available

The schema helps in two cases. First, it enables columns to be unambiguously associated to tables (assuming the SQL query is semantically well-formed, ambiguous columns will be flagged by the SQL compiler). So each column can be associated to a table tree. When the schema is not available, a special table tree, called the *unknown* table tree is introduced. During table tree construction (line 7 in Algorithm 1) a column that lacks a table name or variable is associated to the *unknown* table tree. In the guard, the highest weighted column is chosen to serve as the root of the *unknown* table tree. Second, the schema is used to prune columns associated with joins on foreign keys. But when the schema is not available foreign keys are not known, so such pruning cannot take place.

3.5 Complexity Analysis

Let n be the length of the SQL query, m be the number of columns involved in the SQL query, f be the number of foreign key relationships in the query between tables, and t be the number of tables. Then the guard inference algorithm has the following cost.

- **Parsing:** Parsing the query is $\mathcal{O}(n)$.
- **Assigning Weights to Columns:** Iterates over the extracted columns and assigning weights based on their presence in different clauses. The complexity is $\mathcal{O}(m)$, where m is the number of columns involved in the query.
- **Determining the Table Relationships:** Analyzing the relationships between tables, for JOIN operations and subqueries, involves parsing and understanding the structure of the query. This complexity is $\mathcal{O}(f)$, where f is the number of foreign key relationships or JOIN conditions in the query.

- **Building Table Trees:** This step costs $\mathcal{O}(m)$ as each column is assigned to a single tree, and summing the weights requires iterating over each tree.
- **Building the Hierarchy:** Constructing the hierarchical guard structure involves choosing trees which costs $\mathcal{O}(t)$, since there is one tree per table.
- **Pruning**: Iterates over the guard, which is $\mathcal{O}(m + t)$ in size.

Combining these, the time complexity for the algorithm is $\mathcal{O}(n + m + f + t)$.

4   Conclusions and Future Work

Ae query guard is a specification of the query's input type, that is, the structure or shape of the data that the query needs in order to correctly evaluate. The combination of query guard and query creates a plug-and-play query. Plug-and-play queries are more portable, more reliable because they are input type safe, and are potentially easier to write.

In this paper we showed how to infer a query guard from an SQL query. We also described how a guard can be pruned during the inference to create a smaller guard. Guard inference is important to help ensure that the query guard in is sync with the query. The inferred guard can be generated as the query is constructed, providing guidance to a user constructing a query. The automatically inferred guard can also be compared to a manually constructed guard to check for correctness of the latter.

In the future we plan to investigate whether there is a better way to express a query guard, *i.e.*, what is the best conceptual model to use? Concurrent with this effort we will conduct a user survey to help evaluate the effectiveness of plug-and-play SQL in lowering the time and effort to write queries. The user survey will investigate the use of different conceptual models using a randomized approach [7]. The user survey requires a separate treatment than this paper, which focuses on conceptual modeling. We also plan to expand the range of queries we handle to include subqueries, relational operations (union, intersection, and difference), and data modification.

Acknowledgements. This work was supported in part by the National Science Foundation under Award No. DBI-1759965, *Collaborative Research: ABI Development: Symbiota2: Enabling greater collaboration and flexibility for mobilizing biodiversity data.*

References

1. Ahadi, A., Prior, J., Behbood, V., Lister, R.: A quantitative study of the relative difficulty for novices of writing seven different types of SQL queries. In: Proceedings of the 2015 ACM Conference on Innovation and Technology in Computer Science Education, ITiCSE 2015, pp. 201–206 (2015)
2. Codd, E.F.: A relational model of data for large shared data banks. CACM **13**(6), 377–387 (1970)

3. Dyreson, C.E., Bhowmick, S.S., Grapp, R.: Virtual exist-db: liberating hierarchical queries from the shackles of access path dependence. PVLDB **8**(12), 1932–1943 (2015)
4. Poulsen, S., Butler, L., Alawini, A., Herman, G.L.: Insights from student solutions to sql homework problems. In: Proceedings of the 2020 ACM Conference on Innovation and Technology in Computer Science Education, pp. 404–410 (2020)
5. Swami, S., Aryal, S., Bhowmick, S.S., Dyreson, C.E.: Using a conceptual model in plug-and-play SQL. In: Conceptual Modeling - 42nd International Conference, ER 2023. Lecture Notes in Computer Science, vol. 14320, pp. 145–161. Springer (2023). https://doi.org/10.1007/978-3-031-47262-6_8
6. Taipalus, T., Siponen, M., Vartiainen, T.: Errors and complications in SQL query formulation. ACM Trans. Comput. Educ. **18**(3) (2018)
7. Uesbeck, P.M., Peterson, C.S., Sharif, B., Stefik, A.: A randomized controlled trial on the effects of embedded computer language switching. In: ESEC/FSE '20: 28th ACM Joint European Software Engineering Conference and Symposium on the Foundations of Software Engineering, pp. 410–420. ACM (2020)
8. Weiss, Y.Y., Cohen, S.: Reverse engineering spj-queries from examples. In: Sallinger, E., den Bussche, J.V., Geerts, F. (eds.) Proceedings of the 36th Symposium on Principles of Database Systems, PODS, pp. 151–166. ACM (2017)

Automated Duplicate Bugs Detection: Do We Really Need All Bug Report Sections?

Lobna Ghadhab[1], Ilyes Jenhani[2], Montassar Ben Messaoud[3(✉)],
and Mohamed Wiem Mkaouer[4]

[1] LARODEC, Higher Institute of Management of Sousse, Sousse, Tunisia
lobna.ghadhab@larodec.rnu.tn
[2] University of Doha for Science and Technology, Doha, Qatar
ilyes.jenhani@udst.edu.qa
[3] University of Tunis, LARODEC, Tunis Business School, Tunis, Tunisia
montassar.benmessaoud@tbs.u-tunis.tn
[4] University of Michigan, Flint, USA
mmkaouer@umich.edu

Abstract. Duplicate bugs pose a significant challenge that consumes substantial resources and can complicate the bug triage process, requiring extra work to identify and merge duplicates. Several automated duplicate bug detection methods use Natural Language Processing to handle this problem. Bug reports are often long and contain multiple sections that can show some textual (dis)similarities. This disparity may affect the duplicate bug detection process and hence results in inefficient resource utilization. In this work, we study the impact of bug report sections on the detection of duplicates especially when these sections show some (dis)similarities. Filtering out the most pertinent sections can greatly alleviate computational load and reduce the chances of overlooking potential duplicate bugs. Using less sections would also reduce the cost of the duplicate bug detection system as less tokens may be used. To achieve our objective, we developed and analyzed two types of models. One section-based models are used to analyze the individual impact of bug report sections, whereas cross section-based models are used to analyze their collective impact. These models leverage a siamese network constructed from pretrained DistilRoBERTa [1] and fine-tuned for classification by the Multi-Layer Perceptron (MLP). Our findings reveal that the "title" and "description" sections show the highest relevance in duplicate bug detection, achieving f1-scores of 98.93% and 98.29% respectively. Conversely, the "steps to reproduce" and "actual results" sections tend to cause confusion when distinguishing between duplicate reports, which often results in a high misclassification rate.

Keywords: Duplicate Bug Reports · Section Analysis · Pre-trained Neural Language Model · Distil-RoBERTa

---

I. Jenhani and M. Ben Messaoud—Equal contribution.

1 Introduction

Bug Tracking Systems (BTS) are essential tools in managing software bugs and facilitating collaboration among users. A major challenge in this process is the frequent submission of duplicate bug reports (BRs), which increases maintenance costs and resource usage. Identifying duplicates manually is often more challenging than submitting new reports, which underscores the need for automated detection. To address this, researchers have investigated approaches using Natural Language Processing (NLP), Information Retrieval (IR) [2] and Deep Learning (DL) [3,4]. Several of these methods have been applied in real-world systems. For instance, Bugzilla, a popular BTS, uses a mix of Duplicate Bug Report Detection (DBRD) techniques, such as full-text search, similarity matching, machine learning (ML) models, and keyword/metadata analysis.

As DBRD techniques evolve, understanding subtle differences between duplicate BRs is crucial for accurate detection, highlighting the importance of explainability in DBRD system design. Several studies have explored factors such as textual quality and dissimilarity to improve detection outcomes [5].

BRs consist of various components, including title, description (Desc), steps to reproduce the bug (S2R), actual results (AR) and expected results (ER). Although duplicate BRs often address the same issue, inconsistencies in these components, such as vague descriptions or missing S2R, can complicate detection. Additionally, non-duplicate BRs may contain similar content, further challenging DBRD models in distinguishing between duplicates and distinct reports.

In this study, we aim to investigate the challenges involved in detecting duplicate BRs, with a particular emphasis on the role of textual similarities and differences across core report sections (i.e., Title, Desc, S2R, AR and ER). Our central objective is to generate in-depth explanations and generate informed recommendations that can inform and inspire future research on the effective handling of these challenges.

We analyze the individual and combined effects of each BR section on DBRD performance, identifying conditions where misclassifications may occur. Our approach includes training models based on one section and based on cross sections, with similarity scores to distinguish BR pairs.

We also highlight the limitations of DBRD tools, which often produce false duplicates when critical BR information is missing. This study explores the impact of BR section analysis on reducing computational overhead, especially in real-time pre-submission scenarios, without sacrificing performance. By focusing on high-impact sections, we aim to improve efficiency and reduce time complexity in DBRD systems.

Our study differs from that of Patil et al. [6] in that their work employs an Information Retrieval (IR) approach to evaluate various methods for generating BRs to retrieve similar reports, whereas our focus is on the classification of duplicate BRs. Specifically, we investigate the impact of (dis)similarities within BR sections on classification performance. Our research aligns more closely with that of Jahan et al. [5].

This paper builds on an earlier version [7] by including the completed experiments and reporting extended results.

2   Methodology

This paper provides a granular analysis based on the use of individual (resp. various combinations of) BRs' sections, and their respective impacts on the DBRD classification performance. As depicted in Fig. 1, our study comprises two primary phases: data preparation and section-based analysis. To gain a better understanding of our model's predictions, we adopted LIME explainer [8] to provide interpretable explanations of how our models detect duplicate bug reports when featuring (dis)similar sections.

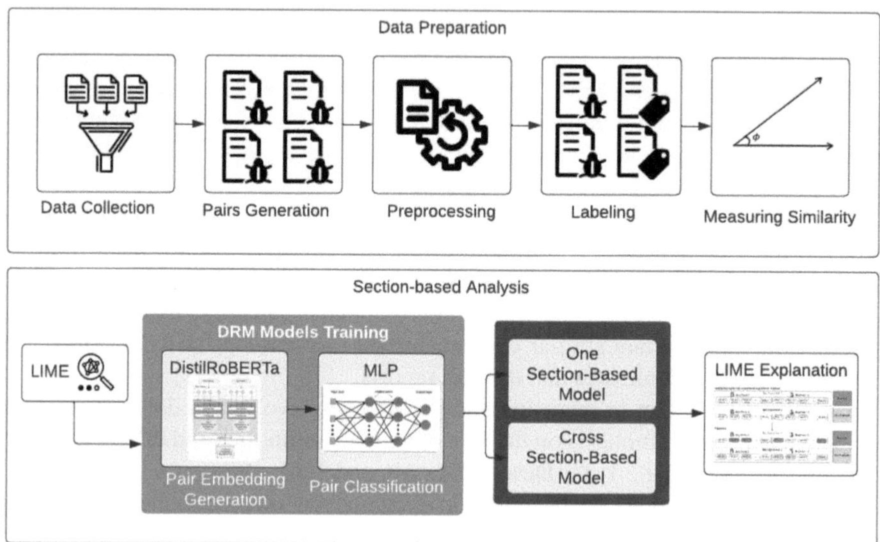

Fig. 1. Process of DBRD (dis)similarity analysis.

2.1   Data Preparation

We collected bug reports from three Mozilla datasets (Firefox, Core, Thunderbird), retaining only complete reports with all sections (Title, Desc, S2R, AR, ER), as summarized in Table 1. Duplicate and non-duplicate pairs were generated, preprocessed, and labeled. Their distributions are presented in Table 2. To measure textual (dis)similarities, we used SBERT (stsb-mpnet-base-v2) with cosine similarity, applying a threshold of 0.6 to distinguish similar vs. dissimilar sections.

2.2   Section-Based Analysis

As a primary contribution, our research aimed to investigate the specific impact of each section on the classification of BRs having (dis)similar sections. We made use of Distil-RoBERTa-MLP (DRM) model on each single section (i.e., Title, Desc, S2R, AR, and

Table 1. Total Number of bug reports vs. number of complete bug reports.

Project	Total number of BRs	Number of Complete BRs
Mz-Firefox	115029	57638
Mz-Core	201648	40278
Mz-Thunderbird	32501	15382

Table 2. Duplicate and Non-Duplicate Pairs Distributions.

Dataset	#Duplicate	#Non-Duplicate	Total
Mz-Firefox	3502	3444	6946
Mz-Core	3418	3858	7672
Mz-Thunderbird	3652	3558	7210

ER). For ease of comprehension, we have categorized these models as one section-based models (namely, @DRM_Title, @DRM_Desc, @DRM_S2R, @DRM_AR and @DRM_ER).

Building on the findings gained from our previous analysis relative to individual sections using one section-based models, we now extend our investigation to examine the effects of combining specific BR sections. This analysis aims to complement our initial contribution by identifying which sections, when combined, can show promise in identifying duplicate bug reports.

Our main contention, here, is that a better understanding of which sections should be combined can lead to more accurate, context-aware, and adaptable duplicate detection. From a software engineering perspective, this can help identify better patterns in reported issues. Specifically, it can assist users in entering only the sections that could aid bug tracking systems when recommending potential duplicates or at least ensuring that confusing sections are reported in a better way. Concretely speaking, we have tested three DRM models categorized as cross section-based models, with each model using a specific combination of bug report sections. Below is the list of these models along with their used sections.

- *@DRM_Full_BR:* uses all bug report sections,
- *@DRM_BR-AR* takes all bug report sections except AR,
- *@DRM_BR-[S2R+AR]:* eliminates S2R And AR from bug reprt pairs.

Embeddings Generation. The first step in training our proposed DRM models consists of generating BR embeddings. To do this, we used all-distilroberta-v1 variant of the DistilRoBERTa model to transform BRs into a contextual representation and help capturing their semantic relationships in a more dense vector format. Here, BRs are encapsulated by a token layer, transforming each BR into a sequence of subwords. These tokens are then fed into the model's encoder, which consists of multiple layers of self-attention and feed-forward neural networks. The encoder processes each BR separately, allowing each token to have its contextual embedding. Each of those output embeddings is then fed into a pooling layer. The pooling layer aggregates each of them to yield the final contextual representation of the entire BR pair.

Pairs Classification. This step consists of determining whether a pair should be flagged as duplicate or distinct. To do this, a classification process is performed where output embeddings derived from DistilRoBERTa are fed into an MLP classifier alongside with their corresponding labels (i.e., duplicate (1) or non duplicate (0)). To prevent overfitting, we employed a 5-fold cross-validation when training our models. During the classification process, the input data is divided into 5 subsets, while maintaining a stratified instance distribution across both duplicates and non duplicates. So, in each iteration, 4 folds are used for training the MLP classifier, while the remaining fold is reserved for testing. Both one section and cross section-based DRM models are trained using the training subset, with adjustments to weights and biases made through backpropagation to minimize classification errors. Cross-validation enables the automatic optimization of MLP hyperparameters, including the number of hidden layers, neurons per layer, and activation functions, through an automated search for optimal performance. Following training, the model performance is evaluated using the validation fold. The cross-validation process is iterated 5 times, with each fold serving as a validation set once.

Producing LIME Explanations. To explain the predictions made by a DRM model, we have used the LIME explainer. To proceed, we implemented a prediction function that takes a BR pair as input and returns their corresponding predictions. This function serves as our black box DRM model, which begins by transforming BR pairs into embeddings using DistilRoBERTa and then uses MLP for classification. The function representing our DRM model is fed into LIME along with the BR pair instance to be explained. At this point, LIME generates a new dataset of perturbations around the input instance and uses the trained DRM model through the prediction function to predict whether each perturbed instance is duplicate or not. The instances in the new generated dataset are weighed based on their distance to the original instance being explained. Finally, the original pair representation is transformed into a discrete binary vector, where words of BR pair are included or excluded. This transformation is achieved by fitting a simpler model (i.e., linear regression) with inherent interpretability. The final output is a comprehensible prediction of the DRM model that reveals the pivotal words within the BR pair that probably influenced its classification as either duplicate or non-duplicate.

3 Experimental Results and Analysis

3.1 RQ1: How Do One Section-Based Models Perform in The Detection of Duplicate Bug Reports When Sections Are Dissimilar?

When a DBRD system misses duplicates (i.e. incorrectly classifies duplicate bug reports as non duplicate), this can result in redundant efforts for developers and QA teams. This inefficiency results in the unnecessary allocation of resources to address the same issue multiple times, thereby diverting attention from other distinct and unresolved problems. This RQ aims to delve into a Type II errors (i.e. false negatives) where duplicate BRs are misclassified as non duplicate. We aim to examine the individual contributions of BR section dissimilairty towards this type of error. To pinpoint pairs having dissimilar sections and contributing to false negative classifications, we start by selecting all duplicate instances misclassified as non duplicates. Next, we set a similarity threshold of 0.6 to differentiate between similar and dissimilar sections, retaining only those misclassified instances that fall below this threshold.

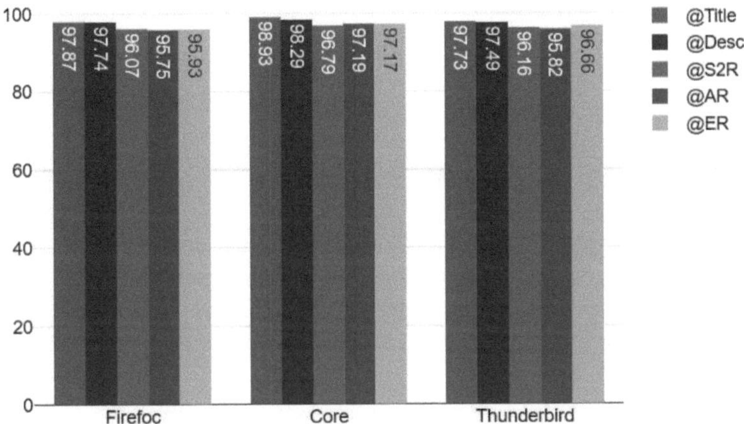

Fig. 2. Accuracices of one section-based models.

To evaluate the overall DBRD performance using individual BR sections, we train and test the five one section-based models (i.e. @DRM_Title, @DRM_Desc, @DRM_S2R, @DRM_AR and @DRM_ER) on each project separately. Results depicted in Fig. 2 and Table 3 reveal that the highest scores across metrics relevant to duplicate classifications (i.e., accuracy, precision (Prec.), recall and F1-score) are attained by the @DRM_Title model (f1-score ranging between 97.73% and 98.93%), closely followed by @DRM_Desc (f1-score ranging between 97.49% and 98.29%). Notably, both models almost perform equally well. Furthermore, the @DRM_S2R, @DRM_AR, and @DRM_ER models demonstrate notably similar performance across all three projects. These initial findings suggest that Title and Desc sections have a more pronounced individual impact compared to the S2R, AR, and ER sections.

Table 3. Precision, recall and f1-score of one-section based models.

Models	Mz-Firefox			Mz-Core			Mz-Thunderbird		
	Prec.	Recall	F1-score	Precision	Recall	F1-score	Precision	Recall	F1-score
@DRM_Title	97.88	97.87	97.87	98.94	98.93	98.93	97.76	97.73	97.73
@DRM_Desc	97.75	97.74	97.74	98.32	98.29	98.29	97.53	97.49	97.49
@DRM_S2R	96.11	96.07	96.07	96.86	96.79	96.8	96.23	96.16	96.16
@DRM_AR	95.78	95.75	95.75	97.26	97.19	97.19	95.89	95.81	95.81
@DRM_ER	95.97	95.93	95.93	97.24	97.17	97.17	96.71	96.66	96.66

Table 4. Average numbers over type II errors: dissimilar duplicate bug reports misclassified as non duplicate for one section based models (over the 5-fold cross validation).

Models	Mz-Firefox	Mz-Core	Mz-Thunderbird
@DRM_Title	8	1.4	6
@DRM_Desc	7.4	4.4	7
@DRM_S2R	12.2	8.4	9.6
@DRM_AR	17.2	7.6	14.2
@DRM_ER	14.6	7.2	12.6

Results in Table 4 show that the misclassifications of duplicate pairs having dissimilar titles occurs less frequently than with the other sections. Consequently, textual differences in titles have a relatively minor adverse effect on the classification of duplicate pairs compared to the other sections of BRs. Notably, @DRM_Desc ranks second after @DRM_Title in the number of misclassifications. However, @DRM_S2R and @DRM_AR demonstrate the highest rates of confusion. As a consequence, dissimilar S2R and dissimilar AR could pose a significant challenge in accurately detecting duplicate BRs.

The frequent dissimilarities observed in the S2R within duplicate BRs can be elucidated by the inherent variability in how duplicate bugs are reproduced. Different testing scenarios may employ distinct methods and steps to replicate identical issues. This variability introduces nuances in the reported steps, contributing to the observed dissimilarities.

As discussed earlier, frequent dissimilarities are often encountered in AR of duplicate BRs. The nature of AR associated with each BR might differ due to diverse factors such as the specific conditions under which the user encountered the bug, the software version being tested, or variations in which users articulate the AR.

3.2   RQ2: How Do One Section-Based Models Perform in the Detection of Non Duplicate Bug Reports Having Similar Sections?

The classification of non-duplicate bug reports as duplicates carries significant implications, notably leading to an increased number of unassigned bugs. In this RQ, we focus on this particular type I of errors, (i.e., false positives). More specifically, we aim to investigate the individual contributions of each section in propagating this error when similarities exist between them. To identify pairs having similar sections and contributing to false positive classifications, we first selected all non-duplicate instances misclassified as duplicates. Then, we used the threshold of 0.6 to keep only those misclassified instances that rise above that threshold.

To address this research question, we initiate our analysis by examining the overall performance of the models in identifying non-duplicate BR pairs, as summarized in Table 3. The @DRM_Title model consistently demonstrates superior performance across all three projects, followed by the @DRM_Desc model with slight variances. Conversely, in MZ-Core, the @DRM_S2R model demonstrates lower scores compared to the other models. As for Firefox and Thunderbird, @DRM_AR has the lowest scores.

Furthermore, according to results in Table 5, @DRM_Title model has minimal instances of non-duplicate BRs with similar sections being misclassified as duplicates, with the exception of the Mz-Thunderbird project where a very low occurrence rate of 0.2 is observed. This indicates that the likelihood of a DBRD model being misled by non-duplicate BRs sharing title similarities is exceedingly rare. Additionally, we note that ER and Desc are both ranked at the second level. However, across all three projects, the @DRM_S2R model demonstrates the highest misclassification rate compared to other models. This highlights the significant role of S2R section as the primary contributor negatively impacting the classification of non-duplicate BRs due to their similarities. The frequent resemblance in S2R among non-duplicate BRs may be attributed to the possibility that reproducing two distinct issues could involve shared or similar steps.

Table 5. Average numbers of type I errors: similar non duplicate bug reports misclassified as duplicate for one section-based models (over the 5-fold cross validation).

Models	Mz-Firefox	Mz-Core	Mz-Thunderbird
@DRM-Title	0	0	0.2
@DRM-Desc	0.2	0.4	0.6
@DRM-S2R	2.6	1.2	3.2
@DRM-AR	1.2	0	0.8
@DRM-ER	0	0.2	0.4

3.3 RQ3: How Does Excluding Confusing Sections from BRs Impact the Overall DBRD Performance?

Based on the findings observed when S2R and AR are used individually, this RQ aims to comprehensively investigate how the absence of these two sections, which are often the most confusing, affects the detection of duplicate and non-duplicate BRs with dis(similar) sections. To achieve this, we conducted tests on three section combinations by training cross section-based models. These model selections are configured by sequentially eliminating S2R and AR from the full BR.

As indicated in Fig. 3, the three cross section-based models have close accuracy performances. However, we aim to specifically focus on per-class misclassifications by these models for the two error types investigated in RQ1 and RQ2. Table 6 shows the average numbers of non duplicate BRs featuring similarities that are erroneously classified as duplicate (tupe I of errors) by cross section-based models. In both Firefox and Thunderbird projects, using the @DRM_Full_BR for DBRD, which involves using the full BR, results in a notable increase in misclassifiying similar non duplicate BRs. However, excluding AR first and then both AR and S2R leads to a significant reduction in this type of misclassification. This indicates that the similarity between S2R increases model confusion. This is also observed with the AR section.

Furthermore, @DRM_Title model, which has the best individual performance reported in Table 3, has fewer instances of misclassifications for similar non duplicates

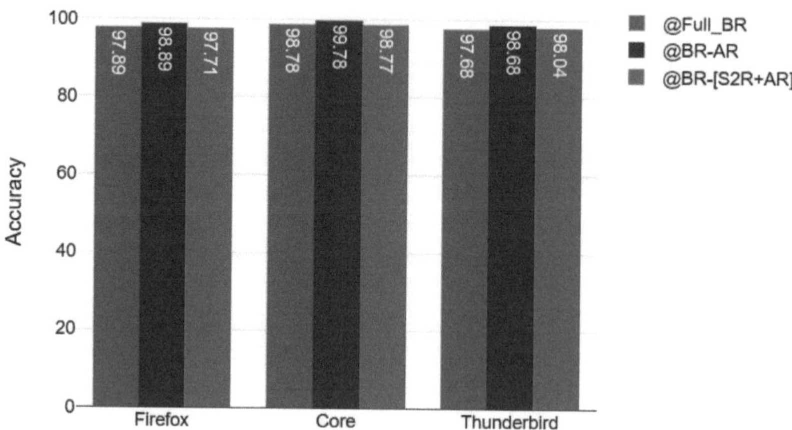

Fig. 3. Accuracy of cross-section-based models.

Table 6. Average numbers of type I errors: similar non duplicate BRs misclassified as duplicate for cross section-based models (over the 5-fold cross validation).

Models	Mz-Firefox	Mz-Core	Mz-Thunderbird
@DRM_Full_BR	28.2	0.6	24.2
@DRM_BR-AR	0	0.6	0.6
@DRM_BR-[AR+S2R]	0.2	0.2	1.2

compared to @DRM-Full_BR model. This suggests that using only the Title section for classifying non duplicate BRs proves to be more effective than employing all BR sections.

Moreover, for this type of error, the behaviors of @DRM_Title and @DRM_Desc models closely resemble those of @DRM_BR-AR and @DRM_BR-[AR+S2R]. This implies that using either Title or Desc section alone produces comparable effectiveness when eliminating AR and S2R sections from the BR. Since eliminating AR and S2R preserves Title, Desc, and ER, this further validates the significant role of these sections within DBRD, particularly in the detection of non duplicate BRs having some similarity. Notably, the impact of Title and Desc sections outweighs that of ER section, despite the frequent number of similar ER sections previously showed by @DRM_ER results.

Table 7. Average numbers over type II errors: dissimilar duplicate BRs misclassified as non duplicate for cross section based models (over the 5-fold cross validation).

Models	Mz-Firefox	Mz-Core	Mz-Thunderbird
@DRM_Full_BR	0	1	0
@DRM_BR-AR	4.8	1.8	4
@DRM_BR-[AR+S2R]	4.6	2.2	3.2

Unlike type 2 of errors (i.e., false positives), when examining the average numbers of duplicate BRs with dissimilarities classified as non-duplicate by cross-section-based models in Table 7, excluding S2R and AR from the BR leads to an increase in misclassifications for dissimilar duplicate BRs. Conversely, including these sections, along with other BR sections like Title, Desc and ER (Full BR), aids in decreasing the chances of misclassifying duplicate BRs with dissimilarities.

4   Discussion and Conclusion

In this study, we introduce a fine-grained analysis based on BR sections, wherein we investigate the impact of these sections through the evaluation of two categories of DBRD models: one section and cross section-based models.

This analysis uncovered notable (dis)similarities between BR sections, which significantly impacts DBRD. Specifically, although the general performance of one section and cross section-based models may be comparable, their error rates differ markedly when using a full BR versus individual sections. Notably, the Title and Desc sections demonstrate positive effects by decreasing both false positives and negatives for cases exhibiting (dis)similarities, whereas the S2R and AR sections emerged as particularly confusing. Consequently, it could be feasible to use either Title or Desc sections as queries within BTSs because they are sufficiently helpful in accurately identifying duplicate BRs.

Identifying the most contributing sections in DBRD could help to streamline the detection process by reducing the time complexity, thereby enabling prioritization of beneficial BR sections. In turn, this opens up prospects for future work aimed at developing efficient real-time DBRD algorithms capable of adapting dynamically according to the relevance of each section. For instance, large BRs, which can be quite lengthy, may exceed the computational capabilities of neural language networks, leading to truncations. As a result, informative sections may be lost, which potentially compromises the accuracy of DBRD tools. This limitation could be addressed by exploring strategies that consider these findings to optimize model architectures and minimize truncations. By doing so, the integrity of relevant sections such as Title and Desc would be preserved. Additionally, implementing ensemble one-section-based models could be a powerful strategy for improving DBRD. Ensemble models combine the strengths of models using a single section, and allow for overcoming the negative impact of some sections, like S2R and AR.

References

1. Sanh, V., Debut, L., Chaumond, J., Wolf, T.: Distilbert, a distilled version of bert: smaller, faster, cheaper and lighter. ArXiv, arXiv:1910.01108 (2019)
2. Rahman, M.M., Roy, C.K.: Improving ir-based bug localization with context-aware query reformulation. In: Proceedings of the 2018 26th ACM joint meeting on European software engineering conference and symposium on the foundations of software engineering, pp. 621–632 (2018)
3. Messaoud, M.B., Miladi, A., Jenhani, I., Mkaouer, M.W., Ghadhab, L.: Duplicate bug report detection using an attention-based neural language model. IEEE Trans. Reliabil. (2022)

4. Messaoud, M.B., Chekaya, R.B., Mkaouer, M.W., Jenhani, I., Aljedaani, W.: Pr-duplichecker: detecting duplicate pull requests in fork-based workflows. Int. J. Syst. Assur. Eng. Manag. **15**(7), 3538–3550 (2024)
5. Jahan, S., Rahman, M.M.: Towards understanding the impacts of textual dissimilarity on duplicate bug report detection. In: IEEE International Conference on Software Analysis, Evolution and Reengineering, SANER (2023)
6. Patil, A., Han, K., Jadon, A.: A comparative study of text embedding models for semantic text similarity in bug reports. *CoRR* (2023)
7. Ghadhab, L., Amor, P.N.B.: Impact of textual (dis)similarities of bug report sections on duplicate bug report detection performance. In: Kallel, S., et al. (eds.) Service-Oriented Computing - ICSOC 2024 Workshops - ASOCA, AI-PA, WE-SOACS, GAISS, LAIS, AI on Edge, RTSEMS, SQS, SOCAISA, SOC4AI and Satellite Events, Tunis, Tunisia, 3–6 December 2024, Revised Selected Papers, Part II, volume 15834 of Lecture Notes in Computer Science, pp. 188–194. Springer (2024)
8. Garreau, D., von Luxburg, U.: Explaining the explainer: a first theoretical analysis of LIME. In: Chiappa, S., Calandra, R. (eds.) The 23rd International Conference on Artificial Intelligence and Statistics, AISTATS 2020, 26–28 August 2020, volume 108 of Proceedings of Machine Learning Research, pp. 1287–1296. PMLR (2020)

Author Index